Frederik Ebbesen Grue   *Study of Oriental Porcelain and Lemons*

A GRAND TRADITION:
THE ART
AND ARTISTS
OF THE
HOOSIER SALON,
1925-1990

Harry A. Davis   *The Bals-Wocher House*

A GRAND TRADITION:
THE ART
AND ARTISTS
OF THE
HOOSIER SALON,
1925-1990

by
Judith Vale Newton
and Carol Weiss

Hoosier Salon Patrons Association
Indianapolis, Indiana
1993

Library of Congress Catalogue Card Number

ISBN Number: 0-9638360-0-5

Published by the Hoosier Salon Patrons Association, Inc.
6434 North College Avenue, Suite C
Indianapolis, Indiana 46220
(317) 253-5340

Distributed by the Hoosier Salon Patrons Association, Inc.

Editor: Robert A. Newton
Designer: Charles Neumeyer
Typesetter: Metropolitan Printing Service, Inc., Bloomington, Indiana
Printer: Edwards Brothers, Incorporated

Edition: 2,000

CONTENTS

ACKNOWLEDGMENTS

Since the spring of 1990, we have been researching the art and artists of the Hoosier Salon with the intent of producing a definitive work on this historic exhibition as well as a biographical dictionary of its nearly twenty-five-hundred artists. A work of this magnitude required the assistance of a great many people to whom we are very much indebted.

We would like to thank Frank Stewart, an art collector and Hoosier Salon Patrons Association Board member who first entertained the notion of such a book. He was supported in his vision by an enthusiastic Board of Directors that commissioned the project as well as by the former Executive Director, Evelyn Wellman, and the current Executive Director, Bonnie Carter. Both women were invaluable in helping us gather information and in giving us ongoing encouragement.

Other Board members offered their talents in furthering the creation of *A Grand Tradition*. Retired *Indianapolis Star* editor Corbin Patrick penned the Foreword for the book, and writer T. Randall Tucker demonstrated his copyediting skills in helping to fine-tune its text. Eugene L. Henderson unearthed a vital, out-of-print source for us, and Pam Hicks shared her well-organized scrapbooks of pertinent newspaper articles. Martha Van Sickle furnished us with information on hard-to-find artists, and Richard E. Ford detailed the Salon's special relationship with Wabash, Indiana. We are grateful, as well, to Joseph B. Davis of Marion, Indiana, for his engaging anecdotes about the artists of yesteryear.

To the hundreds of artists, their families and their friends who thoughtfully responded to our questionnaires, we say "thank you!" Many provided us with a wealth of additional information. Among them were Marianne Miller, Mary C. Craigmile, Chad J. Davis, Jean Templeton, Frederik Grue, Mildred Niesse, E. Gaye Eilts, Carolyn and Stephen L. Taflinger, Folger Brown, Judy Plimpton, Sonny Pearson, Willa Bowen Van Brunt, Evelyn Forsyth Selby, Robert Selby, Jay Vawter, Alice San Pietro, Sister Rita Ann Roethele, S.P., Mary Ann Michau, Merri Leffel, Karen Bixler Steves, Jean Vietor, Harry and Lois Davis, Margery Gates, Paul T. Gilliatt, Nancy Meyer, Ruth Baker, Cynthia Blasingham, Betty Fisher, Jo Money and Thelma Frame.

We are especially grateful to painter Ruth Anderson and printmaker Evelynne Mess Daily for their prodigious memories and vivid descriptions of artistic life from another time. Through their keepsakes as well as their reminiscences, we were able to authenticate the activities of earlier Salons. From the elegant Preview Parties to the tasteful Teas, from the critical commentaries to the artwork on display, we learned much about the exhibition from our hours spent with these two gracious ladies.

Many thanks go to Claudia Kheel, formerly of the Indiana State Museum, for allowing us the use of questionnaires gathered by that museum from artists working during the 1960s and 1970s. Martin Krause, curator of Prints, Drawings and Photographs at the Indianapolis Museum of Art, deserves our gratitude, in addition. He provided us with unwavering support for *A Grand Tradition* as well as ready access to his files. Anne Marie Quets and Ursula Kolmstetter of that same institution were exceptionally efficient as they cheerfully canvassed the IMA's records to track down little known information about artists few people recognize.

We are particularly appreciative of those librarians and staff personnel who became intrigued by our research and worked with us to check "just one more place" or locate that obscure bit of information. Among them are: Julia Muney Moore and Joyce A. Sommers of the Indianapolis Art League, Steven J. Schmidt of IUPUI University Libraries, Frances Friedman of Herron School of Art, Carmen Manuel and Ellen Fischer of the Greater Lafayette Museum of Art, Betty Fishman of Artlink and Elizabeth Petrulis of the Sheldon Swope Art Museum.

Also sharing our search for additional information were Susan P. Colaricci of the Evansville Museum of Arts and Science; Sister M. Rosaleen Dunleavy, C.S.C., of the Cushwa-Leighton Library at Saint Mary's College; Brother Laurian LaForest, C.S.C., of the St. Joseph Spiritual Life Center in Valatie, New York; Sister M. Maurella, O.S.F., of St. Francis College; Sister Ann Kathleen, S.P., of St. Mary-of-the-Woods College; and Brother Wilbert of Holy Cross Brothers' Center in Notre Dame, Indiana.

Others who were most helpful include: Marsha J. Eilers of the Elkhart Public Library, Nan Esseck Brewer of the Indiana University Art Museum, Christina Kuhns of *Arts Indiana,* Diane Hammill of the Crawfordsville District Public Library, Margaret Fette of the Brown County Public Library, Rai Goerler of the University Archives at Ohio State University and Susan Wyngaard of the OSU Art Library. The men and women behind the "Research Desk" at the Monroe County Public Library, the Indianapolis-Marion County Public Library, the Indiana State Library and the Fine Arts Library of Indiana University were notably courteous as they answered our litany of questions.

Over the course of the last three years, we have been aided by the efforts of many on our behalf. Keith Norwalk, president of Crown Hill Cemetery in Indianapolis, verified the death dates of various artists for us, and Barbara Judd of Nashville, Indiana, provided us with key information from her personal files on the Brown County painters. Librarian Chuck Gillespie of Lilly Endowment, Inc., combed that institution's archives for documentation concerning the Hoosier Salon, and David McDaniel of the Indiana State Museum furnished us with architectural facts about the historical building in which the Salon is currently being shown.

To the gallery owners and art aficionados who sought nothing more than to advance the cause of art history, we are most appreciative. Thanks go to the people at Eckert Fine Art—G. Dianne Wright, Henry and Jane Eckert—for the generous use of their extensive art library. We are indebted to Mike Byron of Byron and Sons Galleries for important research leads, Riley Humler and Michele Sandler of the Cincinnati Art Galleries for supplying us with details about the Ohio River painters, and Bill Engle of the William Engle Gallery for providing much-needed data. Thanks, too, to Rosemary Ball Bracken, Leland Howard, Kenneth P. McCutchan, William E. Taylor, John Rardon, Joan D. Weisenberger, Mildred Stilz Haskens and Sue S. Rice for pointing us in the right directions and to Larry Zimpleman for sharing his prized information about the painter John Zwara.

It would have been impossible to undertake a project of this proportion without the love, support, good humor and assistance of our families. Kent, Adam and Erin Newton tirelessly shared their insights and abilities while helping to move *A Grand Tradition* along to its conclusion. Jay Weiss' computer skills proved to be invaluable to this undertaking, and Ivan and Ben Weiss continued to remind us that there was, indeed, a world beyond the book.

For the two of us, this odyssey through the resources of museums, libraries and cultural institutions across the Midwest has been one of discovery. We have sorted through scrapbooks and microfilmed files. We have consulted books, journals and magazine articles, and sifted through stack after stack of crinkled clippings taken from early-twentieth-century publications. Through questionnaires, interviews and endless hours at the library table, we have become convinced that the Hoosier Salon's heritage is decidedly a rich one. As determined as we have been to present the reader with reliable information on our findings, however, we acknowledge that sources may be inexact and memories may be imprecise. Nonetheless, we trust that the reader will know that *A Grand Tradition* has received our best efforts.

*—Judith V. Newton
and Carol Weiss*

ACKNOWLEDGMENTS

Behind any successful venture, there are scores of unsung heroes, and while their names may go unrecognized by some, their contributions are undisputed by all. To those artists and academicians who have ever served on a jury for the Hoosier Salon, we express our gratitude. Drawn from across the country, they have been providing the exhibition with their very best in critical discernment and artistic judgment since 1925. It is to them that we owe much of what the Salon is today.

To the generous patrons of *A Grand Tradition: The Art and Artists of the Hoosier Salon, 1925-1990*, we are deeply indebted. These individuals and businesses have chosen to indicate their support for the book by sponsoring two of our Hoosier Salon artists with an honorary gift. In 1990, they underwrote the project with a donation of at least $250 to the Hoosier Salon Patrons Association, to be used in the research and writing of *A Grand Tradition*. We wish to extend our sincere appreciation for their support.

DONORS

The Hoosier Group, Inc.
by Steve Fess, President
Zionsville, Indiana

Byron and Sons Galleries
Indianapolis, Indiana

John Rardon Associates
Indianapolis, Indiana

Dr. and Mrs. Henry N. Wellman
Indianapolis, Indiana

Mary V. Gallagher
Indianapolis, Indiana

Dr. Jamia Jasper Jacobsen
Zionsville, Indiana

Mr. and Mrs. Herbert B. Feldmann
Indianapolis, Indiana

Charles E. Lanham
Indianapolis, Indiana

Mr. and Mrs. Thomas W. Binford
Indianapolis, Indiana

James W. Brown
Indianapolis, Indiana

Guernsey Van Riper, Jr.
Indianapolis, Indiana

Park and Marjorie Wiseman
Muncie, Indiana

Mrs. Colby S. van Westrum
Indianapolis, Indiana

HONORED ARTISTS

In Support of the
Hoosier Group Artists

Ada Walter Shulz
Lucie Hartrath

Jeffrey C. Burris
Gustave Baumann

Clifton Wheeler
Delita Alvarez Piercy

Theodore C. Steele
Kanwal Prakash Singh

Theodore C. Steele
J. Ottis Adams

Harry A. Davis
William F. Kaeser

Frederik Ebbesen Grue
James Curtin Lentz

Emel Doner
Floyd D. Hopper

Steven Redman
Adolph Robert Shulz

Wayman Adams
Donna Rosser

Glen Cooper Henshaw
Nancy A. Noël

Frank V. Dudley
Robert E. Hartsock

THE HOOSIER SALON, 1925-1990

DONORS	HONORED ARTISTS
Leland G. Howard Rockville, Indiana	George Ames Aldrich Wilbur Meese
Christine N. Carlson Indianapolis, Indiana	William A. Eyden Rich Ernsting
Mrs. Charles Moulin Indianapolis, Indiana	Carl C. Graf Rob O'Dell
Mr. and Mrs. Richard E. Bonsib Fort Wayne, Indiana	Louis W. Bonsib Homer G. Davisson
Josephine Van Fleet, M. D. Indianapolis, Indiana	Phyllis Whitworth John C. Templeton
Mr. and Mrs. Richard L. Alexander Noblesville, Indiana	George Jo Mess Rosemary Browne Beck
Richard M. Atwell Richmond, Indiana	John Elwood Bundy Randolph LaSalle Coats
Mack P. McKinzie Zionsville, Indiana	Jacob Cox Jean F. Vietor
Mrs. Harold W. (Elise Parke) Jordan Bloomington, Indiana	C. Curry Bohm Paul Hadley
Ruth and Greg Woodham Indianapolis, Indiana	Cecil F. Head
Oak Grove Gallery Philip and Susan Desch Nashville, Indiana	L. L. Von Williamson Otto Stark
Nancy and Dick Beatty Princeton, New Jersey	Daniel Garber Donald M. Mattison
Jay Vawter Princeton, New Jersey	Will Vawter
A. Everette James, Jr., Sc.M., J.D., M.D. Nashville, Tennessee	Louis O. Griffith
Joseph M. Shea The Hermitage Brookville, Indiana	Winifred Brady Adams Francis F. Brown
Richard H. Love Chicago, Illinois	Florence White Williams Francis Clark Brown
Frank and Betty Stewart Spencer, Indiana	Ruth B. Anderson Frank Vietor

ACKNOWLEDGMENTS

DONORS

Mitch and Betsy Russ
Indianapolis, Indiana

F. G. and Kathy Summitt
Bloomington, Indiana

Mrs. Grant W. Christian
Indianapolis, Indiana

Dr. Stephen N. Butler
Dr. Linda Ronald Butler
Richmond, Indiana

George and Jane Williston
Wooster, Ohio

Mr. and Mrs. Tad Wilson
Spencer, Indiana

Aileen H. Borough
South Bend, Indiana

Mr. and Mrs. A. M. Bracken
Muncie, Indiana

Mr. and Mrs. Richard Wise
Union City, Indiana

Lorraine H. Davis
Fort Wayne, Indiana

Mr. and Mrs. Eugene Glick
Indianapolis, Indiana

Mr. and Mrs. Henry B. Blackwell
Zionsville, Indiana

Pam and Dave Hicks
Greenwood, Indiana

Martha R. Van Sickle
Indianapolis, Indiana

Mr. and Mrs. Charles H. Moore
Carmel, Indiana

Elaine and Steve Fess
Zionsville, Indiana

Northern Indiana Art Association, Inc.
Munster, Indiana

Ray H. French
Greencastle, Indiana

HONORED ARTISTS

Beulah Brown
William Clusmann

Lois Davis
Harry Davis

Grant W. Christian
Evelynne Mess Daily

John Wesley Hardrick
William Edouard Scott

Janet Scudder
Diana Miller Pierce

Marie Goth
Ken R. Bucklew

Dale P. Bessire
Alexis Jean Fournier

J. Ottis Adams
Winifred Brady Adams

In Support of All Artists

John Frederic Ross
Clara M. Hamilton

Leah S. Traugott
Chicqiela S. Broyles

Thea Clarke
Jerry F. Smith

V. J. Cariani
Jack D. Cowan

Paul A. Wehr
Robert F. Van Sickle

Barbara Beck
Henry Bell

William Forsyth

In Support of All Artists

Henrik Mayer
David K. Rubins

THE HOOSIER SALON, 1925-1990

DONORS	HONORED ARTISTS
Service Supply Co., Inc., of Indiana Indianapolis, Indiana	E. Roger Frey Edmund Brucker
Service Supply Co., Inc., of Indiana Indianapolis, Indiana	Vernon B. Cristee Douglas M. Daniel
Mr. and Mrs. Thomas E. Husselman Zionsville, Indiana	J. Edgar Forkner Ida Nash Gordon
Randall and Evelyn Tucker Columbus, Indiana	Georges LaChance
Mr. and Mrs. Robert H. Selby Austin, Texas	William Forsyth Robert H. Selby
Sally Brant Kriner Nashville, Indiana	In Support of All Artists
Richard E. Ford Wabash, Indiana	In Support of All Artists
Ford Meter Box Foundation, Inc. Wabash, Indiana	In Support of All Artists
Jack and June Beasley Indianapolis, Indiana	Olive Rush George Jo Mess
Eugene L. and Mary L. Henderson Indianapolis, Indiana	In Support of All Artists
Mrs. Glenn W. (Mary Helen) Foster Indianapolis, Indiana	Raymond V. Cradick Helen C. Craig
Mr. and Mrs. Donald W. Goodwin Indianapolis, Indiana	In Support of All Artists
Psi Iota Xi Sorority Indiana	In Support of All Artists

—Frank Stewart, Chairman,
Publications Committee,
Hoosier Salon Patrons Association

PREFACE

Imagination, passion and optimism stimulate new ideas while time, alone, determines their merit. Only with the objectivity that time brings can decisions be evaluated with a wisdom honed by experience. Truths eventually become self-evident.

The truth here is that the Hoosier Salon was created in 1925 by a farsighted group who dreamed of showcasing Indiana's art in an annual exhibition. Its members hoped:

*To inspire Indiana artists, the novices as well as the experts, to develop their collective talent,

*To call attention to those artists who immortalize Indiana's beauty, its characters and its history, and

*To furnish an outlet and profitable market for those artists, a market which would encourage the beginner and reward the professional.

Nearly seventy years later, it is undeniable that the Salon has, very successfully, achieved these original goals. With a singular mind and an abiding grace, its parent organization—the Hoosier Salon Patrons Association—has guided the show during some of life's most daunting circumstances. Through the Great Depression, World War II, the Korean War, the Vietnam War, devastation by fire and almost non-stop criticism, the Salon has persevered. And still, through time, it has influenced nearly twenty-five hundred artists and distributed to them hundreds of thousands of dollars in merit awards, purchase prizes and the sale of their artwork.

What the founders of the Salon may not have foreseen with this undertaking was the breadth of their vision and the scope of their rich legacy. With its participants—artists, patrons and volunteers alike—cutting across social, economic, racial and political lines, the show draws a mixture of diverse individuals. Historically, such notables as the Hoosier Group artists, the Brown County landscapists and members of the Southwestern art colonies of Taos and Santa Fe were on hand for the early shows. American Impressionist Daniel Garber took his place on the Salon's roster along with "Little Orphan Annie's" creator Harold Gray, lithographic revivalist Garo Antreasian, international sculptor Janet Scudder, Pulitzer Prize-winning cartoonist John McCutcheon and Victor Higgins of the "Taos Ten."

With the passage of decades, though, the offerings of more contemporary artists began to take center stage at the Salon. James Cunningham's otherworldly acrylics shared wall space with Harry Davis' architectural renderings, Frederik Ebbesen Grue's exquisite still lifes, Ellie Siskind's social commentaries, Nancy Noël's sensitive portraits and Martha Slaymaker's primitive abstractions.

While attracting the celebrated artists, the Salon has managed, at the same time, to appeal to a wide variety of people, pursuing a wide variety of professions. Insurance agents and doctors enter the show as do gallery owners and lawyers, theater directors and dentists, postal workers and singers, clothing manufacturers and journalists, factory workers and designers, homemakers and musicians, decorators and architects, professors and soldiers, accountants and vagabonds. And the list goes on. The creative spirit moves through them all, and the yearly showing serves to exhibit and pay homage to the result of that dynamic energy.

The Hoosier Salon has passed the most crucial test . . . the test of time. It continues to gather an eclectic group of artists, to elicit financial and moral support from a loyal following and to speak to a large, varied audience. While these champions of the Salon may sometimes brush against the darker sides of life, they continue to uphold artwork that suggests the world can be a place of beauty, pleasure, tenderness, poignancy and good fortune. An organization with the history and integrity of the Hoosier Salon is most certainly entitled to its opinion.

—*J. V. N. and C. W.*

FOREWORD

Art, we like to think, is better than a circus. Without bragging, it really offers the greatest show on earth. No other medium brings so many of the beauties and wonders of the world under one roof.

In a Hoosier Salon exhibit, we have scenes of summer, winter, spring and fall, town and country, mountain and seashore, fact and fancy, today, yesterday and tomorrow fixed in a moment of perfection for the everlasting pleasure of all who care to give them a second look.

In this scientific age, we need the humanizing influence of art more than ever. Science without art could have frightening consequences. Like so much of modern life, science is a highly organized group activity. Art is still the best way individuals have to express themselves and the beauty and truth they see.

Because the Hoosier Salon preserves the finest traditions of Indiana art, it makes a magnificent contribution to our civilized ideal of the good life. If its exhibit were the only activity of the year, the Salon would serve the public admirably.

But the Hoosier Salon also provides Indiana artists with a permanent showcase at its gallery as well as affords members of the Hoosier Salon Patrons Association an unusual opportunity to own works of art that grace both office and home with distinction.

Long may the Hoosier Salon thrive!

—Corbin Patrick
The Indianapolis Star
January, 1959

*   *   *

This is just as true today in 1993 as it was thirty-four years ago, and the potential for service to Indiana artists at the new Broad Ripple gallery is even greater.

—C. P.
Retired Arts & Leisure Editor
The Indianapolis Star
June, 1993

(Reprinted in part from the 1959 Hoosier Salon catalogue)

Illustrations are reproductions of those originally appearing in the Hoosier Salon exhibition catalogues.

The Hoosier Salon

January 26 to February 13 at the

Picture Galleries of

Marshall Field & Company

28 East Washington Street

Second Floor

The Hoosier Salon
January 28 to February 15 at the
Picture Galleries of
Marshall Field & Company
28 East Washington Street
Second Floor

The Twenties

1925 While Texan Miriam "Ma" Ferguson was assuring a place for herself in the record books as the country's first female governor, the 160 members of the Daughters of Indiana were creating their own spot in history. What had begun as a modest study of Hoosier painters during an Art Tea[1] in May of 1924 had become a major project for the women from Chicago. "They realized that the artists of Indiana were not getting the recognition due them," observed Ruth G. Grimes in the *Hoosier Magazine,* "[and] [w]hat was needed was the stamp of approval of the outside world. . . . It was decided that Chicago, being the logical art center of the Middle West and a metropolis, should be the location for the first exhibition of Indiana artists sponsored by them."[2]

In selecting a name for their ambitious undertaking, the Daughters borrowed freely from French tradition. They decided that their show should be known as the Hoosier Salon. The women "evidently wished to emphasize the importance of the event by including in their name the word, 'salon' which when spelled with a capital 'S' had always referred to the famed exhibition of pictures held annually in May and June at the Grand Palais des Champs-Élysées in Paris—up until modernistic schools established a second Salon in the autumn. If Paris could have two celebrated art shows, known as the Spring Salon and the Autumn Salon, why might not the Hoosiers have a third one?"[3]

Under the leadership of Mrs. (Clarence B.) Estella King—a native of Peru, Indiana, who had been appointed as chairman of the Art Committee—a pamphlet announcing the event was circulated. Like the name the Daughters had selected for their show, the goals of the women were lofty and high-reaching. With the Salon scheduled to open in early March of 1925, the members hoped:

*"To accord to struggling artists, sympathetic hearing, liberality and impartial treatment so as to encourage and inspire the development of any latent talent they possess.

*To bring added renown to those artists who by their work have immortalized Indiana's many beauty spots, its famous characters, and history.

*To place Indiana art on the same high plane that its literature now occupies.

*To furnish an outlet and profitable market to Indiana artists that will encourage and develop the beginner and substantially reward those of acknowledged merit."[4]

With its generous purse—awards were to range from $25 to $200 in each prize category—the upcoming show demanded attention. Encouraged to submit work in oil, watercolor, pastel, drawing, etching, miniature and cartoon, Indiana artists or those who had lived within the state for one year were saving their best pieces for the Salon. The new Chicago exhibition, to be held in the art galleries of Marshall Field & Company, promised its entrants increased recognition. It also presented them with an unusual sales opportunity because the department store staff—working on a commission of 33 1/3 percent[5]—had been instructed to promote the purchase of Salon artwork.

As the show's March 9 opening neared, cartoonist John T. McCutcheon and humorist George Ade, members of the Indiana Society of Chicago, handled much of the publicity. Another in their group, publishing magnate John C. Shaffer, spearheaded the fund-raising. He was the first to donate money to the cause, pledging $1,000 and the support of his newspapers in Illinois and Indiana. Others from the Society helped the Daughters with a myriad of last-minute details. Volunteers from the Earlham Alumni Association of Chicago were also enlisted in the effort by Mrs. Ruth Barnard Griffiths, president of the Daughters of Indiana and an Earlham alumna.[6]

The last painting was barely in place before the gallery doors were thrown open to a private reception on Saturday night. Hundreds of people came from across Indiana; many of them had arrived on the morning and afternoon trains from Indianapolis. They were welcomed to the Preview Party by the serenading of an ensemble whose members had been drawn from the Chicago Symphony Orchestra. Among the Indiana tunes offered by the musicians were "On the Banks of the Wabash" and "We're Coming Back to Indiana."[7]

Artists and patrons, club members and guests mingled in the five art galleries at Marshall Field's while waiting for the announcement of awards. Daniel Garber had sent a big landscape entitled *May Evening, A Phantasy* from Philadelphia for the show. Born on a farm in North Manchester, Indiana, "amid surroundings which he describe[d] as hideous rather than merely ugly,"[8] Garber was teaching at the Pennsylvania Academy of the Fine Arts. Noted for picturing "spots one would like to visit, mellow places in which every incidental white horse or red roof are like words in a lyric,"[9] the philosophical painter identified with his lush landscapes. "It is our duty, he [held], to try to render back to the world the blessings that we receive from it; and an artist must try to make his fellow creatures share in the pleasure which he has received from Nature."[10]

Theodore C. Steele was on hand with his wife Selma. Initially reluctant to come, he was convinced to make the journey from his Brown County studio by repeated pleas from Mrs. King. In August of 1924, she had written: "We want the best and we want a comprehensive exhibit. . . . And we surely want Mr. T. C. Steele as no exhibit is complete without your work."[11] Then, in February of 1925, she had tried again: "Nothing has been heard from you in regard to the Hoosier Salon. Have you forgotten all about it? We are most anxious to know how many pictures we are to have from you and whether you will be here during the exhibit?"[12]

Many in the crowd lingered in the center gallery. Filled mostly with landscapes, it had been designated as a place of honor for the paintings of Indiana's senior artists: J. Ottis Adams, William Forsyth, Otto Stark and Steele. Other art patrons gathered around Wayman Adams' portrait of his baby son, Wayman, Jr., done when the namesake was but a few months old. The first painting ever exhibited of his boy, *Ella, Wayman Junior, and Naomi Priscilla* was among the four canvases shipped from the New York City studio of the distinguished Hoosier portraitist.[13]

Three *Little Orphan Annie* cartoons, entered into the Salon by the creator of the nationally known waif, also drew appreciative onlookers. Since starting the comic strip in 1924, cartoonist Harold Gray had been entertaining readers across the country with the exploits of Orphan Annie, her dog Sandy and the fabulously wealthy Daddy Warbucks. In drawing the popular comic, this Purdue University graduate of 1917[14] called upon his midwestern experiences to flavor his work with homely virtues and small-town values.[15]

By all accounts, the first Hoosier Salon was judged a success. A steady stream of visitors had trooped through the Marshall Field galleries to view 253 pieces of art by 132 artists. More than two hundred exhibition entries had been rejected by the jury.[16] Merit awards totaling $4,375 had been given, and special prizes of $100 each had been presented to painters J. Ottis Adams, Otto Stark and G. Ames Aldrich.[17]

Even the *Chicago Daily News* art critic was impressed. Applauding the Hoosier artists for highlighting the natural beauty of their state, Marguerite B. Williams noted: "Look in this exhibition at the work of the most brilliant of this group . . . and you may fancy something like an art tradition is being built up here. . . . In Indiana, practically every one is said to have a flair for writing, and it would seem that some of this desire for self-expression has overflowered into painting for there is probably no other state that could show as many and such a high average of practically unknown painters."[18]

* * *

1926 Hoosier novelist Meredith Nicholson[19] was heartened by the interest shown in the artists of his home state. "One important purpose served by last year's Salon," he wrote in the Foreword to the 1926 Hoosier Salon catalogue, "was the disclosure of so much more artistic talent among the sons and daughters of Indiana than any one had dreamed of. Indiana's literary industry[20] long obscured the state's quiet endeavors in the field of painting, sculpture and illustration. . . . I think I speak for all the Indiana writing folk in saying that we are anxious for our brothers and sisters who paint or draw or sculpt to have their day in court, just as we have had it."[21]

Drawn by the promise of substantial prizes and public notice, artists from around the country were anxious to be included in the second Hoosier Salon. It again was being sponsored by the Daughters of Indiana. Entries for the show were shipped to Marshall Field's from studios in New York City, Santa Fe, Atlanta, St. Louis, Long Beach, Minneapolis, Seattle, San Diego, New Orleans and Washington, D.C., as well as from towns throughout Indiana, Michigan and Illinois. Only 149 of the hopefuls were admitted by the jury, and 339 pieces of their artwork were displayed in the galleries of the department store giant.[22] Crowds, both curious and admiring, packed the exhibition space as more than fifty thousand people from every state in the nation visited the show during its two-week run.[23]

This was the first year in which sculptors had been invited to enter, and the internationally known Janet Scudder won the $300 award for "Outstanding Piece of Sculpture." Her prizewinning *Victory*,[24] a nude figure of a maiden upholding in her right hand a beribboned laurel wreath, was said to symbolize the contributions of women throughout the world during World War I. Scudder had submitted the piece, also known as *Feminine Victory*, as a model for the proposed National Suffrage Fountain in Washington, D. C.

With her fountain sculptures appearing in such collections as the Metropolitan Museum of Art, the Luxembourg Museum, the Peabody Institute and Chicago's Art Institute, the artist who had been born in Terre Haute, Indiana, was in great demand for commission work. Nonetheless, she made time for the Hoosier Salon, returning from Paris, France, to speak at a gallery tea and share the festivities with longtime friends.[25]

Wayman Adams was again in the spotlight as his *The Art Jury* took the $500 top prize for "Outstanding Picture of the Exhibition." The piece was a life-size portrait of the four surviving members of the Hoosier Group—T. C. Steele, Otto Stark, J. Ottis Adams and William Forsyth—standing in a row as if passing judgment on a painting. Started in the upper gallery at the John Herron Art Institute,[26] the canvas never failed to get a reaction from the feisty Forsyth. "Every time I look at the picture, my foot hurts," the artist complained. "You see, when the picture was being painted I had to stand so long on a hard concrete floor, holding that pose, that my foot got terribly cramped. The result is that I begin to suffer sympathetically every time I look at it."[27]

One of the first African-American artists[28] to participate in the Hoosier Salon, William Edouard Scott had an established reputation overseas by the time he entered his *Lights on a Summer Night* in the 1926 show. A pupil of Otto Stark at Manual Training High School in Indianapolis, he had followed in his teacher's footsteps; Scott had won a scholarship under Stark's tutelage to the Académie Julian in Paris. "We cannot do too much for Mr. Stark," the former student had written in a tribute to his favorite teacher during February of 1925. "All I am I owe to him," he noted, remembering how supportive Stark had been in turning over his studio to the younger painter so that Scott might hold an exhibition there.[29]

* * *

1927 Flattered by the reception given the first two Salons but overwhelmed with all the details, the Daughters of Indiana finally had to look outside their organization for help. They had been pushed in this direction by both artists and patrons who, at a meeting held on the opening day of the 1926 Salon, had urged the formation of a permanent group that would oversee the interests of Indiana's artists.[30] In accordance with those wishes, the Hoosier Salon Patrons Association had been created in time to take over the sponsorship of the 1927 show. Planning for the exhibition was made easier because many of the new patrons were also members of the Daughters of Indiana or the Indiana Society of Chicago who brought experience from the first two Salons.

John C. Shaffer, editor and publisher of the *Chicago Evening Post* as well as the *Indianapolis Star* and its sister newspapers in Terre Haute and Muncie, was elected president of the Association. A Board of Trustees was created in addition to a panel of Chicago Vice-Presidents and another of Indiana Vice-Presidents. Mrs. Mary Q. Burnet, author of *Art and Artists of Indiana*, agreed to serve as the membership chairman for Indiana, while Mrs. Estella King, chairman of the Art Committee from the first Salon, took over as the executive chairman.[31]

During its first few months, the Association endured some difficult days. Concerned that several of its patrons were failing to honor their pledges of support, Mrs. King had confided to Selma Steele: "If everyone acts as [they have] done, how are we going to get money to send out our literatures, pay our postage and stenographer's fees? . . . Mr. Shaffer insisted on having our Board of Trustees chosen from Chicago businessmen because he said they would act when the time came, they would answer letters promptly and they would furnish the prize money. I believe he is right after trying this out all summer and giving my entire time to the work."[32]

The artists, though, were unaware of any financial problems; they knew only that the Hoosier Salon was going to become an annual event. In its short two-year history, the show already had become a gathering place for them, a forum where they could meet and talk and exchange ideas about their work. One Indiana painter explained, "It is the great bright light of our entire year. We look forward to it, save money to go, plan to show our very best work there and spend the rest of the year in retrospective reminiscence."[33]

Thanking the Daughters of Indiana for their foresight in staging the earlier Salons, playwright George Ade[34] wrote in the Foreword to the 1927 catalogue: "The women Hoosiers of Chicago who arranged for an annual exhibition of the work of artists living in Indiana did something out of the ordinary and showed a most friendly spirit. They proved in a hurry that Art with a capital A was simply throbbing, back at the old birthplace.

"There have been two Salons and they have been so successful that now they have been taken over by an organization solemnly christened as The Hoosier Art Patrons' Association. The idea is not merely to permit a great many Chicago people to drop in . . . and look at certain commendable specimens of paintings and sketches and models. The real purpose of the Association, as I understand it, is to give direct encouragement to artists of all degrees, permitting them to show their work to the public and stand out in plain sight, ready to be discovered by dealers and buyers."[35]

The 1927 Hoosier Salon was the largest yet: 378 works were displayed by 168 artists in the Marshall Field galleries that had been expanded, since the last show, from five to six. More than $4,000 was given in prizes.[36] With an ever-increasing number of entries came an effort on the part of the Association to distribute the award money among the most artists possible. The 1927 catalogue alerted gallery-goers to the change: "The attention of the public is called to the rule maintained by the . . . Association that no artists may receive the same award in the same class or a similar award in a lower class two successive years. No artist may take the outstanding prizes for three years after having received them."[37]

In assessing the big show, Marguerite B. Williams of the *Chicago Daily News* pointed to the "high state of perfection" in the development of Hoosier landscape art by saluting William Forsyth, Clifton Wheeler and a group of younger men following in their trail. "This is the one great achievement of the Hoosier artists," she wrote, "one which I fancy has gained strength by its gradual growth and isolation from other groups and schools, but more particularly by its separation from the meretricious taint of advertising art. If I could place side by side the best work of landscape painters of Chicago and Indiana, I believe it would be found that though the Chicago artists outstrip the Indiana artists in technical cleverness, the Hoosier artists have that freer, less untrammeled spirit of the artist."[38]

The critic was troubled, however, by the appearance in the show of several "spineless landscapes which ramble around in the weeds and never get anywhere."[39] This, she concluded in her "Here and There in the Art World" column, "seems to be the result of a too close and worn-out pursuit of [I]mpressionism. But, on the other hand, there is that strong sense of form and pattern that Clifton Wheeler has imported to Hoosier landscape art,

and it is not without its influence in the work of Francis Brown, Carl Graf, Simon Baus and V. J. Cariani."[40]

What the press concluded about the landscape offerings mattered little to the throngs of people jamming the galleries to see the work of some of the country's best cartoonists. In addition to Harold Gray of *Little Orphan Annie* fame, Kin Hubbard, John T. McCutcheon, Gaar Williams and Fontaine Fox had been juried into the third Salon. Creator of a philosophical loafer from Brown County named Abe Martin, *Indianapolis News* cartoonist Hubbard had established his reputation by penning the antics of the rustic fellow, along with his pithy sayings. Hubbard had become a household name, and his *Abe Martin* series was syndicated in newspapers across the country.[41]

McCutcheon and Williams shared not only a Hoosier birthright but editorial cartooning responsibilities at the *Chicago Tribune* as well. The older of the two, McCutcheon made his point with cartoons that amused rather than reformed. The best-known American cartoonist of the first quarter of the twentieth century, he would win a Pulitzer Prize in 1931 for his *The Wise Economist,* a cartoon chronicling the psychological effect of the bank failures of 1930.[42]

A member of the Association's Chicago Vice-Presidents, McCutcheon was unflagging in his support of the Salon. In an article illustrated with one of his cartoons, he had written: "It (the exhibition) seems to be stimulating art interest all over the country. Everyone is getting interested in the idea. College presidents are writing that they are beginning to think of establishing art galleries. Other states are agitating salons like this one in their own localities, and requests are now being received from museums and dealers for exhibitions of the work of our artists."[43]

Gaar Williams' hometown of Richmond, Indiana, provided this nationally syndicated cartoonist with the subject matter for his best-loved work, *Among the Folks in History.* He recalled the customs and traditions of small-town living and turned them into homespun images that offered a nostalgic look at the 1880s and 1890s.[44] Several panels from his *Folks in History* series were displayed in the 1927 show, prompting visitors to wonder how this hard-hitting illustrator from Chicago could so adeptly touch the concerns of the common man.

The winner of the $100 award for "Best Group of Cartoons or Illustrations," however, was none of these celebrated artists. The Salon prize went to Fontaine Fox, a former Indiana University student and creator of the syndicated *Toonerville Folks* comic. Visitors to the show were delighted with the entries submitted by this New York-based cartoonist. For the exhibition, he had chosen nine pieces depicting the cast of characters in his popular series; among them were *Terrible Tempered Mr. Bang, Aunt Eppie Hogg, Powerful Katrinka, Mickey (himself) McGuire* and *Toonerville Trolley.*[45]

* * *

1928 As unemployment figures crept upward and the stock market seesawed wildly, members of the Association looked for inventive ways to increase their numbers and fund awards for the 1928 show. The Daughters of Indiana of Chicago suggested a novel solution. They offered to donate $250 for the purchase of a painting to be given to the city or town in Indiana that enrolled the largest number of members, pro rata with its population, in the Hoosier Salon Patrons Association.[46] The competition among Hoosier towns was spirited, but New Castle would win the prize—*June Garden* by Maude Kaufman Eggemeyer—by recruiting twenty-two new patrons for the Association. At the close of the show, the floral landscape would be placed in the city's permanent art collection that was displayed in the library and in various New Castle public schools.[47]

The Art Prize Fund Committee redoubled its efforts to increase the awards for the show. Former donors were encouraged to continue funding their favorite prizes, and new categories were created. As one of the incentives to support the Salon during the increasingly trying times, the Committee announced that "[e]very prize donor [would be] given the privilege of purchasing the picture which wins his prize by paying the listed price less the amount of the prize."[48]

Kappa Kappa Kappa Sorority of Indiana responded by contributing $200 to be given to the "Outstanding Picture by a Woman Artist," after the "Outstanding Picture of the Exhibition" prize had been named. The Board of Trustees of Indiana University voted to give $200 to underwrite a prize category for the "Picture Possessing Unusual Artistic Merit." The Art League of State Normal School in Terre Haute, Indiana, agreed to fund two new awards: "Best Landscape in Oil by Full-time Paid Public School Teacher in Indiana" and "Best Still Life in Oil by Full-time Paid Public School Teacher in Indiana."

Even the limestone industry in southern Indiana got involved in putting its resources behind the three-year-old art show. The Indiana Limestone Company pledged a $200 prize to be given for "Best Creative Work in Indiana Limestone Which Can Be Embodied in an Architectural Design,

Either Exterior or Interior." According to the size limitations stated in the 1928 exhibition catalogue, pieces entered in this category could weigh no more than 150 pounds.[49]

With its customary fanfare, the Association kicked off the 1928 Salon by hosting a Preview Party on Saturday night before the public opening on Monday. Artists, patrons and special guests "were greeted by a liveried doorman and treated to the luxury of an elevator ride"[50] to the second-floor galleries. There they assembled with friends, while waiting to learn which of the 342 pieces on display had won the evening's top awards. Formal wear was *de rigueur* as both women and men—a few were in full dress and others, in tuxedos—offered a colorful complement to the paintings in the show.

The Saturday night affair was kept purely social; the Association had asked that no paintings be sold or commissions be placed. On Monday morning, though, as soon as Marshall Field's had opened, several from the department store staff were on the floor to help sell Salon paintings. They were aided in their efforts by a sales committee from the Daughters of Indiana "who work[ed] like Trojans, and they [were] paid not one penny."[51]

Shortly before the close of the Salon, *Indianapolis Star* art critic Lucille E. Morehouse chastised Hoosier visitors for admiring—but not purchasing—work featured in the show. "[You] must buy some of the things [you] enjoy in the galleries," she urged in her "In the World of Art" column. "What would Indianapolis merchants do if the people who came into their stores only looked at their goods? What would Indianapolis manufacturers do if people came only to watch the wheels go round? What would Indianapolis professional men do if clients only sat in the easy chairs of their offices and read the diplomas on their walls? Get busy, O ye of little faith in your own artists of your own state—get busy and buy exhibited art from the exhibitions!"[52]

* * *

1929 The maintenance of a year-round gallery had been one of the first items on the agenda at the Association's annual meeting in May of 1928. This proposal had been heartily endorsed by the membership, and space for a downtown office had been donated by *Evening Post* publisher and Association president John C. Shaffer. Located in Room 724 of the Chicago Evening Post Building at 211 West Wacker Drive,[53] the Hoosier Art Gallery—designed to display only the artwork of those artists who had been juried into one of the Salons—opened on October 15, 1928.[54]

In the following months, shows were held featuring the work of John Elwood Bundy, Homer Davisson, Ralph Fletcher Seymour, Charles Dahlgreen, Frederick Polley, L. O. Griffith and five of the Brown County artists. By May 1, the Association had sold nearly $4,200 in paintings through the new gallery. Policies were put in place, as well, that offered a ten percent discount to patrons for purchases made in the Hoosier Gallery and in individual studios where artists had given their consent. A special Christmas Purchase Plan was also initiated, enabling buyers to make small monthly payments and possess their paintings while doing so.[55]

Despite the additional work brought on by overseeing the gallery, Mrs. King and her colleagues expanded the activities that were associated with the annual Salon. For an Artists' Tea, held in the Hoosier Gallery on Sunday before the public opening on January 28, they lined up two special speakers. Mrs. Mary Q. Burnet traveled from Indianapolis to talk about "The Art Survey and Its Results," and Mrs. Frank Ball of Muncie, Indiana, spoke on "The Influence of Organized Art Effort on Local Communities."[56]

Later in the year, another kind of creative expression—music—would be championed by the Association. At the direction of the Board of Trustees, the Hoosier Program Bureau would be formed in May of 1929 "to aid, as far as possible, struggling musicians in appearing before clubs and in securing engagements."[57] Despite its intent of helping enterprising Hoosier musicians, the Association had limited success in this arena. Upon moving to Indianapolis after the 1941 Salon, the group concluded that its energies were better spent upon bolstering the visual arts.

The 1929 Hoosier Salon was another blockbuster show, boasting of $5,450 in prize money, 166 artists, and 328 paintings and pieces of sculpture.[58] New awards had been added as well. One of the more intriguing was the category created by Lawrence A. Downs. As president of the Illinois Central Railroad, he had donated $100 to be given to the "Best Industrial Scene (Painted in Oil, Preferably a Railroad Scene) Painted Anywhere Along the Route of the Illinois Central."

Hoosier-born Victor Higgins, a prominent member of the group of painters working in Taos, New Mexico, took the $500 "Outstanding Picture of the Exhibition" prize with a flower composition entitled *Zinnias*. Attracted to the simplicity of the southwestern landscape, much as his colleagues in Indiana were being drawn to Brown County by its rusticity, Higgins had settled in Taos in 1915.[59] In explaining the attraction of the place, this artist from Shelbyville, Indiana, said: "There is in the mind of every member of the Taos art colony the knowledge that here is the oldest of American civilizations. The manners and customs and style of architecture are the same today that they were before Christ was born. They offer the painter a subject as full of the fundamental qualities of life as did the Holy Land of long ago."[60]

Attendance at the Salon was again sparked by the Association's practice of setting aside time for teas, lectures and luncheons for members of various clubs. The women from the Daughters of Indiana turned out in force for their special day as did those from such groups as Kappa Kappa Kappa Sorority, the Rogers Park Women's Club, the Lake County Clubs of Indiana and the Englewood Women's Club. Always popular, Indiana College Day brought alumni from Earlham College, Butler University, Franklin College and DePauw University each year. Sometimes noisy, always enthusiastic, they took over Marshall Field's Tea Rooms to share stories and participate in the artist-led tours of the galleries.

Purdue University even had its own day. After welcoming the school's "Boilermakers" to the show, Mrs. King—serving as the luncheon speaker for the group—thanked them for their support of the Salon art movement: "When we wanted to have something else than the usual formal engraved invitation to invite people to an art exhibition, it was John T. McCutcheon, a Purdue alumnus, who drew a cartoon for the invitation," she said. "It was a picture of father and mother and brother and sister and the dog, all interested in painting, and this helped everybody know that the Hoosier Salon would not be a stiff, formal affair. For this year's card of invitation, Harold Gray, another Purdue man, drew an 'Annie' cartoon which brought many expressions of commendation."[61]

Pleased that the showings in the Association's display space seemed to appeal to a wide audience, Mrs. King told the Purdue alumni about some recent guests in the gallery. "The largest number of men visitors in our new Hoosier [A]rt [G]allery, which was opened in the Chicago Evening Post Building in the fall, is from the body of engineers," she explained. "An engineer came in by himself one day to see the pictures and, in a few days, he returned, bringing twenty-five more engineers with him."[62]

The Hoosier Salon
January 25 to February 12 at the
Picture Galleries of
Marshall Field & Company
28 East Washington Street
Second Floor

When the Hoosier Settin' Room couldn't hold all their Art, they invaded Chicago

The Thirties

1930 Three months after "Black Thursday" and the stock market crash of 1929, the sixth Hoosier Salon opened with its traditional festivities. Both donors and details had been in place for months, so little about the weekend celebration was affected by the financial chaos sweeping Chicago. Artists, patrons and special guests were treated to an elegant Saturday night reception in the Marshall Field Picture Galleries. On Sunday evening, Frank Dudley—known for his paintings of the Indiana dunes—and his wife hosted a "Bohemian" party for the artists.

The exhibition itself, however, was smaller. Only 253 paintings and pieces of sculpture were on display, and prizes for "Best Group of Cartoons," "Best Group of Miniatures"[1] and "Best Landscape in Oil Painted by a Full Time Public School Teacher of Indiana" had been eliminated. In their stead, the Third District of the American Legion Auxiliary of Illinois had agreed to underwrite a new award category for $50: "Best Picture in Oil by an Ex-Serviceman."[2] For the first time, too, Hoosier Salon catalogues were sold instead of being distributed free of charge. Sales from the little booklets brought enough money to buy Leota Williams Loop's *Calla Lilies* for $200. The flower painting was presented to the town of Marion, Indiana, for enrolling the largest number of patrons in the Association.[3]

The highlight of the 1930 Salon was a special exhibit of sixty-one wood-block prints by the nationally known Gustave Baumann. The artist had worked in Brown County for seven years before moving to Santa Fe, New Mexico. There he would spend more than a half century applying what he had learned in the gentler Hoosier terrain to the more dramatic New Mexican landscape. "I went (to Brown County) to investigate art possibilities," explained Baumann, who had been a commercial artist working in Chicago in 1909. "[It] was easy to commute to and I found that restful something we all yearn for. Life was simple; I could stay two months for $100.[4]

"I liked the place," he continued. "Someone has said that literature and art flourish wherever people give themselves time to think. Indiana was one of those places. The artist was accepted with amused tolerance (in Brown County). As such, he could move around freely without being exploited as a strange creature who radiated publicity value."[5]

Shortly before the Salon's opening on January 25, Baumann returned to Chicago from his studio in Santa Fe to catch up with his midwestern colleagues and take part in the show's activities. To him, the exhibition was as much a time to teach as it was to study the latest work of his fellow artists. "The Hoosier Salon idea," he had written earlier, "as I grasp it out here in my western home, is to teach great numbers of people who have not had advantages of special training the fundamental idea behind various phases of art, and to teach them to appreciate and enjoy art so that it may become a part of their everyday life. This cannot be done without some knowledge of the woodblock, which has been termed 'great grandfather of the graphic arts."[6]

Salon-goers were duly appreciative of Baumann's talent, buying several of his color woodblock prints during the first day of the exhibition.[7] By the show's closing on February 12, nearly $6,100 of artwork had been sold, with the most sales in any one division coming from the group of wood-block prints.[8] According to Mrs. King, the gallery workers from Marshall Field "are jubilant over our success and acknowledge that, in view of the Depression which exists at the present time, it is an outstanding event so far as sales are concerned. They also compliment the show very highly as the best held in the galleries."[9]

One art critic was troubled by the possible impact of the modern art movement upon the exhibition. Favoring a representational style that had characterized the work of earlier Salons, Lucille E. Morehouse of the *Indianapolis Star* urged artists to "stick to your Hoosier landscapes. . . . [I]nterpret them in terms of atmosphere and warm sunlight and cool shadows, rather than in terms of an assortment of geometrical figures to be found in a book on higher mathematics.

"But if you feel a wild, mad urge within you to let your paint brush drip cubes and prisms and parallelepipeds upon the canvas," she warned, "then it may be to your interest to quit the conservative ranks and rush along on all fours to the modern front. You'll find many confreres there, making whoopee in an effort to be popular. And, land o' livin', they may be popular now! But wait until after the deluge is over. Sometimes popularity wanes and an obliging waste basket or ash heap stands conveniently nearby."[10]

* * *

1931 The jury's selection of avant-garde artwork, along with more traditional offerings for the 1931 Hoosier Salon, failed to satisfy one art critic who unabashedly favored modernism. Outspoken and liberal, C. J. Bulliet of the *Chicago Daily News* made few friends with a diatribe that dismissed a number of the 269 pieces in the show. "[T]he present Salon—the seventh—is still akin in spirit to the old family album that persists as an ornament of Hoosier rustic homes,"[11] he wrote in a review that later was carried by the *New York Times*.

"The Indiana painters, for the most part, are still untutored except by their like of yesterday, and their 'Salon' is still a matter of rustic fields along the Wabash and the Ohio and of the wooded slopes of the Brown County hills, which the late T. C. Steele made famous all over Indiana," he declared. ". . . The fields and forests are honestly of Indiana, and if this honesty could be maintained until there grew up some native genius powerful enough to take the Hoosier 'motifs' and make of them great art, then it would come to pass that 'American art' would be born in Brown County, Indiana, and not in Woodstock or Taos."[12]

Agreeing that "the jury admitted works of art which constitute[d] an exhibition of unusual interest,"[13] the *Star's* more conservative Lucille Morehouse came to the defense of the traditional work selected by the jury for the exhibition. "[S]uch pictures are the ones we most like to hang in our homes, to bring us rest and quiet when we turn from the busy office and store and the noisy street and factory,"[14] she noted in her "In the World of Art" newspaper column.

"It might be argued that the main purpose of the Hoosier Salon is not merely to amuse and entertain the gallery visitor, but to sell the work of Indiana artists," she added. "And, the argument might continue, if the pictures which are desired in the home are not on display, just what is apt to be the decision of the would-be purchaser? This argument by the one who is all for beech tree paintings and hazy autumn scenes might be clinched by his

statement that one does not find so many 'Sold' tags tucked in at the edges of frames (of more modern paintings) this year, as might be observed after a few days had passed in former Hoosier Salons."[15]

For the most part, those who visited the Salon ignored the torrent of words being unleased by the critics. What did attract the attention of gallery-goers, though, were the canvases that had been shipped from New Mexico by several Hoosier artists living in Santa Fe and Taos. Like Victor Higgins and Gustave Baumann before them, Olive Rush, Wood Woolsey and Carl Woolsey had been drawn to the brilliant landscape and simple lifestyle of these art colonies in the Southwest.

"Many of us came out here to find ourselves . . . [in the] environment of great spaces,"[16] explained Rush, a native of Fairmount, Indiana, and a pioneering resident of Santa Fe. Her *The Mountain Road, Autumn* won the $400 "Outstanding Picture By a Woman Artist After the Shaffer Prize Has Been Awarded" category. A repeat winner in the Salon, the noted muralist and landscapist had been awarded several prizes in the "Best Watercolor" category: $150 for her *Judging Horses* in 1930 and $50 for *County Fair, the Aeroplanes* in 1926.

Miss Rush had left Indianapolis during 1920 to settle in New Mexico. "Santa Fe has a rarefied atmosphere which has not yet been invaded by factory whistles and grimy smokestacks," she later would say of her move to the region that had fascinated her as a child. "Here I am near the Sangre de Cristos, the Pueblo Indians and the Spanish-speaking people whose ancestors settled the region. It is from these forces, these influences, that I derive the peace which I find necessary to creative effort."[17]

Applauding her success in the 1931 Salon, an *Indianapolis Star* critic wrote: "I am glad that Olive Rush has come into her own and is now receiving the recognition that I thought was her due when her delightfully decorative Santa Fe landscapes were hung over the door or in an out-of-the-way corner when the Hoosier Salon was but a year or two old. Since then Miss Rush has done some important mural decorations in Chicago and the Salon jury now sits up and takes notice of the things she enters in the Hoosier show."[18]

Olive Rush was not the only Indiana artist working in the Southwest to find favor with the jury; one of her colleagues from New Mexico, Wood Woolsey, won $200 for the "Best Figure Composition" with his *Romance and Potatoes*. A large composition, the canvas depicts a young girl who rests on weather-beaten porch steps, while her wrinkled grandmother sits nearby peeling potatoes.

Formerly a commercial artist with an engraving company in Indianapolis, Wood had left the city during the summer of 1928 to join his brother Carl who was working in Taos.

The younger of the two, Carl had been living there since 1927 when he had bundled his wife and two small children into an automobile and headed to New Mexico. Upon his arrival, he had been befriended by Walter Ufer, one of the members of the famed "Taos Ten," who had given him free rein in his studio while on visits to New York during the winter.[19] Soon after getting settled, Carl had begun growing a beard, "partly for the fun of it and partly for the purpose of fitting more properly into the Western atmosphere of high-top boots, bandannas and overalls. When winter came," he said, "I found that the beard came in very handy while painting snow scenes in zero weather. So I decided to keep it."[20]

* * *

1932 Even the most ardent of Salon supporters found it difficult to focus on planning the 1932 exhibition. Unemployment figures were soaring into the millions, and Congress was responding with a series of relief bills to prop up industry and create new jobs. Despite widespread economic hardship, Association members were determined to maintain the high standards that had been established by the Salon committees in former years.

Those serving on the Art Prize Fund Committee could do little about the donors who declined to sponsor a prize, however, and the number of merit awards dropped by nearly a half. The 1932 show opened with only fourteen prize categories. Among the missing were: $400 for "Best Picture by Woman Artist After the Shaffer Prize Award," $200 for "Best Still Life in Oil," $200 for "Best Figure Composition," $100 for "Best Pastel," $200 for "Best Landscape by Woman Artist," $200 for "Best Portrait in Oil by Woman Artist," $100 for "Best Garden Scene," $100 for "Best Portrait of a Child" and $200 for "Best Work, Made of Limestone, Which Can Be Embodied in Architectural Design."

Faced with the reality of a smaller Salon, Mrs. King had little choice but to put cost-cutting measures into force. Guests to the Preview Party on Saturday evening found themselves attending a scaled-down reception that was limited to several guest speakers and the announcement of awards. Later in the week, visitors to the show would discover that the practice of holding teas in the gallery had been ended at the suggestion of the executive chairman.

One newspaper reporter felt that this change, in fact, resulted in a better exhibition. "This doing away with a seven-years' precedent means that the time which was given to sipping tea can now be given to a closer study of art," she explained. "It is evident that the serving of tea is not always a necessary adjunct of hospitality: Never has there been a greater spirit of friendliness at a Hoosier Salon than that which now irradiates the six galleries given over to Indiana art."[21]

In breaking yet another tradition, a special attraction had been added to the Salon with the hope of boosting attendance. Choosing the work of a widely popular artist, the Association had filled its sixth gallery with thirty-four oil paintings and eight etchings by Will Vawter of Nashville, Indiana. Hosting such a one-man show within the larger exhibition appeared to be a wise decision as gallery-goers crowded to see the painter's work. Well known as the illustrator for many of James Whitcomb Riley's poems, Vawter was also closely identified with the Brown County art colony since moving there in 1904.[22] From his studio home high atop a ridge outside Nashville, he had a commanding view across the valley floor for his landscape work.

Aside from his painting, "Bill"—as Vawter was affectionately called by his southern Indiana neighbors—had an "insatiable love for chess. He played checkers, of course, but chess was his *pièce de résistance*. He would drop any chore or task to plunge into a thrilling and 'speedy' game of chess. He would sit at a chess board for hours, eyeing the pawns, castles, queens and bishops, and there was never an interruption in the players' concentration aside from an occasional 'Oh,' 'Huh?' or 'Now, let's see.'"[23]

At the close of the Salon, Vawter's unsold paintings were returned to Nashville, and, as had been the practice for several years, many of the 273 exhibition pieces were tagged to be sent on tour. Mrs. King shipped all of the stone sculpture and watercolors to Bloomington, Indiana, where they were to be shown at the university there. A number of the remaining artworks were slated for display in Bozeman, Montana, and then at the University of North Dakota.[24] Another large group of Salon paintings was to be hung in Terre Haute, Indiana, for two weeks before traveling to the Fort Wayne Woman's Club and the Spink-Arms Hotel in Indianapolis.

A collection of selected paintings from the eighth Hoosier Salon opened at the Spink-Arms in early May of 1932. Commending the hotel management "for the interest it has shown in furthering the Indiana art movement by generously sponsoring this exhibition,"[25] one reporter was particularly impressed with the variety of activities that had been organized to complement the two-week exhibition. In addition to the customary art talks, gallery tours and programs of music that were scheduled each day during the show, a demonstration of "the modeling in clay of a portrait head by (sculptress) Mrs. Emma Sangernebo"[26] was held for the education of hotel visitors.

* * *

1933 Still in the depths of a Depression that was ravaging the country, Association members struggled to keep the Salon on track. Because of John Shaffer's generosity, their Hoosier Gallery on Wacker Drive stayed open; with the support of long-standing patrons, their show was able to continue as in years' past. Saluting those who had worked to this end, Eva Gough—a member of the Indiana Women's Press Association—wrote in the Foreword to the catalogue for the 1933 show: "By foresight, by ability, by unselfish effort, the foundation laid in happier times has proved adequate to sustain the peak of the load in the present frantic confusion of external conditions."[27]

The Saturday night reception at Marshall Field gave a gala send-off to the guests who had assembled for the opening of the 1933 Hoosier Salon. Nearly eight hundred people—the largest crowd ever in attendance at an opening party—forgot their troubles for a few hours as they mixed and mingled to admire the 254 pieces on display and find out who had won prizes from the $2,050 purse. They were pleased to learn that, despite the weakened economy, cartoonist Harold Gray of New York City had agreed to sponsor a new award. He had donated $150 in the name of his *Orphan Annie* character for the category: "Outstanding Portrait of a Child in Oil."

Heartened by public response to last year's "show-within-a-show" by Will Vawter, Association members had set aside their sixth gallery for another one-man exhibition. For the 1933 Salon, they had offered the space to Frank V. Dudley who hung thirty-nine of his landscapes and lake views in a solo show there. Known throughout the Midwest, the Chicago artist had been painting the dune land of Indiana along Lake Michigan since 1911. "For the weary, they (the dunes) offer an ideal place to rest; for the energetic, an opportunity to try out the limits of physical endurance; for the dreamer, a fairyland; for the scientist, an almost unequalled spot for study; and for the artist, inspiration for unlimited endeavor,"[28] Dudley had said, in describing his fascination with the place.

A methodical painter, he first would walk over the dunes to find a view that interested him. Later he would go back with his brushes, canvas and easel to work. "I never take my outfit with me the first day; I hike around until I find a scene I like. Then I put up a stick to mark the spot and study the scene carefully for fifteen or twenty minutes. I never look further for fear of being confused," Dudley explained. "After I have studied the scene, I come home and dream about it. By the next day, I have it already painted in my mind. I arrive with my outfit about two or three hours early, so I won't have to hurry with the shadows. I put them in as I remember them. Then as they come, I see them as they are. Sometimes I like what I painted better than what is there."[29]

As it had the prior year, the Salon's Feature Room—billed as "A Special Gallery of Paintings by Frank V. Dudley, Celebrated Dunes Painter"— proved effective in attracting people to the show. In a wrap-up meeting after the show had closed, Mrs. King noted that twenty-four works of art had been sold, bringing in $2,476 for the Association and its artists. Eight Dudley paintings had been purchased, and a ninth had been reserved for sale as soon as the bank situation stabilized.[30]

"We feel, in view of the unfavorable weather and the general business conditions, that we have made a marvelous record," the executive chairman of the Association reported. "We found, in checking up the purchasers, that few pictures had been returned to Indiana. Most of them went to former Hoosiers living in and near Chicago. One picture was purchased for a Wisconsin family.

"The three-day extension (after the scheduled closing date of the Salon on February 11) brought many more out-of-town visitors," she continued. "The interest and the gallery visitors continued until the very last hour. Mr. Dudley is receiving a number of requests for exhibitions outside of Chicago as a result of his one-man show."[31] So many people were interested in his paintings of the Indiana dunes, in fact, that Marshall Field & Company asked Dudley if he would allow his canvases to hang in the gallery space until March 1.

* * *

1934 Grateful for having survived the hard times, the Association dedicated the 1934 Salon to those sponsors who had supported the show since its inception. It invited President William Cullen Dennis of Earlham College to make the principal address at Saturday night's Preview Party. On behalf of the Earlham alumni in Chicago who had helped the Daughters of Indiana establish the Hoosier Salon, he asked—and answered— the question of "What Makes Indiana Great?"[32]

The Association also honored Kappa Kappa Kappa Sorority, a group of Indiana women whose interest centered on educational and philanthropic work, for its involvement by including a section on the club's history in the 1934 catalogue. In addition, Tri Kappa's past grand president Dorothy Donald was asked to compose the Foreword for the catalogue. Lavish with her praise, she wrote: "With the advantages from organization (through the Association), many clubs of the state are contributing much to the artistic life of their communities. Perhaps no participation among the Patrons is so generous and so effective as is that of the Tri Kappa Sorority. From the time that one of its members, as president of the Daughters of Indiana in Chicago, had much to do with the launching of the Hoosier Salon movement, the support of this great charitable organization has been constant."[33]

Since 1931, Tri Kappa had been holding art exhibitions "in various parts of the State; art was promoted in every possible way; pilgrimages made to art colonies; with the result that great art appreciation was developed."[34] The group also had funded significant merit awards during the early years of the Salon's existence and then had switched to underwriting purchase prizes in 1932. Paintings selected in this manner became part of the club's collection and were circulated from chapter to chapter after the Salon closed each year.

As in past shows, members of Tri Kappa were instrumental in shaping the 1934 Salon. They planned the Saturday night Preview Party, handled the arrangements for all receptions during the two-week run, helped staff the sales committee and stood ready to provide gallery tours at a moment's notice. The club's art chairman Josephine Davis of Marion, Indiana, was doubly involved after her painting *A Sunny Lane* had been juried into the show. An artist as well as an art advocate, she had exhibited in earlier Salons, drawing critical notice with her entry in the 1932 Salon. Writing for the *Indianapolis Star,* Lucille Morehouse had noted of this piece: "Josephine Davis, well known as an enthusiastic worker in the Municipal Art Association of Indiana and other art movements of the state, is represented with a charming little landscape, *Greasy Creek, Brown County.*"[35]

Convinced that their "show-within-a show"— used during the 1932 and 1933 Salons—had drawn additional crowds, Association members decided to enlarge the "special gallery" concept. Instead of limiting it to one person, though, they opted to "favor as many artists as possible in this exhibition space."[36] Because there was a large number of landscape painters in the Association, an invitation was sent to each one of them whose work had been admitted into prior Salons. They were encouraged to enter two pictures for the Feature Gallery of "The Beauty Spots of Indiana."

Not surprisingly, the tenth Hoosier Salon was dominated by canvases portraying the Hoosier countryside. Gallery-goers delighted in the pastoral scenes, but C. J. Bulliet of the *Chicago Daily News* found several of them to be "trite, as trite as a village preacher or as a lecturer on art before a woman's club, but also in as deadly earnest."[37] Despite his disappointment with such work, this art critic was encouraged by many of the Salon's offerings. "Sentiment is a part of the spirit of rustic Indiana," he declared, after singling out some of the pieces for an approving nod. "It is in painting Hoosier rusticity that the Indiana artists are at their most promising."[38]

* * *

1935 In the Foreword to the 1935 Hoosier Salon catalogue, George T. Buckingham—one of the Association's Chicago Vice-Presidents—applauded his organization for its ongoing efforts to bring "art creators and art lovers" together. "In its permanent home on Wacker Drive and in its other exhibits throughout the land," he wrote, "the Hoosier Salon carries on its work three hundred and sixty-five days in the year, but its annual exhibit here is the climax of its year and the major event on the calendar of its art-loving clientele."[39]

Aware of the necessity of attracting new patrons and being visible year-round, the Association had expanded its practice of booking exhibitions in venues across the Midwest. Every season, between twenty-five to thirty shows were sent from the Hoosier Art Gallery to schools, colleges, universities, libraries and women's clubs upon request. Although the Salon never circulated intact, many of its prizewinning paintings were included if the permission of the artist or purchaser had been obtained.

Requests for such bookings had even come from the East Coast. The alumni associations of both Indiana University and Purdue University as well as a club of some three hundred members within the New York Telephone Company had expressed an interest in bringing a Salon showing to the Northeast. They were prepared to finalize the plans "when financial conditions [were] more favorable to such a venture."[40]

With increasing its roster as an ever-present goal, the Association nurtured the good-natured competition between Indiana cities and towns that were vying to win a Salon painting for enrolling the largest number of new members each year. It funded the project, as it had in earlier shows, by the sale of exhibition catalogues for fifteen cents. The Association, in addition, encouraged the participation of groups from across the state in its activities. In 1935, it was proud to extend a special welcome to the Indiana Federation of Clubs whose members were visiting the Salon as a group for the first time.[41]

"Club Days" continued to play an important part in the Salon, just as they had since the opening of the first exhibition in 1925. The galleries were especially crowded at those times as club members joined their friends for private luncheons, gallery tours and other special programs. The events planned for the DePauw Alumni Association of Chicago, for example, included a luncheon in the Wedgwood Room at Marshall Field's, a musical recital, an art talk about "The Beauty at DePauw" and a gallery tour led by one of the artists.

The 1935 show, still suffering from the effects of the Depression, was a modest one. Choosing not to set aside space for a Feature Room, the Association, instead, used all six galleries for the 192 works that had been juried into the Salon. Carolyn G. Bradley, an artist whose work had appeared in every Salon, was again singled out by the jury for special merit. She won the $50 "Best Watercolor" award with her entry *The Studio*.

Formerly a teacher at Emmerich Manual Training High School in Indianapolis, Miss Bradley had taken the position of assistant professor in the Department of Fine Arts at Ohio State University in 1932. Widely recognized for her vivid watercolors, this native of Richmond, Indiana, would go on to be appointed as an art consultant with the Inter-American Educational Foundation in 1946. She also would be named as a visiting professor in art to the University of Chile in 1946 and to the University of Costa Rica in 1951.

While in Santiago, Chile, Miss Bradley taught a group of university students that met for ten hours each week. "During the course, which I conducted in Spanish, emphasis was placed on originality, and much of the work executed was from memory or from imagination," she later wrote in a report detailing her experiences at the university. "This method of self-expression was stressed because it would enable the students to work by themselves later. The students were very proud of these paintings for it was different, in most cases, from some of the copy-work they had previously done."[42]

Like Miss Bradley, Lillie Fry Fisher was another of the familiar faces in the Salon; she won a purchase prize given by the Chicago Associate Chapter of Tri Kappa Sorority for her oil *The Landing*. A scene of the New England coast, this landscape

was a new venture for the painter who usually displayed still lifes and flower subjects. "I threw away yards of canvas until I was satisfied with my boats," explained the artist who was known professionally as Fry Fisher. "I even had a bonfire back of my studio. My still life has been accepted in Philadelphia and New York, and I wished to bring my boat pictures to the same standard."[43]

* * *

1936 The 1936 Hoosier Salon opened on a thoughtful note. During the past year, the art world of Indiana had lost William Forsyth and Gaar Williams, and a memorial exhibition for each of them had been incorporated into the show. In a room adjoining one of the main galleries, the Association had set up a small display honoring Forsyth who had died in March of 1935. Hung on its damask-covered walls were three paintings—*Broken Country, Self Portrait* and *Still Life Flowers*—that were representative of Forsyth's efforts in landscape, portraiture and still life. The work had been selected from his studio in Irvington by Wilbur D. Peat, the director of the Herron Museum of Art, and lent to the Salon by his widow, Mrs. Alice Forsyth.[44]

In addition, the Salon catalogue carried an "In Memoriam" that was dedicated to this painter who had trained two generations of Indiana's artists. George Chambers Calvert, in writing for the Indianapolis Art Association, said of Forsyth, the last surviving member of the Hoosier Group:[45] "If it were sought to epitomize his character in one word, that word would be vitality. Inevitably, such a man is positive; and Forsyth was strongly assertive in his convictions and aggressive in his activities. He held staunchly to his artistic creed and in denunciation of fads and frauds gave no quarter. This same intensity pervaded all the relations of his life. . . . To his students, he gave entire devotion."[46]

The Salon's second memorial, a tribute to cartoonist Gaar Williams who had died in June of 1935, was installed in the Feature Room. There gallery-goers were treated to a lively retrospective of this Richmond, Indiana, native whose work was syndicated in newspapers across the country at the time of his death. Among the 113 pieces on display were six drawings completed after Williams had visited an exhibit of Japanese prints. Entitled *Six Caricatures in a Japanese Print Manner*, they had been done as the result of a wager won by Williams that he could forego his cartooning techniques to turn out a series of Japanese-style illustrations.[47]

After studying the 237 works admitted to the

show, the jury selected *Frightened Horses* by W. Karl Steele as the "Outstanding Picture of the Exhibition." The $500 prize was especially welcomed by the artist who, as a penny-stretching art student, had traded one of his paintings for an appendectomy some months earlier. In his last year at Herron Art School, Steele had done the prizewinning oil in his advanced composition class. In order to enter it in the Salon, he had to obtain special permission to finish the painting in advance of other classwork and guarantee its return for the senior exhibit in June.[48]

As soon as the last piece from the 1936 show had been shipped for the traveling exhibitions, Association members plunged into organizing a Summer Hoosier Salon. They had been talking about little else since the management of the Spink-Wawasee Hotel at Lake Wawasee, Indiana, had approached them with the idea. Initially planned as an exhibition of Hoosier paintings to be held in conjunction with the opening of the hotel's new convention hall,[49] the show was later enlarged to include crafts.

The first—and only—Summer Salon opened on June 27, 1936. It was a race with the clock for sculptor C. Warner Williams, who volunteered to act as a one-man hanging committee, to have everything in its place for the Saturday night celebration.[50] The jury—composed of Elmer Taflinger of Indianapolis, L. O. Griffith of Nashville, and Emil Jacques, head of the art department of the University of Notre Dame—was rushed as well. Dodging construction workers who were hurrying to finish the one-story building in time for the dedication, the three sorted through several hundred entries to choose 105 pieces of fine art for display.

Following the tradition established in Chicago, artists, patrons and cottagers from around the lake were invited to a Preview Party in the barely completed hall next to the Spink-Wawasee Hotel. As in the Winter Salon, they were treated to welcoming speeches, a short musical concert and the presentation of awards. Among the artists who split the $1,125 purse were Wilbur Peat with his *Summer Afternoon* ($100, "Outstanding Painting of Lake Wawasee"), Simon P. Baus with *Florence* ($100, "Outstanding Portrait in Oil") and C. Curry Bohm with his *Valley of June* ($50, "Outstanding Summer Landscape").[51]

In addition to the fine art awards, four bronze medals were presented to the winners in different divisions of the art crafts. The forty-two pieces of handicraft in the Salon had been assembled by the Indiana Federation of Art Clubs whose members were vocal proponents of the "crafts movement."[52]

Soliciting pieces from eleven artists, they had pushed batik hangings, copper and silver jewelry, ceramics, hooked rugs and decorated screens to the forefront of the summer-long exhibition. "We know that the public will buy original handicraft for the home if such things are presented to them at reasonable prices," explained Federation president Mrs. Leonidas F. Smith.[53]

* * *

1937 It was hard to ignore the devastating floods that left nearly a million people homeless three days before the opening of the 1937 Salon. Thousands upon thousands of people living along the Mississippi and Ohio rivers were evacuated, and property damage was estimated to be over four hundred million dollars. Providing a stark contrast to the destruction of the rampaging waters were the creative offerings on display in the Marshall Field Picture Galleries.

The disparity between the two was noted by art critic Lucille E. Morehouse in her commentary on the show for the *Indianapolis Star*. Expressing sympathy for the tragedies unfolding across the Midwest, she wrote: "There is an undercurrent of sorrow in the heart of all of us who have come from Indiana or from other flood-stricken states to attend the . . . Hoosier Salon. I sincerely wish that all the homeless and the suffering ones might be transported here to have a glimpse of the many beautiful paintings that are displayed."[54]

In addition to the 213 artworks that had been chosen from over six hundred entries, Association members decided to hasten spring with a showing of floral scenes in their sixth gallery. According to the 1937 exhibition catalogue: "As it has been our custom to set aside one gallery for a special exhibition, this year we have made a Gallery of Flower Paintings. These pictures are exhibited by invitation. They have been judged by the jury and are offered to the public with the hope that many of them will find permanent places in private homes or public buildings."[55] Among the thirty-nine artists whose paintings were admitted to this special room were Simon P. Baus, Dale Bessire, C. Curry Bohm, Karl C. Brandner, Charles Dahlgreen, Edgar Forkner, Marie Goth, Carl Graf, L. O. Griffith, Lucie Hartrath, Will Vawter and John Zwara.

The Feature Room was the hit of the show for the weather-weary crowds. According to one writer, "In this gallery, men—as well as women—were rested and refreshed and sometimes thrilled by the bouquets of blossoms that brought a breath of the outdoors and the fragrance of old-fashioned gardens. . . . It was a treat to watch the expression of pleasure and delight that came into the face of a 'tired businessman' as he stood not far from me and looked at Marie Goth's beautiful large picture of peonies—pink and white and deep rose-red—in a setting of velvety dark green. Here he comes back again. I hope he is deciding to buy the canvas for an over-mantel picture!"[56]

Upon the close of the thirteenth Salon, Association members congratulated themselves. Not only had they kept their show going through the Great Depression, but they had taken it to new heights: exhibition crowds were increasing, and enthusiastic new patrons had been enlisted into the Salon art movement. Unknown to them, however, Meier S. Block—president of the William H. Block Company in Indianapolis—had approached an Indianapolis woman's club with a novel idea.

In a letter to Mrs. (Walter S.) Lottie Lyons Grow, chairman of the Art Department of the Woman's Department Club, he had suggested: "I would like to give you a luncheon announcing the first showing of the first Hoosier Salon in our store. I have been wanting to do something like this to dedicate our new auditorium to honor my mother. Invite as many as you like. You will be my guests. You may choose your date."[57]

After outlining Block's notion to Mrs. King of the Association, Mrs. Grow received nothing but delighted support from Salon headquarters in Chicago. Arrangements were made for mounting an exhibition in the Hoosier capital. Invitations were sent to art aficionados in both Indiana and Illinois, and seventy-three Salon artists selected one or two of their paintings from the most recent show for inclusion. The Indianapolis version of the Chicago Hoosier Salon opened at Block's department store on April 26, 1937. Sponsored by the Art Department of the Woman's Department Club, the project proved a worthy achievement for the group that had been founded in 1912 to promote artistic and educational growth in Indianapolis.

"No one would have dreamed that the big auditorium on the sixth floor of Block's could be transformed into a number of delightful art galleries. . . . But to find a series of intimate little galleries, where everything could be just as cozy and homey as a Hoosier welcome itself, was almost as much of a surprise as to find a fairy queen ruling her court," marveled a newspaper reporter. "Some of these galleries afford four wall surfaces, instead of three, for the hanging of pictures. Tinted a deep cream, these built-in walls have a continuous line of overhead lights, so arranged that the light is thrown upon the pictures and not into the eyes of the gallery visitors. The narrow baseboard line is painted black."[58]

Borrowing the idea of a "Popularity Prize" from the first Salon in Chicago, the sponsors of the show at Block's decided to give a "popular vote" award. Each visitor was given a ballot upon entering the galleries and encouraged to indicate his or her favorite artwork before leaving. The votes were counted on the closing day of the exhibition. The artist whose work had received the highest number of ballots during the two-week show was awarded the "Popular Prize" of $100, donated by the president of Block's.[59]

* * *

1938 Good-natured fun abounded when the Preview Party for the 1938 show featured a musical tour of those Indiana schools that had helped with the Salon art movement. Collegiate rivalries were put aside, as alumni guests from Purdue, Wabash, DePauw, Indiana, Butler, Earlham, Franklin, Indiana State Teachers and Notre Dame gathered at Marshall Field's for the Saturday night event. They were entertained by a musical concert presented by the Interfraternity Glee Club of Chicago. Starting with "Back Home Again in Indiana" and ending with "On the Banks of the Wabash," the group—representing twelve fraternities and eight colleges in the Midwest—hit all the right notes with its sentimental performance.[60]

Particularly proud that evening were the alumni of Culver Military Academy; information about their school and its lengthy involvement with the Salon had been recorded in the exhibition's program. "For many years, Culver has given a prize at the Salon, and apparently the stimulation to young artists has been fruitful in their later work," Colonel F. L. Hunt had written in the catalogue. "Over the years, there have been showings of Salon exhibits at the Academy. . . . This year's prize is on the Selection Purchase plan, so that another work of some young Hoosier artist will be added to the other paintings at Culver."[61]

Dominating the wall space in the first gallery were four life-size portraits of men who were closely identified with the growth of Culver.[62] Painted by Wayman Adams, the oils—*Edwin Raymond Culver, Bertram B. Culver, Admiral Hugh Rodman* and *General Leigh Robinson Gignilliat*—had been lent to the Salon for its two-week run by the school's Board of Trustees. The remaining 220 pieces in the show were divided among four galleries, and a "Gallery of Watercolors" with thirty paintings was designated as the Feature Room. Each of the artist members had been invited to submit one additional watercolor that was passed on by the jury for inclusion in this year's "show-within-a-show."

16

The offerings of the 1938 Salon drew varied reactions from the art critics. Helen Magner of the *New Castle Courier-Times* pointed out that "[t]he jury selected rather conservative types of pictures, with a pleasant balance of landscape and portraits."[63] Eleanor Jewett of the *Chicago Daily Tribune* found the display to be "a pleasant exhibit, with somewhat the same type of pictures to which previous Hoosier Salons have accustomed us."[64] And C. J. Bulliet of the *Chicago Daily News* concluded that the Hoosier artists "are sacrificing honest observation and smell of the soil for the deadly humdrum of American cut-and-dried 'contemporaryism.' It's a disheartening show to those of us who still yearn for 'rugged individualism.' Formerly the Hoosiers had something to say, even though they said it badly. Now they have nothing to say that somebody hasn't said better heretofore."[65]

One of the pieces singled out for critical approval was *Scottish Piper* by Charles Sneed Williams. Winner of the $200 "Best Portrait in Oil" prize, it was praised for being a "startlingly brilliant canvas, . . . a magnificent piece of painting and an intriguing study of a personality. The piper fairly comes alive as you look at him."[66] Ironically, after being rejected by the Salon jury of 1937, the *Piper* had been shipped to Washington, D. C., instead, for display in an American art exhibition at the Corcoran Gallery.[67]

Following the close of the 1938 Salon, most of the paintings were crated and sent to Fort Wayne, LaPorte and Terre Haute for limited showings. By mid-March, though, the artworks were reassembled for the April 4 opening of the second annual Hoosier Salon in Indianapolis. Again sponsored by the Art Department of the Woman's Department Club, the exhibition— showcasing 125 pieces by ninety-eight painters and sculptors—was held for twelve days in the auditorium of the William H. Block Company. For the second year, Meier S. Block had underwritten the "popular vote" prize, increasing his support from $100 to $200 and renaming it the "William H. Block Award."[68]

The members of the Art Department were relieved that the details had fallen into place for another outstanding show. The artists were pleased with the venture, too. Marie Goth had written from her home in Brown County: "The showing of the . . . Hoosier Salon has come and gone. . . . For me, it has been a very happy experience. . . . I cannot help but hope that the Woman's Department Club will continue to sponsor the Hoosier Salon in Indianapolis, just as the Daughters of Indiana have done in Chicago."[69]

The management at Block's was also in favor of the notion of an Indianapolis Hoosier Salon. After the show was over, the department store president had commended the chairman of the Art Department: "In bringing these outstanding exhibits of art to our city and state, I feel that you are making definite cultural progress, . . . and we appreciate your giving the William H. Block Company the opportunity to help you accomplish this project. Please be assured we shall do everything we can in our power to continue this excellent work."[70]

* * *

1939 Association members and their friends fêted the 1939 Hoosier Salon with an especially elegant Preview Party. One guest recalled the Saturday night affair: "Together we set out in a drizzling rain with slush underfoot. We arrived just a few minutes before eight. We thought we'd be the first ones there, but we saw others alighting from taxis. This time, the invitations were asked for as we entered the Marshall Field's store, and I very proudly produced mine.

"After having divested ourselves of coats and galoshes, we proceeded by elevator to the second floor," she continued. "Above the arched entrance were the words, 'Hoosier Salon.' Through another arch wreathed in smilax, we could see into a second room where hung the first prize picture of the exhibition with a garland of smilax about it and the coveted old gold badge of distinction in the lower left corner. . . . As the evening wore on, more and more people crowded into the rooms until they were full to overflowing. The gowns of the women made a lovely picture. There were shimmering satins of all shades, rustling taffetas with bouffant skirts like those of our great-grandmothers, brocaded velvets and black lace and chiffons. The high head dress was in evidence but did not predominate."[71]

The glittering crowd reflected the high spirits of Salon patrons; the exhibition was larger than it had been for several years. Five of the galleries were turned over to a display of 254 paintings, etchings and pieces of sculpture, and the sixth was set aside as a "Gallery of Landscapes." As in past Salons, an invitation had been sent to artist members—this year to the outstanding landscapists in the group— asking them to submit one picture for the Feature Room. Among the twenty-three whose work had been juried into this show-within-a-show were Dale Bessire, C. Curry Bohm, V. J. Cariani, Frank V. Dudley, Edgar Forkner, Carl C. Graf, Lucie Hartrath, Leota Loop, Edward K. Williams and Will Vawter.

Focusing on the oil paintings in the Feature Room, Association members made an extra effort to help market this artwork. Publicity material for the fifteenth annual show was straightforward about their expectations: "We trust that the general public and friends of this Association who visit this room (Gallery of Landscapes) will show their personal appreciation by purchasing these canvases. This room affords a very unusual opportunity for comparison in values, also, an opportunity to add another picture to your already established Indiana collection or to begin a collection if you do not have one."[72] The exhibition catalogue even carried an advertisement for these landscapes as well, reminding gallery-goers that "every picture in the room is for sale."[73]

The art critics were pleased with the offerings of the 1939 Salon. After applauding the show for being one which "embraces many stunning paintings,"[74] Eleanor Jewett of the *Chicago Tribune* devoted a portion of her review to chastising the art lovers in the state of Illinois: "There is no exhibition held in Chicago that has the list of prize donors which the Hoosier Salon boasts. Indiana schools, universities, societies, business firms, newspapers and individuals contribute to swell the number and amounts of prizes each year.[75]

"Were even one-half of the names to back an All-Illinois Society of the Fine Arts (our nearest organization in kind to the Hoosier Salon) exhibit, the president and officers of that society would probably swoon. It just isn't done in Illinois—this taking a genuine interest in Illinois art," she scolded. "And a pity it is this should be so. You will find that many of the artists in the Hoosier Salon are from or are associated with Illinois. They must go out of their state, however, to find encouragement."[76]

The painter who took the $500 "Outstanding Work in Oil of the Exhibition" prize had definite Hoosier ties, though. He was a member of the faculty at John Herron Art School in Indianapolis. Winning the award on the day of his wedding, the twenty-six-year-old Edmund Brucker had been secretive about his marriage plans. His friends had been vague as well. "I know that Brucker was married yesterday, and that's about all anybody knows about it," explained Donald Mattison, director of Herron and one of Brucker's closest associates. "Mr. Brucker said he didn't want any fuss over the ceremony."[77] The newlyweds did manage to get to Chicago after their 3 p.m. wedding in Indianapolis; they were sitting in the front row when Brucker's name was announced at the Preview Party.[78]

At the close of the Salon on February 11, the artwork was prepared for smaller shows around Indiana. One group was sent to Terre Haute, another to South Bend, and a third was displayed at the Ball State Teachers College in Muncie and the Museum of Fine Arts and History in Evansville.[79] During the last two weeks of March, a large part of the Chicago exhibit was on view at the third annual Hoosier Salon in Indianapolis. Sponsored by the Art Department of the Woman's Department Club, the show—featuring most of the prizewinning pieces— again was held in the auditorium galleries of the William H. Block Company.[80]

18

1942
Clifton Wheeler
A Rainy Morning
Outstanding Painting by Public School Teacher

1943
Frederick Polley
Old Houses, Charleston, South Carolina
Outstanding Landscape in Oil

1944
David Rubins
Garden Piece
First Prize—Sculpture

1945
C. Curry Bohm
Gray Hills of Winter
Outstanding Work in Oil

1946
Edmund Brucker
Planting the Seed
Outstanding Work in Oil

The Forties

1940 The Saturday night Preview Party for the 1940 Salon was a dramatic departure from the stately receptions of the past. As soon as the formalities of the evening were over, "a cowbell came ringing from the rear entrance and in ambled five shor-nuff hillbillies, the WLS Hoosier Hot Shots, out for an airing between broadcasts."[1] Sharing ten instruments among them, the musicians—who were dressed in overalls—brought the party to a standstill with their artistry on a mechanical washboard and a down-home rendition of "I Wish I Was Back in Indiana."

Despite the best efforts of this comical group, the mood was far from upbeat as the exhibition opened to the thunder of war in Europe. The crowds continued to come, however, and by show's end, more than twenty thousand people had streamed through the six Marshall Field galleries. Twenty-six paintings had been sold, as well, for a total of $3,365.[2] Slightly smaller than the 1939 show, the regular exhibition featured 230 juried artworks and a prize purse of $3,500. A new $100 award—"Outstanding Flower Painting" given by Mr. and Mrs. James Irving Holcomb of Indianapolis in memory of their daughter Jessie Mae—also had been added.[3]

As it had for the last several years, the Association had specified that one of its galleries be used as the Feature Room. For the second time, a "Gallery of Landscapes" had been set up in response to numerous requests for a repeat performance. After applauding some of the landscapists for their "sparkling and vivacious" work, one Chicago writer complained about the relatively large size of the canvases in the special gallery.

"[I]t would have made for a far more popular room had the painters sent in little pictures for variety," she noted in her coverage of the show. "One can think of any number of subjects that would lend themselves easily to a small canvas. The visitor would fall in love with these on the spot and carry them off. After all, it is the purpose of these shows to put pictures from the studio into the home or school or club, so why not ask the artists to con-

tribute the little canvas for which there is always room? A large painting is something of a problem in these days of apartments and low ceilings."[4]

Singled out as a crowd favorite, especially with the local visitors, was Wayman Adams' entry entitled *Duet*. A portrait of Chicago's sculptor Albin Polasek and painter Rudolph Ingerle, the piece had been sketched from life. "It began at a party where these two Czechs made the welkin ring with the songs they sang and the dances they danced," explained one newspaper account. "Mr. Adams, a guest, was fascinated by the picture the two men made. He had them come later to his studio where he painted this canvas, brushing it in broadly but capturing both personalities. Nor did he let them off lightly; he had them sing every moment of the time he painted."[5]

Deemed a show that "gets better and better each year,"[6] the Salon "has become one of the important features of Chicago's art winter," declared the *Chicago Tribune* critic. "In character, it is always more or less conservative, and because of that it lays itself open each year to scourging whips of vituperation on the part of modernist critics and to a surfeit of praise from the anti-modernist. . . . This year probably a similar play will be enacted, but this by-product of art exhibits is part of the fun. How deadly if all shows were alike, if all critics thought alike, if all visitors followed like sheep in each other's steps, unopinionated and softly complacent!"[7]

The Hoosier Salon closed on February 10 in Chicago; and fourteen days later, a more modest version opened in Indianapolis. Of the 230 pieces that had been displayed in the original exhibition, 187 paintings and works of sculpture had been collected for the showing at the William H. Block Company. Once again, the Indianapolis Hoosier Salon was sponsored by the Art Department of the Woman's Department Club; and once again, Block's department store had turned its sixth floor auditorium into a maze of cozy galleries for the two-week showing.

Guests to the evening preview on February 24

were treated like Hollywood film stars. "There were the spotlights, the movie camera, and one autograph seeker among those present," reported an *Indianapolis News* writer. "As artists and guests crowded through the entrance, they were faced with a battery of lights and artist Randolph Coats in the new role as cameraman. Randy, who has made a successful movie on the art colonies of the New England coast, was busily collecting many celluloid feet for his next box office hit on Indiana artists. Although reticent and modest about it all, the painters finally consented to be shot."[8]

"Th[at] series of scenes," indicated the *Indianapolis Star* critic, "will constitute a sequence to be used in a new movie in full color by Mr. Coats, a history of Indiana art, to be entitled *One Hundred Years of Art and Artists of Indiana*, on whose script he has been at work for three months. He will be assisted in a check-up of the data by Director W. D. Peat of the John Herron Art Museum. That Mr. Coats's first movie venture *New England Art Colonies*, filmed last summer at Cape Cod and Cape Ann, has been viewed by enthusiastic audiences over the state augurs well for the success of the movie in which Indiana artists will figure."[9]

* * *

1941 In a move that undoubtedly drew criticism, the Association's executive chairman asked C. J. Bulliet of the *Chicago Daily News* to write the Foreword for the 1941 Salon catalogue. As an advocate for the modern art movement, the feisty critic had rarely been sympathetic with the more traditional work of the Salon, and even he seemed surprised by the invitation. "I have been looked upon, in many quarters, in years past as a renegade in the matter of art in Indiana," he admitted in his note, "so much so that the rank-and-file of Hoosier artists probably will think Mrs. King should visit a psychiatrist for inviting me to do this foreword."[10]

Nonetheless, he held his biases in check to focus on the Association as a group, applauding it for a job well done. "The executive and her associates have not been content merely with seeing that the State of Indiana puts its best foot forward in the way of exhibiting its art to the world in the Hoosier Salon and in the year-round gallery it maintains at 211 West Wacker Drive," he wrote, "but they also have worked tirelessly and astutely at the task of raising prize money, so that annually the amount for distribution among native artists at the Salon is almost as large as the combined amounts in all other shows of the fine arts in Chicago, including the Art Institute's. Also, the Hoosier Salon ranks first as a selling organization

among the exhibiting societies, again including the Art Institute in any one of its annual shows."[11]

In his role as art critic, though, Bulliet was back in character as the strident liberal. According to his review of the 1941 show, "[t]he 17th annual Hoosier Salon is like unto its 16 predecessors in the mediocrity of paintings on display. With the most powerful and most generous art organization of its kind in the world back of them, the Indiana artists, somehow, can't 'make the grade.' . . . Can Hoosiers paint? The charitable answer is: Not yet. Maybe sometime.

"The one hopeful sign is that the Hoosiers are stubborn. They paint what they see, the way they see it, and not in accordance with 'Expressionism,' 'Cubism,' 'Surrealism,' or any other strange 'ism' that has made so much of our American art 'phony'—see any American or Chicago show, any season of the year at the Art Institute," he continued. "If ever a painting genius arises in Indiana—in Brown County, for example, or on the Lake Michigan dunes or in the Ohio River hills, he will find a way prepared for him, paved with honesty. Maybe Mrs. King and her Hoosier Salon Patrons Association are justified in keeping the candle light in the window."[12]

Undaunted by Bulliet's musings, more than seven hundred people braved a winter storm to attend the Preview Party on January 25. The highlight of the evening's program was the presentation of the life-size *Portrait of John T. McCutcheon* by Marie Goth. Commissioned by the Indiana Society of Chicago to execute a portrait of this dean of American cartoonists, Miss Goth and her painting were presented to a round of applause. Speaking in place of McCutcheon whose health was failing, the artist stood next to her portrait that had been displayed on a platform easel by the lectern. "I am grateful for this honor in the form of a commission," she said, "to paint this great man whose splendid co-operation has made this possible."[13] First as a member of the Art Prize Fund Committee and then as one of the Association's Chicago Vice-Presidents, McCutcheon had been involved with the Salon since its founding in 1925.

The show itself was the smallest yet. Only 120 artists were juried into the 185-piece Salon, and the Feature Room—a "Gallery of Flower Paintings"—added but twenty-five paintings to the exhibition total. The roll call of prize donors was changing as well. Lawrence A. Downs had died since the last Salon, and his $100 "Best Landscape in Oil Painted Along the Route of the Illinois Central Railroad in Indiana" award had been omitted. In its place, Psi Iota Xi Sorority of Indiana had stepped to the forefront. This women's group, founded in 1897 for the development of charitable, cultural and social activities, formally became a sponsor of the Salon by voting at its convention to underwrite three $100 purchase prizes.[14]

Sixteen days after closing in Chicago, the fifth annual Indianapolis Hoosier Salon opened under the auspices of the Art Department of the Woman's Department Club. As before, the management of the William H. Block Company worked long hours to turn the store's auditorium into attractive gallery space; this year the rooms were painted a soft, warm gray as background for the paintings. In addition, Block's display staff had installed a new lighting system for the exhibit. One newspaper reporter remarked "that [it] is as much like sunlight as scientific invention has been able to produce. As one looks at the white light coming down from the concealed electric fixtures, the first thought is that the sunlight is coming in from a skylight in the ceiling. I am told that the correct name of this particular kind of lighting is 'sunlight fluorescent.'"[15]

For the first time, almost all the pieces from the Chicago show had been shipped to Indianapolis with the exception of those that had been sold. Sales were down, and the artists were disappointed that so few of their paintings had been purchased during the Salon. After noting that the receipts—including purchase prizes—from Chicago amounted to little more than $3,000, Lucille Morehouse of the *Indianapolis Star* challenged the art-lovers of Indiana to top the record of their Chicago brethren in buying artwork from the Salon.

"It would seem that, in the capital city of the home state of the Hoosier artists, the total sales should average somewhere near that amount," she suggested. "When the United States government is spending billions of dollars for war equipment, certainly individual citizens of Indiana should be willing to spend something for that which refreshes and builds up the human soul rather than that which depresses and tears it down."[16]

Less than four months after the Woman's Department Club had closed its yearly show at Block's, the headquarters of the Hoosier Salon Patrons Association was moved from Chicago to Indianapolis. Several years in the making, the change was not unexpected. In 1939, Mrs. King had retired from her day-to-day duties as executive chairman of the Hoosier Art Gallery and had gone to Minneapolis to live with her son. From a distance, she had tried to supervise Association activities with the help of Mrs. Edward C. Twells as manager of the gallery.[17] Long-standing Salon lead-

ers George T. Buckingham, Lawrence A. Downs and John T. McCutcheon, all members of the Association's Chicago Vice-Presidents, had put their energies behind her attempt to manage from afar. During 1940, however, Buckingham and Downs had died, and McCutcheon had become infirmed with ill health.

When Association members were told their president, John C. Shaffer, wished to retire so that he might spend time in the West, discussions about relocating the Salon in Indianapolis became serious. On June 30, 1941, the Association's Board of Trustees voted to transfer both the annual exhibition and the year-round gallery to the Hoosier capital. The resignations of Shaffer and Mrs. King, who planned to move to California, were accepted; he was named president emeritus, and she was designated as counselor.[18]

Since Block's had been mounting the Indianapolis Salon on behalf of the Woman's Department Club for the preceding five years, the department store management offered its facilities to the Association on a permanent basis. It also donated two rooms in the State Life Building on Washington Street for the Hoosier Art Gallery.[19] Preserving much of the graciousness of the gallery on Wacker Drive, the new space used the hangings of taupe velvet taken down during the move from Chicago. Sections of the fabric covered the walls in the front gallery; and, in the back, they formed draperies for the large windows. A sturdy oak table and several filing cabinets from Chicago were incorporated into the decor as well.[20]

The gallery still needed furniture, though, and Mrs. (Leonidas F.) Katherine McLeod Smith of Indianapolis—named to replace Mrs. King as the Association's executive chairman and gallery director—responded to the challenge. According to an *Indianapolis Star* account, "the financial outlay (for furnishing the galleries) was comparatively small. . . . All but one of the upholstered chairs were bought from an unclaimed freight storage house of the New York Central Railway. The remaining upholstered chair cost only five dollars when selected from a trade-in group at a northside furniture store."[21] Even the artists were impressed. Complimenting her thriftiness, Randolph Coats told Mrs. Smith: "If you can sell like you buy, the Hoosier Gallery is going to be a great success."[22]

In honor of the Hoosier Salon's "homecoming," Mark C. Honeywell—assuming the office of vice-president with the turnover in Association leadership—invited the group to take part in a "Garden Festival." The industrialist from Wabash, Indiana, planned to open his eighty-acre estate during the middle of August for the benefit of the

Garden Club of Indiana, the Indiana State Symphony Society, the Hoosier Salon Patrons Association and the Indiana Society of Chicago. One journalist concluded that the event would be a time in which "[f]lowers, music, art and literature, one of the finest foursomes of man's existence, [would harmonize] for one week to delight"[23] those who could attend.

The Association's responsibilities for the affair were relatively simple: the group was to mount an art exhibition in the motion picture studio that had been built by Honeywell on the grounds of his estate. Within weeks of receiving the invitation, Mrs. Smith and her volunteers had put together a show that had been drawn in large part from last winter's Hoosier Salon. Five pieces of sculpture, sixty-four paintings and more than fifty etchings were arranged on the first three floors of the five-story building. Most of the work was for sale. The price tags ranged from a low of forty dollars for a Paul Beem piece to a high of $600, set by Frank V. Dudley for his *Under Changing Skies*. Etchings by Frederick Polley and George Jo Mess were also available for as little as one dollar.[24]

More than fifteen thousand people enjoyed the hospitality of the Hoosier philanthropist who scheduled a variety of special activities during his week-long "Garden Festival." Fabien Sevitsky, conductor of the Indianapolis Symphony Orchestra, led the State Symphony Orchestra in a performance; 164 members of the Black Horse Troop from Culver Military Academy passed in review before Indiana Governor Henry F. Schricker; and the Indiana Youth Orchestra of eighty-five youngsters presented a concert.[25]

The visual artists of Indiana had their day in the limelight as well. During an impassioned speech at the Festival, Mrs. Smith set forth her vision of the Association's role in developing Hoosier art. "Mr. Honeywell has provided us with a most auspicious beginning," she said. "And if the organization does not succeed with such a start, we will have failed miserably to make the most of the prestige and the statewide recognition which the Association is receiving through this fine festival.

"This is the weak link in the art history of Indiana: we produce more than we have been able to consume," she continued. "It is this public which must be reached, whose sales resistance to works of art must be annihilated in this campaign. Exhibitions are not enough. People meet their friends, drink a cup of tea and depart to await the next one.

"I intend to be as persistent as a book agent or as an insurance salesman. If a person says to me again, as many have in the past, 'I would love to own a picture but cannot afford it,' we will have a picture he or she can afford, at terms to suit the budget, notwithstanding the government's proposed restrictions on installment selling. With restrictions on the production of automobiles and washing machines, perhaps we'll have better luck."[26]

* * *

1942 Whether or not a painting sold seemed of little consequence as Association members—shaken by the bombing of Pearl Harbor some five weeks earlier—gathered to host their first Salon in Indianapolis. Instead of the joyful celebration they had envisioned during the summer, the show that opened in the Auditorium Galleries of the William H. Block Company was rather somber. The Preview Party was still crowded, though, as guests were welcomed to the event by Block's controller Samuel B. Walker. "We are grateful that in this time when ambition, savagery and barbarism are rampant in the world," he told the more than seven hundred party-goers, "we can offer a quiet retreat where Hoosier artists may display their creations and their self-expression and that we can enjoy an evening given over to culture, refinement and the enduring things of life."[27]

Talk of the nation's entry into the war dominated the night as well as set the tone for the Salon during its two-week run. The Veterans of Foreign Wars had teamed up with the Ladies Auxiliary to give a $300 purchase prize for a painting to be hung at the Indianapolis Veterans' Hospital, and a $100 Defense Bond had been offered by J. Wallace Barnes for the "Outstanding Still Life." Several of the exhibition's 145 artists had explored the subject in their work as well. Among the 261 pieces on display were Lillian Alt's *Men and Guns* and William A. Eyden's *Steel for Defense*.

One clubwoman even based her talk upon the topic at the Indiana Federation of Clubs "Special Day" on January 19. After paying tribute to Carole Lombard—the actress who had been killed in an airplane accident while flying home from a defense bond rally in Indianapolis—Federation president Mrs. Oscar A. Ahlgren told the assembled members. "It is up to the women of America to preserve the arts during the next few years," she said, "for if we do not do it, it will not be done. We are out to win this war. Everything we have will go into it. Demand upon demand will be made upon our time. . . . [It] is up to us to find new ways of living, and it is up to us to keep that which we have. The beautiful in life has been forgotten by the rest of the world, and when we say 'Remember Pearl Harbor,' let us remember what it is we are fighting for."[28]

As the speaker for the Federation luncheon, artist Randolph Coats steered his address away from thoughts of war. Instead, he selected artwork from the Salon with which to illustrate his ideas on how to compose a painting. "The moment you place an arrangement of forms upon a canvas, you make a composition," he explained. "And good pictures are organized and constructed—by consideration of line, dark and light masses and color—just as scientifically as an automobile or any other manufactured article. It is not difficult to recognize a bad composition. Most painters find it easy to avoid the obviously wrong, but there is a great gulf between what is not bad and what is really distinguished."[29]

By show's end, Association members were relieved to find that the Hoosier Salon had survived the difficulties of relocating; their transplanted show was declared a triumph. It had been an exhibition of changes, the most noticeable of which was a new look for the catalogue. In addition to an updated cover design that featured a pen-and-ink drawing of palette and brushes, the small booklet listed the names of the prizewinning artists along with the titles of their work. For the first time, photographs of many of these pieces were included as well as biographical information relating to the jurors. Addresses of the exhibitors were added, too, as was an advertisement that had been placed by the John Herron Art Institute.

A Hoosier Salon Executive Committee had also been formed by women from five of the organizations that were supporting the exhibition. With its members drawn from Psi Iota Xi Sorority, the Woman's Department Club, Tri Kappa Sorority, the Indiana Federation of Art Clubs and the Indiana Federation of Clubs, the Committee had handled the day-to-day details of the show. In Chicago, such responsibilities had been shouldered by the Daughters of Indiana. Each woman on the Executive Committee had served as a "Special Day Hostess" for at least one day during the Salon.[30]

* * *

1943 Under the direction of Mrs. Smith and Mrs. (J. E. P.) Beryl Holland—elected to the presidency of the Association upon Shaffer's retirement some eighteen months earlier—plans for the 1943 show stayed on course despite the burdens of war. Applauding their decision to proceed, Herman B Wells, president of Indiana University, had written in the Foreword to the Salon catalogue: "In the midst of a world aflame with the hatreds and destruction of war, there are groups and institutions on which must fall the responsibility of maintenance of those cultural values without which our

eventual victory would be hollow and without its full meaning. One of these groups which happily is continuing its work is the Hoosier Salon Patrons Association.

"This Association last year opened its first Indianapolis exhibit only a few days after this country entered the war. It had prepared for that exhibit in the days of peace. Now we have been at war for more than a year, and our thoughts and our energies have been devoted to the prosecution of the war. For that reason, there may be some who may have thought that the patrons of art in Indiana would consider abandonment of this exhibit. But such a thought never has entered the minds of those to whom an appreciative citizenry has entrusted the guardianship of a sacred fire and a consecrated trust."[31]

Although the number of guests for Saturday night's Preview Party had dropped from the highs of prior years, those who attended were welcomed by a profusion of spring flowers and the cascading sounds of harp music. According to a newspaper account of the evening, "[t]ables were decorated with bouquets of rose, orchid and white tulips and with yellow jonquils and acacia blossoms. Palms and low boxes of magnolia foliage decorated the auditorium. An attendance of 350 at the dinner party taxed Block's tea rooms to capacity and an additional twenty-five or more had to be taken care of at the Claypool Hotel."[32]

Of the 253 pieces in the show, those which depicted nude figures prompted close consideration by one art critic. "There are not many nude subjects in the exhibition," she noted in her "Books Plus Art" column, "but the largest picture in the watercolor gallery is a pastel group of three wholly nude figures and two others that are partly draped. A horizontal design, measuring about three by four feet, it represents a studio scene in a life class. An almost infinitesimal signature, the one word, 'Elmer,' (Taflinger) tells us who did this unusual composition. . . . There was a time when painting of the nude did not find favor with the Hoosier Salon management. Why the painted nude design did not find favor, while the one that was modeled in clay was accepted and exhibited, is more than I can explain."[33]

With the close of the Salon, Mrs. Smith and her volunteers turned their attention toward overseeing an ambitious traveling schedule for the paintings. They also began hanging a series of two-week shows in the Hoosier Art Gallery. Featured in this display space during the spring and summer months were the works of artists Frederick Polley, Edgar Forkner, Edna Cathell, Randolph Coats, Leota Williams Loop, Edmund Brucker, Sister

Rufinia, Clifton Wheeler, Johann Berthelsen and William A. Eyden.

In her review of Eyden's one-man exhibition, Lucille Morehouse of the *Indianapolis Star* dismissed the notion that the Richmond, Indiana, native could paint nothing but beech trees. "There are many who have associated Mr. Eyden's name with a particularly prolific period of popular beechwood landscapes," she explained. "The term 'potboilers' might well be applied to an inartistic but saleable type of beech tree painting that is turned out by artists because there is a demand from laymen who have had no art training and are not fitted by nature to be discriminating judges.

"A few years ago," the critic continued, "when I had a long illness and was unable to visit the exhibitions for many weeks, William A. Eyden was one of several obliging artists who brought their pictures to my home in order that comment might be made for the art department of the *Sunday Star*. Then were my eyes opened to the fact that the 'atrocious' beech tree pictures were, more or less, a commercial stunt. I also had the pleasure of viewing some exceedingly artistic work with other subjects by the so-called beech tree painter."[34]

In early October, Association members were saddened to hear of the death of John C. Shaffer in Chicago at the age of ninety. Even after the Salon had moved to Indianapolis, their former president had remained interested in the efforts of the group he had helped to found. The newspaper magnate, in addition, had continued to underwrite the "Outstanding Work in Oil of the Exhibition" award until 1943 when Block's had picked up the sponsorship under the name of the William H. Block Memorial.

Winner of Shaffer's $500 award during the 1942 Salon, Henrik Mayer remained grateful to this patron of the arts. "The prize was generous, to be sure," the painter said, "but most important of all, it meant that here was an important prize which allowed an established and nationally known jury of practicing artists to recognize and mark with distinction an outstanding picture without any of the biases or the demands of the donor. It was also an added mark of distinction when Mr. Shaffer sometimes agreed with the jury's selection and kept the picture for his own collection."[35] Such was the case with Mayer's prizewinning entry *Clara*; the portrait of a young girl in braids was the last piece to be added to Shaffer's art collection in this manner.

* * *

1944 As the war ground on, any thoughts of hosting special festivities to mark the twentieth

anniversary of the Salon were abandoned. Nonetheless, a scaled-down Preview Party—an informal buffet because of wartime rationing—kicked off the 1944 show with a flourish. "Artistry went hand in hand with Indiana fried chicken and 'trimmings,' for the tables were masterpieces of beauty, with fragrant gardenias on feathery greenery forming the center decorations which extended the full length of the long tables. Bowls of yellow daffodils and white tulips, like breaths of spring, were used on the round tables, and each guest received a gardenia which added zest to the fête."[36]

The exhibition of 305 artworks was influenced by the war as well. Of the 157 artists juried into the show, a number had tackled war-related subjects in their work. Among them were Vin Adams with his *Food Fights for Freedom* and *Fighters for American Freedom;* Claude Y. Andrews with *Democracy;* Garo Z. Antreasian with *Coast Guard Station, Metomkin;* William A. Eyden with *Steel for War;* Augustus C. Gondring with *Landscape, Northern Australia;* Marie Goth with *General Robert H. Tyndall;* and Donald M. Mattison with *War Show.*

Sgt. Gondring had shipped his painting—it later would win the $100 award for "Outstanding Landscape in Watercolor"—from his post in Australia, and S. F. C. Antreasian had sent his pieces from the Metomkin Inlet Coast Guard Station near Accomac, Virginia. "Another entry, from Karl Steele, stationed at Jackson, Michigan, was accompanied by a letter explaining he had just returned from a tour of army camps where he worked with chaplains and Red Cross members, drawing pictures at chapel and in the hospitals."[37]

For the first time, the Salon catalogue carried a notice regarding the sale of war bonds. Gallery-goers were invited "to help with the current Bond Sale for which the state of Indiana is asked to buy $233,000,000 worth of bonds and stamps. The Hoosier Salon Patrons Association will have a booth at the Auditorium entrance where Bond and Stamps may be purchased during the Hoosier Salon. Paintings by Indiana Artists will be given as Prizes to the Organization and Individual buying the largest number of Bonds and Stamps during the two weeks of the Salon."[38]

The War Bond prizes had been made possible by the generosity of Wayman Adams and Dale Bessire. Adams had contributed an oil painting entitled *Mother and Child* to be given to the individual making the largest bond purchase, and Bessire had made his *Chimney Peaks and Rhododendra* available to the organization buying the most bonds. During the final hours of the show, Bessire's offering was awarded to the American United Life

Insurance Company by Salon officials. Block's "purchased the painting from the artist and gave it to the Hoosier Salon as a gesture of co-operation with the Salon's sale of war bonds. Mr. Bessire, anxious to make a substantial contribution to the Fourth War Loan (Drive), set a very nominal price on this work, in view of the patriotic use to which it was to be put."[39]

Despite shortages due to the war, the Salon continued to attract thousands of visitors. Two days before the close of the show, attendance figures were at seventy-eight hundred people, and total sales amounted to $1,875. The exhibition, too, had remained a favorite of art fans living in Chicago. In a letter to the editor of the *Chicago Tribune*, one enthusiast had written: "As the standards of the Art Institute dropped during the past years, Chicago was privileged to view the annual Hoosier exhibit. This exhibit always measured up to a high standard. Indiana artists seem to have something on the ball when it comes to creating real works of art, the kind you can live with.

"Is it possible the Hoosiers have mastered the fundamentals of color and expression while their Chicago artist friends have been led down the wrong path? . . . Hoosier art sells as the records will show, while we hear the usual complaints of the Chicago exhibitors of 'no sale.' For some unknown reason, the annual Hoosier exhibit in Chicago has been discontinued. Can this exhibit not be revived here so we can have something to look forward to in the field of art each year? I am sure the Hoosier artists will give full cooperation."[40]

While the prospect of organizing a second exhibition in Chicago may have intrigued some in the Association, most were far too busy expanding the Hoosier Art Gallery to give it serious thought. During a fall remodeling project, two rooms were added to the suite, and a second assistant was appointed to help Mrs. Smith and her associate Mrs. (George A.) June H. Jobes. The extra space on the sixth floor of the State Life Building, donated by the William H. Block Company as owner of the building, was turned "into an attractive and altogether modern art gallery."[41]

According to one newspaper account, "the dusty-rose carpet of prewar quality—yards of it—covers the floor completely. . . and the fixtures for the indirect lighting system meant the only expense for the new gallery. . . . The two Italian carved pieces, a high-backed chair and a settee, both antiques that were in Mrs. Smith's family, and the two upholstered arm chairs had all been used in other rooms since the opening of the galleries more than three years ago. . . . Mrs. Smith wished to preserve the spacious effect, and thus put in few pieces of furniture. A small table holds the guest book for names of those who visit the exhibitions."[42]

* * *

1945 Even as the Salon again opened to the sounds of war, victory was in sight. General Douglas MacArthur had returned to the Philippines with the largest armada ever to sail the Pacific Ocean, and the Auschwitz death camp was within days of being liberated. The subject of war, though, continued to be uppermost on the minds of several of the 130 artists who had been juried into the show of 207 pieces. Like Paul Ashby with his *Safety Amid Destruction*, Ruth Pratt Bobbs with *The Commando* and Edmund Brucker with *Machinist's Mate, First Class, Robert Gardner*, Wayman Adams had sent a war-related painting. It was entitled *Young Lieutenant*.

Much to the delight of Salon patrons, the noted New York-based portraitist—"a continuous exhibitor who, for several years, has generously disregarded his right to enter paintings in competition for prizes"[43]—had presented them with a recent likeness of his son in this entry. The young man was a favorite with many of the gallery-goers, as they had watched Wayman Adams, Jr., mature through his father's paintings. They had seen him as a baby in *Ella, Wayman Junior, and Naomi Priscilla* in the 1925 show, a toddler in 1929, a teenage cadet at Culver Military Academy in 1942, and now as a second lieutenant with the United States Army.

Another Indiana artist of renown, C. Curry Bohm was making his contribution to the war effort while staying on the home front. The Brown County painter—whose *Gray Hills of Winter* took the "Outstanding Work in Oil of the Entire Exhibition" prize—"has been in war work at Allison's (Allison Division of General Motors in Indianapolis), commuting from Nashville every day, accompanied by his wife who also was employed in town. They ferry back and forth in their station wagon, their car pool boasting a full passenger list of neighbors similarly employed."[44]

For yet another Salon entrant, however, the war being waged was a very personal one. Battling mental illness while living on the streets and as a patient at Central State Hospital in Indianapolis, the European-trained John Zwara painted surprisingly serene landscapes. A reclusive man who had been diagnosed as schizophrenic upon admission to the hospital in 1938, he earned money for both food and art materials by selling work to Lyman Brothers, Inc. and the H. Lieber Company[45] of

Indianapolis. During his six-month stay in the hospital, his supplies were provided by Dr. Walter Bruetsch,[46] one of the staff doctors.

"I never knew what [Zwara] was going to do or what we were going to get back," said Carl Lyman who furnished a place for the artist to work during bad weather. "He had a lot of ability. . . . He made pencil sketches in his workbooks and put numbers in areas for colors he wanted. I don't know how many numbers he had in his head, but he knew exactly what colors to use when he came to the studio (at Lyman Brothers). It was an original paint-by-number system that he developed himself."[47]

In spite of the hardships imposed by wartime restrictions, the Hoosier Salon persevered under the guidance of Mrs. Smith and her Association volunteers. Continuing in their financial support of the show, too, were clubwomen from Tri Kappa Sorority, the Woman's Department Club, Psi Iota Xi Sorority, the Daughters of Indiana of Chicago and the Indiana Federation of Clubs. In addition, members of Delta Sigma Kappa Sorority, a national organization founded in Lafayette, Indiana, had joined the Salon ranks in 1942 with the sponsorship of a purchase prize.

Largely because of the efforts of these groups, the annual exhibition remained one that few artists cared to miss. "This year's Hoosier Salon was not only the usual artistic success," reported one newspaper, "but it also broke all records as a financial success where exhibitors were concerned. More than $4,600 worth of pictures were sold to the visiting public, as against last year's $2,200 and the 1943 total which was under $1,400. Awards and purchase prizes amounted to $4,500, too, which adds up to a total of $9,100 garnered this year. . . . Attendance of 10,108 this year soared beyond records of all previous Salons"[48] (in Indianapolis).

With the close of the show, the yearly traveling schedule began as Salon paintings were tagged for smaller exhibitions around the state. A number of pictures was sent to Ball State Teachers College in Muncie for display and then on to the Anderson Civic Art Association. Another group went to Indiana University in Bloomington and the Sheldon Swope Gallery in Terre Haute. By late March, all but seventy-three pieces had been brought together for an April showing in Gary. Sponsored by the local chapter of Altrusa International, the ten-day show was booked into that city's Memorial Auditorium.

C. J. Bulliet of the *Chicago Daily News*, the art critic who repeatedly had been critical of the Salon during its years in Chicago, complimented the show. This exhibition, he noted in his column, "is made up of 134 pictures, all that are left after heavy sales in Indianapolis in January from the annual Hoosier Salon, now a capital city event. The sales amounted to $4,425, showing that Indiana is supporting its Salon in a big way, as it used to do in Chicago when the phenomenal out-of-state show outdistanced the Art Institute's local exhibitions in both sales and prize money awarded."[49]

* * *

1946 The Preview Party for the 1946 Salon— the invitational affair had been switched from Saturday evening to late Sunday afternoon—was truly a celebration. The war was finally over, and more than 650 guests braved a mid-winter snowstorm to share in the revelry at Block's galleries. These hearty souls were treated to a buffet tea served from tables decorated with bouquets of red "Better Times" roses and white sweet-peas. A trio of musicians playing the violin, cello and piano serenaded them as well. For the first time, "WIBC, the Indianapolis news station, [gave] a half-hour program directly from the galleries . . . from 5 to 5:30 in connection with the tea."[50]

The exhibition of 203 pieces was dominated by the traditional work that had characterized the Hoosier Salon in prior years. Applauding these "paintings of serene loveliness," Helen Magner of the *New Castle Courier-Times* noted: "The beauty of the hills was there long before the war filled the world with horror, and this eternal beauty is what the Hoosier artists paint. Sincerely, and with skill of hand, they have put on canvas the landscape that is so intimate a part of Indiana life. And it may be that when pictures provoked by war have become dated or forgotten, these pictures will be loved for their simple beauty. They do not demand attention, but win it because they deserve it."[51]

Another art critic, Anton Scherrer of the *Indianapolis Times*, handled his commentary of the show in a more tongue-in-cheek fashion. In his critique, he provided gallery-goers with "A Dictionary for Patrons of Art." ART, he suggested was "[a]nything turned out in Brown County; and, for want of a better word, everything produced outside of Brown County is generally classified under 'Modern Art.'" A LANDSCAPE, for the purposes of his Hoosier Salon review, was "[c]olloquially, a slice of Hoosier scenery (or reasonable facsimile thereof) preferably cut to dimensions to fit the space over the mantel-piece and skillfully treated to suit the predilections of the painter's clientele." An EXIT, to Scherrer, was "[a] sign over the door and, oftentimes, the only emblem of hope for a patron of the arts. Have no fear, however. For the next two weeks, you don't have to make a quick get-away"[52] (from the Salon).

During those two weeks of the show's run, a number among the fifteen thousand people who visited its galleries bought artwork. By the exhibition's close, sales had amounted to $4,555, with landscapes outselling all other subject matter and oils winning in customer appeal. Even a reporter from the *Chicago Tribune* grudgingly had to admit: "There must be something about Indiana air which makes the selling of pictures in Indiana a larger industry than in Illinois."[53]

The merit awards for the 1946 Salon were generous, too, as patrons put together a prize list in excess of $5,400. In addition, the Estella M. King Memorial was given in honor of the former executive chairman who had died in Pasadena, California, in May of 1944. Marie Goth was awarded the $200 prize for her portrait of *Fabien Sevitsky*, the conductor of the Indianapolis Symphony Orchestra.

Winner of another of the Salon's memorial awards—the D. C. Elliott prize given in the "Outstanding Portrait in Oil" category—was Randolph Coats with his entry *Yvonne*. A familiar figure at the Salon, he had been exhibiting in the show since its early days in Chicago. Always busy with landscape work, portraiture or the details of a movie project cluttering his Indianapolis studio, the painter liked nothing better than to unwind with a good game of chess. One of his favorite opponents had been the late Will Vawter. "Will usually wore me out," Coats explained. "He could sit twenty minutes over one move and plan two hundred ahead. Although I never seemed able to prove it, I always thought I would be able to beat him some time."[54]

Like Coats, Edgar Forkner had been a steady presence in the show since 1925. Known primarily as a watercolorist, the Richmond, Indiana, native had been shipping paintings to the Salon for years from his studio in Seattle, Washington. In a tribute to Forkner after his death in July of 1945, one newspaper reporter remembered: "As a young man, he occasionally sold pictures that he considered mere pot-boilers, and he had an amusing way of avoiding the need for having his name connected with that he did not think of too highly. He simply signed his name backwards, so if a painting turns up with the signature 'Renkrof,' the chances are that it is one of these."[55] Forkner's work was exhibited posthumously in the 1946 and 1947 shows.

Soon after the Salon ended, Mrs. Smith initiated a series of two-week exhibitions held in the display space at the Hoosier Art Gallery. Among the more intriguing of these shows was one mounted by Garo Z. Antreasian. An Indianapolis painter of Armenian-American heritage, he had served in the South Pacific as a combat artist with the U. S. Coast Guard. Considering his watercolors of war-torn Manila to be "[e]specially arresting," Filomena Gould of the *Indianapolis News* pointed out that "[h]is work, heralded in *Life* magazine, is in a permanent collection of the Coast Guard Academy at Groton, (Connecticut)."[56] Antreasian would go on to become a pioneer of the lithographic revival that would begin in the United States during the early 1960s.

* * *

1947 As the nation settled into a peace-time economy, Mrs. Smith continued to keep the Salon at the forefront of artistic life in Indiana. Always looking for more sponsors to underwrite the yearly event, she and her volunteers raised more than $6,000 to be apportioned among thirty-two merit awards and seventeen purchase prizes for the 1947 show. Submissions for the exhibition were up as well. After placing an advertisement in the "Where to Show" section of an art magazine published in New York City, the Association received 760 entries from three hundred artists throughout the country.[57]

Taking nearly two days for its deliberations, the jury finally settled on 211 pieces of artwork that had been sent to Indianapolis from artists representing fourteen states. For the most part, the five-person jury selected a conservative show in which the "artists have painted, honestly and in the lovely colors that are all about us, the things they really see. On the whole, they are not introspective and given to digging up dark dismal meanings in hidden thoughts. . . . Rather, they interpret what they see with a poet's understanding, and an appreciation of simple beauty."[58]

There was, though, "a slight leaning toward so-called modernism on the part of many of the exhibitors."[59] Herbert P. Kenney, Jr., of the *Indianapolis News* noted that "[f]or what may be the first time in its history, the Salon harbors an abstract painting—Ralph F. Thompson's *Happy New Year*. Another out-of-the-ordinary work is Dorothea T. Swander's *Undermined*, a stark, bleak, provocative picture which is in contrast to the efforts at 'prettification' evident in so many of the routine landscapes or paintings of flowers."[60]

While Ernest R. Roose's prizewinning entry, *The Famous "500," Indianapolis*, was a landscape, it was hardly a bucolic rendering of the rambling countryside. Instead the piece was an urban scene, done from beneath a canopied grandstand at the Indianapolis 500 Mile Race. A self-described "nut on race cars,"[61] Roose had sketched the finish of the 1946 race from his seat and had worked it into an oil painting for the Hoosier Salon. His picture was purchased during the first week of the show by Mrs. Anton Hulman, Jr., of Terre Haute, Indiana, wife of the owner of the Speedway track. The cityscape was a birthday present for her husband.[62]

The Salon scarcely had opened before gallery-goers learned of Carl C. Graf's unexpected death from complications of influenza. With studios in Indianapolis and Nashville, the artist—"known as 'Shorty' all around the hills of Brown County because of his extreme height and lanky form"[63]—had missed only one Salon since its inception in 1925. First interested in art by his mother who "used to amuse us children by drawing pictures,"[64] Graf later experimented on his own. "In school, I filled up my textbooks with pencil sketches," he explained. "It was not until I was in the eighth grade that the teaching of art was introduced in the public schools.

"When I started to work on a newspaper there in Bedford, my home town, the 'boss' noticed my ability to sketch and encouraged me to take up cartooning. With the idea of becoming a cartoonist, I came to Indianapolis and entered the John Herron Art Institute. But the general education I got there in art made me lose sight of my ambition to draw caricatures. I studied portrait painting, but later confined myself to landscape work. Oh, of course, I break over into other subjects, but landscape makes the strongest appeal."[65]

One of Graf's forays into something other than his lyrical landscapes came as the result of a commission for sculpture work. Hired by an Indianapolis architect, Graf fashioned the figures of a miner and a laborer for the Mary Harris "Mother" Jones Memorial, located in the miners' cemetery at Litchfield, Illinois. According to an account of his contribution to the monument dedicated to this crusading union organizer: "The contract for sculpture was made with Mr. Graf early in April, and it called for working models to be approved within three weeks. . . . The figures were modeled in nondrying modeling clay and required about ten days each in casting plaster. The casts weigh[ed] 125 pounds each. The bronze castings [were] done in New York."[66]

* * *

1948 Even though 245 artists submitted 672 works of art to the Salon, only 143 paintings and pieces of sculpture were juried into the show. It was one of the smallest exhibitions in memory. Lucille Morehouse of the *Indianapolis Star* suggested that the cutback might have been due, in part, to a tightening of the eligibility rules. Additional guidelines had been added to the requirement that an artist be born in Indiana or have been a resident of the state for at least one year.

"Hard and fast rules have been made even harder and faster this year, with regard to non-admittance of entries by 'any amateur or professional artist who attends an art class regularly,'" she noted in her column. "And the following statement (set out in the Call for Entries) has clamped the lid down, good and tight, on the heads of pretenders who might try to edge their way in: 'If any entry is proven to be a copy, and not original in composition and execution, it will be eliminated from the Salon any time during the showing.'

"It so chanced that I was in one of the galleries in Block's auditorium last year," the art critic continued, "when that very thing was being taken care of by the executive chairman, Mrs. Leonidas F. Smith, who very kindly—but nonetheless firmly—requested the winner of a prize to remove a large canvas from the gallery after it had been proved a copy of a color reproduction in a magazine."[67]

For the 109 artists whose work was admitted to the show, however, the Salon offered one of its richest purses. After noting that $3,175 had been contributed for merit awards and $3,055 had been provided for purchase prizes, one reporter took care to distinguish between the two categories: "Prizes, according to custom, are classified first as cash prizes, given as awards of merit in accordance with jury decision," she wrote, "each winner receiving the entire amount of the prize. . . . [S]econd [are] selection purchase prizes—which are subject to the regular commission charge for all sales of art—the selection being made by prize donors or by specially appointed committees."[68]

As they had in the past, the pieces on view "remain[ed] quietly conservative and definitely on the optimistic side."[69] The artists, it seemed, had responded to Mrs. Smith's recommendation in the Call for Entries. Setting forth her vision of the Salon in the admission materials, she had depicted the show as "an annual assembling and display of the best works of art which are suitable to hang in homes—paintings which cannot only be lived with, but which will bring happiness and an uplift of spirit to the owner.

"The Hoosier Salon," she stated, "is not meant to be a fashion show of 'trends in art,' which emphasize the disordered and confused political and economic world affairs of today. We wish to have shown pictures painted on sound fundamental art principles, but not necessarily to have this the end or purpose of the artist, but only the method of expressing the hopeful, and, if possible, the beautiful promise for the future."[70]

With the close of the Salon at Block's came the start of the traveling schedule and the enthusiasm that had become associated with the stopover in Gary. The northern Indiana show—sponsored by Altrusa International since 1945—was an ambitious endeavor, opening on April 4 in Memorial Auditorium. Drawing crowds, critics and media attention during its ten-day run, the Gary version of the Salon highlighted a significant number of prizewinning paintings from Indianapolis.

Calling the display in Gary "the finest exhibit our Indiana painters have ever shown,"[71] Helen Ruth Huber of the *Gary Post-Tribune* praised its offerings. "There is just enough break from the conservative tradition to provide excitement, aesthetically, to the gallery patrons," she declared. "No longer is wall after wall banked with flower paintings and no longer are we surfeited with the autumnal charms of 'Brown County.' To replace this doubtful loss, we are shown 121 of the best paintings Gary has ever been privileged to see. The Hoosier [Salon] this year is superb."[72]

* * *

1949 As Association members finalized the details for the 1949 show, they did so with considerable anticipation. It was an important year for their Salon. The exhibition was celebrating its twenty-fifth anniversary as well as an invitation to Washington, D.C., for a special showing in the spring. As announced by the Indianapolis press some weeks earlier: "This winter's exhibits will be taken intact to Washington where they will be shown next April at the new National Museum. This will be the first time the Washington museum has given space to an exhibition representing one state exclusively and will give eastern critics an insight into Indiana's expression of regional art."[73]

Almost before the finishing touches were in place for the Indianapolis show, opening day was upon Mrs. Smith and her volunteers. This year's Preview Party, they had promised, would be an especially lovely event, unlike the Salon's twentieth anniversary that had gone largely unheralded during the war. More than six hundred guests crowded into Block's Terrace Tea Room—decorated with Peret roses, gardenia sprays and ivy in Florentine statuettes and urns—for an elegant buffet. During the supper, a small orchestra played. The galleries, too, were lavishly bedecked with window boxes of white azaleas and bouquets of forsythia and roses.

From the eight hundred entries that had been delivered to the Association, the jury had narrowed the field to 168 pieces by 112 artists. The resulting show, declared Corbin Patrick of the *Indianapolis Star*, "seems to be a fairly even balance between the kind of pictures meant for a museum and the kind you'd like to take home with you. There's a tinge of 'significance' but charm predominates."[74] The work in sculpture, he noted, was particularly impressive; Patrick found it "the most striking . . . displayed in many years."[75]

Ed Sovola of the *Indianapolis Times* also was pleased with the artwork. "Frankly, it's rather strange to shuffle through the [show] and recognize most of the stuff inside of fancy frames," the critic admitted. "When Salvador Dali's name was on the tip of everyone's tongue several years ago and modern art had exponents of same splashing paints, my hopes for mankind went down to zero. When artists had made their thoughts 'visible' on canvas and I couldn't understand them, I got scared. . . . Then along comes the 25th Hoosier Salon. . . . It's great to be able to go to an art exhibit again without getting into an argument with some character about the 'movement' of parabola No. 4."[76]

Even in the midst of the party, talk was of the upcoming exhibition in Washington, D. C. Being invited to mount a show on the East Coast was an honor for the Association, but the undertaking did necessitate additional efforts on the part of the other two sponsors: the William H. Block Company and the Indiana State Society of Washington, D. C. Six weeks after the Salon had ended, the Society sponsored a style show at the Mayflower Hotel in the nation's capital. Held to raise money for the Salon project, the group highlighted fashion ensembles using the Hoosier state colors of yellow gold and blue as well as "clothes appropriate for a day at the Indianapolis Speedway Race."[77]

The Society staged yet another fund-raiser, a dance in the ballroom at the Shoreham Hotel. "Bloomington-born Hoagland Howard Carmichael and his wife Ruthie flew to Washington from their Hollywood home especially for the dance," reported one newspaper. "It was Old Home Week for Hoagy and former Hoosier contemporaries. Following graduation from Indiana University, Hoagy had a dance orchestra in Indianapolis where he lived in the Columbia Club. . . . Indiana University alumni occupied a ringside table [and] Hoosier Congressmen were special guests at a party held before the dance."[78]

The invitational preview on the evening of April 7 drew five hundred people from Indiana and the Washington, D.C., area. Arranged in the foyer of the National Museum—the repository for the fine arts collection of the Smithsonian Institution—the show featured all 168 pieces from Indianapolis as well as thirty paintings chosen from the Hoosier Art Gallery. "For the first time, a piano was moved into the gallery and soft music was played during the preview," observed a writer on assignment from the *Indianapolis Star*. "It was also the first time that refreshments ever had been served there."[79]

The Washington, D.C., press was supportive. That city's *Sunday Star* proclaimed the show's "[t]echnical competence [to be] high, and subject matter is pleasing. . . . Generally fresh and colorful, these are paintings one imagines the great majority of homeowners would like to hang on their walls. They are good decorations and have no unhappy implications."[80] Jane Watson Crane of the *Washington Post* concluded "[t]he work is, for the most part, conservative in treatment, the approach objective rather than subjective. It gives a general impression of competence and vigor. There are few experiments in technique, relatively few deviations from straight representation. . . . [T]he artists have stuck to themes close to their own experience which is one reason why the show carries conviction."[81]

1953
Robert Laurent
Daphne
First Prize—Sculpture

1955
Louis Bonsib
Snow on Mount Lemon
Purchase Prize

1956
Wayman Adams
Little Johnny Rudd
Outstanding Work in Oil

1959
Rosemary Browne Beck
Still Life
Outstanding Work in Oil

The Fifties

1950 Buoyed by the success of the Salon's showing in Washington, D.C., Mrs. Smith and her volunteers turned to planning their upcoming exhibition. Nearly seven hundred people had placed reservations for the Preview Party at Block's, and a collection of donors had funded a prize purse totaling $5,000. The jury, composed of three artists living outside Indiana, had been busy as well. Taking two full days to deliberate, the trio had selected 182 pieces from a field of seven hundred entries submitted by 265 artists working in eighteen states.

According to Lucille Morehouse, an arts feature writer for the *Indianapolis Star*, the appointment of Rudolph Ingerle to the jury had helped the Salon maintain its standing as a conservative show. "Mrs. L. F. Smith . . . told me," she wrote, "that Ingerle would repeatedly advise, as the jurying progressed: 'Don't ever let down on your policy'— referring to the Salon's loyalty to the fine traditional work of Indiana artists—'for this is an oasis in the desert.' Mrs. Smith continued: Mr. Ingerle even intimated that the Hoosier Salon is watched by other artist groups over the country to see if we will hold out against modernism."[1]

The tendency of the jurors to prefer upbeat, more realistic artwork was confirmed once again by the art critics of Indianapolis. Herbert Kenney, Jr., of the *News* decided that "[t]he show itself has a sunnier face to it than has been the case at any time since the end of the war, as if the artists again are seeing with a brighter vision."[2] Corbin Patrick of the *Star* found that "[w]hile the tone of the show is conservative, it also includes a brilliant splash of the modern."[3] And Marjorie Turk of the *Times* concluded that "[t]here's an art that's strictly Hoosier. It's straightforward, workmanlike and painterly—hangable, pleasing and unsensational. [In the Salon], there's little that's shocking and much that's ownable. The oils, prints, watercolors and pastels would fit into the average living room."[4]

With the Salon's conservative bent in mind, William Eyden had carefully chosen his entries. He had been working from a studio on West 13th Street in New York since 1947 and was enamored with the hubbub of the big city. "I love it—the dazzling lights of Broadway, Grand Central Station, Times Square, 42nd Street, the warm air blasts from a subway entrance, the roaring of trains you cannot see," Eyden had written to a friend. "This is New York from the Bowery to Park Avenue, a pattern of gaiety, tragedy and hope. . . . I have tried to capture this of New York in my paintings."[5]

Drawing his inspiration from more rustic settings was C. Curry Bohm, whose *Heavy Seas* was awarded the $500 "Outstanding Work in Oil of the Exhibition" prize. The award-winning marine was done from sketches he had made the prior September while visiting York, Maine. "First impressions are most vivid, and we rely on self-discipline later for tone-quality," said the artist, in explaining how he was able to finish up a landscape in his studio. "If I have the feeling of a picture and don't lose it, it can be completed in as little time as four hours. But if the feeling comes and goes, as I'm afraid it often does, I return to the picture and do and re-do sections for as long as five months."[6]

Absent from the Salon were any paintings by Edward K. Williams. A favorite with gallery-goers through the years, this long-time Brown County resident had died in his Nashville home four weeks earlier. Fondly remembered by his colleagues, he was described by Simon P. Baus as being "one of the finest artists in the state," by Effie Carter as being "always kind and understanding," and by Evelynne Mess as being "a fine friend!"[7] Indianapolis gallery director Damien J. Lyman recalled that "[i]n his landscape work, [Williams] always painted directly from nature and never resorted to photographs and quick sketches."[8]

* * *

1951 Despite the best efforts of Salon artists to render the world in bucolic terms, the horrors of war again touched their show. Prompted by the mobilization of U. S. troops for the Korean War, the management at Block's "welcome[d] the opportunity to help maintain the traditions of

Indiana art . . . in this era of our history, when alien forces are attempting to destroy the traditional and cultural heritages of people in many parts of the world."[9]

Of particular interest to many show-goers were the eighteen examples of sculpture being set out, for the first time, on solid block-like supports rather than on small pedestals. Applauding the color that was being introduced "with beautiful effect,"[10] an *Indianapolis Star* critic noted that the sculptors were deserting the less durable plaster medium to work in stone and wood. Sy Perszyk's *Boy with Rabbits* was one of the most admired pieces of stone carving, the reviewer said, and it won a $75 prize being offered by Hoosier songwriter Hoagy Carmichael in his debut as an Indiana art patron.

Most of the exhibition's 204 offerings—declared by another critic to be "familiar and conservative,"[11]—were of a type "suitable for taking home, particularly of a size that would not seem outlandish in a small modern room."[12] Presenting this kind of marketable art had continued to be a high priority with Salon leaders despite the remarks of a New York artist that had been printed earlier in the *Indianapolis News.* In a letter to the editor of the *News*, painter John Bernhardt had chided the Association for holding—in its efforts to sell artwork—"a concept of art which is so narrow that little of the true nature of Indiana art has been represented by it.[13]

". . . In most of the paintings which pass the juries of the Hoosier Salon, there is very little in which the man of the Indiana city or country can find his identity," Bernhardt had asserted from his East Coast studio. "In how many paintings in these Salons could the spectator say to himself: 'This art deals with something I really know about. This is of my city, my countryside, my job, my friends. This speaks of the street I know, the tree in my yard, the people I know, the emotions I feel.' It is time that the Hoosier Salon comes to realize that its standards for art are biased in a way which is not only reactionary but spells the death of art expression."[14]

Despite Bernhardt's claim that Salon art was not "alive art,"[15] those crowding the galleries at Block's appeared to disagree; they continued to seek out the familiar work of time-honored Hoosier favorites. For the second year in a row, Wayman Adams walked off with the top "Portrait in Oil" prize, winning $150 with his study of a shabby vagabond. Another of the painters from the show's early days, Frederick Polley, was well represented by three pieces. His *Gate Tree and St. Michaels, Charleston, S. C.* was awarded a $150 purchase prize by the Indiana Soldiers' and Sailors' Children's Home.

As comfortable with etching as with painting, this former head of the Graphic Arts Department at Arsenal Technical High School in Indianapolis had given examples of his artwork to the school some years before. "I hope that this group of etchings will form a nucleus for an outstanding art collection for Technical high school," he had said of his gift of twenty-five etchings and drypoints. "My thought in giving these works is that it may inspire other artists and collectors to present other gifts to the school in order that it may have a truly fine collection of art objects. Such a collection not only would add to the prestige of the school, but would be a real help to the artistically inclined pupils."[16]

* * *

1952 The passage of time did nothing to quell the controversy among art patrons about what kind of work the jurors of the Hoosier Salon should encourage. With the opening of the twenty-eighth show, battle lines were again drawn; the first shot was fired on the editorial page of the *Indianapolis Star.* In an unsigned article, a writer declared of the 232 pieces chosen for display: "What appeals to us most about the Hoosier Salon is the fact that no one has to explain it. Our Indiana artists do not look at things upside down, or inside out. There is nothing in this exhibit to baffle or confuse anybody. . . . What (John) Ruskin called 'furniture pictures,' the kind most people would like to wrap up and take home, predominate. They remind us that art can be a source of real pleasure."[17]

Franz Schulze, an instructor in the Department of Applied Design at Purdue University, was quick to take up the banner of modernism in response. In a letter to the editor of the *Star*, he noted: "The reason this show is a vapid mess of pottage, as its twenty-seven predecessors have invariably been, is clear from your writing. You speak glowingly of the predominance of 'furniture pictures, the kind most people would like to wrap up and take home.' You also deplore the artists who 'look at things upside down, or inside out,' which is an implied rejection of abstract painting. It is out of these diluted, provincial values that a diluted, provincial art arises, and the present Salon demonstrates this as surely as it has consistently in the past."[18]

Not content to let the matter go unanswered, the *Star's* Corbin Patrick used his "As the Day Begins" column to plead a case for traditional art. "At the risk of being considered awfully bourgeois, we confess to a secret admiration for the way our limners of the Hoosier scene combine the art of pleasing with that of painting. In fact, we like it just fine, . . . There is, of course, another school of thought expressed by the advanced thinker who called the current Hoosier Salon 'a vapid mess of pottage.'

"But we'll string along with the original curmudgeon, Samuel Johnson," Patrick concluded. "[Johnson] said, 'I had rather see the portrait of a dog that I know than all the allegorical paintings . . . in the world.' Substitute 'abstract' for 'allegorical' and you have, substantially, our thought."[19] Columnist Ed Sovola of the *Indianapolis Times* agreed. In his "Inside Indianapolis," he championed the Salon's conservative offerings, noting that "[i]t isn't necessary to walk around and ask repeatedly, 'Now, what in tarnation is this supposed to represent?'"[20]

Causing almost as much comment as the press coverage devoted to the Salon was the Saturday afternoon Preview Party. Nearly 650 guests were treated to an impressive buffet supper served from long tables covered with white organdy cloths over pink satin. On the dessert table in the center of Block's Tea Room were three cakes, decorated with pink satin candy icing and surrounded by colored fruit ices on silver trays. "The center cake, composed of six tiers, is seventy inches high and valued at $500," reported Thelma Machael of the *Indianapolis News*, "[and] each of the smaller cakes weighs twenty pounds and is valued at $50."[21]

Among the honored artists was Sister M. Rufinia, O. S. F. Her entry *Summer* took one of two prizes given for "Outstanding Work by an Instructor in a Catholic High School, College or University." This year would be the last in which merit awards in the category would be given. Part of the Salon purse since 1935, they had been underwritten for eighteen years by Peter C. Reilly of Indianapolis. An alumnus and trustee for the University of Notre Dame, he had funded the prizes "in order to stimulate greater interest in the study of art in the universities and parochial schools of the Catholic church in Indiana."[22]

A teacher at St. Francis College in Lafayette, Indiana, Sister Rufinia had exhibited her first painting in the Salon in 1927. Focusing primarily on floral paintings and landscapes, she had collected a string of prizes through the years for her delicate work. "It is my sincere wish to reproduce, at least in a miniature way, something of the world around me," the German-born nun had written when asked to contemplate her art. "I thank the good God for the talent He has given me in the line of paints and brushes, and I hope to make good use of this gift of God by inspiring all who

gaze upon my works of art to think of the Greater and Original Masterpieces."[23]

Like the Salon, exhibitions held in the Association's year-round gallery tended to focus on more traditional art. In addition to solo shows featuring the work of Simon P. Baus, Effie F. Carter, Francis Clark Brown, Burling Boaz, Virginia O'Fallon, Edmund Brucker and Edward Nicholson, the 1952 season offered visitors to the Hoosier Art Gallery a look at pieces being done by "The Twenty."[24] This group of Indiana artists, organized in 1948,[25] was described by Walter Whitworth of the *Indianapolis News* as "men and women . . . [who] are not interested in the psychoanalyst's symbolism, in the aberrations discovered by the psychiatrist, [or] in the theories of those who practice the various 'isms'. . . . They have a strength of their own, a strength that lies in their imaginative perceptions."[26]

* * *

1953 As the opening of the 1953 Salon neared, Mrs. Smith was mindful of the concerns that had been voiced during a recent Board of Trustees' meeting at the Honeywell Memorial in Wabash, Indiana. Even though the Association had erased a deficit from the prior year, several trustees had been alarmed by a weakening of donor support. Missing from the roll-call of prizes for the upcoming show were those underwritten by the Indianapolis Newspaper Publishers Association and Peter C. Reilly. In addition, the monies given by Mrs. Arthur B. Wright and C. B. Ober for the provision of merit awards had been switched to the funding of purchase prizes.

Nearly as troublesome for the Board was "the manner in which the [ongoing] conflict between modern and classic art was affecting the organization and the annual Salon."[27] Mrs. Smith was able to reassure the members on this point, though, suggesting that the friction may well have been advantageous to the sale of artwork. "During the eleven years in which the Salon has been held in Indiana," she told them, "nearly $152,000 has been turned over to Indiana artists . . . in prizes and in purchases of [the] artists' work."[28]

Not unexpectedly, the twenty-ninth Salon was considered once more to be a showcase of traditional art. From the more than seven hundred entries that had been submitted to the jury, only 193 pieces by 121 artists had been chosen for display. Corbin Patrick of the *Indianapolis Star* described the exhibition as being "mildly conservative . . . with only a few entries that will cause any genuine eyebrow-lifting"[29] and Walter Whitworth of the *Indianapolis News* found it to be "sometimes nostalgic, but always serene and reflective."[30] Hertha Stein Duemling of the *Fort Wayne News-Sentinel* agreed. "The Salon always has been and still remains conservative," she noted, "with only a few trickles of modern thought."[31]

Crowding into Block's to admire the artwork and enjoy the afternoon were 775 invited guests. A buffet supper of assorted salad molds, ham canapes, French fried shrimp and creamed chicken in toasted bread cups awaited them, along with a dessert table with its horn-of-plenty centerpiece. The cornucopia had been created by the pastry chef at Block's. Working with hot spun sugar, he had blown "fragile red apples, yellow bananas and other fruits [which tumbled] from the horn of plenty."[32]

Awarded $100 for the "Best Still Life" from a total prize purse of $4,500 was Evelynne Mess. She had painted her winning *Cucurbita,* a still life in oil of squashes and gourds in a basket, after harvesting the colorful assortment from her garden in Brown County. Later, the artist would engage in a spirited correspondence with *Indianapolis News* reporter Wayne Guthrie regarding a question about gourds that had been posed in his "Ringside in Hoosierland" column.

"In the February 10th *News,* you asked, 'Will wrens shun painted gourds?'" the wife of artist George Jo Mess would write Guthrie. "Last summer, I made a few wren gourd houses with gourds I grew. . . . I have tried both artificial and natural colors and notice the birds seem to like the natural tones—shellacked for preservation—perhaps because it is a bird's instinct to camouflage among its natural surroundings in order to hide from its enemies. I, for one, think the ones right from nature are the most artistic."[33]

* * *

1954 Inspired by the elegance that had characterized the well-publicized wedding of Jacqueline Bouvier to John Fitzgerald Kennedy, Mrs. Smith and her committee outdid themselves in organizing the thirtieth Salon. More than seven hundred guests made reservations to attend their gala Preview Party. Those who sampled the buffet supper in Block's Tea Room were not disappointed; the restaurant staff again had demonstrated its culinary artistry.

Creativity had been given free rein for the afternoon. It was evident in the 203 pieces of artwork on display as well as in the spun-sugar figures that adorned the dessert table. "Decorations of the table represented both air and water with four swans floating on a fluffy pool of pale yellow spun sugar candy. . . . [At the] center of the table was a five-foot tiered epergne, fashioned of satin candy, topped with a satin candy basket holding fresh-cut flowers. Each tier of the epergne held petit fours, almond macaroons and truffles, while scattered over the spun water and the backs of the swans were pastel mints in all colors."[34]

Even the Tea Room looked grander than it had in prior shows. "More sophisticated in theme this year were the floral touches in the dining room," one newspaper reporter indicated. "White and gold flowers were accented with touches of black-velvety black wooden shoes hung to hold painting brushes or abstract white drawings on sooty black backgrounds. One of the most charming touches on the walls, though hung as a backdrop for the flowers, were large gold palettes in coarse wire mesh."[35]

Although artist Helen Humphrey failed to win any of the twenty-one merit awards or ten purchase prizes from a combined purse of nearly $5,000, she was pleased to have her *Memories of Autumn* included in the show. Partially paralyzed after an automobile accident, the twenty-nine-year-old had worked on her entry from a wheelchair in her home. Moving her arms with difficulty, she had held her brush with both hands while painting. Despite her handicap, this student of Elmer Taflinger, Edmund Brucker and Ruth Anderson was known for being optimistic. "Life is wonderful," she said, after being notified of her acceptance in the Salon, "especially when you feel that you are accomplishing something."[36]

Missing from the 1954 show was the familiar face of Clifton Wheeler, an exhibitor in the Salon since the first show in Chicago; he had died in his Irvington, Indiana, home the preceding May. A welcomed presence every year, this Indianapolis painter had taken prize after prize with his thoughtful landscapes. Passionate about nature and the beauty of the out-of-doors, he had taught at John Herron Art Institute for almost twenty-five years and at Shortridge High School for ten years.[37]

Attracted by rugged subject matter, Wheeler had spent his vacation time working in scenic areas around the country. In addition to climbing and sketching the Colorado Rockies, he made excursions to the Catskills and Seneca Lake regions of New York, the Black Mountains of North Carolina and the Smoky Mountains of Tennessee. Of his outings in the Smokies, he had written to an acquaintance: "I wish you could see the mountains there. Some of the peaks are so high that clouds are often about the tops of them. The valleys are steep and narrow, and people are living there much as their grandfathers and grandmothers did. Many of the side roads are too steep and rocky for automobiles, and all of the traveling is done on foot or on horseback."[38]

As the closing date for the Salon approached, Mrs. Smith had little time to accept applause for a job well done. Preparing the traveling exhibitions for their stop-overs throughout Indiana was a task yet ahead of her. Almost as pressing, though, were the decisions that needed to be made by the Salon's Board of Trustees. In June of 1953, the William H. Block Company had ended its practice of donating space for the Hoosier Art Gallery.[39] For the last nine months, the Association had been paying rent on its suite in the State Life Building, and the additional outlay was starting to take a toll on programming. Deeply concerned, the Board instructed Mrs. Smith to seek philanthropic support.

In a grant proposal prepared for submission to Lilly Endowment, Inc., Mrs. Smith requested an annual award of $15,000. She pointed out that it was needed "[t]o obtain necessary space to continue, extend our efforts and maintain an adequate staff at modest salaries."[40] She indicated, too, that the Association wished to relocate if the grant were given. "[W]e need quarters on the ground floor, farther out from the downtown congestion where the public will have easier access to our gallery and adequate parking facilities," she explained. ". . . We plan to enlarge our maintenance income in a new location, by inviting club groups to hold their meetings in some of our space, for which they will pay a modest fee for each meeting."[41]

Rallying behind Mrs. Smith and the Board were artists from around the country who had written to share their thoughts about the Hoosier Salon Patrons Association. C. Curry Bohm praised the Salon for bringing "together an audience that normally does not attend exhibitions in Museums and commercial galleries. It has removed from Art Exhibitions the snobbishness that is so often found in Exhibitions."[42] Johann Berthelsen was "certain it (the Salon) has been an impetus for artists to aspire to do that which adheres to the highest ideals in the interpretation of the arts."[43] And Gianni Cilfone felt that "[t]he Salon has had not only a great influence on culture in the Midwest but has done much to develop and encourage native talent."[44] Despite the testimonials from Salon patrons who had joined the artists in backing the proposal, the grant application—and its supporting documentation—was never submitted to Lilly Endowment, Inc. for action.[45]

* * *

1955 Knowing that the operations of the

Association would remain on the sixth floor of the State Life Building for the foreseeable future, Mrs. Smith looked for ways to trim expenses. In the meantime, she and her volunteers prepared for the thirty-first annual Salon. It was a slightly larger exhibition than those of prior years. The jury—composed of three out-of-state artists as well as four honorary lay members representing Tri Kappa Sorority, Psi Iota Xi Sorority, the Indiana Federation of Clubs and the Woman's Department Club—sifted through hundreds of entries to put together a show of 218 pieces.

Borrowing a tradition established during the Salon's run in Chicago, Mrs. Smith set aside space for a "show within a show," hoping to draw new spectators into the galleries. Taking center stage in this small display were three paintings by "Mr. John" (John P. John), a popular hat designer who had once worked in an Indianapolis department store. Although the milliner had missed the entry deadline for the exhibition, "Salon personnel felt that paintings by Mr. John would add an extra fillip to the show, and so they are in the show but are not a part of it."[46]

The trio of John's oil paintings did, in fact, add spice. A newspaper reporter from the *Indianapolis News* labeled one of them—a still life of a watermelon with real seeds imbedded in the canvas—as a "novelty hit."[47] Another writer on assignment for the *Indianapolis Star* declared John's work to be "splash[ing] with bright but beautifully blended colors." His paintings, the journalist indicated, "show a diversity of talent and interest . . . [and every] painting bears the same signature in script that appears in bold black on white in his fabulous hats."[48]

Just as "Mr. John" juggled oil painting with hat designing, so too did John Frederic Ross balance sketching with a bus schedule. Employed as a driver for the Indianapolis Transit System for seven years, he had requested night routes so that he might attend art school during the day. Winning the $75 prize for "Outstanding Flowers in Oil" with his *Fröliche Weinachten 1954*, Ross had based his piece on a bouquet he had purchased for his wife for Christmas. "Many people ask me," said Ross after winning his award, "where do you get the patience to paint after a full day's work? [I tell them] you don't need patience to do what you like to do the most."[49]

Although failing to take a prize in the 1955 Salon, Donald M. Mattison had won more than a few of them since his first show in 1936. Dean of the John Herron School of Art, this painter was as well known for his portraiture as he was for his academic pursuits. "A portrait," he had explained during the unveiling of his rendering of Allen W. Clowes, "unlike other kinds of art, is an art of the specific—of a certain person—and it can be for a given place and for a definite purpose. Yet it must be handsome as a picture and interpretive of the subject and, in the case of the official portrait, it [must] reflect also the office it honors."[50]

Like Mattison, artist Dale Bessire used the language of portraiture; he applied it, however, to his landscape work. "In the same way that a good portrait should portray the character or personality of the subject, I feel, more and more, that a good landscape must characterize the material painted rather than be a mere superficial likeness," noted this recorder of idyllic scenes around the state of Indiana. "Brown County has a definite character of its own, differing from other sections of the country I have seen. It is this indefinable thing that has made me want to live and paint there.

". . . This word 'characterize' is very important, from my point of view," Bessire continued. "A good example of what I mean is in the work of Jean François Millet, whose *Gleaner* and *The Man with the Hoe* characterize the French peasant. When I graduated from . . . school in Indianapolis, quite a long time ago, I was given the subject 'Millet' for a talk at commencement, and, from a study of his life, I was impressed with the sincerity of his attempt to characterize."[51]

* * *

1956 While the national art scene was buzzing about the impact of Jasper Johns, artwork within the Salon remained largely unaffected. Visitors to the thirty-second show found no Pop Art, and, in fact, were reassured to see displayed the recognizable landscapes, portraiture and still lifes of years past. According to one newspaper reporter, the exhibition of 228 pieces was "a bright and colorful display filled with fine work in many forms, mediums and techniques. . . . While there are brilliant exceptions, the conservative modes of painting are dominant."[52]

Little about the Preview Party had changed as well. More than 650 guests savored such delicacies as filet mignon and chicken mousse before heading to an elaborately decorated dessert table for mocha ice cream meringues. Winning the afternoon's top award—the William H. Block Company $500 prize for "Outstanding Work in Oil of the Entire Exhibition"—was Wayman Adams with his *Little Johnny Rudd*. A whimsical portrayal of a blond, blue-eyed boy in red overalls holding a parakeet in a cage, the painting seemed a startling departure from Adams' more formal work in adult portraiture.

Despite his youthful subject, "[t]here's just as much character in the delicacy of a child, as there is in any amount of strength that a man might have,"[53] explained this painter of Presidents and the social elite. "[I] gave them all the best that was in them (when he did their portraits). I didn't smooth up their portraits or take years off their lives," Adams said, "but I did something that really flattered them more. I put into each portrait all the intelligence that the person had. I haven't been harsh with anybody. I've just been honest."[54]

To the delight of art lovers in northern Indiana, Adams' award-winning *Johnny Rudd* was included in the group of paintings that traveled to Gary after the Salon closed on February 18. Again sponsored by the local Altrusa Club, this collection drew rave reviews from Helen Ruth Huber of the *Gary Post-Tribune*. "[It] is a superb exhibit," she declared. "This Hoosier (Salon) smacks of the old days, when the artists of Southern Indiana were discussed as one of the important schools of the Midwest. The work is not of the international movement, but it is good and solid—a type standing on its own."[55]

Other communities within the state also welcomed the offerings from Indianapolis. As the paintings circulated among Fort Wayne, Terre Haute, Delphi, Kentland, Kokomo, Anderson and Muncie, townspeople in each venue put on special events that drew attention to the visiting exhibition. In Anderson, the Civic Art Association held a dinner meeting and gallery talk to fête the Salon's showing there. In Kokomo, members of the area chapter of the American Association of University Women poured at an "Opening Day" tea as did local clubwomen in Delphi when the Salon was set up in their town.

As the artwork traveled throughout Indiana, Mrs. Smith turned her attention to a new fundraising venture at Association headquarters. She had asked Wayman Adams—a friend since her dentist husband had treated the artist during his student days at Herron Art School[56]—to do a portrait demonstration. "Offered as the first in a series of joint projects by the Hoosier Salon Patrons Association and the Indiana Artists Club, Inc. to procure funds for a professional art center, Mr. Adams, selecting the subject for his portrait at random from the audience, will begin painting at 2:30 p. m. in the World War Memorial Auditorium," reported Louise Symons of the *Indianapolis Times*. "Tickets may be purchased at the Hoosier Salon Gallery; Lyman Brothers; H. Lieber Company; Danner Art, Inc; and at the door."[57]

* * *

1957 For some of those who followed Hoosier art, the Salon opened with a measure of sadness. L. O. Griffith, among the first to have established a home and studio in Nashville, had died three months earlier; and Homer G. Davisson of Fort Wayne had passed away only five days before the show was set to start. To the delight of their admirers, though, paintings by both men appeared in the exhibition. In addition, Griffith's *October Light* was honored by a $300 purchase prize sponsored by Mr. and Mrs. Henry Lester Smith.

As it had in prior years, the Salon drew artwork from around the country. Taking two days to sort through the seven hundred entries, the jury put together a show of 218 pieces by 132 artists. Many of the offerings were serene in character. According to Helen Magner of the *New Castle Courier-Times*, "The Hoosier Salon has always been an exhibition in which strange or moody pictures are rare, for the emphasis has always been on the beauties of Indiana landscape. . . . This has been its character from the beginning in Marshall Field's galleries in Chicago, thirty-three years ago, and it is still keeping to the tradition of truly expressing the beauty of Indiana."[58]

Reflecting the creativity of the artwork on display were the "Valentine's Day" table decorations, chosen for the February Preview Party. "A cake of white and red 'satin' spun sugar and topped with a giant red valentine heart attracted the attention (of gallery-goers)," reported the *Indianapolis News*. "Within the heart a doll, gowned in the glistening red and white spun sugar, revolved. The cake, which stood on a table in the center of the Tea Room, was flanked by two urns of spun sugar which held American Beauty roses. It proved that artistry may be achieved in spun sugar as well as oils."[59]

During the afternoon awards ceremony, Louis W. Bonsib of Fort Wayne took one of the forty prizes from a purse of $4,500. Head of an advertising agency, this native of Vincennes looked forward to the weekends when he could pursue his painting without interruption. Winning the Indiana Federation of Clubs' $200 purchase prize with his *Morning in Nikko (Japan)* was especially meaningful for the largely self-taught artist; Bonsib had done the oil after visiting his son who had been on duty with the armed forces in Japan. During his stay, Bonsib had explored the Japanese countryside, gathering sketches and photographs that were later used as reference material for his paintings at home.[60]

Missing scarcely a minute of the thirteen-day Salon were members of the organizations that had helped to support it through the years. The Tri Kappas had been backers of the show since 1928 when the sorority had pledged $450 for three merit awards to be given to women artists. In 1932, the group had begun funding a purchase prize instead. By 1957, the Tri Kappa art collection—the major portion of which was hanging in the Brown County Art Guild galleries—boasted forty-six pictures by forty different artist members of the Hoosier Salon.[61]

Psi Iota Xi, with thirty-two chapters and 4046 members across Indiana,[62] had been involved with the Salon since 1941 when the sorority had first begun giving money for purchase prizes. Because artwork purchased in this fashion was given to the individual chapters, it was often donated to schools and libraries within their local communities. "The paintings are the chapters' to do with what they want," noted Ann Rein of the *Indianapolis News*. "A number rotate theirs between members' homes. . . . Others are given to such hospitals as Riley Hospital for Children in Indianapolis and Parkview Memorial Hospital in Fort Wayne."[63]

Delta Sigma Kappa Sorority, in its sixteenth year of participation, continued to underwrite another of the show's significant purchase prizes. Even the Daughters of Indiana from Chicago were still committed to the exhibition that had moved from the "Windy City" some sixteen years before. Not only were they generously maintaining annual awards, but the Hoosiers from Illinois were also sending a large delegation from their club to the Salon each year.

Joining the women from these groups were patrons from the Woman's Department Club, the Indiana Federation of Art Clubs and the Indiana Federation of Clubs. Furnishing financial aid as well as countless hours,[64] they had kept the Salon going in the midst of uncertain times. Through the years, too, members from all seven organizations had taken their turns serving as hostesses for the show's various "Special Days." By the time the 1957 exhibition had opened, they were sharing the load with volunteers from such associations as the Contemporary Club, the Sunnyside Guild and the Indiana University Women's Club.[65]

* * *

1958 In a nation that was dancing to Pat Boone and applauding "Father Knows Best," the artwork of the thirty-fourth Salon seemed quite in fashion. Nearly two hundred seventy artists—natives of Indiana as well as present or former residents for at least one year—had submitted 676 paintings and sculptures for inclusion in the show. After spending a day and a half examining the entries, the three-person jury settled on an exhibition of 261 pieces by 150 artists.[66] An additional painting, *Metropolitan Suburbs* by juror Floyd Gahman, was borrowed for the show from the Frank C. Dailey Collection at Indiana University.

Assigned to cover the Preview Party for her newspaper, Kathleen Van Nuys of the *Indianapolis Times* reported that "[g]uests jammed the auditorium to hear the announcement of the artist awards, then turned to the Tea Room for an exquisite buffet supper. . . . Patrons, returning to browse in the auditorium, commented on the wide variety of work exhibited this year, and the modern trend it has taken."[67] A journalist from the *Indianapolis Star* agreed, pointing out that "it's the brightest and most varied Salon in several years. More than usual boldness is displayed in the use of colors, materials and techniques, although its dominant tone is traditional."[68]

Despite the examples of contemporary work noted by Ms. Van Nuys, the majority of prizewinning pieces remained solidly conservative. One such painting was *Daily Barn* by Robert Selby; he was awarded $500 for the "Outstanding Work in Oil of the Entire Exhibition." Like his son-in-law Selby, Hoosier Group artist William Forsyth had used a barn motif with great success. Nearly fifty years earlier, Forsyth had submitted a painting entitled *Twilight, Moon over Red Barn* to the 1910 International Fine Arts Exposition and had been rewarded by taking the bronze medal.[69]

One art critic declared Selby's landscape—done when the artist took his paints to a barn lot owned by a friend—to be "remarkable for its charming simplicity."[70] Another from the *Gary Post-Tribune* suggested that "Robert Selby's *Daily Barn*, the winner of the outstanding ribbon, evokes the question from viewers, 'Why did this picture win?' [A]nd it could be answered that he has pattern and plane color, worked for the value of spatial areas—the relationship of one part to another."[71]

Selby, who handled watercolor illustrations for the advertising department at L. S. Ayres & Company, was a painter without a studio. "I have so little time to paint [and] with no studio, it's hard to do any night work," explained the artist, who routinely set up his easel in his backyard whenever weather permitted. "Often, when some thought comes along at a time when I'm not free to paint, it's hard to shelve it until I'm ready to get to it." Sometimes, though, that works to his advantage, Selby admitted. "When time *is* available, you jump into it and the results come easier and are much better."[72]

Although there was nothing by Louis Bonsib displayed in the 1958 Salon, the Fort Wayne artist was very much in the news. "The Allen County Home for the Aged has been made a brighter place in which to live [because] Louis W. Bonsib . . . has donated twelve oil paintings and one watercolor to the home," reported the *Fort Wayne News-Sentinel*. "'I can't think of a finer gift,' said Mrs. Orville Miller, who is a superintendent with her husband at the home. 'Most of the paintings are landscapes. When they are hung in the rooms of shut-ins, they will give those people some visual contact with the out-of-doors.'"[73]

* * *

1959 To the more than seven hundred visitors who "thronged to the galleries and the entire sixth floor"[74] of Block's for the opening of the thirty-fifth Salon, the world of technology seemed far away. The world's first atomic submarine had cruised under the polar ice cap some six months before, and the Soviets had sent a rocket hurtling past the moon several weeks earlier. But for visitors to the exhibition, the pastoral landscapes and delicate still lifes were delightful reminders of simpler times.

The Preview Party was again a fun-filled affair. Promoting the upcoming event, an *Indianapolis Times* writer had promised: "Gold cupids, thirty inches high, and tall white figurines will dominate the buffet tables, setting the Italian motif. . . . Desserts will be placed on an Italian *gelato* dessert cart decorated in spun sugar in party colors of pink, gold and white. An Italian attendant in costume will push the Italian ice cream vendor's cart. . . . The main menu will include ham and chutney canapes, cucumber and shrimp mold with Lamays dressing, olives, chicken mousse with sauce, lattice potatoes, orange, grapefruit and avocado salad with red currant jelly dressing and croissant rolls."[75]

Guests to the buffet supper were not disappointed with the fare. It served to set a gracious tone for the afternoon as art-admirers mingled, pausing before one painting or another in the Auditorium Galleries. During the presentation of awards held earlier in the day, they had watched twenty-five artists—from among the 111 whose work had been admitted to the show—split thirty-two merit awards and purchase prizes.

C. Curry Bohm's *Village of Nashville* stood out among the 193 exhibition pieces, winning the painter $150 for "Outstanding Landscape in Oil." An outdoorsman of long-standing, Bohm was alarmed by the development that was overtaking his beloved Brown County. "It's getting harder and harder to find a place to paint," complained the former president of the Brown County Art

Gallery Association. "So many little trees have been grubbed out, and things are getting too slicked up. Country roads are so full of traffic, and more and more places are being posted against trespassing."[76]

Despite the threat of bulldozers, Bohm took students from his summer landscape classes deep into the Brown County hills. Sometimes, though, his emphasis on working in the out-of-doors created a problem. "Last year, we had a student (from another state) who came to my home the day after her first class session and tore me apart because she got chiggers," he confided. "She wanted to know why I had not told her Indiana was covered with chiggers and said that I could be sued. It was news to me that Indiana has a corner on chiggers."[77]

As had been the practice since the early years in Chicago, community organizations and clubs continued to hold "Special Days" at the Salon. Much of their programming, however, had advanced well beyond the luncheons and gallery tours of prior times. The Indiana Artists Club, for example, planned a panel discussion titled "Educating the Artist" for its Salon program, and "The Twenty"—a group of Indiana professional artists—scheduled its annual business meeting in the Block's Tea Room before viewing the show.[78]

Two months after the Salon had closed and the traveling exhibitions were well under way, the Association suffered a tremendous loss. Wayman Adams, one of the show's most loyal supporters, died at the age of seventy-five in his Austin, Texas, home. Not only had he been a steady presence in the exhibition since 1925, but the portraitist had been generous with his time and talent in furthering the cause of Hoosier art.

Mrs. Smith was especially saddened by his passing; she had lost a dear friend as well as an ally in her Salon work. "Very early in my husband's and my acquaintance with him, he painted my portrait," remembered the executive chairman. "I was very shy, which accounts for the slightly awestruck expression in the picture. He was very shy, too, and my husband, who believed in him, had one constant battle with him over the years of their acquaintance to try to bring him out a little. He never did get over his shyness," she added, "but I did."[79]

1961
Marie Goth
Joel W. Hadley
Outstanding Work in Oil

1962
William A. Eyden
Old Friends
Jury Prize of Distinction

1964
Floyd Hopper
Gill's Rock
First Prize—Watercolor

1966
Ruth Anderson
The Beckoning Wind
Purchase Prize

The Sixties

1960 The first Preview Party of the new decade remained committed to the dignified way in which its Salon guests were entertained. This year, reported the *Indianapolis Times,* visitors to the winter exhibition found that "[l]avender orchids were at the feet of white bisque cupids centering two long buffet tables. The cupids held aloft arrangements of greenery with purple-throated white orchids and white tapers. Orchids in champagne glasses, candlelighted, were used about the recesses in the Terrace Tea Room."[1] This year, too, guests were treated to yet another sumptuous smorgasbord of hot and cold entrees, tasty salads and an assortment of fancy pastries.

There were changes within the workings of the Salon itself, however. "We are doing something a little different . . . in order to let everyone have an opportunity to study the paintings before making their purchase prize selections," stated Mrs. Smith. "On Saturday, when committees from various organizations view the entries at 11 a. m. at Block's, we have arranged for a one-half hour viewing period before any permanent selection [from the 230 entries admitted into the show] may be made. In past years, immediate selections were permitted."[2]

In addition to admitting nearly forty more artworks than it had in 1959, the Salon also had lengthened its list of prizes. New merit awards—from a total purse of $4,300—included the $100 "Best Marine in Oil," given by Mrs. Albert E. Uhl for the Albert E. Uhl Memorial Prize; a $150 "Jury Prize of Distinction," given by Psi Iota Xi Sorority; the $25 "Outstanding Landscape Composition, Any Medium," given by the Frederick W. Rigley Studios; and the $50 "Outstanding Watercolor, Any Subject," given by the American Institute of Decorators.

Winning the "Best Marine in Oil" prize was Ruth Anderson with her *Morning Comes to Monhegan.* Recognized for her seascapes, this Indianapolis painter maintained that "the beauty of getting to live by the ocean is getting to know it."[3] For one of her paintings done during a summer sketching trip to Monhegan Island, she sat in the middle of the shoreline rocks to let the waves break around her. "I was trying to feel a part of the water," she would later explain. "Denims dry quickly, so I had grabbed my sketchpad and just sat there, getting wet and working." Several of her other marine scenes were inspired by boat trips along the Maine coast. "When I could find a ride to sea, I would take my camera and hold it over my head to get photographs of the wave patterns," Miss Anderson continued. "Then I would come back and work from my slides."[4]

Anthony Buchta was another of the artists to be singled out for an award; he was given the Rigley Studios Prize for his *Rustic Charm in the Ozarks.* A presence in the Salon since 1935, the painter had lived and worked in Chicago before building a studio-home in Brown County upon his retirement. "After many years at commercial art, I ventured into the realm of fine art, and somehow I became involved in teaching art to various art clubs in and around Chicago,"[5] Buchta recalled. To those pupils, he had cautioned: "Never expect to reach perfection; you never will. Do not expect an easy road or some magic formula for success; they don't exist. It takes plain, unadulterated years of hard work."[6]

Even though Louis W. Bonsib's name was missing from the roll call of prizewinners in the 1960 Salon, this advertising executive would later command his share of headlines with a gift of eighteen oils and watercolors to Indiana Technical College. Described as "Fort Wayne's artist laureate . . . [on a] one-man crusade to enhance the community's appreciation of the fine arts,"[7] he would be praised for his generosity to the local school of science and engineering. "Long a practitioner of palette and pigments," a reporter from the *Fort Wayne Journal-Gazette* would note, "Bonsib has brightened the corners in numerous Fort Wayne and Indiana schools, churches and other social-service organizations."[8]

* * *

1961 Borrowing an idea from the founders of the first Salon, Mrs. Smith reinstated a "Popular

Prize" for the 1961 exhibition. The award had been used off and on during the show's thirty-seven-year history. In 1925, "[t]he Popularity Prize, of two hundred dollars, was given by Mr. Walter P. Murphy to the picture receiving the greatest number of votes by visitors to the Galleries during the exhibit. Ballots [were] had at the Exhibition Desk."[9] In 1937, the Indianapolis host of the Woman's Department Club showing of the Salon had used this prize. And in 1961, the "Popular Prize" of $150 was being offered by artist Leota Loop of Nashville, Indiana.

"She (Mrs. Loop) has been wanting to do this for some time," explained the Association's executive chairman. "It will work in this way. During the days the exhibition is open to the public, visitors will be given slips of paper on which to note the picture they like best. A tally of the ballot box slips will be made at the close of the show, and the artist awarded Mrs. Loop's prize."[10] V. J. Cariani, also of Nashville, Indiana, would win the most votes—and the prize—with his still life *White Peonies*.[11]

To streamline the process of choosing purchase prizes, a set of chimes had been added to the proceeding; it was to be sounded at the end of the "hands-off" selection period. "Prize donor committees found it annoying to have pictures flying all over the place when none had completed their selection," said Mrs. Smith, remembering the chaotic selection period of the prior year. "A new ruling set[s] an 11 a.m. 'doors open' [policy] in Block's Auditorium, and committees [are] permitted a thirty-minute looking period in cubicles where pictures in designated price ranges are hung. At the sound of the chimes, pictures [can] be removed by the donors."[12]

With 282 pieces admitted from a field of eight hundred entries, the Salon was the largest in recent memory. Its Preview Party caterers followed suit, setting out a buffet supper that would tempt the most demanding gourmet. Even the artwork in the show seemed a bit more adventuresome. Herbert Kenney, Jr., of the *Indianapolis News* noted that "[while the] tone is predominantly traditional, . . . there is evident a good deal of experimentation in materials and techniques, with some surprisingly unusual and pleasurable results."[13]

Among the artists to share in a purse of over $4,000 was Burling Boaz, Jr. His *1905 Model* won an "Outstanding Watercolor, Any Subject" merit award of $50, and it was designated by the Psi Iota Xi selection committee as one of the sorority's three purchase prizes. Recognized for his skill in tempera and opaque watercolor, the self-taught painter ran a bustling sign-painting business in Indianapolis. He had also served at Herron Art School as a part-time instructor in poster design and commercial lettering at one point in his career.

"I had no formal art training, as such," recalled Boaz. "But I really learned much just by being associated (at Herron) with such greats as William Forsyth, who taught life and portrait classes; Clifton Wheeler, famous for his landscapes, and Paul Hadley, a master with watercolors. If you keep your eyes and ears open, [and] ask a few questions, you can't miss in whatever you're seeking to accomplish. Some of it is bound to rub off on you."[14]

Robert Laurent, a prizewinner in the Salon since 1945, took an "Honorable Mention for Sculpture" with his *The Birth of Venus*. After the awards ceremony, news of this world-famous sculptor was shared because of his work on a commissioned piece at Indiana University. While serving as the Resident Professor of Sculpture there, Laurent had been asked to submit sketches for a fountain to be located in the center of the Bloomington campus. His design of a reclining figure of Venus, surrounded by several fish spouting streams of water, had been chosen. This massive version of *The Birth of Venus* would be dedicated as the centerpiece of Showalter Fountain later in the fall.[15]

Despite working in New York City, Johann Berthelsen rarely missed a Salon. This year, he had shipped two entries to Indianapolis in time for the judging: *59th St. and 5th Ave., New York City* and *Upper 5th Ave., New York City*. An exhibitor since the show's start in Chicago, the renowned artist had left a successful musical career in 1932 to devote himself to painting. Trained in voice at Chicago Musical College, he had toured the United States and Canada—singing the leading baritone roles in Grand Opera in English—upon his graduation. Later he had served as head of the Voice Department of the Indianapolis Conservatory of Music for six years before moving to New York in 1920.[16]

Praised for his poetic interpretations of the urban landscape, Berthelsen had been hailed by the local press upon returning to town for an exhibition of his work. "[K]nown to the Indianapolis public as a musician," wrote an *Indianapolis News* critic, "[h]e is now a painter of no little reputation, and he has brought with him a group of ten small pastels painted in and about New York City. They are charming bits, handled with nice feeling for atmospheric values. . . . It is interesting to find paintings of such high order produced by a man who is also a skilled musician and an actor of recognized ability."[17]

* * *

1962 The thirty-eighth Salon opened on anxious times: Berlin had been divided by a massive wall, hundreds of U. S. military advisors were being drawn into Vietnam, and, here at home, Freedom Riders had been savagely beaten in Alabama. Even the writer of the Foreword to the exhibition catalogue, like many others in the general populace, was apprehensive. "In the midst of world turbulence and dire prophecies for the future," observed Mrs. Hugh J. Baker, a patroness of the Salon from Indianapolis, "we are grateful to our artists for the truth and beauty which they give us in American art which one art lover calls 'The Pageant of America.' So we salute this 1962 Hoosier Salon which gives us this pageant with its message of hope."[18]

With "something for everyone," the show of 311 artworks was applauded by one critic for letting "gallery-goers see a spectrum of painting styles rather than limit[ing] the entries to one general style."[19] Focusing on three of the more contemporary pieces on display, Herbert Kenney, Jr., of the *Indianapolis News* wrote, "Rocketry, much in the news lately, inspired the title of one painting, *Flowers in Orbit* by Grace Payne. . . . The picture is a splash of color, an effect apparently achieved by using (Jackson) Pollock's technique of allowing paint to drip from a can, thus forming random patterns. Other paintings which caused much comment and scrutiny were one made of grain glued to the surface and the surrealistic *Tic Tac Tortoise* by Robert Holzapfel."[20]

Capturing two of the prizes from the $4,500 purse were Helen Duckwall and Jane Messick, both of Indianapolis. A portraitist as well as a still-life painter, Miss Duckwall won the $100 "Outstanding Pastel" with *Suzanne*, a piece she had borrowed from its owner who had commissioned the portrait. "It seems like [I've been doing portrait work] forever," she explained after her win. "I'm working on the second generation. When people call me and say, 'You did my father when he was a little boy,' I know I've been around a while. The first time I heard that, I was taken aback, but now I look on the comment with pride."[21]

Jane Messick painted her watercolor, *Women in Patzcuaro, Mexico,* after returning from a summer trip to Mexico where she visited Cuernavaca, Mexico City and Patzcuaro. "The picturesque village (Patzcuaro) and beautiful lake, where fishermen use butterfly nets, is one hundred fifty miles west of Mexico City," the artist said. "I did the painting of the women from sketches made while I was there."[22] Her portrayal of four women in native garb was chosen as one of the W. H. Starbuck-Julia Magill Starbuck Memorial purchase prizes.

Voted as the most popular painting of the show was *Winter in Brown County* by Clayson Baker. This housepainter who had packed up his ladders to pursue the fine arts won $100 from Lyman Brothers of Indianapolis. The company had agreed to continue the "Popular Prize" initiated in 1961 by the late artist Leota Loop. Although Baker's landscape failed to get a nod of approval from the jurists for a merit award, it was selected as the $200 Delta Sigma Kappa Sorority purchase prize.

Also underwriting several purchase prizes— *Afternoon at the Assisi* by Josephine McGee, *Flowers in Orbit* by Grace Payne and *Hillside Fantasy* by Thelma L. Knarr—was Kappa Kappa Kappa Sorority.[23] Long a booster of Hoosier art, the group owned sixty-four paintings, many of which were housed at the Brown County Art Guild galleries in Nashville, Indiana. Proud of the collection, Tri Kappa had produced a slide presentation of its art holdings as well as a history of its participation in the Salon some three years earlier.[24]

While the women of Delta Sigma Kappa and Tri Kappa were buying Salon artwork, the members of the Indiana Federation of Clubs had decided to end their custom of funding a purchase prize. After declining to be involved in the 1962 show, the organization announced that it was disbanding its art collection. The money raised from the sale of its paintings was to be used in establishing a summer art workshop for high school students. "Of the thirty-seven pictures by Indiana artists purchased by the Indiana Federation of Clubs over a period of years, twenty-five have yet to be sold,"[25] reported an Indianapolis newspaper. Priced by Mrs. Smith, the paintings were displayed for sale at the Hoosier Art Gallery in the State Life Building.

* * *

1963 With the Salon set to start in four days, artists and art patrons throughout the Midwest were saddened to learn of the death of Adolph Shulz at the age of ninety-three. Even though this venerable leader of the Brown County art colony had last appeared in the Salon in 1942, he had been a faithful exhibitor during the show's stay in Chicago. Particularly admired for his landscapes, Shulz remembered his excitement upon first exploring the hill country of southern Indiana. "Never before had I been so thrilled by a region," he had explained during one of his last interviews. "It seemed like a fairyland with its narrow winding roads leading the traveler down into the creek beds, through water pools and up over the hills. . . . [A]t last, [I had] found the ideal sketching ground."[26]

Seven months earlier to the day, Indiana's art community had suffered another loss with the untimely death of George Jo Mess on June 24, 1962. Skilled in aquatints as well as oils, this Cincinnati-born etcher had been, in addition, a sought-after illustrator during his multi-faceted career. In 1943, he had provided the artwork for Jeannette Covert Nolan's *Hoosier City, the Story of Indianapolis.* "I expected that an historical book would require pictures of pioneers in the wilderness, but there is only one of those," he had said to a reporter. "I had one month to do all the work! There were no photographs in the early days, and I had to do considerable research on costumes to make the drawings authentic. There were forty altogether."[27]

The 1963 Preview Party focused on the present, however, charming guests to the Salon's opening with imaginative offerings. Chef Fritz Faude of Block's had put forth his best efforts, creating "a four-foot-high windmill made of white and gold spun sugar for a table centerpiece. It [was] complete with tulips in the balconies, large sugar bows and Dutch characters in costume."[28] The paintings on view in the Auditorium Galleries were especially upbeat, too. One critic pointed out that "[t]here is a brightness of palette, as if the jurors were attracted by high-keyed color."[29]

In the exhibition of 237 pieces—chosen from a field of more than seven hundred entries submitted by artists working in twelve states—"Hoosier scenes are less in evidence than formerly. [B]ut those present are of excellent quality," noted Herbert Kenney, Jr., of the *Indianapolis News.* "[B]oth the modernists and the traditionalists have their places on the walls of the gallery. The jurors seem to have decided that Hoosiers should be given a chance to view examples of both schools. The result is a stimulating show, one that will provoke some controversy."[30]

Winning two awards from a total purse of $4,630 was Joel W. Reichard with his *Pemaquid Point Light.* The rock-strewn seascape earned this Bourbon, Indiana, native $100 for the "Outstanding Landscape Composition, Any Medium;" the painting also was selected by the Indiana Union Board of Directors at Indiana University as one of its two purchase prizes. A wanderer at heart, Reichard spent his winters in a permanent studio on the outskirts of Silver Springs, Florida. Every spring, he journeyed to North Truro, Massachusetts, and the rest of each year found him in Brown County, Indiana. During his travels, the bachelor shared a house trailer-turned-studio with his dachshund named Waldo.[31]

Unnoticed by many Salon-goers were the changes that had taken place in the Association staff prior to the start of the 1963 show. Mrs. Smith had relinquished her duties as executive chairman to Mrs. (Keith A.) Dorothy H. Weston of Indianapolis. Her decades of Salon experience were not wasted, though; the veteran had agreed to stay on with the Association and act as its business manager. Sharing office space with the two of them was Mrs. Herbert Bayliff who served as their executive secretary.

Seeking to encourage more visitors to the Hoosier Art Gallery, Mrs. Weston had contacted a local newspaper soon after assuming her post. "Everyone knows of the annual Hoosier Salon," she told Ann Fellows of the *Indianapolis Times,* "but how many art lovers know the Salon has permanent gallery and office space and year-round shows in the State Life Building? The trouble is that this (the annual show) dies in the public mind from year to year. People aren't aware of our permanent facilities; we're always open 9 a. m. to 4:30 p. m. daily, except in August."[32]

* * *

1964 The three women had barely settled into their jobs before Board members undertook a major reorganization of the Association. At the group's meeting in October of 1963, Mrs. Beryl S. Holland of Bloomington, Indiana, stepped down as president of the group. She had been elected to the position in June of 1941. The eighty-one-year-old, also a founder of Tri Kappa Sorority, was named president emeritus by the Board, grateful for her many years of devotion to the Salon. Chosen to take her place was Dr. Joseph B. Davis, a trustee from Marion, Indiana. He first had attended the show as a youngster when his parents had taken him to the event in Chicago.[33]

With the restructuring came an end to the shared leadership of the Chicago Vice-Presidents and the Indiana Vice-Presidents. Created in 1927 to link Hoosiers living in the "Windy City" with those staying in the home state, the twin boards had outlived their usefulness. In their stead, the Association's Board of Trustees—calling itself a Board of Directors—had merged the two panels into one; it became known as the Honorary Vice-Presidents. An Advisory Council was set up as well. In this group were the presidents and art chairmen of those organizations that had supported the Salon through the years. Even Mrs. Weston was given another title. No longer the "executive chairman," she was designated as the "executive director."

Despite this reshuffling, the exhibition remained remarkably consistent. In reviewing the 283 pieces on display, Helen Magner of the *New Castle Courier-Times* noted that the Salon "is one time when the paintings are always the kind that are understandable, with no second-hand Picassos to make you wonder what the artist was trying to do."[34] While another critic labeled the show as "conservative in tone,"[35] he did point out that "[o]ne of the unusual works included . . . is Huckleberry Hawkins' *Still Life*, made of colored yarn glued to the canvas. And there is an illuminated work of varicolored glass which has been fused into a landscape."[36]

The Preview Party, as had been the custom, offered hundreds of by-invitation-only guests a tempting buffet in the Block's Tea Room. Again the room was bedecked with decorations; this year, they highlighted the Salon's fortieth anniversary. According to an advance story about the show in the *Indianapolis News*, the "[c]enterpiece of the central table is a six-foot-tall replica of a pink, tiered birthday cake covered with wide satin ribbons of spun sugar. Two pink candy baskets of the spun sugar will be at each end of the table and will be filled with live pink carnations."[37]

Capturing the $500 "Outstanding Work in Oil of the Entire Exhibition" prize—from a total purse of $5,400—was Edward Nicholson with his *And Alice Said to the Rabbit*. The award-winning piece was a portrait of a mother with her daughter. An exhibitor who had missed only three Salons since his first appearance in Chicago in 1940, this traditional painter had little use for contemporary art. "What is there in Pop Art that you can call art?" he had asked a writer for the Bloomington, Illinois, *Pantagraph* during an interview. "And what do paintings of Dick Tracy have to do with art? They aren't even good cartoons. It amounts to nothing. . . . [T]hese 'Pop' artists are just destroying art. They're being different for the sake of being different."[38]

Even though Adelee Wendel left the Preview Party without a prize for her paintings, she was not disappointed. She had already been well rewarded by the enthusiasm of her art students at the Indiana Women's Prison. "For years, I'd been driving past the prison every day on my way to and from the East Side Art Center," explained this painter who had moved to Indianapolis from Newark, New Jersey, some fourteen years earlier. "I got to thinking that perhaps some of the women would like to take up painting. So, one day, I stopped in to see the superintendent who immediately approved of the idea."[39] There was such interest in her weekly art class that a second teacher, Harold Buck, was recruited as an instructor in portrait painting. Mrs. Wendel and Buck volunteered their

time, and all of the supplies were donated by the Art Center and several of its students.

As it had in the past, the Association continued to receive plaudits for its practice of loaning Salon artwork to the membership. According to a policy developed during its stay in Chicago, "[t]hree pictures a year [could] be loaned to a patron with the limit of sixty days on the retention of each, after which time there [would] be a lapse of sixty days before another picture [could] be borrowed. The artist reserve[d] the right to recall a picture after two weeks."[40] By 1964, though, the lending service was available only for "paintings by Hoosier artists for schools, libraries and community-used buildings."[41]

* * *

1965 Protest, violence and change continued to dominate the news as Mrs. Weston and her corps of volunteers prepared for the forty-first Salon. The nation was still reeling from the assassination of President Kennedy some fourteen months earlier, and the war in Vietnam continued to absorb ever-increasing numbers of American troops. This turbulence was not lost on Elsie Irwin Sweeney as she penned the Foreword for the show's catalogue. "Our world has never been more in need of beauty and sanity," she wrote. "However, the greatest music was created during the stress and strain of revolution and wars. May our contemporary struggles and frustrations bear the same kind of fruit."[42]

Association volunteers worked closely with the personnel at Block's, setting up galleries in the department store Auditorium for the 1965 Salon. There were only two alterations in the well-established proceedings. For the convenience of out-of-town guests, the starting hour of the Preview Party had been switched from 4:30 p. m. to 3:30 p. m.,[43] and an additional rule, governing the submission of entries, had been added. "[N]o picture may be entered that has been in any juried downtown Indianapolis show," reported Helen Magner of the *New Castle Courier-Times*. "This will make the Salon better, for it will not be made up of things already familiar."[44]

Considered by art aficionados around the state to be one of the premier events of the season, the Salon and its Preview Party promised an afternoon of fun, friendship and fine artwork. Lines were long to the buffet tables that were laden with colossal ripe and green olives, cucumber ring molds filled with jumbo shrimp and Lamays dressing, chicken Newburg in patty shells, spiced meat wedges, brandied peaches, petite yeast rolls and a variety of pastries. A string quartet serenaded the nearly eight hundred guests during their supper.[45]

According to Association officials, the show was one of the largest in the Salon's history. Hoosiers from ten states were represented in the galleries that featured 288 artworks; they had been selected from more than one thousand entries submitted by 268 artists.[46] Many of these hopefuls were new exhibitors who sought to match their abilities against such regulars as Marie Goth, V. J. Cariani, Sara Kolb Danner and William A. Eyden, all of whom had been on the Salon's roster since the first year in Chicago.

As a young child, Eyden—a second-generation Hoosier artist—was uncertain "whether he would become a painter or a violinist. He had talent for both, and studied both seriously. His art teacher was his father, William A. Eyden, Sr.; his violin teacher [was] Frederick Hick, professor of music at Earlham College. . . . Art finally won."[47] The violin, however, was never far from the painter's reach; he owned four, among them a Guarnerius. It was that valuable violin, in fact, which he used as a model for creating his prizewinning *Old Friends* for the 1962 Salon.[48]

The record-breaking show was described by Herbert P. Kenney, Jr., of the *Indianapolis News* as "an electric display of 'strong' paintings, watercolors and sculpture."[49] Its range, he wrote, "is from conventional to such modernistic techniques as 'drip' painting, in which the artist forms a pattern of color by letting paint drip from a container."[50] The *Indianapolis Star* critic agreed, noting that "the current exhibition is among the most interesting and varied in recent years. It has a little of everything, from conventional landscapes to collages."[51]

Winning $500 for the "Outstanding Work in Oil of the Entire Exhibition" prize, from a combined purse of $5,000, was Earl Oshier with his landscape *Lost Mail*. This "husky red-haired factory worker from Anderson [had] taught himself to paint."[52] Living with his wife and three-year-old daughter in a house trailer, the twenty-seven-year-old shared the secret of his success with an Indianapolis reporter. "I wanted to learn," he modestly explained, "so I borrowed books from the library and studied."[53]

With the summer slowdown of the Hoosier Art Gallery came an announcement that surprised many in the Association. After less than three years as the group's executive director, Mrs. Weston made known her wish to retire by September 1. Under her leadership, the Salon had thrived. Large numbers of new artists had entered the show, and more cities than ever had been scheduled to host one of the traveling exhibitions. Prior to relocating in Florida with her husband, Mrs. Weston admitted that she had been resisting the move for more than a year because of her commitment to the Salon.[54]

* * *

1966 In addition to underscoring the Salon's twenty-five-year relationship with Block's, the 1966 exhibition also coincided with the Sesquicentennial Celebration for the state of Indiana. It was a time of historical reflection. Writing for the *Indianapolis Star*, Harold Sabin traced the Hoosier art heritage to pioneer painters who had "receded so far into the past that their names and work today are known only to those who have had some incentive to study the history of art indigenous to this state. . . . The first artists hereabout, in fact, were itinerant portrait painters whose work usually was not signed."[55]

While Indiana's early artists may not have created new styles with their work, they did launch regional trends with their rendering of things local. "Previously," continued Sabin, "it had always been considered fashionable to buy French and German works, but artists such as T. C. Steele began to paint Hoosier scenes and, eventually, Hoosiers began to buy their works. This set the spark that brought many painters to Indiana, making it a well-known haven for artists. . . . The first exhibition by home artists in Indianapolis was held in 1877, on the second floor of a building at Pennsylvania and Court streets."[56]

Eighty-nine years later, the practice of exhibiting the work of "home artists" continued with the opening of the forty-second Salon. In the Foreword to the exhibition catalogue, Harold W. Jordan—director of the Indiana Memorial Union at Indiana University in Bloomington and a member of the Association's Board of Directors—saluted this precedent set long ago. "Though the Hoosier Salon Patrons Association cannot boast as long an existence (as Indiana), it can say with pride that it has served the cause of art in our Hoosier State since 1924," he noted. ". . . Let us perpetuate the past through the greater canvases of our artists and let us, our children and their children develop an even greater appreciation of the Arts so that we can encourage the artists of tomorrow."[57]

Despite zero-degree weather, hundreds of Salon patrons braved the winter winds to view one of the smallest shows in recent years. Only 162 pieces of artwork were on display in the Block's Galleries. An extra bit of excitement "was created by the mid-afternoon arrival of five fire trucks outside the store," remarked an Indianapolis reporter who had been invited to the Preview Party. "But hostess Mrs. Sterling Riley informed two guests . . . that 'it was a false alarm.'"[58] Among the party-goers was Governor Roger D. Branigin. Approached for his autograph by Rushville, Indiana, artist Dorothy DeArmond, he obliged but playfully warned her, "[I]f you sell it, I get half. I'm getting greedy in my old age."[59]

Martha Slaymaker won $500—from a combined purse of more than $5,000—when her geometric painting, *Image,* was named the "Outstanding Work in Oil of the Entire Exhibition." "I'm so delighted I won," exclaimed the artist as she waved her check. "This will help us get back to Mexico this spring."[60] Earlier in the fall, she and her husband had taken their children to South America to visit several archaeological sites. The result of her study among the ruins was readily seen in her work. One critic described Mrs. Slaymaker as an abstractionist whose "'abstractions' are really quite explicit, even if they do deal with such esoteric topics as pre-Columbian civilizations and ancient alphabets. Trips through the Southwest, Mexico and South America have piqued and reinforced her archaeological enthusiasm."[61]

Relieved to have mounted the Salon with the help of Mrs. Smith and a cadre of seasoned volunteers, the Association Board moved to fill a vacancy left the prior September by the departure of Mrs. Weston. Named to succeed her as executive director was the newly married Mrs. (David J.) Constance Burkhart Shea of Indianapolis. Mrs. Shea, who had taken course work at the University of Colorado, Butler University and John Herron Art School, had recently returned from a year's study in Barcelona, Spain.[62]

Secure in the knowledge that, once again, the Association was in steady hands with the appointment of another director, Mrs. Smith retired from her position as business manager. "I'm not sure how I feel being retired from the Salon after twenty-five years; I suppose I'll miss it a lot," she told Mary Waldon of the *Indianapolis Star.* "Through [this] experience, I have found that art is a personal matter. You can't take a definite stand and say one kind of art is good and another kind is bad.

"The older people like conservative and traditional art because they have lived through it. It is the young ones who like contemporary art," she continued. "My husband was always interested in art and artists so it was natural for me to be, too. Many Indiana artists were our friends. I will always follow the careers of Hoosier artists and be interested in the Salon."[63] The woman, who was heralded as "Mrs. Hoosier Salon," said that she

intended to keep busy by taking care of her house and writing a book about her involvement with art through the years.

* * *

1967 Less than six weeks before the opening of the forty-third Salon, Walt Disney, the man who had devoted a lifetime to the art of animation, died in California. Miniskirts were shaking the foundations of fashion, centuries-old art was being ravaged by floods in Italy, and the New York Metropolitan Opera House was closing its doors after eighty-three years of making music. The Sixties were a time of change: in the world at large, in art and in the Hoosier Salon.

After noting that the 1967 show contained "fewer than usual of the oils of the hills and woods of southern Indiana,"[64] one reviewer suggested a spirit of experimentation could be seen emerging from a number of the 273 pieces on display. "There are many ways to paint that were seldom done only a few years ago. New materials have been tested and found good, and ways of using them tried out," she observed. "The prints are of unusual interest for they have so much variety and thought in them. . . . In the sculpture, a number are of metal used in large pieces twisted to give the form rather than cast in the shape. . . . Many are finding ways of working on beautiful patterns in collages in which almost anything can be used."[65]

What remained constant, however, was the elegance with which the Preview Party would entertain its nine hundred anticipated guests. "The focal point of decor on service tables will be three-foot high French pitchers filled with spring flowers," promised Bertha Scott of the *Indianapolis News* in her preview of the Salon's upcoming "French Garden" party. "In the background, [a local florist] is planning a gazebo or outdoor trellised garden covered with vines and greenery for a cool, summery effect. In the Tea Room proper, a large willow tree, full of white doves with a pink carnation in the beak of each bird, will center the room. Topiary trees will be spaced around the outer walls."[66]

As reservations poured in for the big party, the untested Mrs. Shea "face[d] her first big show where the final decisions [were] hers."[67] She was particularly grateful when the former executive director, Mrs. Weston, decided to pay a timely visit to Indianapolis "just to be useful where needed."[68] Pulling together plans for the buffet supper was made easier for the young woman with the help of Paul Rizzo, director of Block's restaurants. He reassured Mrs. Shea that "[t]here'll be no problem with Tea Room personnel being on hand. They feel such a loyalty; they're hurt if not asked to serve."[69]

In selecting the award-winners for the February show, the jury chose Harry A. Davis' painting, *La Rues,* as the "Outstanding Work in Oil of the Entire Exhibition." Davis had taken a once-splendid mansion in the 1100 block of North Pennsylvania Street as subject matter for his solemn commentary on the shifting urban landscape. According to the *Indianapolis Star,* the painter had "pictured the house as it [stood] at present in a state of decay awaiting demolition for the proposed inner loop highway"[70] through downtown Indianapolis.

With his entry *Butterfly Weed,* Lester W. Gallagher—like Davis—had attempted to freeze a moment in time before it was lost. "I paint mostly the Dunes now, hurrying, before it is too late," explained this Navy veteran who had kept up with his painting while on duty in the Pacific during World War II. "I've walked over the Dunes from the Gary mills to Michigan City. So much is gone now. It is hard to find the water holes of cattails and lilies, and it is very hard to find butterfly weed to paint. So much of my beloved Dunes is now just a beautiful memory."[71]

For those involved in the administration of Association affairs, change seemed to be the only constant. Once again, the Board of Directors was faced with the task of finding someone to assume the duties of executive director; Mrs. Shea had resigned her post after the close of the 1967 show. By the fall board meeting, though, Mrs. (Philip B.) Margaret G. Reisler had been appointed to the position. A member of the National Society of Arts and Letters, she had graduated from Brenau College and had studied at Columbia University. Mrs. Reisler had been a teacher of speech and drama at Brenau College, Marian College and Butler University.[72]

* * *

1968 The forty-fourth Salon "could be called a year of superlatives," observed a writer from the *Indianapolis Star Magazine.* "More artists entered, more spectators visited, and donors offered more prize money than ever before in the exhibition's history."[73] Welcoming guests to an especially exuberant Preview Party were Indianapolis Mayor Richard Lugar, Hugh J. Baker, Jr.—who had replaced Dr. Joseph B. Davis as president of the Association at the board meeting in the fall of 1967—and Maurice Block, Jr. During the afternoon, they saw thirty-three artists share in a purse of more than $7,000, the richest ever offered at the midwinter show.

Corbin Patrick, long an advocate for the arts in the capital city, was pleased to learn of the record sum of prize money. In his *Indianapolis Star* column, "As the Day Begins," he wrote approvingly of the increased funding. "While arts enjoy increasingly wide-spread popularity, it has not been correspondingly rewarding to artists in terms of apparel, housing [or] fish and chips. For that reason, we find greater financial support of the Hoosier Salon most encouraging," stated Patrick.

"Part of the problem in all the arts, but especially in painting, is the proliferation of the artists. It's one field of creative activity in which expression is free," he continued. "You don't need a license or degree. You don't have to pass all kinds of bothersome exams designed in part to limit competition, if you want to practice art. . . . Consequently, the field is overcrowded. It's as bad as a traffic jam on weekends in summer. Another part of the problem, then, is to gain suitable recognition for outstanding talent, and the generous prize list for the Hoosier Salon is a step in that direction."[74]

As they had done for many years, representatives from Tri Kappa, Psi Iota Xi and Delta Sigma Kappa sororities joined with other purchase prize donors for the typically frantic selection period, held before the start of each Salon. Deciding the procedure "was rather like a little treasure hunt," *Indianapolis Star* reporter Donna Snodgrass wrote: "After witty words of advice offered by Donald Mattison, dean of Herron School of Art of Indiana University, and A. Reid Winsey, head of DePauw University's art department, the participants had an hour—until the musical gong was sounded—to view the 238 pieces accepted (for the show)."[75]

The various groups wove through the Auditorium galleries at Block's, pausing before one painting or another. They appeared to be asking themselves—as they had been encouraged to do by Winsey—"Does [this piece] give me a new pair of glasses? Will I see something in a way I've never seen it before?"[76] or "When I look at it, do I see paint? I don't want to see paint."[77] With twenty minutes to go, "the (Tri Kappa) committee convened informally for a quick trip around again," noted Snodgrass, who had been invited to watch the process from start to finish.

"This year, they seemed to agree that they wanted two or three less expensive works rather than one of the higher price. So the final decision, to be made public Sunday at the Salon's premiere, was all wrapped up in a typical female juggling of figures: 'Now, let's see; that one's $250 and this one's $175, that leaves—no, that one costs more than we have left.' The musical gong sounded."[78] The women of Tri Kappa finally settled on *What If the Sun Shone Not* by Lee Coblentz, *Summer* by Patricia Eberhart Victor and *Rock Structures, Mesa Verde* by Martha Slaymaker.

Rosemary Browne Beck took the day's number-one merit award for the "Outstanding Work, Any Medium, in the Entire Exhibition." Among the ninety-five women whose work had been admitted into the Salon, this Indianapolis artist won $500 with a portrait in oil entitled *Blanche*. Her piece was described by a critic from the *Indianapolis News* as "an arresting portrait of Blanche Stillson, Indianapolis author, art patron and nationally known naturalist and bird-lover. Painted in a woodland setting, the portrait captures the subject's singularity of character."[79]

Attracted by the Salon's generous purse, a handful of Hoosier artists admitted to entering the show for a chance at the prize money. "If one's work is fairly well known and has received prizes in the past, the artist will enter with the hope of getting the top award," explained Claudine Paluzzi, a painter as well as a printmaker. "One isn't happy with the small 'honorable mention.'"[80] The amateur, though, "enters to get exposure," added Martha Slaymaker, a Salon regular who had been awarded last year's $500 Franklin College purchase prize. "At the very first, it is important just to get into the show."[81] Lois Davis, along with her artist-husband Harry Davis, had exhibited in earlier Salons with great success. "I enter all local shows when I have a buildup of work so I have a choice. I don't paint for a specific show," observed this president of the Indiana Artists Club. ". . . Artists do progress in 'plateaus.' There may be those times when their work is not appealing to judges, and they are completely rejected. New growth may appear, and one may receive several prizes. It's a matter of changing and development. One must keep trying."[82]

* * *

1969 Even though the Salon had expanded its categories of prizes to accommodate more contemporary artwork, the show retained a conservative reputation. In writing the Foreword for the catalogue, Talitha Peat, wife of the former director of Herron Museum, commented upon the nature of the exhibition. "The world of art needs and must have the experimenters, the innovators, the expositors to be vital and valid," she declared. "But, at the same time, there is a commensurate place for the traditionalism in art forms. [W]e might call it representationalism or naturalism. The Hoosier Salon, though perhaps traditionalism was not the prepotent of the earliest exhibitions, has become the bastion of the realists in the artistic field of Indiana."[83]

Tradition, indeed, did reign when William A. Eyden won two merit awards and one purchase prize—for a record-setting total of $2,150—with his stately *Self Portrait*. The show's combined purse was attention-getting, too, as over $10,000 was presented to prizewinners by Mrs. Edgar D. Whitcomb, wife of the governor of Indiana. She confided to one of the reporters on the scene that she "was doubly happy the event was at Block's [because she had] ruined her hose on a door . . . alighting from a car and [had] stopped on the first floor to get a new pair."[84]

Pleasing Eyden almost as much as the honors accorded his work was the acceptance into the Salon of a painting—*Mother and Child, No. 1*—by his friend Joseph Holiday. He had been championing the cause of this talented African-American artist from Indianapolis for some time. "Joe's a dandy painter," Eyden said. "His heads are just remarkable; they're out of this world. But he's had a hard time getting ahead. When you're alone in art and when you're colored, well . . . ."[85]

Holiday, among the few African-American artists to have exhibited in the Salon,[86] was grateful to Eyden for his encouragement. "He helped me a lot with money and canvases, and I think it was he who got me into the Hoosier Salon," explained Holiday, a former student at Herron School of Art and the Art Institute of Chicago. "Sometimes I get kind of disgusted with the whole bit. I see other painters, with less talent than I, getting ahead. But then I say, 'Well, what else would I rather do?' And I just go on."[87]

"Going on" was one thing V. J. Cariani[88] had mastered. This Italian-born painter—who had embraced Brown County, Indiana, as his adopted home—had missed only two Salons since the start of the exhibition in 1925. He added to his already long string of awards by taking the show's $100 "Outstanding Flowers in Oil" prize with a still life entitled *Summer Bouquet*. Painting from a studio near one owned by artist Marie Goth, Cariani relaxed by tending the gardens around both buildings. He also made the frames for his paintings as well as for Miss Goth's. A dabbler in the kitchen, too, this World War I veteran loved to cook; spaghetti and apple pie were his specialities.[89]

Foregoing the use of a three-person jury, the forty-fifth show—composed of 201 artworks—had been put together by a panel of two: Jay Connaway, a Vermont-based Hoosier known for his marines and landscapes, and Joseph J. Rishel, the Assistant Curator of Painting and Sculpture at the Art Institute of Chicago. Both men had been surprised by the number of non-traditional entries they had encountered during the judging process. "[T]he show is not as provincial as I expected," said Connaway. "It is quite rare to see something significantly innovative. So much of art is imitative.

But that should be no reflection upon our age. The same was true through history. For every hundred artists, there may have been one who was really painting."[90]

Shepherding the show to its conclusion had been another new president of the Board of Directors. Harold W. Jordan had been elevated from his office of second vice-president to that of president upon the unexpected death of Hugh J. Baker, Jr., earlier in December of 1968. Later, at the 1969 fall board meeting, Jordan would be reelected president of the Association. At that same October session, Mrs. (Victor C.) Stella Hackney of Indianapolis would be named as the new executive director. She would replace Mrs. Reisler, who had resigned the previous June.[91]

1972
Rob O'Dell
Offspring
Outstanding Work—Any Medium

1975
Lois Davis
Neighbors
Outstanding Work—Any Medium

1972
Jean Vietor
Edge of Summer
Jury Prize of Distinction

1977
Nanci Blair Closson
Out of Element
Outstanding Work—Any Medium

The Seventies

1970 Fans of traditional art continued to spar with advocates of the avant-garde as the new decade began. Gently mocking the feud between the followers of the Salon and the more contemporary Indiana Artists Exhibition, A. Ian Fraser—Curator of Research of the Clowes Fund Collection at the Indianapolis Museum of Art—decried the stereotypes held of each. "It seems to be a popular misconception that those people who are champions of Barry Goldwater and the D. A. R. (Daughters of the American Revolution) are also devotees of the Hoosier Salon," he wrote in the *Downtowner Indianapolis,* "while on the other side of the fence sit the friends of Senator (Edmund) Muskie, Civil Liberties and the Indiana Artists."[1]

Noting that "the Indiana Artists tend to fancy themselves as being the heralds of tomorrow's artistic trends, and the Hoosier Salon may think of itself as the guardian of yesterday's,"[2] Fraser maintained that both exhibitions played a vital role in the city's cultural life. Each of the shows provided an occasion for celebration, he said, although their respective openings looked as different as the art they featured.

At the museum, where work by the Indiana Artists was displayed, art-lovers "turn[ed] up in droves, often dressed in a manner calculated to upstage the most *outré* work of art in the exhibition," Fraser declared in his magazine article. "[At] the Hoosier Salon or 'Saloon' as some wags are wont to call it, . . . they have a similar annual winging, albeit in a different location. . . . The turnout for this event is quite as impressive as the turnout for the Indiana Artists Exhibition, although one might note a shift in emphasis from blue jeans to blue rinses.[3]

". . . Critics complain about the prevalence of 'covered bridges' and 'bowls of peonies,' among the (Salon's) exhibits, though they often give scant consideration to the skill and imagination with which the familiar theme may have been handled by the artist, or to the fact that these subjects are part of the traditional character of the Indiana scene," he continued. "Perhaps the Hoosier Salon is guilty of encouraging too many variations on a not very original theme, but why should they be castigated for that? How many of us, after all, have a spot in our living room that is crying out to be filled with a throbbing incandescent plastic bag?"[4]

The offerings of the forty-sixth Salon remained predominantly traditional, in spite of "a vivid scattering of work in contemporary media and techniques."[5] Despite having a field of nearly eight hundred entries from which to choose, the jury appeared to have been drawn to the conservative when it finalized the show of 235 pieces. The two jurors did not even "make a merit award in the '[N]ew [T]rends, [A]ny [M]edium' category, established by the Salon recently to encourage experimental work."[6]

Indianapolis painter and Herron Art School professor Harry A. Davis split the show's top merit award—from a combined purse of $9,445—with himself. "Two of his landmark paintings, *The Athenaeum* and *Westside Drug Store,* were declared co-winners by the jury," reported the *Indianapolis Star.* "They are part of a series of paintings in which Davis has undertaken to preserve for posterity at least the look of many familiar old buildings, some of which already have been razed for 'progress.'"[7] Although Davis had been exhibiting in the Salon since 1947, his double victory would signal the start of a twenty-year pattern in which he would win at least one award every year.

Allen Hackney of Terre Haute, Indiana, was another who collected several awards at the Preview Party. In addition to taking the $200 Psi Iota Xi Sorority purchase prize with his *The Robber,* the junior high school art teacher won a $300 "Jury Prize of Distinction" with his egg tempera, *The Song Sparrow.* This painting also received the most votes among gallery visitors, winning its artist the $100 "Popular Prize."

Enthused about working with the medium of egg tempera—used "by the oldest Old Masters in the 13th and 14th centuries, before the discovery of oil"[8]—Hackney felt that "[p]igment is pigment. The difference in kinds of paints comes from the material used to bind the pigment together. In egg tempera," he noted, "it's the yolk of an egg plus water."[9] Striving for clarity of detail in his realistic paintings of nature, Hackney ignored "[t]he traditional rule . . . that the rest of your composition must subordinate the central theme. I've reversed that rule as it is reversed in nature," he explained. "You have to hunt for my birds and my mushrooms buried in the foliage. But my titles give you the theme."[10]

Demanding an ever-increasing share of attention at the Salon was the work in sculpture. While a metal abstract—*Iron Reflection III* by Steve Wooldridge—won the $300 "Outstanding Work in Sculpture" prize, a marble head entitled *Temujin* won a record $1,500 purchase award for its creator, Don DeWitt. One Salon artist, though, appears to have been singularly unimpressed with the state of contemporary sculpture. After describing one of the pieces from a sculpture exhibit set up on the lawn of the Herron Art Museum as a "hunk of redwood," Elmer Taflinger belittled the remainder of the display. "I guess they put this stuff out there to be hauled away,"[11] he remarked to a security guard upon leaving the show.

Busily writing an autobiographical text that he hoped would put young artists "back on the right track,"[12] the seventy-nine-year-old Taflinger wanted to rekindle in the younger generation the love of art as the Old Masters saw it. He believed that "[a]rt won't be reborn until people need it. Nobody needs it now. People are satisfied. They worship machines. They worship their automobiles."[13] According to the Indianapolis artist, "[a]rt is like a woman: it must be wanted and needed. We need means to make people believe in paintings; today it's only a plaything."[14]

The Hoosier Salon Patrons Association was flourishing under the dynamic leadership of Harold W. Jordan as president; talk of new ventures dominated the group's Board meetings. Among the ideas that had been acted upon was the publication of a *Hoosier Salon Newsletter.* First mailed during October of 1969, this circular was directed to members and prospective members of the Association. It contained "[n]otices of exhibitions, sales, acknowledgements of appointments, gifts, awards, invitations to membership, and calls for volunteers, as well as personal items pertaining to the membership."[15]

Another agenda item that was prompting lengthy discussions by the Board was the need for gallery space in a more accessible location. Ever since 1954, when Mrs. Leonidas Smith had first proposed having "quarters on the ground floor,"[16] the group had been aware of the benefits of securing street-level accommodations. In late spring of 1970, the Board had begun negotiations with the Indianapolis Hilton Hotel for space on its first floor to be used for Salon sales. By early September, a ten-year lease with the hotel had been signed, and plans were underway to furnish the new showroom. A report issued by the Executive Committee indicated that "[a]n expenditure of $3,695 was required to furnish the room and equip it for exhibitions, with space for display of one hundred to 125 paintings."[17]

The acquisition of an additional Hoosier Art Gallery, to be located in the main lobby area of the hotel, was a dream come true for Jordan and members of the Association. Supplementing their office and display area on the sixth floor of the Thomas Building, formerly known as the State Life Building,[18] this added space would only enhance the group's ability to publicize Hoosier art. Its permanent collection would remain in the Thomas Gallery, while the Hilton would be used to feature the artwork of selected painters, watercolorists, printmakers and sculptors.

"We feel the opening of this new showroom will further our goal in promoting the work of Hoosier artists by making them accessible to thousands of visitors to Indianapolis,"[19] explained Jordan. According to the president, artists represented in three or more yearly Salons would be given consideration for solo shows at either the Hilton or the Thomas Building display rooms, or both. In addition, he said, the Association would accept paintings on consignment from artists represented in at least one annual.

In preparation for the official opening, the new executive director adopted an idea that had been popular during the Salon's years in Chicago. Reviving the notion of "Special Day" hostesses, Mrs. Stella Hackney enlisted the participation of clubwomen whose organizations were represented on the Association's Advisory Council. The honor of welcoming guests to the Hilton Gallery on its first day—Monday, October 19—went to members from the Woman's Department Club because "they were most helpful in bringing the Hoosier Salon to Indianapolis from Chicago."[20] The hostesses on duty for the rest of the week included: Indiana Artists Club and Daughters of Indiana, Tuesday; Psi Iota Xi Sorority, Wednesday; Kappa Kappa Kappa Sorority, Thursday; Indiana Federation of Clubs and Indiana Federation of Art Clubs, Friday; and Delta Sigma Kappa, Saturday.[21]

After the excitement of the first week had diminished, members of the newly created Volunteers for the Hoosier Salon were available to handle responsibilities in the gallery. Recruited by Mrs. Hackney—who had sent out invitations for membership that promised "a pretty, interesting and pleasant place to be"[22]—they staffed the showroom Tuesdays through Saturdays. Coordinating the schedules of the sixty charter volunteers[23] was Mrs. (Thomas E.) Marilee Husselman who had been appointed manager of the space at the Hilton.[24]

With the Hilton Gallery came the realization of the Board's dream; it had finally found that convenient location for displaying Hoosier artwork. After a visit to this space in Indianapolis, Helen Magner of the *New Castle Courier-Times* had written: "The new gallery is bringing art to a place where it is more easily seen by the public and where more people can enjoy it. It is a spot of beauty easy to reach. Last week, a mother and two of her children came in at the request of the twelve-year-old boy. He came along on a shopping trip on [the] condition that they would stop to see the pictures. He is growing up an art lover."[25]

* * *

1971 Paying his respects to the history of both the Association and the city in which it was based, George S. Diener, chairman of the Indianapolis Sesquicentennial Commission, had written in the Foreword to the Salon catalogue: "We celebrate our city in this year of 1971, a city now tenth in size in the nation and one hundred and fifty years old. From almost the beginning—even when our town was a 'scraggly little village' and 'its streets filled with mud and tree stumps'—we had an awareness of the value of art as a force in our lives.

"We gave encouragement and provided stimulus to a long list of Indiana and Indianapolis artists," he continued. "As early as the 1840s, Indianapolis boasted a small art gallery for the exhibition and sale of paintings. It was an enclave of beauty in a town that was still part of a rugged frontier. . . . The Hoosier Salon, now in its forty-seventh year, carries on [that] great tradition."[26]

While young Kay McCrary had yet to be born during the early years of the Salon, the Morgantown, Indiana, painter and printmaker made history upon her admission into the show. Even though she appeared in the Salon only once, this exhibitor earned an award for each of her two entries. In addition to winning $500 for the "Outstanding Work, Any Medium, Entire Exhibition" with a contemporary piece entitled *Enterprise*, Mrs. McCrary was given a L. G. Balfour "Honorable Mention" medal for her second entry, *Rolling Circles, Square*.

Another who left the Preview Party with two awards was long-time participant Elizabeth Dodds Shaffer. She won a $150 "Jury Prize of Distinc-

tion" as well as a Psi Iota Xi purchase prize with her landscape entitled *One Afternoon*. At ease with a variety of mediums, the New Castle, Indiana, artist relished painting with oils, acrylics, oil pastels and watercolors. When asked if it were difficult to part with one of her pieces, once completed, Mrs. Shaffer told Susan Lennis of the *Indianapolis Star Magazine*, "I'm sure a beginning painter is so intrigued and thrilled with each production that it is painful to part with the results of each effort. However, after a few years, the painter realizes the greatest pleasure is in the 'doing' of the work."[27]

Nearly one thousand artists and guests previewed the collection of work from which Mrs. McCrary and Mrs. Shaffer had won their prizes. Four hundred and thirty-four artists had entered the show, hoping for a portion of the $7,700 prize purse or, at least, some recognition of their talent. Of the 802 pieces of artwork submitted to the two-person jury, 222 had been selected for display.[28] William G. Ashby had won the $100 "Popular Prize," given at the conclusion of the exhibit for his portrait *Lupe, the Cook, Called Him "Señor Taffee."* "*Señor Taffee*, more familiarly known in art circles here as 'Taf,' is the artist and teacher, Elmer Taflinger," explained Corbin Patrick of the *Indianapolis Star*. "He sat for the portrait by Ashby, a former pupil.[29]

At the end of two weeks, the Salon was dismantled, and the movable gallery walls were stored at Block's for another year. The entries that had remained unsold during the show were separated into smaller groups and sent on their way to various Indiana cities. Selection of the pieces for every stopover on the exhibition calendar was carefully made; when possible, representative work of artists living in each of the ten scheduled venues was included. The 1971 tour would last for four months as towns throughout Indiana hosted their own versions of the parent Salon in Indianapolis.[30]

With the traveling shows underway, Association volunteers were able to concentrate on completing plans for a Memorial Exhibit, slated to open March 8 in their gallery at the Hilton. Designed to highlight the city's sesquicentennial birthday, this special display would "feature artists whose names and paintings are associated with the 'early years' of the Hoosier Salon when the annual exhibit was still being held in Chicago."[31] Among those whose works were to be on view during the month-long show were William J. Forsyth, Clifton Wheeler, Edward K. Williams, Edgar Forkner, J. Ottis Adams, L. O. Griffith, Genevieve Goth Graf, George Jo Mess and Wayman Adams.

In a year that saw a twenty percent increase in the sale of Salon artwork over 1970,[32] the Association was involved in another move. Less than twelve months after opening the Hilton salesroom, the group exchanged its out-of-the-way office space on the sixth floor of the Thomas Building for spacious, well-lighted quarters on the second floor.[33] Upon inspecting the new accommodations in Room 201, *Indianapolis Magazine* writer Marion Adams remarked, "The building itself has been handsomely refurbished since it was bought in 1969 by Mr. and Mrs. Frank P. Thomas, whose public-spirited assistance has encouraged numerous cultural activities in this area during the past decade.

"Recognizing the need of the Hoosier Salon Patrons Association for a larger showroom, the Thomases offered the handsome quarters, formerly occupied by their own Gallery of Today, at the same rental fee the art group had been paying for its tiny room on the sixth floor," she continued. "This was a tremendous shot-in-the-arm for the Salon, which subsists on dues from patrons and artists, supplemented by fees from pictures sold on consignment. Now they can display their paintings on walls prepared for that purpose and under proper lighting conditions. Comfortable chairs, good carpeting and panel display racks are effective aids."[34]

* * *

1972 As the musical *Jesus Christ Superstar* was shaking up theater audiences and the film *A Clockwork Orange* was playing to stunned moviegoers, Salon committee members were preparing for the show's January opening. The artwork chosen by the two Salon jurors, however, appeared to have been unaffected by this spirit of experimentation that was being reflected elsewhere in the arts.

After studying the work selected for the forty-eighth show, Marion Simon Garmel of the *Indianapolis News* concluded: "Overall, there is nothing terribly exciting about the exhibit. There is an overabundance of flowers in pots, some interesting, some not so interesting—few inspired. There are no big, bold paintings."[35] Bothered about the manner in which art was listed in the catalogue, she told her readers of "some caveats to be noted concerning the exhibition. First, no identification cards are provided for the paintings, so that unless one has a program one can't tell the players at all. Worse yet, even the program does not specify the medium of any work. What looks like a print may be an oil or an egg tempera. Who would know? It is a major deficiency which, hopefully, will be corrected in future Salons."[36]

Ms. Garmel may have needled the Association for its handling of the exhibition catalogue, but it was Hoosier artist Riley Bertram who attacked the group with pit-bull ferocity. Having exhibited in only the 1968 Salon, Bertram attended the 1972 show while pretending to be an art reviewer. "Appearing as a critic, notebook in hand,"[37] he wandered through the galleries, discussing the merits of various pieces with the hostesses who were on duty to answer any questions. Compiling his thoughts in what he billed as a "Press Release: The Forty-Eighth Annual Hoosier Salon, Criticism and Review," Bertram sent his missive to newspapers throughout Indiana.

The *Brown County Democrat* seems to have been the sole publication to have given Bertram a forum. "The once-proud standard bearer of Indiana Art, the Hoosier Salon, has inched closer to death," the self-proclaimed critic opined in the Letters to the Editor section of that paper, "its bones once again picked clean by the 'select clientele' in its annual society raid on the show. Little is left of what the Salon was, or could be. It is racked with apathy, abuse, poor judgment, bad art, crass commercialism and high-powered inner-art snobbery that has reduced this once nationally important show to nothing more than a method used by the monied to enhance their collections without having to rub elbows with the 'public.'"[38]

Angered by Bertram's rambling assault and its gross inaccuracies, Harold Jordan—in his capacity as president—prepared to confront Bertram in any newspaper that had printed the artist's letter. In a memorandum advising the Association's leadership of the situation, Jordan explained, "to our knowledge, only one paper published the (four-page) letter. This was the *Brown County Democrat,* which naturally had to publish the letter since Mr. Bertram has a shop in Nashville."[39]

In the Letters to the Editor section of the *Democrat,* therefore, Jordan penned a lengthy response in which he, point-by-point, refuted Bertram's allegations. "I know of no other salon that attempts to more fairly represent the local artists and provide every opportunity for their exposure and success," he wrote. ". . . [W]e go out of the way and at great expense to use an out-of-state jury with a wide spectrum of interest in various forms of art and no particular 'friends' to serve. None of the Hoosier Salon Board of Directors has any contact with the jury until after the selections are made. The Board has no input, nor does it want any.

". . . [T]he statement that this is a 'society' affair is certainly out of line as we don't have that kind of money to waste," continued Jordan. "You realize that we are solely dependent on income from membership fees and a twenty-five percent commission on sales in the Thomas Building Gallery and Hilton Hotel Showroom, both in Indianapolis. With rent, supplies, printing and minimum salaries, it is still difficult to operate within our restricted income. . . . We are indeed grateful for the support of over a thousand individuals, organizations, schools and business memberships. They make our year-long operation possible."[40]

Bertram's harangue failed to affect the number of Salon guests; hundreds of them assembled at Block's for a preview of exhibition artwork. Four hundred and eight artists had submitted 778 pieces to the show; and, from this field, the jury had selected 133 works representing 107 artists. Thirty-seven of them were first-time exhibitors.[41] Submissions to the Salon had poured in from studios across the country. In addition to having come from cities and towns throughout Indiana, work had been shipped from New Mexico, Arizona, New Hampshire, Illinois, Virginia, Pennsylvania, Wisconsin, New York, Maryland, California, Ohio, Georgia, Connecticut, Michigan and Washington, D. C.[42] Merit awards totaling $2,875 were presented to twenty-four artists, and $4,535 in purchase prizes was awarded to twenty-three artists.[43]

Watercolorist Rob O'Dell won the $500 "Outstanding Work, Any Medium, Entire Exhibition" award with *Offspring,* a realistic portrayal of three weathered tree stumps that were sprouting new growth. "O'Dell, who has entered two previous Hoosier Salons and won something in each of them, is one of the state's most competent and original artists, if the number of people who lately have taken to painting like him is any indication," observed the critic from the *Indianapolis News.* "Imitation, they say, is the sincerest form of flattery."[44]

This lanky, red-haired artist from Ladoga, Indiana, never imagined when he was growing up in Decatur, Illinois, that he would become a prizewinning artist. As the son of a cabinet-maker, he was expected, as were his three brothers, to take up his father's trade. "So naturally after high school," O'Dell explained, "I became a cabinetmaker. It took me three years to find out I didn't like it. I quit and joined the Army."[45] His military duty was not particularly demanding, and the artist found himself with leisure time. "Since I always had liked to draw, I did a couple of drawings and entered them in post shows and, well, I came out smelling like a rose."[46]

It was in the American Academy of Art in Chicago where O'Dell, studying under Irving Shapiro, had discovered watercolor. "You either like it or you don't," he said of the medium with which he had become associated. "I like it because it's so fluid. And I like the craftsmanship you have to have from beginning to end. You have to start with a good drawing and then everything must be well thought out. You can't make a mistake in watercolor.

"But because it's watercolor, because it's so fluid, lots of things can happen that are unplanned. That's what makes it so exciting," maintained O'Dell. "Most watercolorists are preoccupied with the medium. They fall in love with color. I used to paint that way, but now I just use watercolor as my medium, not as my goal. When I stopped painting like a watercolorist and let the subject dominate me, that's when I began having real success."[47]

Like Rob O'Dell, Rosemary Browne Beck—who won a $100 "Jury Prize of Distinction, Traditional" with her portrait *Chuck Tehan*—was in tune with the way color influenced her paintings. "Although color may be an exciting and sensual element, I think my work is stronger when reproduced in black and white," she observed. "Evidently, color is so distracting sometimes as to weaken the design elements. . . . [A]ll in all, color is the least important of all things which make up a painting. More important is tonality, subtle and strong gradations that make us feel—as in music—the mood."[48]

Recognized especially for her work in still life, Mrs. Beck was quick to defend the genre. "[S]till-life painting has come to have a bad connotation," she said, "like 'dullsville.' For one thing, so many dull ones have been painted. More important, still-life painting has been used in art school as an exercise, guiding the student in his evolution from student to artist. From here he goes on to something more imaginative, more challenging. In my own case, I've never evolved out of it; my evolution has taken place within its narrow confines.

"I shouldn't apologize for painting still life because I feel strongly that within it are all the possibilities for interpretive expression, and it can be creative," continued this Indianapolis artist who had been a steady prizewinner in the Salon since 1955. "Through the simple device of painting objects and their surroundings, my purpose is to make people see in it that which they might not otherwise find. . . . No messages here—excepting love for life."[49]

* * *

1973 "In the . . . Salon, each of us has an outstanding cultural event which brings honor to our great state through the considerable talent of its artists," observed Indiana Governor Otis R. Bowen, M. D., in writing the "Foreword" of the exhibition catalogue for the 1973 show. "With the heritage of nearly a half-century of Hoosier art, and the limitless future of countless tomorrows, the forty-ninth annual Hoosier Salon stands before us as a signal tribute to Hoosier culture."[50]

Looking ahead to those "countless tomorrows," Mrs. Hackney and her volunteers entered the new year, prepared to chart the future of the Salon as its fiftieth anniversary drew nearer. "The concept and activities of the Association have, over the years, been of such value to the state that the Board hopes to promote an understanding of its cultural impact throughout Indiana," explained Mrs. Henry Lester Smith, a member of the Board of Directors from Bloomington, Indiana. "To this end, the president [of the Board has] appointed the following special committees: Fiftieth Anniversary Planning Committee, Study Committee of the Future of the Hoosier Salon Patrons Association and Membership Development Committee."[51]

In September—as a way of introducing Salon art to a broader audience—would come the Association's participation in the Home Fashion Fair '73 at the Indiana Convention-Exposition Center in downtown Indianapolis. Mrs. Hackney would set up a fifteen-by-eighteen-foot display of artwork at the Indianapolis show that was "exclusively for exhibits of 'home fashion, home furnishings and home living.'. . . The [presentation would] contain original oils, watercolors, acrylics and sculptures . . ., exclusively by Indiana artists."[52]

Later, in mid-October, would come a project that had been developed from a suggestion made by the committee charged with long-range planning. The Association again would maintain an art rental service as it had done at various times in both Chicago and Indianapolis. According to a report issued by the committee: "Pictures for rent would hang exclusively in the Thomas Building Gallery. A sign giving this information would be placed in the Hilton Gallery. Renters would have to belong to the Hoosier Salon Patrons (Association). Artists would be asked to submit three pictures for the Rental Gallery which would be judged for acceptance by a jury of artists. . . . The Committee hope[s] that such a gallery would increase the membership of the Patrons Association because there are a number of people who cannot rent traditional art at present."[53]

With plans being made to honor its past and preparations underway to insure its future, the Salon opened on January 21 to an enthusiastic crowd gathered in the Block Auditorium Galleries. Almost a thousand guests were on hand to applaud the awarding of a $9,310 purse—$3,000 in merit awards and $6,310 in purchase prizes—to deserv-

ing artists. "All in all, the show (of 210 pieces) is noted for a contemporary flavor missing in past years," remarked Marion Simon Garmel of the *Indianapolis News,* "and for the large number of really good works on display."[54]

Among those "really good works" were the entries of the three top winners; all were women, adding yet another distinction to the already distinctive exhibition. Nanci Blair Closson's contemporary watercolor-and-ink design, *Squares II,* won the artist $500 by taking the "Outstanding Work, Any Medium, Entire Exhibition" prize. Martha Slaymaker captured the $400 "Outstanding Painting, Any Medium" prize with her *Bedford Soliloquy,* and Ruth Anderson received the $150 "Best Landscape, Oil" for her cityscape *Sanctuary.*

Encouraged by the warm reception given the 1973 Salon, Mrs. Hackney—along with members of the Fiftieth Anniversary Planning Committee— began to finalize details for next year's celebration. All of their ambitious plans literally went up in smoke on November 5. "A three-alarm fire turned an historic stretch of downtown Indianapolis into an inferno . . ., destroying two buildings, damaging five others and forcing evacuation of an estimated five thousand persons," reported a front-page story in the *Indianapolis Star.*[55] "Fire officials said they believed total damage would be at least fifteen million dollars, although the figure could be considerably higher. . . . Destroyed were the twelve-story Thomas Building . . . and the old four-story Grant Building."[56]

According to Mrs. Hackney, a noon-time shopper had been browsing in the Hoosier Art Gallery when she heard the sound of sirens stop outside the building. The executive director remembered that she had gone to the front of the gallery and had "heard things popping, and I knew it was kind of serious."[57] She had hurried down to the street and stood, with the hundreds of others who had been evacuated, to watch flames licking out of the windows on the fourth and fifth floors of the Thomas Building.

"I don't really know how many paintings were there," Mrs. Hackney said. "I had just finished getting ready to open our rental gallery, and my next job was to count the paintings. That day never came. I know we must have had close to three hundred paintings in the gallery," she continued. "I was sick. We had almost fifty years of memories in that gallery. It was the only home of the Salon we had ever had (in Indianapolis). All of our scrapbooks and records and everything we had gathered for our golden anniversary next year were in there."[58]

When Mrs. Hackney returned to the fire-ravaged building with president Jordan the following week, she automatically took out her door key. "But there wasn't any door there to unlock," she recalled. "Unless you see it, you can't imagine what happened. Whole walls are missing. . . . And where a wall does remain, a wall that served for hanging pictures, there now are just the outlines of the paintings that once hung there. The paintings have been transformed into ashes at the foot of the wall.

". . . For living artists, the loss, while personally wrenching, will not be great. The works were insured for fifty percent of the sale price, and the sale price included the gallery's thirty-three percent commission," she added. "Our biggest loss, besides the gallery itself and a very fine location, is the small but valuable collection of paintings by pioneer Indiana artists that we had on consignment from the artists' relatives or early collectors. With living artists, you know they will keep on painting, but the T. C. Steeles, the William Forsyths, the Otto Starks, they're just gone."[59]

Given refuge in a corner of the backstage area of the Auditorium at Block's, Mrs. Hackney set up a temporary office for the Association. Surrounded by crates packed with artificial Christmas trees for the upcoming holiday, she and Jordan sorted through their options. "We're just going to put the facts on the table and see what they think," said the president, after notifying the directors of an emergency Board meeting. "It's a little rough coming at the end of our forty-ninth year when we had such grand plans for a fiftieth anniversary celebration."[60]

In the weeks following the fire, Jordan contacted key people among the Association's constituency. In a letter to Frank P. Thomas, the group's former landlord, the Board president offered his sympathy. "I want to express to you our sincere regrets for your loss," he wrote. "I greatly appreciate the kindness you have shown our organization. The facilities on the second floor were a great asset to our organization, . . . [and we] appreciate the help you have given us in the modest rent for these facilities. We know that we will never have an opportunity to secure space of equal quality."[61]

Unsure about the long-range future of the show, he informed Katherine Wright, art chairman of the Daughters of Indiana in Chicago, that the Board had decided to proceed with the fiftieth Salon only. "Where we go after that is dependent on the artists and patrons of the Association," he said. "I am sending out a special letter in a few days asking for their opinion and help. It will take

considerable financial support and a lot of hard work to bring back what has been lost. We will need the cooperation of many people. Our Board is dedicated to go ahead if that is what is wanted, but we feel that we should not make the decision (alone)."[62]

Less than five weeks after the fire, Lilly Endowment, Inc.—a philanthropic organization located in Indianapolis—came to the rescue of the Association with a $5,000 emergency grant.[63] In addition, Jordan sought the advice of the members in determining the group's future. In a late-November message to them, he reported: "As you no doubt heard or read, our Indianapolis headquarters was completely destroyed in the multi-million dollar fire which gutted downtown Indianapolis the first of the month. Everything in the headquarters and in the main gallery of the Hoosier Salon Patrons Association was lost. This included 311 paintings.

". . . Because of this catastrophe, the future of the Association is in serious doubt. Your Board of Directors, in a special session [on] November 16, decided to proceed with the 50th Hoosier Salon Annual Exhibit,"[64] the president continued. "All other 50th Anniversary events have been postponed—and no action insofar as the future of the Association will be taken until we have heard from our membership."[65] Jordan went on to ask the members to complete an enclosed card on which they were to state their interest in the continuation of the Association. They were also questioned about their ability to contribute to the rebuilding of the Association, should the decision be made to go forward.

* * *

1974 "As we stood on the threshold of the fiftieth year, the Hoosier Salon Patrons Association was hit by the tragic fire of November 5, 1973, in downtown Indianapolis,"[66] recalled the Association's president as he shared his thoughts about that devastating day in the Foreword of the Salon catalogue. "For a while all seemed to be lost. With the courage of our founders and the firm foundation built these past fifty years and with the assurance given us by our Indiana artists and members, *we shall go ahead.*"[67]

Under Jordan's strong leadership and with the aid of loyal supporters, the group did, indeed, move onward. Stepping up with a timely contribution of $1,000 each, the Woman's Department Club and Kappa Kappa Kappa Sorority helped to guarantee that celebration plans for the Salon's golden anniversary could be made. Even with such backing, "[a] host of gala dinners and receptions, originally scheduled to complement the show, had to be canceled because of the fire."[68] Despite the lack of festivities, though, attention throughout the state was directed to the Salon when Indiana Governor Otis R. Bowen, M. D., proclaimed January 20 through January 26 as "Hoosier Salon Week."[69]

One of the highlights of the "show which is lucky to be a show at all,"[70] was the honoring of two of the Salon's favorite painters. Artists and other guests gathered at the Preview Party to salute a lifetime of work by Marie Goth and William E. Eyden. "In recognition of participation in that first show (in Chicago) and continued interest and participation these fifty years, the Board of Directors presented . . . Goth and . . . Eyden with special engraved medallions commemorating the occasion."[71]

Marie Goth had exhibited in every Hoosier Salon since its beginning in 1925. After studying at the Art Students' League in New York for ten years, "[s]he rocketed to prominence after her return to Indiana. It happened when she was spending the summer at her parents' summer home in Nashville, (Indiana). Charles W. Dahlgreen, [a] famous Chicago artist, was visiting nearby. Miss Goth talked him into giving her a sitting one Sunday afternoon. When he arose, he surprised her by taking the wet canvas off the easel, telling her he wanted to take it with him to the hotel to show to some other artists. When he brought it back the following Sunday, he told Miss Goth to finish the portrait and enter it in the next Hoosier Salon. She did; it won the portrait prize (in 1926)."[72]

Not only was the prizewinning *Charles W. Dahlgreen* the first in a lengthy string of Salon awards for her, but this painting started the Indianapolis-born artist on a career of portraiture. Such a devoted artist was Miss Goth that, when asked by an *Indianapolis Star Magazine* reporter what occupied her spare time, she told him she painted, adding that it was flowers she painted for fun. "I think flowers are prettier than people, don't you?" she waggishly asked the writer. "Flowers have a great deal of character in their faces, and it's hard to catch their exact expression. But it's fun trying."[73]

Also sharing the spotlight with Miss Goth and Eyden at the Preview Party was Mrs. (Henry Lester) Johnnie Rutland Smith of Bloomington, Indiana. A member of the Board of Directors, she had written *The Hoosier Salon, 1925-1974: A Dream of Farsighted Men and Women* in recognition of the Salon's having reached the half-century mark. A concise history of those organizations and individuals who were responsible for the development of the exhibition, the thirty-two-page booklet —and its author—were presented at the party. Mrs. Smith was available during the late-afternoon affair to autograph her publication.[74]

Mrs. (Walter S.) Lottie Lyons Grow, considered by some to be the matriarch of the Salon, announced the award winners. Named an honorary life member of the Association in 1970, the ninety-one-year-old Mrs. Grow had been instrumental in bringing the Salon to Indianapolis in 1937. As chairman of the Art Department of the Woman's Department Club, she had helped stage the first Hoosier Salon at Block's after the show had closed its run in Chicago. Since then, Mrs. Grow had been active with the yearly exhibitions, in addition to having written several books.[75]

Although "[t]he Preview of the fiftieth anniversary Hoosier Salon art show . . . was a triumph for its sponsors," reported an Indianapolis newspaper, "[it was] pretty much a family affair for the Davises of Indianapolis and the Polomchaks of Gary, (Indiana). Harry A. Davis, a member of the faculty of the Herron Art School who makes a habit of winning, was awarded the $500 Block merit prize for the 'Outstanding Work, Any Medium, Of the Entire Exhibition.' Lois Davis, his wife, took home the $150 first prize for 'Portrait or Figure Composition.' The Polomchaks, Steve and Mark, father and son, collected four prizes between them."[76]

In this landmark year, six hundred works were submitted by more than three hundred artists; the single juror chose 163 pieces by 117 artists, twenty-two of whom were accepted for the first time. Twenty-three artists were given a total of $3,125 in merit awards, and seventeen artists received $3,865 in purchase prizes.[77] Quite a few of these artworks were included in a special exhibition that was mounted in Chicago after the close of the Salon. Sponsored by the Indiana Society of Chicago and the Daughters of Indiana in Chicago, the Golden Anniversary Show hung for about three weeks at the Continental Bank and Trust Company on South LaSalle Street. The paintings then went on tour to selected venues within the state of Indiana.[78]

Despite the devastation caused by the fire, Mrs. Hackney did her best to continue with Association activities. In addition to overseeing the traveling exhibitions that were circulating throughout Indiana, she hosted a series of teas to honor those organizations that had faithfully stood behind the Salon. "We're really heartened by the support we've received," said the executive director who had been working out of a temporary office in the basement of her home. "In addition, we're getting pledges of financial support over three years to help get set on a firm basis again."[79]

Also involved in thanking volunteers was Mrs. Husselman, manager of the showroom at the Hilton Hotel. "At the moment, I am in the midst of planning a luncheon for all those ladies who have so generously given of their time in our gallery in the Hilton Hotel,"[80] she wrote to artist Kenneth J. Reeve. She had hoped that she might encourage him—as well as the other twenty-six artists she had approached with her idea—to donate some artwork to be presented to the women in appreciation of their efforts.

"Without their volunteer services, the Hoosier Salon would not have been able to maintain this gallery," she continued. "In view of this, I feel they are deserving of a great deal of thanks. One manner of doing this is through the artists who are helping by the donation of some sort. This is my reason for contacting you—would you be willing to give for this cause? I thought it would be nice if we could have seven of your prints."[81]

During the Board of Directors' annual meeting on September 6, it became apparent that the fire had taken its toll on Stella Hackney and Harold Jordan. Both tendered their resignations to the Association Board. Of her years of Salon leadership, Mrs. Hackney remarked: "I took the job for the fun of it, but the fun's over. I'm tired."[82] Appointed to take her place was Miss Kristin E. Blum, a native of Ohio who had attended Butler University before graduating from the University of Colorado. "She's working right along with me on plans for the annual exhibition," assured the outgoing executive director, "so that this will be done when we do get into our new gallery."[83] Upon Mrs. Hackney's departure, effective October 1, she was presented with an honorary life membership in the Association.

The president of the Association, Harold W. Jordan, had been drained by the demands put upon him after the fire. According to a newspaper account of the fall meeting, Jordan "had asked to be relieved [of his duties] at the end of the Hoosier Salon's fiftieth year."[84] Pursuant to his wishes, his resignation was reluctantly accepted, and Mrs. (Gordon G.) Philippa C. Hughes of Indianapolis had been elected to the position. She had been serving on the Association's Advisory Council—as president of the Woman's Department Club—along with sitting on its Board of Directors.

In early November, with the help of a $20,000 matching grant from Lilly Endowment, Inc., plus $20,000 raised from 350 members, the Association found a new home. It bought the Bals-Wocher mansion, "one of the finest examples of Italianate Victorian architecture in Indianapolis,"[85] at 951 North Delaware Street. On each of the mansion's two floors, there were two small rooms and a large one that could be used for galleries or meeting rooms. "That way," explained Miss Blum, "[people] can use our facilities and tour our galleries at the same time."[86]

Delighted with the space, the newly elected president, Mrs. Hughes, wrote Lilly Endowment to thank the philanthropic group for its generous assistance. "After the tragedy of the fire . . . and the loss of our possessions," she related in her letter, "we were almost too discouraged to go on. Now we look forward to our second fifty years with hope and enthusiasm. With the acquisition of this new building, . . . we will be able to expand our services to Indiana artists. . . . Being able to have a part in the preservation of an historic building seems really exciting to us. Thank you for giving us this opportunity."[87]

The Bals-Wocher mansion, built in 1869, housed the Hisey & Titus Funeral Home from 1916 until being purchased by the Association. Its prior owners seemed eerily close at hand as Miss Blum readied the downstairs rooms for a holiday open house on December 1. To transform a funeral parlor into an art salon was challenging, she remarked, after struggling to get rid of casket imprints in the carpeting. The young executive director discovered, in addition, that the room which had been used as a chapel was still wired for music. "Can you imagine 'Rock of Ages,' wafting out of the fireplaces?"[88] she asked after urging workmen to disconnect the wires.

For the first-floor galleries, "[m]ember artists have been asked to bring works for display on consignment in the rooms," wrote Marion Simon Garmel of the *Indianapolis News*. "Miss Blum also is accepting delivery at the house of donated goods, pledged by member artists immediately after the Thomas Building fire."[89] Additional inventory for the Delaware Street galleries would come from the showroom at the Hilton Hotel; that space would be closed permanently on December 21 because the Association "[was] simply not affluent enough now to be able to manage it."[90]

* * *

1975 In composing the Foreword for the fifty-first Salon catalogue, Mrs. Hughes, as president of the Association, likened the future of the Salon to the Arabian myth about the five-hundred-year-old Phoenix bird. "[T]he only bird of its kind, . . . [it] sets fire to its shelter and is completely consumed," she wrote. "Miraculously, it rises again from the ashes—complete and beautiful and strong—ready to fulfill its destiny for another five hundred years.

"How like the Phoenix is the Hoosier Salon!" she continued. "We too are unique, for we are the only organization whose only purposes are to promote art in Indiana and to encourage artists in our state. Consumed by fire in our fiftieth year, we rise again, ready to fulfill our destiny for another fifty years. We have found new strength from many friends, who have contributed time and money for our well-being. We have found new confidence from many artists who have reaffirmed their belief in us. We look forward from this rebirth to a time of growing."[91]

Within weeks of settling into the Delaware Street building, the Association was beginning to enjoy the fruits of its "rebirth." Artists from around Indiana had "contributed forty paintings to re-establish the Hoosier Salon Patrons Association gallery, helped hang the works in new headquarters and now look forward to using a 'homey' Bals-Wocher mansion,"[92] noted Kathleen Van Nuys in her *Indianapolis News* column "Lightly Speaking." In the historic, red-brick house, "[w]e have one large gallery, two smaller ones and office space (on the first floor), and we hope to transform the large garage into a gallery for special shows," explained Mrs. Hughes. "Upstairs space will be for the use of art groups, special demonstrations and art exhibits, and for meetings by small clubs."[93]

One such event was a student art exhibition being organized for May by Miss Blum. "The juried show, this spring, will be open to university and college students as well as art school students," explained the executive director. "Prizes will be awarded to these new, young artists who may exhibit works done in class."[94] The Association's first All-College Student Art Show would be held May 10 through May 17; Professor Robert Fabe of the College of Design, Architecture and Art at the University of Cincinnati would be the only juror.[95]

Scarcely before Association members were ready, the yearly Salon was upon them. The eye-catching cover for their exhibition catalogue was taken from a lithograph of the Bals-Wocher mansion, executed by Harry Davis and given to the group to promote fund-raising. An acknowledgment of the artist's thoughtful gift appeared in the catalogue, along with the notice that "[s]igned, numbered prints of this limited edition lithograph are for sale through the Hoosier Salon."[96]

The Salon proved to be a successful one for Davis and his wife, Lois. While Mrs. Davis was the winner of the $500 "Outstanding Work, Any Medium in the Entire Exhibition" prize, her husband took the $100 "Realistic or Impressionistic Landscape, Any Medium" award. According to Marion Simon Garmel of the *Indianapolis News,* "Mrs. Davis specializes in painting people. Her prizewinning work, *Neighbors,* is a large, lovely study of an old grandmother shelling peas in a rocking chair on her front porch. One grandchild plays with two cats at her feet, and another waves to a passing man out walking his dog.[97]

". . . Because it is such a venerable institution, wrapped in Hoosier art history and tradition, the Salon show often produces some interesting anomalies," continued Ms. Garmel. "This year, for instance, the third prize, $150, for 'Outstanding Landscape, Oil,' was awarded to Frank Vietor's *Nostalgia.* It is a lovely work picturing an old rural town with a train passing through, but it happens to be painted in acrylic."[98] Even though this acrylic took a prize designated for works in oil, there was no error. "[T]he sole juror for the show—watercolor master Chen Chi—determined that the techniques used in oil and acrylic painting are similar enough to include acrylics in the oil category," explained the reporter from the *News,* "especially since the award categories were established before artists ever heard of acrylic paints.[99]

"Another embarrassing complication," she observed, "occurred when, thanks to the monastic secrecy that surrounds Salon openings, rejection notices were somehow mailed to many of the artists whose works actually won prizes in the show. That was better than to have mailed acceptances to artists whose works were rejected, Miss Blum said, but, as a result, only three of the prizewinning artists were on hand to accept their awards."[100] A smaller purse than in prior years, the combined merit and purchase awards totaled $3,685.

Of the 186 artists who had their work juried into a show of 249 artworks, sixty-three of them were first-timers. "Overall the show this year is an extremely varied one, with art ranging from ultra-traditional to hard-edge and comic-book style," wrote an art critic from Indianapolis. "There are an uncommon number of nostalgia works, including a lot of painted quilts and quilted paintings. There also is more sculpture than usual, excellently displayed in little sculpture clusters in the centers of the Salon's traditional picture alcoves."[101]

Casting a shadow over the exuberance of a rejuvenated Salon were the deaths of Marie Goth on January 9 and Stella Hackney on January 26. Each had made a significant contribution to the development of the show. A formidable presence in the Salon since its early days, Miss Goth—"[t]he delicately structured little lady with the sparkling eyes"[102]—had died from injuries suffered in a fall down a short flight of stairs.[103] Mrs. Hackney, the executive director who had brought the Association through its darkest days after the fire in 1973, had died in her Indianapolis home.[104]

* * *

1976 Once again, several of the state's artists managed to make prizewinning at the fifty-second Salon a family affair. As they had in the past, Harry and Lois Davis passed the show's top award between them. In 1974, Davis had won the "Outstanding Work, Any Medium, Entire Exhibition" prize with his *Princeton, Gibson County Seat,* and in 1975, Mrs. Davis had done likewise with *Neighbors.* In 1976, it had become his turn again as he won the $500 award with an urban landscape entitled *Esse Warehouse.*

Joining the Davises in the roll call of winners were two other Hoosier "art families": the Vietors, a husband-and-wife team from Indianapolis, and the Polomchaks, a father and son from Gary. Frank Vietor took a $100 "Jury Prize of Distinction, Traditional" with *Class of '49,* and Jean F. Vietor captured a $50 "Jury Prize of Distinction" with *The Personality Plant.* Both of the Polomchaks were given a $100 "Jury Prize of Distinction, Traditional," Mark for *Between Six* and Steve for *NC-101.* Steve also won the $100 "Popular Prize," underwritten by Lyman Brothers, Inc. of Indianapolis,[105] with his seascape.

On display at the yearly show were 246 paintings, prints and pieces of sculpture that had been drawn from a field of 653 entries. Twenty-two artists—of the 185 who made their way into the show—shared $3,125 in merit awards from a combined purse of over $5,700. "It is a curious exhibit," observed an Indianapolis art critic. "[W]hen it is good, it is very, very good, and when it is bad, it is horrid. Looking at some of the paintings (judge Charles A.) Mahoney picked, not for prizes but just to get in, one wonders what his criteria could have been. Some of them are strictly amateur. On the other hand, one hardly remembers another recent show with as many surprisingly lovely works."[106]

The Association's Italianate mansion continued to be a busy place. The Hoosier Salon's Second Annual All-College Art Show—made possible, in part, by a grant from the Indiana Arts Commission—was held from April 4 through April 24 in what had become known as the Main Gallery. Billy Morrow Jackson, a professor of art from the University of Illinois, served as juror for the event.[107] Several weeks later, the Association mounted a more modest exhibition there. In a salute to the country's Bicentennial, the group put together a display of gifts that a bride in 1876 might have received. The idea for such an historical exhibit had been chosen, explained Miss Blum, because the original owners of the house "had one daughter who was of marrying age in 1876."[108]

Adding to the bustle at the Bals-Wocher were the activities of the Indiana Artists Club. In mid-August of the prior year, the group had become the Association's first tenant when it had signed a lease for two of the second-floor rooms.[109] Pleased with the accommodations, Neil E. Dunnigan, as the club's president, had spoken of the move into the historic building. "We've been working on this for quite a while," he had said. "This will be our first permanent home in over forty years. We're doing this really to support the downtown, and, of course, the Hoosier Salon needs support. We feel it is a step in the right direction."[110]

On May 16—a week after the opening of the Association's exhibit on antique wedding gifts—the Indiana Artists Club sponsored its first event at the mansion. In its new headquarters, the club hosted a tea in conjunction with a preview of an exhibit featuring the work of its associate members. Also being held that day at the house was a reception for Psi Iota Xi Sorority. The group had become the Association's second tenant by locating its national offices in the remaining room on the second floor.[111]

Sharing Mrs. Hughes' dream of "mak[ing] our location an art building and art center of Indianapolis,"[112] the youthful executive director put together a questionnaire that was mailed to all of the Salon's artists. In it, they were asked their opinions about the running of the annual exhibition. The results were published in the October *Hoosier Salon Newsletter.* According to the findings, seventy-eight percent of the artists wanted a panel of two to three judges to jury the Salon (instead of using a single juror as had been the practice for the prior three years). Fifty-six percent preferred that the jurors be from outside the state, and eighty-seven percent did not object to having their work tour, once the Indianapolis exhibit had closed.

Responding to their suggestions, the Association leadership indicated that a jury of at least two persons would be used for the 1977 show. In addition, it agreed that all prizewinners, henceforth, would be notified before the Preview Party buffet. Only the category in which the artists had won would be left unknown until the official presentation at the awards ceremony.[113] With the disclosure of these changes printed in the October newsletter also came an article that helped clarify the judging process:

"Myth: A representative of the Hoosier Salon

sorts through all entries to the annual show and allows the jury to see only these works.

Truth: The jury views every entry individually. All pieces are shown with a neutral background and good light.

Myth: The jury studies the name and information about the artist before making a selection.

Truth: No information about artists is available nor can his [or her] name be seen on the first viewing.

Myth: The jury is pressured by an artist's 'claque.'

Truth: No one is present at the judging except the Executive Director who acts as secretary and [an] errand-person and the Block employees who handle the artworks.

Myth: All entries accepted for the Salon must go on tour.

Truth: At the time they submit their entries, artists must give their permission for work to go on tour. While we feel that the tour broadens an artist's exposure, we do not insist on the educational aspect of our tour.

Myth: Pictures of all sorts are welcomed at the annual show but sculpture is a step-child.

Truth: In 1975, when we had no money specifically for sculpture, many exceptional pieces were submitted. However, in 1976, after we had made a concerted effort to get over $200 for sculpture prizes, very few pieces were submitted. We would like to see sculpture get the recognition it deserves and will continue to try to find awards for this category. We hope this will encourage more sculptors to enter."[114]

As the winter season approached, Mrs. (David A.) Pam Hicks—who had been elected by the Board to replace Mrs. Hughes as president in April of 1976—directed a letter to all Association members. After explaining that the purchase of the Bals-Wocher mansion had depleted the group's funds, she announced that an art auction had been planned to benefit the Salon. "In order to have a successful auction," she wrote, "we need items to sell and are asking for donations from you or your friends.

"We need paintings, sculpture, antiques and other valuable art objects. 'Old School' works of art are in demand. Let's keep them in circulation through this auction," continued the new president from Indianapolis. "This is simply a fund-raising project. Our membership money in the past provided adequate funds to operate, but now with rising costs, this is no longer sufficient. The proceeds from this auction will be used for our operating budget which includes utilities, repairs, maintenance, etc. and in addition will stimulate exposure and sales of our Hoosier Art."[115]

On December 5—"a good time to Christmas shop,"[116] observed Mrs. Hicks—Hugh Miller of the Curran-Miller Auction Company of Evansville, Indiana, supervised the first auction ever held at Salon headquarters. Among the donated work were pieces by V. J. Cariani, William Forsyth, Edgar Forkner, Homer Davisson, Randolph Coats, L. O. Griffith, George Jo Mess, Otto Stark and Clifton Wheeler.[117] The sale, under the co-chairmanship of Mrs. Husselman and Mrs. Hicks, raised $7,586.[118]

* * *

1977 "Overall this may be the finest Hoosier Salon in years," declared Marion Simon Garmel of the *Indianapolis News* after viewing the Salon in its thirty-sixth year at the Block's Auditorium Galleries. "Primarily traditional to be sure, . . . it is traditional in the best sense of that word—high in quality and, yes, even beautiful to look at. It is a show dominated by watercolors, pastels, pen and pencil drawings, the kind of work that once was not really considered 'painting,' and it is a show in which the architectural element is especially evident. There are many pictures of buildings, farms, bridges; few of people—a legacy of the [B]icentennial and the conservationists."[119]

Nanci Blair Closson captured the $500 "Outstanding Work, Any Medium, Entire Exhibition" award with an acrylic watercolor entitled *Out of Element*, "an abstract design of perfect rectangles and indistinct other shapes in grays, browns and creams."[120] She also took a $100 "Jury Prize of Distinction" with another of her geometric pieces, *Butte Perspective*. "[Much of my work] is a problem in design more than anything. You work on it like a jigsaw puzzle, filling in this space and that, and whatever turns out, turns out," explained the artist from Logansport, Indiana. "Art hasn't any particular meaning for me. It's just there, something I have to do."[121]

Noblesville, Indiana, artist Floyd Hopper, "who for years has been painting some of the best watercolors in the state with little recognition,"[122] won the Salon's second prize, "Outstanding Painting, Any Medium," with his watercolor *Derelict*. The $400 award was another Salon honor for the artist who, during World War II, had exchanged his brushes for the tools necessary to operate a foundry in Noblesville. Hopper had left the business in 1958 to return full-time to art. "I thought I could paint during that twelve-year period," explained this graduate of Herron School of Art, "but as the business got bigger, the less painting I could do."[123]

In response to the artists' strong preference for a

two- or three-person jury (as noted in the 1976 Survey of Artists), the Association had engaged three out-of-state artists to serve as judges; they selected 189 works by 150 artists from a field of 711 entries. Thirty-eight of those artists admitted to the Salon were first-time exhibitors.[124] Presenting the awards from a combined purse of $5,730 were Indianapolis Mayor William H. Hudnut III and Association President Mrs. Hicks.[125]

A newcomer among the sponsors of the Salon's merit awards was the Bloomington chapter of the Hoosier Salon Patrons Association. Organized in time to offer a $50 "Best Watercolor" prize for the 1977 show, the southern Indiana group watched its award go to Warren Sprunger for his *Fresh Snow*. Later, in mid-June, another auxiliary service group—the Hoosier Salon Guild—would be formed in Indianapolis; its purpose would be "to promote, support and assist with the aims and activities of the Hoosier Salon."[126] With Mrs. (Robert) Martha R. Van Sickle as president, Guild members would meet the fourth Monday of September, November, April and June to make plans for their volunteer assignments.[127]

Despite the growing interest in Salon work, Mrs. Hicks and the Board of Directors were increasingly burdened by the upkeep of the Bals-Wocher building. On September 1, the president called an emergency meeting of the Board for September 17 at the mansion. "Many of you may be aware of the fact that there is some controversy within our Board about our current location at 951 N. Delaware Street,"[128] she admitted in her notice to the members. "We have, without question, a heavy financial obligation brought about [by] the lease-acquisition of the property. Within the past few weeks, we have had an offer to sell our interest in the property to a commercial firm. There are many pluses and minuses to be considered relative to this offer. . . . I feel any action taken by the Board should represent the full accord of all the members in the interest of the Hoosier Salon."[129]

While the pros and cons of the proposed sale were being debated, the October *Hoosier Salon Newsletter* carried some surprising news. "[Next] year, for the first time, L. S. Ayres & Company will host the Annual Exhibit," Mrs. Hicks revealed in her "A Message from the President" column. "This will be a monumental change for the Salon. The Wm. H. Block Company has hosted the show for thirty-six years. We have had a marvelous rapport with them and thank them for so many years of dedicated service."[130] The president went on to explain that the Association had been urged for years to hold a spring show so the weather would not interfere with attendance. Ayres department store, unlike Block's, had been able to satisfy that request, she said. In addition, it had offered to double the "Best of Show" award from $500 to $1,000, beginning with the 1978 exhibition.[131]

* * *

1978 "It was a good idea that went sour. Street traffic never developed. Artists stopped bringing in their best work. Maintenance costs were monstrous, and the boiler blew," reported an Indianapolis newspaper. "So the Hoosier Salon has sold (in January of 1978) the Bals-Wocher mansion at 951 N. Delaware which it bought in 1974 as a home and gallery. Record Data, Inc., of Indiana is the new owner, and the Salon has moved to a second-floor room in the old building which it is renting for office space only."[132]

"We just felt we did not want to continually put the Salon's resources into maintenance of an old building like that . . . ," explained Mrs. Hicks. "Three years ago, a very bad mistake was made in buying that property. We've poured money ($5,000 to replace the boiler and $6,000 to repair the roof) into something we should never have done. Obviously, the Board feels we came out as well as we could on it or we would never have made the sale. We have money, and this money we want to use on promoting Indiana art and artists.[133]

". . .We are renting (space in the mansion) along with the Indiana Artists Club and Psi Iota Xi," continued the president of the Association. "We will not have the gallery space we had—we are sorry about that—but, financially, we felt this was the best thing to do. . . .We will continue to have solo shows for our artists. We are handling all the shows at the Hyatt Regency's Eagle's Nest, and we are putting our solo shows there. Right now, our big concern is our spring show coming up, and we are channeling every effort into this show."[134]

The "spring show coming up" was the fifty-fourth Salon; it was being held, for the first time, in the eighth-floor Auditorium of L. S. Ayres & Company in downtown Indianapolis. "Of all the reasons (for the change in location), the best may have been the increased prize money," observed one writer assigned to cover the exhibition. "This is the richest Hoosier Salon in history. Talk about inflation. The top Salon prize, '[B]est of [S]how in [A]ny [M]edium,' traditionally has been a $500 award given by Block's. This year, there are three '[B]est of [S]how' awards, each carrying a cash prize of $1,000. One was given by Ayres, and the other two were donated anonymously."[135]

According to the *Indianapolis Star*, more than fifty merit and purchase prizes totaling over

$11,000, "an all-time high for the state's premier competitive annual exhibition, were distributed among the 130 artists represented by 165 pieces in various media selected for display."[136] Despite the lavish prize money, a new locale and balmy April weather, Marion Garmel of the *Indianapolis News* was lukewarm in her assessment of the Salon's offerings.

"[T]his is not one of the Salon's better exhibits," the critic concluded. "Originally designed as a showcase for Indiana artists, the annual Salon show has tended in recent years to be a showcase for traditional artists. But even with that proviso, the quality of much of the art seems down. Either the judges were too lenient letting works in . . . or not much better [among the 864 entries] was submitted. Yet there are outstanding pieces. And one of the nicest surprises is the number of new works and new artists who pop up, and some old ones whose work has been included."[137]

Robert E. Weaver, a professor at Herron School of Art who had developed a reputation for his circus paintings, won one of three $1000 "Best of Show, Outstanding Work, Any Medium" awards with a piece entitled *Double O-7*. Explaining that he had worked on the atypical, abstract watercolor as a respite from his circus art, Weaver expressed surprise when it took a top prize. "It must have been the title,"[138] he guessed.

When asked about his fondness for the circus, the artist from near Peru, Indiana, said that it had been "all my mother's fault. She was a circus fiend when I was a kid; she saw that I got to every circus in traveling distance."[139] Because Weaver's grandfather had been employed by a circus headquartered in Peru, the youngster had spent time with many of the people working in the Hagenbeck-Wallace Circus there.

"During his junior year at the Herron School of Art (in Indianapolis), Weaver talked director Donald M. Mattison into letting him leave school early to join the Hagenbeck-Wallace Circus and continue research into painting circus life."[140] From his vantage point as a ticket-taker for the sideshows, he was in an ideal spot to observe the activities under the big top. His resulting interpretations of the circus "have been well accepted by critics and art judges."[141]

Another big winner in the Salon was William Zimmerman whose *Arctic Fox and Brant* won a $500 "Jury Prize of Distinction." Known for his paintings of nature, especially birds, the artist said that he thought "of Audubon all the time. He was a fantastic naturalist and a courageous explorer, so to speak. Anybody who specializes in birds has to think about him a lot."[142] Creator of *The Waterfowl*

of North America , a weighty volume that features forty-two full-size plates, Zimmerman admitted that he did "have a pleasant following"[143] for his artwork.

"I spend more time in the studio than outdoors, but the studio is outdoors," explained this illustrator who was also recognized for his work on another book titled *The Birds of Indiana*. "I have every nuance of nature pegged and labeled somewhere, but the outdoors is my inspiration. I am always doing sketches in the woods that I file under 'paintings I am going to do someday.' The problem is that what I do doesn't always look like work."[144]

Missing from the show at Ayres was the Salon's historian, Mrs. (Henry Lester) Johnnie Rutland Smith. Author of *The Hoosier Salon, 1925-1974: A Dream of Farsighted Men and Women*, she had died in July of 1977. With her dedication to the Salon, she would have considered the show a triumph despite the problems that had surfaced with the move. As noted in one account of the show, "[t]he paintings, hung three and four-deep along the outside walls of the auditorium, appear[ed] crowded and not displayed to their best advantage. [Also the] auditorium in spring was hotter than many would have liked. But these are problems that time and experience can solve."[145]

To the relief of the Board of Directors, the appointment of a new executive director shortly before the opening at Ayres had gone smoothly. Mrs. Kristin Blum Lord—married to Joseph Thomas Lord during the summer of 1976—had resigned in January of 1978 to accept a position with Big Sisters of Indianapolis. She had been replaced by Indianapolis resident Mrs. (T. O.) Mary Beck in time for the yearly show. Another changeover in Salon leadership would occur later that fall when Mrs. Hicks would step down as president of the Association. Mrs. Ardath Y. Burkhart, the group's first vice-president for the last seven years, would assume the post.

Soon after her election, Mrs. Burkhart outlined her plans for the Association in the October issue of the *Hoosier Salon Newsletter*. According to the new president from Indianapolis, a Promotion Committee—chaired by Board member John Walsh of Indiana National Bank—would be responsible for securing prize money, promoting the show and seeking corporate memberships. In addition, a Gallery Search Committee would be charged with the responsibility of finding a downtown location with pedestrian traffic.

Furthermore, she wrote: "Since membership fees supply funds for our day-to-day operation, we are going to make a new effort to increase the number of people belonging to the Patrons' Association.

Our plan is to organize Hoosier Salon chapters or Guilds all over the state. Their one and only project will be to supply money, by whatever method they choose, for a merit or purchase prize."[146]

* * *

1979 The year dawned brightly as Mrs. Beck finished unpacking the crates used during a late-December move from the rented upstairs room in the Bals-Wocher mansion. The Association had found a home on the fourth floor of the Board of Trade Building at 143 N. Meridian Street in Indianapolis. As John Shaffer had done in Chicago and Block's in Indianapolis, L. S. Ayres & Company was helping pay the bills as the Association settled into its modest new space. "They [have] two rooms, each ten by sixteen; Ayres [is] doing the decorating free because they are interested in everything about the Salon," reported Helen Magner of the *New Castle Courier-Times*. "When the show travels in May or June, Ayres wants to have a tea and style show in the cities where they have stores—Fort Wayne, South Bend and Lafayette."[147]

Expectations were high as the opening of the fifty-fifth Salon approached. More than eight hundred people had attended last year's Preview Party, membership in the Association had surpassed the twelve-hundred mark,[148] and the prize purse for 1979 promised to be the largest in history. To the delight of Mrs. Beck and her Association volunteers, their hopes for the show were justified. A record number of people visited the exhibition, and a staggering $16,489.99—$9,550 in merit prizes and $6,939.99 in purchase prizes—was distributed among the winners. The show featured 174 artworks by 128 artists, chosen from a field of 665 entries submitted by 354 artists.[149]

The Salon, for the first time, awarded five $1,000 "Best of Show, Outstanding Work, Any Medium" awards. "[T]he money must have attracted the talent," observed the *Indianapolis News* art critic, "for the exhibit is a pleasant surprise in many respects. For one, as the top winners indicate, it is not dominated by the 'Old Guard' but has more than a fair share of new names and images. For another, there is more contemporary art than one might expect in an exhibit with a reputation for upholding the traditional in Indiana art."[150]

Clinching a "Best of Show" award was Jan R. Martin, a thirty-one-year-old production coordinator from an Indianapolis metal contracting firm. His winning entry was a stainless-steel piece entitled *Model for Large Sculpture*. A slim young man with glasses and a mustache, Martin was one of those rare first-time exhibitors who enter a show and take the top prize. Graduating with a Master of Fine Arts degree from the Art Institute of Chicago, Martin had switched from painting to sculpture upon returning to his home in Indianapolis. There he had joined the family business and "began to fall in love with steel, literally."[151]

Vying for attention in this Salon of superlatives was a reception for seven of the exhibition's senior artists. During the gala Preview Party, they were honored by Sister Kathryn Martin, S.P.—chairman of the Indiana Arts Commission[152]—for their years with the Association. Applauded for being among the longest participating artists in the show, they included: Evelynne Mess Daily, William F. Kaeser, Floyd D. Hopper, Esther Nusbaum, Edmund Brucker, Harry A. Davis and William A. Eyden, Jr.[153]

The success of the second exhibition at Ayres was the result of extensive preparation, observed Mrs. Hicks, who had served as chairman of the event. "Preliminary meetings were held with Ayres to alleviate past problems so that we would have a smooth-running show," noted the former president in her report to the Board of Directors. "Four things that we stressed in our meetings were: The works of art in the show were to be placed on all four sides of the auditorium, the sound from the auditorium podium was to be piped into the [T]ea [R]oom so all guests could hear the awards presentation, more decoration, including flowers, was to be prevalent and poor lighting checked. The first three became reality. The lighting problem, Ayres is very much aware of, and they hope to be able to remedy this situation in future years."[154]

Despite the enthusiastic reception given the Salon, Association members remained aware of the need to locate their operations in a more spacious setting. Even their borrowing of a gallery in Zionsville, Indiana—for a "Salon-artists-only" show from May 15 through June 15[155]—only served to remind them that roomier quarters were necessary. Their fourth-floor rooms, however, would continue to serve for a time. Mrs. Burkhart assured them that "[w]e have been told we have another year in the Board of Trade Building. That is a big help since we have not as yet found a satisfactory spot for a downtown gallery. . . . When we sold the property on North Delaware, the Board decided our future location would be downtown with built-in traffic. That is still the plan, but affordable space is hard to find."[156]

1981
Ellie Siskind
Uncle Stan
Outstanding Work—Any Medium

1989
Leah Traugott
Vases with Shadows
$500 Outstanding Work Prize

1981
Wilbur Meese
Green Primitive Farm
Jury Prize of Distinction

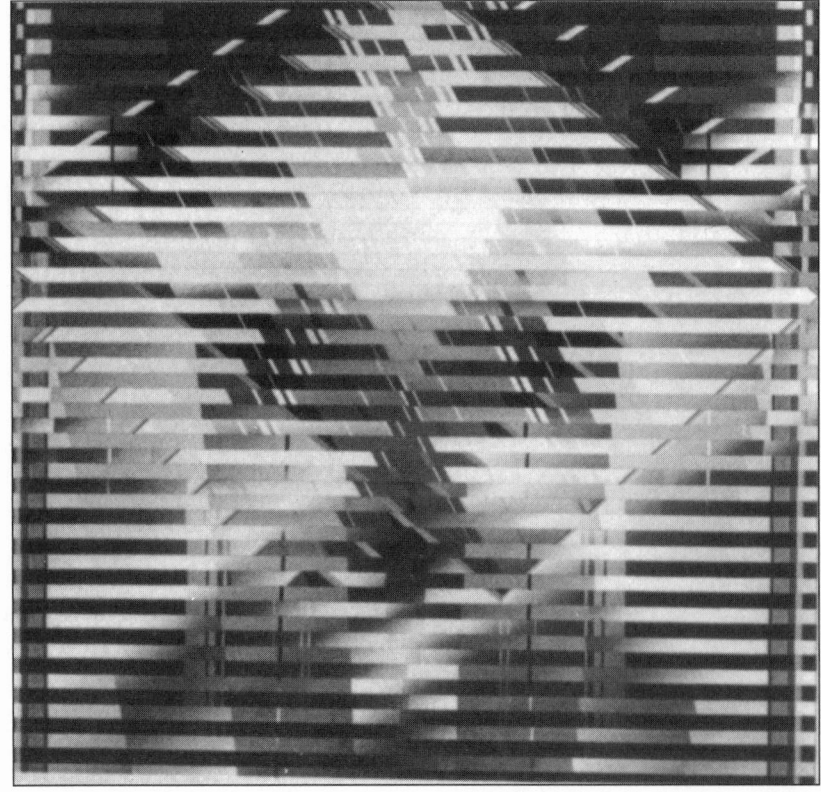

1983
James Cunningham
Arum Ascent
Best of Show

The Eighties

1980 The fifty-sixth Salon was set up, for the third year, in the L. S. Ayres Auditorium "with what one of its judges said was the richest purse of any competitive exhibit he knew of in the United States."[1] A total of $16,445—split among twenty-nine merit awards and twenty-two purchase prizes—was presented to the winners by Janet Harris, executive director of the Indiana Arts Commission. "Certainly the organizers of this exhibition are to be congratulated," observed Marion Garmel of the *Indianapolis News.* "To collect that kind of money is no mean feat. . . . [T]his is all private money. It illustrates that support for the visual arts in Indiana has a strong civic base."[2]

According to Mrs. Burkhart, the increase in award money began with the Salon's move from Block's to Ayres in 1978. While the "host prize" had doubled from $500 to $1,000, she felt that the new Ayres award was not the only factor involved in the expanding purse. The Association president explained that the increase was also due to several "anonymous donations" that had been given for the past two years by Mr. and Mrs. Robert Van Sickle. The couple had contributed $1,000 for a "Best of Show, Outstanding Work, Any Medium" award on the condition that another prize, of like amount, would be funded by money obtained elsewhere.

In 1978, this combination resulted in three $1,000 "Best of Show" awards, and in 1979, there were five such prizes. "[A] limit of five was put on [B]est-of-[S]how awards so that the (1980) show would not become top heavy," reported an Indianapolis newspaper. "This year, those five were acquired without any help from 'anonymous.' Unfortunately, at the last minute, one of the top prizes fell through. So only four [B]est-of-[S]hows were awarded."[3]

William Ashby, a retired photographer who was teaching portraiture at both the Indianapolis and Southside Art Leagues, won one of those "Outstanding Work, Any Medium" awards for his *Portrait of David Rubins.* The prizewinner had chosen a distinguished subject for his painting; Rubins,

also a Hoosier Salon artist who had been honored with a series of awards during the early 1940s, was one of the state's premier sculptors.

Chairman of the Department of Sculpture at Herron School of Art from 1935 until 1968, Rubins was recognized among academics for his bust of the late Indiana Governor Henry Schricker and for his statue of Abraham Lincoln as a young boy.[4] The public, however, knew him best for a twelve-hundred-pound bronze cherub he had fashioned for Ayres department store. From 1947 through 1991, Rubins' cherub—considered by many to be the symbol of Christmas for downtown Indianapolis—would appear the day after Thanksgiving atop the clock outside Ayres at Washington and Meridian streets. There it would remain until Christmas Day.[5]

In Ashby's portrait of Rubins, the noted sculptor was posed "beside an open wood-framed window, his body slightly at an angle but his eyes staring straight ahead. It is the most compelling work in the show," commented Ms. Garmel in her critique of the Salon. "But wait a minute. Isn't this man seventy-eight years old? Could this painting have been done from life?" she wondered in her "Brush Strokes" column. "Yes, says the artist, the painting is newly done, and from life. Only a few wrinkles have been removed. It is this juxtaposition of the wrinkleless flesh and the eyes that seem lost in space that gives the work its remarkable intensity."[6]

As intrigued as the columnist was with Ashby's entry, her review of the exhibition—composed of 165 pieces by 132 artists[7]—was less enthusiastic. "[T]he sad fact is that as the prize money has risen, the overall quality of the Hoosier Salon has dipped," she observed. "There are some wonderful works in this show—most of them among the prizewinners—but there are as many bad ones at the other end. And the show, intended to be a showcase of all Indiana art, has sadly lost touch with the more contemporary."[8]

Far more complimentary was Charles A. Barnes, chairman of the Indiana State Chamber of Commerce; he applauded the Salon for being a leader in the arts. "The Indiana business community is increasingly aware of the great treasury of artistic talent that our state possesses," he wrote in the exhibition catalogue. "More and more of us are gracing our office and corridor walls with the creations of Hoosier artists. That we do this does not occur by accident. We are educated, and reminded, and inspired to do it by many activities—such as the Hoosier Art Salon Preview—that showcase the beautiful things produced by people who are our own friends and neighbors."[9]

* * *

1981 By the time Salon-goers gathered for the fifty-seventh Preview Party, the world had witnessed the murder of John Lennon by a crazed fan, an assassination attempt on the life of President Ronald Reagan and the killing of three nuns in El Salvador. In the midst of such upheaval, it seemed somehow appropriate that Ellie Siskind—who would go on to become one of Indiana's leading painters of social commentary—took a $1,000 "Outstanding Work, Any Medium" prize for her portrait entitled *Uncle Stan*.

In an interview with the artist a decade later, she would remember that "[a]t that time entering shows was the only way I could let myself know where I was."[10] Admired for her penetrating artwork, Ms. Siskind would talk of the difficulty of striking a balance between art and commerce. "Growing up in a family-run business, it has been very difficult for me not to measure my work by my sales," she explained. ". . . I have begun to understand, however, that people choose quiet work for their private spaces, not work that jumps off the wall trying to get you involved. The work I want to make, strong work with clear statements about society, is not going to fit in most people's homes."[11]

Walking off with the largest prize from the show described as "probably the largest of any juried exhibition in the country"[12] was Rich Ernsting. This thirty-three-year-old designer for Herff Jones, Inc. captured the $1,500 "Best of Show" from a purse of $15,550. His entry was "an unusual work for any prize: *Forgotten Wheels*, a close-up pencil drawing of the gears and crossbars of the old steam engine at Broad Ripple Park (in Indianapolis)."[13] Joining him in the winner's circle was Nanci Blair Closson whose *White Sails* was chosen from 204 pieces for the $1,200 "Outstanding Work, Any Medium" award.

According to Ms. Garmel of the *Indianapolis News*, the Ayres staff had corrected several problems in order to mount the big spring exhibition more attractively. "The show itself is both more varied and better displayed than any Hoosier Salon of the recent past," she wrote in her column. "Gone are the spare white walls and subdued lighting of last year. Brown linen panels paralleling the walls and beige linen columns closer to the center provide more and better viewing space. Track lighting has been added."[14]

After the Salon closed on May 23, thirty of its blue-ribbon paintings were shipped to Washington, D. C., where they were placed in the rotunda of the Cannon House Office Building. As in 1949, when the Indiana State Society of Washington, D. C., had helped sponsor a Salon showing at the Smithsonian Institution, the group again took part. This time, the Society worked with Mrs. Burkhart and Representative Bud Hillis, R-Ind., to bring a sampling of the Salon to the nation's capital for a week-long exhibit.

Nearly five hundred people attended the invitation-only reception, held in the Caucus Chamber of the Cannon Building on June 8. Members of Congress mixed with those from the Midwest at the affair sponsored by the Society, L. S. Ayres & Company and the Hoosier Salon Patrons Association. According to Ben Cole of the *Indianapolis Star's* Washington, D. C., Bureau, "Senators Richard G. Lugar, R-Ind., and Dan Quayle, R-Ind., both arrived with their wives . . . [and] Representative Lee H. Hamilton, D-Ind., was there, as was Representative John T. Myers, R-Ind. Their wives, [along] with Mrs. (Marilyn) Quayle and Mrs. (Charlene) Lugar, had a part in arranging the display."[15]

Due to the demands of hosting two exhibitions in two cities during May and June, the Association's executive director postponed until mid-fall the official opening of the group's new headquarters. The preceding February, after receiving word that the Board of Trade Building was to be torn down, Mrs. Beck had "packed her paintings and materials from her tiny fourth-floor office and moved it all to the rehabilitated Morrison Opera Place (once People's Furniture)"[16] at 47 S. Meridian Street.

"The Salon has the smallest space in the building," remarked an Indianapolis journalist during a preview look at the premises. "[It is] little more than a plush office with a lot of paintings on the walls. But what a building it is. Brick interior walls rising four floors from the lobby, a curving wooden staircase, brass lights and coat hangers and even a brass mailbox."[17] After settling into the accommodations on the third floor, the executive director was well satisfied with the Association's new location. "We're doubly excited because this is such an exciting building to be in," said Mrs. Beck, "and we're glad we could remain downtown instead of moving somewhere out in the suburbs."[18]

October 25 signaled the public opening of the Morrison Opera Place gallery as well as the first exhibition to be held there. The occasion was marked by "an exhibit and sale of (eighty-one) paintings by Louis W. Bonsib, [a] Fort Wayne artist who [had] left his collection to the Salon when he died at eighty-seven in 1979."[19] "We were bequeathed half of his collection (one thousand paintings), and another one hundred will be released," explained Mrs. Beck. "Bonsib . . . was a prolific painter, and he had about two thousand of his own works. The other half of his collection went to a Vincennes art group."[20]

Bonsib, the founder of Bonsib, Inc.—an advertising agency in Fort Wayne, Indiana—"was referred to as a Sunday painter. But that didn't stop him [from] turning out a prodigious number of landscapes, seascapes and even one floral, or capturing more than twenty-five awards in juried exhibitions. . . . Originally self-taught, he picked up pointers in painting at art colonies from Brown County to the coast of Maine. He vacationed in Switzerland, Austria, Germany, France, Italy, rural England, Scotland, Ireland and Japan, making sketches or taking photographs to be turned into paintings in his studio at home."[21]

* * *

1982 "To some people, the Hoosier Salon is the last bastion of integrity in an art world going slowly mad," reflected Ms. Garmel of the *Indianapolis News*. "To others, it is the boneyard of traditionalism—the place where Sunday painters and Brown County Artists find brief spots in the sun for art that is lackluster, unimaginative, at best, adequately painted. Both judgments are unfortunate, as the fifty-eighth Hoosier Salon . . . makes abundantly clear," she wrote in her "Brush Strokes" column. "According to one viewer, who is used to thinking of the Salon as a backward show, 'I'm always surprised by how many good paintings there are.' Said another, 'Maybe I am old-fashioned, but there is something to be said for beauty.'"[22]

Adding to the refinements of its Auditorium space, already fitted with track lighting and linen wall panels from the prior Salon, the management at Ayres installed earth-toned carpeting before the 1982 show. "These improvements [will] greatly enhance the exhibit setting," said Mrs. Beck. "Our catalogue was printed in brown and beige for the first time last year, and we have decided to maintain that soft effect. We have chosen a permanent

logo [too]. Designed as a palette with brushes, it incorporates the whole name but centers on [the] Hoosier Salon."[23]

The resulting exhibition bore the effects of the pre-show fine-tuning; its 213 pieces were applauded by New Castle, Indiana, critic Helen Lair. "It is the consensus that this year's Salon ranks with the best of the past for quality and variety of interest," she declared. "It is an enlightening show. . . . Almost all styles and eras are represented."[24] Even the two jurors who narrowed the field from 650 submissions were particularly impressed with the first-rate entries. "This was the best art together under one roof that we have been privileged to judge," they told Mrs. Beck. "We are impressed with the fine quality of the art."[25]

Ms. Garmel agreed, deciding that the show included "more good paintings than in the four years it has been at Ayres. Furthermore, it has found room for such unusual works as Mike Helbing's *Introspect,* a (Alberto) Giacometti-like welded metal sculpture of a stick-thin man with fragments of mirrors for a face."[26] She felt that the jurors had "selected a show that is full of winsome watercolors, rich oils, exquisite pencil drawings and traditional and non-traditional sculpture. To win [B]est of [S]how in such an exhibit, a work would have to be very good indeed."[27]

Named "Best of Show" was a pensive portrait entitled *Matriarch* by Edmund Brucker; the oil painting won its artist both critical acclaim and the top prize of $1,500. He was given his award during a "Polynesian" Preview Party by Harry E. Riser of Indianapolis. As the Association's new president who had assumed the post from Mrs. Burkhart, Riser oversaw the distribution of more than $15,000 in merit awards and purchase prizes for the year.

At the close of the exhibition, Thelma Confer with her *Muscatatuck River III* and Nancy Noël with her *Sisters by the Window* were tied for the $100 "Popular Prize," determined by the votes of the visiting public. Instead of splitting the award, the Hoosier Salon Patrons Association, Inc.—the group had been underwriting the prize since 1981—gave each artist the full amount.[28] Both women had already won merit awards for their work: Ms. Confer had taken the $250 "Outstanding Landscape, Oil or Acrylic" and Ms. Noël, the $100 "Outstanding Traditional Painting, Any Medium."

That Nancy Noël's work would be a favorite among gallery-goers came as no surprise. She was widely acclaimed for her portraiture of children as well as for her life-size renderings of exotic wildlife, domestic animals and vivid florals. According to the Indianapolis-born artist, "[m]y desire to paint is clearly and simply an outgrowth of my need to communicate. As there are many sides to my personality, so too, there are many styles and subjects to my work. I paint what moves me," she explained in a commentary on her artwork, " . . . I paint for the excitement of color or composition, to relate a feeling or a mood, to share a moment, to make a contribution, to fulfill a curiosity, and finally, at times, as an obligation."[29]

As had been the case for nearly six decades, the driving force behind the Salon was its volunteers. In addition to the loyal support of members from Kappa Kappa Kappa, the Woman's Department Club, Psi Iota Xi, the Indiana Federation of Clubs, Delta Sigma Kappa and the Indiana Federation of Art Clubs, new people had been recruited to assist with the Salon. "We appreciate [the] women in thirty-four organizations who support culture in the city by serving as hostesses during the two-week exhibit," said Mrs. Beck.

"One [of the groups] is in Hamilton County, another in Zionsville and three are service-oriented: Women's Rotary and Zonta and Pilot clubs," she continued in a tribute to those who were helping to make the Salon possible. "Matinee Musicale and Women's Committee, Indiana State Symphony Society, are music-oriented organizations helping us. Sunnyside Guild and Daughters of the American Revolution, Caroline Harrison Chapter, are other strong patrons."[30] Missing from the roster of supporters, though, was the Daughters of Indiana of Chicago club. One of the Salon's founders, the organization had voted to disband in November of 1981, leaving a savings account of $6,000 to the Association "to invest for the future of the Salon."[31]

* * *

1983 Indianapolis artist James L. Cunningham, under contract with the National Aeronautics and Space Administration (NASA) to interpret its launch program through his artwork, took the $1,500 "Best of Show" award with *Arum Ascent.* His winning piece was described by one art critic as "a dazzling geometric abstract . . . that looks a little like the portrait of a space ship lifting off behind Venetian blinds."[32] The fifty-ninth Salon was a good exhibition not only for this Herron School of Art-trained painter but for his wife as well. Kate Cunningham left the gala Preview Party at Ayres with a $100 "Jury Prize of Distinction" for her delicate batik, *Toy Kisses/Sweet Sorrows.*

The two artists owned and operated Cunningham Gallery, an early arrival to the Indianapolis art district that carried only their work: Jim's large acrylics on canvas and Kate's smaller batiks. An

advocate for the development of a downtown art community, Jim maintained that "[i]f an artist keeps at it long enough, he will enjoy a certain measure of success. The longer artists paint, compete and exhibit, the greater the chances that they will eventually end up in the right place at the right time."[33]

While Jim's acrylics were characterized in *Arts Insight* as being "subjective . . . [and] a methodical consideration of color and composition,"[34] Kate Cunningham used mixed-media batiks to communicate her feelings. She even dyed the fabrics herself for a more precise effect. "I want them to be as pretty, as precious as they can be," the self-taught artist said of her softly colored abstractions. "Art conveys the essence of an emotion. These paintings come from special moments in my life."[35]

Tragically, the couple's "special moments" would be cut short with Jim's death in a 1991 helicopter crash. The affectionate regard in which the affable painter was held, though, would be remembered by *Indianapolis Star* art critic Steve Mannheimer. "Jim Cunningham's art and personality had a quality of endless sunny skies," Mannheimer would write in his review of A Memorial Exhibition: The Works of James L. Cunningham (1948-1991). "As a man, he may have been the nicest, most mild-mannered artist you'd ever hope to meet outside of a retirement home. He was always ready with a smile or kind, encouraging word—and the skies he painted were not cloudy all day. They were ethereal or interstellar, as sweetly tinted as dawn's pastel promise or blackly stark as the infinite."[36]

Jim Cunningham's prizewinning acrylic injected a modern note into the 1983 exhibition that consisted of 203 pieces. "This year's show is a stunner in many ways," observed an Indianapolis newspaper reporter. "Known primarily as a showcase for Indiana's traditional artists, the show again is dominated by watercolors and drawings of which Indiana has no lack of masters. But many of the works are unexpectedly contemporary, and there is more fine oil and acrylic painting than in decades past."[37]

Several of the other leading prizes went to more conventional paintings. William G. Ashby won the $1,200 "Outstanding Work, Any Medium" with his *Portrait of Robert Frist,* and Harry A. Davis took the $1,000 "Outstanding Work, Any Medium" with his cityscape *A Segment of Canal Street.* Both men were cited for their lengthy participation in the Salon as they were handed their prizes—from a purse totaling $16,360—by Robert A. Yassin, director of the Indianapolis Museum of Art, and Harry Riser, president of the Association. Also present at the awards ceremony were Esther Waterman, a former president of the Daughters of Indiana of Chicago, and seven other members of that organization which had helped to found the Hoosier Salon.[38]

Helping Mrs. Beck with those last-minute details for the Preview Party were members of the Hoosier Salon Guild. Under the leadership of Marilee Husselman of Zionsville, Indiana, the Guild raised funds for merit awards as well as assisted with clerical work in the Association office. According to Guild vice-president and chairman of volunteers, Pam Hicks, the "[m]embers' work is vital when entries are received, during purchase and selection days, in setting up and taking down the exhibition and [in] handling the paintings when they return from a statewide tour. They (the Guild members) also serve as hostesses"[39] [and] oversee "the one-man shows held in the Hoosier Salon Gallery"[40] on the third floor of the Morrison Opera Place.

Soon after his reelection as Association president, Riser turned his attention to monetary matters that were confronting the group. In the August *Hoosier Salon Newsletter,* he reminded readers that their annual dues had remained the same for over twenty-five years and recommended an increase of five dollars in several of the membership categories. "In order for us, as a non-profit organization, to continue our efforts for Hoosier artists, we must elevate our dues structure," he told them. "Consequently, your Board of Directors [has] passed a resolution stating that the dues for the coming year will be: Artists, $10; Members, $15; and Patrons, $30."[41] The Business Membership rate was raised as well, from $25 to $30.

* * *

1984 "It is difficult and largely beside the point to label a show like the Hoosier Salon's 60th Annual Exhibition either good or bad. It simply is important,"[42] observed art critic Steve Mannheimer of the *Indianapolis Star.* Mrs. Beck and the Board of Directors agreed. They commissioned the production of an "anniversary" poster that would commemorate the Salon's long history of showcasing the art and artists of Indiana. With graphics that featured a painting of the 1935 Salon by the late Louis W. Bonsib, the poster was "available for sale in both limited and regular editions."[43] According to Mrs. Hicks, who had taken over the presidency of the Hoosier Salon Guild from Mrs. Husselman, "it seem[ed] to capture the essence of the event."[44]

Marion Garmel, writing for the *Indianapolis News,* found the 1984 Salon to be unusually diverse. "Gone, for the most part, are the covered bridges and winter barns of traditional Hoosier paintings," she observed after studying the 217 pieces juried into the show. "In their place are classical statues, Oriental vases, flashing ribbons of color and the intricate, spiraling lines of Medieval drawing. Gone, too, are the familiar names of artists who have dominated the show for decades. In their place is a new, less homogeneous generation. The result is an exciting and varied exhibition in which every visitor is sure to find something fine."[45]

Among the relative newcomers to the May show was Füsun Gülen, an artist-in-residence with the West Lafayette, Indiana, school system. This native of Turkey, who had left her homeland to study art at Purdue University, took the top prize from a purse of $21,435, the richest in Salon history. She won the $1,500 "Best of Show" with an opulent oil entitled *Gate to the Unknown.* Another artist with scant few years in the Salon was Stephen P. Wheat of Indianapolis. He was awarded the $500 "Outstanding Landscape, Oil or Acrylic" for his intricate *Thy Kingdom Come,* "an acrylic and ink drawing of mind-boggling complexity that required more than four hundred hours of labor."[46]

It was a first-time exhibitor, though, whose work caught the attention of both jury and gallery-goers. Frederik Ebbesen Grue took the $1,000 "Outstanding Painting, Traditional, Any Medium" with his elegant still life, *Study of Oriental Porcelain and Lemons.* That piece—"painted in the style of the seventeenth-century Dutch masters"[47]— would later be tapped for the $100 "Popular Prize" at exhibition's end. Gratified by such an assortment of artwork, Mrs. Beck maintained that this show had "more variety, more excitement and more non-traditional work"[48] than the six other exhibitions she had overseen. "It's more of an educational experience,"[49] she explained.

Whether or not the Salon did provide its audience with an educational experience was considered in Mannheimer's analysis of the exhibition. "What the show teaches us," he wrote in the *Star,* "is open to debate. Certainly it reveals a side of Indiana art that other large, local, competitive shows rarely display to [an] adequate degree. Shows like the Indianapolis Museum of Art's Indiana Artists Show and the Indianapolis Art League's Regional tend to draw entrants more watchful of national trends.

"This is not to say that the Salon's artists are less sophisticated, less talented or less anything. Works like Frederik Ebbesen Grue's *Study of Oriental Porcelain and Lemons* or Rosemary Browne Beck's *Green Apples under Glass* are as good as eye-to-hand realism gets," he continued. ". . . And all the works attuned to 'Back Home in Indiana' are generally well designed and executed. . . . What the show lacks, if anything, is the equally mythic American spirit of adventure. These artists are not interested in boldly going where no artist has gone before. They're having enough of a good time where they already are. The avant-garde proceeds from the premise that art should poke holes in the fabric of culture. The Hoosier Salon seems contentedly intent on patching it up."[50]

Some six weeks after the Salon closed, the art world of Indiana suffered the loss of Floyd Hopper. Almost every watercolorist in the state had studied with him in either his Cherry Tree Hill Studio in Noblesville, Indiana, or at the Indianapolis Art League. "Floyd was one of the pre-eminent practitioners of watercolor painting and continued the Indiana tradition in this medium,"[51] recalled Robert Yassin, director of the Indianapolis Museum of Art. Hopper unquestionably had an affinity for transparent watercolor. "I like the facility of [that] medium," he had told an interviewer. "You can push colors around and determine almost immediately whether you're right or wrong."[52]

With the fall art season approaching, Riser announced plans for a fund-raiser to be sponsored by the Association during October. In his "President's Message" in the *Hoosier Salon Newsletter,* he invited members to a retrospective exhibition of oils and watercolors from the Association's collection of Louis Bonsib paintings. Riser also promised a surprise for the October 24 opening. "On this . . . Sunday," he noted in the newsletter, "there will be an auction of a Paul A. Randall oil painting currently owned by the Salon. . . . (Randall's) *Winter Morning* . . . will be sold to the highest bidder."[53]

* * *

1985 The three top winners in the sixty-first Salon—Frederik Ebbesen Grue, James L. Cunningham and James Curtin Lentz—were back in the eighth-floor Auditorium at Ayres, celebrating repeat victories. The thirty-four-year-old Grue, who had moved from Southern California to Muncie, Indiana, nearly three years earlier, carried off the $1,500 "Best of Show" award with *Prairie Creek Reservoir.* He also won a $100 "Jury Prize of Distinction" with "a larger and showier work,"[54] *The Bronze Scholar.*

Characterized as "a jewel-like miniature landscape"[55] by Marion Garmel of the *Indianapolis News,* the winning oil was done at a spot on the outskirts of Muncie. "He painted it at sunset," she wrote in her "Brush Strokes" column, "facing a ridge of trees, with the light of the fading sky reflected in a small river. It is one of his first Indiana landscapes."[56] Largely self-taught, Grue looked

with pride to one particularly artistic ancestor, Baron François Gérard; works by this early nineteenth-century French painter appear in collections around the world.[57]

The Indianapolis-based Cunningham, with a national reputation for his paintings of aerospace, was the second of the threesome to take a significant Salon prize. He earned the $1,000 "Outstanding Work, Any Medium" award with his linear *Shoreline/Winter Skies.* Influenced by Cunningham's trips to NASA launch sites, the expansive acrylic was singled out by one art critic who described it as catching the "hard-edge, abstract reflections of the Florida coast."[58]

Lentz, the third artist in the prizewinning trio, won with a landscape entitled *Cypress Point.* This Indianapolis high school teacher was given the $1,000 "Outstanding Painting, Traditional, Any Medium" award for his "blue-tinted watercolor of rocks, river and mountains."[59] A familiar presence in the Salon since 1972, he was well accustomed to the winner's spotlight, having taken four other merit awards in earlier years.

The paintings by these three were among 166 pieces chosen by the two-man jury from nearly seven hundred entries. Because of its purse of more than $20,000, the exhibition continued to be one of the richest juried competitions in the country. "The sad thing was that out of thirty-six individual artists capturing forty-one merit and purchase awards," noted an *Indianapolis News* reporter, "only thirteen showed up to claim their prizes. Time was when artists came from all over the state—in the depths of January, too—to participate in the Salon opening."[60]

To boost attendance at the Preview Party, the opening had been scheduled for a weekend in April so as not to compete with Mother's Day celebrations in May. "Our crowd was smaller (in 1984) because of [that] date conflict," said Mrs. Beck. "We usually have between 375 and 450 people."[61] The different time, however, had failed to increase the crowd, and columnist Garmel was not surprised. She thought that perhaps another factor was involved. "[T]imes being what they are," she wrote in the *News,* "with dozens of art organizations holding openings and ceremonies almost every weekend, the Salon has come to be taken for granted. The young have taken over the territory, and the more traditional artists are considered 'passé.'"[62]

* * *

1986 Although the sixty-second Hoosier Salon was given little coverage by the Indianapolis press, *News* columnist Marion Garmel remarked that the jurors had "picked a show full of color and surprises—new artists, new styles and a wonderful variety of images."[63] In its ninth year of being held at Ayres department store, the Salon featured 240 paintings, prints, drawings and pieces of sculpture—drawn from a field of 523 entries—by 174 artists.[64]

Eleanor Lewis collected the "Best of Show" award for her oil painting of *Sculptor Hermann Gurfinkel,* "an unorthodox 'portrait' of the northwestern Indiana sculptor at work at his studio near Valparaiso."[65] She was presented the $1,500 prize by Lee Theisen, executive director of the Indiana State Museum, and Eugene L. Henderson, an attorney from Indianapolis who had taken over the presidency of the Board of Directors from Harry E. Riser. An art teacher at Merrillville High School for thirty years, Dr. Lewis had been entering the Salon since 1972 and had picked up two awards in the process. "But [they were] never anything like this,"[66] the Crown Point, Indiana, artist said after the awards ceremony.

Rich Ernsting's *The Lovers of Lauren Macaw,* a watercolor of gaily plumed birds, was named for a $250 "Jury Prize of Distinction." Employed by Herff Jones, Inc., he scrambled to find the hours after work in which to paint. By June of 1987, this Indianapolis-born artist would give up the security of his full-time job for a career as a free-lance artist. As one of his first ventures, Ernsting would produce a poster entitled *Indianapolis, Movin' Up.* "In one month, [he would sell] five hundred prints . . . , making as much as he had selling fine art in the first eleven months of the year."[67]

Working on this project would prove to be thought-provoking for the young man. "It really has kind of changed my thinking," he would later say of his piece that featured a stylized view of downtown Indianapolis at night. "[I]t wasn't fine art which was my first love. [B]ut if I can get some enjoyment out of doing this, and it does sell—why not? This may be my favorite all-time work; it may keep me in the art field."[68] Like many of his colleagues in the Hoosier capital, Ernsting maintained that "[m]aking it in fine arts is difficult in this city. You almost have to make it in decorator arts. Indianapolis has improved," he said, "but it hasn't improved nearly enough to support a lot of fine artists."[69]

Frederik Ebbesen Grue, however, was one of those fine artists who did find support for his work; both his still-life paintings and landscapes sold quickly. Once again, in the 1986 Salon, Grue was in line for one of the show's foremost awards. This year, the artist from Muncie, Indiana, would win the $1,000 "Outstanding Painting, Traditional, Any Medium" prize—from a purse totaling $17,200—

for his *Study of Porcelain and Lemons.* This oil would also win the $100 "Popular Prize," given by the Hoosier Salon Guild to the piece receiving the greatest number of votes from gallery-goers.

Within five weeks of the Salon's closing on May 3, fifty-four paintings from the exhibition were assembled for a special showing at the Honeywell Center in Wabash, Indiana. In August of 1941, the Association had displayed artwork on the grounds of the Wabash estate of the group's first vice-president, Mark C. Honeywell. Some forty-five years later, in June of 1986, another vice-president, Richard E. Ford, was involved in bringing Salon art back to the area for a summer show.[70] Other stops on the Salon touring calendar included the Indiana towns of Greencastle, Kokomo, Portland, Lewisville, Rochester, Lafayette and Linton.[71]

* * *

1987 From her cramped quarters on the third floor of the Morrison Opera Place, Mrs. Beck continued to supervise the sale of "paintings, sculpture, prints and lithographs by Hoosier Salon artists."[72] An advocate for Indiana art and its artists, she was pleased to learn that another organization in town shared her vision. The newly formed Arts Council of Indianapolis was holding a series of public meetings to develop a long-range plan for the promotion of the arts within the city. "We're looking at the arts in Indianapolis as they exist today and what they might be in the future,"[73] explained Gerald L. Ness, director of the fledgling group. The first workshop was held at the downtown World War Memorial during mid-January.

While the Arts Council was mapping out possibilities, Association members continued with their decades-long support of Hoosier art. Another exhibition was soon upon them with the opening of the sixty-third annual Salon. "While the basic tone of the show . . . is traditional," remarked a writer from the *Indianapolis Star,* "contemporary art is well represented. The exhibition suggests a blurring of the line between traditional and contemporary in the mix of themes and techniques. It also indicates a sharp difference of opinion between the professional jurors who make the merit awards and the selection committees and individuals responsible for the purchase prizes. Few artists came up winning in both categories."[74]

Of those who did come up winning the Salon's larger prizes, all were men. Called to the podium to receive the first eight awards were Frederik Ebbesen Grue, Donald Lee Hadley, Bud Jamison, Grant Christian, Rob O'Dell, James Curtin Lentz, Harry Davis and Mark W. Bratovich. They were given their checks—from a purse totaling

$19,525—by Lee Theisen, executive director of the Indiana State Museum, and Eugene Henderson, president of the Association. Both were back for a second year to present awards at the invitational Preview Party.

From the 238 paintings, prints and pieces of sculpture that had been chosen from more than six hundred entries, Grue again garnered the $1,500 "Best of Show." Even though his paintings had been consistently among the prizewinners in recent years, he was delighted, nevertheless, when his name was called. "I'm really honored and grateful," said the thirty-six-year-old artist to several of the guests assembled in the eight-floor Ayres Auditorium. "There's some very fine work in this show."[75]

Grue's *Wheat Fields,* observed art critic Marion Garmel of the *Indianapolis News,* "is not your typical Brown County landscape. A simple painting of two small fields of golden wheat divided by a placid stream, it has a clarity and precision that are largely unknown in the twentieth century. Each staff of wheat, each blade of grass seems to be made from a separate stroke. There's depth to the water and body in the surrounding trees."[76] At the end of the exhibition, *Wheat Fields* would be voted the favorite painting of visitors to the Salon, and Grue would be given—for the fourth consecutive year—the Hoosier Salon Guild's $100 "Popular Prize."[77]

Among the "fine work" to which Grue referred upon winning his prize was Donald Lee Hadley's *Small World.* This acrylic won the $1,000 "Outstanding Work, Any Medium" award that was underwritten by L. S. Ayres & Company. Hadley, an art teacher from Terre Haute, Indiana, said that he used his art "to represent the life of people through their objects."[78] Though declining to classify his paintings as being within the *trompe l'oeil* tradition, he had no problem in defining his artwork for himself.

"I've tried working in other styles, but I just keep coming back more and more to details," the brown-haired, bespectacled artist explained. "I can't help it. An artist must paint what's valid for him."[79] According to Ms. Garmel, "[w]hat's valid for Hadley are man-made objects that tell him something about the people who once owned them: the old newspaper clippings that reflect past glory, the abandoned bugles once joyfully blown, now left to gather dust and history in the attic."[80]

Within weeks of the show's conclusion, Salon artwork was being circulated to cities around the state. Patrons in many of those venues were planning to host smaller versions of the big exhibition in Indianapolis. On the touring calendar for 1987 were stops at the Picture Show Gallery in Linton, the Guyer Opera House in Lewisville, the Public Library in West Lafayette, the Central National Bank in Greencastle, the Citizens' Bank in Portland, the Honeywell Center in Wabash, the Fulton County Public Library in Rochester and the Kokomo Public Library in Kokomo.[81]

Included among the pieces that were displayed in the Kokomo show was a watercolor entitled *Snowscape with Young Boy* by local artist Jerry G. Stephens. An art instructor at the Kokomo High School for twenty-two years, he declared that the Salon offerings in his city presented "one of the strongest shows I have seen. I was very impressed with the winning landscape picture and the entire show. Artists are returning to more realism with less abstract painting."[82] Another Kokomo artist, Debbie Edwards, decided that "the exhibit just makes you itch to go home and start painting."[83]

The October issue of the *Hoosier Salon Newsletter* carried some exciting news for Association members who were eager to increase the renown of Salon artwork. In her "Executive Director's Report," Mrs. Beck announced that "[s]ome of the Blue Ribbon winners from the last Exhibit will have work hanging at the Circle Theatre (in Indianapolis) for the opening of the (Indianapolis) Symphony (Orchestra) season, . . . The Theatre has asked if it would be possible to make this an annual affair—our Board has consented—and, once again, our Indiana artists will have work on display before a new audience!"[84] Among the twenty artists whose paintings were chosen for the month-long showing were Frederik Ebbesen Grue, Harry Davis, Rob O'Dell, James Curtin Lentz and Mary Jane Bell.[85]

* * *

1988 "This was the year the new Indianapolis Zoo opened in White River State Park, and the Eiteljorg Museum of Native American and Western Art began rising from the wasteland that was the corner of West and Washington streets (in Indianapolis)," recounted an article in the *Indianapolis News.* "This also was the year the Indianapolis Museum of Art cancelled its biennial Indiana Artists Show and the Indianapolis Art League tried to pick up the slack.

". . . But the big news on the arts scene was the fight to obtain increased funding from the City-County Council (of Indianapolis)," the report continued. "Led by the barely one-year-old Arts Council of Indianapolis, the city's performing and visual arts organizations banded together to lobby for one million dollars in city funds. When the dust cleared, they had obtained $624,000, up $100,000 from the $524,000 appropriation that had been standard for years."[86]

Great hopes for the future were vested in the Arts Council and its president, Robert Beckmann, Jr. He had been asked to officiate at the Salon's late-afternoon awards ceremony along with Richard E. Ford, the newly elected president of the Association. Named to succeed Henderson after the 1987 show, Ford had first become active with the group at the suggestion of the late Ardath Burkhart. "In 1980, [she] was the president of the Board," explained this resident of Wabash, Indiana, "and she asked me to become involved in it. I was in the process of moving back to Indiana at that time from the Washington, D. C., area."[87]

Together, Beckmann and Ford distributed a hefty $22,360 in merit awards and purchase prizes to the 174 artists whose work had been juried into the show. It was the richest purse in the Salon's sixty-four-year history. Contributing to this goodly sum was the Hoosier Salon Guild. Formed in June of 1977 to "help with clerical work and assist in hosting the annual exhibit,"[88] it had been able to increase its donation for merit awards from $800 to $1,000 for the 1988 show. The additional $200 had enabled the group to underwrite a prize for "Best Drawing,"[89] in addition to funding the $400 award for "Outstanding Watercolor," the $300 "Best Work, Any Medium, to First Time Exhibiting Artist" and the $100 "Popular Prize."

Joining the Guild in its financial support of the Salon were several organizations that had been participating in the show for over a half-century. Among the loyal donors were Kappa Kappa Kappa, a group that had funded both merit awards and purchase prizes since becoming connected with the Salon in 1927; Delta Sigma Kappa, a sorority that had assisted the Association's efforts with monies and volunteer hours since 1937; and Psi Iota Xi, a collection of women who had been counted among the mainstays of the exhibition since 1941.

The Woman's Department Club, along with its Art Department, had continued to back the exhibition through the years. In 1937, the Club had begun sponsoring—in the Hoosier capital—a showing of Salon art from Chicago until the show itself had been moved to the William H. Block Company in Indianapolis after the 1941 exhibition. Also dependable help-mates in Salon work were members from both the Indiana Federation of Clubs and the Indiana Federation of Art Clubs. Many of those who belonged to art clubs across the state had been involved with the annual shows as well as with the first—and only—Summer Hoosier Salon at Lake Wawasee, Indiana, in 1936.

The winners of two of the Salon's merit awards were familiar to most of the gallery-goers who had gathered at Ayres for the exhibition. Harry A. Davis again stood center stage, taking the $1,500 "Best of Show" with *10th and Connor,* another in his series of paintings devoted to historical architecture. His wife, Lois, was honored with a $300 "Jury Prize of Distinction" for her acrylic entitled *Recovery Room, Back to Consciousness.*

"Davis . . . make[s] precise paintings of buildings his speciality, particularly endangered Indiana buildings," observed one art critic from Indianapolis. "[He] has always had a passion for composition, and his precisely rendered architectural paintings . . . are models of clarity and composition. . . . Mrs. Davis concentrate[s] on people . . . on expression, and her paintings [become] more collages of mood than particular character studies. She fills her canvases with the faces of age and youth, angels and mythological figures, even people on the picket line."[90]

As a teenager in Brownsburg, Indiana, Harry Davis knew that he wanted to become an artist, and World War II only contributed to that end. He had served as a combat artist with the 5th Army Historical Section in Italy from 1942 to 1946.[91] "I made watercolors in the Army," the painter explained in an interview with *Arts Indiana* magazine. "That was the only medium we could use. The experience made me realize that I could change events in a sense; I didn't have to carry a gun.

"I learned there that you had to get an idea on the spot, so a camera was my best bet," he continued. "I learned composition through the lens, and that is how I compose my paintings now so that there is a dynamic thrust when you look at them. Beyond the photograph is where I take off. I feel that light has a certain sparkle in it. I want the vibration to give the eye a little bit of excitement."[92]

Claiming a spot in the prizewinner's circle with Harry and Lois Davis was Frederik Ebbesen Grue who, once again, captured a major award: the $1,000 "Outstanding Painting, Traditional, Any Medium." According to columnist Marion Garmel, though, the big winners of the exhibition were not these three artists but rather two art patrons, Mr. and Mrs. Thomas E. Husselman. "[They] picked a watercolor by an unknown artist at a preview for purchase award donors and bought it for $275.

"The painting, *River Market* by Diane Ubelhor Wunderlich, went on to win the $1,000 award for 'Outstanding Work, Any Medium' and the $300 award for 'Best Work, Any Medium by a First Time Exhibiting Artist,'"[93] continued Ms. Garmel.

Inspiration for the piece had come from a photograph in which a woman was pictured as she sat in a market skiff that had been pulled up to a riverbank in Thailand. The artist had spent several years in the country as a child when her father had been stationed there with the Air Force.[94]

The *Indianapolis News* critic gave the 235-piece Salon a rave review, describing it as "a wonderful show, full of strong paintings and fine drawings, representing still life, portrait, landscape, seascape, sculpture and just about everything in between."[95] When the exhibit closed on May 7, selected artworks from the show toured the Indiana cities of Linton, Lewisville, West Lafayette, Greencastle, Portland, Wabash, Rochester and Kokomo.[96] In addition to these summer showings, announced Mrs. Beck, "[t]wenty paintings by our Merit Award artists in the Indianapolis area will be hanging at the Circle Theatre during the month of October, the opening month of the Indianapolis Symphony Orchestra."[97] This was the second year in which the Salon would be honored with such a display.

* * *

1989 "History teaches us that no society has experienced economic and scientific progress without commensurate progress in artistic achievement," wrote Indiana Governor Evan Bayh in his greeting to gallery-goers who were attending the late-spring show. "As governor of the State of Indiana, I am proud to welcome patrons and members of the Hoosier Salon to your sixty-fifth Annual Exhibit and to thank you for your contributions to artistic progress and excellence in Indiana."[98]

Mindful of the Association's distinguished history, Mrs. Beck decided to put together a modest "show-within-a-show" that would highlight special moments from the group's past. "The catalogue from the first Hoosier Salon in 1925 and that for last year will be among several on display to mark the (sixty-fifth) anniversary,"[99] explained the executive director. "I think it's important to remember that there has been no deviation through the years from the Association's initial purpose of presenting the finest of Indiana art to the public."[100] Also reinstated for the anniversary celebration was the traditional "receiving line" of earlier days. Hoosier Salon Guild members hoped that it might "help to revive some of [the Salon's] former elegance."[101]

Handing out checks from a purse totaling $22,180 were Robert Beckmann, Jr., president of the Board of the Arts Council of Indianapolis, and Richard E. Ford. Both men were back for a second turn at the podium, set up for the Sunday-after-noon Preview Party in the eight-floor Auditorium at Ayres. Tapped for an award from among the 245 artworks that had been juried into the show—from a field of 598 entries—was *A Hundred in the Shade* by Rosemary Lawton Thomas. This portrait of a farmer and the tools of his trade was awarded the $1,000 "Outstanding Work, Any Medium" prize.

Born in Mulberry, Indiana, Ms. Thomas was a graduate of the Herron School of Art and, at one time, had headed the Display Department at L. S. Ayres & Company. "I am much concerned with color and its relation to form," said the artist as she contemplated her work. "Having been a rather poor draftsman, I have found it necessary to depend on color and its tonal values rather than line in order to draw."[102] She went on to explain that her particular interest in color "has opened up an approach to creative painting. . . . It has helped me become a more avid student of composition and to delve into the more scientific aspects of light and its relationship to color."[103]

K. P. Singh, "whose drawings and prints of Indiana architecture also are popular with viewers,"[104] won $100 for the "Outstanding Drawing" with his *Tippecanoe Courthouse, Lafayette, Indiana.* A favorite among those who appreciated fine draftsmanship, Singh had been a regular exhibitor in the Salon since 1972. He had taken a prize in only one other year, though, when he had claimed the award for "Outstanding Drawing" with his *Golden Temple, Amritsar, India,* in 1985.

Later Singh would tell John Shaughnessy of the *Indianapolis Star* how he, as an eight-year-old, and his family had fled India during 1947 while the country was being partitioned. Driven from the area by bloodshed and violence, Singh's family had left their homes "with whatever we had on our backs. . . . We had to start life all over again," he said. "As late as 1953, we had a single room for all of us (his parents and five children). I [know] what true pain and suffering [are] about, so little things don't bother me. I was told long ago, 'Knock [on] lots of doors. and one of them will definitely be open to you.' I've always pursued that thought."[105]

Settling in Indianapolis after studying at the University of Michigan, Singh began a career that celebrated the architecture of Indiana. "[My] drawings essentially began as a journey to discover the state I call home," he explained. "Then [they] evolved to re-evaluating and rethinking how these historic buildings add beauty and elegance to our neighborhoods, our streets, our city. To me, it seemed very important that what our ancestors left behind as landmarks, as fabrics of our thought and society, should be preserved."[106]

Within weeks of the conclusion of the eight-city tour of Salon artwork came the news that Mrs. Mary Beck had submitted her resignation. "After eleven years, our Executive Director . . . has decided to retire," announced the Association president, Richard E. Ford, in the *Hoosier Salon Newsletter.* "The Salon is much indebted to Mary; her devotion to the work of the Salon, her good nature, and her countless friendships with artists and supporters have made her an ideal Director."[107] Members of the Association paid tribute to this dedicated woman at a dinner during which Ford presented her with a "Sagamore of the Wabash" commendation, issued by Indiana Governor Evan Bayh.[108]

Replacing Mrs. Beck as executive director was Mrs. (Henry N.) Evelyn M. Wellman of Indianapolis. Almost as soon as she stepped into the position in September of 1989, Mrs. Wellman was faced with her first big challenge: working with the Board of Directors to find another place in which to mount the annual Salon. Ever since the family-run L. S. Ayres & Company had been purchased by an out-of-state owner in 1983, rumors had been circulating that the downtown department store would end its policy of hosting art shows in the Auditorium.[109]

Ford informed Association members of the new venue for the Salon in the December issue of the *Hoosier Salon Newsletter.* "Those of you who have met Evelyn know that innovations will be coming in 1990. Due to changes at Ayres, we shall be having the annual exhibition at the Indiana State Museum,"[110] he wrote in his "President's Message." Mrs. Wellman, the new executive director, explained more fully. "This move was necessitated by L. S. Ayres' withdrawing the use of their facility," she said. "I believe you will find the [new] location beautifully appointed and well suited for the Annual Hoosier Salon Exhibition."[111]

1990
James Curtin Lentz
Union Stationaries
Outstanding Painting—Traditional—Any Medium

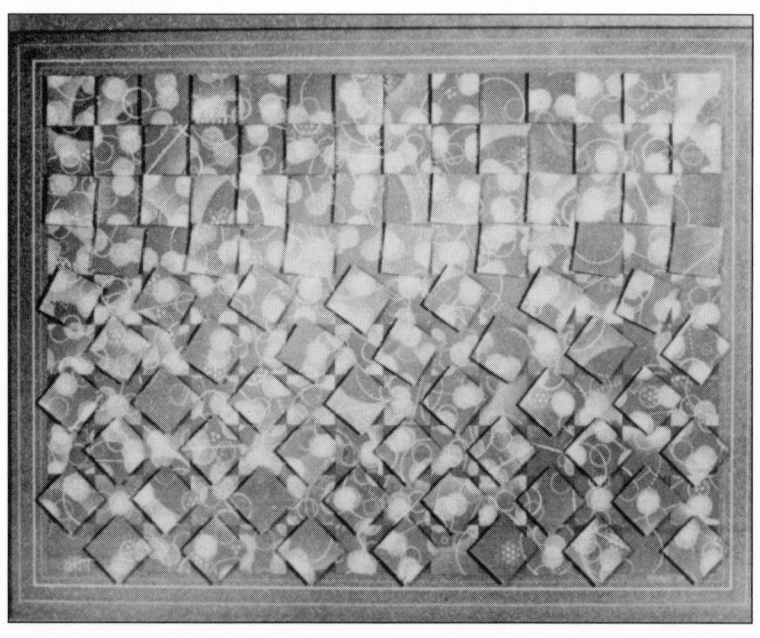

1990
Steven Redman
Eclectic Mix
Outstanding Work—Any Medium

The Nineties

1990 "The oldest and richest show in Indiana (and maybe the nation) gave away $27,370 in merit and purchase awards," reported Marion Garmel of the *Indianapolis News*. "And the Hoosier Salon . . . is ready to crow."[1] With more of its prizes going "to abstract or contemporary art than in any Salon in recent memory,"[2] the exhibition itself had turned in a new direction. After sixty-five years of being held in department stores—Marshall Field & Company, 1925-1941; William H. Block Company, 1942-1977; and L. S. Ayres & Company, 1978-1989—the Salon was being displayed at the Indiana State Museum[3] for the first time.

Pleased to welcome gallery-goers to this regal building, Richard A. Gantz, director of the downtown Indianapolis museum, offered his greetings in the Salon's catalogue. "Without a doubt, Indiana possesses a rich artistic heritage," he wrote, "[and] [o]ver the years, the State Museum has continually exhibited the works of both historic figures and contemporary artists. . . . The Hoosier Salon show is a significant element of the state's artistic calendar. We are happy that the Indiana State Museum can be part of such a worthwhile project."[4]

Spirits were high at the late-afternoon Preview Party as Salon guests chatted beneath the "Tiffany Era" stained-glass dome that towers above the inlaid marble floor of the museum lobby. Later they crowded into a gallery to watch Robert Beckmann, Jr., again team up with Ford to pass out prizes from the attention-getting purse. From the 547 entries that had been submitted for the show, two out-of-state jurors had chosen 207 artworks by 162 artists. Thirty-three of them were first-time exhibitors.[5]

Among those newcomers was the winner of the $1,500 "Best of Show" award, Jack D. Cowan. "[A] twenty-seven-year-old stringbean with streaked short hair, who never went to art school, captured the prize for his oil painting, *Before the Symphony at Capriccios*, which combines the sensibilities of Manet's *The Bar at the Folies-Bergère*

with those of a pin-up magazine," declared Ms. Garmel in her review of the Salon. "Cowan moved here two years ago from Orlando, Florida, where he was born and raised."[6]

Despite his lack of formal art training, Cowan said that he had been drawing since the age of three. "I like to paint formal scenes from memory," he explained. "I have this ability to sit down and draw somebody out of my head."[7] His prizewinning piece, the young man noted, had been inspired by a restaurant in which he had worked while living in the South. According to Ms. Garmel, Cowan had neither shown nor sold any of his paintings. The Salon, he said, was the first show in which he had entered his artwork.

Unlike Cowan, Wilbur Meese—winner of the $400 "Outstanding Watercolor" with his *Patchwork and Pink Pitcher*—was a regular exhibitor in the Salon. He had first been accepted into the show in 1948. Meese, who had been employed as an art director at Eli Lilly & Company, began developing his artistic skills while in high school. It was only in the late-1960s, however, that he seriously began to work in watercolor. "For a number of years, I didn't do too much work in the fine arts, maybe two or three watercolors a year," Meese admitted. "Most of my work was in the commercial arts field. Then I decided I'd better start something I could do when I retired so I began working in watercolor in earnest."[8]

With the decade's first show had come a number of changes: a new executive director, a new exhibition site and the election of Indianapolis attorney Henry B. Blackwell as the new president of the Board of Directors. "I look forward to [the] challenges,"[9] he wrote after assuming his post at the annual meeting in June. Among those issues he wished the Board to consider were "the renewal of our lease or relocation, further adjustments of our membership and dues structure, finding a permanent location for our award exhibition, developing programs to get greater corporate and public support, and [the] expansion of our Advisory [Council] to make the Hoosier Salon more statewide and more inclusive."[10]

As the Association looked ahead, with Blackwell at the helm, its focus never shifted from its early goals of inspiring, promoting and rewarding the artists of Indiana.[11] Capturing best this decades-long mission, novelist Booth Tarkington had marveled at the Salon's genius for joining art with appreciation. "By handsomely bringing paintings and audience together," he had mused in 1940, "the Hoosier Salon provides opportunity for that most satisfying of miracles to occur: the miracle of a painter's finding for his canvases the ideal beholder that was in the back of his mind as he worked. When this happens, as sometimes it does, all that we variously mean when we use the word 'art' has complete being."[12]

EXHIBITION RECORDS
Juries of Award and Admittance

1925
Ralph Clarkson, Joseph H. Defrees, Frank V. Dudley, Pauline Palmer, Beaumont Parks, Edward Rector, Adolph Schulz, John C. Shaffer, Clifton Wheeler

1926
Edward S. Carry, Mrs. Catherine C. Cherry, Frank S. Cunningham, Charles W. Dahlgreen, Oliver Dennett Grover, Miss Lucie Hartrath, Wilson Irvine, Emory P. Seidel, Gaar Williams

1927
Gerald Frank, Harold Gray, Miss Emily Groom, James R. Hopkins, Carl R. Krafft, Arvid Nyholm, Miss Nellie Walker; *(Lay Members)* William G. Edens, Beaumont Parks

1928
Wayman Adams, John David Brcin, Karl Buehr, Edward T. Grigware, Miss Anna Lynch, John Ellsworth Weis; *(Lay Members)* Eugene Buffington, Clement Studebaker, Mrs. William G. Valentine

1929
Oscar E. Berninghaus, Oskar Gross, E. Martin Hennings, Miss Irma Rene Koen, Albin Polasek, John Spelman; *(Lay Members)* Mrs. Lawrence A. Downs, Mrs. J. M. Kleppinger, Harry Kurrie

1930
Claude Buck, Otto Hake, Mrs. Bertha E. Jaques, Mrs. Lucy Perkins Ripley, Rolf Stoll, James Topping; *(Lay Members)* Alexander F. Banks, Hoyt King, Mrs. James L. Sayler

1931
Francis Chapin, Mrs. Grace Rhoades Dean, Frederic V. Poole, Otto J. Schneider, Miss Ruth Sherwood, Charles A. Wilimovsky, Charles Sneed Williams; *(Lay Members)* Mrs. Ross J. Beatty, Scott Brown, Fritz B. Ernst

1932
Joseph Allworthy, J. Jeffrey Grant, Edward T. Grigware, Miss Viola Norman, Leon R. Pescheret, John F. Stacey; *(Lay Member)* Mrs. Frank F. Hummel

1933
Mrs. Eugenie Glamann, Alfonso Iannelli, Rudolph Ingerle, John Nolf, Lee Sturges, Grant Wood; *(Lay Member)* Mrs. John F. Craig

1934
Wilbur G. Adam, Edgar S. Cameron, Allen Philbrick, Tunis Ponsen, Mrs. Anna L. Stacey, Miss Nellie Walker; *(Lay Member)* Mrs. Harry G. Nye

1935
W. Russell Button, Elmer A. Forsberg, Edward T. Grigware, F. R. Harper, Charles Killgore, Robert W. MacBeth, Edward J. Snyder; *(Lay Member)* Mrs. Leon Stern

1936
Karl Buehr, Miss Elizabeth Haseltine, Holger W. Jensen, Walter Krawiec, Gasper J. Ruffolo, Ralph Fletcher Seymour; *(Lay Member)* Mrs. Lawrence J. Lindsay

1937
Miss Frances Foy, Oskar Gross, Morris H. Hobbs, Mrs. Sylvia Shaw Judson, Karl Preussl; *(Lay Members)* Mrs. William D. Coon, Mrs. W. C. Lemke, Jr.

1938
Ruth VanSickle Ford, Louis Grell, Edward T. Grigware, Harriet Krawiec, Hubert Morley, Fred M. Torrey; *(Lay Members)* Mrs. J. M. Kleppinger, Mrs. Lester F. Murphy

1939
Averil Conwell, Frances Farrand Dodge, Antonin Sterba, James Swann, Mable Landrum Torrey, Herman Wessel; *(Lay Members)* Mrs. Clifford Rogers, Mrs. Joseph Spurgeon

1940
Randolph Brooks, Richard Chase, C. Lynn Coy, Jeffrey Grant, Benjamin Kanne, Beatrice Levy; *(Lay Members)* Mrs. Earl Moore, Mrs. Arthur B. Wright

1941
Edouard Chassaing, Frances Farrand Dodge, Charles Killgore, Hubert Morley, Elmer Taflinger, A. Reid Winsey; *(Lay Members)* Miss Catherine Davis, Mrs. Frederick Tice

1942
John F. Carlson, Sidney E. Dickinson, Harvey Emrich, H. H. Wessel

1943
Wayman Adams, Jerry Farnsworth; *(Lay Members)* Mrs. Garland F. Retherford, Miss Helen Whitcomb

1944
Carl F. Gaertner, Alexander Reid Winsey, Adolph Wolter; *(Lay Members)* Mrs. Garland F. Retherford, Mrs. E. W. Sherwood

1945
Allen D. Albert, Rudolph F. Ingerle, James Topping; *(Lay Members)* Mrs. E. J. Hancock, Mrs. Lynn Miller

1946
Gianni Cilfone, J. Scott Williams; *(Lay Members)* Miss Leah Flint, Mrs. Lester F. Murphy

1947
J. Jeffrey Grant, Naomi Northam, Louis Ritman; *(Lay Members)* Mrs. Lester F. Murphy, Mrs. J. D. Young

1948
James Murray Haddow, Marie Evelyn Stuart, Carl Wuermer

1949
Felecie Mixter Howell, Lee H. B. Malone, Gasper J. Ruffolo

1950
Allen D. Cochran, Rudolph F. Ingerle, Roy E. Wilhelm; *(Lay Members)* Mrs. C. H. Cox, Mrs. J. D. Young

1951
Mrs. Ingrid Buchinger *(Honorary Member)*, Richard A. Chase, Niccolo Cortiglia, Antonin Sterba; *(Lay Members)* Mrs. John Ellis Fell, Mrs. Claude S. Steele, Mrs. John W. Thornburgh

1952
John Bacus, Robert Philipp, Paul Riba

1953
Julius Moessel, Walter Parke, Leon R. Pescheret

1954
Paul Chidlaw, Ken Gore, Roy E. Wilhelm

1955
Frank B. Nuderscher, Francis Speight, Santos Zingale; *(Honorary Lay Members)* Mrs. Helen Talge Brown, Mrs. John E. Fell, Mrs. Henry P. Humphrey, Mrs. Borden R. Purcell

1956
William C. Libby, Gerry Peirce, Frank H. Young; *(Honorary Lay Members)* Mrs. Dorothy Doles, Mrs. John E. Fell, Mrs. Henry P. Humphrey, Mrs. Carl M. Sauer

1957
Emerson C. Burkhart, William H. Mosby, Lewis Eugene Thompson; *(Honorary Lay Members)* Mrs. John E. Fell, Mrs. Marie North, Mrs. Carl M. Sauer, Mrs. Henry Lester Smith

1958
Donald J. Anderson, Floyd Gahman, Salvatore Salla

1959
Peter Paul Dubaniewicz, Stephen G. Maniatty, Walter Parke

1960
W. F. McCaughey, Irving Shapiro, Paul Strisik

1961
Erwin George Kummer, William H. Mosby, E. Stanley Turnbull

1962
Edward R. Burroughs, Joseph Newman, Reynold H. Weidenaar

1963
Rupert Kilgore, Herbert Stoddard, Richard Yonkers

1964
Leon A. Makielski, John C. Pellew

1965
Albert Alfredson, Phil Austin, Maxwell Starr

1966
Edward Betts, Larry Quakenbush, George Schwacha

1967
Hilton Leech, Elmer Ladislaw Novotny, Reid Winsey

1968
Arthur Helwig, Gerry Peirce, Ben Stahl

1969
Jay Connaway, Joseph J. Rishel

1970
Hereward Lester Cooke, Richard Wengenroth

1971
Norman Ackroyd, Virginia Webb

1972
Addison Franklin Page, Ulfert Wilke

1973
Herb Olsen, Alex F. Yaworski

1974
Edward Betts

1975
Chen Chi

1976
Charles A. Mahoney

1977
Ken Gore, Angelo J. Grado, Joseph McCullough

1978
Mario Cooper, Rudy Pozzatti

1979
Peter Bermingham, Rolland Golden

1980
Glenn R. Bradshaw, William D. Gorman

1981
Mark Freeman, Frank Webb

1982
James M. Auer, Reta Soloway

EXHIBITION RECORDS

1983
Rolland Golden, Roswell Weidner

1984
Edmund J. Fitzgerald, Howard C. Schroedter

1985
J. Everett Draper, Mervin Honig

1986
Judi Betts, Robert MacDonald Graham, Jr.

1987
Georg Shook, Roger Williams

1988
David Berreth, Charles Movalli

1989
William D. Gorman, Reta Soloway

1990
Suzanne Kaufman, Jim Striby

Hoosier Salon Jurors

ACKROYD, Norman	1971	FORD, Ruth VanSickle	1938
ADAM, Wilbur G.	1934	FORSBERG, Elmer A.	1935
ADAMS, Wayman	1928, 1943	FOY, Frances	1937
ALBERT, Allen D.	1945	FRANK, Gerald	1927
ALFREDSON, Albert	1965	FREEMAN, Mark	1981
ALLWORTHY, Joseph	1932	GAERTNER, Carl F.	1944
ANDERSON, Donald J.	1958	GAHMAN, Floyd	1958
AUER, James M.	1982	GLAMANN, Eugenie	1933
AUSTIN, Phil	1965	GOLDEN, Rolland	1979, 1983
BACUS, John	1952	GORE, Ken	1954, 1977
BERMINGHAM, Peter	1979	GORMAN, William D.	1980, 1989
BERNINGHAUS, Oscar E.	1929	GRADO, Angelo J.	1977
BERRETH, David	1988	GRAHAM, Jr., Robert MacDonald	1986
BETTS, Edward	1966, 1974	GRANT, J. Jeffrey	1932, 1940, 1947
BETTS, Judi	1986	GRAY, Harold	1927
BRADSHAW, Glenn R.	1980	GRELL, Louis	1938
BRCIN, John David	1928	GRIGWARE, Edward T.	1928, 1932,
BROOKS, Randolph	1940		1935, 1938
BUCK, Claude	1930	GROOM, Emily	1927
BUEHR, Karl	1928, 1936	GROSS, Oskar	1929, 1937
BURKHART, Emerson C.	1957	GROVER, Oliver Dennett	1926
BURROUGHS, Edward R.	1962	HADDOW, James Murray	1948
BUTTON, W. Russell	1935	HAKE, Otto	1930
CAMERON, Edgar S.	1934	HARPER, F. R.	1935
CARLSON, John F.	1942	HARTRATH, Lucie	1926
CHAPIN, Francis	1931	HASELTINE, Elizabeth	1936
CHASE, Richard A.	1940, 1951	HELWIG, Arthur	1968
CHASSAING, Edouard	1941	HENNINGS, E. Martin	1929
CHI, Chen	1975	HOBBS, Morris H.	1937
CHIDLAW, Paul	1954	HONIG, Mervin	1985
CILFONE, Gianni	1946	HOPKINS, James R.	1927
CLARKSON, Ralph	1925	HOWELL, Felecie Mixter	1949
COCHRAN, Allen D.	1950	IANNELLI, Alfonso	1933
CONNAWAY, Jay	1969	INGERLE, Rudolph F.	1933, 1945, 1950
CONWELL, Averil	1939	IRVINE, Wilson	1926
COOKE, Hereward Lester	1970	JAQUES, Bertha E.	1930
COOPER, Mario	1978	JENSEN, Holger W.	1936
CORTIGLIA, Niccolo	1951	JUDSON, Sylvia Shaw	1937
COY, C. Lynn	1940	KANNE, Benjamin	1940
DAHLGREEN, Charles W.	1926	KAUFMAN, Suzanne	1990
DEAN, Grace Rhoades	1931	KILGORE, Rupert	1963
DICKINSON, Sidney E.	1942	KILLGORE, Charles	1935, 1941
DODGE, Frances Farrand	1939, 1941	KOEN, Irma Rene	1929
DRAPER, J. Everett	1985	KRAFFT, Carl R.	1927
DUBANIEWICZ, Peter Paul	1959	KRAWIEC, Harriet	1938
DUDLEY, Frank V.	1925	KRAWIEC, Walter	1936
EMRICH, Harvey	1942	KUMMER, Erwin George	1961
FARNSWORTH, Jerry	1943	LEECH, Hilton	1967
FITZGERALD, Edmund J.	1984	LEVY, Beatrice	1940

94

LIBBY, William C.	1956	STRIBY, Jim	1990	
LYNCH, Anna	1928	STRISIK, Paul	1960	
MacBETH, Robert W.	1935	STUART, Marie Evelyn	1948	
MAHONEY, Charles A.	1976	STURGES, Lee	1933	
MAKIELSKI, Leon A.	1964	SWANN, James	1939	
MALONE, Lee H. B.	1949	TAFLINGER, Elmer	1941	
MANIATTY, Stephen G.	1959	THOMPSON, Lewis Eugene	1957	
McCAUGHEY, W. F.	1960	TOPPING, James	1930, 1945	
McCULLOUGH, Joseph	1977	TORREY, Fred M.	1938	
MOESSEL, Julius	1953	TORREY, Mable Landrum	1939	
MORLEY, Hubert	1938, 1941	TURNBULL, E. Stanley	1961	
MOSBY, William H.	1957, 1961	WALKER, Nellie	1927, 1934	
MOVALLI, Charles	1988	WEBB, Frank	1981	
NEWMAN, Joseph	1962	WEBB, Virginia	1971	
NOLF, John	1933	WEIDENAAR, Reynold H.	1962	
NORMAN, Viola	1932	WEIDNER, Roswell	1983	
NORTHAM, Naomi	1947	WEIS, John Ellsworth	1928	
NOVOTNY, Elmer Ladislaw	1967	WENGENROTH, Richard	1970	
NUDERSCHER, Frank B.	1955	WESSEL, Herman H.	1939, 1942	
NYHOLM, Arvid	1927	WHEELER, Clifton	1925	
OLSEN, Herb	1973	WILHELM, Roy E.	1950, 1954	
PAGE, Addison Franklin	1972	WILIMOVSKY, Charles A.	1931	
PALMER, Pauline	1925	WILKE, Ulfert	1972	
PARKE, Walter	1953, 1959	WILLIAMS, Charles Sneed	1931	
PEIRCE, Gerry	1956, 1968	WILLIAMS, Gaar	1926	
PELLEW, John C.	1964	WILLIAMS, J. Scott	1946	
PESCHERET, Leon R.	1932, 1953	WILLIAMS, Roger	1987	
PHILBRICK, Allen	1934	WINSEY, Alexander Reid	1941, 1944, 1967	
PHILIPP, Robert	1952	WOLTER, Adolph	1944	
POLASEK, Albin	1929	WOOD, Grant	1933	
PONSEN, Tunis	1934	WUERMER, Carl	1948	
POOLE, Frederic V.	1931	YAWORSKI, Alex F.	1973	
POZZATTI, Rudy	1978	YONKERS, Richard	1963	
PREUSSL, Karl	1937	YOUNG, Frank H.	1956	
QUAKENBUSH, Larry	1966	ZINGALE, Santos	1955	
RIBA, Paul	1952			
RIPLEY, Lucy Perkins	1930	**Lay Members**		
RISHEL, Joseph J.	1969	BANKS, Alexander F.	1930	
RITMAN, Louis	1947	BEATTY, Mrs. Ross J.	1931	
RUFFOLO, Gasper J.	1936, 1949	BROWN, Scott	1931	
SALLA, Salvatore	1958	BUFFINGTON, Eugene	1928	
SCHNEIDER, Otto J.	1931	CARRY, Edward S.	1926	
SCHROEDTER, Howard C.	1984	CHERRY, Mrs. Catherine C.	1926	
SCHULZ, Adolph	1925	COON, Mrs. William D.	1937	
SCHWACHA, George	1966	COX, Mrs. C. H.	1950	
SEIDEL, Emory P.	1926	CRAIG, Mrs. John F.	1933	
SEYMOUR, Ralph Fletcher	1936	CUNNINGHAM, Frank S.	1926	
SHAPIRO, Irving	1960	DAVIS, Miss Catherine	1941	
SHERWOOD, Ruth	1931	DEFREES, Joseph H.	1925	
SHOOK, Georg	1987	DOWNS, Mrs. Lawrence A.	1929	
SNYDER, Edward J.	1935	EDENS, William G.	1927	
SOLOWAY, Reta	1982, 1989	ERNST, Fritz B.	1931	
SPEIGHT, Francis	1955	FELL, Mrs. John Ellis	1951	
SPELMAN, John	1929	FLINT, Miss Leah	1946	
STACEY, Anna L.	1934	HANCOCK, Mrs. E. J.	1945	
STACEY, John F.	1932	HUMMEL, Mrs. Frank F.	1932	
STAHL, Ben	1968	KING, Hoyt	1930	
STARR, Maxwell	1965	KLEPPINGER, Mrs. J. M.	1929, 1938	
STERBA, Antonin	1939, 1951	KURRIE, Harry	1929	
STODDARD, Herbert	1963	LEMKE, Jr., Mrs. W. C.	1937	
STOLL, Rolf	1930	LINDSAY, Mrs. Lawrence J.	1936	

MILLER, Mrs. Lynn	1945	VALENTINE, Mrs. William G.	1928
MOORE, Mrs. Earl	1940	WHITCOMB, Miss Helen	1943
MURPHY, Mrs. Lester F.	1938, 1946, 1947	WRIGHT, Mrs. Arthur B.	1940
NYE, Mrs. Harry G.	1934	YOUNG, Mrs. J. D.	1947, 1950
PARKS, Beaumont	1925, 1927		
RECTOR, Edward	1925	**Honorary Member**	
RETHERFORD, Mrs. Garland F.	1943, 1944	BUCHINGER, Mrs. Ingrid	1951
ROGERS, Mrs. Clifford	1939		
SAYLER, Mrs. James L.	1930	**Honorary Lay Members**	
SHAFFER, John C.	1925	BROWN, Mrs. Helen Talge	1955
SHERWOOD, Mrs. E. W.	1944	DOLES, Mrs. Dorothy	1956
SPURGEON, Mrs. Joseph	1939	FELL, Mrs. John E.	1955, 1956, 1957
STEELE, Mrs. Claude S.	1951	HUMPHREY, Mrs. Henry P.	1955, 1956
STERN, Mrs. Leon	1935	NORTH, Mrs. Marie	1957
STUDEBAKER, Clement	1928	PURCELL, Mrs. Borden R.	1955
THORNBURGH, Mrs. John W.	1951	SAUER, Mrs. Carl M.	1956, 1957
TICE, Mrs. Frederick	1941	SMITH, Mrs. Henry Lester	1957

Hoosier Salon Exhibition Schedule

Picture Galleries,
Marshall Field & Company,
Chicago, Illinois

1925   Preview Party, March 7
March 9 - 19

1926   Preview Party, March 6
March 8 - 20

1927   Preview Party, January 29
January 31 - February 12

1928   Preview Party, January 28
January 30 - February 15

1929   Preview Party, January 26
January 28 - February 13

1930   Preview Party, January 25
January 27 - February 12

1931   Preview Party, January 24
January 26 - February 7

1932   Preview Party, January 23
January 25 - February 6

1933   Preview Party, January 28
January 30 - February 11

1934   Preview Party, January 27
January 29 - February 10

1935   Preview Party, January 26
January 28 - February 9

1936   Preview Party, January 25
January 27 - February 8

Summer Hoosier Salon,
Spink-Wawasee Hotel,
Lake Wawasee, Indiana
June 27 - September 27

1937   Preview Party, January 30
February 1 - February 13

1938   Preview Party, January 29
January 31 - February 12

1939   Preview Party, January 28
January 30 - February 11

1940   Preview Party, January 27
January 29 - February 10

1941   Preview Party, January 25
January 27 - February 8

Auditorium Galleries,
William H. Block Company,
Indianapolis, Indiana

1942   Preview Party, January 17
January 19 - January 31

1943   Preview Party, January 16
January 18 - January 30

1944   Preview Party, January 15
January 16 - January 29

1945   Preview Party, January 20
January 21 - February 3

1946   Preview Party, January 20
January 21 - February 2

1947   Preview Party, January 26
January 27 - February 8

1948   Preview Party, January 25
January 26 - February 7

1949   Preview Party, January 30
January 31 - February 12

National Museum,
Smithsonian Institution,
Washington, D. C.
April 7 - April 28

1950   Preview Party, January 29
January 30 - February 11

1951   Preview Party, January 28
January 29 - February 10

1952   Preview Party, January 27
January 28 - February 16

1953   Preview Party, January 25
January 26 - February 7

1954   Preview Party, February 7
February 8 - February 20

1955   Preview Party, February 6
February 7 - February 19

1956   Preview Party, February 5
February 6 - February 18

1957   Preview Party, February 10
February 11 - February 23

1958   Preview Party, February 9
February 10 - February 22

1959 Preview Party, January 25
January 26 - February 7

1960 Preview Party, January 24
January 25 - February 6

1961 Preview Party, January 29
January 30 - February 11

1962 Preview Party, January 28
January 29 - February 10

1963 Preview Party, January 27
January 28 - February 9

1964 Preview Party, January 26
January 27 - February 8

1965 Preview Party, January 31
February 1 - February 13

1966 Preview Party, January 30
January 31 - February 12

1967 Preview Party, January 29
January 30 - February 11

1968 Preview Party, January 28
January 29 - February 10

1969 Preview Party, January 26
January 27 - February 8

1970 Preview Party, January 25
January 26 - February 7

1971 Preview Party, January 24
January 25 - February 6

1972 Preview Party, January 23
January 24 - February 5

1973 Preview Party, January 21
January 22 - February 3

1974 Preview Party, January 20
January 21 - February 2

1975 Preview Party, January 19
January 20 - February 1

1976 Preview Party, January 25
January 26 - February 7

1977 Preview Party, January 23
January 24 - February 5

Auditorium Galleries,
L. S. Ayres & Company,
Indianapolis, Indiana

1978 Preview Party, April 9
April 10 - April 22

1979 Preview Party, April 29
April 30 - May 12

1980 Preview Party, April 27
April 28 - May 10

1981 Preview Party, May 10
May 11 - May 23

1982 Preview Party, May 2
May 3 - May 15

1983 Preview Party, April 24
April 25 - May 7

1984 Preview Party, May 13
May 14 - May 26

1985 Preview Party, April 28
April 29 - May 11

1986 Preview Party, April 20
April 21 - May 3

1987 Preview Party, May 10
May 11 - May 23

1988 Preview Party, April 24
April 25 - May 7

1989 Preview Party, April 16
April 17 - April 29

Fine Art Galleries,
Indiana State Museum,
Indianapolis, Indiana

1990 Preview Party, May 6
May 7 - May 19

Merit Awards and Prizes

1925

OUTSTANDING PICTURE OF THE EXHIBITION
Recessional by Eugene Savage
   John C. Shaffer ($500)

PORTRAIT IN OIL
Portrait of Booth Tarkington by Wayman Adams
   The Indianapolis Star ($200)
Portrait of Mrs. Baus by Simon P. Baus
   Clement Studebaker ($100)
The Portrait of George Ade by Robert W. Grafton
   Leroy Goddard ($50)

LANDSCAPE IN OIL
A Soothing Morning by Charles W. Dahlgreen
   Thomas M. Butler Memorial
   by Mrs. Thomas Butler ($200)
Wilton Lake in Winter by Charles Reiffel
   Mrs. Daniel R. Hanna, Jr. ($100)
Frosty Morning, Southern Indiana
by Dorothy Morlan
   Mrs. Preston M. Nolan ($50)

STILL LIFE
Glory of Autumn by William Forsyth
   Honoring Margaret Ball Petty
   by Mrs. F. C. Ball ($100)
A Chicago Beauty Spot by William Clusmann
   Francis W. Jones ($50)

STILL LIFE (NOT FLOWERS)
Yarn Dolls by Randolph LaSalle Coats
   C. M. Kittle ($100)

FIGURE COMPOSITION
Eleanor by Lucy M. Taggart
   Mr. & Mrs. Frank Hummell and
   Mr. & Mrs. Isaac Powell ($100)

ETCHING
(Information regarding award not available)
   Cadet Corps of Culver
   Military Academy ($200)
(Information regarding award not available)
   Earlham Alumni Association
   of Chicago ($100)

WATERCOLOR
The Cathedral at Old Vincennes
by Edward T. Grigware
   Edward Rector ($200)
Oriental Things by Paul Hadley
   Lida A. Ryan Memorial
   by Mrs. Mildred Beatty ($100)
Marooned by John Dukes McKee
   Social Committee of the
   Daughters of Indiana ($50)

PASTEL
Mardi Gras by Hugh M. Poe
   Frank Cunningham ($100)
A Shaft of Sunlight by Laura A. Fry
   Honoring Jean Elliot Richard
   by Edward Daniel Crilly ($50)

GROUP OF MINIATURES
(Information regarding award not available)
   Mrs. George Fawley, Mrs. Albert Jones,
   Tri Kappa of Newcastle, P. E. O. Sisterhood
   of Newcastle ($100)
(Information regarding award not available)
   Herbert Griffiths ($50)

CARTOON
Not a Brain Cell Workin' and
A Strain on the Family Tie by Gaar Williams
   Joseph H. Defrees ($200)
Three Cartoons: The Bean Family by Chic Jackson
   Dr. Clarence Bruce King ($50)
Little Orphan Annie by Harold Gray
   Dr. Clarence Bruce King ($50)

MOST TYPICAL INDIANA SCENE, ANY MEDIUM
Morning in the Hollow by L. O. Griffith
   Daughters of Indiana ($200)

PICTURE PAINTED BY WOMAN ARTIST
The Valley, Morning by Lucie Hartrath
   The Terre Haute Star ($200)

PICTURE BY WOMAN UNDER 21 YEARS OF AGE
(Information regarding award not available)
   Auxiliary of Daughters of Indiana ($25)

PICTURE PAINTED BY MAN OVER 60 YEARS OF AGE
Winter Morning, First Snows by T. C. Steele
   Edward F. Carry ($200)

PICTURE PAINTED BY
MAN UNDER 35 YEARS OF AGE
Resting by J. Murry Wickard
George T. Buckingham ($200)
Daddy Bucks' Place by Francis F. Brown
The Muncie Star ($100)

GARDEN SCENE
A Garden by Maude K. Eggemeyer
DePauw University Alumni
Association of Chicago ($100)

WINTER SCENE
Our Alley by J. W. Vawter
Frank T. Cunningham ($100)

MARINE SCENE
Mussel Rocks by Louise E. Zaring
Daughters of Indiana,
Cass County Group ($50)

ANIMAL PICTURE
(Information regarding award not available)
Indianapolis Group ($50)

PAINTING IN OIL BY ARTIST
ASSOCIATED WITH EARLHAM COLLEGE
(Information regarding award not available)
Board of Trustees of Earlham College ($150)

1926

OUTSTANDING PICTURE
OF THE EXHIBITION
The Art Jury by Wayman Adams
John C. Shaffer ($500)

WORK OF SCULPTURE
Victory by Janet Scudder
Mrs. Howard Spaulding, Jr. ($300)

PORTRAIT IN OIL
Charles W. Dahlgreen by Marie Goth
The Indianapolis Star ($200)
Mrs. W. by John M. King
Margaret Ball Petty ($100)
My Mother by Susan M. Ketcham
Herbert Griffiths ($50)

LANDSCAPE IN OIL
Norwalk River in Winter by Charles Reiffel
Thomas Butler Memorial ($200)
The Wood Lot, October by William Forsyth
Albert G. Jones ($100)
River Clouds by Francis F. Brown
Jean Elliot Richard ($50)

STILL LIFE
Still Life, Roses by Winifred Adams
Frank S. Cunningham ($200)

STILL LIFE (NOT FLOWERS)
Cretonne, a Decoration by Sallie Hall Steketee
Lucy Ball Owsley ($100)

FIGURE COMPOSITION
A Mother from the Hills by Ada Walter Shulz
Edward S. Carry ($200)
Childhood Days by George Rich
Mildred Beatty ($100)

ETCHING
Street Gossip, New Orleans, La by L. O. Griffith
George Ade ($100)

ILLUSTRATION AND LITHOGRAPH
A Tale of County Clare by John Dukes McKee
Donald Defrees ($100)

WATERCOLOR
Summer Flowers by J. Edgar Forkner
C. M. Kittle ($100)
County Fair, the Aeroplanes by Olive Rush
Beaumont Parks ($50)

PASTEL
In the Park by Ralph M. Britt
Mr. & Mrs. F. F. Hummel ($100)
The Mischief-Maker by Lawrence Flammang
Mr. & Mrs. Isaac N. Powell ($50)

GROUP OF MINIATURES
Awarded to Edward W. Carlson
Edward Daniel Crilly ($50)

CARTOON AND
GROUP OF WOOD BLOCK PRINTS
Awarded to Gustave Baumann
Dr. Clarence Bruce King ($100)
High Finance by Wils Berry
John T. McCutcheon ($50)

MOST TYPICAL INDIANA
SCENE, ANY MEDIUM
Morning in the Hills by Will Vawter
Daughters of Indiana ($200)

PICTURE PAINTED BY WOMAN ARTIST
Carnival by Lucy M. Taggart
The Terre Haute Star ($200)

WORK OF ART BY MAN
UNDER 35 YEARS OF AGE
Portuguese Whaler by Randolph Coats
George T. Buckingham ($200)
Park Folks by Reynolds L. Selfridge
The Muncie Star ($100)

WORK OF ART BY MAN
UNDER 25 YEARS OF AGE
Sandy Selfridge by Hugh M. Poe
Culver Military Academy ($200)

INDIANA LANDSCAPE IN OIL
BY INDIANA MAN WHO IS NOW
RESIDENT OF THE STATE
The Hill Country, Brown County
by Theodore C. Steele
Edward Rector Memorial
by Mrs. Edward Rector ($200)

GARDEN SCENE
A June Garden, "Rose City," Indiana
by Helen M. Goodwin
Joseph Defrees ($200)

WINTER SCENE
St. Joe River, Winter by G. Ames Aldrich
Indiana University Alumni Association ($100)

DECORATIVE COMPOSITION
Theft of the Grapes by Beth Driggs Bacon
DePauw University Alumni Association ($100)

PORTRAIT OF A CHILD
Florence by Simon P. Baus
Muncie Art Students' League ($100)

HISTORICAL PAINTING
Decoration for European History Classroom
by Elmer E. Taflinger
L. G. Peed ($100)

DRAWING IN
BLACK AND WHITE
The Phantom Hunter by Wayne B. Colvin
Muncie Art Students' League ($50)

PICTURE BY INDIANAPOLIS
ARTIST NOT RECEIVING PRIZE IN
GENERAL CLASSIFICATIONS
Gray Misty Morning by Carl C. Graf
Butler College ($50)

HONORABLE MENTION: SCULPTURE
Nymph by Walter R. Williams

HONORABLE MENTION: PAINTING
Barnes Barn by Adolph Shulz

1927

OUTSTANDING PICTURE
OF THE EXHIBITION
My Mother by Randolph Coats
John C. Shaffer ($500)

WORK OF SCULPTURE
Ideal Head by Robert Davidson
Mrs. Howard Spaulding, Jr. ($300)
"Aum" Dr. Bhagat Singh Thind of Amritsar, India
by John G. Prasuhn
Mildred Veronese Beatty ($100)

PORTRAIT IN OIL
Miss Guthrie by Charles Sneed Williams
The Indianapolis Star ($200)
Portrait Lt. Cros by Hugh M. Poe
Charles M. Kittle ($100)

LANDSCAPE IN OIL
Over the Hills from Weed Patch by Carl Graf
Thomas M. Butler Memorial
by Mrs. Thomas Butler ($200)
November Song by Frank Dudley
Beaumont Parks ($100)
Autumn by Simon P. Baus
Herbert Griffiths ($50)

STILL LIFE (FLOWERS)
Pitcher of Flowers by Edgar Forkner
Lucy Ball Owsley ($100)

STILL LIFE (NOT FLOWERS)
In the Chinese Room by P. R. McIntosh
Albert R. Erskine ($100)

FIGURE COMPOSITION
Tea in the Studio by J. Murry Wickard
Dr. Clarence Bruce King ($100)

GROUP OF ETCHINGS
Awarded to Ralph Fletcher Seymour
Frank Cunningham ($200)

GROUP OF ILLUSTRATIONS OR
WOOD BLOCK PRINTS
Awarded to Ernest T. Thompson
John T. McCutcheon ($50)

WATERCOLOR
Chadwick Fisheries by Carolyn G. Bradley
Clement Studebaker ($100)

PASTEL
Bill Spoon's House by Paul Hadley
George B. McCutcheon ($100)

GROUP OF MINIATURES
Awarded to Bertha Lacey
Progress Club of South Bend ($50)

GROUP OF CARTOONS OR ILLUSTRATIONS
Awarded to Fontaine Fox
Joseph Defrees ($100)

MOST TYPICAL INDIANA SCENE
Woodland Brook by John E. Bundy
Daughters of Indiana of Chicago ($200)

PICTURE PAINTED BY WOMAN ARTIST
On the Terrace by Marie Goth
The Terre Haute Star ($200)

PICTURE BY MAN OR WOMAN
OVER 60 YEARS OF AGE
September Morning by William Forsyth
Edward S. Carry ($200)

PICTURE BY MAN UNDER
35 YEARS OF AGE, ANY MEDIUM
Portrait of Mrs. W. by Guy Brown Wiser
George T. Buckingham ($200)
Indiana Woodland by W. E. Musick
The Muncie Star ($100)

PICTURE BY MAN
UNDER 25 YEARS OF AGE
The Card Table by George Dietrich
Culver Military Academy ($200)

PICTURE BY WOMAN 25 OR UNDER
WHOSE WORK SHOWS ARTISTIC MERIT
Still Life by Mary Alys Polk
Earlham Alumni Association, Chicago ($50)

INDIANA LANDSCAPE IN OIL
BY NATIVE INDIANA MAN WHO IS
NOW RESIDENT OF THE STATE
The Bridge by Clifton Wheeler
Edward Rector Memorial by
Mrs. Edward Rector ($200)

GARDEN SCENE
The Old Arbor by Ralph Britt
Muncie Art Students' League ($100)

AUTUMN SCENE
Autumn in the Hills by Lucie Hartrath
Donald Defrees ($100)

MARINE SCENE
La Jolla Shore by Charles Reiffel
Tri Kappa Sorority ($50)

PORTRAIT OF A CHILD
Portrait "Brownie" by John King
Margaret Ball Petty ($100)

PICTURE BY RICHMOND
ARTIST WHO HAS NEVER
RECEIVED HOOSIER SALON PRIZE
Sunlight and Shadows by Lawrence McConaha
Earlham College ($50)

1928

OUTSTANDING PICTURE
OF THE EXHIBITION
Mill in Winter by Charles Reiffel
John C. Shaffer ($500)

PICTURE BY WOMAN ARTIST
AFTER THE SHAFFER AWARD PRIZE
Summer Flowers by Sallie Hall Steketee
Tri Kappa Sorority of Indiana ($200)

WORK OF SCULPTURE
Water (for Drinking Fountain) by Seth M. Velsey
Mrs. Howard Spaulding, Jr. ($300)
Portrait of Gladys by Ruth Kerr
Mildred Veronese Beatty ($100)

PORTRAIT IN OIL
Fred L. Pettijohn, M. D. by Marie Goth
The Indianapolis Star ($200)
Portrait of a Young Lady by Simon Baus
Charles M. Kittle ($100)

LANDSCAPE IN OIL
Along the Sandy Way by Frank Dudley
Thomas Meek Butler Memorial
by Mrs. T. M. Butler ($200)
Blossom Time by Will Vawter
Beaumont Parks ($100)
Old Ships, Puget Sound by Edgar Forkner
Herbert Griffiths ($50)

STILL LIFE (FLOWERS)
Still Life by Victor Higgins
Brema Jones Memorial by
Mrs. Albert G. Jones ($100)

STILL LIFE (NOT FLOWERS)
Still Life by Fry Fisher
Mr. & Mrs. Edward C. Twells ($50)

FIGURE COMPOSITION
Oak by Harvey Emrich
Walter P. Murphy ($200)

ETCHING
An Old Court, Sachsenhausen by John C. Sandefur
Frank Cunningham ($200)

GROUP OF ILLUSTRATIONS
The Squirrel, Do You Like Butter?,
Spring, Bunny's Breakfast, and
Mary' Lamb by Mary Anderson
Muncie Art Students' League ($50)

WATERCOLOR
Late Afternoon by George Dietrich
Clement Studebaker ($100)

PASTEL
In the Park by Johann Berthelsen
Albert R. Erskine ($100)

GROUP OF MINIATURES
The Late Mrs. Carlson, Mr. J. C. Shaffer,
Margot Hedman, Raymond Ostergreen,
and *Katherine Hedman* by Edward Carlson
Olive Maine School of Opera,
South Bend ($50)

GROUP OF CARTOONS
Cartoon (Nos. 323 to 331) by Gaar Williams
Joseph Defrees ($100)

LANDSCAPE BY WOMAN ARTIST
The Creek in October by Lucie Hartrath
The Terre Haute Star ($200)

PICTURE BY MAN OR WOMAN
OVER 60 YEARS OF AGE
Brown County Court House by Charles Dahlgreen
Edward F. Carry ($200)

PICTURE BY MAN 35 YEARS
OF AGE OR YOUNGER
An Old Red Dress by John M. King
George T. Buckingham ($200)
Architectural Head by Robert Davidson
The Muncie Star ($100)

PICTURE BY MAN
UNDER 25 YEARS OF AGE
Todd's Head by E. H. Sharp
Culver Military Academy ($200)

PICTURE BY WOMAN 25
YEARS OF AGE OR YOUNGER
Still Life by Helen Woodward
Tri Kappa Sorority of Indiana ($150)

INDIANA LANDSCAPE IN OIL
BY NATIVE INDIANA MAN WHO IS
NOW RESIDENT OF THE STATE
The Creek in Summer by Carl Graf
Edward Rector Memorial
by Mrs. Edward Rector ($200)

PICTURE BY NATIVE INDIANA
MAN OR WOMAN WHO IS NOW
RESIDENT OF THE STATE, 25 YEARS
OF AGE OR YOUNGER
Lower LaGaude, France by Stanley Crane
State Kiwanis of Indiana ($200)

GARDEN SCENE
The Blue Shawl by W. E. Fager
Lucy Ball Owsley ($100)

PORTRAIT OF A CHILD
The Pet Duck by Ada Walter Shulz
Margaret Ball Petty ($100)

DRAWING
The Gravel Washer by Constance Forsyth
Muncie Art Students' League ($50)

LANDSCAPE IN OIL BY
FULL-TIME INDIANA PUBLIC
SCHOOL TEACHER
The Clouds by Francis F. Brown
Art League of State Normal
School, Terrre Haute ($30)

STILL LIFE IN OIL
BY FULL-TIME INDIANA
PUBLIC SCHOOL TEACHER
(Information regarding award not available)
Art League of State Normal
School, Terre Haute ($25)

PICTURE BY WOMAN WHO HAS
NEVER EXHIBITED AT HOOSIER SALON
A Town by the Sea by Bertha Baxter
Tri Kappa Sorority of Indiana ($100)

BAS-RELIEF HEAD
OF CHILD, SCULPTURE
Peggy Goodwin by C. Warner Williams
Rosemary Ball ($100)

WORK, MADE OF INDIANA
LIMESTONE, WHICH CAN BE EMBODIED
IN ARCHITECTURAL DESIGN
Stone Grill by J. E. Jordan
Indiana Limestone Company ($200)

PICTURE POSSESSING UNUSUAL
ARTISTIC MERIT
The Silo by Clifton Wheeler
Board of Trustees, Indiana University ($200)

1929

OUTSTANDING PICTURE
OF THE EXHIBITION
Zinnias by Victor Higgins
John C. Shaffer ($500)

PICTURE BY WOMAN ARTIST
AFTER THE SHAFFER PRIZE AWARD
Across the Valley by Lucie Hartrath
Tri Kappa Sorority of Indiana ($200)

WORK OF SCULPTURE
Robert Pelzl by John David Brcin
Catherine B. Spaulding ($300)

PORTRAIT IN OIL
Irving R. Wiles by Wayman Adams
The Indianapolis Star ($200)
Peg by John M. King
Eugene Buffington ($100)

LANDSCAPE IN OIL
Taos House-Tops by Carl Woolsey
Thomas M. Butler Memorial
by Mrs. T. M. Butler ($200)
Autumn Symphony by Oscar B. Erickson
Beaumont Parks ($100)

STILL LIFE
Wild Flowers by Sallie Hall Steketee
Progress Club of South Bend ($50)

FIGURE COMPOSITION
Hoosier Pioneer by Randolph Coats
Edward Hines ($200)

ETCHING
Florence by Ernest T. Thompson
Frank S. Cunningham ($200)

GROUP OF ILLUSTRATIONS
IN BLACK AND WHITE
Awarded to Howard Leigh
John T. McCutcheon ($50)

WATERCOLOR
Coming into the Harbor by Sara Bard
Clement Studebaker ($100)

PASTEL
Autumn by Francis F. Brown
Charles M. Kittle Memorial by
Mrs. Charles M. Kittle ($100)

GROUP OF MINIATURES
Awarded to J. VanCleave Fish
Olive Maine School of Opera,
South Bend ($50)

GROUP OF CARTOONS
Bruce Vance by Paul A. Plaschke
Joseph Defrees ($100)

LANDSCAPE BY
WOMAN ARTIST
The Old Live Oak by Sara Kolb Danner
The Terre Haute Star ($200)

PICTURE BY MAN OR WOMAN
OVER 60 YEARS OF AGE
The Hills of Morgan by William Forsyth
Edward F. Carry ($200)

PICTURE BY MAN 35 YEARS
OF AGE OR YOUNGER
One of the Barkers by Guy Brown Wiser
George T. Buckingham ($200)
The Six-Fifteen by Marques Reitzel
The Muncie Star ($100)

PICTURE BY MAN
UNDER 25 YEARS OF AGE
Understanding I by Gilbert B. Wilson
Culver Military Academy ($200)

PICTURE BY WOMAN 25
YEARS OF AGE OR YOUNGER
Still Life by Helen M. Woodward
Tri Kappa Sorority of Indiana ($150)

INDIANA LANDSCAPE IN OIL
BY NATIVE INDIANA MAN WHO
IS NOW RESIDENT OF THE STATE
Cedars by Lawrence McConaha
Edward Rector Memorial
by Mrs. Edward Rector ($200)

PICTURE BY NATIVE INDIANA
MAN OR WOMAN WHO IS NOW
RESIDENT OF THE STATE, 25 YEARS
OF AGE OR YOUNGER
Max and Jawn by Everett Hill Sharp
State Kiwanis of Indiana ($200)

GARDEN SCENE
Morning Mists, Hanover by Estelle Peel Izor
Lucy Ball Owsley ($100)

PORTRAIT OF A CHILD
Portrait of Francesca and Angelica W.
by Frank Hugh Wagner
Margaret Ball Petty ($100)

DRAWING IN BLACK AND WHITE
Xmas Eve (Fanny May Candy ad)
by J. Murry Wickard
Muncie Art Students' League ($50)

LANDSCAPE IN OIL BY
FULL-TIME INDIANA PUBLIC
SCHOOL TEACHER
Memories by Una Ann Greenwood
Art League of State Normal
School, Terre Haute ($50)

PICTURE BY WOMAN WHO HAS
NEVER EXHIBITED AT HOOSIER SALON
Zinnias by Florence B. Smithburn
Tri Kappa Sorority of Indiana ($100)

BAS-RELIEF HEAD
OF CHILD, SCULPTURE
William Henry Failey by Robert Davidson
Rosemary Ball ($100)

WORK, MADE OF INDIANA
LIMESTONE, WHICH CAN BE EMBODIED
IN ARCHITECTURAL DESIGN
Stone Pilaster for Fireplace by Stephen A. Snape
Indiana Limestone Company ($200)

INDUSTRIAL SCENE, IN OIL,
PAINTED ALONG ROUTE OF
ILLINOIS CENTRAL RAILROAD
Steel by G. Ames Aldrich
Lawrence A. Downs ($100)

PICTURE POSSESSING UNUSUAL
ARTISTIC MERIT
Noon by Harvey Emrich
Board of Trustees, Indiana University ($200)

1930

OUTSTANDING PICTURE
OF THE EXHIBITION
Hills of Kelp by L. O. Griffith
John C. Shaffer ($500)

PICTURE BY WOMAN ARTIST
AFTER THE SHAFFER PRIZE AWARD
Mountaineers by Marie MacPherson
Tri Kappa Sorority of Indiana ($250)

WORK OF SCULPTURE
Negro by George Adams Dietrich
Catherine B. Spaulding ($300)

PORTRAIT IN OIL
The Costume by J. Murry Wickard
The Indianapolis Star ($200)
Portrait of Lois S. by Gerald Mast
Eugene Buffington ($100)

LANDSCAPE IN OIL
From Hanover Campus by Frank V. Dudley
Thomas M. Butler Memorial
by Mrs. T. M. Butler ($200)
Carolina by Clifton Wheeler
Alexander F. Banks ($100)

STILL LIFE
My Window Sill by Edgar Forkner
Edward Hines ($200)

STILL LIFE, MODERNISTIC
IN TREATMENT
Lamp-Light by Helen A. King
J. C. Stewart ($50)

FIGURE COMPOSITION
Faculty Club No. 1 by Guy Brown Wiser
George T. Buckingham ($200)

GROUP OF ETCHINGS
Awarded to Frederick Polley
Frank S. Cunningham ($200)

BLOCK PRINT
An Alley by Maude K. Eggemeyer
Olive Maine School of Opera,
South Bend ($50)

WATERCOLOR
Judging Horses by Olive Rush
Tri Kappa Sorority of Indiana ($150)

PASTEL
> *Margaret* by Hugh M. Poe
> Clement Studebaker, Jr. ($100)

LANDSCAPE BY WOMAN ARTIST
> *Autumn Pageant* by Lucie Hartrath
> *The Terre Haute Star* ($200)

WORK OF ART BY MAN 35
YEARS OF AGE OR YOUNGER
> *Late January Afternoon* by Karl C. Brandner
> *The Muncie Star* ($100)

PICTURE BY MAN UNDER
25 YEARS OF AGE
> *Jacob and the Angel* by Lotan Welshans
> Culver Military Academy ($200)

WORK BY WOMAN 25
YEARS OF AGE OR YOUNGER
> *Pot of Flowers* by Florence Smithburn
> Tri Kappa Sorority of Indiana ($100)

INDIANA LANDSCAPE IN OIL
BY NATIVE INDIANA MAN WHO
IS NOW RESIDENT OF THE STATE
> *Hills of Brown County* by Carl C. Graf
> Edward Rector Memorial
> by Mrs. Edward Rector ($200)

PICTURE BY NATIVE INDIANA
MAN OR WOMAN WHO IS NOW
RESIDENT OF THE STATE, 25
YEARS OF AGE OR YOUNGER
> *Sunny Hollow* by Alton P. Coffey
> State Kiwanis of Indiana ($200)

GARDEN SCENE
> *New Hampshire* by H. R. MacGinnis
> Lucy Ball Owsley ($100)

WINTER SCENE IN OIL
> *Oaks in Winter* by Edward K. Williams
> Frances Hall Davis Memorial
> by Mrs. R. Heinrichs ($200)

AUTUMN SCENE IN OIL BY ARTIST
WHOSE TRAINING HAS BEEN
RECEIVED IN INDIANA
> *Deepening Shadows* by Dale Bessire
> Mr. & Mrs. E. M. Morris ($50)

PORTRAIT OF A CHILD
> *Marjory* by Seth M. Velsey
> Margaret Ball Petty ($100)

DRAWING IN BLACK AND WHITE
> *Black and White Drawing* by Dorothy Eisenbach
> Muncie Art Students' League ($50)

BAS-RELIEF HEAD
OF CHILD, SCULPTURE
> Awarded to C. Warner Williams
> Rosemary Ball ($100)

WORK, MADE OF LIMESTONE,
WHICH CAN BE EMBODIED
IN ARCHITECTURAL DESIGN
> *Carved Panel for Bank* by Hobart B. Smale
> Indiana Limestone Company ($200)

GARDEN SCULPTURE
MADE OF LIMESTONE
> Awarded to Robert Davidson
> Harry Johnson ($100)

ARCHITECTURAL ORNAMENT IN
THE ROUND, MADE OF LIMESTONE
> *Architectural Ornament* by Harley D. Clark
> Harry Johnson ($100)

INDUSTRIAL SCENE PAINTED
ALONG ROUTE OF ILLINOIS
CENTRAL RAILROAD
> *Hoosier Saw Mill* by Charles F. Surendorf
> Lawrence A. Downs ($100)

LANDSCAPE IN OIL OF
INDIANA BEAUTY SPOT
> *Edge of Town* by Will Vawter
> Harry R. Kurrie ($100)

PICTURE IN OIL PAINTED
BY AN EX-SERVICEMAN
> *In Connecticut* by Lawrence McConaha
> Third District, American Legion Auxiliary,
> Dept. of Illinois ($50)

1931

OUTSTANDING PICTURE
OF THE EXHIBITION
> *Portrait of Anna Sargent Smith* by Howard Leigh
> John C. Shaffer ($500)

PICTURE BY WOMAN ARTIST
AFTER THE SHAFFER PRIZE AWARD
> *The Mountain Road, Autumn* by Olive Rush
> Tri Kappa Sorority of Indiana ($400)

WORK OF SCULPTURE
> *Lorraine* by Leslie T. Posey
> Catherine B. Hickox ($300)

PORTRAIT IN OIL
> *Bobby Cotton* by Roy A. Ketcham
> *The Indianapolis Star* ($200)

LANDSCAPE IN OIL
> *Banner Gorge, Southern California*
> by Charles Reiffel
> Thomas M. Butler Memorial
> by Mrs. T. M. Butler ($200)
> *After the Frost* by Lucie Hartrath
> Alexander F. Banks ($100)

STILL LIFE IN OIL
> *Still Life* by Harry Engel
> Edward Hines ($200)

FIGURE COMPOSITION
Romance and Potatoes by Wood W. Woolsey
George T. Buckingham ($200)

GROUP OF ETCHINGS
Awarded to Ralph Fletcher Seymour
Frank S. Cunningham ($100)

WATERCOLOR
Yacht Club by George Dietrich
Margaret Ball Petty ($100)

PASTEL
Portrait by George Yater
E. J. Buffington ($100)

GROUP OF LITHOGRAPHS
Awarded to Wayman Adams
John T. McCutcheon ($50)

LANDSCAPE BY WOMAN ARTIST
Maine Coast by Sara Bard
The Terre Haute Star ($200)

PORTRAIT IN OIL BY WOMAN ARTIST
The Wash Lady by Dorothy B. Harford
Tri Kappa Sorority of Indiana ($200)

WORK OF ART BY MAN 35
YEARS OF AGE OR YOUNGER
Church of Montigny by George Jo Mess
The Muncie Star ($100)

PICTURE BY MAN
UNDER 25 YEARS OF AGE
Spring by Edward H. Dunlap
Culver Military Academy ($200)

INDIANA LANDSCAPE IN OIL
BY NATIVE INDIANA MAN WHO
IS NOW RESIDENT OF THE STATE
A Rainy Day at Nashville by Homer G. Davisson
Edward Rector Memorial
by Mrs. Edward Rector ($200)

PICTURE BY NATIVE INDIANA
MAN OR WOMAN WHO IS NOW
RESIDENT OF THE STATE, 25 YEARS
OF AGE OR YOUNGER
The Pink Drape by Paul E. Beem
State Kiwanis of Indiana ($200)

GARDEN SCENE
A Rock Garden by Sallie Hall Steketee
Lucy Ball Owsley ($100)

AUTUMN LANDSCAPE
Autumn Day by Lawrence McConaha
Rosemary Ball ($100)

WINTER LANDSCAPE IN OIL
Awarded to Karl C. Brandner
Muncie Art Students' League ($50)

PORTRAIT OF A CHILD
Oliver Ormsby Annan by C. Warner Williams
Clement Studebaker, Jr. ($100)

WORK, MADE OF LIMESTONE,
WHICH CAN BE EMBODIED
IN ARCHITECTURAL DESIGN
Cresting for Pylon, Indiana Limestone
by John Jackson
Indiana Limestone Company ($200)

GARDEN SCULPTURE
MADE OF LIMESTONE
Bear Cubs by Jon Magnus Jonson
Harry Johnson ($100)

ARCHITECTURAL ORNAMENT IN
THE ROUND, MADE OF LIMESTONE
Native by Elmer H. Daniels
Harry Johnson ($100)

INDUSTRIAL SCENE PAINTED
ALONG ROUTE OF ILLINOIS
CENTRAL RAILROAD
The Gary Steel Mills by Art Sprunger
Lawrence A. Downs ($100)

PICTURE IN OIL BY
EX-SERVICEMAN
Richmond's Greenwich Village by Roy Hirshburg
Third District, American Legion Auxiliary,
Dept. of Illinois ($50)

1932

OUTSTANDING PICTURE
OF THE EXHIBITION
The Wood Vender by Wood W. Woolsey
John C. Shaffer ($500)

WORK OF SCULPTURE
Lewis Conner Newman by C. Warner Williams
Catherine B. Hickox ($300)

PORTRAIT IN OIL
Miriam by Marie Goth
The Indianapolis Star ($200)

LANDSCAPE IN OIL
From Mt. Jackson by Frank Dudley
Thomas M. Butler Memorial
by Mrs. T. M. Butler ($200)

GROUP OF ETCHINGS
Awarded to Frederick Polley
Frank S. Cunningham ($100)

WATERCOLOR
My Studio Window by Helen King
John T. McCutcheon ($50)

WORK OF ART BY MAN 35
YEARS OF AGE OR YOUNGER
Coleus Plant by Paul E. Beem
The Muncie Star ($100)

PICTURE BY MAN UNDER
25 YEARS OF AGE
And Models Call This Work by J. M. Henninger
Culver Military Academy ($200)

INDIANA LANDSCAPE IN OIL
BY NATIVE INDIANA MAN WHO
IS NOW RESIDENT OF THE STATE
High Lights and Shadows by William T. Turman
Edward Rector Memorial
by Mrs. Edward Rector ($200)

PICTURE BY NATIVE INDIANA
MAN OR WOMAN WHO IS NOW
RESIDENT OF THE STATE, 25 YEARS
OF AGE OR YOUNGER
Still Life by Mary Adele Ziegler
State Kiwanis of Indiana ($200)

AUTUMN LANDSCAPE IN OIL
BY NATIVE INDIANA ARTIST
Autumn's Last Touch by Carl Graf
Edward Holloway Memorial
by Indiana Society of Chicago ($100)

WINTER LANDSCAPE IN OIL
Mid-Winter, Indiana by G. Ames Aldrich
Alexander F. Banks ($100)

GARGOYLE DOWNSPOUT, MADE
OF INDIANA LIMESTONE
(Information regarding award not available)
Shawnee Stone Co. ($100)

LANDSCAPE IN OIL PAINTED ALONG
ROUTE OF ILLINOIS CENTRAL
RAILROAD IN INDIANA
The Village Church by Karl C. Brandner
Lawrence A. Downs ($100)

PICTURE IN OIL BY
EX-SERVICEMAN
Portrait by Guy Brown Wiser
Third District, American Legion Auxiliary,
Dept. of Illinois ($50)

1933

OUTSTANDING PICTURE
OF THE EXHIBITION
Dan by J. M. Henninger
John C. Shaffer ($500)

WORK OF SCULPTURE
Dancing Lesson and *Else* by Robert Davidson
Catherine B. Hickox ($300)

PORTRAIT IN OIL
Mrs. Chandler in Her Grandmother's Dress
by Guy Brown Wiser
The Indianapolis Star ($200)

LANDSCAPE IN OIL
New England Winter by Samuel F. Hershey
Thomas M. Butler Memorial
by Mrs. T. M. Butler ($200)

GROUP OF ETCHINGS
Awarded to Karl C. Brandner
Frank S. Cunningham ($50)

WORK OF ART BY MAN 35

YEARS OF AGE OR YOUNGER
The Finding of Moses by Lotan Welshans
The Muncie Star ($100)

INDIANA LANDSCAPE IN OIL
BY NATIVE INDIANA MAN WHO IS
NOW RESIDENT OF THE STATE
Winter by Clifton Wheeler
Edward Rector Memorial
by Mrs. Edward Rector ($200)

PICTURE BY NATIVE INDIANA
MAN OR WOMAN WHO IS NOW
RESIDENT OF THE STATE, 25 YEARS
OF AGE OR YOUNGER
Birth Control by Gilbert Wilson
State Kiwanis of Indiana ($100)

AUTUMN LANDSCAPE IN OIL
The Catskill Mountains by Harvey Emrich
Edward Holloway Memorial by
Indiana Society of Chicago ($100)

PORTRAIT OF A CHILD IN OIL
Jimmie by John M. King
Honoring Orphan Annie
by Harold Gray ($150)

LANDSCAPE IN OIL PAINTED ALONG
ROUTE OF ILLINOIS CENTRAL
RAILROAD IN INDIANA
Red Mill by Harold McWhinney
Lawrence A. Downs ($100)

PICTURE IN OIL BY
EX-SERVICEMAN
A Century of Progress, Madison Bridge
by George Jo Mess
American Legion Auxiliary,
Cook County Council ($50)

HONORABLE MENTION
The Unfinished Picture by Elmer E. Taflinger
Autumn, Nashville, Brown County by Frank Sohn
Rubber Plant and Pears by Paul Beem
Busy Day by Lawrence McConaha
Old Vase of Flowers by Edgar Forkner
The Original Mutt by Carolyn Bradley

HONORABLE MENTION: SCULPTURE
Eve by Seth Velsey
Black Adam by Theodore Randall

SPECIAL HONORABLE MENTION
Awarded to Walt Louderback
for a group of drawings

1934

OUTSTANDING PICTURE
OF THE EXHIBITION
Procession by Edward H. Dunlap
John C. Shaffer ($500)

WORK OF SCULPTURE
Jung by Forrest F. Stark
Catherine B. Hickox ($200)
Bob Tschaegle by Seth M. Velsey
Catherine B. Hickox ($100)

PORTRAIT IN OIL
Tenant Farmer by Paul A. Plaschke
The Indianapolis Star ($200)

LANDSCAPE IN OIL
Between Showers by Alexis Jean Fournier
Thomas M. Butler Memorial
by Mrs. T. M. Butler ($200)

STILL LIFE IN OIL
Pots and Pans by Cecil Head
Mr. & Mrs. Ross J. Beatty ($50)

FIGURE COMPOSITION IN OIL
Lady in Red by J. Murry Wickard
Daughters of Indiana of Chicago ($50)

GROUP OF ETCHINGS
Awarded to Lee Sturges
Frank S. Cunningham ($50)

WATERCOLOR
The Cove by Sara Bard
John T. McCutcheon ($50)

WORK OF ART BY
WOMAN ARTIST
The Architect by Marie Goth
The Muncie Star ($100)

INDIANA LANDSCAPE IN OIL
BY NATIVE INDIANA MAN WHO IS
NOW RESIDENT OF THE STATE
The Lane in Autumn by George Mock
Edward Rector Memorial
by Mrs. Edward Rector ($200)

AUTUMN LANDSCAPE IN OIL
Autumn Tapestry by Edward K. Williams
Edward Holloway Memorial by
Indiana Society of Chicago ($100)

PORTRAIT OF A CHILD IN OIL
Jerry Tressler Hause by E. Hill Sharp
Honoring Orphan Annie
by Harold Gray ($100)

LANDSCAPE IN OIL PAINTED ALONG
ROUTE OF ILLINOIS CENTRAL
RAILROAD IN INDIANA
The Creek, Late September by V. J. Cariani
Lawrence A. Downs ($100)

PICTURE IN OIL BY
EX-SERVICEMAN
Will Haney by Guy Brown Wiser
Honoring Orphan Annie
by Harold Gray ($50)

1935

OUTSTANDING PICTURE
OF THE EXHIBITION
Tornado by Will Harvey Hunt
John C. Shaffer ($500)

WORK OF SCULPTURE
Mother and Child by Jon M. Jonson
Catherine B. Hickox ($300)

PORTRAIT IN OIL
Portrait, John C. Shaffer by Wayman Adams
The Indianapolis Star ($200)

LANDSCAPE IN OIL
Coast of Devon by Charles Sneed Williams
Thomas M. Butler Memorial
by Mrs. T. M. Butler ($200)

STILL LIFE IN OIL (FLOWERS)
Gladiolas by William Liepse
Honoring Orphan Annie
by Harold Gray ($50)

FIGURE COMPOSITION IN OIL
Snow Maiden by Henrik M. Mayer
Daughters of Indiana of Chicago ($100)

GROUP OF ETCHINGS
Awarded to Charles W. Dahlgreen
Frank S. Cunningham ($50)

WATERCOLOR
The Studio by Carolyn Bradley
John T. McCutcheon ($50)

WORK BY TEACHER OR PUPIL FROM
INDIANA PAROCHIAL SCHOOL
San Andres, Cholula, Mexico by John E. Miller
Peter C. Reilly ($100)
Indian Woman, Guanahuato, Mexico
by W. L. Newberry
Peter C. Reilly ($75)

WORK OF ART BY WOMAN ARTIST
Hillside by Lucie Hartrath
The Muncie Star ($100)

INDIANA LANDSCAPE IN OIL BY
NATIVE INDIANA MAN WHO IS
NOW RESIDENT OF THE STATE
Road to Trevlac by L. O. Griffith
Edward Rector Memorial
by Mrs. Edward Rector ($200)

AUTUMN LANDSCAPE IN OIL
Autumn's Tapestry by Carl Woolsey
Frank F. Hummel Memorial
by Mrs. F. Hummel ($150)

PORTRAIT OF A CHILD IN OIL
Mother and Child by Marie Goth
Honoring Orphan Annie
by Harold Gray ($100)

LANDSCAPE IN OIL PAINTED ALONG
ROUTE OF ILLINOIS CENTRAL
RAILROAD IN INDIANA
Morning Light in Woods by Will Vawter
Lawrence A. Downs ($100)

PICTURE IN OIL BY
EX-SERVICEMAN
Coke Otto by Lawrence McConaha
American Legion Auxiliary,
Cook County Council ($50)

HONORABLE MENTION
Reflections by Stanley Sessler
Huncky Murray's Place by Helen A. King

HONORABLE MENTION: SCULPTURE
Taos Group by Paul J. Baus

1936

OUTSTANDING PICTURE
OF THE EXHIBITION
Frightened Horses by W. Karl Steele
John C. Shaffer ($500)

WORK OF SCULPTURE
George Ade by C. Warner Williams
Mrs. Charles V. Hickox ($200)
Sonneteer by John David Brcin
Mrs. Charles V. Hickox ($100)

PORTRAIT IN OIL
Dr. Wm. B. Hesseltine by Hill Sharp
The Indianapolis Star ($200)

LANDSCAPE IN OIL
Edge of Town by Grant Christian
Thomas M. Butler Memorial
by Mrs. T. M. Butler ($200)

STILL LIFE
Rubber Plant by William Kaeser
Harold Gray ($50)

GROUP OF ETCHINGS
Awarded to George Jo Mess
Frank S. Cunningham ($50)

WATERCOLOR
Island Homes by Sara Bard
George T. Buckingham ($50)

WORK BY INSTRUCTOR IN CATHOLIC
HIGH SCHOOL, COLLEGE OR UNIVERSITY
Sun Play by Emil Jacques
Peter C. Reilly ($100)
Mixed Bouquet by Sister Rufinia
Peter C. Reilly ($75)

WORK OF ART BY WOMAN ARTIST
"V" by Marie Goth
The Muncie Star ($100)

INDIANA LANDSCAPE IN OIL
BY NATIVE INDIANA MAN WHO IS
NOW RESIDENT OF THE STATE
Awarded to Floyd D. Hopper
Edward Rector Memorial
by Mrs. Edward Rector ($200)

AUTUMN LANDSCAPE IN OIL
Hardin's Holler, Brown County
by Joe Spurgeon
Frank F. Hummel Memorial
by Mrs. F. Hummel ($200)

MARINE IN OIL
Morning Surf by Samuel Hershey
Daughters of Indiana of Chicago ($100)

PORTRAIT OF A CHILD IN OIL
Betty Louise by Vera Griffith
Honoring Orphan Annie
by Harold Gray ($100)

LANDSCAPE IN OIL PAINTED ALONG
ROUTE OF ILLINOIS CENTRAL
RAILROAD IN INDIANA
Wintry Road by Dale Bessire
Lawrence A. Downs ($100)

HONORABLE MENTION
Rain Fell on Alabam by G. Ames Aldrich
The Willows by Alexis Fournier
Lazy Day by Adolph Shulz
The Old Elm by Oscar B. Erickson
Sunlight, Symphony by William A. Eyden
Mother by Lucy Drake Marlow
Girl in the Red Blouse by John M. King
Drying Sails by Lillie Fry Fisher
Snow Scene by Sister M. Edna
Flowers and Drapery by Edgar Forkner
Tree Dotted Hill by Carolyn Bradley
The Still Life Painter by George Yater
The Black Tower by Glen Mitchell
Group of etchings by J. H. Euston

HONORABLE MENTION: SCULPTURE
Life by Seth M. Velsey

1937

OUTSTANDING WORK IN OIL
OF THE EXHIBITION
Hills of the Middle West by Carl Woolsey
John C. Shaffer ($500)

WORK OF SCULPTURE
Sketch, Negro by Mahlon B. Payne
Mrs. Charles V. Hickox ($200)
Kneeling Figure by Robert Davidson
Mrs. Charles V. Hickox ($100)

PORTRAIT IN OIL
The Long Grey Line by Roy A. Ketcham
The Indianapolis Star ($200)

LANDSCAPE IN OIL
Along the Ohio by W. Karl Steele
Thomas M. Butler Memorial
by Mrs. T. M. Butler ($200)

STILL LIFE
Garden Bouquet by Mattie Lietz
Harold Gray ($50)

GROUP OF ETCHINGS
Awarded to J. H. Euston
Frank S. Cunningham ($50)

WATERCOLOR
Rainy Day by Charles G. Yeager
George T. Buckingham ($50)

WORK BY INSTRUCTOR IN CATHOLIC
HIGH SCHOOL, COLLEGE OR UNIVERSITY
Contentment by Sister Esther
Peter C. Reilly ($100)
Fruit and Flowers by Sister M. Laureen
Peter C. Reilly ($75)

WORK OF ART BY WOMAN ARTIST
Misty Morning by Lucie Hartrath
The Muncie Star ($100)

WORK BY MAN 25 YEARS
OF AGE OR YOUNGER
Henry by William B. Peed
Culver Military Academy ($50)

INDIANA LANDSCAPE IN OIL
BY NATIVE INDIANA MAN WHO
IS NOW RESIDENT OF THE STATE
Winter Morning by George A. Mock
Edward Rector Memorial
by Mrs. Edward Rector ($200)

AUTUMN LANDSCAPE IN OIL
The End of the Trail by Edward K. Williams
Frank F. Hummel Memorial
by Mrs. F. Hummel ($200)

WINTER LANDSCAPE IN OIL
January 17th by Karl C. Brandner
Delta Sigma Kappa Sorority,
Eta Chapter ($25)

PORTRAIT OF A CHILD IN OIL
Ruth by Marie Goth
Honoring Orphan Annie
by Harold Gray ($100)

LANDSCAPE IN OIL PAINTED ALONG
ROUTE OF ILLINOIS CENTRAL
RAILROAD IN INDIANA
Snow of Hardan Hollow by C. Curry Bohm
Lawrence A. Downs ($100)

PRIZE GIVEN FOR FEATURE
FLOWER PAINTING ROOM
Summer Bouquet by Samuel Hershey
Margaret Bridwell Memorial
by Tri Kappa of Chicago,
Associate Chapter ($75)

HONORABLE MENTION
The Foot Bridge by Roy Trobaugh
Pigeon Hill by Grant Christian
Glaciers of Govotnie by Carolyn G. Bradley
Across the Ceek by Francis F. Brown
Summer Bouquet by Samuel Hershey
Flowers by Olive H. Skemp
Snow of Hardan Hollow by C. Curry Bohm

HONORABLE MENTION: SCULPTURE
Sigrun by J. M. Jonson

1938

OUTSTANDING WORK IN OIL
OF THE EXHIBITION
Nogales, Mexico by Charles Reiffel
John C. Shaffer ($500)

WORK OF SCULPTURE
Study by John David Brcin
Mrs. Charles V. Hickox ($200)
Tall Buffalo by John G. Prasuhn
Mrs. Charles V. Hickox ($100)

PORTRAIT IN OIL
Scottish Piper by Charles Sneed Williams
The Indianapolis Star ($200)

LANDSCAPE IN OIL
Down on the Farm by William B. Peed
Thomas M. Butler Memorial
by Mrs. T. M. Butler ($200)

STILL LIFE
Aztec God, Cactus, Virgin and Birds
by Samuel F. Hershey
Harold Gray ($50)

GROUP OF ETCHINGS
Awarded to George Jo Mess
Frank S. Cunningham ($50)

WATERCOLOR
My Son by Walt Louderback
George T. Buckingham ($50)

WORK BY INSTRUCTOR IN CATHOLIC
HIGH SCHOOL, COLLEGE OR UNIVERSITY
Dressed up Canadian by Sister Rufinia
Peter C. Reilly ($100)
Malagas by Stanley S. Sessler
Peter C. Reilly ($75)

WORK OF ART BY WOMAN ARTIST
The Black Hat by Helen L. Briggs
The Muncie Star ($100)

INDIANA LANDSCAPE IN OIL BY
NATIVE INDIANA MAN OR ONE WHO
HAS BEEN A RESIDENT OF THE STATE
FOR AT LEAST FIVE YEARS
The Gentle Breeze by V. J. Cariani
Edward Rector Memorial by
Mrs. Edward Rector ($200)

AUTUMN LANDSCAPE IN OIL
Autumn Lustre by W. Karl Steele
Frank F. Hummel Memorial
by Mrs. Frank Hummel ($200)

PORTRAIT OF A CHILD IN OIL
Cynthia by Hill Sharp
Honoring Orphan Annie
by Harold Gray ($100)

LANDSCAPE IN OIL PAINTED ALONG
ROUTE OF ILLINOIS CENTRAL
RAILROAD IN INDIANA
Home of the Red Fox by Edward K. Williams
Lawrence A. Downs ($100)

PRIZE GIVEN FOR FEATURE
WATERCOLOR ROOM
Sunshine and Shadow by Clay Kelly
Margaret Bridwell Memorial
by Tri Kappa Sorority, Chicago
Associate Chapter ($100)

WORK SUBMITTED BY RESIDENT
OF CHICAGO OR SUBURBS
R. R. No. 3 by Karl C. Brandner
Town and Country Arts Club, Chicago ($50)

HONORABLE MENTION: SCULPTURE
Awarded to Jon Jonson

1939

OUTSTANDING WORK IN OIL
OF THE EXHIBITION
Slave Block by Edmund Brucker
John C. Shaffer ($500)

WORK OF SCULPTURE
Mr. B by John G. Prasuhn
Mrs. Charles V. Hickox ($200)
Goose Herder by Nancy Bixby Edwards
Mrs. Charles V. Hickox ($100)

PORTRAIT IN OIL
Self Portrait by Marie Goth
The Indianapolis Star ($200)

LANDSCAPE IN OIL
November Hills by Karl C. Brandner
Thomas M. Butler Memorial
by Mrs. T. M. Butler ($200)

STILL LIFE
The Church, the Cardinal and Angel
by Paul E. Beem
Harold Gray ($50)

GROUP OF ETCHINGS
Awarded to Hill Sharp
Frank S. Cunningham ($50)

WATERCOLOR
Cold and Lonesome by Joseph Spurgeon
George T. Buckingham ($50)

WORK BY INSTRUCTOR IN CATHOLIC
HIGH SCHOOL, COLLEGE OR UNIVERSITY
Mr. Smith by Sister Esther
Peter C. Reilly ($100)
Marguerite by Sister Immaculee
Peter C. Reilly ($75)

WORK OF ART BY WOMAN ARTIST
The Valley in November by Lucie Hartrath
The Muncie Star ($100)

INDIANA LANDSCAPE IN OIL
BY NATIVE INDIANA MAN OR ONE
WHO HAS BEEN RESIDENT OF THE
STATE FOR AT LEAST FIVE YEARS
The Hills of Arcady by Frank Dudley
Edward Rector Memorial by
Mrs. Edward Rector ($200)

PORTRAIT OF A CHILD IN OIL
Jackie by William Latz
Honoring Orphan Annie
by Harold Gray ($100)

LANDSCAPE IN OIL PAINTED ALONG
ROUTE OF ILLINOIS CENTRAL
RAILROAD IN INDIANA
Beside the Still Waters by Lucie Hartrath
Lawrence A. Downs ($100)

PRIZES GIVEN FOR FEATURE
LANDSCAPE ROOM
Lonely Road by Georges LaChance
Frank F. Hummel Memorial
by Mrs. Frank Hummel ($150)
Abundance by L. O. Griffith
Delta Sigma Kappa Sorority of Indiana ($50)

WORK BY ARTIST NEVER BEFORE
RECEIVING PRIZE IN HOOSIER SALON
Heavenly Blue Morning Glories by Leota W. Loop
Margaret Bridwell Memorial
by Tri Kappa Sorority, Chicago
Associate Chapter ($50)

HONORABLE MENTION
Meditatin' the Word by Helen King
Cactus Plants by William F. Kaeser
Winter Wind by Carl Woolsey
Son, Albert by Paul A. Plaschke
Research by Sister Rufinia
Shoson Screen and Sansevieria by Stanley S. Sessler

HONORABLE MENTION: SCULPTURE
Wayman Adams by C. Warner Williams

1940

OUTSTANDING WORK IN OIL
OF THE EXHIBITION
Morning Concert, Aix Les Thermes, France
by Walt Louderback
John C. Shaffer ($500)

WORK OF SCULPTURE
David by Frances Johnson Moody
Mrs. Charles V. Hickox ($150)
Portrit of Dr. Comstock by Robert Davidson
Mrs. Charles V. Hickox ($100)
Study in Opposing Forces, Boxing by David Parsons
Mrs. Charles V. Hickox ($50)

PORTRAIT IN OIL
Chinese Art Student by Edmund Brucker
The Indianapolis Star ($200)

LANDSCAPE IN OIL
Rustic Simplicity Down in the Holler
by Anthony Buchta
Thomas M. Butler Memorial
by Mrs. T. M. Butler ($200)

FLOWER PAINTING
Tulips by Rena A. Hostetler
Jessie M. Holcomb Memorial by
Mr. & Mrs. J. I. Holcomb ($100)

STILL LIFE (NOT FLOWERS)
Fall Harvest by William F. Kaeser
Mr. and Mrs. Harold Gray ($50)

GROUP OF ETCHINGS OR OTHER
WORK IN BLACK AND WHITE
Awarded to Ella Fillmore Lillie
Frank S. Cunningham ($50)

WATERCOLOR
Taxco by Glen Mitchell
George T. Buckingham ($50)

WORK BY INSTRUCTOR IN CATHOLIC
HIGH SCHOOL, COLLEGE OR UNIVERSITY
Sung and Samurai by Francis J. Hanley
Peter C. Reilly ($100)
Clown by Sister Rufinia
Peter C. Reilly ($75)

WORK OF ART BY WOMAN ARTIST
Mr. E. H. K. McComb by Marie Goth
The Muncie Star ($100)

INDIANA LANDSCAPE IN OIL
BY NATIVE INDIANA MAN OR ONE
WHO HAS BEEN RESIDENT OF THE
STATE FOR AT LEAST FIVE YEARS
Song of the Hoosier by C. Curry Bohm
Edward Rector Memorial by
Mrs. Edward Rector ($200)

PORTRAIT OF A CHILD IN OIL
Portrait of a Boy by Elton Krafft
Honoring Orphan Annie by
Mr. & Mrs. Harold Gray ($100)

LANDSCAPE IN OIL PAINTED ALONG
ROUTE OF ILLINOIS CENTRAL
RAILROAD IN INDIANA
Agoin' Home by Georges LaChance
Lawrence A. Downs ($100)

PRIZE GIVEN IN FEATURE
LANDSCAPE ROOM
The Old Road by James Topping
Frank F. Hummel Memorial
by Mrs. F. Hummel ($150)

WORK BY ARTIST NEVER BEFORE
RECEIVING HOOSIER SALON PRIZE
Indian Still Life by Mary Spencer
Margaret Bridwell Memorial
by Tri Kappa Sorority, Chicago
Associate Chapter ($50)

LANDSCAPE BY ARTIST NEVER BEFORE
RECEIVING HOOSIER SALON PRIZE
A Brown County Road by H. J. Garceau
Delta Sigma Kappa Sorority of Indiana ($50)

HONORABLE MENTION
Pigeon Point Light House by Marques E. Reitzel
Dad and His Pipe by Edward Nicholson
An Old-Fashioned Bouquet by Genevieve Goth Graf
Blue Pitcher by Forrest F. Stark
Soloot Valley by Charles G. Yeager
The Harbor by Sara Bard
Group of etchings by George Jo Mess

HONORABLE MENTION: SCULPTURE
Alec Templeton by Warner Williams
Torso de Jeune Fille by Nancy Bixby Edwards

1941

OUTSTANDING WORK IN OIL
OF THE EXHIBITION
The Valley Road by Edward K. Williams
John C. Shaffer ($500)

WORK OF SCULPTURE
Head Study by C. Warner Williams
Mrs. Charles V. Hickox ($200)
Nanene by Frank L. Engle
Mrs. Charles V. Hickox ($100)

PORTRAIT IN OIL
Ruth by Hill Sharp
The Indianapolis Star ($200)

LANDSCAPE IN OIL
Under Changing Skies by Frank V. Dudley
Thomas M. Butler Memorial
by Mrs. T. M. Butler ($200)

FLOWER PAINTING
Still Life by Frank V. Hoffman
Jessie M. Holcomb Memorial by
Mr. & Mrs. J. I. Holcomb ($100)

STILL LIFE (NOT FLOWERS)
Femme Qui Se Chauffe by Paul Beem
Mr. & Mrs. Harold Gray ($50)

GROUP OF ETCHINGS
Awarded to George Jo Mess
Frank S. Cunningham ($50)

WATERCOLOR
Fall Landscape with Figures by Clifford E. Jones
The Indianapolis News ($50)

WORK BY INSTRUCTOR IN CATHOLIC
HIGH SCHOOL, COLLEGE OR UNIVERSITY
Waterfront by John J. Bednar
Peter C. Reilly ($100)
Offerings to Kwan-Yin by Stanley S. Sessler
Peter C. Reilly ($75)

INDIANA LANDSCAPE IN OIL
BY NATIVE INDIANA MAN OR ONE
WHO HAS BEEN RESIDENT OF THE
STATE FOR AT LEAST FIVE YEARS
Kids by Georges LaChance
Edward Rector Memorial by
Mrs. Edward Rector ($200)

WORK OF ART BY WOMAN ARTIST
Just Off Main Street by Lucie Hartrath
The Muncie Star ($100)

WINTER SCENE IN OIL
Snow of Ephraim by C. Curry Bohm
Daughters of Indiana of Chicago ($150)

PORTRAIT OF A CHILD
Mary by Georges LaChance
Honoring Orphan Annie by
Mr. & Mrs. Harold Gray ($100)

PRIZE GIVEN IN FEATURE
FLOWER PAINTING ROOM
Cyclamen and Sweet Peas by Samuel Hershey
Mark C. Honeywell ($200)

WORK BY ARTIST NEVER BEFORE
RECEIVING HOOSIER SALON PRIZE
Be It Ever So Humble by W. Wils Bell
Margaret Bridwell Memorial
by Tri Kappa Sorority, Chicago
Associate Chapter ($50)

LANDSCAPE BY ARTIST NEVER BEFORE
RECEIVING HOOSIER SALON PRIZE
Church Street, Charleston, S. C. by Ethel Stout
Delta Sigma Kappa Sorority of Indiana ($50)

INDIANA SOCIETY OF CHICAGO AWARD
Portrait of John T. McCutcheon by Marie Goth

HONORABLE MENTION
Snow of Ephraim by C. Curry Bohm
The Valley Road by Edward K. Williams
Cari by Marie Goth
Upper 5th Ave., New York by Johann Berthelsen
Awarded to Wood Woolsey
Becky by Hill Sharp
Linda by Ruth Pratt Bobbs
Still Life with Mandolin by Edmund Brucker
Yesterday, Today, and Tomorrow: Taos
by Esther Ruble Richardson
Flowers by Johann Berthelsen
Zero Weather by Edward K. Williams
Group of etchings by William Schaldach

1942

OUTSTANDING WORK IN OIL
OF THE EXHIBITION
Clara by Henrik Mayer
John C. Shaffer ($500)

WORK OF SCULPTURE
Portrait of J. Edwin Kopf by Elmer H. Daniels
Mrs. C. V. Hickox ($200)
Seated Nude by David K. Rubins
Mrs. C. V. Hickox ($100)

PORTRAIT IN OIL
Ruth by Floyd Hopper
Indianapolis Publishers Association ($200)

COMMISSIONED PORTRAIT OF WILL H. HAYS
Awarded to Marie Goth
Indiana Society of Chicago ($500)

LANDSCAPE IN OIL
Landscape in Winter by Charles M. West, Jr.
Mark C. Honeywell ($200)

LANDSCAPE IN WATERCOLOR
Montana Hills by Floyd Hopper
Mrs. E. M. Morris ($100)

FLOWER PAINTING
Flowers and Figurine by Marie Stewart
Jessie Mae Holcomb Memorial
by Mr. & Mrs. J. I. Holcomb ($100)

STILL LIFE
Still Life by Edwin Fulwider
Renee Barnes Memorial
by J. Wallace Barnes ($100)

INDIANA CHARACTER STUDY
Odd Jobs Man by Lee Detchon
Hoosier Salon Patrons Association ($50)

GROUP OF ETCHINGS
Adirondack Roadway; Cemetery Oaks;
and *San Juan Mission, San Antonio*
by Frederick Polley
The Muncie Star ($50)

PRINT
Waiting Room by David K. Rubins
Indianapolis Publishers Association ($50)

WATERCOLOR
Taxco Street Scene by Marion L. Patterson
Margaret G. Bridwell Memorial
by Tri Kappa, Chicago ($50)

PAINTING IN OIL BY TEACHER
IN INDIANA PUBLIC SCHOOLS
A Rainy Morning by Clifton Wheeler
William H. Block Memorial
by Amelia S. Block ($100)

PAINTING IN WATERCOLOR BY TEACHER
IN INDIANA PUBLIC SCHOOLS
Still the Seasons Change by Mildred K. Walker
William H. Block Memorial
by Amelia S. Block ($100)

WORK BY INSTRUCTOR IN CATHOLIC
HIGH SCHOOL, COLLEGE OR UNIVERSITY
Phlox by Sister Mary Jane
Peter C. Reilly ($100)
Head of a Negro by John J. Bednar
Peter C. Reilly ($75)

HONORABLE MENTION
Man with the Red Nose by Glenn Mitchell
Hoosier Winter by Edwin Fulwider
The Studio Stove by Lee Detchon
Still Life by B. E. Neff

1943

OUTSTANDING WORK IN OIL
OF THE EXHIBITION
The Narrows by Charles M. West, Jr.
William H. Block Memorial
by Amelia S. Block ($300)

WORK OF SCULPTURE
Ruth by Jon Jonson
Mrs. C. V. Hickox ($150)
Head Study by Warner Williams
Mrs. C. V. Hickox ($150)

PORTRAIT IN OIL
Portrait Julie by Henrik Mayer
Indianapolis Publishers Association ($150)

LANDSCAPE IN OIL
Old Houses, Charleston, S. C. by Frederick Polley
Mark C. Honeywell ($100)
Deserted by James W. Taylor, Jr.
Seventh District Federation of Clubs ($25)

INDIANA LANDSCAPE IN OIL
Christmas by Clifton Wheeler
Indiana University ($100)

LANDSCAPE IN WATERCOLOR
Iowa Village by Joe H. Cox
Mrs. E. M. Morris ($100)

FLOWER PAINTING
Flowers in Old Pitcher by Edgar Forkner
Jessie M. Holcomb Memorial by
Mr. & Mrs. J. I. Holcomb ($100)

PEONY PAINTING IN OIL
By the Window by Carl Graf
Renee Barnes Memorial
by J. Wallace Barnes ($50 Bond)

STILL LIFE
Antique Jar by Charlotte Sidman
Frank Elliott Ball Memorial
by Mr. &. Mrs. Frank C. Ball ($100)

INDIANA CHARACTER STUDY
Aunt Jenny by Bessie H. Wessel
Hoosier Salon Patrons Association ($50)

PRINT
The Station by Paul Wehr
Mrs. Mark A. Brown ($50)

WATERCOLOR
Beach Scene by Anne West
Daughters of Indiana, Chicago ($100)

PASTEL
Menagerie by Edmund Brucker
Margaret G. Bridwell Memorial
by Tri Kappa, Chicago ($50)

PAINTING IN OIL BY TEACHER
IN INDIANA PUBLIC SCHOOLS
At the Window by Edmund Schildknecht
William H. Block Company ($100)

PAINTING IN WATERCOLOR BY
TEACHER IN INDIANA PUBLIC SCHOOLS
Pear Still Life by Charles Yeager
William H. Block Company ($100)

WORK BY INSTRUCTOR IN CATHOLIC
HIGH SCHOOL, COLLEGE OR UNIVERSITY
Dried Out Potato Field by Sister Rufinia
Peter C. Reilly ($100)
Jane by Sister Esther
Peter C. Reilly ($75)

PAINTING OF SUBJECT
RELATING TO THE WAR
Industrial Horizon, 1942 by Hill Sharp
Journal-Gazette Company ($100)
The Welder by Paul Wehr
Woman's Department Club ($50)

1944

OUTSTANDING WORK IN OIL
OF THE EXHIBITION
Pastoral Indiana by Henrik Mayer
William H. Block Memorial
by Amelia S. Block ($300)

WORK OF SCULPTURE
Garden Piece by David K. Rubins
Mrs. C. V. Hickox ($300)

PORTRAIT IN OIL
Little Susan by Edmund Brucker
Indianapolis Publishers Association ($150)

LANDSCAPE IN OIL
Village by the Sea by Edmund Schildknecht
Mark C. Honeywell ($100)

LANDSCAPE IN WATERCOLOR
Landscape, Northern Australia
by Augustus C. Gondring
Mrs. E. M. Morris ($100)

LANDSCAPE IN OIL BY
NATIVE BORN INDIANA ARTIST
Mountain Solitude by Randolph Coats
Indiana University ($250)

FLOWER PAINTING
Zinnias by Simon P. Baus
Jessie Mae Holcomb Memorial
by Mr. & Mrs. J. I. Holcomb ($100)

PEONY PAINTING IN OIL
White Peonies by V. J. Cariani
Renee Barnes Memorial
by J. Wallace Barnes ($50)

STILL LIFE
Indian Craft by Roy B. Trobaugh
Frank Elliott Ball Memorial
by Mrs. Frank C. Ball ($100)

FLOWER STILL LIFE BY
NATIVE BORN INDIANA ARTIST
Lovers Interlude by June Burkholder
Journal-Gazette Company ($125)
Nubian Rhapsody by Jane Messick
Journal-Gazette Company ($125)

INDIANA CHARACTER STUDY
Portrait, Loretta by Ernest R. Roose
Hoosier Salon Patrons Association ($50)

GROUP OF ETCHINGS
*Four O'Clock, A New Dawn, and
The Handy Pump* by George Jo Mess
The Muncie Star ($50)

PRINT
Gloucester Houses by Ella Fillmore Lillie
Mrs. Mark A. Brown ($50)

WATERCOLOR
The Red Caboose by Paul A. Wehr
Daughters of Indiana, Chicago ($100)

PASTEL
Child's Portrait by Clara Epstein
Margaret G. Bridwell Memorial
by Tri Kappa, Chicago ($50)

PAINTING IN OIL BY TEACHER
IN INDIANA PUBLIC SCHOOLS
The Edge of Town by Clifton Wheeler
William H. Block Memorial ($100)

PAINTING IN WATERCOLOR BY TEACHER
IN INDIANA PUBLIC SCHOOLS
Tulip Tree Blossom by Eva May Yoder
William H. Block Memorial ($100)

WORK BY INSTRUCTOR IN CATHOLIC
HIGH SCHOOL, COLLEGE OR UNIVERSITY
Heroes Unsung by Sister M. Dolorita
Peter C. Reilly ($100)
Head of Christ by Bro. Loyola Christoph
Peter C. Reilly ($75)

PAINTING OF AN INDUSTRIAL SUBJECT
OR RELATING TO WAR
Southwest Industry by Floyd D. Hopper
Homer E. Capehart ($100)

WORK OF ART FOR
COMMERCIAL PURPOSE
Abuela Mexicana by Edward Nicholson
Keeling Company ($100)

HONORABLE MENTION
Art Appreciation by Mahrea C. Lehman
Critic by Mahrea Cramer Lehman
"Making Up," Cover Design for the May Issue of
the Eli Lilly Company Wholesaleman Magazine
by Paul H. Wehr
Bathers by Henrik Mayer
Red Barn by James W. Taylor, Jr.
Boats and Nets, Eastern Shore by Garo Z. Antreasian

1945

OUTSTANDING WORK IN OIL
OF THE EXHIBITION
Gray Hills of Winter by C. Curry Bohm
William H. Block Prize ($300)

WORK OF SCULPTURE
Salome by Robert Laurent
Mrs. C. V. Hickox ($150)
St. Jerome by John J. Bednar
Mrs. C. V. Hickox ($100)
Night Mares by Bette Graham
Mrs. C. V. Hickox ($50)

PORTRAIT IN OIL
Dr. Floyd Boys by Marie Goth
Indianapolis Publishers ($150)
Jenny by William A. Eyden
M. C. Honeywell ($100)
Portrait of a Young Girl by Donald M. Mattison
Indianapolis Publishers ($50)

LANDSCAPE IN OIL
Enchanted Hills by Karl C. Brandner
Keeling & Co., Inc. ($150)
In the Harbor by Georges LaChance
Daughters of Indiana ($100)
Winter Solitude by Edward K. Williams
Woman's Department Club ($50)

LANDSCAPE, ANY MEDIUM
The Lily Pond by Paul T. Sargent
Keeling & Company, Inc. ($100)
Snow on Williams Creek by Ernest Roose
Mr. & Mrs. Lawrence Carter ($25)

FLOWERS IN OIL
Phlox and Wedgewood by Frances R. Tranbarger
Jessie Mae Holcomb Memorial
by Mr. & Mrs. J. I. Holcomb ($100)
Petunias by Rena A. Hostetler
Jessie Mae Holcomb Memorial
by Mr. & Mrs. J. I. Holcomb ($75)
Phlox by V. J. Cariani
Jessie Mae Holcomb Memorial
by Mr. & Mrs. J. I. Holcomb ($25)

STILL LIFE IN OIL
Still Life by Bessie H. Wessel
Anderson Art Association ($100)
Fruit and Ivy by Fred A. Eilers
Anderson Art Association ($50)

FIGURE CHARACTER STUDY
Parade by Donald M. Mattison
Mr. & Mrs. Dudley Williston ($150)
The Bashful Muchacha by Edward Nicholson
Chester Cleveland ($50)

PRINT
Adirondacks by George Jo Mess
The Muncie Star ($50)
High on a Hill by Ella Fillmore Lillie
Benjamin Blumberg ($25)
Clifty Falls In Winter by Paul W. Ashby
Samuel B. Walker,
Alpha Chi Omega ($20)

WATERCOLOR
Aspiration by M. Wright Witmer
Mr. & Mrs. E. M. Morris ($75)
Marian's Stove by Catherine M. Mattison
Mr. & Mrs. E. M. Morris ($50)
Few Guest Artists by Mahrea Cramer Lehman
Mr. & Mrs. E. M. Morris ($25)

WATERCOLOR (FLOWERS)
Begonia by Eva May Yoder
L. G. Balfour ($75)
From Leila's Garden by Margaret Adams
L. G. Balfour ($50)
Variety by Francis F. Brown
L. G. Balfour ($25)

PASTEL
Petunias by Winnie H. Harvey
Margaret G. Bridwell Memorial
by Tri Kappa, Chicago ($50)
Skylight Etude by Elmer E. Taflinger
Jean Coler Memorial ($25)

PAINTING IN OIL BY TEACHER
IN INDIANA PUBLIC SCHOOLS
Rip Van Winkle Country by Clifton Wheeler
William H. Block Prize ($100)

PAINTING IN WATERCOLOR BY TEACHER
IN INDIANA PUBLIC SCHOOLS
Echoes in Glass by Jane Messick
William H. Block Prize ($100)

WORK BY INSTRUCTOR IN CATHOLIC
HIGH SCHOOL, COLLEGE OR UNIVERSITY
Sunshine and Shadow by Sister Rufinia
Peter C. Reilly ($100)
Madonna by Brother Etienne Cooper
Peter C. Reilly ($75)

1946

OUTSTANDING WORK IN OIL
OF THE EXHIBITION
Planting the Seed by Edmund Brucker
William H. Block Prize ($500)

WORK OF SCULPTURE
St. Francis by Eugene Kormendi
Mrs. C. V. Hickox ($150)
Girl and Mandolin by Robert Laurent
Mrs. C. V. Hickox ($100)
Struggle by A. G. Wolter
Mrs. C. V. Hickox ($50)

PORTRAIT IN OIL
Nancy by Edward Nicholson
Indianapolis Publishers ($150)
Marisue by Simon P. Baus
Indianapolis Publishers ($100)
Yvonne by Randolph Coats
D. C. Elliott Memorial ($50)

LANDSCAPE IN OIL
Seeking Shelter by C. Curry Bohm
Keeling & Co., Inc ($150)
The Promise by George Jo Mess
Mark C. Honeywell ($100)

LANDSCAPE, ANY MEDIUM
Connecticut River Wharves by Henrik Mayer
Keeling & Co., Inc. ($100)

FLOWERS IN OIL
Angel Trumpets by Leota W. Loop
Jessie Mae Holcomb Memorial
by Mr. & Mrs. J. I. Holcomb ($100)
The Plaza, New York City by Johann Berthelsen
Jessie Mae Holcomb Memorial
by Mr. & Mrs. J. I. Holcomb ($75)
From October's Garden by Robert Selby
Jessie Mae Holcomb Memorial
by Mr. & Mrs. J. I. Holcomb ($25)

FIGURE CHARACTER STUDY
Toshi by Joel W. Reichard
Katherine Langdon Memorial ($100)
Reminiscence by Lawrence Trissel
Chester Cleveland ($50)

PRINT
Maine by Ella Fillmore Lillie
The Muncie Star ($50)

GROUP OF PRINTS
Living Better Without, Flashes in the Harbor, and
Lullaby of the Leaves by George Jo Mess
Mrs. Mark A. Brown ($50)

WATERCOLOR
White River Fisher by Ernest R. Roose
Mr. & Mrs. E. M. Morris ($75)
Bradford Street in Winter by George Yater
Mr. & Mrs. E. M. Morris ($50)
The Belt by Floyd D. Hopper
Mr. & Mrs. E. M. Morris ($25)

PASTEL
Roberta Sancrant by Elmer E. Taflinger
Tri Kappa, Chicago ($50)

ESTELLA M. KING MEMORIAL PRIZE ($200)
Fabien Sevitzky by Marie Goth

PAINTING IN OIL BY TEACHER IN INDIANA PUBLIC SCHOOLS
Red House by the Sea by Edmund Schildknecht
William H. Block Prize ($100)

PAINTING IN WATERCOLOR BY TEACHER IN INDIANA PUBLIC SCHOOLS
Flower Study by Gladys A. Denney
William H. Block Prize ($100)

WORK BY INSTRUCTOR IN CATHOLIC HIGH SCHOOL, COLLEGE OR UNIVERSITY
Flora et Fauna by Sister M. Itta
Peter C. Reilly ($100)
Woman with Pearls by Bro. Etienne Cooper
Peter C. Reilly ($75)

1947

OUTSTANDING WORK IN OIL OF THE EXHIBITION
Windy Night by Clarence W. Staley
William H. Block Prize ($500)
Phantasmagoria by Lorena Phemister
Estella M. King Memorial ($200)

WORK OF SCULPTURE
Mimi by Robert Laurent
Mrs. C. V. Hickox ($150)
Soldiers by Eugene Kormendi
Mrs. C. V. Hickox ($100)
Head Design by Warner Williams
Mrs. C. V. Hickox ($50)

PORTRAIT IN OIL
Portrait by Donald M. Mattison
Indianapolis Newspaper Publishers ($150)
Pattie by Edmund Brucker
Indianapolis Newspaper Publishers ($100)
Seventeen by Rosa Lee
I. C. Elston ($50)

LANDSCAPE IN OIL
Love by George Jo Mess
Keeling & Co., Inc. ($150)
January by Mattie Lietz
Daughters of Indiana ($100)
Across the Fields by Stella C. Coler
Mark C. Honeywell ($100)
Michigan Winter by Wilna B. Barrickman
Mark C. Honeywell ($50)

LANDSCAPE, ANY MEDIUM
Assault by Jay Hall Connaway
Keeling & Co., Inc. ($100)
The Famous "500," Indianapolis
by Ernest R. Roose
Mr. & Mrs. Joseph Daniels ($100)

LANDSCAPE, AQUARELLE
River at Allegan by Helen Aldrich Hare
Mr. & Mrs. Joseph Daniels ($100)

FLOWERS IN OIL
Pitcher of Flowers by Martha H. Mosier
Jessie Mae Holcomb Memorial
by Mr. & Mrs. J. I. Holcomb ($100)
The Yellow Scarf and the Monarch
by Robert Selby
Jessie Mae Holcomb Memorial
by Mr. & Mrs. J. I. Holcomb ($75)
July Variety by Wilna B. Barrickman
Jessie Mae Holcomb Memorial
by Mr. & Mrs. J. I. Holcomb ($25)

STILL LIFE
Legerdemain by Alma L. Steinmetz
Arthur B. Wright ($100)
Still Life by Bessie H. Wessel
Mark C. Honeywell ($50)

FIGURE CHARACTER STUDY
The Duke of Hollywood by Elmer Spenner
Katherine Keene Langdon Memorial
by Dr. H. K. Langdon ($100)
Capt. Caleb and Patience by Henrik Mayer
Chester Cleveland ($50)

PRINT
Falls, McCormick's Creek Canyon by Paul W. Ashby
The Muncie Star ($50)

GROUP OF PRINTS
The Country Church and *Nature's Lace Work*
by Evelynne Mess
Mrs. Mark A. Brown ($50)

WATERCOLOR
Conservatory by Catherine Mattison
Mr. & Mrs. E. M. Morris ($75)
Ward, Colorado, Post Office by Gladys A. Denney
Mr. & Mrs. E. M. Morris ($50)
Brilliant Bisbee, Arizona by Frances Failing
Mr. & Mrs. E. M. Morris ($25)

PASTEL
Judy by Alice Cook
Tri Kappa, Chicago ($50)

PAINTING IN OIL BY TEACHER IN INDIANA PUBLIC SCHOOLS
Junction with 431 by Edmund Schildknecht
William H. Block Prize ($100)

PAINTING IN WATERCOLOR BY TEACHER IN INDIANA PUBLIC SCHOOLS
Old Ladies' Home by Virginia Rice Parker
William H. Block Prize ($100)

WORK BY INSTRUCTOR IN CATHOLIC
HIGH SCHOOL, COLLEGE OR UNIVERSITY
Mother and Child by Lorena Phemister
Peter C. Reilly ($100)
Torso by John J. Bednar
Peter C. Reilly ($75)

1948

OUTSTANDING WORK IN OIL
OF THE EXHIBITION
Morning by Clifton Wheeler
William H. Block Prize ($500)
Lobster Dories by Edward E. Herrmann
Estella M. King Memorial ($200)

WORK OF SCULPTURE
Duck by Robert Laurent
Mrs. C. V. Hickox ($200)
Head Study by C. Warner Williams
Mrs. C. V. Hickox ($100)

PORTRAIT IN OIL
Edgar F. Kiser, M. D. by Marie Goth
Indianapolis Newspaper Publishers ($150)
Old Man Small by Joel Reichard
Chester W. Cleveland ($100)
Angel Without Wings by Simon P. Baus
Indianapolis Newspaper Publishers ($50)

LANDSCAPE IN OIL
Back Porch by James Taylor
Keeling & Company, Inc. ($150)
University Park by Ernest Roose
Daughters of Indiana ($150)
The New Day by Georges LaChance
Mark C. Honeywell ($100)
A Sunday Afternoon by Karl C. F. Brandner
Mark C. Honeywell ($50)

LANDSCAPE, ANY MEDIUM
Out of Business by Burling Boaz, Jr.
Two Art Patrons ($125)
Babe in the Woods by Evelynne Mess
Keeling & Company, Inc. ($100)

FLOWERS IN OIL
Morning Glories by Cloa Ginney
Jessie Mae Holcomb Memorial
by Mr. & Mrs. J. I. Holcomb ($100)
Peonies by V. J. Cariani
Jessie Mae Holcomb Memorial
by Mr. & Mrs. J. I. Holcomb ($75)
Pansies by A. Noel
Jessie Mae Holcomb Memorial
by Mr. & Mrs. J. I. Holcomb ($25)

STILL LIFE
Copper and the Conch Shell by Robert H. Selby
Mr. & Mrs. T. C. Werbe ($100)
Store for the Winter by Leo R. Weeks
Mark C. Honeywell ($50)

FIGURE CHARACTER STUDY
Parrhesia by Hugh Poe
Katherine Keene Langdon Memorial
by Dr. H. K. Langdon ($100)
New Orleans Gossip by Wayman Adams
Woman's Department Club ($50)

WATERCOLOR
Snowscape by Lawrence Trissel
Mr. & Mrs. E. M. Morris ($75)
Bridge Across the Wabash by D. Omer Seamon
Mr. & Mrs. E. M. Morris ($50)
Little Engine by Gene Lacy
Mr. & Mrs. E. M. Morris ($25)
In Brown County by E. K. Williams
Birdie B. Steele ($25)

PASTEL
My Mother by Alice Dimmick Cook
Tri Kappa, Chicago ($50)

JURY CHOICE
The Old Place by Harriet E. Rynerson
Hugh J. Baker Memorial ($50)
The Farewell by David Blower
Mrs. Mark A. Brown ($50)

PAINTING IN OIL BY TEACHER
IN INDIANA PUBLIC SCHOOLS
Woodland Fungus by Oakley Richey
William H. Block Prize ($100)

PAINTING IN WATERCOLOR BY TEACHER
IN INDIANA PUBLIC SCHOOLS
Chichicastenango, Guatemala
by Marion L. Patterson
William H. Block Prize ($100)

WORK BY INSTRUCTOR IN CATHOLIC
HIGH SCHOOL, COLLEGE OR UNIVERSITY
Chrysanthemums by Sister Mary Edna
Peter C. Reilly ($100)
Ballet Boheme by Sister M. Dolorita
Peter C. Reilly ($75)

1949

OUTSTANDING WORK IN OIL
OF THE EXHIBITION
Summer Tapestry by Henrik Mayer
William H. Block Prize ($500)
Winter Glory by Francis Clark Brown
Estella M. King Memorial
by Anna D. McFann ($100)
and Arthur B. Wright ($100)

WORK OF SCULPTURE
Pitcher Plant by Robert Laurent
Mrs. C. V. Hickox ($200)
Mother and Child by Eugene Kormendi
Mrs. C. V. Hickox ($100)
Mother and Child by Jon Jonson
Woman's Department Club ($50)

PORTRAIT IN OIL
Brother by Edward Nicholson
Indianapolis Newspaper Publishers ($150)
Bomar Cramer by Marie Goth
Chester W. Cleveland ($100)
Eternal Triangle by Frances Norris Streit
Indianapolis Newspaper Publishers ($50)

LANDSCAPE IN OIL
The Widower by Harriet Rex Smith
Keeling & Company, Inc. ($150)
Deserted Strip Mine by George Jo Mess
Daughters of Indiana ($150)
Old Ruins, Columbia by Charles Surendorf
Mark C. Honeywell ($100)
October Snow by Olive Rush
Mark C. Honeywell ($50)

LANDSCAPE COMPOSITION, ANY MEDIUM
Fresh Snow by Stuart Eldredge
Arthur B. Wright ($50)

FLOWERS IN OIL
Home in Indiana by Robert Selby
Jessie Mae Holcomb Memorial
by Mr. & Mrs. J. I. Holcomb ($100)
Geraniums by Harriet Rynerson
Jessie Mae Holcomb Memorial
by Mr. & Mrs. J. I. Holcomb ($75)
California Bouquet by David Blower
Jessie Mae Holcomb Memorial
by Mr. & Mrs. J. I. Holcomb ($25)

STILL LIFE
Wedgewood Ware and Cluny Lac by Roy Trobaugh
Mrs. T. C. Werbe ($100)
Still Life by Louise Fults Agnew
Mark C. Honeywell ($50)
Grandmother's Treasures by Edmund Brucker
Indiana Federation of Art Clubs ($25)

FIGURE CHARACTER STUDY
Portrait: Meta P. Lieber by Simon P. Baus
Katherine K. Langdon Memorial
by Dr. H. K. Langdon ($100)

PRINT
The Shrimp Plant by Margaret Powell
Hugh J. Baker Memorial ($50)

GROUP OF PRINTS
*Stairway, New Orleans; St. Louis No. 1,
New Orleans;* and *Courtyard, New
Orleans* by Charles Surendorf
Mrs. Mark A. Brown ($50)

WATERCOLOR
The Music Strange by Catherine Mattison
Mr. & Mrs. E. M. Morris ($100)
Sidewalk Artist by Garo Z. Antresian
Mr. & Mrs. E. M. Morris ($50)
Indiana Spring Flowers by Thurman Nicholson
Birdie B. Steele ($25)

CHALK AND WATERCOLOR
Flowers by Constance Forsyth
Margaret Bridwell Memorial
by Tri Kappa, Chicago ($50)

PAINTING IN OIL BY TEACHER
IN INDIANA PUBLIC SCHOOLS
An Old Estate by Sy Perszyk
William H. Block Prize ($100)

PAINTING IN WATERCOLOR BY
TEACHER IN INDIANA PUBLIC SCHOOLS
Quiet Harbor by Max Howard
William H. Block Prize ($100)

WORK BY INSTRUCTOR IN CATHOLIC
HIGH SCHOOL, COLLEGE OR UNIVERSITY
House in the Woods by Sister Edna
Peter C. Reilly ($100)
Winter Recollection by Francis J. Hanley
Peter C. Reilly ($75)

1950

OUTSTANDING WORK IN OIL
OF THE EXHIBITION
Heavy Seas by C. Curry Bohm
William H. Block Prize ($500)

WORK OF SCULPTURE
Dancer by Paul J. Baus
Mrs. C. V. Hickox ($200)
Sandstone Bear by W. E. Moore
Mrs. C. V. Hickox ($100)

PORTRAIT IN OIL
Abraham Walkowitz by Wayman Adams
Indianapolis Publishers ($150)
Old Sheriff by Edward Nicholson
Mark A. Brown ($100)
Teena by Joel W. Reichard
Indianapolis Publishers ($50)

LANDSCAPE IN OIL
Quiet Winter Mood by Gianni Cilfoni
Keeling & Company, Inc. ($150)
Fifth Avenue, New York City by Johann Berthelsen
Daughters of Indiana ($150)
Factory District by Roland D. Osborne
Mark C. Honeywell ($100)
Paradise Valley by George Jo Mess
Mark C. Honeywell ($50)

LANDSCAPE COMPOSITION, ANY MEDIUM
A Rocky Pasture by Clifton Wheeler
Anonymous ($100)

FLOWERS IN OIL
Peonies in Blue Vase by V. J. Cariani
Jessie Mae Holcomb Memorial
by Mr. & Mrs. J. I. Holcomb ($100)
The Blue Scarf by Charlotte Sidman
Jessie Mae Holcomb Memorial
by Mr. & Mrs. J. I. Holcomb ($75)
From the Chrysanthemum Show
by Jane Anderson Fowler
Jessie Mae Holcomb Memorial
by Mr. & Mrs. J. I. Holcomb ($25)

STILL LIFE
Samovar No. 2 by Harry Engel
Mrs. T. C. Werbe ($100)
Arrangement with Lemons by Jean Swiggett
Mark C. Honeywell ($50)
Oriental Symphony by Margaret W. Powell
Indiana Federation of Art Clubs ($50)

FIGURE CHARACTER STUDY
Uptown by Robert E. Weaver
Katherine K. Langdon Memorial
by Dr. H. K. Langdon ($100)
Net Mender's Resting Time by Mattie Lietz
Woman's Department Club ($50)

PRINT
Main Street by George Gawehn
Hugh J. Baker Memorial ($50)

GROUP OF PRINTS
Atlanta to the Sea; Pink Chapel,
St. Simon's Island; and Siamese Oak,
Sea Island by Ella Fillmore Lillie
Mrs. Mark A. Brown ($50)

WATERCOLOR
Prelude to Rain by Edward E. Herrmann
Mr. & Mrs. E. M. Morris ($100)
Goldie by Joel W. Reichard
Mr. & Mrs. E. M. Morris ($50)
Sweet Gum by Paul Hadley
Edward K. Williams Memorial
by Tri Kappa Sorority ($50)
Negro Baptism by Elizabeth D. Ashton
Birdie B. Steele ($25)

PASTEL
The Window Washer by Francis E. Holt
Margaret Bridwell Memorial
by Tri Kappa, Chicago ($50)

PAINTING IN OIL BY TEACHER
IN INDIANA PUBLIC SCHOOLS
Interlude by Oakley E. Richey
William H. Block Prize ($100)

PAINTING IN WATERCOLOR BY
TEACHER IN INDIANA PUBLIC SCHOOLS
Fisherman's Cove, Puget Sound
by Gail C. McDonnell
William H. Block Prize ($100)

WORK BY INSTRUCTOR IN CATHOLIC
HIGH SCHOOL, COLLEGE OR UNIVERSITY
Second Eve by Sister M. Dolorita
Peter C. Reilly ($100)
Ohio River Banks by Sister M. Itta
Peter C. Reilly ($75)

1951

OUTSTANDING WORK IN OIL
OF THE EXHIBITION
Lambertville, N. J. by Sara Kolb Danner
William H. Block Prize ($500)

WORK OF SCULPTURE
Moses by Richard Peeler
Mrs. C. V. Hickox ($200)
Last of the Herd by W. E. Moore
Mrs. C. V. Hickox ($100)

PORTRAIT IN OIL
Not a Member of This Club by Wayman Adams
Indianapolis Newspaper Publishers ($150)
Cari by Marie Goth
Anonymous ($100)
Steno by Joel W. Reichard
Indianapolis Newspaper Publishers ($50)
Portrait of Julie by Donald M. Mattison
C. Ober ($50)

PORTRAIT
Paul Dresser by Edmund Brucker
Indiana Society of Chicago ($350)

LANDSCAPE IN OIL
Warning at Nausett by Joel W. Reichard
Keeling & Company, Inc. ($150)
Peaceful Valley by Karl C. Brandner
Daughters of Indiana ($150)
Dusk by Gladys F. Buschmann
Mark C. Honeywell ($100)
From My Window, No. 2 by Clifton Wheeler
Mark C. Honeywell ($50)

FLOWERS IN OIL
Mallow by Robert Selby
Jessie M. Holcomb Memorial by
Mr. & Mrs. J. I. Holcomb ($100)
Summer's Blend, Zinnias by June Burkholder
Jessie Mae Holcomb Memorial
by Mr. & Mrs. J. I. Holcomb ($75)
Driftwood Still Life by G. W. Martin
Jessie Mae Holcomb Memorial
by Mr. & Mrs. J. I. Holcomb ($25)

STILL LIFE
The Green Thumb by William F. Kaeser
Mrs. T. C. Werbe ($100)
Speedway Still Life by Ernest R. Roose
Mark C. Honeywell ($50)
Decoys by Henrik Mayer
Indiana Federation of Art Clubs ($50)

FIGURE CHARACTER STUDY
  Doc by Elizabeth Dodds Shaffer
    Katherine K. Langdon Memorial
    by Dr. H. K. Langdon ($100)
  Spanish Ballet Student by Edward Nicholson
    Woman's Department Club ($50)

PRINT
  Toadstools by Evelynne Mess
    Hugh J. Baker Memorial ($50)

GROUP OF PRINTS
  Cordelle, Deserted Cabin, and
  Fossils by August Mead
    Mrs. Mark A. Brown ($50)

WATERCOLOR
  The Wall by Donald Allen Peters
    Mr. & Mrs. E. M. Morris ($100)
  Rice Paddy Field and *Huts* by Aulie Kurtz
    Clarence A. Cook ($50)
  Depot at Three Rivers, Michigan
  by Roy F. Thompson
    Anonymous ($50)

PASTEL
  Autumn Time by Lillian M. Davidson
    Margaret Bridwell Memorial
    by Tri Kappa, Chicago ($50)

PAINTING IN OIL BY TEACHER
IN INDIANA PUBLIC SCHOOLS
  Pan Fish by Robert W. Crawford
    William H. Block Prize ($100)

PAINTING IN WATERCOLOR BY TEACHER
IN INDIANA PUBLIC SCHOOLS
  Study in Color by Maurice D. Frost
    William H. Block Prize ($100)

WORK BY INSTRUCTOR IN CATHOLIC
HIGH SCHOOL, COLLEGE OR UNIVERSITY
  Landscape by Sister M. Edna
    Peter C. Reilly ($100)
  City Park at Noon by Francis J. Hanley
    Peter C. Reilly ($75)

OUTSTANDING WORK, ANY MEDIUM
  Boy with Rabbits by Sy Perszyk
    Hoagy Carmichael ($75)

1952

OUTSTANDING WORK IN OIL
OF THE EXHIBITION
  Low Tide by Edmund Brucker
    William H. Block Prize ($500)

WORK OF SCULPTURE
  Girl with Biwa by Ralph N. Hurst
    Mrs. C. V. Hickox ($200)
  Pigeon by Robert Laurent
    Mrs. C. V. Hickox ($100)

PORTRAIT IN OIL
  Gus Parker by Wayman Adams
    Indianapolis Newspaper Publishers ($150)
  Young Pastor Pinkston by Joel Reichard
    Mrs. Arthur B. Wright and
    Chester W. Cleveland ($100)
  Mrs. Ballman by Marie Goth
    Indianapolis Newspaper Publishers ($50)
  Little Old Lady by Helen Woodward Woods
    C. Ober ($50)

LANDSCAPE IN OIL
  Central Park by Johann Berthelsen
    Keeling & Company, Inc. ($150)
  Pacific Night by David Blower
    Daughters of Indiana ($150)
  Near Danby, Vermont by Gianni Cilfone
    Mark C. Honeywell ($100)

LANDSCAPE COMPOSITION, ANY MEDIUM
  Election by Jane VanSickle
    Mark C. Honeywell ($50)

FLOWERS IN OIL
  Composition No. 2 by Louis Dimitroff
    Jessie Mae Holcomb Memorial
    by Mr. & Mrs. J. I. Holcomb ($125)
  Flowers at the Edge of Night
  by Martha Hinkle Mosier
    Jessie Mae Holcomb Memorial
    by Mr. & Mrs. J. I. Holcomb ($75)

STILL LIFE
  White Pitcher by Jane VanSickle
    Mrs. Arthur B. Wright ($100)
  The Green Case by Robert L. Ochs
    Mark C. Honeywell ($50)
  Still Life by Leon R. Walker
    Indiana Federation of Art Clubs ($50)

FOR AN INTERIOR
  Farm Weather Outlook by Gifford Hansell
    American Institute of
    Decorators, Indiana ($50)

FIGURE CHARACTER STUDY
  Hoosier Blacksmith by Edmund Brucker
    Katherine K. Langdon Memorial
    by Dr. H. K. Langdon ($100)
  Family Group by Donald Mattison
    Woman's Department Club ($50)

GROUP OF PRINTS
  Highway No. 1, Off the Main Highway,
  and *Coffee Time* by George Jo Mess
    Charles A. Segner ($50)
  Mardi Gras, N. O.; St. Peter Street, N. O.;
  and *Madison Street, N. O.* by Charles Surendorf
    Mrs. Mark A. Brown ($50)

WATERCOLOR
Lake Freeman, Indiana by Gene Lacy
Ernest M. Morris Memorial
by Mrs. E. M. Morris ($150)
Steam by Edward E. Herrmann
Hugh J. Baker Memorial by
Mrs. Hugh Baker and Sons ($100)
Excavation by Walter Crowl
Clarence A. Cook ($50)

PASTEL
Baby Lawrence by Clara Epstein
Margaret Bridwell Memorial
by Tri Kappa, Chicago ($50)

PAINTING IN OIL BY TEACHER
IN INDIANA PUBLIC SCHOOLS
Against the Light by Genevieve Goth Graf
William H. Block Co. Prize ($100)

PAINTING IN WATERCOLOR BY TEACHER
IN INDIANA PUBLIC SCHOOLS
Night Estuary, San Francisco Bay
by Miriam T. McVeigh
William H. Block Co. Prize ($100)

WORK BY INSTRUCTOR IN CATHOLIC
HIGH SCHOOL, COLLEGE OR UNIVERSITY
Wilderness by Sister Dolorita
Peter C. Reilly ($100)
Summer by Sister Rufinia
Peter C. Reilly ($75)

HONORABLE MENTION
Group of Color Wood Engravings
Shantyboats, The Round Barn,
and *Heritage* by August Mead
Group of Lithographs
Madrugada; Ancient Bridge,
Mexico; and Mexican Rhythm
by Ella Fillmore Lillie

1953

OUTSTANDING WORK IN OIL
OF THE EXHIBITION
Sunday Morning by Joel W. Reichard
William H. Block Prize ($250)
Hillside Spring by Oakley E. Richey
William H. Block Prize ($250)

WORK OF SCULPTURE
Daphne by Robert Laurent
Mrs. C. V. Hickox ($150)
Mother and Baby by Richard Peeler
Mrs. C. V. Hickox ($100)
Head of Mr. Davisson by Forrest F. Stark
Mrs. C. V. Hickox ($50)

PORTRAIT IN OIL
Lonesome Cowboy by Helen Briggs Duckwall
Mrs. Edmund B. Ball ($150)
Self Portrait by Simon P. Baus
Mr. & Mrs. Charles A. Segner ($100)
Jo-Ann, Art Student by Stella C. Coler
Mrs. Edmund B. Ball ($50)

LANDSCAPE IN OIL
A Fair Breeze by C. Curry Bohm
Keeling & Company ($150)
Harbor Impressions by Gianni Cilfone
Daughters of Indiana ($150)
Last Rehearsal of the Four Robins by Jane Ziegler
Mark C. Honeywell ($100)

LANDSCAPE COMPOSITION, ANY MEDIUM
Gray Spring Day by Marion Boyd
Mark C. Honeywell ($50)

FLOWERS IN OIL
Yellow Still Life by Miles R. Hodson
Jessie Mae Holcomb Memorial
by Mr. & Mrs. J. I. Holcomb ($125)
Angel Trumpets by Leota Loop
Jessie Mae Holcomb Memorial
by Mr. & Mrs. J. I. Holcomb ($75)

STILL LIFE
Cucurbita by Evelynne Mess
Foster Miles,
Smith Alsop Paint Co. ($100)
Still Life by June Burkholder
Mark C. Honeywell ($50)
White Poinsettias and Fruit
by Helen Woodward Woods
Indiana Federation of Art Clubs ($50)

FIGURE CHARACTER STUDY
Alcalde Artiaga by Wayman Adams
Katherine K. Langdon Memorial
by Dr. H. K. Langdon ($100)
The Actor by Francis E. Holt
Woman's Department Club ($50)

PRINT
Painting the Station by Laura J. Thompson
Hugh J. Baker Memorial by
Mrs. Hugh Baker and Sons ($25)

WATERCOLOR
Palms by Dorothy Short Paul
Ernest M. Morris Memorial
by Mrs. E. M. Morris ($150)
Winter on Rockingham Road by Stuart Eldredge
F. B. Bernard ($100)
Elevator in Winter by Grace L. Lay
Clarence A. Cook ($50)
Snow on the Catalinas by Helen P. Shaver
Mrs. Mark A. Brown ($50)
Beckoning by Dyna Cammack
Hugh J. Baker Memorial by
Mrs. Hugh Baker and Sons ($25)

PASTEL
Christopher by Helen Briggs Duckwall
Margaret G. Bridwell Memorial
by Tri Kappa, Chicago ($50)

HONORABLE MENTION
For Still Life in Oil to Roy Trobaugh
For Still Life in Watercolor
Southern Indiana by Charles G. Yeager

1954

OUTSTANDING WORK IN OIL
OF THE EXHIBITION
Gull and Buoys by George Yater
William H. Block Prize ($500)

WORK OF SCULPTURE
Stone Sheep by W. E. Moore
Mrs. C. V. Hickox ($300)

PORTRAIT IN OIL
Little Old Lady by Joel W. Reichard
Mrs. Edmund B. Ball ($150)
Self Portrait by Carl E. Jones
Charles A. Segner Memorial by
Mrs. Charles A. Segner ($100)
Adolescent Dream by Stella C. Coler
Mrs. Edmund B. Ball ($50)

LANDSCAPE IN OIL
Light and Shadow by Frederick Rigley
Keeling & Company ($150)
Peace and Quiet by Derk Smit
Daughters of Indiana ($150)
Quiescence by Pauline Briggs
Mark C. Honeywell ($100)

LANDSCAPE COMPOSITION, ANY MEDIUM
United Nations, New York City
by Johann Berthelsen
Mark C. Honeywell ($50)

FLOWERS IN OIL
George Hiding by William Kaeser
Jessie Mae Holcomb Memorial
by Mr. & Mrs. J. I. Holcomb ($125)
Garden Royalty by Robert Selby
Jessie Mae Holcomb Memorial
by Mr. & Mrs. J. I. Holcomb ($75)

STILL LIFE
By Man's Hands by Ernest Roose
Mark C. Honeywell ($50)
Milk Glass with Citrus by Helen Canaday
Indiana Federation of Art Clubs ($50)

FIGURE CHARACTER STUDY
Old Tom by Mary Hunter
Katherine K. Langdon Memorial
by Dr. H. K. Langdon ($100)
Telegram for the Funny Man by Grace Dickerson
Woman's Department Club ($50)

PRINT
Lode Lynching by Charles Surendorf
Hugh J. Baker Memorial by
Mrs. Hugh Baker and Sons ($50)

BEST GROUP OF PRINTS
Brown County Estate and
Brown County by George Jo Mess
Mrs. Mark A. Brown ($50)

WATERCOLOR
Flower Arrangement by Catherine Mattison
Ernest M. Morris Memorial
by Mrs. E. M. Morris ($150)
November Day by Edward Basker
F. B. Bernard ($50)
Sylvania Store Front by F. Raymond Jenkins, Jr.
Clarence A. Cook ($50)

PASTEL
Native of Old Natchez by Mary Hunter
Margaret Bridwell Memorial
by Tri Kappa, Chicago ($50)

JURY HONORABLE MENTION
Barn Dance by Harry A. Davis
Construction in Orange by Oakley E. Richley

1955

OUTSTANDING WORK IN OIL
OF THE EXHIBITION
Dry Dock by Edmund Brucker
William H. Block Prize ($500)

WORK OF SCULPTURE
Child by Paul Baus
Mrs. C. V. Hickox ($300)
Horseplay by Marjorie Peeler
Mrs. C. V. Hickox ($150)

PORTRAIT IN OIL
Uncle Jim Hayes by Wayman Adams
Mrs. Edmund B. Ball ($150)
Gertrud by Rosemary Browne Beck
Charles A. Segner Memorial
by Mrs. Charles A. Segner ($100)
Mary's New Dress by Elizabeth Dodds Shaffer
Mrs. Edmund B. Ball ($50)

LANDSCAPE IN OIL
Eve of Winter by Paul W. Zimmerman
Daughters of Indiana ($150)
Lonely House by James McBride
Mark C. Honeywell ($100)
Cape Cod Landscape by Bruce McKain
Foster Miles, Smith-Alsop
Paint & Varnish Co. ($100)

LANDSCAPE IN WATERCOLOR
Carousel by Al LaToor
Margaret Bridwell Memorial by
Tri Kappa, Chicago ($50)

LANDSCAPE COMPOSITION, ANY MEDIUM
Lake Near Bean Blossom by George Jo Mess
Mark C. Honeywell ($50)

FLOWERS IN OIL
Flowers and Apple by Mildred D. Cutler
Jessie Mae Holcomb Memorial
by Mr. & Mrs. J. I. Holcomb ($125)
Froliche Weinachten 1954 by John Frederic Ross
Jessie Mae Holcomb Memorial
by Mr. & Mrs. J. I. Holcomb ($75)
Arrangement with Mask and Fan by Stella C. Coler
Mark A. Brown ($50)

STILL LIFE
Harvest by Helen Humphrey
Mark C. Honeywell ($50)
Still Life by Miles R. Hodson
Hazel Murray Memorial
by Tri Kappa, Chicago ($50)

FIGURE CHARACTER STUDY
Roadside Fruit Stand by Harry A. Davis
Katherine K. Langdon Memorial
by Dr. H. K. Langdon ($100)
Patti by Carl E. Jones
Woman's Department Club ($50)

PRINT
Morphotic Cells by Elizabeth C. Stouder
Hugh J. Baker Memorial by
Mrs. Hugh J. Baker and Sons

WATERCOLOR
This Ol' House by Joel W. Reichard
Ernest M. Morris Memorial
by Mrs. E. M. Morris ($150)
Portrait of a Smoke House by Karl Warren
F. B. Bernard ($50)
Little Red Hen by Paul J. Sweany
Chester W. Cleveland ($50)

1956

OUTSTANDING WORK IN OIL
OF THE EXHIBITION
Little Johnny Rudd by Wayman Adams
William H. Block Prize ($500)

WORK OF SCULPTURE
Beach Bird by Ralph Hurst
Mrs. C. V. Hickox ($300)
Stone Loons by W. E. Moore
Mrs. C. V. Hickox ($150)

PORTRAIT IN OIL
Hoosier Farmer by Elizabeth Dodds Shaffer
Mrs. Edmund B. Ball ($150)
Christina by Harriett Rex Smith
Charles A. Segner Memorial
by Mrs. Charles A. Segner ($100)
Julie by Henrik Mayer
Mrs. Edmund B. Ball ($50)

LANDSCAPE IN OIL
Nashville, Indiana by Gianni Cilfone
Daughters of Indiana ($150)
River, Flow Gently by Henrik Mayer
Mark C. Honeywell ($100)
Boats in the Sun by Edmund Brucker
Mark C. Honeywell ($50)

LANDSCAPE COMPOSITION, ANY MEDIUM
Winter Patterns by George Jo Mess
Foster Miles, Smith-Alsop
Paint & Varnish Co. ($100)

FLOWERS IN OIL
Still Life by Rosemary Browne Beck
Jessie Mae Holcomb Memorial
by Mr. & Mrs. J. I. Holcomb ($100)
Early Fall, Chrysanthemums by June Burkholder
Jessie Mae Holcomb Memorial
by Mr. & Mrs. J. I. Holcomb ($50)

STILL LIFE
The Black Jug by Roland D. Osborne
Katherine K. Langdon Memorial
by Dr. H. K. Langdon ($100)
The Meadow by Harry F. Breen
Mark C. Honeywell ($50)

FIGURE CHARACTER STUDY
Mrs. West by James McBride
Mrs. Mark A. Brown ($50)

FIGURE COMPOSITION STUDY
The Apple Pickers by Harry Davis
Woman's Department Club ($100)

PRINT
Scarecrow by George Jo Mess
Hugh J. Baker Memorial by
Mrs. Hugh J. Baker and Sons ($50)

WATERCOLOR
Winter Afternoon, Provincetown by George Yater
Ernest M. Morris Memorial
by Mrs. E. M. Morris ($150)
Spring Bouquet by May Guckelberg
F. B. Bernard ($50)

PASTEL
Lunch at Block's by Helen Briggs Duckwall
Margaret G. Bridwell Memorial
by Tri Kappa, Chicago ($50)

HONORABLE MENTION
Ohio Homestead by Francis Clark Brown
October Day by Derk Smit
Country Still Life by Edward Nicholson
Rural Harmony by James McBride
Devil's Gulch by Edward Basker
For of Such by Donald Mattison

1957

OUTSTANDING WORK IN OIL
OF THE EXHIBITION
Country Girl by Joel W. Reichard
William H. Block Prize ($500)

WORK OF SCULPTURE
Horse Sale by W. E. Moore
Mrs. C. V. Hickox ($300)
Foxes by Henrik Sueberkrop
Mrs. C. V. Hickox ($150)

PORTRAIT IN OIL
V. J. C. by Marie Goth
Herman B Wells ($100)
Polly by Marie Goth
Ernest M. Morris Memorial
by Mrs. E. M. Morris ($50)
Member of the "Polar Bears" by Edward Nicholson
Charles A. Segner Memorial
by Mrs. Charles A. Segner ($25)

LANDSCAPE IN OIL
Brew Weather by C. Curry Bohm
Daughters of Indiana of Chicago ($150)
Red Georgia Clay by Francis Clark Brown
Charles A. Segner Memorial
by Mrs. Charles A. Segner ($75)
Spring by Roland Donovan Osborne
Ernest M. Morris Memorial
by Mrs. E. M. Morris ($25)

LANDSCAPE COMPOSITION IN OIL
Greasy Creek by D. C. Donaldson
Katherine K. Langdon Memorial
by Dr. H. K. Langdon ($100)
Lazy Days by Georges LaChance
Foster Miles, Smith-Alsop
Paint & Varnish Co. ($50)

LANDSCAPE COMPOSITION IN WATERCOLOR
Birchwoods by Lilian Fendig
Brown County Art Gallery Association ($50)

FLOWERS IN OIL
Last Year's Bird Nest by Jane Ziegler
Jessie Mae Holcomb Memorial
by J. I. Holcomb ($100)
Fantasy by Rena A. Hostetler
Jessie Mae Holcomb Memorial
by J. I. Holcomb ($50)
Life's Blessings by Ruth K. Hibbs
Foster Miles, Smith-Alsop
Paint & Varnish Co. ($25)

STILL LIFE IN OIL
Holiday by Edward Nicholson
Mark C. Honeywell ($100)
The Lantern by Jean Unversaw
Mr. & Mrs. Frank B. Hunter ($50)
Behind the Green Door by Frank R. Myslive
Mrs. Mark A. Brown ($25)

FIGURE CHARACTER STUDY, ANY MEDIUM
Brother Simon by Wayman Adams
Woman's Department Club ($50)

PRINT
Far Into the Hills by Anne M. Duncan
Hugh J. Baker Memorial by
Mrs. Hugh J. Baker and Sons ($50)
Limestone Creek by Paul W. Ashby
Foster Miles, Smith-Alsop
Paint & Varnish Co. ($25)

WATERCOLOR
Rainbow Rocks by Lilian Fendig
Mark C. Honeywell ($100)
The Sightless One by Francis E. Holt
Mr. & Mrs. Carl M. Sauer ($50)
Three-Wheeled Buggy by Karl Warren
Mrs. Mark A. Brown ($25)

PASTEL
Portrait by Harriet E. Monteith
Ernest M. Morris Memorial
by Mrs. E. M. Morris ($75)
Friend in Silk Shirt by Helen Briggs Duckwall
Margaret Bridwell Memorial
by Tri Kappa, Chicago ($50)

1958

OUTSTANDING WORK IN OIL
OF THE EXHIBITION
Dairy Barn by Robert Selby
William H. Block Company ($500)

WORK OF SCULPTURE
Wedding Dance of the Whooping Cranes
by Richard Kishel
Mrs. C. V. Hickox ($300)
Strand Birds by Henrik Sueberkrop
Mrs. C. V. Hickox ($150)

PORTRAIT IN OIL
Jeanie by Joel W. Reichard
Herman B Wells ($100)
Dr. Allen D. Albert by Marie Goth
Woman's Department Club ($50)

LANDSCAPE IN OIL
City Snow by James F. McBride
Daughters of Indiana of Chicago ($150)
Cape Cod Landmark by Francis C. Brown
Charles A. Segner Memorial
by Mrs. Charles A. Segner ($100)
Low Tide by Frederick Rigley
Ernest M. Morris Memorial
by Mrs. E. M. Morris ($25)

LANDSCAPE COMPOSITION IN OIL
Walla Walla by Thelma F. Pearson
Katherine K. Langdon Memorial
by Dr. H. K. Langdon ($100)
Early Spring Patterns by George Jo Mess
Foster Miles, Smith-Alsop
Paint & Varnish Co. ($50)

FLOWERS IN OIL
The Contender by Gertrude Harbart
Jessie Mae Holcomb Memorial
by J. I. Holcomb ($100)
Carolyn's Marigolds by Jane Fowler
Jessie Mae Holcomb Memorial
by J. I. Holcomb ($50)
Field Flowers by Evelynne Mess
Foster Miles, Smith-Alsop
Paint & Varnish Co. ($25)

STILL LIFE IN OIL
Still Life by Rosemary Browne Beck
Mark C. Honeywell ($100)
Still Life With Cabbage by Harriet E. Monteith
Art Department, Woman's
Department Club ($50)

FIGURE CHARACTER STUDY, ANY MEDIUM
The Gates Brothers by Wayman Adams
Mark A. Brown ($50)

PRINT
The Great Draft of Fishes by Arthur Sprunger
Hugh J. Baker Memorial by
Mrs. Hugh J. Baker and Sons ($50)
Winter Work by Ella Fillmore Lillie
Foster Miles, Smith-Alsop
Paint & Varnish Co. ($25)

WATERCOLOR
Winter Mood by Edward Basker
Mark C. Honeywell ($100)
Rainy Day in the Studio by Karl Warren
Margaret Bridwell Memorial
by Tri Kappa, Chicago ($50)

PASTEL
Mother and Child by Virginia Murdock
Ernest M. Morris Memorial
by Mrs. E. M. Morris ($75)
Isle of St. George, Venice by B. Bailey Bemis
Ernest M. Morris Memorial
by Mrs. E. M. Morris ($50)

HONORABLE MENTION
Don't Fence Me In by Floyd D. Hopper
Portrait of the Artist's Wife by Norbert Smith
Covered Bridge No. 3 by D. Omer Seamon

1959

OUTSTANDING WORK IN OIL
OF THE EXHIBITION
Still Life by Rosemary Browne Beck
William H. Block Company ($500)

WORK OF SCULPTURE
Bears by Henrik Sueberkrop
Mrs. C. V. Hickox ($300)
Pixie by Mildred Helmuth
Mrs. C. V. Hickox ($150)

PORTRAIT IN OIL
Connie by Joel W. Reichard
Mark C. Honeywell ($100)
Portrait by Edmund Brucker
Woman's Department Club ($50)

LANDSCAPE IN OIL
Village of Nashville by C. Curry Bohm
Daughters of Indiana of Chicago ($150)
Brown County Panorama by Mary Ann Gibson
Foster Miles, Smith-Alsop
Paint & Varnish Co. ($100)
Mt. Adams Houses by Charles Townsend
Art Department, Woman's
Department Club ($25)

LANDSCAPE COMPOSITION IN ANY MEDIUM
Approaching the Market, Guatemala
by Ruth K. Hibbs
Charles A. Segner Memorial
by Mrs. Charles A. Segner ($100)
March Storm by Stuart Eldridge
Mrs. Mark A. Brown ($50)

FLOWERS IN OIL
June Bouquet by Mary Hunter
Jessie Mae Holcomb Memorial
by J. I. Holcomb ($100)
Still Life by Bruce McKain
Jessie Mae Holcomb Memorial
by J. I. Holcomb ($50)

STILL LIFE IN OIL
Attic Tenant by Edward Nicholson
Mark C. Honeywell ($100)

GRAPHIC
Mother and Child by Max Altekruse
Hugh J. Baker Memorial by
Mrs. Hugh J. Baker and Sons ($50)

WATERCOLOR
St. George Street by Joel Reichard
Ernest M. Morris Memorial
by Mrs. E. M. Morris ($100)
Chill November by Edward J. Basker
Ernest M. Morris Memorial
by Mrs. E. M. Morris ($50)

PASTEL
Lynn Gatti by Helen Duckwall
Margaret Bridwell Memorial
by Tri Kappa, Chicago ($50)

JURY'S CHOICE
Cosmos by Lilian Fendig
Indiana Federation of Art Clubs ($50)

1960

OUTSTANDING WORK IN OIL
OF THE EXHIBITION
Flood Scene, West Terre Haute by John Laska
William H. Block Company ($500)

WORK OF SCULPTURE
Totem by Alice F. Usher
Mrs. C. V. Hickox ($300)
Weasel by Don Moore
Mrs. C. V. Hickox ($150)

PORTRAIT IN OIL
Portrait by Marie Goth
Mark C. Honeywell ($100)
Charlynne by Elizabeth Dodds Shaffer
Woman's Department Club ($75)
Bon Vivant (Self Portrait) by Edward Nicholson
Indiana Federation of Art Clubs ($50)

LANDSCAPE IN OIL
Monday Club Meeting by Ruth K. Hibbs
Daughters of Indiana of Chicago ($150)

LANDSCAPE COMPOSITION, ANY MEDIUM
Winter Romance by Derk Smit
Mark A. Brown ($50)
Rustic Charm in the Ozarks by Anthony Buchta
Frederick W. Rigley, Rigley
Studios, Nashville ($25)

MARINE IN OIL
Morning Comes to Monhegan by Ruth Anderson
Albert E. Uhl Memorial
by Mrs. Albert E. Uhl ($100)

FLOWERS IN OIL
Golden Moment by Charles Untulis
Jessie Mae Holcomb Memorial
by J. I. Holcomb ($100)
Late Gathering by Catherine Mattison
Jessie Mae Holcomb Memorial
by J. I. Holcomb ($50)

STILL LIFE IN OIL
Little White Pitcher by Genevieve Goth Graf
Mark C. Honeywell ($100)
Still Life in Oil by Harriett Monteith
Mark C. Honeywell ($50)

PRINT
River Barge by Sarah Hurt
Hugh J. Baker Memorial by
Mrs. Hugh J. Baker and Sons ($50)

WATERCOLOR
October Morning by Karl Warren
Ernest M. Morris Memorial ($100)
Sycamore by Lilian Fendig
Ernest M. Morris Memorial ($50)
January Rain by James McBride
American Institute of Decorators ($50)

PASTEL
Where Next? by Mary Hunter
Margaret Bridwell Memorial
by Tri Kappa, Chicago ($50)

JURY PRIZE OF DISTINCTION
Weather Beaten by C. Curry Bohm
Psi Iota Xi Sorority ($150)

1961

OUTSTANDING WORK IN OIL
OF THE EXHIBITION
Joel W. Hadley by Marie Goth
William H. Block Company ($500)

WORK OF SCULPTURE
Venus (Without Wings) Flying by Richard Peeler
Mrs. C. V. Hickox ($300)
Leah by Claudine Paluzzi
Mrs. C. V. Hickox ($150)

PORTRAIT IN OIL
Girl in White Hat by Billie Cothran
Mark C. Honeywell ($100)
Mary by John Laska
Woman's Department Club ($75)
Girl with Fan by Edmund Brucker
Indiana Federation of Art Clubs ($50)

LANDSCAPE IN OIL
The Haunt of the Red Dragger by C. Curry Bohm
Daughters of Indiana ($150)
First Weekend in November by Joseph A. Trover
Albert E. Uhl Memorial
by Mrs. Albert E. Uhl ($100)

LANDSCAPE COMPOSITION, ANY MEDIUM
Church in the Hills by Frederick W. Rigley
Foster Miles, Smith-Alsop
Paint & Varnish Co. ($100)
Old Landmark by Ruth Anderson
Mark A. Brown ($50)

FLOWERS IN OIL
Climbing Roses by Mildred Blair
Jessie Mae Holcomb Memorial
by J. I. Holcomb ($100)
Glass and Flowers in Sun by Helen Woods
Jessie Mae Holcomb Memorial
by J. I. Holcomb ($50)

STILL LIFE IN OIL
Still Life by Derk Smit
Mark C. Honeywell ($50)
The Begonia by Donna Rector
Rigley Studios, Nashville ($25)

PRINT
Early Morning by Marion Maxon Healy
Hugh J. Baker Memorial by
Mrs. Hugh J. Baker and Sons ($50)

WATERCOLOR
The Clam Digger by Joel W. Reichard
Ernest M. Morris Memorial ($100)
Jackson Bridge, Parke County by D. Omer Seamon
Ernest M. Morris Memorial ($50)
1905 Model by Burling Boaz, Jr.
Indiana Chapter of American
Institute of Decorators ($50)

PASTEL
> *Mrs. Reefer* by Helen Duckwall
> Margaret Bridwell Memorial
> by Tri Kappa, Chicago ($50)

JURY PRIZE OF DISTINCTION
> *Cowboy* by Ann DeMun
> Psi Iota Xi Sorority ($125)

HONORABLE MENTION FOR SCULPTURE
> *The Birth of Venus* by Robert Laurent
> *Youth* by Helen Devoe
> *Faun* by George Stephans
> *Concerned Prophet* by Arthur Sprunger

HONORABLE MENTION FOR PRINT
> *Falling Figure* by Claudine Paluzzi
> *Haunted Valley* by Constance Forsyth
> *Old Kentucky Home* by Georgiabelle Clark

1962

OUTSTANDING WORK IN OIL
OF THE EXHIBITION
> *Harbor* by Edmund Brucker
> William H. Block Company ($500)

WORK OF SCULPTURE
> *Child with Bird* by Paul J. Baus
> Mrs. C. V. Hickox ($300)
> *Phrygian Sybil* by John J. Bednar
> Mrs. C. V. Hickox ($150)

PORTRAIT IN OIL
> *Rastus* by Edmund Brucker
> Mark C. Honeywell ($125)
> *School Girl* by Elizabeth Dodds Shaffer
> Mark C. Honeywell ($75)

LANDSCAPE IN OIL
> *Snow and the Development* by Robert Selby
> Daughters of Indiana of Chicago ($150)
> *Grey Hills of Indiana* by C. Curry Bohm
> Albert E. Uhl Memorial
> by Mrs. Albert E. Uhl ($100)

LANDSCAPE COMPOSITION, ANY MEDIUM
> *Early Snow* by Roland Donovan Osborne
> Foster Miles, Smith-Alsop
> Paint & Varnish Co. ($100)
> *Street Urchins* by Charles R. Untulis
> Mark A. Brown ($50)

FLOWERS IN OIL
> *Nicotina and Chinese Lanterns* by Grace L. Lay
> Jessie Mae Holcomb Memorial
> by J. I. Holcomb ($150)
> *The Piano Stool* by Betty Muhl
> E. Kirk McKinney Memorial
> by Mrs. E. Kirk McKinney ($75)

STILL LIFE IN OIL
> *Plant Life in Moonlight* by George Jo Mess
> Indiana Federation of Art Clubs ($100)
> *Still Life with Chair* by Carolyn Smaltz
> Rigley Studios, Nashville ($25)

PRINT
> *What I Live For, Thoreau* by Max Altekruse
> Hugh J. Baker Memorial by
> Mrs. Hugh J. Baker and Sons ($50)

WATERCOLOR
> *Tropical Mood* by Anna M. Jones
> Ernest M. Morris Memorial
> by Mrs. E. M. Morris ($100)
> *Early Spring* by Edward L. Basker
> Ernest M. Morris Memorial
> by Mrs. E. M. Morris ($50)

PASTEL
> *Suzanne* by Helen Duckwall
> Art Department, Woman's
> Department Club ($100)
> *Ballerina* by Harriet Monteith
> Margaret Bridwell Memorial
> by Tri Kappa, Chicago ($50)

JURY PRIZE OF DISTINCTION
> *Old Friends* by William A. Eyden
> Psi Iota Xi Sorority ($115)

1963

OUTSTANDING WORK IN OIL
OF THE EXHIBITION
> *Arrangement of Chairs*
> by Marilyn Osborn Feighner
> William H. Block Company ($500)

WORK OF SCULPTURE
> *Torso* by John D. Julian
> Mrs. C. V. Hickox ($300)
> *Rhinoceros* by Harry F. Breen
> Mrs. C. V. Hickox ($150)

PORTRAIT IN OIL
> *Beautiful Dreamer* by Marie Goth
> Mark C. Honeywell ($125)
> *Portrait* by Harriet E. Monteith
> Mark C. Honeywell ($75)

LANDSCAPE IN OIL
> *Stone Quarry* by Marie E. Lutz
> Daughters of Indiana of Chicago ($150)
> *Fragment of a City* by Alan Patrick
> Albert E. Uhl Memorial
> by Mrs. Albert E. Uhl ($100)

LANDSCAPE COMPOSITION, ANY MEDIUM
> *Pemaquid Point Light* by Joel W. Reichard
> Smith-Alsop Paint &
> Varnish Company ($100)
> *Sea Mist Collage* by Lenore K. Whitmore
> Mrs. Mark A. Brown ($50)

FLOWERS IN OIL
> *Tranquillity* by Frances Norris Streit
> Psi Iota Xi Sorority ($100)
> *Lilies and Companions* by Carrie Dyar Smith
> Psi Iota Xi Sorority ($50)

STILL LIFE IN OIL
My Mother Loved Amaryllis by Harriet E. Monteith
Indiana Federation of Art Clubs ($100)
En Glace by Mary Jo Hackett
Art Department, Woman's
Department Club ($50)
The Cardinal by Stella Coler
Rigley Studios, Nashville ($25)

PRINT
Boy Reading by John Laska
Hugh J. Baker Memorial
by Mrs. Hugh J. Baker and Sons ($75)
Bird and Waves by Constance Forsyth
Mr. & Mrs. Hezzie B. Pike ($25)

WATERCOLOR
City by Mary C. Dill
Ernest M. Morris Memorial
by Mrs. E. M. Morris ($100)
Mike by Jane Wendt
Ernest M. Morris Memorial
by Mrs. E. M. Morris ($50)

PASTEL
Robin by June B. Feltz
E. Kirk McKinney Memorial
by Mrs. E. Kirk McKinney ($75)
Portrait by June Boone
Margaret Bridwell Memorial
by Tri Kappa, Chicago ($50)

JURY PRIZE OF DISTINCTION
Excavation by Edmund Brucker
Psi Iota Xi Sorority ($100)

1964

OUTSTANDING WORK IN OIL
OF THE EXHIBITION
And Alice Said to the Rabbit by Edward Nicholson
William H. Block Company ($500)

WORK OF SCULPTURE
Hemipteran by Don Moore
Mrs. C. V. Hickox ($300)
Johnny by Claudine Paluzzi
Mrs. C. V. Hickox ($150)

PORTRAIT IN OIL
Rosina by Bruce Kimberling
Mark C. Honeywell ($125)
Me by Marie Goth
Mark C. Honeywell ($75)

LANDSCAPE IN OIL
The Sudden Squall by C. Curry Bohm
Daughters of Indiana of Chicago ($150)
Route 67 by Edmund Brucker
Albert E. Uhl Memorial
by Mrs. Albert E. Uhl ($100)

LANDSCAPE COMPOSITION, ANY MEDIUM
Between the Tides by Joel W. Reichard
Woman's Department Club ($100)
Early Snow by William A. Eyden
Indiana Federation of Clubs ($50)

FLOWERS IN OIL
Tropical Plants by William F. Kaeser
Psi Iota Xi Sorority ($100)
Bouquet Rouge by Stella Coler
Psi Iota Xi Sorority ($50)

STILL LIFE IN OIL
Antiques with Fruit by Derk Smit
E. Kirk McKinney Memorial
by Mrs. E. Kirk McKinney ($75)
Still Life by Amanda Eller Kirby
Indianapolis Federation of Art Clubs ($50)
Pleasant View by Mary Lienert
Art Department, Woman's
Department Club ($25)

PRINT
Flower Patterns #4 by Sarah Hurt
Hugh J. Baker Memorial by
Mrs. Hugh J. Baker and Sons ($75)
Mother and Babes by Evelynne Mess
Rigley Studios, Nashville ($35)

WATERCOLOR
Gill's Rock by Floyd D. Hopper
Ernest M. Morris Memorial
by Mrs. E. M. Morris ($100)
Gossip by Edward Basker
Ernest M. Morris Memorial
by Mrs. E. M. Morris ($50)
Street Scene, Paris by V. F. Bannon
Art Department, Woman's
Department Club ($25)

PASTEL
Karen Hansen by Helen Duckwall
Mrs. John E. Fehsenfeld, Sr. ($100)
Carolyn Sleeping by Mary Harrell McIntyre
Margaret Bridwell Memorial by
Tri Kappa, Chicago ($50)

JURY PRIZE OF DISTINCTION
Backbone of the Nation by Frank Myslive
Psi Iota Xi Sorority ($125)

HONORABLE MENTION
Torso by John D. Julian
Unicorn from the Garden by Harry F. Breen

1965

OUTSTANDING WORK IN OIL
OF THE EXHIBITION
Lost Mail by Earl Oshier
William H. Block Company ($500)

WORK OF SCULPTURE
Girl on a Stool by John Chase Lewis
   Mrs. C. V. Hickox ($300)
A-Marketing by Howard Demyer
   Mrs. C. V. Hickox ($150)
Pluto Offering Persephone
a Pomegranate Seed by Ronald R. Tracy
   American Institute of Interior
   Designers, Indiana Chapter ($50)

PORTRAIT IN OIL
Barbara by Marie Goth
   Mark C. Honeywell Memorial ($125)
Karl with Bird by John Laska
   Mark C. Honeywell Memorial ($75)

LANDSCAPE IN OIL
Cape Ann Boats by Edmund Brucker
   Daughters of Indiana of Chicago ($150)
Deserted by William A. Eyden
   Albert E. Uhl Memorial
   by Mrs. Albert E. Uhl ($100)

LANDSCAPE COMPOSITION, ANY MEDIUM
The Mushroom Hunt by Allen Hackney
   Woman's Department Club ($100)
Summer by the Sea by Grace Payne
   Indiana Federation of Clubs ($50)

FLOWERS IN OIL
Compliments by Robert Selby
   Psi Iota Xi Sorority ($100)
Magnolias by Joel W. Reichard
   Psi Iota Xi Sorority ($50)

STILL LIFE IN OIL
Fruit of the Garden by Lester Gallagher
   E. Kirk McKinney Memorial
   by Mrs. E. Kirk McKinney ($75)
Summer Ballet by Louise Gray Symons
   Indiana Federation of Art Clubs ($50)
Still Life with Fruit by Derk Smit
   Art Department, Woman's
   Department Club ($25)

PRINT
Print No. 94 by James A. Walker
   Hugh J. Baker Memorial by
   Mrs. Hugh J. Baker and Sons ($75)
Woodland Echoes by Sister Mary Ignatia
   Rigley Studios, Nashville ($50)

WATERCOLOR
Across the Park by Edward Basker
   Ernest M. Morris Memorial
   by Mrs. E. M. Morris ($100)
White Horses by Floyd D. Hopper
   Ernest M. Morris Memorial
   by Mrs. E. M. Morris ($50)
Shrimp Boat by Stephan Polomchak
   Art Department, Woman's
   Department Club ($25)

PASTEL
Kelly by Helen B. Duckwall
   Mrs. John E. Fehsenfeld, Sr. ($100)
Abandoned Mine by Charles J. Cady
   Margaret Bridwell Memorial
   by Tri Kappa, Chicago ($50)

JURY PRIZE OF DISTINCTION
Studio Table by Lu Kek
   Psi Iota Xi Sorority ($125)

1966

OUTSTANDING WORK IN OIL
OF THE EXHIBITION
Image by Martha Slaymaker
   William H. Block Company ($500)

WORK OF SCULPTURE
Crab by Don Moore
   Mrs. C. V. Hickox ($300)
The Central Nervous System by John Chase Lewis
   Mrs. C. V. Hickox ($150)

PORTRAIT IN OIL
Girl in Blue by Edmund Brucker
   Mark C. Honeywell Memorial ($125)
Deena with Cat by John Laska
   Mark C. Honeywell Memorial ($75)

LANDSCAPE IN OIL
A Day in Summer by William A. Eyden
   Daughters of Indiana of Chicago ($150)
The Station at Atlanta by Harry A. Davis
   Albert E. Uhl Memorial
   by Mrs. Albert E. Uhl ($100)

LANDSCAPE COMPOSITION, ANY MEDIUM
Comber at Herring Gut by William G. Ashby
   Woman's Department Club ($100)
Summer in Brown County by Genevieve English
   Indiana Federation of Clubs ($50)

FLOWERS IN OIL
Roadside Loveliness by Olif Pegg
   Psi Iota Xi Sorority ($100)
Flowers in White Vase by Mary Michau
   Psi Iota Xi Sorority ($50)

STILL LIFE IN OIL
Two Apples on a Platter by Ida Gordon
   Art Department, Woman's
   Department Club ($100)
Mr. Gottlieb's Chair by Barbara Cotton Kysar
   E. Kirk McKinney Memorial
   by Mrs. E. Kirk McKinney ($75)
Still Life with Fruit by Helen I. Sarber
   Indiana Federation of Art Clubs ($50)

PRINT
Print No. 82 by James A. Walker
   Hugh J. Baker Memorial by
   Mrs. Hugh J. Baker and Sons ($75)

WATERCOLOR
>   *Galena* by Edward Basker
>   Ernest M. Morris Memorial
>   by Mrs. E. M. Morris ($100)
>   *Newport, R. I.* by Zygmund S. Jankowski
>   Ernest M. Morris Memorial
>   by Mrs. E. M. Morris ($50)
>   *Dry Dock* by Floyd D. Hopper
>   Mrs. John E. Fehsenfeld, Sr. ($100)
>   *The Buddy System* by Virginia P. Ziels
>   Margaret Bridwell Memorial
>   by Tri Kappa, Chicago ($50)

JURY PRIZE OF DISTINCTION
>   *Still Life with Brown Bottle*
>   by Rosemary Browne Beck
>   Psi Iota Xi Sorority ($100)

1967

OUTSTANDING WORK IN OIL
OF THE EXHIBITION
>   *La Rues* by Harry A. Davis
>   William H. Block Company ($500)

WORK OF SCULPTURE
>   *April Chapeau* and *Lamentation* by Barbara Gray
>   Mrs. C. V. Hickox ($300)
>   *Non-Objective* by Don Moore
>   Mrs. C. V. Hickox ($150)

PORTRAIT IN OIL
>   *Sandy* by William G. Ashby
>   Mark C. Honeywell Memorial ($150)
>   *Peacock Curtain* by Lois Davis
>   Mark C. Honeywell Memorial ($100)

LANDSCAPE IN OIL
>   *Relic* by Earl Oshier
>   Daughters of Indiana of Chicago ($150)
>   *On the Rock Stood the Tree* by Al Todd
>   Albert E. Uhl Memorial
>   by Mrs. Albert E. Uhl ($100)

LANDSCAPE COMPOSITION, ANY MEDIUM
>   *Under Burnt Head* by William G. Ashby
>   Woman's Department Club ($200)
>   *Tranquility* by William A. Eyden
>   Indiana Federation of Clubs ($50)

FLOWERS IN OIL
>   *Herald of Spring* by C. Curry Bohm
>   Psi Iota Xi Sorority ($100)
>   *Still Life with Flowers* by Helen B. Duckwall
>   Psi Iota Xi Sorority ($50)

STILL LIFE IN OIL
>   *Goblet and Apples* by Rosemary Browne Beck
>   Indiana Federation of Art Clubs ($100)
>   *Homage to Degas* by Edmund Brucker
>   Art Department, Woman's
>   Department Club ($75)
>   *Abundance* by Lucille Dennis
>   E. Kirk McKinney Memorial
>   by Mrs. E. Kirk McKinney ($75)

PRINT
>   *Print No. 100* by James A. Walker
>   Hugh J. Baker Memorial by
>   Mrs. Hugh J. Baker and Sons ($75)

WATERCOLOR
>   *One Night* by Shurle Lee
>   Ernest M. Morris Memorial
>   by Mrs. E. M. Morris ($100)
>   *Winter, Lake Michigan* by Floyd D. Hopper
>   Ernest M. Morris Memorial
>   by Mrs. E. M. Morris ($50)

PASTEL
>   *Flores Bonitas* by Leah S. Traugott
>   Mrs. John E. Fehsenfeld, Sr. ($100)
>   *Kent Morse* by Helen B. Duckwall
>   Margaret Bridwell Memorial
>   by Tri Kappa, Chicago ($50)

JURY PRIZE OF DISTINCTION
>   *Delta* by Joan Brams
>   Psi Iota Xi Sorority ($100)

HONORABLE MENTION
>   *Scavi* by Claudine Paluzzi
>   *Poster* by Mary C. Dill
>   *Winter Morning* by Patricia Montgomery
>   *Winter Solstice* by John D. Julian
>   *Girl with Her Skirt Caught on a Stump*
>   by Edith Steinkraus
>   *European Atmosphere* by Anne Duncan

1968

OUTSTANDING WORK, ANY MEDIUM,
OF THE EXHIBITION
>   *Blanche* by Rosemary Browne Beck
>   William H. Block Company ($500)

OUTSTANDING PAINTING, ANY MEDIUM
>   *The Window* by Allen Hackney
>   Beryl Showers Holland Memorial
>   by Tri Kappa Sorority ($400)

WORK OF SCULPTURE
>   *Vincent* by Peter Bruning
>   Mrs. C. V. Hickox ($300)
>   *Swinger* by Maxine Keene
>   Mrs. C. V. Hickox ($150)

PORTRAIT OR FIGURE COMPOSITION IN OIL
>   *Portrait* by Harriet E. Monteith
>   Mark C. Honeywell Memorial ($150)
>   *Want* by Mary Curry
>   Mark C. Honeywell Memorial ($100)

LANDSCAPE IN OIL
>   *Smutty Nose* by William G. Ashby
>   Daughters of Indiana of Chicago ($150)
>   *The Windmill* by Edward E. Herrmann
>   Albert E. Uhl Memorial
>   by Mrs. Albert E. Uhl ($100)

LANDSCAPE COMPOSITION, ANY MEDIUM
America the Beautiful by Marilyn O. Feighner
Woman's Department Club ($200)
Campbell by Zygmund S. Jankowski
Indiana Federation of Clubs ($50)

FLOWERS IN OIL
Fruit and Flowers by P. Raney Newman
Psi Iota Xi Sorority ($100)
What If the Sun Shone Not by Lee Coblentz
Psi Iota Xi Sorority ($50)

STILL LIFE OR FLOWERS, ANY MEDIUM
Poppies by Anna M. Jones
Indiana Federation of Art Clubs ($100)
Still Life by Amanda Eller Kirby
Art Department, Woman's
Department Club ($100)
Recollections of Childhood by Randall Morgan
E. Kirk McKinney Memorial
by Mrs. E. Kirk McKinney ($75)

PRINT
Self Portrait by Virginia Piersol
Hugh J. Baker Memorial by
Mrs. Hugh J. Baker and Sons ($75)

WATERCOLOR
Salt Air by Joel W. Reichard
Ernest M. Morris Memorial
by Mrs. E. M. Morris ($100)
Lonesome Landmark by Wilbur Meese
Ernest M. Morris Memorial
by Mrs. E. M. Morris ($50)

PASTEL OR DRAWING
Girl with Flowers by Will Lamm
Mrs. John E. Fehsenfeld, Sr. ($100)
Golden Bouquet by Leah S. Traugott
Mr. and Mrs. Carl M. Sauer ($50)

JURY PRIZE OF DISTINCTION
Fishing Shack by Irene Mitchell
Delta Theta Tau, Iota Kappa Chapter ($200)
Still Life by Will Lamm
Psi Iota Xi Sorority ($100)

HONORABLE MENTION
Appalachia by Lois Davis
Print No. 103 by James A. Walker
Leonardo Fragmenta by Edmund Brucker
The Studio by Marilyn O. Feighner
The Green Shawl by Elizabeth Shaffer
Contraluce by Randall Morgan
Medals given by Mr. and Mrs. L. G. Balfour

1969

OUTSTANDING WORK, ANY MEDIUM,
OF THE EXHIBITION
Self Portrait by William A. Eyden
William H. Block Company ($500)

OUTSTANDING PAINTING, ANY MEDIUM
Sea at Dusk by William G. Ashby
Beryl Showers Holland Memorial
by Tri Kappa Sorority ($400)

WORK OF SCULPTURE
Meditation by Don DeWitt
Mrs. C. V. Hickox ($300)

PORTRAIT OR FIGURE COMPOSITION IN OIL
Self Portrait by William A. Eyden
Mark C. Honeywell Memorial ($150)
Nancy Jane by Charles C. Crawford
Indiana Federation of Art Clubs ($100)

LANDSCAPE IN OIL
Melting Snow by Theodore Fox
Daughters of Indiana of Chicago ($150)
Snowscape by Ruth Anderson
Albert E. Uhl Memorial
by Mrs. Albert E. Uhl ($100)
Indiana Farm by William F. Kaeser
Indianapolis Business and
Professional Women's Club ($50)

LANDSCAPE COMPOSITION, ANY MEDIUM
Gateway to Crown Hill by Harry A. Davis
Mr. & Mrs. Herman Krannert ($100)
The Tree That Came Home by Hal Kinder
Indiana Federation of Clubs ($50)

FLOWERS IN OIL
Summer Bouquet by V. J. Cariani
Psi Iota Xi Sorority ($100)
Potted Plants by Ida Gordon
Psi Iota Xi Sorority ($50)

STILL LIFE OR FLOWERS, ANY MEDIUM
The Black Pitcher by Clotilde Embree Funk
Art Department, Woman's
Department Club ($100)
Apothecary's Still Life by Lilian Fendig
E. Kirk McKinney Memorial
by Mrs. E. Kirk McKinney ($75)

PRINT
Landscape with Figures by Virginia Piersol
Hugh J. Baker, Sr. and Hugh
J. Baker, Jr. Memorial ($75)

WATERCOLOR
Provincetown Dories by Joel Reichard
Ernest M. Morris Memorial
by Mrs. E. M. Morris ($100)
Mykonos by Floyd D. Hopper
Ernest M. Morris Memorial
by Mrs. E. M. Morris ($50)

PASTEL OR DRAWING
In April by Andrea Porter Koch
Mrs. John E. Fehsenfeld, Sr. ($75)
The Balloon Man by Carol Lynn Smith
Mr. and Mrs. Carl M. Sauer ($50)
Young Girl in Landscape by Will Lamm
Mrs. John E. Fehsenfeld, Sr. ($25)

EXHIBITION RECORDS

JURY PRIZE OF DISTINCTION
Path to Holly Hill by Thomas Thiery
    Psi Iota Xi Sorority ($125)
Mountain Snow and Flowers by Paul A. Wehr
    Mark C. Honeywell Memorial ($100)

JURY PRIZE OF DISTINCTION, TRADITIONAL
Cairo by Floyd D. Hopper
    Woman's Department Club ($200)

NEW TRENDS, ANY MEDIUM
Ganglion by Bruce Bobick
    Mr. and Mrs. John Burkhart ($100)

HONORABLE MENTION
Basket of Eggs by Vivian M. Hauser
Jean in Gold by Richard Scheid
Watchtower #2 by Genevieve English
High View by James McBride
Decay and Delight by Allen Hackney
Scrap Pile Bound by George Sperl
    Medals given by
    Mr. and Mrs. L. G. Balfour

1970

OUTSTANDING WORK, ANY MEDIUM,
OF THE EXHIBITION
Westside Drug Store and
The Athenaeum by Harry A. Davis
    William H. Block Company ($500)

OUTSTANDING PAINTING, ANY MEDIUM
Tattered Glory by Donald L. Hadley
    Beryl Showers Holland Memorial
    by Tri Kappa Sorority ($400)

WORK OF SCULPTURE
Iron Reflection III by Steve E. Wooldridge
    Mrs. C. V. Hickox ($300)

PORTRAIT OR FIGURE COMPOSITION IN OIL
Portrait of a Happy Man by Marie A. Miles
    Mark C. Honeywell Memorial ($150)

LANDSCAPE IN OIL
The Fortress by Steve DeSanto
    Daughters of Indiana of Chicago ($150)

LANDSCAPE COMPOSITION, ANY MEDIUM
Afterglow by Opal F. Shuman
    Mr. & Mrs. Herman Krannert ($100)
Queen's Lace by Jene D. Burns
    Indiana Federation of Clubs ($50)

FLOWERS IN OIL
Grandma's Pitcher by Shirley Goodman
    Psi Iota Xi Sorority ($100)
Out by the Cellar Door
by Rosemary Lawton Thomas
    Psi Iota Xi Sorority ($50)

STILL LIFE OR FLOWERS, ANY MEDIUM
Bird Seed by Amanda Eller Kirby
    Art Department, Woman's
    Department Club ($100)
Flaming Persimmons with Flowers
by Leah S. Traugott
    E. Kirk McKinney Memorial
    by Mrs. E. Kirk McKinney ($75)

PRINT
Sequestrum by Marilyn Price
    Hugh J. Baker, Sr. and Hugh
    J. Baker, Jr. Memorial ($75)
Life Is Full of Fruition and Intuition
by Melanie Alter
    Hugh J. Baker, Sr. and Hugh
    J. Baker, Jr. Memorial ($25)

WATERCOLOR
Cascade by Louise B. Hansen
    Indiana Federation of Art Clubs ($100)

PASTEL OR DRAWING
In October by Andrea Porter Koch
    Mrs. John E. Fehsenfeld, Sr. ($75)
Self Portrait with Status Symbol by Delbert Michel
    Mr. and Mrs. Carl M. Sauer ($50)
Deserted by Opal Merritt
    Mrs. John E. Fehsenfeld, Sr. ($25)

JURY PRIZE OF DISTINCTION
The Song Sparrow by Allen Hackney
    Mrs. C. V. Hickox ($300)
Two Generations by Thomas Thiery
    Psi Iota Xi Sorority ($150)
Balancing Rock at Hidden Lake by Frances Stuebe
    Albert E. Uhl Memorial
    by Mrs. Albert E. Uhl ($100)
Dusty Stairs by Rob O'Dell
    Mark C. Honeywell Memorial ($100)

JURY PRIZE OF DISTINCTION, TRADITIONAL
Portrait by Edmund Brucker
    Woman's Department Club ($100)

NEW TRENDS, ANY MEDIUM
(No award in this category)
    Mr. and Mrs. John Burkhart ($100)

BALFOUR MEDAL AWARDS
Apples and Honey by Thomas Midkiff
Attic Retirement by Thelma L. Knarr
Urban Encroachment by William Kaeser
Approaching Storm by James McBride
St. Phillips, Charleston by Joel Reichard
The Jade Merchant by David Hockensmith
    Medals given by Mr. and Mrs. L. G. Balfour

HONORABLE MENTION
Temujin by Don DeWitt
Ochre by Lance Baber
Joe's Grandmother by John Laska
Mom by Thelma Confer
The Royal Hawker by Gerald Boyce
An Afternoon in Winter by Jan Scott Boyer
Composition No. 1 (Winter)
by Patricia F. Montgomery
A Day in Winter by William A. Eyden
Composition by L. W. Gallagher
Generation Gape by Robert Holzapfel
The Acoma Jar by Clotilde Embree Funk
Inhabitants of the House by Patricia Eberhart Victor

1971

OUTSTANDING WORK, ANY MEDIUM,
OF THE EXHIBITION
Enterprise by Kay McCrary
William H. Block Company ($500)

OUTSTANDING PAINTING, ANY MEDIUM
Mountain Mist by Roxie Remley
Beryl Showers Holland Memorial
by Tri Kappa Sorority ($400)

WORK OF SCULPTURE
Miss Lacey by Arlene Seitzinger
Mrs. C. V. Hickox ($300)
Dairy Queens by John W. McNaughton
Mrs. C. V. Hickox ($150)

PORTRAIT OR FIGURE COMPOSITION IN OIL
Waiting by Barbara Brookie White
Mark C. Honeywell Memorial ($150)

LANDSCAPE IN OIL
The River's Edge by Elton G. Krafft
Daughters of Indiana of Chicago ($150)

LANDSCAPE COMPOSITION, ANY MEDIUM
Vanishing Era by E. Gaye Eilts
Mrs. & Mrs. Herman Krannert ($100)
The Waning Light by Harry A. Davis
Indiana Federation of Clubs ($50)

FLOWERS IN OIL
Hollyhocks by Lydia S. Schaefer
Psi Iota Xi Sorority ($100)

STILL LIFE OR FLOWERS, ANY MEDIUM
Flowers by Judy Armstrong Baker
Art Department, Woman's
Department Club ($100)

PRINT
Three Poems by Kathryn H. Clark
Hugh J. Baker, Sr. and Hugh
J. Baker, Jr. Memorial ($75)
Lois by Virginia Piersol
Hugh J. Baker, Sr. and Hugh
J. Baker, Jr. Memorial ($25)

PASTEL OR DRAWING
Bark by Val Walters
Mrs. John E. Fehsenfeld, Sr. ($75)

JURY PRIZE OF DISTINCTION
One Afternoon by Elizabeth Dodds Shaffer
Psi Iota Xi Sorority ($150)
Study in Profile by Margaret Kennedy
Psi Iota Xi Sorority ($50)
Untitled by Nanci Blair Closson
Indiana Federation of Art Clubs ($100)
Getting Straight by James Guy Miller
Mr. and Mrs. Carl M. Sauer ($50)
Hanikraft by Mildred D. Hanika
Mrs. John E. Fehsenfeld, Sr. ($25)
Red Maple by Margaret Kennedy
Mark C. Honeywell Memorial ($100)
Alterpiece #7 by David Hockensmith
Albert E. Uhl Memorial
by Mrs. Albert E. Uhl ($100)
Chain of Sierras by Jennie Roche Saunders
E. Kirk McKinney Memorial
by Mrs. E. Kirk McKinney ($75)

JURY PRIZE OF DISTINCTION, TRADITIONAL
Over the Hill by Bernard Wynne
Woman's Department Club ($100)
White Reflected White by Rob O'Dell
Mr. & Mrs. Bayham Memorial by
Mr. & Mrs. William Eyden ($100)

HONORABLE MENTION
Representation by Nanci Blair Closson
Desert Rain by Louise B. Hansen
Rolling Circles, Square by Kay McCrary
Red Eyed Pig by Rodney R. Peabody
Arrangement by Nancy Gloh Rosenthal
Car Bank by Robert G. Venn
Medals given by Mr. and Mrs. L. G. Balfour

1972

OUTSTANDING WORK, ANY MEDIUM,
OF THE EXHIBITION
Offspring by Rob O'Dell
William H. Block Company ($500)

OUTSTANDING PAINTING, ANY MEDIUM
View of Greensburg by Harry A. Davis
Beryl Showers Holland Memorial
by Tri Kappa Sorority ($400)

PORTRAIT OR FIGURE COMPOSITION
Girl Reading by Tim Engelland
Mark C. Honeywell Memorial ($150)
Joey by James Gross, Jr.
Mark C. Honeywell Memorial ($100)

LANDSCAPE IN OIL
Sun on the Brush by Elton G. Krafft
Daughters of Indiana of Chicago ($150)
Country Green by Joe Shell
Albert E. Uhl Memorial
by Mrs. Albert E. Uhl ($100)

LANDSCAPE COMPOSITION, ANY MEDIUM
Thrush by Allen Hackney
 Mr. & Mrs. Herman Krannert ($100)
Old Farm Home by Jennie Roche Saunders
 Indiana Federation of Clubs ($50)

FLOWERS IN OIL
October Song by Michiko Boorman
 Psi Iota Xi Sorority ($100)
Petunias by Lydia Schaefer
 Psi Iota Xi Sorority ($50)
(No award made by Jury)
 Charles Untulis Memorial
 by Mrs. Charles Untulis ($100)

STILL LIFE OR FLOWERS, ANY MEDIUM
Mums by Virginia Warfield
 Art Department, Woman's
 Department Club ($100)
October Melange by Lilian Fendig
 E. Kirk McKinney Memorial
 by Mrs. E. Kirk McKinney ($50)

PRINT
Labna by Martha Slaymaker
 Hugh J. Baker, Sr. and Hugh
 J. Baker, Jr. Memorial ($75)
Circle in Arch by W. Steven Luther
 Hugh J. Baker, Sr. and Hugh
 J. Baker, Jr. Memorial ($25)

PASTEL OR DRAWING
Split Image by Val Walters
 Mrs. John E. Fehsenfeld, Sr. ($75)
Hooverville by William F. Kaeser
 Mr. and Mrs. Carl M. Sauer ($50)
Child Outside by Peter Bruning
 Mrs. John E. Fehsenfeld, Sr. ($25)

JURY PRIZE OF DISTINCTION
Late Afternoon by Charles Hirsch
 Psi Iota Xi Sorority ($150)
A Thing of Beauty Is . . . by Donald L. Hadley
 Indiana Federation of Art Clubs ($100)
Edge of Summer by Jean F. Vietor
 Mr. & Mrs. Bayham Memorial by
 Mr. & Mrs. William Eyden ($100)
Alterpiece #9 by David Hockensmith
 Frank Wiedemann, M. D. Memorial
 by Mrs. Frank E. Wiedemann ($50)
The Sensuous Woman by Bill Shane Ware
 Kappa Kappa Kappa Sorority ($125)
Flower Patterns #7 by Leah S. Traugott
 Elba L. Branigin, Jr. Memorial ($150)

JURY PRIZE OF DISTINCTION, TRADITIONAL
Chuck Tehan by Rosemary Browne Beck
 Woman's Department Club ($100)

BALFOUR MEDAL AWARDS
The Secret Place by Jo Beck
The Dove by James Gross, Jr.
Winter Evening by Floyd Hopper
Anderson Courthouse by Earl Oshier
Gemini by Ann Scott
East Coast Fishing Boats by W. Karl Steele
 Medals given by Mr. and Mrs. L. G. Balfour

HONORABLE MENTION
Snowshoe Hare by Jeanette Chupack
Watch Fob by Earl James Killy
Oscar Banfi by Michael Kitkowski
Through the Looking Glass by James Curtain Lentz
Dolls by Nancy A. Noel

1973

OUTSTANDING WORK, ANY MEDIUM, OF THE EXHIBITION
Squares II by N. Blair Closson
 William H. Block Company ($500)

OUTSTANDING PAINTING, ANY MEDIUM
Bedford Soliloquy by Martha Slaymaker
 Beryl Showers Holland Memorial
 by Tri Kappa Sorority ($400)

PORTRAIT OR FIGURE COMPOSITION IN OIL
Barbara Zimmer by Rosemary Browne Beck
 Mark C. Honeywell Memorial ($150)
Nature Children by Lois Davis
 Mark C. Honeywell Memorial ($100)

LANDSCAPE IN OIL
Sanctuary by Ruth Anderson
 Daughters of Indiana of Chicago ($150)
Old Buoys by Grant W. Christian
 Albert E. Uhl Memorial
 by Mrs. Albert E. Uhl ($100)

LANDSCAPE COMPOSITION, ANY MEDIUM
Door County, Winter '72 by Steve Polomchak
 Mrs. Herman C. Krannert ($100)
Dark Woods by Anne K. H. Cleaver
 Indiana Federation of Clubs ($50)

REALISTIC OR IMPRESSIONISTIC LANDSCAPE, ANY MEDIUM
Memory Mix by Frank Persell
 Judge & Mrs. Hutchinson Memorial
 by Mrs. Florence Lonsford ($100)

FLOWERS IN OIL
Tea and Trumpets by Mildred D. Cutler
 Charles Untulis Memorial
 by Mrs. Charles Untulis ($100)

PRINT
Petroglyph by Doris J. Brinkman
 Hugh J. Baker, Sr. and Hugh
 J. Baker, Jr. Memorial ($75)
Walrus Dance by Jenny Lind
 Hugh J. Baker, Sr. and Hugh
 J. Baker, Jr. Memorial ($25)

PASTEL OR DRAWING
Vintage Past by Evelyn McConnell
Mr. and Mrs. Carl M. Sauer ($50)

JURY PRIZE OF DISTINCTION
Tools of Yesteryear by David E. Kinney
Mr. and Mrs. John Burkhart ($200)
New Tenants by David E. Kinney
Psi Iota Xi Sorority ($150)
Gothic Sentinels by J. Huston Bain
Frank Wiedemann, M. D. Memorial
by Mrs. Frank E. Wiedemann ($50)
A Block of the 1800's by Harry A. Davis
Kappa Kappa Kappa Sorority ($125)
Stars and Stripes Forever by Robert E. Weaver
Indiana Federation of Art Clubs ($100)

JURY PRIZE OF DISTINCTION, TRADITIONAL
Yesterday by Frank Vietor
Art Department, Woman's
Department Club ($100)
Tall Tales by Patricia Hawkins
Mr. and Mrs. E. Kirk
McKinney Memorial ($75)
McNarney's by William Parker Stouffer
Woman's Department Club ($100)

Two Odd Buoys by Joel W. Reichard
Mr. & Mrs. Bayham Memorial
by William A. Eyden ($100)
Gingerbread and Weeds by Douglas Henry
Lucille Weller Eyden Memorial
by William A. Eyden ($100)

HONORABLE MENTION
Terre Haute Scene by Peter Bruning
Back Street in Avallon by Carol Elrod
Portrait in Organic Shapes
by Richard R. Patterson
Waiting for the Tide by Thomas Thiery
Medals given by Mr. and Mrs. L. G. Balfour

1974

OUTSTANDING WORK, ANY MEDIUM,
OF THE EXHIBITION
Princeton, Gibson County Seat by Harry A. Davis
William H. Block Company ($500)

OUTSTANDING PAINTING, ANY MEDIUM
Indiana National by Edmund Brucker
Beryl Showers Holland Memorial
by Tri Kappa Sorority ($400)

PORTRAIT OR FIGURE COMPOSITION
Masque by Lois Davis
Mark C. Honeywell Memorial ($150)
Girl Gazing by Marie Miles
Mark C. Honeywell Memorial ($100)

LANDSCAPE IN OIL
Indiana Limestone by Eleanor Lewis
Daughters of Indiana of Chicago ($150)

LANDSCAPE COMPOSITION, ANY MEDIUM
October 1950 by Frank Vietor
Mrs. Herman C. Krannert ($150)
Spring by Sister Rita Ann Roethele
Indiana Federation of Clubs ($50)

REALISTIC OR IMPRESSIONISTIC
LANDSCAPE, ANY MEDIUM
You Can't Go Back by Rob O'Dell
Judge & Mrs. Hutchinson Memorial
by Mrs. Florence Lonsford ($100)

STILL LIFE OR FLOWERS, ANY MEDIUM
Glass by Ann Scott
Art Department, Woman's
Department Club ($100)

PRINT
Dispossessed by Dorothy J. Adams
Hugh J. Baker, Sr. and Hugh
J. Baker, Jr. Memorial ($75)
Erie Station by Connie Bishop
Hugh J. Baker, Sr. and Hugh
J. Baker, Jr. Memorial ($25)

PASTEL OR DRAWING
Floral Elegance by Leah Traugott
Mr. and Mrs. Carl M. Sauer ($50)

JURY PRIZE OF DISTINCTION
Behind Is Yesterday by Peggy Brown
Albert E. Uhl Memorial
by Mrs. Albert E. Uhl ($100)
Hoosier Classified by James McBride
Mrs. John Burkhart ($200)
Still Life by Rosemary Browne Beck
Frank Wiedemann, M. D. Memorial
by Mrs. Frank E. Wiedemann ($50)
*Dry Creekbed, Little Raccoon Creek,
Parke County, Indiana* by Fred H. Montague, Jr.
Psi Iota Xi Sorority ($150)
Wooded Terrain by Evelyn McConnell
Kappa Kappa Kappa Sorority ($125)
Shale by Nanci Blair Closson
Indiana Federation of Art Clubs ($100)
Great Wall by Robert E. Weaver
Ralph N. Tirey Memorial
by Mrs. Ralph N. Tirey ($100)

JURY PRIZE OF DISTINCTION, TRADITIONAL
The Ol' Watertower: Chicago by Thomas J. Cushing
Woman's Department Club,
Indianapolis ($100)
Root of Life by Michiko Boorman
American Association of University
Women, Franklin Branch ($25)
Study of the Cottonwood by Louise Johnson
Mr. and Mrs. Bayham Memorial
by William A. Eyden ($100)
Gail Plus Two by Steve Polomchak
Lucille Weller Eyden Memorial
by William A. Eyden ($100)

EXHIBITION RECORDS

HONORABLE MENTION
Silver Grasshopper by Beth Carrel
Hide-away by Helen C. Craig
Through the Looking Glass by Nanci Blair Closson
Fading Era by Ken Whipple

1975

OUTSTANDING WORK, ANY MEDIUM,
OF THE EXHIBITION
Neighbors by Lois Davis
William H. Block Company ($500)

OUTSTANDING PAINTING, ANY MEDIUM
No Swimming Allowed by Allen Hackney
Beryl Showers Holland Memorial
by Tri Kappa Sorority ($400)

LANDSCAPE IN OIL
Nostalgia by Frank Vietor
Daughters of Indiana of Chicago ($150)

LANDSCAPE COMPOSITION, ANY MEDIUM
Kids Play by Douglas Henry
Indiana Federation of Clubs ($50)

REALISTIC OR IMPRESSIONISTIC
LANDSCAPE, ANY MEDIUM
A Segment of New Harmony by Harry Davis
Judge & Mrs. Hutchinson Memorial
by Mrs. Florence Lonsford ($100)

STILL LIFE OR FLOWERS,
TRADITIONAL, ANY MEDIUM
Bearded Iris by Leah S. Traugott
Art Department, Woman's
Department Club ($100)

PRINT
Snow Birds by Anne Hoffman Cleaver
Hugh J. Baker, Sr. and Hugh
J. Baker, Jr. Memorial ($75)
Bull Shoals by Betty Muhl
Hugh J. Baker, Sr. and Hugh
J. Baker, Jr. Memorial ($25)

JURY PRIZE OF DISTINCTION
Portholes by Nanci Blair Closson
Mrs. Ardath Burkhart ($200)
Hedgerow by Louise B. Hansen
Frank Wiedemann, M. D. Memorial
by Mrs. Frank E. Wiedemann ($50)
Railway Pylon by Max Howard
Psi Iota Xi Sorority ($150)
Only the Wind by Rod Peabody
Kappa Kappa Kappa Sorority ($125)
Cross Section: Retina with Optic Nerve
by Bruce Bobick
Mr. and Mrs. R. O. Clutter ($150)
Super Stripe by Ann Leech
Ralph N. Tirey Memorial
by Mrs. Ralph N. Tirey ($100)
Sunlit by Pamela Lang Redick
Mr. and Mrs. Carl M. Sauer ($50)

JURY PRIZE OF DISTINCTION, TRADITIONAL
Last Testament by Donald Lee Hadley
Woman's Department Club ($100)
Night Session by J. Huston Bain
Indiana Federation of Art Clubs ($100)
Neighbor by Marie Goth
Mr. and Mrs. Bayham Memorial
by William A. Eyden ($100)
Remembrance Imagery by James McBride
Lucille Weller Eyden Memorial
by William A. Eyden ($100)

HONORABLE MENTION
Lion in the Rocks by Robert E. Weaver
Petunias in a Rose Room by Anna Jones
April by Peter Bruning
L. G. Balfour Memorial

1976

OUTSTANDING WORK, ANY MEDIUM,
OF THE EXHIBITION
Esse Warehouse by Harry A. Davis
William H. Block Company ($500)

OUTSTANDING PAINTING, ANY MEDIUM
Afternoon Shadows by James McBride
Beryl Showers Holland Memorial
by Tri Kappa Sorority ($400)

PORTRAIT OR FIGURE
Dyan by Mike J. Desatnick
Hugh J. Baker, Sr. and Hugh J.
Baker, Jr. Memorial ($100)
Little Girl by Füsun Gülen
American Association of
University Women, Franklin Branch ($25)

LANDSCAPE IN OIL
Roof Tops by Francis Clark Brown
Daughters of Indiana of Chicago ($150)

REALISTIC OR IMPRESSIONISTIC
LANDSCAPE, ANY MEDIUM
Lunar Landscape by Kathleen Graham
Judge and Mrs. Frank E. Hutchinson Memorial
by Mrs. Florence Lonsford ($100)

LANDSCAPE COMPOSITION, ANY MEDIUM
Interstate Construction Downtown
by E. Roger Frey
Indiana Federation of Clubs ($50)

STILL LIFE OR FLOWERS,
TRADITIONAL, ANY MEDIUM
Homage to Heroes of Two Centuries
by Anna M. Jones
Art Department, Woman's
Department Club ($100)

PRINT
Red, White & Blue #2 by Dorothy J. Adams
Mr. and Mrs. Robert Fair ($100)

JURY PRIZE OF DISTINCTION
Sand Creek Church: Freedom,
Friendship and Charity by Tom Greene
 Mrs. Ardath Burkhart ($200)
The Personality Plant by Jean F. Vietor
 Frank Wiedemann, M.D. Memorial
 by Mrs. Frank E. Wiedemann ($50)
Squander by Shelia K. Burchett
 Psi Iota Xi Sorority ($150)
Floral Composition by Marilou Crisman
 Kappa Kappa Kappa Sorority ($100)
Morning Comes Softly by Ruth Anderson
 Mr. and Mrs. R. O. Clutter ($150)
Anasazi Structures by Martha Slaymaker
 Mr. and Mrs. Carl M. Sauer ($50)
Fish Kite by Doug Henry
 Mrs. Victor Hackney Memorial ($200)
Decaying Grid by Tom Platt
 Anonymous ($100)

JURY PRIZE OF DISTINCTION, TRADITIONAL
NC-101 by Steve Polomchak
 Woman's Department Club ($100)
Abel's Showroom by Harry A. Davis
 Indiana Federation of Art Clubs ($100)
Class of '49 by Frank Vietor
 Mr. and Mrs. Bayham Memorial
 by William A. Eyden ($100)
Between Six by Mark Polomchak
 Lucille Weller Eyden Memorial
 by William A. Eyden ($100)

JURY PRIZE OF DISTINCTION, SCULPTURE
Coach by Thomas M. Bryce
 Mrs. Victor Hackney Memorial ($100)

JURY PRIZE OF DISTINCTION,
CONTEMPORARY
Pillows by Nanci Blair Closson
 Mr. & Mrs. Donald Holmquist ($100)

HONORABLE MENTION
On Ice by Margery M. Gates
Colors on Parade by Joan Rudman
 L. G. Balfour Memorial

1977

OUTSTANDING WORK, ANY MEDIUM,
OF THE EXHIBITION
Out of Element by Nanci Blair Closson
 William H. Block Company ($500)

OUTSTANDING PAINTING, ANY MEDIUM
Derelict by Floyd Hopper
 Beryl Showers Holland Memorial
 by Tri Kappa Sorority ($400)

JURY PRIZE OF DISTINCTION, SCULPTURE
Portrait of Andrea by Marjory Wood
 Mrs. Ardath Burkhart ($200)

PORTRAIT, ANY MEDIUM
Dinky Dawn by Phyllis Wicker
 Bertha Crosley Ball Memorial
 by Mrs. Edmund F. Ball ($100)

FIGURE, ANY MEDIUM
Elf in the Garden by Ann Kane
 Hugh J. Baker, Sr. and Hugh
 J. Baker, Jr. Memorial ($100)

LANDSCAPE IN OIL OR ACRYLIC
Barner House, Circa 1860 by Mildred Niesse
 Daughters of Indiana of Chicago ($150)

REALISTIC OR IMPRESSIONISTIC
LANDSCAPE, ANY MEDIUM
Another Time, Another Place by Peggy Brown
 Judge and Mrs. Frank E.
 Hutchinson Memorial by
 Mrs. Florence Lonsford ($100)

STILL LIFE OR FLOWERS,
TRADITIONAL, ANY MEDIUM
Fence Row by Louise Hansen
 Art Department, Woman's
 Department Club ($100)

WATERCOLOR
Fresh Snow by Warren Sprunger
 Hoosier Salon Patrons
 Association, Bloomington ($50)
Victorian Primitive by Wilbur Meese
 American Association of
 University Women, Franklin Branch ($25)

JURY PRIZE OF DISTINCTION
Between the Sky and I by Val Walters
 Psi Iota Xi Sorority ($150)
Matter of Life and Death by Eleanor Lewis
 Frank Wiedemann, M. D. Memorial
 by Mrs. Frank E. Wiedemann ($50)
Forked Trunk by Rob O'Dell
 Mr. and Mrs. Harry Riser ($125)
Butte Perspective by Nanci Blair Closson
 Tri Kappa Sorority ($100)
Figure #1 by John Habela
 Reid Winsey Memorial
 by Mrs. Lawson Clark ($50)
Sanctuary by Harry A. Davis
 Mr. and Mrs. R. O. Clutter ($150)
Innocence by Mike Hamman
 Mr. and Mrs. Donald Holmquist ($100)

JURY PRIZE OF DISTINCTION, TRADITIONAL
Laced Curtains by Crawford Donnelly
 Indiana Federation of Art Clubs ($100)
Twilight by Allen Hackney
 Woman's Department Club ($100)
Three Blue Ducks by James C. Lentz
 Mr. and Mrs. Bayham Memorial
 by William A. Eyden ($100)
Summertime by Frederick W. Rigley
 Lucille Weller Eyden Memorial
 by William A. Eyden ($100)

JURY PRIZE OF DISTINCTION, PRINT
Merrymobile Route by Roger Sills
Mr. and Mrs. Robert Fair ($100)

1978

BEST OF SHOW, OUTSTANDING
WORK, ANY MEDIUM
Double O-7 by Robert E. Weaver
L. S. Ayres & Company ($1,000)
Still Waters Run by Peggy Brown
Anonymous ($1,000)
Into the Valley by Grant Christian
Anonymous ($1,000)

OUTSTANDING PAINTING, ANY MEDIUM
Bastet by Nancy Hancock Cummins
Beryl Showers Holland Memorial
by Tri Kappa Sorority ($400)

WORK OF SCULPTURE
Oolite II by David L. Rodgers
Mr. and Mrs. Hugh Baker, Sr. and
Hugh Baker, Jr. Memorial ($100)

CONTEMPORARY WORK, ANY MEDIUM
Idle Blue by J. Huston Bain
Mary B. Nichols Memorial by
Mr. & Mrs. Gordon G. Hughes ($50)

LANDSCAPE IN OIL OR ACRYLIC
October Evening, 1952 by Frank Vietor
Daughters of Indiana of Chicago ($150)

REALISTIC OR IMPRESSIONISTIC
LANDSCAPE, ANY MEDIUM
Quiet Snow by Wilbur Meese
Judge and Mrs. Frank E.
Hutchinson Memorial by
Mrs. Florence Lonsford ($100)

STILL LIFE OR FLOWERS,
TRADITIONAL, ANY MEDIUM
Fall Elegance by Leah S. Traugott
Art Department, Woman's
Department Club ($100)

WATERCOLOR
Winter Trees by Stan Obermueller
Johnnie Rutland Smith Memorial
by Hoosier Salon Patrons
Association, Bloomington ($75)
75 Gourds by Joyce Stouder
American Association of University
Women, Franklin Branch ($25)

JURY PRIZE OF DISTINCTION
De-Tourism by Nanci Blair Closson
Indianapolis Power and Light Company ($500)
Arctic Fox and Brant by William Zimmerman
Mr. and Mrs. Harry Riser ($500)
Pastel Desert by Jean Unversaw
Beatrice P. Morell Memorial by Robert,
Stephen and William Morell, Jr. ($300)
The City Market and Arena by Harry A. Davis

Mr. and Mrs. Robert Batton ($150)
Off Palmetto Dunes by Andrea Koch
Mr. and Mrs. R. O. Clutter ($150)
John by Helen Craig
Psi Iota Xi Sorority ($150)
Still Life by Rosemary Browne Beck
Mr. and Mrs. Harrison Eiteljorg ($100)
Old Homestead by Michael Martin
Senator and Mrs. Robert J. Fair ($100)
On a Clear Day by Elton G. Krafft
Stella L. Hackney Memorial
by Dr. Victor C. Hackney ($100)
Rockport Quarry by Edmund Brucker
Mr. and Mrs. Donald Holmquist ($100)
Arizona Night I by Marilyn Feighner
Indiana National Bank ($100)
Nelly Has Crash-Landed! by Max Howard
Tri Kappa Sorority ($100)
Delores Horns by Charles Spear
Merchants National Bank ($100)
Cedar Sun 106 Years Old by Denice Goldschmidt
National Bank of Greenwood ($100)
4 p. m., January 26 by Thomas Thiery
Johnnie R. Smith Memorial by
Friends of Johnnie Smith ($100)
History by Douglas Henry
Frank Wiedemann, M. D. Memorial
by Mrs. Frank E. Wiedemann ($100)
Puffballs by Allen Hackney
Snodgrass Studios ($100 in framing)
Flower Out of Wilderness by Lee Coblentz
Indianapolis Water Company ($75)
Grandpa's Tractor by Warren Sprunger
Indiana Federation of Clubs ($50)
Cathedral at Taxco by Floyd D. Hopper
Mrs. Arthur Overbay Memorial by
Mr. & Mrs. Leonard Sullivan ($25)

JURY PRIZE OF DISTINCTION, TRADITIONAL
Indiana Barns XI by James Patterson
Mr. and Mrs. Bayham Memorial
by William A. Eyden ($100)
Telling of Raw Eyes and Bloody Bones
by Shelby Harding
Lucille Weller Eyden Memorial
by William A. Eyden ($100)
Sunset at Udaypur by Daksha J. Patel
Indiana Federation of Art Clubs ($50)

BEST WORK REPRESENTING A SIMPLE
STATEMENT TAKEN DIRECTLY FROM NATURE
The Porch in Winter Sunlight
by Stephen Charles DeSanto
Dixie Ben-Nett ($25)

BEST WORK, ANY MEDIUM, TO
FIRST TIME EXHIBITING ARTIST
Halifax, Nova Scotia by Bob Griffitt
Hoosier Salon Guild ($250)

1979

BEST OF SHOW, OUTSTANDING
WORK, ANY MEDIUM
Model for Large Sculpture by Jan R. Martin
L. S. Ayres & Company ($1,000)
Partytime by Nancy Hancock Cummins
Anonymous ($1,000)
Earth, Sky, Water by Nanci Blair Closson
Ardath Y. Burkhart ($1,000)
The Circle Theatre by Harry A. Davis
Anonymous ($1,000)
Wheel & Disk by Max Howard
Mr. and Mrs. John A. Hillenbrand II ($1,000)

OUTSTANDING PAINTING, ANY MEDIUM
Resting in Oakland by William Borden
Beryl Showers Holland Memorial
by Tri Kappa Sorority ($400)

TRADITIONAL PAINTING, ANY MEDIUM
A Summer Afternoon by Crawford Donnelly
Woman's Department Club ($100)

WORK OF SCULPTURE
X-Ray Fish Form by Charles R. Schiefer
Hoosier Salon Guild ($300)
The Relationship by Helen Caldwell
Hugh J. Baker, Sr. and Hugh
J. Baker, Jr. Memorial ($100)

LANDSCAPE IN OIL OR ACRYLIC
Martinsville & Franklin R. R. by Frank Vietor
Daughters of Indiana of Chicago ($250)

REALISTIC OR IMPRESSIONISTIC
LANDSCAPE, ANY MEDIUM
Under the El by William A. Eyden
Judge and Mrs. Frank E.
Hutchinson Memorial by
Mrs. Florence Lonsford ($100)

STILL LIFE OR FLOWERS,
TRADITIONAL, ANY MEDIUM
Still Life (Green & White)
by Rosemary Browne Beck
Art Department, Woman's
Department Club ($100)

STILL LIFE OF FLOWERS
Oriental Roses by Kerry Holsapple
Bernardine Grow Memorial
by Lottie Grow ($100)

DRAWING IN BLACK AND WHITE
Punkin by Michael Martin
Anonymous ($100)

JURY PRIZE OF DISTINCTION
As Cold As Ice by Peggy Brown
Mr. and Mrs. Harry Riser ($500)
Barriers to Understanding by Kathleen Graham
Mr. and Mrs. Harrison Eiteljorg ($200)
Saturday Night Fisherman by Shelby Harding
Franklin College ($200)
High Society by Diana Sowder

Mr. and Mrs. Robert Batton ($150)
Untitled by Stephen Paul Wheat
Mr. and Mrs. R. O. Clutter ($150)
Grandmother Melville's Quilt,
Made for Young Herman by Bruce Bobick
Psi Iota Xi Sorority ($150)
Looking East, Nova Scotia by Bob Griffitt
American Association of University
Women, Franklin; Dixie Ben-Nett,
Indiana Federation of Art Clubs, and
Indiana Federation of Clubs ($150)
Melting Snow by Theodore Fox
Mrs. E. B. Ball Memorial
by Mrs. E. F. Ball ($100)
Vanity Fair by James Curtain Lentz
Mr. and Mrs. Robert Fair ($100)
Untitled by Peggy Lovett
Gene B. Glick Company ($100)
Sacrament of Sea & Sun by Lee Coblentz
Stella L. Hackney Memorial by
Victor and Jerry Hackney ($100)
Southern Comfort by Joel W. Reichard
In honor of Mrs. H. L. Smith
by Anonymous ($100)
The Uprighting by Myron Finchum
Indianapolis Newspapers, Inc. ($100)
Turn On by Michael J. Moore
Indianapolis Water Company ($100)
Grandma Flo's Private Gallery
by Florence Z. Jagger
Tri Kappa Sorority ($100)

A-6 by Betty Muhl
National Bank of Greenwood ($100)
Leaf Patterns by Joe Traugott
Kay Haines Memorial by Mrs. Elba
Branigan and Ardath Burkhart ($100)

JURY PRIZE OF DISTINCTION, TRADITIONAL
One Way by Raymond Melevage
Mr. and Mrs. Bayham Memorial
by William A. Eyden ($100)
C'ulture? by Arthur F. Lindberg
Lucille Weller Eyden Memorial
by William A. Eyden ($100)

BEST WORK, ANY MEDIUM, TO
FIRST TIME EXHIBITING ARTIST
Closet Clutter by Bryant Whitted
Hoosier Salon Guild ($200)

1980

OUTSTANDING WORK, ANY MEDIUM
The Beauchamp Complex by Harry Davis
L. S. Ayres & Company ($1,000)
The Flowering by Will Lamm
Ardath Y. Burkhart ($1,000)
Portrait of David Rubins by William Ashby
Mrs. William Cooling ($1,000)
Reflection Principle by N. Blair Closson
Ruth Lilly VanRiper ($1,000)

OUTSTANDING PAINTING, ANY MEDIUM
For Evermore by Peggy Brown
Beryl Showers Holland Memorial
by Tri Kappa Sorority ($500)

TRADITIONAL PAINTING, ANY MEDIUM
Tranquil Solitude by W. Ray Stevens
Woman's Department Club ($100)

WORK OF SCULPTURE
The Bride by Harold Langland
Anonymous ($500)
Metamorphosis by Bruce Reines
Hoosier Salon Guild ($300)
Sundial by Richard Lemberg
Merrill S. Davis, M. D. Memorial
by Dr. Joseph B. Davis and
Mrs. Merrill S. Davis ($250)

LANDSCAPE IN OIL OR ACRYLIC
The Swing by Stephen C. DeSanto
Daughters of Indiana of Chicago ($250)

REALISTIC OR IMPRESSIONISTIC
LANDSCAPE, ANY MEDIUM
Overflow of Riverbank by Theodore Fox
Judge and Mrs. Frank E.
Hutchinson Memorial by
Mrs. Florence Lonsford ($100)

STILL LIFE OR FLOWERS,
TRADITIONAL, ANY MEDIUM
Going Hunting by Barbara Beck
Art Department, Woman's
Department Club ($100)

STILL LIFE OF FLOWERS
823 by Michael D. Macomber
Bernardine Grow Memorial
by Lottie Grow ($100)

JURY PRIZE OF DISTINCTION
Portrait of Cynthia by Alan Larkin
Mr. and Mrs. Thomas Husselman,
Mr. and Mrs. R. O. Clutter ($600)
City in Winter by Floyd Hopper
Mr. and Mrs. Harry Riser ($500)
Sleeping Lion by Robert E. Weaver
Mr. and Mrs. Fred Adams ($400)
The Pink Boa by Nancy Hancock Cummins
Mr. and Mrs. Joseph Cain ($200)
Waiting by Jeanne McLeish
American Association of University
Women, Franklin; Indiana
Federation of Clubs; Tri Kappa,
Epsilon Sigma Chapter ($175)
Indiana Barns XVI by James Patterson
Franklin College ($150)
Louie's Bar by John T. Hodgin
Psi Iota Xi Sorority ($150)
Reverie by Marlene Coble
Bertha Crosley Ball Memorial by
Mr. & Mrs. Edmund F. Ball ($100)

Patches by Rob O'Dell
Indianapolis Newspapers, Inc. ($100)
The Cauliflower by Barb Jones
Indianapolis Water Company ($100)
Glass Fusion by Myron Finchum
Indiana Federation of Art Clubs ($100)
Susan at Thirteen by Ruth A. Baker
National Bank of Greenwood ($100)
Spring by Robert Matthews
F. C. Tucker Company, Inc. ($100)

JURY PRIZE OF DISTINCTION, TRADITIONAL
Farm Boy by Michael Martin
Mr. and Mrs. Bayham Memorial
by William A. Eyden ($100)
Pat by Rosemary Browne Beck
Lucille Weller Eyden Memorial
by William A. Eyden ($100)

BEST WORK, ANY MEDIUM,
TO FIRST TIME EXHIBITING ARTIST
Old Shoe and Lace Hanky Landscape
by Hilary Jackson Edwards
Hoosier Salon Guild ($200)

1981

BEST OF SHOW
Forgotten Wheels by Rich Ernsting
Mr. & Mrs. William Cooling ($1,500)

OUTSTANDING WORK, ANY MEDIUM
White Sails by Nanci Blair Closson
Ardath Y. Burkhart ($1,200)
Uncle Stan by Ellie Siskind
L. S. Ayres & Company ($1,000)
Night Launch by James Cunningham
Ruth Lilly VanRiper ($500)

OUTSTANDING PAINTING, ANY MEDIUM
A Segment of the Old Northside by Harry Davis
Beryl Showers Holland Memorial
by Tri Kappa Sorority ($500)

TRADITIONAL PAINTING, ANY MEDIUM
Goblet Makes Nine by Rosemary Browne Beck
Woman's Department Club ($100)

WORK OF SCULPTURE
Crystal by Ingrid Toebes
Hoosier Salon Guild ($300)
Facade by James Miller
Merrill S. Davis, M. D. Memorial
by Dr. Joseph B. Davis and
Mrs. Merrill S. Davis ($100)
Third Class Carriage by Joe Rohrman
Mrs. Robert D. Orr ($100)

NON-REPRESENTATIONAL WORK
Frozen Hues by Myron Finchum
Winthrop Art Place ($100)

LANDSCAPE IN OIL OR ACRYLIC
Fantasia by Elton Krafft
Daughters of Indiana of Chicago ($250)

REALISTIC OR IMPRESSIONISTIC LANDSCAPE, ANY MEDIUM

The Banks of White River by Mark Stevenson
Judge and Mrs. Frank E.
Hutchinson Memorial by
Mrs. Florence Lonsford ($100)

STILL LIFE OR FLOWERS, TRADITIONAL, ANY MEDIUM

Let's Have Cake by Anne Horwedel
Art Department, Woman's
Department Club ($100)

STILL LIFE OF FLOWERS

Backyard Bouquet by Thomas J. Cushing
Bernardine Grow Memorial
by Lottie Grow ($100)

JURY PRIZE OF DISTINCTION

Calliope by Robert Weaver
Mr. and Mrs. Harry Riser ($500)
Look Inside My Fantasy by Peggy Brown
Mr. and Mrs. Fred Adams ($400)
Special Times by Rob O'Dell
Mr. & Mrs. Thomas Husselman
and Mr. & Mrs. R. O. Clutter ($300)
Square Times 5 by John DeCosta
Mr. and Mrs. Joseph Cain ($200)
Early Portrait by Cecil Head
Dr. and Mrs. Arthur C. Jay ($200)
Miss Herron by Kerry Holsapple
Psi Iota Xi Sorority ($150)
Sequel by Phyllis Wicker
Indianapolis Newspapers, Inc. ($100)
The Underpass by Floyd D. Hopper
National Bank of Greenwood ($100)
Antique Car by Karen Shand
Indiana Federation of Art Clubs ($100)
The Promise by Donald Hadley
Mrs. Wilbur E. Ford ($100)
Entwined by Hilary Jackson Edwards
Bertha Crosley Ball Memorial by
Mr & Mrs. Edmund F. Ball ($100)
Carlos by Lester Swartz
Tri Kappa, Epsilon Sigma;
American Association of
University Women, Franklin ($75)

JURY PRIZE OF DISTINCTION, TRADITIONAL

Abandoned Forms by Max Howard
Mr. and Mrs. Bayham Memorial
by William A. Eyden ($100)
Green Primitive Farm by Wilbur Meese
Lucille Weller Eyden Memorial
by William A. Eyden ($100)

BEST WORK, ANY MEDIUM, TO FIRST TIME EXHIBITING ARTIST

Landscape with Arclight by Archie Williamson
Hoosier Salon Guild ($200)

1982

BEST OF SHOW

Matriarch by Edmund Brucker
Mr. & Mrs. William Cooling ($1,500)

OUTSTANDING WORK, ANY MEDIUM

Once, My Own by Donald Lee Hadley
Mrs. Ardath Y. Burkhart ($1,200)
A Monument in Crawfordsville by Harry Davis
L. S. Ayres & Company ($1,000)
Wicker 'n Baskets by Willa Howell Bullock
Mrs. Ruth Lilly ($1,000)

TRADITIONAL PAINTING, ANY MEDIUM

The Quiet Room by Gladys Rae Flynn
Beryl Showers Holland Memorial
by Tri Kappa Sorority ($500)
Sisters by the Window by Nancy Noël
Woman's Department Club ($100)

WORK OF SCULPTURE

Bernadine Oliphint, Soprano by Harold Langland
Hoosier Salon Guild ($300)
Mine Shaft by Michael Michele
Gertrude J. Connor Memorial
by Philippa C. Hughes ($100)
Fish by Helen Caldwell
Merrill S. Davis, M. D. Memorial
by Dr. Joseph B. Davis and
Mrs. Merrill S. Davis ($100)

NON-REPRESENTATIONAL WORK

Desert Return by James L. Cunningham
Winthrop Place of Art ($100)

LANDSCAPE IN OIL OR ACRYLIC

Muscatatuck River III by Thelma Confer
Daughters of Indiana of Chicago ($250)

REALISTIC OR IMPRESSIONISTIC LANDSCAPE, ANY MEDIUM

Let It Snow by Mark Polomchak
Judge and Mrs. Frank E.
Hutchinson Memorial by
Mrs. Florence Lonsford ($100)

STILL LIFE OR FLOWERS, TRADITIONAL, ANY MEDIUM

Clematis by Mary Eggert
Art Department, Woman's
Department Club ($100)

FLORAL PAINTING

From My Neighbor's Garden by Crawford Donnelly
Lottie Grow Memorial by Friends
Through Hoosier Salon ($100)

JURY PRIZE OF DISTINCTION

Rose Cascade #2 by Sylvia Worman
Mr. and Mrs. Harry E. Riser ($500)
Hoosier Farmer: The Man and His Creation
by Roslynn Webb Cady
Mr. & Mrs. Thomas Husselman and
Mr. & Mrs. R. O. Clutter ($300)

Susan in Light by Ruth A. Baker
  Dr. and Mrs. Arthur C. Jay ($200)
Navajo Trace #1 by Bill Grams
  Mr. and Mrs. Fred Adams ($200)
Meeting Adjourned by James Curtin Lentz
  Tri Kappa Sorority, Epsilon Sigma and
  Alpha Iota Chapters; American
  Association of University Women,
  Franklin; Mr. & Mrs. Robert Fair ($200)
Tree View by Steve Polomchak
  Psi Iota Xi Sorority ($150)
Gooslings by Karen Shand
  Indianapolis Newspapers, Inc. ($100)
Chantilly Lace by Stephen P. Wheat
  National Bank of Greenwood ($100)
Ocean City Urn by Stephen DeSanto
  Indiana Federation of Art Clubs ($100)
First Santa Cruz Escape by Jan Tenenbaum
  Mrs. Wilbur E. Ford ($100)
The Leo Northrop by William P. Stouffer
  Mr. and Mrs. Bayham Memorial
  by William A. Eyden ($100)
Blue Victorian by Wilbur Meese
  Lucille Weller Eyden Memorial
  by William A. Eyden ($100)

BEST WORK, ANY MEDIUM,
TO FIRST TIME EXHIBITING ARTIST
  First Crush by Verdale Forget
  Hoosier Salon Guild ($200)

1983

BEST OF SHOW
  Arum Ascent by James Cunningham
  Mr. & Mrs. William Cooling ($1,500)

OUTSTANDING WORK, ANY MEDIUM
  Portrait of Robert Frist by William G. Ashby
  Mrs. Ardath Y. Burkhart ($1,200)
  A Segment of Canal Street by Harry Davis
  L. S. Ayres & Company ($1,000)
  Where the Wheel Stopped by Max Howard
  Mrs. Ruth Lilly ($500)

TRADITIONAL PAINTING, ANY MEDIUM
  Over the Hill by Margaret Kessler
  Beryl Showers Holland Memorial
  by Tri Kappa Sorority ($1,000)
  Boxed Forms by Kathryn Jarrett
  Woman's Department Club ($100)

WORK OF SCULPTURE
  Static Blue by Gary E. Voreis
  Mr. and Mrs. Harry E. Riser ($500)
  The Exotic Family by Michael Michele
  Hoosier Salon Guild ($300)

NON-REPRESENTATIONAL WORK
  Skirting the Issue by Nanci Blair Closson
  Winthrop Place of Art ($100)

LANDSCAPE IN OIL OR ACRYLIC
  Garden at No. 22 by Hilary Jackson Edwards
  Daughters of Indiana ($250)

REALISTIC OR IMPRESSIONISTIC
LANDSCAPE, ANY MEDIUM
  The Elevator by Joe Mayberry
  Judge and Mrs. Frank E.
  Hutchinson Memorial by
  Mrs. Florence Lonsford ($100)

STILL LIFE OR FLOWERS,
TRADITIONAL, ANY MEDIUM
  Eggs by Rosemary Browne Beck
  Art Department, Woman's
  Department Club ($100)

FLORAL PAINTING
  Ginger Peachy by Patsy Surh O'Connell
  Lottie Grow Memorial by Friends
  Through Hoosier Salon ($100)

WATERCOLOR
  Le Grande Tractor by Dean Davis
  Dr. and Mrs. Hanus J. Grosz ($200)

WORK IN PENCIL
  Another View by Michael Martin
  Robert VanSickle Memorial by
  Hoosier Salon Friends ($200)

JURY PRIZE OF DISTINCTION
  Wings of Fire (Flight of Fantasy)
  by Myron Finchum
    Mr. & Mrs. Thomas E. Husselman
    and Mr. & Mrs. R. O. Clutter ($300)
  Entry Way by Floyd D. Hopper
    Mr. and Mrs. Edmund F. Ball ($250)
  Did I Tell You That My Chicken Is Dead?
  by Michael Martin
    Psi Iota Xi Sorority ($250)
  Honey Wagon by Barbara Jones
    Indiana National Bank ($250)
  Self Portrait with Straw Hat by Peggy McCarty
    Dr. and Mrs. Arthur C. Jay ($200)
  Winter Escape by Barbara Meeker
    Mr. and Mrs. Robert Fair ($200)
  Torso by Gregory Ziesemer
    Indianapolis Water Company ($100)
  Toy Kisses/Sweet Sorrows by Kate Cunningham
    Indianapolis Newspapers, Inc. ($100)
  Vegetable Stand by Judy Olive
    National Bank of Greenwood ($100)
  Which Way to Morgantown?
  by Raymond V. Cradick
    Mrs. Robert D. Orr ($100)
  Master Design for Indianapolis by Jan Boyer
    Indiana Federation of Art Clubs ($100)
  The Children's Nation, Will It Remain Indian?
  by David Labrum
    Mr. and Mrs. Wilbur Ford ($100)

BEST WORK, ANY MEDIUM,
TO FIRST TIME EXHIBITING ARTIST
1723 N. Penn by Douglas Daniel
Hoosier Salon Guild ($200)

1984

BEST OF SHOW
Gate to the Unknown by Füsun Gülen
Mr. & Mrs. William Cooling ($1,500)

OUTSTANDING WORK, ANY MEDIUM
Attic Reverie by Catherine Mills Royer
L. S. Ayres & Company ($1,000)
To A Joker by Sharon J. Montgomery
Mrs. Ruth Lilly ($500)

TRADITIONAL PAINTING, ANY MEDIUM
Study of Oriental Porcelain and Lemons
by Frederik Ebbesen Grue
Beryl Showers Holland Memorial
by Tri Kappa Sorority ($1,000)
Priorities by Lorna R. Swartz
Woman's Department Club ($100)

WORK IN OIL
My Mother by Edmund Brucker
Ardath Y. Burkhart Memorial by
Robert and the late Emily Fair ($200)

WORK OF SCULPTURE
African Woman by Harold Langland
In honor of Robert & Sandra Borns
by Mr. & Mrs. Sidney Mishkin ($350)

JURY PRIZE OF DISTINCTION, SCULPTURE
Young Acrobat by Alison R. Adams
Bertha Crosley Ball Memorial by
Mr. & Mrs. Edmund F. Ball ($250)

NON-REPRESENTATIONAL WORK
Different Places/One by Peggy Brown
Winthrop Place of Art ($100)

LANDSCAPE IN OIL OR ACRYLIC
Thy Kingdom Come by Stephen P. Wheat
Anonymous ($500)
Maine-ly Blue by Jeffrey C. Burris
Daughters of Indiana ($250)

REALISTIC OR IMPRESSIONISTIC
LANDSCAPE, ANY MEDIUM
Twilight by William Hancock
Judge & Mrs. Hutchinson Memorial
by Mrs. Florence Lonsford ($100)

STILL LIFE OR FLOWERS,
TRADITIONAL, ANY MEDIUM
Green Apples Under Glass
by Rosemary Browne Beck
Art Department, Woman's
Department Club ($100)

FLORAL PAINTING
Prelude to Spring by Anna M. Jones
Lottie Grow Memorial by Friends
Through the Hoosier Salon ($100)

WATERCOLOR
The Knightstown Academy by Harry A. Davis
Ardath Y. Burkhart Memorial
by Hoosier Salon Guild ($300)

DRAWING
The Skeleton Who Came to Dinner
by Rick Schroeder
Dr. & Mrs. Hanus J. Grosz ($100)

JURY PRIZE OF DISTINCTION
Spacey Spring by Barbara M. Meeker
Mr. and Mrs. Harry Riser ($500)
Arum Fire by James L. Cunningham
Mr. and Mrs. R. O. Clutter and
Mr. and Mrs. T. E. Husselman ($300)
Buns Boogying to Beethoven's #1 by Gloria Fischer
Indiana National Bank ($250)
Spanish and Sweet Bermuda by Louise B. Hansen
Psi Iota Xi Sorority ($250)
Torso Twisting by C. R. Schiefer
Mrs. Robert D. Orr ($100)
Indianapolis Futureplex Jan Scott Boyer
Epsilon Sigma Chapter of
Tri Kappa Sorority ($100)
Meridian Street Bridge/Portland, Indiana
by Mark A. Mullen
Indianapolis Water Company ($100)
Still Life by Candi Grandidier
Indiana Federation of Art Clubs ($100)
Saanen Specialty by Chicquiela S. Broyles
National Bank of Greenwood ($100)
Closing Time by George Bredewater
Indianapolis Newspapers, Inc. ($100)
Daybreak at Rocky Point by Ruth Baker
Mr. and Mrs. Wilbur Ford ($100)

BEST WORK, ANY MEDIUM,
TO FIRST TIME EXHIBITING ARTIST
Grandpa's Tractor by J. Anna Roberts
Hoosier Salon Guild ($200)

1985

BEST OF SHOW
Prairie Creek Reservoir by Frederik Ebbesen Grue
Mr. & Mrs. William Cooling ($1,500)

OUTSTANDING WORK, ANY MEDIUM
Shoreline/Winter Skies by James L. Cunningham
L. S. Ayres & Company ($1,000)
Secrets of the Earth by Teri Jonas
Mrs. Ruth Lilly ($500)

TRADITIONAL PAINTING, ANY MEDIUM
Cypress Point by James Curtin Lentz
Beryl Showers Holland Memorial
by Tri Kappa Sorority ($1,000)
Our Daily Bread by Donald Hadley
Woman's Department Club ($100)

WORK OF SCULPTURE
Aurora by Gary Voreis
In honor of Robert & Sandra Borns
by Mr. & Mrs. Sidney Mishkin ($350)

JURY PRIZE OF DISTINCTION, SCULPTURE
Venus Natarani (Dance of Creation)
by Harold Langland
Bertha Crosley Ball Memorial by
Mr. & Mrs. Edmund F. Ball ($300)

NON-REPRESENTATIONAL WORK
Piece by Piece by Sue Freudenberg
Winthrop Place of Art ($100)

LANDSCAPE IN OIL OR ACRYLIC
Vanishing Scene by Frederick Rigley
Anonymous ($700)
Red Winged Blackbirds by Jan Davis
Daughters of Indiana ($250)

REALISTIC OR IMPRESSIONISTIC
LANDSCAPE, ANY MEDIUM
Red Brick by Jerry Smith
Judge & Mrs. Hutchinson Memorial
by Mrs. Florence Lonsford ($100)

STILL LIFE OR FLOWERS,
TRADITIONAL, ANY MEDIUM
Gold Fold by Rosemary Browne Beck
Art Department, Woman's
Department Club ($100)

FLORAL PAINTING
Bouquet Series #385 by Sylvia Worman
Lottie Grow Memorial by
Woman's Department Club ($200)

WATERCOLOR
Silent in the Snow by Stephen Edwards
Hoosier Salon Guild ($200)

DRAWING
Golden Temple, Amritsar, India by K. P. Singh
Dr. & Mrs. Hanus J. Grosz ($100)

JURY PRIZE OF DISTINCTION
The White Iron Gate by Harry A. Davis
Mr. and Mrs. Harry E. Riser ($500)
Flowers in the Old French Inn by Jean Garro
Mr. & Mrs. R. O. Clutter,
Mr. & Mrs. Wilbur Ford, and
Mr. & Mrs. T. E. Husselman ($400)
Chins Up by Henry Bell
Psi Iota Xi Sorority ($250)
Corinthian by Donna Rosser
Indiana National Bank ($250)
The Bronze Scholar by Frederik Ebbesen Grue
Mrs. Robert D. Orr ($100)

MERIT AWARD
Utah Road 128 by Mark Mullen
Indianapolis Newspapers, Inc. ($100)
Indiana Limestone by Jerry Smith
Epsilon Sigma Chapter of
Tri Kappa Sorority ($100)
Blacksmith & Apprentice by Ralph E. Willson
Indianapolis Water Company ($100)
Sentinel by Michael Martin
Indiana Federation of Art Clubs ($100)

BEST WORK, ANY MEDIUM,
TO FIRST TIME EXHIBITING ARTIST
Marble Canyon by Paul Crane
Hoosier Salon Guild ($300)

1986

BEST OF SHOW
Sculptor Hermann Gurfinkel by Eleanor Lewis
Mr. & Mrs. William Cooling ($1,500)

OUTSTANDING WORK, ANY MEDIUM
735 Chartre Street by James Curtin Lentz
L. S. Ayres & Company ($1,000)
Portrait of Ronelle by William G. Ashby
Mrs. Ruth Lilly ($500)

TRADITIONAL PAINTING, ANY MEDIUM
Study of Porcelain and Lemons
by Frederik Ebbesen Grue
Beryl Showers Holland Memorial
by Tri Kappa Sorority ($1,000)
Lynn by Mark Dillman
Woman's Department Club ($100)

WORK OF SCULPTURE
Moon Dial II by Harold D. Langland
In honor of Robert & Sandra Borns
by Mr. & Mrs. Sidney Mishkin ($350)

JURY PRIZE OF DISTINCTION, SCULPTURE
The Law Givers by Charles R. Schiefer
Bertha Crosley Ball Memorial by
Mr. and Mrs. Edmund F. Ball ($300)

NON-REPRESENTATIONAL WORK
Seeing Red by Sylvia Worman
Indianapolis Newspapers, Inc. ($150)

LANDSCAPE IN OIL OR ACRYLIC
Eagle Creek Visitors by Myron Finchum
Anonymous ($700)
Blue Shadows by Thelma Confer
Daughters of Indiana ($250)

REALISTIC OR IMPRESSIONISTIC
LANDSCAPE, ANY MEDIUM
Alone with Two Trees by Donna Rosser
Judge & Mrs. Hutchinson Memorial
by Florence Lonsford ($100)

STILL LIFE OR FLOWERS,
TRADITIONAL, ANY MEDIUM
Walk with the Roses by Donna Rosser
Art Department, Woman's
Department Club ($100)

FLORAL PAINTING
Spring Splendor by Leah S. Traugott
Woman's Department Club ($200)

WATERCOLOR
Blue Steps by Jerry Smith
Hoosier Salon Guild ($350)

DRAWING
Vigo County Court House by John Laska
Dr. & Mrs. Hanus J. Grosz ($100)

JURY PRIZE OF DISTINCTION
Rain by Robert Hoffman
Mr. and Mrs. Harry E. Riser ($500)
The Shrine on the Avenue by Harry A. Davis
Mr. & Mrs. R. O. Clutter,
Mr. & Mrs. Wilbur Ford, and
Mr. & Mrs. T. E. Husselman ($400)
Strange Pursuit by Max Howard
Psi Iota Xi Sorority ($250)
The Lovers of Lauren Macaw by Rich Ernsting
Indiana National Bank ($250)
Sunlight and Leaves by Connie J. Deering
National Bank of Greenwood ($100)
Grandmother's Kitchen by Lynne Gilliatt
Indianapolis Water Company ($100)
Portrait of Sherri by Phillip E. Monteith
Mr. and Mrs. Frank Owings ($100)

MERIT AWARD
Aftermath by Lois Davis
Epsilon Sigma Chapter,
Tri Kappa Sorority ($100)
Past Pleasures by Barbara M. Meeker
Indiana Federation of Art Clubs ($100)

BEST WORK, ANY MEDIUM,
TO FIRST TIME EXHIBITING ARTIST
Blue Ribbon by H. R. Almquist
Hoosier Salon Guild ($250)

1987

BEST OF SHOW
Wheat Fields by Frederick Ebbesen Grue
Mr. & Mrs. William Cooling ($1,500)

OUTSTANDING WORK, ANY MEDIUM
Small World by Donald Lee Hadley
L. S. Ayres & Company ($1,000)
Oak Creek by Rob O'Dell
Mrs. Ruth Lilly ($500)
*A Segment of the Court House Square,
Covington, Indiana* by Harry Davis
Mrs. Ardath Burkhart Memorial by
Mr. and Mrs. William Cooling ($500)

TRADITIONAL PAINTING, ANY MEDIUM
The Gathering Place by Bud Jamison
Beryl Showers Holland Memorial
by Tri Kappa Sorority ($1,000)
Portrait of Stephanie by William Ashby
Woman's Department Club ($200)

WORK OF SCULPTURE
Facade I by Harold Langland
In honor of Robert & Sandra Borns
by Mr. & Mrs. Sidney Mishkin ($350)

JURY PRIZE OF DISTINCTION, SCULPTURE
SOUL (Search of Universal Life) by William Snapp
Bertha Crosley Ball Memorial by
Mr. and Mrs. Edmund F. Ball ($300)

NON-REPRESENTATIONAL WORK
Victorian Grid III by William H. Messer
Indianapolis Newspapers, Inc. ($150)

CONTEMPORARY PAINTING
Passion by Hilary Eddy
Richard E. Ford ($250)

LANDSCAPE IN OIL OR ACRYLIC
This Too Shall Pass by Grant Christian
Anonymous ($700)
Sunset by Gerald Pearcy
Daughters of Indiana ($250)

REALISTIC OR IMPRESSIONISTIC
LANDSCAPE, ANY MEDIUM
Natchez Trace by Ruth Pritchard
Judge & Mrs. Hutchinson Memorial
by Florence Lonsford ($150)

STILL LIFE OR FLOWERS,
TRADITIONAL, ANY MEDIUM
Pastel Bouquet by Sylvia Worman
Art Department, Woman's
Department Club ($150)

FLORAL PAINTING
Neoregelia #2 by Emel Doner
Woman's Department Club ($300)

WATERCOLOR
Sun Patterns by Mary Jane Bell
Hoosier Salon Guild ($400)
After the Storm by William Smoot
Floyd D. Hopper Memorial by
Dr. & Mrs. Hanus J. Grosz ($100)

JURY PRIZE OF DISTINCTION
Rose by James Curtin Lentz
Mr. and Mrs. Harry E. Riser ($500)
Summer's Prisoners by Mark W. Bratovich
Mr. & Mrs. R. O. Clutter,
Mr. & Mrs. Wilbur Ford, and
Mr. & Mrs. T. E. Husselman ($400)
Early A. M. at Irnies by A. T. Solomon
Psi Iota Xi Sorority ($250)
The Corn Harvest by Charlene George
Indiana National Bank ($250)
Battered Kettle and Turnips by Dennis M. Jones
Floyd D. Hopper Memorial by
Frank and Patte Owings ($250)

MERIT AWARD
One Sunday Afternoon by Stephen Paul Wheat
Epsilon Sigma Chapter,
Tri Kappa Sorority ($100)
Palm Patterns by Rich Ernsting
Indiana Federation of Art Clubs ($100)

EXHIBITION RECORDS

BEST WORK, ANY MEDIUM,
TO FIRST TIME EXHIBITING ARTIST
Autumn Garden Visitors by Leslie E. Williamson
Hoosier Salon Guild ($300)

1988

BEST OF SHOW
10th and Connor by Harry A. Davis
Mrs. William P. Cooling ($1,500)

OUTSTANDING WORK, ANY MEDIUM
River Market by Diane Ubelhor Wunderlich
L. S. Ayres & Company ($1,000)
Golden Glimpse by Grant Christian
Mrs. Ruth Lilly ($500)
The Big 'A' by James C. Borden
Mrs. Ardath Burkhart Memorial
by Mrs. William P. Cooling ($500)
Lair of the Green Dragon by Marilyn Kruger
Mr. and Mrs. Wilbur Ford ($400)

TRADITIONAL PAINTING, ANY MEDIUM
Persimmons by Frederik Ebbesen Grue
Beryl Showers Holland Memorial
by Tri Kappa Sorority ($1,000)
Oriental Vase by W. Ray Stevens
Woman's Department Club ($200)

WORK OF SCULPTURE
It Is So Cold by Alison Adams
In honor of Robert & Sandra Borns
by Mr. & Mrs. Sidney Mishkin ($350)

JURY PRIZE OF DISTINCTION, SCULPTURE
Femme d'Afrique by Tuck Langland
Bertha Crosley Ball Memorial by
Mr. and Mrs. Edmund F. Ball ($300)

NON-REPRESENTATIONAL WORK
Untitled A by William Messer
Indianapolis Newspapers, Inc. ($150)

LANDSCAPE IN OIL OR ACRYLIC
Wayne County Afternoon by Dennis Jones
Anonymous ($750)
Sacred Lake by Bill Cross
Daughters of Indiana ($250)

REALISTIC OR IMPRESSIONISTIC
LANDSCAPE, ANY MEDIUM
Saint Mary's River by Isabel White
Judge & Mrs. Hutchinson Memorial
by Florence Lonsford ($150)

STILL LIFE OR FLOWERS,
TRADITIONAL, ANY MEDIUM
Prelude to Summer by Leah Traugott
Art Department, Woman's
Department Club ($150)

FLORAL PAINTING
Waterlilies Against the Sky by Carolyn Jagodits
Woman's Department Club ($300)

WATERCOLOR
Knockout No. III by Rush Cole
Hoosier Salon Guild ($400)

DRAWING
Portrait of Marcy by Mark Dillman
Hoosier Salon Guild ($200)
Summer in the Smokies by Tracy J. Thurman
Mr. & Mrs. Gordon Hughes ($100)

JURY PRIZE OF DISTINCTION
Radiance by Hilary Eddy
Mr. & Mrs. Harry E. Riser ($500)
Recovery Room, Back to Consciousness by Lois Davis
Mr. & Mrs. R. O. Clutter and
Mr. & Mrs. T. E. Husselman ($300)
Good Morning Cincinnati by Sandy Day
Psi Iota Xi Sorority ($250)
We Sold 'Em All This Morning
by Diana Miller Pierce
Pleasant Run Gallery ($275)
Torch Ginger by Phillip Monteith
(Information unavailable)

MERIT AWARD
Daisy and Dolly by Rosemary Lawton Thomas
Epsilon Sigma Chapter,
Tri Kappa Sorority ($150)
Warm on Cool by Gentry Day
Indiana Federation of Art Clubs ($100)

BEST WORK, ANY MEDIUM,
TO FIRST TIME EXHIBITING ARTIST
River Market by Diane Ubelhor Wunderlich
Hoosier Salon Guild ($300)

1989

BEST OF SHOW
1st Lutheran Church by Harry A. Davis
Mrs. William P. Cooling ($1,500)

OUTSTANDING WORK, ANY MEDIUM
A Hundred in the Shade
by Rosemary Lawton Thomas
L. S. Ayres & Company ($1,000)
The Journey by Mark Bratovich
Mrs. Ruth Lilly ($500)
Vases with Shadows by Leah S. Traugott
Mrs. Ardath Burkhart Memorial
by Mrs. William Cooling ($500)
Early Light by Robert A. Maxam
Mr. and Mrs. Wilbur Ford ($400)

TRADITIONAL PAINTING, ANY MEDIUM
Susan E. Mauck & Daughter "Nikko"
by William G. Ashby
Beryl Showers Holland Memorial
by Tri Kappa Sorority ($1,000)
Window Series, Charleston, South Carolina
by Denise Anne Horne-Kaplan
Woman's Department Club ($200)

JURY PRIZE OF DISTINCTION, SCULPTURE
Waiting for the Light to Change, VI
by C. R. Schiefer
Bertha Crosley Ball Memorial by
Mr. & Mrs. Edmund F. Ball ($350)

NON-REPRESENTATIONAL WORK
Painting, Teaching: Our Living Legacy
by Eleanor Lewis
Indianapolis Newspapers ($150)

LANDSCAPE IN OIL OR ACRYLIC
Rice Paddy in Japan by James Dormann
Anonymous ($750)
Shades of Winter by Hilary Eddy
Daughters of Indiana ($250)

REALISTIC OR IMPRESSIONISTIC
LANDSCAPE, ANY MEDIUM
Blessed Sunlight by Grant Christian
Judge & Mrs. Hutchinson Memorial
by Florence Lonsford ($150)

STILL LIFE OR FLOWERS,
TRADITIONAL, ANY MEDIUM
Orchid Composition, VI by Paul J. Sweany
Art Department, Woman's
Department Club ($150)

FLORAL PAINTING
Hidden Beauty by Emel Doner
Woman's Department Club ($300)

WATERCOLOR
Night Light by Keith Kline
Hoosier Salon Guild ($400)

DRAWING
Two for the Show by Chicquiela Broyles
Hoosier Salon Guild ($200)
Tippecanoe Courthouse, Lafayette, Indiana
by Kanwal Prakash Singh
Mr. and Mrs. Gordon Hughes ($100)

WORK OF ART
Lost in Space, Challenger Disaster
by Kenneth G. Ryden
Hoosier Salon Guild ($350)

JURY PRIZE OF DISTINCTION
Horse Power by Nancy R. Owen
Mr. and Mrs. Harry E. Riser ($500)
Inventory Reduction by Lois Davis
Mr. & Mrs. R. O. Clutter and
Mr. & Mrs. T. E. Husselman ($300)
White Lace Floating Over Crazy Quilt
by Teresa Staley
William F. Kaeser and
Floyd D. Hopper Memorial
by Pleasant Run Gallery ($275)
Thief in My Patch by Louise Hansen
Psi Iota Xi Sorority ($250)
Wild Goose Chase by Marjorie Davoust
Indiana National Bank ($150)

MERIT AWARD
Afternoon Coffee, A Self Portrait
by Peggy McCarty
Epsilon Sigma Chapter,
Tri Kappa Sorority ($150)
Duneland Grasses by Robert Hoffman
Indiana Federation of Art Clubs ($100)

BEST WORK, ANY MEDIUM,
TO FIRST TIME EXHIBITING ARTIST
Room at Night by Ronald Monsma
Hoosier Salon Guild ($300)

1990

BEST OF SHOW
Before the Symphony at Capriccios by Jack D.
Cowan
Mrs. William P. Cooling ($1,500)

OUTSTANDING WORK, ANY MEDIUM
Eclectic Mix by Steven Redman
L. S. Ayres & Company ($1,000)
Nature Series #15 by Julieta Higgins
Mrs. Ruth Lilly ($500)
River Banks Remembered by George Elliott
Mrs. William P. Cooling ($500)
Martha's Time by Keith Kline
Mrs. Wilbur Ford ($400)

TRADITIONAL PAINTING, ANY MEDIUM
Union Stationaries by James Curtin Lentz
Beryl Showers Holland Memorial
by Tri Kappa Sorority ($1,000)
#5 Men Working Series, Guitar Player
by Ann T. Solomon
Woman's Department Club ($200)

JURY PRIZE OF DISTINCTION, SCULPTURE
Autumn by Harold Langland
Bertha Crosley Ball Memorial by
Mr. & Mrs. Edmund F. Ball ($350)

NON-REPRESENTATIONAL WORK
Emerging Order by Donna Ozbun
Indianapolis Newspapers ($150)

LANDSCAPE IN OIL OR ACRYLIC
One Way by Harry A. Davis
Anonymous ($750)
Metamora Grist Mill by Robert Hartsock
Daughters of Indiana ($250)

LANDSCAPE IN OIL
Urban Pattern by Vernon B. Cristee
Frank and Patte Owings ($250)

REALISTIC OR IMPRESSIONISTIC
LANDSCAPE, ANY MEDIUM
Gull Bay, Maine by Val Walters
Judge & Mrs. Hutchinson Memorial
by Florence Lonsford ($150)

EXHIBITION RECORDS

REALISTIC OR IMPRESSIONISTIC
LANDSCAPE IN OIL
> *Road from Goshen Pass* by Jeff Burris
> Grant W. Christian Memorial ($150)

STILL LIFE OR FLOWERS,
TRADITIONAL, ANY MEDIUM
> *Pleasant Under Glass #2* by Willa Howell Bullock
> Art Department, Woman's
> Department Club ($150)

FLORAL PAINTING
> *Deep Woods* by Jean Vietor
> Woman's Department Club ($300)

WATERCOLOR
> *Patchwork and Pink Pitcher* by Wilbur Meese
> Hoosier Salon Guild ($400)

DRAWING
> *Dorthea* by Marty Montgomery
> Hoosier Salon Guild ($200)

WORK OF ART
> *Sculptural Form* by George Debikey
> Hoosier Salon Guild ($350)

JURY PRIZE OF DISTINCTION
> *Time Out* by Nancy R. Owen
> Mr. & Mrs. T. E. Husselman ($300)
> *(Untitled #1) As the Wheel Turns*
> by Stephen Edwards
> Mr. & Mrs. Harry E. Riser ($250)

> *Fractured Panes II* by Birgit Stewart
> Psi Iota Xi Sorority ($250)
> *Repose* by Ann-Marie Korczyk
> Epsilon Chapter, Psi Iota Xi Sorority ($200)
> *Pledge/Revenge* by Lois Davis
> Indiana National Bank ($150)

MERIT AWARD
> *Don't Be Silly, Cows Can't Fly*
> by Kelley Griffith Daniel
> Indiana Federation of Art Clubs ($100)

BEST WORK, ANY MEDIUM,
TO FIRST TIME EXHIBITING ARTIST
> *Country Still Life* by Paulette McGriff
> Hoosier Salon Guild ($300)

A

Index by Artist
(An * indicates merit award winner)

ABBETT, BETTY
1989 1.   Jo's Lilacs

ABELL, D. L.
1990 1.   Polyneices

ABRAHAM, JAMES R.
1934 1.   Self Portrait
      2.   St. John's Cathedral

ADAMS, ALISON R.
1984 1.   Young Acrobat*
1988 1.   It Is So Cold*
      2.   Let Me Out

ADAMS, C(harles) B.
1976 1.   Closed on Sunday
1977 1.   Sarah

ADAMS, DOROTHY J.
1967 1.   Russian Family
      2.   Private Worlds
1974 1.   Disentangled
      2.   Dispossessed*
1976 2.   Storm Scarred
      3.   Red, White & Blue #2*
1979 1.   Opticle Shapes #2

ADAMS, J. OTTIS
1925 5.   Scene on White Water
1926 3.   Clouds
      4.   Winter Time in Florida

ADAMS, JOY HARBOURT
(See Harbourt, Joy Adams)
1970 1.   Untitled

ADAMS, JUANITA R.
1977 2.   Poppies

ADAMS, MARGARET
1945 1.   From Leila's Garden*
1946 1.   Grandma's
1947 1.   Mystic River
1950 1.   Southern Bouquet
1955 1.   Pale Flowers
1959 1.   Little Brown Jug

ADAMS, MARTHA
1947 2.   Howard's Paint Cans
      3.   Wabash Station

ADAMS, SONDRA
1979 2.   Sloan's Mill

ADAMS, VIN
1944 1.   Food Fights for Freedom
      2.   Fighters for American Freedom
      3.   Spring

ADAMS, WAYMAN
1925 1.   Uncle Randolph Jones
      2.   Ella, Wayman Junior, and
            Naomi Priscilla
      3.   Portrait of Booth Tarkington*
      4.   Portrait of J. E. Bundy
1926 5.   The Art Jury*
1927 1.   108 W. 57th Street, New York
1928 1.   Cynthia
1929 1.   Wayman Adams, Jr.
      2.   Irving R. Wiles*
1930 1.   Little Old Mexico
1931 1.   Madonna on the Ass
      2.   Mouthing
      3.   The Offering
      4.   The Alibi
      5.   The Hymn
      6.   The Clinging Vine
1932 1.   The Sphinx
      2.   Mrs. Alexander Cameron
1933 1.   John Larkin
      2.   Portrait of Mrs. Adams
1935 1.   Portrait, John T. McCutcheon
      2.   Portrait, John C. Shaffer*
1936 1.   Jose
1937 1.   Portrait, Mrs. William Wallace Gaar
1938 1.   Edwin Raymond Culver
      2.   Bertram B. Culver
      3.   Admiral Hugh Rodman
      4.   General Leigh Robinson Gignilliat
            (Invited entries)
1939 1.   Mrs. Charles Deering
1940 1.   Duet
1941 1.   Three in the South
1942 1.   Wayman Adams, Jr.
1943 1.   The Red Cloak
1944 4.   The Young Miner
      5.   Winfred Merrill
1945 2.   Young Lieutenant
      3.   Mrs. Alexander Gersen
1946 2.   Woody
1947 4.   Creole Cabbage

1948	1.	New Orleans Gossip*
	2.	Saltillo Doorway
1949	1.	Ninety-six
1950	2.	Abraham Walkowitz*
1951	1.	Not a Member of This Club*
1952	1.	Years After
	2.	Gus Parker*
1953	1.	Old Fiddler
	2.	Alcalde Artiaga*
1954	1.	In New Orleans
	2.	Three in Mexico
1955	2.	Episode in the Park
	3.	Uncle Jim Hayes*
1956	1.	Little Johnny Rudd*
1957	1.	Brother Simon*
1958	1.	The Gates Brothers*
1959	2.	Little Miss Barbara

ADAMS, WINIFRED BRADY

1926	6.	Flowers
	7.	Still Life, Roses*
1929	3.	Wayside Weeds, Cape Cod
1930	2.	Still Life
1945	4.	Resignation

ADNEY, CAROL

| 1978 | 1. | Luminous Blue |

AGAR, EDNA

| 1941 | 2. | Our House |

AGNEW, LOUISE FULTS
(See Fults, Louise Christin)

| 1949 | 2. | Still Life* |
| | 3. | Lunch on Friday |

AGUET, HENRY A.

| 1982 | 1. | Lost Layers Found |

AILES, CURTIS

| 1976 | 4. | Evening South Wind |

AKER, REBECCA

| 1983 | 1. | South of Hazelwood |
| 1984 | 2. | Homeward |

ALATZA, GEORGE E.

| 1954 | 3. | The Red Cup |
| | 4. | Self Portrait |

ALDRICH, G. AMES

1925	6.	Christmas Eve
	7.	Winter, The Brandwyne
1926	1.	Moulin du Port, Pont Aven
	2.	St. Joe River, Winter*
1927	2.	Misty Morning
	3.	On a Winter Day
	4.	Incoming Tide
1928	2.	Brittany Mill
	3.	Frankenstein
	4.	St. Joe River, Winter

1929	4.	Winter Morning
	5.	Winter, Brittany
	6.	Steel*
1930	3.	The Pit
	4.	Sugar Creek, Winter
	5.	Market Day, Candebec
1932	3.	Mid-Winter, Indiana*
	4.	Roofs
	5.	Bye-Street, Normandy
1933	3.	Gloucester Harbor
	4.	Quimperle
1935	3.	Old Houses, Candebec
	4.	In the Yellowstone
1936	2.	Rain Fell on Alabam*
	3.	Where the West Begins, Bad Lands
1937	2.	Market Place Honfleur
	3.	Old Houses, Cherbourg
1938	5.	Court Yard, Caudebec-En-Caux
	6.	Winter Stream
1939	2.	The Fountain
	3.	Sailors Church, Honfleur
	4.	Winter Streams, Normandy

ALEXANDER, MARTHANN

| 1943 | 2. | Inglescomb Yellow |

ALIG, MARY JEAN

| 1989 | 2. | Beyond Alpha Centuri |
| | 3. | Encounter in Space |

ALLEN, BETTE SIMONSON

| 1958 | 2. | Thistles |

ALLEN, BLANCHE I.

| 1953 | 3. | Chrysanthemum |

ALLEN, JANET (Stewart)

1958	3.	Grapes
1959	3.	Lolita
	4.	Drama
1962	1.	Gwendolyn

ALLEN, MARIAN

1964	1.	Still Life with Pomegranates
1967	4.	View from a Small Hill
	5.	Cellar Door
1969	1.	The Tea and Crumpet Society
	2.	Prairie
1972	1.	Muskrat Pond
1976	5.	Star Magnolia, October

ALLMAN, NORMAN

| 1962 | 2. | No title |
| | 3. | No title |

ALMQUIST, H. R.

1986	1.	Blue Ribbon*
1987	1.	In for Repairs
	2.	Backyard Games
1988	3.	Auction at Old Towne

ALT, LILLIAN

1931	7.	Still Life
1932	6.	The Black Cat
	7.	Aspidistra
1933	5.	Phlox
1934	3.	Early Autumn
	4.	Old Norwegian Pot
1935	5.	Emma
1936	4.	The White Teapot
1937	4.	Irene's Mother
	300.	Shasta Daisies
1938	7.	Little Angel
1941	3.	Summer Bouquet
1942	2.	Men and Guns
1952	3.	The Blue Pitcher with Flowers and Fruit

ALTEKRUSE, MAX

1947	5.	Iron Horse Dismantled
	6.	Keep a Livin'
	7.	Across the Tracks
1959	5.	Mother and Child*
	6.	Study
1962	4.	Barnyard Pisa
	5.	November Study
	6.	Silo and Textures
	7.	What I Live For, Thoreau*
1964	2.	Fragment

ALTER, MELANIE

1968	1.	Still Life with a Pear
1970	2.	Life Is Full of Fruition and Intuition *

ALTGELT, ELINOR

1945	5.	In My Neighbor's Garden
1947	8.	Marigolds

AMIES, PATRICIA

1977	3.	Seven Hogs and a Frog

AMMERMAN, JOHN M.

1969	4.	Harvest Wake

ANDERSON, ALLAN ARTHUR

1927	5.	Apache Trail, Arizona

ANDERSON, CHARLES O.

1930	6.	Reverie

ANDERSON, GARNETHA

1962	8.	Mardi Gras

ANDERSON, GARY

1981	1.	The Bearer

ANDERSON, IDA P.

1930	7.	Among the Hills
1932	8.	Sunset Glow

ANDERSON, MARY

1928	5.	The Squirrel*
	6.	Do You Like Butter?*
	7.	Spring*
	8.	Bunny's Breakfast*
	9.	Mary's Lamb*
1929	7.	Old-Fashioned Roses
	8.	The Song
1930	8.	The Green Singing Book
	9.	Nell and Tarbaby
	10.	Bubbles
1931	8.	The Red Jar
1933	6.	Rock-A-Bye Baby
1937	5.	Bittersweet
	301.	Spring Bouquet

ANDERSON, RUTH (B.)

1944	6.	After the Rain
1946	3.	Desert Afterglow
1948	3.	Desert Barrier
1950	3.	The Barren Land
1951	2.	Afternoon Shadows
	3.	Morning on the Desert
1953	4.	Solitude
	5.	Morning in Leland
1954	5.	Monument of Time
	6.	Gloucester Docks
	7.	Cloud Drifts
1955	4.	Gaspesian Holiday
1956	2.	Late Afternoon
1957	2.	Side Street, Rockport
	3.	In For the Night
1958	4.	Evensong
	5.	Morning Caprice
1959	7.	Windward Cove
	8.	The Tender Years
1960	1.	Flowers of the Fields
	2.	Morning Comes to Monhegan*
	3.	Homing
1961	1.	Old Landmark*
	2.	Well of the Sea
	3.	Morning Breakers
1962	9.	The Singing Surf
	10.	Evensong
1963	1.	Along the Creek
1964	3.	Clearing
1965	1.	Deep Calls Unto Deep
1966	1.	The Beckoning Wind
1967	6.	My Brother's Keeper
1968	2.	High Tide
1969	5.	Snowscape*
1970	3.	Rising Sea
1973	1.	Sanctuary*
1974	3.	The Power and the Glory
1976	6.	Morning Comes Softly*
	7.	Impressions in the Rain
1986	2.	Music Hath Charms

THE HOOSIER SALON, 1925-1990

ANDERT-BASHOVER, PAULA
1978 7. Floral Observation No. 12

ANDIS, HELEN
1964 4. Time Takes Its Toll

ANDREWS, CLAUDE Y.
1944 7. Democracy

ANDREWS, FLAVIA K.
1937 6. In a June Garden

ANTREASIAN, GARO Z.
1944 8. Boats and Nets, Eastern Shore*
      9. Coast Guard Station, Metomkin
      10. Sentinel, Dam Neck
1949 4. Slum Clearance
      5. Sidewalk Artist*
      6. New York City Arrangement
1950 4. Stone Yard
      5. The Dance
1952 4. The Pit
      5. Milkweed
1953 6. The First Snow

APPLEGATE, R. C.
1926 8. Youth's Dream
      9. Portrait of Mr. Rotti
      10. Portrait of Dr. Brunner
      11. Portrait of Dr. Hayworth
      12. Portrait of Dr. Johnson
      13. Portrait of Lawrence Flammang
      14. Playmates

APPLETON, JACK
1973 2. Turkey Mushrooms

ARBOGAST, VAN DARRELL
1961 4. Louisville, City Library
1964 5. La Petite Jeune Fille

ARCHER, JOSEPH
1925 8. Once Upon a Time
1926 15. The Stag at Eve

ARD, CAROLYN
1981 2. Computer Terminal

ARDELEAN, CHRISTINE
1983 2. Li'l Tomboy
1987 3. Waiting for the Wind
      4. The Inside Story
1989 4. Teller House, Central City,
          Colorado

ARMSTRONG, CATHARINE B.
1925 9. Mountains
1926 16. November
      17. Late Afternoon
1927 6. Late Autumn

ARNOLD, ANN (M.)
1984 3. Lunarscape
      4. Birds of a Feather
1986 3. Helican Pelicans
      4. In Depth
1988 4. September Morn

ARNOLD, CAROL
1978 2. Untitled

ARRICK, THERESSA
1959 9. Hollywood Polka

ARTHUR, JUDITH E.
1986 5. This Old House

ASHBROOK, CAROLYN S.
1928 10. Cypress Trees, Carmel, California
1943 3. Gulls at Perce
      4. Old Barn, Rockport
      5. Under the Bridge

ASHBY, PATRICIA E.
1971 1. Hamilton County Barn
      2. The Old Water Pitcher

ASHBY, PAUL W.
1940 2. Dreary Day
      3. Log Cabin, Spring Mill State Park
1941 4. October Night
1942 3. Lincoln Tower, Ft. Wayne
      4. Seven Pillars of Mississinewa
1943 6. Bridge and Mill
      7. Winter Night
      8. Falling Star
      9. Promises
      10. Out the Back Window
1944 11. Getaway
1945 6. Safety Amid Destruction
      7. Stone Mill, Spring Mill State Park
      8. Winter Night
      9. Charmer
      10. Landscape
      11. Clifty Falls in Winter*
      12. Mexican Cloister
      13. Forsaken
1946 4. Over Lake James
      5. Toadstools and Stump
      6. Escape
      7. The Marsh
      8. Monastery Corridor
      9. Dogwood Berries
1947 9. Falls, McCormick's Creek Canyon*
1949 7. Blow-out, Dune State Park
      8. Abandoned
      9. Cataract Falls, Owen County
      10. Ah! Make Up
1950 6. Candlelit Altar
      7. City Glow
      8. Grandpa's Barn
      9. Indiana University Union Building

154

1951	4.	Houlton Bridge, DeKalb County
1952	6.	Tunnelton Bridge
	7.	Three Dancers
	8.	Covered Bridge, DeKalb County
	9.	Night in the Dunes
	10.	Toadstools and Trillium
	11.	Evening Mist
	12.	Covered Bridge, Brown County
	13.	Lichen
	14.	Bright Lights, Rain on the Highway
1954	8.	Prophet
	9.	Maestro
	10.	The Inscrutible Dunes
	11.	Powers of Light and Darkness
	12.	Puffball
	13.	Incoming Rollers
	14.	Wave Tracks
	15.	Il Pensee
	16.	Storm Beaten
1955	5.	Spots and Shadows No. 2
1956	3.	Dune Labyrinth
1957	4.	Light
	5.	Limestone Creek*
1958	6.	Cataract, Dam and Bridge
	7.	Bivouac
	8.	Winter Dawn in the Dunes
1961	5.	Carillon, Butler University
	6.	Light and Shadow
	7.	Toadstool and Puffball
	8.	Car Lighted Bridge
	9.	Dune Pathway
	10.	Winter Dusk in the Dunes
1962	11.	Observatory, Butler University
	12.	Foggy Morning
	13.	Counter Currents
1963	2.	Phantasmagoria
	3.	When Icicles Hang on the Canyon Wall
1964	6.	Sweeping Clouds
	7.	Millstone Cabin
1965	2.	Lower Falls Cataract
	3.	Lock Ness Monsters
1967	7.	Counter Currents
1968	3.	Covered Bridge
1970	4.	U. F. O.'s
1971	3.	Hilltop House
	4.	Deserted

ASHBY, WILLIAM G.

1966	2.	Washer Woman
	3.	Comber at Herring Gut*
1967	8.	Sandy*
	9.	Devil's Point
	10.	Under Burnt Head*
1968	4.	Norton's Ledge
	5.	Portrait of Lynn
	6.	Smutty Nose*

1969	6.	Sea at Dusk*
	7.	Under Burnt Head
1970	5.	Maine Sea
	6.	Christmas Cove
1971	5.	Lupe, the Cook, Called Him "Señor Taffee"
	6.	Consider the Subtleness of the Sea
1973	3.	Burning Off
1976	8.	Ronelle
1978	3.	Portrait of Bishop Craine
1979	3.	Gray Sea
1980	1.	Morning Coffee
	2.	Portrait of David Rubins*
1981	3.	Mrs. Ashby
1982	2.	Juli
1983	3.	Portrait of Robert Frist*
1984	5.	Ronelle
1985	1.	Tuscan Haystack
	2.	Portrait of Ellen Frist
1986	6.	Portrait of Ronelle*
1987	5.	Portrait of Stephanie*
1988	5.	Portrait of Ronelle
1989	5.	Susan E. Mauck and Daughter, "Nikko" *
1990	.	Drew & Alex Frist

ASHDOWN, ENID

1959	10.	Lilacs
	11.	Kelp and Shells
1961	11.	Whitby, England
1962	14.	Twilight on the Moors

ASHTON, ELIZABETH DOUGHERTY
(See Dougherty, Elizabeth H.)

| 1950 | 10. | Negro Baptism* |

AULL, DIXIE

| 1989 | 6. | Bouquet Canyon Wall |

AUSTIN, DON

| 1976 | 9. | Wandering Hill Ky. |
| | 10. | Body and Soul |

AUSTIN, RUTH

| 1955 | 6. | Quiet Harbour |
| | 7. | The Cruel Mountains |

AYRES, LESLIE F.

1947	10.	Life
	11.	Junk
	12.	University Park
1949	11.	Sustenance
	12.	Very Early Sunday Morning on the Circle
1950	11.	Ever with Us
	12.	St. John's, Indianapolis
	13.	St. Patrick's, Indianapolis

B

BABCOCK, PAT(ricia)
1955	8.	Madonna 1954
1960	4.	Dune Grass
	5.	The Endless Tide
1962	15.	Somebody's Dog

BABCOCK, R. FAYERWEATHER
1933	7.	A Night in Burma
1934	5.	Whoo-Whoo-Hoosier
1935	6.	Portrait of my Grandmother
1936	5.	Back of the Barn
	6.	Springtime in Minnesota
	7.	The Autumn Road
1937	7.	October Sun
1939	5.	Flying High
	6.	Voices in the Night

BABER, LANCE
| 1970 | 7. | Ochre* |

BACHMAN, WILLIAM J.
| 1938 | 8. | Still Life |
| 1939 | 7. | Still Life |

BACON, BETH DRIGGS
1925	10.	The Apple Tree
1926	18.	Theft of the Grapes *
1927	7.	Gazelles
1928	11.	The Boar Hunt

BADGER, LENORE WEYBURN
1937	8.	Tony
	9.	The Cobbler
	302.	Yellow Tulips
1946	10.	Peonies

BAHLS, RUTH
1928	12.	Still Life
	13.	The Chinese Background
1929	9.	Alice Ann
	10.	Napping
1930	11.	From the Studio Window
	12.	Compassion
1931	9.	Side Street, Provincetown
1934	6.	First Street, Madison
	7.	Autumn Morning
1939	8.	Indiana Home
1942	5.	Antiques
	6.	Garden Flowers
1944	12.	Lafayette in November
	13.	Potomac Tureen and Flowers
1945	14.	Old Homestead
	15.	Cottage in the Woods
1946	11.	So Many Springs

BAIDINGER, ROBERT
| 1960 | 6. | Nightscape |

BAILEY, ELISABETH
| 1965 | 4. | October |

BAILEY, KATHERINE
| 1988 | 6. | Hollyhocks |

BAILEY, LORENE
| 1989 | 7. | Lady |

BAILEY, LOUISE G.
| 1978 | 4. | Rachel |

BAIN, J. HUSTON
1973	4.	Gothic Sentinels*
1974	4.	Demotivation
	5.	Mis-match
1975	1.	Night Session*
1976	11.	Goldie's Rainbow
	12.	Fishbowl
1978	5.	Idle Blue*
1979	4.	Gothic Bird

BAIR, DOROTHY (H.)
1976	13.	Amtrak's Ancestor
1982	3.	Erosion
1984	6.	Remnants
1985	3.	Equinox I, II
1986	7.	Early Snow
	8.	Sticks and Stones

BAKER, CLAUDIA GRIFFIN
| 1950 | 14. | The Justice |

BAKER, CLAYSON
1957	6.	The Old Red Barn
	7.	Bean Blossom Overlook, Brown County
1960	7.	Bear Wallow Hill
1961	12.	Mid-November, Brown County
	13.	Rocky Coast
1962	16.	Snow Flurries
	17.	Winter in Brown County
1964	8.	Early Spring
1966	4.	Greasy Creek

BAKER, GEORGE H.
1925	14.	A Clear Winter Day
	15.	November Afterglow
	16.	Shortcreek Hillside
1926	19.	The Farm Road
	20.	Snow-Clad Hills
	21.	Lingering Snow
1930	13.	Light Triumphant
1931	10.	Young Persimmon Tree
	11.	Waning Winter
1932	9.	Farm Home

BAKER, GLORIA
1990   3.   The Dedicated #5

BAKER, HELEN SEYMOUR
(See Baker, Seymour and Seymour, Helen)
1929   11.   Giovanna
1930   14.   Portrait of Roszika
1933   8.   Myself

BAKER, JINNIE
1982   4.   Heron's Nest
1983   4.   Nappanee Morning

BAKER, JUDITH (Ann Armstrong)
1969   8.   George #3
          9.   Victory
1970   8.   Hired Gun
1971   7.   The Astronaut
          8.   Flowers*

BAKER, RUTH (A.)
1979   5.   Newborn
          6.   Winnie the Pooh II
1980   3.   Susan at Thirteen*
1982   5.   Susan in the Light*
          6.   Boy in the Red Cap
1984   7.   Daybreak at Rocky Point*

BAKER, SEYMOUR
(See Baker, Helen Seymour and Seymour, Helen)
1935   7.   Mary

BAKKEN, JOSEPHINE
1976   14.   Summers Ending
1977   4.   Under the Sea

BALDWIN, JOSEPH N.
1929   12.   The Ranger

BALES, GEORGE C.
1954   17.   Lt. Gen. William E. Kepner

BALKIN, MAXIM
1943   11.   Lone Tree

BALL, WALTER N.
1978   6.   Grey Square with Two Figures

BALLARD, HORTON
1952   15.   Alley Approach
          16.   Contact
1958   9.   Weaver's Supplies
          10.   Mt. LeConte
1960   8.   Old Neighborhood
1962   18.   Rivertown
1963   4.   The Ozarks

BALOGH, BEATA M.
1980   4.   Gallop

BANNING, DOROTHY
1980   5.   R. R. Greensfork
1983   5.   The Crossing

BANNON, VIOLET F.
1956   4.   From Here to There
          5.   Preparation
          6.   Little People
1962   19.   On Deck
1964   9.   Street Scene, Paris*
1969   10.   Queen Ann's Lace and Mums

BANTA, DAVID A.
1976   15.   Wild Raspberries
          16.   Cabbage I
1977   5.   Dr. Eustus Philpott's Electric
                 Calliope
1990   4.   Zebra Swallowtail

BARD, SARA (F.)
1927   8.   Play Time
          9.   The Yellow Tavern
          10.   Daily Papers
1928   14.   The Harbor
          15.   Foxgloves
          16.   Early Morning
1929   13.   Maine Coast
          14.   The Yellow House
          15.   Coming into the Harbor*
1930   15.   The Fire House
          16.   The Gas Station
          17.   Maine Village
1931   12.   Maine Coast*
          13.   The Harbor
          14.   The Storm
1932   10.   Henderson's
1934   8.   High Street
          9.   The Cove*
1936   8.   Island Homes*
          9.   Harrisville
          10.   Gertie Cooper's Garden
1937   10.   Eastport
          11.   Parker's Landing
          12.   Pembroke
1938   9.   Red Houses
          10.   Fishing Boats
          300.   Wisconsin River
1939   9.   Across the Tracks
          10.   The Elm Tree
1940   4.   Christmas Eve
          5.   The Harbor*
1942   7.   Easter
1944   14.   The Station
1945   16.   The Frederick Snow House

BARKER, E. A.
1974   6.   Totem: Americana
          7.   Death of a Superstar

BARLOW, IRENE
(See Sipe, Irene Barlow)
1969	11.	Old Wharf
	12.	Moonglow
1970	9.	The Peaceful Valley
1971	9.	Around the Corner
1973	5.	Atlantic Symphony
1974	8.	Autumnal Shadows
1975	2.	Untitled Symphony

BARNES, CHARLES E.
| 1940 | 6. | Indiana Landscape |
| | 7. | Rural Route No. 1 |

BARNES, RENEE
1927	11.	Delphiniums
1929	16.	Childhood Treasures
	17.	Blue Delphinium
1931	15.	The Chicken Man
1932	11.	Old Churn Glorified
1939	11.	Zinnias

BARNES, ROY
| 1942 | 8. | Nan |
| | 9. | October |

BARNHART, KATHERINE MONGER
| 1971 | 10. | Judith |

BARNSTONE, HELLE
| 1976 | 17. | Grand Lady |
| | 18. | Underwater Life |

BARR, CARROLL BAILEY
1947	13.	Rubber Plant
1952	17.	Cherry Trees
	18.	Willows

BARR, PAUL E.
1927	12.	Woodland, Early Autumn
1938	11.	Bullion Butte
1939	12.	Landscape, South Roosevelt Park
1940	8.	West from Mt. Lassen
1941	5.	Abandoned Barns
1943	12.	Palacio Del Obispado, Monterrey, Mexico
1944	15.	El Popo from Cuernavaca, Mexico

BARR, THELMA A(dams)
1943	13.	50th Anniversary
	14.	Sunlight and Shadows
1946	12.	House of Seven Gables on the Hudson
1951	5.	Reflection Incarnadine
1955	9.	Snow Bound

BARRICKMAN, WILNA B(eaver)
1946	13.	Spring Glory
1947	14.	Reflections
	15.	July Variety*
	16.	Michigan Winter*

1948	4.	The Dunes
1953	7.	White Peonies
	8.	Still Life, Squash & Lemons
1956	7.	Roseate Cockatoos, Detroit Zoo

BARTILOTTA, SAMUEL
| 1933 | 9. | Grand Central |
| 1936 | 11. | Winter Scene |

BARTLETT, JAN
| 1983 | 6. | An Afternoon with Freeman's Sculpture |

BARTLEY, RUTH A.
| 1988 | 7. | Up the Corporate Ladder |

BARTLOW, CATHERINE (B.)
1965	5.	Bouquet in Blue
	6.	Atomic City
	7.	Tipsy Teakettle
1967	11.	Airy Castles
1968	7.	South of the Border

BARTOLINI, MYRTLE F.
1975	3.	Black Diamond #2
	4.	Vibrations
1977	6.	Anteres II

BASKER, EDWARD (J.)
1952	19.	Station B.
	20.	Sunflower Lane
1953	9.	Winter Thaw
	10.	The Road to Galien
1954	18.	November Day*
	19.	Lazy Brook
1955	10.	Pigeon Cove
	11.	Winter
	12.	Fall in Indiana
1956	8.	Devil's Gulch*
	9.	Indiana Autumn
1957	8.	The Red Barn
	9.	Fall Road
1958	11.	Down Fog Road
	12.	Sunday Morning
	13.	Winter Mood*
1959	12.	Chill November*
	13.	The First Snow
	14.	Winter Road
1960	9.	Early Spring
	10.	Snowland
1961	14.	Sunday Gossip
	15.	Sixteen Below
	16.	At Road's End
1962	20.	Fog Road
	21.	Early Spring*
	22.	Mississippi Lowland
1963	5.	A Rainy Day
	6.	Misty Morning
	7.	Fall's End

1964	10.	After the Storm
	11.	Gossip*
	12.	Early Spring
1965	8.	Across the Park*
	9.	Frosty Morn
	10.	Stream's End
1966	5.	Whistle Stop
	6.	Galena*
	7.	Pennsylvania
1967	12.	Spring Thaw
	13.	St. Phillips
1968	8.	Dubuque
	9.	Homeward Bound
1969	13.	Snug Harbor
	14.	Edwardsville
1970	10.	Lead City
1971	11.	Tyler Street

BASS, LYNDALL

| 1979 | 7. | Milkweed Pods |
| | 8. | Still Life with Cabbage |

BASTIAN, CAROLYN WEBER

| 1949 | 13. | Coulee Country |

BASTIN, PATRICIA T.

| 1988 | 8. | Sunday Morning |

BATES, VICTORENE G.

| 1973 | 6. | Morning on the Creek |
| 1975 | 5. | The Linotype Operator |

BATTEN, LUCY ARTHUR

| 1927 | 13. | Dunes Country |
| | 14. | At the Edge of the Dunes |

BATTEN, RONAL A.

| 1926 | 22. | Still Life |
| 1927 | 15. | Sycamores |

BATZKA, STEPHEN (A.)

1964	13.	The Harborage
1965	11.	The Harborage
1967	14.	Umber Landscape #2

BAUGH, (Jr.), ETHERIDGE B.

1976	19.	Summer Bouquet
1981	4.	Jesse
1982	7.	Independence Hall
1985	4.	Amazing Grace
1989	8.	Prairie Fire Sunset
1990	5.	Sunday Afternoon at Meeting House

BAUM, ELIZABETH L.

1943	15.	God's World
1946	14.	At the Bend of the River
1949	14.	Grey Monday
	15.	Summer Vista
1950	15.	October Mood
1952	21.	Tying in to Dock

1953	11.	Earth and High Heaven
	12.	Harbor Reflections
1960	11.	At the Creek's Edge
	12.	Fishermen in Port
	13.	Flame of Autumn
1961	17.	The Touch of Autumn
	18.	Back Country
	19.	Suddenly It's Spring
1962	23.	Clouds over Point Labos
1963	8.	A Breath of Spring
	9.	Bright Water
	10.	Clouding Over
1964	14.	Unfoldment
	15.	Morning on a Western Ranch
1965	12.	After the Rains, California

BAUM, GEORGE C.

1956	10.	Golden October
1957	10.	The Back Road, Smokies
1960	14.	Down Cosby Way
	15.	Weare Valley
1961	20.	Down Schooner Valley
	21.	The Winter's Mirror
	22.	Rural Route #2
1963	11.	Old Road to Cosby
1964	16.	Late October
	17.	Autumn Glory

BAUMANN, GUSTAVE

1926	23.	Mountain Gold
	24.	Summer Rain
	25.	Summer Clouds
	26.	Pinch Hunting Chipmunks
	27.	Atalaya Peak
	28.	Summer Breezes
	29.	Three Pines
	30.	Rain in the Mountains
	31.	Ridge Road
1928	17.	El Velorio
	18.	Bishops Garden
	19.	Summer Rain
	20.	Indiana Red Gum
	21.	Grandma Battin's Gardens
	22.	Talaya Peak
	23.	Harden Hollow
1929	18.	Singing Woods
	19.	Pelican Rookery
	20.	Windswept Eucalyptus
	21.	Coast Range
1930	18.	Sixty-one Wood Blocks (Invited)

BAUS, PAUL J.

1934	10.	Portrait
1935	8.	Taos Group*
1938	12.	Madonna
1948	5.	Karen
1950	16.	Dancer*
1951	6.	Carmella
	7.	Portrait
1955	13.	Child*
	14.	Mr. John Flint

1958	14.	Dr. Dubois
	15.	Anico
1959	15.	Figures
1960	16.	Mr. Edward McGehee
1962	24.	Child with Bird*
	25.	Head Study

BAUS, SIMON P.

1925	11.	Portrait of Mrs. Baus*
	12.	Rabbi Messing
	13.	California
1926	32.	Portrait of Mrs. Baus
	33.	Florence*
	34.	Hoosier Winter
1927	16.	Geraldine
	17.	Autumn*
	18.	Self Portrait
1928	24.	Portrait of a Young Lady*
	25.	William Dudley Foulke
	26.	Autumn Still Life
1929	22.	Portrait of Gen. Gignilliat
	23.	Portrait of Violin Maker
	24.	October
1930	19.	Gen. Gignilliat
1931	16.	Nude
	17.	Betty Hassler
1932	12.	Crecita
1933	10.	Portrait of a Girl
	11.	California Mountain Stream
	12.	Nude
1934	11.	Portrait of a Young Lady
1935	9.	Julie
1936	12.	Miss Florence
	13.	Summer Bouquet
	14.	October Haze
1937	303.	Summer Bouquet
1938	13.	Spanish Lady
1939	13.	Dr. Frank S. C. Wicks
1940	9.	Sylvia
1941	6.	Rose Marie
	7.	Symbols of Autumn
1942	10.	Paul
1943	16.	Marginal Land
	17.	Blackstone
1944	16.	The New Order
	17.	Still Life
	18.	Zinnias*
1945	17.	Autumn Bouquet
	18.	Paul
1946	15.	White River
	16.	Hoosier Autumn
	17.	Marisue*
1947	17.	Deborah No. 2
1948	6.	Angel without Wings*
1949	16.	Portrait: Meta P. Lieber*
1950	17.	Wayman Adams
1951	8.	Pottery Vendor
	9.	Flowers
1952	22.	Polley
	23.	October

1953	13.	Self Portrait*
	14.	Still Life
	15.	Southern Indiana
1955	15.	Doc and Smokie
1956	11.	An Old Friend
	12.	Hoosier Salon
1958	16.	Autumn
	17.	Anne Baker
1959	16.	Karin
	17.	Fishing Weather
1960	17.	Clay Creek Road
1961	23.	Little Lady
1962	26.	Town Hall
1963	12.	Brandywine River
	13.	October
1964	18.	Near Spearsville
	19.	Portrait

BAXTER, BERTHA

1928	27.	A Still Harbor
	28.	A Town by the Sea*
1929	25.	Flowers
	26.	Interior
1930	20.	Indian Still Life
	21.	Interior

BEALS, GEORGE F.

1977	7.	Surf and Rocks
1979	9.	Evening Surf

BEATTY, MARY

1976	20.	Portrait of Linda
1977	8.	Twenty One
1981	5.	Still Life
1982	8.	Still Life with Apples
1988	9.	Pastel in White

BEAUCHAMP, JOHN W.

1931	18.	Interlude in Cold Weather
	19.	Mardi Gras
	20.	Last Chance Gulch

BECK, BARBARA

1975	6.	Still Life with Blue
	7.	Gray Velvet
1976	21.	Green Apples
	22.	Autumn Treasure
1977	9.	Bicentennial
	10.	Copper's Warm Elegance
1978	8.	Winter Apples
1979	10.	Still Life with Eggs
	11.	Yellow and Orange
1980	6.	Going Hunting*
	7.	Sparkle Green
1981	6.	Vertical
	7.	Carol's Flute
1982	9.	Flowers
1987	6.	Brass Bowl with Apples

BECK, JO
| 1972 | 2. | The Secret Place* |
| 1973 | 8. | Untitled |

BECK, LEOLA E.
1967	15.	Ruffled Petunias with Unruffled Friends
1968	10.	Spring Reunion
1969	15.	Mirror, Mirror!?
1975	8.	Time for Reflection
	9.	Roses

BECK, ROSEMARY BROWNE
1955	16.	Still Life
	17.	Pears
	18.	Gertrud*
1956	13.	John Michael Murphy
	14.	Still Life*
1958	18.	Portrait
	19.	Still Life*
	20.	Trees
1959	18.	Still Life*
1962	27.	Still Life
1964	20.	Trees
	21.	White Still Life
1965	13.	Lemons
1966	8.	Brian Beck
	9.	Still Life with Brown Bottle*
	10.	Little Gray and White
1967	16.	Goblet and Apples*
1968	11.	Blanche*
	12.	Pears
1969	16.	Still Life
	17.	Ann Rohn
1970	11.	Pears
1971	12.	Tom Johnson
1972	3.	Portrait
	4.	Chuck Tehan*
1973	7.	Barbara Zimmer*
1974	9.	Bea Smale
	10.	Still Life*
1975	26.	Frederick Browne
	27.	Winter Light
1976	23.	Still Life
	24.	Charley Kirk
1977	22.	Winter Light-2
1978	9.	Still Life*
1979	12.	Still Life (Green & White)*
1980	8.	Pat*
1981	8.	Dominique's Pat
	9.	Goblet Makes Nine*
1982	10.	Still Life
1983	7.	Lemons and Blue
	8.	Eggs*
1984	8.	Green Apples under Glass*
1985	5.	Gold Fold*

BECK, WILLIAM J.
| 1935 | 10. | Snowy Roofs |
| 1941 | 8. | Sails |

BECKMAN, FREDERICK S.
1952	24.	Auction
1954	20.	Carriage Trade
	21.	Angulas Ridet

BECKSMITH, LUISE VEACH
| 1950 | 18. | Janie |
| 1951 | 10. | Bob |

BECVAR, ARTHUR N.
| 1932 | 13. | And See the Holy Edifice of Stone |

BEDNAR, HERMINA BEIDINGER
(See Beidinger, Hermina)
| 1947 | 18. | Zinnias |
| | 19. | New Carlisle, Indiana, Railroad Station |

BEDNAR, JOHN J(ames)
1941	9.	Waterfront*
1942	11.	Head of a Negro*
1945	19.	St. Jerome*
1947	20.	R. R. Station, New Carlisle, Indiana
	21.	Torso*
1960	18.	Seated Woman
	19.	Summer Idyll
1962	28.	Mississippi Eel Fish
	29.	Phrygian Sybil*
1963	14.	Rudolph, Ex-Sergeant
	15.	Buffalo
1965	14.	Floral

BEEBE, OLIVE ANDERSON
| 1968 | 13. | Old Fashioned Garden |

BEEM, OLIVE C.
| 1936 | 15. | The Christmas Snow |
| 1943 | 18. | The Red Pitcher |

BEEM, PAUL E.
1931	21.	The Pink Drape*
1932	14.	Coleus Plant*
1933	13.	Rubber Plant and Pears*
1935	11.	Black and Gold No. 1
	12.	Gardenias
1939	14.	The Church, the Cardinal and the Angel*
	15.	Ambrose
1941	10.	Femme Qui Se Chauffe*
	300.	Senior Rose
1943	19.	Father and Son

BEHR, ROBERT
1939	16.	Roselon
1945	20.	Frozen Creek
	21.	A Covered Bridge

BEIDINGER, HERMINA
(See Bednar, Hermina Beidinger)
| 1940 | 10. | Saugatuck Wharf |

1941	11.	St. Mary's on the South Shore
	12.	The Ferry Store, Saugatuck, Michigan
1944	19.	Chapin Street
	20.	Boogie Woogie Piano
	21.	House on the Bremen Road

BELDING, ANN H.
| 1947 | 22. | Maine Seas |
| | 3. | Indiana Snow |

BELL, HENRY
1980	9.	Swamp Grove
1981	10.	Grandmother McKenzie
1982	11.	Overlook
	12.	Afternoon Notice
1983	9.	The Ellen Keen
1984	9.	Just Once, on a Sunday Morning
	10.	Coaster
1985	6.	Chins Up*
1986	9.	#18 of a Series
	10.	Seven White Tulips
1988	10.	#26 of a Series
	11.	67 Degrees
1989	9.	Say Goodbye
1990	6.	#60 in a Series
	7.	So Early

BELL, MARY JANE
1978	10.	Country Club
	11.	Guardian
1980	10.	Island Gold
1982	13.	Down East
	14.	Pastorale
1983	10.	Still Life
	11.	Blushing Ladies
1984	11.	Image
	12.	Time Out
1985	7.	George
	8.	Ford and Twenty Blackbirds
1986	11.	Island Gold
	12.	The Sun Is a Lacemaker
1987	7.	Sun Patterns*
1989	10.	The Sun Is a Lacemaker
	11.	Susan

BELL, RON
1982	15.	The Waiting
1984	13.	Kasey's Crayons
1985	9.	Marbles on Foil
1989	12.	Reflections

BELL, W. WILS
1941	13.	Be It Ever So Humble*
1944	22.	Storm Clouds
	23.	The Pride of a Pioneer

BELSER, JEAN M.
1975	10.	Painted Canyon
	11.	Nancy
1976	25.	Island Shoreline

1986	13.	Judy
1989	13.	Nancy
1990	8.	Jacob

BEMIS, B(eatrice) BAILEY
1955	19.	Rainy Night Bloom
1958	21.	Isle of St. George, Venice*
1961	24.	Plum Tree Gothic
1962	30.	Red House, Venice
1963	16.	First Snow
1964	22.	Boats at Lucerne, Switzerland, Mt. Pilatus in the Background
1968	14.	Summer

BENDIT, RUTH
| 1978 | 12. | Bright Bouquet |

BENHAM, CHRISTINA M.
| 1977 | 11. | Indiana Landscape |

BEN-NETT, DIXIE
| 1973 | 9. | The Later Years |

BENNETT, HELEN FREEMAN
| 1929 | 27. | Euphorbia |

BERGSTROM, CHARLES J.
1946	18.	The Last Glow
	19.	Virgin Stream
1947	24.	Mt. Harvard
1950	19.	Rocky Mountain Stream

BERKSHIRE, DON
1960	20.	Shadows on the Snow
1961	25.	The Thaw
1962	31.	After the Snow
1964	23.	Winter
1965	15.	Stream, Winter

BERLYN, JEAN
1983	12.	The Quilters
	13.	Caroling for Ol' "Miss Peeby"
1986	14.	Mom, the Flag and Apple Pie
	15.	Sunday Evening in Spring

BERNARDIN, MAREN N.
| 1972 | 5. | Untitled Drawing |

BERNHARDT, JOHN
| 1950 | 20. | The Poles |

BERNSTEIN, BLANCHE
| 1952 | 25. | Indiana Scene |

BERRY, WILS
| 1926 | 35. | High Finance* |

BERTHELSEN, JOHANN
1928	29.	Edge of Park
	30.	Lake in the Park
	31.	In the Park*

1929	28.	In the Park
	29.	Across the Park
1941	14.	Flowers*
	15.	Still Life
	16.	Upper 5th Ave., New York*
1942	12.	Brooklyn Bridge Tower, N. Y. C.
	13.	Fifth Avenue, N. Y. C.
1943	20.	Little Church Around the Corner
	21.	Winter, New York City
1944	24.	Nocturne, New York City
	25.	Connecticut Landscape
	26.	Winter, New York City
1946	20.	Flowers
	21.	The Plaza, New York City*
1947	211.	Central Park, New York
1948	7.	Winter, New York City
	8.	5th Avenue, New York City
1950	21.	5th Avenue, New York City*
	22.	Little Church Around the Corner
1951	11.	5th Avenue, New York, N. Y.
	12.	Winter, New York, N. Y.
	13.	Spring Evening, the Plaza, New York City
1952	26.	Central Park*
	27.	5th Avenue, Looking South at 60th St., N. Y.
1954	22.	The Lake, Central Park
	23.	United Nations, New York City*
	24.	The Plaza, New York City
1955	20.	East River Drive
	21.	5th Avenue, New York
1957	11.	Chanson Grise
	12.	Washington Square, New York City
1958	22.	Gramercy Park, New York
	23.	Evening, Central Park, New York City
	24.	Summer Evening, Washington Square
1959	19.	East 42nd St.
	20.	United Nations, New York
	21.	The Old Fifth Avenue Bank, 1955
1960	21.	"The Mall," Central Park
	22.	"The Plaza," New York, New York
1961	26.	59th St. and 5th Ave., New York City
	27.	Upper 5th Ave., New York City
1962	32.	Belvedere Fountain
	33.	Central Park, New York

BERTRAM, LUCILE

1955	22.	Spring Flowers
1965	16.	Serigraph No. 1

BERTRAM, RILEY

1968	15.	Studio Study

BESSIRE, DALE (P.)

1925	17.	Peaceful Valley
	18.	Snowbound Village
1926	36.	A Brown County Cabin
	37.	Early Morning in the Hills

1927	19.	Fog and Tide, Provincetown
	20.	A Street in Provincetown
1928	32.	Our Hillside
	33.	The Valley at Evening
1929	30.	A Road in the Hills
	31.	October Hills
	32.	October Galaxy
1930	22.	Wintry Sky
	23.	Deepening Shadows*
1931	22.	November Haze
1932	15.	A Road in the Valley
	16.	Hills in Haze
	17.	In the Valley
1933	14.	Hills of Story
	15.	Sunlight Hills
1934	12.	Blue Valley
	13.	Sunset Glow
1935	13.	Sage Grass
1936	16.	Locust Hill
	17.	Wintry Road*
1937	13.	Tranquility
	304.	Red Bud and Blossoms
1938	14.	Quietude
	15.	Reflections
1939	17.	October Comes
	300.	A Bright Spring Morning
1940	11.	White Mantled Hills
	300.	Valley of Peace
1941	17.	Hills of April
	301.	Lavender and Lace
1942	14.	Road to Greenbriar
1943	22.	After a November Rain
1944	27.	The Roadside Maple
	28.	December Stream
1945	22.	Blossoms
1946	22.	Quebec Waterfront
1947	25.	January Thaw
1948	9.	Hoosier Landmark
1950	23.	Winter Peace
1951	14.	Smoky Mountain Stream
1952	28.	Hidden Valley
1954	25.	Oaks of Maumee
1955	23.	Spring in Brown County
1956	15.	Pioneer Cabin

BESSMER, HAL

1961	28.	Coventry

BEST, PHILIP H.

1971	13.	Two Riders
	14.	Two Barns

BEVAN, JOCK S. B.

1960	23.	Civic Progress
	24.	R. M. S. Queen Mary
	25.	LaPorte Neuve Vezelay

BEVER, ROBERT C.

1975	12.	Remains of Prince
1977	12.	Kingman Hotel

1982	16.	Reflections
1986	16.	Comfortable

BEYER, EARL
1931	23.	Helen's Story (Portrait of Helen Barry)
1932	18.	One and Two
1938	16.	Shadow Green

BHAT, MADHUKAR BALIRAM
1975	13.	Horizon

BIELECKY, STANLEY
1935	14.	Clown Resting
	15.	Monks
	16.	Circus Zebras
1936	18.	The Sledge Men
1937	14.	Portrait of C
1938	17.	La Mercado Merced
1939	18.	Flowerpiece with Zinnias
	19.	Portrait of Pierrot

BIESEL, CHARLES
1925	19.	Mount Tom
1926	38.	Mt. Tom, Indiana
1927	21.	Early Morning
1929	33.	Swordfishermen
1938	301.	Winter Morning

BIGELOW, JOHN M.
1968	16.	Pigeons in the Park

BIGGERSTAFF, MYRA
1947	26.	A Pot of Flowers

BIGLER, MARY JANE (White)
(See White, Mary Jane)
1943	23.	Weeds and a Mandolin
1948	10.	Bouquet Bleue
1949	17.	Pink Flowers

BILLINGSLY, ROBERT A.
1987	8.	A Sea of Umbrellas
	9.	Hoosier Panorama
1988	12.	The Water Gap

BINGMAN, TERESA
1987	10.	Jake's
	11.	Alex
1988	13.	Dad

BIPPUS, ANNE
1955	24.	Water: Smooth But Pliable

BIRD, PETER F.
1969	18.	Rev. Martin Luther King

BIRDSONG, JOAN
1976	26.	Memory Lane

BIRGE, EVELYN C.
1953	16.	No Admittance

BIRREN, DONALD H.
1949	18.	Delphine
	19.	Kansas, 1935

BIRREN, JOSEPH (P.)
1927	22.	Eagle Hollow
	23.	Indian Creek
1928	34.	Indian Summer
1929	34.	Willow Lace
	35.	Days Ending
	36.	A Glorious Day
1930	24.	Gilding Sunshine
1933	16.	Sassafras Trees
	17.	The Manor House Beyond

BISHOP, CONNIE
1974	11.	Sidetracked
	12.	Erie Station*

BISHOP, DEE
1982	17.	Wild Grapes
	18.	Winter Go Round
1986	17.	I Ain't Got No Body
1987	12.	"912 North Street"
	13.	Palm

BISHOP, LOUISE NEVIUS
1973	10.	Down East Fisherman's Shack
1981	11.	Sheffield Tankard

BIXLER, HELEN
1987	14.	Chapeaux Circa 1910
1989	14.	Young Bananas

BLACK, JEAN
1968	17.	Cuernavaca, Mexico
1969	19.	Rogues Hollow
1970	12.	Cadadupa, Jamaica

BLACK, LEAH J.
1963	17.	Souvenirs of Summer
1964	24.	Bean Blossom Bridge

BLACK, LEE
1962	34.	La Poire Murissante

BLAIR, MILDRED
1961	29.	Climbing Roses*
	30.	Peonies and Shadows

BLAKER, HELEN S.
1961	31.	Sunrise over Mt. Eagle

BLANKENSHIP, DIANE
(See Day, Gentry)
1980	11.	Bill

BLASE, PANSY
1960	26.	The Lone House
1962	35.	On Petersburg Road
1963	18.	Sandra's Mandolin
1965	17.	Lilacs

BLASINGHAM, KATHERINE GROH
1931	24.	Jonquils and Stock
1932	19.	Lilacs
1933	18.	Zinnias
1934	14.	Winter Flowers
1937	15.	On the Coffee Mill Steps
1938	18.	On the Red Tablecloth
1939	20.	Flowers with Shell
	21.	On a White Table Cloth
1941	302.	Phlox
1942	15.	On the Blue Table Cloth
	16.	Spring Flowers
1943	24.	Marigolds and Love-in-the-Cup
	25.	On the Red Tablecloth
1945	23.	White Chrysanthemums
1947	27.	Flowers in the Staffordshire Teapot
1948	11.	White Pinks, Pink Roses
1949	20.	Summer White
1951	15.	Flowers in Victorian Vase
	16.	Garden's End
1952	29.	Nostalgia
1955	25.	White Roses
1956	16.	Spring Enchantment
1957	13.	Tigers
1959	22.	Angel Trumpets
1961	32.	Nostalgia II
1962	36.	White Flowers from a Summer Garden
	37.	Spring Fragrance
1963	19.	Brocade and Paisley
1969	20.	Marigolds

BLATZ, JAMES (E.)
1973	11.	The Wood Box
1977	13.	Autumn Peacock

BLEVINS, PATRICIA
1966	11.	Sun Life
1967	17.	The River
	18.	The Flowers #1

BLODGETT, JOHN W.
1990	9.	Mother Hawk

BLOOMHORST, KENNETH
1965	18.	A Study of Barns and Planes

BLOWER, DAVID
1948	12.	The Farewell*
1949	21.	California Bouquet*
1951	17.	Opening Act, Back Stage
	18.	The Picture Window
1952	30.	Quiet Inlet, Lake Mead
	31.	Pacific Night*
	32.	Moonlight Dance

1954	26.	Ghost Town, Rhyolite, Nevada
1955	26.	Low Tide, Newport Beach
	27.	Surf Fishing, Malibu
1956	17.	House by the Pacific
1960	27.	Tin Can Beach
1962	38.	Bunker Hill House

BLUHM, MARIE
1983	14.	Lunch Hour

BOAZ, (Jr.), BURLING
1947	28.	Serenity
1948	13.	Out of Business *
	14.	Storm Clouds
1949	22.	Brand New Pump
1950	24.	Dyer's Bay
	25.	Jack's Shack
1951	19.	Corn
	20.	Boat House Tall Timbers
1952	33.	News Broadcast
	34.	Sunday Morning and the Sexton
1953	17.	Super Market
	18.	Carroll County
	19.	Monticello
1954	27.	T. E. "Pop" Myers
1956	18.	The Scavengers
	19.	Grand Circuit
1957	14.	Mrs. Procter
1958	25.	Collapidated
	26.	The Last Load
1959	23.	Snow Slide
	24.	Secretaries of Agriculture
1960	28.	Main Street
1961	33.	Abandoned
	34.	1905 Model*
	35.	Snow Sled
1962	39.	The Decoys
	40.	9 Degrees Below
	41.	T in Tennessee
1963	20.	Turn Around
	21.	Collapidated
1964	25.	On Georgian Bay
	26.	Shadow Patterns
1965	19.	Depressed Area
	20.	Detour
1966	12.	Along the Canal
1967	19.	Sunday Morning
	20.	Old Coal Mine
1968	18.	Snowed In

BOBBS, RUTH PRATT
1925	24.	Portrait Walter L. Milliken
	25.	Mary
	26.	Alice
1926	39.	Betsy
	40.	Irma
1940	12.	The Scientist
1941	18.	Linda*
1942	17.	Judy
	18.	Mrs. G. H. A. Clowes

1944	29.	Portrait
1945	24.	Objects on a Table
	25.	The Commando
1946	23.	Christopher
1947	29.	J. P. Frenzel, Jr.
1951	21.	Portrait Sketch
1956	20.	Tinkie

BOBICK, BRUCE

1969	21.	Ganglion*
	22.	Beacon
1970	13.	Neuroglia
	14.	Barium Traces
1972	6.	Cirriped Larvae
1973	12.	Shaft Mine with Strata
1974	13.	Milkweeds
1975	14.	Cross Section: Retina with Optic Nerve*
	15.	Ritual Arrangement: Talismans and Phalanges
1978	13.	Butterfly Woman V: In the Garden of Orchids
1979	13.	Grandmother Melville's Quilt, Made for Young Herman*
	14.	Remnant of the Black Bean Quilt

BODELL, MARK ROBINSON

1930	25.	River Edge

BOHLANDER, JOAN (S.)

1964	27.	Spring Flood
1967	21.	Winter Pears
1968	19.	The Three Sisters, Katoomba
1974	14.	From Orchard & Field
1976	27.	Collectors Items

BOHM, C. CURRY

1928	35.	October Morning
	36.	Brown County Landscape
	37.	In the Valley
1929	37.	The Picnickers
	38.	Brown Co., Landscape
1930	26.	When October Comes
	27.	Early Spring
1931	25.	Look Up
	26.	The Wet Road
1932	20.	Light o' Morn
	21.	A Kentucky Mt. Road
1933	19.	Late October
	20.	The End of the Street
1934	15.	To the Field
	16.	East Chicago
	17.	Early Monday Morning
1935	17.	A Dewy Morning
	18.	Storm in the Smokies
	19.	Wet Snow
1936	19.	Morning
	20.	The Harvest
	21.	Woman's Song of Color

1937	16.	Resurrection
	17.	Valley of Contentment
	18.	Snow of Hardan Hollow**
	305.	Zinnias and Old Glass
1938	19.	Early Winter
	20.	Silver Morning
	302.	Angry Mountain
1939	22.	Drifting Snow
	23.	Spring Melody
	24.	Symphony in Pink and White
	301.	Young Winter
1940	13.	Hills of Summer
	14.	Mountain Man's Gold
	15.	The Thaw
	301.	Song of the Hoosier*
1941	19.	Autumn Rhythm
	20.	Cauldron of the Smokies
	21.	Snow of Ephraim**
1942	19.	For Better, For Worse
	20.	Rain on the Fishing Village
	21.	Winter's Lace
1943	26.	Wet Autumn
	27.	Approaching Storm
	28.	Virgin Snow
1944	30.	Wind Swept
	31.	The Young Oaks
1945	26.	Spring Symphony
	27.	Gray Hills of Winter*
	28.	The Twins
1946	24.	Seeking Shelter*
	25.	Family Industry
	26.	Magic of an April Shower
1947	30.	Snow Clad Hills
	31.	The Sudden Squall
	32.	Northern Vermont
1948	15.	Clearing
1949	23.	Hills of Winter
1950	26.	Heavy Seas*
	27.	Winter Grays
1951	22	Winter Ends
	23.	Watching the Frenzy
1952	35.	Conflict
	36.	Edge of the Village
1953	20.	A Fair Breeze*
	21.	The Heart of the Village
	22.	A Snug Harbor
1954	28.	Foul Weather
	29.	The Last Glow
	30.	Fish Industry
1955	28.	Clearing
	29.	March Snow
	30.	Mackerel Boats
1956	21.	November Hills
	22.	Eastern Blow
	23.	Salvaging
1957	15.	Brew Weather*
	16.	Melancholy Day
	17.	The Men Who Man the Boats
1958	27.	Young Spring
	28.	Preparation
	29.	The Blow

1959	25.	Village of Nashville*
	26.	Fog on a Grey-Green Sea
	27.	Springtime on a Fence Row
1960	29.	Resistance
	30.	Galosh Weather
	31.	Weather Beaten*
1961	36.	Home of the Vermonter
	37.	Quietude
	38.	The Haunt of the Red Dragger*
1962	42.	Grey Hills of Indiana*
	43.	Grey-Green Sea of Monhegan
	44.	Winter Conversation
1963	22.	Spring Symphony
1964	28.	The Sudden Squall*
	29.	Wind in the Sky
	30.	Fisherman's Wharf
1965	21.	Coming Fury
	22.	Burning Off
	23.	When the Green Mountains Turn Gray
1966	13.	White Water of the Morning
	14.	Lobstermen's Lane
1967	22.	Herald of Spring*
1972	7.	Lobstermen Gathering Their Gear

BOHNER, MARIAN (A.)

1943	29.	Mexican Peon Farmer
1944	32.	Siesta Time in Taxco
	33.	Po Po, the Great White Warrior

BOLESKY, JOHN

| 1980 | 12. | Series #5 |

BOLINGER, INEZ RUSSELL

1938	21.	October Reflections
1944	34.	Marjories Alley
1946	27.	Blue Coat and Asters
	28.	White Bowl

BOLLER, CAROLE

1988	14.	Cat Napping
1989	15.	Levitating Spirit
1990	10.	Tool Bag

BOMBARD, FLOYD (W.)

1957	18.	Gladiolas
	19.	Autumn at Shakamak
1958	30.	"Adoration," at Brown County
1959	28.	Companions
1960	32.	Surf in Storm
	33.	Stormy Day
1961	39.	Let the Sea Roar
	40.	Queechee Forest
1963	23.	Fog, Cape Elizabeth, Maine
1964	31.	Eventide
	32.	Makapun Point on Island of Oahu
1965	24.	Portrait, Mary
1967	23.	At Renoirs, "Les Collettes"
1968	20.	Waiting

BOND, BYRON LELAND

| 1928 | 38. | Low Tide, Provincetown |
| 1929 | 39. | Indiana World War Memorial |

BONIFIELD, CHARLES

| 1961 | 41. | Pilings against the Surf |

BONSIB, LOUIS W.

1932	22.	Evening in Autumn
1934	18.	The Apple Tree
1936	22.	Indian Gap, Great Smokies
	23.	The First Snow
1937	19.	Cloudy Afternoon
1938	22.	Snow Time
1939	25.	Snow in Tennessee
	302.	Afterglow
1940	302.	Autumn Tapestry
1941	22.	Home in the Hills
1942	22.	Winter Mood
1944	35.	Storm at Tucson
	36.	Washday in Tennessee
1945	29.	Sunlight after Rain
1946	29.	Cabin in the Corn
1947	33.	October Gold
1948	16.	Beeches in Snow
	17.	Crossroads Church
1951	24.	The Old Mill
	25.	Eucalyptus Trees
1953	23.	Busy Mill at Auburn
1954	31.	Along the St. Mary's
1955	31.	Snow on Mount Lemon
1956	24.	Storm at Carmel
	25.	The Great Smokies
1957	20.	Rainy Day in Japan
	21.	Morning in Nikko (Japan)
	22.	Tennessee in Afternoon
1959	29.	Mediaeval Bruges
1960	34.	Winter Wonderland
	35.	Mountain Park
1961	42.	Old Kentucky Home
	43.	Mountain Vista
	44.	Snowbound
1962	45.	Alpine Majesty
	46.	Spring Bouquet
1963	24.	Hazy Day
1964	33.	Autumn Tapestry
	34.	Old Saw Mill
1965	25.	Winter on Cedar Creek
1967	24.	Happy Valley
1969	23.	Mount Moran
1970	15.	Evening in Tennessee
1971	15.	Tennessee River

BOOMER, FRANCES E.

| 1946 | 30. | Windows in the Sky |

BOONE, GARRET J.

| 1963 | 25. | Head |

BOONE, JUNE (Elvina)
1960	36.	Brenda
1961	45.	A Study
	46.	Kitty
	47.	Annette
1962	47.	Portrait No. 1
	48.	Portrait No. 2
1963	26.	Mother and Child
	27.	Portrait*
1964	35.	Diana
	36.	Jane
1965	26.	Portrait No. 2
1967	25.	Young Pocahontas
	26.	Fur Hat
1968	21.	My Neighbor's Daughter
1970	16.	Pastel No. 2

BOORMAN, MICHIKO
1970	17.	Window
1972	8.	October Song*
1973	13.	Abandoned Memories
1974	15.	Root of Life*
1976	28.	The Last Embers
1977	14.	Winter Harmony
1984	14.	Milkweed
1986	18.	Corn Field
	19.	Affection
1989	16.	Nature's Beauty
1990	11.	Cornfield
	12.	Old Log

BOPP, CHERYL H.
| 1975 | 16. | Ray: Time-Life |

BORDEN, JAMES C.
1972	9.	Terry
1985	10.	A Man
1986	20.	From the Sea
1987	15.	Boat Out East
	16.	Those Chickens Are Loose Again
1988	15.	Out East
	16.	The Big 'A'*
1990	13.	Man with Beard
	14.	Festival

BORDEN, WILLIAM
1975	17.	At the End of the Line
	18.	Marion Grain Company
1976	29.	Heading Out
1977	15.	Aunt Maude's
	16.	Farwell Mills
1979	15.	Michigan Winter
	16.	Resting in Oakland*
1980	13.	Venerable Veteran
1981	12.	Near Silver Lake
	13.	Travelers Reprieve
1983	15.	Winter River

BOSKO, CAROL
| 1989 | 17. | An Aerobic Dancer |

BOTKIN, PENELOPE
1963	28.	Lone Cabin
1964	37.	Glory Street
1965	27.	Moon Lace
	28.	A Dreamer's Dream
1966	15.	Two's Company
1969	24.	Autumn Symphony
1972	10.	Autumnal Pagentry

BOTT, EARLE WAYNE
1925	27.	Farm House, Montoir, France
1933	21.	A Peasant's Cottage, LaRochelle, France
1963	29.	Bird

BOTT, MABEL SIEGELIN
| 1926 | 41. | Still Life Group |
| | 42. | Still Life Group |

BOTT, OREN EARLE
| 1967 | 27. | Turbulence |

BOUILLET, JULES A.
| 1971 | 16. | Spencer County |

BOWDEN, A. J.
| 1939 | 26. | Spring |

BOWE, MARY E.
(See Osterday, Mary B.)
1960	37.	Stay, Sam
1961	48.	Charlie's Sam
	49.	Good Friday in the Rocky Mountains

BOWEN, DOROTHY J.
| 1947 | 34. | Isolation |

BOWEN, RUTH
| 1965 | 29. | My Little Vase |

BOWERS, DOROTHY A.
| 1946 | 31. | Portrait of Magnolia |

BOWMAN, MARY ANN
| 1968 | 22. | Vase with Dry Flowers |
| 1970 | 18. | Overstuffed |

BOYCE, GERALD G.
| 1970 | 19. | The Royal Hawker* |
| | 20. | San Marco Vittoria |

BOYD, MARION (McBroom)
1948	18.	The Matriarch
1951	26.	Magnolia
1953	24.	Gray Spring Day*
1954	32.	Forsythia
1955	32.	The Nisqually
1956	26.	Fall Chores
1957	23.	Yesterday's Relic
	24.	Picnic for the Birds

1958	31.	Smoky Mountain Torrent
1959	30.	Sunlit Beach
1960	38.	Spring along the Creek
	39.	Path in the Park
1961	50.	Play's End
1962	49.	Early Morning
1963	30.	Band Boat
1964	38.	Early Color
1967	28.	The Rink at Night

BOYER, DWIGHT O.

1956	27.	Reaching High
1960	40.	Indian Summer
	41.	Misty Morn
1962	50.	Autumn Mist

BOYER, JAN SCOTT

1967	29.	After a Snowy Winter Day
1968	23.	Old Fashioned Winter
1969	25.	Wisconsin Winter
	26.	Kurt's Corner
1970	21.	An Afternoon in Winter*
1973	14.	Town with Bridge
	15.	A Winter Long Past
1974	16.	Twin Cities
1975	19.	Kneeling Goddess with Bird
1976	30.	Yaotzin
1980	14.	The Tenth Realm
1981	14.	Jungle
1982	19.	Indianaplex
1983	16.	Master Design for Indianapolis*
	17.	Computerplex
1984	15.	Kingdom of the Imagination
	16.	Indianapolis Futureplex*
1985	11.	My Kingdom
	12.	Blue City

BOYKIN, J. N.

1963	31.	Lonely Sands

BOYLE, BETTY C.

1970	22.	Two with Mustard
	23.	Patterns
1973	16.	Passing Parade
1976	31.	Nassau Blue
	32.	The Circle, A. M.
1977	17.	Corner Shadows
1984	17.	The Walls Come Tumblin'
	18.	Landmark
1986	21.	Tomorrow's Blossoms
1987	17.	Downtown
	18.	Sea Wall
1988	17.	The Park Dancers
1990	15.	View Point

BRACKMIER, HERBERT W.

1935	20.	Roger's House
1938	23.	Arabian Horse and Rider

BRADFIELD, ROD (M.)

1982	20.	Stereo #2
	21.	Paint Tubes and Templates #1
1983	18.	Petroglymph Series #1
	19.	Petroglymph Series #2

BRADFORD, ELGIN

1978	14.	Floral No. 3
1980	15.	Open Window

BRADLEY, CAROLYN G.

1925	20.	Zinnias
1926	43.	The Fairy Festival
	44.	The Gitana Maid
	45.	A Still Life of Flowers
1927	24.	The Deserted Barn
	25.	The Green Bottle
	26.	Chadwick Fisheries*
1928	39.	Dahlias
	40.	Boothbay Harbor
	41.	A Flower Garden
1929	40.	Garden Flowers
	41.	Repairing the Boat
	42.	Escadinhas
1930	28.	Habitant House
	29.	Drying Sails
	30.	Still Life of Flowers
1931	27.	A Grey Day
	28.	Chinese Lanterns
1932	23.	In the Court
1933	22.	Cascade
	23.	Clothes Line Ghosts
	24.	The Original Mutt*
1934	19.	Beached
	20.	High Tide
1935	21.	Tropical Sun
	22.	The Studio*
1936	24.	Tree Dotted Hill*
1937	20.	Luis Jose
	21.	Glaciers of Govotnie*
1938	24.	Nopal Cactus
	25.	A Basque
	303.	Mexican Market
1939	27.	Matea and Inez
	28.	Lilies for Sale
1940	16.	Landscape, Guatemala
1941	23.	Cecelia at Market
1942	23.	Guatemalan Mother and Child
	24.	Sam Marcos
1943	30.	San Miguel
1944	37.	Midwest Station
1945	30.	Farm Buildings
1950	28.	The Balcony
	29.	The Grain Market
	30.	The Mountain Road

BRADLEY, NORMAN

1966	16.	Untitled

BRADSHAW, DEL(ores)

1977	18.	African Women in Rhythm

BRADSHAW, MARTHA

1961	51.	Garden Variety
1963	32.	The Cornfield
1964	39.	Within the Cave
1968	24.	Sunset
	25.	Hydrangeas
1970	24.	Sunlight and Shadows
1974	17.	Golden Glow

BRADY, HAROLD

1969	27.	Pencil Drawing
	28.	Goldenrod

BRAMS, JOAN

1967	30.	Japanese Landscape
	31.	Landscape in the Pale
	32.	Delta*

BRANCH, KAY

1961	52.	Eagle Star Taos Chief
1963	33.	Peonies

BRANDNER, GLADYS D(ecker)

1931	29.	Delphiniums
1933	25.	From the Garden Wall
	26.	A Son of the East
1934	21.	A Window Bouquet
1935	23.	Portrait
1949	24.	A Summer Bouquet
1950	31.	Dogwood and Redbud

BRANDNER, KARL C. (F.)

1929	43.	Mid-summer Day, Fairfield, Indiana
	44.	Hillside Barn
	45.	Tumble-Down Barn
1930	31.	Monday
	32.	Snowbound
	33.	Harvest
	34.	Boyhood Haunt
	35.	Old Covered Bridge
	36.	Late January Afternoon*
1931	30.	Mid-Summer Fields
	31.	An Old Landmark
	32.	Abandoned
	33.	Old Barn
	34.	The Well House
	35.	The Trysting Place
	36.	Old Covered Bridge
	37.	Snow Bound
	38.	Winter
1932	24.	The Grist Mill
	25.	The Wind
	26.	The Village Church*
1933	27.	The County Seat (Nashville, Indiana)
	28.	Springtime at the Mill

	29.	The Trackless Deep
	30.	The Village Church
	31.	Boyhood Memories
	32.	Wintery Solitude
	33.	Brown County Idyll
1934	22.	The White Mantle
	23.	Phlox and Hydrangia
	24.	A Friendly Road
1935	24.	Green Shutters
	25.	Sunlite and Shadow
1937	22.	January 17th*
	23.	Red Flannels
	24.	Softly Falling Snow
	306.	Zinnias and Cosmos
1938	26.	R. R. No. 3*
	27.	Across the Valley
	28.	Spring Awakening
	304.	Summer Fields
1939	29.	Lace
	30.	November Hills*
1940	17.	Christmas Eve in the Old Neighborhood
	18.	Silence
	303.	Mid Summer
1941	24.	Sunlight and Shadow, Grand Canyon
1942	25.	Early Morning, Grand Canyon
	26.	February
	27.	Snow Covered Hills
1943	31.	July
	32.	A Winter Poem
	33.	October, Brown County
1945	31.	The Back Road
	32.	January
	33.	Enchanted Hills*
1946	32.	Over the Valley
	33.	The Sugar Shack
1947	35.	Hempfield
	36.	February 12th
1948	19.	The Patriarch
	20.	A Sunday Afternoon*
1949	25.	Undefiled
1950	32.	Over the Valley
	33.	The Red Barn
1951	27.	December 24th
	28.	Peaceful Valley*
1953	25.	Sunlite & Shadows, Grand Canyon
	26.	October, Nashville, Indiana
1955	33.	A Memento of Other Days
	34.	One Winter Day

BRATOVICH, MARK (W.)

1985	13.	Renewal
1987	19.	Summer's Prisoners*
1988	18.	Quarry Heat
1989	18.	The Journey*
	19.	Broadside
1990	16.	Crossing the Line
	17.	The Last Fourth

BRCIN, JOHN DAVID
1929	46.	Robert Pelzl*
	47.	Caroline
	48.	Centaur of the Steppes, Razin of the Cossack Bandit
1931	39.	Fantasy
	40.	Distaff Memories
	41.	The Bullwhacker
1933	34.	Woodrow Wilson
	35.	Portrait of a Friend
1935	26.	Sioux Warrior
	27.	Jean
1936	25.	Sonneteer*
	26.	Nancy
1938	29.	Study*
1939	31.	Echo
1940	19.	Mark Twain

BREDEWATER, GEORGE
| 1984 | 19. | Closing Time* |

BREEN, HARRY F.
1956	28.	A Portrait of Juno
	29.	The Meadow*
1957	25.	The Blowout
	26.	Sand And Sky
1959	31.	Ripening Wheat
1960	42.	The Cloud
1961	53.	Midwest Prairie
	54.	The Fence
1963	34.	Rhinoceros*
1964	40.	Unicorn from the Garden

BREEN, MARTHA
| 1976 | 33. | Pears and Bagels |
| | 34. | Self Portrait |

BREEN, MILDRED
1970	25.	Little Boxes
1972	15.	Pueblo DeLos Montanas
	16.	Ring Around the Circuit
1975	20.	Labyrinth '74
	21.	Bellerophon Slaying the Chimera
1976	35.	Genesis
1980	16.	Pueblo
1981	15.	Agamemnon
1982	22.	Jerusalem
1985	14.	Oriental Composition
1986	22.	Composition-October-December
	23.	West Window
1990	18.	Evelyn's Peonies

BREHM, GEORGE
| 1927 | 27. | Unhappy Day |

BRENTLINGER, MIRIAM
| 1966 | 17. | Mabel |

BRETHAUER, MARY (M.)
| 1958 | 32. | Lighthouse near Daytona |
| 1963 | 35. | Portrait of Young Artist |

BREWER, ELEANOR K.
| 1988 | 19. | Hope & Faith |

BRIDGE, MORTON
| 1933 | 36. | Eve |
| | 37. | Portrait of a Dowdy Lady |

BRIGGS, HELEN L.
(See Duckwall, Helen Briggs)
1938	30.	The Black Hat*
	31.	Tomorrow's Ballerina
1939	32.	First Day of School

BRIGGS, PAULINE
1954	33.	Quiescence*
	34.	Abandoned
1955	35.	Day's End
1963	36.	Percé

BRILL, SHARON
| 1966 | 18. | Virgin Timber Land |

BRINDEL, CAROLYN S.
| 1971 | 17. | Continuum |

BRINKMAN, DORIS J.
1970	26.	Americana
	27.	Remnant
1971	18.	Moment in a Mexican Cathedral
1973	17.	Morning at the Point
	18.	Petroglyph*
1974	18.	Caribbean Patterns
1979	17.	Storm Warning
1980	17.	Morning's First Light
1983	20.	Wind-Swept
1984	20.	Remnants of Power
1986	24.	Ancient Sentinels
	25.	Frozen Forms
1989	20.	Along an Ancient Way
	21.	Patterns of Time and Wind
1990	19.	Land of Rock & Wind

BRINTON, H. DOSWELL
| 1938 | 33. | Hay Stack, Straw Stack |

BRITT, RALPH M.
1926	46.	Sleepy Time
	47.	In the Park*
1927	28.	The Old Arbor*
	29.	Corner of Studio
1928	42.	Gray Day
	43.	Along the Street
1929	49.	Monday Parade
1930	37.	Self Portrait
1951	29.	Pottery Maker
1952	37.	Young Bacchus
	38.	Clouds on the Hill
1954	35.	Georgia Road

BROCKENBROUGH, ELEANOR
1925	28.	Main Street
	29.	Drying Sails, Gloucester
1926	48.	Zinnias
	49.	Along the Wabash
	50.	A Summer Morning
1927	30.	The Red Boat
	31.	Gloucester Street
	32.	The Garden Gate
1929	50.	Gloucester Flowers
1930	38.	Old Houses in Gloucester
1931	42.	Gloucester from the Hill

BROSS, JANIS
1970	28.	Still Life, Three = One

BROTHER ETIENNE COOPER, C.S.C.
1944	38.	Filipino
1945	34.	Head of Christ
	35.	Madonna*
1946	34.	Interlude
	35.	Woman with Pearls*
1950	34.	St. Francis

BROTHER LOYOLA CHRISTOPH, C.S.C.
1944	39.	Head of Christ*

BROWER, JOE H.
1954	36.	Old Man
1957	27.	The Cove
	28.	Schuylkill River Locks

BROWN, BEULAH H(azelrigg)
1958	33.	Spring Fragrance
1964	41.	Summer Treasures
	42.	Indiana Hill Country
	43.	Summer Splendor

BROWN, FRANCIS CLARK
1935	28.	Dwelling
1939	33.	Blue Ridge Mountains
	34.	Indiana Wheatfield
1943	34.	The Frozen Pump
	35.	Elkinsville, Brown County
	36.	A Spring Day
1947	37.	General Store
	38.	Snowbound
1948	21.	Other Side of the Tracks
1949	26.	Winter Glory*
1951	30.	Treaty Creek
1956	30.	Ohio Homestead*
	31.	Snow Hill
1957	29.	Red Georgia Clay*
	30.	Winter Sentinel
	31.	Old Covered Bridge
1958	34.	Cape Cod Landmark*
1959	32.	By the Side of the Road
	33.	Boat's End
	34.	Port Isabel, Texas
1960	43.	Old Gasoline Wagon

1961	55.	Traders Point Bridge
	56.	Boats in the Sun
	57.	The First Snowfall
1962	51.	Arnold's Wharf
	52.	Old Mill in Winter
1963	37.	Pigeon Cove
	38.	Ice Wagon
	39.	Lanesville Harbor
1964	44.	Pears
1967	33.	The Wishing Gate
1968	26.	Lone Mail Box
1969	29.	Flowering Crab Apple
1970	29.	Bridge at Friendship
	30.	Lobster Shanty
1971	19.	Crooked Creek Bridge
1972	11.	Snow on Lick Creek
1973	19.	Winter of '72
1975	22.	Nashville Landmark
	23.	Kelly Hill
1976	36.	Roof Tops*
1977	19.	Old Blackiston Mill
1979	18.	Stillwater River
1980	18.	Pattern of Winter
1982	23.	The First Snow

BROWN, FRANCIS F.
1925	21.	Across the Field
	22.	Fairy Land
	23.	Daddy Bucks' Place*
1926	51.	Beginning of Autumn
	52.	Winter
	53.	River Clouds*
1927	33.	Autumn
	34.	Cloud Sand
1928	44.	The Clouds*
1929	51.	Fairyland
	52.	Landscape
	53.	Autumn*
1930	39.	Horse Shoe Point
1935	29.	Factory Buildings
	30.	Flowers
1936	27.	An Indiana Landscape
1937	25.	Across the Creek*
	26.	The Stone Crusher
1938	32.	Ball Factory
1939	35.	Autumn in Westwood
1943	37.	The Creek
	38.	Spring
1945	36.	Variety*
	37.	Fall Flowers
1946	36.	Flowers
1951	31.	Folger's Point
1955	36.	New York
	37.	Fishing Boats
1964	45.	Springtime

BROWN, HELEN M.
1968	27.	Inner Earth

172

BROWN, MARGARET JAMES
| 1941 | 25. | Zinnias and Delphinium |
| 1942 | 28. | Japanese Peonies |

BROWN, MARY JOHNSTON
| 1943 | 39. | Plant Park, Tampa Jungle |
| | 40. | Road to Carlisle |

BROWN, PEGGY
1968	28.	Purely Imaginative Flowers
1969	30.	The House on the Hill
1971	20.	Patriarch II
1973	20.	Variations
1974	19.	The Poet's Hour
	20.	Behind Is Yesterday*
1975	24.	Beyond Memory II
	25.	Voice of Winter
1977	20.	Another Time, Another Place*
	21.	Cross Currents
1978	15.	Fading Fast
	16.	Still Waters Run*
1979	19.	As Cold As Ice*
	20.	This Moment in Time
1980	19.	Somewhere Before
	20.	For Evermore*
1981	16.	Look Inside My Fantasy*
1982	24.	Remembering
1983	21.	A Place Visited
1984	21.	Somewhere in Time
	22.	Different Places/One*

BROWN, RO ZELMA
| 1986 | 26. | The Sentinel |
| 1989 | 22. | Whistle Peddler |

BROWN, SARAH
| 1965 | 30. | Dingeys |
| | 31. | Yellow Weeds in a Window |

BROWN, WILLIAM F.
1981	17.	Box Series, #4
	18.	A Winter Plaque
1982	25.	Audubon Park, Summer (1982)

BROYLES, CHICQIELA S.
1975	28.	Amiable Pigs
1976	37.	Portrait of Plowhorse
1978	17.	Spot
1982	26.	Paul's Spotted Pig
1983	22.	Amiable Hogs
1984	23.	Saanen Specialty*
1989	23.	Hooded Chevoit
	24.	Two for the Show*

BRUBAKER, ROBERT L. (Bob)
1965	32.	Still Life
1966	19.	Gypsy Girl
	20.	Seascape
1967	34.	The Young Painters

BRUBECK, JEANNE D.
1976	38.	Kings Crowns
1977	23.	Hillside Foliage
	24.	Greenhouse Plantings

BRUCE, BLANCHE (C.)
1927	35.	Sand Dune Country
1928	45.	Landscape
1929	54.	View at Riverside
1930	40.	Taos Mountain
	41.	California Playground
1933	38.	Hollyhock & Daisies
	39.	Zinnias

BRUCE, BONNIE
| 1982 | 27. | Pops |
| | 28. | Happy |

BRUCE, PATTY McNAIR
1976	39.	April Showers
1977	25.	My Window
1982	29.	Solstice
1985	15.	Sarajevo

BRUCKER, EDMUND
1939	36.	Portrait of the Painter
	37.	Portrait of R. G. Jones
	38.	Slave Block*
1940	20.	Chinese Art Student*
	21.	The Green Cloth
1941	26.	Barbara
	27.	Still Life with Mandolin*
	28.	View of Nashville
1942	29.	Hoosier Woman
	30.	Allegory: Europe and Asia
	31.	Negro Art Student
1943	41.	Homage to Titian
	42.	Menagerie*
	43.	Patty
1944	40.	Marcelline
	41.	Little Susan*
1945	38.	Sisters
	39.	Machinist's Mate, First Class, Robert Gardner
1946	37.	Planting the Seed*
	38.	Aviation Cadet
	39.	Barbara Ann
1947	39.	Pattie*
	40.	Sober Eighties
	41.	Street Corner
1948	22.	Babs
1949	27.	Grandmother's Treasures*
	28.	Young Baseball Player
1950	35.	Victorian Lady
	36.	Portrait of Ginny
1951	32.	Paul Dresser*
1952	39.	Low Tide*
	40.	Blue Ribbon Percherons
	41.	Hoosier Blacksmith*
1953	27.	Morning Light
	28.	The Gray Cloth

1954	37.	Rockport
	38.	John O. Beasley
1955	38.	Portrait
	39.	End of Winter
	40.	Dry Dock*
1956	32.	The Old Mill
	33.	Boats in the Sun*
	34.	Victorian Portrait
1957	32.	Industrial Indianapolis
	33.	The Red Scarf
1958	35.	Bobby
	36.	Repose
1959	35.	The Sober Eighties
	36.	Portrait*
	37.	Rockport Revisited
1960	44.	Bass Rocks
1961	58.	Girl with Fan*
	59.	Portrait
1962	53.	Rastus*
	54.	Nocturnal Beach
	55.	Harbor*
1963	40.	Gloucester Pier
	41.	Excavation*
	42.	Paula
1964	46.	Rural Silhouette
	47.	Portrait
	48.	Route 67*
1965	33.	Cape Ann Boats*
1966	21.	Boats Ashore
	22.	Lobster Floats
	23.	Girl in Blue*
1967	35.	The Pier
	36.	Homage to Degas*
1968	29.	Portrait
	30.	Old Mining Town, Colo.
	31.	Leonardo Fragmenta*
1969	31.	Slave World or Free World
	32.	Negress
1970	31.	Untitled
	32.	Portrait*
1972	12.	Portrait
	13.	Untitled
1973	21.	Cape Ann Quarry
1974	21.	Portrait of Kathy
	22.	Indiana National*
1976	40.	Interior
1977	26.	Woman In Gray
1978	19.	Rockport Quarry*
	20.	Debbie Lynn
1979	21.	Portrait of Bob
1980	21.	Energy and Pollution
1981	19.	Country Girl
1982	30.	Matriarch*
1983	23.	Reflecting
1984	24.	Nude Composition
	25.	My Mother*
1985	16.	Portrait of a Young Man in Brown Jacket
1986	27.	White River Abutment
	28.	Portrait Study

BRUNDAGE, ETHEL (A.)

1986	29.	Sticks and Stones No. 2
	30.	Cosmic Energy
1988	20.	Queen Ann's Lace
	21.	Autumn Floral
1989	25.	Camelia
1990	22.	Still Life

BRUNING, PETER

1960	45.	Self Portrait
1967	37.	On Christmas Morning
	38.	Dutch Scene
1968	32.	Vincent*
	33.	Portrait of M. B.
1969	33.	Girl with Cat
	34.	Miriam
1972	14.	Child Outside*
1973	22.	Terre Haute Scene*
1975	29.	April*
	30.	Quiet Moment
1986	31.	The Kiss
1989	26.	Corsican Landscape
	27.	Still Life

BRYAN, RUTH GLASER

| 1948 | 23. | Still Life, Geranium |

BRYANT, JACQUELIN

1976	43.	Experience
	44.	A Touch of Blue
1978	18.	Reflections

BRYCE, THOMAS M.

| 1976 | 41. | Coach* |
| | 42. | John |

BRYDENTHAL, DOROTHY

| 1970 | 33. | Squall |

BUCHSBAUM, ELIZABETH M.

1931	43.	Fish
1932	27.	Flower Study
	28.	Owl
1933	40.	Opossum
1934	25.	Peonies
1936	28.	Heron and Turtle
1937	27.	Adobe House, Las Vegas, New Mexico

BUCHTA, ANTHONY

1935	31.	Corn in the Hollow
	32.	October's Robe of Scarlet
	33.	In the Grape Arbor
1936	29.	The Autumn World
	30.	October's Morning Robes
1938	34.	Evening Solitudes
	305.	A Humble Estate
1939	39.	Winter in Cincinnati
	40.	A Bit of Cincinnati
	303.	Spring at Bean Blossom

1940	22.	Rustic Simplicity Down in the Hollow *
	23.	Summer's Mantle of Peace
	304.	Summer's Childhood Play Days
1941	29.	Mother Earth Rewards Her Toiling Sons
1943	44.	Glorious America
1945	40.	Bounty from the Soil
1947	42.	An Old Courtyard in Old New Orleans
	43.	In the Peaceful Valley
1948	24.	Bean Blossom Overlook
	25.	Indiana's Fertile Fields
1951	33.	Young Corn and Cloudy Skies
	34.	The Great Smokies, Tennessee
1952	42.	O'er the Dreaming Knoll
1953	29.	Cotton Picking in the Delta
1954	39.	Fleeting Clouds of Summer
	40.	Springtime along Stonehead Creek
1955	41.	The Summer Clouds
	42.	A Rainy Day
1956	35.	The Veil Shrouded Cumberlands
	36.	The White Countryside
1957	34.	Sharecropper's Cottage
	35.	Winter Comes Again
	36.	Spring Baptism of the Good Earth
1958	37.	Spring Comes to the Hills
	38.	Jimmy Has a Bite
	39.	Milking Time
1959	38.	Summer Pastures
	39.	My Neighbor and His T. V. Program
	40.	The Happy Fisherman
1960	46.	Rustic Charm in the Ozarks*
	47.	Spring Lyric to Brown County
1961	60.	Jimmy Gives Sis a Ride
	61.	Summer's Boyhood Joys
	62.	Autumn Hunt
1962	56.	Milking Time
	57.	After the Rain
	58.	Winter Glorifies the Hills
1963	43.	This Alley Has Charm
1964	49.	Winter's Robes of White
	50.	Harvesting Hay in June
1965	34.	Majesty of Winter Robes
1966	24.	The Hills Covered with White
	25.	Summer Tranquility

BUCK, HAROLD (L.)

1976	45.	Aggregates
1977	27.	Fishing Pier, Virginia Beach
1978	21.	Indiana Barn
	22.	Face
1979	22.	Prismatic Impressions
1980	22.	Along Salt Creek
	23.	Virginia Beach
1985	17.	Railroad Pass
1986	32.	Old Iron Bridge on Driftwood River
1987	20.	Johnson County Sycamores

BUCK, LUKE (Luther A.)

1969	35.	Gloucester
1970	34.	The Sound of Summer
	35.	Study and Self Portrait
1972	17.	Winter Thaw
1973	23.	Red Mills
1979	23.	The Wave Inn
1981	20.	Sweetwater Trail Schoolhouse
	21.	Isle in the Field
1982	31.	Foxes Corner Indiana
1983	24.	Riverfront Home, Aurora, Indiana
1984	26.	Birth of the Blues
	27.	Goshen Church

BUCKLEW, KEN R.

1990	23.	February Cottonwoods
	24.	Bluebird Country

BUCKLEY, PATRICIA MORRISON

1967	39.	Mexican Boy

BUDDENBAUM, F. C.

1944	42.	Sunlit Bank

BUDDENBAUM, RALPH L.

1959	41.	The Ruffled Feathers

BUESCHER, HELEN A.

1990	20.	Earth Mother IV
	21.	Earth Mothers

BUFFINGTON, JULES O.

1988	22.	Thistles
	23.	Studs

BULLOCK, RAY E.

1962	59.	Geese in Flight
1964	51.	Architectural Forms
	52.	Affinity
	53.	Matinal Harbor
1965	35.	Stratification
	36.	Totem
	37.	Mardigras
1970	36.	Proclamation

BULLOCK, WILLA HOWELL

1981	22.	The Brass Bed
1982	32.	Wicker 'n Baskets*
1983	88.	Trash 'n Treasures No. 5
1984	104.	Baker's Clearing
	105.	A Touch of Elegance
1986	33.	Blue Skies and Blue Jeans
1988	24.	The Music Room
1990	25.	Pleasant under Glass #2*

BUNDY, FULTON A.

1929	55.	Jamb

BUNDY, JOHN ELWOOD

1925	30.	Among the Hills in Winter
	31.	The Passing Cloud
	32.	Beech in Autumn
1926	54.	Moonrise at Sunset
	55.	After Rain
	56.	Grey Day
1927	36.	Woodland Brook*
	37.	Reflections
	38.	Golden Tints of Autumn
1928	46.	The Oaks
1930	42.	Late October (Invited)
	43.	Blue and Gold (Invited)

BURCHETT, SHEILA K.

1976	46.	Squander*
1977	28.	Hellooo
1978	23.	Skylight
	24.	Scarecrow

BURDEN, ELIZABETH (Flagg)

1963	44.	Sunflower House
1984	28.	Shades of Spring

BURFORD, STANLEY L.

1975	31.	Christy
	32.	Owen County
1978	25.	Trees

BURGAN, BETH A.

1970	37.	Series #1, 1970

BURKE, FLORA M.

1956	37.	Mischief
1958	40.	Empty Saddles
1959	42.	Little Annie
1960	48.	Liberry Books
	49.	Thank Heaven for Little Girls
1961	63.	Don't Call Me Freckles

BURKE, RICHARD

1967	40.	Toil

BURKE, ROBERT E.

1926	57.	An Opal Afternoon
1927	39.	An August Arabesque
1928	47.	Plum Bloom

BURKETT, PEGGY

1964	54.	Daybreak
1965	38.	Winter Shadows
1968	34.	Population Explosion

BURKHART, HELENE S.

1968	35.	Autumn
1971	21.	I'm Hungry
	22.	Symphony of Fall
1973	24.	Through the Window

BURKHOLDER, JUNE

1938	35.	The Phlox
	36.	Apple Blossom Time
1939	41.	Autumn Glory, the Dahlia
1940	24.	Autumn's Prize
	25.	The Peony Supreme
1941	30.	Choice Varieties, Peonies
	31.	Purple Glory, Lilac
1942	32.	Summer's Gift, Petunia
1943	45.	Lilac-Time
1944	43.	Lilac's Fragrance
	44.	Lovers Interlude*
1945	41.	The Orchid of the Chrysanthemum
	42.	Fragrance of Spring Lilac
1946	40.	Symphony in Pink
1947	44.	The Glass Ball
1948	26.	Petunia Lore
1950	37.	Gold Muse
1951	35.	The Chant of Fall, Chrysanthemums
	36.	Summer's Blend, Zinnias*
1952	43.	Lilacs and Apple Blossoms
1953	30.	Still Life*
1954	41.	Still Life
1955	43.	Spring's Hyacinth
	44.	The Copper Jug
1956	38.	Early Fall, Chrysanthemums*
	39.	Still Life
1957	37.	Flower Market, Copenhagen
1958	41.	Still Life, Cabbage Like a Rose
	42.	Rhythm In Color: Tulips, Roses and Fruit
1961	64.	The Mystery of Glass
1962	60.	The Old Churn
1964	55.	The Broken Egg
	56.	The Golden Marigold
1965	39.	Sunny Marigolds
	40.	Peaches and Grapes
1966	26.	Butter and Eggs

BURNS, JENE D.

1964	57.	The Canine Place
1970	38.	Forgotten Elegy
	39.	Queen's Lace*
1971	23.	Winter Keep
	24.	String Beans
1972	18.	Ike's Place
1973	25.	End of Winter
1980	24.	February 14th
	25.	George Kircher's Spring House

BURNS, MARGARET

1970	40.	Always on New Years

BURRIS, J(effrey C.)

1975	33.	The Colonnade
1982	33.	Lazy Gray-Sunday Afternoon
1984	29.	Maine-ly Blue*
1985	18.	View Toward the Presidio

1986	34.	Opening of the Crew
	35.	By the Dock at the Bay
1987	21.	An American Heritage
	22.	Halloween Afternoon
1988	25.	Maalea Bay
	26.	Lunch Hour
1989	28.	Circle Sights
	29.	Smith's Cove
1990	26.	A Day at the Dunes
	27.	Road from Goshen Pass*

BURROWS, MARY

| 1956 | 40. | Apples and Nuts |

BURTON, RON

| 1975 | 34. | Champions Dueling |
| 1976 | 47. | Official Poster, "Indianapolis 500" |

BUSCHMANN, GLADYS F.

1951	37.	First Snow
	38.	Dusk*
1952	44.	Early Morning Light
1953	31.	Winter Valley
	32.	Silent Hills
1955	45.	Season's End
	46.	Side Street
	47.	Farmstead

BUSHMAN, LEO N.

| 1941 | 32. | Four Fish |

BUTLER, DEAN

1988	27.	The Cook
	28.	Deer
1989	30.	Buffalo Hunt
	31.	Gruff & Tough
1990	28.	Park Bench People

BUTTON, DAVID

| 1971 | 25. | Old School in the Sunset |
| 1972 | 19. | The Sacrifice |

BUTTS, CLEMENCE N.

| 1984 | 30. | Santa Fe Warehouse |
| 1986 | 36. | The Home Pier |

BYRUM, RUTHVEN H.

1929	56.	Mt. Hood
	57.	Dollar Day
1931	44.	Red Umbrella
	45.	Girl on the Lounge
	46.	Crumbling Walls
1932	29.	Swimming Pool
1933	41.	Old Timer
	42.	Irene
1934	26.	County Court House
	27.	Old Green House
1935	34.	Maggie
1936	31.	His Majesty
	32.	Depot
1937	28.	Unloading Salmon
	29.	Turkey Farm
	307.	Asters
1938	37.	Mother
	306.	Smugglers Cove
1939	42.	End of a Soldier's Dream
	43.	Shelved
	44.	Where Mound Builders Roamed
	304.	Entrance to Beauty
1940	26.	Breaking Clouds
	27.	Skyline Drive, Virginia
	305.	Winding Road
1942	33.	Grandfather Mountain
	34.	Nubble Light House
1943	46.	Lake in the Cumberland
	47.	Bear Wallow
1944	45.	Grand View
	46.	Heart of the Blue Ridge
1945	43.	Blowing Rock
	44.	Wisconsin Lake
1946	41.	Sunset Trail
1947	45.	Girl in Red
1952	45.	After the Storm
1953	33.	Leaning Sycamore
	34.	Philadendron
1954	42.	Smoky Mountain Highway
1957	38.	Storm in the Rockies

C

CADY, CHARLES J.
1957	39.	Deep Woods
1962	61.	They Also Die, Waiting
1963	45.	Cactus
	46.	Circus Elephants
1965	41.	Abandoned Mine*
	42.	November
1966	27.	Ravine
1970	41.	Chromalude
1971	26.	Rock Bound

CADY, ROSLYNN WEBB
1981	23.	Indiana State Fair Collage
1982	34.	Hoosier Farmer: The Man and His Creation*
1986	37.	Dark and Shining
1987	23.	Grandmother Ellis, An Artist and a Lady
	24.	Not Down, Just Out
1990	29.	Steamtrain Maury Salute

CAIN, ROSS B.
1939	45.	Clayton B.

CALDWELL, HELEN
1979	24.	TAO
	25.	The Relationship*
1982	35.	Matt
	36.	Fish*
1984	31.	Form One
	32.	Head
1986	38.	Rhythm
1987	25.	Old Memory
1989	32.	Balance I

CALDWELL, JOAN
1954	43.	Snow and Sand

CALVERT, TRUDY L.
1990	30.	January Juncos

CAMBRIDGE, STEPHANIE
1970	42.	Memory of a Rose
1971	27.	Dark Shadows
1976	48.	Celebrate
1978	26.	Summertime
	27.	Wild Crocus Heralds Spring

CAMERON, S. N.
1973	26.	Mary Noble

CAMMACK, DYNA
1953	35.	Beckoning*
1954	44.	Hope

CANADAY, HELEN D.
1951	39.	December at New Belleville
1952	46.	July Bouquet
1954	45.	Milk Glass with Citrus*
1957	40.	Whoppers
1958	43.	Autumn Still Life
1965	43.	Bean Blossom Bridge

CANADAY, READ B.
1963	47.	Sturbridge Inn
	48.	Alaskan Railroad
1964	58.	Ships at Rest
	59.	Alaskan River

CANNON, ALISON R.
1978	28.	Windowsill Still Life

CANNON, CATHY
1987	26.	The Bubble
1988	29.	Woman of Achievement

CANNON, VIOLA
1961	65.	Winter Landscape
1962	62.	Bowl of Roses

CAPEK, LOREN LEE
1975	35.	Porch Chair
	36.	Creek

CARDWELL, JO ANN
1986	39.	Waiting for Spring
1987	27.	Sunday Morning
1990	31.	Nature's Patterns

CAREY, JERRY L.
1973	27.	Steller's Shelf

CARIANI, V. J.
1925	33.	Vine Clad Trees
	34.	Moonrise at Sunset
	35.	June Clouds
1926	58.	October
	59.	In the Hills o' Brown
1927	40.	Indian Summer
	41.	The Sycamore
	42.	Zinnias
1928	48.	Autumn's Glory
	49.	Vineclad Trees
	50.	Cloudland
1929	58.	October in the Hills
	59.	September Clouds
1930	44.	Autumn's Mantle
	45.	The First Snow
1931	47.	Over Hill and Dale
1932	30.	November Haze
	31.	Fleeting Shadows

1933	43.	A Spring Bouquet
1934	28.	The Creek, Late September*
1935	35.	The Golden Mantle
1936	33.	When Tulip Trees are Golden
	34.	Snow Clad
1937	30.	Beanblossom Valley
	31.	Sunlight and Shadow
	32.	White Peonies
1938	38.	The Red Maple
	39.	The Gentle Breeze*
1939	46.	Spring Enchantment
	305.	October along the Creek
1940	29.	Peonies
	30.	Sailing Heigh
	306.	The Golden Tulip
1941	33.	Sunlight and Shadow
	303.	Blue and Gold
1942	35.	White Peonies
	36.	Cloud Shadowed Hills
1943	48.	The First Snow
	49.	The Valley in October
1944	47.	Banners of the Frost
	48.	White Peonies*
1945	45.	Phlox*
1946	42.	October's Golden Interlude
1947	46.	Peaceful Autumn
	47.	Winter Stream
	48.	Marigolds
1948	27.	Peonies*
	28.	Winter Afternoon
1950	38.	Peonies in Blue Vase*
	39.	Plum Blossom Time
	40.	The Gold of Autumn
1951	40.	Late Autumn
	41.	Golden Tulip
1953	36.	Lilac
1954	46.	Shifting Shadows
1955	48.	Peonies
1956	41.	Zinnias
	42.	Autumn Pageant
1957	41.	Autumn Pageant
	42.	A February Afternoon
1958	44.	Under An October Sky
1959	43.	Zinnias in a Blue Vase
	44.	Old Covered Bridge
	45.	Early Snow
1960	50.	Afternoon in October
1961	66.	Marigolds
	67.	The Ford In Winter
	68.	White Peonies
1962	63.	Peonies
	64.	Snow Clad
1963	49.	In White Mantle
1964	60.	Under an October Sky
1965	44.	Lilacs
	45.	Chrysanthemums
	46.	Early October
1966	28.	The Creek in Winter
1967	41.	Autumn's Glory

1968	36.	Sunlight and Shadows
1969	36.	Summer Bouquet*
	37.	The Monarch

CARLOCK, VERNON THORWALD

| 1939 | 47. | Elaine |
| | 48. | Torso |

CARLSON, CHRISTINE N.

| 1974 | 23. | Golden Abstract |

CARLSON, EDWARD (W.)

1926	60.	Mrs. Mary Dittman
	61.	The Bather
	62.	The Late Mr. Frederick Waskow
	63.	Miss Ruth Larson
	64.	My Daughter Marjorie
	65.	Mr. W. S. Taylor
1927	43.	John Lindstrom
	44.	Mary Elaine
	45.	The Late Mr. C. M. Hedman
	46.	Mr. J. M. Westerlin
1928	51.	The Late Mrs. Carlson*
	52.	Mr. J. C. Shaffer*
	53.	Margot Hedman*
	54.	Raymond Ostergreen*
	55.	Katherine Hedman*
1929	60.	Mrs. Herbert Hedman
	61.	Mr. Georg North
	62.	Mr. C. B. Dorchester
	63.	Mrs. Georg North
1930	46.	Miniature
	47.	Virginia and Mrs. Garard, Ed. Hines, Jr.
1931	48.	The Late Mr. F. P. Gibson
	49.	The Late Mr. Rouse
	50.	Katherine

CARMACK, JEAN (E.)

1972	20.	Big Four Station
1973	28.	Apache Junction
	29.	Round Barn, Indiana

CARMICHAEL, DON

| 1970 | 43. | Elk Creek in Winter |

CARMIN, TIM

1972	21.	In God We Trust, Number Two
1973	30.	New Castle Courthouse
	31.	Opus Three
1974	24.	E Pluribus Unum
1975	37.	Baseburner
	38.	Untitled

CARR, ELMER B.

| 1962 | 65. | Iron Kettle |
| 1964 | 61. | Louisa |

CARR, SHIRLEY WERNER
(See Werner, Shirley J.)

| 1970 | 44. | Images of Yesterday |

1972	22.	Masts and Sails
1979	26.	The Last Piece of Chalk

CARREL, BETH

1964	62.	Heritage
	63.	Etude
1965	47.	The Promise
1966	29.	Sleepy Hollow
	30.	Watusi
	31.	Kismet
1967	42.	Cloisonne
1970	45.	Mother Earth
1973	32.	Papillon
1974	25.	Silver Grasshopper*
1976	49.	Search for the Tao
	50.	Forest Floor
1977	29.	The Wind Was Born
1979	27.	Tung Yuan
1981	24.	O-What A Web We Weave

CARROTHERS, GRACE NEVILLE

1932	32.	The Edge of the Canyon
	33.	Drying Fish Nets
	34.	Old Fish Houses, Charlevoix

CARTER, ALAN L.

1981	25.	My Son, Myself
1983	25.	Paul's Bakery
	26.	America
1984	33.	The Parade
	34.	The Royal

CARTER, EFFIE F.

1942	262.	In the Shelter of the Matterhorn
1946	43.	Fog in the Harbor
1951	42.	Lands End
1955	49.	Shadows
1956	43.	A Bit of New England

CARTER, GEORGIA

1981	26.	Solitude

CARTER, MARY JO

1939	49.	Asters
1941	304.	Hollyhocks
1953	37.	Blue & Gold, Still Life
1957	43.	Peace: On Deercreek
1959	46.	Yellow Roses
1960	51.	Peonies
1962	66.	Historical Landmark

CARTON, WINIFRED

1931	51.	Petunias
1932	35.	The Stone Pitcher
	36.	Peonies
	37.	Marigold

CASEY, WARREN (Vale)

1949	29.	Head of St. John the Baptist
	30.	Meditation

1951	43.	DeHirsh Margules
1952	47.	Prophet

CASS, PAUL

1979	28.	Landscape

CASSELL, MARIAN SIMON

1955	50.	Winter Fun
1958	45.	Gravel Pit
	46.	Old Barn
1959	47.	White House
1960	52.	Jim

CASWELL, GLADYS

1944	49.	A Workman's Shack
1946	44.	Ferris Wheel
1948	29.	Bouquet
1950	41.	Vase of Flowers
1954	47.	Anemones

CATHELL, E(dna) S.

1925	36.	Flowers
	37.	Calendulas
1926	66.	Still Life, Chinese Things
	67.	Still Life, Italia
	68.	Flowers, Calendulas
1927	47.	Marigolds
1929	64.	Flowers
1930	48.	Phlox
1937	308.	Blue and Yellow
1941	305.	Study in Yellow

CAUBLE, MARCELLA

1987	28.	Ashland Oil Inc. on Ohio
1990	32.	Ohio Tug & Barges

CAULDWELL, CHERRI

1983	27.	Potter's Window
1989	33.	Sandra's Shadows

CHALLINOR, MURIEL

1948	30.	Portrait of the Artist

CHAMBERLIN, GEORGE L.

1926	69.	From the Hills
	70.	The Old St. Joe

CHANNELS, VERA G.

1986	40.	Grandma's Scissors

CHAPPELL, JOANNE

1966	32.	Indian Summer
	33.	Still Life
1967	43.	Girl with Still Life #2

CHASE, JAMES K.

1973	33.	Emergence
	34.	Senior Citizen

CHATTIN, LOU-ELLEN
(See Showe, Lou-Ellen Chattin)
1926	71.	Autumn
1927	48.	Dogwood
	49.	Abundance
1928	56.	Patterns
1930	49.	Morse's Studio

CHESNUL, CHARLES
1969	38.	Harbor

CHICKADAUNCE, LOUETA
1975	39.	Joanne
	40.	Self-Portrait
1980	26.	Two Women

CHINWORTH, LOUESE (Gypsy)
1958	47.	Red Oaks in Fall
1960	53.	Zinnias
	54.	Sycamores at Winona Lake
1961	69.	Nostalgia

CHIPMAN, C. DEAN
1935	36.	Tiger Lilies
1937	33.	March, Monticello College

CHLEBEK, MICHELE
1990	33.	Lift Me to the Light

CHOGAS, JOHN A.
1975	41.	Trees in a Park

CHRISTEL, LEO C.
1956	44.	Meditation
	45.	Father and Child

CHRISTENSEN, SUE (Susan M.)
1967	44.	All Things New
	45.	Trees
1968	37.	Nipples #14
1970	46.	Nipples #15, Orange Circle
	47.	Dyptic III Positive & Negative
1976	51.	Eye Form

CHRISTIAN, GRANT W.
1936	35.	Edge of Town*
	36.	Woodcutters
	37.	Portrait of Elizabeth Jean
1937	34.	Portrait of Martha
	35.	Pigeon Hill*
1938	40.	Early Autumn
	41.	Evening
1973	35.	Old Buoys*
1974	26.	Patience & Impatient
1975	42.	Sunday Morning, Hong Kong Island
1978	29.	Into the Valley*
1979	29.	Landscape
1980	27.	Peggy's Cove
1982	37.	A Winter Evening

1984	35.	Beauty and the Beast
1987	29.	This Too Shall Pass*
	30.	Girl with Her Dog
1988	30.	Golden Glimpse*
	31.	The Littlest Witch
1989	34.	Blessed Sunlight*

CHRISTOPHER, ROSEMARIE
1988	32.	Sunday Afternoon

CHRISTY
1970	48.	Ann

CHUPACK, JEANETTE
1972	23.	Snowshoe Hare*
	24.	Broomstick Hill II
1974	27.	Double Birch

CILFONE, GIANNI
1949	31.	Italian Docks, Gloucester
	32.	Covered Bridge
1950	42.	Birches in Autumn
	43.	Quiet Winter Mood*
	44.	Village Street, Nashville, Indiana
1951	44.	Winter Idyll
	45.	Covered Bridge, U. S. A.
1952	48.	Autumn in Skokie
	49.	Near Danby, Vermont*
1953	38.	New England Village
	39.	Fishing Boats, Gloucester
	40.	Harbor Impressions*
1956	46.	Nashville, Indiana*
	47.	Rainy Sunday
	48.	Rockport
1958	48.	Hillside
	49.	Greasy Creek
	50.	North Country

CLAPP, MARCIA
1932	38.	Primitive
	39.	Negro
	40.	Marcia
1934	29.	William Beebe

CLARK, C. OLIN
1936	38.	Still Life

CLARK, GEORGIABELLE
1954	48.	Quaint Castles
1955	51.	Dahlias
1958	51.	Potted Poinsettia
1961	70.	Old Kentucky Home*
1962	67.	Down Gilbert Ave.
1963	50.	Roses
1964	64.	Summer on Hackberry Street
	65.	Jonquil
1965	48.	Miami River at Dayton
1966	34.	White Ramblers
1968	38.	Camelback in Phoenix
1971	28.	Mt. Adams

THE HOOSIER SALON, 1925-1990

CLARK, HARLEY D.
1930 50. Architectural Ornament*
1931 52. Carved panel for a radio industry, creative design

CLARK, KATHRYN H.
1971 29. Three Poems*

CLARK, MARION
1969 39. Portrait of Olive

CLARK, MERRILL WARD
1945 46. Near Brookville
1946 45. Hill Country Store
1947 49. St. Augustine Shrimp Boats
1948 31. Fall Creek in Winter
1949 33. Building Our Cabin
1952 50. San Antonio's Mexican Quarter
1953 41. The Back Way
1958 52. Old Mt. Carmel Church

CLARK, OPAL
1975 43. Lace Fan

CLARK, VIRGINIA KEEP
1938 42. The White Rabbit

CLARK, VIVIAN D.
1945 47. Salem

CLARKE, THEA
1987 31. Across the Bay
32. Tropical Fragrance
1988 33. Columns and Curves
34. Palm Streamers
1989 35. Filtered Fronds
1990 34. Green Piece
35. Beached

CLAY, KAY
1969 40. Soft Shadows Peer into Silent Soul

CLEAR, STEVE(n)
1979 30. Rainbow
1981 27. in the Clouds

CLEAVER, ANNE (K.) HOFFMAN
1969 41. Biafra
1971 30. Where Have All the Flowers Gone?
1973 36. Kate
37. Dark Woods*
1975 44. Snow Birds*
45. In the Park
1976 52. The Bean Patch
53. Family Album
1977 30. Street in Kyoto
31. Polly Eliza
1981 28. The Verger
1982 38. The Star
1985 19. Study in Red, Grey and Gold

CLEMENTS, EILEEN
1984 36. Gates of Peace

CLEVELAND, ROBERT W.
1960 55. Sleepy Sycamores
1963 51. Spring Valley

CLOETINGH, JAMES H.
1934 30. Gloucester
1940 31. Quebec
1941 34. Church at Zimapan, Mexico
35. Santa Prisca Church, Taxco
1942 37. Calle en Taxco
1961 71. Sponge Boat
72. Market in Mexico
1962 68. Nassau Market
69. Indiana Dunes
70. Evening
1964 66. Nassau Fisherman
67. Hoosier Farm
68. The Little Bayou

CLOSSON, NANCI BLAIR
1970 49. The Arrangement
50. Abandoned
1971 31. Untitled*
32. Representation*
1972 25. Faces
1973 38. Yellow Is
39. Squares II*
1974 28. Shale*
29. Through the Looking Glass*
1975 46. Portholes*
47. Untitled
1976 54. Coat with Macrame
55. Pillows*
1977 32. Out Of Element*
33. Butte Perspective*
1978 30. De-Tourism*
31. Loopholes
1979 31. Earth, Sky, Water*
32. Window Rock
1980 28. Clues
29. Reflection Principle*
1981 29. Morning, Cheops Pyramid
30. White Sails*
1982 39. Free Float
40. Sycamores in Shadow
1983 28. Skirting the Issue*
1984 37. Hidden Conch

CLOUD, C. CAREY
1931 53. Marigold
54. Queene
55. Autumn Evening
1932 41. Old Bean Blossom Bridge
42. September Hills
1933 44. Autumn Comes to the Village
1947 50. Midsummer Rural
1958 53. Beanblossom, Ind.
1968 39. A Neglected Antique

182

CLUSMANN, WILLIAM

1925	38.	A Chicago Beauty Spot*
	39.	Indian Summer
	40.	Clearing Up
1926	72.	Morning on the River
	73.	September Morning
	74.	Hillside Heather
1927	50.	Way in October
	51.	Sunday Morning

CLUTE, IDA MARTIN

| 1944 | 50. | Snow in Early Spring |

COATES, RUTH ALLISON

1949	34.	Pink Cyclamen
1954	49.	Still Life with Red Apples
1975	48.	Delphiniums

COATS, RANDOLPH (LaSalle)

1925	41.	Yarn Dolls*
	42.	La Cote Finisterre
	43.	An Indiana Idyll
1926	75.	Portrait of Mimi
	76.	Helen
	77.	Portuguese Whaler*
1927	52.	My Mother*
1928	57.	Nature's Tapestry
	58.	Laughing Beggar
	59.	Lazy April
1929	65.	Girl in Coolie Coat
	66.	Hoosier Pioneer*
1930	51.	Peggy
1940	32.	An Early Snow
1941	36.	A Wintry Greeting
	37.	Hollyhocks
1942	38.	High Horizon
	39.	Isolation
1943	50.	Total War
	51.	Winter in the Smokies
1944	51.	Mountain Solitude*
	52.	Red Kelly, Boss Riveter
1945	48.	A Bit of Old Madison
	49.	Turbulent Waters
1946	46.	Yvonne*
	47.	Jerrie
1948	32.	Greenbrier Pinnacle

COBB, CAROLYN

| 1982 | 41. | Dandelion |

COBB, THEA

| 1971 | 33. | Sabrina's Sleigh Run |
| | 34. | Migration |

COBLE, DAN R.

| 1977 | 34. | Coconut Grove |

COBLE, MARLENE

1974	30.	Ladies Awaiting
1980	30.	Reverie*
1982	42.	Poppies

COBLENTZ, LEE

1968	40.	What If the Sun Shone Not*
1978	32.	Nightly Singing Owls
	33.	Flower out of Wilderness*
1979	33.	Flowers Loved-Fade
	34.	Sacrament of Sea & Sun*

COFFEY, ALTON P.

1929	67.	Salt Creek Valley
1930	52.	Sunny Hollow*
1932	43.	A Roadside Sugar
1934	31.	The Chubby Hole
1962	71.	Winter Woodland
	72.	Snow Clad Hills
1963	52.	Winter Solitude
1964	69.	Midwinter
	70.	Winter in Brown Co.
1965	49.	Winter Along Salt Creek
	50.	McClarys Grove, Nashville

COFFMAN, DORIS J.

| 1969 | 42. | Solitude |
| | 43. | Frustration |

COHAN, BEVERLY

| 1977 | 35. | Zionsville, USA |

COLE, RUSH

1986	41.	Gladys
1987	33.	Lainie: Portrait of the Artist's Daughter
	34.	Karl's Garden
1988	35.	Winter Still Life
	36.	Knockout No. III*
1989	36.	Widow's Market Stand, Trsteno, Yugoslavia

COLER, STELLA C.

1939	50.	Mr. Bokedis on Relief
1942	40.	After the Ball
1943	52.	Seven A. M.
	53.	Summer Blooms
1944	53.	The First Snow
	54.	Still Life with Stone Jug
1946	48.	Arrangement with Banjo & Mexican Shoe
1947	51.	Across the Fields*
1952	51.	Flower Still-Life
	52.	Grease Wagon
1953	42.	Jo Ann, Art Student*
	43.	Two Teapots
1954	50.	Adolescent Dream*
1955	52.	Beauty Salon
	53.	Arrangement with Mask and Fan*
1956	49.	After the Wedding
	50.	The Back Yard Next Door
1959	48.	Job Hunting
1961	73.	The Blue Dresser
	74.	The Tall Vase
1962	73.	Tragedy and Comedy
	74.	Fontevarault

1963	53.	Anybody Home
	54.	The Cardinal*
1964	71.	Bouquet Rouge*
1966	35.	The Wedding Ring Tea Pot, No. 1

COLLINS, LYNDA

1982	43.	Motion
1983	29.	Pull
1986	42.	Howard
1988	37.	Christy and Heather

COLVIN, WAYNE BENSON

1926	78.	A Strange Port
	79.	Illustration for "Old Gods"
	80.	The Phantom Hunter*
	81.	To the Moon
1927	53.	Cathedral, Santiago de Cuba
	54.	Bo's'n of the Caravelle
	55.	Cafe, Santiago de Cuba
	56.	The Call of the Conch Shell
	57.	Native Boatmen, Haiti
1928	60.	Study of a Cuban
	61.	Off Tortuga

CONFER, THELMA

1964	72.	Pat Rose
1968	41.	The Little Woman
1969	44.	Mrs. Beckeridge
1970	51.	Mom*
1978	34.	Pokagon
1980	31.	Clifty Falls
	32.	The Confers
1981	31.	Laughery Creek II
1982	44.	Muscatatuck River III*
	45.	Strahl Lake III
1984	38.	Governor's Residence
1985	20.	Laughery Creek IV
1986	43.	Blue Shadows*
	44.	McCormick's Creek "Mini-Falls"
1987	35.	Flamingos and Friend
	36.	Indpls. Zoo Entrance, 30th Street
1988	38.	Lake Kickapoo II
1989	37.	They Say......

CONNAWAY, JAY HALL

1926	82.	Maine Coast
	83.	Mountain White
	84.	Coast Moonlight
1947	52.	Assault*
	53.	Winter
1948	33.	Storm
	34.	New England

CONNELL, MARTHA J.

| 1977 | 36. | Marianne and Jason |

CONNELL, SYBIL H.

1939	51.	Cosmos
	52.	Golden Hickories
1940	33.	The Old Studio

1941	38.	Springtime in Greasy Creek Valley
	306.	Petunias and Ageratum
1942	41.	Chrysanthemums
1944	55.	The Last Petunias
	56.	Calendulas in a Pottery Pitcher
	57.	Zinnias with Cosmos
1945	50.	Snowswept
	51.	Ruffles
1946	49.	Cosmos with Hydrangeas
	50.	Marigolds & Orange Cosmos
1947	54.	Petunias With Zinnias and Delphinium
	55.	Azalia Mums
1951	46.	Little Mums in the Teapot
	47.	Blue and Gold

CONNER, A. F.

| 1927 | 58. | Still Life |

CONNER, NINA

1976	56.	Mother Earth
	57.	Laveda of Delpha
1977	37.	Colonial Metal

CONNER, PAUL

1925	44.	San Capistrano Mission
1926	85.	San Gabriel Mission Steps
	86.	Sand Dunes
	87.	Mt. San Jacinto in Winter
1927	59.	Guardians of the Valley

CONNORS, CAROLYN SIHLER

1982	46.	Joy of First Flower
	47.	Grandfather's Dress
1983	30.	Basket of Joy
1984	39.	Noah's Ark

CONSTABLE, CATHERINE

| 1945 | 52. | Picnic |

CONWELL, WILLIAM J.

| 1972 | 26. | The House on Dandelion Hill |

COOK, ALICE D(immick)

1944	58.	Peggy
1945	53.	Roberta
	54.	Barbara
1946	51.	Nancy
1947	56.	Judy*
1948	35.	My Mother*
1954	51.	Vicki
1960	56.	Brother and Sister
1970	52.	Gentlefolk
1976	58.	Ring Around
1977	38.	The Oldest Member

COOK, EDITH ROSE

| 1963 | 55. | Interlude |

COOLER, Jr., HARRY E.
1951   48.   Last Stop
          49.   Station No. 13

COONEY, MILDRED KELLER
1961   75.   Mother and Child

COOPER, DANIEL R.
1988   39.   Jupiter over Indianapolis

COOPER, LUCILLE N.
1987   37.   Barefoot Is Better
1989   38.   Coconut Palm

COOPER, WAYNE
1977   39.   Covered Bridge

CORRELL, IRA A.
1929   68.   Carved panel in limestone

CORTELLINI, CONRAD
1975   49.   Christy

CORYN, C(elest) E.
1925   45.   The Old Fishing Wharf
1927   60.   With the Flow of the Tide
          61.   Mending of Nets
          62.   A Lone Sail
1929   69.   Indiana War Memorial

COTHRAN, BILLIE
1958   54.   Lady in Red
1960   57.   Patricia
1961   76.   Three Lemons and Violets
          77.   The Turquoise Ribbon
          78.   Girl In White Hat*
1962   75.   Pears and Daisies
          76.   Mid-Summer Mood
          77.   Still Life with Pink Violet
1963   56.   Girl in Red Jumper
          57.   Elmer
          58.   Pears and Apples
1965   51.   Dianne
          52.   Melon and Marigolds
1966   36.   Circus Girl

COURET, HORTENSIA
1989   39.   Santiago de Compostela Cathedral

COVARRUBIAS, JOY
1981   32.   Mexican Evening

COWAN, JACK D.
1990   36.   Before the Symphony at Capriccios*

COX, JACOB
1925   46.   Portrait Nancy A. Cox
          47.   Portrait Nancy A. Cox
                  (Loaned by Mr. D. R. Peck)

COX, JOHN ROGERS
1955   54.   Summer

COX, JOSEPH (Joe) H.
1943   54.   Frame Maker
          55.   The Landlady
          56.   Iowa Village*
1950   45.   The Priest

COX, KERMIT O.
1969   45.   Empty House

CRADICK, RAYMOND V.
1983   31.   Which Way to Morgantown?*
          32.   Special on Celery
1985   21.   Family Gathering at Uncle Ralph's
1986   45.   And There Was Pearl and Harvey
          46.   Cow Path Superintendents
1987   38.   A Brew for E. K. U., Richmond, Kentucky
          39.   Colts 0 - St. Johns 3
1988   40.   Urban Tycoon
          41.   Fillet Crochet

CRAIG, HELEN (C.)
1969   46.   Forest Primeval
          47.   Clowning Around
1970   53.   A Then in a Now World
1971   35.   Flowerlike Foliage
1973   40.   Winter Fantasy
1974   31.   Hide-away*
1975   50.   Hope Springs Eternal
1978   35.   John*

CRAIG, LUCILE KIRK
1949   35.   Cornfield on the Prairie

CRAIG, RALPH
1932   44.   Boats
          45.   Misty Day
          46.   Figure
1934   32.   Paris Roofs
          33.   Apples

CRAIG, ROBERT (C.)
1927   63.   Creek in Rain
          64.   Creek in Sunlight
1931   56.   Fish Dock
          57.   McNichols Cove
1942   42.   Black Schooner
1944   59.   Eastport Street
          60.   Circus Day

CRAMER, MABEL
1954   52.   Home in Brown County Hills
1956   51.   Lilacs

CRANE, PATRICIA
1982   48.   Horse
          49.   Classic Lines

1983	33.	Well Chosen
1984	40.	The Last Waltz

CRANE, PAUL

1985	22.	Marble Canyon*
1987	40.	Midwestern Bounty
1988	42.	With Their Heads in the Clouds
	43.	Mt. McKinley
1989	40.	Mogollan Mountains
	41.	A Child's Cathedral

CRANE, STANLEY W.

1928	62.	Cactus No. 1, France
	63.	Alpes Maritimes, France
	64.	Lower LaGaude, France*
1953	44.	G. San Martini

CRÁPO, DOE

1969	48.	March at Geist Reservoir
	49.	Blue Spruce Cove
1973	41.	The Crooked Tree
1974	32.	Up, Up and Away
1975	51.	Only Yesterday
1986	47.	Spring Growth

CRAWFORD, CHARLES C.

1965	53.	Lynda
1968	42.	The Red Blouse
1969	50.	Nancy Jane*

CRAWFORD, ROBERT W.

1951	50.	Pan Fish*
1964	73.	Three Plants on a Red Cloth
1965	54.	St. Francis
1968	43.	Summer Idyl
	44.	Quietude
1980	33.	The Flow

CRESSY, WILLIAM

1971	36.	Stone Quarry
	37.	Gloucester, Massachusetts

CRICK, MARY L.

1970	54.	Pleasant Acres
	55.	Mackinac Island, Michigan

CRIMSON, LINDA

1989	42.	Suzanna and the Elders
1990	37.	The English Lawyer

CRISMAN, MARILOU

1958	55.	Little Brother
1962	78.	Four Children
1963	59.	Jane
	60.	Harbor
	61.	The Neighborhood
1964	74.	Still Life
1965	55.	Swamp-Fire
	56.	Orange Sails

1967	46.	Somewhere
	47.	Road Construction
	48.	Trick or Treat
1968	45.	Argos Quarry
1969	51.	The Door
1971	38.	Wild Rice
	39.	The Village
1974	33.	Indiana Rural Scene
1975	52.	Tattered Sails
1976	59.	Floral Composition*
	60.	The Dunes
1977	40.	Untitled
	41.	Untitled
1981	33.	Untitled
1982	50.	Earth Images

CRISTEE, VERNON B.

1961	79.	Bottles and Jugs
1966	37.	Wharf Scene
1978	36.	Fred
1979	35.	Dorothea
1982	51.	Across the Park
	52.	Family Reunion
1983	34.	Interior
	35.	Desert Industry
1985	23.	Visit to New Harmony
1986	48.	Old Grain Elevator
	49.	Across the Tracks
1990	38.	Early Morning
	39.	Urban Pattern*

CRITCHLOW, JOSEPH P.

1988	44.	The Forgotten Game
1989	43.	Streamers

CROOK, THELMA

1967	49.	Roadside Beauty
	50.	Mackinac
1971	40.	Queen of the Brush

CROSS, ADELYNE SCHAEFER

1931	58.	A Pot of Flowers
	59.	The Begonia
1933	45.	A Study
	46.	Threatening Clouds

CROSS, KAREN HODGIN

1988	46.	Barbados

CROSS, WILLIAM (Bill)

1988	45.	Sacred Lake*

CROUSE, JANET E.

1932	47.	Cappellini
	48.	Head of a Girl

CROWDER, MARGARET PEG

1968	46.	The Pebble Trace

CROWL, WALTER
1948	36.	Shaffer's Place, January
1949	36.	Dunes
1952	53.	Excavation*

CROWN, KEITH
| 1938 | 43. | Busker |
| | 44. | The Peacock Fan |

CRYSLER, E. L.
| 1940 | 34. | Gardenias in Blue Vase |

CUMMINS, JEANNE
1986	50.	Magnolia by Moonlight
	51.	Sunbeam, October 10
1987	41.	Surfside Breeze
	42.	Sunbeam at Eagle Creek
1988	47.	Ice Mania
1989	44.	Hoosier Hallmark
	45.	Spring Sunbeam, Indiana

CUMMINS, NANCY HANCOCK
1978	37.	Bastet*
1979	36.	Laughing Jumeau
	37.	Partytime*
1980	34.	The Pink Boa*
1987	43.	Lost Mountain Store

CUNNINGHAM, JAMES L(ee)
1970	56.	Evalen Flow Time
1981	35.	Whale Singing to the Stars
	36.	Night Launch*
1982	53.	Florida Coast
	54.	Desert Return*
1983	36.	On the Edge of the Forest
	37.	Arum Ascent*
1984	41.	Shore Line, near the River
	42.	Arum Fire*
1985	24.	Shoreline/Winter Skies*
	25.	2,900 Views of EDO
1986	52.	Arum/Requiem
1987	44.	Pineiro Brazilianus

CUNNINGHAM, (D.) KATE
1981	34.	Letters/As Dreams Begin and End
1983	38.	Toy Kisses/Sweet Sorrows*
	39.	Paris Night/Swept Away Again
1984	43.	Star Tramp, Take Me with You
	44.	Snow White, Along the Way to Wonderland
1985	26.	Abandoned Glitter/Tender Ambitions

CUNNINGHAM, LOIS HAWN
1967	51.	Bottoms Up
1983	40.	Encounter
1985	27.	Interim

CUPKA, NANCY IRVINE
| 1970 | 57. | Forsythia at One-Thirty |
| 1989 | 46. | Shimmering Moments |

CURRY, MARY (M.)
1968	47.	The Garden
	48.	Want*
	49.	Woman
1970	58.	Stack in Rose
	59.	Blue-Yellow
1971	41.	Peach on Green
	42.	Blue Stack #30

CURRY, TIM S.
| 1979 | 38. | The Winker |

CURTIS, NORMAN S.
| 1947 | 57. | Waders |

CUSHING, THOMAS J. (Tom)
1974	34.	The Ol' Watertower: Chicago*
1975	53.	Ship Shape, Gloucester
1976	61.	Friendship Gardens, Michigan City, Indiana
1977	42.	Lighthouse, Michigan City, Indiana
1978	38.	Sturgeon Bay: Entry to Door County
1979	39.	Leprechaun
1980	35.	Story, Indiana
1981	37.	Backyard Bouquet*
1983	41.	On Seacrest Lake, Indiana
1985	28.	Pigeon Forge
	29.	Broken Gate
1986	53.	Indiana Dunes Beach
1987	45.	Unkie
	46.	Clean Switch

CUTLER, MILDRED D.
1955	55.	Flowers and Apple*
	56.	Red Pitcher
1956	52.	Summer Bouquet
1957	44.	Stone Crock and Companions
1959	49.	J. F.'s Arrangement, Flowers
1961	80.	Winter Bouquet
1964	75.	Autumn with Old Jug and Last Year's Bird's-nest
	76.	Petunias and Contemplation
	77.	October Day
1965	57.	No Vacancy
1966	38.	From Jessie's Garden
1967	52.	Old Jug, Teakettle and Fruit
1968	50.	Fruit and Wine
1969	52.	Daisies
	53.	Over-Night Guests
1970	60.	Hoosier Recollections
1973	42.	Tea and Trumpets*

D

DAHLGREEN, CHARLES W.
1925	48.	The Old Oak
	49.	A Soothing Morning*
	50.	The Spirit of Brown County
1926	88.	Early Snow
	89.	The Old Hickory
	90.	Oak and Sycamore
1927	65.	The Old Sycamore
	66.	By the Creek
	67.	Winter in Brown County
	68.	Down to the Creek
	69.	The Five Elms
	70.	On a Mountain Road
	71.	Winter in the Woods
	72.	A Chicago River
	73.	Big Pines
1928	65.	The Road to Bear-Walla
	66.	Brown County Court House*
	67.	Edge of the Pines
	68.	The Pond
	69.	In the Mountains
1929	70.	By the Creek
	71.	Hills of Brown County
	72.	A Poem
	73.	Reflections
	74.	The Old Sycamore
	75.	The Tribune Tower
1930	53.	In the Valley
	54.	Tribune No. 3
	55.	The Island 1st State
	56.	December Thaw
1931	60.	The Island No. 2
	61.	Early Snow
	62.	In the Hills
1932	49.	A Vista
	50.	A Home in the Aspens
	51.	The Old Cottonwood
1933	47.	Snaring Trout
	48.	The Proposal
1934	34.	The Old Sugar Maple
	35.	Homeward Bound
	36.	Aspen and Pines
	37.	A Note in Pattern
	38.	Across the Lagoon
1935	37.	The Spur
	38.	A Note in Pattern
	39.	Western Pines
	40.	Morning Shadows
	41.	The Ford
1936	39.	Old Homestead
	40.	Barn Yard
	41.	Rail Fence
	42.	Back Door

1937	36.	Beavers Farm
	37.	Meeting Branches
	38.	Enchantment
	309.	Flowers
1938	46.	Indian Still Life
1939	53.	Frosty Morning

DAHLSTROM, DOROTHY
| 1958 | 56. | Covered Bridge |
| 1967 | 53. | Blue Treasure Trove |

DAHM, JO
| 1982 | 55. | Rio Taos |

DAILEY, DON
1962	79.	Maestro
	80.	Upstream
	81.	Steel Stallion

DAILEY, MELBA
1963	62.	The Dancer
1968	51.	The Lancer
	52.	Oriental Fisherman
1970	61.	Out of the Depths
1973	43.	Noah and the Dove
1975	54.	Picasso People
	55.	Let's Catch Kokoutek
1977	43.	Sit!
	44.	Miss 1914
1981	38.	Pomposity

DAILY, EVELYNNE (Mess)
(See Mess, Evelynne C.)
1970	62.	Stone Quarry Incident
	63.	Illusive Ones
1971	43.	Butterfly Weeds
1973	44.	Winter Wonderland
1980	36.	Down on the Farm

DAILY, LENORA
| 1967 | 54. | Charlie's Farm |
| | 55. | Midwest Farm |

DANCE, MARY
| 1974 | 35. | Dissolving Lake Shore |
| | 36. | Brown Co. State Park |

DANIEL, DOUGLAS M.
1983	42.	1723 N. Penn*
1984	45.	Kelly
	46.	I-70 West
1987	47.	Japanese Aurelia
	48.	Portrait of Artist's Father
1988	**48.**	**Pat and Louise**
	49.	Portrait

| 1989 | 47. | Lady in Blue |
| 1990 | 40. | The Politician's Land |

DANIEL, KELLY GRIFFITH

| 1990 | 41. | Don't Be Silly, Cows Can't Fly* |
| | 42. | Keystone |

DANIELS, E(lmer) H.

1928	70.	Helen
	71.	Nathalia
1931	63.	Italian Girl
	64.	Native*
1932	52.	The Brothers, Karamazon
	53.	Portrait of Joseph Conrad
1940	35.	A. Lincoln
1941	39.	Medusa
	40.	Portrait of Evans Woollen
1942	43.	Figure Study
	44.	Nature
	45.	Portrait of J. Edwin Kopf*
1943	57.	Portrait of Hilton U. Brown
	58.	Adage Satana
1944	61.	Father Fedilis, the Builder

DANKERT, MARLA (K.)

| 1968 | 53. | Composition |
| 1969 | 54. | Composition |

DANNER, SARA KOLB

1925	51.	Summer Flowers
1929	76.	Fiesta, Santa Barbara
	77.	The Old Live Oak*
	78.	The Green Jar
1930	57.	In the Patio Garden of George Washington Smith, Santa Barbara, California
1931	65.	Autumn Sycamore
1932	54.	A Village on the Hill
	55.	Sycamore Canyon, Santa Barbara
1936	43.	Santa Barbara Artists' Fair
	44.	Flowers
1938	45.	Model Posing
1940	36.	Sunny Hillside
1941	41.	Oyster Cove
1942	46.	Picking Plums
	47.	At the Nursery School
1949	37.	Amaryllis and Zinnias
	38.	California Coast
1950	46.	Snowy Street
1951	51.	Lambertville, N. J.*
	52.	Across the River at New Hope, Pa.
1952	54.	Santa Barbara
1953	45.	Hollywood Boulevard
1954	53.	Dahlias
1955	57.	Philadelphia Parkway
	58.	Santa Barbara from My Window
1956	53.	Manayunk Hill
1957	45.	On Germantown Pike
1958	57.	On The Embankment
1962	82.	Monterey Wharf
	83.	Naples Street

1964	88.	Along the Delaware
1965	58.	In the Studio No. 1
1966	39.	Snow in Fairmount Park
	40.	Spring on Bowman's Hill

DARROW, PAUL W.

1927	74.	Cabin, Turkey Run
	75.	Sand Dunes
1928	72.	Wet Sands
	73.	Side Street
	74.	The Tugboat, Sketch
1929	79.	Scraping Hulls
	80.	Stone Barn
	81.	Jersey Flats
	82.	Catfish Row, South Philadelphia
1930	58.	Run-Down Farm

DARST, ROSE MARIE

| 1937 | 39. | Roots |

DAUM, BARBARA TRESTER

| 1962 | 84. | Saundra Kay Daum |
| 1971 | 44. | 23 Ps. |

DAUMER, MIKE

1964	78.	Dune, Early Morn
1965	59.	Growing Dune
	60.	Lonely Dune
1966	41.	January Day

DAVIDSON, LILLIAN M.

1944	62.	Spring Landscape
	63.	Old Quaker Home
1946	52.	The House in the Valley
	53.	Late Fall Landscape
1950	47.	The Old Homestead
1951	53.	Early Autumn
	54.	Autumn Time*
1952	55.	The Hamlet
	56.	January Sunlight
1953	46.	The Sunday Hobby
	47.	Landscape near Oldenburg
1954	54.	The Church on the Hill
	55.	Earlham May Day
1956	54.	Old Sol
	55.	Wayside House

DAVIDSON, ROBERT

1927	76.	Holy Family
	77.	Portrait of Frances Cheney
	78.	Ideal Head*
1928	75.	Architectural Head*
1929	83.	Memories III
	84.	William Henry Failey*
1930	59.	Wave Head
	60.	"Io"
	61.	Garden Fountain
1932	56.	Eve
	57.	Garden Figure
	58.	Figure Study

1933	49.	Dancing Lesson*
	50.	Else*
1935	42.	Charles B. Millholland, Playwright
1937	40.	Kneeling Figure*
1938	47.	Ceramic Fountain Figure
	48.	Figure Study
	49.	Reading Girls
1939	54.	Terra Cotta Fragment
	55.	Edward Dunlap
1940	37.	Jockey
	38.	Portrait of Dr. Comstock*
1943	254.	Sketch for a Garden Figure
1945	55.	Boy with Ball

DAVIDSON, WILLIAM S.

1948	37.	Prairie Storm

DAVIS, DEAN (H.)

1979	40.	Texas City
1980	37.	Iroquois
1982	56.	Plain People
1983	43.	Le Grande Tractor*
	44.	Magnolia Metamorphosis
1984	47.	Race to Oblivion
1985	30.	Amish Frieze
1986	54.	Tractor/Tractor
1987	49.	Bett's Reverie
1988	50.	Wall Chairs

DAVIS, ELIZABETH

1987	50.	Koi I

DAVIS, EVERETT

1928	76.	The Old Barn-Lot
1929	85.	The Creek Road
1944	64.	Two Horses

DAVIS, FRANCES

1928	77.	April, Cover Design
	78.	September, Cover Design
	79.	October, Cover Design

DAVIS, HARRY A.

1947	58.	The Adulteress
1948	38.	Washington Park
1949	39.	The Pond, Midwinter
	40.	The Railways, Gloucester
1950	48.	Picnic
1951	55.	The Dead Tree
	56.	Farmers in Town
1953	48.	View of Orvieto
	49.	Along White Lick Creek
	50.	Red Fish Boats
1954	56.	Little Town
	57.	Grain Elevator
	58.	Barn Dance*
1955	59.	Main Street, Hillsboro
	60.	Waiting for a School Bus
	61.	Roadside Fruit Stand*
1956	56.	An Autumn Evening
	57.	The Apple Pickers *

1957	46.	The Refugees
	47.	Reverie
	48.	The Hired Hand
1958	58.	The Swimmers
	59.	The Beach Party
1959	50.	Fall Near Holliday Park
	51.	Head of a Girl
1960	58.	Autumn Landscape
	59.	Conversation
1966	42.	The Station at Atlanta*
	43.	The Crossing
1967	56.	La Rues*
1968	54.	A Segment of the Inner City
1969	55.	Gateway to Crown Hill*
1970	64.	Westside Drug Store*
	65.	The Athenaeum*
1971	45.	A Segment of Indiana Avenue
	46.	The Waning Light*
1972	27.	View of Greensburg*
	28.	West Michigan Storefront
1973	45.	Terre Haute Courthouse
	46.	A Block of the 1800's*
1974	37.	1000 N. Delaware St.
	38.	Princeton, Gibson County Seat*
1975	56.	A Segment of New Harmony*
	57.	Station at Mt. Vernon
1976	62.	Abel's Showroom*
	63.	Esse Warehouse*
1977	45.	The Marion Building
	46.	Sanctuary*
1978	39.	The City Market and Arena*
	40.	The Indiana State Museum
1979	41.	The Circle Theatre*
	42.	Urban Contrasts
1980	39.	The Beauchamp Complex*
1981	39.	A Segment of the Old Northside*
	40.	The Old Black Curtain Theatre
1982	57.	The Stumpf House
	58.	A Monument in Crawfordsville*
1983	45.	The Joggers #3
	46.	A Segment of Canal Street*
1984	48.	The Kappel House
	49.	The Knightstown Academy*
1985	31.	The White Iron Gate*
	32.	The Depew Fountain
1986	55.	The Shrine on the Avenue*
1987	51.	The Zocalo, Mexico City
	52.	A Segment of the Courthouse Square, Covington, IN*
1988	51.	122-24 S. Meridian
	52.	10th and Conner*
1989	48.	The Antelope Club
	49.	1st Lutheran Church*
1990	43.	Central Christian Church
	44.	One Way*

DAVIS, JAN R.

1981	41.	Cats
1982	59.	Juli
1983	47.	Tyann No. 12 and the Chimney
1985	33.	Red Winged Blackbirds*

DAVIS, JOSEPHINE
1931	66.	Road to Spencer
1932	59.	Greasy Creek, Brown County
1933	51.	Artist Studio and Garden
	52.	Red Gums on Weed Patch
1934	39.	A Sunny Lane
1936	45.	Fresh from Market

DAVIS, LOIS
1949	41.	Studio Row, Gloucester
	42.	Unloading Redfish, Gloucester
	43.	Summer Afternoon
1967	57.	Peacock Curtain*
	58.	Pine Lake
1968	55.	The Prisoners
	56.	Appalachia*
1969	56.	Reflection
1971	47.	Buttercup Fields Forever
	48.	Fringe Benefit
1973	47.	Revolution and Counter-Revolution
	48.	Nature Children*
1974	39.	The Music in the Park
	40.	Masque*
1975	58.	Facades
	59.	Neighbors*
1976	64.	Queve
1977	47.	Malcontents
1980	38.	The Flowers That Bloom in the Spring
1981	42.	Work Break
1983	48.	Big Daddy
1985	34.	Safeguards
1986	56.	Punk Rockers
	57.	Aftermath*
1987	53.	Threat to Dominance
1988	53.	Giants on Parade
	54.	Recovery Room, Back to Consciousness*
1989	50.	Inventory Reduction*
1990	45.	Pledge/Revenge*

DAVIS, MARY ELSIE
| 1953 | 51. | Western Eagles |

DAVIS, ROSALIE
| 1988 | 55. | The Last Morning Glory |

DAVISSON, HOMER G.
1925	52.	Beechwoods in Autumn
	53.	A Squall at Pemaquid, Maine
	54.	October Afternoon
1926	91.	The Edge of the Woods
	92.	Under the Willows
	93.	An Autumn Afternoon
1927	79.	October in Brown County
	80.	Market Day at Dournenez
	81.	A Fisherman's Home, Brittany
1928	80.	In Nick Robest's Woods
1929	86.	The Fish Wharf
	87.	A Summer Morning

1930	62.	Landing the Catch
1931	67.	A Rainy Day at Nashville*
1932	60.	The Boter House at Bruges
1933	53.	The First Snow
1934	40.	At Conner's Mill
	41.	Rainy Day at Nashville
1936	46.	The First Snow
1937	41.	At Conner's Mill
1938	50.	Market Day at Honfleur
	51.	Springtime at Somerset
1939	307.	The First Snow
1940	39.	November
	307.	Summer Evening at Syracuse
1941	42.	Erie Stone Crusher
1942	48.	Indiana Sugar Camp
1943	59.	Hilltop Farm
1944	65.	Rainy Day in Spring
	66.	In the Gaspe Country
1945	56.	Rainy Day at Jalapa
	57.	Early Spring
1946	54.	September
	55.	The Causeway
1947	59.	On Ten Mile Creek
1948	39.	Autumn on the Slocum Trail
1950	49.	The Tide Mill
1952	57.	Upland Pasture
1953	52.	On Ten Mile Creek
	53.	Spring on Pipe Creek
1954	59.	Pool in the Katerkill
	60.	October in the Catskills
1955	62.	In My Backyard
1956	58.	Brittany Fishing Village
1957	49.	The Approaching Storm

DAVOUST, MARJORIE
| 1989 | 51. | Wild Goose Chase* |

DAWSON, ETHEL
1943	60.	Fragrance
1944	67.	A Cold Morning
	68.	Peonies

DAWSON, LEON
| 1963 | 63. | Arizona Sky |

DAY, CHARLES C.
| 1977 | 48. | Abandoned |

DAY, DICK
| 1975 | 60. | Peaceful Afternoon |
| 1977 | 49. | Autumn Glade |

DAY, ELNORA
1964	79.	Granny's Kitchen
1965	61.	Reflections
1966	44.	Fruits of Summer
1977	50.	Hot Peppers

DAY, GENTRY
(See Blankenship, Diane)
| 1981 | 43. | Michelle |

1984	50.	Sunshine Star
1988	56.	Warm on Cool*

DAY, HERBERT J.

1930	63.	Reflections

DAY, SANDY

1988	57.	Good Morning, Cincinnati*
1989	52.	Nourishment

DEAHL, BETTY JEAN

1965	62.	Antique Glass
	63.	Zinnias
1967	59.	Autumn Gold
	60.	Zinnias in White Pitcher
1969	57.	Geraniums

DEAN, FRANCES

1943	61.	New House

DeARMOND, DOROTHY

1967	61.	Fall Mushrooms

DeATLEY, GERTRUDE

1962	85.	The Dreamer's Paradise

DEBIKEY, GEORGE

1984	51.	Cranes
1985	35.	Pas de deux
1986	58.	Ecstasy II
1987	54.	Emancipation
	55.	Dream
1988	58.	Uprising
	59.	Momentum
1989	53.	Unraveled
1990	46.	Sculptural Form*

DEBIKEY, ILANA

1989	54.	Tranquil Motion

DECHART, DONNA M.

1961	81.	Sunset Meditation

DECIL, DEL

1973	49.	Microcosm

DeCOSTA, JOHN

1979	43.	Golden Cubes
1980	40.	Chain Reaction
1981	44.	Square Times 5*
1982	60.	Outburst
1983	49.	Fortress of Sanity

DEERING, CONNIE J(o)
(See Wallpe, Connie Deering)

1973	50.	Summer in Tipton County
1975	61.	The Door of Perception
1977	51.	Victorian Composite
1978	41.	House on County Line
	42.	Winter Sunset
1979	44.	Rural Indiana

1980	41.	Winning
1981	45.	Where Lilacs Grow
	46.	A Familiar Sight
1982	61.	Atlanta's Summer Garden
1983	50.	California Vacation
1984	52.	Circle City Monument
1985	36.	View from University Park
1986	59.	Sunlight and Leaves*
1987	56.	Bridge on Crooked Creek #1
	57.	Window on My World
1988	60.	Country
	61.	Morning

DeMUN, ANN P.

1959	52.	Portrait of Phillip
	53.	Sonata
1960	60.	The Blue Plate
	61.	Mrs. Hamilton Hunter
1961	84.	Cowboy*
	85.	Winter Woods
1964	80.	Spring
	81.	The Artist's Mother

DEMYER, EVELYN

1960	62.	Construction

DEMYER, HOWARD

1960	63.	Tenement
1961	86.	Haitian Harbor
	87.	Woman Of Haiti
1965	64.	A-Marketing*
	65.	The Bull Fighter
	66.	Lincoln's Desk in Illinois
1966	45.	Spanish Fishermen

DENNEY, GLADYS A.

1942	49.	Midsummer Flowers
	50.	The Abandoned Stone-Crusher
1944	69.	In for Repair
	70.	Portrait of a Stove
	71.	Colorado Mountain Stream
1945	58.	Our Backyard
1946	56.	Flower Study*
1947	60.	Ward, Colorado, Post Office*
1948	40.	Tuberous Begonia
	41.	Ducks
1949	44.	Fye's Ranch
1950	50.	The High Range
1951	57.	North St. Vrain, Colorado
1954	61.	Colorado Mining Town

DENNEY, LYLE

1989	55.	Calling Time
1990	47.	Indian Summer Evening

DENNIS, GRETCHEN M(arkle)

1961	88.	Street Scene
1963	64.	Melrose Abbey
1964	82.	Jimmy
	83.	Bottles

EXHIBITION RECORDS

DENNIS, LUCILLE
1958	60.	Peaceful Valley
1959	54.	Tempo
	55.	L'Apertif
1963	65.	Two Faces of Eve
1965	67.	Exodus
	68.	Emerging Forms
1967	62.	Abundance*
	63.	Portrait Study
1971	49.	Waiting
1975	62.	Encore

DENTON, HOWARD H.
1968	57.	Totem

DEPAUL, VESTA V.
1958	61.	From A Garden

DeSANTO, STEPHEN (Charles)
1970	66.	The Fortress*
	67.	Abandoned Door
1978	43.	The Porch in Winter Sunlight*
1979	45.	Last Winter
1980	42.	Fig Buckets
	43.	The Swing*
1981	47.	Ocean City Awning
	48.	Front Steps, Mid-Winter
1982	62.	Ocean City Urn*
1985	37.	Umbrella in Miami
	38.	Ocean City Railing

DESATNICK, MIKE J.
1976	65.	Dyan*
1977	52.	Still Life with Milkglass Vase

DESPOT, SHIRLEY (Ann)
1962	86.	Clown
	87.	Street Scene
	88.	Still Life
1965	69.	Summer Still Life
1970	68.	Latent-3
1974	41.	Requiem for Summer '73
1975	63.	Bouquet
	64.	Survivor
1976	66.	Autumn Repose
1980	44.	Fence Row
1981	49.	Waiting

DETCHON, (Irwin) LEE
1942	51.	Odd Jobs Man*
	52.	The Alley Comber
	53.	The Studio Stove
1943	62.	Flower Arrangement
	63.	Spring Design
	64.	The Model Stand
1948	42.	Dunes of Indiana
1949	45.	Drying the Nets
1980	45.	My Sister, Esther

DEUITCH, BRYAN
1981	50.	Untitled

DEUKER, FREDRIK
1933	55.	Argentine Tango
	56.	The Woman Tempted Me
	57.	Godiva
	58.	Big Parade
	59.	Pan Gone Jazz
	60.	Sweet Adeline

DEUTSCHMAN, LOUANNA
1987	58.	Peachy
1989	56.	Sumac in Scarlet
	57.	Winter Sun, Milkweed

DEVANEY, NANCY
1961	89.	Rescue Race

DEVOE, HELEN
1961	90.	Youth*
	91.	Portrait of a Girl

DeWESTER, LEANNE J.
1983	51.	Early Spring
1986	60.	The Canal with Scarlet Vine
1987	59.	Salt Creek Bridge
	60.	Gentleman with Arcs and Intersections

DeWITT, DON
1969	58.	Meditation*
1970	69.	Temujin*

DICKERSON, GRACE LESLIE
1946	57.	Negro Head
1954	62.	Telegram for the Funny Man*
1955	63.	Joyce
1956	59.	Norma
1957	52.	Mary and Her Goats
1958	62.	Seated Figure
1960	64.	Muchachas
1961	92.	Madonna and Child
	93.	Mexican Peasant
1965	70.	Los Mexicanos
	71.	Charlotte
1967	64.	Tropical San Blas
1968	58.	Lost Sparrow
1971	50.	Tropical Zihuatanejo
	51.	Flower Market
1976	67.	Nine Fifty One North Delaware
	68.	The Marina, Marbella, Spain

DICKHAUS, JOHN ROBERT
1981	51.	Portrait (Barbara, the Artist's Wife)
1982	63.	Portrait of Mrs. Jim Kartes
1983	52.	Portrait of Mr. Steven M. Dickhaus
1985	39.	T. C. Steele's "House of the Singing Winds"
1986	61.	Still Life, Apples and Bottles
	62.	Portrait of Robin
1987	61.	Still Life, Apples and a Duck
	62.	Bounteous Harvest

1988	62.	Silver Goblet, Orange and Grapes
1989	58.	Oak Creek Canyon
	59.	Blue Nude

DICKINSON, BARBARA

1948	43.	Amaryllis
	44.	Homestead
1949	46.	November Morning

DICKINSON, H. O.

1946	58.	Thoroughbred

DIEDRICH, GAIL

1987	63.	Hillside

DIEMAN, CLARA (Leonard Sorensen)

1927	82.	Architectural Fragment
	83.	Study for Memorial
1931	68.	Relief, detail of Terra Cotta doorway of Denver National Bank
	69.	Portrait Bust of Charles Cassidy

DIETRICH, GEORGE ADAMS

1927	84.	The Stairway
	85.	Willy's Chapel Church
	86.	The Card Table*
1928	81.	The Doctor
	82.	I. U. Mitchell Hall
	83.	Late Afternoon*
1929	88.	Negro
	89.	Water Color Interior
	90.	Portrait of Miss Dorothy Laverne Meredith
1930	64.	After the Shower
	65.	Farmers' and Gardeners' Market
	66.	Negro*
1931	70.	Yacht Club*
1933	54.	Bunker Hill
1934	42.	Greene's Corner
1937	42.	Kathleen
	43.	Artist's Wife
1939	56.	Rima
1942	54.	Sunday Afternoon

DILL, MARY C.

1963	66.	City*
	67.	Lakeside
1965	72.	Marina
1967	65.	Bridge
	66.	Poster*
1968	59.	Night Theme
	60.	Untitled
1970	70.	Five-Part Invention
1971	52.	Earth Construction II
	53.	Fragment
1973	51.	This Old House
1977	53.	River Series I

DILLINGHAM, JERRY

1976	69.	Untitled

DILLMAN, MARK

1986	63.	Untitled
	64.	Lynn*
1987	64.	Foreshortened Foot
	65.	Lynn with Degas Bather
1988	63.	Portrait of Marcy*
1989	60.	The Artist's Wife

DIMITROFF, LOUIS

1941	43.	Still Life with Jug and Apples
1952	58.	Composition No. 2*
1953	54.	Houses

DIMITROFF, LUBEN

1952	59.	St. Joan Church, Macedonia
	60.	Ships at Rest
1955	64.	Boats In Bay
1956	60.	Citadel-City
	61.	Winter
1957	50.	Old Fishermen's Point
	51.	Sailing After The Rain
1961	82.	Winter in Adirondacks
	83.	Approaching Storm

DiPALMA, JOHN M.

1981	52.	Summer Bouquet

DITMIRE, JEFFREY J.

1988	64.	Summer Garden

DITZENBERGER, PAUL E.

1955	65.	Seventeen
1970	71.	Laura
1971	54.	The Group

DODDS, (Mary) ELIZABETH
(See Shaffer, Elizabeth Dodds)

1937	44.	Still Life
1938	52.	Still Life
1943	65.	The Blue Cup

DOERSCHEL, MARGARET (R.)

1947	61.	Strictly Juvenile
1948	45.	An Apple A Day?
1955	66.	Reminder of a Forgotten Era
1956	62.	Buildings, Lawrence

DOLT, MARY BELLE

1946	59.	Mexican Costume
	60.	February 14th, Any Year
1947	62.	Summer Shadow

DOMROESE, EWALD F.

1939	57.	Study in Brown
	58.	Zinnias

DONALDSON, D(aniel) C.

1957	53.	Greasy Creek*
1958	63.	On Madeline Island
1960	65.	Sycamores
	66.	Kelly Hill

1961	95.	Whitewater Canal
1962	89.	Fisherman's Bay
1963	68.	A Day of Showers and Flowers

DONALDSON, HILDEGARDE

| 1961 | 94. | Mary's Window |

DONATO, C. D.

| 1938 | 53. | Festival |

DONER, EMEL

1984	53.	Cyclamens
	54.	Winter at Lake Superior
1986	65.	Patterns in Bromeliad
	66.	Winter's Bloom
1987	66.	Shadows on Poinsettia
	67.	Neoregelia #2*
1988	65.	Full Glory
	66.	The Patio
1989	61.	Amish Girls of Sarasota
	62.	Hidden Beauty*

DONNELLY, CRAWFORD (F.)

1972	29.	Monhegan Dinghy
1973	52.	Old Mill Bridge
1974	42.	The Captain's Skiff
1975	65.	The Fishin' Hole
	66.	#4466 Retired
1976	70.	The Town Dock
1977	54.	Laced Curtains*
1978	45.	This Arid Land No. 1
1979	46.	A Summer Afternoon*
1981	53.	A Moment to Reflect
1982	64.	From My Neighbor's Garden*
	65.	Acadian Waves
1984	55.	Of Many Winters
1986	67.	Summer Reflections
1987	68.	Notre Dame de Paris
1990	48.	Autumn
	49.	Woodstock Bridge

DORMANN, JAMES

1981	54.	Over-Look
1987	69.	Savanna Waterfront
1989	63.	Mill at Mansfield, Indiana
	64.	Rice Paddy in Japan*

DORSEY, HOLLAND

1963	69.	Parisian Bouquet
	70.	Song of Autumn
1964	84.	Study in Red

DOTY, ELLEN

1970	72.	Petunias
1974	43.	Blossoms
	44.	Augsburg
1975	67.	Hauptstrassa
	68.	Without Love, I Am a Noisy Gong
1976	71.	After the Rain
1978	44.	Flowers and Rain
1981	55.	Hibiscus

DOUGHERTY, ELIZABETH H.
(See Ashton, Elizabeth Doughterty)

| 1949 | 47. | Antique Show, New Orleans |
| | 48. | Hot Dog Haven |

DOUGLAS, LANCE

1967	67.	Owl
	68.	Madonna
1968	61.	A Friend
1982	66.	Gibbet
	67.	Screen Play
1983	53.	Birth of a Nation

DOVERSBERGER, JAMES

| 1958 | 64. | Awakening |
| 1959 | 56. | By a Window in Venice |

DOYLE, R. J.

| 1934 | 43. | November Snow |

DRAGSTREM, BON B.

| 1969 | 59. | Apts. For Rent, Naptown, U. S. A |

DRISKELL, DOROTHY L.

| 1952 | 61. | Tired House |
| 1953 | 55. | Take It Easy, Portrait of Kelly |

DROEGE, ANTHONY J.

| 1982 | 68. | Female Torso |
| 1988 | 67. | Black and Blue |

DuCHATEAU, ROY

| 1962 | 90. | Mrs. Roy DuChateau |

DUCHEMIN, IRVIN P.

1955	67.	Commuter
	68.	Antique
	69.	Showers
1958	65.	My Dog
1970	73.	Dora

DUCKWALL, HELEN B(riggs)
(See Briggs, Helen L.)

1953	56.	Jeannette
	57.	Lonesome Cowboy*
	58.	Christopher*
1954	63.	Gail
	64.	Backyard Garden
1955	70.	Carol Anne
1956	63.	Lunch at Block's*
	64.	Chris
	65.	Trick or Treat
1957	54.	Christopher
	55.	Friend in Silk Shirt*
1958	66.	Little Leaguer
	67.	Flowers In The Window
	68.	Ann
1959	57.	Melancholy Clown
	58.	Lynn Gatti*
	59.	Miriam Callahan

1960	67.	Mrs. Callahan
	68.	The Restaurant
	69.	The Bus
1961	96.	Mrs. Reefer*
	97.	Rainy Dark
	98.	Lisa
1962	91.	Suzanne*
	92.	Young Girl
1963	71.	Harriet
	72.	Rodney Brown
1964	89.	Karen Hansen*
1965	73.	Kelly*
1966	46.	Young Girl
	47.	Sisters
1967	69.	Kent Morse*
	70.	Still Life with Flowers*
1969	60.	Little Girls

DUDLEY, FRANK V.

1925	55.	Shadow Swept
	56.	Drifting Shadows
	57.	Treasures of the Trail
1926	94.	One September Day, Dunes
	95.	Across Shaded Sands
	96.	Dune Creek in Winter
1927	87.	November Song*
	88.	Indian Summer
	89.	At the Turn of the Trail
1928	84.	Along the Sandy Way*
	85.	From a High Dune
	86.	Thru Drifted Snow
1929	91.	A Woodland Trail
	92.	Where Winds Have Played
	93.	The Foreboding Calm
1930	67.	From Hanover Campus*
	68.	When Autumn Comes to Waverly
	69.	Spring
1931	71.	Hills of Sandland
	72.	Sand Cherries in Gay Attire
1932	61.	From Mt. Jackson*
	62.	In the Wake of High Winds
	63.	Butterfly Weed
1933		(Nos. 300-338 were displayed in a special Dudley gallery)
	300.	Duneland in Winter
	301.	Summer Days
	302.	In Lupine Time
	303.	Lupine and Puccoon
	304.	Butterfly Weed
	305.	Dune Meadow Flowers
	306.	When Swamp Maples Turn
	307.	Autumn Passes
	308.	Through Drifted Dunes
	309.	The Conquest
	310.	Spring Fever
	311.	The Silhouette
	312.	At the Turn of Day
	313.	Storm Clouds
	314.	Sunny Hours of Winter
	315.	A Salutation

	316.	Golden Days of Autumn
	317.	Sunlight and Shadow
	318.	Cloud Shadows
	319.	A Sunny Autumn Day
	320.	Juniper and Pine
	321.	Shadows at Eventime
	322.	Under Moonlit Skies
	323.	Off Duneland Shores
	324.	A Clear Day
	325.	When Summer Wanes
	326.	The Magic Touch of Autumn
	327.	A Grey Day
	328.	Across Sunny Sands
	329.	Sandcherries and Juniper
	330.	Over the Tree Tops
	331.	The Sunlit Cloud
	332.	Dune Grasses
	333.	A Sunny Day
	334.	The Moving Dune
	335.	Skies at Even'
	336.	The Blowout
	337.	A Windy Day
	338.	The Last of the Forest
1934	44.	The Call of the Dunes
	45.	A Dune Meadow Song
1935	43.	The Wind Worn Hollow
	44.	The Far Horlizon
	45.	Cool Shadows Steal Along
1936	47.	After Winter's Winds
	48.	A Dune Meadow
	49.	Lazily Drifting Shadows
1937	45.	Autumn Comes to the Dunes
	46.	The Magic of Autumn
	310.	Butterfly Weed
1938	54.	Sand Cherries in Blossom Time
	55.	Where Dunes and Waters Meet
1939	59.	The Hills of Arcady*
	60.	The Trail Goes Down
	61.	Where Waves and Shoreline Meet
	308.	From Mount Holden
1940	40.	From Mt. Jackson
	41.	Sun Swept Sands
	42.	The Old Stage Coach Trail
	308.	Autumn
1941	44.	Jack Pine and Company
	45.	Song of Sun and Shadow
	46.	Under Changing Skies*
	307.	Lupine
1942	55.	Thru the Pine Tops
1943	66.	Wind Tossed Pines
1944	72.	Under Winter's Snowy Mantle
	73.	Ol' Faithful

DUDLEY, GEORGE

1939	62.	Blue and Gold
	63.	The Red Bowl

DUFF, CHARLES T.

1989	65.	Sunday Afternoon

DUNBAR, DAVID W.
1987   70.   A Sunday Drive

DUNBAR, JERRY (A.)
1982   69.   Overlooking Chicago
      70.   Spanish Flavor
1983   54.   Welcome Home
1985   40.   A Quiet Sanctuary
1986   68.   Porch Talk
1987   71.   The Laura B
1990   50.   When the Fog Lifts

DUNCAN, ANNE (M.)
1956   66.   Hoosier Gardener
      67.   Nort's Place on Little Sand
      68.   Symphony
      69.   Down Mexico Way
1957   56.   Fisherman's Cove
      57.   Meditation
      58.   Far Into The Hills*
1958   69.   Ke Kali Nei Au
      70.   Na Pali Coast
      71.   City Ducks
1959   60.   Trees and Beyond
1960   70.   Pale Moon
      71.   Distant Hills
1961   99.   Abandoned Bird Nest
     100.   Something About Spring
     101.   Beyond the Trees
1962   93.   Tropicana
      94.   Weeping Tree
      95.   Wheat
1963   73.   Light Fragments Descending
      74.   Echo the Sound
      75.   Flower Motif
1965   74.   Gulls Swooping Down
      75.   Up Hill Sensation, San Francisco
1967   71.   Big G-Little G
      72.   European Atmosphere*
1968   62.   Of Ancient Rome #2
      63.   Landscape Composition
1969   61.   Landscape Composition
1970   74.   Flowers Afield
      75.   My Castle Came Tumbling Down

DUNCAN, JENNEE STRATTON
1945   59.   Spring Melody
1946   61.   Jean's Knobby Vase
      62.   Gladiolus & Graffie
1954   65.   The Old Pilcher Place
      66.   Across the Tracks
1955   71.   Old House
1956   70.   Captain Dick's Retreat
1957   59.   Road Construction Ahead
1959   61.   Along Sargent Road
1960   72.   Along Sargent Road
      73.   Ice Rings
1961   102.   Old Roberts Place
1962   96.   Dreary Morning
      97.   Beckett's Barn

1963   76.   Circuitous Lines
      77.   Three Rocks and Dirt
1964   85.   Indiana Sycamores
      86.   Winter at Home
      87.   Bridle Path Fantasy
1965   76.   Pulcinella
      77.   Curing Time
      78.   Frozen Lagoon
1973   53.   Saltbox House
1987   72.   Castleton Depot
1988   68.   Smokie Mountain Farm
1989   66.   Victorian House on Geist
1990   51.   Abandoned

DUNLAP, BERNICE N.
1939   65.   Ranchos de Taos
      66.   Street Scene, Taos, N. M.

DUNLAP, CATHERINE (Alice)
1929   94.   Still Life
1932   64.   Cosmos
      65.   Still Life
1933   61.   Still Life

DUNLAP, DAVID (W.)
1944   74.   Pool in the Woods
      75.   The Wrestlers
      76.   Into the Valley
1945   60.   Yucca: Theme and Variations
      61.   Autumn Bouquet
1947   63.   Old Cabin and Orchard
      64.   Winter in the Park
      65.   Street Scene, Mexico
      66.   Winter in the Park

DUNLAP, EDWARD HUBER
1929   95.   Girl in Rose
1931   73.   Spring*
      74.   Wagley's Cabbage Patch
1934   46.   Procession*
1936   50.   Nocturne
      51.   Catherine
1939   64.   Going Home
1943   67.   On the Rocks

DUNLAP, WILLIAM D.
1941   47.   Rock Fence and Tree
1942   56.   Spring Landscape, New Mexico
      57.   Watchers of the Sea

DUNLEVY, ETHEL F. BALL
1937   47.   Bowl of Fruit
      48.   Still Life
      49.   Still Life
     311.   Summer Flowers
1939   67.   Still Life
1944   77.   Still Life
1947   67.   Still Life

DUNN, DELPHINE

1926	97.	Gloucester Sketch
1927	90.	A Summer Morning
1930	70.	Gloucester
	71.	Gloucester Harbor

DUNNIGAN, LILLIAN R.

1972	30.	Debbie
1973	54.	Boggstown Mill
1976	72.	Meditation
1977	55.	Old Sycamore
1982	71.	Muchacha de San Miguelle
	72.	Dietrich's Barn
1984	56.	Indiana Summer
1986	69.	First Signs of Autumn
	70.	Afternoon Shadows
1987	73.	Doe Run Creek
	74.	The White Teapot

DUNNIGAN, NEIL (E.)

1962	98.	A Bit of the Past
1964	90.	Flower Seller
1967	73.	The Prophet
1968	64.	Red Coal Bucket
	65.	March Rain
	66.	Surplus
1969	62.	Rose
1971	55.	The Window
1972	31.	Boy of Mine
1975	69.	Cora
1980	46.	Sleepy Head
1981	56.	Pigeon Lady
1984	57.	Dry Dock
1985	41.	Yugoslav Bridge
1986	71.	House on Mound St.
1987	75.	Klompin Dancers
	76.	Brown County Barn

E

EASON, DANA RAE
1982	73.	Under the Violets
1986	72.	Raccoon Spy
1990	52.	Snort, Sniff

EATON, JUDITH S.
| 1986 | 73. | Field Fantasia |
| | 74. | Joy, at 6 Weeks |

EATON, RUTH
| 1961 | 103. | Idaho Grain Elevators |
| 1964 | 91. | Glacial Stream |

EBERG, MARILYN
| 1989 | 67. | Memories |
| | 68. | Lunch |

ECCLES, JAMES
1949	49.	Willows along the Creek
1950	51.	Sloppy Weather
1951	58.	A November Day
	59.	On Salt Creek
1953	59.	Creeping Shadows
	60.	The Old Homestead
1954	67.	Isle of Sunshine, Trinidad
	68.	Sloppy Weather
1956	71.	Storm Clouds
1957	60.	A Spring Day
	61.	Purple And Gold
1958	72.	The White Road
1959	62.	Storm Clouds
	63.	The Golden Hickory
	64.	Cloud Reflections
1960	74.	Market in Barbados
1961	104.	Souvenir Shop, St. Clair, Virgin Islands
	105.	In Port Antonio
	106.	Market, St. Thomas, Virgin Islands
1962	99.	Summer Skies
	100.	Smokies
1963	78.	A Winter Day
1964	92.	A Summer Sky
	93.	River Commerce
1965	79.	Old Road in Winter
1966	48.	Old Cottonwoods
1967	74.	Yesterday

ECHELBARGER, BERTHA
| 1963 | 79. | Garden Zinnias |

EDDY, HILARY A. (Jackson)
(See Edwards, Hilary Jackson)
1984	58.	Living Room
1986	75.	Sunlit Rhododendrons
	76.	Snapdragons
1987	77.	Passion*

1988	69.	Radiance*
	70.	Translucence
1989	69.	Flowers Afloat
	70.	Shades of Winter*
1990	53.	Transient Light

EDWARDS, HILARY JACKSON
(See Eddy, Hilary A. Jackson)
1980	47.	Old Shoe and Lace Hanky Landscape*
1981	57.	Entwined*
1983	92.	Garden at No. 22*
	93.	Roses

EDWARDS, NANCY BIXBY
1936	53.	Greedy Imp No. 1
	54.	Greedy Imp No. 2
	55.	Denyse
1937	50.	Little Sister
	51.	Terra Cotta Garden Piece
1938	58.	Mother and Child
	59.	Portrait of Bobby Davey
1939	70.	Goose Herder*
	71.	Portrait of Robert David
	72.	Wall Panel
1940	44.	Sheba in Shawl
	45.	Torso de Jeune Fille*
1941	48.	The Clod
1944	78.	The Treasure

EDWARDS, STEPHEN E.
1984	59.	Daisy Quilt and Spring Tea Still Life
1985	42.	Silent in the Snow*
1986	77.	South of Milroy, Winter Hill
1988	71.	Handyman's Dream 1988
	72.	February Winds/Blue Tarps
1989	71.	Too Early for the Spring Thaw
	72.	Pulteney Bridge on the River
1990	54.	Untitled #2
	55.	(Untitled #1) As the Wheel Turns*

EGGEMEYER, MAUDE KAUFMAN
1925	58.	Hoosier Beeches
	59.	A Garden*
1926	98.	The Garden of the Blue Door
	99.	Old Willow
1927	91.	February Thaw
	92.	Blue and Gold
	93.	Willows and Sunshine
1928	87.	June Garden
1930	72.	An Alley*

EGGERT, MARY
| 1982 | 74. | Clematis* |
| 1985 | 43. | Evening Dogwood |

EGLOFF, (Rita) EVANNE
1975 70.   Curiosity

EILERS, (A.) FRED
1945 62.   Fruit and Ivy*
1962 101.   Self Portrait
      102.   Sun and Storm
      103.   Small Boat Harbor

EILTS, E. G(aye)
1968 67.   An Old Pitcher
1970 76.   Untitled
1971 56.   Vanishing Era*
1973 55.   Sentry
      56.   Broken Pitcher
1976 74.   Last Flowers
1978 46.   Lost Time
1985 44.   Italliante Circa 1872
1988 73.   Untitled Floral

EISENBACH, D(orothy) LIZETTE
1927 94.   Lying Idle
      95.   The Paint Shop
      96.   Gloucester Doorway
1928 88.   Ruth
1930 73.   Black and White Drawing*
      74.   Summer School Office
      75.   Decorative Still Life
      76.   Drawing
1937 52.   Central City, Colo.
      53.   House in Central City, Colo.
1943 68.   Still Life
      69.   Street Scene, No. 3
      70.   After the Ball Is Over
1944 79.   Flotsam and Jetsam
      80.   Elsie, Our Phi Beta Kappa
      81.   Landscape

EISENHUT, MARIESUE
1936 56.   Jonathans

ELDREDGE, STUART
1933 62.   Still Life with Tools
      63.   The Brass Horse
      64.   March Evening
      65.   Flowers and Feather
      66.   Marigolds and Shell
1934 47.   Willow Road
      48.   Distant Farm
1936 57.   Potato Field
      58.   A St. Joseph County Farm
1949 50.   Fresh Snow*
      51.   Winter
1950 52.   The Village in Winter
1951 60.   Important Occasion
1952 62.   Annunciation
      63.   The Connecticut River at Bellows Falls
      64.   The Elms in October
1953 61.   Winter View from Eureka
      62.   Winter on Rockingham Road*

1954 69.   Early in March
      70.   Snow Patches
      71.   The Connecticut near Weathersfield Bow
1955 72.   Chrysanthemums
      73.   November Storm
      74.   Early Evening
1956 72.   A March Morning
      73.   Bare Winter
1957 62.   The Road Home
      63.   Spring In West Granby
      64.   Dark Winter
1958 73.   Cold
      74.   Two Apples and a Quince
1959 65.   Dark Morning
      66.   March Storm*
1960 75.   Wintry View
1961 107.   In St. Joseph County
     108.   The River in July
     109.   The Village in March
1962 104.   St. André Chartres
     105.   March
     106.   Winter Light
1964 94.   Spring Bouquet
      95.   On the Palatine
      96.   May Showers

ELETSON, BARBARA F.
1973 57.   Grain Elevator
1976 73.   Rainy Night, Bell Street
1978 47.   Detached Symmetry

ELKINS, DANIEL L.
1983 55.   Yesterday's Images
      56.   Cassidy's Barn

ELLINGHAM, Mrs. MILLER
1958 75.   Patti's December Child
1961 110.   Zurich From the Dolder

ELLIOTT, G(eorge) C.
1979 47.   Expressions from Hamburg
      48.   The Pig
1981 58.   Merry Go
      59.   Expressions from Masai
1982 75.   Ambassadors of Ambigui
      76.   Bound to Be Heard
1983 57.   Calico Tablecloth
      58.   The Marriage of Meranda
1984 60.   Viviapolis
      61.   Palm Beach Party
1985 45.   He Who Laughs at Such a Thing
1986 78.   Penny for Your Thoughts
1987 78.   Man's Consumption, Mother Nature's Threat
1988 74.   The Meeting
      75.   Invitation to a Voyage
1989 73.   Cats and Old Lace
      74.   Chief Hawk and Friends
1990 56.   River Banks Remembered*

ELLIOTT, MARY W.
1958	76.	Mary Jo
1960	76.	Slim
1962	107.	Martha
1963	80.	Boy
1964	97.	Stanhope
	98.	Cornflowers
1968	68.	Marty
1970	77.	Rachael

ELLIS, JEFFREY THOMAS
| 1985 | 46. | Wed. Storm! |

ELLIS, LINDA J(ane)
1965	80.	We Live Only to Give
1967	75.	He Restoreth My Soul
1969	63.	Walk in the Meadow
1970	78.	Crimson Vase
1971	57.	Vase-of-Flowers

ELLYSON, MARTHA
| 1946 | 63. | Rhythm in Bronze |

ELMORE, JOHN M.
| 1987 | 79. | A White Dog |

ELROD, CAROL
| 1973 | 58. | Back Street in Avallon* |

ELROD, EDWARD
| 1971 | 58. | The Great Plains |

EMERICK, CLARA L.
| 1944 | 82. | Macey's Slip, Wawasee |

EMRICH, HARVEY
1928	89.	Oak*
	90.	Bouquet
	91.	Dream of Youth (over mantel)
1929	96.	Noon*
	97.	The Mighty Hunter
	98.	Old Fashioned Bouquet
1930	77.	Fruit
1931	75.	Hard Times
	76.	Spring in the Orchard
1932	66.	Betty
1933	67.	The Catskill Mountains*

ENGEL, HARRY
1931	77.	Still Life*
	78.	Annunciation to Joseph
1933	68.	Abandoned Quarry
	69.	Quarry
1934	49.	Portrait of Dad
1937	54.	Portrait
1939	73.	Cornshocks
	74.	Deep Cut
	75.	Hillside
1940	46.	Quarry

1942	58.	Mail Boxes
	59.	Smoked Herring
1944	83.	Self Portrait
	84.	Maine Rain
	85.	Still Life
1946	64.	Provincetown Waterfront
1947	68.	Clam Diggers
	69.	Provincetown Seascape
	70.	Fisherman
1950	53.	Samovar No. 2*

ENGELLAND, TIM
1971	59.	Portrait of Paul (Study)
	60.	Still Life After Onions
1972	32.	Girl Reading*

ENGLE, FRANK L.
1941	49.	A Tucson Sky
	50.	Nanene*
1943	71.	The Woman

ENGLE, HARRY L.
1925	60.	Nashville, Brown County
	61.	Cabin on Greasy Creek
1926	100.	Shore Silhouettes
	101.	Aerials
	102.	Hillside Rhythm
1927	97.	The Heath of Amneran
	98.	Summer Wanes
	99.	Vacation

ENGLE, NANENE QUEEN
| 1984 | 62. | Thunderstorm |
| | 63. | Morning Frost |

ENGLISH, GENEVIEVE
1961	111.	Boulder Canyon
1962	108.	Arapaho Basin
	109.	Calumet Harbor
1963	81.	Buffalo Creek
	82.	Canal Lights
1964	99.	The Sportsman
1965	81.	Flowers on the Patio
	82.	Garden Bouquet
	83.	Western Slope
1966	49.	Summer in Brown County*
	50.	Rock and Bramble #2
	51.	Rendezvous
1967	76.	Fruitbasket
1968	69.	Tippecanoe Flowage
1969	64.	Watchtower #2*

ENGLISH, JEAN
| 1975 | 71. | Forever |
| 1978 | 48. | Spirit of Atlanta |

ENOCH, MARK (P.)
1980	48.	A Fashionable Affair
1981	60.	Lemon Tea with Your Still Life
	61.	Jacki's Surprise

ENSFIELD, MICHAEL R(obert)
1989	75.	Grandpa
	76.	Betty
1990	57.	Horse & Buggy
	58.	Irish Farmer

EPSTEIN, CLARA
1942	60.	Avenue
	61.	Beech Trees
	62.	Boats
	63.	Boats on the River
	64.	Early Spring
	65.	Park
1944	86.	Flowers
	87.	Ernestine Jane
	88.	Child's Portrait*
1945	63.	Portrait of a Young Girl
1946	65.	Brother and Sister
1947	71.	Sunshine in Fall
1948	46.	Fall Creek Boulevard
1949	52.	Spring
1950	54.	Gale G
	55.	Little Girl's Head
1952	65.	Cathedral, Taxco, Mexico
	66.	Market Scene, Mexico
	67.	Baby Lawrence*
1953	63.	Rolling Country
1955	75.	Fall at Turkey Run

ERBAUGH, MELODY
1983	59.	Vanishing Herd
1985	47.	Pigmented Lace Laceration
	48.	Shadow Dancing

ERICKSON, OSCAR B.
1927	100.	Simon's Barn
	101.	The Willows
	102.	Three Block Prints
1928	92.	Reflections
1929	99.	Clearing Skies
	100.	Autumn Symphony*
	101.	Indian Summer
1930	78.	From the Hilltop
	79.	The Last Rays
1931	79.	Indiana Hills
	80.	Early October
1932	67.	A Touch of Autumn
	68.	Autumn Begins
1933	70.	Cloud Shadows
	71.	Across the Valley
1934	50.	The Sun Spot
1935	47.	Autumn
1936	59.	The Old Elm*
	60.	Beside a Country Lane
1941	51.	Peaceful Valley
1942	66.	Black Mts. Ozarks

ERNESTI, ETHEL H.
1943	72.	This Flower from My Garden

ERNSTING, RICH
1981	62.	Forgotten Wheels*
	63.	Grave Sight
1982	77.	Floral Fantasia
1983	60.	Ship Shapes
1984	64.	Twilight of Discussion
1985	49.	Radiant Walls
1986	79.	The Lovers of Lauren Macaw*
1987	80.	Palm Patterns*
1988	76.	Victorian Tracery
1989	77.	Chust for Nice
	78.	Circles
1990	59.	Too Tired

ERVIN, JOYCE
1973	59.	Basement Still Life

ESKENAZI, LOIS
1990	60.	Memories

ESSLING, CINDEE
1989	79.	Calling All Poppies

ETLER, VERNON
1938	60.	Red Feed Barn
	307.	Long White House

EUSTON, J. H.
1930	80.	Duneland Trees
	81.	Dune Pines
	82.	Duneland Vista
1931	81.	Black Oaks
	82.	White Pine
	83.	Duneland Sunset
1932	69.	Ridge Trail
	70.	Pines Along the Shore
	71.	Stately Sequoia
	72.	At Dawning
	73.	On Mt. Holden
1933	72.	Willows in Winter
	73.	Orchard Shade & Sunny Fields
	74.	Aspen in Snow
	75.	Over the Pine Tree Tops
	76.	Mt. Tom
1934	51.	Dudley Blowout
	52.	Juniper Valley
	53.	The Citadel
	54.	Dunes Hinterland
1935	48.	White Silence
	49.	Sandy Shorelands
1936	61.	November
	62.	San Gabriel Divide
	63.	High Dune Country
	64.	Trees of the Sand Hills
	65.	Winter Holds the Hills
	66.	Verdugo Woodland
	67.	Folded Hills
	68.	Ramparts of Duneland

1937	57.	Piegan Mountain
	58.	Black Mesa
	59.	Winter's Etching
	60.	Snow in the Hills
	61.	Delaware River
1938	61.	Big-Cone Spruce
	62.	Edge of the Wood
	63.	Indiana Shore
	64.	Pond at Evening
	65.	Toward the West
1939	78.	Blackfoot Country
	79.	Clay Lick Valley
	80.	Divide
	81.	Eagle Aerie
	82.	Lake Vista
	83.	Sierra Graybeards
	84.	Torrey Pine
1940	49.	Breath of Keewaydin
	50.	Orchard Gate
	51.	Pines of Duneland
	52.	Snow Bound
1941	52.	Duneland Sentinel
	53.	Hillside Home
	54.	Snow in the Hills
	55.	White Hills Farm

EVANS, W. JEROME
| 1967 | 77. | Untitled |
| | 78. | Cap D'Azure |

EVERETT, DOROTHY M.
1976	75.	Watermelon
1978	49.	Monarch
1979	49.	Huntington Cemetery
1983	61.	Summer
1984	65.	Sea and Sky

EVERETT, WALKER
| 1940 | 48. | Pigs |

EVERHART, JANE
1976	76.	Studio Interior
1979	50.	Monroe County Fieldscape I
	51.	Monroe County Fieldscape II

EWELL, PATRICIA P.
| 1962 | 110. | Sun-flowers |
| | 111. | Roof-tops |

EWING, DEBORAH A.
| 1984 | 66. | Bare Feet |

EYDEN, (Jr.), WILLIAM A.
1925	62.	An Autumn Lane
1926	103.	In the Heart of the Beechwoods
	104.	A Misty Morning
1927	103.	The Storm
1928	93.	Brown County Hills
1936	69.	Sunlight, Symphony*
1938	66.	Indiana Landscape
	308.	On the Bridge

1939	306.	Sunlight Vista
1940	309.	Winter's Mood
1942	67.	Steel for Defense
1943	73.	Snowing
1944	89.	Steel for War
	90.	November Day
1945	64.	Jenny*
1946	66.	Autumn Creek
1949	53.	Under the El, New York
1950	56.	Monday's Wash
	57.	Patty
1952	68.	Steel Mills
1953	64.	Winter Glow
1954	72.	Gently Falls the Snow
	73.	Moonlight
1956	74.	Manhattan Skyline
	75.	Storm
1957	65.	Farm News
1958	77.	Lucille
	78.	East Side, New York
1959	67.	Central Park, N. Y.
1960	77.	Winter Valley
	78.	Weather-Beaten
1961	112.	Carnival
	113.	Winter-Hills
	114.	High Surges
1962	112.	Covered Bridge
	113.	Tranquility
	114.	Old Friends*
1963	83.	Winter Solitude
1964	100.	Morning in the Valley
	101.	Early Snow*
1965	84.	Frosty Morning
	85.	Deserted*
1966	52.	Eventide
	53.	Shadow in the Valley
	54.	A Day in Summer*
1967	79.	Blue Winter
	80.	Tranquility*
1968	70.	Quaker Woman
	71.	Old Harbor
	72.	The Good Earth
1969	65.	Self Portrait**
1970	79.	A Day In Winter*
1971	61.	Winter
	62.	Old Harbor
1972	33.	In the Valley
1973	60.	Autumn Hills
1974	45.	A Day to Remember
1975	72.	Evening Sky
1977	56.	Evening Tide
	57.	My Two Loves
1978	50.	Berry Pickers
1979	52.	Under the El*
1981	64.	Winter Woods

EZELL, SANDY
1973	61.	Hard Times
1975	73.	The Village Smithy
1983	62.	Flowers of My Mind

F

FACKERT, O. W.
1925	63.	Nina
	64.	Red Kimono
	65.	Harvest
1926	105.	The Blue Robe
	106.	Fancy's Flight
	107.	Nehemiah (". . .and viewed the walls. . .")
1927	104.	Palos Hills
	105.	Indiana Dunes
	106.	The Green Room

FAGER, W. E.
1928	94.	The Evening Song
	95.	The Blue Shawl*
	96.	Kids
1929	102.	Sunny Stories
	103.	Gypsy Lure
1931	84.	One Fine Day
	85.	Woodland Fantasy
1933	77.	Fawns and Foliage
	78.	Exodus

FAGERBURG, LORENE K.
1954	74.	"Fall"
1955	76.	Reflections
1961	115.	Winter Dunes

FAILING, FRANCES
1934	55.	Along Cape Cod Bay
	56.	Three Nudes
1935	50.	Along the Cape
1936	70.	Veterans
1942	68.	Puenta De Ixtla, Mexico
1947	72.	Brilliant Bisbee, Arizona*
	73.	Ranchito (Arizona)

FARMER, EVELYN
1958	79.	Shadows
1963	84.	Columbus Falls
1964	102.	Greasy Creek
1967	81.	The Falling Snow
1982	78.	Majesty Unadorned

FARNHAM, JULIA C.
1936	71.	Portrait of a Gentleman
	72.	Joyce
1938	67.	Alan
1940	53.	All in the Family

FARRELL, RON
1974	46.	Vanderburg Co. Barn
1975	74.	Indiana Gold
	75.	West of Winchester
1985	50.	The Yoder Farm
1986	80.	Blue Door

| 1987 | 81. | Spring in Shelby County |
| | 82. | The Yoder Farm |

FAUCETT, JULIA (Ashton)
1971	63.	Landscape with Flowers
1974	47.	Mary's Flowers
	48.	Warm Flowers
1979	53.	Autumn
	54.	Country
1980	49.	Seascape-Cloudscape
1984	67.	Flowers & Grasses
1985	51.	Strati

FECHTMAN, HELEN L(ogan)
| 1947 | 74. | Head |
| 1967 | 82. | Simon |

FECHTMAN, HUGO W(illiam)
| 1968 | 73. | In the Beginning |

FEHSENFELD, BECKY
| 1986 | 81. | Gramaggie's Gone |

FEHSENFELD, MARGUERITE K(ern)
1961	116.	In The Studio
1965	86.	Safe Harbor
1967	83.	Grandmother's China
1976	77.	Despair

FEIGHNER, MARILYN (Osborn)
1954	75.	"Flower Riot"
1955	77.	Composition in Red and Blue
	78.	Red Roofs on Gray Day
1956	76.	Steel Mill
	77.	Carnival
1957	66.	Boyne Mountain, Winter
	67.	Stanyard Cay, Nassau
1958	80.	Monument Circle
	81.	Yacht Harbor, Nassau
1960	79.	Carnival
	80.	Rooftops
1961	117.	Circus
1963	85.	Arrangement of Chairs*
	86.	Main Street at Dusk
	87.	Night Buildings
1965	87.	Lily and Red Stools
1967	84.	Duomo
	85.	Notre Dame Cathedral
	86.	Madrid
	87.	Narcissus
1968	74.	America the Beautiful*
	75.	The Studio*
	76.	The Alps
1970	80.	American Landscape
	81.	Bondage
1971	64.	Night and Day
1972	34.	Interior Landscape

1975	76.	American Artifacts
1976	78.	Pueblo Bird
	79.	Original American Forms
1977	58.	Vertical Forms
1978	51.	Arizona Night I*
1979	55.	Arizona Landscape II
	56.	Repetitions

FELDMAN, LUCINDA PIERSOL

| 1969 | 66. | 85th Street |

FELTS, MAIDIE CRANDALL

| 1931 | 86. | Study |
| | 87. | Jap-O-Lanterns |

FELTZ, JUNE B.

1962	115.	Girl with Book
1963	88.	Robin*
1964	103.	Chris
1965	88.	Young Student
1966	55.	Pat
1967	88.	Apples
	89.	Still Life with Pears

FENDIG, LILIAN

1950	58.	Northport, Michigan
	59.	The Barnlot
1951	61.	View from the Jury Room
	62.	Rockport Harbor, Mass.
1952	69.	Prairie Spires
	70.	Beside an English Stream
1953	65.	Fishermen's Shacks
	66.	English Sidestreets
	67.	Corfe Castle
1954	76.	Winter in Patagonia
1955	79.	Arizona Landscape
	80.	Corfe Castle
1956	78.	Arizona Gold
	79.	Landscape near Patagonia
1957	68.	Rainbow Rocks*
	69.	April Afternoon
	70.	Birchwoods*
1958	82.	Winter Mesquite
	83.	The Village Store
	84.	The Short Cut
1959	68.	Barn by the Road
	69.	French Lick
	70.	Cosmos*
1960	81.	Summer Morning
	82.	Sycamore*
	83.	Brown County Barns
1961	118.	Bottles
	119.	Jackson Branch Road
	120.	Red Barn
1962	116.	Woodland Path
	117.	Red Petunias
	118.	Village Street with Castle
1963	89.	Early Spring
	90.	Sycamores
	91.	Lower Town, Quebec

1964	104.	Gloriosa Daisies
	105.	The Picnic
	106.	Arizona Woodland
1965	89.	The Coppice
	90.	Azalea
1966	56.	Dorset Village
1967	90.	Corner Drug Store
1969	67.	Apothecary's Still Life*
	68.	Dairy Barn
1970	82.	Phlox
	83.	Market Day, St. Anne's Bay
1972	35.	October Melange*
	36.	Forsaken Barn
1974	49.	Gourds
1975	77.	Church Lane
1977	59.	Brixham Harbour
	60.	Low Tide

FENIMORE, KRESZENTIA S.

| 1955 | 81. | Reflections of Spring |
| 1956 | 80. | Sycamore Snag |

FENIMORE, R. A.

| 1947 | 75. | Winter |

FENTZ, LARRY R.

| 1979 | 57. | Old Hancock School |

FERGUSON, SARAH H.

| 1967 | 91. | Kapp's Barn |

FERGUSON, WILLIAM R.

1987	83.	Summer House
1988	77.	Zuni Polychrome Jar
1989	80.	Trio

FERRARA NELLE

| 1974 | 50. | Edge of the Woods |
| | 51. | Hard Hat |

FIELD, T. V.

| 1929 | 104. | Meddow Run |

FIELDS, W. DAVID

| 1980 | 50. | Country Fresh Eggs |
| 1981 | 65. | Betty's Brown Eggs |

FINCH, F.

| 1925 | 66. | Cartoons |

FINCH, LEWIS E.

| 1928 | 97. | Red Dragon |
| | 98. | Indiana Memorial |

FINCHUM, MYRON

1975	78.	Glass Space
	79.	London Road
1979	58.	Encased Landscape
	59.	The Uprighting*

1980	51.	Glass Fusion*
1981	66.	Aurora
	67.	Frozen Hues*
1982	79.	Afterglow
	80.	Merging Conflict
1983	63.	Chromatics
	64.	Wings of Fire (Flight of Fantasy)*
1984	68.	Night Flight
1985	52.	Sunday Stroll in Newburgh
1986	82.	Evening Flight
	83.	Eagle Creek Visitors*
1987	84.	Green-backed, Sunny Morning

FINK, ROBERT R.
1936	73.	Salt of the Earth
1937	62.	Katie
1939	85.	A Study
1941	56.	Grandmother
1942	69.	Elsie, Chinese Girl

FINNAN, FLORENCE
1978	52.	Les Fleurs
1981	68.	Rockport Garden
	69.	Anniversary Bouquet
1984	69.	Lilies of the Field

FINNEY, SUE
1977	61.	Gill Net

FISCHER, GLORIA
1984	70.	Interior Landscape II, #5
	71.	Buns Boogying to Beethoven's #1*
1985	53.	What's Holding Up the World and the Neighborhood #4
	54.	Chinese Baroque Fish Tune #6
1986	84.	Portal of Italian Stairs and Stares #3
	85.	Well, Feelings, Pienza #5

FISCHER, MILDRED
1951	63.	Midwest Downtown
1952	71.	Table in Garden

FISCHER, TERRI
1976	80.	American Heritage

FISCUS, GORDON W.
1945	65.	October Morning
	66.	Brown County
1946	67.	First Touch of Autumn
1947	77.	Along the Road
1978	53.	Monterey Bay

FISH, J(ulia) VanCLEAVE
1927	107.	The Bride
	108.	Mrs. Ann C. Shevill
	109.	Portrait of a Child
	110.	The Late Rev. T. M. S. Kinney
	111.	My Mother
	112.	My Father
	113.	Portrait of a Lady in Lace
	114.	Eva
	115.	Portrait of a Child
1928	99.	Mrs. Alice Price Bell
	100.	Mrs. Ottillie Holstein
	101.	Copy from Beatrice Tounesen's Negative
	102.	Copy of an Old Portrait
1929	105.	Orlando Miller
	106.	Mary Myers
	107.	Mrs. Woodruff
1930	83.	Dr. Gray
	84.	Mrs. Eckert
	85.	Mrs. J. W. Lees
	86.	Jones Boy
1931	88.	Mr. M. L. Redfield
	89.	Mrs. Arthur Davis
	90.	Rosemary Beck
1932	74.	Mrs. J. W. Lees
	75.	Late Mr. J. W. Lees, Indiana Harbor
	76.	Mrs. Ann Sheville

FISHER, HELEN E.
1975	80.	Mums
1976	81.	Misty Morn
1980	52.	Silence After First Snow
1982	81.	Canoeing on the Maumee

FISHER, (Lillie) FRY
1925	67.	Donarnenez, France
1926	108.	Oriental Still Life
1927	116.	Flowers
1928	103.	Still Life*
1929	108.	Arrested Attention
1932	77.	Foggy Day
1933	79.	Cashmere Shawl
	80.	White Roses
1934	57.	Every Day Things of Life
	58.	Nasturtiums
1935	51.	In the Harbor
	52.	Ships in the Harbor
	53.	The Landing
1936	74.	Village of Grand Pre
	75.	Mending Nets
	76.	Drying Sails*
1937	63.	The Wanderbird
	64.	Flowers
	65.	Clam Diggers
1939	86.	From the Artist's Garden
	87.	The Yankee and Tar Baley
1940	54.	Fishing Boat
1941	57.	Fishing Boats
1942	70.	Fisherman's Pride
1943	74.	Sail Boat

FISHER, WILLIAM R.
1926	109.	Portrait, Mr. Howard Petty

FITZGERALD, FRANCIS E.
1945	67.	Dusk in New Guinea

FLAMMANG, LAWRENCE
1926	110.	The Mischief-Maker*
1929	109.	When We Were Kids
1930	87.	Slush
	88.	The Washerwoman's Kid

FLANAGAN, EM
1963	92.	Water's Edge
1964	107.	The Light of Day
1966	57.	Cold and Storage
1970	84.	East of Needham
1971	65.	The Edge of Night
	66.	The Forest's Invitation
1974	52.	Center Stage

FLECK, MARY E.
| 1965 | 91. | Tangible Reward |

FLOCK, BARBARA
1987	85.	The Ol' Oaken Bucket
1989	81.	House in Mecca
	82.	Cabbage
1990	61.	County Fair

FLOWERS, WINIFRED
| 1956 | 81. | The Red Gown |

FLYNN, GLADYS RAE
1975	81.	The Spring Festival
1976	82.	The Showalter Fountain
1982	82.	The Quiet Room*
1987	86.	Anna Savage

FOGG, F. B.
| 1980 | 53. | Attitudes and Aryshires |

FOGLE, ARNOLD B.
1954	77.	Brookville Hills
1957	71.	Fisherman's Path
1958	85.	Mellow Memories
	86.	Morning Greetings
1961	121.	Winter's Fleecy Blanket

FOLSON, JOWELL
| 1976 | 83. | Boonville Mill |

FORGET, VERDAYLE (M.)
1982	83.	The Loner
	84.	First Crush*
1983	65.	The Bounty Hunter
	66.	Andy
1984	72.	Once Upon A Rodeo
	73.	Love Song
1986	86.	Gretchen
	87.	Day's End

FORKNER, (J.) EDGAR
1925	68.	Indiana Roadway
	69.	The Blue Bowl
1926	111.	Summer Flowers*
	112.	The Old Deck
	113.	The First Snow, Indiana
1927	117.	Old Boats, Puget Sound
	118.	Lake Union, Seattle
	119.	Pitcher of Flowers*
1928	104.	Golden Sail
	105.	Old Ships, Puget Sound*
	106.	Old Fashioned Bouquet
1929	110.	The Roman Vase
	111.	A Glimpse of Lake Union
	112.	Boats of Lake Union
1930	89.	Shacks and Boats
	90.	My Window Sill*
	91.	Zinnias and Marigolds
1931	91.	Peonies
	92.	Flowers of Summer
	93.	Iris
1932	78.	Late Summer Flowers
	79.	Drying Sails
	80.	Gay Sails
1933	81.	Old Vase of Flowers*
	82.	Puget Sound Boats
	83.	Peony & Fox Gloves
1934	59.	Flowers of Spring
	60.	Along the Lake
	61.	Boats on Lake Union
1935	54.	Journey's End
	55.	Peonies
	56.	Flowers, Blue and Gold
1936	77.	A Seattle Dock
	78.	Flowers and Drapery*
	79.	Alley Hollyhocks
1937	66.	Pitcher of Peonies
	67.	Seaman's Home
	312.	Daisies and Delphinium
1938	68.	Fishing Boats at Bridge
	69.	Flowers in Window
	70.	Tulips in Old Pitcher
	309.	On the River
1939	88.	Journey's End
	89.	Old Pitcher of Zinnias
	90.	Red and White Flowers
	309.	On Hood Canal
1940	55.	Oriental Poppies
	56.	Pink Poppies
	57.	Flowers Against Curtain
1941	58.	Hill and Sail
	59.	Old Maple Pitcher
	308.	Mixed Bouquet
1942	71.	Around the Lake, Seattle, Washington
	72.	Peonies, A Still Life
1943	75.	Group of Boats on Lake
	76.	Flowers in Old Pitcher*
	77.	Anemones and Old China
1944	91.	Gay Flowers in Old Pitcher
	92.	Around the Lake
	93.	Peonies
1946	68.	Morning Mist, Lake Union
1947	76.	Autumn Sunset

FORSYTH, CONSTANCE

1928	107.	At the Docks
	108.	The Gravel Washer*
	109.	The Wood Pile
	110.	The Grotto
1929	113.	The Bridge
	114.	Water Front
	115.	Indiana Dunes, Lake Michigan
1933	84.	Delaware Bridge
	85.	The Tree
	86.	Inside the Boat House
1944	94.	Valley Town
	95.	Sangre de Cristo Peaks
1949	54.	Flowers*
	55.	Birds
1950	60.	Brother Law's Wife
1951	64.	And in the End
1953	68.	The Cheerful Mountain
1955	82.	Bright Land
1956	82.	The Mesa
	83.	The Lake
	84.	Small Clouds
1957	72.	Island Birds
1958	87.	Susie, 1957
	88.	Into The Storm
1961	122.	Haunted Valley*
	123.	Surf
	124.	A Place With Birds
1962	119.	Summer Garden
	120.	Backyard Cowboys
1963	93.	Bird and Waves*
	94.	Gay Cloud

FORSYTH, W(illiam) (J.)

1925	70.	Reverie
	71.	Glory of Autumn*
	72.	The Pool, Evening
1926	114.	Early Spring
	115.	The Painter Man
	116.	The Wood Lot, October*
1927	120.	Portrait Miss Stover
	121.	Dahlias
	122.	September Morning*
1928	111.	At the Edge of a Wood
	112.	Tide Coming In
	113.	Resting a Moment
1929	116.	The Edge of Winter
	117.	The Hills of Morgan*
	118.	Janice
1930	92.	October, Southern Indiana
	93.	Winter Brook
1931	94.	Bass Rock, Gloucester
1932	81.	A New Street
	82.	Dahlias
	83.	The Brook
1933	87.	Orchard, Still Life
	88.	By the Side of the Road
1936	238.	Broken Country (Special invitation)
	239.	Self Portrait (Special invitation)
	240.	Still Life Flowers (Special invitation)

FOSTER, BETTY

1933	89.	Garfield Park
1937	68.	Where Wagner Wrote Siegfried
1940	58.	Carol and her Carollers
1942	73.	Beautiful Confusion

FOSTER, ERNEST B.

| 1939 | 91. | Mrs. Maud Lucas Rumpler |

FOSTER, O(rion) L.

1927	123.	California Hills
	124.	Laguna
1929	119.	Our Garden
	120.	Monday
1930	94.	The Pink House

FOUREMAN, NANCY

| 1979 | 60. | For Idle Hands |

FOURNIER, ALEXIS J(ean)

1926	117.	Clouds and Hills
	118.	Morning in Venice
	119.	Moonlight, Cape Cod
1927	125.	Clouds and Shadows, Catskills
	126.	Summer's Offering
1928	114.	Indian Summer Morning
	115.	In April
1929	121.	A Home in the Hills
	122.	Clearing of the Catskills
	123.	Summer Skies
1930	95.	The Mill by the Sea Picardie
1931	98.	October Sunlight
	99.	Morning in the Hills
1932	84.	Wolf Creek Letchworth Park, N. Y.
	85.	Clearing Skies, Normandy
1934	62.	A Home in the Hills
	63.	Between Showers*
1935	57.	Passing Storm in Junetime
	58.	Shadows Come and Go
1936	80.	Peaceful Valley
	81.	The Willows*
1938	71.	Clearing Weather
	72.	Glorious Autumn
	310.	Summer Clouds

FOWLER, DAVID (L.)

1932	86.	Houseboat on the Ohio
1933	90.	Sunday Morning
1935	59.	Baptism in Evansville
1937	69.	Goose Island
	70.	Still Life
	71.	Fishing Shacks
1942	74.	Country Back Yard
	75.	Room Without Board

FOWLER, JANE ANDERSON

1950	61.	From the Chrysanthemum Show*
1951	65.	Autumn Bouquet with Dancing Boy and Girl
1958	89.	Carolyn's Marigolds*
	90.	Harbingers Of Spring

FOX, FONTAINE
1927	127.	Terrible Tempered Mr. Bang
	128.	Tomboy Taylor
	129.	Aunt Eppie Hogg
	130.	"Stinky" Davis
	131.	Powerful Katrinka
	132.	Little Stanley
	133.	Toonerville Trolley
	134.	Mickey (himself) McGuire
	135.	Toonerville Trolley

FOX, THEODORE
1969	69.	Melting Snow*
1970	85.	October Day
1971	67.	Pine Trees
1975	82.	Barn Yard
	83.	Landscape in April
1977	62.	Grim Winter
1978	54.	The Morgen Farm in Illinois
1979	61.	Changing Season
	62.	Melting Snow*
1980	54.	Last Snow in Brown County
	55.	Overflow of Riverbank*

FRAIN, NELLIE M.
| 1928 | 116. | Mrs. Temple |

FRAIN, TIMOTHY C.
| 1988 | 78. | Blueberry Hill |
| | 79. | Dawn Departure |

FRAME, THELMA
| 1982 | 85. | Hill's Bros. |

FRANTZ, DOROTHY (M.)
1962	121.	June Ectasy
	122.	Afternoon on Bay Street
1963	95.	Spring Comes to Nashville
1965	92.	Church in the Valley
	93.	Along the Ridge

FRASER, KATHRYN E.
| 1982 | 86. | Interrupted Flight |

FRAZELL, THOMAS G.
| 1975 | 84. | River Clams |
| 1976 | 84. | Vanda Orchid |

FREDERICK, LOUIS J.
| 1940 | 59. | Desolation |

FREED, ERNEST B.
1931	95.	Mildred Gerrish
	96.	Prof. W. T. Turman
	97.	Pauline Freed
1932	87.	Into the Night
	88.	Mignonette
1933	91.	Still Life
	92.	Dorothy Cornthwaite

FREELAND, ANNE
1962	123.	Thistledown
	124.	Pot of Hyacinths
	125.	Lotus
1963	96.	Window Box

FREEMAN, PEGGY DALTON
| 1986 | 88. | Last of Winter |
| 1987 | 87. | "What's Next?" |

FREER, RAY(mond)
1988	80.	Z-Scape Eve
	81.	Z-Scape
1989	83.	Giza Z-Scape
1990	62.	Bovine March

FRENCH, RAY H.
1958	91.	The Patriarch
	92.	Elephant
	93.	The Swan

FREUDENBERG, SUE
1980	56.	Morning Fresh
	57.	Almost Home
1981	70.	Molly, Polly and Peter
1985	55.	Piece by Piece*
1986	89.	Linen and Lace

FREY, E. ROGER
1932	89.	Old Homestead
1944	96.	Colored Boy Fishing
	97.	Still Life Composition
1976	85.	Interstate Construction Downtown*
1980	58.	Streetwork, Lockerbie Square
1981	71.	Restoration, A Landmark
1982	87.	Transformed Houses
1983	67.	Construction, Hoosier Dome
1985	56.	Construction, White River Bridge
1986	90.	The Red Sled
	91.	Time to Remember, Indiana Avenue
1987	88.	Museum Home
	89.	Picnic Grounds
1988	82.	The White Ghost
1989	84.	Washington & Illinois Street in 1988
1990	63.	Antique Franklins to Go
	64.	Roots

FROST, MARGUERITE
| 1946 | 69. | Rag Dolls & Their Pets |

FROST, MARTHA L(ee)
1934	64.	Portrait of a Child
	65.	Lottie
1935	60.	Blanch Stillson
1953	69.	Jean
1956	85.	Backyard Winter
1957	73.	Winter Smoke
1960	84.	Winter Evening
	85.	The Blue Hills

FROST, MAURICE D.
1951   66.   Silver Plume
        67.   Study in Color*

FROULA, JOSEF
1934   66.   Dunes
        67.   Sun and Snow
1936   82.   Somebody's Alley

FRY, LAURA A.
1925   73.   A Shaft of Sunlight*
        74.   A Corner of the Greenhouse

FUGATE, LINDA
1979   63.   Buckeye

FULLEN, HERSCHEL E.
1958   94.   Solitude
1960   86.   Back Road
1965   95.   Checker Board Square
1966   58.   #7
1967   92.   Paint Rags
1968   77.   Back Street
1969   72.   Once Was
        73.   Impression

FULLER, BARBARA J.
1975   85.   Convocation

FULTS, LOUISE C(hristin)
(See Agnew, Louise Fults)
1942   76.   Scarf and Flowers
1943   78.   Victory Village
1947   78.   Miniature in Oil
        79.   Out of Service

FULWIDER, EDWIN (L.)
1937   72.   Cape Race
1938   73.   Mrs. Franklin T. Brodix
1939   92.   The Artist's Home
1940   60.   Country Bridge
        61.   Woodsmen
1942   77.   Hoosier Winter
        78.   Still Life*
1946   70.   Evening
        71.   Triple Header
1947   80.   Depot
        81.   Country Sawmill
1950   62.   Holiday Special
        63.   Passing Track
        64.   Waterfront

FUNK, ARLENE NELSON
1983   68.   Floral Chinese Lanterns

FUNK, CLOTILDE EMBREE
1968   78.   Cloisters in Bayonne
1969   70.   The Black Pitcher*
        71.   From Mexico
1970   86.   The Acoma Jar*
        87.   Blow Torch 1909 A. D.

FUSON, BARB(ara)
1987   90.   Abandoned
        91.   Autumn Barns
1988   83.   Spring's Beauty
1990   65.   Midnight Crossing
        66.   Trail Hand

GAALEMA, MARY
1974 53. Broken Beech
1976 86. Whispering Winds
        87. Salute to '76

GAHMAN, FLOYD
1958 ** Metropolitan Suburbs
           (Invited Work by Jury
           Member from Frank C.
           Dailey Collection)

GALBRAITH, DALLAS A.
1965 96. Early Autumn
        97. Milkweed, Goldenrod and Foxtail

GALBRAITH, R. KARL
1925 75. Gas Plant at Twilight
        76. Late Winter at Broadripple

GALLAGHER, L(ester) W.
1961 125. Indiana Dunes
1963 97. Twilight
1965 98. Fruit of the Garden*
1967 93. Butterfly Weed
1970 88. Composition*
1971 68. Back Yard View

GALLOWAY, WILLIAM
1985 57. Oracle at Delphi
1986 92. La Fille Des Fleurs
        93. Ozymandias
1989 85. Venus
        86. 864 C. I.

GAMBILL, WOODROW J.
1975 86. Dance Hall Lillies
        87. The Road Home
1976 88. Milk Barn

GANT, ELSIE
1967 94. Seashore
1973 62. Spring Flowers

GARBER, DANIEL
1925 77. May Evening, A Phantasy

GARCEAU, H. J.
1934 68. Winter Woods
        69. Farm Lane
1936 83. In Brown County Hills
        84. Where the Road Turns
1937 73. Early Snow
        74. Low Tide
1939 93. Mountain Farms
        94. Winter Pattern

1940 62. A Brown County Road*
1941 60. Winter
1946 72. Cherry Valley
        73. Road to Bean Blossom
1948 47. Indiana Winter

GARNER, OPAL
1966 59. Hollyhock Garden

GARRIOTT, MICHELE
1977 63. German Town of Rhens

GARRISON, ANNIE DYE
1938 74. Old Cotton Picker

GARRO, JEAN COVAL
1981 72. The Captive
1983 69. We'll Be Back Next Summer
        70. The End of November
1984 74. Fall Creek
1985 58. Flowers in the Old French Inn*
1986 94. Observation Post
        95. A Cool and Shaded Place
1987 92. Helsinki Flower Market
1990 67. Prime Acreage, Suburban

GARSON, ETTA CORBETT
1940 63. The Catskill Mountains
1942 79. Old Street, Ipswich, Mass.

GARVIN, EVELYN
1954 78. Tired Sentinel and Long Road
           Home
1956 86. Majesty Unadorned

GASKINS, LETHA (H.)
1941 61. Leland, Michigan, Fishing Harbor
        62. Willow Banks
1943 79. Mountain Mist, Taos
        80. Fishing Tugs at Dock
1947 82. Snowy Roof Tops
        83. Pennsylvania Patchwork
1973 63. Turbulent Cloud

GATES, MARGERY M.
1958 95. Gloucester
1960 87. City Reflections
        88. Winter Day
        89. Beach Party
1961 126. On A Winter Day
        127. Sentinels
1963 98. Minus Two
        99. Market Place
1965 99. Day in December
1966 60. Winter Reverie
1967 95. Refuge

1968	79.	February's Day
	80.	Vale Town
1970	89.	Dawn
1971	69.	Another Winter Day
	70.	Weather or Not
1975	88.	Winter's Touch
1976	89.	On Ice*
1984	75.	Winter Blanket

GATEWOOD, ROBERT
| 1954 | 79. | Bridge to Town |

GAUCHAT, NOLA C.
| 1970 | 90. | Grandmother |

GAWEHN, GEORGE
1950	65.	Architectual Contrast
	66.	Double Reflection
	67.	Main Street*
	68.	Whistling Boy
1951	68.	Hoosier St. Marks

GAYNES, ROSELLA R.
| 1970 | 91. | Double or Nothing |

GEHLERT, WILLIAM
| 1972 | 37. | Gentle Flow |

GEIER, SHIRLEY
| 1970 | 92. | Island Flowers |
| 1971 | 71. | Lace and Lobster Buoys |

GENDERS, RICHARD A.
| 1955 | 83. | Liberty Express |

GENTRY, REX
| 1958 | 96. | Relativity No. 1 |

GEORGE, CHARLENE
1981	73.	Indiana Cornfield
1982	88.	Daybreak
1983	71.	Dad's Old Bull
1984	76.	Summer Harvest
	77.	An Old Neighbor
1987	93.	The Corn Harvest*
1989	87.	Ruby and Bluebell (1925)

GEORGE, FAY AKIN
| 1956 | 87. | Mugfull |

GERARD, ALLEE W.
1944	98.	Indiana Corn Field
	99.	Red and White Gladiolas
	100.	Near the Everglades
1945	68.	Tippecanoe R. Bend
	69.	Delphinium and Lilies
1946	74.	Sleepy Hollow
1948	48.	June Reflections
1950	69.	November
1951	69.	A Bowl of Iris

1956	88.	Cherry Creek
1957	74.	The Old Hotel
	75.	Tippecanoe River
1958	97.	Tippecanoe River
1959	71.	Zinnias
1960	90.	Autumn at the Lake
1962	126.	Rust and White Mums
1963	100.	The O'conolufte
1964	108.	Falling Leaves, Tippecanoe River
1965	100.	River Hideaway

GERHART, CHARLES
| 1928 | 116A | The Nativity |

GERST, MARILYN B.
1981	74.	Atlantis
1983	72.	Our Holly in First Snow
1984	78.	Sea Wall
1985	59.	The Monolith
	60.	Summer's Breeze
1989	88.	Summer Tree, Series III
	89.	Magnolia II

GESNER, KATHLEEN
| 1987 | 94. | Got Carried Away on Valentine's Day |

GIBBONS, NANNETTE
| 1962 | 127. | Portrait of Jim |

GIBSON, CARLTON
1951	70.	The Night Switchman
1952	72.	Behind Schedule
1954	80.	The Nocturnal Nativity
1956	89.	The Old Harbor
1957	76.	Hydrangeas
1960	91.	The Nun
1961	128.	Flora
	129.	Young Pranksters
1962	128.	Respite from Labor
1963	101.	The Builders
1966	61.	A Segment of Delapidation
1967	96.	Street Scene, Halloween
	97.	From My Studio Window

GIBSON, CHARLES (Charlie)
| 1974 | 54. | To-Lynn-with-Love |

GIBSON, MARY ANN
1958	98.	Weatherbeaten Barn
1959	72.	Woodland Walk
	73.	Brown County Panorama*

GIFFIN, LYDIA
1971	72.	A Pleasant Pasture
	73.	Genesis
1973	64.	Sights and Sounds of Woods

GILES, MARY CASEY
| 1945 | 70. | Fruit |

GILLIATT, KATHLEEN
1971   74.   Moon Glow

GILLIATT, LYNNE
1986   96.   Remember That Long Velvet Couch
       97.   Grandmother's Kitchen*

GILLIATT, MICHAEL T.
1970   93.   George
       94.   Kathy

GINNEY, CLOA
1945   71.   Mums
1946   75.   White Petunias
       76.   Regals and Hollyhocks
       77.   Phlox
1947   84.   Dogwood
1948   49.   Morning Glories*
1949   56.   Morning Glories

GINTHER, JERRY L.
1975   89.   Untitled
       90.   Untitled

GIORGINI, ALDO
1973   65.   Craters
       66.   Metamorphosis
1975   91.   Collision of Worlds
       92.   Moonscape

GLASEL, LOLLY KACKLEY
1989   90.   Woman with Red Scarf

GLOBENSKY, LOUIS JAMES
1931   100.   Still Life

GLORE, CHARLES FRANKLIN
1951   71.   First Snow

GLOVER, JACK DONUS
1964   109.   East College
       110.   No Exit
1965   101.   The Show Boat
       102.   Robert T. Blickenstaff
       103.   River Street

GODWARD, SUZANN WATT
1963   102.   The Channel
1964   111.   The Plain People
1965   104.   The Dooryard
1967   98.   The River Man
1968   81.   Tua res agitur
       82.   The Barn

GOEDE, HELEN L.
1975   93.   Foggy Day at the Dunes

GOEHL, GEORGE
1978   55.   Splitting Apart
1981   75.   Summer Storm
       76.   Equanimity

GOETHE, JOE (Joseph Alexander)
1935   61.   Standing Nude
       62.   Seated Nude

GOLDSCHMIDT, DENICE
1978   56.   Cedar Sun 106 Years Old*
1982   89.   Barn Shadow
1984   79.   Snow Casted Brambles
       80.   Dance of the Leaves
1985   61.   The Uttermost Parts of the Sea

GONDRING, AUGUSTUS C.
1942   80.   Classic Pillars, 1941
       81.   Local Industry
1944   101.   Landscape, Northern Australia*

GOODE, VINNIE REAM
1925   78.   Portrait of Paul McCormick
       79.   A Group of Miniatures

GOODMAN, SHIRLEY
1970   95.   Grandma's Pitcher*

GOODRICH, MARGARET G.
1945   72.   Old Cypress Tree

GOODWIN, DORIT
1976   90.   The Bitter Cost

GOODWIN, FRANCES M.
1926   120.   Benjamin S. Parker

GOODWIN, HELEN M.
1925   80.   The Pepper Berry
       81.   Miniatures
1926   121.   A June Garden, "Rose City," Indiana*
       122.   The Bitter Sweet
1927   136.   Christmas at the Old Home
1928   117.   Still Life
1932   90.   Japanese Lanterns
1937   75.   Springtime
1946   78.   The Angel & the Flowers

GORDON, IDA NASH
1953   70.   Out of the Basket
1957   77.   Americana
1958   99.   The Patient One
1959   74.   The Quiet Place
1960   92.   Adoration
       93.   Girl in Red Jacket
1961   130.   Landscape, Beside the Still Waters
       131.   The Girl Next Door
1962   129.   Still Life with Potatoes
       130.   White Roses
1964   112.   Early Snow
       113.   Coffee Break
1965   105.   Nature's Gift
1966   62.   Two Apples on a Platter*
       63.   Autumn Bouquet
1967   99.   Falling Leaves

1969	74.	Potted Plants*
1970	96.	Still Life with Flowers
1973	67.	Summer Flowers
1975	94.	Patio Bouquet
1976	91.	October in Brown County
1977	64.	Hint of Spring
	65.	Vining Geranium

GORDON, THOMAS L.
1961	132.	Oedipus Rex

GORDON, VIRGINIA O.
1969	75.	Untitled

GORMAN, JAMES G.
1976	92.	Dragon Pot
	93.	Clay Form #11

GOTH, MARIE
1925	82.	The Spanish Lady
	83.	Portrait of Clarence W. Nichols
1926	123.	Charles W. Dahlgreen*
	124.	Babie's Breakfast
	125.	Mrs. Herbert Griffiths
1927	137.	On the Terrace*
	138.	Wanda
	139.	Portrait
1928	118.	Embers
	119.	Fred L. Pettijohn, M. D.*
1929	124.	My Father
	125.	Mrs. C. S. Jr.
1930	96.	Grafton Johnson
	97.	"Helen"
1931	101.	Florence
	102.	A Brown County Artist
	103.	Charlotte
1932	91.	Mary Jane
	92.	Miriam*
	93.	Colonel Paul V. McNutt
1933	93.	Mrs. Paul V. McNutt
	94.	Charlotte
1934	70.	Reflection
	71.	The Architect*
1935	63.	Portrait
	64.	Mother and Child*
	65.	The Bride
1936	85.	"V"*
1937	76.	Lady in Silver Shawl
	77.	Ruth*
	313.	Peonies
1938	78.	Jean
1939	95.	Mr. J. W. Piercy
	96.	Self Portrait*
	97.	Martha
1940	68.	Mr. E. H. K. McComb*
	69.	Wilma
1941	63.	Cari*
	64.	Prof. W. A. Cogshall
	309.	Roses
	200.	Portrait of John T. McCutcheon*

1942	82.	Betty
	83.	Little Linda
	84.	Samuel B. Walker
	263.	Will H. Hays*
1943	81.	Elizabeth
1944	102.	Mary Frances
	103.	General Robert H. Tyndall
	104.	V. J. Cariani
1945	73.	Portrait Sketch
	74.	Dr. Floyd Boys*
1946	79.	Hazel
	80.	Fabien Sevitzky*
1947	85.	Louise
1948	50.	Edgar F. Kiser, M. D.*
1949	57.	Bomar Cramer*
	58.	Silver Earrings
1950	70.	Annie
	71.	Fermor Cannon
1951	72.	Fairy Tales
	73.	Cari*
1952	73.	Mrs. Ballman*
	74.	Portrait
1953	71.	Triana
	72.	James De W. Kline
1954	81.	Mr. Kenneth M. Kunkel
1955	84.	Angelina
	85.	Miss Elizabeth Osborn
1956	90.	Roses
	91.	Cari
1957	78.	Polly*
	79.	Jeannette
	80.	V. J. C.*
1958	100.	Douglas
	101.	Jeannette
	102.	Dr. Allen D. Albert*
1959	75.	Elizabeth
	76.	Ruth
	77.	Brother and Sister
1960	94.	Gift of Spring
	95.	Portrait*
	96.	Mother and Child
1961	133.	Yellow Roses
	134.	Lilacs
	135.	Joel W. Hadley*
1962	131.	Cynthia
	132.	Mrs. William G. Turnbull
1963	103.	Two Below
	104.	Beautiful Dreamer*
1964	114.	Me*
	115.	Roses
	116.	Harley-Rhodehamel III
1965	106.	Barbara*
	107.	Kathy
	108.	Roses
1966	64.	Portrait
	65.	Joan
	66.	Cari
1967	100.	Sally
1968	83.	Self Portrait
1969	76.	"Cari" in his Studio

1970	97.	Portrait, Linda
	98.	Clarence H. Marchant, M. D.
1971	75.	Roses
1972	38.	Gypsy
1975	95.	Neighbor*
	96.	Spring Miracle

GOTHELF, LOUIS
1952	75.	Landscape
	76.	Myself
1961	136.	Red Barn
	137.	The Orange Hat
	138.	Juanita
1963	105.	Self-Portrait

GRABENHOFER, VIRGINIA
| 1990 | 68. | Salt Creek Valley |

GRADY, AUDRE
| 1968 | 84. | Cove Retreat |

GRAF, CARL C.
1925	84.	Early Autumn Afternoon, (Brown County, Indiana)
	85.	Under the Summer Sky
1926	126.	Winter Shadows
	127.	Gray Misty Morning*
	128.	Where Lengthy Shadows Fall
1927	140.	Late Afternoon Sunlight, Autumn
	141.	Lights and Shadows of Early September
	142.	Over the Hills from Weed Patch*
1928	120.	The Bend in the Creek, Autumn
	121.	The Creek in Summer*
	122.	The Sentinels
1929	126.	Early October Morning
	127.	Up Owl Creek, Brown County
1930	98.	Hills of Brown County*
	99.	The Shadowed Stream
1931	104.	In Salt Creek Valley
	105.	Under Summer Skies, Weedpatch
1932	94.	Mirrored Sycamores
	95.	Autumn's Last Touch*
1933	95.	Reflections, Winter
1934	72.	Opalescent Day
	73.	Winter Bound
1935	66.	Dahlias
1936	86.	Into the Light
	87.	The Waning Winter
1937	78.	Summer Greens
	314.	Peonies
1938	75.	Autumn Tapestry
	76.	Harp of the Winds
1939	310.	Epic of Autumn
1940	66.	Early Morning
	67.	Graying October
	310.	Autumn Vice-Clad
1941	65.	Autumn in the Valley
	310.	Peonies, Pink and White

1943	82.	By the Window*
	83.	Sycamore Shadows
1944	105.	Late Afternoon Glow
1945	75.	The Flower Shop
1946	81.	Winter Bound
	82.	A Bowl of Peonies
1947	86.	Spring Comes Again
	87.	Silent Winter
1948	51.	Welcome Spring

GRAF, GENEVIEVE GOTH
1937	79.	On the Pantry Shelf
	315.	Asters
1938	77.	Gold, Amber and Brass
1939	98.	Bittersweet
	99.	Zinnias
1940	64.	An Old-Fashioned Bouquet*
	65.	The Blue Pitcher
1942	85.	On the Studio Table
1943	84.	The Tintype
	85.	Hollyhocks
1944	106.	Parted Curtains
	107.	The Clock Shelf
	108.	By the Window
1945	76.	Things of Yesterday
1947	88.	Sweet William
	89.	Roses
1948	52.	Lace Weed and Zinnias
1950	72.	Asters
1951	74.	Still Life
	75.	Tea Things
1952	77.	Still Life
	78.	Against the Light*
1954	82.	Still Life
1955	86.	The Blue Pitcher
1956	92.	Asters
1957	81.	Still Life
	82.	Straw Flowers
1958	103.	On The Chimney Shelf
1959	78.	Still Life
	79.	From the Orient
	80.	The Antique Pitcher
1960	97.	From An Old Fashion Kitchen
	98.	Little White Pitcher*
1961	139.	Lilacs and Dog-Wood
1962	133.	Mixed Bouquet
	134.	Zinnias

GRAFTON, ROBERT W.
1925	86.	Portrait of Anne
	87.	The Portrait of George Ade*
	88.	Portrait of Mrs. M. F. Johnston
1926	129.	Portrait of Stanton Jabncke
	130.	Portrait of Mrs. Truesdale Vail
	131.	Portrait of Commodore Ernest Lee Jabncke (Invited)
1927	143.	Portrait Mrs. G.
	144.	Portrait Patsy
1929	128.	French Market

GRAHAM, BETTE
1945	77.	Night Mares*
1964	117.	Gloucester Harbor
	118.	Hoosier Gothic

GRAHAM, EDWARD B.
1926	132.	Cartoon
	133.	Cartoon
	134.	Cabby

GRAHAM, KATHLEEN
1976	94.	Lunar Landscape*
1979	64.	Barriers to Understanding*
	65.	Paperdoll

GRAMS, BILL
| 1982 | 90. | Summer Dream |
| | 91. | Navajo Trace #1* |

GRANDIDIER, CANDI(de Y.)
1983	73.	Tony
1984	81.	Still Life*
	82.	Study

GRAVES, ARDIS D.
| 1976 | 95. | Steve |

GRAVES, Mrs. C. E.
| 1937 | 80. | A Pioneer |

GRAY, BARBARA
1958	104.	White Water
1967	101.	April Chapeau*
	102.	Lamentation*
1968	85.	Pro Forma
	86.	Lunch Counter
1969	77.	Gemini
	78.	Windsong

GRAY, H. MAXWELL
| 1968 | 87. | Circus, Circa 1920 |

GRAY, HAROLD
1925	89.	Little Orphan Annie, Cartoon*
	90.	Little Orphan Annie, Cartoon*
	91.	Little Orphan Annie, Cartoon*
1927	145.	We're on Our Way Home
	146.	More Blessed to Give
	147.	A Good Sign
	148.	This Suspense
	149.	' Twas the Night Before Xmas
	150.	Good Ol' Santa Claus

GRAY, MARY CHILTON
(See Mendenhall, Mary Chilton Gray)
1925	92.	Still Life
1933	96.	Portrait of George Henderson
1935	67.	Portrait of Norma Lovelace

GRAY, MURIEL
1969	79.	Guatemala Flower Lady
1970	99.	Helping Hands
	100.	Ninety-Two Candles

GREATHOUSE, Mrs. R. V.
| 1943 | 86. | Back-Yard Splendor |

GREEN, HERSCHEL S.
| 1946 | 83. | Winter |
| 1947 | 90. | Nocturne |

GREENE, JAMES A.
| 1950 | 73. | A Winter Morning |
| | 74. | Boat Harbor |

GREENE, JO
(See Raymond, Jo Greene)
1967	103.	Fenwyck Street
	104.	Shacks and Shadows
1968	88.	Serenity

GREENE, TOM (Thomas)
1962	135.	Cripple Creek Mine
	136.	Salve Regina
1965	109.	Land's End
	110.	Spring Mill
1975	97.	Old Oak
1976	96.	Sand Creek Church: Freedom, Friendship and Charity*
1979	66.	Mary V. Totem

GREENWOOD, UNA ANN
1929	129.	Memories*
1937	81.	Sunny Days
1938	79.	In the Nursery

GREENWOOD, W. RUSSELL
| 1929 | 130. | An Indian Pueblo of the Colorado |

GREER, GERALD N.
1956	93.	Overcast
1957	83.	Hand Of Progress
1958	105.	Young Girl
1959	81.	Looking Southeast
1960	99.	Snowscape Off 37
	100.	Thru the Park
1961	140.	Circus Horses

GREGG, F. D.
1958	106.	Local Scene, Richmond
	107.	An Hour's Ride and a Short Walk
	108.	Late Summer

GREPP, JOHN A.
1943	87.	Ohio Afternoon
	88.	Carolina Morning
1949	59.	View of Franklin
	60.	Indianapolis Skyline

1951	76.	Still Life with Printing Press
	77.	Martyr
1952	79.	Mardi Gras
1955	87.	January Evening
	88.	Mountain Stream

GRESHAM, BARBARA H.

1985	62.	Fly Change
	63.	Earthworks
1986	98.	Beaver Dam

GRIEB, ELEANOR

1988	84.	Colors and Shapes
	85.	Chair and Carpet
1989	91.	Lilies and Hyacinths
	92.	Come Around to the Front
1990	69.	The Impressionist

GRIEB, TIMOTHY

1988	86.	Hilbish Nursery
1989	93.	Illini Bovines

GRIFFIN, WORTH D.

1938	80.	Little Yellow Wolf
1940	72.	Two Indians

GRIFFITH, ELAINE MARIE

1975	98.	Mother and Son
	99.	Sagging Fields

GRIFFITH, KATHARINE PATTON

1933	97.	Tom McClure, Cattleman
1934	75.	Ranunculu and Delphinium

GRIFFITH, L(ouis) O.

1925	93.	Garden Time
	94.	Morning in the Hollow*
1926	135.	Indiana Autumn
	136.	Hillside Aglow
	137.	Giant Elm, Brown County, Indiana
	138.	Street Gossip, New Orleans, La.*
	139.	Old Spanish Court
1927	151.	Sunlit Valley
	152.	Indian Summer
	153.	Promise (decoration)
1928	123.	Bending Boughs
	124.	Beacons of the Weed Patch
	125.	The Patriarch
	126.	The Late Snow
	127.	Brown County Cabin
1929	131.	In the Valley
	132.	The Cool Marsh
	133.	One Morning
1930	100.	Hills of Kelp*
	101.	Old Basin, New Orleans, La.
1931	106.	Little Mexico
	107.	Hill Top Maze
1932	96.	Old Quebec
	97.	Spring Clouds

1933	98.	Scarce o' Fat Ridge
	99.	Sorghum
	100.	Along the I. C.
1934	74.	Road to Blue Bluff
1935	68.	Villa Santiago
	69.	Road to Trevlac*
1936	88.	Drifting Leaves
	89.	A Sunny Hollow
1937	82.	Old Schooners
	316.	In Season
1938	81.	Leaf Laden Stream
	311.	The Sunny South
1939	100.	Clearing
	101.	Edge of the Village
	311.	Abundance*
1940	70.	Oak Grove Road
	71.	Orange and Blue
1941	66.	Hoosier's Retreat
	67.	Lower Forty
	68.	Stone Head Store
	311.	Miscellaneous
1942	86.	Avenue of the South
	87.	Greasy Creek Ford
1943	89.	Fleeting Light
	90.	The Afterglow
1944	109.	In the Town
	110.	St. Andrews Parish, S. C.
1945	78.	From the Heights
	79.	Thawing Weather
	80.	Fall Vista
1946	84.	Season's Close
1947	91.	Southern Suburbs
1948	53.	Return to Contentment
1949	61.	Ending Day
1951	78.	Open Gateway
1954	83.	Morning Promise
	84.	Sunny Roadway
	85.	Along the Creek
1955	218.	Cricket Chorus
1956	94.	Cabin in the Hollow
	95.	Morning Muse
1957	84.	New Mexico
	85.	October Light

GRIFFITH, ROSA B.

1925	95.	Zinnias
1926	140.	A Precise Arrangement
1927	154.	Lenox and Old Lace

GRIFFITH, VERA A.

1936	90.	Betty Louise*
1939	102.	Mary
1944	111.	Summer Serenity
	112.	Peonies
	113.	Mildred
1967	105.	Debra

GRIFFITT, BOB

1978	57.	Early Morning Catch, Nova Scotia
	58.	Halifax, Nova Scotia*
1979	67.	Looking East, Nova Scotia*

1980	59.	Patterns Under a Pier, Nova Scotia
1981	77.	Highlands, Nova Scotia
1983	74.	Outer-banks, Outpost
1984	83.	Sonya and the Sand Dollar
1985	64.	Lunch on the Circle
1987	95.	Calabash, North Carolina
1988	87.	Just Looking Things Over

GRIGSBY, PIETER R.

1974	55.	The House Isn't There Anymore

GRIGSBY, T(obey) D(iane)

1979	68.	Bloomington Lights
	69.	Plastic Circles
1981	78.	We
1988	88.	A Prayer for South Africa

GRIGWARE, EDWARD T.

1925	96.	Along the Wabash
	97.	The Cathedral at Old Vincennes*

GRISEZ, E. A.

1933	101.	LaPorte, New York Central Tracks
1937	83.	The Hot Sun

GROSJEAN, MARY

1931	108.	Dimity

GROSS, Jr., JAMES

1972	39.	The Dove*
	40.	Joey*

GROSS, Sr., JAMES M.

1972	41.	7th Street Warehouse

GRUE, FREDERIK EBBESEN

1984	84.	Still Life with Japanese Doll
	85.	Study of Oriental Porcelain and Lemons*
1985	65.	Prairie Creek Reservoir*
	66.	The Bronze Scholar*

1986	99.	Study of Apples
	100.	Study of Porcelain and Lemons*
1987	96.	Wheat Fields*
	97.	Study of Grapes
1988	89.	Oxblood Porcelains and Mums
	90.	Persimmons*
1989	94.	June, Madison County, HWY 69
1990	70.	Canton Porcelain & Lemons
	71.	Persimmons

GRUELLE, JUSTIN C.

1942	88.	Mother

GRUENINGER, LIBBY JONES

1982	92.	2 p.m. at the Ferry Building
1984	86.	Jud

GUCKELBERG, MAY

1952	80.	Summer on the Farm
1954	86.	Glorious Colors of Winter
1955	89.	White River at 38th
1956	96.	Spring Bouquet*
1957	86.	Indiana Farmer's Home
1961	141.	Protection
1964	119.	Flower Arrangement
1968	89.	The Hunting Lodge
1976	97.	Helen

GÜLEN, FÜSUN

1975	100.	Busy Hands
	101.	Old Turkish Lady
1976	98.	Little Girl*
1977	66.	Still Life with Roses
	67.	The Purses
1981	79.	Untitled
	80.	Untitled
1983	75.	The Alley
1984	87.	Gate to the Unknown*
1985	67.	Inevitable

HAAG, CARL H.
1958   109.   Passing Shower

HAAG, O. O.
1939   103.   Halloween
1946   85.   Hoosier Agriculturist
1950   75.   Dollie
1958   110.   Mel

HAAS, MARY M.
1973   68.   Black and Silver

HAAS, PAULINE ANDERSON
1946   86.   Jimmy
1947   92.   Perkin's Cove
         93.   Pensive

HABELA, JOHN J.
1977   68.   Self-Portrait
         69.   Figure #1*

HACKER, OLLIE
1975   102.   Field of Wildflowers
1976   99.   Carpenter's Lace

HACKETT, GENEVIEVE
1955   90.   The Blue Vase

HACKETT, J.
1966   67.   Fleur de Lis
1973   69.   Enigma

HACKETT, MARY JO
1962   137.   Printemps
1963   106.   En Glace*

HACKNEY, ALLEN
1965   111.   Sacrifice II
         112.   The Mushroom Hunt*
1967   106.   A Barn at Fairbanks
         107.   The Trap
         108.   The Forgotten Grave
1968   90.   The Window*
         91.   The Fox Den
         92.   The Locker
1969   80.   The Lightning Flashes
         81.   Decay and Delight*
1970   101.   The Robber
         102.   The Song Sparrow*
1971   76.   Flushed Covey
         77.   Sack of Nails
1972   42.   Thrush*
1973   70.   The Mockingbird
         71.   Delight and Decay
1974   56.   Amanita
         57.   Song Sparrow, II
1975   103.   No Swimming Allowed*
         104.   Odds and Ends
1976   100.   The Fox Den II
         101.   Hide and Seek
1977   70.   Twilight*
1978   59.   Puffballs*
1986   101.   The Laboratory
1988   91.   Blue Bird
1989   95.   Les Grandes Dimensions du Bird

HADLEY, ALICE ROSS
1927   155.   Still Life

HADLEY, DONALD LEE
1968   93.   Ann's Barn
         94.   Painter's Niche
1970   103.   Tattered Glory*
1971   78.   Long Distance
1972   43.   A Thing of Beauty Is . . .*
         44.   Lord I'm One
1973   72.   Last Payment
1975   105.   Last Testament*
1981   81.   The Promise*
         82.   Evanescence
1982   93.   Once, My Own*
1985   68.   Our Daily Bread*
1986   102.   Threshold
1987   98.   Small World*

HADLEY, PAUL
1925   98.   Dream City
         99.   Oriental Things*
         100.   Mountain Stream
1926   141.   Waterfall
         142.   Lea Garden
         143.   After the Shower
1927   156.   Along Bear Creek
         157.   In the Rockies
         158.   Bill Spoon's House*
1928   128.   Autumn in the Hills
         129.   Autumn
1929   134.   Morgan County Cedars
         135.   Windy Day
1931   109.   Tinker Shop
         110.   Whitewashed Cabin
1932   98.   Southern Garden
         99.   Madison Ind. Doorway
1942   89.   Busy Corner, Maysville, Ky.
         90.   Full Bloom
         91.   Old Place, November
1943   91.   Town Pump
         92.   Daybreak on the Wabash
         93.   Ivory-Green and Gray
1946   87.   River-bank
         88.   Rose o'Sharon & Sweet Gum
1948   54.   Clifty Falls

1950	76.	Peach Blossoms and Church
	77.	Sweet Gum*
1952	81.	Still Life

HADLEY, SENORA RIEKE

1950	78.	The Grain Elevator
1951	79.	The Grain Elevator, Fremont, Ind.
1953	73.	A Century of Milling
	74.	Tekonsha Flour Mill
1956	97.	The Stone Quarry
1958	111.	Playmates
	112.	French Quarter, New Orleans
1961	142.	Old Covered Bridge, Lancaster, N. H.
	143.	St. John's Church, Fullersborg
1963	107.	The Old Sawmill
1969	82.	The Country Church

HAGEDORN, VALENTINE OKO

1961	144.	Out of the Night
1963	108.	Shebui
	109.	Boy with Green Hair

HAGEN, GRACE ROWLAND

| 1936 | 91. | Sunset on Lake Linden |

HAGEN, GREG (L.)

1976	102.	Barbeque
1977	71.	Pumphouse
1978	60.	House on Chigger Hollow Road
1981	83.	Mueller's Drugs
	84.	Crossroads

HAGENBOOK, EDNA (Slagle)

1958	113.	Petunias and Green Glass Bottle
1960	101.	Grandmother's Treasures
1976	103.	Canadian Glacier and Wellington Lakes
	104.	Still Life with Blue Bottle

HAHN, LEANN

1983	76.	Dave's Parlor
	77.	Thelma
1984	88.	Play
	89.	Andy

HAINES, FRANCES
(See McVey, Frances H. and Sweeney, Frances H.)

1933	102.	The Circus
	103.	Portrait of My Husband
1934	76.	Miriam

HALBROOKS, DARRYL

| 1975 | 106. | G's with Landscapes |
| | 107. | Where Is the Train Station |

HALL, THOMAS

| 1930 | 102. | Sentinels of the Woods |
| | 103. | Twilight |

HALL, W. PINK

1928	130.	A By Road, Brown County
	131.	A Glimpse of a Creek in Brown County
1929	136.	The Morning After the Night Before

HAMILTON, CLARA M.

1940	73.	Still Life
1945	81.	Still Life
1946	89.	Wash Day

HAMILTON, DOROTHY GALLAHUE

| 1976 | 105. | Untitled II |

HAMILTON, EILEEN (R.)

1971	79.	Alone
1972	45.	Waiting
1974	58.	Traces
1976	106.	"Returning"
	107.	"This Land"
1986	103.	Moon Cat

HAMM, RUSSELL

1942	92.	Grandad's Study
	93.	Still Life
	94.	Still Life

HAMMAN, MIKE

| 1977 | 72. | Innocence* |

HAMMOND, EMILY M.

| 1987 | 99. | West Hill, 1800's |
| 1988 | 92. | Beneath the Sea |

HANCOCK, G. MICHAEL

| 1977 | 73. | Doc's Lake |

HANCOCK, W. HAROLD

1951	80.	The Lighthouse
1952	82.	The Shrimp Boats
1955	91.	Ft. Myers Shrimp Dock
1957	87.	North Michigan Avenue
	88.	Ridge Road
1960	102.	Lonesome Barn
	103.	Late Afternoon Shadows
1961	145.	Mt. Zun Road
	146.	Road to Gatesville
1962	138.	Carnival
1963	110.	Rainy Evening
1964	120.	Glow of Twilight
	121.	Bean Blossom Bridge
1965	113.	Autumn Gold
1975	108.	Winter in the Valley
1976	108.	Golden Hind II at the Golden Gate
	109.	Bean Blossom Bridge
1977	74.	Indiana Farm in Winter
	75.	Winter's Eve

EXHIBITION RECORDS

HANCOCK, WILLIAM
1974	59.	Blue Ridge
1976	110.	Indiana Wheat Field
1978	61.	Still Life
1984	90.	Still Life
	91.	Twilight*
1985	69.	Shadows
1987	100.	Booth Bay

HANES, JUDITH M.
| 1966 | 68. | Gray Mood |

HANIKA, MILDRED D.
| 1971 | 80. | Hanikraft* |

HANLEY, FRANCIS J(oseph)
1939	104.	Sophomore of Notre Dame
1940	74.	Sung and Samurai*
1941	69.	The Tang Horse
1948	55.	Palermo Anchorage
1949	62.	Winter Recollection*
1951	81.	City Park at Noon*

HANNELL, HAZEL
| 1975 | 109. | Queen Anne's Lace |

HANNIN, NANCY H.
| 1965 | 114. | Jessica |

HANSBERRY, LUCILLE K.
| 1954 | 87. | Poppies with Brass Bowl |

HANSELL, GIFFORD
1951	82.	Retired Farmer
	83.	Kitchen from Away Back
1952	83.	Farm Weather Outlook*

HANSEN, LOUISE B.
1969	83.	Ghost Town
1970	104.	Estuary
	105.	Cascade*
1971	81.	Desert Rain*
1973	73.	The Grasshopper
	74.	Abandoned
1974	60.	Queen Ann's Lace
	61.	Desert Storm
1975	110.	Hedgerow*
	111.	Retirement
1976	111.	Of Seasons Past
	112.	Jake's Orchard
1977	76.	Patchwork
	77.	Fence Row*
1978	62.	Indiana Heritage
	63.	Sanctuary
1979	70.	Sunlit Interior
1982	94.	Hiding Place
1984	92.	Spanish and Sweet Bermuda*
1985	70.	Hiding Place
1986	104.	Late Season
	105.	Morning Shadows

HARBART, GERTRUDE (F.)
1988	93.	Rearview
1989	96.	Thief in My Patch*
	97.	In High Country
1950	79.	Fennville
1951	84.	Main Street
1952	84.	The Storm
	85.	The Clown
	86.	The Fish
1953	75.	Birds and Cage
	76.	The Square Dance
1954	88.	Highway No. 6
	89.	Mixed Bouquet
1955	92.	May Baskets
	93.	Flowers and Fruit
1956	98.	Trading Post
	99.	Geraniums
1957	89.	The Old Way
	90.	Shadow Box
1958	114.	The Contender*
	115.	Pomeroy On Ohio River
1959	82.	The Party
	83.	With Love
	84.	Elfreth's Alley

HARBOURT, JOY (Adams)
(See Adams, Joy Harbourt)
1969	84.	That's My Bag
	85.	Untitled
1971	82.	Clark's Upholsterers
	83.	Untitled

HARCOFF, LYLA MARSHALL
1930	104.	Persimmons
	105.	Helen
1931	111.	Green Apples
1932	100.	Sleeping Negress
1935	70.	Calla Rhythmus
	71.	Green Bananas

HARDING, SHELBY
1976	113.	Rhubarb Wine
	114.	Flea Market
1977	78.	Outlook
1978	64.	Ennui
	65.	Telling of Raw Eyes and Bloody Bones*
1979	71.	Saturday Night Fisherman*
1980	60.	Last Winter
	61.	Intrusion
1981	85.	The October Stories
1982	95.	Dogtrot Liar
	96.	Out of Season
1983	78.	Never, Ever Cut a Churchyard Yew
1984	93.	Moon Rise

HARDRICK, JOHN W(esley)
| 1929 | 137. | Golden Glow |
| | 138. | Child of the Wildwood |

221

1931	112.	The Light of the World
1934	77.	No Suh
	78.	Aunty

HARDY, MAUDE F.

| 1944 | 114. | Sword Fish Boats |
| | 115. | Calla Lillies |

HARE, HELEN ALDRICH

1934	79.	Studio
1935	72.	The Studio
	73.	No School Today
1936	94.	Brimming Bowl
1937	317.	Easter
1938	82.	Found in the Attic
	312.	Home Spun
1939	105.	Sunny Window
	106.	Studio
1947	94.	River at Allegan*
	95.	Shelter
1948	56.	Plowed Field
1950	80.	City at Dawn
1952	87.	Patriarch of the Orchard
	88.	Minnesota Farm
1953	77.	Night

HARFORD, DOROTHY B(ethel)

1931	113.	The Wash Lady*
1933	104.	My Father
1934	80.	The Marmelade Maker
1935	74.	Mrs. Walden Mitchel Harford
1936	92.	Portrait
1938	83.	Helen M. Goodwin

HARGRAVES, EMILY RAINBOLT

| 1955 | 94. | Asters |

HARLAN, ROMA C.

| 1942 | 95. | Portrait of Mrs. Edith Roberts |

HARPEL, ALICE

| 1977 | 79. | Homecoming |
| 1979 | 72. | Cityscape |

HARPER, HARRIETT (J.) ECKEL

1950	81.	Fisherman's Luck
1952	89.	Sunset Hours
1962	139.	Grandpa Eckel, A Wise Old Fellow
1965	115.	In the High Country
1967	109.	Alberta Falls

HARRINGTON, BARBARA

| 1973 | 75. | Attic Mirror |

HARRINGTON, GREGORY S.

| 1987 | 101. | Umbrella #3 |

HARRISON, HARLEY F.

| 1969 | 86. | Floral Spectrum |
| 1970 | 106. | Garden Gate |

HARROD, AMY L.

1948	57.	Gladiolus
	58.	Zinnias
1949	63.	Mother's Corner

HARROLD, CON

| 1964 | 122. | Steve |
| | 123. | Elsie |

HART, DRENNAN W.

| 1945 | 82. | Village Post Office |
| 1947 | 96. | Model |

HART, JOHN PATRICK

1961	147.	Storm over the Dunes
1964	124.	Student '64
1965	116.	Bedford Quarry

HART, JOSEPHINE
(See McGee, Josephine Hart)

1973	76.	Street Urchins
1974	62.	Steeplescape
1975	112.	Jeffery
1977	80.	Spring Tapestry

HARTH, EMMA E.

1942	96.	Grandma F.
	97.	Grandpa W.
1945	83.	Lena

HARTLEY, MARY

| 1981 | 86. | Jaquita |
| 1982 | 97. | A Mother's Love |

HARTMAN, BETSY

| 1989 | 98. | Bronco |
| 1990 | 72. | Lost Ball |

HARTMAN, LAVERN

| 1963 | 111. | West of Yuma |

HARTRATH, LUCIE

1925	101.	The Valley, Morning*
	102.	September Morning
	103.	Houses in Sunshine
1926	144.	The Green Hat
	145.	October Morning
	146.	Young Oaks in November
1927	159.	Snowy Roofs
	160.	Autumn in the Hills*
	161.	Morning on the Hilltop
1928	132.	The Clearing
	133.	The Creek in October*
	134.	The Red Oak
1929	139.	Peonies
	140.	The Oaks
	141.	Across the Valley*
1930	106.	Hillroad in November
	107.	Tapestry
	108.	Autumn Pageant*

1931	114.	After the Frost*
1932	101.	From the Hilltop
	102.	Still Life
	103.	Willows Along the Creek
1933	105.	September Haze
	106.	A Hoosier Home
1934	81.	Garden Flowers
	82.	Hilltop Apple Trees
	83.	Blue Days and Fair
1935	75.	Hillside*
	76.	Autumn Glory
	77.	The Yellow Vase
1936	95.	The Alley
	96.	October Woodland
1937	84.	Misty Morning*
	318.	Still Life
1938	84.	Orchard Road
	85.	September
	86.	Tranquil Day
1939	107.	Beside the Still Waters*
	108.	November
	109.	The Valley in November*
	312.	Noon
1940	75.	A Village Home
	76.	From My Window
	77.	Our Alley
	311.	Sunlite Valley
1941	70.	Autumn Harmony
	71.	Just Off Main Street*
	312.	Flowers in Sunshine

HARTSOCK, ROBERT E.

1984	94.	Radiance
1985	71.	Old Smokie
	72.	Winslow Homer's "Breezing Up"
1987	102.	Pastoral
1988	94.	Jenny
1989	99.	University Square
	100.	Refuge
1990	73.	Metamora Grist Mill*

HARVEY, HOMER

1931	115.	Head of A. W. Harvey

HARVEY, WINNIE H.

1940	78.	Late Bouquet
1942	98.	Dogwood Blossoms
	99.	White Petunias
1943	94.	Late Summer Still Life
1944	116.	Flowers in Cranberry Pitcher
	117.	Peonies
	118.	Christmas Begonia
1945	84.	Petunias*
	85.	Old Lustre
1947	97.	White Petunias
1949	64.	The Beach
1950	82.	Hibiscus
1951	85.	Prickly Poppies
1952	90.	Sabino Canyon

1953	78.	Flower Still Life
	79.	Spring Cleaning
	80.	Hibiscus
1954	90.	Soy Bean Field
1956	100.	East Meets West
1957	91.	Still Life with Flowers
1958	116.	Hedge-Row Harvest
	117.	Iris

HASSELMAN, ANNA

1925	104.	Laid Up
1929	142.	A Gloucester Street
	143.	The Saint Peter
	144.	The Wharf House
1931	116.	Port du Jersual, Dinan
1934	84.	Surf, Goose Rocks
1935	78.	Gray Day Boats

HASWELL, LEONA H.

1937	85.	Primitive Baptists
1938	87.	Rhododendron

HATCH, SARA

1989	101.	The Guardian
	102.	The Handmaiden
1990	74.	3 Horses on a Hill
	75.	Women Flying

HAUSER, VIVIAN M.
(See Hauser-Smithhart, Vivian)

1968	95.	Apples with Basket
	96.	Markle Mill
1969	87.	Still Life in the Colors of Leo
	88.	Basket of Eggs*

HAUSER-SMITHHART, VIVIAN M.
(See Hauser, Vivian M.)

1990	169.	Pristine

HAWK, BARBARA L.

1963	112.	Captured Garden

HAWKINS, HUCKLEBERRY

1964	125.	Still Life
1965	117.	Nag's Head No. 2

HAWKINS, PATRICIA

1973	77.	Curiosity
	78.	Tall Tales*

HAYES, BRENDA

1966	69.	Prairie

HAYES, HAZEL BARKER

1944	119.	Oddities in Pitchers
	120.	This and That
1946	90.	Tulip Tree Blossoms
1968	97.	Natures Own

HAYES, ROBERT T.
1954	91.	Gloucester Harbor
	92.	Sunday at East Dover
1955	95.	Gloucester Harbor
	96.	Bass Rocks Surf
1956	101.	The Sadie M. Nunan
1957	92.	Seine Boats In Repair
	93.	Ebb Tide At Rocky Neck
1958	118.	Clam Diggers
	119.	Terrible Tom
1959	85.	The Orange Dory
1961	148.	The Holdouts
	149.	Atlantic Street, Rockport
1962	140.	Pulp Mill
1975	113.	Indian Corn and Gourds
	114.	Water Wagon

HAZINSKI, HARRIET M.
| 1942 | 100. | Still Life |

HEAD, CECIL F.
1934	85.	Pots and Pans*
1935	79.	Back Yard
	80.	Strolling Boy
1936	93.	Indiana Potato Planters
1937	86.	A Winter Day
	87.	Buildings in Winter
1938	88.	Evening Light
1941	72.	Still Life
1942	101.	Kitchen Crockery
	102.	Street Corner at Night
1981	87.	Early Portrait*
1983	79.	The Shack Woman
1984	95.	Light on My Wood Pile
1986	106.	Down on the Farm
	107.	Sunflowers with Bee
1987	103.	Rest and Lunch Time
1989	103.	Industrial

HEADY, CONSTANCE
1984	96.	Eagle Creek Park
1986	108.	Golden October
	109.	Almost Home

HEALY, MARION MAXON
1958	120.	The Arch At Alamos
	121.	Early Morning
1960	104.	Tree in the Courtyard
	105.	Only Weeds
1961	150.	Abandoned Quarry
	151.	Early Morning*
	152.	Mason-Dixon Line
1964	126.	Dark Magic
	127.	The Matterhorn
	128.	Church in the Valley
	129.	Mason-Dixon Line

HECKLER, WILLIAM C.
| 1970 | 107. | Romantic Figure |

HEDGES, JAMES
| 1986 | 110. | Pete |

HEINICKE, JANET HART
1957	94.	Restraint
1958	122.	Ice Fishers
	123.	The Maze
	124.	Hawthornes
1959	86.	Night Bridge

HEINSEN, L(inda) LEE
| 1989 | 104. | The Vineyard |

HEISKELL, NANCY S.
| 1987 | 104. | Carrousel, Oh Carrousel |

HEISLER, JULES
| 1963 | 113. | Thank Thee |
| | 114. | At Eventide |

HELBING, MICHAEL G.
1981	88.	Grandfather and Son on a Park Bench
	89.	The Scream
1982	98.	Painted Lady Pulltoy for Grownups
	99.	Introspect
1984	97.	Salome

HELMUTH, MILDRED (C.) NORTON
1959	87.	Pixie*
	88.	Purdue '59
1960	106.	In Agony
	107.	Little Mike
1961	153.	Snaps and Snails
	154.	Sugar and Spice
1964	130.	Matthew
1965	118.	Another Pixie
1968	98.	Mischief
1970	108.	Matthew
	109.	Major Lewis
1975	115.	Three Score and Ten

HEMENWAY, LUDY
1984	98.	Forest Floor Fascination
1986	111.	Rekindled Memories in Coulters Barn
1988	95.	Mushroom Tapestry II
1989	105.	It's Spring
	106.	Tropical Codiaeum
1990	76.	Peace on the Pond II

HENDERSON, RAY
| 1957 | 95. | Spring along Salt Creek |

HENDRICKSON, NILA
| 1971 | 84. | Our National Guard |

HENGEN, NONA
| 1979 | 73. | Tired |

HENLINE, FLOYD H.
  1938   89.   Trees in Late Autumn
  1939   110.   Indian Summer
  1940   79.   Fair and Colder

HENNINGER, J. M.
  1932   104.   And Models Call This Work*
  1933   107.   Dan*
  1936   97.   Danica

HENRY, DOUG(las)
  1973   79.   Gingerbread and Weeds*
  1974   63.   The Fieldchair
          64.   October Bouquet
  1975   249.   Kids Play*
  1976   115.   Duck Decoy
          116.   Fish Kite*
  1977   81.   Summer Wharf
          82.   Beached Skiffs
  1978   66.   History*
          67.   Cathedrals
  1979   74.   Domed Plaza
  1980   62.   Small Town, Last Summer
          63.   Grandma's House
  1981   90.   Late October
          91.   Childhood Days

HENRY, OUIDABON
  1931   117.   Olden Provincetown

HENSHAW, GLEN COOPER
  1925   105.   William
          106.   Little Hallie
  1926   147.   Little Giovanni
          148.   Rio Della Guerra, Venice
  1927   162.   Old Woman
          163.   Old Sailor
  1928   135.   Sunrise and Mist
          136.   Old Man

HERITIER, JULES R.
  1983   80.   Hoosier Woodland Scene #2
  1984   99.   Ex Forti Dulcedo
  1986   112.   Hard Luck Story

HERMAN, CAROL M.
  1979   75.   Jan
          76.   Untitled

HERMAN, LORETTA
  1976   117.   Wintery Scene

HERRMANN, EDWARD E.
  1948   59.   Lobster Dories*
          60.   Portent of Spring
  1949   65.   White Grass
          66.   River Mist at Madison
  1950   83.   Prelude to Rain*
  1951   86.   Country Home
  1952   91.   Steam*

  1953   81.   House of White
          82.   Reflections
  1954   93.   Modern Sunlight
          94.   Blue Pitcher
  1968   99.   The Windmill*
          100.   Gray Day
          101.   Early Light

HERSHBERGER, ABNER
  1971   85.   Red Environs #2

HERSHEY, SAMUEL F.
  1933   108.   Eleanor
          109.   New England Winter*
  1934   86.   Byway
          87.   Portrait of Compris
          88.   Winter Coast, Cape Ann
  1935   81.   The Cove, October Evening
          82.   The Smokehouse
  1936   98.   Rockport Doorway
          99.   Morning Surf*
  1937   319.   Summer Bouquet**
  1938   90.   Aztec God, Cactus, Virgin and
                Birds*
  1939   111.   Still Life
  1940   80.   Jane
  1941   313.   Cyclamen and Sweet Peas*
  1942   103.   Still Life
  1947   98.   Still Life
          99.   Essex Shipyard

HERTEL, ELSA
  1948   61.   Minnesota Fall
  1949   67.   Minnesota Border Lake
          68.   Sumac and Old Copper
  1951   87.   Duluth Harbor
  1977   83.   Flames of Autumn
          84.   Minnesota Winter

HERTENSTEIN, DeWITT
  1989   107.   Space Odyssey

HEYMAN, MARTHA J(osephine)
  1962   141.   Tree Face
  1964   131.   Fragments of Spring
  1965   119.   Fragments of Summer
  1967   110.   Linear Landscape No. 3
          111.   Linear Figure Composition
  1968   102.   Circular Comp

HIBBEN, THOMAS E.
  1925   107.   Stanford Union
          108.   Just Winter
  1926   149.   Lisieux, France
          150.   Tangiers
          151.   Magdalen College, Oxford
          152.   Chinon, France

HIBBS, RUTH K(erlin)
  1938   92.   Meditation
          93.   Yodeling

1939	112.	Sunflowers
1940	81.	From Shaggy Hills
1950	84.	Slave Quarters, New Orleans
1951	88.	Haunted House, New Orleans
	89.	Winter Came Early
1955	97.	New Orleans' Top of the Tree
1956	102.	Breakfast for One
	103.	A Full Window
	104.	Hostelry, Guatemala
1957	96.	Remembering All
	97.	Life's Blessings*
1958	125.	Greeting Strangers, Guatemala
	126.	Low Tide, Provincetown
	127.	Equality
1959	89.	Sharing Equally
	90.	Approaching the Market, Guatemala*
	91.	Side Street, Central City
1960	108.	Monday Club Meeting*
	109.	Transportation Unscheduled
	110.	Old Cathay
1961	155.	Seeking New Frontiers
	156.	A Weed Patch
	157.	A Pause That Refreshes
1962	142.	Togetherness
	143.	Before the Harvest
1963	115.	Autumn Returns
1965	120.	Queen Ann and Lowly Dock
	121.	Bewildered
1966	70.	A Florist's Shelf
1967	114.	Spread of Autumn
	115.	Ancient History
	116.	Devotion to Beauty
1970	110.	Evolution of Decay

HICKOK, CONDE WILSON

1926	153.	Old Orchard, near Cedar Lake
1927	164.	Peonies
	165.	Weatherworn Patriarchs of the Dunes
1928	137.	Edge of Blow-out
	138.	Hiding in Hollyhocks
1929	145.	Old Red Bridge
	146.	Marsh Land

HIGDON, PHIL

1971	86.	Ritual by Moonlight
	87.	Portrait of a Clown

HIGGINS, BARBARA DUNCAN

1967	117.	Dusk
	118.	Serendipity
	119.	Winter Loneliness
	120.	Untitled
1968	103.	Hollow Souls
	104.	And He Speaks

HIGGINS, HERBERT C.

1960	111.	Stevie
1963	116.	Little Dorothy
1980	64.	Mid-Winter

HIGGINS, JULIETA

1985	73.	Fall
	74.	Clear Stream in the Woods
1986	113.	Nature Series No. 6
1988	96.	Kaleidos No. 3
	97.	Nature Series No. 12
1989	108.	Orchids
1990	78.	Nature Series, #15*

HIGGINS, MARIAN

1946	91.	Old Stone Quarry

HIGGINS, REBECCA MOORE

1984	100.	Untitled (Canadian Goose)
1985	75.	October
1990	77.	Morning Florals

HIGGINS, VICTOR

1928	139.	Still Life*
	140.	A Mountain Ceremony
1929	147.	Zinnias*
	148.	Stubble Pasture
	149.	A Cabin in the Aspens
1930	109.	Cloth of Gold

HILL, LARRY

1968	105.	The Kormelink Barn

HILL, LAURA

1984	101.	The Marsh: Great Blue Heron
1985	76.	New Beginnings: Mallards
1986	114.	Wyland Pond
	115.	Down Where the May Apples Grow

HILL, MARIAN J.

1961	158.	Things of Yester Year
	159.	Summer Lilacs
1962	144.	The Bisque Horses
1964	132.	San Jose Mission
	133.	Amaryllis

HILL, WAYNE W.

1939	113.	Head of Woman
	114.	Dr. Walter E. Dove

HIMELICK, LUANA

1967	112.	Winter's Blanket
1968	106.	Winter Pasture
1969	89.	No. 56

HINDMARCH, ALAN W.

1967	113.	Diagonal Street Galena

HINER, JOHN

1975	116.	Skeye-Crack

HINKLE, BEN(jamin)

1985	77.	Winter Afternoon
1987	105.	Happy Hollow
1989	109.	Woodland Trail

HINKLE, JAMES ROBERT
1972 46.   The Storm
1973 80.   The Quiet Storm

HINNEFELD, A. JEAN
1959 92.   Clown III

HIRSCH, CHARLES
1972 47.   Late Afternoon*

HIRSCH, IONE
1937 88.   The Battery
        89.   House Tops
1938 94.   The Hartzel Home
1939 115. Low Tide
1940 82.   Missouri Hills
1941 73.   Blast Furnace
        74.   Green Hill

HIRSHBURG, ROY
1931 118. Richmond's Greenwich Village*

HOBBS, FLORENCE RYAN
1943 95.   Wagon Shed
        96.   Hoosier Barn
1944 121. Old Hundred
1947 100. Spring
1948 62.   February Thaw

HOCHMAN, JACQUIE
1967 121. Blue City
1970 111. Sea Tangle

HOCKENSMITH, DAVID
1969 90.   January 1st
1970 112. Early Autumn Event with Castor,
             Pollux and Unidentified Female
             Companion
       113. The Jade Merchant*
1971 88.   Alterpiece #6
        89.   Alterpiece #7*
1972 48.   Alterpiece #9*
        49.   Alterpiece #10

HODAPP, MARY L.
1969 91.   White-Gold
        92.   Resting Sycamore
1970 114. Pastels of Spring
1973 81.   White Beauty

HODGIN, JOHN T.
1973 82.   Door of Steins
1980 65.   Louie's Bar*
1982 100. Postcard, 1927
1983 81.   Troll Bridge
        82.   Toys & Trinkets

HODGIN, MARSTON D(ean)
1925 109. Mid-Winter
       110. Among the Hills

1926 154. Winter
       155. Creeping Fog
1930 110. The Dory
       111. Marblehead

HODSON, MILES R.
1953 83.   Yellow Still Life*
        84.   Five
1955 98.   Still Life*

HOERGER, GRACE E.
1946 92.   Dreamer
        93.   Smiling David
1948 63.   The Blind Will Be Told

HOFFLER, OTHMAR
1933 110. Mimi
       111. Barnyard Animals
1935 83.   Still Life
1936 100. Betty
       101. Deborah of Bean Blossom

HOFFMAN, ARTHUR
1968 107. Sketch for Grass City

HOFFMAN, FRANK V.
1938 95.   Orte, Hill Town
        96.   Volterrain Permanence
1939 116. Portrait
       117. Transylvania
1940 83.   Still Life with Harp
1941 75.   Charlestown, Street Scene
        76.   Still Life*
1942 104. River Town
1943 97.   Still Life with Squash
        98.   Old Bills and Flowers

HOFFMAN, P. D.
1975 117. Adam and Eve

HOFFMAN, ROBERT
1986 116. Rain*
       117. Misty Winter Morning
1987 106. Tides Out
       107. Favorites
1988 98.   Pelican's Rest
        99.   Sycamores
1989 110. Duneland Grasses*

HOGUE, SARA JAYNE
1964 134. Scent of Spring
1969 93.   October Objects
1976 118. Friends of the Fields

HOLIDAY, JOSEPH
1969 94.   Mother and Child, No. 1
1970 115. Mother and Child
       116. The Leader
1978 68.   In Memory Of

HOLLETT, CLARE FERGUSON
1982   101.   Of Edges

HOLLINGSWORTH, ALICE CLAIRE
1929   150.   Black and white pen drawing
       151.   Black and white pen drawing
       152.   Black and white pen bookplate
       153.   Black and white pen drawing

HOLLINGSWORTH, JOSEPHINE A.
(See Poulson, Josephine Hollingsworth)
1928   141.   The Sheep Herders
       142.   Book Plates and Christmas Cards
       143.   Book Plates and Christmas Cards
       144.   Illustration
1929   154.   Nursery Rhymes
       155.   Drawing of San Juan Tenements
       156.   Book Plate
       157.   The Pool

HOLLIS, FREDERIC L(ee)
1954   95.   Former Gov. H. F. Schricker
1959   93.   Dust Storm

HOLME, MAUD
1926   156.   Lake Gage
       157.   Sunrise on Lime Lake

HOLMES, MARY J.
1969   95.   Patches of Light

HOLMES, PALMER Z.
1943   99.   Winter Fantasy
1944   122.   Shower Coming
1955   99.   River Town

HOLSAPPLE, KERRY
1979   77.   Oriental Roses*
1980   66.   A-Major
       67.   Spring Morning II
1981   92.   Miss Herron*
1983   83.   Little Geisha
1986   118.   Morning Glory
1988   100.   Harmony in Orange and Blue

HOLT, FRANCIS E.
1949   69.   The Tea Tasters
       70.   Dejeuner
1950   85.   The Author
       86.   The Window Washer*
1952   92.   The Ingenue
1953   85.   The Actor*
1954   96.   Hikers, Turkey Run
       97.   The Connoisseur
       98.   Summer Afternoon
1956   105.   The Nurse
       106.   The Hat
1957   98.   The Record Player
       99.   The Sightless One*
1958   128.   Have Gun, Will Travel
       129.   Navajo Ponies

HOLTMAN, FLORENCE
1934   89.   An Old Foundry
       90.   Morning Shadows

HOLTMAN, HOLLY
1937   90.   Girl on Divan
       91.   Ballet Girls

HOLZAPFEL, ROBERT
1961   160.   August Auction
1962   148.   New Blue Silo
       149.   Tic Tac Tortoise
1964   135.   County Fair
1965   122.   Farm Cad
1970   117.   Generation Gape*
1971   90.   American Landscape with Still Life
1975   118.   Scene in a Mirror
       119.   Comb for the Aged
1977   85.   Bosch's Rose Garden

HOOVER, TODD
1971   91.   Orgiastic #2
       92.   Orgiastic #3
1972   50.   Corner

HOPPER, FLOYD D.
1936   102.   Deserted House
       103.   A Summer Rain
       104.   Summer Night
1937   92.   To Dust Returneth
       93.   Blue Horizon
1938   97.   Blue Hills
       98.   Morning in the Knobs
       99.   Winter Landscape
       313.   Landscape
1941   77.   Fisherman's Cove
       78.   Great Lake Industry
1942   105.   Montana Hills*
       106.   Ruth*
       107.   Under Clouded Skies
1943   100.   Sun and Snow
       101.   Humble and Mighty
       102.   River Town
1944   123.   Southwest Industry*
       124.   Perce
       125.   University Park
1945   86.   White Sands at Alamogordo, N. M..
       87.   Mexican Market
1946   94.   The Belt*
1947   101.   Lowly Mansions
       102.   Indiana Winter
1958   130.   Santiago, Chile
       131.   Don't Fence Me In*
1959   94.   Fishing Boats
1961   161.   White Horses
       162.   Two Black Cats
       163.   The Hunter
1962   145.   Portrait of Jo
       146.   Red Mills
       147.   I Remember Manhattan

1963	117.	In the Greek Islands
	118.	Remnants of the Past
1964	136.	Gill's Rock*
	137.	Market in Haiti
	138.	Sunset After the Rain
1965	123.	White Dove of the Desert
	124.	White Horses*
1966	71.	Wild Geese
	72.	Rainy Day
	73.	Dry Dock*
1967	122.	Mexican Street
	123.	Stinesville in Winter
	124.	Winter, Lake Michigan*
1968	108.	Peggy's Cove
	109.	Near Allisonville
	110.	Wisconsin Barn
1969	96.	Cairo*
	97.	Mykonos*
1970	118.	White Boats
	119.	Snow in Aurora
1972	51.	Winter Evening*
	52.	Street in Tangier
1973	83.	Mykonos Stairway
	84.	Monday
1974	65.	Past Elegance
	66.	Winter Evening
1975	120.	First Touch of Autumn
	121.	It Rained Last Night
1976	119.	Door County
1977	86.	Derelict*
1978	69.	Cathedral at Taxco*
	70.	Unloading The Catch
1979	78.	Blue Wall
	79.	Townscape
1980	68.	City in Winter*
1981	93.	The Underpass*
	94.	Indiana Town
1982	102.	Siesta Time
1983	84.	Entry Way*
	85.	Retired From Service

HORNE-KAPLAN, DENISE ANNE

1989	119.	Window Series, Charleston, South Carolina*
	120.	Floral Series, Clemantis

HORTON, MARTHA (L.) POWELL
(See Powell, Martha L.)

1986	119.	String of Pearls II
1987	108.	Sisters
1988	101.	Portrait of Jessica

HORWEDEL, ANNE

1980	69.	Scarves
	70.	Ribbon Boxes
1981	95.	Let's Have Cake*

HORWITZ, HAROLD I.

1936	107.	Evening Express

HOSACK, MARY

1985	78.	Night Song

HOSTERMAN, N(aomi) S.

1935	84.	Cosmos
	85.	Hydrangeas
1936	108.	Calla Lilies
1937	94.	Forsythia

HOSTETLER, RENA A.

1937	320.	Peonies
1938	100.	Autumn Glory
	101.	Peonies
1940	84.	Snow Scene
	85.	Tulips*
1941	314.	Peonies
1945	88.	Petunias*
1947	103.	Marilyn Bottomley, Lafayette, Indiana
1948	64.	Peonies
1950	87.	Dahlias
1951	90.	Gold Jar
1953	86.	Lilacs
1956	107.	Gladiolias
1957	100.	Fantasy*
1958	132.	Petunias
	133.	Zinnias
1959	95.	Spring Flowers
1962	150.	Skokie Valley

HOUCK, ELIZABETH D.

1955	101.	March in Mineral Point
	102.	Living in the Sun
1956	108.	La Perla, San Juan

HOUGH, BERENICE

1959	96.	The Favorites

HOUGLUM, JONATHON W.

1980	71.	Linda

HOUSE, MARTY

1980	72.	Malta Boat Repair

HOWARD, (F.) MAX

1946	95.	Warming Her Back
1947	104.	Landscape
1949	71.	Quiet Harbor*
1950	88.	Remains
1951	91.	Old Barn
	92.	Country Church
1953	87.	Custard Apples
1954	99.	From the Orient
1955	100.	In the Quiet of the Night
1974	67.	Winter Sun
1975	122.	Railway Pylon*
1976	120.	Late Afternoon
1977	87.	Autumn Sunlight
1978	71.	Nelly Has Crash-Landed!*
1979	80.	Rear Exit
	81.	Wheel & Disk*

1980	73.	Dead
	74.	A Man & His Shadow
1981	96.	Abandoned Forms*
	97.	Dark Idol
1982	103.	The Last Scream
	104.	Lumber Yard
1983	86.	Down by the River
	87.	Where the Wheel Stopped*
1984	102.	Where People Once Lived
	103.	Silent Watcher
1985	79.	Wounded Warrior
1986	120.	Strange Pursuit*
	121.	View Thru Opening
1987	109.	Encirclement
	110.	Wheels at Rest
1988	102.	Cool Accent
	103.	151
1989	111.	Decapitated
	112.	Wheels and Things
1990	79.	Rust-Rest

HOWARD, FRANK A.

1970	120.	Untitled

HOWE, PHILIP

1982	105.	The Balance of Man
	106.	After the Sea

HOWE, SUSAN R.

1936	105.	Cosmos
	106.	Chrysanthemums
1937	321.	Hybiscus
1940	86.	Heavenly Blue Morning Glories

HUBBARD, J. F.

1951	93.	Feed Mill

HUBBARD, KIN

1927	166.	Cartoon
	167.	Cartoon
	168.	Cartoon

HUBER, HELEN RUTH

1934	91.	Sunlight on the Haunted

HUDSON, BARBARA A.

1964	139.	Portrait of Phil
1965	125.	The African
1967	125.	The Old Fisherman
1976	121.	Confection 109
1977	89.	Sleep Soft My Son

HUFFORD, BERNIECE (M.)

1959	97.	Snow View
1962	151.	Country Snow
1967	126.	Winter at Water's Edge
1969	98.	Untitled
1970	121.	Untitled No. 1
	122.	Untitled No. 2
1973	85.	Planter Plate Flowers

1977	88.	Autumn Dried Okra, Cocklebur and Weeds
1978	72.	Bursting Free
1981	98.	Fenceline Floral
1984	106.	Grandma's Butter Churn

HUGHES, LEIGH E.

1946	96.	Jerry

HULL, STEVE

1983	89.	Cincinnati City Hall

HUMKE, CAROLYN J.

1989	113.	Bennington, Vermont
1990	80.	Arizona Mission

HUMMEL, REBA LAYMAN

1942	108.	Sketch of Woman Quilting

HUMMER, ED (J.)

1961	164.	Tennessee Waterfall
	165.	Gloucester Ships
1963	119.	Temporal Cycle
1964	140.	Edgar Hiatt, Retired Hunter
	141.	Mexican Washday
1970	123.	Autumn Air

HUMPHREY, HELEN

1954	100.	Memories of Autumn
1955	103.	Harvest*
1956	109.	Grandpa's Corner
	110.	Fruit Arrangement, No. 2
	111.	Souvenirs of the Sea
1957	101.	The Green Jug
	102.	Fruit Arrangement, No. 3
1958	134.	Gourds and Bittersweet
	135.	The Copper Teakettle
1959	98.	The Blue Pitcher
	99.	Harvest #2
1960	112.	The Sound of Music
	113.	Wood Ducks
1961	166.	Fascination
1962	152.	Black Magic

HUNT, LOIS

1984	107.	Earthborn
1986	122.	Landscape

HUNT, WILL HARVEY

1935	86.	Tornado*
1936	109.	Siesta
1938	102.	Emily Lemcke
	103.	Nipponese

HUNTER, EDWIN E.

1945	89.	Salt Market
1972	53.	Shawmucky Bridge
1973	86.	Manlove Park
1975	123.	Street, Tiburon, California

HUNTER, MARY
1954	101.	The German Girl
	102.	Old Tom*
	103.	Native of Old Natchez*
1955	104.	The Cotton Pickers
	105.	Mister John Hopabout
1956	112.	Morning Visitor
1957	103.	Karen
1958	136.	Roadside Bouquet
	137.	The Matriarch
1959	100.	Annie
	101.	June Bouquet*
1960	114.	Self-Portrait
	115.	Spring '59
	116.	Where Next?*
1961	167.	Paul
	168.	Still Life With Tulips
1962	153.	Portrait of a Painter
	154.	Ruth's Doorstep
1963	120.	Nooning
1964	142.	Rowena
	143.	Woman with a Fan
1967	127.	Still Life
1968	111.	Look around in the Now
	112.	Paul
1969	99.	Still Life
1970	124.	Studio Still Life

HURD, MAXINE
1982	107.	Samantha's Family
1983	90.	Cape Elizabeth, Maine
1984	108.	Patrick
1986	123.	Hello Out There
1987	111.	The Captain's Chair
1988	104.	The Sentinel

HURST, RALPH N.
| 1952 | 93. | Girl with Biwa* |
| | 94. | Meditation |

| 1956 | 113. | Beach Bird* |
| | 114. | Toreador Goddess |

HURT, SARAH
1960	117.	River Barge*
	118.	Flowers #3
1961	169.	Dancing Trees
	170.	Print
	171.	Print
1962	155.	Color Sprites
	156.	Emphasis
	157.	Salad Bowl
1964	144.	Nightly Spectacular
	145.	Flower Patterns #4*
	146.	Fevillage #4
	147.	Fevillage #8
1966	74.	Collage Still Life #11
	75.	Birds in Flight
	76.	Collage Still Life #12
1967	128.	Progress
	129.	Blue Mood
	130.	Dried Plum and Friends
1970	125.	Collage Still Life #27
	126.	Hot Line #2

HUTCHINSON, ROBERT F.
| 1961 | 172. | Anne |

HUTCHISON, CONNIE
| 1975 | 124. | Indian Pottery |
| 1978 | 73. | Sycamore Fall |

HUTTO, BLANCHE
1943	103.	The Steam Shovel
	104.	Cactus Garden
1944	126.	Boat for Sale

HUTTON, ALBERT N.
| 1962 | 158. | Entoning |

I

IANUCILLI, FRANK J.
    1957   104.   Gray Barn In May

ILES, MINNIE ELLEN
    1964   148.   Jugs & Fruit

INCE, NANCY CROCKETT
    1983   91.   Spring Glory
    1990   81.   Autumn Leaves

IZOR, ESTELLE PEEL
    1925   113.   Path to the River
    1928   145.   Zinnias
    1929   158.   Morning Mists, Hanover*
    1932   105.   Plow Handle Point, Hanover

J

JACKLEY, (F.) DANO
1940 88. Ellicott City

JACKS, SUSAN
1975 125. Silvery Bromeliad

JACKSON, CHIC
1925 114. Three Cartoons: The Bean Family*

JACKSON, GERTRUDE
1937 95. Old Ironsides
1941 315. Flowers in Blue Bowl

JACKSON, JOHN
1928 146. Carved Stone Panel for Over Mantel
1929 159. Balustrade for Stair or Balcony Rail
1930 112. Cement Cast, Lion and Lioness
    113. Sculpture, Fountain Figure
1931 119. Cresting for Pylon, Indiana
        Limestone*
    120. Bas relief of young child in Hoosier
        Soapstone
1932 106. Gargoyle Downspout, Indiana
        Limestone

JACKSON, LOIS M.
1972 54. Glorious Cross

JACQUES, EMIL
1930 114. On the Pacific Shore
    115. Flirtation on the Beach
1931 121. The Flower Lover
1932 107. Sirens
1933 112. Magdalen
1936 110. Sun Play*
    111. Peaceful Hour
1937 96. Summer Reflections
    322. Fall Flowers

JAGGER, FLORENCE Z.
1963 121. Crystal Creek
    122. Summer's Palette
    123. Old Wound
1964 149. Peaches
1965 126. Demise
    127. Sanctuary
    128. White River
1966 77. River's Edge in Winter
1967 131. Hufford's Hill
1970 127. Woodland Wake
1972 55. Boston Afternoon
1974 68. Early Autumn
1975 126. Boggstown, USA
1976 122. Flora of Fantasy
1979 82. Grandma Flo's Private Gallery*
    83. Too Much
1980 75. Out Front

1981 99. Sunny Knoll
1982 108. Sunday Afternoon, Between Runs
1983 94. Cabin Fever
    95. Segment of Autumn #2
1986 124. The Many Facets of the Heart, with
        Strings Attached

JAGODITS, CAROLYN
1988 105. Waterlilies against the Sky*
    106. A Touch of the Past
1990 82. Wild Beauty
    83. The Woodpile

JAMES, EIZABETH E.
1990 84. Midnight Tide

JAMES, EVA GERTRUDE
1926 159. Blue Vase and Green Bowl

JAMES, EVALYN GERTRUDE
1926 160. The Culvert
1927 169. Soldiers' and Sailors' Monument
1929 160. Frog Hunters
1930 116. Blue Reflections
    117. A Caledonian Still Life

JAMISON, BUD
1987 112. The Gathering Place*
1988 107. Florence

JANKOWSKI, ZYGMUND S.
1966 78. Gloucester, Mass.
    79. Newport, R. I.*
1968 113. Annie
    114. Campbell*
    115. Turk

JARRETT, JAMES E.
1978 74. Madonna of the Flowers

JARRETT, JUDY
(See Olive, Judy)
1990 85. I Shout Your Name
    86. She Billed Herself As Child
        Entertainment

JARRETT, KATHRYN
1975 127. Still Life No. 7
1983 96. Boxed Forms*
    97. Opened Boxes

JARVIS, (Sr.) LEON F.
1966 80. Venice
1967 132. Water Front

JARVIS, PHILIP M.
1986 125. Hollyhocks

JEFFERSON, ORVILLE
1925 115. October
1926 161. An October Snow
1927 170. The Brook, at Twilight
1929 161. Old Jerome

JEFFRIES, HARRIET H.
1944 127. Indian Summer
1952 95. Midland Underpass
96. Landscape Motif
1953 88. Haunted by Memories
1954 104. Snow in the Valley
1955 106. Abandoned Factory

JENKINS, CONNIE (S.)
1980 76. Seventeen
1981 100. Pinecones

JENKINS, Jr., F. RAYMOND
1953 89. January Production
90. Storefront
91. Winter Thaw
1954 105. Sylvania Store Front*

JENKINS, JAN
1976 123. Snow Berries

JENNINGS, EDNA C.
1977 90. Lone Tree

JILBURG, LLOYD
1984 109. Solitude
1986 126. Lonely

JOHNS, MARY ANN
1976 124. Self-Portrait #7
125. Untitled

JOHNSON, CAROLYN W.
1986 127. Standing on the Promises
1987 113. Under the Old Oak Tree
1988 108. The Lowly Potato
1989 114. Fish Town

JOHNSON, FRANCES GOLDRICK
1930 118. Diana

JOHNSON, F(rancis) M.
1929 162. Dorothy Hayes
1934 92. Portrait

JOHNSON, GRACE
1952 97. Parrot Tulips

JOHNSON, GUY (D.)
1951 94. Wind in the Alley
1954 106. Roman Still Life
1956 115. Wine Bottles

JOHNSON, JESSAMINE (I.)
1925 116. Zinnias
1926 162. Garden Flowers
1927 171. The Old Barn
1928 147. Flowers from our Garden
1929 163. Reflected Skies
1930 119. Sunlit Hills
120. Indiana Hills
1932 108. The Scarf

JOHNSON, LOUISE
1964 150. The Country Store
151. Unexpected Snow at Lamb Time
1966 81. Top of the World
1967 133. City Slickers
1968 116. Advance Platoon
1970 128. Winter in Iowa
1974 69. Study of the Cottonweed*
1975 128. Studio Still Life
1976 126. Salt of the Earth
127. Autumn Visitor
1978 75. Clop of Wooden Shoes
1980 77. San Francisco
1981 101. Dancing Tulips
1982 109. Best Friends
1984 110. A Quiet Place
1987 114. Point Betsie
1988 109. Dancing Petunias
110. Her Profile
1989 115. The Amish Mother
1990 87. "Old Master" Boston Harbor

JOHNSON, MAXINE
1967 134. Winter Wonderland

JOHNSON, NEOLA
1929 164. Umbrellas of the Wood
165. Poison Ivy
166. White Wings

JOHNSON, PAMELA
1989 116. Portrait of Marcus
117. Myopic Girl

JOHNSON, ROBERT R.
1956 116. Morning Shadows

JOHNSON, THELMA
1987 115. See Jesse James

JOHNSTON, F.
1967 135. The Earth Is Red
136. Blue and White

JONAS, TERI
1981 102. Nesting
1985 80. Life Flow
81. Secrets of the Earth*
1987 116. Reflections
1988 111. Gingerbread Summer

EXHIBITION RECORDS

JONES, ANNA M.
1959	102.	Basket O' Gold
	103.	Colorado's Late October
1960	119.	Flower Show Arrangement
1961	173.	At Dusk
1962	159.	The Pacers, Indiana State Fair
	160.	Tropical Mood*
1963	124.	Deserted
	125.	Deep in the Forest
1964	152.	Nymphs of the Trees
1965	129.	First Flight
	130.	Gray Dawn, Neuvo Laredo, Mexico
	131.	Mother Hen and Chick
	132.	A Warm Day in May
1967	137.	Night Beat
	138.	Spring Floods
	139.	Late Summer
	140.	Autumn in My Garden
	141.	Cliff Dwellers
1968	117.	Shrove Tuesday
	118.	Poppies*
	119.	Market Place
1973	87.	Victorian Arrangement with Lace
1975	129.	Petunias in a Rose Room*
1976	128.	Homage to Heroes of Two Centuries*
1977	91.	The Letter
	78.	Side Porch
1983	98.	Fourth of July
1984	111.	Prelude to Spring*
1986	128.	Open Window
1987	117.	Treasures from the Past
1990	88.	Alice's Room

JONES, BARBARA
1980	79.	The Cauliflower*
1982	110.	Sycamore
1983	99.	Honey Wagon*

JONES, BEAUFORD FLOYD
| 1932 | 109. | Indiana Hill Side |
| | 110. | Square Rigger |

JONES, CARL E.
1954	107.	Self Portrait*
	108.	Demise and Despair
1955	107.	Patti*
	108.	Afternoon Sun
1956	117.	Piazza San Marco
	118.	The Annunciation
1975	130.	Sun Volley Vent on the Bay
	131.	Maryknoll Seminary, Los Altos Hills

JONES, CLIFFORD E.
1940	89.	Riviera at Rapallo
	90.	Tuscan Landscape
1941	80.	Fall Landscape with Figures*
	81.	T-corner
1942	109.	Pink Rider
	110.	Street Scene
	111.	Village Scene

1948	65.	Scituate Yacht Club
	66.	Beached
1950	89.	Sea Harvest
1952	98.	Main Street
	99.	Fish Market
	100.	American Baroque

JONES, DENNIS M.
1985	82.	Copper & Mums
1986	129.	Brass and Onions
	130.	Delaware County Afternoon
1987	118.	Battered Kettle and Turnips*
	119.	Spring Mill Park
1988	112.	Wayne County Afternoon*
1989	118.	Sunset, Delaware County
1990	89.	Ouabache State Park

JONES, DORIS D.
1962	161.	On 5th Street
	162.	Still Life
1963	126.	Frost
1965	133.	New England Shore
	134.	Painted Daisies
	135.	Feathered Friends
1966	82.	Cadmium Daisies

JONES, GLADYS
| 1975 | 132. | Downtown Fire 1973 |

JONES, HARRY DONALD
| 1935 | 87. | Drought |
| | 88. | Hitch-Hiker |

JONES, JACQUELYN JUDITH
1933	113.	Neysa McIllwaine
1934	93.	The African Fire Dancer
1935	89.	Julie Weber
	90.	Bobie Weber
1938	104.	Roman Athlete
	105.	Torso

JONES, KENNETH
| 1971 | 93. | Autumn on the Kankakee |

JONES, L(oran) RAYMOND
1932	111.	Pattie
1933	114.	Hoosier Farmer
1936	115.	Home Work
1938	106.	Dorothy
	314.	Busy Fingers

JONES, MELVIN T.
| 1953 | 92. | Wandering Three |
| | 93. | Winterscape |

JONES, MICHAEL L.
| 1980 | 80. | Nags Head Dunes |
| 1981 | 103. | Summer Refuge |

JONSON, JON (Magnus)
| 1931 | 122. | Bear Cubs* |

1932	112.	The Pelican Family
1933	115.	John Alden & Priscilla
1934	94.	After the Fair
	95.	Mrs. Jonson
1935	91.	Rearing Horse
	92.	Mother and Child*
1937	97.	Sigrun*
1938	107.	The Cloud
	108.	Norn
	109.	Work Horses
1939	121.	Adam and Eve
1940	91.	Dr. Edward C. Elliott
1943	105.	Ruth*
1949	72.	Mother and Child*
	73.	Lot's Wife

JORDAN, J. E.
1928   148.   Stone Grill*

JORDAN, JANE
1971   94.   Small Part of November
1973   88.   Hobbit Flowers #5
1976   129.   Impossible?
1977   92.   Past and Future Pleasures

JOSEPH, Jr., ROBERT H.
1969   100.   First Snow
1970   129.   Walton's Pond
1971   95.   Evenfall Beeches

JOSLIN, IRENE SHELLY
1990   90.   Charlie and Fanny's Girls

JOSSEL, LEONARD
1975   133.   Bottles #2

JOURDAN, FRANCES
1975   134.   Patty
        135.   Diana (The Best Years of Her Life)

JOYCE, PATRICK M.
1981   104.   Bridge at Garfield

JUBELL, ALBERT (E.)
1929   167.   Portrait of Carter Manny
        168.   Still Life
1936   112.   Merry-go-round
        113.   View of Michigan City

JUDD, PATRICIA
1973   89.   Interruption
        90.   Summer

JUERLING, GAIL
1987   120.   Turnips

JULIAN, JOHN D.
1963   127.   Bird
        128.   Torso*
1964   153.   Torso*
1967   142.   Winter Solstice*
1969   101.   Proud Forest
1971   96.   Tribute to Ryder
1975   136.   Untitled

JUNGE, CARL S.
1935   93.   Black Forest, Century of Progress
1936   114.   Dante Gabriel Rossetti
1937   98.   The Old Homestead
1938   110.   The Blue Vase
        111.   Rubber Plant
1939   122.   Fishing Boats, Boothbay Harbor
        123.   Fisherman's Shack
        124.   The Fisherman's Boat
1940   92.   Street Scene
        93.   The Farm Yard
1941   82.   Gloucester Street Scene

KACHEL, NANCY JEAN
1977   93.   Untitled

KACKLEY, SALLY ANN
1960 120.   Portrait
        121.   Self Portrait

KAESER, WILLIAM F.
1931 123.   Portraits in Oil
1936 116.   Mississippi Levee
        117.   Rubber Plant*
        118.   An Indiana Backyard
1937   99.   Begonia Plant
1938 112.   Two Plants and Fruit
        315.   An Old Barn
1939 125.   Cactus Plants*
        126.   Rosemarie Kaesar
        127.   The Big Top
1940   94.   Fall Harvest*
1942 112.   Cactus and Fruit
        113.   Flowers and Apples
        114.   The Attack
1946   97.   Riding High
1947 105.   Ready for Action
        106.   The Letter
1949   74.   She Too, Helps
1950   90.   For Us and You
1951   95.   The Green Thumb*
1952 101.   The White Mask
        102.   Dieffen Bachia
        103.   Palm and Maranta
1953   94.   Walking Iris
         95.   Ballerinas
1954 109.   George Hiding*
1956 119.   African Violets
        120.   Elephants and Clown
1957 105.   News Stand
        106.   Bird's Nest Fern
        107.   The Circus
1958 138.   Anthurium
1960 122.   On the Levee
1961 174.   Circus Elephants
1962 163.   The Final Payment
1963 129.   Circus
        130.   Carol
1964 154.   Bird Feeder
        155.   Tropical Plants*
1965 136.   American Indian Blend
1967 143.   Birdnest Fern
        144.   Calla Lily
1968 120.   Peeling Fruit
1969 102.   Indiana Farm*
1970 130.   Urban Encroachment*
1972   56.   Louisiana Bayou
         57.   Hooverville*
1973   91.   Arrangement
1974   70.   Woodland

1979   84.   Circus
1980   81.   Carmine Red
1981 105.   Daffodils
1982 111.   Self Portrait
1983 100.   Out of the Past
1985   83.   Unemployed
1986 131.   Americans All
        132.   Christmas Dinner at Grandma's
1987 121.   Woman in Pink

KAKUTANI, MITSUO
1978   76.   "D" Shape

KANE, ANN (C.)
1977   94.   Elf in the Garden*
1984 112.   Grandma's Garden Nymph
        113.   I Remember How She Listened

KANG, HELEN
1972   58.   Composition

KAPLAN, BARBARA
1972   59.   Iris
1973   92.   Woman Speaking

KARN, RON
1972   60.   My Ups and Downs

KASUBJAK, NAOMI
1971   97.   Marsh Melody
1973   93.   Study in Chartreuse

KECK, LOUISE HOPKINS (Lu)
(See Kek, Lu)
  1944 128.   Cile (Portrait)
         129.   My Boy (Portrait)
  1945   90.   Robert A. Keck
          91.   Lorene
  1946   98.   Cry-Baby
  1948   67.   Portrait of Mahala

KEENE, MAXINE M.
1968 121.   Horse I
        122.   Swinger*
1969 103.   Sorry

KEENER, ANNA ELIZABETH
1931 124.   Autumn Reflections

KEESLING, ELIZABETH
1964 156.   Mary's Attic
1968 123.   Signal Tower

KEK, LU
(See Keck, Louise Hopkins)
1959 104.   La Niche
1961 175.   Peonies

1962	164.	Study in Blue and White
1963	131.	Flowers
1964	157.	LaProcesion
1965	137.	Mother and Child
	138.	Studio Table*
1968	124.	Third & Main
	125.	Flowers #1
	126.	Flowers #2
1970	131.	First Light

KELLEY, BONNIE
1970 132. Tell Me the Story of Jesus

KELLEY, JOHN R.
1932 113. Lynn Beach, Mass.
114. Farmhouse in Normandy
115. French Hill Town
116. Wharf in Rockport, Mass.

KELLOGG, JOAN HARLAN
1985 84. Our Barn
1986 133. Image Skylight

KELLY, CLAY
1930 121. Fish Market under Delancy St. Bridge
1932 117. Grey Blanket
1933 116. A Crust of Bread
1934 96. New Orleans Court
1938 113. Free as the Air, Pittsburgh
316. Sunshine and Shadow*
1939 128. Minus Worry

KELLY, GORDON R.
1947 107. Winterlude

KELLY, JOANNE
1989 121. 1933 Duesenberg
1990 91. Silver Duzy

KELLY, RUTH T.
1933 117. Water Lilies

KELSEY, CLAUDINE PALUZZI
(See Paluzzi, Claudine)
1984 157. Leah, 1984
1988 113. Second Generation

KEMPF, (F. P.) TUD
1928 149. I Will
150. The Chief, Early Indiana
1937 100. Flower Plant
101. Head Beaver
1938 114. Indiana Indian
1939 129. Fish Sunning

KEMPF, ROMAN
1940 95. Primitive Americana

KEMPF, THOMAS M.
1925 117. The Red Book
1926 163. Still Life

KEMPTON, ELMIRA
1926 164. Out of the Attic
165. In Lick Creek
1927 172. Old Home and Garden
173. In Centerville
1928 151. A Doorway Garden, Milton, Indiana
1929 169. Spring in Milton
1930 122. From Garden Beautiful
123. The Statuetto
1937 102. Peonies and Brass
103. Before Night
1939 130. Finale, Autumn
1942 115. From Mitchell Garden

KENADY, NANCY (A.)
1957 108. Two Boats
1968 127. Blue Flowers

KENDALL, YVONNE
1934 97. Provender
1952 104. Miss B's Property

KENNEDY, MARGARET
1971 98. Study in Profile*
99. Red Maple*

KERCHEVAL, DALE (O.)
1973 94. Dale
1974 71. Farm House
72. Barn on Circle St.
1990 92. Megan

KERR, RUTH
1928 152. Portrait of Gladys*
153. Figurine
154. Portrait, Adam

KERSEY, CONNIE
1982 112. Roadside Bouquet

KERSTETTER, BARBARA (A.)
1971 100. Winter Solstice
101. The Horsetraders
1972 61. The Netmenders

KESSLER, JAMES B.
1975 137. Memory of Half Moon Bay

KESSLER, MARGARET
1982 113. Buckingham Estates, Winter
1983 101. Winter's Last Rays
102. Over the Hill*
1984 114. Liquid Sunshine
115. Old Bossy

KETCHAM, ROY ANDERSON
1931	125.	Bobby Cotton*
1932	118.	Wabash Avenue Bridge
	119.	Girl in a Blue Blanket
1935	94.	Head of a Boy
	95.	Bonnie
1936	119.	Libby
	120.	Ruth Van Sickle Ford
1937	104.	The Long Grey Line*
	105.	Sissie
	106.	Sailor
1938	115.	Aunt Tardy
	116.	The Pilgrim
	117.	Lobster
1939	131.	Portrait of Little Girl
1945	92.	'Teen Age

KETCHAM, SUSAN M.
1926	166.	Mother (Invited)*
	167.	The Headland, Maine Coast
1927	174.	Evening, Maine Coast
	175.	Ogunquit River at Full Tide
1928	155.	A Young Model

KIESS, G. M.
1929	170.	The Toy Giraffe

KIGHTLINGER, HELEN E.
1962	165.	Arrangements with Fruit
1963	132.	The Town
1964	158.	Goblets
1965	139.	Rush Hour
	140.	Willows
1967	145.	The Window
	146.	My Son
	147.	The Sisters
1968	128.	A Moment and the Artist
1970	133.	Compartments
1971	102.	Red Bouquet
	103.	A Merry-Go-Around for Cathy

KILGORE, RUPERT
1966	83.	Tragic Friday
	84.	And Found Wanting

KILLY, E(arl) JAMES
1972	62.	Watch Fob*
1973	95.	Kinetic Mechanism #9

KIMBERLING, BRUCE
1958	139.	Red Flower
	140.	Violinist
1963	133.	Portrait of the Artist
1964	159.	Rosina*
	160.	Bal Masque
	161.	The Prophet
1965	141.	La Bohemienne
	142.	The Letter

KINCAID, JAMES A.
1967	148.	Venice
	149.	The Sea
1971	104.	Through My Window
1973	96.	Summer Tears
1974	73.	Forgotten Yesterdays
1975	138.	In My Time
1976	130.	Holding On

KINDER, HAL
1969	104.	Flying Fisherman
	105.	The Tree That Came Home*

KING, CLARA W.
1931	126.	Self Portrait
1932	120.	Old Cracker Jar

KING, EDWIN W.
1931	127.	Winter

KING, EMMA B.
1925	118.	A Quiet Hour
1926	168.	The Old Bridge, Evening
	169.	Coast at Ogunquit, Maine
1927	176.	Homewards
	177.	The Farmyard
	178.	On the River
1928	156.	The Barnyard
1929	171.	Portrait of Miss K.
1931	128.	Alice

KING, HELEN A.
1930	124.	A Fishing Boat
	125.	Lincoln Park Lagoon
	126.	Lamp-Light*
1931	129.	The Corner Grocery
	130.	The Nelson Home
	131.	Jenkins' Junction
1932	121.	Breton Fishing Boats
	122.	My Studio Window*
1933	118.	July Afternoon, Fiesole
1934	98.	The Rittenhouse Home
1935	96.	Huncky Murray's Place*
	97.	Village Center
1936	121.	The Green-Front Grocery
	122.	Liz
1937	107.	Rock-Port Boats
	108.	Old-Timers (Still-life)
1938	118.	Hill Street
	119.	Morning Silhouette
	120.	Postle-Town
	317.	4 South Fourth
1939	132.	High-Tide
	133.	Granny
	134.	Meditatin' the Word*
1940	96.	Land Poor
1941	83.	Top of First Street Hill
1942	116.	Dicky's Coal Yard
	117.	Johnson's Tonsorial Parlor
	118.	Uncle Bill's Service Station

1943	106.	Morgue House
	107.	Viaduct Bridge
1944	130.	Saturday Night
	131.	Wade's Cafe for Colored
	132.	Back Yards

KING, JOHN (M.)

1925	119.	Retrospection
1926	170.	The Easter Bonnet
	171.	Mrs. W.*
	172.	Pets
1927	179.	Portrait "Brownie"*
	180.	A Little Old Lady
1928	157.	An Old Red Dress*
	158.	The Gardener
1929	172.	Memories
	173.	Portrait
	174.	Peg*
1930	127.	Mrs. Clara King, Portrait
	128.	Mrs. Virginia Meredith, Portrait
1931	132.	Jim Tree
	133.	Portrait "Fred"
1932	123.	Billy
1933	119.	Katheryn
	120.	Mrs. L. W. Sprague
	121.	Jimmie*
1934	99.	Brown House
1935	98.	Sally
	99.	Peonies
1936	123.	Girl in the Red Blouse*
1939	135.	Beulah
	136.	Portrait of Kathryn

KING, MYRA P.

| 1928 | 159. | Portrait Relief |
| | 160. | Plaster Head from Life |

KING, PATRICK

| 1979 | 85. | Water Lilies |

KING, SHARON

| 1985 | 85. | Feminine |

KINGSBURY, EDNA A.

| 1925 | 120. | Winter Day |

KINNAMAN, LISA A.

| 1983 | 103. | Calla Lily |
| | 104. | Transparent Flowers |

KINNEY, DAVID E.

1972	63.	Grandfathers Things
1973	97.	New Tenants*
	98.	Tools of Yesteryear*
1976	131.	Home Sweet Home
1977	95.	Time for Repairs

KINSEY, (Horace) GAWAYNE

| 1942 | 119. | Autumn |
| 1947 | 108. | April Snow |

KINZ, ROBERT

| 1977 | 96. | Here's Looking at Ya |

KIRBY, AMANDA ELLER

1961	176.	Potter's Bridge
	177.	Interior with White Table
1962	166.	Summer Collection
1964	162.	Still Life*
	163.	Still Life with Bottles
1965	143.	Snapdragons
1966	85.	Summer Bouquet
1967	150.	Autumn's Magic
	151.	Seated Figure
1968	129.	Deserted
	130.	Winter Bouquet
	131.	Still Life*
1969	106.	Still Life
	107.	Dahlias
1970	134.	Bird Seed*
1976	132.	Summertime
1978	77.	St. Marten Fisherman

KIRK, (Mary) ELIZABETH

1982	114.	Double Check
1984	116.	Chilean Plums
1987	122.	Italian Lemons
1990	93.	Pair of Pears

KIRKPATRICK, BLAINE E.

| 1945 | 93. | Cape Cod Dune |

KIRN, FRANCIS EDWARD

1929	175.	White Eagle
	176.	Doc. Tom
1930	129.	Robin Hood
	130.	Two Feathers
1931	134.	Rainbow's End
	135.	Meeting

KIRSCHNER, HARRY A.

| 1972 | 65. | South Side, Indianapolis |

KISHEL, RICHARD F.

1958	141.	Wedding Dance of the Whooping Cranes*
	142.	Bird
1959	105.	Quay Bird
	106.	Bull
1965	144.	Kathy
1966	86.	Birds

KISKOWSKI, ROBERT G.

1960	123.	After the Rain
1961	178.	Monnickenwerf, Marken, Holland
1964	164.	Still Life
1965	145.	View, St. Joseph River
	146.	View, Thierville, France
	147.	Head

KISNER, JOAN KING
1971 105. Seaside Solitude
1972 64. Has Anyone Here Seen Tony?
1974 74. The Critics
1975 139. The Bear Fact Is....!

KITKOWSKI, MICHAEL
1972 66. Oscar Banfi*

KITTERMAN, ALMEDA H.
1958 143. Pleasant Valley
1963 134. A Bouquet

KLAUS, MAE B.
1955 109. Delectable

KLINE, DAVID
1989 122. Bygone Days

KLINE, KEITH
1988 114. Toys in the Attic
115. Portrait of Lauren
1989 123. Picking Petunias
124. Night Light*
1990 94. Kate Reading
95. Martha's Time*

KLINTWORTH, ANNE SHIER
1981 106. Summer Roses

KNARR, THELMA L.
1962 167. Hillside Fantasy
168. A Dreamy Day
1963 135. Ode to Winter
1964 165. Demolition
1965 148. Mushrooming
1966 87. Tangled
1967 152. Off the Beaten Path
1970 135. I Remember Grandma
136. Attic Retirement*

KNECHT, KARL KAE
1927 180-A. Cartoon
1928 161. Cartoon
162. Cartoon
163. Cartoon
164. Cartoon

KNIESE, KATHERINE
1942 120. Red Buds
1943 108. Hillside in October
1944 133. Snow

KNIGHT, KENNETH E.
1987 123. Final Dignity

KOCH, ANDREA (Porter Carter)
1969 108. In April*
1970 137. In October*
1972 67. Untitled #1

KOCH, T. J.
1932 124. Thawing Snow
1934 100. Winter Afternoon
101. Wolf Creek

1973 99. Migratory Pass
100. The Outpost
1974 75. Morning Break
1976 133. Woods Edge
1978 78. Off Palmetto Dunes*
79. By Hickory Cove
1979 86. Calibogue Greenery
87. Port Royal
1980 82. Spring Baskets
83. Frosted
1981 107. Garden Friends
108. Carriage House Home
1983 105. The Reef, Harbour Island
1984 117. Eminence Front

KOCHMAN, LEE
1970 138. Dream #3 Turned Inside Out,
Version I

KORBLY, PATAREKA
1967 153. The Brown Earth

KORCZYK, ANN-MARIE
1990 96. Panther on the Prowl
97. Repose*

KORMENDI, ELIZABETH
1943 109. Still Life
110. St. Francis
111. Baptizing of Jesus
1949 75. Station of the Cross
76. Station of the Cross

KORMENDI, EUGENE
1943 112. Madonna
113. Kneeling Woman
114. Walking Woman
1946 99. St. Francis*
1947 109. Soldiers*
1949 77. Mother and Child*
78. War Mothers
79. Young Women

KRAFFT, ELTON G.
1940 97. Portrait of a Boy*
1947 110. Summer Pastures
1950 91. Man in Hockey Cap
1953 96. Still Life with Lamp
1960 124. White Steeple
1971 106. Yellow Rocket
107. The River's Edge*
1972 68. Sun on the Brush*
1973 101. Pink Steepled Church
102. Sienna Spring
1974 76. The Shriner

1975	140.	Big Country
	141.	Willow Gray Island
1977	97.	The Pink Tree
1978	80.	On a Clear Day*
1979	88.	Alpine Valley
1981	109.	Fantasia*
1985	86.	Over and under the Bridge
	87.	Mirror Lake
1988	116.	Winter Road
1989	125.	North of Monroe

KRINER, SALLY B.

1961	179.	Pansies
1965	149.	Siberian Iris
1967	154.	Iris
1968	132.	Me
1973	103.	Portrait
1975	142.	Violets
1976	134.	Friends
	135.	Forsythia
1977	98.	Forsythia
1982	115.	Roses
	116.	Lilacs
1986	134.	Geraniums
1987	124.	Summer Bouquet
	125.	White Cyclamen

KRUGER, MARILYN

1987	126.	Jack in the Pulpit
1988	117.	Lair of the Green Dragon*
1989	126.	May Apple I
1990	98.	Wild Apples

KUHN, DAVID PAUL

1972	69.	Family Dinner
	70.	Warrior
1975	143.	Fly

KULA, NANCY

1987	127.	Of Yesterday
1988	118.	Calm Before the Storm
1990	99.	La Iglesia del Santo

KULIK, LUBA

| 1970 | 139. | Metamorphosis Minus One |

KURTZ, AULIE

1950	92.	Autumn Morning, Holliday Park
1951	96.	Rice Paddy Field and Huts*
1961	180.	Moss and Trees Make a Mountain Scene
1963	136.	Ghost-Town Storm

KYSAR, BARBARA JEAN (Cotton)

1961	181.	Herman Holiday
1965	150.	Flower Study
1966	88.	Mr. Gottlieb's Chair*
1967	155.	Essence of Northampton
	156.	Composition
1971	108.	Queen Size
	109.	Composition #9
1976	136.	Autumn Landscape
	137.	In the Round
1981	110.	By the Sea

L

LABRUM, DAVID
1981	111.	Northern Cheyenne Girl
1983	106.	The Children's Nation, Will It Remain Indian?*
	107.	Rose Medicine Elk Has Told Me Many Stories About Her Past (Northern Cheyenne Series)

LACEY, BERTHA (J.)
1925	121.	Zinnias
	122.	A Bit of Florence
1926	173.	Mountain Snow
	174.	Old French Woman
	175.	Lillian
	176.	Mr. Simons
	177.	Rowena
1927	181.	Portrait
	182.	Constance
	183.	Dorothy
1929	177.	Portrait of Miss Laura Munger

LaCHANCE, GEORGES
1926	178.	Silhouette, Moonlight on the Wabash
1927	184.	Moonlight Fantasia
1929	178.	Gray Skies
	179.	A Misty Night
1931	136.	Mrs. William Wilkes
1932	125.	Late Afternoon LaJolla
	126.	Portrait Sketch
	127.	Mother Penrose
1933	122.	Old Carpet Loom
1934	102.	Hugh Tom
	103.	Autumn Colors
1935	100.	Home in the Hills
1936	124.	Run-a-way Brook
	125.	Frannie
1937	110.	Solitude
1938	121.	A Portrait Sketch
1939	137.	Adolph Shulz
	138.	In the Shade of the Old Apple Tree
	139.	Morning Light
	313.	Lonely Road*
1940	98.	The Young Equestrian
	99.	When Day Is Done
	312.	Agoin' Home*
1941	84.	Kids*
	85.	Mary*
	86.	Thin Ice
	316.	Water Lilies
1942	121.	Prelude to Winter
1943	115.	Coming Home
1944	134.	The Guardians
	135.	Little By Little
1945	94.	In the Harbor*
	95.	Over the Hills
	96.	Breaking the Trail
1946	100.	A Cape Ann Harbor
	101.	A Load for Our House
1947	111.	Rose Colored Vista
	112.	Three Workers
1948	68.	The New Day*
1949	80.	Snow-bound
1950	93.	Away to Work We Go
1951	97.	Winter Idyll
	98.	Peaceful Valley
1953	97.	Red Shoes
	98.	Hillside Pasture
	99.	The Long Road Home
1954	110.	Hard Pull
	111.	Late Afternoon
	112.	Top O' The Morning
1955	110.	Day's End
1956	121.	Peaceful Moment
	122.	Silvery Morning
1957	109.	Lazy Days*
	110.	Shades Of Evening
1958	144.	Patience Plus Age
	145.	Quiet After Storm
1960	125.	Pull in Home
1961	182.	The Flaming Oak

LACY, GENE
1946	102.	Clouds & Pineapple, Oahu, Hawaii
1947	113.	Mt. Kaya, Hawaii
1948	69.	Little Engine*
1949	81.	White River
1950	94.	Shrimpers
1951	99.	Intruders
1952	105.	Lake Freeman, Indiana*
1955	111.	Picture Frames
1986	135.	Chicago
	136.	Starfish

LAIDLAW, ROBERT C(harles)
| 1967 | 157. | Arthropod |
| 1968 | 133. | Woman in Repose |

LAIN, MAXINE
1985	88.	October Happenings
1986	137.	Fall Foliage Festival
1987	128.	Sunday School Class Picnic
1989	127.	Once Upon a Summer's Day
	128.	The County Seat
1990	100.	Busy Busy Bonnieville
	101.	A Bright New Day

LAKE, MARY E.
| 1964 | 166. | Polynesian Girl |

LAMM, WILL
1957	111.	Girl Standing
1968	134.	Still Life*
	135.	Girl with Flowers*

1969   109.   Young Girl in Landscape*
1980   84.   The Flowering*
1983   108.   The Gift
          109.   Muttley and Friend
1988   119.   Scotch Beltie

LANDON, JOY
1968   136.   Athena's Way
1969   110.   Serenity
          111.   Mist
1970   140.   Ground Fog

LANE, MARSHALL H.
1928   165.   Boats Near Kentucky

LANGLAND, HAROLD (Tuck) (R.)
1980   85.   The Bride*
          86.   Watching Woman
1981   112.   Prelude
          113.   The Letter
1982   117.   Bernadine Oliphint, Soprano*
          118.   Two Swimmers: Meet
1983   110.   Head of Venus
1984   118.   African Woman*
          119.   Swimmer: Alone
1985   89.   Venus Natarani (Dance of Creation)*
          90.   The Shower
1986   138.   Stella Maris
          139.   Moon Dial II*
1987   129.   African Girl
          130.   Facade I*
1988   120.   Femme d' Afrique*
1989   129.   African Girl
          130.   Israeli Soldier
1990   102.   Autumn*

LANGLEY, EDWARD
1927   185.   Seven Palms, Colorado Basin, California

LANPHEAR, HELEN M.
1959   107.   Collington Oaks

LARKIN, ALAN
1980   87.   My Apartment
          88.   Portrait of Cynthia*
1981   114.   Revelations

LARKIN, TERI
1982   119.   The Venus of Urbino

LARRANCE, WINNIFRED
1942   122.   May Roses
          123.   Spring Beauties
1943   116.   A Dahlia Portrait
1944   136.   Lilacs

LARROWE, HERMANN L.
1927   186.   Still Life (Zinnias)

LARSH, S. A.
1979   89.   Crystal Ball of Destiny
          90.   Elisha's Garden of Delight

LARSH, THEODORA
1925   123.   The Butterfly (Mme. Pavlowa)
          124.   Ilka
          125.   Blue Gauze
1926   179.   Group, Five Studies
          180.   A Study
          181.   Spring
1927   187.   Violets
          188.   A Study
1930   131.   One Gentleman from Indiana
          132.   Head of a Boy
          133.   Julia

LaRUE, GENE
1953   100.   Shimbashi Street Scene
1962   169.   Shimbashi Shops
1964   167.   Pool Room
          168.   Conversation
1965   151.   Still Life with Flowers
          152.   Portrait of Linda
1968   137.   Guitar Player
1969   112.   Two Nuns
1976   140.   Flower Lady
1977   99.   Turquoise Eagle
1979   91.   Reflections
1980   90.   Hauling Logs
1981   115.   Autumn Afternoon
1982   120.   Long Winter's Night
          121.   Afternoon Shadows
1983   111.   Rainy Afternoon
1988   121.   Rhino
          122.   Leavin' Town
1989   131.   April Showers
1990   103.   Indiana Barn

LASKA, JOHN (J.)
1960   126.   "Trail 1," Turkey Run State Park
          127.   Flood Scene, West Terre Haute*
          128.   Sue with Hat
1961   183.   Skating at Deming Pond
          184.   Mary*
1962   170.   The Launderesses
          171.   Sue with Flowers
          172.   Early Spring Bathers
1963   137.   Boy Reading*
          138.   Autumn's Past Adrift
1964   169.   Smoke, Steam & Steel
1965   153.   Karl with Bird*
          154.   Self Portrait
1966   89.   Deena with Cat*
1967   158.   Strip Pit #1
          159.   Strip Pit
1968   138.   Warehouse Work
          139.   Negro American
1969   113.   Tournament at Recess
          114.   Still Life

1970	141.	Young Potter
	142.	Joe's Grandmother*
1971	110.	Warm-Up-Ballet
1972	71.	Family
1973	104.	Managua, 1972
1974	77.	Jim
1975	144.	Triva Feeding Jonah
1976	138.	Jonah and His Chickens
	139	Still Life
1978	81.	Bubby
1980	89.	Cove's End
1982	122.	Marina at New Mystic
1983	112.	Panoramscopic
1984	120.	Be Well, Child
1985	91.	Lydia
1986	140.	Vigo County Court House*
1988	123.	Karen and Nate at the Lake
	124.	Milford Center, Connecticut
1990	104.	Massachusetts Cove with Lobster Pots

LATHROP, RUTH M.

1960	129.	Girl with Plums

LaTOOR, AL

1955	112.	Carousel*
	113.	Shopper's Lane
1956	123.	Bridle Path
	124.	The Faithful Village
1957	112.	Back Yard
	113.	The Sycamores
	114.	Oil Refinery
1958	146.	Shrimp Nets

LATZ, WILLIAM

1939	140.	Jackie*

LAUCK, ANTHONY

1949	82.	Saint John beside the Cross
1955	114.	Finned Form

LAURENT, ROBERT

1944	137.	Kneeling Figure
	138.	Bantam Rooster
1945	97.	Hero and Leander
	98.	Salome*
	99.	Music
1946	103.	Dawn
	104.	Anxiety
	105.	Girl and Mandolin*
1947	114.	Hen and Chicks
	115.	Girl With Doc
	116.	Mimi*
1948	70.	Duck*
	71.	Girl With Dove
1949	83.	Pitcher Plant*
1950	95.	Sue
	96.	Woman with Dove
1951	100.	Rest
	101.	Kneeling Figure
1952	106.	Pigeon*

1953	101.	Daphne*
1954	113.	Kneeling Figure
	114.	Girl with Fawn
1957	115.	Repose
1961	185.	The Birth of Venus*
1964	170.	Spring

LAUTER, FLORA

1927	189.	Spires
	190.	Two by Two
1934	104.	Winter: A Decorative Study
1937	323.	Peonies

LAVENGOOD, GINEVRA J.

1943	117.	February Gray Day
	118.	Old Faithfuls

LAWLOR, WILLIAM P.

1962	173.	Study of An Old Man

LAWRENCE, MARIA A.

1984	121.	Inspiration Point
1987	131.	Down in Brown County
1989	132.	Brown County Hills

LAWRENCE, ROBERT (D.)

1973	105.	Barn by the Bayou
	106.	Iroquois River
1981	116.	Untitled
1982	123.	Blue Harvest

LAWSON, LENORE CONDE

1936	126.	Nature's Design
	127.	Isle of Dreams
	128.	Cottage in the Dunes
	129.	Moonlight in Winter
1937	111.	Mills at Night
	112.	The Haven
	113.	Shadows in Yosemite
	324.	Tulips in My Window
1938	124.	Tranquillity
1939	141.	Balconies in Old New Orleans
	142.	Blue Monday
	143.	Covered Bridge
	144.	The Bohm Barn
1940	100.	Desolation
	101.	Under the Street Light
	102.	With the Wind
1941	87.	Chicago's Midnight Magic
	88.	Superior Shores
	317.	On My Cottage Table
1942	124.	A Song
	125.	Mansfield
	126.	Old Rail Fence

LAY, GRACE L.

1950	97.	The Blue Roof
	98.	The White Bridge
1952	107.	Clouds over Northport
1953	102.	Elevator in Winter*

1955	115.	January Thaw
	116.	Winter Chores
1956	125.	Withered Plants
	126.	Side Street
	127.	Farm Buildings
1958	147.	Condemned
1959	108.	The Money Plant
1960	130.	The River in Winter
	131.	The Red Pump
	132.	An Old Mill
1961	186.	Decadence
	187.	Areaway
1962	174.	Smoke and Sunlight
	175.	Rainy Day
	176.	Nicotina and Chinese Lanterns*
1965	155.	Winter Mood
	156.	Smog

LEBHERZ, VICKI
1983   113.   Keeping a Lid on It

LEDBETTER, DON
1989   133.   Forged Extruder

LEE, GENNIE
1981   117.   Garden Monarch

LEE, MARIE
1974	78.	Wild Roses & Spiderwort
	79.	Wood Frog & Boletus Edulis
1975	145.	Egg and Dominecke Feathers
1976	141.	October Woods
1978	82.	Allez Oop

LEE, NANCY
1990   105.   The Keeper

LEE, ROSA
1944	139.	Hat a Courting Goes
	140.	Little Boy of the Mountains
1945	100.	Little Miss Grown-up
1947	117.	Seventeen*
1948	72.	Lady in Blue
1951	102.	Dolly and Bozo
1952	108.	One White Rose
	109.	Kazu
1958	148.	Golden Days
1960	133.	Storm at Sea
1961	188.	Lady Clown
1962	177.	Summer Model
1964	171.	Star of Cape Cod Playhouse
1965	157.	A Walk in the Woods

LEE, SHURLE
1967	160.	Soft is the Morn
	161.	In the Stillness
	162.	One Night*

LEECH, ANN
1971   111.   Circle with Blue Line

1975	146.	Relief with Stripes
	147.	Super Stripe*
1980	91.	Fantasy Mountain

LEFF, HENRY H.
1987   132.   Fine Tuning

LEFFEL, DOROTHY S.
1972	72.	Garden Flowers
1974	80.	Molly's Garden
	81.	Jane's Garden
1975	148.	Amy's Garden

LEFFLER, D. R.
1978   83.   Still Life for Two Carlos

LEHMAN, DIANE TRACY
1990   106.   Best Friend

LEHMAN, MAHREA CRAMER
1938	125.	Dimples
	126.	Mister
	127.	Missus
	318.	The Red Dress
1940	103.	Gold
	104.	Silver
	105.	The Shadow
1941	89.	Mother and Daughter
1942	127.	Music
	128.	The Shadow of the Cross
1943	119.	Sheltered
	120.	Scold
	121.	Daisies Won't Tell
1944	141.	Art Appreciation*
	142.	Critic*
	143.	Mumsy
1945	101.	Few Guest Artists*
	102.	My Mom
	103.	My Cookie Dunkers
1946	106.	Portrait of Paul Lehman
	107.	The Bombsight
1948	73.	See Em
1950	99.	It's Me
	100.	Young Man
1951	103.	Blonde in Black and Blue
	104.	Poetry Reading

LEICH, CHESTER
1937	117.	Pine Grove at Holland
	118.	Village Street, Bedford
	119.	Norwegian Village
	120.	In Connecticut

LEIGH, HOWARD
1925	126.	A Back Canal
1928	166.	Pont a Avignon
	167.	Aqueduct, Segovia, Spain
	168.	Head of a Girl
	169.	Pont du Gard, Avignon

	170.	Arch of Septimus Severus, Rome
	171.	Old Cloisters, Palermo
	172.	Rue do L'Epicerie, Rouen
1929	180.	Gate to Utrera, Spain
	181.	The Gypsy Quarter, Setenil, Spain
	182.	Roman Bridge, Ronda, Spain
	183.	Head of French Girl
1931	137.	Chloe
	138.	Portrait of Anna Sargent Smith*
1932	128.	Peruvian Lady

LEIST, DORIS
1960	134.	On the Porch
	135.	Fitting Room
1962	178.	Jenny
	179.	Dream
	180.	Pomeroy

LEMBERG, RICHARD
1978	84.	Nutcracker
1979	92.	This Bomb Makes Rainbows
	93.	Say What
1980	92.	Sundial*
1981	118.	Living Rainbow
1982	124.	Her Rainbow
	125.	His Rainbow

LENHARDT, M. JOHN
1942	129.	The Organ Grinder

LENNART, ESTHER
1941	90.	Woods in Spring

LENNOX, JOHN C.
1989	134.	Self Portrait
1990	107.	Imperial Dragon

LENTZ, JAMES CURTIN
1972	73.	Through the Looking Glass*
	74.	Sara
1973	107.	Monroe County
1974	82.	Rorschach Landscape
	83.	George
1976	142.	Double Sol
1977	100.	Three Blue Ducks*
1978	85.	The Historian
	86.	Chiaroscuro
1979	94.	Vanity Fair*
1980	93.	Boston Pop
	94.	Dangling Conversation
1981	119.	First Mate
1982	126.	Meeting Adjourned*
	127.	Portrait of Mr. Floyd J. Campbell
1983	114.	Red-headed King Fisher
	115.	Cape Brehal
1984	122.	From Greyhavens Farm
	123.	Cut Flowers
1985	92.	Cypress Point*
1986	141.	735 Chartre Street*
	142.	Buddha and Brass
1987	133.	Rose*

1988	125.	Turnburry, No. 10
	126.	Cooling Out
1989	135.	Our Lady
1990	108.	Union Stationaries*
	109.	Dahlias

LENTZ, VIVIAN (C.)
1973	108.	Fall Creek
1975	149.	Pisces Person
1977	101.	Patty
1978	87.	Susie
	88.	Fall Creek, July
1980	95.	Susie Pence
1983	116.	The Cousins
1984	124.	Lick Creek
1986	143.	Reflections, Ripples
1987	134.	Jim
1990	110.	Sausalito
	111.	Dare Devil

LEONARD, BEATRICE
1929	184.	Mischief

LEONARD, GERALD L.
1979	95.	Fission Reactor

LEONARD, JAMES B.
1968	140.	Old Man with a Beard

LETT, GLADYS B.
1942	130.	A Mid-Night Lunch
1945	104.	Before Rationing

LEVITON, FLORIE (Florence)
(See Williams, Florie)
1971	112.	Owl III
	113.	Old City of Jerusalem
1990	112.	The Settler
	113.	A Little Fishy

LEWIS, BETSE
1954	115.	Self Portrait

LEWIS, ELEANOR
1972	75.	East on Indiana 2
1973	109.	Boxes
	110.	Old Friends
1974	84.	High Rise, Low Rent
	85.	Indiana Limestone*
1975	150.	Tammy
1977	102.	Collection of the Artists
	103.	Matter of Life and Death*
1980	96.	Down-to-Earth-Tones
1981	120.	Oh, What a Beautiful Stump
1982	128.	Tammy
1983	117.	Tiffany
1984	125.	Inside, Out
1986	144.	Sculptor Hermann Gurfinkel*
1987	135.	Old Friends
1988	127.	Curio Crystal

1989 136. Painting, Teaching: Our Living
         Legacy*
1990 114. French Creek

LEWIS, JOHN C(hase)
1954 116. Jewell School House
1955 117. The Red Coat
1965 158. Judith
     159. Janet
     160. Girl on a Stool*
1966 90. The Central Nervous System*

LEWIS, LORENE S.
1950 101. The Mandarin Coat

LEWTON, BONNIE
1968 141. Landscape #1
     142. Winter Landscape
     143. Boy
1970 143. Seated Figure
     144. Mirkwood
1972 76. Coward's Way Out
1973 111. Geraniums IV

LEY, MARY HELEN
1943 122. Spring's Corsage

LIAS, TOM
1953 103. Subjectivity
     104. The Yellow Vase

LICHTENSTEIN, ESTHER FRIEND
1954 117. Very Old and Proud
1955 118. Emily

LIDDELL, ALBERTA B.
1931 139. The Old Home
1933 123. My Studio Window

LIENERT, MARY (Smyrnis)
(See Smyrnis, Mary)
1958 149. Sandy
1964 172. Pleasant View*
1965 161. Portrait Sandy

LIEPSE, WILLIAM
1934 105. Along the Roadside
     106. Orange and Yellow Flowers
     107. The Pink Apron
1935 101. Flowers
     102. Gladiolas*

LIESS, TIM
1987 136. Sounds of Sunset
     137. December Moods

LIETZ, MATTIE
1934 108. John Nolf
1935 103. Sky Eagle
1936 130. By Our Window

1937 114. Indian Still Life
     115. Garden Bouquet*
     116. Dean
1938 128. Flower Arrangement
     129. Hints o' Sunshine
1939 145. Portuguese Fishermen
     315. Happy Hollow
1940 106. Sea Gleaners
     313. June Morning
1941 91. Eager Anticipation
1942 131. Humming Bird
1943 123. Lifting Fog
1946 108. Old Sugar Maple
1947 118. January*
     119. Flying Fishes Play
1948 74. A White Blanket
1949 84. The Road Home
1950 102. Leaves Falling
     103. Net Mender's Resting Time*
1951 105. After Chores
1955 119. Ever Tomorrow

LIGOCKI, MICHAEL
1957 116. Marty
1962 181. Rose Hlodnicki

LIGOCKI, RAY
1958 150. Letitia
     151. Lavonne
1962 182. Ann
1963 139. Lavonne

LIGOCKI, REGINA
1963 140. Afternoon at the Beach

LILLIE, ELLA FILLMORE
1939 146. Sugar House, Vermont
     147. Vermont Landscape
     148. 30 Below
     149. Road Home
     150. Light Snow
1940 107. Lym Hannie Fish House
     108. Old Wood
     109. The Beam Trawler
     110. The Open Door
1941 92. Champlain Valley
     93. Twin Pines
     94. Unspoiled Vermont
     95. Where Junie Lives
1942 132. Nine-O'clock
     133. Marble Head
     134. Waiting
     135. Old Town Square
     136. April Morning
1943 124. Winter Fruit
1944 144. Nadine
     145. Gloucester Houses*
     146. Rolling Hills
1945 105. High on a Hill*
     106. Tranquility
     107. New Harbor, Maine

1946	109.	Maine*
	110.	Night
	111.	Lane to the Lake
1947	120.	The Trespasser
	121.	Free Enterprise
1950	104.	Atlanta to the Sea*
	105.	Pink Chapel, St. Simon's Island*
	106.	Siamese Oak, Sea Island*
	107.	Tabby Ruins Retreat Plantation
1952	110.	Madrugada*
	111.	Ancient Bridge, Mexico*
	112.	Mexican Rhythm*
1954	118.	Coon in the Cornpatch
	119.	The Secret Place
1958	152.	Vermont
	153.	Slow Motion
	154.	Winter Work*
	155.	Long Trail
1959	109.	Lupita, LaLavandera
	110.	Lago De Patzcuaro

LIMBACH, RAY
1975 151. Depression Playground

LIMBAUGH, LORENE
1973 112. Sutton Farm
1974 86. The Skojac Home on Sherman Drive

LIND, JENNY
1973 113. Land of Challenge
 114. Walrus Dance*

LINDBERG, ARTHUR F.
1979 96. C'ulture?*

LINDLEY, AUDNA J.
1952 113. Winter Warning

LINDWALL, MARIE
1957 117. Sand, Sun & Shadows of the Dunes

LINK, JOHN J.
1962 183. Father J. J. Gruetter

LITTELL, JUNE
1985 93. Fiesta Holiday
1986 145. Cities' Roots
 146. Tapestry

LITTLE, SHIRLEY (A.)
1970 145. Old Chair with Mums
1973 115. Joy
1976 143. Still Life
1982 129. Joy
1984 126. Roses

LLOYD, ROSEMARY
1968 144. Summer Bouquet
 145. Studio Arrangement

| 1971 | 114. | Winter Wonderland |
| 1973 | 116. | Peace on Earth |

LOBSIGER, EVELYN
1978 89. Hoosier Hysteria
1979 97. Frames

LOBSTEIN, MIRIAM
1975 152. Out of Myself
 153. Shofar

LOCHMUELLER, MICHAEL
1965 162. The Intruder

LOCKER, THOMAS
1965 163. Rising of the Cold Dew

LOCKHART, GLADA TRENCHARD
1931 140. Yellow Roses
 141. Dove with Calla Lilies
1936 131. The Blue Vase
 132. Still Life Group
 133. Still Life
1937 121. Gladiolas
 325. Dune Flowers
1938 130. Indiana Wild Flowers
1940 111. The Bronze Figure

LOCKMAN, ROBERT (H.)
1946 112. Spared
1988 128. Savannah

LOGSDON, NICH(olas)
1974 87. Metamorphal Appleton
 88. Anascoca

LOHMAN, ROBERT
1952 114. Horseback

LOKOTZKE, JOSEPHINE
1960 136. Red and White Bouquet

LOMASNEY, ETHEL
1945 108. Zinnias
 109. Autumn Leaves
1959 111. Autumn Bouquet

LONG, ESSIE
1930 136. A Flower Garden
1933 124. The Boathouse
 125. Industry along the Monon
1942 137. Light and Age
1944 147. Closed for Duration
1947 122. Ohio River Tugboat
1948 75. Bourbon Street, New Orleans

LONSFORD, FLORENCE (Hutchinson)
1959 112. Chrysanthemums
1967 163. Mining Town
1968 146. Inlet
1974 89. Lenore

1986	147.	Wild Flower Walk
	148.	Regatta

LOOP, LEOTA W(illiams)

1925	127.	Through the Maples
1926	182.	After the Shower
1927	191.	The Birds' Retreat
	192.	Old Glory on Sycamore Pike
1929	185.	White Peonies
1930	134.	Calla Lilies
	135.	Hollyhocks
1931	142.	Peonies
1932	129.	Peonies
1933	126.	Marigolds
	127.	Burning Bush
1934	109.	Peonies
1935	104.	Autumn's Offering
	105.	Phlox on the Studio Steps
1936	134.	Hollyhocks
	135.	Heavenly Blue
1938	131.	Indian Summer
1939	151.	Heavenly Blue Morning Glories*
	152.	Peonies
	314.	The First Snow
1940	112.	Blue Morning Glories and Pewter
1941	96.	Quietly Tucking Us In
	318.	Heavenly Blue and Red Bowl
1942	138.	Bluebells in Bloom
1944	148.	Heavenly Blue Morning Glories
	149.	Regal Lillies
	150.	Angel Trumpets
1945	110.	November
	111.	Red Magnolias
1946	113.	Angel Trumpets*
1947	123.	Delphiniums
	124.	Melting Snow
1948	76.	One Winter Day
1949	85.	Winter Wonderland
1951	106.	Mums in Old Copper
1952	115.	Marigolds
1953	105.	Angel Trumpets*
1954	120.	Hollyhocks
	121.	Zinnias in Copper
1955	120.	Summer Wild Flowers
1956	128.	Red Asters and Petunias
1957	118.	Lilacs
1959	113.	Summer Wild Flowers

LOPEZ, H. COURET

1969	115.	Evelyn

LOUDERBACK, WALT(er)

1931	143.	Gypsy Band, Spain
	144.	Cafe Singers, Malaga, Spain
	145.	Threshing in Andalucia, Spain
1932	130.	The Potters of Palma de Mallorca
	131.	Spanish Fishermen in Port
	132.	Fish Wives, Malaga, Spain
	133.	Drying Sails, Valencia, Spain
	134.	Production of French Art

1933	128.	Lottery Ticket Venders
	129.	Entrance of the Picadore
	130.	Luck of Some People
	131.	Wine Delivery
	132.	Traffic Problems
	133.	Fisherman's Return
	134.	Lunch Time in Algiers
1934	110.	British Fleet at Pollensa
	111.	The Loafers
	112.	Flirtation
	113.	Morning Chores
	114.	Rainy Market Day in Madrid
	115.	The Fruit Peddler's Lunch
	116.	The Unemployed of Spain
1935	106.	Spanish Woman
1937	122.	New Telephone Co. Exchange
1938	132.	Barges at Work
	133.	Seine Fisherman
	134.	Sunday Afternoon, Suburbs of Paris
	319.	My Son*
1939	153.	Mediterranean Fisherman
	154.	Wind and Spain
1940	113.	Morning Concert, Aix Les Thermes, France*

LOUNSBURY, LAVERGNE I.

1940	114.	Dunes Glory
1941	97.	Dunes in Winter

LOVE, DANE L.

1985	94.	Oregon

LOVE, EMMA JEAN

1953	106.	Sunflowers
	107.	Industry

LOVE, JOAN S.

1984	127.	The Great Progenitor

LOVETT, PEGGY

1976	144.	Just Anglin' off the Old Pad, Folks, for a Little Midnight Rumble
	145.	Untitled
1979	98.	Untitled*
	99.	Untitled
1982	130.	Bridge II

LOWE, DON

1989	137.	Apostile Island, Winter

LOWENGRUB, CAROL

1985	95.	Black White Gray #2
1986	149.	Black White Gray III
	150.	Garden
1987	139.	Woods

LOWES, SADIE H.

1932	135.	Still Life
	136.	Zinnias
	137.	Asclepias

1933	135.	Emily Weaver Joy
1934	117.	Helen
	118.	Heirlooms
1935	107.	First Snow
1937	123.	Spring
1938	135.	Still Life
1939	155.	On the Table
	156.	The White Bird
1940	115.	Still Life
1941	98.	Still Life
1942	139.	Still Life
	140.	Still Life with White Bird
1943	125.	Still Life
	126.	The White Cat

LUCAS, GEORGETTA

1954	122.	Arachne
1956	129.	Evening Walk
1962	184.	Queen Anne's Lace
	185.	Fall Composition
1963	141.	Leaves and Ivy
1964	173.	A Touch of Moonlight
1965	164.	Ethereal Season
1967	164.	Autumnal Arabesques
1968	147.	Flowers Unnamed
	148.	Jugs and Jars #2
1970	146.	Chawanders
1972	77.	Wait For No Man
1987	138.	Mythical Tales
1988	129.	Hiding
	130.	Unlatched Coop

LUEDEMANN, DOROTHY

| 1947 | 125. | Fisherman |

LUND, BELLE JENKS

| 1926 | 183. | Sand Dune Blow Out |
| 1927 | 193. | Glimpse of Dunes |

LUNDY, ROBERT

| 1969 | 116. | Entrada I |

LUNN, W(illiam) H. W.

| 1967 | 165. | The Musician |

LUPRESTO, JOYCE M.

| 1987 | 142. | Sun Dance |

LURIE, BARBARA

| 1952 | 116. | Rhythm |

LUSHER, SUZANNE E.

1985	96.	Sunday Afternoon
1987	140.	Grandma and Grandpa Price
	141.	Maple Melody II

LUTHER, W. STEVEN

| 1972 | 78. | Circle in Arch* |

LUTTRELL, KAREN MILLER

| 1985 | 97. | "The Light Is the First of the Painters," Emerson |

LUTZ, MARIE E.

1951	107.	Early Spring
1952	117.	Blossom Time
	118.	Deserted
1955	121.	Boathouse
1958	156.	Trumpet Flowers
	157.	Old Timers
	158.	Sentinels of Deer Lick Lane
1959	114.	Sunflower Still Life
	115.	Landscape Composition
	116.	New Neighbor
1961	189.	Old Man Cave, Athens, Ohio
1962	186.	Fish Boy
1963	142.	Stone Quarry*
	143.	Leaves and Berries
1968	149.	Trees
1969	117.	Composition #2
	118.	Yesterday's Memories
1970	147.	Dancing Shadows
1971	115.	A Little Acorn Grew
1973	117.	Misty Morn

LUTZ, TIMOTHY GEORGE

| 1975 | 154. | Rearwindow |

LUZZI, MARTHA M.

| 1966 | 91. | After the Storm |

LYBARGER, JOHN T.

| 1971 | 116. | The Jeffersonian |

LYLES, JAMES L.

| 1978 | 90. | Palm |

LYNCH, JAMES

1972	79.	Mourning Dream
1987	143.	The Workman
	144.	The Musician

LYNCH, KATHLEEN M.

| 1961 | 190. | Sanibel |

LYNN, KAY (Kathryn)

| 1962 | 187. | Carnival |
| 1968 | 150. | Life |

LYON, CHARLES K.

| 1967 | 166. | Transfiction |

LYTLE, JOYCE EDWARDS

| 1989 | 138. | Healing Plant I |

M

MacCOLLUM, ELIZABETH GETZ
1940	116.	Judy
	117.	Dr. J. Ambrose Dunkel
1941	99.	Sissy
	100.	The Art Critic
1942	141.	Handy Andy
	142.	Janet
1943	127.	Dr. Roy Ewing Vale
1944	151.	Col. Reed G. Landis
	152.	Karen
	153.	Mrs. L. M. Ceaser
1945	112.	Betty
1946	114.	Major Ralph Stevens
1948	79.	Mary Elizabeth
1949	88.	Randy

MacDANIEL, DONALD L.
1962	188.	Winter Landscape II
	189.	Winter Landscape III
1967	173.	Whitewater Canal

MacGINNIS, H. R.
1930	144.	New Hampshire*
	145.	Jane Erwin
1931	149.	Jane
1932	138.	New Hampshire Rocks
1933	138.	Flowers
	139.	Silver Kimoni
1934	119.	Delphinium

MacINNIS, PATTY
| 1984 | 130. | One of John's Toys |
| 1988 | 131. | Chim-Chimney |

MACK, RONALD P.
1981	125.	Pyramid
1982	131.	Concaved Images
1983	123.	Silver Onions
1984	131.	Blue Shadows
1987	146.	Wedding Vase
	147.	Table Delight
1988	132.	Reflections
1989	143.	Silver Pots
1990	121.	Rocklane

MacKENZIE, JACQUELINE (Jackie)
1987	148.	Coconut Concession
1989	144.	Harvest Time
1990	115.	Greenhouse Series, Caladiums

MacMILLAN, DAVID
1958	159.	City Roofs
	160.	Stein And Pitcher
1959	117.	Still Life With Shield

MacNABB, ELEANOR
| 1967 | 174. | Night Engagement |
| | 175. | Gay Blooms |

MACOMBER, MICHAEL D.
1979	101.	Tulips
1980	101.	822
	102.	823*

MacPHERSON, MARIE M.
| 1930 | 146. | Mountaineers* |
| 1932 | 139. | Chastity |

MacPHERSON, MARIE R.
| 1952 | 119. | Homeward Bound |
| | 120. | Going Home |

MADINGER, SELENA
| 1953 | 108. | Antique Cooky Jar |
| | 109. | Still Life with Fruit |

MAGAW, JEANNE
| 1978 | 92. | Goddess Serpet '78' |

MAGAW, WILLIAM (P.)
1975	160.	Swinging Duo
1976	146.	Frontiers
	147.	Fountain of Roses

MAGLINGER, CALVIN
| 1971 | 123. | Bottom Land |

MAGNER, HELEN (E.)
1926	184.	The Little Pool
1927	194.	The Greenhouse
1929	186.	The Foundry
1930	137.	Coal Yard
	138.	The Green Pool
1944	157.	Spring
1956	130.	The Porch

MAHLER, ANNEMARIE
| 1984 | 132. | Tree |

MAHONEY, MURIEL
| 1952 | 121. | Lighthouse on Cape Cod |

MAINES, MARIE
| 1980 | 103. | Finity I |

MAKIELSKI, BRONISLAW A.
| 1925 | 128. | Landscape |
| 1926 | 185. | Clouds |

MAKIELSKI, LEON A.
| 1926 | 186. | Portrait Study |
| | 187. | In the Studio |

| 1940 | 118. | M'Shadow and M'Shoes |
| | 119. | Pink Peonies |

MAKIELSKI, THEODORA B.
1940	120.	Before Sundown
1941	321.	Dull Day Cheer
1948	80.	Summer at Notre Dame

MALICOAT, PHIL(ip)
1931	150.	Betty
	151.	Provincetown Fishing Boats
1932	140.	The White Bowl
	141.	Dusk

MANETTA, EDWARD
1955	122.	Skyline
1956	131.	Industrial Backyard
1961	191.	Energy and Smoke

MANGUS, BARBARA
| 1971 | 124. | Green Summer |

MANN, (Jr.), JOHN (L.)
1952	122.	Wabash Fisherman
1953	110.	Kaleidoscopic Kilns
1962	190.	Old North School
1963	144.	January Moment
	145.	Sycamore over Sand Creek
1965	165.	Nostalgic Myth
	166.	Solitude
1974	93.	Early American Prosperity

MAPEL, JEAN
| 1987 | 149. | The Toppled Vase |

MARCHETTI, VASCO
| 1929 | 187. | Flower Panel |

MARINE, RICHARD (M.)
1957	123.	Evening in the Woods
1961	192.	Willows by Moonlight
	193.	Autumn Shades
1962	191.	Silver Creek Bridge
1975	161.	Song of the Eagle

MARKER, ANNA S.
| 1927 | 195. | Dune Woodland |
| 1929 | 188. | Still Life |

MARKEY, PATRICIA CONDO
| 1969 | 119. | Anarchist |
| 1970 | 148. | Croesus |

MARKS, ELIZABETH
| 1970 | 149. | October Poppies |

MARLOW, CHERI
| 1979 | 102. | The Journey |
| 1981 | 126. | White Masked Thief |

MARLOW, LUCY DRAKE
1933	143.	Mrs. Peter D. Overfield
	144.	Blossie
1934	123.	The Teacher
1935	109.	Close Quarters
1936	136.	Mother*
1937	124.	Yaqui Indian Woman
	326.	Glozinia
1939	157.	Anna May
	158.	Ocotilla and Mexican Grass
1940	121.	Marigolds
	122.	Petunias
1941	101.	Portrait of Mary Cecile Duncan
	320.	California Poppies
1942	148.	Picacho Peak, Arizona

MARSDEN, HELEN M.
1979	106.	Companion to Owls
1982	132.	The Artist in the World
1984	133.	No Hunters Allowed

MARSH, ALIDA
| 1933 | 145. | Bachelor Buttons |

MARSH, J. P.
| 1928 | 173. | Snails |

MARSH, SUSAN R.
1925	129.	Classic Madison
1926	188.	Spring and the River Nearby
1929	189.	Miniatures
1932	142.	A Mediterranean Vision
1933	146.	Peonies
1938	136.	Episode of County Fair

MARSISCHKE, FLONA (A.)
1954	123.	Flowers of the Field
1960	137.	Nature's Bouquet
1964	179.	Still Life with Oil Pot
	180.	Still Life with Highbush Cranberry

MARTENS, CHRISTIANE T.
| 1972 | 83. | Landscape 747 |
| | 84. | Musical Landscape |

MARTIN, G(ail) W.
1950	108.	Pomegranate Still Life
	109.	Still Life
1951	109.	Driftwood Still Life*
	110.	Helianthus
1952	123.	Under the "El"
	124.	Landscape

MARTIN, JAN R.
| 1979 | 103. | Model for Large Sculpture* |

MARTIN, LORINE
1968	151.	Whispering Waves
1971	125.	Falling Shadows
1976	148.	Downtown
1989	145.	High Tide

MARTIN, MARY E.
1958	161.	Bob
1960	139.	"Flo" Portrait
	140.	Fishing Haven
	141.	Florida Hibiscus
1961	194.	Ann
1967	176.	Farm Buildings
	177.	Girl with Hat
1971	126.	Afternoon in a Forest
1973	123.	Petunias in Blue Vase

MARTIN, MICHAEL
1978	93.	The Sentinel
	94.	Old Homestead*
1979	104.	Brushrow
	105.	Punkin*
1980	104.	Circle of Friends
	105.	Farm Boy*
1981	127.	Spring Snow
1982	133.	Easy Rider
	134.	Sesame II
1983	124.	Another View*
	125.	Did I Tell You That My Chicken Is Dead?*
1984	134.	Long Way Home
	135.	Morning Mist
1985	100.	Down on the Rocks Where the Waves Thunder, the Green Curl Over and the White Curl Under
	101.	Sentinel*
1987	150.	Melissa
	151.	Emily

MARTIN, ROBERT E.
1975	162.	Fruit Basket

MARTIN, WES
1989	146.	Summer Breeze

MARTIN, WILLIAM EDWARD
1968	152.	Decanter
	153.	Eggs
1969	120.	Mateus

MARTINDALE, MONTA V.
1935	110.	Saw Mill along the I. C.

MASCHER, HERMINE (E.)
1974	94.	From Our Deck
1976	149.	In Perpetuity
	150.	Rustication
1978	95.	Lahaina Beach, Hawaii
	96.	Ravages of Time
1980	106.	Treasure Hunt
1981	128.	Roof Tops
1982	135.	New Bridge, Ronda, Spain

MASON, GLADYS
1934	124.	In Shanty Town

MASSEY, DOROTHY HARDIN
1960	138.	Blue River Bridge
1961	195.	Girl at Work
1962	192.	On the Wharf
1963	146.	Amber Woods
	147.	Figures and Sky
1964	181.	Dunes & Wind

MAST, GERALD
1930	139.	Portrait of Lois S.*
	140.	Ideal Head
	141.	Nude Standing
1931	152.	Drawing
	153.	Drawing

MAST, S. P.
1926	189.	The Road to London

MATCHETTE, ADA B.
1956	132.	The Striped Tablecloth
1957	124.	Autumn Gold
	125.	October Reflections
1959	123.	Treaty Creek
1960	142.	Autumn Color
1961	196.	Sunlight and Shadow
1963	148.	Midsummer
1965	167.	Symphony of Spring

MATHIS, A. W.
1986	151.	Kick the Can
1987	152.	Yuppie Up Town
1988	133.	The Old Neighborhood

MATHIS, RUTH
1964	182.	In The Garden
	183.	Beckman's Place
	184.	Back of Main Street
1965	168.	Golden Weeds

MATTHEW, NEIL E.
1962	193.	Lake Constance Landscape

MATTHEWS, ROBERT
1980	107.	Spring*

MATTICE, HELEN
1932	143.	Billie
	144.	Forrest
1933	142.	Mary Adele McNally

MATTINGLY, TOMMIE (Mary Agnes)
1960	143.	Sisters
1962	194.	Joe

MATTISON, CATHERINE (M.)
1945	115.	Marian's Stove*
1946	115.	Hyannisport
1947	126.	Conservatory*
1948	81.	Spring Forecast

1949	89.	"Of a Stone, a Leaf, a Door and of all the Forgotten Faces"
	90.	The Music Strange*
1950	110.	Flower Setup
1951	111.	Flower Panel
1952	125.	The Shrimp Plant
	126.	Still Life with Flowers
	127.	Picnic Ground
1954	124.	Flower Arrangement*
	125.	Landscape
1957	126.	The Shell
	127.	Landscape
1960	144.	Trackside
	145.	Late Gathering*

MATTISON, DONALD M.

1936	137.	Carnival
	138.	Storm
	139.	Davico Sisters
1942	149.	Portrait of Mrs. Earl Barnes
	150.	Summer
	151.	The Island of Hatteras, N. C.
1944	158.	War Show
	159.	River Landing
	160.	Portrait of Miss Madden
	161.	Good-by
1945	116.	Portrait of a Young Girl*
	117.	Parade*
1946	116.	Concert
1947	127.	Kite Flyers
	128.	Saugatuck Landscape
	129.	Portrait*
1948	82.	Conversation
	83.	Skaters
	84.	Summertime
1949	91.	Hatteras
1950	111.	Low Tide
1951	112.	Portrait of Julie*
1952	128.	Family Group*
1953	111.	Morning
1954	126.	Portrait
	127.	Costume Party
1955	123.	Friends
1956	133.	Friends
	134.	Seaside
	135.	For of Such*
1957	128.	Portrait of Mary
	129.	Portrait

MAXAM, ROBERT A.

1989	147.	Early Light*
	148.	Apples

MAXWELL, C(onstance) V.

1938	137.	I, Jerry
1950	112.	End of the Garden

MAY, MARION E.

1946	117.	House Mountain
	118.	Old Friends
1947	130.	Monday

MAYBERRY, ELIZABETH S.

1982	136.	Going
1983	126.	Little Kitty & Sis
1985	102.	Spencer
1987	153.	Alexandria

MAYBERRY, JOE (Joseph)

1970	150.	Coffee and Tea
1973	124.	Big Brown Jug
	125.	Pour Power
1975	163.	Mousetrap
1976	151.	Iron in the Round
1977	107.	Patina
	108.	Flea Market
1980	108.	Pier Patterns
	109.	Methodist Church, Wexford, Ireland
1981	129.	Cameo House
1982	137.	Pitcher Personalities
	138.	Once It Was a Wagon
1983	127.	Tin Dominoes
	128.	The Elevator*
1984	136.	Oshkosh B'gosh
	137.	Cat Nap
1985	103.	Have You Looked in the Barn?
1986	152.	Back Door to Three Rivers
1987	154.	This & That
	155.	Milk Glass Medley
1988	134.	Inside Out
1989	149.	Campaign Torches & Mousetrap
	150.	Yo-Ho's
1990	122.	Calico on Calico

MAYER, HENRIK (M.)

1935	111.	Gossiping Wives, Monhegan Island
	112.	Snow Maiden*
	113.	North Wind, Monhegan Island
1941	102.	Pony Trek
	319.	Flowers
1942	152.	Afterglow
	153.	Clara*
	154.	Hallowe'en Carnival
1943	130.	March Wind
	131.	Regatta
	132.	Portrait Julie*
1944	162.	Pastoral Indiana*
	163.	Picnic New Haven
	164.	Bathers*
1945	118.	Clam Diggers
	119.	Portrait, Jessie
	120.	Beachcombers
1946	119.	Portrait, Mr. I. Richard Wagner
	120.	Connecticut River Wharves*
1947	131.	Capt. Caleb and Patience*
	132.	North Cove
1949	92.	Lynde Point Bell
	93.	Summer Tapestry*
1951	113.	Decoys*
	114.	Sentinels

1952	129.	Interval
	130.	Hunter and His Dog
	131.	Portrait of Jim
1956	136.	Per Astra
	137.	Julie*
	138.	River, Flow Gently*
1957	130.	September Sun

MAYES, ANN

| 1982 | 139. | Home Sweet Home |

MAYS, SUZANNE

1986	153.	In the Window
	154.	Summer Shadows
1987	156.	Another Day
	157.	His and Hers
1988	135.	Rue de Monvinet
1989	151.	Waiting
	152.	L'entree
1990	123.	107 Buckeye Street

McALLISTER, SUE

| 1983 | 118. | Wonderland |
| 1985 | 98. | Gold Fish Bowl |

McAULIFFE, MICHELLE

| 1981 | 121. | Rock Concert |

McBRIDE, JAMES (J.)

1948	77.	Valley With Barns
1953	119.	January Hunt
1955	142.	Lonely House*
	143.	Rooftops
1956	156.	Rural Harmony*
	157.	Mrs. West*
1957	119.	Hoosier Hampshires
	120.	Afternoon Patterns
1958	181.	City Snow*
1959	118.	Sneider's Shack
	119.	The Two Nuns
	120.	Evening's Preview
1960	157.	January Rain*
	158.	Morning Thaw
	159.	Holy Man
1961	206.	Winter Thaw
	207.	Rain in Fort Wayne
	208.	Jamacian Musician
1962	220.	February Homecoming
1963	159.	Lonely House
	160.	February Farm
1965	187.	Farm Scene
	188.	Apple Orchard
1966	92.	Farm Patterns
1967	167.	Summer Mountain Rain
	168.	Glen Valley, Ind.
1968	154.	Street Scene
	155.	Valley Patterns
1969	121.	High View*
	122.	Hill City
1970	151.	Approaching Storm*

1971	117.	Autumn Chores
1972	80.	Carriage House
1973	118.	Winter's Rest
1974	90.	Hoosier Classified*
1975	155.	Remembrance Imagery*
	156.	Village Patterns
1976	152.	By the Bay
	153.	Afternoon Shadows*
1977	104.	Abandoned Boat, Ireland
	105.	Rock of Cashel, Ireland
1978	165.	Wayne Junction
1980	97.	Moongrass
	98.	Whitehurst House

McCAIN, SUSAN

1958	182.	Strange Gift, Twenty-Three
	183.	Strange Gift, Sixteen
	184.	Strange Gift, Four

McCARTY, ARTHUR L.

1953	120.	Self Portrait
	121.	Negro Head
1954	143.	Still Life with Onion

McCARTY, PEGGY

1983	119.	Self Portrait with Straw Hat*
1984	128.	The Artist's Studio
1989	139.	Afternoon Coffee: A Self Portrait*
1990	116.	Bus 24
	117.	Cowscape

McCONAHA, LAWRENCE

1926	190.	January Day
	191.	Sunset, Lick Creek
1927	196.	Sunlight and Shadows*
	197.	Gray Day
1929	190.	Cedars*
	191.	Misty Morning
1930	142.	Gold and Orange
	143.	In Connecticut*
1931	146.	Nearing Spring
	147.	Autumn Day*
	148.	A Connecticut Valley
1933	136.	Students
	137.	Busy Day*
1934	120.	Mt. Vaimu, Tahiti
	121.	Mt. Opunohi, Moorea
	122.	Mt. Paruoro, Moorea
1935	108.	Coke Otto*
1936	160.	Farm Buildings
1937	135.	Springtime
	136.	Autumn Afternoon
1938	150.	Summer Afternoon
1942	143.	Early Morning
	144.	Farm Buildings
1945	113.	Harvest Time
1946	133.	Swimming Hole
1947	144.	Winter
	145.	Railroad Crossing

McCONNELL, EVELYN
1969   123.   Landscape
1972   81.   Garden View
1973   119.   Nature Patterns
        120.   Vintage Past*
1974   91.   Patterns
        92.   Wooded Terrain*
1975   157.   Flower Pattern
        158.   Woodland
1977   106.   Blossoms
1978   91.   Blossoms
1981   122.   Floral Patterns
        123.   Changing Vistas
1989   140.   Flowers Patterns
1990   118.   Shapes in Nature

McCOY, MARTI
1971   118.   Hair
1976   154.   Uncle Santa

McCRARY, KAY
1971   119.   Enterprise*
        120.   Rolling Circles, Square*

McCULLOCH, HARRIET F.
1926   192.   Florida
1927   198.   Bay of Naples

McCUTCHEON, JOHN T.
1925   130.   Cartoons (three sets)
1926   193.   Two newspaper cartoons
1927   199.   Hoosier Salon Stimulating Art in Indiana
        200.   The Changing World
        201.   Their Landing Field
        202.   Switzerland, the Asylum of Kings
        203.   The Round the World Flight
        204.   The Women Are Uniting against War
        205.   Mother Is Becoming Worried
        206.   Drawing
        207.   Drawing

McDERMED, ED
1962   221.   St. Francis
1967   169.   Rooster

McDONALD, HAROLD
1942   145.   Jill Hallingberry
        146.   Still Life
1943   128.   Jill
1949   86.   County Court House
        87.   Silver Hills

McDONALD, VIRGINIA PERRY
1983   120.   Wealth
        121.   Drunkard's Path

McDONNELL, GAIL CARNEFIX
1948   78.   Bucks County, Pennsylvania

1950   121.   Fisherman's Cove, Puget Sound*
1951   108.   Madrona Tree

McDUFFEE, RUBY
1969   124.   Wonderment

McFARLAND, E. A.
1929   192.   New Beads

McGEE, JOSEPHINE HART
(See Hart, Josephine)
1957   121.   Apples, Plums & Porcelain
1960   160.   Eunice
        161.   Rue De St. Germain
1961   209.   Vieux Carre
1962   222.   Afternoon at Assisi
        223.   Moment of Grace
1963   161.   St. Louis and Royal
        162.   Just Ripe
1964   175.   Handful of Summer
        176.   Reflection of an Artist
1965   189.   Pinks and Apples
        190.   Gloucester
        191.   Josette and the Muses
1967   170.   The Storm
        171.   Chinatown Alley

McGREGOR, JAMES
1971   121.   Coho Fishers Off Chicago
1975   159.   Public Service

McGRIFF, PAULETTE
1990   119.   Country Still Life*

McGUINESS, ANN
1952   149.   Piazza Barbarini, Rome
1954   144.   Italian Street

McHUGH, JOHN W.
1945   114.   The Great American Painting

McILRATH, JAMES E.
1973   121.   Echoes

McINTOSH, P. R.
1925   131.   Winter in Control
1926   194.   The Christening
1927   208.   In the Chinese Room*
1929   193.   Idle Morning

McINTYRE, MARY (Harrell)
1964   177.   Carolyn Sleeping*
        178.   Barbara
1965   192.   Sleeping Child
1967   172.   Summer Afternoon
1969   125.   Adventure

McKAIN, BRUCE
1955   144.   Cape Cod Landscape*
        145.   Lumber Yard, Winter
1957   122.   Spring

1959 121. Still Life*
122. Dyer Street
1961 210. Summer Cottage
211. Old Wharf

McKEE, JOHN DUKES
1925 132. Lights o' the Bog
133. Smoke Fancies
134. Marooned*
1926 195. Never-Never Land
196. A Tale of County Clare*
197. The Moon Maker
1927 209. The Impossible Adventure
1928 174. Music Hath Charms
175. The Gossips
176. Peer Gynt and the Troll Imps

McKENZIE, RHEA
1984 129. Cameron with Ducks
1985 99. Zinnias in a Small Basket

McLAUGHLIN, ANN
1989 141. Show-Off

McLEISH, JEANNE
1979 100. Sunlit Brick
1980 99. Baskets
100. Waiting*
1981 124. Tin Lantern
1983 122. Pierrot
1987 145. Glimpse of Gothic
1988 137. The Edge of Winter
138. Wintergreen
1989 142. Genevieve

McMANUS, ONNA
1927 210. Old Mother Beech
211. Bit o' Brown County

McMATH, NELLIE
1942 147. Music in Air, Mexican Market
1943 129. San Juan River, Mexico
1944 154. Withered Chrysanthemums
1947 146. The Old Red Mill on Sugar Creek
1952 150. Jade Vase and Antiques

McMILLAN, LAURA B.
1927 212. Shadows of Evening
213. Late Winter

McNAGNY, ROB R.
1950 122. The Lone Ranger

McNAMEE, DOROTHY DAVIS
1944 155. W. S. Davis, A Hoosier
156. October: Santa Fe

McNAUGHTON, JOHN W.
1971 122. Dairy Queens*
1972 82. Baby's Got a New Pair of Shoes
1973 122. The Eagle Squats on Friday

McNURNEY, PATRICK L.
1990 120. Glacier Sands

McQUARIE, ELLEN
1947 147. The Return

McVEIGH, MIRIAM T.
1952 151. Night Estuary, San Francisco Bay*
1953 122. The Glad Bouquet

McVEY, FRANCES HAINES
(See Haines, Frances and Sweeney, Frances Haines)
1939 171. Portrait, Mary Timms

McWHINNEY, HAROLD
1933 140. Sunlight and Shadows
141. Red Mill*
1937 137. North of Morgantown

MEAD, AUGUST
1951 115. Cordelle*
116. Deserted Cabin*
117. Fossils*
1952 132. Shantyboats*
133. The Round Barn*
134. Heritage*

MEADOWS, HARVEY
1929 194. Portrait in June
195. Mostly Van Vechten
196. A Record
1931 154. The Little Stern Wheeler

MEADOWS, HELEN A.
1955 124. Monday Morning
125. The Pink Petunia
126. Art Critic
1956 139. The Bird's Nest
140. My Neighbor
1957 131. Antique Pitcher
132. Must I Wear A Hat?
1958 162. Rosalind

MEDERNACH, RUTH
1968 156. Silent Winter

MEEKER, BARBARA M(iller)
1961 197. Daisies
1963 149. Les Bouteilles
1981 130. Big Digger
1983 129. Winter Escape*
1984 138. Lily and Fern
139. Spacey Spring*
1985 104. Woven Woods
1986 155. Cuenca Revisited
156. Past Pleasures*
1988 139. America the Beautiful

MEEKS, DONALD J.
1988 140. Kennebunkport Gulls II
141. Country Shop Window

MEESE, MARYANN
1975   164.   Pewter

MEESE, WILBUR
1948   85.   The Old Mill
1949   94.   Village Church
1962   195.   Church in the Snow
1967   178.   Midwestern Storm
        179.   The Alps
1968   157.   Great Society
        158.   Lonesome Landmark*
        159.   Sunset in City
1969   126.   Victorian
        127.   Zero at Bay Village
1970   152.   Snowy Day
1971   127.   January
1972   85.   Reflections
        86.   Winter
1973   126.   Vermont Snow
        127.   Gingerbread
1974   95.   Vermont Barns
        96.   White House
1975   165.   Victorian Winter
        166.   Stone & Wood Barn
1976   155.   Victorian Splendor
        156.   Ohio Barns
1977   109.   Victorian Primitive*
1978   97.   Primitive In The Round
        98.   Quiet Snow*
1979   107.   Victorian Primitive
1980   110.   Victorian Grace
1981   131.   Green Primitive Farm*
        132.   Yellow Victorian
1982   140.   Light House
        141.   Blue Victorian*
1983   130.   Foggy Day
        131.   Gray Victorian Primitive
1985   105.   Floyd's Mill
1986   157.   Light House
        158.   Gray Lady No. 2
1988   142.   Rail Road Station Primitive
        143.   Christmas Angels Quilt
1989   153.   Red Barn Reflections
        154.   Victorian Winter
1990   124.   Patchwork and Pink Pitcher*
        125.   English Mill

MEESE, WILLIAM
1939   159.   Dark Skies
        160.   Lizton

MEIS, BARBARA M.
1966   93.   October Still Life
1967   180.   Rock Flowers
        181.   Tegerhi
1970   153.   Flower Garden

MELCHIONE, HUGO
1936   140.   Arrangement

MELEVAGE, RAYMOND (P.)
1978   99.   Store Front
1979   108.   Feelings
        109.   One Way*
1985   106.   Union of Elements
1987   158.   In My Father's Footsteps
        159.   Gentle Tim

MENDENHALL, MARY CHILTON GRAY
(See Gray, Mary Chilton)
1931   155.   Pueblo of the Taos Indians

MERIDITH, I. W.
1936   141.   October Morning
        142.   Autumn
1937   125.   Phlox
        126.   The River Road
1938   138.   Morning
1939   161.   Before the Storm
        162.   Hydrangea
        163.   Sunshine and Shadows
1940   123.   October Sunshine
1941   103.   Winter Morning
        322.   Yellow Chrysanthemums
1943   257.   Scene in Brown County

MERKEL, ROGER
1982   142.   Ford's Antiques
1984   140.   Too Wet to Plow
        141.   First Monday in October
1988   144.   The Blacksmith
        145.   Just Keep Your Shirt On
1990   126.   Spring Floods

MERRILL, ALTA
1944   165.   Virginia Lee

MERRITT, OPAL
1965   169.   Reflections
1966   94.   Winter Moment
1967   182.   Sweetpeas
1968   160.   Net Boat
1970   154.   Deserted*
        155.   A Drawing
1971   128.   Summer of '70
1973   128.   P. Kline's Old Barn

MESS, BETTY (ELIZABETH) JANE
1944   166.   Onekama Village
        167.   Resting
1945   121.   Coffin Stones on Millbeck Moors
1957   133.   King Salmon
1958   163.   Misty Pine
        164.   Mrs. Irene Goldberg

MESS, EVELYNNE (C.)
(See Daily, Evelynne Mess)
1929   197.   The Old Barn
        198.   The Mountain Barnyard
1931   156.   Rainy Day in Fontainebleau
        157.   Etching for Book Plate

	158.	Trees of Fontainebleau	1935	114.	Romantic Aurora
	159.	In the Alps	1936	143.	Metamora
	160.	Porte de Samois		144.	Summertime
1934	125.	Trees		145.	Lightning
	126.	A Courtyard in Moret		146.	Edge of the Forest
	127.	A Church in Brookville		147.	Nestled in the Hills
	128.	Church in China, Indiana		148.	Aurora
	129.	Queen Anne's Lace		149.	Abode of the Boatmaker
1942	155.	A Water Fantasy		150.	The Barren Plum Tree
	156.	Biloxi Bay		151.	Prevailing Winds
	157.	Boats on Lake Lugano	1937	127.	The Passing of the Monarch
	158.	Christmas Tree	1938	139.	Back Yard Romance
	159.	Creepy Hollow		140.	Ed Luckey's Farm
	160.	Inspiration from a Frosted Window		141.	Ever So Humble
	161.	Night Club Lights	1939	164.	Winter Moonlight
	162.	Tangled Branches	1940	124.	Hill Top
	163.	Under a Blanket of Snow		125.	Sand Dunes Cabins
1943	133.	Arrangement		126.	Work Shed
1945	122.	Mountain Valley Farm	1941	104.	Ever So Humble
	123.	Barnyard		105.	Neighbors
	124.	White Mountain Flowers		106.	Tangled Branches
1946	121.	Foot Bridge to the Forest		107.	Winter in the Hills
1947	133.	The Country Church*		108.	Wishing Gate in Winter
	134.	Nature's Lace Work*	1942	164.	Sunset Hill
1948	86.	Flower Arrangement	1943	134.	Summer Romance
	87.	Babe in the Woods*		135.	Where Bridges Meet
1949	95.	The Branching Willow		136.	Summer Solitude
	96.	Towers		137.	Summer Kitchen
1951	118.	Mushroom Hollow		138.	Glorious Day
	119.	Toadstools*	1944	168.	Four O'Clock*
1952	135.	December		169.	Indiana Quarry
1953	112.	Cucurbita*		170.	A New Dawn*
1955	127.	Lazy River		171.	The Handy Pump*
	128.	Water Fantasy	1945	125.	Landmark
	129.	Herbs in My Garden		126.	Salt Creek
1957	134.	In My Little Studio		127.	The Goat Farm
1958	165.	Field Flowers*		128.	Adirondacks*
	166.	Aquarium	1946	122.	The Promise*
1959	124.	Variations		123.	Living Better Without*
1961	198.	Flowers and Fruit		124.	Flashes in the Harbor*
1964	185.	Evergreen Hills		125.	Lullaby of the Leaves*
	186.	Mother and Babes*	1947	135.	Love*
1965	170.	Fall Landscape		136.	Hill Top Pond
1967	183.	Woodland Treasures		137.	Just A Fishin'
	184.	Hide-Away	1948	88.	The Old Mill
				89.	Population 514
MESS, GEORGE JO(seph)			1949	97.	Deserted Strip Mine*
1926	198.	October Sunshine		98.	To the Beach
1929	199.	Among the Hills	1950	113.	All Is Quiet
	200.	In the Valley		114.	Paradise Valley*
1930	147.	Mill of Montigny		115.	Snow in My Valley
	148.	Across the Canal of Episy	1951	120.	Time to Play
1931	161.	Brown County Farm Yard	1952	136.	Highway No. 1*
	162.	Canal Moret		137.	Signs of a Good Time
	163.	Church of Montigny*		138.	Off the Main Highway*
1932	145.	The Last Snow		139.	Coffee Time*
	146.	The Mystery Shack		140.	Stormy Weather
1933	147.	A Century of Progress, Madison Bridge*	1953	113.	Sympathetic Scarecrow
				114.	Summer Home among the Trees

1954	128.	Brown County Estate*
	129.	Brown County*
	130.	Weathervane
	131.	Bit of Dill
	132.	Branching Out
1955	130.	Little Water Falls
	131.	Lake near Bean Blossom*
	132.	The Lighted Way
	133.	Dramatic Masks
1956	141.	Reelfoot Lake Bridge
	142.	Scarecrow*
	143.	Main Street
	144.	An Enchanted Evening
	145.	Winter Patterns*
1957	135.	In Full Moon
	136.	To Sail Beyond
1958	169.	Dwarf's Pass Over
	170.	Early Spring Patterns*
1959	125.	Echo Hills
1960	231.	Stone Head
1961	199.	Way of Life
	200.	Faith
1962	196.	Beside the Still Waters
	197.	Rural Patterns
	198.	Plant Life in Moonlight*

MESS, GORDON BENJAMIN

1933	148.	Laurel
1934	130.	Reflections in the Water
	131.	Valley of Contented People, Aurora
	132.	Madison Hills
1940	314.	The Valley Road
1941	109.	The Passing Storm
1942	165.	Gloucester Fishing Boats
	166.	Stage-Coach Tavern
1943	139.	Home Again
	140.	Sunlight Day
1944	172.	Atlantic Avenue
	173.	Mid-Day
1945	129.	Waiting for Fair Weather
1952	141.	Sunlight Day
	142.	Along Sleepy Hollow Road
1953	115.	First Boat In
	116.	Early Start
1954	133.	Indian Summer
	134.	In the Still of the Morning
1955	134.	Colorful Blue Rocks Nova Scotia
1956	146.	Change in the Weather
1957	137.	New Arrival
	138.	Gloucester
1958	167.	Morning Shadows
	168.	Captain's Paradise
1959	126.	Along the Shore
	127.	Sunlight Serenade

MESSER, LAURIE

| 1971 | 129. | Tumbledown Mill |
| 1973 | 129. | Summer Sunshine |

MESSER, WILLIAM (H.)

| 1987 | 160. | Victorian Grid III* |

| 1988 | 146. | Untitled A* |
| 1989 | 155. | Victorian Grid VIII |

MESSICK, JANE

1942	167.	El Pilluelo
	168.	Miguel
1943	141.	Chartreuse and Shadows
1944	174.	Nita
	175.	Hadji
	176.	Nubian Rhapsody*
1945	130.	Echoes in Glass*
	131.	April
1946	126.	Reflections
1947	138.	Old Adobe
1950	116.	Museum Pieces
1951	121.	Still Life
1952	143.	Morning Light
1953	117.	Derelict Houses
1955	135.	Maria
	136.	Study
1956	147.	The Spell of the Carousel
	148.	Chuck
	149.	Zinnia and Pears
1957	139.	Memorabilia
	140.	On the Road to Lisbon
1959	128.	Flowers for Winter, Drying on My Doorstep
	129.	Outside the Bullring
1960	146.	Early Spring
	147.	Alicia and the China Bird Cage
1962	199.	Women in Patzcuaro, Mexico
	200.	Megnolia Blossoms
	201.	From Our Garden
1963	150.	Pears
1964	187.	Avila
1965	171.	Mexican Boy

METZGER, DAVID F.

| 1970 | 156. | The Engagement |

MEYER, THOMAS

| 1987 | 161. | Waiting for Tomorrow |

MEYNCKE, G(retchen) D.

| 1933 | 149. | Leaden Skies |
| 1934 | 133. | A Light in the Window |

MICHAU, MARY

| 1966 | 95. | Flowers in White Vase* |

MICHEL, DELBERT

| 1970 | 157. | The Alumni |
| | 158. | Self Portrait with Status Symbol* |

MICHELE, MICHAEL

1982	143.	Mine Shaft*
	144.	Tuxedo
1983	132.	The Exotic Family*
	133.	Ann & Friend
1984	142.	Mystic Imagery
1985	107.	Taliesin Spirit

1986	159.	Odyssey
	160.	Pegasus
1988	147.	American Splendor

MIDDENTS, JOHN R.
1949	99.	Jean Lafitte, Renegade Hero
	100.	John Henry, Steel-driven Man
	101.	Landscape with a Red Pony

MIDKIFF, THOMAS C.
1969	128.	The Sentinels
	129.	Morning Chores
1970	159.	Adellas Walk
	160.	Apples and Honey*
1971	130.	Last Voyage
	131.	John Wilson's Place
1973	130.	Worked Out

MIKUS, PAUL A.
| 1969 | 3. | Looking Beyond |

MILES, MARIE (A.)
1963	151.	Rye Whiskey
1965	172.	Woodbine Twineth
1966	96.	Midnight Lace
1967	185.	110 in the Shade
	186.	On a Clear Day
1968	161.	Hoosier Sabbath
	162.	Revive Us Again
1969	130.	The Night Is Dark, and I Am Far from Home
1970	161.	Hope Town Harbor Light
	162.	Portrait of a Happy Man*
1973	131.	Still Life
1974	99.	Girl Gazing*
1975	167.	Neptune's Daughter

MILLER, DIANNA THORNHILL
| 1981 | 133. | Kabuki |
| | 134. | Three Rivers |

MILLER, EMERY M.
| 1929 | 201. | Wall Fountain |
| 1932 | 147. | Gargoyle |

MILLER, ISABEL J.
| 1946 | 127. | Spring Harmony |
| | 128. | Back Door in Summer |

MILLER, JAMES GUY
| 1965 | 173. | Stare |
| 1971 | 132. | Getting Straight* |

MILLER, JAMES H.
| 1981 | 135. | Facade* |

MILLER, JOHN EDWARD
1935	115.	San Andres, Cholula, Mexico*
	116.	At Coyoacan, Mexico
	117.	The Pyramid, Cholula, Mexico

| 1936 | 152. | The Sorrento Road |
| | 153. | Paper Mill, Valle de Molini, Amalfi |

MILLER, LEE E.
1962	202.	Still Life
	203.	Becoming (Spring)
	204.	Still Life

MILLER, MELVIN T.
| 1966 | 97. | Folk Singer |
| 1967 | 187. | Point of View |

MILLER, MURILE
| 1925 | 135. | Petunias |
| 1927 | 214. | Jonquils and a Lady |

MILLESON, HOLLIS E.
| 1926 | 199. | Sea Shore, Marble Head |

MILLHOLLAND, DORIS B.
| 1990 | 127. | Once Upon a Time |

MILLS, PANSY
| 1944 | 177. | Non-Objective |

MILONADIS, KONSTANTIN
| 1971 | 133. | UFO Tracking Station |

MILROY, HARRIE C.
| 1925 | 145. | A Hoosier Village |

MINKLER, THOMAS
| 1969 | 131. | Balloon Man |
| | 132. | Owl |

MITCHELL, GLEN
1928	177.	Pont de Suspice, Venice
	178.	Pont Neuf, Paris
	179.	Portrait, Jerusalem
	180.	By the Seine
	181.	Bedouin Girl
1929	203.	Moret-sur-Loing
1930	149.	Montreux
	150.	Old Granada
1931	164.	Fishing Boats, Venice
	165.	Mount of Olives
1936	154.	The Black Tower*
	155.	Hag's House
1938	142.	Kings Crown Squash
1939	165.	Onions
	166.	Street in Taxco
1940	127.	Taxco*
1941	110.	El Cabrigo
1942	169.	Man with a Red Nose
	170.	Old Man with a White Rooster
1949	102.	Zocale, Taxco

MITCHELL, IRENE F.
1968	163.	Victorian Table
	164.	Fishing Shack*
1969	133.	Shades of Yellow

MITCHELL, JERRY L.
| 1989 | 156. | Perennial Mind |
| 1990 | 128. | Sky & Danny |

MITCHELL, LUCY
1967	188.	Eggs in a Blue Dish
1968	165.	Teapot with Lemons
1969	134.	Geranium
1973	132.	Racing Chariots

MOCK, GEORGE A.
1925	136.	October Morning
	137.	Winter in Hoosier-land
1926	200.	Gray Beaches
	201.	The Low Lands
	202.	The Creek in Winter
1927	215.	The Lane in Winter
	216.	Farm Buildings in Winter
1928	182.	Pyramid of Trees
	183.	Winter Evening
1929	204.	Tall Trees
	205.	The Light Snow
1930	151.	Gray Day in Winter
	152.	Winter Morning
1932	148.	Winter in the Orchard
	149.	The Lane in Winter
	150.	Old Apple Tree in Winter
1933	150.	Winter Morning
1934	134.	Winter Afternoon
	135.	The Lane in Autumn*
	136.	Willows in Winter
1935	118.	The Barn Yard
	119.	Frosty Morning
	120.	Old Farm Buildings
1936	156.	New Year's Day
	157.	Golden Willows
	158.	Sleighing Time
1937	128.	Late October
	129.	Winter Morning*
	130.	Melting Snow
1938	143.	Hazy Morning
	144.	Frosty Morning
1939	167.	A Bright Morning
	168.	High Tide
	169.	Hill Top
	316.	The Winding Road
1940	128.	The First Snow
	315.	In Brown County
1941	111.	Peace and Quiet
	323.	Dogwood
1942	171.	November Morning
	172.	Old Boats, Key West
1943	142.	Willows in Winter
	143.	Water Front, Key West
	144.	October Sunlight
1944	178.	Key West
	179.	The Lonesome Road
	180.	When the Sun Is Low
1945	132.	Sleighing Time
	133.	The Winding Stream
1946	129.	Winter in Brown County
	130.	Late Afternoon
1947	139.	The Lane in Winter
1948	90.	Creek in Winter
1949	103.	After the Blizzard
1951	122.	Winter
1953	118.	Corn Stalks in Snow

MOLL, MARY (H.)
1967	189.	Abandoned House on Dandy Trail
	190.	Sunflowers
1971	134.	Wisconsin Landscape
1973	133.	The Coleman Place
1974	97.	Dandelion Seed Cluster
	98.	Squash
1975	168.	Five Senses
	169.	Orange-Pink Composition

MONEY, JO
| 1973 | 134. | Still Life with Green Air |
| 1990 | 129. | Whitney, Reading |

MONNINGER, IRENE
| 1944 | 184. | Gloria |

MONSMA, RONALD
| 1989 | 160. | Room at Night* |

MONTAGUE, (Jr.), FRED (H.)
1974	100.	Trillimum & Bloodroot along Big Creek
	101.	Dry Creekbed, Little Raccoon Creek, Parke County, Indiana*
1976	157.	Silent Snow
	158.	Winter Feast II
1978	100.	Barred Owl
1980	111.	Shell Study I
1982	145.	Ladyslippers

MONTEITH, HARRIET E.
1940	129.	Bethany Bridge
1942	173.	China Rooster
1943	145.	My Studio
	146.	Rodeheaver's Summer Home
	147.	Sunflowers
1944	181.	Nancy
	182.	My Mom
	183.	All Is Well
1947	140.	Sun Flowers
1956	153.	Sunflowers
1957	141.	Portrait*
	142.	Pixie Head
1958	171.	Sister Act
	172.	Still Life with Cabbage*
	173.	Portrait of a Little Girl
1959	130.	Just Weeds
	131.	Easter At Ziesels
	132.	Fall Still Life
1960	148.	Ann
	149.	Still Life in Oil*

1961	201.	Meg
	202.	Geraniums
	203.	Carol
1962	205.	Ballerina*
	206.	Hat Bar
	207.	Jenifer
1963	153.	Our Willow
	154.	Portrait*
	155.	My Mother Loved Amaryllis*
1964	188.	Fall Flowers
	189.	Nora
1965	174.	Butch
	175.	Vicki
	176.	Still Life
1966	98.	Artesha
1967	191.	Julia
	192.	For the Birds
1968	166.	Portrait*

MONTEITH, PHILLIP E.

1986	161.	Portrait of Sherri*
	162.	Five Iris
1987	162.	Life's Cycle
	163.	Daybreak
1988	148.	Torch Ginger*
1989	157.	New Snow
1990	130.	The Angelique

MONTGOMERY, MARTY

| 1990 | 131. | Dorthea* |

MONTGOMERY, PATRICIA A. (Fenton)

1960	150.	Stephanie
1962	208.	Four Square Quilt
	209.	Seaside
1963	152.	Portrait of Cynthia
1964	190.	Portrait of Sarah
1965	177.	March
1966	99.	Mr. Tyner's Cows
	100.	Women with Children
1967	193.	Winter Morning*
1969	135.	Pontoon Boat
1970	163.	Composition No. 1 (Winter)*
1971	135.	Landscape
1972	87.	Figure Composition
1973	135.	Amish Autumn
1974	102.	Landscape
	103.	Suzanne
1975	170.	Summertime
1979	110.	Figure Composition
1983	134.	Easter Sunday
	135.	Amish Family
1984	143.	Winter Sky
	144.	April Evening
1985	108.	After the Storm
	109.	Winter Morning
1986	163.	Dawn
1987	164.	Sarah
1988	149.	Houlihan's

1989	158.	Endangered
	159.	Arabian Room
1990	132.	December Evening

MONTGOMERY, SHARON J.

1983	136.	Iris
1984	145.	To a Joker*
	146.	For a Joker

MOODY, FRANCES J(ohnson)

1935	121.	Dolores
	122.	Neo-classic figure
1937	131.	Girl with Fawn
1938	145.	Jeanie
	146.	Young African
1940	130.	David*
1957	143.	Granny J.
1960	151.	Mary Gordon

MOONEY, JOHN DAVID

| 1970 | 164. | Crucifixion |

MOORE, DON

1959	133.	Predator and Victim
	134.	Kneeling Figure
	135.	Sandstone Head
1960	152.	Warrrior
	153.	Weasel*
	154.	Rhino
1962	210.	Bison
1964	191.	Stag Beetle
	192.	Mantis
	193.	Hemipteran*
1965	178.	Fish
	179.	Bug
	180.	Lobster
1966	101.	Crab*
	102.	Peacock
	103.	Iguana
1967	194.	Insect No. 1
	195.	Insect No. 2
	196.	Non-Objective*
1968	167.	Lizard

MOORE, HELEN ARNOLD

| 1925 | 138. | Snapdragons |

MOORE, M. JAYNE

| 1982 | 146. | Serene and Grand |
| 1984 | 147. | Welcome to Lockerbie Square |

MOORE, MICHAEL J.

| 1979 | 111. | Turn On* |

MOORE, W. E.

1950	117.	Pumas
	118.	Sandstone Bear*
1951	123.	Family Portrait
	124.	The Old Oaken Bucket
	125.	Last of the Herd*

1952	144.	Sandstone Otter
1954	135.	Helen
	136.	Stone Sheep*
1955	137.	Cinnamon Bears
1956	150.	Red Moose
	151.	Stone Loons*
	152.	Coyotes
1957	144.	Otter
	145.	Eagle
	146.	Horse Sale*
1958	174.	Beavers
	175.	Stone Foxes
1962	211.	Winter Cattle
	212.	Sam
1965	181.	Tree Frog

MOORMAN, BONNIE BAKER

1974	104.	Heart of the Plant
1975	171.	Wood Ducks and Willow
	172.	Silken Butterfly
1976	159.	Peach Flowers
1977	110.	Iris Blue
1978	101.	If the Breath of Spring Was Caught
1980	112.	Mermaids Wine Glasses
1981	136.	View of the Sea Flowers
	137.	The Cradle of the Sea
1982	147.	Fish Heads

MOOTS, (M.) MAXINE

1952	145.	"Pan" from the antique cameo
	146.	"Bacchus" from the antique cameo
1954	137.	Jewel for January
	138.	Jewel for May

MORGAN, LYNN T.

1925	139.	The Glen
1926	203.	A Peaceful Summer's Day
1927	217.	The Last Boom
1928	184.	An Old English Street
	185.	Le Gros Horloge
1934	137.	Fishing Boats of Gaspe
	138.	Warging In
	139.	Through the Open Door

MORGAN, RANDALL

1955	138.	Alberobello
	139.	Amalfi Coast
1968	168.	Recollections of Childhood*
	169.	Contraluce*
	170.	Voyeur
1969	136.	Ophelia

MORGAN, ROSE ANN DAVIS

| 1957 | 147. | Harrison County |

MORLAN, DOROTHY

1925	140.	Frosty Morning, Southern Indiana*
1926	204.	Spirit of Winter
1930	153.	Twin Poplars

1944	185.	Glade in the Rockies in May
	186.	Rocky Mountain Solitude
1945	134.	October

MORRIS, ELLWOOD

| 1925 | 141. | A Misty Morning |
| | 142. | Quiet Valley |

MORRIS, ELSA

| 1988 | 150. | Morning Blue |
| 1989 | 161. | Bromeliad, Pink |

MORRIS, RAYMOND L.

1938	147.	Before the Gong
	148.	One in Every Neighborhood
1940	131.	Kitchen Still Life
	132.	Still Life

MORRIS, ROBERT C.

1929	206.	Still Life
1946	131.	Bob
1947	141.	Fluffy, Peter and Cerberus

MOSER, LLOYD V.

1957	148.	Along The Wabash
	149.	All Steamed Up
1959	136.	Hanging Moss
	137.	Santa Prista-Taxco
	138.	Backyard
1973	136.	Old House, Rockville

MOSIER, MARTHA HINKLE

1947	142.	Pitcher of Flowers*
1952	147.	Flowers at the Edge of Night*
1958	176.	Spring Bouquet
1959	139.	Indian Summer

MOTZ, GRACE LESLIE

1936	159.	A Filling Station at Davidson and Wells
1938	149.	Study of Cacti
1940	133.	My Boy

MOWREY, HELEN

| 1946 | 132. | Blue-Purple |
| 1980 | 113. | Portrait of a Young Girl |

MUDGETT, MARCIA GARDNER

| 1927 | 218. | Rocky Neck Avenue |
| 1929 | 207. | Gross Mutter |

MUELLER, JO FROHBIETER

| 1982 | 148. | The French Lieutenant's Woman |

MUELLER, KARL

| 1984 | 148. | Spanish Gold |

MUELLER, LOUIS (F.)

1925	143.	The Old Fisherman
	144.	Brown County Cabin
1928	186.	Winter Landscape

1929	208.	A Market Basket
1938	320.	The Old Mill
1944	187.	Jugs
1945	135.	A Decorator
1951	126.	Lest We Forget

MUHL, BETTY

1962	213.	Building the Temple
	214.	The Piano Stool*
1963	156.	Vase of Flowers
	157.	Bugaboo Swamp
1965	182.	The Forest
	183.	Girl Reading
1973	137.	Pajama Girl
1974	106.	Shades of Winter
1975	173.	Bull Shoals*
	174.	Mary's Garden
1976	160.	Wayne County Court House
1977	111.	Studio Stimuli
1978	102.	Sundown at the Dovecote
1979	112.	A-6*
	113.	Third Theme

MUHL, ROBERT

| 1971 | 136. | Potter's Dock |

MULLEN, MARK A.

1979	114.	The Wind Up
1984	149.	Meridian Street Bridge/Portland, Indiana*
1985	110.	Utah Road 128*
	111.	Winchester Library
1986	164.	The Davis Building
1987	165.	Auburn-Cord-Duesenberg Museum
	166.	Downtown Escape

MULLEN, NORMA

1973	138.	Gathered
1976	161.	Azaleas for Easter
1977	112.	Hold On To Autumn

MULLIN, CHARLES EDWARD

| 1930 | 154. | Indiana Fishermen |
| | 155. | Fish Shack in the Dunes |

MUNDY, C. W.

| 1990 | 133. | Rebecca's Floral |

MURDOCK, VIRGINIA

1952	148.	Lime Quarry
1954	139.	Nina Jo
	140.	Brad
	141.	Lynn
1956	154.	Harriet
	155.	Pitcher and Peaches
1958	177.	Mother and Child*
	178.	Fruit
	179.	That Old House
1962	215.	Iris
	216.	Old Place

1964	194.	Still Life #1
	195.	Still Life #2
	196.	Portrait
1965	184.	Still Life

MURPHY, MARIAN (R.)

1973	139.	The Beach House
1974	105.	Two Calves
1975	175.	Memory Lane
1984	150.	Sea Harvest
1985	112.	Low Tide

MURPHY, WILLA

| 1948 | 91. | Oriental Fan & Poppies |

MURRAY, MARIA C.

1962	217.	Madison, Indiana
	218.	Still Life
	219.	Inland Steel

MURRAY, ROSANNE (Rose Ann)

1978	103.	Shells of Sanibel, II
1984	151.	Your Place or Mine
1986	165.	Meeting Adjourned
	166.	The Farmer's Market

MUSICK, W. E.

1926	205.	Paw Paw River
	206.	Down by the St. Joe
1927	219.	Fisherman's Shanty
	220.	By the Mississippi
	221.	Indiana Woodland*
1928	187.	The Green House-boat
1929	209.	Lily
1930	156.	Mexico Patio
	157.	A Street in Vera Cruz
	158.	Along the Trail
1931	166.	Mexican Canary
	167.	Mexican Vendor
	168.	Lily
1933	151.	Early Morning in the Tropics
1937	132.	The Bay
	133.	Deserted Cabin

MUSSELMAN, KEITH DON

| 1927 | 222. | Shadow Canyon |
| 1929 | 210. | Chinese Junks |

MYERS, DORIS B.

1986	167.	Iris #2
1987	167.	Adam's World
1989	162.	Roses & Iris #5

MYRICK, RUTH KEALING

| 1925 | 146. | The Brass Bowl |

MYSLIVE, FRANK R(ichard)

1937	134.	Mid-Winter Nite
1939	170.	Looking South
1940	134.	Twin Forks
1945	136.	Antiquated

EXHIBITION RECORDS

N

NASH, GRACE
1938   151.   Billie

NATHAN, MARILYN
1980   114.   Home

NAUMAN, HAZEL M.
1965   193.   Study of John
        194.   Composite

NAYLOR, ALICE L.
1977   113.   Old Barn, Lafayette, Indiana

NEEDHAM, RAY CLAY
1932   151.   Low Tide
1935   123.   The Make-up
1937   138.   Sumac
        139.   Gray Day at Boothbay Harbor
1944   188.   China Town
        189.   At Rest
1950   123.   Deserted
        124.   Snowed Under
1951   127.   Dusk
1954   145.   Design
        146.   Stranded
1955   146.   Winter
        147.   New England Harbor
1956   158.   Pal
1957   151.   Early Spring
        152.   Oil Refinery
1958   185.   Composition
        186.   Still Life
1961   212.   Deserted
        213.   Early Fall
1962   224.   Gray Day
        225.   Early Snow

NEELD, C. E.
1926   207.   Looking for Crawdads
1927   223.   Early Winter
        224.   Morning Toilet
1928   188.   The Old Lithographer
        189.   Old Indiana Home
1929   211.   The Fisherman
1932   152.   Winter in Glen Ellyn
1935   124.   First Mountain
1940   135.   Edge of Town

NEFF, B. E.
1942   174.   Cat's Cradle
        175.   Still Life

NELSON, GERTRUDE WISER
1935   125.   From Grandmother's Garden
1937   140.   Tea Time
1939   172.   Still Life, Flowers

NELSON, WILLIAM (J.)
1930   159.   December Afternoon
1932   153.   March Morning
1940   136.   Late Afternoon Dunes
1946   134.   Prelude to Autumn (Dunes)

NESSLAGE, F. HELEN
1948   92.   Magnolia Leaves
        93.   The Day Begins

NETHERCUTT, RONNA A.
1973   141.   Bluegill

NEUFELD, LEO
1990   134.   Irene with Bluegreen Scarf

NEWBERRY, W. L.
1935   126.   Guanahuato, Mexico
        127.   Indian Woman, Guanahuato, Mexico*

NEWMAN, ANNA MARY
1925   147.   Azaleas, with Woman in White
        148.   Knee Deep in June
1927   225.   Woods Interior
1928   190.   A Worker in the Palette Club

NEWMAN, CLARA G.
1927   226.   In Estes Park
1937   141.   Winter Day
        327.   Friend's Bouquet
1943   148.   At the Window

NEWMAN, HELEN
1951   128.   Night Highway
1962   226.   Tom
1966   104.   Facade 1865

NEWMAN, PAULA RANEY
1955   148.   Blue Hills
1956   159.   Early Spring
1957   153.   New England Coast
1958   187.   The Breakers
        188.   Seacrest
1959   140.   Sea and Surf
        141.   Restless Seas
1964   199.   Chapel in the Hills
        200.   Pounding Surf
1965   195.   Rocky Shore
        196.   Sea and Surf
1966   105.   Breaking Seas
1967   197.   High Tide
1968   171.   Roses
        172.   The Tides
        173.   Fruit and Flowers*
1969   137.   Orchids

EXHIBITION RECORDS

1970 165. Fruit Basket
1973 142. Fruit Basket

NEWTON, KATHERINE
1944 190. Memories
     191. Flemish Teapot
1945 137. The Old Lantern
     138. Plans
1946 135. The Discovery

NICHOLLS, M(erle) R.
1936 161. The Old Hay Barn
1951 129. Sunlight and Shadow
1954 147. Duneland Meadow
1956 160. Valley Road
1957 154. Seed Time
     155. At Miller Beach
1960 162. Aspen and Sage
     163. Autumn's Touch
     164. Morning Light
1961 214. Somebody's Alley
1963 163. Monument Valley Maid
1964 201. Navajo Mother
     202. February Solitude
     203. Seed Time
1967 198. Butterfly Weed
1969 138. Atop a Dune

NICHOLSON, EDWARD
1940 137. Dad and His Pipe*
     138. Mexicana
     139. Morro Boat Yard
1941 112. Carmelita
     113. Honey
1942 176. Gloucester, Harbor
     177. Portrait of Dorothy
1943 149. Musical Beach Comber
1944 192. Abuela Mexicana*
1945 139. The Bashful Muchacha*
1946 136. Nancy*
1947 148. Little Mother
1949 104. Brother*
1950 125. Old Sheriff*
     126. Spanish Dancer
1951 130. Spanish Ballet Student*
     131. Jean
1952 152. Maxine
1953 123. Wayne and Tuffy
     124. The Patriarch
     125. Jose Manero
1954 148. Lynne at Art School
1956 161. Country Still Life*
     162. Miss Audrey Suffield
     163. Laurie
1957 156. Holiday*
     157. Member of the "Polar Bears"*
1958 189. Artist's Son
     190. Mountaineer
     191. Helen Spennetta

1959 142. The Doll Maker
     143. Cheta
     144. Attic Tenant*
1960 165. Little Miss Chatterbox
     166. Bon Vivant (Self Portrait)*
1962 227. Teryuko
1963 164. Portrait in Yellow
1964 204. And Alice Said to the Rabbit*
     205. Claude Buck
1965 197. Mary and Billy
     198. Becky
1966 106. California

NICHOLSON, THURMAN
1947 149. Moses in the Bullrushes
1949 106. Indiana Spring Flowers*
1950 127. Skunk Cabbages

NICOLAI, C(harles) A.
1925 149. Fall Creek

NICOLAI, HELEN
1946 137. Young Girl

NIESSE, MILDRED
1946 138. Still-Life, Iris
1955 149. Dixie Highway
1956 164. Country Sale, 1955
1959 145. Empress of the Night
1960 167. Salvaged Treasure
1962 228. China Cove, Calif.
     229. The Wayfarer
1963 165. Spring Countryside
1964 206. My Lucky Find
1966 107. Indianapolis Speedway, View 5
1967 199. Wills Landmark
1968 174. Indiana Classic
     175. The Famous Race
1969 139. House of Destiny
1970 166. Golden Marigolds
     167. Weathering the Storm
1971 137. Assemblage #5
1973 143. Indiana Landmark #2
1975 176. St. Mark's Cathedral
     177. Old Murphy Barn
1977 114. Golden Years
     115. Barner House, Circa 1860*
1979 115. Indiana Farm House
1982 149. Circus City, Peru, Indiana
1987 168. Barr Brothers Barn, Route 70
     169. Murphy's Place
1989 163. Elephant Ears and Caladium
     164. Indiana Primitive Farm
1990 135. Primitive, Memories

NIXON, FLOYD
1961 215. Rain Clouds
     216. Summer Sky

NOEL, A.
1948 94. Pansies*

269

NOËL, NANCY (A.)
1972	88.	Dolls*
1981	138.	Images in a Field
	139.	The Mechanics
1982	150.	Portrait of Amey
	151.	Sisters by the Window*

NOLF, JOHN T.
| 1925 | 150. | The Hoosier Smoker |

NORTHWAY, ANN
| 1976 | 162. | The West Coast |

NORTON, JAMES C.
| 1975 | 178. | Soft Blend #1 |
| 1976 | 163. | Evolution |

NUSBAUM, ESTHER C(ommons)
1934	140.	Still Life
1935	128.	Ivy Plant
1942	178.	Old Pitchers
1944	193.	Still Life with Grapes

1947	150.	Old Fish House, Key West
1948	95.	Spring Rain
1949	107.	Children in the Rain
1951	132.	Lobsterman's Shacks
1952	153.	Willow Pond, Cape Ann
1953	126.	The Sycamore Log
1959	146.	After the Storm
	147.	Fall Fantasy
1961	217.	Wyoming Forest
	218.	Toward The Tetons
1962	230.	The Long View
	231.	Wayside Wonders
1963	166.	Italian Hilltown
	167.	Alpine Afternoon
1964	207.	Portofino, Italy
	208.	Fortified City
1965	199.	Red Barns
1970	168.	Nor'easter
1973	144.	September Song #5
	145.	Windswept
1974	107.	Winter Valley
	108.	Foothills

OBER, ELEANOR VEE
1962   232.   Madonna in the Garden

OBERGFELL, MARY JANE
1971   138.   Jamaica, Wish You Were Here

OBERHOLTZER, TAMIKO
1990   136.   Recurrence

OBERMUELLER, STAN
1977   116.   Big Horn Canyon
1978   104.   Winter Trees*
1981   140.   Sycamore Stand
        141.   Sails
1982   152.   Indiana Woods

O'BRIEN, BEA
1983   143.   Santorini

OCHS, ROBERT L.
1952   154.   Winter City
        155.   The Green Case*
1953   127.   The City and the River

O'CONNELL, PATRICIA ELLIOTT
1983   137.   Balloons for Sale

O'CONNELL, PATSY (Patricia) SURH
1981   142.   Paradise Lost
1982   153.   On the Prowl
1983   138.   Ginger Peachy*
        139.   Moonlight Sonata

O'CONNOR, JOANNE
1972   89.   The Old Grandmother
1975   179.   Down at the Corner of Lincoln and
                Halsted

O'CONNOR, KATIE C.
1927   227.   The Red Fox

O'CONNOR, VINCENT L.
1940   140.   High-Hat

O'DELL, ROB
1970   169.   Dusty Stairs*
        170.   Wind Dance
1971   139.   White Reflected White*
        140.   A Sense of Winter
1972   90.   Arrangement in Gray
        91.   Offspring*
1974   109.   Winters Way
        110.   You Can't Go Back*
1977   117.   The Beginning
        118.   Forked Trunk*
1978   105.   The Whited Air
        106.   Hash Marks

1979   116.   Arrangement in White
        117.   Go Big Red
1980   115.   Patches*
1981   143.   Special Times*
        144.   Newberry Storefronts
1982   154.   Adventure
1983   140.   Somebody's Grandma Lives Here
        141.   Intruder
1984   152.   36' Ward Canvasback
        153.   Meandering
1985   113.   Indiana Roadscape
        114.   Snow Blind
1986   168.   In the Beginning
        169.   Take Me Home
1987   170.   Oak Creek*
        171.   Winter Magic
1988   151.   Time Teller
1990   137.   Almost Perfect Day
        138.   February Fields

O'FALLON, VIRGINIA
1941   114.   The Spider
1942   179.   Katherine Davis
1957   158.   The Desponder

OFFUTT, LEE P.
1960   168.   A Deer
1963   168.   Rush County Home

O'HARA, MICHAEL
1977   119.   Shattered Summer

O'HAVER, MARIAN (Johnson)
1973   146.   Rhyolite, Nev.
1976   164.   Industrial Site
1977   120.   Therapy
1978   107.   Shattered Windows, Shattered
                Dreams
1986   170.   Ribbons and Lace
1989   165.   Croton

OLIVE, JUDY
(See Jarrett, Judy)
1983   142.   Vegetable Stand*
1984   154.   Caldonia

OLIVER, LOREN
1956   165.   Still Life
        166.   Uncle Willie's Room

O'LOUGHLIN, THOMAS
1949   108.   Joey
        109.   One Sunday Morning
1950   128.   Floral Still Life
        129.   The Westerner
1951   133.   Shepherd's Dream

OLSON, EARL B.
1933   152.   The Delta Vase

OLSON, MILDRED A.
1976   165.   Teen-Ager
        166.   Stavros

ORR, CAROLYN (Grabhorn)
1976   167.   Chief Tintinmeet
1978   108.   Young Girl
1982   155.   Limberlost Child

ORR, CYNTHIA A.
1981   145.   A Forgotten Touch
1982   156.   Spring Promise
        157.   The Sentry

ORR, (Jr.) R. B.
1976   168.   Alley Scene
        169.   Blue Skies, Blue Water
1980   116.   Elmer's Place

OSBORN, MARIAN
1970   171.   Body Shop Revisited

OSBORNE, BETTY LOCKE
1963   169.   Going Home
        170.   Still Life with Basket

OSBORNE, ROBERT
1962   233.   Pigtail

OSBORNE, ROLAND DONOVAN
1949   110.   Center Street, U.S.A.
1950   130.   Factory District*
        131.   Still Life With Pears
1951   134.   Finlayson's Farm, Ontario
        135.   Winter Magic
1952   156.   House of Six Gables
1953   128.   A December Morning
        129.   Wet Snow
1954   149.   November Snow
1955   150.   October
        151.   End of the Season
        152.   Snow
1956   167.   The Black Jug*
1957   159.   Spring*
1958   192.   The Jug
1960   169.   The Bridge
1961   219.   Winter Along the Still Water
1962   234.   Early Snow*

OSHIER, EARL
1965   200.   Lost Mail*
1966   108.   The Observer
        109.   Inheritance
1967   200.   From the Bridge
        201.   Self Portrait
        202.   Relic*
1968   176.   Miss Linville
        177.   The Wait

1969   140.   The Collector
        141.   Sylvia
1970   172.   Inherit the Wind
1971   141.   The Ritual
1972   92.   Anderson Courthouse*
1973   147.   Mark
        148.   Intruder
1974   111.   Lingering Spirit
1975   180.   The Messenger
1977   121.   Melvin
        122.   Separate Realities
1978   109.   The Window
1979   118.   Bernard
1980   117.   Gisela

OSHRAIN, JOAN
1963   171.   Eighth Child

OSTEN, MARY
1935   129.   Ladywood School

OSTERDAY, MARY BOWE
(See Bowe, Mary E.)
1963   172.   Author of Liberty

OVERHOLSER, JOAN F.
1988   152.   Anderson Island Ferry
1989   166.   Temple of Artemis at Ephesus

OVERLEY, BRIAN D.
1978   110.   Cogito, ergo sum

OVERMAN, DARIS J.
1965   201.   Country Lane, Brown County
1966   110.   Vintage

OVERMAN, FRANCES
1968   178.   Teapot and Fruit
        179.   Lonely Sycamore
        180.   Suspended in Space and Time

OVERMAN, WENDELL F.
1947   151.   Afternoon of a Farm

OVERPECK, (L.) GAIL
1989   167.   Cactus Flower

OVERSTREET, ANNA
1957   160.   Sunset on White River

OWEN, NANCY R.
1987   172.   My Country Store
1988   153.   Upper Quarters
1989   168.   A Stitch in Time
        169.   Horse Power*
1990   139.   Time Out*

OWINGS, PATRICIA L.
1988   154.   She Wants a Young American

OZBUN, DONNA (M.)

Year	No.	Title
1977	123.	The Dreamer
1978	111.	Dreamless Sleep
	112.	Reflections in Green
1979	119.	Metamorphose
1980	118.	Beneath the Surface
1981	146.	Manuscript Garden
	147.	Testament
1982	158.	Fortuna's Fallout
	159.	Bronze II
1983	144.	Early Spring II
	145.	Meaning Obscure
1984	155.	Thor's Puzzle
	156.	Foundation
1985	115.	Yet, Another Door
1986	171.	A Sense of Direction
1988	155.	Everyman
	156.	Passage Through
1989	170.	Primordial Dawn
1990	140.	Emerging Order*
	141.	Bird House City

P

PADDACK, JULIE
1976   170.   Michigan Shaft House

PAGE, CARRIE O'HARA
1956   168.   Just Plain Bill
       169.   Roses in the News
1960   170.   Lilacs in the Sun
1962   235.   A Sunny Window

PAGE, EDSON WARD
1961   220.   Der Tod, das ist die kuhle Nacht

PAGE, Jr., GROVER
1949   111.   Fuzzie-Wuzzie
       112.   Wango, Squire?

PAIDRICK, RUSSELL E.
1929   212.   Old Fashioned Still Life

PALUZZI, CLAUDINE
(See Kelsey, Claudine Paluzzi)
1961   221.   Apple Still Life
       222.   Falling Figure*
       223.   Political Gathering
       224.   The Tumblers
       225.   Leah*
1962   236.   Nursing Child
       237.   Eric
       238.   Boy with Bird
       239.   Eucalyptus
1964   209.   Johnny*
1965   202.   Still Life, Butterfly
       203.   Still Life on a Table
       204.   Ceremony
       205.   Earth Forms
1966   111.   Apple Still Life
       112.   Untitled
1967   203.   Scavi*
       204.   Root Formation No. 2
       205.   Youngest Daughter
1970   173.   Still Life on Black
1975   181.   Portrait Study

PALUZZI, RINALDO R.
1957   161.   Gravel Pit

PARCELS, SAM
1988   157.   Natural Abstractions

PARKER, VIRGINIA RICE
1947   152.   Old Ladies' Home*
       153.   Hoosier Station

PARKER, WENTWORTH
1925   151.   A Legend
       152.   Winter in the Thickets
1926   208.   In the Lowlands

       209.   Late Fall
       210.   Autumn Days
1927   228.   In June

PARKS, ROBERT OWEN
1944   194.   Rented Room: A Still Life

PARSONS, DAVID G.
1935   130.   Psalm
1940   141.   Study in Opposing Forces, Boxing*
       142.   Study in Opposing Forces, Football
       143.   Unity

PATEL, DAKSHA J.
1976   171.   Quiet Corner
1978   113.   In the Natures Lap
       114.   Sunset at Udaypur*
1979   120.   The Abode in the Valley
       121.   Ras Leela (Indian Folk Dance)
1980   119.   In the Toy Shop

PATRICK, ALAN
1962   240.   Behind the Scenes
1963   173.   Banner
       174.   Fragment of a City*
1964   210.   Fragment of a City
1990   142.   Phalaenopsis #1

PATRICK, MILDRED
1971   144.   The Old Glass Mill

PATTERSON, JAMES K. (Jim)
1977   124.   Indiana Barns X
1978   115.   Indiana Barns XI*
1979   122.   Farm House
       123.   Indiana Barns XII
1980   120.   Indiana Barns XIV
       121.   Indiana Barns XVI*
1981   148.   Indiana Barns XIX
1982   160.   Indiana Barns XXI
       161.   Indiana Barns XX
1985   116.   Indiana Barns #22

PATTERSON, MARION L.
1942   180.   Taxco Street Scene*
1943   150.   Old Church at Ranchos de Taos
       151.   Talpa Hill, New Mexico
1944   195.   Carlotta's Pool
1946   139.   Storm Brewing
1948   96.   Chichicastenango, Guatemala*

PATTERSON, RICHARD R.
1973   149.   Portrait in Organic Shapes*

PATTON, JACK D.
1970   174.   Protest 1969
       175.   Untitled

1975	182.	Linthicum House, Georgetown
1977	125.	Old Tombstone Courthouse
1980	122.	Detail: Nutt's Folly

PAUL, DOROTHY SHORT
1951	136.	Edie
	137.	The Next Farm Up
1953	130.	Palms*
	131.	Mud Flats

PAUL, EVA E.
| 1938 | 152. | Shasta Daisies |

PAUL, FRANK K.
| 1933 | 153. | Walnut Plants |

PAULSON, REBECCA
| 1981 | 149. | Chicken Lady |

PAXSON, CONNIE J.
| 1975 | 183. | ECKS |

PAYNE, GRACE
1958	193.	Green Apples in Iron Bowl
1960	171.	Galla Evening
1962	241.	Flowers in Orbit
	242.	Flower Composition
	243.	Swamp Patterns
1963	175.	Florida Swamp Land
1965	206.	Fruit and Flowers
	207.	Summer by the Sea*
1967	206.	Fish
1969	142.	Autumn in Indiana
1971	142.	Scenery #6
	143.	Tension Headache

PAYNE, MAHLON (Bayley)
1936	162.	Miriam
1937	142.	Sketch, Negro*
1939	173.	Friends
	174.	Wood Carving
1940	144.	Spring
1942	181.	Jimmie
	182.	Kittens
	183.	Mrs. Pennybacker
1943	152.	Francine
	153.	Undine
1944	196.	Mardi
	197.	Margaret

PAZOL, BETTY
| 1959 | 148. | October Hillside |

PEABODY, ROD(ney) (R.)
1970	176.	Ladies Aid
1971	145.	Red Eyed Pig*
1975	184.	Only the Wind*
1976	172.	The New and the Old
1980	123.	Winter Sunshine

PEARCY, GERALD
1973	150.	Flower Basket
1987	173.	Sunset*
	174.	Roses
1988	158.	Grapes

PEARSON, THELMA FORSYTH
1952	157.	Manhattan, Tower
	158.	Afternoon Sun
1953	132.	Red Hen Family
1958	194.	Walla Walla*
	195.	Indian Nets
	196.	Indian Dug Outs
1960	172.	Feeling of Summer

PEDDLE, JULIET A.
| 1930 | 160. | Corpus Christi College, Oxford |

PEDEN, DONNA MOORE
| 1971 | 146. | The Clearing |

PEED, WILLIAM B.
1936	163.	Coming of the Storm
	164.	Evening Train
	165.	Country Kitchen
1937	143.	Henry*
1938	153.	Down on the Farm*
	154.	Grandma's Basement

PEELER, MARJORIE M.
1950	132.	Three Fish
1951	138.	Toadstools
	139.	Turtle
1955	153.	Horseplay*
1959	149.	Dancer

PEELER, RICHARD
1950	133.	Grock
1951	140.	Moses*
1953	133.	Mother and Baby*
1954	150.	The Family
1956	170.	The Prophet
1957	162.	Father And Son
1958	197.	Fish
	198.	King Solomon and the Disputed Child
1960	173.	Moses
	174.	Salome and Head of John the Baptist
1961	226.	Venus (Without Wings) Flying*
1964	211.	Beach Birds

PEELING, FLORENCE
| 1943 | 154. | Harbingers of Spring |
| 1944 | 198. | Studio Corner |

PEGG, OLIF
1959	150.	The Lone Beech
1961	227.	Spring Song
1964	212.	Dainty Wild Flowers

1966	113.	Dark Water
	114.	Roadside Loveliness*
1967	207.	Flowers of the Field
1976	173.	Autumn

PEKELSMA, JUDY
| 1981 | 150. | Indiana Skies |

PELHAM, ELEANOR Y.
| 1964 | 213. | Head of Child |

PENN, EVA
| 1951 | 141. | Woman in the Sun |

PENNISTON, DAVID R.
| 1977 | 126. | Ron |

PEREIRA, MARGARET
| 1937 | 144. | Rest Before Dinner |

PERKINS, F. ALIDA
| 1941 | 115. | The Dome at Notre Dame |

PERSELL, FRANK
1967	208.	Nature is Basic
	209.	Gothic
1973	151.	Memory Mix*
1974	112.	The Alphabet
1975	185.	Construction #1
1976	174.	1776-1976
1977	127.	Script Alphabet
1980	126.	Hills at Twilight
1982	162.	Churches
1983	146.	Tornado
	147.	Mystique
1984	158.	Mystique #2
1989	171.	Basics

PERSOV, ANNEMARIE
| 1961 | 228. | Diane |

PERSZYK, SY
1949	113.	An Old Estate*
1951	142.	Boy with Rabbits*
	143.	Torso
	144.	Fisherman's Dream
1952	159.	Study in Stone
1953	134.	Martin
	135.	On the Run

PESAVENTO, ERIN
1976	175.	Lilacs
	176.	Cicero Bridge
1984	159.	Ruby Falls

PESTA, MAUREEN
1989	172.	Slygo Knobs
	173.	Three Horses
1990	143.	The Memory

PESTOW, FRANCES E.
| 1968 | 181. | Shanty Town |
| 1970 | 177. | Still Life (Flowers) |

PETERS, DONALD ALLEN
1951	145.	The Wall*
	146.	First Star
	147.	Past Perfect
1952	160.	The Web of Time
	161.	A Far Corner

PETERS, DONOVAN W.
1969	143.	Diamond Sunset
	144.	Moonlight
1983	148.	A Deer in the Woods
1984	160.	The Big Tree
1986	172.	Filling Station on Route 52
	173.	Back Yard
1987	175.	Grape Vine in Spring
1988	159.	That's Indiana
1989	174.	Soy Bean Field in the Sun

PETERS, MARI
| 1967 | 210. | Reflections |
| | 211. | Backstage |

PETERS, STEVE
1983	149.	Crawling Paislies
1987	176.	Niche
	177.	Self Portrait as a Fat Snob

PETERSON, ELIZABETH F.
| 1967 | 212. | The City Weeps |
| 1972 | 93. | Grounded |

PETERSON, HERMAN
| 1940 | 145. | Portrait, Gordon Taylor |

PETTY, MARGARET BALL
1926	211.	The Sentinels
1927	229.	After Glow
	230.	Hollyhocks
1928	191.	Flowers
1930	161.	The Skaters
	162.	The Toiler

PHEMISTER, LORENA
1947	154.	Mother and Child*
	155.	Phantasmagoria*
1949	114.	Twilight Free-for-All
1956	171.	Autumn Leaves

PHILLIPS, CONNIE (L.)
| 1977 | 128. | Zebras Two |
| 1979 | 124. | Masai Child Bride |

PICKENS, BARBARA ALLEN
| 1985 | 117. | Cogent Copper |

PIEPER, LOIS
1968	182.	Violet and Friends
1971	147.	Down by the Station
	148.	Fragmented Fish
1972	94.	Flower Garden
1973	152.	Quiet Summer
1974	113.	Facade
	114.	Beached
1975	186.	Weeds, Seeds & Pods
	187.	Sumac
1976	177.	The Earth Sleeps
	178.	Autumn in Arkansas

PIERCE, DIANA (Miller)
1984	161.	The Wheel of Fortune
1986	174.	Places and Spaces
	175.	The Seventh Day
1988	160.	Dora's Poppies
	161.	We Sold 'Em All This Morning*
1989	175.	What about Those Crazy Tulips
	176.	Up at the Corner
1990	144.	Up the Waterspout
	145.	Vespers

PIERCE, JENNIE S.
1951	148.	Gauley Mill
1953	136.	In Autumn Dress

PIERCY, DELITA A(lvarez)
1985	118.	Chicago, Rainy Day
1986	176.	Light & Reflections
	177.	Evening Approaches in the Greenhouse
1987	178.	A Garden of Roses
	179.	Lion in the Fog
1988	162.	Lovers in the Garden
1990	146.	Observatory
	147.	Flower Shopping

PIERSOL, VIRGINIA
1968	183.	Self Portrait*
	184.	Girl in Doorway
1969	145.	Landscape with Figures*
1971	149.	Lois*
	150.	Spacescape

PIKER, HELEN B.
1968	185.	Frolic at Forty Fathoms
	186.	Tired Dolls
1973	153.	Go Forth, My Child
1974	115.	Pity the Earthbound
1983	150.	Brother Sun
	151.	Grandpa's Song

PILLE, HELEN S.
1927	231.	Zinnias

PIPPENGER, ROBERT
1940	146.	Bathers
	147.	Edward

PIRKLE, B.
1964	214.	Picnic

PITLUCK, DORRIE
1975	188.	Dorrie's Lunch

PIUNTI, KATHLEEN
1973	154.	Queen Anne's Lace

PLAAS, JOANNE
1971	151.	Circle of the Flowers
	152.	Generation

PLASCHKE, PAUL A.
1925	153.	Nocturne, Silver Creek, Southern Indiana
	154.	Nocturne, Ohio River
	155.	Wind Blown
1926	212.	Early Moon
	213.	Rainy Day, Ohio River
1927	232.	Clifty Creek, State Park, Madison
	233.	The President' Message (cartoon)
	234.	The Prodigal Son (cartoon)
	235.	The Semaphore (cartoon)
1928	192.	Spring
1929	213.	Charles Sneed Williams
	214.	Bruce Vance*
	215.	Lieut.-Col. Arnold Strode-Jackson, A. N. S.
	216.	In Dry Dock, Back Bay Biloxi
1930	163.	Southern Indiana Hills
	164.	Annette
1931	169.	Cartoon
	170.	Chuckling Boy
	171.	Moonlight
1934	141.	Tenant Farmer*
	142.	Myself
1935	131.	Mister Anteek
	132.	Nocturne, Southern Indiana
1936	166.	Nocturne, Spring
	167.	Southern Indiana Moon
1937	145.	Uncle Mose
	146.	Southern Indiana Farm
1939	175.	Water Color Caricature
	176.	Son, Albert*
1940	148.	Tante Ida
1941	116.	Spring, Southern Indiana

PLATT, TOM
1976	179.	Decaying Grid*

PLATTER, LOUISE M.
1955	154.	March
1962	244.	Melting Snow
	245.	Daybreak
1967	213.	The Catch
	214.	Wind Dried

PLEASANT, GLENNA
1987	180.	Self Portrait #1

PLOEGER, DOLORES
1959	151.	Gestalt, Southern Indiana
1960	175.	Otrabanda

PLUMMER, NELL
1962	246.	January
1963	176.	Deep River
1971	153.	Night Lights
	154.	Italian Hill Town

PNEUMAN, MILDRED YOUNG
1928	193.	An Old Fashioned Bouquet
1929	217.	Spanish Galleon
	218.	In the Sierras
1930	165.	Bear Lake, Colorado
	166.	San Juan Capistrano
	167.	Out for a Stroll
1931	172.	Bear Lake, Colorado
1933	154.	Showmass Lake, Colorado
1934	143.	Loch Vale, Colorado
1940	149.	From the Presidio, San Francisco
	150.	Loch Vale, Colorado
	151.	Indiana Dunes in Autumn
	152.	Lower Manhattan

POE, HUGH M.
1925	156.	Lorene, Reading
	157.	Herman and Vermin
	158.	Mardi Gras*
1926	214.	Composite Sweethearts
	215.	Portrait of H. W. B.
	216.	Sandy Selfridge*
1927	236.	The Costume Ball
	237.	The Last-Lite
	238.	Portrait Lt. Cros*
1928	194.	Mr. Bradburn
	195.	The Revelers
	196.	The Celebration
1929	219.	Costume Ball
1930	168.	Before Sunset
	169.	Margaret*
1933	155.	Betty
	156.	Mother
1937	147.	Old Man and His Stick
1941	117.	Celebration
	118.	Charlotte Leasure
1942	184.	Industrial Valley
	185.	Mrs. Hugh M. Poe
1944	199.	Self-Portrait
1945	140.	Rita
1948	97.	Parrhesia*
1950	134.	Color Reflection
1955	155.	The Mourners
1960	176.	Moonlight
1961	229.	Obit
1964	215.	Morning Riders
	216.	Queen Street South

POEHLMANN, THEODORE
1926	217.	Summer of Life

POINTS, JERRY W.
1969	146.	Relief Study #1

POLK, MARY ALYS
1925	159.	Flowers
	160.	Frogs
1927	239.	Swan
	240.	Still Life*
	241.	Toads
1928	197.	Vegetables
	198.	Kettle and Flowers
	199.	The Gravel Pit

POLLEY, FREDERICK (M.)
1925	161.	The Monument, Indianapolis
	162.	State House Dome, Indianapolis
	163.	The Towers, Brookville, Indiana
1926	218.	Illustration, Tech High School Tower
	219.	Illustration, Lower Broadway
	220.	Illustration, Madison Avenue, New York
	221.	Illustration, Old State House
	222.	Illustration, I.U. Campus
	223.	Illustration, Municipal Tower, N. Y.
	224.	Highlights and Shadows, New York
	225.	Library of Congress, Washington, D. C.
	226.	The Volcano, Pittsburg
1928	200.	Provincetown Street
	201.	The Volcano, Pittsburgh
	202.	Cortlandt Street, N. Y.
	203.	Highlights and Shadows
	204.	A Clump of Trees
	205.	Broadway from the Battery, N. Y.
1929	220.	Old Houses and New
	221.	Charleston Courtyard
	222.	Cliff-Dwellers
	223.	Broadway at 23rd
	224.	Dying Oak
	225.	Shadow Hill Farm
	226.	A Charleston Gateway
1930	170.	Fairy Glen
	171.	Mountain Retreat
	172.	Scottish Rite Cathedral
	173.	Village Road
	174.	Paradise Valley
	175.	Old Cart Road
	176.	Slopes of Mt. Hurricane
	177.	Rugged Adirondack Road
	178.	Paradise Hills
1931	173.	Avenue Market
1932	154.	Cemetery Oaks
	155.	The Capitol, Washington
	156.	Ferry Wharfs, Charleston, S. C.
	157.	End of Road
1933	157.	Early Autumn, Adirondacks
1934	144.	Cortlandt Street, N. Y.
	145.	Meadow Pathway
	146.	Old Dock, Gloucester

1935	133.	Pirate's Patio, New Orleans
	134.	Towers, Brookville, Ind.
	135.	The Volcano, Pittsburg
1936	168.	Trees and Birds
	169.	My Lower Meadow
	170.	Bean Blossom Bridge
	171.	San Antonio Mission, Night
1937	148.	In the Adirondacks
	149.	A Gnarled Veteran
	150.	Canal Footbridge, Metamora
1938	157.	Autumn in Brown County
1939	177.	Carolina Oak
	178.	From Battery, N. Y. C.
	179.	Market House, Charleston, S. C.
1940	158.	Inner Cove
1942	186.	Adirondack Roadway*
	187.	Cemetery Oaks*
	188.	San Juan Mission, San Antonio*
1943	155.	Old Houses, Charleston, S. C.*
	156.	My Studio in Winter
1944	200.	Paradise Valley
	201.	Old Cart Road
	202.	Wedding at Beaufort
1945	141.	Cathedral and the Gables
1946	140.	The Monument
	141.	Church on the Circle
1947	156.	Young Maple in Autumn
1948	98.	Approaching Storm
1951	149.	Gate Tree and St. Michaels, Charleston, S. C.
	150.	Out of Work
	151.	University Park
1952	162.	Black Horse Troop
	163.	Indiana Pottery

POLOMCHAK, MARK

1973	155.	L. H. 1973
1974	116.	Hodges Place
	117.	Ace & Deuce
1975	189.	Mike's Boat House
1976	180.	Old Friend
	181.	Between Six*
1977	129.	Just A Can
1978	116.	Clinton 1939
1979	125.	Lonesome Pine
1980	124.	Cities Escape
1982	163.	Let It Snow*
	164.	It's Only a Dream
1985	119.	Reflections
1986	178.	Left Out
1987	181.	Cool & Crisp
	182.	Milk Cans & Buckets
1988	163.	Little Hoosier

POLOMCHAK, STEPHAN (Steve)

1965	208.	Cathedral Arch
	209.	Shrimp Boat*
	210.	Lonesome Junction
1967	215.	Lost Path
	216.	Farm Scene Study #13

1968	187.	Old Mikes Place
	188.	Chicken Coop
1969	147.	Winter 1967
	148.	Stephan's Point
1970	178.	Fisherman's Morning
1971	155.	Idle Wagon
1972	95.	Door County, Wisc.
	96.	Sometimes in Winter
1973	156.	The Pump
	157.	Door County, Winter '72*
1974	118.	Early Snows
	119.	Gail Plus Two*
1975	190.	The Old Mill
	191.	Lobster Traps
1976	182.	Worn Out
	183.	NC-101*
1977	130.	Pieces of Dreams
1980	125.	Salty Air
1981	151.	Wagon Cover
	152.	Lower Dock
1982	165.	Tree View*
	166.	Cape Ann
1985	120.	Missing Spoke
	121.	Icewater
1986	179.	Vanishing Stairs
1988	165.	On a Cold Sunday Morning

POMPA, GLADYS

1956	172.	Summer
1957	163.	Zinnias
	164.	Spring Dilemma
1958	199.	Treasures
1960	177.	Iris

PONADER, LEATHE CARMAN

1941	119.	Betty
1942	189.	A Small World, Three China Horses, Stretching Shadows, and Hope
	190.	Gaudy Spring
	191.	Joan

PONCE, ANN

1979	126.	By the Water

POOL, KAYE

1971	156.	Winter's Shadow
1976	184.	Winter Witchery
	185.	Those Bittersweet Days

POOR, BARB(ara) F.

1967	217.	Wintery Estate
1984	162.	Mansfield Mill in Winter

POPE, W. L.

1982	167.	Sheller-19 M

PORTER, E(lmer) JOHNSON

1929	227.	University of Chicago Chapel
	228.	Stella
	229.	Christmas

1930	179.	Still Life
1931	174.	Primroses
1932	158.	Small Point, Maine
1937	151.	Lobster Pots
	152.	Rock Pools
	153.	Illinois Central Turn Table
1938	155.	The Green House
	156.	The Tar Pot
	321.	Red Lobster Buoys
1939	180.	Phippsburg Meeting
	181.	Pink Hydrangea
	182.	Union County Bridge
1940	153.	A Bit of Old Centerville
	154.	Fish House Cove
1941	120.	Grasselli Chemical Plant, East Chicago, Ind.
	121.	Walt's Dock
1942	192.	Story Book House

PORTER, MARY LOUISE
1955	156.	The Red Tablecloth

POSEY, LESLIE T.
1931	175.	Lorraine*
	176.	Mrs. Joy C. Yee
	177.	Simplicity
1932	159.	Portrait, Laura Slobe
	160.	Non Sibi, Sed Patriae
	161.	Portrait, Georges Rosier
1933	158.	Portrait Relief
	159.	Moses
	160.	Churning

POTTENGER, ZEB E.
1928	206.	A March Landscape

POULSON, JO(sephine Hollingsworth)
(See Hollingsworth, Josephine A.)
1932	162.	Illustration (11)
	163.	Friends
	164.	Spotty
	165.	Illustration (3)
	166.	Book Plate
	167.	Illustration (2)
	168.	Who's Afraid
	169.	Illustration (1)
1940	155.	Sunlit Pines
	156.	Destroyer 396
	157.	Caribou
1941	122.	The Grey Barn
1942	193.	Mountain Stream
	194.	Water Street
1943	157.	Windy Days
	158.	Wilmette Harbor
	159.	Saugatuck
1949	115.	Vermont Village
	116.	Mont St. Pierre Gaspe P. Q.

POVALAC, JAN ERRINGTON
1980	127.	Three Phases of a Woman
	128.	Once Upon a Time

POWELL, MARGARET (W.)
1947	157.	U. S. Coast Guard, Michigan City
	158.	The Oasis
1949	117.	The Shrimp Plant*
1950	135.	Oriental Symphony*
	136.	Snow Caps
1951	152.	Boutique Fantasque
	153.	End of the Race

POWELL, MARTHA L.
(See Horton, Martha Powell)
1989	177.	Larder Shelf
1990	148.	Early Racers

POWERS, JANET T. (Tommy)
1973	158.	Summer's End
1974	120.	Untitled
1975	192.	Out of the Sea
1976	186.	Up to the Ridge
1977	131.	Santuary
1978	117.	McClellan's Woods
1984	163.	Side by Side with Sorghum
1985	122.	Shelf Top Sandpiper

PRASUHN, JOHN G.
1926	227.	James Whitcomb Riley at 35
	228.	Portrait
	229.	Riley Roses
1927	242.	"Aum" Dr. Bhagat Singh Thind of Amritsar, India*
1928	207.	Portrait, Judge B.
	208.	Job
1930	180.	Young Philosopher
1931	178.	Portrait Study
1932	170.	The Eskimo Kid
1933	161.	Rocena
	162.	Portrait Charles A. Corwin
1934	147.	Bah-Mary, Navajo
1935	136.	Portrait, Harrietta R.
1936	172.	Marie E.
	173.	Ramon G.
1938	158.	Tall Buffalo*
1939	183.	Mr. B*
	184.	Original Pot, Two Famous Indians

PRATT, ROSALIND JEAN
1978	118.	Chippewa Beach

PRETZ, RICHARD
1930	181.	A Chinese Horse, Wong Dynasty

PRICE, CAROLYN
1977	132.	Marshy Landscape

PRICE, GENE
  1953 137. Vintage of Harmony
  1973 159. Self Portrait

PRICE, GLENN
  1936 174. Sternberg Farm near Glenview
      175. Barnyard
      176. Farm Dooryard

PRICE, MARILYN
  1970 179. Sequestrum*
  1971 157. His Habits, Phase I
  1981 153. Internal Forces
      154. Stages

PRICE, ROLLAND
  1946 142. Winter Haven

PRILIK, CHARLES RAPHAEL
  1925 164. Copenhagen Harbor
      165. In the Mohawk Valley
      166. Scotty

PRITCHARD, RUTH W.
  1987 183. Ohio at Madison
      184. Natchez Trace*

PROUT, G. MORTON
  1940 159. Saturday Night
  1942 195. Los Pregoneros

PROW, HALLIE PACE
  1926 230. My Garden in June

  1927 243. Woodland Spring Blossoms
      244. A Summer Bouquet
  1928 209. A June Bouquet
  1930 182. Late Summer Flowers
  1932 171. Peonies
      172. Hardy Phlox
  1937 154. Broom Sedge and Clak
  1942 196. A Garden Bouquet
  1943 160. Gathered from the Roadside

PRUITT, VERNISE IRENE
  1938 159. Adam and Eve
      160. Daniel in the Lion's Den
      161. Hoosier Milk Maid
      162. Tiger
      322. Lilies

PUCKETT, HENRY
  1938 163. Fire
      164. Flight into Egypt
      165. Sea Shore
  1939 185. Job
  1940 160. Salt Creek

PUTNAM, FANNY GIBBS
  1943 161. Hucsache

PUTTY, HELEN
  1986 180. Sarah

Q

QUAKENBUSH, SHIRLEY
1990 149. Hoosier Flower

QUEAR, EDNA
1962 247. My Gardner's Tools

QUILLIN, EMERSON
1971 158. Silkscreen People
        159. Untitled

1972 97. Discover America
         98. Crystal

QUILLIN, WILLIAM
1969 149. Painting
1970 180. RISDI

RAADE, KAY
1980 129. Dakota
1981 155. Hooking Worms
1982 168. Stag

RAEMAEKERS, ANTOINE
1953 138. Egypt

RAFERT, MILLIE
1973 160. Winter Weeds

RAINEY, JUDITH A.
1983 152. Geometric Magnification
1985 123. Black of Night/Gold of Day

RAMSEY, SHERI J.
1973 161. Tree in Mist
162. Self Portrait
1974 121. At Crossroads

RANDALL, PAUL A.
1928 210. Hollyhocks
1930 183. Winter Morning

RANDALL, THEODORE
1933 163. Black Adam*
1934 148. Old Jake

RANS, JON (W.)
1979 127. Minimum Daily Requirement II
1980 130. Envelopes

RANSTEAD, PEARL
1941 123. Stocks
124. White Cockatoo

RARICK, DOROTHY
1985 124. Still Life with Green Bottle

RATLIFF, LOUISE G.
1946 143. Natalie

RATLIFF, PAT STAPF
1985 125. Trees in Sienna
1988 166. Wood Ducks

RAY, MELVILLE
1955 157. Sentinels, Kennebunkport, Maine
1958 200. Brixham Harbor (England)

RAYMOND, JO GREENE
(See Greene, Jo)
1970 181. The Bribe

REARICK, RUSSELL
1936 177. The Widowed One

REASON, MARILOU SMITH
1989 178. Cass Country

REASONER, DAVID
1928 211. Sawkill in Winter

RECTOR, DONNA
1957 165. Ante-Bellum
1958 201. Citrus Still Life
1960 178. While Viewing Television
1961 230. The Begonia*
1964 217. Still Life in Fives
218. First Thaw

REDICK, JOHN
1975 193. Thirties Buckel

REDICK, PAMELA LANG
1975 194. Textile
195. Sunlit*

REDMAN, STEVEN
1989 179. King Me
180. Irish Chain
1990 150. Deco Network
151. Eclectic Mix*

REED, DOEL
1925 167. Spring Morning
1926 231. Spring in Arcadia
232. A Land of Romance and Tree Study
233. Autumn Sun
1927 245. Rainy Evening (Boulevard Montparnesse, Paris)
246. Liebestraum
1942 197. Black Bear Creek Country
198. Evening after the Rains
199. Romanza

REED, FORREST J.
1960 179. House on Top of the Hill
180. Still Life
1961 231. Early Stoneware
1962 248. Falling Monarch
1964 219. Fall's Bounty
1965 211. Found Beauty
212. Fall's Bounty
1969 150. Wedgwood Pitcher

REED, MATTHEW M.
1979 128. Still Life with Gesso Jar
1985 126. Untitled II

REED, MAY
1968 189. Red Square

REED, ROBERT BROWNING
| 1977 | 133. | Green Pears |
| 1979 | 129. | Traveler II |

REENTS, HENRY A.
1934	149.	Evening at the Dunes
	150.	Wind Swept Leaves
1937	155.	Mount Round Top
	156.	Sand Turrets
1939	186.	By the Sand Hollow

REEVE, KENNETH J.
1952	164.	Church at New Bellsville
1953	139.	Indian Summer
	140.	Streamside Sycamore
1954	151.	Back Yard
1955	158.	Country Church
	159.	Early October
1956	173.	Brown County Farm
	174.	Brown County, Group of Prints
1957	166.	Country Store
	167.	Winter Wonderland
	168.	The Old Pump
1958	202.	Winter In Brown County
	203.	The Covered Well
	204.	Autumn Evening
1960	181.	Old-Timers
	182.	Along the Creek
1962	249.	Afternoon Shadows
1963	177.	Snow Blanket
1965	213.	Caribbean Morning
	214.	Brown County Roadside
1966	115.	Cargo from St. Kitts
1967	218.	Winter Day, Brown County
	219.	After-Glow
	220.	The Brass Lock
1970	182.	Morning at Nubble Light
1971	160.	Winter Weather
1972	99.	The Old Oak
	100.	Bear Wallow Road
1973	163.	Brown County Winter
1976	187.	Snow Blanket
	188.	Sun and Snow

REEVES, LARRY G(ene)
| 1976 | 189. | The Window |
| 1979 | 130. | Winter Intrusions |

REEVES, PAUL B.
1957	169.	In Dry-Dock
1970	183.	Portrait in Water Color #1
	184.	Portrait in Water Color #2

REGAN, MARY
| 1986 | 181. | Multifloral |
| | 182. | House Next Door |

REGESTER, ALICE
| 1927 | 247. | Wild Roses |

REIBEL, BERTRAM
1935	137.	Sunlight in Antigua
	138.	Seated Japanese
	139.	Shadows
1936	178.	Diggers

REICHARD, JOEL W(arner)
1946	144.	Sponge Boats
	145.	Toshi*
	146.	Side Yards, Florida
1947	159.	Uncle Dave
	160.	Shell Gatherers
1948	99.	Old Man Small*
	100.	Lady on a Green Bench
	101.	Provincetown Gossip
1949	118.	Banana Tree
1950	137.	Goldie*
	138.	Sunday A. M., Wellfleet
	139.	Teena*
1951	154.	Warning at Nausett*
	155.	Hea' Bi'y Bi'y
	156.	Steno*
1952	165.	The Cellist
	166.	Steps to the Church
	167.	Young Pastor Pinkston*
1953	141.	North of Lido
	142.	Sunday Morning*
	143.	The Blacksmith's Son
1954	152.	Little Old Lady*
	153.	Boat Yard
	154.	Man in the Park
1955	160.	Tom
	161.	This Ol' House*
	162.	Recess
1956	175.	The Skipper
	176.	Along the B. & O.
1957	170.	The Sentinels
	171.	Street In Madison
	172.	Country Girl*
1958	205.	LaParade
	206.	Boat Repairs
	207.	Jeanie*
1959	152.	St. George Street*
	153.	Memorial Park
	154.	Connie*
1960	183.	Miss Heady of Muncie
	184.	Tourist Rooms
	185.	The Net Mender
1961	232.	The Clam Digger*
	233.	Rena
	234.	Mill Pond Farm
1962	250.	Derelict
	251.	Autumn in Vermont
	252.	Oyster Harbor
1963	178.	Eurasian Girl
	179.	Pemaquid Point Light*
	180.	Old House at Bristol
1964	220.	Between the Tides*
	221.	Claire
	222.	The Lobster Pound

1965	215.	Magnolias*
	216.	Treasure Cove
	217.	The Red Flyer
1966	116.	Julie
	117.	Seaward
	118.	Low Tide
1967	221.	October
	222.	Wellfleet Flats
1968	190.	Salt Air*
	191.	Beached
	192.	Jody
1969	151.	Provincetown Dories*
	152.	Pemaquid
1970	185.	Beachwalk
	186.	St. Phillips, Charleston*
1971	161.	Crossing at Bremen
	162.	Derelict
1973	164.	Derelict II
	165.	Two Odd Buoys*
1974	122.	Morning Mail
	123.	End of an Era
1978	119.	Elkhart Opera
	120.	Past Elegance
1979	131.	Southern Comfort*
	132.	Sunday Afternoon

REID, JOANNE

| 1986 | 183. | Untitled |
| 1988 | 167. | Summer's Morning |

REIDER, JOHN HENRY

| 1970 | 187. | Homecoming of Tommy Rose |

REIFERS, ANNE

| 1953 | 144. | Summer's Glory |
| 1958 | 208. | Arizona Skies after the Storm |

REIFFEL, CHARLES

1925	168.	The Harbor Entrance
	169.	Wilton Lake in Winter*
	170.	Booth Bay Harbor
1926	234.	Across the Valley
	235.	Rockport
	236.	Norwalk River in Winter*
1927	248.	La Jolla Shore*
	249.	Midsummer
	250.	Autumn
1928	212.	Mill in Winter*
	213.	Melting Snow
	214.	The Pool in Winter
1930	184.	Mountain Ranch after Rain
	185.	Morning, Nogales, Arizona
1931	179.	Banner Gorge, Southern California*
	180.	Still Life
	181.	The Sketching Class
1932	173.	Mountain Dairy
1938	166.	Nogales, Mexico*
	167.	The Trout Stream
1939	187.	Late Afternoon Glow
	188.	Sun Up

REINES, BRUCE

| 1980 | 131. | Metamorphosis* |

REITH, L(yle)

| 1974 | 124. | After the Snowfall |

REITZEL, MARQUES E.

1925	171.	High Point
1927	251.	Foothills
	252.	Spring Clouds
	253.	Moose Ear Creek
1928	215.	The Morning Shift
1929	230.	Across the Bridge
	231.	The Six-Fifteen*
1930	186.	Loch Vale
	187.	On the Road to Milner Pass
	188.	In the Calumet District
1932	174.	Sawtooth Mountain
1934	151.	Before the Storm
	152.	Presque Isle, Marquette, Michigan
1935	140.	Whistling Boy
1936	179.	Winter Evening
	180.	Behind the Loaf
1937	157.	The River Road
	158.	Autumnal Showers
1938	168.	The Burning Barn
	169.	Railroad Siding
1940	161.	Blue Shadows
	162.	Pigeon Point Light House*
1943	255.	Rocky Shore
	256.	Swamp Shadows
1954	155.	Winter, Pescadero, Cal.

REMLEY, ROXIE

| 1971 | 163. | Mountain Mist* |
| | 164. | Red Landscape |

RENNER, CHARLES H.

| 1952 | 168. | Homeward Bound |

RENT, WILLIAM A.

| 1962 | 253. | Fruit |
| | 254. | Rita's Bath |

REVEAL, JAMES RODNEY

| 1981 | 156. | Concrete Landscape |
| 1988 | 168. | Ladder Company #10 |

REX, RUBY M.

| 1943 | 162. | Californis Rannunculus |

REYNERSON, JUNE

| 1932 | 175. | Relief |

RHOADES, JACK

| 1944 | 203. | "E." Award |

RICH, GEORGE

| 1925 | 172. | Southern Indiana |
| | 173. | Hills of Genoa |

1926	237.	Childhood Days*
1931	182.	Sid Walton
1932	176.	Introspective

RICHARDS, MYRA REYNOLDS

1926	238.	The Idealist
1927	254.	Jazz Idol

RICHARDS, VIOLET

1973	166.	Sierra DelCarmen

RICHARDSON, CONSTANCE

1949	119.	Hot Sun

RICHARDSON, ESTHER RUBLE

1933	164.	Philodendron
1934	153.	Matrimony and Bittersweet
1935	141.	Bean Blossom Valley
1936	181.	Lace Cloth
1937	328.	Two Windows
1938	170.	Tall Pines
1939	189.	Summer in Arcady
1940	163.	Etude: Pink Phlox
1941	125.	The Endless Hills
	126.	Yesterday, Today, and Tomorrow: Taos*

RICHARDSON, LaMONTA

1969	153.	Barnyard
1971	165.	New Orleans Courtyard
1975	196.	Catamarans

RICHARDSON, MILDRED

1976	190.	Queen Anne's Fantasy
	191.	Blossoms of Spring
1977	134.	The Call of Spring

RICHEY, OAKLEY E.

1930	189.	The Tempest
	190.	The Workers
1935	142.	The Concrete Mixer
	143.	Suggestion of Marblehead
1937	160.	Gas Tank
	161.	Leland Reels
	162.	Green Kitchen
1940	164.	Alcatraz Twilight
	165.	Ferris Wheel
	166.	Golden Gate Bridge
1941	127.	Evening Light
	128.	Noon Heat
1942	200.	Night Fair
1948	102.	Woodland Fungus*
1949	120.	Accent in Black
	121.	The Wading Pool
1950	140.	Interlude*
1951	157.	Promenade
1953	145.	Hillside Spring*
	146.	Green Sections
1954	156.	Construction in Orange
1970	188.	Golden Pen

RICHMAN, JEANNE P.

1971	166.	Ecology
	167.	Snow Bird

RICHMAN, MARGARET (A.) VOGEL

1965	218.	Waiting for Cue
1967	223.	Collage No. 5
	224.	Still Life
1975	197.	Rag Alley
1976	192.	Sally Vogel

RIDGWAY, MARIFRANCES

1961	235.	Ozark Mountain Village
1974	125.	Feedlot
1975	198.	Holiday
1978	121.	Braid

RIFFLE, ELBA L.
(See Vernon, Elba Riffle)

1928	216.	Assembly
	217.	Treasures
1931	183.	Old Apple Butter Kettle
	184.	Gladflowers
	185.	Portrait of a Child
1932	177.	Tulips
	178.	Forsythia
1933	165.	Still Life
	166.	Late October, Morning
1934	154.	Play
	155.	Before Daylight
1935	144.	Boarding House, Saturday Night
1937	159.	Orientals
1938	171.	Busy Corner
	172.	Still Life, Flowers
1939	190.	Water Front
1940	167.	6 A. M.
1941	129.	Allegory, Any Man

RIFNER, BEN O.

1942	201.	Greek Revival

RIGLEY, FREDERICK W.

1954	157.	Evening Light
	158.	Light and Shadow*
	159.	Overlook
1955	163.	In the Center Ring
1956	177.	A Link with the Past
	178.	Side by Side
1957	173.	Pigeon Cove
	174.	Dancing Sycamores
	175.	Treasure Island
1958	209.	Down Brown County Way
	210.	Squall's End
	211.	Low Tide*
1959	155.	Along the Street
	156.	Kelp's Place
	157.	Early Leaves
1960	186.	Greasy Creek Road
	187.	After Glow

1961	236.	Church in the Hills*
	237.	Grandma Barnes Road
	238.	South Street Rockport
1962	255.	Autumn's Foliage
1963	181.	Light and Shadow
1964	223.	Going Back
	224.	Spring
	225.	Shifting Sands
1965	219.	Winter Light
	220.	Duneland
1966	119.	Evening Glow
1967	225.	Yesterday's Way
	226.	February 1st
1970	189.	Back Bayou
	190.	No Return
1971	168.	Stem and Stern
	169.	Tide and Time
1973	167.	Bayou Boats
1974	126.	Grains of Time
1975	199.	Solitude
	200.	Old Port
1976	193.	Free Enterprise
	194.	A Bridge with a Past
1977	135.	Cedar Key
	136.	Summertime*
1985	127.	Vanishing Scene*
1986	184.	Blue Boat
	185.	Weeds

RIGSBY, JON
1975 201. Mop Top

RILEY, HARRIETT F.
1939 191. Mary
1940 168. Mehala
     169. Michigan Hills

RITZ, JO
1973 168. Sycamore Hat

RITZI, ELLEN
1970 191. A Munich Gate

ROBBINS, BELLE BOGARDUS
1953 147. Jeanne

ROBERTS, EDWARD J.
1986 186. "I" House, Metamora
1987 185. End of Winter

ROBERTS, GEORGINA F.
1955 164. On the Garden Table
     165. Monday Afternoon
1958 212. Old Hillside House

ROBERTS, HERMINE
1940 170. Coal Dock
     171. Montana Snowstorm
     172. Mountain Camp
     173. The Mill

ROBERTS, J. ANNA
1984 164. Grandpa's Tractor*
1985 128. A Bike of Another Color
1986 187. Mill Machinery, View II
     188. Before the Fall
1988 169. Excalibaro
1989 181. Irish Chain
1990 152. Farm Aid
     153. Untitled

ROBERTS, PATRICIA M.
1967 227. Storm a Coming

ROBERTSON, DONALD L.
1970 192. Vertical Rods 84 C
1971 170. Wild and Free
1976 195. Sunday Cyclist
     196. Life's Journey

ROBERTSON, W. A.
1956 179. Boy and Stilts

ROBINSON, R. H.
1938 173. Portrait

ROCKE, GILBERT
1929 232. Sunday Afternoon

RODGERS, DAVID L.
1978 122. Oolite II*
     123. Trisectrix III
1989 182. Plaza with Two Tan Towers

ROESENER, ELIZABETH TAUER
1933 167. Cyclamen Plant
     168. A Japanese Study

ROGERS, NELLE C.
1934 156. Sunny Morning in Brown County
     157. Side Road
1936 182. Across the Street
1947 161. Any Autumn
1948 103. The Cowgill House

ROHRMAN, JOE
1978 124. Lineup
1979 133. Park
1980 132. Vacation
1981 157. Killing Time
     158. Third Class Carriage*
1982 169. Night Hawks
1983 153. Line
     154. Street Artists
1985 129. Bathers
1988 170. Shriners

ROLLF, E. FIRTH
1961 239. Garden Flowers
1963 182. The Green Bottle
1964 226. Steps in Glen Miller Park

ROOSE, ERNEST R.
1944	204.	Portrait, Loretta*
	205.	The Riffle
	206.	Portrait, Camilla
1945	142.	Snow on Williams Creek*
	143.	Still Life with Peace Maker
1946	147.	Stella
	148.	White River Fisher*
1947	162.	The Famous "500," Indianapolis*
1948	104.	Speed Maestro Henning
	105.	University Park*
	106.	Lap 183, Indianapolis
1949	122.	The Wet Road
1950	141.	Indiana
	142.	Speed Artist
1951	158.	Along Billy Creek
	159.	Speedway Still Life*
1952	169.	Pit Fire
1954	160.	By Man's Hands*

ROPKEY, ERNEST C.
1939	192.	The Old Barn
1944	207.	A Winter Evening

ROSE, PATRICIA E.
1968	193.	Flowers on a Kitchen Chair
1969	155.	The Berkshires

ROSEBROCK, WAHNITA C.
1984	165.	Playing, Self Portrait

ROSENTHAL, NANCY GLOH
1971	171.	Arrangement*
1972	101.	Venice in Blue

ROSS, CHARLES A.
1947	163.	November Evening

ROSS, JOHN FREDERIC
1955	166.	Interlude
	167.	Froliche Weinachten 1954*

ROSS, JOSEPH
1965	221.	Lisbon, Portugal
	222.	Old Fisherman

ROSSER, DONNA
1979	134.	Marsh
1980	133.	Souvenirs
1982	170.	Conversation Piece
1983	155.	Early Morning Boathouse
1984	166.	To Climb A Hill
	167.	Indiana Stream
1985	130.	Corinthian*
	131.	Santorini
1986	189.	Alone with Two Trees*
	190.	Walk with the Roses*

ROTH, AMANDA
1958	213.	Grain Elevator
	214.	Through The Shed

ROTHENBERGER, GARY L.
1970	193.	Mary

ROUSH, CATHERINE
1961	240.	Roses
1962	256.	Peonies
	257.	Grandmother's Roses
1969	156.	Old Homasassa

ROUSH, J. J.
1962	258.	Twilight (Mt. Nebo Overlook, Morgan Co.)
	259.	May Apple Jungle (Morgan County)

ROYCE, JAN
1987	186.	Pensive
	187.	The Reader

ROYER, CATHERINE MILLS
1984	168.	Attic Reverie*

ROYSTER, Sr., GEORGE M.
1961	241.	An Artist First Studio
1962	260.	Winter Sky

RUBENKOENIG, IRMA
1944	208.	Beside the Road
1945	144.	Winter's Decoration

RUBINS, DAVID K.
1942	202.	Prairie Farmer
	203.	Seated Nude*
	204.	Seated Nude
	205.	Waiting Room*
1943	163.	Standing Nude
	164.	The Cloud
1944	209.	Garden Piece*
1952	170.	Seated Nude

RUDDER, S(tephen) W. D.
1929	233.	From My Window
1930	191.	Pink House
1931	186.	Fourth Presbyterian Church, Chicago
	187.	Encroachment
1932	179.	Near North Side, Chicago
	180.	Street in Algiers
	181.	St. Mark's Square, Venice
1933	169.	Monon Station, Salem

RUDIN, ALBERT
1928	218.	Pen and Ink Motif of Switzerland
	219.	Pen and Ink Motif of Switzerland

RUDMAN, JOAN (Combs)
1971	172.	Silver Dunes
	173.	Mud, Rocks and Water
1972	102.	After the Storm
1973	169.	Biddeford Poo!, Maine
	170.	The Road Not Taken

1974	128.	Autumn
1975	202.	Oriental Still-Life
	203.	The Sentinel
1976	198.	Colors on Parade*
	199.	Fall Motif
1986	191.	End of Summer

RUDOLPH, JOAN V.
1970   194.   Kirsten

RUEFF, JINI
1987   188.   Psyche Renewed by TV
            189.   Fall Pathways on Indiana Farm
1989   183.   Inner Resource
1990   154.   The Invitation

RUEL, TED
1984   169.   Richmond Rest Stop

RUMLEY, LUCILLE
1931   188.   Seven Elms
1933   172.   The Student
            173.   Fruit
1934   158.   Sentinels

RUNDELL, ORA E.
1976   200.   Q. E. D.

RUSH, OLIVE
1925   174.   Food Bearers, Shalako Dance
            175.   Sun-Basket Dance
            176.   Portrait of Mrs. A.
1926   239.   County Fair, the Aeroplanes*
            240.   Men in the Chorus
1927   256.   Fawn at Daybreak
            257.   The Buffalo Stampede
1928   220.   Landscape with Barnyard
            221.   Goats on the Road

1929   236.   Thoughts
            237.   Helen
            238.   Forest Family
1930   192.   Judging Horses*
            193.   Deer in the Garden of Eden
1931   189.   The Mountain Road, Autumn*
            190.   Landscape with Deer
1932   182.   Forest Rhythms
1934   159.   The Weird Land
1940   175.   Autumn Sunset
1943   165.   The Wooden Horses
            166.   Putting Up the Big Tent
1946   149.   The Empty Foodpots
1949   123.   October Snow*
            124.   Holy Night
1950   143.   Black Rock & Deer
1951   160.   Geese and Spring Blossoms
            161.   Merry Go Round
1952   171.   Spring Will Come Again

RUTSCHMANN, NANCY ANDER
1985   132.   From Time to Time
            133.   Blind Devotion (Braille Symbol: LOVE)
1988   171.   Lunar Phases & Mythical Grecian Faces

RYDEN, KENNETH G.
1988   172.   Wisdom's Fleeting Glance
1989   184.   Lost in Space, Challenger Disaster*
            185.   Guardian of Peace

RYNERSON, HARRIET (E.)
1948   107.   The Old Place*
1949   125.   The Wind-swept Hill
            126.   Geraniums*

S

SAGER, GERALDINE
1988   173.   Ann's Flowers

SALMON, CLORADEL D.
1943   167.   Orientals
       168.   My Kingdom for a Horse
       169.   The Sleuth
1944   210.   Straw Flowers
       211.   Bouquet of Peonies
       212.   A Spot of Sunshine
1945   145.   Yes: We Have No Bananas
1946   150.   The White House in Danville

SALTZ, LARRY
1971   174.   Oriental Fire

SAMPLE, ROSAMOND
1965   223.   Three Figures
       224.   White Design No. 2,
              Incompatibility

SAMPSON, JOHN H.
1937   165.   Quietude
       166.   Interlude
1938   177.   Snowbound

SANBORN, JAMES
1987   190.   The Rutting Season
1989   186.   For Herb Domination

SANDEFUR, JOHN COURTNEY
1927   258.   Street of David, Jerusalem
       259.   Federal Building from Quincy Street
       260.   A Flanders Doorway
       261.   An Old Town Gate, Cairo
       262.   The Shepherd
       263.   Sam's Junk Yard
       264.   Le Marchand de Mouron
       265.   An Old Court, Sachsenhausen
       266.   Ca D'Oro and the Grand Canal
1928   222.   Sam's Junk Yard
       223.   A Dutch Mill
       224.   Marchand de Mouron
       225.   An Old Court, Sachsenhausen*
       226.   Elevated Road
       227.   Dobbins Retreat
1929   239.   Old Fine Arts Bldg., Chicago
       240.   Towers, Michigan Boulevard
       241.   Maxwell Street Market, Chicago
1930   194.   Maxwell Street Market, Chicago
       195.   Spiral Stairway, New Orleans
       196.   Rue Madison at Chartres, New
              Orleans
       197.   Old French Quarter, New Orleans

1932   183.   Rue Madison Street, Chartres, New
              Orleans
       184.   Spiral Stairway, New Orleans
       185.   Old French Quarter, New Orleans
       186.   A Bit of Brown County
       187.   Sailing
       188.   Old Beauregard House, New
              Orleans

SANDERSON, HARRIET
1982   171.   Marigold Featherstone

SANFORD, W. DeLACEY
1963   183.   Alley 19

SANGERNEBO, EMMA EYLES
1925   179.   Mrs. Walter Flawdorf
1927   267.   Tapestry
1928   228.   Zinnias
1943   170.   An Historic Sunday Morning

SAN PIETRO, ALICE K.
1976   201.   Pears
1977   137.   Impression
1985   134.   Patterns
1986   192.   Fuchsias
1987   191.   Cyclamen
1989   187.   Cactus Flower
1990   155.   Among the Sycamores

SARBER, HELEN I.
1960   188.   Tools of the Trade
1963   184.   Landscape Finger Painting
1964   227.   Winter Landscape
1965   225.   Sunflowers and Apples
1966   120.   Still Life with Fruit*
1967   228.   Spring Landscape

SARGENT, PAUL (T.)
1925   177.   In the Beech Woods
       178.   Woods' Shadows
1926   241.   Over the Hilltop
       242.   Sunset After Rain
       243.   Three Trees
1927   268.   Afternoon in the Beech-Woods
1928   229.   Beeches in October
       230.   Wood Interior
       231.   Clearing Weather
1929   242.   Trees in Winter
       243.   The Yellow Tree
1930   198.   A Corner of the Wheatfield
       199.   In the Orchard
       200.   Shade
1931   191.   Sketch
       192.   Snowy Morning

1932	189.	Creek in Winter
1933	174.	Autumn
	175.	Across the Valley
1934	160.	Clouds of Afternoon
1935	148.	In the Heat of the Day
1936	184.	Gray Mountain
1938	178.	Frosty Morning
1939	194.	A Hint of Spring
	317.	The Oak
1940	176.	The Creek in Winter
1941	131.	Sycamores
1942	206.	October Sunlight
	207.	The Harvest
1943	171.	October
	172.	The Barn Lot
	173.	Hillside Farm
1944	213.	Spring Time
	214.	The Oak Tree
1945	146.	The River
	147.	The Lily Pond*
	148.	Zinnias
1946	151.	Sunset in Florida

SAUNDERS, JENNIE ROCHE

1970	195.	Grandson Fishing
	196.	Simpson Chapel, Methodist Church
1971	175.	Chain of Sierras*
1972	103.	Old Farm Home*
	104.	Primitive Home
1973	171.	Simpson Chapel
1974	129.	Sea of Galilee

SAVAGE, EUGENE FRANCIS

1925	180.	Recessional*
1926	244.	Resorgimento
1928	232.	They Shall Be Filled
	233.	They Shall Receive Mercy
	234.	Symbol Bearers, Fidelity
	235.	They That Suffer Persecution
	236.	They Shall Be Called the Children of God
	237.	Symbol Bearers, Justice
	238.	Theirs Is the Kingdom of Heaven
	239.	They Shall Be Comforted
	240.	Symbol Bearers, Charity
	241.	They Shall Inherit the Earth
	242.	They Shall See God
	243.	Symbol Bearers, Brotherly Love

SAVIDGE, HENRIETTA

| 1942 | 208. | Street in San Miguel |

SCAHILL, MARY MONSCHEIN

1984	170.	Alice, A Tribute
1985	135.	Still Life Composition by Candlelight
1987	192.	Food for Thought
1988	174.	Candle Lit Bounty

SCHAEFER, HAROLD

| 1974 | 130. | John |
| 1975 | 204. | Coltrane's Peace |

SCHAEFER, LYDIA (S.)

| 1971 | 176. | Hollyhocks* |
| 1972 | 105. | Petunias* |

SCHALDACH, WILLIAM J.

1941	132.	A Fresh-run Fish (Atlantic Salmon)
	133.	'Possom up de 'Simmon Tree
	134.	Spring Note (Brook Trout)
	135.	The Hot Corner (Ruffled Grouse)

SCHAUB, MARY HALL

| 1947 | 164. | Algonquin Highway |

SCHEERER, BILLIE MARIE

| 1964 | 228. | School Girl |

SCHEID, RICHARD

| 1969 | 157. | Jean in Gold* |

SCHELL, J. E.

1926	245.	Portrait of an Artist Friend
	246.	Melting Snow
	247.	Self Portrait
1927	269.	Edgebrooke in Winter

SCHEPMAN, FRANCES BERNHARDT

| 1962 | 261. | Narcissis |
| | 262. | Ducks |

SCHERSCHEL, DORETTA

| 1984 | 171. | Woods Poppies, Blue Eyed Marys |

SCHIEFER, C(harles) R.

1975	205.	Modified Ax Form
	206.	Wings Plus
1976	202.	Modified Indian Art Form
	203.	Head
1977	138.	Three Friends
1978	125.	Chameleon
	126.	Fertility Stella
1979	135.	Thin Lady
	136.	X-Ray Fish Form*
1981	159.	W-O-M-A-N
	160.	Fish
1983	156.	Waiting for the Light to Change
	157.	Contemplating Baby
1984	172.	Fertility Goddess
	173.	Torso Twisting*
1985	136.	Thinking Twins
	137.	Waiting for the Light to Change
1986	193.	The Guardians
	194.	The Law Givers*
1987	193.	The Lovers
1988	175.	Dancers Onstage

1989	188.	Waiting for the Light to Change, VI*
1990	156.	Hoosier Hysteria

SCHILDKNECHT, EDMUND (G.)

1927	270.	Sunny Meadows
	271.	Little Anne
1942	209.	Indiana Barnyard
1943	174.	At the Window*
	175.	An Indiana Orchard
	176.	Still-Life with Fan
1944	215.	Bob
	216.	An Indiana Farm
	217.	Village by the Sea*
1945	149.	South End Crossing
1946	152.	Red House by the Sea*
1947	165.	The Merrill Wilson Farm
	166.	Junction with 431*
1948	108.	Maine Village
	109.	Midwestern Gold
1955	168.	The Black Pool
	169.	Maine Landscape

SCHILL, ALICE E.

1934	161.	A Yellow House
	162.	Portrait of Old Man
	163.	Country Backyard

SCHILLER, DOROTHY

1973	172.	Solitude
1975	207.	Winter Scene
1976	204.	Abstract No. 1
	205.	Abstract No. 2
1981	161.	Broken Thread

SCHLEMMER, F. LOUIS

1927	272.	Composition
	273.	Study
	274.	Portrait
1928	244.	Old Fritz
	245.	My Palette
	246.	Evalyn
1929	244.	Rogue
	245.	Rag Picker
	246.	Flowers
1930	201.	Mixed Bouquet
	202.	Spring Comes to the Crazy Mountain
1931	193.	Julia
	194.	Mrs. Hunter Leaming
	195.	Ruggles of Red Gap
1932	190.	Eros
	191.	Yvonne
1942	210.	Flowers
	211.	Last Chance Gulch
	212.	Retrospection

SCHMIAT, WALT

1975	208.	Handbuilt Landscapes
	209.	Occult Cross

SCHMIDT, WALTER (C.)

1976	206.	Handbuilt Cover Jar
1978	127.	Fall in the Marsh Cover Jar

SCHOLER, WALTER

1960	189.	Red Barn

SCHROEDER, RICK

1983	158.	Mustard Gas
1984	174.	Saturday Night, Sunday Morning
	175.	The Skeleton Who Came to Dinner*
1985	138.	The First of the Heart

SCHULTZ, GENE P.

1975	210.	Buffalo Indian Dancers

SCHULTZ, JOSEPH L.

1988	176.	A Child's Salon
	177.	The Practice

SCHULTZ, TERRI

1988	178.	James
	179.	Maureen

SCHULZ, DOROTHY H.

1981	162.	Landscape
	163.	Flower Sprite Emerging
1982	172.	Waterlily
1983	159.	Flowers in the Abstract
	160.	Joy
1984	176.	Composition with Flower Forms
	177.	Refractions
1985	139.	Cityscape: The Pennants
1986	195.	Lotus
	196.	Iris
1989	189.	Sun-Drying in Maine

SCHULZ, (Jr.), EDWIN A.

1951	162.	Stinesville Quarry
	163.	The Next Morning
1956	184.	Atlantic Mist
1957	176.	Still Life

SCHULZ, MARJORIE D.

1952	172.	Mountain Music
1953	148.	Per Pound
1954	161.	November Bouquet
1956	185.	Prelude to Autumn
1957	177.	Fishing Boats

SCHUSTER, HELEN MARIE

1953	149.	Blue Platter

SCHWEHM, RAY F.

1961	242.	Summer Bouquet

SCOTT, ANN

1971	177.	Green Still Life
1972	106.	Gemini*
1973	173.	View into Another Room

1974	131.	Cat in a Window
	132.	Glass*
1975	212.	Mr. and Mrs. Smith
1976	207.	Patchwork Cape
1977	140.	Interior with Balloons
	141.	Still Life with Fruit
1978	128.	Boy on a Stool
1979	137.	Telephone Call

SCOTT, DAVID O.
1986   197.   Jacob

SCOTT, GERALDINE ARMSTRONG
1927   275.   Autumn in Glory
        276.   December Symphony
1928   247.   Tranquil Woodland
1929   247.   Winter Calm
1932   192.   Into the Woods

SCOTT, NANCIE
1986   198.   Union Pacific 4442
1987   194.   Destinations Unknown
1988   180.   Estella's Iris
1989   190.   Hugo

SCOTT, VERNON R.
1934   164.   Sunny Side Church
1944   218.   Train Smoke and Tracks
        219.   Five After Five
        220.   Prof. Frederick Ingersol

SCOTT, WILLIAM EDOUARD
1926   248.   Lights on a Summer Night
1927   277.   Portrait, Mrs. Welling R. Chavis
        278.   The Witching Hour
1928   248.   Wrigley Reflections

SCUDDER, JANET
1926   249.   Frog Fountain
        ——.   Victory*
1927   279.   Figure for Bird Bath
        280.   Youth
        281.   Frog Baby
1933   176.   Flowers
1934   165.   Still Life

SEAFORD, JOHN ALBERT
1926   250.   Tremont Street, Boston, with King's Chapel
        251.   Fishing Boats at Old T Wharf

SEAMON, D. OMER
1947   167.   New Guinea Natives
        168.   Cape Sahsapor, N. E. I.
1948   110.   Along the Wabash
        111.   Bridge across the Wabash*
1949   127.   College Chapel
1950   144.   First Snow
        145.   Streets of Taxco, Mexico
        146.   Sugar Creek, Shades State Park

1951	164.	Signs of Winter
	165.	Roustabouts
1952	173.	Old Barn
	174.	Hoosier Sawmill
1953	150.	Autumn
	151.	Raccoon Creek
1954	162.	Owen County
	163.	Governor of Taos
1955	170.	Bay at Salina Cruze
	171.	Sidewalk Cafe, Mexico
	172.	Siesta
1957	178.	Pemaquid Point, Maine
	179.	High Surf, off the Coast Of Maine
	180.	Monhegan Island, Maine
1958	215.	Covered Bridge No. 1
	216.	Covered Bridge No. 3*
	217.	Covered Bridge No. 2
1961	243.	West Union Bridge, Parke County
	244.	Jackson Bridge, Parke County*
	245.	Campus Colors, DePauw
1962	263.	Pots
	264.	Big Raccoon Creek
1963	185.	Along the County Line
	186.	Deer Mills Bridge, Crawford County
	187.	Little Old Barn
1964	229.	Winter at Spring Mill
	230.	White River
1965	226.	Wabash at Merom
	227.	Giants along Old Sugar
1966	121.	Floating Leaves
	122.	Swimmers, Sugar Creek
1967	229.	Mansfield Mill
1968	194.	Spiral Staircase, Merom, Indiana
	195.	Empty Classroom, Merom, Indiana

SEARS, NELSON
1969   158.   Floral

SEET, MARY P.
1968   196.   Still Life
        197.   The Girl

SEIFERT, BERTHA
(See Watkins, Bertha Seifert)
1936   185.   In the Valley
1937   167.   Alexander Avenue

SEIPEL, MARY
1960   190.   Buzzard Hill

SEIPEL, VIRGINIA (L.)
1960   191.   Wood and Stream
1961   249.   Retreat
1962   265.   Mountain Storm
1963   188.   Memories
        189.   Silent Setting
1964   231.   Country Church
1987   195.   Cabbage Roses

SEITZINGER, ARLENE (Miller)
1967 230. The Wedding Dance
1971 178. Miss Lacey*
1975 213. Freedon

SELBY, ROBERT (H.)
1931 196. Cyclamen
     197. Landscape
     198. Nude
1943 177. The Old Pump
     178. The Forgotten Apple
     179. Gaillardia and Japonica Apples
1944 221. Summer Bouquet
1945 150. Mabel
1946 153. From October's Garden*
     154. J. D. Brown
     155. Spire of Our Lady of Lourdes
1947 169. Spring
     170. The Yellow Scarf and the Monarch*
1948 112. Copper and the Conch Shell*
1949 128. Field Flowers
     129. Home in Indiana*
     130. Figure in Blue
1950 147. Spring Monday
1951 166. Survivor of the Past
     167. Mallow*
1952 175. June Apples
1953 152. Pressed Glass
     153. Cannelton Ferry
1954 164. Morning at the Stables
     165. Garden Royalty*
1955 173. Spider Plant
1956 186. 1910 South Third
1957 181. Boy With A Yoyo
     182. Business Bridges the Alley
1958 218. Bayou Beauty
     219. Dairy Barn*
     220. The Third Party
1960 192. Ice Boats
     193. Early Spring in the Meadows
1962 266. Skyline on the Passaic
     267. Snow and the Development*
1964 232. Summer Afternoon
     233. Last Stop Dover
1965 228. Compliments*
1966 123. Storm Contrast
1967 231. Heart of the City
1968 198. Lobster Wharf
1971 179. Golden Evening
     180. On the Rocks
1986 199. Spring Bouquet
1988 181. Reflections

SELFRIDGE, R(eynolds) L.
1925 181. The Jug-Vase
     182. Cape Cod, Boats
     183. Low-tide
1926 252. Winter Evening
     253. Park Folks*
     254. Drying Nets
1927 282. Calle Vecchio, Napoli

1928 249. The Old Cathedral
     250. Early Morning Notre Dame
     251. The Church on the Circle, Indianapolis
1929 248. Water-Tank
     249. Morning
1931 199. Sara's Garden
     200. The River House
     201. The Hermit's House
1934 166. Fallow Farm
1935 149. September Surf

SELLERS, LYDIA ROBERT R.
1931 202. Still Life No. 1

SEN
1933 177. Marionette Prince

SENSENY, SCOTT M.
1978 130. Untitled
     131. Untitled

SENTER, GRACIE O.
1954 166. Contentment
1961 250. Winter Enchantment

SESSLER, STANLEY S.
1931 203. Oriental Symphony
1932 193. Mums
     194. The Grotto, Notre Dame
1933 178. Arrangement in Blue
1934 167. October's Kitchen Chorus
1935 150. Reflections*
1936 186. A Full Table
1938 179. Angry Hoosier Skies
     180. Archer-Hunter, Self Portrait
     181. Malagas*
1939 195. Shoson Screen and Sansevieria*
1940 177. Nocturne, Notre Dame
     178. Robert Peggs, Esquire
1941 136. Bishop John F. O'Hara, C. S. D., D. D.
     137. Offerings to Kwan-Yin*
1949 131. Cho-Cho-San and Bittersweet
1951 168. Kitchen Chore
1969 159. Judas Duck #3
     160. Teruko

SEVIN, WHITNEY
1962 268. Seal

SEYBERT, DIANE (Pierce)
1977 142. Kate, Oriental Style
     143. Echinops
1979 138. 1935
     139. Spring Day
1980 134. Before School

SEYMOUR, HELEN
(See Baker, Helen Seymour and Baker, Seymour)
1931 204. The Fisherman's Mother

SEYMOUR, RALPH FLETCHER

1927	283.	Bells of Montcourt
	284.	The Skokie
	285.	Pilgrims at Sanctuario
	286.	Baking Bread, Santa Clara
	287.	La Poterne, Moret
	288.	Lake Bluff at Ravinia
	289.	Old Mill House
	290.	The Shack
	291.	Courtyard Paris
1928	252.	Concarneau
	253.	Rothenburg Turin
	254.	Rag Picker's Court, Segovia
	255.	Old Frankfort
1929	250.	Point Lobar, California
	251.	North Shore Bluffs at Ravinia
	252.	Out to Sea
	253.	From the Rock of Gilbraltar
	254.	Church in Burgas
	255.	The Bridge to Toledo, Madrid
1931	205.	Cabaret in Paris
	206.	Golden Bough
	207.	Big Drop
1940	179.	Cenema in Tasco
	180.	Cervante's House, Toledo
	181.	More Trouble
	182.	Steamboat at the Landing
	183.	The Supreme Court of the United States

SHAFFER, ELIZABETH DODDS

(See Dodds, Mary Elizabeth)

1951	169.	Doc*
1952	176.	Mrs. Floyd Stout
	177.	Sally
1953	154.	Still Life Impression
1955	174.	Mary's New Dress*
	175.	Margaret
1956	187.	Hoosier Farmer*
	188.	The Pink Blouse
1957	183.	Perry
1958	221.	Charlynne
	222.	Old Charley
	223.	Louise
1959	158.	Barbara
1960	194.	Barbara
	195.	Milkweed and Queen Anne's Lace
	196.	Charlynne*
1961	246.	Milkweed
	247.	Sunday Best
	248.	Strawflowers
1962	269.	School Girl*
	270.	Blue Arrangement
	271.	Green Pears
1963	190.	Karen
	191.	Still Life
1964	234.	Winter Arrangement
1965	229.	Lisa
	230.	March Life
	231.	Still Life

1966	124.	Tommie and the Bongo Drums
	125.	Morning at Hatteras
1967	232.	The Lone Fisherman
	233.	In the Marina
1968	199.	The Green Shawl*
	200.	Model in Blue Sweater
1969	161.	A Student of Mathematics
1970	197.	Then
	198.	Linda
1971	181.	Early Morning
	182.	One Afternoon*
1973	174.	At Grandma's House
1976	208.	Debbie
1977	144.	Howdy
1980	135.	Fishermen Three

SHAFFER, ELLEN E.

1988	182.	Windflowers II
1989	191.	Violets, Trillium and Morel
	192.	Joe-Pye-Weed
1990	157.	Peppers
	158.	A Year in the Life

SHAND, KAREN L.

1981	164.	Indian Brave
	165.	Antique Car*
1982	173.	Apache Chief
	174.	Gooslings*
1984	178.	Touring Fish
1985	140.	Tiger Lily
1986	200.	Penguin Parade
1989	193.	Apples in Transition
	194.	High Noon Rhino
1990	159.	Carnation Fascination

SHANNON, CLARA J.

1976	209.	Still Life

SHARP, (Everett) HILL

1928	256.	Todd's Head*
	257.	Joe Socobasin's
1929	256.	Max and Jawn*
	257.	The Framer
	258.	Chris Carsten's
1931	208.	The Guide
1933	179.	Self Portrait
1934	168.	Watching the Pot
	169.	Pollensa Fishing Boats
	170.	Jerry Tressler Hause*
1935	151.	Portrait
	152.	Portrait
1936	187.	Dr. Wm. B. Hesseltine*
	188.	John Van and Charles
1937	168.	A-Tsu-Que-Ta and Pah-Gee
1938	182.	Cynthia*
1939	196.	Country Auction
	197.	On Top
	198.	San Vincente
	199.	Summer Visitors
	200.	Main Street Merchants

1941	138.	Becky*
	139.	Evelyn
	140.	Ruth*
1942	213.	Mr. Tingle
1943	180.	Industrial Horizon, 1942*
	181.	The Editor
1944	222.	Back Porch
	223.	Becky & Billy
1945	151.	Mrs. R. E. Hanson
1946	156.	Carolyn
1947	171.	Col. Philip W. McAbee
1948	113.	Great Grandmother's Dress
1956	189.	Dr. R. C. Scarf
1958	224.	Dr. Robert Hargreaves

SHARP, G. MARTY

| 1974 | 133. | Strawberries |

SHARP, JAMES W.

| 1968 | 201. | Poetic People |
| 1970 | 199. | Grandpa's Store |

SHATTUCK, JULIA C.

| 1977 | 145. | Good Eating |

SHAVER, HELEN PUTNAM

1952	178.	Lake Gulls
1953	155.	Snow on the Catalinas*
	156.	Foothills of Tucson

SHAW, ROBERT M.

1932	195.	Deer Creek
1937	169.	October Rain
	170.	Bird Haven
	171.	Lugar Creek

SHEARER, PEG

1965	232.	The Orchard
	233.	November Afternoon
1968	202.	Sunflowers #2
	203.	Sand Bar
1971	183.	In the Park
1973	175.	Red Table
1974	134.	In the Park
1975	214.	Rocks at Lobster Cove
1976	210.	East of Darlington
1978	132.	Brenda
	133.	Lane of Tickle Grass

SHEEHAN, EVELYN STEVENS

| 1960 | 197. | Ghostly Victorian |
| | 198. | Spring Light |

SHELINE, LEROY M.

| 1965 | 234. | Of Ships and Things |

SHELL, JOE

| 1971 | 184. | Summer Depths |
| | 185. | Summer Dusk |

1972	107.	Country Green*
	108.	West-Central Indiana Summer Time
1974	135.	Summer Creek-side

SHERLOCK, EDWARD (W.)

1927	292.	Treasures
1928	258.	On a Studio Shelf
1929	259.	Still Life
1934	171.	Still Life
	172.	Mexican

SHERRILL, LOIS M.

| 1933 | 180. | Indiana Autumn |
| | 181. | Sunlight and Shade |

SHERROW, STEPHEN

1952	179.	Palette Alley
1955	176.	Butler's Alley
1957	184.	Ragpicker
1959	159.	Nite Lite
1960	199.	Alley on Green Street
1961	251.	Brown House
1963	192.	Swamp Ice

SHERWOOD, IDA G.

1963	193.	Nancy
1964	235.	My Friend Emily
	236.	Carol
	237.	Mary

SHICK, OLIVE J.

| 1954 | 167. | Gourds |

SHIDELER, PAUL

1931	209.	The Barrister
	210.	The Editor
	211.	Romance
	212.	Kin
1932	196.	Old Timer
	197.	Apprehensive
	198.	The Quest
	199.	Possum in de Pen
	200.	Nearing Port
	201.	Capt'n
	202.	Hajj
	203.	Easy Pickin
	204.	Singapore Sam
1933	182.	Dave
	183.	Lou
	184.	The Problem
	185.	Pete

SHIELDS, NANCY

| 1989 | 195. | Purple & Patches |

SHORR, WINIFRED

| 1972 | 109. | Assemblage II |

SHORT, BONNIE K.

| 1989 | 198. | Martha's Garden |

1990 160. My Summer Garden
161. Honeybee Hideaway

SHORT, JEANNE
1989 199. Now
1990 162. Mill at Mansfield

SHOVER, EDNA MANN
1925 184. Still Life

SHOWE, LOU-ELLEN CHATTIN
(See Chattin, Lou-Ellen)
1925 185. Lifting Mist, Catskills

SHULER, DAVID
1946 157. Summer Rhapsody
1947 172. Hester Street Merchant
173. Sara's Bouquet
1948 114. Reminiscences
115. Morning Light
1949 132. Full Moon

SHULZ, ADA (Walter)
1925 186. Young Mother
187. Paul and Dorothy
188. Sycamores
1926 255. A Mother from the Hills*
256. The Pet Gobbler
257. The Yellow Hen
1927 293. A Cabin Child
294. A Mother's Lap
295. The Pet Guinea
1928 259. On Mother's Lap
260. The Pet Duck*
1930 205. Helen and Gobba (Invited)
206. The Gray Goose (Invited)

SHULZ, ADOLPH (Robert)
1925 189. June Time
190. Foots of the Bear Waller
191. Rocky Hill Top
1926 258. Barnes Barn*
259. The Hills of Brown Co.
260. Blossoming Hillside
1927 296. Gentle Hills O' Brown
297. Summer Quiet
1928 261. Plumed Dancers
262. Mild October
263. Happy Hunting Grounds
1929 260. A Bunch of Willows
261. The Yellow Tree
1930 203. Road to the Village
204. Cabin in the Holler
1931 215. Main Street, Pikes Peak, Indiana
216. Back to Nature
1932 205. On the Road to Nashville
206. In the Bay Holler
1936 189. Lazy Day*
190. Autumn Hillside

1938 183. In the Violet Flame
184. Silence of Eventide
185. Spring Idyl
1939 201. The Grateful Shade
1940 184. Back Water
316. Spring Peepers Concert Hall
1941 141. Autumn Twilight
1942 214. Hilltop Cabin

SHULZ, ALBERTA REHM
1938 186. Bittersweet
1939 202. I Love Thy Templed Hills
203. Long May Our Land Be Bright
1940 185. My Country, 'Tis of Thee I Sing
1943 182. Into the Light
183. Peace
1944 224. Wild Plum Blossoms
225. The Sunny Window
1945 152. I Love Thy Rocks and Rills
153. My Own, My Native Land
1946 158. Schooner Valley

SHUMAN, OPAL F.
1963 194. Early Autumn Snow
1967 234. Village Streets
235. Road to the Hills
1970 200. Up from the Valley
201. Afterglow*
1973 176. Lake Tippy

SHUMATE, ELLA (A.)
1925 192. The Top of the Wall, St. Paul du Var
1926 261. Noon, September
262. Sunny Morning in the Alps
1927 298. The Blue Stein
299. Old and New
1931 213. Figure
214. Still Life
1933 186. The Old Ice Plant, Lebanon
187. Red Front Grocery Stores, Lebanon
188. Looking out over Lebanon
1935 153. White Zinnias
154. The Little White Hen
1939 204. Street Walkers, Sally-Port
205. White Peonies

SIDDIQ, PATRICIA FOLEY
1968 204. Three Figures

SIDMAN, CHARLOTTE
1943 184. Antique Jar*
185. Morning Blue and Scarlet
1944 226. A Spring Study
1945 154. My Kitchen Table
1946 159. Old Leaves, Old Vase
160. Glories in Fall
1949 133. Rose Patterns
1950 148. The Blue Scarf*
1951 170. Heirloom

1952 180. November Snow
      181. Flower Composition
1955 177. The Blue Vase

SILEIKIS, MICHAEL J.
1940 186. When Leaves Turn Yellow
1942 215. A Day in October
      216. Tailor
1943 186. Dune Landscape
1944 227. Beach House Blowout
1945 155. Butterfly Weed and Sand
1952 182. Spring Morning

SILLS, ROGER
1977 146. Merrymobile Route*

SILVER, IRENE
1953 157. Landscape

SIMMONS, ROBERTA F(ay)
1970 202. Ronnie
1975 215. Lea

SIMPER, LEW
1968 205. Delilah's Sheds
1969 162. Back Cove
1970 203. At the Foot of Mt. Mansfield
      204. Bench Street, Galena
1972 110. Rocks at Schoodic Point, Maine

SIMPSON, HARRY
1944 228. Tawas Bay
      229. Autumn

SINCLAIR, BERNICE
1933 189. First Gleam across the River
      190. December Fog

SINCLAIR, MARTHA WRIGHT
1968 206. Pink Eye
      207. Red Bird

SINGH, K(anwal) P(rakash)
1972 111. James Whitcomb Riley House
1973 178. Tippecanoe Co. Courthouse
1975 216. Indiana Historic Architecture
      217. The Bals-Wocher Mansion
1976 211. Monument Circle II
1977 147. Knightstown, Indiana
      148. East College, DePauw University
1979 140. Chennakesava Temple, India
1980 136. DePauw University, Greencastle,
            Indiana
      137. Indianapolis IV
1981 166. Tippecanoe County Courthouse
1982 175. State Capitol Building, Indianapolis
1983 161. Medieval Clock, Czechoslovakia
1984 179. A Landmark, St. Patrick's
            Cathedral, NY

1985 141. Knox County Courthouse,
            Vincennes, Ind.
      142. Golden Temple, Amritsar, India*
1986 201. St. Mark's Basilica, Venice, Italy
1987 196. Golden Temple, Amritsar, India
1988 183. Along the Canal, Venice, Italy
      184. The Duomo, Como, Italy
1989 200. Tippecanoe Courthouse, Lafayette,
            Indiana*
      201. Golden Temple, Amritsar, India

SINICK, GARY
1973 177. Elsalyn Shop

SINNETT, LOIS BROWN
1980 138. Where Pan Plays

SIPE, IRENE B(arlow)
(See Barlow, Irene)
1978 134. The Hideout
1990 163. Autumn

SIRKO, HELEN
1988 185. Variable Emergence
1990 164. Visionary Forms
      165. Sensitive Harmony

SISKIND, ELLIE
1972 112. Steerforth
1975 218. The Sweet Gum Tree
1976 212. Tide Pool I
1977 149. Old Bird in Paradise
1978 135. Tide Pool IV
      136. The Babysitter
1981 167. Teaq Room
      168. Uncle Stan*
1983 162. Stanley: A Study
      163. Maggie
1984 180. Leanne
1986 202. Anguished Woman
      203. The Leaders

SISTER CAMILLE, S.P.
1940 28. Lady in Blue
1947 174. Pioneer
      175. Ohio River Boat, 1840

SISTER ESTHER, S.P.
1937 55. Contentment*
      56. The Copper Jug
1939 76. Laid Off
      77. Mr. Smith*
1940 47. Negress
1943 187. Jane*
      188. Mother of Sorrows

SISTER IMMACULEE, S.P.
1939 118. Still Life
      119. Marguerite*
      120. Still Life
1940 87. God Sees Me

EXHIBITION RECORDS

SISTER M. DOLORITA, O.S.F.
1943	189.	Sunflowers Below
1944	230.	Lilac Time
	231.	Hill Country
	232.	Heroes Unsung*
1945	156.	Rainy Day
1948	116.	Ballet Boheme*
1949	136.	Night Shift
1950	150.	Second Eve*
1952	183.	Wilderness*
	184.	St. Francis and the Birds

SISTER M. IMMACULATA, C.S.C.
1925	111.	Still Life
	112.	The Pond
1926	158.	Cyclamen

SISTER M. ITTA, O.S.F.
1943	190.	Stencil Study
1945	157.	Gaiters
	158.	Interpretation
1946	162.	Flora et Fauna*
	163.	The Mallards
1950	151.	Ohio River Banks*
1955	178.	Oldenburg Towers

SISTER M(ary) LAUREEN, C.S.C.
1937	109.	Fruit and Flowers*
1938	122.	On the Table
	123.	Yellow Lily

SISTER (M.) RUFINIA, O.S.F.
1927	255.	Marguerites and Sweet Peas
1929	234.	Flowers
	235.	Still Life
1933	170.	Golden Glow
	171.	Autumn Glow
1935	145.	Indian Chief
	146.	White Peonies
	147.	Autumn Glory
1936	183.	Mixed Bouquet*
1937	163.	Old Cunning
	164.	Relaxed
1938	175.	Dressed up Canadian*
	176.	Still Life
1939	193.	Research*
1940	174.	Clown*
1941	130.	Study in White
1943	192.	Flax
	193.	Dried Out Potato Field*
1944	234.	Singing Colors
	235.	Still Life and Fruit
	236.	Single Peonies and Delphiniums
1945	160.	Sunshine and Shadow*
	161.	Phlox
1946	165.	Autumn Glory
	166.	From My Little Garden Patch
1947	176.	Autumn Colors
1948	118.	Indiana's Beauties

1950	152.	Shell Flowers
	153.	Spring Song
1951	173.	Mixed Bouquet
1952	186.	Autumn
	187.	Color Symphony
	188.	Summer*
1955	180.	St. Gregorian
1958	225.	For A Dr.'s Lab
1959	193.	Venite Adoramus

SISTER MARIE ROSAIRE, C.S.C.
1938	174.	The Fourth Station
1956	181.	I Am Black But Beautiful
	182.	King and Queen
	183.	Epiphany

SISTER MARY dePAUL SCHWEITZER, O.S.F.
1975	211.	Jay
1977	139.	Yellowwood Tree
1978	129.	Diamond

SISTER (Mary) EDNA, C.S.C.
1935	46.	Historic Statue
1936	52.	Snow Scene*
1938	56.	Autumn
	57.	Madeline
1939	68.	Arrow Flight
	69.	Puzzled
1940	43.	Fruit and Flowers
1946	161.	Pauline Chapel
1948	117.	Chrysanthemums*
1949	134.	House in the Woods*
	135.	Mount Adam
1950	149.	Two Ways Meet
1951	171.	Landscape*
	172.	Portrait, Madeline
1952	185.	View from Kentucky
1954	168.	Reverend Gerrer
1955	179.	Flowers and Fruit
1956	180.	White Flowers
1964	238.	Madeline
1966	126.	Bridge
	127.	Landscape

SISTER MARY IGNATIA, S.P.
1965	235.	Forest Fairies
	236.	Woodland Echoes*
	237.	Three Faces of Eva
1966	128.	Mediterranean Sunset
	129.	Salute to Ialf
1967	236.	Memory Lane

SISTER MARY JANE, O.S.F.
1941	79.	Candle-Light
1942	217.	Phlox*
1943	191.	Still Life
1944	233.	The White Hat
1945	159.	Time-worn
1946	164.	Genius & Poverty

SISTER RITA ANN ROETHELE, S.P.
1969	154.	Abstraction II
1974	127.	Spring*
1976	197.	Snow from TWA

SITZMAN, E(dward) R.
1925	193.	County Line
	194.	Bit of New Orleans
	195.	Snow and Sunshine
1926	263.	Beech Woods
	264.	Through the Woods
	265.	Winter Evening
1927	300.	Autumn Symphony
	301.	The Haunt of the Quail
1928	264.	Sleeping Branches
	265.	Early Winter
1929	262.	Morning After Night of Storm
1930	207.	Sunshine in the Woods
	208.	Mining Town in Tennessee
1941	142.	Lunch Time
1947	177.	Country Store

SKEMP, OLIVE H.
1937	172.	Burrowers
	173.	Woman of Bavaria
	329.	Flowers*

SKEMP, ROBERT O.
| 1937 | 174. | Laughing Baby |

SKINNER, (R.) CAROL
1981	169.	Duplicate in Design
	170.	Good Morning Spring
1986	204.	Reclined Figure
1987	197.	White River Bridge at 10th Street
1989	202.	Evening at the Station
	203.	Patterns in Color
1990	166.	Morning in Amsterdam

SLAYMAKER, GENE
1964	239.	Mayapan
	240.	Maya
1976	213.	5-Star Banner
1978	137.	Borg: Fifteen-Love at the National Clay Tournament
	138.	Pyramids

SLAYMAKER, MARTHA
1962	272.	Survivors of Warsaw
	273.	Serenade
1965	238.	Maya X
1966	130.	Fragment
	131.	Cuneiform Tablet V
	132.	Image*
1967	237.	Inca
1968	208.	Rock Structures, Mesa Verde
	209.	Aerial View, Jupiter
	210.	Rock Structures
1969	163.	Aerial View of a Small Planet
1970	205.	Sacsayhuaman

1971	186.	Bedford Quarry
	187.	Springmill, Indiana
1972	113.	Labna*
	114.	Canaanite Woman
1973	179.	Bedford Monoliths
	180.	Bedford Soliloquy*
1974	136.	Yanabito
1975	219.	Anasazi Cliff Dwelling
1976	214.	Anasazi Structures*

SLUSSER, CECILIA
1981	171.	Reflections
1982	176.	Volcanic Landscape
1983	164.	When Winter Comes
1985	143.	Frost Patterns
1986	205.	Sycamore Patterns

SMALE, HOBART B.
| 1929 | 263. | A Rosette |
| 1930 | 209. | Carved Panel for Bank* |

SMALTZ, CAROLYN
1962	274.	Rooftops
	275.	Still Life with Chair*
1963	195.	July 1962

SMEAD, VIRGINIA M.
| 1959 | 160. | Autumn Textures |
| | 161. | And in a Quiet Place |

SMILEY, WALLACE J.
| 1951 | 174. | Torso |
| | 175. | Beverly |

SMIT, DERK
1953	158.	Dogwood and Redbud
	159.	Sunny Day
	160.	Red Barn, Nashville
1954	169.	Winter in Indiana
	170.	Spring Flowers
	171.	Peace and Quiet*
1955	181.	White Peonies
1956	190.	Brown County Barn
	191.	October Day*
1957	185.	October In Brown County
	186.	Tennessee Smokies
1958	226.	Still Life With Urn
	227.	Cove Mountain, Great Smokies
1959	162.	Great Great Granny
	163.	Old Mill
	164.	Back Road, Bean Blossom
1960	200.	Still Life, A Dutch Relic
	201.	Mount Hood, Oregon
	202.	Winter Romance*
1961	252.	Laguna Canyon Road
	253.	Snow on Greasy Creek
	254.	Still Life*
1962	276.	Fish House
	277.	Still Life with Antique Urn
	278.	Palm Desert

1963	196.	October Day Smokies
	197.	Laguna Canyon
1964	241.	Laguna Canyon
	242.	El Toro Road
	243.	Antiques with Fruit*
1965	239.	Still Life with Fruit*
	240.	Windy Day, Carmel Coast
1966	133.	The Broken Plate, Persimmons
1967	238.	Mixed Bouquet
	239.	Taxco Street Scene
1968	211.	Rainy Day

SMITH, CAROL LYNN
1969	164.	The Balloon Man*
	165.	All Salt Shakers Two Fifty

SMITH, CARRIE DYAR
1963	198.	Lilies and Companions*
1964	244.	August Party

SMITH, DEBORAH A.
1987	198.	Easter Morning

SMITH, DOROTHEA E.
1952	189.	Cider Time in Indiana

SMITH, DOROTHY
1968	212.	Let the Waters Cover the Land
1969	166.	My Love Is a Yellow Rose

SMITH, F. HAROLD
1949	137.	The Lamplighter
1951	176.	April Sunshine
1955	182.	Pesce Fresche

SMITH, HARRIET REX
1949	138.	Winter, Late Afternoon
	139.	The Widower*
1956	192.	Wayside Grasses
	193.	Christina*
1958	228.	Suki
	229.	Young Forest
	230.	Flowering Milkweed
1975	220.	Window

SMITH, HOWARD E.
1965	241.	South of Deedsville
1970	206.	On The Hill

SMITH, JERRY (F.)
1976	215.	Parsonage
	216.	Summer Grass
1977	150.	Down Home
	151.	Class of '62
1978	139.	Companions
1980	139.	Nine in a Row
1981	172.	Warming Trend
	173.	Winter Break
1984	181.	Side Street
	182.	Lady in Waiting

1985	144.	Indiana Limestone*
	145.	Red Brick*
1986	206.	Blue Steps*
1987	199.	Harbor Gray
	200.	Stubble Patterns
1988	186.	Gateway
	187.	Country View
1989	204.	Weather Check
	205.	Homestead
1990	167.	Red White & Blue
	168.	Roll On By

SMITH, LUCILLE
1933	191.	Navajo Country
	192.	The Nomad
	193.	Ninobah

SMITH, NELLE ADAMS
1937	175.	Early Autumn, Indiana

SMITH, NORBERT
1950	154.	Knock and It Shall Be Opened
1951	177.	City Tree
1956	194.	City Landscape
1958	231.	Portrait of the Artist's Wife*
	232.	The Back View

SMITH, RICHARD F.
1980	140.	Water Wagon
1981	174.	Woodburn Cemetery
1982	177.	Midsummer
1986	207.	Watching
	208.	First Snow

SMITH, SAMUEL EDWARD
1971	188.	Soliloquy
	189.	I Remember J C

SMITH, SHIRLEY
1956	195.	Offshore Ballet

SMITH, TERRY LLOYD
1984	183.	Tera at the Grill
1986	209.	Reflections on "I" Street

SMITH, THOMAS P.
1963	199.	Earth
	200.	Triumph
1964	245.	Mind over Matter

SMITH, WILMA ALE
1938	187.	Night Blooming Cereus

SMITHBURN, FLORENCE (Bartley)
1929	264.	Zinnias*
1930	210.	Pot of Flowers*
	211.	Still Life
	212.	Dam, Landing
1933	194.	Fleur-de-Lis
	195.	On the Kitchen Table
	196.	Portrait of Ruth

SMOCK, WILLIAM D.
1972   115.   Mint Farmer

SMOOT, WILLIAM
1965   242.   The Porch
1983   165.   Abandoned
1987   201.   Port of Indiana
        202.   After the Storm*

SMYRNIS, MARY
(See Lienert, Mary Smyrnis)
1952   190.   Elaine
        191.   Distraction
1954   172.   Carol
1955   183.   After the Thaw
        184.   Christy
1956   196.   On Train to Megalopoli

SNAPE, S(tephen) A.
1929   265.   Stone Swag Panel for Fireplace
        266.   Stone Pilaster for Fireplace*
        267.   Stone Monk Head
1930   213.   Stone Monk Head
        214.   Stone Monk Head
        215.   Stone Monk Head
        216.   Stone Window Spandrel
1932   207.   Agriculture and Industry Mantel
                Clock

SNAPP, WILLIAM
1987   203.   SOUL (Search of Universal Life)*
1989   206.   Talk to Me

SNETHEN, MERRILL F.
1936   191.   At the Dunes
        192.   Old Church in Oberammergau
1941   143.   Kent
        144.   Market Place
        145.   Mountain Station
1942   218.   Cherry Street
        219.   Curb Service
        220.   Island Queen
1943   194.   Little Jog
        195.   The Inner Circle
1944   237.   Passing Storm
        238.   River Front
1945   162.   Lobster Cove
        163.   Still Life
        164.   River Town
1946   167.   Ballet Dancer
        168.   At the Piano

SNIDER, DOLLY
1976   217.   Bermuda Seascape

SNYDER, ROBIN A.
1989   207.   Peek-a-boo Blush Poinsettia

SOHN, FRANK
1930   217.   Indiana Farm
1931   217.   Signscape
        218.   Autumn in Brown County
        219.   Boatyard, Chicago River
1932   208.   Nashville, Brown County
1933   197.   Miller's Pharmacy, Nashville
        198.   Autumn, Nashville, Brown County*
        199.   On Court House Square, Madison,
                Indiana
        200.   Corner Stores, Nashville, Brown
                County
        201.   On Court House Square,
                Columbus, Indiana
1934   173.   Piecefield's Back Yard
        174.   Edge of Town, Nashville
        175.   Back of Mill, Columbus, Indiana
1935   155.   Nashville, Indiana, in 1933
1936   193.   Sycamores
        194.   Echo Lake
1937   176.   Back Yard
        330.   Fantasy in a Flower Garden
1938   188.   Paris Sketch
        323.   Edge of Town
1948   119.   Weeds and Butterflies
        120.   Street Corner, Nashville, Ind.

SOLICH, LUCILLE KATHRYN
1956   197.   La Femme
1960   203.   Ossmanius

SOLOMON, A(nn) T.
1986   210.   On the Rocks
1987   204.   Early A. M. at Irnies*
        205.   Indian Custom
1988   188.   In Zion National Park
        189.   Victorian Mementos
1989   208.   Frosty Autumn Morning
1990   170.   #5 Men Working Series, Guitar
                Player*

SOMMERKAMP, SHERYL
1990   171.   Traveling Light

SONGER, GENE
1967   240.   Les Alpes
1969   167.   Mid-Morning in the Smokies
1973   181.   Mid-morning in the Hills

SONNEFIELD, WILMA
1946   169.   Chrysanthemums
1948   121.   Spring Shower
1949   140.   Magnolias
1975   221.   Spring Bouquet
1978   140.   Dubrovnik Impressions
1980   141.   Moroccan in the Casbah

SORENSON, ERIC
1971   190.   Portrait of a Mood
        191.   Grein Building

SOTOLONGO, BERTHA C.
1977	152.	Iris
1978	141.	Iris
1979	141.	Blue Iris

SOWDER, DIANA
| 1979 | 142. | High Society* |
| | 143. | Huston and Edna Mae |

SPANNUTH, SHARON
1988	190.	Her Presence Lingers
	191.	If These Chairs Could Talk
1990	172.	Waiting for Washday

SPAULDING, WILLIAM A.
| 1967 | 241. | Old Stage Stop |

SPEAR, CHARLES
| 1977 | 153. | Abandoned |
| 1978 | 142. | Delores Horns* |

SPENCER, MARY(belle)
1934	176.	Enchanted Isle, Summer 1933
1935	156.	Still Life
	157.	Study with Masks
1936	195.	Shoe Shiner
1937	331.	Silhouette
1938	189.	Matinee at the Zoo
	190.	Mexicana
1939	206.	Flower Pattern
	207.	Mei-Mei and Her Public
1940	187.	Indian Still Life*

SPENNER, E(lmer) E.
1933	202.	Panther Woman
	203.	Rhythm in Harlem
1934	177.	Adele
1935	158.	Fisherman
1947	178.	The Duke of Hollywood*
	179.	Gamecock
1961	255.	Bird Watcher
1962	279.	Carnival
	280.	The Philosophers
	281.	Once upon a Time
1964	246.	Gypsy Mary
1965	243.	Juanita
1972	116.	Adele

SPERL, GEORGE
1966	137.	Chicago Skyway
	138.	Grandma's Coffee Grinder
1969	168.	Wharf's End
	169.	Scrap Pile Bound*
1970	207.	Side Tracked
1975	222.	Fore and Aft
1987	206.	Gone Forever

SPICKA, WALTER R.
| 1933 | 204. | From My Window |

SPIEGEL, DOROTHY A.
1937	177.	Whirling Movement, Oleanders
	178.	A Watercolor
	332.	Heads of Gold
1942	221.	Desert Dancers
	222.	Evening
1944	239.	Late Afternoon Glow
	240.	Flowers

SPIER, LINDA L.
| 1971 | 192. | Zinnias |
| | 193. | Portrait of a Boy |

SPINKS, WAYNE F.
1962	282.	The Awakening
	283.	The Hand-Off
1963	201.	Balthasar
	202.	Silent Sentry
1964	247.	Second Generation

SPRAGUE, RACHEL J.
| 1986 | 211. | Brown County |

SPRAGUE, ROBERT B.
1933	205.	Iowa Monolith
	206.	Floria
	207.	Graves

SPRUNGER, ARTHUR L.
1928	266.	Under the Willow
	267.	The Amish Mint Still
	268.	The First Snow
1929	268.	Winter, West Goshen
1930	218.	Late Snow
1931	220.	The Gary Steel Mills*
	221.	Bonneyville Mill
	222.	Winter, West Goshen
	223.	The Farmyard in Winter
1932	209.	By An Old Dam-Site
	210.	Rural Symphony
	211.	A Winter Morning
	212.	On a Gray Winter Day
	213.	Landscape No. 9
1934	178.	Open Forum
	179.	The Amish 'Mint' Still
1936	196.	Lilies
1937	179.	Celery Weeders
	180.	Quarry No. 2
1939	208.	Amish Family
	209.	Cockscomb
	210.	Courthouse Lawn
	211.	Ice Fishermen of Lake Wawasee
	212.	The Old Tile Mill
1940	188.	The Wawasee Slip
	189.	Farmyard
	190.	The Boat Slip at Wawasee
1943	196.	September, '42
	197.	Bristol Hills
	198.	Autumn Glory
1945	165.	Bonneyville Mill

1958	233.	White Water
	234.	The Great Draft of Fishes*
1959	165.	Dr. S. C. Yoder
	166.	Fall Symphony
1961	256.	Concerned Prophet*
1968	213.	The Chapel of Light
	214.	Flame of Learning

SPRUNGER, WARREN

1974	137.	Bygone
	138.	Arthur Dove Farm
1976	218.	Quiet Place
1977	154.	Fresh Snow*
1978	143.	Grandpa's Tractor*
1979	144.	For Future Use
	145.	Ladder to the Beach House
1981	175.	October Afternoon
	176.	White Water
1983	166.	Gayle
	167.	Retired
1988	192.	Dark/Light
	193.	Road Sign

SPURGEON, JOSEPH

1936	197.	Hardin's Holler, Brown County*
1937	181.	Dream Lake
	333.	Water Lilies
1938	191.	Grand Marais
	192.	Mock Orange
	193.	Ole's Place
	324.	Wind Point
1939	213.	Cold and Lonesome*
	214.	High and Dry
	215.	Farm in Chicago
1940	191.	Hoosier Souvenirs
	192.	Red Hills
	317.	Schooner Valley

ST. HELENS, PAX

| 1945 | 170. | Head |
| | 171. | Carving |

ST. JOHN, LOLA ALBERTA

| 1928 | 277. | Winter |
| 1944 | 250. | Chrysanthemums |

STAGE, ELIZABETH G.

| 1965 | 244. | The Sportsman |

STAIR, MARY ELI

| 1962 | 284. | The City |
| 1963 | 203. | Milkweed |

STALEY, C(larence) W.

1938	194.	Sun Kissed Hills
1942	223.	Winter, Early Snow
1943	199.	Snow Bound Village
	200.	Winter Symphony
1944	241.	The Road Home
	242.	Winter on Goose Creek

1945	166.	The Haunted House
	167.	Old Willows
1946	170.	The Fisherman's Moon
1947	180.	Windy Night*

STALEY, TERESA

| 1989 | 209. | White Lace Floating over Crazy Quilt* |

STARBUCK, JULIA MAGILL

1943	201.	The Pool in the Rocks
	202.	Fisherman's Sunday
	203.	Timber Island
1945	168.	The Silver Tree
1950	155.	The Long Road
1952	192.	Black Lace
1953	161.	Morning Glories
1955	185.	Village in the Valley
1956	198.	By the Side of the Road
1957	187.	Lilacs in the Moonlight
	188.	Duet
1958	235.	Look Homeward, Angel

STARK, BARBARA

1982	178.	German Classic
1989	210.	Wellfleet Harbor
1990	173.	Past Finder

STARK, FORREST F.

1934	180.	Mrs. Hunt
	181.	Jung*
1940	193.	Blue Pitcher*
	194.	Pastel Portrait
1953	162.	Head of Mr. Davisson*

STARK, OTTO

1925	196.	The Forest at Sunset
	197.	Twilight
	198.	Meal Time
1926	266.	Decorative Still Life
	267.	Self Portrait
	268.	Pyramid Point

STARKEN, NADINE

| 1973 | 182. | The Critic |

STARLIN, RUTH

| 1964 | 248. | Happy Randy |
| | 249. | Empty |

STARR, JANE

| 1971 | 194. | Melissa |

STEADHAM, TERRY

| 1969 | 170. | Stencil II |
| | 171. | Declaration |

STEDRON, FRANK

| 1931 | 224. | Garden Sculptor |

STEELE, SALLY
1977 155. Tomorrow Rain

STEELE, THEODORE C.
1925 199. Hunnicutt Valley in Autumn
     200. Winter Morning, First Snows*
     201. Summer Morning
     202. James Whitcomb Riley
1926 269. The Hill Country, Brown County*
     270. Sunlight in the Forest
     271. Winter Afternoon
1927 302. An Autumn Day
     303. The Peony Bed
     304. The Forest Veteran

STEELE, W. KARL
1931 225. The Elm
1932 214. Autumn Beeches
1933 208. Lingering Snow
1934 182. Across the Valley
1935 159. The Ohio, Late October
1936 198. Autumn Afternoon
     199. Frightened Horses*
1937 182. Along the Ohio*
     183. Lake Fishermen
1938 195. Autumn Lustre*
     196. North Country
1939 216. Marsh Stream
     217. Michigan Afternoon
     318. Rock Bound Coast
1940 195. Sorghum Making
1941 146. Winter Sun
1942 224. Dune Ridge
     225. Spring Sketch
     226. Village Mill
1943 204. Spring Willow
     205. Front Yard
1944 243. Winter Sunlight
     244. Grey Day
     245. Early Snow
1945 169. Sunlit Maple
1946 171. Marsh Willows
1947 181. Old House on the Hill
1948 122. Birch Grove
1949 141. Quebec Farmhouse
1950 156. Road to the Bay
1951 178. Mountain Home
     179. River in January
1952 193. Farm Wagons
1953 163. Northwest Landscape
     164. Late Autumn
1954 173. Reservation Home
1955 186. Rythmic Rocks
1957 189. December Freeze
     190. Shrimp Boats
1959 167. Rocky Creek Bed
1960 204. Pascagoula Water Front
1965 245. Of Days Past
     246. White Herons
1966 135. Forty-nine Windows
1967 242. Afternoon along the Gulf

1970 208. Along the Waterfront
1971 195. Carolina Spring
1972 117. East Coast Fishing Boats*
1973 183. Guadalupe River
1976 219. Portuguese Fishing Boats
1977 156. Early Spring
     157. Mending the Net

STEFFEN, JOE
1980 142. Log Cabin
     143. Milky Way
1981 177. Autumn Winds
1985 146. Dream Weaver

STEFFLER, ALVA
1962 285. Al Hutton
     286. Barb

STEINKRAUS, EDITH
1967 243. Singing Hill
     244. Girl with Her Skirt Caught on a
          Stump*

STEINMETZ, ALMA L.
1940 196. Heirlooms
1947 182. Legerdemain*

STEKETEE, CRAIG
1976 220. Pass Form I

STEKETEE, SALLIE HALL
1925 203. Flowers
1926 272. A Bowl of Flowers
     273. A Grey Day
     274. Cretonne, a Decoration*
1927 305. A Snowy Day
     306. Garden Flowers
1928 269. Flowers and Still Life
     270. Summer Flowers*
     271. January in Mexico
1929 269. Wild Flowers*
     270. Phlox
1930 219. The Pink Table Cover
1931 226. A Rock Garden*
     227. A Yellow Vase
     228. A Trout Stream, Michigan
1932 215. In a Green House
1933 209. A Mountain Home, Palm Springs,
          Cal.
     210. Anne
1936 200. A Small Bouquet
1938 197. A Summer Bouquet

STEPHANS, GEORGE
1958 236. Surprised
1959 168. Harness Shop
1961 257. Faun*

STEPHENS, JERRY G.
1981 178. Liberty Still Life
1982 179. Deercreek Crossing

1983	168.	Still-Life with Nutcracker
1987	207.	Snowscape with Young Boy
1988	194.	Yesterday

STEPHENSON, GRIFFIN

1940	197.	Stone Quarry
	198.	Linie Kiln

STEPHENSON, JOHN G.

1925	204.	Nude

STEUERWALD, DOROTHY (Schnitzius)

1962	287.	Indian Wedding Jug
1963	204.	Baking Bread
	205.	Pottery and Bulbs
	206.	Dad

STEVENS, MARGI

1970	210.	Three for the Money
1982	180.	Puppet Workshop

STEVENS, MARTIN

1970	209.	Portrait

STEVENS, W. RAY

1978	144.	Love You
1979	146.	Early Light
1980	146.	Tranquil Solitude*
1981	179.	Winter Lane
1983	169.	Victorian Beauty
1985	147.	Night on the Town
1986	212.	Festival I
1987	208.	Blue Granite Sauerkraut
	209.	Ralph Lauren's No Lens
1988	195.	Spring Barn
	196.	Oriental Vase*
1989	211.	Oriental Series #8
1990	174.	Evening Light

STEVENS, WILL H.

1925	205.	The River
	206.	Springtime Landscape
1926	275.	Spring in a Valley
	276.	Pastel
1927	307.	Misty Woods
	308.	Street in Turmoil
	309.	Somber Hills
1928	272.	House-boat
	273.	Cabin in the Woods
	274.	Bayou

STEVENSON, CLAUDIA

1928	275.	Portrait Sketch
1929	271.	John
	272.	Study of Old Man
1930	220.	A Hoosier
	221.	Peggy
1932	216.	Portrait
	217.	Peggy
	218.	Head of a Woman

STEVENSON, MARK

1979	147.	Welcome to Tomorrowland
1980	144.	Rooted Dancer
1981	180.	Rhythms in Moonlight
	181.	The Banks of White River*

STEVENSON, MARTHA

1973	184.	The Face of Loneliness
1974	139.	Left Behind
1976	221.	Fifteen
1980	145.	Other Spaces III, Escape
1981	182.	Still Life with White Lilac
1983	170.	The Student
1984	184.	Early April at the Cleavers
1985	148.	The Legacy
1986	213.	Dockside
1987	210.	On the Way to Wabash
	211.	Sunset at the Frog Pond
1988	197.	Pooh's Tree III
	198.	Branches
1989	212.	Hot Stuff

STEWART, BIRGIT (I.)

1982	181.	Birds of a Feather
1989	213.	Patterns & Planes
1990	175.	Fractured Panes II*
	176.	Reflections

STEWART, FENTON (E.)

1962	288.	Day Begins
1965	247.	Steel and Stone
1966	136.	High Noon
1967	246.	Lonely Hill
1968	215.	Time Passed This Way
1969	172.	A Face of the City
1970	211.	A Part of Yesterday

STEWART, MARIE H.

1941	147.	Bowl of Lilies
1942	227.	Flowers and Figurine*
1944	246.	Spring Snow
1946	172.	Winter
1948	123.	After the Storm

STILLSON, BLANCHE

1925	207.	The Squall
	208.	Interior with Figure
1926	277.	Still Life, Flowers
	278.	Mary Lou
	279.	Low Tide
	280.	Old Wharf
	281.	Unloading Fish
1927	310.	Zinnias
	311.	Betty
	312.	Tranquil Day
	313.	The Depew Fountain
	314.	The Federal Building
1928	276.	Still Life, Jug, and Apples

STINEBURG, WILLIAM E.
1980 147. Rubins
148. Taflinger

STIPANOVICH, DEBORAH
1982 182. Starlight
183. Progression

STIPANOVICH, MATZIE
1982 184. Cook Stove

STIPANUK, BARBARA
1978 145. Untitled

STIREWALT, MARY T.
1960 205. Below Zero

STOCKING, CURTIS M.
1950 157. Mountain Pasture

STOCKWELL, JILL AULT
1977 158. Gen. Lew Wallace, Study in Autumn

STODDARD, (Beatrice) MUSETTE OSLER
1925 209. A Spot of Color
210. Panel, God is Love
211. Panel, Fairy Story Lady
1926 282. A Fantasy
1927 315. Village by the Sea
1929 273. Rose Glow
1933 211. Hooked Rug Shop
1934 183. Morning Glow
184. A Brown County Cabin
1936 201. A Provincetown Street Scene
1937 184. Up Greasy Creek
1939 218. Gov. Claiborne Courtyard, New Orleans
1943 206. Mission Peak, California
1945 172. The Green Shutter Tea Room, New Orleans
173. The Wayside
1951 180. Chicago Northwestern, 1888

STOEFFLER, AILEENE HOCH
1943 207. Old Houses
208. Along Fall Creek

STOKES, CRESTON
1981 183. Generation Gap
1984 185. Monday's Washday
1989 214. Tea Leaf & Apples
215. A Crowning in Winter
1990 177. Collection

STOKESBERRY, C. L.
1963 207. Cottage Trail

STONGE, CARMEN
1978 146. Visions of Color

STOODY, CLYDE A.
1939 219. The Emerald House
220. Ramchae
1940 199. Norway
1941 148. Sunday Morning
1942 228. Chicago Waterfront
1944 247. Wind and Rain
248. Twilight at Drumlins

STOOPS, CAROL K.
1984 186. Time II
187. Reverse Images IV
1985 149. Contained II

STOTTS, RUSSELL
1929 274. Symphony

STOUDER, ELIZABETH C(henoweth)
1954 174. Vibrations
1955 187. Morphotic Cells*
188. Still Life
1956 199. Geo-Fractures
1957 191. Fishermen's Wharf
1958 237. Waterfront
1962 289. Apothecary
1966 134. Berlin Wall
1967 245. Cellocut No. 3

STOUDER, JOYCE A.
1975 223. The Tin Shop
1978 147. 75 Gourds*
148. Appleton's Book Store
1980 149. Sergeant at Arms
150. Summer at the Beach
1981 184. Passing Through
1982 185. Tiger Lilies
186. Farm Boy Market
1983 172. Reflections of the Past
1985 150. Seascape No. 1
1988 199. Corner of 6th and W. 10th St., NYC

STOUFFER, WILLIAM PARKER
1973 185. McNarney's*
1974 140. Ericson Street
141. Recluse
1975 224. Omaha Restaurant
1977 159. Tiffany
1979 148. Connecticut Puzzle
149. Pointed Pulled
1982 187. The Leo Northrop*
1983 171. The Mamie Lee
1984 188. The Blue Egyptian
1988 200. The Exhibition
201. Heir to the Family Business
1989 216. Portrait of a Painting
217. Portrait of a Man with a Mortgage

STOUT, ETHEL
1941 149. Church Street, Charleston, S. C.*

STOUT, FORREST A.
1951   181.   Winter Garden

STOUT, KARYL DANIEL
1983   173.   Electric Plant #4

STOVER, WALLACE (P.)
1925   212.   Still Life, Fruit
1927   316.   Chief Longfeather
        317.   Flowers
1929   275.   Portrait of an Old Woman

STRACK, MARY E(llen) CALLAND
1979   150.   Plant Life
1980   151.   Wild Flowers

STRANGE, JENNIFER A.
1984   189.   Along the Thames
        190.   Road in Raffina
1987   212.   I Saw It through the Grapevine

STREIT, FRANCES NORRIS
1949   142.   Eternal Triangle*
1963   208.   Tranquillity*

STRONG, CONSTANCE (J.) GILL
1928   281.   Bowl of Fruit
1961   258.   Sunshine and Shadows
1964   250.   Montana Mountains
1966   139.   The Gab Session
1968   216.   Sunflowers

STROUSE, ELVA
1944   249.   After the Rain

STUEBE, FRANCES
1962   290.   July Bouquet
        291.   Sentinel
1965   248.   Rural Landscape
        249.   Lure of the City
1967   247.   For Many Years
        248.   In the Valley
1968   217.   Pink Roses
        218.   Hills in October
1969   173.   Rock Mountain Canyon
        174.   Zinnias in a Brown Jug #2
1970   212.   Variation in Yellow
        213.   Balancing Rock at Hidden Lake*
1971   196.   Power Lines
1974   142.   Deep in the Woods
1975   225.   House on the Ridge
        226.   Mountain Road
1980   152.   High Altitude
        153.   Urban Windows

STUMP, CAROL
1982   188.   Nature's Way
1983   174.   Touch of Spring

1989   218.   The Gathering Place, Indianapolis
                Zoo
        219.   Old Legacy of San Francisco

STURGEON, LEA A.
1929   276.   In the Kitchen
        277.   Helen

STURGEON, THELMA M.
1962   292.   Mountain Town
1963   209.   Angry Sea

STURGES, LEE
1934   185.   Midsummer on the Tippecanoe
        186.   Corn Stubble Indiana
        187.   Winter Cornfield Indiana
        188.   Nature's Architecture
        189.   The High Country
        190.   Elmhurst
        191.   Locating the Blind
        192.   An Alaskan Husky
        193.   The Sourdough's Friend
1935   160.   Sentinels
        161.   Indiana Marsh
        162.   Mount Hood
1936   202.   The Seine
        203.   Young Crows
        204.   The Jungfrau
1937   185.   Indiana Corn
        186.   Swiss Village
        187.   Jung Frau

SUEBERKROP, HENRIK
1956   200.   Bison
        201.   Cow
        202.   Mountain Lion
1957   192.   Foxes*
        193.   Seal
1958   238.   Strand Birds*
        239.   Beaver
        240.   Otters
1959   169.   Bears*
        170.   Nanook Is Awaiting
1960   206.   Polar Bear
        207.   Caribou
1961   259.   Raven
        260.   Horse
        261.   Lynx
1962   293.   Owl
        294.   Rattlesnake
1963   210.   Mandan, Buffalo Dance
        211.   Bear Cub
1964   251.   Foxes
        252.   Dancing Indian Women

SUGARMAN, S. JENNIFER
1989   220.   Interior Forty-Seven: Marge Truly
                Understood the Importance
1990   178.   Exterior Sixty-One: Dancing
                through the Dream
        179.   I Will Think of You Whenever

SUGGS, ISABELLE
1963 212. Tim
1964 253. The Principal
       254. My Daughter, Nancy

SULLIVAN, JANET
1975 227. Tofte Point

SUMMERFIELD, BRUCE
1981 185. In the Duckweed
       186. Grants Zebra
1982 189. Chipmunk
       190. African Lion Cubs

SUMMERS, MAURICE
1953 165. The Strike
       166. Old Logging Road in New Mexico

SURENDORF, Jr., CHARLES FREDERICK
1928 278. The Section Foreman
       279. Portrait of an Old Lady
       280. Pen and Ink Work
1930 222. Hoosier Saw Mill*
       223. Portrait of a Girl
       224. Pleasant Hill
1931 229. Studio Plant
1949 143. Snow, Columbia
       144. Old Ruins, Columbia*
       145. Stairway, New Orleans*
       146. St. Louis No. 1, New Orleans*
       147. Courtyard, New Orleans*
1952 194. Mardi Gras, N. O.*
       195. St. Peter Street, N. O.*
       196. Madison Street, N. O.*
       197. Ghost Town
       198. Driftwood
       199. Fallon House
       200. Miner's Cabin
1953 167. Hills House
1954 175. Lode Lynching*
       176. Boatyard Junkyard
       177. Old Fire Engine
       178. Mother Lode Covered Bridge
       179. State Street
       180. Mother Lode Landscape
       181. Stage Driver's Retreat
       182. Wells Fargo Building
       183. Old School House

SWABEY, LAURA C.
1938 198. Endymion Dreams of the Moon Goddess
       199. Figure No. 1 from "The Blessed Damozel"
       200. Figure No. 2 from "The Blessed Damozel"
1939 221. Pegasus and the Poet
       222. Dancer

SWAN, RETA
1946 173. Petunias

SWANDER, DOROTHEA T.
1947 183. Undermined

SWARTZ, LESTER (L.)
1981 187. Carlos*
1984 191. Sunny Day

SWARTZ, LORNA R.
1983 175. King Oil
1984 192. Priorities*
1986 214. Pegasus
1987 213. Pastimes Past

SWEANY, PAUL J.
1955 189. Still Life
       190. Little Red Hen*
1956 203. Arrangement from Autumn
       204. Fred's Place
1964 255. Wings of the Sea
1988 202. Snow Bunting
1989 221. Orchid Composition, VI*

SWEENEY, FRANCES HAINES
(See Haines, Frances and McVey, Frances Haines)
1932 219. Lilacs
       220. Self-Portrait

SWIGGETT, JEAN
1950 158. Arrangement with Lemons*
       159. Recuerdo De Mexico
1951 182. Harlequin with Melon
       183. San Miquel
1952 201. Geranium
1954 184. Luz and the Birdcage

SWITZER, JOHN E.
1971 197. Archimedian Family

SWOPE, H. VANCE
1925 213. The Little Harbor
       214. Afternoon Light
       215. Full Surf

SYLVESTER, AGUSTUS M.
1976 222. Untitled #2

SYLVESTER, STEPHEN L.
1977 160. Madison County Monuments

SYMONS, LOUISE GRAY
1951 184. Going Fishing at Leland's Dam
1952 202. The Introvert and the Extrovert
       203. Summer Bouquet
1954 185. Foothills, Jasper, Indiana
1955 191. Indiana Horizons
       192. Nellie's Garden
       193. Memorial Peonies
1956 205. Jeff's Bouquet
       206. The Corn Is Blowing
1957 194. Moonlight and Peonies
1960 208. Early Morning

1961	262.	Bringing in the Catch		**1966**	140.	Around the Harbor
1962	295.	Rainy Day			141.	Chinatown
1964	256.	Miss Morton's Weeds			142.	Everybody Loves a Garden
1965	250.	Number 1559		**1967**	249.	Cathedral No. 2
	251.	Brown County Moonlight				
	252.	Summer Ballet*				

SZERDAHELYI, GEORGE V.

    1964   257.   Don Quixote

TAFLINGER, ELMER E.
1926 283. Over blackboard decoration for European History classroom, left end*
      284. Over blackboard decoration for European History classroom, center*
      285. Over blackboard decoration for European History classroom, right end*
1927 318. Once in August
      319. Decoration for a Child's Room
      320. Decoration for a Child's Room
1933 212. The Unfinished Picture*
1934 194. Reflections, Romanesque
1943 209. Francis Finds a Pose
      210. Through the Looking Glass
1944 251. Light and Shade along Pogue's Run
      252. Studio Light
      253. Jane Messick
1945 174. Skylight Etude*
1946 174. Roberta Sancrant*
1953 168. A Disciple of Audubon

TAGGART, BARBARA
1981 188. Flight
1983 176. Lara
1984 193. Earthen Harmony

TAGGART, EDWIN LYNN
1925 216. Studio Shelf
      217. Japonesque

TAGGART, LUCY M.
1925 218. Still Life
      219. Eleanor*
1926 286. Carnival*
1927 321. Summer
1929 278. Young Girl in Green
1931 230. Janet

TANNER, RUSSELL
1973 186. February Path
1974 143. Brook in Winter
      144. A Touch of Fall

TARR, MARIE
1951 185. We Have Television
1952 204. Steel Mills
1953 169. Skyline Dawn
1955 194. Big Storm

TASKEY, HARRY LEROY
1931 231. Sion, Switzerland

1932 221. Le Pont Fortifie, Kayersberg, Alsace
      222. Les Blanchisseries, Chartres, France
      223. La Maison Pfister, Colmar, Alsace

TAYLOR, B. L.
1972 118. Worlds Ends
1975 228. Repose

TAYLOR, D. CODER
1940 200. Building

TAYLOR, HAROLD E.
1968 219. 500 Miles
      220. Moses
1969 175. Meditation

TAYLOR, JAMES EARL
1940 201. Summer Night

TAYLOR, Jr., JAMES W.
1940 202. Morning Fog near Ludlow, Vermont
      203. Snow Clouds over U. S. 2, Indiana
1941 150. Farm between Thorn Hill and Bean Station
1942 229. Irish Hills, November
1943 211. Peaceful Valley
      212. Deserted*
1944 254. Late September
      255. Red Barn*
1945 175. Blue Wagon
1946 175. Zero Day
1947 184. End of Summer
1948 124. Back Porch*
1949 148. Indiana Home
      149. Snow Flurries Tonight
1950 160. Old Timer

TEMPLETON, J(ohn) C(owan)
1938 201. Duneland
1939 223. Autumn Shadows
      224. Indiana Shoreland
1940 204. The Two Sentinels
1941 151. Along the Beach
1945 176. Afternoon Shadows
      177. A Glimpse of the Lake
1946 176. Dunes Grandeur
      177. Dunes Fantasy
1947 185. Sandy Glen
      186. Dune Acres
1948 125. Sandland Shadows
1949 150. Dunes Park, Indiana
1950 161. Lakeside Shores
1951 186. Ogden Dunes
      187. Late Fall
1952 205. Autumn Idyll

1953	170.	An Old Barn
	171.	The First Snow
	172.	Dune
1954	186.	Winter
	187.	Ogden Dune
1955	195.	Winter in the Valley
1956	207.	Winter
	208.	Sunny Afternoon
1957	195.	Tremont Beach
	196.	In Duneland
	197.	December
1958	241.	In Dune Land
	242.	Winter Afternoon

TEMPLETON, LOIS M.

1980 154. September Sun

TENENBAUM, JAN

1982 191. North Soy Field
192. First Santa Cruz Escape*

TERRY, WAYNE

1970 214. The Cross

THIERY, THOMAS

1969	176.	Northeaster
	177.	Path to Holly Hill*
1970	215.	Two Generations*
1971	198.	Rome Center Road
1972	119.	Joel's Mackinaw
1973	187.	Grand Masters of Washington Square
	188.	Waiting for the Tide*
1977	161.	American Gothic Revisited
	162.	Charlotte's Ridge
1978	149.	Edge of Camelot II
	150.	4 p.m., January 26*

THOMAS, DIAN BUDKO

1970 216. Isometric Freeze

THOMAS, MARYBETH

1981	189.	Spring Seclusion
1983	177.	In Port
1984	194.	Just off Bourbon Street
1988	203.	Roots in the Sand
1990	180.	Seclusion

THOMAS, ROSEMARY LAWTON

1964	258.	Herein Is My Father Glorified
1965	253.	September Afternoon
1967	250.	Summertime
1968	221.	Mixed Bouquet
1970	217.	Out by the Cellar Door*
	218.	Gretchen's Flowers
1971	199.	The Innocents
1973	189.	Orientale
	190.	Study in Textures
1975	229.	The Queen and Her Court

1976	223.	Nearly Home
1977	163.	East Bank
1980	155.	Back Porch Morning
1981	190.	The Sound of Light II
1984	195.	Profile
1985	151.	Papa's Old House
1986	215.	The Garden Club II
1987	214.	Adventure
1988	204.	Daisy and Dolly*
	205.	The Craftsman
1989	222.	Dolly and the Dark Horse
	223.	A Hundred in the Shade*

THOMAS, SHIRLEY

1973	191.	Shining Moment
1976	224.	Weed Study
1977	164.	The Garrulous Guards
1984	196.	Forever Violets
	197.	Sunny Nasturtiums

THOMAS, WILLIAM

1931	232.	Louis
1932	224.	Ted Shawn
	225.	Aurora
	226.	Ralph

THOMPSON-SHOLTY, BEVERLY

1988	206.	Toward Eastern Skies
1989	196.	Grandiose
	197.	Iridescent Fans Dancing in the Clouds

THOMPSON, DOROTHY

1952 206. Calla Lilies

THOMPSON, EDNA

1961 263. Sunlight and Shadows

THOMPSON, ERNEST THORNE

1925	220.	Indiana Snows
1926	287.	"Elaine the Fair, the Lily Maid, Cometh to Camelot"
1927	322.	Marken in the Zuyderzee
	323.	The Black Spot
	324.	The Top of the Street, Chester
	325.	On the Dyke, Volendam
	326.	Water Mills of Alkmaar
	327.	Massachusetts Hills at Dusk
	328.	Cocoa Mill at Zaandam
	329.	Chimney Pots and Slates, Chester
	330.	The Plumed Hat
1928	282.	Cockington Cottage
	283.	Hoosier Mint Still
	284.	Afterglow, Stonehenge
	285.	Curato's Cottage, Cockington
	286.	Drying Nets, Marblehead
	287.	John Halifax Mill, Tewksbury
	288.	Clipper Graveyard, Boston

1929 279. Net Mender's Yard, Marblehead
280. Tete Serieux
281. Chapelle St. Auberle, Mont St. Michel
282. Chimney Pots and Slates, Vitre
283. Florence*

THOMPSON, FLORENCE M.
1928 289. The Apparition
290. Tristran and Isolde
291. Avarice

THOMPSON, JEAN
1990 181. Good Ole Days

THOMPSON, LAURA J(ones)
1941 152. The Old Barn
1942 230. Anchored, Larsons Boat Yard
231. Circle Tent, Belleville, Kansas
1943 213. Red Door
1944 256. Hoosierscape
257. Boskey Dell
258. Iris and Peony
1945 178. Peonies
1952 207. Reflections
208. Lady with a Lamp
209. Boat Patterns
1953 173. Digging for Bait
174. Painting the Station*
1954 189. The Pot Shop

THOMPSON, MABEL GRACE
1954 188. Marie
1956 209. Old House

THOMPSON, MARIE J.
1960 209. Boy in the Red Coat
210. The Captain
1962 296. Mother's Little Hero
297. Collector's Items
1964 259. Fruit and Nuts
1965 254. Mary's Iris
1967 251. Still Life with Jug
1969 178. Christie
1970 219. Young Girl with Tulips
1974 145. Pensive Moment
1976 225. Growin' Wild
1982 193. Pensive Moment
1987 215. Mums for Sale
1988 207. Down East
1990 182. Fall Harvest

THOMPSON, NORMAN E.
1971 200. Golgotha

THOMPSON, RALPH F.
1936 205. Living Gems
1938 204. Old Aunt Mary
325. Self Portrait
1945 179. Ye Gods, The Artist
1947 187. Happy New Year

THOMPSON, ROY F.
1950 162. Whistle Stop
1951 188. Depot at Three Rivers, Michigan*
1952 210. Spring Plowing

THORNBER, MIRIAM H.
1934 195. Rillito Wash. Tucson
196. Cliffs, Point Loma

THORNTON, H. LaVERNE
1936 206. Lolita
1937 188. Terra Cotta Head
1938 202. Figure
203. Mrs. Robert Gunnell
1939 225. Decorative Head
226. Gerald A. Clark
227. Simplicity
1940 205. Michael Ligochi
206. Virgil Hiermeier
1941 153. Pat
154. Rev. Thomas James Simpson

THORWARD, CLARA (Schafer)
1929 284. Indiana Sycamores
1942 232. Madonna and Child

THUNDERE, O. D.
1947 188. Low Tide

THURMAN, TRACY J.
1987 216. Dad's Side of the Family
217. Melon Maze
1988 208. Summer in the Smokies*
1989 224. Harry and Lily

TIMBERMAN, ANN GILLIS
1973 192. Abracadabra
1974 146. Two Bicycles for 5 People
147. Chelonia

TIMMINS, ABBIE
1989 225. To View through a Wall: The Bakery

TINGLEY, JOHN K.
1935 163. Chinese Pots
164. Brass and Fruit

TIPTON, DAVID N.
1986 216. Winter Solitude
1987 218. Landmark on 421, Boone County
219. Grandma's House
1988 209. Hendricks Co. Farm
210. Mathena's Barn, Johnson Co.
1989 226. Grandpa Tipton's Place, Monroe Co.
1990 183. Snow on the Way

TIRMENSTEIN, MARTIN S.
1950 163. The Other Side of the Tracks
1958 243. Miscellany

TODD, AL
1967 252. On the Rock Stood the Tree*
      253. This Too Shall Pass

TODD, DIANE
1976 226. Lobster Shell
      227. Bloom
1977 165. Relic from New Orleans House

TODDERUD, SARA
1976 228. Crab-apples
1983 178. Boats of St. Michael
1985 152. For Sale
      153. St. Michael's
1986 217. Tonala Mk
1987 220. Los Hombres
      221. Untitled
1990 184. Approaching Storm

TOEBES, INGRID
1981 191. Crystal*

TOMPKINS, BARBARA
1983 179. Butterflies and Mayan Ruins
1984 198. Jaguar
      199. Raccoon in the Mangrove
1986 218. Cautious Marsh Rabbit

TOOLE, DONALD C.
1963 213. Heritage
1965 255. Afternoon Light
      256. Gifts of Gold
1975 230. Summer Oak

TOOLE, KATHY (Katherine A.)
1987 222. Golden Corner
1988 211. Dogwoods

TOPPING, JAMES
1931 233. Wind Swept Sky
      234. From the Helmsburg Road
      235. Indiana Hillside
1932 227. Drifting Clouds
      228. Autumn Sunlight
      229. Across the River
1933 213. A Breeze from the West
      214. The Old Homestead
1935 165. From Bean Blossom Ridge
1938 205. Blue Valley
      206. The Village from the Hill
      207. Wandering Clouds
1939 228. Roving Clouds
      229. Old Farm
      319. Old Willows
1940 207. Flying Clouds
      318. The Old Road*
1941 155. Passing Clouds
1942 233. Late Afternoon
1947 189. Frolicking Clouds

TORNOW, KENN
1943 214. A Trail through Beech and Maple

TOTH, GENEVIEVE HARTIG
1944 259. The Down Beat
      260. Summertime
      261. Prelude
1950 164. Mary

TOWN, CAROL (M.)
1982 194. Parent to the Kay
1983 180. Cast Off Cast Iron
      181. Fran's Toys
1984 200. Vulcan's Feet

TOWNSEND, CHARLES
1957 198. Chrysanthemums
      199. Ohio River
      200. Winter Hills
1959 171. Tulips
      172. Mt. Adams Houses*
1960 211. Big Sycamore
      212. Fourth Street, Cincinnati

TOWNSEND, HARRY R.
1928 292. Backwater at Webster Lake
1929 285. Along the Whitewater
      286. The Barn Lot
1930 225. Pine Crest
1931 236. The Pool
1932 230. First Snow
      231. Winter Evening
1937 189. Across the River
      190. Winter Morning
1940 208. Fall Glow
1941 156. Carpenter Mill
1942 234. Winter Sunshine
1943 215. Summer Day
1944 262. Late Afternoon
      263. Grey November
1945 180. Winter in Indiana
1950 165. One Evening
1951 189. Michigan Shore Line
1958 244. Shadows
1959 173. Edge of Pool

TRACY, JAMES (Jim) LEON
1975 231. Naked
1976 229. A Winter Barn
      230. Homage to Rosseau
1977 166. Meditation

TRACY, RONALD (R.)
1963 214. Slumber
1965 257. Pluto Offering Persephone a
            Pomegranate Seed*
      258. Portrait with a Mandolin
1966 143. The Green Nude

TRANBARGER, FRANCES (Roe)
1942	235.	Zinnias and Marigolds
1943	216.	Color Splashes
	217.	Hollyhocks and Daisies
1944	264.	Double Feature
	265.	October Blossoms
1945	181.	Phlox and Wedgewood*
1971	201.	Winter Fun, Lake of the Hills
1972	120.	The Big Dipper

TRAUGOTT, DALE ELLEN
1971	202.	Mayan God

TRAUGOTT, JOSEPH (Joe) HENRI
1969	179.	Study No. III, Serenity
	180.	The Couples
1970	220.	Study #VII
	221.	Study #V
1976	231.	Crab
1978	151.	Nature Suite
1979	151.	Crab Metamorphosis
	152.	Leaf Patterns*

TRAUGOTT, LEAH S.
1965	259.	Poplars in Spring
	260.	Tulips
1967	254.	Flores Bonitas*
	255.	Resplendent Fruit
1968	222.	The Orange Cloth
	223.	Pitcher with Flowers
	224.	Golden Bouquet*
1970	222.	Autumn Garden
	223.	Flaming Persimmons with Flowers*
1972	121.	LeGrande Bouquet
	122.	Flower Patterns #7*
1973	193.	Blazing Tulips
1974	148.	Floral Elegance*
1975	232.	Bearded Iris*
	233.	Strange That So Few Ever Come to the Woods
1976	232.	Patio Pansies
	233.	Golden Flower Patterns
1977	167.	Spring Bouquets
1978	152.	Fall Elegance*
	153.	Shell Landscape
1979	153.	Roots
	154.	Summer Vases
1980	156.	Hydrangia
1981	192.	Spring Bouquets
	193.	Shell Scape #7
1982	195.	Vibrant Iris
1983	182.	Bearded Iris
1984	201.	The White Door
1986	219.	Spring Splendor*
	220.	Vases on Glass Top Table
1987	223.	Fall Basket with Vases
1988	212.	Bearded Iris #7
	213.	Prelude to Summer*

1989	227.	Vases with Shadows*
	228.	Spring Reflections
1990	185.	Basket with Shadows

TREES, JULIA
1945	182.	Hollyhocks
1946	178.	July Bouquet

TRIMBLE, RAY
1982	196.	Forbidden Shore

TRIPLETT, THELMA
1965	261.	Still Life

TRISSEL, LAWRENCE E.
1941	157.	Frances
	158.	The Alley
1942	236.	Crucifixion
	237.	Rain on Sunday
	238.	Winter Landscape
1943	218.	Urban Night
	219.	Indiana Landscape
	220.	Thursa-Jean
1944	266.	Winter
	267.	Ancient House
	268.	Village Street
1945	183.	Snow Valley
	184.	21st At Oak
1946	179.	Winter
	180.	Reminiscence*
1947	190.	Landscape, Winter
	191.	Maria
	192.	Sunday Morning
1948	126.	Traders Point Hunt
	127.	Landscape, Summer
	128.	Snowscape*
1949	151.	Sledding
1951	190.	Snowland
	191.	Winter Afternoon
1952	211.	Seascape

TRITCH, FAITH
1934	197.	Old, New Orleans

TROBAUGH, ROY (B.)
1925	221.	October Day
	222.	Midwinter on Deer Creek
1926	288.	Way Side Beech
	289.	Snow Flurry
1927	331.	Springtime on Deer Creek
1928	293.	The Winding Tippecanoe
1929	287.	Vevey Ferry
1932	232.	Hilltop Pasture
1936	207.	Snow Storm
1937	191.	Winter Landscape
	192.	The Foot Bridge*
1940	209.	New Snow
	319.	Winter Magic
1941	159.	Indiana Hills

1944	269.	Indian Craft*
	270.	Abandoned Schoolhouse
1945	185.	Still Life
1947	193.	Boothbay Harbor, Me.
1949	152.	Wedgewood Ware and Cluny Lace*
1952	212.	Old Houses, Eastport, Maine
1953	175.	Bachelor Run Creek
	176.	Indian Craft
1954	190.	Indian Craft Design

TROTTNOW, BERT MORRIS

1936	208.	North of Truro
1937	193.	Barn in Shady
1939	230.	Cook Street
1941	160.	Zocalo, Taxco, Gro.

TROVER, JOSEPH A.

1957	201.	The Red Barn
1959	174.	Back of Town
1960	213.	Back of the Mills
	214.	Snow on Raccoon Creek
1961	264.	First Weekend in November*
1962	298.	The Red Bridge
1964	260.	Winter on Big Leatherwood Creek
1965	262.	Clear and Cold
	263.	Pursuit of Happiness
1966	144.	My Friend John
	145.	A Rural Scene
1967	256.	Low Tonight-Zero
	257.	Deep Into Spring

TRUCKSESS, F. C(lement)

1925	223.	Dusk
	224.	Feeding Time
1929	288.	Night
	289.	Sagittarius
	290.	The Indian

TRUE, VIRGINIA

1925	225.	Monday Morning
1926	290.	Suzanne
	291.	Helen's Baby
1927	332.	Autumn Along the Bluffs
1928	294.	Top o' the Hill
1929	291.	Pajarita Canyon, N. M.
	292.	Up the Arroyo
	293.	We Dwell in the Desert
1931	237.	Boulder Canyon
1933	215.	Wood Chopper
	216.	Autumn Landscape

TRUEBLOOD, SUSAN

| 1978 | 154. | Our Birth Is But a Sleep and Forgetting |

TRUEMPER, Jr., JOHN W.

| 1976 | 234. | Autumn Stillness |
| | 235. | Banks of the Wabash |

TRUITT, JANE

| 1956 | 210. | Self Portrait |
| | 211. | Barb |

TSCHAEGLE, ROBERT

1926	292.	Albert Edward Wiggam
	293.	Magdalene
1927	333.	Clarence Darrow
	334.	Smiling Grandmother
1928	295.	Lilith

TUCK, RICHARD

| 1975 | 234. | Head of Barbara |

TUCKER, IRENE (W.)

1984	202.	Slides Eye View
1985	154.	Sentinel
1986	221.	Patterns
1987	224.	Le Hangout
	225.	The Neighborhood
1988	214.	Pioneer Memory
1989	229.	Flotsam-Jetsam

TURMAN, WILLIAM T.

1925	226.	Winter Morning
1926	294.	November Sunshine
	295.	Long Shadows on the Snow
1927	335.	Emerald Bay, Lake Tahoe
1928	296.	October
1929	294.	Over and beyond Penn. Acad., Chester Springs
1930	226.	Mt. Soledad Sunset, Mojave Desert, Calif.
1931	238.	Strip Mining
	239.	By Deep Waters
1932	233.	High Lights and Shadows*
1933	217.	Mount Moran, Teton, Wyoming
1935	166.	Big Sycamores
1936	209.	California Glories
1941	161.	Entrance to the Woods
1944	271.	Fog Coming Inland
	272.	Desert Girl
1945	186.	Self Portrait
1950	166.	Vain October
1951	192.	Across the Valley
1952	213.	October's Farewell
1955	196.	Cataract Lake
	197.	Deep Dark in the Woods
1956	212.	Out From the Woods

TURNBAUGH, DORIS (O.)

1975	235.	Queen Anne
1977	168.	Roadside Riches
	169.	#19
1978	155.	Fishy Waters
1979	155.	Americana
	156.	Time to Throw My Hat In
1982	197.	Paula
1983	183.	Yesteryears

1984	203.	Burlington Route
1987	226.	We'll Be All in Clover
	227.	Summer
1988	215.	Pulling Together
	216.	Fall

TURNER, MARY CLEMENT

1926	296.	Before Dusk

TURTLE, ARNOLD E.

1951	193.	Salome

TYREE, JEANNINE

1965	264.	Blue Flowers

U

UHL, MARY A.
1976   236.   Flurries Predicted

UNTHANK, GERTRUDE
1928   297.   Monterey Cypresses
       298.   Winter on Lake Superior
1932   234.   Toboggan Trail, Chester Park, Duluth
       235.   Rue de la Grande Mesure, Rouen, France

UNTULIS, CHARLES R.
1956   213.   Autumn Glory
1957   202.   Early Morn
1958   245.   Barbi
       246.   Serenity
1959   175.   Blackfoot Squaw
       176.   Bittersweet
       177.   Circus
1960   215.   Still Life
       216.   Rhapsody in Blue
       217.   Golden Moment*
1961   265.   Flowering Quince
       266.   Pussy Willows
       267.   Shepherd Boy
1962   299.   Street Urchins*
       300.   Mixed Flowers
1963   215.   Caleche
       216.   Plant No. 1
       217.   Still Life
1964   261.   Pussy Willows
       262.   Carnival
       263.   Refinery
1971   203.   Carnival

UNVERSAW, JEAN
1955   198.   Self Portrait
1956   214.   Sisters
1957   203.   Sheila
       204.   The Lantern*
1958   247.   Pears And Stripes
1959   178.   Outdoor Flower Planting
       179.   Corner of My Studio
1977   170.   Pastel Creations
       171.   Reflections II
1978   156.   Pastel Desert*
1979   157.   It's Always Greener on the Other Side of the Fence
       158.   Pear and Stripes

UPDEGRAFF, WILLIAM (Bill) R.
1986   222.   Chit Chat
1988   217.   Bus Stop
       218.   The Roost

USHER, ALICE (Fraver)
1960   218.   Totem*
1965   265.   Portrait of Willis
       266.   Child
       267.   Boy
1971   204.   Youth
1975   236.   Abandoned Form
       237.   Child of Giotto
1984   204.   Burnt Coffee

USUL, NURUNNISA
1986   223.   Squares

UUK, MARI
1969   181.   The Holy Family
       182.   Evolution of Thought

V

VAIL, DOROTHY MAKEPEACE
1926	297.	Commuters
	298.	Symphony Night
	299.	Monday

VanBRUNT, WILLA BOWEN
1977	172.	Matrix
1983	184.	Blue, Blue Grotto
1985	155.	Wind Drift
1986	224.	Floral Piece II
1987	228.	Nature's Forces
1989	230.	Interlace
1990	186.	Northern Slope

VANCE, FRED NELSON
1925	227.	Clearing
	228.	Sandy Shores
1926	300.	Sunset and Evening Star
	301.	Cara Italia
1927	336.	Morning Light
	337.	Town Hill
	338.	The Old Walnuts
1928	299.	Springtime

VANDERPOOL, EARL
| 1964 | 264. | Bright Morning |

VanHORNE, ANDREA MEIDINGER
| 1973 | 194. | Church at Helmer |
| 1982 | 198. | Blackberries, Gailardia, and Queen Anne's Lace |

VanLANDINGHAM, MARY
1963	218.	The Timbers
1964	265.	Window Accent
	266.	White Peonies
1968	225.	Gay 90's Bath

VANN, ESSE BALL
| 1934 | 198. | Summer Flowers |
| | 199. | The Chinese Bowl |

VanSELL, PATRICIA ANN
| 1969 | 183. | Trinity of Nuns |

VanSICKLE, JANE HEWITT
1952	214.	The Woods
	215.	Election*
	216.	White Pitcher*
1955	199.	Pewter and Petunias

VanSICKLE, JOSEPH L.
| 1954 | 191. | Embrace of November |

VanSICKLE, ROBERT F.
| 1948 | 129. | November Election |
| 1956 | 215. | Still Creek |

1975	238.	Copper & Bronze Kung Gi
1976	237.	American Bicentennial Eagle
1977	173.	School Bus
1978	157.	Sunlight and Shadow
1979	159.	Spring at Earlham
1981	194.	Earlham Campus

VanVOORHIS, WILMA JEAN
1958	248.	Cornfield
	249.	Treescape
1961	268.	Two Hoots

VAWTER, (J.) WILL
1925	229.	Sifter Sunlight
	230.	Cloud Shadows
	231.	Our Alley*
1926	302.	Asters
	303.	Morning in the Hills*
	304.	Hidden Away
1927	339.	Winter Quiet
	340.	Rocky Coast
1928	300.	The Willows
	301.	Blossom Time*
	302.	The Blue Pool
1929	296.	Summer Morning
	297.	Whispering Spring
	298.	A Song of Summer
1930	227.	A Snowy Road
	228.	Edge of Town*
1931	240.	Deserted Orchard
1932		(Nos. 300-341 were displayed in special Vawter gallery)
	300.	Path Thru Woods
	301.	Snow Bound
	302.	Dream Days
	303.	A Touch of Frost
	304.	Red Gums
	305.	Shady Pool
	306.	Maturity
	307.	Cabin Home
	308.	Rock Bound Coast
	309.	Meadow Brook
	310.	Spring Blossoms
	311.	Flowers
	312.	Twilight
	313.	Sunlit Road
	314.	Spring Sunshine
	315.	Blue Bonnets
	316.	Dredge Boat
	317.	Pearly Waters
	318.	Texas Mesquite
	319.	Snow Clouds
	320.	A Glimpse of the Sea
	321.	The Willows
	322.	The Home in the Hills
	323.	Pals

	324.	Glorious Autumn
	325.	After Glow
	326.	Edge of Town
	327.	Old Fashioned Garden
	328.	The Doorway
	329.	Our Garden
	330.	Blue and Gold
	331.	September Day
	332.	Afternoon Shadow
	333.	Late Summer
	334.	Apple Blossoms
	335.	Greasy Creek
	336.	House Beside the Road
	337.	Mollies Alley
	338.	Bridge
	339.	Beech Tree
	340.	Sycamore
	341.	Edge of Town
1933	218.	Under November Skies
	219.	A Rest on the Hill Top
1934	200.	Poetry of Spring
	201.	Neighbors
1935	167.	Morning Light in Woods*
	168.	Winter Bound
1936	210.	Harvest Days
	211.	Shadowy Pool
	212.	The Bend in the Creek
1937	194.	The Old Mill
	195.	Pageant of Autumn
	334.	Blue and Gold
1938	208.	Lilacs
	209.	Mirror Pool
1939	231.	Serf on Monhegan
	232.	A Load of Sunshine
	233.	The Creek Road
	322.	Indian Summer
1940	210.	Drifting Shadows
	320.	Rocky Stream
1941	162.	After the Storm
	163.	A Quiet Interlude
	164.	Woods in Winter
	324.	Lilacs
1942	239.	Crowned with Glory
	240.	Peonies
	241.	The Storm Subsides
		(Exhibited by special invitation)

VAWTER, MARY H. MURRAY

1929	295.	Portrait, Miss Mary L.
1932	236.	Edge of the Ridge in Spring
	237.	Portrait: Juanita
	238.	Hillside: Early September
1937	196.	Wayside: My Place, Brown County, Ind.

VELSEY, SETH (M.)

1926	305.	Modern Tendencies
	306.	Portrait of T. A. B.
	307.	Lillian
1927	341.	Fakrud-Din Pirzada
	342.	A Mask

1928	303.	Frances
	304.	Water (for Drinking Fountain)*
1929	299.	Study for Memorial
	300.	Sidney Sayers
	301.	West Wind
1930	229.	Marjory*
	230.	Burrell Booth: A Pioneer
1931	241.	The Sybarite
	242.	Head and Hat
	243.	E Paul W.
1932	239.	Gothic
1933	220.	Aspiration
	221.	Eve*
1934	202.	Bob Tschaegle*
1936	213.	Elinor
	214.	Life*

VELVICK-VIGNA, BERNICE

1987	229.	Evening

VENN, ROBERT G.

1971	205.	Car Bank*

VERNON, ELBA (L.) RIFFLE
(See Riffle, Elba L.)

1944	273.	St. Catherine St., Montreal
1946	203.	Aspiration
1950	167.	Gray Day
1952	217.	Street Composition
1955	200.	Ghosts
1957	205.	Early Morning
1962	301.	Old Railroader
1964	267.	The Meadow
1965	268.	A Likely Place
	269.	Composition
1966	146.	Hill Top Road
1967	258.	Daily Chore
1968	226.	Rain Washed Meadow
1969	184.	The Condemned
1970	224.	Morning Break
	225.	Anticipated Weather

VETETO, WILMA

1970	226.	Inner City

VICE, H. STODDARD

1927	343.	Indiana Corn-Field
1928	305.	Purple and Gold
1931	244.	Along Forster Road

VICTOR, PATRICIA EBERHART

1964	268.	The Flowers
1965	270.	Waiting
	271.	Fall
1967	259.	Eve and the Apple
	260.	Leftovers
1968	227.	Summer
	228.	Empty Buildings
1969	185.	Flowers for the Dead
	186.	The Birthday Party

1970	227.	Inhabitants of the House*
1971	206.	Untitled
1972	123.	And Zarathustra Spoke

VIETOR, FRANK

1973	195.	H-10
	196.	Yesterday*
1974	149.	November Morn
	150.	October 1950*
1975	239.	Nostalgia*
	240.	Iron Horse
1976	238.	Class of '49*
1977	174.	End Of An Era
1978	158.	October Evening, 1952*
1979	160.	Later Afternoon
	161.	Martinsville & Franklin R. R.*
1980	157.	County Seat
	158.	Rainy Day in Shoals

VIETOR, JEAN (F.)

1970	228.	Lone Resident
1971	207.	House of Yesterday
	208.	Incompatible Worlds
1972	124.	Edge of Summer*
1973	197.	Fog Bound
	198.	Winter Softness
1974	151.	No Trespassing
	152.	Weed or Wildflower?
1975	241.	Passing Through

1976	239.	Mirror Image #2
	240.	The Personality Plant*
1977	175.	The Bad and the Beautiful
	176.	Love On A Branch
1979	162.	Ice Fantasy
1980	159.	Fluff Explosions
1988	219.	Rock of Ages
	220.	The Happy Dream
1989	231.	Grapes of the Wild
1990	187.	Imprints on Time
	188.	Deep Woods*

VINING, SHIRLEY

1968	229.	The Empty House
1969	187.	Rain for the Parched Land
	188.	Closed on Sundays
1974	153.	Soft Weather
1975	242.	Stonington Grey

VOGL, DON

1972	125.	Ice Cream Pie
	126.	Miss Liberty
1973	199.	Squirrel Hill

VOREIS, GARY E.

1982	199.	Eroded Times
1983	185.	Static Blue*
1985	156.	Aurora*

WADE, BETTY (S.)
1979	163.	Cascade of Mums
1983	186.	By the Window
1984	205.	Sitting on the Edge
	206.	Window Dressing
1985	157.	Things Do Get Complicated
1986	225.	Window Setting
1987	230.	Bright Spot on Winter Day
	231.	Ivy Leaf Morning Glory
1988	221.	Taking a Bow
1989	232.	Banded Together
1990	191.	A Spring Get Together

WADE, ROSSIE S.
| 1955 | 201. | Trees |

WADE, TED
| 1947 | 194. | Temalpais Creek |

WAGNER, FRANK HUGH
1925	232.	Mary Alice
	233.	Angelica Mary Elizabeth
	234.	Portrait of Mr. H.
1926	308.	Silhouette, Napoleon Bonaparte
	309.	Silhouette, Antique Figures
	310.	Silhouette, Antique Figures
	311.	Troubadour
1927	344.	Twilight
1929	302.	Portrait of Francesca and Angelica W.*
1931	245.	Portrait of Mr. B. Gage Leake
1932	240.	Autumn, Saugatuck
	241.	God and the Soldier Man
1933	222.	Evicted
1935	169.	Portrait of Mr. Hinckley
	170.	Portrait of Mrs. Carmichael

WAGNER, MARY NORTH
1927	345.	The Child
	346.	Rose of the World
1930	231.	The First Garden
1937	197.	A Triptych

WAITKUS, E. ALGERD
1962	302.	The Resting Place
	303.	3 Empty Chairs
1964	269.	The Dune Cottage
	270.	Carolina Washday
1966	147.	Rooftop Laundry, Taxco

WALDORF, BARBARA J.
| 1972 | 127. | Bone Study |

WALKER, FERDINAND GRAHAM
| 1926 | 312. | Posing for his Picture |

WALKER, INES D.
| 1941 | 165. | Jean |

WALKER, JAMES A.
1963	219.	Print No. 38
	220.	Fowl Play
	221.	Print No. 41
	222.	Print No. 65
	223.	Print No. 67
	224.	Print No. 70
	225.	Print No. 74
1965	272.	Print No. 90
	273.	Print No. 94*
	274.	Print No. 88
1966	148.	Print No. 55
	149.	Print No. 92
	150.	Print No. 85
	151.	Print No. 89
	152.	Print No. 82*
	153.	Print No. 36
1967	261.	Print No. 99
	262.	Print No. 98
	263.	Print No. 100*
	264.	Print No. 91
	265.	Print No. 90-A
	266.	Print No. 94-A
1968	230.	Print No. 103*
	231.	Print No. 102
	232.	Print No. 101
	233.	Print No. 39
	234.	Print No. 49

WALKER, JUDITH
| 1988 | 222. | Patchwork of Petals |

WALKER, LEON R.
| 1952 | 218. | Still Life* |

WALKER, MARGARET McKEE
| 1935 | 171. | Portrait of My Mother |

WALKER, MILDRED K.
1941	166.	Storm Returning
	167.	Tiger, Tiger Burning Bright
1942	242.	Dark Omen
	243.	Finite Man
	244.	Iscariot
	245.	Still the Seasons Change*
1943	221.	Softly Evening Comes Down
	222.	Spring Comes to Berry Street
1944	274.	Storm Warning
1945	187.	Eternal Vigilance
1946	181.	Dark Mountain
1954	192.	Nor Death Dismay

WALLACE, MICHAELENE R.
| 1966 | 154. | Bay of Naples |

WALLPE, CONNIE DEERING
(See Deering, Connie J.)
1990   192.   Bank Barn

WALTERS, VAL
1971   209.   Bark*
        210.   45 Ways to View a Seashell
1972   128.   Split Image*
        129.   Smallmouth
1975   243.   Beth In The Sun
1977   177.   Between the Sky and I*
        178.   Untitled
1983   187.   750 W/200 N
1990   193.   Gull Bay, Maine*
        194.   Minnesota Birch

WALTON, LARRY (A.)
1962   304.   Susan
        305.   Crowning Glory
        306.   The Orator
1963   226.   Despair
        227.   On Guard
1964   271.   Flight Pattern
1965   275.   The Trio
1968   235.   Sky King

WALTZ, ROBERT
1949   153.   Industrial Scene
        154.   Cement Mixer

WALWORTH, JOHN
1938   210.   Man

WAMPLER, MARYROSE
1973   200.   Sanctuary
1979   164.   Jack and William

WAPPLER, EDWIN
1933   223.   Springtime
1936   215.   At the River's Bend
1938   211.   October
1939   234.   Orchard Place
1940   211.   Down Stonehead Way

WARE, BILL SHANE
1971   211.   Nancy's Grandfather
        212.   Untitled
1972   130.   The Sensuous Woman*
        131.   Winter Woodpile

WARE, JORDAN E.
1963   228.   Barbe
1964   272.   Suzanne

WARFIELD, VIRGINIA
1969   189.   Off with the Old/On with the New
1972   132.   Mums*
1976   241.   Stranded

WARNACUT, CREWES
1928   306.   Awaiting
        307.   Self Portrait
1929   303.   Mother
1930   232.   Grace

WARNER, CLARA E.
1967   267.   Sunflower

WARREN, KARL
1955   202.   Portrait of a Smoke House*
        203.   October in Brown County
1956   216.   Covered Bridge in Fall
        217.   Old House, Brown County
        218.   October in the Dunes
1957   206.   Wash Day in Brown County
        207.   A Warm Day in October
        208.   Three-Wheeled Buggy*
1958   250.   Old Well
        251.   Rainy Day in the Studio*
        252.   October Glory
1959   180.   Old Pump
        181.   October in Brown County
        182.   Greasy Creek
1960   219.   Peace I Give Unto You
        220.   Late Afternoon
        221.   October Morning*
1961   269.   October In Brown County
        270.   In For Repairs
        271.   Gloucester Harbor
1962   307.   Motif No. 1
1963   229.   Afternoon Sunshine
        230.   A Morning in October
1964   273.   Old Sycamore
        274.   Greasy Creek
        275.   Down Greasy Creek Road
1965   276.   A Day to Remember
        277.   It's Autumn Again

WASSON, CAROL
1990   195.   Untitled

WASSON, JEANNE BRUBECK
1983   188.   Midnight Celebration
        189.   Having a Wonderful Time
1984   207.   Three Friends, Ambergris Cay,
                Belize, C.A.
1985   158.   James Whitcomb Riley Home
        159.   Lovers, Observers and Fools
1986   226.   Beach Rivalry
        227.   Cloud Cover
1989   233.   View from Another Place

WATHEN, JOHN ST. JUDE
1971   213.   Truth of Dimension

WATKINS, BERTHA SEIFERT
(See Seifert, Bertha)
1939   235.   Broad Street
1940   212.   Mulberry Town Square

WATKINS, G(ertrude) MAY
1932	242.	Joy
1933	224.	Primrose
1936	216.	Whole Year Through
1937	335.	God's Work

WATKINS, MARY KAY
| 1990 | 196. | Wonderland |

WATT, PHYLLIS
| 1984 | 208. | Twilight |
| | 209. | April Showers & Spring Flowers |

WAVRA, ROBERT J.
| 1980 | 160. | Fruit with Basket |

WEAVER, AVERY B.
1952	219.	Rocks
	220.	Rolling Farm
1953	177.	Field Pattern
1954	193.	Red Roof
1955	204.	Winter Vista
	205.	Harbor Rhythm
1956	219.	Geranium Composition
1957	209.	Winter Came
1958	253.	Ageless Abyss

WEAVER, DOROTHY
1982	200.	Composition No. 8
1983	190.	Sparrow: A Bird for All Seasons
1987	232.	Pastel on Wood #8

WEAVER, ELAINE HARTER
1949	155.	The Orange Door
	156.	Neto
1951	194.	House in San Angel

WEAVER, JACKIE
| 1983 | 191. | Roann Mill |

WEAVER, JAMES W.
| 1987 | 223. | Portrait of Carol |

WEAVER, MARGARITA W.
1925	235.	Portrait of John McCutcheon
1926	313.	Sketch, Ralph
	314.	Sketch
1927	347.	Flowers
	348.	The Green Dress

WEAVER, ROBERT E.
1940	213.	Those Riding Hannefords
1947	195.	First Section
	196.	Little Performer
1948	130.	Red Wagons
1949	157.	Intent
1950	168.	Johnny Cadarro
	169.	Uptown*
1951	195.	Spring Hats
	196.	Boarding House Bath
1952	221.	He Went Up into a Mountain
	222.	The Great Cadarro
1953	178.	Winter Pasture
1956	220.	Gothic Winter
1969	190.	Glory Road
1973	201.	Summer Afternoon
	202.	Stars and Stripes Forever*
1974	154.	Circus Clown
	155.	Great Wall*
1975	244.	Lion in the Rocks*
1978	159.	Send in the Clowns
	160.	Double 0-7*
1979	165.	Strata
1980	161.	Interlude
	162.	Sleeping Lion*
1981	195.	Calliope*
1982	201.	Gemini II
	202.	Aquabed

WEAVER, SYLVESTER V.
| 1952 | 223. | Brown County Log Gaol |

WEBB, LORNA
| 1982 | 203. | Sunflowers |
| 1988 | 223. | Glads and Grandmother's Lace |

WEBER, BETTIE L.
| 1963 | 231. | Attic Treasures |

WEBER, JAN
1965	278.	Lobster
1966	155.	For the Night Is Coming
	156.	Grandmother's Flowers
1967	268.	Life's Beauty
	269.	Flowers
1971	214.	Geranium
1973	203.	Near Here

WEEKS, LEO R.
1939	236.	Sunday Lull, Gloucester
1940	214.	Schooner Creek, Indiana
1941	168.	A Restful Hollow
	169.	Rag Pickers
1942	246.	Settin' a Spell
1943	223.	Rosemary
1944	275.	Dwarf Marigolds
1948	131.	Store for the Winter*
	132.	The Junk Man

WEHR, PAUL A.
1943	224.	The Station*
	225.	Steel Workers
	226.	The Welder*
1944	276.	"Making Up," Cover Design for the May Issue of the Eli Lilly Company Wholesaleman Magazine*
	277.	Brick Mansion
	278.	The Red Caboose*
1969	191.	Fishing Boat
	192.	Mountain Snow and Flowers*

WEISEL, JAN
1976 242. Misty Morning
1981 196. Reflections

WELCH, WILLIE F.
1977 179. Mrs. Hubbard

WELSHANS, LOTAN
1928 308. Grostesque
1929 304. Venus and Adonis
305. The Wheel
306. Blind Sampson
1930 233. Jacob and the Angel*
1932 243. Scarlet
1933 225. The Finding of Moses*

WENDEL, ADELEE (B.)
1950 170. Harbingers of Summer
1953 179. Spring Song
180. Hoosier Gold
1954 194. Light of the Years
1957 210. October's Solitude
211. Autumn's Brief Fling
1958 254. Mama's Daily Bread
1959 183. October Lights a Taper
184. Only a Rose
1960 223. Effie's Studio
1961 272. Lobsterman's Cove, Boothbay
Harbor
273. Mama's Sewing Room
274. Winter in Washington Park
1964 276. Illusion
277. Old Love Letters and Empty Glasses
278. Winter in a City Park
1965 279. Melody of Love
280. Indian Summer on the Ridge

WENDT, JANE
1960 222. Timmy
1961 275. Contemplation
1963 232. Mike*
1969 193. Tools of the Trade

WENGER, SUSAN
1975 245. The Last Frame
246. November's Arrangement

WENTE, TRICIA HEISER
1990 197. Pier Fishing
198. Rainbow River

WENTLAND, FRANK A.
1932 246. Purple Vase

WERNER, SHIRLEY J.
(See Carr, Shirley Werner)
1969 194. Our Heritage

WESNER, KATHLEEN D.
1967 270. Drying Sunflowers

WESSEL, BESSIE H.
1943 227. Myra
228. Aunt Jenny*
1944 279. The Old Fisherman
280. Portrait of H. H. Wessel
1945 188. Mike, The Lobsterman
189. Still Life*
1946 182. The Ruby Necklace
1947 197. Still Life*
1948 133. Ruth Allen
1952 224. Ruth Ellen
1953 181. Eleanor

WESSEL, H(erman) H(enry)
1925 236. Portrait of Mrs. H.
237. Day Dreams

WEST, ANNE WARNER
1943 229. Beach Scene*
230. Centreville Landing
231. Landscape
1944 281. Gourds
282. Pines

WEST, Jr., CHARLES MASSEY
1942 247. Landscape in Winter*
248. Town Creek
1943 232. The Narrows*
233. Old Bridge Crossing
234. Paper Flowers
1944 283. Ocean City
284. Sketch of Monk
285. East River
1959 185. Portrait of Susie

WEST, WILBUR WARNE
1935 172. Eden
1936 217. Barn in Brown County
218. Scherazade

WESTALL, T. C.
1932 244. Lilies
245. Girl in Old Hat
1933 226. Jessie
227. A White Bowl
1938 212. Fall Bouquet

WESTCOTT, L. GEYER
1939 237. Lake Michigan at Ogden Dunes, Ind.

WESTFALL, SONYA A.
1973 204. Thru the Window

WHEAT, STEPHEN PAUL
1979 166. Untitled*
167. Untitled
1982 204. Spring Fever
205. Chantilly Lace*
1983 192. Going Home

1984	210.	Wait for Me!
	211.	Thy Kingdom Come*
1986	228.	Seek, And Ye Shall Find
1987	234.	One Sunday Afternoon*
1988	224.	Watching Over You
1989	234.	On the Other Side

WHEELER, CLIFTON

1925	238.	The Hill Farm
1926	315.	In the Valley
	316.	The Sugar Camp
	317.	Across the Ravine
1927	349.	The Bridge*
	350.	Frosty Morning
	351.	A Road Through the Hills
1928	309.	The Silo*
	310.	Cumberland Gap
	311.	In the Hills
1929	307.	In the Mountains
	308.	Near Madison
	309.	The Picnic
1930	234.	The Barn
	235.	Carolina*
	236.	Dunes
1931	246.	Colorado
	247.	The Pinnacle
1932	247.	Portrait
	248.	An Outcrop
	249.	Rockies
1933	228.	Carolina Mountains
	229.	Winter*
	230.	My Daughter
1934	203.	The New Cabin
	204.	Girl in Red
1939	238.	Morning in the Valley
	239.	Near Madison
1942	249.	A Rainy Morning*
	250.	Through the Trees
1943	235.	Spring Morning
	236.	Christmas*
1944	286.	The Edge of Town*
	287.	Cottage in Autumn
1945	190.	Rip Van Winkle Country*
	191.	A Winter Morning
1946	183.	Winter
	184.	Up Greenbrier
1947	198.	Wandering Mule
	199.	A Ray of Sunlight
1948	134.	Morning*
	135.	Houses and Cedars
1949	158.	Farm Near Gentryville
	159.	Smokies
1950	171.	A Rocky Pasture*
	172.	The Appalachian Trail (Great Smokies)
	173.	Young Woman in Black
1951	197.	From My Window, No. 2*
	198.	The Pinnacle, Martin County
1952	225.	Pennsylvania Barn

1953	182.	The First Snow
	183.	The Trail
	184.	Whither

WHEELER, HILAH DRAKE

1926	318.	Living Room Interior
	319.	Childhood
	320.	The Note of Thanks

WHEELER, RONALD

1989	235.	Talking Hands
1990	199.	The Artist

WHEELING, W(illiam) G.

1983	193.	Early Snow
1986	229.	Myopia

WHIPPLE, KEN

1974	156.	Fading Era*
1975	247.	1894 Circus Litho

WHITAKER, CHRIS

1982	206.	41 Bridges to Home

WHITAKER, PETE

1985	160.	Geronimo
1986	230.	Vino
1987	235.	Picnic at the Indian Museum
1989	236.	Spreading Eagle
	237.	Vino

WHITE, ALAN B.

1971	215.	Still Life

WHITE, BARBARA BROOKIE

1970	229.	Alan White
	230.	Alexander
1971	216.	Waiting*
1973	205.	Girl with Flute

WHITE, CRAIG L.

1983	194.	Too Late to Portage

WHITE, ELAINE

1986	231.	Singapore

WHITE, GRACE TYNER

1926	321.	Decorative Panel
	322.	Flower Studies, A & B

WHITE, ISABEL

1962	308.	The Christening
1963	233.	Home
1964	279.	At the Beach
1965	281.	The Old Farm House
1966	157.	Beached
1971	217.	Unusual Situation
1988	225.	St. Mary's River*
1990	200.	Studio "A"

WHITE, MAPHAJEAN
1988	226.	Sunflowers
	227.	Indian Corn
1989	238.	Fruit of the Vine
1990	201.	American Harvest

WHITE, MARGUERITE G.
| 1963 | 234. | After a Storm |

WHITE, MARY JANE
(See Bigler, Mary Jane White)
| 1933 | 231. | Saugatuck Fish Houses |

WHITESEL, MILDRED (A.)
1967	271.	Terrain Study
1970	231.	The Beach
1971	218.	Mirror on the Lake
1977	180.	The Under Branches

WHITLOCK, WALTER
| 1985 | 161. | A Boat Rests |
| 1986 | 233. | East African Cape Buffaloes |

WHITMIRE, LAVON
| 1944 | 288. | Home in Wyoming |

WHITMORE, LENORE (K.)
1962	309.	Last of Summer
1963	235.	This Old Wall
	236.	Sea Mist Collage*
1967	272.	Bathing

WHITTED, BRYANT
1979	168.	Closet Clutter*
	169.	Root Bound
1980	163.	An Early Spring
1981	197.	Nature's Palette
	198.	First Prize Potatoes
1984	212.	Hang It Any Way
1985	162.	Jedi Jeodes and Julips
	163.	Afternoon Shadows
1986	232.	Hang It Any Way No. 2

WHITWORTH, PHYLLIS
1974	157.	Port Clyde
	158.	And the Woods Was Scattered with Gold
1977	181.	A Bit of Autumn's Glory
1984	213.	Autumn's Golden Glow

WICKARD, J(ohn) MURRY
1925	239.	Eleanor in a Costume
	240.	Resting*
	241.	Danseuse
1926	323.	The Parasol
1927	352.	The Dancer
	353.	Campaspe
	354.	Tea in the Studio*
1928	312.	The Chinese Jar
1929	310.	Xmas Eve (Fanny May Candy ad)*
	311.	Marie Antoinette (Fanny May Candy ad)
1930	237.	The Man in the Moon
	238.	The Costume*
1932	250.	Porcelain Cat
1933	232.	Siesta
1934	205.	Polo Player
	206.	Lady in Red*
1936	219.	Yellow Lily
1937	198.	Afternoon Calle
	336.	Peonies
1940	215.	Great-grandmother's Doll

WICKER, JAMES H.
| 1964 | 280. | Chapel |

WICKER, MARY H.
1933	233.	An Old Courtyard
	234.	Italian Fishing Boats, Chioggia
1934	207.	On My Balcony in Corsica
1935	173.	In a Man's Garden (Dahlias)
1936	220.	Peonies

WICKER, PHYLLIS
1977	182.	Dinky Dawn*
	183.	Beyond Words
1979	170.	Amy
	171.	Ruby
1980	164.	Sisters
1981	199.	Sequel*
1982	207.	Her Turn
	208.	Jon
1983	195.	Beau, Brass Rings & Painted Horses
	196.	Portrait of Daniel Greene
1984	214.	Julie

WIEDENHOEFT, JANICE
| 1990 | 202. | October Snow |

WIGGINS, LINDA A. GLASS
| 1987 | 236. | Favorite Teacher |

WIGGS, CATHY E.
| 1965 | 282. | Self-Portrait |

WILCOX, ROBERT ALLEN
1933	235.	Autumn, Duneland
	236.	Miss Mary Mason, Portrait
	237.	May Harvest

WILD, SYLVIA M.
| 1965 | 283. | La Vielle Prient |

WILDER, BETTY DeVERE
1938	213.	Loamland
	214.	Morning in the Berkshires
	326.	Emerald Lake Reflections

WILDER, LOUISE
1927	355.	Dunes
1928	313.	Wild Flowers
1929	312.	Mary
1931	248.	Shadow Patterns

WILDMAN, E. G.
| 1986 | 234. | Enticing |

WILDMAN, MARILYN
1989	239.	Whitebull's Twins
1990	203.	Nancy
	204.	The Sunshine Kids

WILLIAMS, (C.) WARNER
1927	357.	Francis Johnson
	358.	J. K. Lilly III
1928	317.	Leda and the Swan
	318.	Mrs. John E. Moore
	319.	Peggy Goodwin*
1929	314.	Milford Hall Davis
	315.	Dr. Lucius L. Ball
	316.	John and Shirley Williams
1930	239.	Mary Drake Lamberton
	240.	Patsy Jean Redfern
	241.	Portrait Head
1931	250.	Jean
	251.	Carroll Logan Shaffer
	252.	Tranquillity, Marble
	253.	Oliver Ormsby Annan*
1932	252.	Cadel, Painter
	253.	Portrait of Boy
	254.	Lewis Conner Newman*
1933	239.	Javanese Head
	240.	John T. McCutcheon
1934	208.	Japanese Girl
	209.	Mr. and Mrs. Daniel M. Mead
1935	177.	Fish and Waves
	178.	Portrait
1936	223.	Carolyn K.
	224.	George Ade*
	225.	Anticipation
1937	202.	Dignity of Youth
	203.	Barbara Barton
	204.	Dr. Harry E. Mock
1938	216.	Edwin and Marion
	217.	Head Design
	327.	Workman
1939	240.	Anne Ordway
	241.	Henry Monheimer
	242.	Wayman Adams*
1940	217.	Alec Templeton*
	218.	Head Design
	219.	John Smalley
1941	173.	Head Study*
	174.	Head
1942	251.	Dr. Irving S. Cutter
	252.	Head Study
	253.	Portrait Relief
1943	240.	Portrait in Relief
	241.	Head Study*

1946	186.	Felix Borowski
	187.	Bruce Blythe
	188.	Head Study
1947	202.	Head Design*
	203.	Portrait in Relief
1948	139.	Head Study*
	140.	Study
1949	162.	"Choir Girl"
1951	199.	Only the Dreamer Is Awake
	200.	Sally
1953	185.	Brenda
1954	195.	Portrait
	196.	Bas Relief
	197.	Bird Form
1978	161.	Bear
1979	172.	Animal Form
	173.	Transcendental Meditation

WILLIAMS, CHARLES SNEED
1925	242.	Portrait of My Wife
	243.	Cliffs of Cornwall
	244.	Martha Louise Dunbar
1926	324.	George Arliss, Esq. (Invited)
	325.	Portrait in Black
1927	356.	Miss Guthrie*
1928	314.	The Book of Prints
	315.	Mounts Bay, Cornwall
	316.	Devonshire Fisherman
1929	313.	Ned Mortimore
1931	249.	The Bravo
1932	251.	Senor Antoni Sala
1933	238.	Portrait of a Lady
1935	174.	Coast of Devon*
	175.	Head of Young Girl
	176.	Corfe Castle, Dorsetshire
1936	221.	Ludlow Castle, England
	222.	The Late Marquis of Dufferin and Ava
1938	215.	Scottish Piper*
1939	243.	"1860"
	244.	Youth

WILLIAMS, EDWARD K.
1928	320.	In the Snow Country
	321.	Early April
	322.	The Student
1930	242.	Oaks in Winter*
	243.	Landscape
1931	254.	Norway Pines
	255.	The Stone Chimney
1932	255.	A Hoosier Cabin
	256.	Winter in the North
	257.	An Old Fashioned Homestead
1933	241.	The Open Gate
	241.	Peace and Frugality
1934	210.	The Road to Briar Knob
	211.	The Old Settler's Home
	212.	Autumn Tapestry*
1935	179.	The Barnyard
	180.	The Sentinel
	181.	Valley of the Whippoorwill

1936	226.	The Bridge in Winter
	227.	Morning Light
1937	199.	Southern Indiana Highlands
	200.	The End of the Trail*
	201.	The Lowlands
1938	218.	Home of the Red Fox*
	219.	Road to the Village
	328.	Hills in Shadow
1939	245.	The Trapper's Cabin
	246.	Tranquillity
	320.	In the Land of Snow
1940	216.	Spring in Green Valley
	321.	An Old Homestead
1941	170.	Early April
	171.	The Valley Road**
	172.	Zero Weather*
1943	237.	The Snow Blanket
	238.	Joe's Alley
	239.	The Duck Bill
1944	289.	In the Foothills
1945	192.	Winter Solitude*
	193.	Those Were the Days
	194.	Powell's Alley
1946	185.	Organ Mountain
1947	200.	A Visitor
	201.	The Bridge
1948	136.	In Brown County*
	137.	The Critics
	138.	Old Nashville
1949	160.	November, Sear and Gold
	161.	Home from School

WILLIAMS, FLORENCE WHITE

1925	245.	Spring at the Ford
	246.	Still Life
	247.	Sand Cherries

WILLIAMS, FLORIE (Florence)
(See Leviton, Florie)

1985	164.	French Lick Folks
1986	235.	At My Window
	236.	Gitya & Jacob
1988	228.	Tee for Two
	229.	We Spent the Summer Together
1989	240.	Off the Rack
	241.	Be Seated

WILLIAMS, GAAR

1925	248.	Not a Brain Cell Workin'*
	249.	Among the Folks in History
	250.	A Strain on the Family Tie*
1926	326.	Among the Folks in History
	327.	Among the Folks in History
	328.	Among the Folks in History
	329.	Among the Folks in History
	330.	Among the Folks in History
	331.	Among the Folks in History
	332.	Among the Folks in History
	333.	Among the Folks in History

1927	359.	Something Ought to Be Done about This
	360.	Static
	361.	Among the Folks in History
	362.	How to Keep from Growing Old
	363.	Something Ought to Be Done about This
	364.	Static
	365.	Static
	366.	Among the Folks in History
1928	323.	Cartoon*
	324.	Cartoon*
	325.	Cartoon*
	326.	Cartoon*
	327.	Cartoon*
	328.	Cartoon*
	329.	Cartoon*
	330.	Cartoon*
	331.	Cartoon*
1936		(Nos. 1-113 were exhibited in a Gaar Williams Memorial Gallery)
	1-6.	Six Caricatures in a Japanese Print Manner
	7-12.	Six Illustrations Made for Stories in 1921
	13.	Remember?
	14.	"And He's the War Secretary, Too"
	15.	Some Friends of Ours Say Prosperity Is Entering the Home Stretch
	16.	Some Day When You Feel Pretty Important
	17.	Have You Met the Mysterious Stranger?
	18.	Gee, They Can Be Heartless
	19.	All White Again
	20.	German Militarist
	21.	Now Then
	22.	War Axe
	23.	After All
	24.	Not Greatly Excited
	25-37.	Among the Folks in History
	38-44.	Our Secret Ambition
	45-55.	Wotta Life! Wotta Life!
	56-67.	A Strain on the Family Tie
	68-79.	Something Ought to Be Done about This
	80-91.	Static
	92-94.	When Words Fail Yuh
	95.	How To Keep From Growing Old
	96.	How To Keep From Growing Old
	97.	How To Keep From Growing Old
	98.	How To Keep From Growing Old
	99.	How To Keep From Growing Old
	100.	How To Keep From Growing Old
	101.	How To Keep From Growing Old
	102.	Not a Brain Cell Workin'
	103.	Not a Brain Cell Workin'
	104.	The Artist

105. The Old Swimming Hole
106. An Art Puzzle Solved
107. Mort Green and Wife
108. Thanksgiving Day
109. Something for Dad
110. Household Hint
111. Invited Out for Dinner
112. Colored Cartoon
113. Who Remembers When

WILLIAMS, JEAN
1950   174.   Rooster Design

WILLIAMS, PAULINE
1971   219.   Competence

WILLIAMS, ROBERT S.
1982   209.   Rise and Fall

WILLIAMS, WALTER (R.)
1926   334.   Nymph*
        335.   Flora
        336.   Fantast
1927   367.   Infant Bacchus
1928   332.   Eve
        333.   Simonetta
1930   244.   Portrait Relief of John

WILLIAMSON, ARCHIE
1981   200.   Landscape with Arclight*

WILLIAMSON, (L. L.) VON
1988   230.   Alone
1989   243.   Submission to Autumn

WILLIAMSON, LESLIE E.
1987   237.   Autumn Garden Visitors*
1989   242.   Spice Bush and Lilac

WILLIS, WAYNE
1978   162.   Little White Box

WILLS, JAN
1983   197.   Rabbit

WILLS, VINETTA
1969   195.   Waiting
        196.   Auction #3

WILLSON, RALPH E.
1984   215.   The Thinker
1985   165.   Blacksmith & Apprentice*

WILSON, GILBERT (B.)
1929   317.   Understanding II
        318.   Understanding I*
1931   256.   Sketch for Mural
        257.   My Friend, Max Ehrmann
        258.   The Two of Them

1933   243.   Birth Control*
        244.   Analogy
1934   213.   Study

WILSON, GLENN (L.)
1951   201.   The Picnic
1952   226.   The Parade
1955   206.   Western Village

WILSON, JOHN H.
1964   281.   The Circle

WILSON, JUDI
1983   198.   19th Hole
        199.   Patterns of the Past

WILSON, KEVIN J.
1988   231.   Mr. Personality

WILSON, NELSON
1939   247.   Hutchison's Barn
        248.   The Old Buggy Shed
1940   220.   The Old Barn
1941   175.   Old Houses
1942   254.   Old Kentucky Homestead
1943   242.   Backwoods Cabin
        243.   On Road to Stonehead
        244.   Old Ninth and Cherry St.
1944   290.   Phantom Gold
        291.   Road into the Hills
1946   189.   McCormick's Creek in Springtime
        190.   An Enchanted Bower
        191.   Greise Creek
1950   175.   Gone Are the Years
        176.   Meadow Mid-Autumn

WILSON, N(orman) B.
1934   214.   Blue Mood

WILSON, WINIFRED
1941   176.   Cacti in the Dunes

WILSTACH, GEORGE (L.)
1926   337.   Lobos Point
1935   182.   Young Girl
1937   205.   Gloucester Harbor
        206.   Brookside
1938   220.   Drying Sails
1940   221.   Bickford's Float
        222.   Fisherman's Dock
        322.   The Inner Harbor

WIMMER, ETHEL THORNBURG
1936   228.   Reflections

WINANS, FRANCILLE
1981   201.   Landscape with an Oak Tree

WINGERD, LOREEN
1927   368.   The Lady and the Horse
        369.   Fantasy

1928	334.	Mermaid and Fish
1932	258.	Black and White Drawing
1933	245.	Lilies
1934	215.	Dancing Figures

WINKLER, AGNES CLARK

| 1926 | 338. | Pacific Ocean |
| 1927 | 370. | Scene on Lake Superior |

WINN, ALICE COLLINSBOURNE

1926	339.	Gladiolas
1927	371.	Old Tea Pot and Flowers
1928	335.	Flowers
1930	245.	Flower Market, Paris

WINSLOW, EDWARD L.

1935	183.	Street in "Lovetown"
1936	229.	Lick Creek
1939	249.	Shantytown

WINTON, EFFIE DILL

1939	250.	Pier Cove, Michigan
1940	223.	Peonies
1941	177.	The Ambassador Bridge
1944	292.	Peonies No. 1
	293.	Peonies No. 2
1945	195.	Basket of Grapes
1946	192.	Lilacs in Profusion
1950	177.	June Roses
1951	202.	An Interior

WIPPERMAN, ELFRIEDA

| 1945 | 196. | Texas Oranges |

WISE, BEULAH

| 1967 | 273. | The Lagoon |
| 1971 | 220. | Green Water Hole |

WISEMAN, MINNIE

| 1960 | 224. | Friends of the Field |
| 1961 | 276. | June Morning Occurrence |

WISER, GUY BROWN

1927	372.	Portrait of Mrs. W.*
1928	336.	Portrait of an Old Lady
1929	319.	Parade
	320.	One of the Barkers*
1930	246.	The Panther
	247.	Composition
	248.	Faculty Club No. 1*
1931	259.	Faculty Club No. 2
	260.	"1930"
	261.	Dorothy Cassell
1932	259.	Blanket Counter
	260.	Nancy
	261.	Portrait*
1933	246.	Mae
	247.	Mrs. Chandler in Her Grandmother's Dress*
1934	216.	Will Haney*

1935	184.	The Bohemian Vase
	185.	Sachiko
	186.	William Lehman, Jr.
1936	230.	Beverly Glen
	231.	Amalia

WITHERSPOON, NORMA J.

| 1990 | 205. | Roses |

WITMER, M(ary L.) WRIGHT

1936	232.	Fantasy
1937	207.	Visiting Florida
1938	221.	Good Bye
1945	197.	Aspiration*
	198.	Winter in Vermont
1946	193.	Shadow over the Valley
1947	204.	Village View
1949	163.	Enchantment
1951	203.	Grover Square
	204.	Private Property
1952	227.	Vermont Woods
1955	207.	Near Arkville
1957	212.	Peggy's Cove
1958	255.	East Dorset

WITTENBERG, JET

| 1977 | 184. | Straw Flowers |
| | 185. | Indiana Dunes |

WITTICH, WOLFGANG

1943	245.	Tamarack Swamp
1945	199.	Duneland in Fall
1949	164.	The Graveyard in Indiana State Park
1950	178.	Fairy Cave
1953	186.	Hummingbirds

WITTNER, RUTH

| 1946 | 194. | Matillija Poppies |

WOLTER, ADOLPH G.

1942	255.	College Youth
	256.	General Stonewall Jackson
	257.	Prancing Horse
1946	195.	Steel
	196.	Struggle*
	197.	Spiritual Victory
1965	284.	Owl
	285.	De Profundis
1966	158.	Shepherd
1968	236.	Aiming High
1969	197.	Coral Reef
	198.	Perspective
1975	248.	Gazelle
1976	243.	1776
	244.	Violinist
1977	186.	Head Abstract
1978	163.	Union In Space
1979	174.	Man

WOOD, HARRY E.
1947   205.   Dorns Drugs

WOOD, MARJORY FARLEY
1977   187.   Portrait of Andrea*

WOODRUFF, HALE A.
1927   373.   The Red Blouse
        374.   Garden Idyll
        375.   Glorious Autumn

WOODS, HELEN (M.) WOODWARD
(See Woodward, Helen M.)
1952   228.   Little Old Lady*
1953   187.   Still Life Flowers
        188.   White Poinsettias and Fruit*
1954   198.   And Only the Master Shall Praise
                Them
        199.   Millersville
1955   208.   Still Life
1956   221.   Composition, Figure and Fruit
        222.   Portrait, Sara Ann
1957   213.   Chickens for Sale
1958   256.   Portrait
        257.   Provincetown
        258.   Still Life
1959   186.   Bonnie Bruce
        187.   Girl in Striped Blouse
1960   225.   Barns
1961   277.   Vivian
        278.   Glass and Flowers in Sun*
        279.   Sandra Faye and Brenda Kay
1962   310.   My Grandson Michael
        311.   The Teacher
1963   237.   Vera
1964   282.   Michael
        283.   Flowers
1965   286.   Thomas and Geraldine Scott
        287.   Against the Light
        288.   Still Life with Flowers
1966   159.   Study
        160.   Young Girl

WOODWARD, HELEN M.
(See Woods, Helen M. Woodward)
1928   337.   Still Life*
        338.   Still Life
1929   321.   Still Life*
1930   249.   Drawing, Black and White
        250.   Water Color
1932   262.   Bottles
        263.   Gladiolus
1933   248.   My Windows
1936   233.   Gladiolus
1938   329.   The White Barn
1940   224.   Snow in the Village
1941   178.   Acapulco, Mexico
        179.   Snowballs
1942   258.   Landscape, Peaceful Valley
1943   246.   Still Life, Flowers

1944   294.   Spring
        295.   Keeper of the Old Log Jail
1945   200.   Old Man, Portrait
        201.   The Old Town Hall
1947   206.   Indian Summer, Brown County
1968   237.   The Cyclamen
1969   199.   Portrait of Young Lady
        200.   Pink Hat and Flowers
1970   232.   Child Thou Art Like a Flower
1972   133.   And Then It Was Christmas
1973   206.   Portrait, Barbara
1974   159.   Flowers
        160.   Still Life

WOODWORTH, CHARLES H.
1983   200.   Covered Bridge, Bridgeton, Ind.

WOOLDRIDGE, RUTH
1970   233.   Pretty Things
1971   221.   A Road in the Past
1973   207.   Apples
        208.   Tom

WOOLDRIDGE, STEVE E.
1970   234.   Iron Reflection III*

WOOLF, AMELIA
1936   234.   Window View

WOOLSEY, CARL (Edward)
1927   376.   After the Shower
        377.   Gray Evening
        378.   Winter Morning Haze
1928   339.   Cottonwoods, Taos
        340.   Backway, Taos
        341.   Winter in Taos
1929   322.   Taos House-Tops*
        323.   Winter's Approach
        324.   From Arroyo Seco
1930   251.   Winter Landscape
1931   262.   Houses of Earth
        263.   Autumn Leaves
1932   264.   Blossoms
        265.   Winter Moonlight
1934   217.   The Stream
1935   187.   Autumn's Tapestry*
        188.   Toward the Moon
        189.   Late Afternoon
1937   208.   Hills of the Middle West*
1938   222.   Forbidding Range
1939   251.   Winter Wind*
        252.   Road to the Village
        321.   House on the Hill
1940   225.   Winter Morning
1941   180.   Clear and Cold

WOOLSEY, WOOD (W.)
1929   325.   Through the Greasewood
        326.   El Paseo
1930   252.   Bargaining

332

1931	264.	Penitentes
	265.	Romance and Potatoes*
	266.	Old Mexican of Prado
1932	266.	Pueblo Women
	267.	Snow, Taos
	268.	The Wood Vender*
1935	190.	Pueblo Medicine Man
	191.	The Hired Man
1937	209.	Three Men
1938	223.	Fringe of Town
1939	253.	Hard Winter
1941	181.	Lonely Home
	182.	Self Portrait
1942	259.	Morgan County Man

WORMAN, SYLVIA

1981	202.	A Summer Bouquet
	203.	Wildflowers & Weeds
1982	210.	Rose Cascade #2*
	211.	Rose Cascade #1
1983	201.	Bouquet Series #5
1985	166.	Bouquet Series #385*
1986	237.	Seeing Red*
	238.	Floral Series
1987	238.	Pastel Bouquet*
1988	232.	Naska Universe

1989	244.	Tropical V
	245.	Roses
1990	206.	Image I

WOTTON, JUNE MERKEL

| 1949 | 165. | Connersville Canal |

WROBEL, JOSEPH

1945	202.	Portents of Winter
1946	198.	March
1947	207.	January Morning
1948	141.	After the Rain (Indiana Dunes)
1953	189.	Good Friday, No. 2
1956	223.	October
	224.	Old Salty

WUNDERLICH, DIANE UBELHOR

| 1988 | 233. | Marshall Fields |
| | 234. | River Market** |

WYKOFF, LESTER D.

| 1929 | 327. | Bas-Relief Child's Head |
| 1930 | 253. | Sports and Education |

WYNNE, BERNARD

| 1971 | 222. | Over the Hill* |

YATER, GEORGE (David)

1931	267.	Portrait*
	268.	Still Life
1932	269.	Class Study, Provincetown
1936	235.	The Still Life Painter*
	236.	Gray Mood
1940	226.	New River, Fort Lauderdale
1941	183.	Provincetown Rooftops
	184.	Sunday Morning in Florida
1946	199.	Bradford Street in Winter*
	200.	Figurehead House, Provincetown
1947	208.	Spring Bouquet
1954	200.	Oyster Boats at Wellfleet
	201.	Gull and Buoys*
1955	209.	Nubble Light
	210.	Old Schooners at Wiscasset
1956	225.	Sand Flats, Provincetown
	226.	Winter Afternoon, Provincetown*
1957	214.	The Unicorn
	215.	L. N. A. & C. Caboose at Corydon
1958	259.	Wellfleet in Winter
1959	188.	Provincetown Shed Door
	189.	Drying Nets
1960	226.	Fall Bouquet
	227.	Oyster Shack at Wellfleet
1961	280.	Trap Boat and Weir

YAZEL, MIKE

| 1984 | 216. | Looking Through |

YEAGER, CHARLES G.

1933	249.	The Llewellyn Plazzik Place
	250.	Red and White
1934	218.	Seven Apples
1935	192.	Fruit and Shadows
1937	210.	Goose Creek
	211.	Rainy Day*
1939	254.	Summer Landscape
1940	227.	Soloot Valley*
1942	260.	Iceberg Lake
1943	247.	Pear Still Life*
	248.	Blue Lake
1947	209.	Mountain Shack
	210.	Green Peaks
1949	166.	Fall
	167.	Southern Indiana
1953	190.	Southern Indiana*
1955	211.	Gray Skies
1957	216.	Coast
1960	228.	North Country

YEAMANS, DAVID

| 1990 | 207. | Washington Street |

YODER, EVA MAY

1940	228.	Desert Rose
	229.	Sentinel of the Prairie
1941	185.	The Lily
1943	249.	White Magnolias
	250.	White Flowers
	251.	Summer Flowers
1944	296.	Indiana's Windblown Tulip Tree
	297.	Tulip Tree Blossom*
1945	203.	Dogwood
	204.	Madonna Lily
	205.	Begonia*

YOHLER, KAREN

| 1986 | 239. | Elephants |

YORGEN, DORRIE

| 1977 | 188. | Batik I |
| | 189. | Batik II |

YOUNG, JUDITH

1973	209.	Blue Fantasy
1974	161.	Shadows
	162.	Winter Moon
1982	212.	Emergence

YOUNG, NUY

| 1946 | 201. | Girl Pianist |
| | 202. | Ethel |

YOUNG, RUTH M.

| 1984 | 217. | End of the Falls |

YUNG, JANE K.

1928	342.	Spring Flowers
1929	328.	The Jungfrau from Interlaken
1931	269.	Bacchus
1932	270.	Dahlias
	271.	Color
1933	251.	The Edge of Tyrol
1934	219.	Garden Flowers
1936	237.	Grapes
1937	212.	A Cheerful Corner
	337.	Gay Blossoms
1938	224.	A Mexican Garden
1940	230.	Boat Builders
1942	261.	White Roses

Z

ZARING, LOUISE E.
1925 251. Waiting for the Ebb Tide
      252. The Patio
      253. Mussel Rocks*

ZEIGLER, BILL
1969 201. Desert Shrubs
1970 235. Michigan Lake

ZEIHER, MARGARET
1968 238. "Then this big bear came and...."

ZERWEKH, BEATRICE
1973 210. Car 477
1974 163. Circle of Pears

ZIEGLER, JANE
1952 229. Siesta Key Bayou
      230. Hibiscus
1953 191. Queen of the Night
      192. Last Rehearsal of the Four Robins*
1954 202. Bells of Ireland
      203. Driftwood
1955 212. Going on Four
      213. Tapa
      214. Monkey Business
1956 227. Pony Boy's Dream
      228. Cindy
1957 217. Homogenesis
      218. Last Year's Bird Nest*
1958 260. All Day and All Night
      261. Me Do
1959 190. Easter Morning
      191. Los Turistas
      192. Night Life
1960 229. Donna
      230. Fruit Salad
1961 281. Buttons
      282. Party Hair Do

ZIEGLER, MARY ADELE
1932 272. Portrait
      273. Still Life*
1933 252. Althaea Rosea
      253. Miss Gould

ZIELS, VIRGINIA P.
1966 161. Toe Dippers
      162. The Buddy System*
1976 245. Lupine
      246. Yucca

ZIESEMER, GREGORY A.
1981 204. Serenity amidst Desolation
1982 213. Contours I: Flight
1983 202. Torso*

ZIGROSSI, DOROTHY
1986 240. What's In There?
1988 235. The Budding Artist

ZIMMERMAN, BEATRICE HARTIG
1944 298. Wildermere, on St. Joe River
      299. All Is Not Gold
1948 142. Cove Lake, Tenn.
1949 168. Haven on the St. Joe River
1950 179. Cora
      180. Nancy

ZIMMERMAN, HELEN M.
1933 254. Marigolds

ZIMMERMAN, PAUL W.
1944 300. Death Rides a Pale Horse
      301. Sorrels and Sun
      302. Mrs. R. F. Zimmerman
1948 143. The Circle
1950 181. Melon Vendor
      182. Young Dancer
1952 231. Helios
      232. Ghost Writers
1955 215. Eve of Winter*
      216. Golden Still Life
      217. Old Clown

ZIMMERMAN, WILLIAM
1978 164. Arctic Fox and Brant*
1983 203. Wild Turkeys

ZIMPLEMAN, LARRY
1980 165. October

ZOUMIS, ELIAS
1953 193. Egyptian Scenery

ZWARA, JOHN
1937 213. Creek Bottom, Turkey Run State Park
      338. Peonies
1943 252. Fall Flowers
      253. Kentucky Ave. Bridge
1944 303. Chrysanthemums
      304. Lone Tree
      305. White River
1945 206. White River
      207. Mixed Flowers

BIOGRAPHICAL DICTIONARY
How to Read an Entry

(Each entry may contain as many as eleven categories of information that occur in the following sequence:)

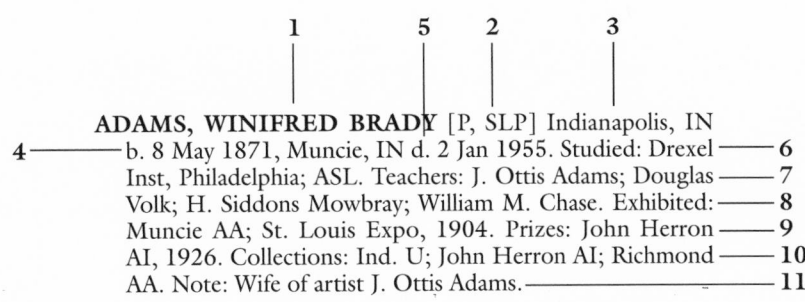

1. **Name:** Last name, first name and middle name or initial are printed in capital, bold-face letters. A married name, brush name or cross reference may appear in parentheses following the proper names. In addition, a nickname or completed initialed name may appear in parentheses. A woman's name may be followed by her husband's if the entry is alphabetized under her married name; for example, BARNES, RENEE (Mrs. J. Wallace).

2. **Professional Classification:** Brackets following the artist's name include his or her professional classification, if known. See following Abbreviations sections.

3. **Last Known Address:** City and state and/or country of artist's last known address are recorded. Sometimes two addresses may be separated by a (/), indicating a summer residence or a second home.

4. **Birth Date/Birth Place:** The artist's date of birth follows the b. and adheres to the form: day, month, year. Months are abbreviated as follows: Jan, Feb, Mar, Apr, May, Jun, Jul, Aug, Sep, Oct, Nov, Dec. The place of birth, if known, follows the date.

5. **Death Date/Death Place:** The death date, when applicable and if known, follows the d. The place of death, if known, follows the death date. If the place of death and the last known address are the same, the information is not repeated.

6. **Studied:** Schools in which the artist studied are listed.

7. **Teachers:** The artist's most significant teachers are listed.

8. **Exhibited:** The artist's most significant exhibitions are listed. If an artist won a prize in an exhibition, the show may be indicated in this section with (Pr) or (Prs) following the exhibition's name. More commonly, prizes may be found in the Prizes category. When (solo) follows an entry, it indicates an artist exhibited alone. Because all artists in *A Grand Tradition* have exhibited in the Hoosier Salon, participation in this particular show is not specified.

9. **Prizes:** The artist's most significant prizes, awards and honors are noted. When a Hoosier Salon (HS) prize is indicated but does not correspond to the Merit Awards and Prizes section, the prize in the biographical entry refers to a purchase prize rather than a merit award.

10. **Collections:** Public institutions, art institutions and corporations that conserve the artist's work are recorded.

11. **Note:** Significant information contributing to the artist's biography was added whenever possible.

Professional Classification Abbreviations

Ab	Abstractionist		HPA	Handmade Paper Artist
Adv. A	Advertising Artist		I	Illustrator
Arch	Architect		JA	Jewelry Artist
Bat	Batik Artist		Ldscp. P	Landscape Painter
C	Craftsperson		Li	Lithographer
Car	Cartoonist		Min	Miniature Artist
Caric	Caricaturist		MM	Multimedia or Mixed Media
Cer	Ceramicist		Mur. P	Mural Painter
Col. A	Collage Artist		P	Painter
Com. A	Commercial Artist		Photo	Photographer
Comp. A	Computer Artist		Por. P	Portrait Painter
Dec	Decorator		Print	Printmaker
Des	Designer		S	Sculptor
Dr	Drawing Specialist		SG	Stained Glass Artist
Edu	Educator		SLP	Still Life Painter
Fiber A	Fiber Artist		SP	Sign Painter
Genre P	Genre Painter		T	Teacher
Glass A	Glass Artist		TA	Textile Artist
Gra. A	Graphic Artist		W	Writer

Association, Museum, Exhibition and School Abbreviations

AAPL	American Artists Professional League		IMA	Indianapolis Museum of Art
ACP or AC Phila.	See Phila. AC		IUPUI	Indiana University-Purdue University at Indianapolis
AFA	American Federation of Arts		JCC	Jewish Community Center
AG	Artists' Guild. Unless preceded by another city name, refers to the Artists' Guild of the Author's League of America in New York City		LOC	Library of Congress
			MMA	Metropolitan Museum of Art
			MOMA	Museum of Modern Art
AGAA	Addison Gallery of American Art		NAC	National Arts Club
AIC	Art Institute of Chicago		NAD	National Academy of Design
Arch. Lg. of Am.	Architectural League of America		NAWA/NAWPS	National Association of Women Artists. Also called National Association (sometimes "Academy") of Women Painters and Sculptors
ASL	Art Students' League. Unless a city name precedes or follows ASL, reference is to the ASL of New York City			
			NEA	National Endowment for the Arts
ASMP	American Society of Miniature Painters		New Haven PCC	New Haven Paint & Clay Club
AV	American Artists for Victory		NGA	National Gallery of Art
AWCS	American Watercolor Society		NYPL	New York Public Library
BAID	Beaux-Arts Institute of Design		PAFA	Pennsylvania Academy of the Fine Arts
Ball State TC	Ball State Teachers College (became Ball State University)		Phila. AC	Art Club of Philadelphia
			PIASch	Pratt Institute Art School
BM	Brooklyn Museum		PMG	Phillips Memorial Gallery
BMFA	Boston Museum of Fine Arts		PMSchIA	Philadelphia Museum School of Industrial Art
Butler Col	Butler College (became Butler University)		P.-P. Expo	Panama-Pacific Exposition, San Francisco, 1915
CAFA	Connecticut Academy of Fine Arts			
CAM	See St. Louis AM		RISD	Rhode Island School of Design (and Museum)
CGA	See Corcoran			
CI	Carnegie Institute		SAE	Society of American Etchers
Cincinnati AM, CM	Cincinnati Art Museum		SAM	Seattle Art Museum
CMA	Cleveland Museum of Art		SC	Salmagundi Club
Corcoran	Corcoran Gallery of Art		Scarab C	Scarab Club
CUASch	Cooper Union Art School		SFMA	San Francisco Museum of Fine Arts
FAP	Federal Art Project		SSAL	Southern States Art League
FMA	Fogg Museum of Art		St. Louis AM	St. Louis Art Museum
GGE	Golden Gate Exposition, San Francisco, 1939		SWA	Society of Western Artists
			TMA	Toledo Museum of Art
Herron AI	John Herron Art Institute, established in 1902 as part of the Indianapolis Art Association (later associated with IUPUI)		USPO	United States Post Office
			VMFA	Virginia Museum of Fine Arts
			WFNY	World's Fair, New York, 1939
Herron AM	Herron Art Museum (eventually encompassed by the IMA)		WMA	Worcester Museum of Art
			WMAA	Whitney Museum of American Art
Herron Sch A	See Herron AI		WPA	Federal Art Project of the Works Progress (later, Projects) Administration
HS	Hoosier Salon			
IHA	Indiana Heritage Arts			

General Abbreviations

A, Ar	Art, Arts, Artist, Artists
AA	Art Association (preceded or followed by a city)
AC	Art Club, Artists' Club (preceded or followed by a city)
A&C	Arts & Crafts
A&CC	Arts & Crafts Club (preceded or followed by a city)
Acad	Academy
Adv	Advertising
AFB	Air Force Base
AG	Artists' Guild (preceded or followed by a city)
A Gal	Art Gallery
AI	Art Institute
AL	Art League
All	Alliance, Allied
Am	American, America
AM	Art Museum (preceded by city or name)
Ann	Annual
App	Applied
Ar, A	Art, Artists
Arch	Architect, Architects, Architectural
Assn	Association
Assoc	Associated
Assocs	Associates
Asst	Assistant
b.	born
Bldg	Building
C, Cl	Club
c., ca.	circa
Cen	Center
Cer	Ceramicist, Ceramic, Ceramics
Ch	Church
Cl, C	Club
Cnty, Co	County
Co	Company, Companies, County
Col	College
Coll	Collection
Com	Commercial
Comp	Competition
Cont	Contemporary
Corp	Corporation

Cr	Craft, Crafts (as part of the organization's name)
d.	died
Dec	Decoration, Decorator
Dept	Department
Des	Design, Designer
Dir	Director
Dr	Drawing
Exh	Exhibition, Exhibited
Expo	Exposition
F & App A	Fine & Applied Art
FA	Fine Arts
Fed	Federation
Fnd, Found	Foundation
Ft	Fort
G	Guild
Gal	Gallery
Hist	History, Historical
HS	Hoosier Salon
H. S.	High School
I, Illus	Illustrator, Illustrators, Illustrated, Illustrations
IA	Institute of Art (preceded or followed by a city)
Inc	Incorporated
Indst	Industrial, Industry
Inst	Institute, Institution
Instr	Instructor
Intl	International
Ldscp. P	Landscape Painter, Landscape Painting
Lg	League
M, Mus	Museum
MA	Museum of Art (preceded or followed by a city or name)
Mem	Memorial, Memorials
MFA	Museum of Fine Arts (preceded or followed by a city)
Mgr	Manager
Min	Miniature, Miniatures
Mod	Modern
Mon	Monument
Mun, Munic	Municipal
Mus, M	Museum
Nat	National
NYC	New York City

P	Painter, Paintings
PCC	Paint & Clay Club (preceded or followed by a city or name)
PM, Pr. M	Printmakers (preceded or followed by a city or name)
Por, Port	Portrait
PPC	Pen & Pencil Club (preceded or followed by a city or name)
Pr	Prize
Pr. M, PM	Printmakers (preceded or followed by a city or name)
Prof	Professional, Professor
Prs	Prizes
PS	Painters and Sculptors (preceded or followed by a city or name)
PS&G	Painters, Sculptors & Gravers
Reg	Regional
S, Soc	Society
SA	Society of Artists (preceded or followed by a city or name)
Sal	Salon
Sc	Science, Sciences, Scientific
Sch	School
SE	Society of Etchers (preceded or followed by a city or name)
SMP	Society of Miniature Painters (preceded or followed by a city or name)
Soc, S	Society
St	Saint
T	Teacher, Teachers
TC	Teacher's College (preceded by city or name)
Tech	Technical
Text	Textile
Twp	Township
U	University
U.S.	United States
WC	Watercolor
WCA	Watercolor Association
WCC	Watercolor Club
WCS	Watercolor Society

State Abbreviations

AL; Ala.	Alabama	IL; Ill.	Illinois	NE; Neb.	Nebraska	SC; S.C.	South Carolina
AK	Alaska	IN; Ind.	Indiana	NV; Nev.	Nevada	SD; S.D.	South Dakota
AZ; Ariz.	Arizona	IA	Iowa	NH; N.H.	New Hampshire	TN; Tenn.	Tennessee
AR; Ark.	Arkansas	KS; Kan.	Kansas	NJ; N.J.	New Jersey	TX	Texas
CA; Calif.	California	KY; Ky.	Kentucky	NM; N.M.	New Mexico	UT	Utah
CO; Colo.	Colorado	LA; La.	Louisiana	NY; N.Y.	New York	VT; Vt.	Vermont
CT; Conn.	Connecticut	ME	Maine	NC; N.C.	North Carolina	VA; Va.	Virginia
DE; Del.	Delaware	MD; Md.	Maryland	ND; N.D.	North Dakota	WA; Wash.	Washington
DC; D.C.	District of Columbia	MA; Mass.	Massachusetts	OH	Ohio	WV; W. Va.	West Virginia
		MI; Mich.	Michigan	OK; Okla.	Oklahoma	WI; Wis.	Wisconsin
FL; Fla.	Florida	MN; Minn.	Minnesota	OR; Ore.	Oregon	WY; Wyo.	Wyoming
GA; Ga.	Georgia	MS; Miss.	Mississippi	PA; Pa.	Pennsylvania		
HI	Hawaii	MO; Mo.	Missouri	PR	Puerto Rico		
ID	Idaho	MT; Mont.	Montana	RI; R.I.	Rhode Island		

A

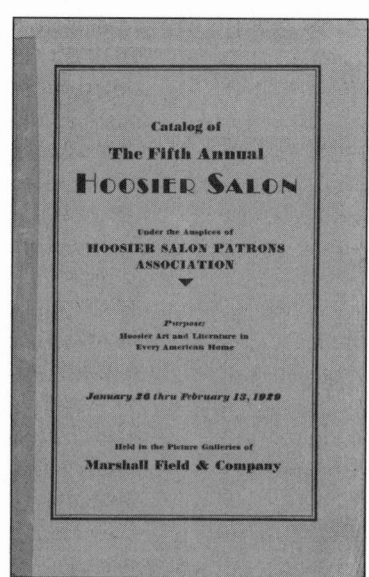

Biographies

ABBETT, BETTY [Ldscp. P, SLP] Morgantown, IN b.19 Nov 1925, Nashville, IN. Studied: East Side A Cen. Teachers: Adelee Wendel; Nanci Scott; Kaye Pool. Exhibited: IHA, 1986-88, 90; Shelby Cnty Circle of A; Greenfield Riley Days, 1987, 88. Prizes: Shelby Cnty Fair, 1974; Riley Days, 1983-86. Collections: Farmers Nat Bank and Merchants Nat Company, Shelbyville, IN.

ABELL, D(aniel) L. Anderson, IN b. 26 Mar 1961, Anderson, IN. Studied: Ball State U. Exhibited: Anderson Area Ann Exh, 1988, 90 (Pr).

ABRAHAM, JAMES R. [Ldscp. P] Indianapolis, IN b. c. 1909. Studied: Cincinnati A Acad; Nat Acad, New York, NY; Herron AI. Teachers: Elmer Taflinger; Leon Kroll. Exhibited: H. Lieber Gal, 1933.

ADAMS, ALISON R. [Dr, S] New Haven, IN b. 30 Apr 1939, Farnham, England. Studied: Ruskin Sch of A, Oxford, England. Exhibited: Jay Cnty A Council (solo), Portland, IN, 1984; Tri Kappa Reg, Ft Wayne, IN, 1983. Prizes: HS, 1984, 88; Ind. A Craftsman Award, NLAPW 5th Annual Show, 1984. Collections: Jay Cnty A Council; West Point Military Acad of the U.S.; Catholic Cemetery of Ft Wayne, IN.

ADAMS, CHARLES B. [P] Lafayette, IN. Studied: Ringling Sch A, Sarasota, FL.

ADAMS, DOROTHY J. [Print, Dr, P] Indianapolis, IN b. NYC. Studied: IUPUI; Ball State U. Teachers: M. Fierke; Jan Tannenbaum. Prizes: Indianapolis AL; HS, 1974, 76. Collections: IMA, rental gal; Evansville M of A&Sc, rental gal. Note: T, Central Elementary Sch, Beech Grove, IN.

ADAMS, J(ohn) OTTIS [Ldscp. P, Por. P, T] Brookville, IN/Leland, MI b. 8 Jul 1851, Amity, Johnson Cnty, IN d. 28 Jan 1927, Indianapolis, IN. Studied: South Kensington A Sch, London; Royal Acad of Munich, Germany. Teachers: John Parker, London; Gyula Benczur, Ludwig von Loefftz, Munich. Exhibited: Five Hoosier Painters, Chicago, IL, 1894; P.-P. Expo, San Francisco, CA, 1915.

Prizes: St Louis Expo, 1904; Soc Western A, Chicago, 1907; Buenos Aires Expo, 1910. Collections: Richmond (Ind.) AA; Herron AI, Indianapolis; AA, Muncie; Indianapolis Athletic Cl; Ind. State M. Note: Joined with several members of the Hoosier Group to teach at the John Herron AI; T, John Herron AI, 1902-06. Husband of artist Winifred Brady Adams.

ADAMS, JOY HARBOURT (*See Harbourt, Joy Adams*) [Por. P] b. England.

ADAMS, JUANITA R. [P] Lebanon, IN.

ADAMS, MARGARET (Boroughs) b. Austin, TX d. c. 1965. Studied: U of Texas; Newcomb College; Tulane U; Columbia U; NY Sch FA&App A. Exhibited: PAFA, 1945; U of Texas, 1930; Texas FA Assn; Dallas Woman's Cl, 1950. Note: Wife of artist Wayman Adams.

ADAMS, MARTHA

ADAMS, SONDRA [P] Greenfield, IN.

ADAMS, VIN Indianapolis, IN.

ADAMS, WAYMAN [Por. P, T] Austin, TX/NYC/Elizabethtown, NY b. 23 Sep 1883, Delaware Cnty, 6 miles from Muncie, IN d. 7 Apr 1959, Austin, TX. Studied: John Herron AI. Teachers: William Forsyth; William M. Chase; Robert Henri. Exhibited: NAD, 1932; Newport (R.I.) AA, 1918; Ind. A Exh, 1916. Prizes: HS, 1925, 26, 29, 35, 48, 50-53, 55-58; Newport (R.I.) AA, 1925; AIC, 1918; Richmond AA, 1915; Muncie AA, 1910; NAD, 1914, 26. Collections: Ind. State Library; Ind. State M; Herron AI; AIC; Ind. U; Lafayette AA; Harvard U; Johns Hopkins U; U of Pa. Note: Painted portraits of Booth Tarkington, James Whitcomb Riley, Sergei Rachmaninoff, Otis Skinner, Alice Roosevelt Longworth, Calvin Coolidge and Warren G. Harding. Husband of artist Margaret Adams.

ADAMS, WINIFRED BRADY [P, SLP] Indianapolis, IN b. 8 May 1871, Muncie, IN d. 2 Jan 1955. Studied: Drexel Inst, Philadelphia; ASL. Teachers: J. Ottis Adams; Douglas

Volk; H. Siddons Mowbray; William Merritt Chase. Exhibited: Muncie AA; St Louis Expo, 1904. Prizes: John Herron AI, 1926. Collections: Ind. U; John Herron AI; Richmond AA. Note: Wife of artist J. Ottis Adams.

ADNEY, CAROL Indianapolis, IN b. 1949, Indianapolis. Studied: DePauw U; Claremont Graduate Sch, Claremont, CA. Exhibited: Art 500, Indianapolis, 1976; S Performance, Columbus, IN, 1974; Post Card Show, Cambridge, MA, 1973; Indianapolis AL, 1978. Prizes: 10th Ann S. Calif Exh; Long Beach MA, 1972; HS, 1978. Note: Curator Herron Sch A, 1978; Asst Curator Educational Programs, IMA, 1974-77.

AGAR, EDNA Valparaiso, IN.

AGNEW, LOUISE FULTS (See Fults, Louise Christin) [P, T, W] Chicago, IL b. Huntington, IN d. Chicago, IL. Studied: Nat U, Mexico; U of Wis.; PAFA; AIC. Exhibited: Okla. A Cen, 1943; Herron AI, 1935-39; PAFA, 1944-46; Erie Theatre (solo), Ft Wayne, IN. Prizes: Midland Acad, South Bend, IN. Note: T, Huntington Col.

AGUET, HENRY A. [T] Indianapolis, IN. Note: T, Visual Communication, Herron Sch A.

AILES, CURTIS [Ldscp. P, SLP] Connorsville, IN b. 11 Jul 1920, Brookville, IN. Studied: Famous A School, Westport, CT; Austria, 1944-45, POW camp. Teachers: Louise Rauch, Hamilton, OH; Mr. Sooy, CA. Exhibited: Evansville MA; Sheldon Swope A Gal, 1973. Prizes: Brown County A Gal. Collections: Everton Elementary Sch; Fayette Memorial Hospital; Stants MFG Co, Connorsville, IN. Note: Developed his artistic skills in an Austrian prisoner-of-war camp during World War II. His plane was shot down over East Germany, 11 Apr 1944.

AKER, REBECCA [Dr, P] Indianapolis, IN b. 22 Nov 1953, Greencastle, IN. Studied: Herron Sch A; Indianapolis AL. Teachers: Robert Berkshire; Holly Sears. Exhibited: Anderson Winter Show, 1984; Ball State Dr&Small S Show; Ind. AC. Prizes: Indianapolis AL Reg, 1983; Whitewater Valley Exh, 1983.

ALATZA, GEORGE E.

ALDRICH, G(eorge) AMES [P, Ldscp. P, Print] Chicago, IL b. 3 Jun 1872, Worcester, MA d. 7 Mar 1941. Studied: ASL; MIT; Académie Julian, Paris; Académie Colarossi, Paris. Teachers: John H. Twachtman; Aman-Jean; James McNeill Whistler; Collin; Thaulow. Exhibited: AIC; Chicago Gal Assn (solo), 1927. Prizes: AIC, 1926; HS, 1926, 32, 36; Ind. U Alumni Pr. Collections: Sioux City A Soc; Purdue U; U of Ill.; Houston MFA; Musée de Rouen, France. Note: I, *Punch* and *London Times*, 1890s.

ALEXANDER, MARTHANN Muncie, IN.

ALIG, MARY JEAN [Ab, Dr, Ldscp. P, Print, I, Por. P] Indianapolis, IN b. 9 Jun 1929, Indianapolis, IN. Studied: Wellesley Col; Indianapolis AL. Teachers: Jeanne Wasson; Tom Mauck; Maxine Masterfield; Roger Frey; Val Thelin. Exhibited: Ind. WCS. Prizes: Indianapolis AL.

ALLEN, BETTE SIMONSON

ALLEN, BLANCHE I. [P] Indianapolis, IN b. 3 Dec 1903, Springfield, OH. Self-taught. Exhibited: Ind. State Fair.

ALLEN, JANET STEWART [P] South Bend, IN. Note: Member, Gary Altrusa Cl.

ALLEN, MARIAN [P] Logansport, IN b. c. 1908, Logansport. Studied: Herron Sch A, 1927; John Pike WC Sch,

Woodstock, NY, 1967. Teachers: Paul Sweany; Robert Weaver. Exhibited: Ind. AC; Ft Wayne Ann; Logansport AA. Collections: Logansport H.S.; Tri State Mental Health Hospital; Winimac Public Library.

ALLMAN, NORMAN

ALMQUIST, H. R. [P, I, T] Nashville, IN b. 8 Feb 1919, Chicago, IL d. 4 Jun 1993, Denver, CO. Studied: Am Acad of A; AIC. Teachers: Rudolph Penn; Hilda Rubins. Exhibited: Oakbrook A Fair, 1975-80; Executive House (solo), Chicago, IL, 1974. Prizes: HS, 1986; Brown Cnty AG, 1989; Brown Cnty A Gal, 1983.

ALT, LILLIAN [P] Chicago, IL b. Kokomo, IN d. ca. 1955. Studied: AIC. Teachers: George Oberteuffer; F. DeForest Schook; Louis Ritman; Frederick Victor Poole.

ALTEKRUSE, MAX [Dr, Ldscp. P, I, Por. P, Print, T] Franklin, MI b. 16 Aug 1920, Ft Wayne, IN. Studied: PAFA; ASL; Ft Wayne A Sch. Teachers: Francis Speight; Frank Reilly. Exhibited: Ind. AA, 1950s; Ann Scarab Cl WC Show, 1961; Soc I, NY, 1979. Prizes: Ann Scarab Cl WC Show, 1962. Collections: Ford Motor Co. Publications, *Ford Times*, Excello Corp; Chrysler Corp.

ALTER, MELANIE Prizes: HS, 1970.

ALTGELT, ELINOR [P] South Bend, IN.

AMIES, PATRICIA [P] Terre Haute, IN.

AMMERMAN, JOHN M. [Ldscp. P, P] Teachers: Paul Sweany; Ruth Anderson; Marie Thompson. Exhibited: Thomas Bldg Gal, 1972; Hilton Hotel, 1972; Wendel Sch A, 1972.

ANDERSON, ALLAN ARTHUR [P] Indianapolis, IN/Taos, NM. Exhibited: Herron MA, 1927.

ANDERSON, CHARLES O. [P] Valparaiso, IN.

ANDERSON, GARNETHA Note: Member, Brown Cnty A Gal.

ANDERSON, GART [Enamel A] Bloomington, IN.

ANDERSON, IDA P. [P] Calumet City, IL b. OH. Teachers: Edgar Forkner; Esterbrook; E. Frederick.

ANDERSON, MARY [P] Jeffersonville, IN. Prizes: HS, 1928.

ANDERSON, RUTH BERNICE [Ldscp. P, T] Indianapolis, IN b. 7 Jul 1914, Indianapolis, IN. Studied: John Herron A Sch. Teachers: Clifton Wheeler; Gerry Pierce. Exhibited: Tucson FA Assn; Washington D.C., 1983. Prizes: HS, 1960, 61, 69, 73, 76; Ind. AC, 1974; All-State Exh, Tucson, 1937; Collections: Brown Cnty A Gal Assn; Kokomo Public Library; Ind. U; Ind. Bell Telephone; Public Service, Plainfield, IN; Ind. State U; DePauw U; Tri Kappa; Ind. Nat Bank; Orchard Sch. Note: T, Indianapolis AL; T, Shortridge High School, Indianapolis.

ANDERT-BASHOVER, PAULA [P, T] Brownsburg, IN b. 29 Sep 1953, South Bend, IN. Studied: Ind. U, South Bend; Northern Ill. U, DeKalb, IL. Exhibited: Jewish Community Center (solo), 1979; Ind. Nat Bank (solo), Indianapolis, 1978; Northern Ill. U (solo), 1977. Prizes: Americana A, Nat A Comp, 1978. Note: T, College Ave Elementary Sch, Brownsbury, IN.

ANDIS, HELEN [P] Evansville, IN b. c. 1914 d. 8 Nov 1985. Studied: Nat Sch FA, Washington, D.C.; Ind. U. Note: Co-founder, A Fair in Garvin Park and A Gal in old courthouse.

ANDREWS, CLAUDE Y. [P] Peru, IN b. 12 Oct 1873, Vermillion Cnty, IN. Studied: Franklin College; U of Mich.

ANDREWS, FLAVIA K. [P] Winnetka, IL.

ANTREASIAN, GARO ZAREH [P, I, Li] Albuquerque, NM b. 16 Feb 1922, Indianapolis, IN. Studied: John Herron AI. Teachers: Stanley William Hayter; Will Barnett. Exhibited: Colog Lithography Biennial, Cincinnati AM; Va. Biennial; Am Prints Today, traveling exh; MMA, NY, 1969; Martha Jackson Gal (solo), NY, 1969; Park Ave Gal (solo), Indianapolis, 1969; Marjorie Kauffman Graphics (solo), Houston, 1972; Malvina Miller Gal (solo), San Francisco, 1971; Editions Ltd Gal (solo), Indianapolis, 1971; IMA, 1974; Lyman-Snodgrass Gal, Indianapolis, 1982. Prizes: Milliken Traveling Fellowship, 1948-49; HS, 1944, 49; Ind. AC, 1953; Ind. State Fair, 1955. Collections: AIC; Boston MFA; Brooklyn M; Cincinnati MA; Cleveland MA; Ind. U; Smithsonian Inst; Guggenheim M; MMA; Notre Dame U. Note: T, Herron Sch A, 1948-64; T, U of N.M., 1964-87. Technical Dir, Tamarind Inst, U of N.M., 1970-72. Co-author, *The Tamarind Book of Lithography*. Antreasian was a pioneer of the lithographic revival that began in the U.S. in early 1960s.

APPLEGATE, R(alph) C. [P, Mural P] Chicago, IL b. 10 Apr 1904, Carmel, IN. Studied: Herron Sch A. Teachers: William Forsyth. Collections: Northwestern U (stained glass windows.) Note: Member art staff, *Chicago Tribune*, 1929.

APPLETON, JACK [P] South Bend, IN b. 27 Dec 1932, Chicago, IL. Studied: Am Acad A, Chicago; Famous A Course, Westport, CT; Southport A Center; Ind. U. Exhibited: Ind. State M; Marshall Field Picture Gal, Americana A of the Year, 1975, Chicago. Prizes: Michiana Biennial; Union AL, Chicago. Collections: South Bend Chamber of Commerce; Beiger Heritage Corp; Nat Bank of South Bend; St Joseph Hospital.

ARBOGAST, VAN DARRELL [Dr, Ldscp. P, I, Por. P] Indianapolis, IN b. 13 Dec 1920, Indianapolis. Self-taught. Exhibited: L. S. Ayres 75th Anniversary A Exh; Ind. A Exh, 1950. Collections: Red Feathers Services FA Catalogue.

ARCHER, JOSEPH [Ldscp. P] Falmouth, IN b. Booneville, MS. Teachers: James E. McBurney.

ARD, CAROLYN [Col. A, P, Installation A, T] Indianapolis, IN b. East Chicago, IN. Studied: Ind. U, Bloomington; Indianapolis AL. Exhibited: 431 Gal, 1991; Art 500; Ind. State Fair. Prizes: Channel 20; Indianapolis AL Student Show. Collections: CCA Gal, Indianapolis; IMA, rental gal.

ARDELEAN, CHRISTINE [Ldscp. P, Genre P] Coatesville, IN b. 10 Sep 1926, Chicago, IL. Studied: AIC. Teachers: Rosemary Lawton Thomas; Joan Cardwell; Clayson Baker. Exhibited: Ind. State Fair, 1987, 89; IHA, 1987, 90. Prizes: Central Ind. A, 1989, 90.

ARMSTRONG, CATHARINE B. [P] Indianapolis, IN/Staunton, VA b. Anaconda, MT. Studied: Lewiston Normal, Lewiston, ID; U of Chicago. Teachers: Avard Fairbanks; George Brandt; Walter Sargent. Exhibited: Ind. A Ann; Herron AM; Ind. AC.

ARNOLD, ANN M. [Ab, Por. P] Cincinnati, OH b. 24 Aug 1926. Teachers: Daniel Green; Fred Eilers; Carol Barnes. Exhibited: Ky. Aqueous '87; Ohio WCS, 1981-89; Middletown A Gal, 1983. Prizes: Strathmore Award, 1986; Outstanding WC Award, 1983. Collections: Zanesville A Gal.

ARNOLD, CAROL [P] Anderson, IN.

ARRICK, THERESSA

ARTHUR, JUDITH E. [Ldscp. P, Por. P, T] Kokomo, IN b. 23 Apr 1933, Kokomo, IN. Studied: Indianapolis AL. Teachers: June Boone; Jerry Smith. Exhibited: Ind. State Fair, 1988, 89. Prizes: HS, 1986; George Yeagy A Show, 1986; Howard Cnty Circuit Court, 1988. Collections: Ball Corp.

ASHBROOK, CAROLYN S. [P, Print, T] Indianapolis, IN b. Paris, KY. Studied: Pratt Inst; Columbia U; Harvard Summer Sch; U of Calif; AIC; Intl Sch A. Teachers: Ralph H. Johonnet; William Forsyth; Marya Werten. Exhibited: Herron AI, 1928. Note: T, Shortridge H.S., Indianapolis; T, Pratt Inst, Brooklyn, NY.

ASHBY, PATRICIA E. Zionsville, IN.

ASHBY, PAUL W(arren) [Print, P, C, T] Kendallville, IN b. 9 Sep 1893, Gunnison, CO. Studied: DePauw U; Ind. U; Evansville Col; Herron A Sch. Teachers: William Forsyth; Otto Stark; Clifton Wheeler; Harold H. Brown. Exhibited: Ind. AC, 1938; LOC, 1943; IMA; Ind. State U (solo); DePauw U (solo); Ball State U (solo). Prizes: HS, 1945, 47, 57; Ind. AC, 1939; Northern Ind. AA; Ind. State Fair. Collections: IMA; Evansville U; DePauw U; Ind. State U; Taylor U. Note: An avid photographer and published writer.

ASHBY, WILLIAM G. [Ldscp. P, Por. P, T] Brownsburg, IN b. 10 Feb 1916. Studied: Herron AI. Teachers: Donald M. Mattison; Henrik M. Mayer; Lucy Taggart. Exhibited: Ind. A Exh, 1988; Ind. State Fair, 1981. Prizes: HS, 1966-69, 80, 83, 86, 87, 89. Collections: Ind. U, Bloomington; Ind. U Medical Sch, Indianapolis; Purdue U, West Lafayette, IN. Note: Retired photographer. T, Indianapolis and Southside ALs.

ASHDOWN, ENID Downers Grove, IL.

ASHTON, ELIZABETH DOUGHERTY *(See Dougherty, Elizabeth H.)* Prizes: HS, 1950.

AULL, DIXIE [Col. A, P, JA, TA] Indianapolis, IN b. 17 Sep 1945. Studied: Indianapolis AL; Arrowmont Sch of A&Cr, U of Tenn. Teachers: Marilyn Price; Edwin Kalker. Exhibited: Evansville MA, 1979; Wabash Valley Exh, 1980. Prizes: Wabash Valley Exh, 1980; Ind. State Fair, 1978, 79.

AUSTIN, DON [P] Anderson, IN b. Anderson. Studied: Ind. U. Teachers: Frederick Rigley; Floyd Hopper. Exhibited: Ind. State Fair; Whitewater Valley; Anderson A Cen.

AUSTIN, RUTH

AYRES, LESLIE F. [Arch, Dr] Indianapolis, IN b. c. 1907 d. Sep 1952. Studied: Princeton, 1926-27. Exhibited: Herron MA; Lyman's Gal, Indianapolis, 1946. Prizes: Ind. State Fair. Note: Designed Garrick Theatre, Chicago, Ill., Hawthorne Room, Indianapolis, Ind. and several buildings on Ind. U medical campus.

B

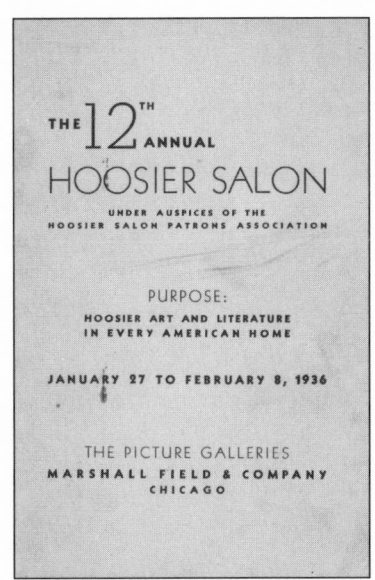

BABCOCK, PATRICIA

BABCOCK, R(ichard) FAYERWEATHER [Des, I, W, P, T] Evanston, IL b. 4 Jun 1887, Denmark, IA d. 23 Feb 1954. Studied: AIC; Herron AI; Weinhold and Eisengraber Sch Painting, Munich; Stätische Gewerbe Schule, Munich. Exhibited: AIC (solo). Collections: Leglar Public Library, mural, Chicago; Evanston Public Schs, Chicago. Note: I, natural history subjects, *Encyclopaedia Britannica*. T, AIC and CAFA.

BABER, LANCE [T] Indianapolis, IN. Prizes: HS, 1970. Note: T, Herron Sch A.

BACHMAN, WILLIAM J. [P] Hammond, IN b. 1914, Hammond. Exhibited: Lake Cnty P&S Lg, 1936-40; Northern Ind. A Salon, 1942-53. Note: Principal architect with William J. Bachman&Partners, Hammond.

BACON, ELIZABETH (Beth) DRIGGS [P, I] Indianapolis, IN b. Indianapolis, IN d. 15 Mar 1928. Studied: AIC; ASL. Teachers: Vanderpoel, AIC; John Johansen; Martha Baker; Frederick Richardson; Charles Freer. Prizes: DePauw U Alumni Assn, 1926; HS, 1926. Note: Staff, John Herron AI. One of the founders of Orchard Country Day Sch, Indianapolis, IN.

BADGER, LENORE WEYBURN [P] Kokomo, IN b. Chicago, IL. Studied: Chicago Acad FA; River Forest AL; Oak Park AL. Teachers: Wellington J. Reynolds; Wayman Adams.

BAHLS, RUTH [P] Lafayette, IN b. 23 Mar 1901, Lafayette. Studied: Purdue U; John Herron AI; Broadmoor A Acad, Colorado Springs. Teachers: William Forsyth; Clifton Wheeler; Charles Hawthorne; Boardman Robinson. Exhibited: Indianapolis A Exh; Herron AM.

BAIDINGER, ROBERT

BAILEY, ELISABETH Logansport, IN.

BAILEY, KATHERINE [Dr, T] New Castle, IN b. 8 Dec 1960, Union City, IN. Studied: Herron A Sch. Teachers: Mildred Whitsel. Prizes: Randolph Cnty A Show, 1986-88.

BAILEY, LORENE [Ldscp. P, Genre P] Muncie, IN b. 7 Feb 1937, Sand Gap, KY. Studied: Kachina Sch A; North Light Sch A, Cincinnati, OH. Teachers: Earlene Ford, Phoenix, AZ; Mark Reed; Barbara Rauf; Mary Farrell, Cincinnati, OH. Exhibited: Ind. State Fair, 1988. Prizes: Ind. State Fair, 1988.

BAILEY, LOUISE G. [Por. P, Ldscp. P] Greenwood, IN. b. Anderson, IN. Studied: Eastside A Cen. Teachers: William Ashby. Exhibited: Greenfield Bank; Riley Days. Prizes: Indianapolis 500 Show.

BAIN, J. HUSTON [P] Indianapolis, IN b. 1928, Akron, OH. Studied: Applied A Acad, Akron, OH. Exhibited: Ind. A, L. S. Ayres, 1972; Ind. State Fair, 1971-73; 500 A Exh, 1973; Tippecanoe Reg Exh, 1973; Wabash Valley Exh; Swope Gal, Terre Haute, 1973. Prizes: HS, 1973, 75, 78.

BAIR, DOROTHY H. [Ab, Ldscp. P, T] Bloomington, IN b. 26 Sep 1925, Lincoln, NE. Studied: U of Neb.; U of Colo. Teachers: Dwight Kirsh, Neb. Prizes: Swope Gal, Wabash Valley Exh, 1986; Ind. WCS, 1985; IHA, 1980. Collections: Ind. U, Bloomington and Gary; Monroe Cnty Bank, Bloomington; Merchants National Bank, Terre Haute.

BAKER, CLAUDIA GRIFFIN [P, Por. P, T] Sheridan, IN b. 16 Sep 1897, Hamilton Cnty, IN d. Mar 1964, Port Arthur, TX. Studied: Herron Sch A. Teachers: Ruth Anderson. Exhibited: Swope Gal, Terre Haute, IN; Hamilton Cnty AA, IN; Plaza de Tubac Gal (solo), AZ; AA of Port Arthur (solo), TX. Note: Known for her illustrated lectures in Ind., Ky., Ariz. and Texas. Painted the Indians of the Southwest.

BAKER, CLAYSON [Ldscp. P, Por. P, T] Indianapolis/Nashville, IN b. 15 Mar 1909, Hillisburg, IN d. 27 Jan 1975. Studied: Indianapolis AL. Teachers: George Jo Mess; Simon Baus. Exhibited: H. Lieber Co (solo), Indianapolis, IN; K. W. Danner A Store; Brown Cnty A Gal; L. S. Ayres&Co Anniversary Exh, 1947. Collections: Danville Christian Church; St Luke Presbyterian Church, Southport, IN. Note: T, East Side A Cen, Indianapolis. Member, Brown Cnty A Gal; Ind. AC.

BAKER, GEORGE H(erbert). [Ldscp. P] Centerville, IN b. 14 Feb 1878, Muncie, IN d. 11 Nov 1943. Studied: Cincinnati AA; Boothbay, Maine A Sch. Teachers: J. E. Bundy. Prizes: Richmond AA, 1913, 15, 30; Muncie,

1910; Ind. State Fair, 1930. Collections: Earlham Col; Miami U; Richmond AA.

BAKER, GLORIA [Genre P] Evansville, IN b. 26 Jun 1943, Petersburg, IN. Teachers: Christopher Schenk; Jeanne Dorie; Miles Batt; Morris Shubin. Exhibited: Evansville MA&Sc, 1986; U of Evansville, 1985; Old Nat Bank, 1981. Prizes: Evansville AG, 1988; Aqueous Nat Exh, 1981. Collections: Bristol-Myers Squibb; Daughters of Charity; United Bank of Louisville.

BAKER, HELEN SEYMOUR (See Baker, Seymour and Seymour, Helen) [P] Whiteplains, NY b. 1 Apr 1900, LaPorte, IN. Teachers: George Elmer Browne; Robert Henri; Sigurd Skou.

BAKER, JINNIE HAMEL [P, T] Anderson, IN b. Portland, ME. Studied: Jackson Col for Women; Indianapolis AL. Teachers: Carl Schmalz; Floyd Hopper; Rob O'Dell; Jean Vietor. Exhibited: A Encounter, FL, 1983-87 (Pr), 89, 90; Fla. WCS, 1984 (Pr); Fla. A Group, 1988; Ind. WCS, 1983, 84, 87, 88. Collections: Merchants Nat Bank; Anderson Banking Company; Banc Fla.; Quail Creek Country Cl.

BAKER, JUDITH ANN ARMSTRONG [SLP] Indianapolis, IN. Prizes: HS, 1971.

BAKER, RUTH A. [Ldscp. P, Por. P, T] Ft Wayne, IN b. 9 May 1927. Studied: Ft Wayne AI. Teachers: Daniel Greene; Barbara Nechis; Peggy Brown. Exhibited: Ventures in Creativity, 1977-88; Wasserberg M, Van Wert, 1980-84. Prizes: HS, 1980, 82, 84. Collections: Ft Wayne AM; Kokomo Public Library; Professional Federal Credit Union.

BAKER, SEYMOUR (See Baker, Helen Seymour and Seymour, Helen)

BAKKEN, JOSEPHINE [MM, P]

BALDWIN, JOSEPH N. Greenfield, IN.

BALES, GEORGE C.

BALKIN, MAXIM Indianapolis, IN.

BALL, WALTER N. [P, Dr, T] DeKalb, IL. Studied: Baker U; Wichita State U; Ohio State U. Exhibited: NOHO Gal, NYC, 1987; Gal X, State and Madison, Rockford, IL, 1987; 29th N.D. Print&Dr Ann, N.D. MA, Grand Forks, ND, 1986; 46th Ann Exh Cont Am P, Soc of the Four A, Palm Beach, FL, 1984. Prizes: 7th Ann Baer A Comp, Beverly A Cen, Chicago, IL, 1983; 30th Ann Mid-States A Exh, Evansville M, Evansville, IN, 1977.

BALLARD, HORTON [Ldscp. P] Exhibited: Herron Sch A; Ft Wayne MA; Friends Fellowship Community Church (solo), Richmond, IN. Note: Former Marion (Ind.) artist.

BALOGH, BEATA M. [Bat] Trafalgar, IN.

BANNING, DOROTHY [P] Modoc, IN b. c. 1926. Studied: Ind. U East, Richmond; Centerville H.S. Exhibited: Whitewater Valley Exh, Ind. U East; Richmond AA. Prizes: Hagerstown A Exh; Richmond AA, 1983. Note: From Centerville, IN.

BANNON, VIOLET F. [P] Indianapolis, IN b. Milwaukee, WI. Studied: Indianapolis AL. Prizes: HS, 1964.

BANTA, DAVID A. [Adv. A] Indianapolis, IN b. 10 May 1937. Studied: John Herron Sch of A. Teachers: Robert Weaver; Harry Davis; David Rubens. Collections: U.S. Navy Permanent Coll.

BARD, SARA FORESMAN [P, T] Indianapolis, IN b. Slippery Rock, PA. Studied: Grand Central Sch A; AIC. Teachers: Henry B. Snell; George Pearse Ennis; Sigourd Skou. Exhibited: Herron AM (two-person), 1946; NAWA, 1931. Prizes: HS, 1929, 31, 34, 36, 40; Baltimore WCC, 1928; N.Y. WCC, 1928, 29; NAWA, 1934. Note: Instructor, FA, Arsenal Tech H.S., Indianapolis.

BARKER, E. A. [S] Westfield, IN.

BARLOW, IRENE (See Sipe, Irene Barlow)

BARNES, CHARLES E. Nashville, IN/Indianapolis, IN b. 1915, Chicago, IL. Studied: Miami U, Oxford, OH; Ind. U, Bloomington; John Herron A Sch; Santa Monica Sch Des; Sch Modern Photography, NYC. Teachers: Eliot O'Hara; Edgar Whitney; Max Kahn; Frances Chapin. Prizes: Ind. A Ann, Herron AM, 1940. Collections: Yale U, New Haven, CT; Ind. Medical Assn. Note: FA Instructor, Park School for Boys, Indianapolis.

BARNES, RENEE (Mrs. J. Wallace) [Por. P, Ldscp. P, SLP] Indianapolis, IN b. 5 Sep 1886, Grand Rapids, MI d. 28 Dec 1940. Studied: John Herron AI. Teachers: William Forsyth; Randolph Coats; Will Vawter. Exhibited: Ind. AC, Herron, 1927; Pettis Gal (solo), 1928; Lyman's Gal (solo), 1928.

BARNES, ROY [S, P] Collections: Mural, Randolf Cnty Courthouse.

BARNHART, KATHERINE MONGER [P, Por. P, Dr] Elkhart, IN b. 20 Feb 1902, Elkhart. Studied: Elkhart H.S. Teachers: Eva Cole. Exhibited: Northern Ind. A Show; Southern Shores Ann A Show. Prizes: Southern Shores Ann A Show, 1964. Note: One of the founders of Elkhart AL.

BARNSTONE, HELLE (Phaedra) TZALOPOULOU [P] Bloomington, IN b. Istanbul, Turkey of Greek parents. Studied: Wellesley Col; U of London; London Sch A&C; École de Louvre; Yale U; Ind. U. Exhibited: Wesleyan U A Gal (solo), 1960; Lynn Kottler Gal, Group Show, NY, 1958; Unicorn Gal (solo), Bloomington, 1972. Prizes: Columbus (Ind.) A Fair, 1973. Collections: Fog Hollow A Cen, VT; Common Place, Columbus, IN; IMA, 1971. Note: I, *Greek Lyric Poetry, Solitudes* by Gongora; I, *The Real Tin Flower, The Stupid Children* by Anamaria Matute.

BARR, CARROLL BAILEY [Print] West Lafayette, IN. Exhibited: All-Wis. Salon; AIC; Corcoran Gal, Washington, D.C. Prizes: GLMA, 1950. Note: Former resident of New Castle, IN. Moved to Miss. where her husband taught at the state university.

BARR, PAUL E. [Edu, Ldscp. P] Grand Forks, ND b. 25 Nov 1892, Tipton Cnty, IN d. 1953. Studied: AIC; U of Chicago; Ind. U; Sorbonne; U of Paris; U of N.D. Teachers: Roda E. Selleck; Albert Krehbiel; Robert E. Burke; G. C. Henshaw; Walter Sargent. Exhibited: IBM Corp, 1940; Rockefeller Center, 1936-38. Prizes: N.D. A Exh, 1940. Collections: Tipton Public Library; Mural, U of N.D.; Municipal University, Wichita, KS. Note: Co-author, *Creative Lettering* and *Art in Dakota*. Head A Dept, U of N.D., Grand Forks.

BARR, THELMA ADAMS Indianapolis, IN. Note: Member of the Ind. chapter of the Nat Soc of A&Letters.

BARRICKMAN, WILNA BEAVER [P] Detroit, MI b. 27 Jun 1896, Orange, Rush Cnty, IN. Studied: Detroit A Acad; Messinger A Sch; Summer Sch P, Saugatuck, MI.

Teachers: Carlos Lopez; Leon Makielski; William Greason. Exhibited: Metropolitan AA, Detroit, 1944; 40th Ann Ind. A Exh, 1947. Prizes: Mich. A Show, 1945, 46; HS, 1947; Palette&Brush AC Show; Detroit Scarab Cl, 1947.

BARTILOTTA, SAMUEL A. [P] Chicago, IL b. 22 Aug 1900, Villarosa, Italy. Studied: AIC; Chicago Acad FA; Piccinelli. Collections: AIC.

BARTLETT, JAN [Ab, Ldscp. P] Indianapolis, IN b. 16 Oct 1941, Clinton, IN. Teachers: Mary Gaalema; Rob O'Dell; Jerry Smith; Marilyn Hughey Phillis. Exhibited: Hendricks Cnty A Show, 1980-84; Indianapolis AL, 1982. Prizes: Hendricks Cnty A Show, 1980, 81, 83. Collections: Avon Library, Avon, IN.

BARTLEY, RUTH A. [P, Ab, Ldscp. P] Indianapolis, IN b. 13 Mar 1929, Butler, PA. Studied: Indianapolis AL. Teachers: Rosemary Lawton Thomas; Henry Bell; Harry Andrews. Exhibited: Ind. A, 1989; Ind. WCS, 1986; Ind. State Fair, 1989, 90; Whitewater Valley A Exh, 1987. Prizes: Central Ind. A.

BARTLOW, CATHERINE B. [Ldscp. P] Carmel, IN b. c. 1908, Winston Salem, NC d. 19 Jul 1983.

BARTOLINI, MYRTLE F. [MM] Griffith, IN.

BASKER, EDWARD J. [P] South Bend, IN b. 12 Nov 1908, South Bend d. 27 Jan 1972. Self-taught. Prizes: Ernest M. Memorial Award, 1965, 66; HS, 1954, 56, 58, 59, 62, 64-66. Collections: Ind. U; Detroit MA; Montreal MA.

BASS, LYNDALL [Dr, P] Bloomington, IN. Studied: Ind. U, Bloomington; PAFA; Philadelphia Col. A. Exhibited: Manufacturers Hanover Trust Gal, NYC, 1976. Prizes: 14th Nat Benedictine A Awards (finals), 1976.

BASTIAN, CAROLYN WEBER

BASTIN, PATRICIA T. [P] Martinsville, IN.

BATES, VICTORENE G. [P] Whitestown, IN b. Indianapolis, IN. Studied: Indianapolis AL; Famous A Correspondence Course; Ind. U Extension. Teachers: George Jo Mess. Exhibited: Anderson Winter Show; Ind. State Fair; Frankfort City Fair; Riley Days, Greenfield.

BATTEN, LUCY ARTHUR [P] New Albany, IN. Wife of artist Ronal A. Batten.

BATTEN, RONAL A(lbert) [P] New Albany, IN. Husband of artist Lucy Arthur Batten.

BATZKA, STEPHEN A. Cambridge City, IN.

BAUGH, Jr., ETHERIDGE B. [Ldscp. P] Lafayette, IN b. 24 Sep 1925, Lafayette. Self-taught. Exhibited: Tippecanoe A All, 1990. Prizes: Delphi A Show, 1989. Collections: Ind. Nat Bank, Lafayette.

BAUM, ELIZABETH L. [P] San Francisco, CA/Brown Cnty, IN. Studied: Ind. U; Am Acad A, Chicago; AIC. Teachers: Harry Engel; Homer Davisson; C. Curry Bohm. Exhibited: Northern Ind. A Salon. Note: Assistant T to C. Curry Bohm for several years. Daughter of artist George C. Baum.

BAUM, GEORGE C. [P] Brown Cnty, IN b. Sweetser, Grant Cnty, IN. Teachers: C. Curry Bohm. Exhibited: Northern Ind. A Salon; Ind. AC. Note: Businessman turned artist. In 1958 he sold his home in Rochester, Ind., moved to Nashville, Ind., to paint. Father of artist Elizabeth L. Baum.

BAUMANN, GUSTAVE [P, Print, C, W] Santa Fe, NM b. 27 Jun 1881, Magdeburg, Germany d. 8 Oct 1971. Studied: AIC; Koenigliche Kunstgewerbeschule, Munich, Germany. Teachers: Maximillian Dasio, Munich. Exhibited: AIC, 1906, 09; Woman's Dept Cl, Indianapolis, 1913; Palette&Chisel Cl, Chicago, 1913; Second Ann Exh by P-Gravers of Am, Milch Gal, NYC; Exh of Block Prints and Wood Engravings, AIC, 1916; Block-Prints in Color by Gustave Baumann, Smithsonian Inst, Washington, D.C., 1926; IMA (solo), 1930. Prizes: P.-P. Expo, 1915; Fifty Books of the Year, 1940; Seventh Ann Intl PM Exh, Los Angeles MA, 1926. Collections: Albuquerque Public Library, NM; BMFA; Fogg AM; IMA; MMA; Nat Gal, Toronto; AIC; Yale U A Gal; LOC; CM. Note: Author/Illustrator, *Frijoles Canyon Pictographs*, 1939. Worked throughout his life to perfect wood-block technique. Named Honorary Fellow in FA, Sch of Am Research, Santa Fe, NM. Worked in Nashville, Ind., 1910-17.

BAUS, PAUL JEAN [S, P] Indianapolis, IN b. 2 Nov 1914, Indianapolis. Teachers: Simon P. Baus; Elmer E. Taflinger, Indianapolis; Erwin F. Frey, Columbus, OH; Millard Sheets and Lawrence T. Stevens, Los Angeles, CA. Prizes: Ind. A, Indianapolis, 1934; HS, 1935, 50, 55, 62; Ind. A Ann, Herron AM. Note: Worked as assistant in the execution of murals and sculpture for the NYC and San Francisco World Fairs, 1939. Son of artist Simon P. Baus.

BAUS, SIMON PAUL [Por, P, SLP, Ldscp. P, T] Indianapolis, IN b. 4 Sep 1882, Indianapolis d. 9 Apr 1969, Ravenna, OH. Teachers: J. Ottis Adams; William Forsyth; Otto Stark. Prizes: Wanamaker, Philadelphia, 1909; Indianapolis AA, 1919; Chicago Exh Am PS, 1923; HS, 1925-28, 44, 46, 48, 49, 53. Collections: Herron AM, Indianapolis; IMA; Dailey Col, Ind. U, Bloomington; State House collection of governors; Richmond AG. Note: T, Indianapolis AL. Painted Ralph F. Gates, Paul V. McNutt and Henry F. Schricker, all former Ind. governors. Studio in Union Trust Bldg while employed as a postal clerk for 45 years in the Indianapolis Post Office. Retired in 1949. Moved to Ohio in 1966.

BAXTER, BERTHA [P] NYC/East Gloucester, MA b. Alexandria, IN. Studied: N.Y. Sch Fine&App A. Prizes: HS, 1928.

BEALS, GEORGE F. [Ldscp. P] Ft Wayne, IN b. 22 Oct 1913, Gary IN d. 14 Aug 1992. Self-taught. Exhibited: Ventures in Creativity, Ft Wayne 1977-90; Glenbrook A Exh, 1976-89. Prizes: James McBride Award, WC, 1990. Collections: Lincoln Corp; Shambaugh Corp; Wayne Metal Co; Chamber of Commerce.

BEATTY, MARY COX [Dr, P] Kokomo, IN b. 1932, Pocahontas, AR. Studied: Ind. U, Kokomo. Teachers: John Chase Lewis; John Howard Sanden; Daniel Greene.

BEAUCHAMP, JOHN W. [P, Print, Mur. P] Provincetown, MA b. 22 Jun 1906, Marion, IN. Teachers: R. E. Miller; L. Kroll; F. L. Schlemmer. Prizes: PAFA, 1935. Collections: WPA murals, USPOs, Millinocket, MA and Muncy, PA.

BECK, BARBARA McDONALD [SLP] Indianapolis, IN b. 26 Sep 1931, Indianapolis. Teachers: Rosemary Browne Beck. Exhibited: Ind. AC, 1978-82; Ind. State Fair, 1975-82; 500 A Show, 1975, 76. Prizes: Ind. AG, Mile of A, 1975; HS, 1980. Collections: Indianapolis Power and Light; Metropolitan A Council of Indianapolis; Hooverwood, Indianapolis.

BECK, JO (Mary Jo Bergin) [P] Indianapolis, IN. Prizes: HS, 1972. Note: Grew up in New Castle, IN.

BECK, LEOLA E. [Ldscp. P, SLP, Por. P, T] Danville, IN b. c. 1905, McCordsville d. Nov 1986. Exhibited: Plainfield Library, 1972.

BECK, ROSEMARY BROWNE [SLP, Por. P, T] Indianapolis, IN b. 1926, Indianapolis, IN. Studied: John Herron AI. Exhibited: Lyman-Snodgrass Gal, 1983; Herbert Benevy Gal, NYC; Herron AM; Ind. Central U (solo), 1986. Prizes: HS, 1955, 56, 58, 59, 66-68, 72-74, 78-81, 83-85; Ind. AC; Ind. State Fair. Collections: Circle Theatre, Indianapolis, portrait of conductor John Nelson.

BECK, WILLIAM J. Chicago, IL.

BECKMAN, FREDERICK S.

BECKSMITH, LUISE VEACH

BECVAR, ARTHUR N. Notre Dame, IN.

BEDNAR, HERMINA BEIDINGER (Mrs. H. B.) *(See Beidinger, Hermina)* [Des, P] South Bend, IN b. 13 Apr 1916, South Bend. Note: Staff A, Bendix Aviation Corp, 1943-44; Adv. A, 1944-45.

BEDNAR, JOHN JAMES [Edu, P, S, Des, Mur P] South Bend, IN b. 1 Jul 1908, Cleveland. Studied: U of Notre Dame. Prizes: HS, 1941, 42, 45, 47, 62. Collections: murals, St Edward's U; U of Notre Dame. Note: T, U of Notre Dame, 1943-1945.

BEEBE, OLIVE ANDERSON (Mrs. Jerry) Peru, IN b. Evansville, IN. Studied: Oakland City Col; John Herron Sch A. Prizes: Miami AG, Peru.

BEEM, OLIVE C. [P] Bloomington, IN b. Mitchell. Studied: Ind. U. Teachers: Robert E. Burke, Harry Engel, Ind. U; Carl C. Graf, Nashville, IN. Exhibited: "25" Gal; Lyman Bros. Collections: Bedford and Odon Libraries; Woman's Dept Cl, Indianapolis.

BEEM, PAUL EDWARD. [Des, I, P, Print, S, SLP] Chicago, IL b. 12 Jan 1908, Indianapolis, IN d. 15 Sep 1979. Studied: John Herron AI; AIC; ASL; Pasadena A Sch. Teachers: Elmer Taflinger; William Forsyth; George Bridgeman. Prizes: Herron AI, 1930-34; HS, 1931-33, 39, 41; AIC, 1932. Collections: Herron AI; U of N.D.; Ind. U.

BEHR, ROBERT [P, Photo Engraver] Indianapolis, IN b. 19 Aug 1913, Indianapolis. Studied: Herron A Sch. Teachers: William Forsyth; Constance Forsyth; Schover. Exhibited: CCA Gal, Indianapolis.

BEIDINGER, HERMINA *(See Bednar, Hermina Beidinger)*

BELDING, ANN H. [P]

BELL, HENRY [Ab, Ldscp. P, T] Noblesville, IN b. 30 Sep 1942, Lansdale, PA. Studied: Purdue U; Ball State U; Indianapolis AL. Teachers: Floyd Hopper; Jean Vietor; Rob O'Dell; Leah Traugott. Exhibited: Ky. WCS "Aqueous," 1981, 83; Pa. State U, Dunmore Campus; Anderson Winter Show; Whitewater Valley; Ind. State Fair; Pen Women Show. Prizes: HS, 1985; Ind. AC, 1986; Ind. WCS, 1983, 85, 87, 88. Collections: Carmel Clay Schools; Pa. State U; State Col Pa.; Ill. Benedictine Col. Note: T, Ind. public schools.

BELL, MARY JANE [P] Aurora, IN b. Cincinnati, OH. Studied: U of Cincinnati affiliate. Teachers: Meyer Abel; Ray Loos; Don Dennis; E. Whitney; Claude Croney. Exhibited: Cincinnati Women's AC. Prizes: Cincinnati AC; Tri Kappa; Viewpoint '82; HS, 1987.

BELL, RON [Dr, P] Hartford City, IN.

BELL, W(illiam) WILS [Ldscp. P] Terre Haute, IN b. 28 Aug 1964, Green County, IL. Studied: AIC. Exhibited: MFA, Little Rock, AR, 1941; Danville's Women's Cl, 1941; Midlands Gal A, South Bend, IN. Prizes: HS, 1941; Ind. AC, 1943.

BELSER, JEAN M. [Por. P, Min. Rooms] Indianapolis, IN b. 18 Oct 1916, Indianapolis. Studied: Herron A Sch; Indianapolis AL. Teachers: Bill Ashby; Billie Cathran; Lois Davis; Harry Davis. Exhibited: Ind. A, 1989; IHA, Nashville, 1988; Ind. State Fair, 1990. Prizes: Ind. State Fair; IHA; Senior Citizens Fair, 1983, 84, 86; Mile of A, 1982.

BEMIS, BEATRICE BAILEY [Por. P, Ldscp. P, SLP] Columbus, OH b. Schenectady, NY. Studied: N.Y. Sch F&App A; Ohio U; Columbus A Sch. Exhibited: England; France; Scotland; Mexico; U.S. Prizes: HS, 1958. Collections: Capital U, Columbus, OH; Banc Ohio Nat Plaza; Col Union, Hiram, OH.

BENDIT, RUTH [P] Lebanon, IN.

BENHAM, CHRISTINA M. [P, T] Indianapolis, IN d. 1990. Studied: Indianapolis AL. Teachers: Frederick Rigley. Note: Member, Woman's Dept Cl.

BEN-NETT, DIXIE [P, T] Kokomo, IN b. 1928, Port Huron, MI. Studied: Ind. U, Kokomo; Herron Sch A. Teachers: Floyd Hopper; Ruth Anderson; Harry Davis. Exhibited: Ball State U; Ind. U; Ind. State Fair; Indianapolis 500. Collections: Warren Wilson College, NC; Kokomo Sch System; portrait of Elvis Presley in Circle G Ranch, home of Elvis Presley Intl Fan Cl. Note: T, Kokomo Schs.

BENNETT, HELEN FREEMAN (Mrs. R. C.) [P] Indianapolis, IN b. Greensburg, IN. Studied: Ft Wayne, IN; AIC.

BERGSTROM, CHARLES J. [Ldscp. P] Furnessville, IN b. Norway. Studied: AIC; Chicago Acad FA. Teachers: Karl Krafft; Stacy. Exhibited: Drake Hotel (solo); Michigan City (solo). Prizes: HS; Northern Ind. A Salon.

BERKSHIRE, DON [P]

BERLYN, JEAN [P] Brownsburg, IN.

BERNARDIN, MAREN N. [Dr] Clifton, VA.

BERNHARDT, JOHN [Print, P] Santa Barbara, CA b. c. 1921, Indianapolis d. 23 Jun 1963. Studied: Herron Sch A; Colorado Springs FA Cen; Columbia U. Exhibited: Ind. AC (solo); McNey AI (solo), San Antonio; Colorado Springs FA Cen (solo); Occidental Col (solo), LA; Santa Barbara MA (solo). Prizes: 1st Ann Intl A Exh, San Miguel de Allende, Mexico, 1959. Collections: Herron MA; Metropolitan MA; NYPL; MFA, Boston; Boston Public Library.

BERNSTEIN, BLANCHE [P]

BERRY, WILS(on) REED [P, Genre P, I, T] Logansport, IN b. 22 Apr 1851, Adamsboro, Cass Cnty, IN d. 28 Apr 1928. Self-taught. Prizes: HS, 1926. Note: His work, *The Dominion Parliament Buildings at Ottawa, Canada,* presented to Queen Victoria, owned by king or queen of Great Britain.

BERTHELSEN, JOHANN [P, T] New Milford, CT b. 25 Jul 1883, Copenhagen, Denmark d. 2 Apr 1972, Greenwich, CT. Studied: Chicago Musical Col. Exhibited: Mun A Committee, New Deal A Projects, NYC, 1936. Prizes:

HS, 1928, 41, 46, 50, 52, 54; Chicago, 1928. Collections: Sembrich Mem, Lake George, NY; Terre Haute M; Texas Tech Col. Note: Toured U.S. and Canada singing lead baritone roles in Grand Opera in English, 1905. Faculty, Chicago Musical College, beginning 1910; Head of Voice Department, Indianapolis Conservatory of Music, beginning 1913. Co-founder, Little Theater Soc, Indianapolis. Met artist Wayman Adams, 1913. They shared a double wedding ceremony in NYC in 1918. Moved to N.Y. in 1920. Between 1943 and 1960, exhibited frequently in NYC and Indianapolis, and occasionally in Chicago.

BERTRAM, LUCILE [S, P, C, Print, T] West Lafayette, IN b. MI d. 29 Aug 1990. Studied: U of Ill.; AIC. Collections: GTE, Lafayette, IN; created plaque at Boonesborough, Ky., marks sight of first Legislative Assembly in Ky.; helped create life-size bronze statue of Ky. race horse. Note: Member, Board of Directors, Lafayette AA.

BERTRAM, RILEY [P, W] Nashville, IN. Exhibited: Am Fletcher Bldg, Indianapolis, 1974; A Alley, Madison, IN, 1972. Prizes: Professional Picture Framers Assn, 1973. Note: As an author, winner of Franklin College Knobe Prize; as a poet, one of Indiana's Sesquicentennial poets elected by the Governor's committee. Owned a frame shop, Franklin, IN.

BESSIRE, DALE P(hilip) [P] Nashville, IN b. 14 May 1892, Columbus, OH d. 5 Jan 1974. Studied: U of Chicago; John Herron AI. Teachers: William Forsyth; Clifton Wheeler; Rhoda Sellic; T. C. Steele; Homer Davisson; Lucie Hartrath. Exhibited: Chicago Gal Assn, 1936-46; H. Lieber Co Gal (solo); Century of Progress Exh, Chicago. Prizes: HS, 1930, 36; Ind. AC; Ind. State Fair. Collections: Ind. U; Ball State Col M; Public Schools of Chicago. Note: President Ind. AC, 1945-1947. Initiated Nashville's First Blossom Festival. Charter member, Brown Cnty A Gal Assn.

BESSMER, HAL Drummond Island, MI.

BEST, PHILIP H. [P, T] West Lafayette, IN d. 1 Mar 1972. Exhibited: Purdue U, West Lafayette, IN, 1972. Note: T, Purdue U, West Lafayette, IN.

BEVAN, JOCK S. B.

BEVER, ROBERT C. [S, P] Hillsboro, IN b. 15 Mar 1915, Danville, IL. Studied: U of Ill., Danville. Teachers: Breen; Walter Johnson; Shultz. Exhibitions: Swope A Gal, Terre Haute, 1985; Wabash Col A Show, 1981. Prizes: HS, 1977; Swope A Gal, 1981; Paris, Ill. A Show, 1982. Collections: First Nat Bank, Terre Haute, IN; Bank of Western Ind., Hillsboro.

BEYER, EARL [P, Por. P, SLP] Indianapolis, IN. b. c. 1906, Indianapolis d. 1977. Studied: John Herron AI; ASL; Butler U. Teachers: Elmer Taflinger; Olinsky; Von Schlegell; Kenneth Hays Miller. Exhibited: Indianapolis Public Library (solo), 1930; Lymans Fireplace Gal. Collections: Union Lg Cl, NY (Portrait President Harrison).

BHAT, MADHUKAR BALIRAM [P] Vincennes, IN.

BIELECKY, STANLEY [P, T] East Chicago, IN b. 12 Nov 1903, near Berlin, Germany d. 1985. Studied: Minneapolis IA; AIC; PAFA; John Herron AI. Teachers: Glen Mitchell; George Oberteuffer; Charles Wilimovsky; Francis Chapin; Boris Anisfeld; Louis Ritman. Exhibited: Springfield MFA; Hoosier Gal (solo), 1935; San Francisco MA, 1938, 39; Albright A Gal, Buffalo, NY; PAFA; AIC, 1948, 52; Toledo MFA; City AM, St Louis; Delgado M, New

Orleans. Prizes: Resident Fellowship, Tiffany Foundation, NY, 1938; Herron AM, 1939; Detroit MA. Collections: Ind. U, East Chicago extension; Public Schools, East Chicago. Note: Co-founder and director, Mackinac Island Summer School of A. T, Calumet Cen of Ind. U, Valparaiso U.

BIESEL, CHARLES [P, Print] NYC b. 20 Oct 1865, NYC d. 5 Aug 1945, Chicago. Studied: NYC. Exhibited: AIC, 1938; Marshall Field Gal, Chicago; The Ten, 1920s-30s; Chicago&Vicinity Exh, 1920-40; No Jury Soc, Chicago, 1922. Note: Employed by the WPA FA Project through 1936.

BIGELOW, JOHN M(errit) [P, Car, Genre P, I, Comp. A, Gra. A] Indianapolis, IN b. 24 Apr 1939, Somerville, NJ. Studied: Ind. U; Kutztown S.T.C., PA. Teachers: Harry Engel; Elmer Taflinger. Exhibited: Indianapolis AL, 1969; Oldfields, 1969. Note: A, *Indianapolis Star*.

BIGGERSTAFF, MYRA [P]

BIGLER, MARY JANE WHITE *(See White, Mary Jane)* [Edu, P] Detroit, MI b. Columbia City, IN. Studied: Ind. U; Wayne State U; Taylor A Sch; Brown Cnty Sch; AIC; Detroit Society of A&C. Teachers: Robert E. Burke; Harry Engel; C. Curry Bohm; Gertrude Hadley. Exhibited: Ind. AC, 1940, 46; Detroit IA; Detroit A Market. Collections: Hanover Col. Note: Instr Wayne State U; I, *Notes in the Wind* by Helen McGaughey.

BILLINGSLY, ROBERT A. [P] Lebanon, IN. Studied: Herron Sch A, c. 1945; Indianapolis AL.

BINGMAN, TERESA [Dr] Marion, IN.

BIPPUS, ANNE

BIRD, PETER F. Indianapolis, IN.

BIRDSONG, JOAN B. [P] Freetown, IN b. 4 Aug 1922, Milan, IN.

BIRGE, EVELYN C.

BIRREN, DONALD H.

BIRREN, JOSEPH P(ierre). [P, I, Li, T] Chicago, IL b. 1864, Chicago d. 5 Aug 1933. Studied: AIC; NY; Philadelphia; Paris; Munich. Exhibited: AIC, 1917-33; PAFA, 1924; Chicago Gal Assn (solo), 1928; Newhouse Gal (solo), St Louis, 1930. Collections: Union Lg Cl, Chicago; Ill. State M; Los Angeles M; Washington U M; Pasadena AI. Note: T, AIC. Wrote *The Art Student*, published by AIC, 1916.

BISHOP, CONNIE [Dr, Print, T] Huntington, IN b. Takoma Park, MD. Studied: Wheaton Col, BA, 1954; Mich. State U MA, 1966; U of Wis.; AIC; U of Wichita; St Francis Col; Corcoran A Sch. Exhibited: Tri Kappa, Ft Wayne; Countryside Gal, Arlington Heights, IL; Ball State U; Taylor U. Prizes: HS, 1974. Collections: Mich. State U; Wheaton Col; Taylor U. Note: T, Huntington, Col.

BISHOP, DEE [Ldscp. P, SLP] Logansport, IN b. 27 Jan 1943, Peru, IN. Self-taught. Exhibited: Pen Women, 1983-84; Ind. State Fair, 1982; Ft Wayne AG, 1987-88. Prizes: HS, 1982; Pen Women, 1984; Logansport, 1989. Collections: Eli Lilly Corp; Ft Wayne AM.

BISHOP, LOUISE NEVIUS [P] Columbus, IN.

BIXLER, HELEN SAYRE [Ldscp. P, P] Anderson, IN b. 2 Nov 1920, Columbus, OH. Studied: Anderson U; Indianapolis AL. Teachers: Floyd Hopper; Daniel Green; Bill

Ashby; Harry Davis; Paul Sweeney; Nita Ingle. Exhibited: Marion Col (solo). Prizes: Ind. State Fair; Indianapolis AL; Anderson FA Cen.

BLACK, JEAN (Mr.) [Ldscp. P] Indianapolis, IN b. 6 Apr 1907, Crawfordsville, IN. Studied: Wabash Col. Teachers: Fritz Schlemmer; Gary Pierce; Robert Wood; John Pike; Tom Hill. Exhibited: Toledo (Ohio) M; Ind. A; Tucson A Show; Ind. WC; Ind. State Fair.

BLACK, LEAH J.

BLACK, LEE

BLAIR, MILDRED (Mrs. A. M.) [P] Tipton, IN. Teachers: Ida Gordon. Prizes: HS, 1961.

BLAKER, HELEN S. [P] Gary, IN.

BLANKENSHIP, DIANE *(See Day, Gentry)*

BLASE, PANSY L. [P] Princeton, IN b. Cynthiana, KY. Studied: Herron A Sch; Cincinnati A Acad. Teachers: William Forsyth; Oakley Richey; Dorothy Eisenbach; Carl Zimmerman. Prizes: Ind. AC, 1939. Note: Supervisor of A, Princeton (Ind.) schools.

BLASINGHAM, KATHERINE GROH (Mrs. H. E.) [Ldscp. P, SLP] Indianapolis, IN b. 4 Aug 1893, Logansport, IN d. 29 Jun 1978. Studied: Herron AI; AIC; Cleveland (Ohio) Sch A; Ind. State TC. Teachers: Carl C. Graf; Wayman Adams; Eliot O'Hara; Francis Chapin. Exhibited: John Herron AI. Prizes: Canton AI, 1936, 38; Ind. AC; HS; Ind. State Fair. Collections: Canton AI.

BLATZ, JAMES E. [P] Indianapolis, IN. Exhibited: Mini Gal, Cincinnati, OH. Note: Worked as a paint and color technician in the laboratories of Perfection Paint and Color Co.

BLEVINS, PATRICIA [Ldscp. P, Dr, Por. P] b. 21 Nov 1938, Hannibal, MO. Studied: U of Mo. Teachers: John Weller. Exhibited: IHA.

BLODGETT, JOHN W. [Dr]

BLOOMHORST, KENNETH (Eugene) [Ldscp. P, Print, Car, I, Gra. A] Noblesville, IN b. 23 Aug 1932, Dayton, OH. Studied: Dayton AI Sch, BFA. Teachers: Alvin Raffel; John King; Edward Burroughs. Exhibited: Beru's Gal, 1970. Prizes: Ind. A Dir Cl, 1970, 83; U.S. Environmental Protection Agency adopted seal designed by Bloomhorst.

BLOWER, DAVID H(arrison) [P] Los Angeles, CA b. 18 Sep 1901, Fontaner, IN d. 1976. Studied: Wieker Sch FA, Detroit. Prizes: HS, 1948, 49, 52; Mich. A, Detroit AI, 1930, 31.

BLUHM, MARIE R. [Ab, Ldscp. P, Com. A] Seal Beach, CA b. 16 Sep 1912, Ft Wayne, IN d. 7 Dec 1990. Studied: Ft Wayne AI; St Francis Col. Exhibited: Pikes Peak A Show, 1967; Tri Kappa Sorority, 1980. Prizes: Van Wert, OH, 1969; Westminster, 1988. Collections: Lincoln Nat Life Insurance Co.

BOAZ, Jr., BURLING [P, Ldscp.P, T] Indianapolis, IN b. 1891, Indianapolis d. 24 Sep 1968. Exhibited: HS (solo), 1952; Ind. A Show; Ind. State Fair. Prizes: HS, 1948, 61. Note: T, Herron Sch A. In 1914, started display and Com. A business. Began art career as designer of stained glass windows for churches while working for the Erkins Co of Cincinnati, OH. Also designed ornamental iron for another Cincinnati firm.

BOBBS, RUTH PRATT (Mrs. William C.) [P, Por. P] Indianapolis, IN b. 3 Sep 1884, Indianapolis d. 16 Jan

1973. Studied: Herron Sch A; Académie Julian, Paris; Chase Sch A; ASL; BMFA Sch. Teachers: Mary Y. Robinson; Charles Hawthorne; Robert Henri; William Merritt Chase. Prizes: Herron AI, 1926; HS, 1941; Ind. AC, 1944, 45. Collections: IMA.

BOBICK, BRUCE [P, C, T] Macomb, IL b. 1941, Clymer, PA. Studied: U of Pa.; Notre Dame. Exhibited: WC USA, Springfield, MO, 1968, 69, 71, 73; Ill. A Council Gal, Chicago, 1972; Ill. State M, Springfield, 1970-72; PAFA, 1969; Purdue U A Gal, West Lafayette, IN, 1969. Prizes: Ill. State M, 1971; HS, 1969, 75, 79; Pittsburgh WCS, 1974. Collections: Ill. State M, Springfield; Mt Mercy Col, Cedar Rapids, IA; Laura Musser AM, Muscatine, IA. Note: T, Associate Professor A, Ill. U, Macomb, IL and West Ga. Col, Carrollton, GA.

BODELL, MARK ROBINSON [P] Glen Ellyn, IL b. 24 Apr 1891, Lafayette, IN. Teachers: John Sloan; Forrest Shook.

BOHLANDER, JOAN S. [P] Indianapolis, IN/Brown Cnty, IN b. Sydney, Australia d. 20 Jul 1989. Teachers: Rosemary Browne Beck; Floyd Hopper; William Ashby. Exhibited: Jefferson Nat (solo), 1974. Prizes: Ind. State Fair, 1963; HS, 1974. Note: Joan Bohlander A Studio, 1975-86, Brown Cnty, IN.

BOHM, C. CURRY [P, T] Nashville, IN b. 19 Oct 1894, Nashville, TN d. 18 Nov 1971. Studied: AIC; Nat Acad A, Chicago. Teachers: Edward Timmins. Exhibited: AIC, annually; Brown Cnty AG (solo), 1971. Prizes: Chicago Mun AL; HS, 1937, 40, 41, 45, 46, 50, 53, 57, 59, 60, 61, 62, 64, 67; Chicago Palette&Chisel Acad FA, 1931 (gold); Chicago Mun AL; Ind. AC, 1945; Brown Cnty A Gal Assn. Collections: Chicago Public Sch Coll; Ill. State M; Swope Gal A; Muncie AA; Ind. U. Note: Director Brown Cnty Sch Ldscp P. Selected by Intl Business Machines Corp for representation in World's Fair, 1940. Son of artist Robert W. Bohm.

BOHNER, MARIAN A. (Mrs. C. B.) [P] Indianapolis, IN b. 30 Aug 1904, Decatur, IL. Studied: Taflinger's A Sch, Indianapolis; Indianapolis ASL. Teachers: Harold McDonald; Wayman Adams. Exhibited: Indianapolis ASL, 1941-1943; Ind. A, 1944.

BOLESKY, JOHN [Dr] Marion, IN.

BOLINGER, INEZ RUSSELL [P] Anderson, IN. Exhibited: Hoosier A Gal, 1945.

BOLLER, CAROLE [Dr, Ldscp. P] Lowell, IN b. 24 Sep 1941, Harvey, IL. Studied: Thornton Col; Drisi Acad of A; Scottsdale A Sch. Teachers: Mohamed Drisi; David Laffel. Exhibited: Intl Exh of Pastels, 1990; Curator's Choice, Ind., 1989; Knickerbocker A 39th Open, 1989. Prizes: 5 State Competition, 1989; Natl West Coast, 1988; Northern Ind. Salon, 1988. Collections: Northern Ind. Public Service Corp; Purdue U; Ind. U; Inacomp Corp; Calumet Sch Corp.

BOMBARD, FLOYD W. [P] Terre Haute, IN. Note: A native of Ill.; his family moved to Ind. in 1935.

BOND, BYRON LELAND [Des, P, Print, I, C] Richmond, IN b. 8 May 1906, Richmond, IN. Studied: Ind. U; John Herron AI; ASL. Teachers: Randolph Coats. Exhibited: Richmond AA; John Herron AI. Note: Des, "Leland Line" bookplates; Dir, Leland Commercial A&Adv Studios, Richmond.

BONIFIELD, CHARLES

BONSIB, LOUIS W. [P, Ldscp. P] Ft Wayne, IN b. 10 Mar 1892, Vincennes, IN d. 29 Oct 1979. Self-taught. Exhibited: Herron AM; Maine AM, Ogunquit. Prizes: HS, 1937; Ind. AA, 1939. Collections: Ft Wayne Women's Cl; YMCA, Ft Wayne; Hanover Col; Ind. U; Ft Wayne A Sch and AM. Note: Chairman Emeritus of Bonsib Advertising Agency of which he was founder and president until his retirement at age 70 when he became Chairman of the Board.

BOOMER, FRANCES E. East Chicago, IN.

BOONE, GARRET J. [Print, P, S, T] Richmond, IN b. c. 1932. Studied: DePauw U; Ind. U, Bloomington. Exhibited: Leeds Gal, Earlham Col, Richmond, IN, 1974, 87; Left Bank Gal, Greencastle, IN, 1976; DePauw U, 1987. Prizes: Fulbright Research Scholar, Italy. Note: T, DePauw U, 1955-71; Earlham Col, beginning1971. Helped establish Great Lakes Col Assn's N.Y. arts program.

BOONE, JUNE C. ELVINA [Por. P, S] Kokomo, IN. Studied: England. Exhibited: HS Gal. Prizes: HS, 1963. Note: I, England for six years. Noted for her portraits of children.

BOORMAN, MICHIKO [Ldscp. P] Indianapolis, IN. b. 2 Mar 1927, Osaka, Japan. Studied: Elementary and Secondary Education, Japan; Indianapolis AL. Teachers: Adelee Wendel; Clayson Baker; Rosemary Lawton Thomas; Floyd Hopper; Jean Vietor; Paul Sweaney. Prizes: HS, 1972, 74; Exhibit 100; Ind. AC; Wabash Valley, 1981; Ind. State Fair; Griffith Parks, 1990. Collections: Jefferson Nat Life Insurance; Indianapolis Power and Light; Farm Bureau Insurance; Wabash Insurance; Ind. Nat Bank; Merchants Nat Bank.

BOPP, CHERYL H. [Dr] Lebanon, IN b. 1948, Terre Haute, IN. Studied: Ind. State U. Teachers: Hiram Williams. Exhibited: Jane Haslem Gals (solo), Madison, WI and Washington, D.C.; The Commons Gal (solo), Columbus, IN; Pine Street Gal (solo), Zionsville, IN; Mark Twain Gal (solo), St Louis; Swope Gal (solo), Terre Haute; New Harmony Gal (solo), New Harmony, IN. Collections: Ind. State U, Terre Haute; Wabash Col, Crawfordsville, IN; Washington Gal, Frankfort, IN.

BORDEN, JAMES C. [Ldscp. P, Genre P, T] South Bend, IN b. 14 Oct 1928, Indianapolis, IN. Studied: American Acad A, Chicago; Famous A Course, Westport, CO; South Bend A Center. Teachers: Harold Zisla; Zig Jankowski; Frank Webb; Tony Couch. Exhibited: A for the Parks, 1988; St Joseph WC Soc, 1985-1989. Prizes: HS, 1988; A for the Parks, Jackson Hole, WY, 1988 (Finalist); Am A Magazine, 1986 (Finalist). Collections: South Bend A Cen; Mem Hospital, South Bend; South Bend Symphony; First Source Bank.

BORDEN, WILLIAM [Ldscp. P, Des] Dearborn, MI b. 29 Jan 1943, Indianapolis, IN. Studied: Cleveland IA. Teachers: John Paul Miller; C. E. Van Duzer. Exhibited: Am WC Soc, 1982, 83, 86-88; WC USA, 1984; WC West, 1986. Prizes: AM WC Soc, 1983; AM Acad of A Award, Midwest WC Soc, 1981; HS, 1979. Collections: Ford Motor Co; Detroit Bank&Trust; DePauw U; Ferris State U; U of Evansville; Mich. Bell Telephone.

BOSKO, CAROL [Dr, Por. P, T] Newburgh, IN b. 3 Feb 1943, Oxford, CT. Studied: U of Evansville. Teachers: Albert Handel; Daniel Green; Dom Petro. Exhibited: Sheldon Swope Gal, 1989; Old Gal, 1986. Prizes: Rose Hulman Inst, Purchase Award; AG, 1989; Evansville AG, 1990. Collections: Rose Hulman Inst; Old Nat Bank; Charles Leich Co.

BOTKIN, PENELOPE [P, Dr, Col. A] Edinburg, IN b. Kansas City, MO d. 24 Sep 1986 (auto accident). Studied: John Herron A Sch; Indianapolis AL. Teachers: Elmer Taflinger; Frederick Polley. Exhibited: Sheldon Swope Gal; Mid-States A Exh, Evansville; Ind. AC. Prizes: Ind. State Fair; Nat Cr Show, Chicago.

BOTT, EARLE WAYNE [P, Des, Print, Car] Brazil, IN b. 1 Jan 1894, Indianapolis d. 19 Jul 1964. Studied: John Herron AI; A Acad, Cincinnati; AIC. Teachers: William Forsyth; Clifton Wheeler; Otto Stark; James R. Hopkins; Frank Duveneck. Exhibited: John Herron AI, 1914, 21-23, 32; Ind. AC, 1922, 33, 35; Richmond AA, 1922-24; Sheldon Swope Gal, Terre Haute, 1964. Prizes: Ind. State Fair, 1921. Collections: Am Legion, Kokomo. Note: Husband of artist Mabel Siegelin Bott; father of artist Oren Earle Bott.

BOTT, MABEL SIEGELIN [T, C, P, Des] Brazil, IN b. 12 Sep 1900, Clay Cnty, IN d. Dec 1967. Studied: John Herron AI. Teachers: William Forsyth; Clifton Wheeler; Otto Stark. Exhibited: John Herron AI, 1926, 27, 29, 30; Ind. AC, 1933, 35, 36. Prizes: Ind. State Fair, 1924-26, 29-33; Ky. State Fair, 1927, 32; Ind. Fed AC, 1936. Note: T, Van Buren Township High School for 25 years. Wife of artist Earle Wayne Bott; mother of artist Oren Earle Bott.

BOTT, OREN EARLE Brazil, IN. Note: Son of artists Earle Wayne Bott and Mabel Siegelin Bott.

BOUILLET, JULES A. [S, Wood Carver] Vincennes, IN b. c. 1940, Knox City. Exhibited: Untamed A Gal, Indianapolis, 1983; Woodson M, Wausau, WI; London M; Ward Foundation World Championship Wild Fowl Carving Competition.

BOWDEN, A(lfred) J. Indianapolis, IN.

BOWE, MARY E. *(See Osterday, Mary Bowe)*

BOWEN, DOROTHY J(eanne). [P, SLP] Delphi, IN. Studied: School of Fine&App A, U of Ill. Prizes: Northern Ind. A Salon, Hammond, 1947. Note: Art Supervisor, Chesterton-Porter Schs.

BOWEN, RUTH

BOWERS, DOROTHY A. [P]

BOWMAN, MARY ANN Louisville, KY.

BOYCE, GERALD G. [P, Silversmith, Silverpoint Dr] Indianapolis, IN b. WI. Studied: Wis. State U, Milwaukee; State U, IA; Milwaukee AI; Americano-Guatemalteco Inst, Guatemala City. Exhibited: MOMA; AIC; Wadsworth Antheneum; Toledo MA; San Francisco MA. Collections: Ball State U; Ind. State U; Evansville U; DePauw U; Wabash Col. Prizes: HS, 1970. Note: Professor of A and Head of A Dept, Ind. Central Col, Indianapolis.

BOYD, MARION McBROOM (Mrs. Ralph), [Por. P, T] Nashville, IN b. Chicago, IL d. 3 Jun 1970. Studied: U of Wis. Teachers: Homer Davisson; C. Curry Bohm; Gianni Cilfone; Katherine Shackleford. Exhibited: Swope Gal, Terre Haute, IN; Anderson A Show; Ft Wayne Woman's Cl Show. Prizes: Anderson A Show, 1954; HS, 1953.

BOYER, DWIGHT O. Indianapolis, IN.

BOYER, JAN SCOTT [P] Indianapolis, IN. Exhibited: New Assocs Gal (solo), Elwood, IN, 1973. Prizes: HS, 1970, 83, 84.

BOYKIN, J(udson) N. Indianapolis, IN d. 5 Oct 1979.

Note: Operated West Side A Cen, 1969-75; proprietor, A Treasures Ltd, Nashville, IN.

BOYLE, BETTY C. [Ab, Ldscp. P, T] Columbus, IN b. 11 May 1927, Yonkers, NY. Self-taught. Exhibited: Am WCS, NY, 1983; Am A Prof Lg, NY, 1982, 83; Audubon A, NY, 1983. Prizes: WSI, 1984; Ky. WC, Aqueous, 1985; Ind. AC, 1986. Collections: IUPUI Conference Center; L. S. Ayres, Lafayette Square, Indianapolis.

BRACKMIER, HERBERT W. [Print, C] Indianapolis, IN b. 29 Jun 1909, Indianapolis. Studied: John Herron Sch A. Teachers: Paul Hadley; Clifton Wheeler; Forrest F. Stark; Ralph Sowell.

BRADFIELD, ROD M. [Dr, P] Brazil, IN.

BRADFORD, ELGIN L. (Mrs. W. J.) [Ab, Ldscp. P] Sun City, AZ b. 19 Mar 1918, Newell, IA. Studied: Butler U, Indianapolis; Indianapolis AL. Teachers: Floyd Hopper; Paul Sweany; Thelma Confer; Claudine Paluzzi; Ed Manetta; Val Thelin. Exhibited: Mid-States A Exh, 1976-78; Wabash Valley Exh, Terre Haute, IN, 1977, 80, 81 (Pr); Art 500, Indianapolis, 1977, 78; Ind. State Fair; Ind. WCS, 1983 (Pr), 84-86; Ariz. WCS, 1987. Collections: Harrison and Moberly law firm, Indianapolis.

BRADLEY, CAROLYN G(ertrude) [P, I, C, Print, T, W] Columbus, OH b. 1898, Richmond, IN d. 8 Dec 1954, Indianapolis, IN. Studied: Earlham Col; Herron AI; Escuela Universitaria de Belles Artes, Mexico; Columbia U; Traphagen Sch of Fashion. Teachers: William Forsyth; Henry B. Snell; George P. Ennis; James Hopkins; Carlos Merida; W. Lester Stevens; Victor Julius. Exhibited: Herron AI, 1928; NAWA, 1928; H. Lieber Co Gal, Ann Solo Exh; Santiago, Chile; U of Chile; Honduras. Prizes: HS, 1927, 33, 35-37; Herron AI, 1930; NAWA, 1934; Ind. AC; Nat Assn Women P&S; Richmond AA; Cincinnati Women's AC. Collections: Richmond AA. Note: T, Manuel Training H.S., Indianapolis; T, Ohio State U, 1932-54. Specialist in art to Chile for the Inter-Am Education Fnd. In 1946, served as visiting professor of art at U of Chile; in 1951, served as visiting professor of fine arts at the U of Costa Rica. Wrote *Costume Design* and *Costume and You.*

BRADLEY, NORMAN [I, T] Ft Wayne, IN b. 1935, Ft Wayne. Studied: Ft Wayne A Sch; Mexico City Col, BFA, 1959; U of the Americas, MFA, 1964. Exhibited: Herron; Wabash Valley Exh, Terre Haute. Prizes: Vincennes U; Los Angeles Home Show. Collections: Ft Wayne MA; Mexican-North Am Inst of Cultural Relations, Mexico; U of the Americas, Mexico. Note: T, Ft Wayne AI; Ind. U, Ft Wayne. I, U.S. Army, 1960-63, Washington, D.C.

BRADSHAW, DEL(ores) [P] Bristol, IN b. 29 Jul 1943, Berrien Springs, MI. Studied: Elkhart AL. Teachers: Nita Engles; Tom Lynch. Exhibited: Thompson Gal, 1986, 87; Midwest M Am A, 1986; Elkhart AL, 1980-90. Prizes: Elkhart AL Prof Juried Competition, 1986, 87; Midwest M Am A, 1986. Collections: Miles, Inc; Robert Weed Corp.

BRADSHAW, MARTHA [Ldscp. P, T] Richmond, IN b. 28 Sep 1906, Richmond. Teachers: Esther Nusbaum. Exhibited: Ball State U; Greenville, OH; Connersville, IN. Prizes: HS, 1970; Ball State U; Union City, IN; Connersville, IN; Richmond, IN.

BRADY, HAROLD [Dr, Ldscp. P, Genre P] Richmond, IN b. 30 Jun 1914, Richmond. Teachers: Esther Nusbaum; Ray Stevens. Exhibited: Richmond AA Ann. Prizes:

Greenville AG; Richmond AA, 1970; Preble AA, Eaton, OH. Collections: U.S. Chemical Co, Greenville, OH; Richmond Bakery Co., Richmond, IN.

BRAMS, JOAN Prizes: HS, 1967.

BRANCH, KAY

BRANDNER, GLADYS DECKER [Por. P] Note: Wife of artist Karl Brandner.

BRANDNER, KARL C. F. [P, Ldscp. P, Photo, Print] Riverside, IL b. 17 Jan 1898, Oak Park, IL. Studied: AIC; Chicago Acad FA; Detroit Sch A. Teachers: Antonin Sterba; Elmer A. Forsberg; John P. Wicher; Myron Barlow; Francis P. Paulas. Exhibitions: AIC; AOPRF AL, 1927; IAFA. Prizes: HS, 1930, 32, 37, 39, 45, 48, 51; Palette and Chisel Cl, 1936. Collections: State MFA, Springfield, IL; Palette and Chisel Cl, Chicago; State Library, Springfield. Note: Husband of artist Gladys Decker Brandner.

BRATOVICH, MARK W. [Ldscp. P] Bedford, IN b. 30 Sep 1953, Salem, IL. Self-taught. Exhibited: Ind. State Fair, 1985-87; IHA Exh, 1984-87. Prizes: HS, 1987, 89; Ind. State Fair, 1987. Collections: Ford Motor Company; Bedford Public Library.

BRCIN, JOHN DAVID [S, T] Chicago, IL b. 15 Aug 1899, Gracac, Serbia. Studied: AIC; U of Chicago; Chicago Acad FA. Teachers: Albin Polasek. Exhibited: AIC, 1920, 45; Mun AL; "A for Victory, " MMA. Prizes: HS, 1929, 36, 38; AIC, Lathrop Fellowship, 1922; AIC, 1923, 26. Collections: Com Cl, Gary, IN; First Unitarian Church, Omaha, NE; Joslyn Mem Bldg, Omaha. Note: Emigrated to Gary, IN, 1914.

BREDEWATER, GEORGE [Com. A] Columbus, IN b. 5 Apr 1925, Indianapolis, IN. Teachers: Wilbur Meese. Prizes: Ind. State Fair; HS, 1984; Brown Cnty AG.

BREEN, HARRY F. [P, T] Gary, IN b. IN. Prizes: HS, 1956, 63. Note: T, Emerson Sch, Gary, IN, and U of Ill.

BREEN, MARTHA [Com. A, Bat] b. 1925. Studied: AIC; Inst Des, Chicago. Teachers: Leon Golub; Paul Weighardt. Note: Her work is included in many museums and private collections throughout the U.S., Germany and India.

BREEN, MILDRED [Com. A, Bat, Print] West Lafayette, IN b. Chicago, IL. Studied: AIC; Inst of Des, Chicago; Kanpur, India. Teachers: Leon Golub; Paul Weighardt; Richard Callner; Robert Reed. Exhibited: Harcourt-Butler Inst, Kanpur, India; Lafayette A Cen, 1967; Sheldon Swope A Gal, Terre Haute, IN, 1968, 69; House of Living Judaism, NY, 1970; Wabash Col, Crawfordsville, IN, 1970; Kretschmer Gal, NY, 1971. Collections: Smithsonian Inst; State Farm Insurance Co, Lafayette, IN; Temple Emmanuel, NYC. Note: Studied batik process in New Delhi, India. Developed program of instruction in batik process at the Lafayette A Cen.

BREHM, GEORGE [I, P] NYC b. 30 Sep 1878, Anderson, IN. Studied: ASL; Ind. U. Teachers: Twachtman; DuMond; Bridgman. Note: I, magazines and advertising.

BRENTLINGER, MIRIAM [Dr, S, T] Terre Haute, IN b. 21 Mar 1924, Terre Haute. Studied: Ind. State U. Teachers: John Laska; Robert Montgomery. Exhibited: Wabash Valley Exh, 1966, 74; Swope Gal. Prizes: Mid-State Exh, 1965; Paris AL.

BRETHAUER, MARY M. [P, T] Mt Dora, FL. Studied: Herron Sch A, 1942-44.

BREWER, ELEANOR K. [Ab, Ldscp. P, S, Por. P, T, HPA, W] Ladoga, IN b. 19 Mar 1939, Ladoga. Studied: Herron Sch A; IUPUI. Teachers: Stanley Burford; Edmund Brucker; Robert Weaver; Lance Baber. Exhibited: Gold Coast A Fair, 1989, 90; Talbott Street A Fair, 1989; Strawberry Festival, Crawfordsville, 1989; Penrod, Indianapolis. Prizes: Strawberry Festival, 1989; Creative A Gal. Collections: IMA, rental gal. Note: Co-authored *Computer Art Discovery—A Renaissance in Education* .

BRIDGE, MORTON [P] Chicago, IL.

BRIGGS, HELEN L. *(See Duckwall, Helen Briggs)* [P, Por. P, SLP] Muncie, IN b. 15 Feb 1912, Sheridan, IN d. 27 Feb 1988, Clearwater, FL. Studied: John Herron AI; PAFA, Chester Springs, PA. Exhibited: John Herron AI; Ball State AM, Muncie. Prizes: HS, 1938, 53, 56, 57, 59, 61, 62, 64, 65, 67; Ind. AC, 1937. Note: Painted portrait of Governor Rodger D. Branigin.

BRIGGS, PAULINE (Mrs. Earl) [P] Indianapolis, IN. Prizes: HS, 1954.

BRILL, SHARON

BRINDEL, CAROLYN S. [S] Anderson, IN b. Louisville, KY. Exhibited: 500 Festival of A; Preview 71, OH; Ind. State Fair; Whitewater Valley Exh. Note: T, Anderson Col.

BRINKMAN, DORIS J. [Ldscp. P, Print] Carmel, IN b. 14 Jun 1926, Indianapolis, IN. Studied: Herron Sch A; U of Colo.; U of Wash. Exhibited: Herron MA, 1963; 2nd Ind. State MFA Exh, 1975; Ball State U Ann Dr&S Show, 1962, 63, 65, 68, 69, 80. Prizes: 36th Ann Ind. AC Exh, 1968; HS, 1973; Ann A for Religion Exh, 1959, 60, 63, 65, 77. Collections: Evansville MA⪼ Ind. State U; Ind. U Mem Union. Note: T, Indianapolis Public Sch.

BRINTON, H. DOSWELL Oak Park, IL.

BRITT, RALPH M. [P] Atlanta, GA b. 19 Jul 1895, Winchester, IN. Teachers: William Forsyth; Clifton Wheeler; Otto Stark; Olive Rush. Prizes: HS, 1926, 27; Atlanta AA, 1927; High M, Atlanta, 1928; Ga. State Exh, 1929. Collections: Purdue Mem Union, West Lafayette, IN. Note: Dir, Britt Sch A.

BROCKENBROUGH, ELEANOR [P, C] Lafayette, IN b. 12 Mar 1880, Lafayette, IN d. 1938. Studied: Ferguson A Colonies, East Gloucester, MA. Teachers: Eric Pape; F. F. Fursman; C. H. Hawthorne; H. H. Breckenridge. Collections: Ft Wayne MA; Lafayette AA; Washington, Ford and Centennial Schools, Lafayette, IN. Note: Elected as first woman president of the Lafayette AA, 1919.

BROSS, JANIS Bloomington, IN.

BROTHER ETIENNE COOPER, C.S.C. [S, P, T] Notre Dame, IN b. 11 Jul 1915, Altoona, PA d. 11 Jul 1990. Studied: U of Notre Dame; Catholic U. Exhibited: John Herron AI, 1945; AM, Evansville, IN. Prizes: HS, 1945, 46. Note: I, *Young Prince Gonzaga*, 1944. T, Cathedral H.S., Indianapolis.

BROTHER LOYOLA (John) CHRISTOPH, C.S.C. [T, P, S] b. 18 Jan 1903, Seattle, WA d. 4 Apr 1981. Studied: U of Notre Dame; AIC. Prizes: HS, 1944.

BROWER, JOE H.

BROWN, BEULAH H(azelrigg) [P, Ldscp. P, TA, Cer, T] Muncie, IN b. 24 Nov 1892, Napoleon, IN d. April 1988. Studied: Cincinnati Conservatory of Music; Ball State U; Herron Sch A. Exhibited: Ball State U; Earlham Col; Rich-

mond, New Castle and Mitchell libraries; Ind. State Fair. Note: T, Springport; T, Mt Summit; T, New Castle State Hospital. Principal, Indiana Village, New Castle. Designed textiles. Wrote and illustrated children's books. Married to artist Francis Focer Brown.

BROWN, FRANCIS CLARK [Mur. P, SLP, Ldscp. P] Nashville, IN b. 7 Aug 1908, New Sharon, IA d. 12 Oct 1992. Studied: John Herron Sch A; Purdue U; Fuller Sch A, St Ives, England; Gruppe School, Gloucester, MA. Teachers: William Forsyth; Clifton Wheeler; Oakley Richey; Al Hibbard; Paul Hadley; Eliot O'Hara; Emile Gruppe. Exhibited: Corcoran Gal, Washington, D.C.; New Kirk Gal, St Ives, England, 1952. Prizes: HS, 1949, 56-58, 76; Richmond AA, 1957, 65, 66, 71, 82; Ind. State Fair, 1934, 39; Richmond P Exh, 1934; Anderson A Soc, 1936. Collections: Public Library, Noblesville; Ind. U; Earlham Col; Richmond AA; Lynchburg Col; murals, Hamilton Cnty Courthouse. Note: Pastor of Society of Friends (Quakers) for 25 years.

BROWN, FRANCIS FOCER [Edu, M Dir, P, T] Muncie, IN b. 19 Jan 1891, Glassboro, NJ d. 14 April 1971. Studied: Earlham Col; John Herron AI; Ball State TC; Ohio State U. Teachers: J. Ottis Adams; William Forsyth; James R. Hopkins. Exhibited: CMA, 1922-25; PAFA, 1922, 23; Worlds Fair, 1933. Prizes: HS, 1925, 26, 28, 29, 37, 45; Richmond AA, 1922; John Herron AI, 1922. Collections: Richmond A Gal; Herron AI; Public Schs, Muncie and Lafayette, IN. Note: T/Dir, A Gal, Ball State TC, Muncie, 1916-46. Married to artist Beulah Hazelrigg Brown.

BROWN, HELEN M. [P] Logansport, IN. Exhibited: Little Gal, Honeywell Community Cen, Wabash, IN.

BROWN, MARGARET JAMES [P] Oak Park, IL.

BROWN, MARY JOHNSTON (Mrs. Dewitt, Jr.) [P] New Augusta, IN b. 4 Feb 1918, Indianapolis. Studied: John Herron AI; Butler U; Ind. U. Exhibited: Witte Mem M, San Antonio, TX, 1945 (Pr); John Herron AI, 1942, 44 (Pr); AIC, 1940, 43.

BROWN, PEGGY [Ab, P] Nashville, IN b. 15 Mar 1934, Ft Wayne, IN. Self-taught. Exhibited: Am WCS; Nat WCS; Allied A of Am. Prizes: Am WCS, 1979; Nat Acad of Des, 1978; HS, 1974, 77-81, 84. Collections: Ft Wayne MA; Ind. U, Bloomington; Standard Oil of Ind. Note: T, Ind. U, Ft Wayne.

BROWN, RO ZELMA [Ldscp. P, Por. P, SG, T] Cumberland, IN b. 22 May 1922, Estancia, NM. Studied: East Side A Cen; AL. Teachers: Rosemary Lawton Thomas; Bill Ashby; Luke Buck. Exhibited: Southside 7 State Show, 1989; Ind. State Fair, 1986-88. Prizes: Ind. State Fair, 1989; HS, 1986; Central Ind. A, 1990. Collections: Old Bethel Methodist; Trilogy Gal; Stuart's Gal.

BROWN, SARAH

BROWN, WILLIAM F. [P, I] IN b. 21 Jun 1947, Evansville, IN. Studied: Ind. State U; AIC. Exhibited: 25th Ann Wabash Valley Exh, 1969. Prizes: 8th Ann Ind. Salon of A, Bloomington, 1969; New Horizons in A, Chicago, 1971.

BROYLES, CHICQIELA S. [Dr, Print, Li, P, T] Gaston, IN b. 10 Jun 1951, Anderson, IN. Studied: Ball State U. Teachers: Ray Bullock; Tom Minkler; John Warner; Charlotte Shay. Exhibited: Three Rural Women, 1982; Sheldon Swope M, Terre Haute, 1980. Prizes: HS, 1984, 89; Ind. State Fair, 1987. Collections: Anderson FA Cen, Anderson, IN; Pay Less Supermarket, Anderson, IN.

BRUBAKER, ROBERT L. (Bob) [Ldscp. P, Genre P, Por. P, P, T] Greenville, OH b. 7 Apr 1921, Union City, IN. Studied: Dayton AI. Teachers: M. Wogaman; John Price; Don Stone; Paul Strisik; G. Condon. Exhibited: Richmond AA Ann; Greenville AG; Central Ohio WC Assn. Collections: 2nd Nat Bank, Greenville.

BRUBECK, JEANNE D. [P] Martinsville, IN. Teachers: Leah Traugott; Floyd Hopper; Claudine Paluzzi; Marilyn Price; Jean Vietor; Amanda Block. Exhibited: Art 500; Lafayette Square Cinema, Indianapolis, 1977; Ind. State Fair.

BRUCE, BLANCHE CANFIELD [P] Terre Haute, IN/Minoquoa, WI b. 29 Sep 1880, Wells, MN d. 26 Aug 1945. Studied: AIC; ASL. Teachers: Charles W. Hawthorne; Hayley Lever; Susan Ricker Knox. Exhibited: Herron AM. Collections: Nat Hist M, Chicago; Ind. State TC, Terre Haute.

BRUCE, BONNIE [Dr, S, Weaver] Indianapolis, IN b. 10 Oct 1946, Indianapolis. Studied: Herron Sch A; Principia Col; Indianapolis AL. Teachers: Patty McNair Bruce; Gianni Cilfone; Paul Sweany; Hank Richter; Elmer Taflinger. Exhibited: Ind. State Fair; Intl Min S, Print, and Engraver's Show; Art 500. Prizes: Ind. State Fair. Note: Daughter of artist Patti McNair Bruce.

BRUCE, PATTI McNAIR [Ldscp. P, Dr, Car, Des] Indianapolis, IN b. 13 Jul 1916, Kinney, MN. Studied: Minezingers A Sch, Detroit; Indianapolis AL; Principia Col. Teachers: Elmer Taflinger; James Green; Gianni Cilfone. Exhibited: Art 500; Midwest WCS; Ind. State Fair; IMA, rental gal; Ind. AC; Ind. WCS. Note: Past coordinator of the Animated Cartoon Dept, Jam Handy Organization, Detroit. Designed and supervised building of 275 Ind. houses, some built by her husband, Robert Q. Bruce. Mother of artist Bonnie Bruce.

BRUCKER, EDMUND [Por. P, T] Indianapolis, IN b. 20 Nov 1912, Cleveland, OH. Studied: Cleveland Sch of A. Teachers: Henry G. Keller; Rolf Stoll; Carl Gaertner; Paul B. Travis. Exhibited: MMA, 1942, 52; PAFA, 1937, 40, 50; Carnegie AI, National, 1941. Prizes: Ill. State Fair, 1958; HS, 1939-41, 43, 44, 46, 47, 49, 51, 52, 55, 56, 59, 61-68, 70, 74, 78, 82, 84; Ind. A, Herron AM, 1941. Collections: Cleveland MA; Indianapolis Motor Speedway, Hall of Fame M; IMA; Evansville MA; Butler Inst Am A; Dartmouth Col; City of Cleveland; DePauw U. Note: Former faculty member, Herron A Sch. Painted portraits for Phillips Petroleum Co, Eli Lilly and Co, Ind. U Law Sch, Butler U, Indianapolis Medical Soc, Ind. War Memorial Commission and Arthur Jordan Foundation.

BRUNDAGE, ETHEL A. [Ab, Ldscp. P, Genre P, S] Evansville, IN b. 27 Aug 1910, Chicago, IL. Teachers: Frank Webb; Virginia Cobb; Carole Barnes. Exhibited: Evansville M of A&Sc. Prizes: HS, 1990; Evansville AG, 1988; Owensboro AA, 1989. Collections: Merchants Nat Bank, Indianapolis.

BRUNING, PETER [Ldscp. P, Por. P] Terre Haute, IN b. 23 Mar 1923, Amsterdam, Netherlands. Studied: Rembrandt, Amsterdam; Bern, Switzerland; Paris, France; Ind. U, Bloomington. Teachers: Leo Steppat; Alton Pickens; Robert Laurent. Exhibited: HS Gal (solo), 1969; North Light Gal (solo), Terre Haute, 1988; Sheldon Swope AM (solo), 1989. Prizes: HS, 1968, 72, 73, 75; Wabash Valley Exh, 1957. Collections: Ind. State U; Pittman Moore Headquarters, General Housewares Corp. Note: T, Ind. State U.

BRYAN, RUTH GLASER Muncie, IN. Studied: Ladywood Sch; St Mary- of-the-Woods. Exhibited: Ball State Teachers Conference.

BRYANT, JACQUELIN Plainfield, IN. Studied: Indianapolis AL.

BRYCE, THOMAS M. [S] Indianapolis, IN. Prizes: HS, 1976.

BRYDENTHAL, DOROTHY

BUCHSBAUM, ELIZABETH M. [Ldscp. P, Print, Li, Por. P] Gary, IN b. U.S. Army Ft, Philippine Islands. Studied: AIC. Teachers: Louis Ritman; Edmund G. Giesbut; Laura Van Pappeldam. Exhibited: Gary A. Prizes: Gary Assn Music and Applied A; Junior Lg Allied A.

BUCHTA, ANTHONY [P] Chicago, IL b. 13 Jun 1896, Cedar Rapids, IA d. 20 Dec 1967, Brown Cnty, IN. Studied: Chicago Acad FA; AIC; Prang Traveling Sch of A&C, NY. Teachers: Charles Schroeder; Johonas Schumacher; Leslie F. Thompson. Exhibited: PAFA; Philadelphia WC Annual, 1934; Group Shows, AIC. Prizes: Ill. State Fair; Palette and Chisel, 1929; HS, 1940, 60; Chicago Gal Assn; North Shore AL; New Orleans AA WC Pr. Collections: AIC; Swope Gal, Terre Haute, IN; Valparaiso AM.

BUCK, HAROLD L. [Ldscp. P, Por. P] Indianapolis, IN b. 1909, Henderson, KY d. c. 1990. Studied: Manual H.S.; John Herron AI. Teachers: William Forsyth; Simon Baus; Effie Carter; George Cherpov; Emil Gruppe. Note: Father of artist Luther Buck.

BUCK, LUTHER A. (Luke) [P, I, T] Nineveh, IN b. 1940, Bridgeport, IN. Studied: Arsenal Technical H.S., commercial art; John Herron A Sch; Indianapolis AL. Teachers: Harold Buck; Floyd Hopper; Gene Lacy. Exhibited: IHA; Wabash Valley A Show, Swope Gal, Terre Haute, IN; Ind. State Fair; Pen Women A Show, Indianapolis. Collections: Shelbyville Bank; Homer A Gal. Note: Son of artist Harold L. Buck.

BUCKLEW, KEN R. [Ldscp. P, P, T] Spencer, IN b. 8 Mar 1957, Greencastle, IN. Self-taught. Exhibited: Phoenix and Dragon Gal, Bloomington, IN; Wildlife West A Festival, CA, 1987; Southside AL, 1986, 89; U.S. Dept of Interior, Nat Tour of Duck Stamp Des, 1990. Prizes: 1st Place, Ind. Game Bird Stamp Comp, 1984; 1st Place, Ind. Duck Stamp Comp, 1990; 1st Place, Ind. DNR Calendar Competition, 1991. Collections: McDonald's Corp, Chicago, IL.

BUCKLEY, PATRICIA MORRISON

BUDDENBAUM, F. C. Indianapolis, IN.

BUDDENBAUM, RALPH L. Indianapolis, IN.

BUESCHER, HELEN A. [S, Cer, Por. P, T] Decatur, IN b. 22 Sep 1920, Ft Wayne, IN. Studied: St Francis Col; Ind. U-Purdue U, Ft Wayne. Teachers: Robert Barnum; Clyde Burt; Hector Garcia. Exhibited: Ind. State Fair, 1989; Ft Wayne Ventures since 1971. Collections: Decatur Public Library; Parkview Hospital; Lutheran Hospital; Decatur Mem Hospital.

BUFFINGTON, JULES O. [P] Peru, IN.

BULLOCK, RAY E. [S, T] Upland, IN b. 1930, Somerset, KY. Studied: Ball State U. Exhibited: Defiance Col (solo); Marion Col (solo); Taylor U (solo); IMA; Ind. A; Ind. A-Craftsman. Collections: Marion Col.

BULLOCK, WILLA HOWELL [Ldscp. P, Genre P] Peru, IN b. 13 Feb 1932, Peru, IN. Studied: John Herron AI. Teachers: Garo Antreasian; Robert Weaver. Exhibited: Ind.

Nat Bank, 1986-88; Honeywell Center, Wabash, 1988. Prizes: HS, 1982, 90; LAA, Logansport, 1988; Woman's A, Ft Wayne, 1989. Collections: Sq D Inc; Nixon Newspapers, Inc; Peru Trust Co.

BUNDY, FULTON A. Bedford, IN.

BUNDY, JOHN ELWOOD [Ldscp. P, Por. P] Richmond, IN b. 1 May 1853, Guilford Cnty, NC d. 17 Jan 1933, Cincinnati, OH. Self-taught. Exhibited: Richmond, 1907, 08; Corcoran A Gal; Nat Gal; AIC. Prizes: HS, 1927; Richmond, 1909, 11; Indianapolis AA, 1917; Herron AI, 1917. Note: Specialty, woodland scenes, especially beeches. Headed Earlham Col A Dept, 1887-1895.

BURCHETT, SHEILA K. [P] Indianapolis, IN b. 20 Jun 1952, Indianapolis. Studied: Herron Sch A. Exhibited: Jefferson Nat Insurance Co (solo), 1977; Logansport Bicentennial, 1976. Prizes: HS, 1976; 500 Festival. Collections: IMA.

BURDEN, ELIZABETH FLAGG [Ldscp. P] Indianapolis, IN b. 22 Aug 1920, Indianapolis. Studied: Arsenal Tech Sch; Herron AI. Teachers: Sara Bard; David Rubens; Edmund Brucker. Exhibited: Ind. WCS, 1985-87. Prizes: Ind. WCS, 1986, 87.

BURFORD, STANLEY L. [P, HPA, T] Indianapolis, IN b. 1936 Martinsville, IN. Studied: Herron Sch A; Butler U; Instituto Allende, San Miguel de Allende, Mexico. Exhibited: Ind. AC, 1970, 71(Pr), 72, 73(Pr), 74; Works on Paper, IMA, 1974; Mid-States A Exh, Evansville, IN, 1967-69, 74; JCC, Indianapolis, 1981. Note: T, Herron Sch A.

BURGAN, BETH A. [TA, S] Buffalo, NY b. 1945, Indianapolis, IN. Studied: Ball State U; Kent State U. Exhibitions: Ball State U, 1967; 500 Festival A, 1968; Akron AI, Akron, OH, 1972; Patteran Soc of Buffalo, 1974. Collections: Coronado Steel Government Sovern Mint Co, Youngstown, OH; Winona Building, Indianapolis, IN.

BURKE, FLORA M. Indianapolis, IN. d. 1985

BURKE, RICHARD

BURKE, ROBERT E. [P, T] Bloomington, IN b. 14 Sep 1884, Winchester, CT. Studied: Pratt Inst, Brooklyn, NY. Note: Head of FA Dept, Ind. U, Bloomington.

BURKETT, PEGGY Indianapolis, IN.

BURKHART, HELENE S0WERS. [P, Col. A, T] Indianapolis, IN b. 21 Jun 1909, Pike Cnty, IN d. 1982. Studied: Herron A Sch; IUPUI; Ind. U; Butler U, Indianapolis. Teachers: Clifton Wheeler; William Forsyth; Paul Hadley; Paul Sweany. Exhibited: 500 Festival of A; Ind. AC; Nat Min A Show of New Jersey; Scottsdale Gal, AZ; Oldfields, IMA. Note: T, Butler U; A Consultant, Indianapolis Public Sch.

BURKHOLDER, (Alyce) JUNE [P, SLP] West Lafayette, IN. b.18 Dec 1892, Westernill, OH. Studied: Ohio State U; Ind.; Ill.; Conn.; Fontainbleau A Sch, France. Teachers: L. O. Griffith; V. J. Cariani, Nashville; Sister Rufinia, Lafayette; Jacque Villon, Fontainbleau A Sch, France; Arnold Turtle, Chicago; Robert Brackman, Noanth, CT; Jerry Farnsworth. Exhibited: Herron AM, 1947; Oklahoma City A Gal, 1965. Prizes: HS, 1944, 51, 53, 56; Swope A Gal, 1957. Collections: Purdue U, West Lafayette; Ind. U, Duncan Hall; Swope Gal; Lafayette MA.

BURNS, JENE D. [P, Dr] Crawfordsville, IN b. 14 Jun 1917, near Richmond, IN. Self-taught. Prizes: HS, 1970. Note: Writer and Illustrator, *Journal Review*, Crawfordsville, IN.

BURNS, MARGARET [P] Brownsburg, IN b. 6 Dec 1918, Brownsburg, IN. Studied: Bendell A Sch, Bradenton, FL. Teachers: William Eyden; Marilyn Bendell; George Burrows; Ruth Anderson; Minnie Wiseman; Bernice Hufford. Prizes: Hendricks Cnty AL Exh, 1962, 65; Bendell Sch&Gal, 1980.

BURRIS, J(effrey) C. [Ldscp. P] Indianapolis, IN b. 21 Jan 1951, South Bend, IN. Self-taught. Exhibited: Eckert Gal (solo), Indianapolis, 1989; Evansville M, rental gal (solo), 1987; Frames & Things Gal (solo), Indianapolis, 1990. Prizes: HS, 1984, 90; Ind. AC, 1984, 85; Southside Reg, 1987; Wabash Valley Exh, 1983. Collections: Indianapolis Athletic Cl; Methodist Hospital, Indianapolis; First Nat Bank, Terre Haute.

BURROWS, MARY

BURTON, RON [P] Indianapolis, IN b. Spiceland, IN. Collections: Wall of Fame, Speedway M, Indianapolis. Note: A race car mechanic; specialized in painting racing art. Owned gallery across from the Indianapolis "500" Speedway racetrack.

BUSCHMANN, GLADYS F. [P, T] Painesville, OH b. Sunman, IN. Studied: Herron Sch A. Exhibited: HS A Gal, 1962; Cleveland MA; Ind. AC; Ohio WCS; Ohio Valley Oil&WC Show. Prizes: HS, 1951. Note: Was display and advertising artist for L. S. Ayres. T, Euclid H.S., Painesville.

BUSHMAN, LEO N. [P, Ldscp. P, Print] Calgary, Alberta b. 18 May 1917, Mishawaka, IN. Studied: AIC. Teachers: Emile Zettler; Edward Ropp. Exhibited: Nickle AM, U of Calgary, 1980; Triangle Gal, Calgary, 1992. Prizes: Intl Dr&WC, AIC, 1939, 41; South West Ann WC&Dr, Dallas, 1957. Collections: AIC; AMACO, Canada; Calgary Cont A Triangle Gal; U of Notre Dame, Snite M; U of Calgary Nickle AM. Note: Curator of A, Arctic Inst of N. Am, U of Calgary.

BUTLER, DEAN [S, T] Decatur, IN b. 7 Sep 1919, Hudson, IN. Studied: Ft Wayne A Sch; Ind. U. Prizes: Wassenberg A Cen, Van West, OH; Jay Cnty A Cen, Portland, IN. Collections: Glenbrook Square, Ft Wayne; Ft Wayne Public Library.

BUTTON, DAVID Kendallville, IN.

BUTTS, CLEMENCE N. [P] Carmel, IN.

BYRUM, RUTHVEN HOLMES [P, Ldscp. P, W, T] Anderson, IN b. 10 Jul 1896, Grand Junction, MI d. 1958. Studied: Ind. U; Académie de la Grande Chaumière, Académie Julian, Paris; AIC. Teachers: Andre Lhote, Paris; Hans Hofmann, Munich. Exhibited: John Herron AI, 1943 (Pr); HS, 1942 (Pr); Ind. State Fair, 1928, 29, 32-36, 38, 39 (Pr); Ind. AC, 1928-38, 39 (Pr), 1940, 41, 42 (Pr); 43-46; AIC, 1931, 39; Corcoran A Gal, Washington, D.C. Collections: Anderson YMCA; Anderson Col; Swope AG; Richmond AA; Ind. U. Note: I, *Mr. Noah's ABC Book*. Head of A Department, Anderson Col.

C

THE
17TH ANNUAL
★ **HOOSIER SALON**

Under Auspices of the
HOOSIER SALON PATRONS ASSOCIATION

JANUARY 27 THROUGH
FEBRUARY 8, 1941

Purpose:
HOOSIER ART AND
LITERATURE IN EVERY
AMERICAN HOME

THE PICTURE GALLERIES
MARSHALL FIELD & COMPANY
CHICAGO

CADY, CHARLES J. [Des, P] Terre Haute, IN b. Farmersburg, IN. Studied: La. Tech U; Aspen Sch Cont A, Aspen, CO. Teachers: Larry Day; Tom Larkin; Edgar Whitney; Milford Zornes; John Laska; Elmer Porter. Exhibited: Swope Gal, 1960, 61 (Pr), 62, 66, 67; M of A&Sc, 1955, 56, 70; Paris AL, 1957, 59, 61-65, 68 (5 Prs); HS, 1965 (Pr). Collections: Ind. State U; Rose Hulman Inst; Marathon Oil Co. Note: Formed Cady Industrial Des, 1967. Retired 1981.

CADY, ROSLYNN WEBB [Ldscp. P, Por. P] Carmel, IN b. 28 May 1943, Philadelphia, PA. Teachers: Alex Yaworski; Rush Cole. Exhibited: IMA, 1983; Knickerbocker A Nat Open, NYC, 1989; Nat Soc of P in Casein&Acrylic, NYC, 1990. Prizes: HS, 1982; IMA, 1983; Ind. State Pen Women Exh., 1980; Earlanger Mem Award, Nat Soc of P in Casein&Acrylic, NYC, 1989. Collections: Indianapolis-Marion Cnty Public Library; Merchants Nat Bank.

CAIN, ROSS B. Brookfield, IL.

CALDWELL, HELEN (W.) [S] Bloomington, IN. Prizes: HS, 1979, 82.

CALDWELL, JOAN [P] Indianapolis, IN. Studied: Herron AI. Exhibited: Nat Acad Gal, NY; Boston MFA; Springfield (Mass.) MFA; Miss. AA, Jackson. Prizes: Ind. State Fair.

CALVERT, TRUDY L. [I, Ldscp. P, SLP, Por. P] Bloomington, IN b. 24 Mar 1951, Salem, IN. Studied: Ind. U, Bloomington. Exhibited: South Side AL, 1990; Fall Foliage Festival, 1979, 87, 88; Depot A Festival, 1988. Prizes: IHA, 1990; Fall Foliage Festival, 1986, 89, 90; Depot A Festival, 1989, 90. Collections: Curtin Imprint, Inc, Logo Design; South Ind. Conference United Methodist Church; Girl Scouts of America; Monroe Cnty Public Library, Bloomington.

CAMBRIDGE, STEPHANIE [P] Frankfort, IN b. Springfield, IL. Teachers: William Eyden; Ruth Anderson; G. S. Robertson. Exhibited: Clinton Cnty Fair; Clayton House Gal, St Louis, MO. Prizes: Tippecanoe Reg. Collections: Brickers Construction Co, Frankfort, IN; Patton Interiors, Coronado, CA; Frankfort Country Cl.

CAMERON, S. N. [P] Indianapolis, IN.

CAMMACK, DYNA [P] Greencastle, IN. Prizes: HS, 1953. Note: Known throughout state as gardener and naturalist.

CANADY, HELEN D. [Ldscp. P, SLP] Anderson, IN. Teachers: Ruthven Byrum; George Jo Mess; Gianni Cilfone. Prizes: HS, 1954. Note: Married to artist Read B. Canady.

CANADY, READ B. Anderson, IN d. c. 1969. Note: Married to artist Helen D. Canady.

CANNON, ALISON R. [P, Por P] b. c. 1958. Studied: Washington U. Teachers: John Laska. Note: She was a high school student briefly at Ind. State U Lab Sch.

CANNON, CATHY (Catherine) [P] Elwood, IN.

CANNON, VIOLA [P] Indianapolis, IN. Deceased. Note: Member, Brown Cnty A Gal.

CAPEK, LOREN LEE [Ab] Chicago, IL b. 1955, LaPorte, IN. Studied: Herron Sch A. Exhibited: Ind. A Show, IMA, 1981.

CARDWELL, JO ANN [P, T] Greenwood, IN b. 14 Nov 1936, Jefferson City, MO. Studied: Kansas City AI; Lincoln U, MO. Teachers: Marilyn Phyllis; Virginia Cobb. Exhibited: Ind. State Fair; 500 A Festival; IHA; Ind. AC, 1978-1990; Anderson WC Show; Ind. WCS, 1986, 87, 90. Prizes: Tippecanoe Reg, 1973; Ind. AC, 1986; Ind. WCS, 1990. Collections: Indianapolis Power and Light; Jefferson Nat Life Insurance Co; Boehringer Mannheim Corp; Emerald Technology, Inc.

CAREY, JERRY L. [P, Print, Photo] Indianapolis, IN b. c. 1944. Studied: U of Md.; Herron Sch A.; Ind. U. Teachers: Paul Sweany. Exhibited: Impressions Gal (solo), Indianapolis, 1979; HS, traveling show, 1972; Herron Gal, 1976-78; Butler Inst Am A 42nd Ann Show, 1978, Youngstown, OH; Mid-States Show, Evansville, 1980. Prizes: Art 500, Indianapolis AL, 1977.

CARIANI, V(araldo) J. (Giuseppe) [Ldscp. P, Por. P, Mur. P] Nashville, IN b. 8 Feb 1891, Renazzo, Italy d. 30 Dec 1969. Studied: N.Y. Acad FA; NAD; ASL. Teachers: Luis Mora; Emil Carlsen; George DeForest Brush; Frank V.

DuMond; Douglas Volk. Prizes: Tiffany Fnd Fellowship, 1922; Springfield AL, 1923; HS, 1934, 38, 44, 45, 48, 50, 69; Brown Cnty A Gal, 1943; Ind. AC, 1945. Collections: Ind. U; Indianapolis Public Sch; Statehouse, IN; Hanover Col, IN. Note: Anglicized his middle name Giuseppe to Joseph giving him the initials V. J. Moved to Brown Cnty where he worked for artist Marie Goth's father until he became sufficiently established to support himself with his art. Cariani built a studio on the Goth property near Marie Goth's studio. He was well known for his cloud and floral paintings. In 1933, one of 20 artists selected from Ind. to exhibit at the Chicago World Fair.

CARLOCK, VERNON THORWALD [S, Des] Dayton, OH b. 2 Aug 1912, Evansville, IN. Collections: Dayton AI; bas relief, USPO, Worthington, OH; WPA A.

CARLSON, CHRISTINE N. [Dr, I] Indianapolis, IN b. 31 May 1948, St Louis, MO. Studied: Herron AI; Indianapolis AL. Teachers: Edmund Brucker.

CARLSON, EDWARD W. [Min, P] Chicago, IL b. 4 May 1883, Chicago. Studied: AIC. Exhibited: AIC. Prizes: HS, Chicago, 1928; Swedish Am AA, Chicago, 1929.

CARMACK, JEAN E. [P, Dr] Anderson, IN b. Anderson, IN. Teachers: Kayton. Exhibited: Anderson FA Cen; Indianapolis 500; Ind. State Fair; Ball State Col.

CARMICHAEL, DON [P] Jackson, TN b. 1922, Elnora, IN. Studied: Herron AI. Teachers: John Taylor; David Friedenthal; Edwin Fulwider; Garo Antreasian. Exhibited: Tenn. Painting Today, 1967; Intl Woodworking Expo (solo), Louisville, KY, 1968; Retrospective 20 Years, Union U, 1969; Exh South '73, Tenn. Valley A Cen, Tuscumbia, AL. Collections: Cheekwood FA Cen, Nashville, TN; Jackson Mental Health Cen; Student Union, U of Tenn., Martin; Union U.

CARMIN, TIM [P, S, Print, T] Marion, IN b. Marion. Studied: Ball State U. Prizes: Ind. State Fair, 1973; Anderson Redbud Show. Collections: Madison Cnty Courthouse; Ind. Supreme Court. Note: T, Northside Jr H.S., Anderson, IN.

CARR, ELMER B. Indianapolis, IN.

CARR, SHIRLEY WERNER *(See Werner, Shirley J.)* [P] Indianapolis, IN. Studied: Purdue U. Teachers: Floyd Hopper; Harry Davis; Paul Sweany; Jean Vietor. Exhibited: IMA; Tippecanoe A Festival; 500 Exh; Ind. State Fair; Ind. AC.

CARREL, ELIZABETH (Beth) [Ab] Angola, IN b. 2 Mar 1916, Terre Haute, IN. Studied: John Herron AI; Indianapolis AL. Teachers: George Jo Mess; Robert Berkshire. Exhibited: Lafayette A Cen, 1973; Art Link (solo), Ft Wayne, 1979-80. Prizes: Am Interior Des, 1966; Lincoln Life, 1980; General Telephone, 1987. Collections: Ft Wayne MA; Lafayette A Cen; Lincoln Life Insurance Co; General Telephone.

CARROTHERS, GRACE NEVILLE [P, Print, T] Tulsa, OK b. Abington, IN. Studied: Bellaire, MI. Teachers: John Carlson; Anthony Thieme. Exhibited: Northwest Pr. M, 1932; Kansas City AI, 1933; N.Y. Mun Exh, 1937. Collections: NYPL; Gibbes A Gal, Charleston, SC; NGA; British M. Note: Instructor, Ldscp. P, Philbrook A Cen, 1940-46; Head, Grace Neville Carrothers Sch Ldscp. P, 1932-46.

CARTER, ALAN L. [Ldscp. P, SLP] Terre Haute, IN b. Lafayette, IN. Self-taught. Exhibited: Franklin Barry Gal, 1982, Zionsville, IN; Gal Frame Des, Indianapolis, 1990.

CARTER, EFFIE F. [P, T] Chesterton, IN b. Sep 1888, Indianapolis, IN d. 7 Feb 1981. Studied: Indianapolis T Col; N.Y. TC; Glouchester, Mass. Sch A. Teachers: Della Brown; Otto Stark; T. C. Steele; J. Ottis Adams; C. Curry Bohm; Emile Gruppe; George Dinkle; J. C. Templeton. Collections: Indianapolis Public Sch. Note: Restored damaged paintings. T, East Side A Cen; T, A Cen AG; T, LaRue Carter Hospital. One of the founding members, Ind. AG.

CARTER, GEORGIA [Print] Greenfield, IN.

CARTER, MARY JO [P, T] Marion, IN b. Marion. Studied: Marion Col A Sch; Ft Wayne Sch A. Teachers: Mary Clark; Lou Charles Marion; Leota W. Loop. Prizes: Federated Cl; Ind. State Fair. Note: Wrote manuscript, *Art of Living* .

CARTON, WINIFRED [P] Earl Park, IN.

CASEY, WARREN VALE [S, T] Muncie, IN. Prizes: Ind. State Fair, 1948; Ohio State Fair, 1948; Intl S Show, Philadelphia.

CASS, PAUL [Ldscp. P, P] Crawfordsville, IN.

CASSELL, MARIAN SIMON [Des] Indianapolis, IN. Studied: Herron Sch A. Note: Designed kitchens for her husband, builder Leo Cassell.

CASWELL, GLADYS [P] Indianapolis, IN. Studied: Herron Sch A; Detroit Sch of App A. Teachers: Zoltan Sepeshy; William Forsyth; Albert Krehbiel. Exhibited: HS A Gal (solo), 1951. Note: Worked in A Dept, Wm. H. Block Co.

CATHELL, EDNA S. (Mrs. J. E.) [P, S] Richmond, IN b. 1 Nov 1867, Richmond, IN d. 1955. Studied: Cumming A Sch, IA. Teachers: John E. Bundy; Randolph Coats; John M. King. Exhibited: Richmond A; Ind. AC.

CAUBLE, MARCELLA [P] Greenwood, IN. Exhibited: United Life Insurance Bldg, 1976. Prizes: Ind. Fed AC.

CAULDWELL, CHERRI Brownsburg, IN. Studied: Indianapolis AL.

CHALLINOR, MURIEL

CHAMBERLIN, GEORGE L. [Ldscp. P] Indianapolis, IN b. Indianapolis. Teachers: G. Ames Aldrich; Leon Makielski.

CHANNELS, VERA G. [Ab, Dr, Ldscp. P, Col. A] Terre Haute, IN b. 28 Jan 1915, Trenton, ND. Studied: Ind. State U. Teachers: Louise Hansen; Catherine Knight. Exhibited: Swope AM, 1988-90; Southside AL, Inc, 1987.

CHAPPELL, JOANNE Note: Owner and operator of Editions Limited Gal, Indianapolis. Moved to Calif.; opened a similar gallery there.

CHASE, JAMES K. [T] Muncie, IN b. Logansport, IN. Studied: Ind. U; Ball State U; Mich. State U; N. M. Exhibited: One-man shows in NYC, Kalamazoo, Midland, Sturgis, Mt Pleasant and Saugatuck, MI. Collections: Randall Publishing House, Detroit; Northwood Inst. Note: Chairman A Dept, Northwood Inst.

CHATTIN, LOU-ELLEN *(See Showe, Lou-Ellen Chattin)* [P] Towson, MD/Chatauqua, NY b. 16 Nov 1891, Temple, TX d. 8 Oct 1937. Teachers: J. F. Carlson; DuMond; G. Bridgman; O. Linde; Kathryn C. Cherry.

CHESNUL, CHARLES

CHICKADAUNCE, LOUETA [Dr, Por. P, P] Terre Haute, IN. Teachers: John Laska. Note: High Sch student, Ind. State U Lab Sch, early 1970s.

CHINWORTH, LOUESE GYPSY (Mrs. Wm. J.) Warsaw, IN.

CHIPMAN, C. DEAN [Print, T, M Dir] Elgin, IL b. 6 Jun 1908, La Porte, IN. Studied: Columbia U; Northwestern U; Kunstgewerbe Schule, Vienna. Exhibited: St Louis AG; St Louis AM; Fox Valley AA, Elgin, IL. Note: T, Monticello Col, Godfrey, IL, 1935-40. T/Dir A Gal, The Elgin Acad.

CHLEBEK, MICHELE [MM] South Bend, IN.

CHOGAS, JOHN A. [P] Logansport, IN.

CHRISTEL, LEO C.

CHRISTENSEN, SUSAN M. [Des] Indianapolis, IN b. 24 May 1936, Chicago, IL. Studied: Bradley U, Peoria, IL; Northwestern U, Chicago Campus; AIC; Indianapolis AL. Exhibited: Eastern Ind. Exh, Muncie; Franklin Col (solo); Jewish Community Center (solo). Prizes: Mid-States Exh, Evansville M of A⪼ 500 Festival A. Collections: Evansville M of A&Sc.

CHRISTIAN, GRANT WRIGHT [P, T] Monhegan Island, ME b. 17 Jul 1911, Edinburg, IN d. 21 May 1989. Studied: Herron A Sch; PAFA. Teachers: William Forsyth; Clifton Wheeler; David Rubins; Frank Schoonover; Donald M. Mattison; Henrik M. Mayer; Hugh Breckenridge; George Harding; Henry McCarter; Daniel Garber. Exhibited: Ind. AC; Herron AM; Ind. A Ann; Grand Central Gal, N.Y.; Corcoran Gal, Washington, D. C.; Swope Gal, Terre Haute, IN. Prizes: HS, 1936, 37, 73, 78, 87-89; PAFA; Ind. State Fair, 1973; Ann Heritage A Exh, Nashville, IN, 1979; PAFA. Collections: USPOs in Indianapolis and Nappanee; WPA A. Note: T, Ind. U, 1936-37. Joined Keeling&Co A Dept, 1937; joined A Dept, Quinlan, Keene, Peck&McShay Advertising Agency, 1969; joined the Mathewson Group Advertising Agency, 1972.

CHRISTOPHER, ROSEMARIE [Ldscp. P, Genre P, Por. P] Knightstown, IN b. 18 Apr 1943, Chicago, IL. Studied: Ind. U, East; AL. Teachers: Luke Buck; Dora Hagge; Tom Thomas; Paul Sweany; Jean Vietor; Joanne Cardwell. Exhibited: Richmond Ann Exh, 1991; Ind. Heritage, Brown Cnty, 1989-90. Prizes: New Castle AA, 1988; Tri Kappa, 1991.

CHRISTY

CHUPACK, JEANETTE [P] Littleton, NH. Prizes: HS, 1972.

CILFONE, GIANNI [P, T] Chicago, IL b. 20 Jan 1908, San Marco, Foggia, Italy. Studied: Chicago Acad FA; AIC. Teachers: Hugh Breckenridge; John F. Carlson; Antonio Pacioni; Mario Caldarelli; J. Wellington Reynolds; DeForest Shook; Abraham Poole; Carl Scheffler. Exhibited: North Shore AA, Gloucester, Summer 1945; Allied A NYC, 1946; Audubon A 6th Ann, NYC, 1947; AIC, 1919, 28; Chicago Gal Assn, 1940-46; SC, 1945, 46. Prizes: HS, 1950, 52, 53, 56; Chicago Gal Assn, 1943, 45; SC, 1943, 44; Mun AL, Chicago, 1946. Collections: Michigan City (Ind.) Library Assn; Midwest AA, Chicago; Hawthorne Public Sch, Elmhurst, IL. Note: HS juror, 1946. Had art studio in Nashville, 1951.

CLAPP, MARCIA (Mrs. Jovan De Rocco) [S, Com. A, T] NYC/Bushkill (in the mountains of PA) b. 7 Dec 1907, Hartsville, IN. Studied: John Herron A Sch; Butler U; ASL. Teachers: Myra Richards; William Zorach. Exhibited: NAD, 1931, 32; PAFA, 1932; Indianapolis (solo), 1934. Prizes: Herron AI, 1931.

CLARK, C. OLIN [SLP] Warren, IN.

CLARK, GEORGIABELLE [P] Cincinnati, OH b. Indianapolis, IN d. c. 1978. Studied: John Herron AI. Teachers: Emma Mendenhall; Carl Zimmerman; William Gebhardt; John Imhoff. Exhibited: Ohio WCS Traveling Show; Zoo A Festival, Cincinnati; Cincinnati A, Cincinnati AM. Prizes: HS, 1961; Woman's AC; Ohio Oil and WC Show, Athens, OH. Collections: Mariemont Recreation Cen; Southeastern Ind. Rehabilitation Cen, Jefferson, IN.

CLARK, HARLEY D. [Des] Bloomington, IN. Prizes: HS, 1930.

CLARK, KATHRYN H(augh) [Print, HPA, T] Brookston, IN b. 25 Jan 1944, Indianapolis, IN. Studied: Wittenberg U, Springfield, OH; Wayne State U, Detroit, MI; San Francisco AI; Master Printer, Collectors Press, San Francisco, CA. Teachers: Richard Graf; Stanley Rosenthal; Aris Koutroulis. Exhibited: PM Gal (solo), San Francisco; Purdue U (solo), West Lafayette, IN. Collections: Oakland M; U of Calif., Berkeley, CA; Calif. Soc of PM; M of Paper Chemistry, Appleton, WI. Prizes: HS, 1971. Note: Owner and paper-maker, Twinrocker, Inc; Director, Purdue Cen for Handcrafted Papers.

CLARK, MARION [Com. A, Por. P] Brownsburg, IN b. c. 1917.

CLARK, MERRILL WARD Indianapolis, IN b. Jessup, Park Cnty, IN. Studied: AIC; John Herron AI. Exhibited: Brown Cnty Gal.

CLARK, OPAL [Quilling] Bedford, IN.

CLARK, VIRGINIA KEEP (Mrs. Marshall) [I, P, Por. P] Winter Park, FL b. 17 Feb 1878, New Orleans, LA. Studied: Ind. Sch A; Chase Sch; ASL. Teachers: William Forsyth; K. Cox; C. Beckwith; H. Pyle. Exhibited: PAFA; Corcoran Gal A; Montross Gal (solo); NAWA. Prizes: AIC, 1923, 26. Note: I, *Live Doll Series*.

CLARK, VIVIAN D. Indianapolis, IN.

CLARKE, THEA [P] Indianapolis, IN b. 21 Nov 1943, Johannesburg, South Africa. Studied: Indianapolis AL. Teachers: Christopher Schink; Paul Sweany; Jerry Smith; Janet Walsh; Jeanne McLeish; Emel Doner. Exhibited: Ind. State Fair, 1986; Ind. AC, 1990. Prizes: Indianapolis AL, 1989; Ind. WCS, 1987, 89, 90; Hamilton Cnty AA, 1989, 90. Collections: Merchants Nat Bank; IMA, rental gal.

CLAY, KAY [P, Cer, Dr, T] Indianapolis, IN. Studied: John Herron A Sch. Exhibitions: Ransburg Gal, Ind. Central U (solo); Jewish Community Cen (solo); IMA, rental gal; Linker Gal, Ft Wayne, IN. Prizes: Ind. A Show; 500 Festival A; DePauw U Cer Show; Ind. A-Craftsmen. Note: T, A Dept Head, Crispus Attucks H.S.; T, John Herron A Sch; T, Indianapolis AL; T, IUPUI.

CLEAR, STEVEN (L.) [P] Indianapolis, IN b. 1954, Indianapolis. Studied: IUPUI. Exhibited: Ind. A Show, IMA, 1979.

CLEAVER, ANNE K. HOFFMAN [Por. P, Print] Westfield, IN b. 1914, Ft Wayne, IN. Studied: Wellesley Col; AIC; Saugatuck Summer Sch of A; Ft Wayne A Sch; John Herron A Sch; Indianapolis AL. Exhibited: Ft Wayne MA; Ind. AC; Davidson Nat Print&Drawing Exh, Davidson, NC; Mich. P&Print Exh, Grand Rapids; Hunterdon A Cen Nat Print Show, Clinton, NJ. Prizes: HS, 1973, 75; Ind. State Fair; Art 500.

CLEMENTS, EILEEN [P] Danville, IN.

CLEVELAND, ROBERT W.

CLOETINGH, JAMES H. [P, Des] South Bend, IN b. 3 Jul 1894, Muskegan, MI d. c. 1965. Teachers: Raymond Weir, England; Emil Jacques, Harry Muir Kurtzworth, Belgium. Exhibited: Northern Ind. A, 1940, 41; Hackley A Gal (solo), 1943; Wawasee A Gal, 1938-40.

CLOSSON, NANCI BLAIR [P] Indianapolis, IN b. Durham, NC. Studied: Purdue U, West Lafayette, IN. Exhibited: WC USA; Am WCS; Nat WCS; San Diego WCS; Western Fed of WCS. Prizes: HS, 1971, 73-80, 81, 83; WC USA; Audubon Artists. Collections: Ind. U, Student Union; Springfield AM, Springfield, MO. Note: Lived also in Logansport, IN and Tucson, AZ.

CLOUD, C. CAREY [P, Des, I] Brown Cnty, IN b. 12 Mar 1899, Whistleville, Wells Cnty, IN d. 9 Nov 1984, Tucson, AZ. Self-taught. Collections: Truman Library, Independence, MO. Note: Designer of toys until 1964. Designed and produced the toys found in "Cracker Jack" boxes. Authored book of memoirs, *Cloud Nine—the Dreamer and the Realist*, 1983.

CLUSMANN, WILLIAM [P, Ldscp. P] Chicago, IL b. 1859, North LaPorte, IN d. 28 Sep 1927. Studied: Royal Acad, Munich. Teachers: Gyula Benczur. Exhibited: P.-P. Expo. Prizes: Stuttgart, Germany, 1884; AIC, 1913, 19; HS, 1925. Collections: AIC; City of Chicago; Evanston (Ill.) Woman's Cl; Governor's Mansion, Springfield.

CLUTE, IDA MARTIN [I] Indianapolis, IN b. Poplar Creek, MS d. c. 1952. Studied: ASL; Chase A Sch. Teachers: John H. Twachtman; Douglas Volk; H. Siddons Mowbray; Frederick W. Freer; William M. Chase; William F. Kaeser. Exhibited: Herron AM; ASL, Indianapolis; Ind. AC. Note: I, *Fern Allies of North America;* Co-illustrator, *Ferns: Agronomy.*

COATES, RUTH ALLISON (Mrs. Robert E. Coates) [SLP, Por. P] Indianapolis, IN b. Mt Carmel, IL. Studied: Ind. U; Bethel Woman's Col. Teachers: Helen Wallace. Note: Worked in Com A Dept, L. S. Ayres, late 1930s. Reporter, *Mt. Carmel Daily Republican Register* and feature writer, *Evansville Courier.*

COATS, RANDOLPH LaSALLE [P, Ldscp. P, Por. P, Li, T] Indianapolis, IN b. 14 Sep 1891, Richmond, IN d. Jun 1957. Studied: Herron Sch A; Cincinnati Acad FA, OH. Teachers: William Forsyth; J. R. Hopkins; Frank Duveneck. Exhibited: Société Nationale des Beaux-Arts, Paris, France; AIC; John Herron AI; Sesquicentennial Expo, Philadelphia; CI; AIC; CM; PAFA; Buffalo AM, NY; Grand Rapids A Gal, MI; AM Toronto, Canada. Prizes: HS, 1925-27, 29, 44, 46; Chicago Gal Assoc, 1928; Ind. State Fair. Collections: Richmond Ind. AA; John Herron AI; Gary (Ind) AA.

COBB, CAROLYN [P, Print, Col. A] Evansville, IN. Exhibited: Mid-States Comp, Evansville M, 1982. Note: Owner, Showcase Studio.

COBB, THEA Bedford, IN.

COBLE, DAN R. [P] Wabash, IN.

COBLE, MARLENE [P] Wabash, IN. Prizes: HS, 1980.

COBLENTZ, LEE [P] Ft Wayne. Prizes: HS, 1968, 78, 79.

COFFEY, ALTON P(owell). [Ldscp. P, Por. P] Brown Cnty, IN b. 3 Jul 1904, Brown Cnty, IN d. 15 Jul 1978, Nashville, IN. Studied: Butler U; Herron Sch A. Teachers: William Forsyth; Clifton Wheeler; Myra Reynolds

Richards; Will Vawter; Edward K. Williams. Prizes: HS, 1930. Collections: Brown Cnty Court House.

COFFMAN, DORIS J. Indianapolis, IN.

COHAN, BEVERLY [Dr, Print, Por. P, T, Photo] Indianapolis, IN b. 17 Apr 1926, N.Y., NY. Studied: Hunter Col, NYC; U of Mexico; Herron A Sch; Indianapolis AL. Teachers: Amanda Block; William Ashby; Fred Wrigley. Exhibited: Hoosier 500; Ball State U; Ind. State Fair; Indianapolis AL. Prizes: Indianapolis AL. Collections: Prithy/Pac, Inc.

COLE, RUSH [Por. P, Ldscp. P, SLP] Indianapolis, IN b. 10 Apr 1951, Vincennes, IN. Self-taught. Exhibited: Am WCS, 1988; Nat AC, NYC, 1987; WC West; Midwest WCS. Prizes: Nat WCS, 1988; HS, 1988; Ind. AC, 1987. Collections: Ind. State M; Eli Lilly&Co; Advak Naval M, Advak, AL; Dean Witter Reynolds; Bayfront Plaza Convention Center, Corpus Christi, TX.

COLER, STELLA C. [P] Indianapolis, IN b. 29 Jul 1892, Grand Rapids, MI. Studied: U of Mich.; John Herron A Sch; ASL. Teachers: Eliot O'Hara; Jerry Farnsworth; Aaron Bohrod; Herbert Stoddard. Exhibited: John Herron AI; TMA, 1941, 44; Rollins Col, 1942-44, 46; Ind. AC, 1946, 50, 51, 54; Sarasota AA, 1951. Prizes: HS, 1947, 53-55, 63, 64. Note: Instructor, Indianapolis AL, 1953-55; President, Sarasota AA, 1955.

COLLINS, LYNDA [Dr, Print] Kokomo, IN. Exhibited: Kokomo Public Library (solo), 1985; World Championship Horse Show, Louisville, 1985; Greater Lafayette MA, Lafayette, IN, 1985; Intl Arabian Horse Show, Albuquerque, NM, 1980, 81, 83, 84. Collections: Ind. U, Kokomo.

COLVIN, WAYNE BENSON [P, Dr] Chicago, IL b. c. 1903, Indianapolis. Studied: AIC. Prizes: HS, 1926.

CONFER, THELMA (Mrs. Byron) [Ab, Ldscp. P, Por. P] Indianapolis, IN b. 15 Nov 1924, Macon Cnty, TN. Studied: Herron Sch of A. Exhibited: Ind. State M, 1974, 82; IMA, 1976. Prizes: HS, 1970, 82, 86; Am Assn State and Local History, 1977; Ind. AC, 1978; Whitewater Valley Exh, 1981. Collections: Ind. State M; IMA; Sheldon Swope Gal, Terre Haute; RCA; Indianapolis Life Insurance Co.

CONNAWAY, JAY HALL [P, T] Dorset, VT. b. 27 Nov 1893, Liberty, Union Cnty, IN d. 18 Feb 1970, Tucson, AZ. Studied: John Herron A Sch; ASL; Académie Julian, Paris; NAD; L'École des Beaux-Arts, Paris. Teachers: William Forsyth; George Bridgman; William Merritt Chase; Laurens. Exhibited: Corcoran Gal A, 1932-43; PAFA, 1926-43; NAD, 1924-46; AIC, 1928-40; Herron AM, c. 1966; MacBeth Gal (solo), NYC; Kennedy Gal (solo), NYC. Prizes: NAD, 1926; HS, 1947; NAC, 1928; Nat Acad A, N.Y., Hallgarten Pr; Schiff Pr; Hans Hinrich Pr; McCutcheon Pr for marine painting, Chicago; New Haven (Conn.) Paint&Clay Cl. Collections: John Herron AI; Sweat Mem AM; Canajoharie AM; Springville, Utah A Gal; Boston MFA. Note: Renowned marine painter. Lived for seventeen years on Monhegan Island, ME. T, Connaway's Monhegan A Sch, ME. Elected Associate, Nat Acad, 1933, Academician, 1943.

CONNELL, MARTHA J. [P] Indianapolis, IN b. Bedford, IN. Studied: Herron AI; IUPUI; Wendell Sch of A. Exhibited: Anderson Sch of A.

CONNELL, SYBIL H. [P, Ldscp. P, Por. P] Nashville,

IN/Bloomington, IN b. 1895, Dana, IN. Studied: Herron A Sch. Teachers: Harold Haven Brown; William Forsyth; Clifton Wheeler; Otto Stark; V. J. Cariani. Exhibited: Herron AM; L. S. Ayres&Co; Wawasee; Cincinnati AM. Prizes: Ind. State Fair. Note: Fashion and Com A at William H. Block Co, L. S. Ayres and H. P. Wasson; Com. A, Indianapolis Engraving Co.

CONNER, A. F. [SLP, P] Indianapolis, IN.

CONNER, NINA [Por. P, Dr] Studied: Herron Sch A. Collections: First Nat Bank, Monticello, IN.

CONNER, PAUL [P] Long Beach, CA. b. 5 Sep 1881, Richmond, IN d. 11 Mar 1968. Teachers: H. L. Richter; A. Clinton Conner. Exhibited: Southern Calif. Eisteddfod, 1926. Prizes: Long Beach AA, 1935. Collections: Athletic Cl, Los Angeles; Rockefeller Fnd, London, England; Ebell Cl, Long Beach.

CONNORS, CAROLYN SIHLER [P] Indianapolis, IN. Exhibited: Jewish Community Cen, Indianapolis, 1978; IMA, rental gal; Lockerbie Gal, Indianapolis.

CONSTABLE, CATHERINE Bloomington, IN.

CONWELL, WILLIAM J. Elwood, IN.

COOK, ALICE DIMMICK [P, T] Indianapolis, IN b. c. 1905, Boswell, IN d. 31 Dec 1990. Studied: Herron Sch A. Teachers: Eliot O'Hara; Gladys Rockmore Davis. Exhibited: Ind. State Fair; Ind. AC. Prizes: HS, 1947, 48; Glendale, 1971. Collections: Indianapolis Public Schs #70, #94; Harcourt Sch; Methodist Home, Franklin. Note: T, Indianapolis Public Schs; Indianapolis AL.

COOK, EDITH ROSE [P] Indianapolis, IN d. North Carolina. Studied: Indianapolis AL. Teachers: Ruth Anderson.

COOLER, Jr., HARRY E.

COONEY, MILDRED KELLER

COOPER, DANIEL R(aymond) [Ab, I, Graphic Design Computer Assisted Visual A] Indianapolis, IN b. 11 Feb 1952, Greensburg, IN. Studied: Arlington H.S.; Ind. U, Bloomington; Ind. Central U, Indianapolis. Teachers: Marjorie Hindman; Joan Simpson. Exhibited: Start with A, 1990; A Creative Affair, 1986.

COOPER, LUCILLE N. (Cille) [P] Anderson, IN/Ft Myers, FL b. 29 Jun 1924, Louisville, KY. Studied: Ohio State U. Teachers: Floyd Hopper; Paul Sweany; Judi Belts. Exhibited: Ind. WCS; Ind. A. Collections: Nyhart Co, Inc, Indianapolis; Eli Lilly, Indianapolis.

COOPER, WAYNE [P] Hebron, IN Studied: Famous A Sch; Valparaiso U. Exhibited: Gilcrease M, Tulsa, OK. Prizes: Ind. A Exh, 1976.

CORRELL, IRA A. [Ldscp. P, Arch, S] Austin, TX b. 2 Feb 1873, Clarksburg, IN d. 4 Feb 1964. Teachers: David Richards; Lorado Taft. Collections: Statue of Abraham Lincoln, Odon, IN; St Joan of Arc, Indianapolis; British and French Embassies, Washington, D.C.; Texas State Centennial, Dallas; Sterling Library, Yale U.

CORTELLINI, CONRAD [Dr, S, P, Arch, T] Indianapolis, IN b. c. 1943, Ancona, Italy. Studied: Herron Sch A. Note: Architectural and commercial designer. Designed several O'Malia Food Markets, Indianapolis.

CORYN, C(elest) E. [P, Com. A] Indianapolis, IN.

COTHRAN, BILLIE [P, Por. P, T] Indianapolis, IN b. 26 Sep 1907, Chillicothe, MO d. 25 Jun 1980. Studied: Jack-

son U; Jerry Farnsworth Sch A; ASL. Teachers: Brackman; Elmer Taflinger; George Jo Mess; Floyd Hopper; Ruth Anderson. Exhibited: Indianapolis AL, 1975; Wabash Valley Exh; Ball State U; Ind. State Fair; Ind. AC. Prizes: HS, 1961. Note: T, Indianapolis AL.

COURET, HORTENSIA Indianapolis, IN.

COVARRUBIAS, JOY [P] Mexico City, Mexico.

COWAN, JACK D.[Genre P] Franklin, IN b. 14 Aug 1962, Orlando, FL. Self-taught. Prizes: HS, 1990.

COX, JACOB [Por. P, Ldscp. P, SLP] Indianapolis, IN b. 9 Nov 1810, Burlington, NJ d. 2 Jan 1892. Studied: NAD, 1860. Collections: IMA; Ind. Statehouse. Note: Started a copper and tinware business with his two brothers in Indianapolis before becoming a full-time artist. Painted six Ind. governor's portraits. Cox's work exhibited at first Hoosier Salon posthumously.

COX, JOHN ROGERS [P] Wenatchee, WA b. 24 Mar 1915, Terre Haute, IN. Studied: PAFA; U of Pa. Exhibited: CI, 1941, 45, 46; PAFA, 1944; AIC, 1944, 45. Prizes: AV, 1942; CI, 1943, 44. Collections: CMA; *Encyclopaedia Britannica* Coll. Note: First Dir, Sheldon Swope Gal.

COX, JOSEPH H. [P, Edu] Raleigh, NC b. 4 May 1915, Indianapolis, IN. Studied: John Herron AI; U of Iowa. Teachers: Donald Mattison; Eliot O'Hara; Jean Charlot; Philip Guston; Leo Lasanski. Exhibited: Grand Central Gal; GGE, 1939; Raleigh Mun Bldg (solo), 1985; Then and Now Retrospective, 1992; N.C. State A Exh; Herron AI; N.C. A Ann, 1965-71. Prizes: HS, 1943; Ind. A Exh, 1939; Knoxville A Cen, 1955; Tenn. State Fair; Achievement in A Award, Raleigh, 1984; Outstanding T&Distinguished Alumni Professor, 1972-75. Collections: Chrysler M, Norfolk, VA; Mint M, Charlotte, VA; Herron AM; Nat Hist M, U of Iowa; murals in USPOs in Garrett, IN and Alma, MI; Denver AM; U of Ill. Note: T, U of Iowa; T, U of Tenn.; T, U of Fla.; T, N.C. State U and Sch of Des. Note: Son of artist Charlotte Sidman.

COX, KERMIT OWEN [Ab, Ldscp. P, I, P, Photo] Carmel, IN b. 10 Oct 1938, Shelbyville, IN. Studied: Herron AI. Teachers: Harry Davis; Renaldo Paluzzi. Prizes: 500 Festival of A, late-1960s.

CRADICK, RAYMOND V. [Genre P] Indianapolis, IN b. 4 Apr 1918, Indianapolis. Studied: U of Cincinnati. Teachers: Sara Bard; Frederick Polley; John F. Simpson; Ruth Kothe; Elizabeth Jasper; Reginald Grooms. Exhibited: AL WCS, 1986, 88; Honeywell Mem Cen, Wabash, IN (solo), 1985; Ann Mid-States Exh, Evansville, IN, 1983-85. Prizes: HS, 1983; Wabash Valley Exh, Swope Gal, 1985; Evansville M, 1987. Collections: Evansville M of A⪼ Mead Johnson Company; Bristol-Myers.

CRAIG, HELEN C. [P, T] Indianapolis, IN b. 1 Oct 1917 Harco, IL d. c. 1990. Studied: Indianapolis AL. Teachers: Floyd Hopper; Rosemary Lawton Thomas; Edward Manetta. Exhibited: Ind. AC; 500 A Show; Ind. State Fair; Washington, D.C. Min A Show, 1970. Prizes: HS, 1978. Collections: Connersville Bank; Farm Bureau Insurance Co.

CRAIG, LUCILE KIRK

CRAIG, RALPH SPANN [P, Des, T] Indianapolis, IN b. 3 Nov 1908, Jefferson Cnty, IN d. 3 Mar 1983. Studied: Herron A Sch; Elmer E. Taflinger Sch; ASL; Beaux-Arts, Paris. Teachers: William Forsyth; Clifton Wheeler; Ralph

Sowell; Oakley Richey; Paul Hadley; Frank V. DuMond; P. A. Laurens. Exhibited: Ind. State Fair, 1928, 29 (Pr), 36. Collections: Children's M, Indianapolis. Note: Head A Dept, Arsenal Tech H.S., Indianapolis. Stained glass artist for 31 years with Capitol Glass.

CRAIG, ROBERT C. [P, Print, Li, T, C] Indianapolis, IN/Eastport, ME b. Spencer, IN. Studied: Bradley Polytechnic Inst. Teachers: William Forsyth; George Pearse Ennis. Exhibited: Herron AM (two-man), 1947; PAFA; AWCS; LOC, 1944, 45. Note: Head A Dept, Arsenal Technical H.S., Indianapolis, 1925-41; Instructor, George Pearse Ennis' A Sch, Eastport.

CRAMER, MABEL (Mrs. Allen) [Ldscp. P, T] Indianapolis, IN b. 16 June 1891, Brown Town, WI d. 23 Oct 1963. Studied: Stevens Point, WI; Northwestern U. Teachers: Marie Goth; Edmund Brucker. Note: T, Rockford, IL, 1919-1925.

CRANE, PATRICIA [S] Anderson, IN.

CRANE, PAUL [Ldscp. P] West Lafayette, IN b. 17 Oct 1925, Clayton, NM. Studied: U of Hawaii; Lafayette MA. Teachers: Barbara Gresham. Exhibited: Watercolor USA, 1985; Ky. WCS Aqueous, 1986; WC West, 1987-89. Prizes: HS, 1985; Monticello AA, 1984, 86; Ind. WCS, 1987.

CRANE, STANLEY WILLIAM [P, Des, I] Woodstock, NY b. 14 Nov 1905, LaPorte, IN. Exhibited: AIC, 1938; VMFA, 1940; PAFA, 1938, 40-42; CI, 1941; NAD, 1942, 44. Prizes: HS, 1928; MOMA, 1942; NAD, 1945. Collections: Albany Inst Hist&A; mural, Eastern Airlines, Jacksonville, FL. Note: I, national magazines.

CRÁPO, DOE SPIESS [Ldscp. P, Photo, T] Indianapolis, IN b. 6 Sep 1924, Dayton, OH. Studied: John Herron AI; DePauw U. Teachers: A. Reid Winsey; Harry Davis; Floyd Hopper; Constance Forsyth. Exhibited: 500 Festival A; Tippecanoe Reg; Ind. AC. Prizes: HS; Eastside Mile of A; Indianapolis AL. Collections: Irvington Hist S; Indianapolis Mayor's Office.

CRAWFORD, CHARLES C. [P, Por. P] Bedford, IN b. 1903, Pinhook, IN. Studied: John Herron A Sch; Hawthorne Cape Sch, Provincetown, MA. Teachers: William Forsyth; Clifton Wheeler; Paul Hadley; Charles Hawthorne; Henry Hensche. Exhibited: Indianapolis AA; Herron M; Sheldon Swope Gal. Prizes: HS, 1969; Ind. State Fair. Collections: Lawrence Cnty Court House, historic murals; Crowe Hospital, Bedford; Bedford Dunn Hospital.

CRAWFORD, ROBERT W. [Ab, Dr, Car, Genre P, S, I, Por. P, T] Whiteland, IN b. 27 Aug 1923, Cleveland, OH. Studied: Ohio State U. Teachers: Frey; Hoyt Sherman; Ralph Fanning. Exhibited: Ind. State Fair; Johnson Cnty Fair; Bethlehem Lutheran Church. Prizes: HS, 1951; Ind. State Fair; Southside AL. Collections: Emmerich Manual H.S., Indianapolis; Our Lady of Greenwood Church; Artcraft Press; Knights of Columbus Hall. Note: T, Indianapolis Public Sch, 39 years.

CRESSY, WILLIAM South Bend, IN.

CRICK, MARY L. [P] Lebanon, IN. Self-taught. Exhibited: HS Gal, Hilton Hotel, 1971.

CRIMSON, LINDA [S] South Bend, IN b. 19 Sep 1946, South Bend. Studied: Ind. U, South Bend. Teachers: Jan Zach; "Tuck" Langland. Exhibited: Ore. Statewide Comp, 1977; Munster A Comp, 1991. Prizes: Catherine Lorillard

Wolfe, NY, 1989; Michiana Reg, South Bend, 1989; Elkhart Reg, 1987.

CRISMAN, MARILOU [P, T] Logansport, IN b. Logansport, IN d. c. 1985. Teachers: Robert Weaver; Paul Sweany; John Pike; Edgar Whitney; Valfred Thelin; N. Reale. Exhibited: Allied A of Am, Inc, NY; Rocky Mt Nat, CO; Ky. WCS Annual, 1981; Ind. AC; Ft Wayne Reg. Prizes: HS, 1976. Collections: Logansport Public Library; First Federal, Logansport; Butler U; Ind. Mem Union, Bloomington, IN. Note: T, Logansport YMCA.

CRISTEE, VERNON B. [Ldscp. P, I] Terre Haute, IN b. 4 Jan 1907, Indianapolis, IN. Studied: John Herron AI. Teachers: William Forsyth; Clifton Wheeler; Paul Hadley; Frank Riley. Exhibited: Wabash Valley, 1950s, 89; Ind. A, 1959. Prizes: HS, 1990; Ind. State Fair; Swope Gal; Wabash Valley. Collections: Rose Hulman Poly Tech, Terre Haute, IN.

CRITCHLOW, JOSEPH P. Indianapolis, IN. Studied: Herron Sch A.

CROOK, THELMA (A.) Indianapolis, IN.

CROSS, ADELYNE SCHAEFER [P, I] East Chicago, IN b. 17 Jan 1905, Columbus, WI. Exhibited: AIC, 1937-39, WFNY, 1939. Collections: Gary and Chicago public schools.

CROSS, KAREN HODGIN [Ldscp. P, T] Lafayette, IN b. 26 Jul 1955, Schnectady, NY. Studied: Purdue U. Exhibited: Wabash A Alliance Exh, 1990-91. Collections: Lafayette Leader Newspaper Office.

CROSS, WILLIAM [Ab] Lafayette, IN b. 25 Jul 1944, Kokomo, IN. Studied: Ind. U; Purdue U. Exhibited: WC USA, 1988. Prizes: HS, 1988; Lafayette MA, 1991; Ind. A Commission Fellowship Exh, 1989-90; WC USA, 1989. Collections: Tippecanoe Cnty Library.

CROUSE, JANET E. South Bend, IN.

CROWDER, MARGARET PEG FL.

CROWL, WALTER Indianapolis/Kendallville, IN b. Hicksville, OH. Self-taught. Exhibited: Audubon A 5th Ann Exh, NY, 1946. Prizes: HS, 1952; L. S. Ayres Anniversary, 1947.

CROWN, Jr., KEITH (Allen) Gary, IN.

CRYSLER, E. L. (Mrs. Frederick S.) [P] Wabash, IN.

CUMMINS, JEANNE [Ldscp. P] Noblesville, IN b. 16 Apr 1931, Cincinnati, OH. Studied: Indianapolis AL. Teachers: Floyd Hopper; Paul Sweany. Exhibited: Ind. WCS; The Seasoned Eye, *Modern Maturity* Magazine. Prizes: HS, 1986; Indianapolis AL, 1985; Ind. WCS, 1990. Collections: Shorewood Corp; Eli Lilly&Co.; Fearrin Insurance.

CUMMINS, NANCY HANCOCK [P] Indianapolis, IN b. 1944, George Field Air Force Base, IL. Studied: Purdue U; Ind. U, Bloomington; Indianapolis AL. Exhibited: Ind. State Fair. Prizes: HS, 1978-80; Wabash Valley Exh, 1979.

CUNNINGHAM, JAMES L. [P, S] Indianapolis, IN b. 21 Sep 1948, Indianapolis d. 24 Jul 1991. Studied: Herron Sch of A. Teachers: Chesley Bonestell. Exhibited: The Artist and the Space Shuttle, Nat Air and Space M, 1982; Partners of the Americas Exh, Paintings of Rio Grande De Sul, (solo), 1987; Visions of Flight: A Retrospective from the NASA Arts Collection, 1989. Prizes: HS, 1981-85; Winner of Nat Sports Center commemorative poster competition, 1982; Winner of competition, WTHR television studio, 1982; Volunteer of the Year, Indianapolis AL, 1990. Collections: Nat Air and Space M, Smithsonian Inst, Washington, D.C.; Nat Aeronautics and Space Administration, NASA Headquarters, Washington, D.C. and Cape Canaveral, FL; Ind. State M, 20th Century Collection. Note: T, A-in-Service, Metropolitan A Council; Visiting A, funded, NEA; Documented nine space program events as a NASA artist by invitation of NASA. Owned and operated Cunningham Gal, Inc. with his wife, artist Kate Cunningham.

CUNNINGHAM, (D.) KATE [P] Indianapolis, IN b. 26 Jan 1949. Self-taught. Exhibited: IMA, Alliance Gal (solo), 1980; Indianapolis AL, 1980 (solo), 84 (group); Cunningham Gal (solo), 1990. Prizes: IMA, Ind. Cr Show, 1979; Indianapolis AL Reg, 1983; HS, 1983. Collections: Bank One, Indianapolis; Simon & Assocs, Indianapolis; St Vincent Hospital, Indianapolis. Note: Owned and operated Cunningham Gal, Inc with her husband, artist James L. Cunningham.

CUNNINGHAM, LOIS HAWN [Ab, Por. P] Indianapolis, IN b. 8 Oct 1928, Washington Cnty, IN. Studied: East Side A Cen; Indianapolis AL. Teachers: Rosemary Lawton Thomas; William Ashby. Exhibited: A for Relgion; Ind. State Fair. Prizes: Ind. State Pen Women Exh, 1980; IHA, 1986; Ind. AC, 1989.

CUPKA, NANCY IRVINE [P, SLP, Ldscp. P] Indianapolis, IN b. 9 Oct 1942, Indianapolis. Teachers: Floyd Hopper; Clay Kent; Sally Stiele. Exhibited: Festival A of Lafayette, 1968, 70; Brown Cnty AG, 1989. Prizes: Festival A of Lafayette, 1968, 70; Kappa Kappa Kappa A Show, 1970. Collections: St Elizabeth Hospital, Lafayette, IN.

CURRY, MARY M(arston) b. Annapolis, MD. Studied: Herron Sch A; Ind. U. Teachers: John Young; Charles Shannon. Exhibited: Wabash Valley Exh; Sheldon Swope Gal, Terre Haute, IN; Eastern Ind. A Show, Ball State U, Muncie, IN; Ind. A Show. Prizes: HS, 1968; Ind. State Fair; Whitewater Valley Exh; Indianapolis AL; Muncie AA; Indianapolis 500 A Exh; Mid-States A Exh.

CURRY, TIM S. [S]

CURTIS, NORMAN S. [Des] Deceased. Studied: Herron Sch A, graduated 1937. Note: Des, Ransburg Corp.

CUSHING, THOMAS J. [Dr, Ldscp. P, Genre P, I, Por. P, Com. A, T] Griffith, IN b. 19 Mar 1939, Chicago, IL. Studied: Governors State U, U Park, IL; American Acad A, Chicago; Wilbur Wright Junior College, Chicago. Teachers: William Mosby; Vernon E. Stake; Bill L. Parks; Walter S. Parke. Exhibited: Ind. State M, 1975, 81; Northern Ind. AA Bicentennial, 1976-77. Prizes: HS, 1974, 81; Northlight/Hallmark A Competition, 1981; Palette&Chisel Acad. Collections: Cultural A Cen, Munster, IN; Northern Ind. AA; Griffith Ind. Sch System. Note: T, Ind. Vocational Technical Col and Purdue U, Calumet.

CUTLER, MILDRED D. [Por. P, Com. A, SLP] Nashville, IN b. Pittsburg, PA. Studied: Carnegie Tech A Sch. Exhibited: Brown Cnty AG (solo), 1971. Prizes: HS, 1955, 73. Note: Com. A in Indianapolis, 12 years.

D

DAHLGREEN, CHARLES W(illiam) [P, Print, Ldscp. P, T] Oak Park, IL b. 8 Sep 1864, Chicago d. Jun 1955. Studied: Dusseldorf A Sch, Dusseldorf, Germany; AIC; ASL; FA Acad, Chicago. Teachers: Henry Walcott; John C. Johansen; Charles F. Browne; William P. Henderson; Wellington J. Reynolds; John H. Vanderpoel; Ralph Clarkson. Exhibited: Paris Salon, 1910; Intl Etching Exh, 1934. Prizes: AIC, 1919, 20, 28, 34, 35; HS, 1925, 28; P.-P. Expo, San Francisco, 1915; Chicago Gal A, 1927; ASL Chicago. Collections: AIC; LOC; Smithsonian Inst; Chicago Gal Assn; NYPL; Intl Soc A&Letters; Chicago public schs.

DAHLSTROM, DOROTHY [T] Anderson, IN. Exhibited: Lynn Kottler Gal, NYC; Ind. A Show.

DAHM, (Mary) JO [P] Wanamaker, IN.

DAILEY, DON LEE [Por. P] Morgan Cnty, IN b. 1932. Prizes: Martinsville Fall Foliage Festival. Note: Lab Technician, Beveridge Paper Co, Indianapolis.

DAILEY, MELBA (Mrs. J. Robert) [Ldscp. P, S, Dr, MM] Nashville, IN b. 28 Apr 1909, Akron, OH. Studied: Ind. U, Kokomo; Purdue U; Indianapolis AL. Teachers: Garo Antreasian; John C. Lewis; Ida Gordon; George Jo Mess; Mastif Nagibg. Exhibited: Ind. A for Religion; Lieber Gal; Nat Ceramic Show, Chicago. Prizes: IHA, 1979; HS, 1977; Ind. AC, 1971. Collections: Arlington Mem Baptist Church, Akron, OH; First Congregational Christian Church, Kokomo; United Methodist Church, Nashville, IN. Note: Self-taught in the art of fused cathedral glass.

DAILY, EVELYNNE MESS (*See Mess, Evelynne C.*) [Ldscp. P, Print, T] Indianapolis, IN b. 8 Jan 1903, Indianapolis. Studied: Herron A Sch; AIC; Bauhaus Sch Des, Chicago; École des Beaux-Arts, Paris, France. Teachers: J. Von Wicht; Achile Ouvré; Andre Strauss; Wayman Adams; William Forsyth; Clifton Wheeler; Frederick Polley. Exhibited: Herron AM, 1934 (solo), 48 (solo); NAD, 1949. Prizes: Ind. AC, 1949; HS, 1947, 48, 51, 53, 58, 64; Herron M, 1958. Collections: LOC, Washington, D.C.; Philadelphia MFA; IMA; Ind. State M; Philadelphia MA; DePauw U; Ft Wayne AM; Richmond AA. Note: Her first husband was artist George Jo Mess with whom she lived in

Brown Cnty. Through that marriage, she was the sister-in-law of artists Gordon Benjamin Mess and Betty Mess.

DAILY, LENORA [P, T] Indianapolis, IN. Studied: Herron Sch A. Teachers: George Jo Mess; John W. Taylor; Francis Chapin; Edward Manetta. Exhibited: Ind. AC; Cinema I&II, Glendale Shopping Cen, Indianapolis.

DANCE, MARY [P] South Bend, IN b. 1927, Chicago, IL. Studied: St Mary-of-the-Woods Col; Ball State U; Ind. U; South Bend A Cen. Exhibited: South Bend A Cen; 57th Street A Fair, Chicago, IL; Michigan City Dunes A Show, IN; 1972 Town and Country Theater Gal (solo). Prizes: Nappanee A Festival, 1969, 70.

DANIEL, DOUGLAS M. [Ldscp. P, I, Por. P] Greenwood, IN b. 9 Apr 1956, Terre Haute, IN. Studied: Herron Sch of A. Teachers: Edmund Brucker. Exhibited: Evansville Mid-States Reg, 1982. Prizes: HS, 1983; Ind. State Fair, 1989. Collections: Ind. U Medical Center; Riley Memorial Assn, Riley Hospital, Indianapolis. Note: Husband of artist Kelly Griffith Daniel.

DANIEL, KELLY GRIFFITH [C, MM] Greenwood, IN b. 30 Dec 1959, Charleston, WV. Studied: Herron Sch A. Exhibited: Start With Art, Indianapolis; Patrick King Gal, Indianapolis. Prizes: HS, 1990, 91; IHA, 1992. Note: Owner, Weird Leaf Design Co, Greenwood, IN. Wife of artist Douglas M. Daniel.

DANIELS, ELMER HARLAND [S, Des] Pasadena, CA b. 23 Oct 1905, Owosso, MI. Studied: John Herron AI; BAID; ASL. Teachers: Leo Friedlander; Edward McCarten; Cleb Derijinski; John Flannigan; Edmond Amateis; Wheeler Williams. Exhibited: Ind. AC, 1931-39. Prizes: HS, 1931, 42; Ind. AC, 1940; Chicago, 1931. Collections: Ind. U; Turkey Run State Park; Ind. State Library, Indianapolis; Ind. Lincoln Union; Ball State TC, Muncie.

DANKERT, MARLA K. [T] Indianapolis, IN. Studied: Oberlin Col; U of Ill. Note: T, A History, Indianapolis AL.

DANNER, SARA KOLB (Mrs. W. M.) [P] Santa Barbara, CA b. 1884, NYC d. c. 1969. Studied: Philadelphia Sch Des; Mass. Normal A Sch; Calif. Col A&Cr. Teachers: G. L. Noyes; Snell. Exhibited: NAWA, 1946; NAD; Los

Angeles MA, 1942-44; Santa Barbara MA, 1943, 45 (solo). Prizes: South Bend A, 1922; HS, 1929, 51; Women P of the West, 1942, 43.

DARROW, PAUL W. [P] Wallingford, PA b. 9 Nov 1902, Indianapolis. Studied: AIC. Exhibited: Intl WC Exh; AIC, 1934-39; PAFA WC Ann, 1938.

DARST, ROSE MARIE [Ldscp. P] Radnor, OH b. Radnor, OH. Studied: AIC; Ohio U; Columbia U. Exhibited: Kansas Soc A, 1936; Ann Midwestern, Kansas City, 1936. Note: Indiana resident for 6 years.

DAUM, BARBARA TRESTER [Por. P, Ldscp. P] Indianapolis, IN b. 10 Mar 1923, Carmel, IN. Studied: Ind. U. Teachers: George Jo Mess; Simon Baus; Stella Coler; Paul Sweany; Fred Rigley. Exhibited: Swope Gal, Terre Haute; Ind. State Fair; Pastel Portrait, Nashville.

DAUMER, MIKE [P, Com. A, Des] Hammand, IN b. Hammond, IN, 1920. Prizes: Northern Ind. A Salon; Gary AL Exh.

DAVIDSON, LILLIAN M. (Mrs. Frank Bowers) [Dr] Richmond, IN b. 27 Jun 1896, Canton, OH d. ca. 1960. Studied: John Herron A Sch; Pa. A Sch, Chester Springs, PA. Teachers: George Jo Mess; Dewin Fulwider; Edmund Brucker; Lawrence McConaha; Ahron Bohrod. Exhibited: Ind. U; Culver Military Acad. Prizes: HS, 1951; Ind. State Fair. Collections: Richmond AA.

DAVIDSON, ROBERT (Robin W.) [S] Rock City Falls, NY b. 13 May 1904, Indianapolis, IN. Studied: John Herron AI; AIC; Munich. Teachers: Myra R. Richards; William Forsyth; Clifton Wheeler; A. Iannali; E. Amateis; Joseph Wackerle. Exhibited: WMAA, 1944; AIC, 1934; PAFA, 1937; John Herron AI, 1928, 33, 39; SFMA, 1928. Prizes: HS, 1927-29, 33, 37, 40. Collections: John Herron AI; Skidmore Col; Minneapolis IA. Note: T, Skidmore Col, 1933-46.

DAVIDSON, WILLIAM S.

DAVIS, DEAN H. [Ab, Por. P, T] Evansville, IN b. 14 Aug 1920, Oxford, NE. Studied: Denver A Col. Teachers: Jeanne Dobie; Alex Powers; Miles Batt. Exhibited: Nat WCS, 1989; Rocky Mountain Nat, 1987, 89; Am WCS, 1983. Prizes: HS, 1983; Rex Brandt WC Award, CA, 1987; New Orleans Nat Exh, 1988; La. WCS, 1989.

DAVIS, ELIZABETH [P, Print] Evansville, IN b. 10 Jan 1946, Evansville. Studied: DePauw U; Sacramento State U; USI, Evansville. Teachers: Ray French; Marga Goodridge; Michael Aakhus. Exhibited: Live Link A Gal, Augusta, KY, 1990; Evansville-Owensboro Invitational, Evansville, 1990; Mid-States Exh, Evansville M of A&Sc, 1987. Prizes: Evansville AG, 1988.

DAVIS, EVERETT [P] Chicago, IL b. Fountain City, IN. Teachers: William Forsyth; George Oberteuffer.

DAVIS, FRANCES [Cover Design A] Chicago, IL.

DAVIS, HARRY A. [P, Dr, Ldscp. P, Por. P, T] Indianapolis, IN b. 21 May 1914, Hillsboro, IN. Studied: Herron Sch of A; Am Acad, Rome, Italy. Teachers: Donald Mattison; Henrik Mayer. Exhibited: Mainstreams Intl Comp, 1968-77; Butler Mid-Year Exh, 1961, 67, 68, 70, 71, 73, 78; WC USA, 1965, 66, 68-76, 84, 85. Prizes: Prix de Rome, 1938; Butler Mid-Year Exh, 1961, 78; WC USA, 1965, 66, 68, 70, 72, 73, 76; HS, 1954-56, 66, 67, 69-90. Collections: Butler Inst Am A; Springfield AM, MO; Evansville M of A⪼ Greater Lafayette AM; Ind. State M; IMA;

Hallmark Inc. Note: T, Herron Sch of A. Noted for paintings of midwestern landmarks. Husband of artist Lois Davis.

DAVIS, JAN R. [P] Converse, IN b. 1955, Marion, IN. Self-taught. Prizes: HS, 1985; IHA; Grant Cnty AA.

DAVIS, (Mary) JOSEPHINE [Ldscp. P, SLP] Marion, IN. b. 24 Jul 1892, Spencer, IN d. 16 Dec 1983. Studied: Marion, Kokomo, Nashville, all in Ind. Teachers: Will Vawter; Leota Williams Loop. Collections: Library, Spencer, IN; Ind. U, Woodburn House; Ind. U, Memorial Union Business Office.

DAVIS, LOIS [Dr, Ldscp. P, Por. P, T] Indianapolis, IN b. 6 Jan 1924, LaPorte, IN. Studied: Herron Sch of A. Teachers: Donald Mattison; Henrik Mayer; David K. Rubins. Exhibited: Rockford Nat Print&Dr, 1983; Nat Small P Exh, 1974, 81, 83; WC USA, 1971. Prizes: HS, 1967, 68, 73-75, 86, 88-90; Nat Small Painting Exh, 1983; Herron Sch of A, 1947. Collections: Ind. State M; Greater Lafayette MA; Ind. U Mem Union; Jay Cnty Center for the A; Summitt Collection. Note: Wife of artist Harry Davis.

DAVIS, MARY ELSIE

DAVIS, ROSALIE [P] Carmel, IN b. 15 Jun 1938, Warsaw, IN. Studied: Ball State U. Teachers: Lois Davis; Sandy Ezell; Jo Ann Cardwell; Emel Doner. Exhibitions: Ind. State Fair, 1988; IHA, 1985. Collections: Merchants Nat Bank.

DAVISSON, HOMER G(ordon) [P, Print, T] Ft Wayne, IN/Somerset, IN b. 14 Apr 1866, Randolph Cnty, IN d. 6 Feb 1957. Studied: DePauw U; PAFA; Corcoran A Sch; ASL; Szbe Sch, Munich; Holland; France. Teachers: Thomas Anshutz. Prizes: HS, 1931; Ind. AC; Swope A Gal, Terre Haute, IN; Northern Ind. Hoosier A Salon. Collections: Ind. U; Ft Wayne AM; Hamilton Cl, Brooklyn, NY; Ind. public libraries in Tipton, Peru and Marion; Herron AI; Swope A Gal. Note: T, Ft Wayne A Sch. Painted frequently in France, Holland and Belgium. As a four-year-old, he was taken with his twin to Blountsville, Ind., to be raised by his grandparents.

DAVOUST, MARJORIE [Ldscp. P, Genre P, T] Evansville, IN b. 22 Sep 1930, Chicago, IL. Studied: AIC. Teachers: Dean Davis; Gerald Brommer; Les Miley. Exhibited: Mid-States Exh, Evansville M, 1987; Wabash Valley Exh, Swope Gal, 1989. Prizes: HS, 1989.

DAWSON, ETHEL [P] Indianapolis, IN. Deceased.

DAWSON, LEON

DAY, CHARLES C. Indianapolis, IN. Exhibited: Fireside A Gal, Metamora, IN, 1976; Homer Gal, Homer, IN, 1977; Wendel Sch A, Indianapolis, 1971.

DAY, DICK [P]

DAY, ELNORA [Ldscp. P, SLP, Por. P] Indianapolis, IN. Studied: Famous A; Herron Sch A; Jerry Farnsworth's Sch A, Sarasota, FL. Teachers: George Jo Mess; Simon Baus; Clayson Baker; Elmer Taflinger; V. J. Cariani. Exhibited: Wendel Sch A, 1971; Homer Gal, Homer, IN, 1977; Fireside A Gal, Metamora, IN, 1976.

DAY, GENTRY (See Blankenship, Diane) [S, Por. P] Noblesville, IN b. 12 Jan 1939, Noblesville, IN. Studied: DePauw U; Southern Methodist U. Teachers: Aaron Shikler; Franz Greisler; Barney Bright. Exhibited: Reg Exh, 1990. Prizes: Pan-Pacific A Show, 1967; Pastels '90; HS,

1988. Collections: Public Service Ind.; Noblesville Library. Note: Also painted under the name of Diane Blankenship.

DAY, HERBERT J. [P] Des Plaines, IL.

DAY, SANDY [Ldscp. P, Por. P, T] Anderson, IN b. 12 Nov 1938, Clinton Cnty, IN. Studied: Minneapolis AI Inc. Teachers: Mary McFarland; Elise Mulvihill. Exhibited: Anderson Winter Show, 1989, 90; Celebrate the City, Muncie, 1989, 90. Prizes: Celebrate the City, Muncie, 1988; HS, 1988; Anderson Area Show, 1989. Collections: Elwood H.S.

DEAHL, BETTY JEAN [SLP, Ldscp. P] Syracuse, IN b. 27 Jul 1919, Goshen, IN. Studied: South Bend A Cen. Teachers: Arthur Sprunger; Harold Zisla; Harriet Monteith. Exhibited: St Joseph WCS, 1983; Northern Ind. A. Prizes: Lakeland AA, Warsaw, IN, 1987; St Joseph WCS, South Bend, IN, 1983; Elkhart AL, 1982, 83, 85. Collections: Goshen Public Library; Park View Hospital, Ft Wayne, IN.

DEAN, FRANCES GLADDING (Mrs. Noble) [Por. P, SLP] Anderson, IN b. Memphis, TN. Studied: Herron A Sch; Florence, Italy.

DeARMOND, DOROTHY [P, Com. A, T] Rushville, IN b. 1919 Fayette Cnty. Studied: John Herron Sch A; Indianapolis AL; East Side A Cen. Teachers: Adele Wendell; Ray Needam; Frederick Rigley; Simon Baus; C. Curry Bohm. Exhibited: Ind. State Fair; Indianapolis AG, Marrott Hotel; Canal House (solo), Metamora; Homer A Gal, Shelbyville, IN. Prizes: Mile of A, Eastgate; Ind. State Fair.

DeATLEY, GERTRUDE Indianapolis, IN. Deceased.

DEBIKEY, GEORGE [Cer, S, Des] Indianapolis, IN. Studied: Ballardini State AI for Cer A, Faenza, Italy; Mengaroni State AI, Pesaro; Acad of FA, Perugia. Teachers: Carlo Zauli; Angelo Biancini. Exhibited: Clay Fest, 1988-90; 500 A Show, 1978; Lafayette AM Show; IMA (solo); Jewish Community Cen (solo); Merchants Plaza Gal (solo). Prizes: HS, 1990; Ind. Now, 1989. Collections: Eli Lilly & Co.; Riley Children's Hospital, Indianapolis, IN; GTE North, IN; Ind. State M, Indianapolis. Note: Head of dept, product research and development, Am. A Clay Co, Indianapolis. Husband of artist Ilana Debikey.

DEBIKEY, ILANA [Des, HPA, JA] Indianapolis, IN. Exhibited: Clay Fest; 500 A Show; Ind. Now; Artforms; Indianapolis AL Reg. Note: Wife of artist George Debikey.

DECHART, DONNA (M.)

DECIL, DEL [P, SLP, Por. P, Ab, T] AZ. Studied: Indianapolis Acad of Com A; John Herron AI. Exhibited: Ariz. State Fair; Glendale Festival of the A; Phoenix Library; Phoenix AM Four Corners Biennial; Town and Country Reg. Note: Staff A, *Indianapolis News*. Named "Advertising Woman of the Year," Advertising Cl, Indianapolis, 1958.

DeCOSTA, JOHN [P] Indianapolis, IN b. 13 Nov 1945, Pensacola, FL. Primarily self-taught. Teachers: Jurgen Peters. Exhibited: Hyatt-Regency, 1979; Indianapolis AG; First Ann A Expo, Indianapolis; Artwork Framers, Indianapolis, 1979. Prizes: HS, 1981.

DEERING, CONNIE JO *(See Wallpe, Connie Deering)* [Ldscp. P, Bat, T] Tipton, IN b. 17 Jul 1930, Tipton, IN. Studied: Indianapolis AL; Ind. U. Teachers: Frederick Rigley; Ruth Anderson; Ruth Ross. Exhibited: Ind. AC, 1990; Marion Col; Ind. State Fair, 1989; 500 Festival A; Hamilton Cnty AA, 1990. Prizes: HS, 1986; Pen Woman,

1984. Collections: Merchants Nat Bank, Indianapolis; Kokomo Public Library; Carmel Public Library; Shorewood Corp, Noblesville. Note: Self-taught batik artist.

DeMUN, ANN P. [Por. P] Indianapolis, IN. Studied: Miami U, Oxford, OH. Prizes: HS, 1961. Collections: Northwood Christian Church, Indianapolis.

DEMYER, EVELYN [P] Philipsburg, Antillean Island, Sint Maarten. Studied: Summer Sch P, Saugatuck, MI. Note: Wife of artist Howard DeMyer.

DEMYER, HOWARD [S] Philipsburg, Antillean Island, Sint Maarten. Studied: Summer Sch P, Saugatuck, MI. Prizes: HS, 1965. Note: Former senior partner in law firm, LaPorte, IN. Husband of artist Evelyn DeMyer.

DENNEY, GLADYS A. [P, C, T] Indianapolis, IN b. 21 Sep 1898, Portland, IN. Studied: CUASch; PMSchIA; John Herron AI; U of Colo. Teachers: E. Warwick; J. Boule. Exhibited: Ind. State Fair, 1935, 36; PAFA, 1937; NAWA, 1942-44; John Herron AI, 1937-40, 42, 44. Prizes: CUASch, 1925; Ind. State Fair, 1937-40, 46; HS, 1946, 47. Note: T, FA, Emmerich Manual Training H.S., Indianapolis, beginning 1930.

DENNEY, LYLE [Ldscp. P] Springport, IN b. 22 Oct 1951, Muncie, IN. Self-taught. Prizes: Muncie AG, 1989.

DENNIS, GRETCHEN M(arkle) Paris, IL.

DENNIS, LUCILLE [Ab, Ldscp. P, Genre P, Por. P] Terre Haute, IN b. 10 Feb 1910, Terre Haute. Studied: U of Chicago; Chicago Acad FA. Teachers: Edmund Geisbert; Laura Van Pappeldam; John Laska. Exhibited: Sheldon Swope AM, 1976; Ind. State U, 1971. Prizes: HS, 1967. Collections: Ind. U, Bloomington; Psi Iota Xi Sorority; *USA Bicentennial* (Publication), 1976.

DENTON, HOWARD H. Madison, IN.

DEPAUL, VESTA V. Indianapolis, IN b. Frankfort, IN d. 23 Dec 1983. Studied: John Herron AI. Teachers: Elmer Taflinger; V. J. Cariani; Carl Graf; Dirk Smit.

DeSANTO, STEVEN CHARLES [P] Ft Wayne, IN b. 1951. Studied: Ball State U, Muncie, IN; Huntington Col, Huntington, IN. Exhibited: Audubon A Nat Open, Nat AC, NYC; Mid-Year Show, Butler Inst Am A, Youngstown, OH. Prizes: Nat Open Exh, Salmagundi Cl, NYC, 1981; Am WCS, NYC, 1980; Allied A of Am, NYC, 1980; HS, 1970, 78, 80, 82. Collections: Witchita AM, KS; Anderson FA Cen, IN; General Telephone, IN; Crosby Gardens, Toledo, OH.

DESATNICK, MIKE J. [Ldscp. P, Por. P, T] b. Hammond, IN. Studied: Am Acad A, Chicago. Prizes: HS, 1976. Note: T, Am Acad A, Chicago.

DESPOT, SHIRLEY (Ann) [P, Cer, T] Greenwood, IN b. 25 Feb 1932, Des Moines, IA. Studied: Herron A Sch; U of Indianapolis; Arrowmont, Gatlinburg, TN. Teachers: George Jo Mess; Ed Manetta; Marcia Goldenstein; Leonard Kosclanski; Judi Betts. Exhibited: IMA, rental gal; Falcon Gal, Louisville, KY, 1987; Ind. AC; Mid-States; Tippecanoe Reg; 500 Festival; Whitewater Valley. Prizes: Ind. AC, 1974; Ind. State Fair, 1985; Wabash Valley A Festival, 1989. Collections: Terre Haute Bank; Gene B. Glick Construction Co, Indianapolis. Note: T, Perry Twp and Center Grove Schs.

DETCHON, IRWIN LEE [Por. P, SLP, Ldscp. P] Crawfordsville, IN b. 1900, Crawfordsville. Studied; NY. Teachers: Ferdinand (Fritz) L. Schlemmer. Exhibited: Ind. AC;

Ind. A Ann, Herron M, 1937; Hist Soc, NYC; Smithsonian Gals, Washington, D.C.; Springfield MA, Springfield, MA. Prizes: HS, 1942. Collections: Wabash Col; Elston Bank&Trust Co; Old Jail M.

DEUITCH, BYRAN [P] Indianapolis, IN b. 1956, Toledo, OH. Studied: DePauw U. Exhibited: Ind. A Show, IMA, 1981.

DEUKER, FREDRIK Chicago, IL.

DEUTSCHMAN, LOUANNA [Genre P] Kewanna, IN b. 21 Feb 1923, Logansport, IN. Studied: the books of Helen Van Wyk and David Leffel. Exhibited: Honeywell Center (solo), Wabash, IN, 1989; Ft Wayne MA, Alliance Gal, 1985. Prizes: HS, 1987; A in the Park, Winamac, IN, 1979, 83. Collections: Soc Bank, Winamac, IN; Pulaski Cnty Treasurer's Office, Winamac, IN.

DEVANEY, NANCY

DEVOE, HELEN Prizes: HS, 1961.

DeWESTER, LEANNE J. [Dr, Ldscp. P, I, Por. P, T] Indianapolis, IN b. 7 Oct 1948, Columbus, OH. Studied: Herron Sch A; U of Chicago. Exhibited: Ind. State Fair, 1985; IHA, 1986.

DeWITT, DON [S] Indianapolis, IN. Prizes: HS, 1969, 70.

DICKERSON, GRACE LESLIE [Ldscp. P, Por. P] Ft Wayne, IN b. 27 Aug 1911, Ft Wayne. Studied: Ft Wayne A Sch; AIC; Cranbrook Acad A; St Francis Col; Instituto Allénde, San Miguel de Allénde, Mexico. Teachers: Homer Davisson; Ritman; Zoltan Szabo; Daniel Green; Claude Croney; Al Bravilette. Exhibited: Ind. Heritage, Nashville, IN, 1989; Intl Platform Assn, Washington D.C., 1987; Herron AI, 1938, 39, 41, 44; Ind. A, 1939-45. Prizes: HS, 1954; Ind. A Show, Ft Wayne Woman's Cl, 1984; Women's A Show, YMCA, 1989; Ft Wayne M, 1944. Collections: Ft Wayne Community Schs; Caylor-Nickel Clinic; Smock Foundation; Anderson Gal A; cathedrals in Ft Wayne, Evansville and South Bend.

DICKHAUS, JOHN ROBERT [P, Por. P, SLP, Ldscp. P] Indianapolis, IN b. 9 Jan 1926, Cincinnati, Ohio. Studied: Indianapolis AL and workshops. Teachers: John S. Sargent. Exhibited: Merchants Bank, Indianapolis, 1982; Ruthven Gal; Hammon Gal. Prizes: Third Ann Heritage A, Inc, Nashville, IN; Indianapolis AL; Ind. State Fair.

DICKINSON, BARBARA

DICKINSON, H. O.

DIEDRICH, GAIL [P] Indianapolis, IN.

DIEMAN, CLARA (Leonard Sorensen) [S, T] NYC b. 29 Nov 1877, Indianapolis, IN. Studied: AIC; Columbia U. Teachers: Ozenfant; Zadkine; Archipenko. Exhibited: AIC, 1917; PAFA, 1943, 45; NAWA, 1945, 46; Philadelphia A All, 1943 (solo); Santa Fe P&S, 1930-46. Collections: Mem Coll in Ind., Iowa, Colo., N.M. and Pa. Note: Specialty was in collaborating with architects on sculpture. T, Shipley Sch for Girls, Bryn Mawr, PA, beginning 1934.

DIETRICH, GEORGE ADAMS [S, Des, P, T] Milwaukee, WI b. 26 Apr 1905, Clark Cnty, IN. Studied: Layton Sch A; AIC. Teachers: Partridge; Garolumo Picolli; Viola Norman; William Owens; Joseph Binder. Exhibited: AIC, 1928, 30, 31; PAFA, 1929, 30. Prizes: HS, 1927, 28, 30, 31; Milwaukee AI, 1929. Collections: Layton A Gal, Milwaukee; Mem, City of Milwaukee; USPO, Lake Geneva, WI. Note: T, Layton Sch A, 1929-37; U of Mich., 1937-

38; Milwaukee Sch Engravers, 1939-43; U.S. Navy, 1943-46.

DILL, MARY C. [P, T] Daleville, IN. Studied: Ind. U; Western Mich U; Parsons Sch Des. Exhibited: Herron Spring Show, 1964; Michiana Biennial, South Bend, 1965; Ind. State Fair, 1964, 66, 67. Prizes: HS, 1963, 67. Note: T, Danville Community Schs and Indianapolis AL.

DILLINGHAM, JERRY [P] Ft Branch, IN.

DILLMAN, MARK [Dr, Genre P, Por. P] Indianapolis, IN b. 20 Feb 1955, Indianapolis. Studied: John Herron AI. Teachers: Edmund Brucker; Harry Davis. Exhibited: Butler Inst Am A, 1988; Wichita Nat Small P, Oil, 1989, 90; Anderson Winter Show, 13 State Reg, 1988, 90. Prizes: Ind. State Fair, 1986, 88, 89; HS, 1986, 88. Collections: Hanover Col; Ind. State Library; Grace Col; Riley Mem Assn.

DIMITROFF, LOUIS [P] Gary, IN b. 1911, Sofia, Bulgaria d. 1977. Studied: AIC. Exhibited: Gary AL Exh; Northern Ind. A Salons; Retrospective, Chesterton A Gal. Prizes: HS, 1952. Note: Helped found Gary AL. Operated artist supply shop, Gary.

DIMITROFF, LUBEN [P] Indianapolis, IN. b. Macedonia d. c. 1962. Studied: U of Sofia, Bulgaria. Prizes: Ind. State Fair. Note: Editor, *Macedonian Tribune*.

DiPALMA, JOHN M. [P] Evansville, IN.

DITMIRE, JEFFREY J. [P] Logansport, IN.

DITZENBERGER, PAUL E.

DODDS, (Mary) ELIZABETH *(See Shaffer, Elizabeth Dodds)* [Dr, Ldscp. P, Por. P, T] New Castle, IN b. 12 Feb 1913, Cairo, IL. Studied: Butler U. Teachers: Jerry Farnsworth; Fritz Schlemmer; Elmer Taflinger; Wayman Adams; George Jo Mess. Exhibited: John Herron AM; 2nd Ann Dr Show, Ball State U, 1956; Knicherbocker A, 1962; Nat Exh Am A, NY; Ind. AC. Prizes: Ind. State Fair, 1949, 52, 54; HS, 1951; Ind. AC, 1953, 54; 7th Ann Michiana Reg, 1956; Wabash Valley Exh, 1965. Collections: Inland Container Corp; Mcguire Gal.

DOERSCHEL, MARGARET R. [P] Indianapolis, IN b. Indianapolis. Studied: ASL, Indianapolis. Teachers: Floyd Bailey; Carolyn Ashbrook; Harold McDonald; Edmund Brucker. Exhibited: ASL, Indianapolis, 1941-46. Note: Member of Ind. Chapter, Nat Soc of A&Letters.

DOLT, MARY BELLE

DOMROESE, EWALD F. [P] Crawfordsville, IN b. 29 Sep 1916 d. 30 Oct 1974. Note: Son of Frederick Carl and Rose Pintzke Domroese. Frederick, professor of German, was Registrar, Wabash College. Ewald, mentally handicapped, had a gift for painting.

DONALDSON, D(aniel) C. [P] Brown Cnty, IN b. Maywood, IL. Studied: Acad FA, Chicago. Teachers: Ezra Winter; J. Wellington Reynolds; Al St. John; E. J. F. Timmons. Exhibited: Swope Gal; Ind. U; Brown Cnty A Gal. Prizes: HS, 1957. Note: Technical representative in reproduction and creative fields with Eastman Kodak Co for 20 years. Husband of artist Hildegarde Donaldson.

DONALDSON, HILDEGARDE [P, Photo] Brown Cnty, IN b. Fond du Lac, WI d. 27 May 1993, Nashville, IN. Studied: Acad FA, Chicago; AIC. Teachers: Elizabeth Dana; Jessie Paynter; George Buehr; Ruth Anderson; Frederick Rigley. Exhibited: Brown Cnty A Gal; Ft Wayne

Women's Cl; Swope Gal; Ind. U. Collections: Lincoln Life; Tri Kappa. Note: Employed by Eastman Kodak Co. Her photographs were accepted and exhibited by international salons. Wife of artist Daniel C. Donaldson.

DONATO, C(rescenzo) D. [P, S] Bloomington, IN b. 1880, Rivisondali, Italy. Collections: St Nicholas di Bari Catholic Church, Rivisondali, Italy. Note: A stone carver. Operated C. D. Donato Stone Co. until 1926. In 1927, he built the Heltonville Limestone Mill; operated it until 1936.

DONER, EMEL [P, T] Carmel, IN b. 8 Feb 1947, Anhara, Turkey. Studied: Indianapolis AL. Teachers: Floyd Hopper; Sara Todderud. Exhibited: Nat Midwest WCS, 1988-90; Nat Aqueous, 1986, 87, 89; Butler Inst Am A, Nat Exh, 1989. Prizes: Ind. WCS, 1988; Ind. AC, 1989; Ind. State Fair, 1989; HS, 1987, 89. Collections: Eli Lilly&Co; Merchants Nat Bank; Ind. Bell Telephone Co; Am United Life Insurance Co; Turkish Embassy.

DONNELLY, CRAWFORD F. [Ldscp. P, I, Por. P] Indianapolis, IN b. 4 Jan 1914, Indianapolis. Studied: Herron Sch A; N.Y. Inst of Photography. Teachers: William Forsyth; Clifton Wheeler; Elmer Taflinger; John Pike; Don Stone; Edgar Whitney. Exhibited: Ind. WCS; Brown Cnty AG; Mainstreams, 1975-77; Cincinnati AC Ann, 1976-79; Ind. WCS. Prizes: HS, 1977, 79, 82; Eli Lilly Award, 1973; Ind. Fed A Cls, 1978; Mary Grismer Award, 1979. Collections: Merchants Nat Bank; Wabash Nat Bank; First State Bank of Lancaster; Statesman Insurance; Tyson Corp.

DORMANN, JAMES ARTHUR [P] Indianapolis, IN b. 10 Apr 1934, Erie, PA. Studied: Adult Education, Washington Township Schs. Teachers: Florence Jagger. Exhibited: CCA Gal; Heritage A Exh; Brown Cnty AM; Ind. State Fair. Prizes: HS, 1989; Ind. State Fair, 1990.

DORSEY, HOLLAND J. (Mrs. Paul E.) [P] Indianapolis, IN/Sarasota, FL b. c. 1908, Effingham, IL d. July 1964. Studied: Indianapolis AL. Teachers: Robert Chase; Jerry Farnsworth; Marilyn Bendell; V. J. Cariani; Helen Sawyer. Exhibited: St Petersburg, FL; Clearwater, FL (solo), 1961, 64; Indianapolis, IN (solo), 1963. Prizes: Indianapolis AL, 1961-63; Longboat Key Show, 1961-63.

DOTY, ELLEN (Mrs. Roger F.) [T] Connorsville, IN. Studied: U of Kan.; Kansas City AI; Nelson Gal A, Kansas City, MO. Exhibited: 500 Festival A; Whitewater Valley Ann Reg Show. Note: T, Connorsville. Worked for Vernon Advertising Co and Nat Wildlife Federation.

DOUGHERTY, ELIZABETH H. *(See Ashton, Elizabeth Dougherty)*

DOUGLAS, LANCE [S] Worthington, IN.

DOVERSBERGER, JAMES [P] Indianapolis, IN b. Tipton, IN. Studied: Herron Sch A; IUPUI; Butler U. Exhibited: Ball State Dr Show; Ind. A Show; Herron AM; Ind. AC; Ind. State Fair. Collections: Am Fletcher Nat Bank; Orchard Sch; Indianapolis Public Sch. Note: Chairman A Department, Lawrence Central H.S.

DOYLE, R(obert) J(oseph) [P, T] Indianapolis, IN b. 25 Jul 1912, Indianapolis. Teachers: Edward R. Sitzman.

DRAGSTREM, BON B. Indianapolis, IN.

DRISKELL, DOROTHY L. [S] Florence, Italy/Aspen, CO. Studied: Tudor Hall, Indianapolis. Exhibited: Environment Gal, NYC, 1978. Collections: Exxon, Rockefeller Center.

DROEGE, ANTHONY J. [Dr, Ldscp. P, S, Por. P, T] New Carlisle, IN b. 22 Sep 1943, Philadelphia, PA. Studied: Pa.

State; U of Iowa. Teachers: Stuart Frost; Joseph Patrick. Exhibited: Butler Inst Am A; State U Col, Potsdam, NY, 1974; Pa. State U, 1974; Speed M, Louisville, KY. Prizes: Michiana Reg, 1972-74. Collections: IMA; Kemper Insurance; Ind. U; Murray State U; U of Iowa. Note: Chairman A Dept, Ind. U, South Bend.

DuCHATEAU, ROY

DUCHEMIN, IRVIN P.

DUCKWALL, HELEN BRIGGS *(See Briggs, Helen L.)*

DUDLEY, FRANK V. [Ldscp. P] Chicago, IL/Chesterton, IN b. 14 Nov 1868, Delavan, WI d. 5 Mar 1957. Studied: AIC; Palette&Chisel Cl. Exhibited: AIC, 1918; Chicago Gal Assn, 1929, 31; Ann A Exh, Chicago, 1902-27; Chicago&Vicinity Exh, 1902-43; MA Cedar Rapids, IA; Union Lg Cl, Chicago; MA, Valparaiso U. Prizes: Chicago P&S; AIC, 1921; Business Men's AC, 1931; Municipal AL, 1907; HS, 1927, 28, 30, 32, 39, 41; Union Lg A Show, Chicago, 1957. Collections: AIC; Municipal Coll, Owatonna, MN; Cedar Rapids AA; Public Sch Coll, St Louis and Chicago; State M, Springfield, IL. Note: Famed painter of the dunes. A tireless supporter of the preservation of Indiana dune land.

DUDLEY, GEORGE [P] Detroit, MI.

DUFF, CHARLES T. [P] Culver, IN.

DUNBAR, DAVID W. [P] Indianapolis, IN.

DUNBAR, JERRY A. [P, Ldscp. P, T] Rochester, IN b. 11 Mar 1929, Indianapolis. Studied: Ind. U. Teachers: John Pike; Judi Betts; Luke Buck. Exhibited: Ind. State Fair, 1980-89; Ind. WCS, 1985-89. Prizes: Second Ventures, Ft Wayne, 1989; First Warsaw, 1990; Logansport Spring Show, 1987. Collections: Purdue U; Kokomo Library.

DUNCAN, ANNE M. [P, Print] Indianapolis, IN b. Buck Creek, IN. Studied: Indianapolis AL; Herron Sch A. Teachers: Garo Antreasian. Exhibited: Sheldon Swope Gal; Burr Gal, NY. Prizes: HS, 1957, 67; Mid-States; Ind. AC; A for Religion; Ind. State Fair. Collections: Ind. U; Nat M of Modern A, Rome, Italy; Indianapolis Athletic Cl.

DUNCAN, JENNEE STRATTON [Ldscp. P, Por. P] Indianapolis, IN b. 27 Sep 1911, West Middleton, IN. Studied: Herron Sch A; IUPUI; Indianapolis AL. Teachers: Clifton Wheeler; Paul Hadley; Oakley Ritchey; Henrik Mayer; Hilton Leech; George Jo Mess; Floyd Hopper; Bill Ashby. Exhibited: Turners A Shows in Indianapolis, South Bend and Ft Wayne (Pr); Glendale A Show, 1961 (Pr); Brown Cnty AG; Franklin A Gal (solo). Collections: Franklin U; Ind. State U.

DUNLAP, BERNICE N. [P] LaPorte, IN.

DUNLAP, CATHERINE ALICE [P, Des] Plymouth, IN b. 13 Aug 1911, Lewisville, IN. Self-taught. Exhibited: Northern Ind. A Exh.

DUNLAP, DAVID W. [P] Indianapolis/Nashville, IN b. c. 1901 d. 14 Mar 1973. Exhibited: Herron A Sch; Bloomington Public Library; H. Lieber Co. Gal, Indianapolis. Note: Trade book manager, Prentice-Hall Publishing Co.

DUNLAP, EDWARD HUBER [Por. P, Ldscp. P, Mur. P] Plymouth, IN b. 24 Feb 1909, Lewisville, IN d. c. 1984. Studied: Herron A Sch; Yale U. Teachers: Robert Davidson; Reynolds L. Selfridge; Eugene Savage. Prizes: North Ind. A, 1929; HS, 1931, 34; Prix de Rome, Honorable Mention; Winchester Fellowship, Yale U.

DUNLAP, WILLIAM D. [Ldscp. P] Nashville, IN.

DUNLEVY, ETHEL F(arrar) BALL [Des, SLP, P, T] Jeffersonville, IN b. Milwaukee, WI d. c. 1955. Studied: Church Sch A, Chicago, IL. Teachers: Emma Church; Forsberg. Exhibited: Wawasee, 1936; Evansville, 1936; Indianapolis, 1936. Note: Also worked in Charlestown, IN.

DUNN, DELPHINE [P, T] Boston, MA b. Rushville, IN. Studied: Colo. Col A Sch; Chase A Sch, NY; AIC; Columbia U; PAFA; Fountainebleau Sch FA. Teachers: Lorado Taft; Artus Van Briggle; Arthur Dow; Daniel Garber; L. Soutter. Note: T, Scott Carbee Sch A.

DUNNIGAN, LILLIAN R. [Ldscp. P, SLP, Por. P, T] Nashville, IN b. 23 Jan 1921, Madison Cnty, IL. Studied: Chicago Professional Sch A; Am Acad A, Chicago; Indianapolis AL. Teachers: Louis Grell; Cliffe Eitel; Frederick Rigley; Simon Baus; William Ashby; Vivian Browne Boron. Exhibited: Ind. AC Exh, 1965-90; Ind. State Fair; Ind. State A Exh, 1980. Prizes: Indianapolis AL, 1960; Ventures in Creativity, 1989, 90. Note: Was affiliated with Beilefeld Studios (Chicago), Gardner Advertising, Datché Advertising and Sprague Studios (St Louis). Wife of artist Neil E. Dunnigan.

DUNNIGAN, NEIL E. [P, Ldscp. P, Print, I, T] Nashville, IN b. 9 Sep 1921, Lansing, MI. Studied: Chicago Professional A Sch; Washington U, St. Louis, MO. Teachers: Vivian Browne Boron; Cliffe Eitel; Louis Grell; Paul Sweany; Simon Baus. Prizes: Lincoln Nat Corp, 1989; Indianapolis AL, 1961; Religious A, Oldenberg, 1979; Ventures in Creativity, Ft Wayne, 1989; Ind. AC, 1974; HS, 1964, 72, 86. Collections: Purdue Campus, Calumet, IN; Am Fletcher Nat Bank, Indianapolis. Note: Former art director, Ayres Budget Store Advertising, Indianapolis, IN. Husband of artist Lillian R. Dunnigan.

EASON, DANA RAE [P, I] Greencastle, IN b. 7 Nov 1954, Noblesville, IN. Studied: John Herron Sch A. Teachers: Floyd Hopper. Exhibited: Jefferson Nat Life (solo), 1988; Ind. WCS, 1983, 85. Prizes: Conner Prairie, 1981; Atlanta New Earth Festival, 1980; Putnam Cnty AL, 1986. Collections: Merchants Nat Bank, Indianapolis.

EATON, JUDITH S. [P] Versailles, IN b. 3 Feb 1941, Anderson, IN. Teachers: Don Dennis; Judi Betts; Alex Powers. Exhibited: Ind. WCS, 1985; Cincinnati AC, Viewpoints, 1986. Prizes: Ohio Valley Reg, 1986; River Valley Reg, 1986. Collections: Quinco Consulting Cen.

EATON, RUTH

EBERG, MARILYN (Mrs. H. R.) [P, Ldscp. P, Por. P] Greenwood, IN b. 8 Nov 1933, Greencastle, IN. Teachers: Ruth Pritchard. Prizes: Tri Kappa.

ECCLES, JAMES [P, T] Oak Park, IL b. 1885, Chicago, IL d. Sep 1983. Studied: AIC; Smith Col A; Chicago Acad FA. Teachers: Walter Clute; Frederick Fursman; Albert Krehbiel; Allen St. John; R. DeForest Shook; Louis Wilson. Exhibited: Business Mens AC, Chicago; Lutheran General Hospital, Park Ridge, IL; Oak Park Public Library; Oak Park Arms Hotel. Prizes: Palette&Chisel Cl. Note: Worked for Continental Bank until 1945.

ECHELBARGER, BERTHA Swayzee, IN.

EDDY, HILARY A. JACKSON *(See Edwards, Hilary Jackson)* [P] Lafayette, IN b. 12 Nov 1948, Epsom, Surrey, England. Studied: Normal Col, North Wales; Purdue U. Exhibited: 54th Mid-Year Nat, Butler Inst Am A, 1990; Realism Today, Evansville M of A&Sc, 1989, 90; 41st Nat A Exh, Nat AC, NY, 1983. Prizes: W&J Nat Painting Exh, 1981; HS, 1980, 81, 83, 87-89; Northern Ind. AA, 1988. Collections: Olin FA Cen, Washington, PA; Hoyt Inst FA, New Castle, PA.

EDWARDS, HILARY JACKSON *(See Eddy, Hilary A. Jackson)*

EDWARDS, NANCY BIXBY [S] Chicago, IL b. 18 Feb 1882, Evansville, IN. Studied: Pratt Inst. Exhibited: Am PS, AIC, 1935, 37, 38; A Chicago Vicinity, AIC, 1939; Cer Exh, Syracuse, 1938, 39. Prizes: HS, 1939, 40.

EDWARDS, STEPHEN E. [Ldscp. P] Sheridan, IN b. 30 Nov 1951, Indianapolis, IN. Teachers: Crawford Donnelly; Floyd Hopper; Phil Austin; Phillip Jamison; Thomas Daly. Exhibited: Rocky Mountain Nat Watermedia Exh, 1988; Ky. WCS Nat Exh, 1988; Pa. WCS Nat Exh, 1988. Prizes: HS, 1985, 90; Ind. AC, 1989; Ind. State Fair, 1983. Collections: Ind. Farmers Mutual Insurance Co; Union State Bank; Summit Bank; Ameritrust Bank; Shorewood Corp.

EGGEMEYER, MAUDE KAUFMAN [P, Por. P] NYC b. 9 Dec 1877, New Castle, IN d. 1959. Studied: Cincinnati A Acad; Earlham Col. Teachers: J. E. Bundy; G. Beal; W. Adams; Margaret Overbeck; H. L. Meakin. Prizes: HS, 1925, 30; Richmond, 1910. Collections: AA, Richmond, IN; Butler University; Earlham Col.

EGGERT, MARY [P] One-time Indianapolis resident. Prizes: HS, 1982.

EGLOFF, (Rita) EVANNE [MM, T] West Terre Haute, IN b. 3 Mar 1948, Seymour, IN. Studied: U of Cincinnati; Ind. U, Bloomington and Indianapolis; Ind. State U, Terre Haute. Exhibited: Ind. State Fair, 1979, 80, 92. Prizes: 48th Wabash Valley Exh, 1992; 37th A Show, Paris, IL, 1991; Ind. State U, 1991. Collections: Registry, Ariel Gal, NYC.

EILERS, A. FRED [Por. P, Ldscp. P, T] Evansville, IN. Prizes: HS, 1945. Note: T, U of Evansville for over 40 years.

EILTS, E. GAYE [Ldscp. P] Wabash, IN b. 28 Mar 1933, Greenbriar Cnty, WV. Teachers: Floyd Hopper; Rob O'Dell; Ida Gordon; James McBride; Francis Clark Brown. Exhibitions: Va. Beach, VA; Ft Wayne AM; Anderson Salon; Brown Cnty AG. Prizes: HS, 1971; Anderson Winter Show; Pulaski Cnty, 1979. Collections: Manchester Col, Student Union; U of Ill.; Container Corp.

EISENBACH, DOROTHY LIZETTE [P, C, Print, T] Lafayette, IN b. 9 Oct 1899, Lafayette. Studied: Herron A Sch; PAFA. Teachers: William Forsyth; Ethel Traphagen; George Harding; Henry Poore. Exhibited: Herron AM; U of Colo.; Colo. State Col; Philadelphia WCC. Prizes: J. I. Holcomb Pr, 1929; HS, 1930; 2nd Michiana Reg, South Bend, 1951. Note: T, Herron Sch A.

EISENHUT, MARIESUE Indianapolis, IN.

ELDREDGE, STUART EDSON [P, T, Des] Brooklyn, NY/Springfield, VT b. 1 Jul 1902, South Bend, IN. Studied: Dartmouth Col; ASL. Teachers: Simon Nicolaides. Exhibited: Grand Cen Gal, 1935; murals, N.Y. Arch Lg, 1936; murals, Textile Bldg, WFNY, 1939. Prizes: HS, 1949, 53, 59; Tiffany Foundation Fellowship. Collections: Dartmouth Col; Butler Inst Am A; Miller A Cen, Springfield; South Bend AA; Fleming M, Burlington. Note: T, CUASch.

ELETSON, BARBARA F. [P, T] Terre Haute, IN b. 23 Dec 1923, Bloomington, IL. Studied: ISU, Normal, IL; Columbia U TC; ASL; AIC; ISU, Terre Haute, IN. Teachers: Mary Parker; Jeanne Mcleish. Exhibited: Ind. WCS Exh, 1991; Wabash Valley A Exh, Swope Gal, 1991. Prizes: Wabash Valley Exh, Swope Gal, 1989; Paris A Exh, Paris, IL, 1988-90.

ELKINS, DANIEL L(ee) [Com. A, Gra. A, Des] Indianapolis, IN b. 26 Feb 1957, Indianapolis. Studied: Bob Jones University. Teachers: Emery Bopp. Exhibited: IMA Alliance Gal, 1984. Prizes: Ind. State Fair, 1979; *Ceramics Monthly*, Best Amateur, 1978; Trenholm AG Award, 1979.

ELLINGHAM, Mrs. MILLER Ft Wayne, IN b. Tipton, IN. Note: Training, Interior Decorating.

ELLIOTT, GEORGE C. [Ab, Dr, Ldscp. P, Genre P, S] Noblesville, IN b. 2 Apr 1940, Indianapolis. Studied: John Herron AI; Ind. U; Indianapolis AL. Exhibited: Indianapolis AL; Ind. State Fair; Anderson Winter Show; Wabash Valley Exh, Swope Gal; Northern Ind. AA Salon Show; IHA; Mid-States A Exh. Prizes: HS, 1990; Celebration of Creativity, Indianapolis, 1985; Ind. AC, 1986; Channel 20 A Auction, 1986. Collections: Indianapolis Athletic Cl; Floyd Cnty M; Indianapolis Chamber of Commerce; Noblesville Public Library; Merchants Nat Bank; Shorewood Corp; Caldwell-Van Riper.

ELLIOTT, MARY W. [Por. P] Muncie, IN b. 2 Jan 1910, Louisville, KY. Self-taught and Famous A courses. Exhibited: Evansville M of A&Sc. Note: Employed by Bell Telephone Co for 26 years.

ELLIS, JEFFREY THOMAS [Ab, Dr, I, Des] Indianapolis, IN b. 11 Mar 1962, Indianapolis. Studied: Ball State U. Teachers: Joan Gee. Exhibited: Jefferson Nat Life, 1985. Prizes: 49th Ann Ball State U Student A Show, 1984; 30th Ann Drawing and Small S Show. Collections: Embassy Suites, North. Note: Creator of constructions of embossed paper and miscellaneous materials, air brushed. Home designer/draftsman.

ELLIS, LINDA JANE [P] Indianapolis, IN. Deceased. Studied: Indianapolis AL.

ELLYSON, MARTHA

ELMORE, JOHN M. [Dr] Nashville, IN.

ELROD, CAROL [Col. A] Indianapolis, IN b. 23 Jun 1934, Indianapolis, IN. Self-taught. Exhibited: 500 Festival of A, 1970; Beech Grove Festival of A, 1976. Prizes: HS, 1973; Beech Grove Festival of A, 1976. Collections: Ind. Sch for the Blind; Typo Service Corp; Beech Grove Union Federal. Note: Wife of artist Edward Elrod.

ELROD, EDWARD Indianapolis, IN b. 24 Feb 1934, Noblesville, IN. Teachers: Henry Holmes Smith. Note: Profession, Insurance Agent. Husband of artist Carol Elrod.

EMERICK, CLARA L. Kendallville, IN.

EMRICH, HARVEY [P, I, Com. A] Woodstock, NY b. 9 Oct 1884, Indianapolis, IN. Studied: Manual Training H.S.; Herron AI. Teachers: Otto Stark. Prizes: HS, 1928, 29, 33. Note: Com A, NYC.

ENGEL, HARRY [P, Edu] Bloomington, IN b. 13 Jun 1901, Romania d. 1970. Studied: Notre Dame U; Columbia U; Académie Ranson, Paris. Teachers: Maurice Denis; Zingg; Serusier; Wayman Adams; Eliot O'Hara. Exhibited: PAFA, 1939; AIC, 1940; John Herron AI (solo), 1933. Prizes: HS, 1931, 50; Ind. AC, 1931, 45, 46; Milwaukee AI, 1946. Collections: Ind. U. Note: Head of A Department, Ind. U; Curator, Ind. U AM, Bloomington.

ENGELLAND, TIM [P] Terre Haute, IN. Prizes: HS, 1972.

ENGLE, FRANK L. [Cer, S] Newburgh, IN b. 1916, near Anderson, IN. Studied: Herron Sch A; U of Calif., Los Angeles. Exhibited: 42nd Ind. A Ann, Herron AM. Prizes: Ind. State Fair, 1939; HS, 1941; Nat Chaloner Competition. Note: Head Ceramic S Dept, U of Ala., Tuscaloosa. Husband of Nanene Queen Engle.

ENGLE, HARRY L(eon) [Ldscp. P] Chicago, IL b. 24 Feb 1870, Richmond, IN d. 1968. Studied: AIC. Exhibited: AIC; Chicago Gal Assn. Prizes: Palette and Chisel Acad FA, 1917, 23. Collections: Chicago A Commission; Long Beach (Calif.) Public Library; mural, Cook Cnty Juvenile Court. Note: Director, Chicago Gal Assoc.

ENGLE, NANENE QUEEN [Ldscp. P, Mur. P, SLP, Por. P] Newburgh, IN b. Evansville, IN. Studied: Bosse H.S., Evansville; U of Southern Calif.; Herron A Sch. Collections: Wheel Sch, Evansville. Note: Author, *Pooky and Pepper*. Wife of artist Frank L. Engle

ENGLISH, GENEVIEVE [P] Nashville, IN. Studied: Valparaiso U; Indianapolis AL. Teachers: Miles Hudson; Manetta. Exhibited: Hoosier Salon Gal, 1966; Ind. A Exh, Herron AM; Chicago A Festival; Cincinnati Zoo A Show; Wabash Valley, 1960s, 70s. Prizes: HS, 1966, 69.

ENGLISH, JEAN [P, T] Sheridan, IN b. 26 Aug 1937, Port Huron, MI. Studied: Famous A Studio, Westport, CT. Exhibited: Ind. State Fair; 500 Exh; Hamilton Cnty AA. Prizes: Brown Cnty AA.

ENOCH, MARK P. [Ldscp. P, I] Carmel, IN b. 1 Oct 1947, Oklahoma City, OK. Studied: Herron Sch A; South Bend, IN. Exhibited: L. S. Ayres. Prizes: HS. Note: Advertising Consultant.

ENSFIELD, MICHAEL ROBERT [Pen&Ink Stibbling] Logansport, IN.

EPSTEIN, CLARA [Dr, Ldscp. P, Print, Por. P, Mur. P, Print] Indianapolis, IN b. c. 1887, Bruenn, Czechoslovakia d. 12 May 1955. Studied: FA Acad, Vienna; Munich; Paris. Teachers: Tina Blau; Hans Meid. Exhibited: Tokyo; Osaka; Prague; Berlin; the Hague; H. Lieber Gal, Indianapolis; Herron AM. Prizes: Vienna; HS, 1944, 52; Ind. State Fair, 1950. Note: Com. A for L. S. Ayres&Co.

ERBAUGH, MELODY [P, SG] Galveston, IN. Studied: Indianapolis AL. Prizes: Monticello AA, 1985, 86; Logansport AA, 1985, 86; Pulaski AA, 1983; Iron Horse Festival, 1986.

ERICKSON, OSCAR B. [P, Ldscp. P] Chicago, IL b. 2 Aug 1883, Milwaukee, WI d. 1968. Studied: Herron AI; Milwaukee AL; AIC; Woodstock, NY, summer school. Teachers: John F. Carlson. Exhibited: Ill. State M. Prizes: State Bank of Chicago, 1926; HS, 1929, 36; Chicago Norwegian Cl, 1929; Palette and Chisel Acad FA, 1917, 23, 32. Collections: Public Library, Long Beach, CA; Chicago A Commission; mural, Cook Cnty Juvenile Court.

ERNESTI, ETHEL H. [P] Seattle, WA. Note: Her husband, Richard, was also a painter.

ERNSTING, RICH [P] Indianapolis, IN b. 31 May 1947, Indianapolis. Studied: Frank Reilly Sch A, NY. Exhibited: Aqueous '89, Ky. WCS; Ind. AC, 1985; Brown Cnty AG; Ind. State Fair; IMA, rental gal. Prizes: HS, 1981, 86, 87; Ind. WCS, 1983, 84.

ERVIN, JOYCE [Dr] Lebanon, IN b. Minneapolis, MN. Studied: U of Minn.; John Herron A Sch. Teachers: Paul Sweany. Exhibited: 500 Festival of A; Frankfort City Fair, 1972.

ESKENAZI, LOIS [Genre P, Por. P] Indianapolis, IN b. 20 Feb 1933, Chicago, IL. Studied: Indianapolis AL. Prizes: Indianapolis AL, 1989.

ESSLING, CINDEE [P, T] Indianapolis, IN b. 2 Dec 1952, Michigan City, IN. Studied: Indianapolis AL; Stuarts A Cen. Teachers: Jo Ann Cardwell; Rosemary Lawton Thomas; Jean Vietor; Kevin Wilson; Judy Jarrett. Exhibited: Ind. State Fair, 1988 (Pr);89. Collections: IMA, Alliance Gal. Note: T, Special Education.

ETLER, VERNON [Arch] Indianapolis, IN b. Battle Creek, IA. Studied: U of Ill. Exhibited: Ind. AC, 1936.

EUSTON, J(acob) H(oward) [Print, P, C] Chesterton, IN b. 4 Oct 1892, Lebanon, PA. Studied: U of Ill.; Cleveland Sch A; AIC. Teachers: A. R. Dyer; J. Allen St. John; Alfred de Sauty. Exhibited: AIC, 1936; NGA, 1935; Chicago SE, 1935-45; Northwest PM, 1935; Southern PM, 1934-41; Ind. Soc PM, 1934-46; HS, 1937 (Pr). Collections: NGA; YMCA, Gary, IN. Note: Dir, Chicago SE.

EVANS, W. JEROME

EVERETT, DOROTHY M. [Print] Indianapolis, IN.

EVERETT, WALKER G. South Bend, IN.

EVERHART, JANE [P] Greencastle, IN.

EWELL, PATRICIA P. [P, Por. P] Monticello, IN b. IN. Studied: Purdue U; St Francis Acad; Guadalajara U, Mexico; Lafayette A Cen; Instituto San Miguel de Allende, Mexico. Exhibited: Lafayette A Cen (Pr); Monticello (solo); Purdue U; Bethlehem Church, Indianapolis.

EWING, DEBORAH A. [Dr, T] Indianapolis, IN b. 2 Dec 1950, Pana, IL. Studied: Northern Ill. U; Herron Sch A. Teachers: Nelson Stevens. Prizes: Joliet AL, 1969.

EYDEN, Jr., WILLIAM A(rnold) [Ldscp. P, Por. P, T] Indianapolis, IN b. 25 Feb 1893, Richmond, IN d. 16 Sep 1982. Teachers: W. A. Eyden, Sr; T. C. Steele; J. E. Bundy; Charles Hawthorne. Exhibited: Richmond AA, 1915-27, 29-44; PAFA; John Herron AI, 1946. Prizes: HS, 1936, 45, 62, 64-67, 69, 70, 79; Richmond Exh, 1927; Richmond AA, 1928; Wawasee A Gal, 1944; Ind. AC, 1945. Collections: Richmond AA; Ball State TC; Ind. U; public schools in Richmond, Muncie, Anderson and Indianapolis, all in Ind. Note: Owned and operated his gallery-studio in Greenwich Village, NYC, for 11 years. Columnist, *The Cornucopia*, publication of The Poet's Corner. Son of artist William Eyden, Sr.

EZELL, SANDY LYNNE [P, Ldscp. P, T] Indianapolis, IN b. 21 Mar 1939, LaCrosse, WI. Studied: St Olaf Col, Northfield, MN; Indianapolis AL. Teachers: Floyd Hopper; Marilyn Hughey Phillis; Maxine Mastefield; Al Broillette; Barbara Nechis. Exhibited: Ind. State Fair; Anderson Winter Show; Ky. WCS; Jefferson Nat Life (solo); Ind. WCS; Wabash Valley Exh, Sheldon Swope Gal. Prizes: Ky. WCS Traveling Show, 1991; Wabash Valley Exh, 1990; Ind. AC; Tippecanoe Exh, Lafayette, IN; LaCrosse Soc A&C; Mid-States A Exh, Evansville; Mile of A, Indianapolis; Wabash Valley AA, Terre Haute; Whitewater Valley AA, Connorsville; Ind. WCS. Collections: U of Louisville, KY; Jefferson Nat Life; Indianapolis Power and Light; Franklin Col; Purdue U. Note: Director A&C Center, Ft Benjamin Harrison.

F

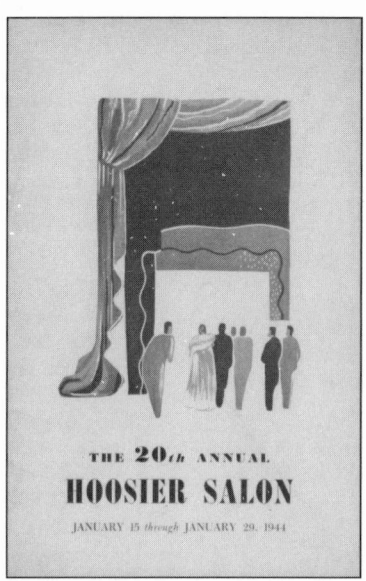

FACKERT, O(scar) W(illiam) [P, I] b. 29 Jul 1891, Jersey City, NJ. Teachers: Schook; Grant; Gottwald; Bentley. Exhibited: Midwest Exh, Kansas City AI, 1924. Prizes: Northern Ind., 1923-25. Note: T, Notre Dame U.

FAGER, W. E(win) [P, Des] Chicago, IL b. New Albany, 1897 d. 1973. Studied: AIC, 1927-28. Prizes: HS, 1928. Note: Established himself in Chicago as an interior designer. Specialized in commissions for lamps, tables and other furniture.

FAGERBURG, LORENE K. Gary, IN.

FAILING, FRANCES E(lizabeth) [P, T] Indianapolis, IN b. Canisteo, NY. Studied: PIASch; Western Reserve; Columbia U; Butler U; Ind. U; Alfred U; Cape Cod Sch A. Teachers: C. Martin; Hawthorne; Frank Wilcox. Exhibited: Cincinnati AM, 1934, 36, 37; PAFA, 1936; AIC, 1937; BM, 1937; NAWA, 1936, 38, 41; John Herron AI, 1933-35, 37, 38, 40-43; Ind. AC, 1932-34, 36; Kansas City AI, 1938; Dallas MFA, 1938; MFA, Houston, 1939; Baylor U, 1938; Ball State A Gal, 1937. Prizes: HS, 1947; NAWA, 1937. Note: T, Head of FA Dept, Washington H.S., Indianapolis, beginning1935.

FARMER, EVELYN [P] Indianapolis, IN. Note: Member, Brown Cnty A Gal.

FARNHAM, JULIA C. Winnetka, IL. Note: Worked in Nashville, IN.

FARRELL, RON [P, Ldscp. P] Bremen, IN b. Jul 1912, Cleveland, OH. Studied: Cleveland Inst of Technology; South Bend A Cen; U of Mich. Teachers: Emil Weddidge; Ed Herrmann; Josef Wrobel. Prizes: HS, 1974; Union Lg Show, Chicago, 1969, 72; Fletcher's A Festival, 1968-70, 73; Fulton Cnty A Festival, 1972; Elkhart AL, 1966; Four Flags A Show, Niles, MI, 1973. Note: Vice President and general manager, Bremen Bearing Co, Inc.

FAUCETT, JULIA ASHTON [Ldscp. P, T] Franklin, IN b. 21 Jun 1903, Boonefield, IN. Studied: John Herron Sch A; Franklin Col; Ind. U. Teachers: Harry Davis. Exhibited: Howard Cnty Public Library, Kokomo. Prizes: Ind. State Fair; Religious Show. Collections: Eli Lilly&Co, Indianapolis; Ind. State U; Franklin Col; Merchants Bank, Indianapolis.

FECHTMAN, HELEN LOGAN [Por. P, Ldscp. P, S] b. 27 Jul 1901, Brookville, IN d. 1985. Studied: Herron Sch A. Exhibited: Indianapolis AL. Note: Wife of artist Hugo W. Fechtman.

FECHTMAN, HUGO W(illiam) b. 12 Sep 1902, Indianapolis, IN d. 1982. Exhibited: A for Religion, Bethlehem Lutheran Church. Note: Self-taught creator of assemblage boxes. Influenced by Joseph Cornell. Husband of artist Helen Fechtman.

FEHSENFELD, BECKY [P, T] Indianapolis, IN. b. 22 Apr 1953, Worthington, OH. Studied: Otterbein Col, Westerville, OH. Teachers: Billie Cothran; Earl Hassenpflug; John Tymitz. Exhibited: Art in Bloom Gal, Naples, FL, 1988-92; Circle Theatre (solo), Indianapolis, 1993; Indianapolis AL (solo), 1990, 92; American United Life Bldg (solo), Indianapolis, 1992; Whitewater Valley Reg; Oil Pastel Assn of Am; Maryland Pastel Assn. Note: T and Board Member, Indianapolis AL.

FEHSENFELD, MARGUERITE KERN [P, S] Indianapolis, IN b. 12 Dec c. 1890 NY d. c. 1985. Studied: MOMA; Cape Ann Sch A; ASL. Teachers: Joseph Floch; Billie Cothran; Floyd Hopper; Sophie Johnstone. Exhibited: Nantucket&Taylor Gal (Pr); Artz Gal, NY. Note: Art patron as well artist who continued to paint into her nineties. Instrumental in development of Indianapolis AL. Moved to Indianapolis from N.Y. when she was in her sixties to marry John Fehsenfeld.

FEIGHNER, MARILYN OSBORN [P, Print] Marion, IN b. 1926, Marion, IN. Studied: Ball State U; Herron AI; DePauw U. Exhibited: WC USA, Springfield, MO, 1964; Ball State U (solo), 1964; Preview '71, Cincinnati, OH, 1970; Ind. State Fair, 1964-73; DePauw U (solo), 1967; Ind. A Exh, IMA, 1964, 66, 67, 69, 71; Works on Paper, IMA, 1972; Sheldon Swope A Gal (solo), 1970; Ft Wayne M (solo), 1973. Prizes: HS, 1963, 68, 78. Collections: Ind. U; DePauw U; Notre Dame U; Indianapolis Public Schs; Ind. State U; Ball State U; Lafayette A Cen; RCA Corp; Taylor U.

FELDMAN, LUCINDA PIERSOL

FELTS, MAIDIE CRANDALL Chicago, IL.

FELTZ, JUNE B. [P, Por. P, S] Indianapolis, IN b. 29 Mar 1916, Indianapolis. Studied: Indianapolis Acad Com A; Cranbrook Acad, MI; Positona, Italy. Teachers: Elmer Taflinger. Prizes: Indianapolis AL, 1970s. Note: Became Mrs. June Feltz Hill.

FENDIG, LILIAN (Mrs. Ralph) [I, P, Por. P, Ldscp. P, T] Rensselaer, IN b. 1 Apr c. 1912, London, England d. 25 Nov 1985. Studied: Hornsey Col A, London, England. Exhibited: William Engle Gal, Indianapolis, 1984, 90-91 (posthumously). Prizes: HS, 1957, 59, 60, 69, 72; Ind. AC; Northern Ind. Salon; Ft Wayne Women's Cl. Collections: Franklin Col; Ind. U Union; Marion AG; Lafayette Gal; Rensselaer H.S.; Ind. Nat Bank; Indianapolis Public Sch; Associated Group, Blue Cross/Blue Shield, Indianapolis. Note: Founding member, Brown Cnty AG. Worked as quick-sketch artist for the Red Cross during the war where she met her husband. Affiliated with the theatre dept, St Joseph's Col, Rensselaer through the 1960s. Painted frequently on location in Cotswold, England; Canada; France; and U.S. Niece of well-known architect, Lord Alfred Bossom who was an early pioneer in the skyscraper movement. Portfolio of Fendig's woodblock prints published by William Engle Gal, 1993.

FENIMORE, KRESZENTIA S.

FENIMORE, R(alph) A. [Ldscp. P] Indianapolis, IN d. c. 1951. Studied: Valparaiso U. Note: Supervising foreman, Ind. Bell Telephone Co.

FENTZ, LARRY R. [Com. A, Dr, P] Indianaplis, IN b. 1954, Greenfield, IN. Teachers: Luke Buck. Prizes: HS, 1979.

FERGUSON, SARAH H.

FERGUSON, WILLIAM R. [P, Com. A] Worthington, IN. Studied: George Washington U, Washington, D.C.; Corcoran Gal, Washington, D.C. Exhibited: Brown Cnty A Gal, Nashville, IN; Ind. State Fair; Owen Cnty Fair; Owen Cnty AG; Shawnee Theatre (solo).

FERRARA, NELLE [P] Indianapolis, IN b. KY. Studied: Indianapolis AL. Teachers: Leah Traugott; Floyd Hopper; Edward Manetta. Exhibited: 500 Exh, Indianapolis, 1973; Ind. State Fair, 1973; Mid-States Exh, Evansville, 1973; Indianapolis AL, 1973.

FIELD, T(homas) V. [Ldscp. P] Chicago, IL b. Dec 1866, Cincinnati, OH. Exhibited: AIC, 1928; Business Men's AC.

FIELDS, W. DAVID [P] Bedford, IN.

FINCH, F. [Car]

FINCH, LEWIS E. [T] Indianapolis, IN b. 19 Apr 1899. Teachers: Henry B. Snell; Walter Beck; William Forsyth.

FINCHUM, MYRON [Com. A, I, Des, P, T] Indianapolis, IN b. 1942, Martinsville, IN d. 9 Nov 1991. Studied: Herron Sch A, graduated in 1964. Prizes: HS, 1979, 80, 81, 83, 86; IHA, Inc. Exh; Wabash Valley Exh. Note: T, Pro A Studios, East Side AL; Adele Wendell Sch A, Indianapolis.

FINK, ROBERT R. [Por. P] Terre Haute, IN b. 10 Jul 1909, Terre Haute. Studied: Herron A Sch; Elmer E. Taflinger A Sch. Teachers: William Forsyth; Clifton Wheeler; Wayman Adams. Prizes: HS, 1936; Ind. State Fair, 1936. Collections: Ind. State TC.

FINNAN, FLORENCE [P] Richmond, IN b. Oswego, NY d. c. 1985. Studied: State U of N.Y., Oswego, NY; Ind. U, East. Teachers: Tom Thomas; Don Dennis; Ray Loos; Doris Turnbaugh. Prizes: Richmond, IN, 1976, 79, 81. Collections: Richmond AA; Kokomo Public Library.

FINNEY, SUE [P] Plainfield, IN.

FISCHER, GLORIA [Ab, Dr, Print, Genre P, T] Indianapolis, IN b. 28 Oct 1941, Houston, TX. Studied: Herron Sch A; IUPUI; Indianapolis AL. Teachers: Jan Tannenbaum; Robert Berkshire; Peg Fierke. Exhibited: Editions Limited Gal, Indianapolis, 1983, 85, 88, 89, 93 (solo); Intl Min Print Show, Talleri Gal, Cadaques, Spain, 1983-92; Indianapolis AL, 1983; AM Rio Grande de Sul, Brazil, 1989; Herron, 1989. Prizes: Pratt Inst, 1986; HS, 1984. Collections: Ontario Corp; Cooper and Lybrand; Kasler and Associates; Radisson Plaza, Indianapolis; Am United Life Insurance; Eli Lilly&Co; Barth Electric; AM, Porto Alegre, Rio Grande de Sul, Brazil.

FISCHER, MILDRED [HPA, T] Cincinnati, OH. Note: T, Ft Wayne A Sch.

FISCHER, TERRI [Woodcut A] Connersville, IN.

FISCUS, GORDON W. [P, Ldscp. P, Com. A, T] Nashville, IN b. 1902, Indianapolis, IN. Studied: AIC; Herron Sch A; San Francisco AL. Teachers: William Forsyth; Elmer Taflinger; Randolph Coats; Maynard Dixon; Walter Ufer. Exhibited: San Francisco AL (solo), 1934; Ind. State Fair; Pleasant Run Gal; Southside AL; Heritage A Gal; Brown Cnty AG. Note: T, John Herron A Sch for 18 years. Des, Rhoades-Humphreys Studio, Indianapolis; Des, Ford, Brown & Mathews, Chicago; Des, Sidener Van Riper; Des, Bozell&Jacobs, Indianapolis.

FISH, JULIA VanCLEAVE [Min. P] Chicago, IL b. Crawfordsville, IN. Teachers: Shunnon; Eda Nemoeda. Collections: Ill. Women's Athletic Cl Salon.

FISHER, HELEN E. [Dr, Ldscp. P, P] Greenwood, IN b. 24 May 1909, Frankfort, IN d. 25 May 1993. Studied: Herron Sch A; Indianapolis AL; Butler U. Teachers: Jon Jonson; Mrya Richards; Rosemary Lawton Thomas; Paul Hadley. Exhibited: Washington WCS; Miniature P, S Soc Show, Watercolor, Smithsonian Inst, Washington, D.C., 1966, 67, 69, 72, 74, 75, 78 (Pr); Brown Cnty AG (Pr). Collections: Ind. State M. Note: Silhouette Collages, original conceptions. Lectured, "Silhouettes in Am," throughout Ind.

FISHER, LILLIE FRY [P, C] Terrace Park, OH b. Monticello, IN d. c. 1943. Studied: Cincinnati A Acad; ASL; Corcoran A Sch; Paris. Teachers: George Elmer Browne; Arthur Wolfe; Guy Wiggins; Emile Gruppe; Cameron Burnside (a student of Claude Monet). Exhibited: Cincinnati Women's AC, 1934; NAWA; Lafayette AA; Ohio State Fair, Columbus. Prizes: HS, 1928, 36. Collections: Cincinnati Public Sch; Permanent Gal, Youngstown, OH. Note: Daughter of woodcarver William H. Fry; granddaughter of Henry L. Fry of Bath, England, one of the pioneers in the development of art in Cincinnati; sister of artist Laura Fry. Associated with the A Dept, Purdue U, for 4 years.

FISHER, WILLIAM R. [Des, P] Winchester, IN. Studied: John Herron AI (completed in 1926); Hartford A Sch; ASL. Exhibited: 47th Ann Ind. A Exh, Herron AM, 1953; Lieber Gal, Indianapolis; Am WCS, NY; 3rd Intl Leica Photography Exh; Morton Gal (solo), NYC.

FITZGERALD, FRANCIS E. Indianapolis, IN.

FLAMMANG, LAWRENCE [I] Evanston, IL b. Evanston, IL. Teachers: William Forsyth. Exhibited: Herron AI.

FLANAGAN, EM(mabelle) (Mrs. J. E.) [Ldscp. P, T] Anderson, IN b. 1 Jul 1915, Sandusky, OH. Studied: Purdue U; Indianapolis AL; Herron A Sch; Ind. AC; Longboat Key A Gal. Teachers: Frederick Rigley; Emile Gruppe; Edward Manetta; Paul Sweany; Marilyn Bendell; Isabelle White; George Burrows. Exhibited: Brown Cnty AG; Ind. State Fair, 1960s; Swope Gal, 1960s. Note: Painted in Bradenton, FL.

FLECK, MARY E.

FLOCK, BARBARA [Dr, Ldscp. P, SLP] Rockville, IN b. 27 Jan 1931, Terre Haute, IN. Teachers: Louise Hansen. Exhibited: Bicentennial Exh, Paris, IL. Prizes: Wabash Valley A Exh, 1984; Parke Cnty Bicentennial Exh, 1973; Ind. State Fair. Collections: Covered Bridge A Gal; Billy Creek A Gal.

FLOWERS, WINIFRED b. Michigan City, IN. Studied: Elmer Taflinger Studios. Exhibited: Ind. State Fair, 1947.

FLYNN, GLADYS RAE [Ldscp. P, Genre P, S, Por. P, T] Russiaville, IN b. 28 Dec 1922, French Lick, Orange Cnty, IN. Self-taught. Prizes: Kokomo AA, 1976, 80; HS, 1982. Collections: Ind. U, Kokomo extension; Showalter Western Sch Library.

FOGG, F. B. [HPA, JA] Muncie, IN. Studied: U of Ariz.; Ind. U; Ball State U; Oregon State Col; U of Notre Dame. Exhibited: Mullaly-Matisse, Birmingham, MI; Fireside Gal; Cain Gal; Jay Cnty A Gal; Wustum AM, Racine, WI, all solo. Prizes: Ft Wayne AG; Fulbright Candidate; Columbus '84. Collections: Marsh, Inc; Foxfire Restaurant; First Nat Bank, Minneapolis, MN; Ball Corp, Muncie. Note: Real name, Annette V. Johnson.

FOGLE, ARNOLD B. [P] Shelbyville, IN b. c. 1898.

FOLSON, JOWELL [Dr] Columbus, IN.

FORGET, VERDAYLE M. [P, Dr] Indianapolis, IN/Seattle, WA b. Alliance, NE. Studied: Famous A Sch. Teachers: Dennis Ramsey. Exhibited: Plaza Gal, 1982. Prizes: HS, 1982. Note: Painted 12 paintings for 1988 Indianapolis Zoo calendar.

FORKNER, J. EDGAR [Por. P, P, T] Seattle, WA b. 31 Jul 1867, Richmond, IN d. 7 Jul 1945. Studied: ASL. Teachers: J. Carroll Beckwith; Irving Wiles; William Merritt Chase; Frank DuMond. Exhibited: Seattle AM (solo); AIC; Chicago World Fair, 1933; PA, 1932. Prizes: HS, 1926-28, 30, 33, 36, 43; Seattle FA Soc, 1918, 23; Philadelphia Acad. Collections: AIC; Seattle AM. Note: Painted boats and flowers primarily. T, Auditorium Tower, Chicago.

FORSYTH, CONSTANCE [Ldscp. P, Print, Li, T] Austin, TX b. 18 Aug 1903, Indianapolis, IN d. 22 Jan 1987. Studied: Butler U; John Herron Sch A; PAFA; Broadmoor A Acad, Colorado Springs, CO. Teachers: William Forsyth; G. Harding; B. Robinson; W. Lockwood; H. McCarter; Clifton Wheeler; Myra Richards. Exhibited: PAFA; MFA, Houston; Dallas MFA; Texas FA Assn; Kansas City AI; Denver AM; NAWA. Prizes: HS, 1928, 49, 61, 63; John Herron AI, 1936, 38; Dallas Print Soc, 1945. Collections: IMA; Joslyn Mem M, Omaha NE; John Herron AI; Ball State TC; Manual Training H.S., Indianapolis; Scottish Rite Cathedral, Indianapolis; Butler U, Indianapolis; Irvington Hist Soc. Note: I, *Lincoln the Hoosier*. T, John Herron AI, 1931-33; T, Western Col, OH, 1939; T, U of Texas, 1940-73, Professor Emeritus of A, 1973. Daughter of artist William Forsyth and sister-in-law of artist Robert Selby.

FORSYTH, WILLIAM J. [P, Ldscp. P, T] Irvington, IN b. 15 Oct 1854, California, Hamilton Cnty, OH d. 29 Mar 1935, Indianapolis. Studied: Ind. Sch A; Royal Acad, Munich. Teachers: Nikolaus Gysis; John W. Love; James F. Gookins; Ludwig von Loefftz; Gyula Benczur; Lietzenmeyer. Prizes: HS, 1925-27, 29; Royal Acad Show, Munich, 1885; La. Purchase Expo, St Louis, MO, 1904; Intl FA Expo, Buenos Aires, 1910; SWA, 1910; P.-P. Expo, San Francisco, 1915; Indianapolis AA, 1924, 25; Richmond AA Ann, 1911, 12. Collections: Indianapolis Athletic Cl; Ind. State M; Indianapolis Public Schs; Herron AI; Indianapolis AA; Public Gal, Richmond, IN; Brooklyn M; Vanderpoel AA, Chicago. Note: Associated with J. Ottis Adams in the teaching of art classes in Muncie and Ft Wayne, IN and with T. C. Steele at the second Ind. Sch of A in 1891. T, John Herron AI, 1906-33. Father of artist Constance Forsyth and father-in-law of artist Robert Selby.

FOSTER, BETTY (Elizabeth Jane) [P, Des, T] Indianapolis, IN b. 16 Jul 1910, Columbus, IN. Studied: Ind. U; Herron A Sch; AIC; Irving Manoir AI, Chicago; Fabir Birren, Color Consultant, Cambridge, England. Teachers: William Forsyth; Robert E. Burke; Clifton Wheeler. Exhibited: Ind. AC, 1932, 33, 38-46; NAC, 1938; John Herron AI, 1934, 35, 38. Prizes: Ind. AC, 1944, 45. Note: A Critic, *Indianapolis News.* T, Emmerich Manual Training H.S., Indianapolis. She became Mrs. Ben Blumberg, moved to Terre Haute. She was elected to the Board of Directors of the HS Patrons Assn in 1971.

FOSTER, ERNEST B. [Por. P, Ldscp. P, Mur. P, Des, T] Indianapolis, IN b. Rush Cnty, IN. Studied: Herron A Sch; Sch of Industrial A, Pa. Mus. Teachers: William Forsyth; Brandt Steele; Herman Deigendesch; Charles Thomas Scott; Philip Muhr; J. Frank Copeland; Helen A. Fox; Charles B. Dunn. Exhibited: Ind. A Ann; Herron AM. Prizes: Joseph F. Temple Foundation Scholarship. Note: T, Herron Sch A. Assistant, H. Hanley Parker, Mur. P.

FOSTER, ORION L. [P] Lafayette, IN b. 12 May 1878, Ogden, IN. Studied: Purdue U. Teachers: Harry Leith-Ross; L. A. Fry. Exhibited: Ind. A Ann; Herron AM. Note: President and founder, Lafayette AA, started in 1908.

FOUREMAN, NANCY [P] Greenville, OH b. 24 Jun 1944, Greenville, OH. Studied: Ind. State TC, Terre Haute, IN; Miami U, Oxford, OH. Teachers: Clear; Wisenhunt; Easton. Exhibited: Am P in Paris, France; Middletown FA Cen, OH; A Train, NY. Prizes: Northshore AA, Glouchester, MA, 1990; Jay Cnty A Council, Portland, IN, 1990; Grumbacher Co Award, 1989. Collections: Moroki, Japan; A Instruction, Minneapolis, MN; Belden Corp, Richmond, IN; Graphic Press, Portland, IN; Second Nat Bank, Richmond, IN.

FOURNIER, ALEXIS JEAN [Ldscp. P, W, T] East Aurora, NY b. 4 Jul 1865, St Paul, MN d. 20 Jan 1948, Lackawanna, NY. Studied: Minneapolis Acad FA; Académie Julian, Paris. Teachers: Henri Harpignies; D. Volk; Laurens. Exhibited: NAD; NAC; Corcoran Gal A; PAFA; AIC; Minneapolis IA; Brown Cnty AA. Prizes: Buffalo, 1911; Minn. Indst Soc; HS, 1934, 36. Collections: Roycroft Salon, East Aurora, NY; Vanderbilt U; Detroit IA; Public Sch, Gary, IN.

FOWLER, DAVID L. [P, Com. A] Chicago, IL b. Memphis, TN. Studied: Chicago Acad A; AIC. Teachers: Ruth Ford; Giesbert; Chapin. Collections: M, Boonville, IN. Note: Son of Evansville architect, Frank Fowler. Worked for Keller Crescent Printing Co. Left Evansville in mid-1930s.

FOWLER, JANE ANDERSON [P] Gary, IN. Prizes: HS, 1950, 58.

FOX, FONTAINE [Car, I] Greenwich, CT b. 1884, Louisville, KY d. 9 Aug 1964. Studied: Indiana U, Bloomington, IN. Collections: Huntington Library, San Marino, CA. Note: Created cartoon, "Toonerville Trolley." Member, Soc I. Worked at the *Louisville Herald*, the *Louisville Times* and the *Chicago Post*.

FOX, THEODORE [Ldscp. P, SLP, Dr] Nashville, IN b. Dec 1900, Gelsenkirchen-Buer, West Germany d. 1988. Studied: Folkvank M, Essen in the Ruhr; AIC; Munich, Germany; U of Ill. Teachers: Hugo Troendle; Schroeder; Krebriel; Guenther; Peter Bodnar; Bradshaw. Exhibited: AIC; Libertyville A Cen; U of Chicago; U of Ill. Prizes: HS, 1969, 79, 80. Collections: Topeka Public Library, Kansas; U of Ill., Urbana; Evansville M of A&Sc.

FRAIN, NELLIE M. [I, W, P] Chicago, IL b. Furnesville, IN. Studied: AIC; Northwestern U; U of Ill. Exhibited: AIC; Century Progress, Chicago. Collections: Northwestern U Library; Presbyterian Hospital; U of Ill. Col of Dentistry. Note: Specialty, medical illustrations; I, *Pathology of the Mouth* by Moorehead and Dewey, *Surgical Anatomy* by Eycleschymer.

FRAIN, TIMOTHY C. [Ldscp. P, T] Wabash, IN b. 12 Mar 1950, Winamac, IN. Teachers: Thad Miller. Exhibited: Jewish Community Cen (solo), 1989; Ft Wayne MA, Alliance Gal, 1987-90; Anderson FA Cen, Winter Show, 1987, 88. Note: Works with cast paper designs and silkscreen.

FRAME, THELMA [Ldscp. P, Print, Dr, T] Richmond, IN b. 7 May 1919, Hebron, IN. Studied: Ind. U; Colo. Col. Teachers: John Nartker; Homer Hacker; Judy Betts; Zoltan Szabo; Don Dennis; Dora Hagge; Bob Brubaker. Exhibited: Anderson Winter Show, 1985; IHA, 1991, 92; Richmond A; Whitewater Valley. Prizes: Ohio WCS, S.W. Reg, 1982; Randolph Cnty, 1981; Richmond AM, 1991. Collections: Richmond AM; City of Springfield, OH; Eaton Nat Bank, Eaton, OH; Minnetrista Cultural Cen, Muncie, IN. Note: Lived in Eaton, Ohio, from 1970-87. T, many years in Ind. public schs in Merrillville, Columbus, Mishawaka and Richmond.

FRANTZ, DOROTHY M. [P, Ldscp. P, T] Midlothian, IL/Nashville, IN b. 1904, Chicago, IL d. 1972. Exhibited: Brown Cnty AG. Prizes: Palette&Chisel Acad, Chicago; Wabash Valley Show. Collections: Ind. U, Bloomington; Ind. and Ill. Schs. Note: T, Ridge Park Fieldhouse.

FRASER, KATHRYN E. [Dr] Elwood, IN.

FRAZELL, THOMAS G. [Print, P, Dr] Indianapolis, IN. Exhibited: Winthrop Gal, 1975.

FREDERICK, LOUIS J. South Bend, IN.

FREED, ERNEST B(radfield) [P, T] Rockville, IN b. 20 Jul 1908, Rockville. Studied: U of Ill.; PAFA; U of Iowa. Teachers: C. E. Bradbury; C. V. Donovan; E. E. Nearpass; D. Garber; G. Harding; H. R. Poore; R. C. Nuse; Grant Wood; Mauricio Lasansky. Prizes: Brooklyn P Ann; Ind. State Fair, 1936, 37, 38. Collections: State TC, Kirksville, MO.

FREELAND, ANNE

FREEMAN, PEGGY DALTON [Ldscp. P, Por. P] New Castle, IN b. 21 Nov 1924, Lenoir City, TN. Teachers: Elizabeth Dodds Shafer; Adele Wendell; Kerry Holsapple; Adrian Hansen; Bill Hughes. Exhibited: Richmond Professional Exh, 1985, 86, 88, 89; Ind. State Fair, 1986, 88, 89. Prizes: New Castle, 1987, 89; Richmond, 1985.

FREER, RAYMOND [Ab, Ldscp. P] Anderson, IN b. 22 Oct 1941, Lexington, KY. Studied: Anderson U; Herron Sch A; Calif. State U, Los Angeles; U of Calif., Riverside Claremont; Boston State U. Exhibited: Nat Drawing and Small S Comp, Ball State U, 1980; Indianapolis 500 Exh, 1974; Indianapolis AL, 1988. Prizes: Anderson Area Ann, 1991; A for Mental Health, St Johns Hospital, Anderson, IN, 1982. Collections: St Johns Hospital, Anderson, IN; Anderson U, Anderson, IN.

FRENCH, RAY H. [Ldscp. P, Print, S, T] Greencastle, IN b. 16 May 1919, Terre Haute, IN. Studied: U of Iowa; John Herron A Sch; Academia di Belle Arti, Florence, Italy. Teachers: M. Mikel Williams; Mauricio Lasansky; Maxil Ballinger; Donald Mattison. Exhibited: Walker A Cen, 1949; MOMA, 1953, 54; Pratt Graphic Cen, 1977-79. Prizes: John Herron AI, 1956; Pennell Purchase Award, 1960; 50 Ind. Prints, John Herron AI, 1958. Collections: MOMA; LOC; Nat M of Am A; Victoria&Albert M, London; Bibliotique Nationale, Paris; Brooklyn M; Denver AM; Philadelphia AM. Note: Professor of A, DePauw U, 1948-84; Head of Dept, 1970-78; Curator DePauw U A Coll, 1978-84; Professor Emeritus of A and Emeritus Curator, 1984.

FREUDENBERG, SUE [Ldscp. P, SLP] Ft Branch, IN b. 4 Aug 1933, Gibson Cnty, IN. Studied: Evansville M, workshops. Exhibited: Evansville M, 1988; Ft Wayne, 1988. Prizes: HS, 1985; Owensboro MFA, 1986; Grumbacher Bronze Medallion, 1984. Collections: Vincennes U; Security Bank and Trust, Vincennes; Cen for Mental Health, Anderson; Progress Printing Co, Owensboro, KY.

FREY, E. ROGER [Ldscp. P, Por. P, T] Indianapolis, IN b. 2 Dec 1908, Indianapolis. Studied: John Herron AI; Elmer Taflinger A Sch; ASL; Indianapolis AL. Teachers: William Forsyth; Elmer Taflinger; George Bridgman; Frank DuMond; William Ashby; Billie Cothran. Exhibited: John Herron AI, 1933; Indianapolis AL, 1986. Prizes: HS, 1976; Ind. WCS, 1986; Ind. AC, 1988. Collections: Indianapolis Public Library; Ind. Bell Telephone.

FROST, MARGUERITE

FROST, MARTHA LEE [S, T] Indianapolis, IN b. Madison, IN. Studied: John Herron Sch A; PAFA. Teachers: William Forsyth; Forrest Stark; Albert Laesslie. Exhibited: Irvington A Exh, 1934. Prizes: HS, 1934; Ind. A Ann, Herron AM, 1933, 36. Note: T, Butler U; T, Greensburg H.S.

FROST, MAURICE D. [P, T] Indianapolis, IN. Prizes: HS, 1951. Note: T, Indianapolis Public Sch.

FROULA, JOSEF [P] Chicago, IL.

FRY, LAURA A. [P, C, T] Loveland, OH b. White County, IN. Studied: ASL; France; England. Teachers: William Fry; Kenyon Cox; William M. Chase; Thomas Noble; Louis Rebisco; Frank Alvah Parsons. Exhibited: Sevres M, Paris; British M, London; Boston MFA; Cincinnati M Assn; St Louis AM; Herron MA. Prizes: HS, 1925; Columbian Expo, 1893; Cincinnati. Collections: Music Hall, Cincinnati. Note: Head of Purdue U's A Dept, early 1900s. Sister of artist Lillie Fry Fisher. Daughter of woodcarver William H. Fry.

FUGATE, LINDA [P] Greenfield, IN. Studied: Indianapolis AL.

FULLEN, HERSCHEL E. [P, Com. A] Plainfield, IN b. c. · 1905 d. 5 Jan 1991. Studied: John Herron AI; Ind. U. Teachers: George Jo Mess; Ruth Anderson; Grace Senter. Note: Com A, William H. Block Co. and H. P. Wasson before he worked in his own Com A business. Author, *These Are My Hands.*

FULLER, BARBARA J. [MM] NY. Note: Worked in Ft Wayne, IN.

FULTS, LOUISE CHRISTIN *(See Agnew, Louise Fults)*

FULWIDER, EDWIN L. [P, Li, T] Idaho b. 15 Aug 1913, Bloomington, IN. Studied: Herron A Sch. Teachers: William Forsyth; Clifton Wheeler; Ralph Sowell; Donald M. Mattison; Henrik M. Mayer. Exhibited: HS, 1942 (Pr); Herron AI, 1936-39, 40 (Pr), 41, 42, 43 (Pr), 44, 45 (Pr), 46; Cincinnati AM, 1939, 41; AIC, 1940, 41; GGE, 1939. Collections: mural, First Methodist Episcopal Church, Bloomington, IN; Herron AM, permanent collection of prints; U.S. embassies in Rome, Italy and Ankara, Turkey. Note: T, John Herron A Sch. Chairman A Dept, Miami U, Oxford, Ohio, 1963-73.

FUNK, ARLENE NELSON [Ldscp. P, SLP, P] Kentland, IN b. Green Bay, WI. Teachers: Shirley Friedman; Sister Rufinia; Hilary Eddy; Zoltan Szabo. Exhibited: Fish Bowl Gal, St Elizabeth's Hospital, Lafayette, IN, 1988; Tri Kappa Sorority (solo), Kentland, IN, 1984; Newton Cnty Fair, 1980, 81 (Pr).

FUNK, CLOTILDE EMBREE (Mrs. C. Douglass) [I, P, T] Indianapolis, IN b. 1893, Princeton, IN d. 10 Nov 1991. Studied: John Herron AI; Women's A Sch of Cooper Union, NYC; ASL; NAD; Columbia U; N.Y. U; Roerick Sch A; Grand Chaumiere, Paris. Exhibited: Ind. State Fair, 1963-65; Mid-States Exh, Evansville, 1963-68; Jewish Community Cen (solo), 1966; Whitewater Valley Exh, Connersville, 1965, 66, 68-70; 500 Festival. Prizes: Whitewater Valley, 1968; HS, 1969, 70. Collections: Walter Library, U of Minn.; Ind. Mem Union Building, Ind. U, Bloomington; William Allen White Library, Wichita, KS. Note: T, Indianapolis AL; T, Jewish Community Cen. I, more than 30 children's books, including *John of Pudding Lane, To See the Queen* and *Ladycake Farm.* One of the first women to be hired in the *New York Times* art department.

FUSON, BARBARA [Print, Genre P, Por. P, T] Syracuse, IN b. 12 Mar 1935, Indianapolis, IN. Studied: DePauw U; Famous A Sch of Com A; N.Y. Sch of Interior Des. Teachers: D. Kingman; Chris Shink; Ed Whitney; Irving Shapiro; Daniel Greene; Rob O'Dell; Floyd Hopper. Exhibited: Ind. Wildlife A, 1990; Ind. WCS, 1990. Prizes: Ventures in Creativity, Ft Wayne, 1989; Ind. WCS, 1985. Collections: GTE, Ft Wayne; Greencastle Central Nat Bank.

G

GAALEMA, MARY [P] Plainfield, IN b. 8 Mar 1920, Hendricks Cnty, IN. Teachers: Elmer Taflinger; Marian Cassel; Clayson Baker; Ruth Anderson; Nadine Starken. Exhibited: Ind. State Fair, 1973. Prizes: Hendricks Cnty AL, 1970, 73.

GAHMAN, FLOYD [P, T] NYC b. 14 Oct 1899, Elida, OH. Studied: Valparaiso U, IN; Columbia U; NAD. Teachers: Hobart Nichols; H. V. Poor; H. Carnohan. Exhibited: All A Am, 1936-41, 43; NAD, 1932-43; WFNY, 1939. Collections: Scarsdale Women's Cl; Penn. State U. Prizes: Tiffany Foundation Fellowship; SC, 1942; All A Am, 1942. Note: Combat pilot, World War I; Air Force Captain, World War II. T, Penn. State U.

GALBRAITH, DALLAS A. b. Peru, IN. Studied: Ind. State Col.

GALBRAITH, R. KARL [P] Indianapolis, IN.

GALLAGHER, LESTER W. [Ldscp. P, S, P] Ogden Dunes, IN d. c. 1974. Studied: Am Acad A, Chicago. Exhibited: Ill. Festival A, McCormick Place; Northern Ind. A Salon. Prizes: HS, 1965, 70.

GALLOWAY, WILLIAM A. [S, Stone Carver, T] Nashville, IN b. 12 Feb 1954, Beech Grove, IN. Studied: Ind. U. Teachers: Clarence "Dick" Hayes; Henry Morris; J. P. Darreau. Exhibited: Ind. Limestone S Contest, 1988, 89 (Pr), 90 (Pr). Collections: Washington Cathedral; Iowa State Capital Building; White River Park; Abercrombie Mansion, Ind. U; Bloomington City Parks.

GAMBILL, WOODROW J. [P] Clinton, IN.

GANT, ELSIE [P] Richmond, IN.

GARBER, DANIEL [P, Print] Lumberville, PA b. 11 Apr 1880, North Manchester, IN d. 6 Jul 1958. Studied: Cincinnati A Acad; PAFA. Teachers: Vincent Nowottny; Thomas Pollock Anshutz. Prizes: NAD, 1909, 15, 17, 27; ACP, 1910; CI, 1910, 24; CGA, 1910, 12, 21; AIC, 1911; Buenos Aires Expo, 1910; PAFA, 1911, 18, 19, 23, 29, 37; P.-P. Expo, San Francisco, 1915; SC, 1916; Newport AA, 1916. Collections: CGA; Cincinnati M; AIC; St Louis AM; U of Mo.; CI; M of A&Sc, Los Angeles; MMA; PAFA; Nat AC; Detroit AI; Mem Hall, Philadelphia;

Albright Gal; Swarthmore Col; NGA and Phillips Mem Gal, both in Washington, D. C.; Herron AI; Woodmere A Gal. Note: T, PAFA.

GARCEAU, HARRY J(oseph) [P, C] Muncie, IN b. 11 Jul 1876, Providence, RI d. 14 Feb 1954. Studied: RISD. Teachers: S. Tolman; F. Mathews. Exhibited: Ind. AA; Herron AM; Ball State TC. Prizes: HS, 1940.

GARNER, OPAL [T] Plainfield, IN b. IN. Prizes: Ind. State Fair, amateur, 1963, 65. Note: Member, Brown Cnty A Gal.

GARRIOTT, MICHELE [P] Beech Grove, IN.

GARRISON, ANNIE DYE Chicago, IL.

GARRO, JEAN COVAL [Ldscp. P, SLP] Indianapolis, IN b. 3 Feb 1922, Indianapolis. Studied: Arsenal Tech H.S.; Ball State TC. Teachers: Elmer Taflinger; Paul Sweany. Exhibited: Wabash Valley Exh, 1990; Ind. State Fair, 1989. Prizes: HS, 1985; Brown Cnty Assn Show, 1980; Mile of A, 1978. Collections: General Motors; Rose Hulman Inst.

GARSON, ETTA CORBETT Oak Park, IL.

GARVIN, EVELYN

GASKINS, LETHA H(eckman) (Mrs. O. K.) [P] Indianapolis, IN b. Indianapolis. Studied: John Herron A Sch; Famous A Sch; Butler U. Teachers: Edward R. Sitzman; C. Curry Bohm; George Jo Mess; Garo Antreasian; Elmer Taflinger; Eliot O'Hara; Charles Burchfield; Francis Chapin. Exhibited: Nevelle M, Green Bay, WI; Louisville, KY; Ohio State Reg, Athens. Prizes: Michiana Reg; Ind. AC; Indianapolis AL; Ind. State Fair. Collections: Butler U, Indianapolis; Indianapolis Public Sch #84.

GATES, MARGERY M. [Ldscp. P] Elkhart, IN b. 12 Feb 1919, Elkhart. Studied: ASL; Ind. U, South Bend. Teachers: Edward Basker; Don G. Kingman; E. A. Whitney. Prizes: HS, 1976; Motorola Nat Amateur A, 1961; Ill. State Fair, 1963; Northern Ind. A Salon, Hammond. Collections: Motorola Corp; Standard Federal Savings&Loan; Tri Kappa; Kokomo Public Library.

GATEWOOD, ROBERT [P, Arch] Chicago, IL. Studied: Terre Haute AL; U of Ill. Teachers: Alice Monday; June

Rynerson; Jane K. Yung; William Kennedy. Exhibited: Nat Gal A, Washington, D.C., 1941; Intl WC Show, AIC, 1943; Herron AM; Whitney M, 1946; Northwestern U, 1945-46. Prizes: Scarab Metal, 1942. Note: Arch, Holabird&Root.

GAUCHAT, NOLA C. New Castle, IN.

GAWEHN, GEORGE [Print] Prizes: HS, 1950.

GAYNES, ROSELLA R. (Mrs. Nicholas J.) [P] Jonesboro, IN d. c. 1981. Studied: Famous A's FA Course; East Side A Cen, Indianapolis. Exhibited: 500 Festival A; Grant Cnty AA; Blackford Cnty AA; Mississinewa A Cl. Collections: Jonesboro Public Library.

GEHLERT, WILLIAM R. [P] New Castle, IN b. 1929, Chicago, IL. Teachers: Austin Fraser; Robert Von Newmann. Exhibited: WC Wis; Tri-States, Evansville. Prizes: Henry Cnty A Exh.

GEIER, SHIRLEY

GENDERS, RICHARD A(THERSTONE) [P, T] Indianapolis, IN b. 1919, London, England. Studied: John Herron A Sch. Teachers: William Genders. Exhibited: Operation Palette, traveling show, U.S. Navy; Norfolk M, 1953. Prizes: 44th Ind. A Exh, Herron M. Collections: South Calvary Baptist Church, Indianapolis. Note: Combat A, U.S. Navy.

GENTRY, REX

GEORGE, CHARLENE [Dr, T] Ridgeville, IN b. 30 Oct 1951, Batesville, IN. Studied: Ball State U. Exhibited: U of Neb. (solo), Lincoln; AG of Columbus (solo). Prizes: Salamonie Reg A Show; Ball State Drawing&Small S Show, 1976; Ind. State Fair, 1978; Randolph Cnty A Show; IHA, 1979; McGuire Hall Show, Richmond, IN, 1979; Sheldon Swope Gal, Terre Haute; HS, 1987. Collections: Ball State U A Gal; McGuire Mem Hall, Richmond, IN; Sheldon Swope Gal, Terre Haute, IN. Note: T, Jay Cnty Schools.

GEORGE, FAY AKIN

GERARD, ALLEE WHITTENBERGER [P] Warsaw, IN b. 9 Feb 1895, Rochester, IN. Studied: Ft Wayne A Sch; Miami A Sch. Teachers: Homer Davisson; C. Sheperd; C. Curry Bohm; Eliot O'Hara; Emile Gruppe. Exhibited: Norton Gal, 1942; John Herron AI, 1943; Ft Wayne AM, 1942, 43, 45, 46; Sheldon Swope Gal, Terre Haute, IN; Miami Beach A Cen, FL; Mayfair A Theater, FL; U of Fla., Gainsville; Purdue U, West Lafayette, IN; Ball State U; Herron M; Ind. U. Prizes: HS, 1944; Northern Ind. Salon, 1944. Collections: Warsaw Public Library; Rochester Public Library.

GERHART, CHARLES Bloomington, IN.

GERST, MARILYN B. [I, P, Dr] Evansville, IN b. Houston, TX. Studied: Washington U, St Louis, MO. Exhibited: Mid-States Exh, Evansville M; WC Intl '85; Owensboro AG Exh, KY; U of Evansville; Totally Transparent, Louisville, KY. Note: Freelance I and Layout A, specialized in newspaper advertising for Evansville retail clients.

GESNER, KATHLEEN [P, Print] Exhibited: CGA Gal, Indianapolis, 1983; Ind. U Law Sch, Indianapolis, 1983.

GIBBONS, NANNETTE Indianapolis, IN.

GIBSON, CARLTON [P] Indianapolis, IN b. Indianapolis. Self-taught. Prizes: L. S. Ayres, 1947.

GIBSON, CHARLES [S] Terre Haute, IN b. 1937, Terre Haute. Studied: U of Detroit, MI; Wayne State U, Detroit, MI; Carrara, Italy. Exhibited: Cleo Rogers Mem Library (solo), Columbus, IN, 1972; St Mary-of-the-Woods Col (solo), IN, 1972; Collectors Show Room, Chicago; Pucker/Safai Gal, Boston, MA; IMA, 1975; Bardstown A Cen, Bardstown, KY; Ind. Repertory Theatre, 1974. Note: Artist-in-residence, Ind. A Commission.

GIBSON, MARY ANN [Ldscp. P] Prizes: HS, 1959.

GIFFIN, LYDIA [Woodcut A] Ft Wayne, IN.

GILES, MARY CASEY Indianapolis, IN.

GILLIATT, KATHLEEN Valparaiso, IN.

GILLIATT, LYNNE [P] Bloomington, IN. Prizes: HS, 1986.

GILLIATT, MICHAEL T. Studied: Ind. U. Note: Was authority on Egyptian art and culture. Faculty member, Va. State U for one year. Note: Lived at one time in Valparaiso, IN.

GINNEY, CLOA [P] Kokomo, IN b. Cass Cnty, IN. Prizes: Northern Ind. A; Ind. A; HS, 1948.

GINTHER, JERRY L. [Dr] Rochester, IN.

GIORGINI, ALDO [P, Comp. A] West Lafayette, IN b. Voghera, Italy. Teachers: Casati, Italy; Ingegneri, Eritrea. Exhibited: 64th Ind. A Show; Tippecanoe Cnty Show, 1973, 74; Washington Gal (solo), Frankfurt; Krannert Lounge (solo), Purdue U. Note: Associate Professor, Civil Engineering, Purdue U.

GLASEL, (Sally) LOLLY KACKLEY [Por. P, Dr] Indianapolis, IN b. 10 Sep 1933, Indianapolis. Studied: John Herron Sch A; Indianapolis AL; England; San Francisco. Teachers: C. Frederick Hobbs; Ellie Siskind; David Rubins; Edmund Brucker; Harry Davis. Exhibited: Gal of Frame Designs, 1990; Indianapolis AL Student Show, 1986-89. Prizes: Indianapolis AL, 1984; Arts Ind. Post Card Series, 1990.

GLOBENSKY, LOUIS JAMES [P] Indianapolis, IN.

GLORE, CHARLES FRANKLIN

GLOVER, JACK DONUS Studied: Herron Sch A.

GODWARD, SUZANN WATT (Sue) [P, Dr, Glass A] Indianapolis, IN. Studied: Shortridge H.S., Indianapolis.

GOEDE, HELEN L. [P] Valparaiso, IN.

GOEHL, GEORGE [S] Brown Cnty, IN b. 1938. Studied: Ohio State U. Exhibited: Badeb-Goehl Gal; Brown Cnty A Gal; Carribean Touch, Inc, Sarasota, FL; Country Harmony, Brownsburg, IN; Tillery Interiors, Indianapolis. Note: Metal Sculptor. Managed a home studio and shop/studio in Nashville's (Ind.) Antique Alley.

GOETHE, JOSEPH ALEXANDER [P, Print, S, W, T] Santa Monica, CA b. 1 Mar 1912, Ft Wayne, IN. Studied: Dayton AI; Phillips Mem Gal, Washington, D.C. Exhibited: CM, 1935, 36; AIC, 1934; NAD, 1943; AC, Washington; Centennial Expo, Dallas, TX; Am M Natural History, NYC; 3rd Intl S Exh, Philadelphia M, 1950; Intl WC Exh, Chicago, 1932; Corcoran A Gal, Washington D.C. Prizes: Calif. State Fair, 1957. Collections: Brooks Mem MA, Memphis, TN; Columbia MA, SC; Evansville M; San Francisco MA; St Mary's Col A Gal, Notre Dame, IN. Note: Author, *Handbook of Commercial Woods*, 1938, *Woods of the World*. T, Los Angeles, 1965-67, Brooks Inst, Sch FA, Santa Barbara, CA.

GOLDSCHMIDT, DENICE [Dr, T] Lafayette, IN b. 5 May 1936, Appleton, WI. Studied: Syracuse U. Teachers: George Benedict; Selby Donnison; Phillip Best; Jeanette Ahern; Robert Reed; Nora Anson. Exhibited: Lafayette A Cen, (three women), 1982; Purdue U (solo), 1979; Ball State U 26th Ann Drawing&Small S Show, 1980; Anderson Winter Show, 1979. Prizes: HS, 1978; Lafayette A Cen, 1975, 77. Collections: United Way, 50 print edition woodcut/lithograph, 1980; St Andrew United Methodist Church, 30 print edition.

GONDRING, AUGUSTUS C. [Ldscp. P, P] Chesterton, IN. Prizes: 37th Ann Ind. A Exh, Herron MA, 1944; HS, 1944.

GOODE, VINNIE REAM [Por. P, Min] Chicago, IL.

GOODMAN, SHIRLEY [SLP, Por. P, Dr] Indianapolis, IN b. Indianapolis. Studied: Herron AI; Indianapolis AL. Teachers: Edmund Brucker; Floyd Hopper; Leah Traugott; Harriett Jeffries; Ruth Anderson; Marilyn Price; Brenda Hayes. Exhibited: Whitewater Valley, 1969; Lafayette Reg, 1969; Ind. State Fair, 1970, 71; Ind. A, 1971, 73. Prizes: HS, 1970. Collections: Public Typographic Service.

GOODRICH, MARGARET G. (Bette) [Ldscp. P, Por. P, T] Lafayette, IN b. 14 Apr 1923, Chicago, IL. Studied: Mills A Sch, Rensselaer, IN. Teachers: Louise Weidman. Exhibited: Wabash A (3-person), 1991; Greater Lafayette MA (solo), 1991; Greater Lafayette MA, 1990. Prizes: Ind. Now, 1984, 90; Monticello AC, 1986-88. Collections: Wolcott Public Library, Wolcott, IN; West Lafayette Public Library, West Lafayette, IN; Bank One, West Lafayette.

GOODWIN, DORIT [Dr] Zionsville, IN.

GOODWIN, FRANCES M. [S] New Castle, IN b. c. 1855, New Castle d. 8 Nov 1929. Studied: Indianapolis AA Sch; AIC; ASL. Teachers: Lorado Taft; D. C. French. Exhibited: Chicago World's Fair, 1893. Collections: Office of the Governor, Indianapolis, IN; bust of Robert Dale Owen, Ind. State House; bust of Vice-President Schuyler Colfax, Senate Chamber, Washington, D. C.; bust of Capt. Everett, Riverhead Cemetery, NY; Public Library, New Castle; Henry Cnty Hist M. Note: Sister of artist Helen Goodwin.

GOODWIN, HELEN M. [Ldscp. P, Min. P] New Castle, IN b. c. 1865, New Castle d. 1955. Studied: Switzerland; Brittany; Holland; Belgium. Teachers: Hoffbauer; Mme. La Forge; Charles Hawthorne; Kenneth Miller. Exhibited: Ind. AC; London; Paris; Chicago; New York. Prizes: HS, 1926. Collections: New Castle Public Sch; Spiceland Acad, IN; Public Library, New Castle. Note: Sister of artist Frances Goodwin.

GORDON, IDA NASH [P, Ldscp. P, Por. P] Nashville, IN b. 1903, Windfall, IN d. Feb 1983, New Smyrna Beach, FL. Studied: Ind. U; Paris Am A Acad. Teachers: Marie Goth; George Jo Mess; Stanley Turnball; Marilyn Bendell; Homer Davisson; Leonard Richmond, England; Legare, Paris, France. Exhibited: Brown Cnty A Gal (solo); Ind. State Fair; Herron AI; IMA; Gal de A, NY; Sherman Hotel Gal, Chicago; Northern Ind. Salon. Prizes: Ind. State Fair; HS, 1966, 69; Herron, 1963; Paris Award, Akademia Raymond Duncan, Paris, France.

GORDON, THOMAS L.

GORDON, VIRGINIA O. Indianapolis, IN.

GORMAN, JAMES G. [C, Cer, T] Vincennes, IN b. 5 Dec 1946, Peoria, IL. Studied: U of Ill., Urbana; Ind. U, Bloom-ington; Bradley U; U of Okla., Norman. Teachers: Don Frith; Don Pilcher; Karl Martz. Exhibited: Marietta Col Crafts Nat; Beaux Arts Des Craftsman; Lake Superior '77 Intl Crafts Exh; Ind. Crafts; Renwick Gal, 1980. Note: T, Coordinator FA, Vincennes U Jr Col, Vincennes, IN. Associate professor and Director, Shircliff Gal, Vincennes U.

GOTH, (Jessie) MARIE [P, Por. P, T] Indianapolis, IN/Nashville, IN b. 15 Aug 1887, Indianapolis d. 9 Jan 1975. Studied: ASL; Herron AI. Teachers: Frank V. DuMond; William Merritt Chase; Luis M. Mora; John C. Johansen; Robert Aiken. Prizes: NAD, 1939; Brown Cnty A Gal, 1933; Ind. AC, 1935, 39, 44, 45; Evansville M A&Hist, 1939; Herron AI, 1924; HS, 1926-28, 32, 34-37, 39, 42, 45, 46, 48, 49, 51, 52, 57, 58, 60, 61, 63-65, 75; Ft Wayne AA, 1923. Collections: Hanover Col, IN; Franklin Col, IN; Purdue U; Ind. U; Butler U, Indianapolis, IN; Herron AI; DePauw U. Note: Sister of artist Genevieve Goth Graf and sister-in-law of artist Carl Graf.

GOTHELF, LOUIS [P, I] Yonkers, NY b. 6 Apr 1901, Russia. Studied: NAD; AIC. Teachers: I. Olinsky; G. W. Maynard; J. W. Reynolds. Collections: Jewish Educational Bldg, Toledo, OH. Note: A Director, Orpheum Theatre, Rockford, IL.

GRABENHOFER, VIRGINIA [Ldscp. P, T] Nineveh, IN b. 5 Jun 1918, Hopkinsville, KY. Studied: Tenn. Temple Col. Teachers: John Hilton; Kaye Poole; Clay Kent; Joseph Fennigs; Sharon Carson; Al Stine. Exhibited: Shelbyville, IN (solo), 1991; Indian Creek A Show, 1991; Wabash Valley Exh, 1990. Prizes: Las Vegas Round Up, 1956; Edinburg Show, 1990, 91. Collections: Brown Cnty Golf&Country Cl; Shelbyville A Gal, Shelbyville, IN; Nashville Frame, Inc; Railroadman Savings&Loan.

GRADY, AUDRE Indianapolis, IN.

GRAF, CARL C(hristopher) [P, S, T, Car] Nashville, IN b. 24 Sep 1892, Bedford, Lawrence Cnty, IN d. 28 Jan 1947, Indianapolis. Studied: ASL; Herron AI; Cincinnati A Acad; Philadelphia; NYC; Boston. Teachers: James R. Hopkins; Herman H. Wessel; J. Ottis Adams; T. C. Steele; Otto Stark; William Forsyth; Merle Allison; Rudolph Schwarz; George Julian Zolnay. Exhibited: Brown Cnty A Assn, annually. Prizes: HS, 1926-28, 30, 32, 43; J. I. Holcomb Prize, 1918; Indianapolis AA, 1922. Collections: Herron AM; Public Sch; contributed to Mother Jones Memorial, Litchfield, IL. Note: Before entering Herron Sch A, Graf did cartoons for three years for the *Bedford Daily Democrat*. Husband of artist Genevieve Goth Graf and brother-in-law of artist Marie Goth.

GRAF, GENEVIEVE GOTH [P, SLP, T] Brown Cnty, IN b. 12 Aug 1890, Indianapolis d. 21 Dec 1961. Studied: Indianapolis Normal Col. Teachers: V. J. Cariani; Marie Goth; Carl Graf. Exhibited: Ind. AC. Prizes: HS, 1940, 52, 60. Note: Sister of artist Marie Goth and wife of artist Carl C. Graf. T, Indianapolis Schs, 41 years. In 1922, she purchased a summer home in Brown Cnty for her family (North on State Rd. 135); later she and her husband established a summer home in Nashville, IN.

GRAFTON, ROBERT W. [P, Por. P, Mur. P] Michigan City, IN b. 19 Dec 1876, Chicago, IL d. 1936. Studied: AIC; Académie Julian, Paris; Holland; England. Exhibited: AIC, 1907; Ft Wayne AA, 1908; Thurber Gal, Chicago, 1919; Delgado M, New Orleans; Brooks Mem M, Memphis. Prizes: Richmond AA, 1910, 1919; HS, 1925. Collections: New Orleans AA; Lafayette AA; Union Lg Cl, Chicago; Northwestern U; Purdue U; Earlham Col. His murals appear in Statehouse, Springfield, IL; Kansas Wesleyan U; Tulane U; Rumely Hotel, LaPorte, IN; Fowler Hotel, Lafayette; Anthony Hotel, Ft Wayne; Bank of Ft Wayne. Portraits: State Library, Indianapolis; Ind. State Capital; Mich. State Capital; U of WI; Dept. of Agriculture, Washington, D.C.; Iowa State Col Agriculture; Paris Embassy, Administration Bldg, Mundelein. Note: Best known for portraits of educators, professional men and public officials. Painted three portraits for Governors' Portrait Coll of State of Ind.: Warren T. McCray, Edward L. Jackson and Harry Guyer Leslie. T, AIC.

GRAHAM, BETTE [Ldscp. P, Print] Muncie, IN b. 17 Jun 1919, Muncie, IN. Studied: MacMurray Col; U of N.C., Greensboro; Ball State U. Teachers: Gregory Ivy; Alexander Achipenko; Frank Webb. Exhibited: Longboat Key A Gal, 1985. Prizes: HS, 1945; BCAA, Montpelier, 1971; Ind. State Fair. Collections: Minnetrista Cultural Cen, Muncie; Wells Cnty A Cen, Bluffton, IN; Am Nat Bank, Muncie.

GRAHAM, EDWARD B. [Car] Chicago, IL.

GRAHAM, KATHLEEN [Print, P, MM] b. Terre Haute, IN. Studied: Ind. State U; IUPUI; Indianapolis AL. Exhibited: DePauw U; Ind. State U; Notre Dame U; St Mary-of-the-Woods Col. Prizes: HS, 1976, 79. Collections: Mural, Children's M, Indianapolis.

GRAMS, BILL [P, MM] Indianapolis, IN. Prizes: Ind. State Fair, 1981; HS, 1982.

GRANDIDIER, CANDIDE Y. [P] Terre Haute, IN. Prizes: HS, 1984.

GRAVES, ARDIS DANNER [Dr, Print, Cer, Por. P, Bat, JA] Indianapolis, IN b. 8 Apr, Knightstown, IN. Studied: Tech H.S.; Herron Sch A. Teachers: Eliot O'Hara; Frederick Polley; George Jo Mess; Edmund Schildknecht; Sara Bard; Floyd Hopper. Exhibited: Indianapolis AL, 1969-71. Prizes: Indianapolis AL, 1972; North Deanery, East Gate, 1972, 73. Collections: IMA, rental gal.

GRAVES, MYRTLE (Mrs. C. E.) [SLP, Por. P] Hammond, IN b. Bridgman, MI. Studied: AIC. Exhibited: Towertown, Chicago, 1936.

GRAY, BARBARA [S, Dr, JA, T] Anderson, IN b. Indianapolis. Studied: Anderson Col; Ball State U. Teachers: Ruthven Byrum; Bradford Lambert; Marian Boyd. Exhibited: Ball State U; Delaware Cnty Exh. Prizes: HS, 1967. Collections: Anderson FA Cen. Note: T, Anderson Sch System, Anderson Col, Anderson FA Cen.

GRAY, H. MAXWELL

GRAY, HAROLD (Lincoln) [P, Car] La Jolla, CA b. 20 Jan 1894, Kankakee, IL d. 10 May 1968. Studied: Purdue U, West Lafayette, IN. Prizes: HS, 1925. Collections: Comprehensive collection of Gray's drawings are preserved in the Mugar Library, Boston U. Note: Creator, "Little Orphan Annie" comic strip. Co-authored, *My Folks*, Little Orphan Annie's autobiography. Gray joined the staff of the *Chicago Tribune* in 1917.

GRAY, MARY CHILTON *(See Mendenhall, Mary Chilton Gray)* [P, Print] Denver, CO b. 22 May 1888, Philadelphia, PA. Studied: John Herron AI. Exhibited: NAWA, 1943, 44; AWCS, 1942; NYC (solo), 1942; Columbus, OH, 1931; Indianapolis, IN, 1931. Collections: murals, Colo. M Natural History.

GRAY, MURIEL (Mrs. Leon) Martinsville, IN. Note: Member, Brown Cnty A Gal, beginning 1966.

GREATHOUSE, R. V. (Mrs.) Indianapolis, IN.

GREEN, HERSCHEL S. Terre Haute, IN.

GREENE, JAMES A. [P]

GREENE, JO *(See Raymond, Jo Greene)*

GREENE, THOMAS [Ldscp. P, Ab, S] Martinsville, IN b. 14 Oct 1918, Audubon, NJ. Studied: U of the Arts; Philadelphia Col of A. Teachers: Morris Blackburn; Gertrude Schell. Exhibited: Third Ann Review P/S, U.S., 1957; A and the Circus, S, Intl Show, 1953; A from Corporate Coll, IMA, 1977. Prizes: Far East A Competition, 1949; HS, 1976; 500 FA Exh, 1972. Collections: RCA; Ind. Bell; Am United Life Insurance Co; Dayton Plaza Hotel, OH; Southeastern Ill. Col; McKesson Corp, San Francisco, CA. Note: Des, Industrial furniture, 33 years.

GREENWOOD, UNA ANN [P, Ldscp. P, T] Gary, IN b. Lewisville, IN. Studied: PMSchIA. Teachers: Krehbiel; Fursman; C. Curry Bohm. Prizes: HS, 1929. Note: T, Indianapolis Public Sch.

GREENWOOD, W(illiam) RUSSELL [P, Print] Lafayette, IN/Colorado Springs, CO b. 25 Jun 1906, Oxford, IN. Studied: Purdue U. Teachers: Sister Rufinia; D. Miller.

GREER, GERALD N. [P] Indianapolis, IN b. Mitchell, IN. Teachers: Max Rauchen, Germany.

GREGG, F. D. Richmond, IN. Prize: Kentland Group, 1958, Kappa Kappa Kappa Purchase Prize.

GREPP, JOHN A. [P] Franklin, IN b. Indianapolis, IN. Studied: John Herron A Sch; State U of Iowa; Ohio State U. Prizes: Butler AI, Youngstown, OH, 1952; Ind. State Fair, 1952, 53, 55; Ind. A Ann, Indianapolis, 1953, 55; Michiana A Exh, South Bend, 1956. Note: Head of A Dept, Franklin Col, Franklin, IN.

GRESHAM, BARBARA H. [P] West Lafayette, IN b. Atlanta, GA. Studied: Agnes Scott Col, Decatur, GA; U of Louisville. Exhibited: Ga. WCS Ann Nat Exh; La. WCS Intl Comp, New Orleans, LA. Prizes: Aqueous, Ky. WCS Nat Exh; WCS of Ind. Ann Juried Exh, Indianapolis; Bluegrass Biennial Art's Cl of Louisville.

GRIEB, ELEANOR [Ldscp. P, SLP, Por. P] Elkhart, IN b. 7 Feb 1925, Ontario, Canada. Studied: Layton Sch A, Milwaukee, WI. Teachers: Martin Stevens; Frederick Rigley; Bob Hoffman; Ronald Monsma; Charles Movalli; Albert Handell; June Cary; Ben Konis. Exhibited: Midwest M of Am A, 1988; Five State Pastel Competition, Krasl A Cen, St Joseph, MI, 1989. Prizes: HS, 1988; Elkhart AL, 1977; Midwest M of AM A, 1989. Collections: Soc Bank, Elkhart; Howard Cnty Public Library, Kokomo, IN; Robt Weed Plywood Corp, Bristol, IN.

GRIEB, TIMOTHY [Ldscp. P, T] Eagle Nest, New Mexico b. 10 Nov 1954, Elkhart, IN. Studied: Ind. U, South Bend. Teachers: Harold Zisla. Exhibited: Midwest M of Am A, Elkhart, IN, Reg Juried Exh, 1980 and Invitational, 1988. Prizes: Elkhart AL, 1979, 82, 88.

GRIFFIN, WORTH D. [P, Print, T] Pullman, WA b. 15 Dec 1892, Sheridan, IN. Studied: Okla. Christian U; U of Ore.; John Herron AI; AIC. Teachers: H. Walcott; G. Bellows; C. Hawthorne; W. Reynolds; Clifton Wheeler; William Forsyth. Exhibited: SFMA, 1940, 42, 45; Oakland A Gal, 1939, 40; SAM, 1939-44. Note: T, Head FA Dept, Wash. State Col, 1925-46.

GRIFFITH, ELAINE MARIE [Ldscp. P, P] Clay City, IN

b. 23 Aug 1951, Worcester, MA. Studied: Worcester AM Sch. Exhibited: Honeywell Community Cen (solo), Wabash, IN, 1976; Clay City Community Cen (solo), 1976; Tri Kappa Show, Brazil, IN, 1976.

GRIFFITH, KATHARINE PATTON [P] Long Beach, CA.

GRIFFITH, L(ouis) O(scar) [Ldscp. P, Print] Nashville, IN b. 10 Oct 1875, Greencastle, IN d. 13 Nov 1956. Studied: St Louis Sch FA; AIC; NAD; Paris. Teachers: Frank Reaugh. Exhibited: Ind. PM; Ind. AC; LOC, 1943; Sesquicentennial Expo, Philadelphia; Intl Print Show, Florence, Italy; Canadian Nat Expo; NAD, 1943. Prizes: P.-P. Expo, 1915; Brown Cnty AA, 1938; Palette and Chisel Cl, 1921; Chicago SE, 1949, 53; HS, 1925, 26, 30, 35, 39; San Antonio AL, 1929. Collections: Delgado MA; Oakland A Gal; Ind. U; Lafayette AA; Vanderpoel Coll; NGA; Witte Mem M; J. B. Speed Mem M. Note: Among the first painters to establish a home and studio in Nashville, IN. A special showing of his prints was held at the Smithsonian Inst, Washington, D. C., 1945.

GRIFFITH, ROSA B. [P, T] Terre Haute, IN b. 18 Apr 1867, Merom, IN d. 23 Feb 1927. Teachers: C. A. Cumming; J. F. Smith; A. Dow. Note: T, Terre Haute Public Sch, 30 years.

GRIFFITH, VERA ALICE [Por. P, Ldscp. P, SLP, T] Anderson, IN b. 2 Dec 1906, Anderson d. c. 1971. Studied: Evansville Acad FA; Herron A Sch. Teachers: Donald M. Mattison; Henrik M. Mayer; K. Scheffler. Prizes: HS, 1936; Ind. State Fair, 1935-38; Anderson Soc of A Exh, 1935-37. Note: T, Aurora Public Sch, IN.

GRIFFITT, Sr., ROBERT (Bob) [Ldscp. P, Por. P] Charlestown, IN b. 28 Jan 1917, Luverne, IA. Studied: Central Acad A, Cincinnati. Teachers: Jackson Storey. Exhibited: Ky. WCS, 1978-87; Mid-America Biennial, 1988. Prizes: HS, 1978, 79; Mid-America Biennial, 1982. Collections: Delaware State M. Note: Artist's brush signature, K. W. S.

GRIGSBY, PIETER R. [P] Indianapolis, IN.

GRIGSBY, TOBEY DIANE [Dr] Indianapolis, IN.

GRIGWARE, EDWARD T(homas) [P, Mur. P, I, Com. A, T] Oak Park, IL/Cody, WY b. 3 Apr 1889, Caseville, MI d. 9 Jan 1960. Studied: Chicago Acad FA. Exhibited: Marshall Fields Gal, Chicago (solo), 1931; Chicago Gal Assn (solo), 1927. Prizes: Palette and Chisel Cl, 1925, 28; HS, 1925; AIC, 1926, 31; Assn Chicago PS, 1931; All Ill. Soc FA, 1933. Collections: U of Chicago; State M, Springfield, IL; Chicago Union Lg Cl. Murals: City Hall, Chicago; Kalif. Shrine, Sheridan, WY; U of Wyo.; Latter Day Saints Temple, Los Angeles. Note: Husband of artist Blanche Lanaghen (d. 1959); T and Founder, Frontier Sch of Western A, Cody, WY, 1937.

GRISEZ, E. A. [P, T] LaPorte, IN b. 29 Apr 1908, LaPorte. Teachers: A. C. Winn.

GROSJEAN, MARY Chicago, IL.

GROSS, Jr., JAMES [Por. P, P] Marion, IN. Prizes: HS, 1972.

GROSS, Sr., JAMES M. Marion, IN.

GRUE, FREDERIK EBBESEN [SLP, Ldscp. P] Indianapolis/Muncie, IN b. 29 Jun 1951, Sherman Oaks, CA. Self-taught. Exhibited: Hillcrest Festival (solo), Whittier, CA; Grand Central Gal, NYC; Stewart Am A Gal, San Francisco; Minnetrista Cultural Cen, Muncie, IN, 1989; Carnegie Cultural A Cen, 1982; Montgomery Gal, San Francisco, 1985. Prizes: HS, 1984-88, 91, 92; Pasadena Festival, 1978-80; Santa Paula Festival of A, 1981, 82.

GRUELLE, JUSTIN C. [P, I] New York, NY b. 1 Jul 1889, Indianapolis, IN. Studied: Herron AI; ASL. Teachers: R. B. Gruelle. Prizes: Richmond, IN. Note: Son of Hoosier Group artist Richard B. Gruelle and brother of Johnny Gruelle who created the *Raggedy Ann* series.

GRUENINGER, LIBBY JONES [Dr, Ldscp. P, Por. P] Indianapolis, IN b. 4 Apr 1932, Indianapolis. Studied: Am Acad A, Chicago; DePauw U. Teachers: Ken Potter; Marjorie Leighton; Edmund Brucker; Irving Shapiro. Exhibited: Ind. A, 1981-83; Anderson Drawing Show, Reg; Ind. State Fair; Marin Cnty Fair, CA; Ball State Dr&Print Show. Prizes: Whitewater Show, 1980. Collections: Detroit Diesel, Indianapolis; Farmers State Bank, Zionsville, IN; Fayette Federal Savings&Loan Assn, Brookville, IN; Ind. Womens Cen, Indianapolis.

GUCKELBERG, MAY [P] Indianapolis, IN b. England d. Feb 1989. Studied: Am H.S., Chicago; Famous A Course; Metropolitan A Seminars. Teachers: Frances de Erdely; Wallace Mitchel; Fred Oswald. Exhibited: Ind. State Fair; Ohio Valley Oil and WC Show; Ala. WCS; Michiana Reg; Ridge A Soc, Chicago; Ind. AC. Prizes: HS, 1956. Collections: Indianapolis Public Sch.

GÜLEN, FÜSUN [Dr, Ldscp. P, Print, S, Cer, Por. P, T] West Lafayette, IN b. 7 Feb 1948, Turkey. Studied: Purdue U, West Lafayette, IN. Teachers: Al Pounders; Brent Crocker. Exhibited: Northern Ind. AA, 1990; Greater Lafayette AM, 1985. Prizes: HS, 1976, 84; Northern Ind. A, 1984; Sheldon Swope Gal, 1983. Collections: Arthur Young Co; Eli Lilly&Co; Marsh Headquarters. Note: T, West Lafayette H.S.

HAAG, CARL H. [P] Middletown, IN b. 1890, Hammond, IN. Note: Paintings included in Kentland Group.

HAAG, O(rval) O. [Por. P] Hammond, IN b. 1881, Peru, IN d. 1978. Exhibited: E. C. Minas Co; Northern Ind. A Salon; South Bend AL; Gary AL Exh. Prizes: All Ill. Exh. Collections: Ind. U, Bloomington; Valparaiso U AM. Note: Instrumental in bringing together the artists of Lake Cnty and developing annual exhibitions at Edward C. Minas Co.

HAAS, MARY M. [P] West Terre Haute, IN.

HAAS, PAULINE ANDERSON [Ldscp. P] Logansport, IN b. 11 Jul 1958, Chicago Heights, IL. Self-taught. Exhibited: Anderson Reg Juried Show, 1990. Prizes: Logansport AA Ann Comp, 1989, 90; Logansport Iron Horse Festival Show, 1988.

HABELA, JOHN J. [Dr, P] Valparaiso, IN. Prizes: HS, 1977.

HACKER, OLLIE [Por. P, P] Greenwood, IN. Prizes: Southside AL, Indianapolis, 1976.

HACKETT, GENEVIEVE [P] deceased.

HACKETT, J.

HACKETT, MARY JO [P, SLP] Indianapolis, IN. Prizes: HS, 1963.

HACKNEY, ALLEN [P, T] Terre Haute, IN b. 13 Aug 1938, Madison, IN. Studied: Ind. State U. Teachers: John Laska; Zoltan Sepeshy. Exhibited: Mainstreams '68, Marietta, OH; Nat Soc P in Casein and Acrylics Ann, NYC. Prizes: HS, 1965, 68, 69, 70, 72, 75, 77, 78; Eli Lilly Grant, 1988. Collections: New England M of Sport, Boston; Chalmer's Gal, London; Brigham Young U, Provo, UT; Ind. State U, Terre Haute. Note: T, Vigo Cnty Schs.

HADLEY, ALICE ROSS [P, C] Indianapolis, IN b. 14 Apr 1854, Indianapolis. Teachers: T. C. Steele; William Merritt Chase; Barton S. Hays. Exhibited: Herron AI; Pettis Gal. Note: Taught china painting, Herron Sch A.

HADLEY, DONALD LEE [P, T] Terre Haute, IN b. 8 Nov 1937, Tangier, IN. Studied: Ind. State U. Teachers: John Laska. Exhibited: Ind. State M Inaugural Exh, Indianapolis, IN, 1974; Ind. A Exh 100, L. S. Ayres, Indianapolis; Paris (Ill.) AL Exh, 1967, 68; Wabash Valley Exh, 1967, 69. Prizes: HS, 1970, 72, 75, 81, 82, 85, 87; Paris (Ill.) AL Exh, 1969, 72; Eli Lilly Award, 1973; Ind. Realist Exh, 1978, 81; Wabash Valley, 1970, 72, 73, 75. Note: T, Woodrow Wilson Jr. H.S., Terre Haute, IN.

HADLEY, PAUL [P, Des, SG, T] Richmond, IN b. 1880, Indianapolis, IN d. Jan 1971. Studied: PMSchlA; PAFA; Philadelphia Acad FA. Teachers: Otto Stark. Exhibited: Ind. AC. Prizes: HS, 1925, 27, 50; Ind. State Fair. Collections: Indianapolis Public Sch. Note: T, Herron Sch A, Indianapolis. Assistant Curator, Herron AI, Indianapolis. Designed Ind. State Flag, 1917. Lived in Mooresville, IN for many years. Cousin of artist Clifton Wheeler.

HADLEY, SENORA RIEKE (Mrs. Richard) [Dr, P, Ldscp. P, T] LaGrange, IL b. Ft Wayne, IN. Studied: AIC. Exhibited: Toledo MA; Toledo Fed A Soc; Herron AI, Indianapolis, IN; Ohio WCS; All-Ill. Soc of FA; LaGrange AL. Note: Created drawings, 1969 Hoosier Hist Calendar, Hoosier State Bank of Ind.

HAGEDORN, VALENTINE OKO

HAGEN, GRACE ROWLAND [Ldscp. P, SLP] Evanston, IL b. Indianapolis, IN. Studied: AIC. Teachers: Ethel L. Coe; Frank C. Peyraud. Exhibited: Ind. AC.

HAGEN, GREG L. [P] Indianapolis, IN. Exhibited: Purdue U, 1977; Wabash Valley Show; CCA Gal, Indianapolis, 1979; Park Cnty A Show.

HAGENBOOK, EDNA SLAGLE [Ldscp. P, SLP] Franklin, IN b. 24 Feb 1904, Lebanon, IN. Studied: AIC. Teachers: Marilyn Bendel; Emile Gruppe; Charles Untulis. Exhibited: Chicago; Clinton Cnty Fair; Boone Cnty Fair; All-Ill. Assn, 1955-63. Collections: Ill. Schs.

HAHN, LEANN [C, MM, P] Columbus, IN. Studied: AIC; Rockford Col. Exhibited: Burpee A Gal, 1967-69, Rockford, IL; IMA Cr Show, 1974, 76, 78; 500 Show, Indianapolis AL, 1976-79; Evansville (Ind.) Cr Show, 1978. Prizes: Artform, Lafayette, IN, 1982.

HAINES, FRANCES *(See McVey, Frances Haines and Sweeney, Frances Haines)* [Por. P, P] Chicago, IL b. Muncie, IN.

HALBROOKS, DARRYL [P, S, Print, T] Richmond, KY b. 1948, Evansville, IN. Exhibited: Ind. State M, Indianapolis; Louisville Biennial, 1972. Prizes: Mid-South, Memphis; Ind. A Exh, 1973; Washington Nat Painting Exh, 1973. Collections: Brooks Mem Gal, Memphis, TN; Louisville Sch A, KY. Note: T, Eastern Ky. U, Richmond, KY.

HALL, THOMAS [P, T] Oak Park, IL b. 23 Apr 1883, Ama, Sweden. Studied: AIC. Teachers: Frederick Freer; Wellington J. Reynolds; Wolcott; Emile Zoir. Exhibited: Swedish-Am Soc, 1920, 23, 24 (Pr), 25 (Pr), 37 (Pr); AIC, 1909-1941; Chicago Soc A, 1913; PAFA. Collections: Englewood H.S., Chicago; Midway Masonic Temple, Chicago; Shimer Col; Vanderpoel AA.

HALL, W(ashington Elwood) PINK [P] Indianapolis, IN b. 13 Jun 1859, Rising Sun, IN d. 6 Feb 1945. Self-taught. Note: Well-known Indianapolis drummer.

HAMILTON, CLARA M. (Laughlin) (Mrs. N. C.) [SLP, Ldscp. P, T] Kokomo, IN b. 8 Apr 1872, Belle Center, OH d. Oct 1968, Evanston, IL. Studied: Wooster Col; Cleveland Sch A. Teachers: Frederic Gottwald; Herman Matson; William Forsyth; Randolph Coats; C. Curry Bohm. Exhibited: Herron MA. Prizes: Ind. AC, 1939. Collections: Kokomo Public Library; Country Cl; Woman's Dept Cl. Note: T, in Kokomo for more than 40 years.

HAMILTON, DOROTHY GALLAHUE [P, Ab] Boca Raton, FL/Columbus and Indianapolis, IN b. 5 May 1914 d. 8 Dec 1991. Teachers: Edward Manetta. Exhibited: HWA Kang M, Taipei, Taiwan, 1979. Prizes: Honorary Doctorate of Arts, Butler U, 1978.

HAMILTON, EILEEN R. PHELAN [P, Ldscp. P, Por. P, MM, T] Bloomington, IN b. 30 Apr 1932, Cincinnati, OH. Studied: U of Cincinnati; Cincinnati A Acad; Central Acad of Com A, Cincinnati. Teachers: Reginald Grooms; Carl Von Volborth; Arthur Helwig. Exhibited: Jefferson Nat Life (solo), Indianapolis, 1981; Monroe Cnty Public Library (solo), 1985; Ind. State Fair, 1970s; 500 Festival of A, Indianapolis; Tippecanoe Reg, Lafayette, 1970s; Showcase for the A, Cincinnati; A for Religion, Cincinnati. Prizes: Nat Lg Am Penwomen, Indianapolis; Ind. State Fair. Collections: PTS Electronics, Bloomington, IN.

HAMM, RUSSELL [SLP, P] Crawfordsville, IN.

HAMMAN, MIKE Prize: HS, 1977.

HAMMOND, EMILY M. [Ldscp. P, Li, Por. P] Edinburgh, IN b. 7 Apr 1923, Edinburgh, IN. Self-taught. Exhibited: Nashville A Gal, IN; Southside AL, 1987, 88; Ind. State Fair. Prizes: Senior A Show, Columbus Commons, 1988; Franklin Fair, 1986; Nashville AG, 1989.

HANCOCK, G. MICHAEL [P] Greensburg, IN.

HANCOCK, W. HAROLD [P, Com. A] Nashville, IN b. 1920, Wasson, IL. Studied: John Herron AI. Exhibited: Brown Cnty A Gal. Collections: G. C. Hillenbrand, Batesville, IN; Abe Martin Lodge, Nashville, IN. Note: Studios in Nashville, IN/Ft Myers Beach, FL/Lake Tahoe, NV. Lived for 35 years in Greensburg, IN.

HANCOCK, WILLIAM [Ldscp. P, I, Por. P] New Albany, IN b. 4 May 1916, New Albany, IN. Studied: U of Louisville A Cen; Famous A Course; Inst of Com A, Inc. Teachers: John Pike; Daniel E. Greene; Albert Handell.

Exhibited: Frame House Gal, 1978; Pastel Soc of Am, NY, 1974, 76, 78; Krempp Gal, Jasper, IN, 1990; Ind. State Fair; Ky. State Fair; Ky. WCS, 1978; Floyd Cnty M. Prizes: HS, 1984; Ky. WCS, 1978. Collections: McNichols A Gal, Naples, FL; Floyd Cnty Schs; St Johns United Presbyterian Church.

HANES, JUDITH M. [P] Middletown, IN b. Henry Cnty, IN. Studied: Sprague A Sch, St Petersburg, FL; Ball State U, Muncie IN; Cont A Sch. Exhibited: Ball State Gal; Anderson, IN. Prizes: Ind. State Fair.

HANIKA, MILDRED D. Owens [Col. A, T] Clay Township, IN b. c. 1922, Connersville, IN d. c. 1978, Indianapolis. Prizes: HS, 1971. Note: Head of A Dept, Carmel H.S.

HANLEY, FRANCIS JOSEPH [P, T] South Bend, IN b. 6 Apr 1913, Providence, RI. Studied: RISD; Brown U; Fordham U. Exhibited: Northern Ind. A, 1939-41, 46; Wightman Gal, Notre Dame, IN. Prizes: HS, 1940, 49, 51. Collections: U of Notre Dame; St Remuald Chapel, Matunuck, RI. Note: T, U of Notre Dame, 1937-46.

HANNELL, HAZEL (Johnson) [P] Chesterton, IN b. 31 Dec 1895, La Grange, IL. Studied: Church Sch A; AIC.

HANNIN, NANCY H.

HANSBERRY, LUCILLE K. [P] New London, NH.

HANSELL, GIFFORD [P] Jefferson Cnty, IN b. 18 Jul 1903, Deputy, IN. Teachers: Mrs. Adolph Shulz; Ralph Sowell; Carl Graf; C. Curry Bohm. Exhibited: Brown Cnty AG Gal. Prizes: Ind. State Fair, 1947; Jeffersonville Exh, 1948; HS, 1952. Note: Pig farmer in Jefferson Cnty.

HANSEN, LOUISE B. [P, T] Terre Haute, IN b. 10 May 1927, Pleasant Grove, UT. Studied: Brigham Young U; U of Utah; Instituto Allende, San Miguel Guanajuato, Mexico. Exhibited: Am WCS Traveling Exh, 1973; Evansville M of A&Sc, 1973. Prizes: Swope Gal, 1973; Springville Nat Invitational, 1965; HS, 1970, 71, 75, 77, 84, 89. Collections: Swope AM, Terre Haute; Rose Hulman Inst; Brigham Young U; Springville AM; Kokomo Library; Fairfax Cnty Library, Arlington, VA. Note: T, Vigo Cnty Schs; T, Ind. State U.

HARBART, GERTRUDE F. [SLP, Ldscp. P, T] Michigan City, IN b. Michigan City. Studied: U of Ill.; U of Calif.; AIC; Summer Sch of P, Saugatuck, MI; U of Ind. Extention, South Bend. Exhibited: John Herron AM, Indianapolis. Prizes: HS, 1958; Northern Ind. A Salon, Hammond, IN, 1952; Michiana Reg, South Bend, IN, 1952; Ind. State Fair, 1948, 1950; Terry Nat, Miami, FL, 1952. Note: T, public schs, Calif. and Ill.

HARBOURT, JOY ADAMS *(See Adams, Joy Harbourt)*

HARCOFF, LYLA MARSHALL [P, T] Santa Barbara, CA b. Lafayette, IN. Studied: Purdue U; AIC; Paris. Exhibited: San Francisco, 1944; San Diego; Los Angeles; Chicago. Prizes: Santa Barbara MA, 1944.

HARDING, SHELBY [Linocut, T] Richmond, IN b. 1937, Loogootee, IN. Studied: Ind. State U; Ball State U. Exhibited: Eastern Ind. Ann, Richmond, 1981, 82; Anderson Winter Show, 1982; Clovis, NM; McGuire Gal, 1982; 5th Ann Ind. A Exh, Ind. State M, Indianapolis. Prizes: HS, 1978, 79; Darke Cnty AA, Greenville, OH, 1981; Ind. Realists, 1981; New Mexico Intl, 1981; Eastern Ind. Ann, 1983; Anderson Winter Show, 1980. Collections: McGuire Gal; Richmond Municipal Bldg.

HARDRICK, JOHN WESLEY [P, Por. P, Ldscp. P, Mur. P, T] Indianapolis, IN b. 21 Sep 1891, Indianapolis d. Oct 1968. Studied: Herron AI. Teachers: William Forsyth; Clifton Wheeler; Otto Stark. Exhibited: FA Gal, Balboa Park, San Diego, CA, 1929; AIC, 1927, 32; Smithsonian Inst, 1929; Am Negro Expo, Chicago, 1941; IMA; Herron AM; Ind. AC. Prizes: Harmon Foundation, NYC, 1928; Indianapolis AA, 1929; Ind. State Fair, c. 1915-1920s; Ind. State Exh, 1933. Collections: Fletcher Savings&Trust Co and YMCA, both in Indianapolis; Wilberforce U; John Herron AI; Tuskegee, AL; IMA; Ind. State M; mural, Allen Chapel A.M.E. Church, Indianapolis, 1929.

HARDY, MAUDE F. [P] Detroit, MI.

HARE, HELEN ALDRICH [P, Ldscp. P] Chicago, IL. Exhibited: HS A Gal, Indianapolis, 1948. Prizes: HS, 1947.

HARFORD, DOROTHY BETHEL [Por. P] Indianapolis, IN b. Ohio. Studied: Cleveland (Ohio) Sch A; Ohio Wesleyan. Prizes: HS, 1931.

HARGRAVES, EMILY RAINBOLT

HARLAN, ROMA C. [Por. P] Lafayette, IN. Studied: AIC. Teachers: Fern McCormick Harlan (mother); Marie Goff; Ralph Clarkson.

HARPEL, ALICE [P] Crawfordsville, IN.

HARPER, HARRIETT J. ECKEL

HARRINGTON, BARBARA WITHHAM [Col. A, P] Martinsville, IN.

HARRINGTON, GREGORY S. [P] Union Mills, IN.

HARRISON, HARLEY F. [P] Indianapolis, IN b. c. 1895, Indianapolis. Studied: Manual H.S. Exhibited: 500 Festival. Note: Made and decorated lamp shades for Indianapolis Power and Light Co. Painted and antiqued floral pictures for L. S. Ayres&Co.

HARROD, AMY L. [P]

HARROLD, CON

HART, DRENNAN W. [I, Com. A] Indianapolis, IN b. 13 Mar 1914, Indianapolis d. 18 Dec 1982. Teachers: Frederick Polley; Elmer Taflinger.

HART, JOHN PATRICK b. Michigan City, IN. Studied: Fordham U; Notre Dame.

HART, JOSEPHINE *(See McGee, Josephine Hart)* [Por. P, SLP, Ldscp. P] Alexandria, VA b. Lafayette, IN. Studied: Purdue U; Madison Sch of A; Indianapolis AL. Teachers: George Brackman; Elmer Taflinger; Frederick Rigley; Edward Nicholson; Paul Sweany; Gianni Cilfone. Exhibited: Wabash Valley Exh; Ind. 20; Brown Cnty AG. Prizes: Ind. State Fair; Indianapolis AL; Ind. AC; Mid-States Exh; Ft Wayne's Women's Cl. Collections: Tri Kappa; Evansville M.

HARTH, EMMA E. [P] Chicago, IL b. 9 Jan 1878, Indianapolis, IN d. 22 Mar 1964. Studied: Herron AI, 1902-03. Teachers: Brandt Steele. Exhibited: North Shore AG. Note: Maiden name Emma Klanke. First signed work E. Klanke, then E. E. Harth.

HARTLEY, MARY [P] Indianapolis, IN.

HARTMAN, BETSY [P] Carmel, IN b. 6 Feb 1947, Camden, NJ. Teachers: Rosemary Thomas; Rob O'Dell; Paul Sweany. Exhibited: Ind. State Fair, 1989; Ind. WCS, 1990.

HARTMAN, LAVERN

HARTRATH, LUCIE [P, Ldscp. P, T] Chicago, IL b. 1868, Boston, MA d. 12 Aug 1962. Studied: AIC. Teachers: Vanderpoel; Coutrois, Rixens, Paris; Rizens; Angelo Jank, Munich. Exhibited: PAFA, 1901-09; Chicago Gal Assn (solo), 1929; Paris Salon. Prizes: AIC, 1911, 12, 15, 16; HS, 1925, 27-31, 35, 37, 39, 41; Assn Chicago PS, 1939; Chicago Mun AL, 1922; Peoria, 1922. Collections: Bryn Mawr Women's Cl; Governor's Mansion, Springfield, IL; Municipal AL, Public Sch A Soc, both in Chicago; Public Sch, Gary, IN; Public Library, Bedford, IN; AIC. Note: One of the founders, Chicago Women's Salon. T, Rockford Col, Rockford, IL, 1902-04.

HARTSOCK, ROBERT E. [Dr, Ldscp. P, Por. P] Indianapolis, IN b. 31 Oct 1919, Brooklyn, NY. Studied: DePauw U; ASL. Teachers: Robert Brackman; Frank Vincent DuMond. Exhibited: Ind. AC, 1986-89; Catholic A of '80s, Washington, D. C., 1986. Prizes: HS, 1990. Collections: Mishkin, Cromer, Eaglesfield&Maher.

HARVEY, HOMER Bloomington, IN.

HARVEY, WINNIE H. [P] Muncie, IN b. 1891, Delaware Cnty, IN d. 1965. Studied: John Herron AI; Ball State TC. Teachers: Wayman Adams; Eliot O'Hara; Jerry Farnsworth; Frances F. Brown. Exhibited: Ball State Col; Century of Progress, Ind. Bldg, Chicago. Prizes: HS, 1945. Note: Known for her floral studies in pastel.

HASSELMAN, ANNA [P, T, Print] Franklin, IN b. 12 Jan 1871, Indianapolis d. 16 Apr 1966. Studied: AIC; ASL; Columbia U; Chase Sch, NY. Teachers: William Forsyth; Charles Hawthorne; Eliot O'Hara; William Merritt Chase. Exhibited: Philadelphia WC Exh; NYC WC Exh; AWCS; Ind. A, annually. Collections: John Herron AI; Meridian Street Methodist Church, Indianapolis; Indianapolis Athletic Cl. Note: T, Mt Vernon Seminary, District of Columbia; T, John Herron AI, 1925-35; Curator, John Herron AI, beginning 1930.

HASWELL, LEONA H(alderman) (Mrs. Ernest Bruce) [P, Des, C, T] Cincinnati, OH b. Hagerstown, IN. Studied: Cincinnati A Acad. Teachers: W. Stevens.

HATCH, SARA [P, T] Bloomington, IN b. 17 Aug 1941, Rushville, IL. Studied: U of Ill.; Western Ill. U; U of S.C. Teachers: Phillip Mullen. Exhibited: U.S. Embassy Gal (solo), Taegu, Seoul; 45th Wabash Exh, Terre Haute, 1989; Southside AL Reg Show, 1988, 89; Greater Lafayette M, 1990. Prizes: Nat Competition, Dickenson State Col, ND, 1970; S.C. State Fair, 1984; HS, 1989. Collections: Cummins Corp; PIP Printing, Bloomington, IN; Municipal Building, Springfield, IL; Urbana AA, Urbana, IL; Springfield Old Capital AA. Note: T, New Era A Sch, Bloomington; T, CCAC, Ind. U, Bloomington.

HAUSER, VIVIAN M. *(See Hauser-Smithhart, Vivian)* [P] Ft Wayne, IN b. 8 Sep 1924, Ft Wayne, IN. Studied: Ft Wayne AI; A Instruction, Inc, Minneapolis, MN; St Francis Col, Ft Wayne; Ox Bow, Saugatuck, MI. Teachers: Jim McBride; Richard Yip; Zolton Szabo. Exhibited: Ft Wayne Womens Cl, 1966-68; Wassenberg A Cen, Van Wert, OH, 1966; Nevada State Fair, Reno, 1975, 76; Nevada AA, State House, Carson City, 1977; Nevada AG, Virginia City, 1976; Pioneer State Bank (solo), Reno, Nevada, 1974; Kitty Jo's Gal (solo), Carson City, Nevada, 1975; Blue Palette Gal (solo), Sparks Public Library, Sparks, Nevada, 1976. Prizes: N.E. Ind. A Fair, 1966; HS, 1969; Latimer AG, Reno Nevada, 1976, 77.

HAUSER-SMITHHART, VIVIAN M. *(See Hauser, Vivian M.)*

HAWK, BARBARA L.

HAWKINS, HUCKLEBERRY

HAWKINS, PATRICIA [Dr] Indianapolis, IN. Prizes: HS, 1973.

HAYES, BRENDA [Dr, P, Print, TA] Indianapolis, IN b. 1941, Rockford, IL. Studied: U of Ill.; Cranbrook Acad A, MI; Ind. U, Bloomington. Exhibited: New Orleans Intl, LA, 1976; Nudes Intl, Wilmington, DE, 1976; Nat Small P Comp, Bloomfield, MI, 1977; Nat A&C Show, Corning, NY, 1970, 71; Ind. A, IMA, 1973; Ind. State Fair, 1965-68, 73; 500 Festival of A, Indianapolis, 1968, 69, 72, 73. Prizes: Los Angeles Nat Print Comp, 1978; Nat Min A Show, Clearwater, FL, 1978; Ball State Nat Dr&Small S Show, Muncie, IN, 1968; Mid-States A&C Show, Evansville, IN, 1969.

HAYES, HAZEL BARKER [P, SLP, Ldscp. P] Indianapolis, IN b. 18 Dec 1894, Amite (Tangipahoa Parish), LA d. c. 1984. Teachers: V. J. Cariani; C. Curry Bohm. Exhibited: Herron AM; Southern States AL. Prizes: Ind. AC; Delgado M, New Orleans. Collections: Dailey Mem; Ind. U, Bloomington. Note: Worked in a Brown Cnty studio for 25 years.

HAYES, ROBERT T. [P]

HAZINSKI, HARRIET M. [SLP] Greencastle, IN.

HEAD, CECIL F. [Ldscp. P, Com. A] Whiteland, IN b. 1 Jul 1906, near Lebanon, IN. Studied: John Herron AI. Teachers: William Forsyth; Clifton Wheeler; Paul Hadley; Dorothy Eisenbach; Oakley Richey; Myra Richards; F. E. Schoonover. Exhibited: CI, Pittsburg, 1941; WFNY, 1939; First Biennial Exh of Cont A, Va. MA, 1938. Prizes: HS, 1934, 81; Ind. A Exh, John Herron AI, 1933, 37; Ind. State Fair, 1934, 40. Collections: IMA; Children's M, Indianapolis; Ind. State M; Franklin Public Library, Franklin, IN.

HEADY, CONSTANCE [Ldscp. P, T] S. Palm Beach, FL b. 14 Apr 1935, Ravenna, OH. Studied: John Herron AI; Indianapolis AL. Teachers: Rosemary Lawton Thomas; Floyd Hopper; Ruth Anderson; William Ashby; Stanley Marc Wright. Exhibited: Whitewater Valley, 1983. Prizes: Ind. WCS, 1987; Nat Lg Am Penwomen, 1985. Collections: Jenn Air Corp; Dow Consumer Products; AT&T; Conseco Insurance Co; Am United Life Insurance Co; Anderson Banking Co.

HEALY, MARION MAXON (Mrs. Rufus Alan) [P, Por. P] Cincinnati, OH b. 5 Oct 1890, Mobile, AL. Studied: Cincinnati Acad A; PAFA; ASL. Teachers: Herman H. Wessel; J. Weis; Daniel Garber; E. T. Hurley; H. Wickey. Prizes: HS, 1961.

HECKLER, WILLIAM C. Indianapolis, IN.

HEDGES, JAMES (R.) [Dr] Arcadia, IN.

HEINICKE, JANET HART [P, T] Indianola, IA b. Richmond, IN. Studied: Northern Ill. U, De Kalb, IL; U of Wis; Wittenberg U; Cleveland Sch A. Exhibited: Harwell M (solo), Poplar Bluff, MO, 1988; Ellsworth Community Col (solo), Iowa Falls, 1986; 87th Richmond A Ann, 1987; Ill. Central Community Col, 1981. Prizes: Richmond A Exh, 1987; Tower Park Gal, Peoria, IL, 1979; Richmond AA, 1978. Collections: Simpson Col; We-toast Corp, Chicago; Richmond AA; Kankakee Community Col; Farm Services Corp, Bloomington, IN.

HEINSEN, LINDA LEE [Ab, P] Winamac, IN b. 25 Apr 1949, Hammond, IN. Studied: AIC; Ind. U, South Bend. Teachers: Irving Shapiro; George Rauch; Judi Betts; Frank Webb; Robert Hoffman; Konrad Juestel. Exhibited: Southside AL, Indianapolis, 1990; Watercolor Ohio '90; Am United Life, Indianapolis; Beverly A Cen, Chicago, 1990; Marc T. Nelson Interiors, 1989, 90; 46th Colo. Springs AG, 1991. Prizes: Elkhart Midwest M Juried Show, 1990; Chesterton Woman Show, Chesterton, IN. Collections: Holliday/Maple Lane Construction Co, Elkhart, IN; Ind. Federal, Chesterton, IN.

HEISKELL, NANCY S. [P] Indianapolis, IN.

HEISLER, JULES

HELBING, MICHAEL G. [P, S, Dr, T] Indianapolis, IN b. 1946, Elmhurst, IL. Studied: Purdue U; Ball State U; Ariz. State U; IUPUI; Indianapolis AL; Herron Sch A. Exhibited: WXTZ Ind. A Series, 1981; Wabash Valley Exh, Swope Gal, Terre Haute, 1981; Midwest Reg, Indianapolis AL, 1981; A Insight Ind. Postcard Series, 1981; 5 Person Exh, Indianapolis AL, 1980; 67th Ind. A Show, 1979; Mid-States Cr, 1974, 76, 77. Note: T, Indianapolis AL, 1979-81; Conner Prairie Pioneer Settlement, research potter, demonstrator, 1974-76.

HELMUTH, MILDRED C. NORTON (Mrs. Dewey J.) [S, P, Por. P] Kokomo, IN b. c. 1903 d. 15 Jun 1978. Studied: Marion College. Teachers: Seth Mast; Ida Gordon; Ancel Costlow; John Chase Lewis; Adolph Wolters; Billy Cothran; June Boone. Prizes: Ind. State Fair; Kokomo AA; Sculptors' Guild; Ind. U FA Exh; HS, 1959. Collections: Kennedy Mem Bldg, Boston. Note: Sculpted bust, Governor Otis Bowen, 1975.

HEMENWAY, LUDY [Genre P, P] Indianapolis, IN b. 12 Sep 1930, Bloomington, IN. Studied: Ind. U; Indianapolis AL. Teachers: Floyd Hopper; Sandy Ezell; Zoltan Szabo; Irving Shapiro; Leah Traugott; Rob O'Dell; Jean Vietor; Paul Sweany. Exhibited: Ind. State Fair; Ind. A; IHA. Prizes: Ind. WCS, 1987; National Penwomen's Show. Collections: Indianapolis Power and Light; Indianapolis Athletic Cl.

HENDERSON, RAY [P] Columbus, IN b. 21 May 1887, Columbus d. 25 Nov 1973. Studied: DePauw U; Cincinnati A Acad; AIC. Exhibited: Brown Cnty AG. Note: Owned and managed Benzol cleaning company in Columbus for 21 years.

HENDRICKSON, NILA Winchester, IN.

HENGEN, NONA [P] Bloomington, IN/Spokane, WA. Exhibited: Spokane Ann Original Western A Show, M of Native Am Cultures. Note: Associate professor of education, Ind. U, Bloomington. I, *Monty's Pal* by Howard Small.

HENLINE, FLOYD H. [P] Ft Wayne, IN.

HENNINGER, J(oseph) M(organ) [P, I, Car] b. 15 May 1906. Studied: Herron AI; Paris. Teachers: Simon, Paris; William Forsyth; I. Olinsky. Prizes: HS, 1932, 33. Collections: Muncie MFA, IN. Note: Car, *Indianapolis Post*; Staff, *Indianapolis News*.

HENRY, DOUGLAS [P] Evansville, IN b. 1934, Spencer, IA. Studied: Brownville Sch A, NE. Exhibited: Evansville M, 1973; Bluegrass Open P Exh, Louisville, KY, 1973.

Prizes: HS, 1973, 75, 76, 78; Wabash Valley Exh, Sheldon Swope Gal, 1973. Collections: Wabash Col; Bell Telephone Co, Indianapolis; Stockwell Sch, Evansville; Carver Community Cen; Keller Cresent Co.

HENRY, OUIDABON [P, T] Connersville, IN/Bay View, MI b. 10 Feb 1907, Connersville, IN. Studied: John Herron AI. Teachers: C. Hawthorne; G. Bridgman; William Forsyth; I. Olinsky. Exhibited: John Herron AI, 1934.

HENSHAW, GLEN COOPER [P, Dr] Baltimore, MD b. 8 Aug 1884, Windfall, IN d. 5 Apr 1946. Studied: John Herron AI; L' École des Beaux-Arts; Académie Julian, Paris; Delacluse Académie. Teachers: Carl Marr, Munich; Jean Paul Laurens; Bonnat; J. Ottis Adams. Exhibited: CGA; AIC; Herron AI; BM (solo); AGAA (solo); Santa Fe M (solo); Md. Inst (solo). Collections: Brown Cnty AG, Nashville, IN; Tipton Library; Anderson AA, IN. Note: Artist changed the spelling of his name from Hinshaw to Henshaw c. 1911.

HERITIER, JULES R(eed) [Ldscp.P] Española, NM b. 1 Dec 1943, St Louis, MO. Studied: Culver Military Acad, Culver, IN. Teachers: Laurence Sisson; Warner Williams. Exhibited: Moondance Gal (solo), Santa Fe, NM, 1993. Note: Moved from Ind. to N.M. in 1986.

HERMAN, CAROL M. [P, Dr] Indianapolis, IN.

HERMAN, LORETTA [P] Exhibited: Am Fletcher Nat Bank, 1974.

HERRMANN, EDWARD E. [P, Des, T] South Bend, IN b. Ft Wayne, IN. Studied: Purdue U; Ind. U; Pa. State Col. Teachers: Eliot O'Hara; John Bednar; George C. Eddinger. Exhibited: Nat and Corcoran Galleries, Washington, D.C.; AIC; Butler AI, Ohio; Herron AM; PAFA; WC USA; South Bend A Cen; Ft Wayne A Cen. Prizes: HS, 1948, 50, 52, 68. Note: T, Ind. U, 1951. Opened design office, South Bend, 1958.

HERSHBERGER, ABNER [P] Goshen, IN b. 1934, Milford, NE. Studied: Washburn U, Topeka, KS; Goshen Col, Goshen, IN; Notre Dame U; Ind. U, Bloomington; U of Mich., Ann Arbor. Teachers: Rudy Pozzatti; Ronald Markman. Exhibited: Works on Paper, IMA, 1972; 3rd Ann N.Y. Exh of P, S, and Graphics, Avanti Gal, NYC, 1970; 16th Ann Dr&Small S Show, Ball State U, 1970; San Salvador and San Jose Bi-Nat Cens, El Salvador (solo) and Costa Rica (solo). Prizes: 30th Ann Northern Ind. AA, 1973; Ann Southern Shores Exh, Gary, IN, 1970; Images on Paper, Miss. AA, Jackson, MS, 1970.

HERSHEY, SAMUEL F(ranklin) [Des, P, T, C] Rockport, MA b. 10 Aug 1904, Peru, IN. Studied: MIT; PAFA; BMFA Sch. Teachers: P. Hale; Hibbard; Stevens. Exhibited: CGA; NAD; PAFA; Rockport AA; North Shore AA; Boston. Prizes: New Haven PCC, 1932; HS, 1933, 36, 37, 38, 41. Note: T, Harvard, 1937-42; RISD, beginning 1946.

HERTEL, ELSA [T] b. Deluth, MN. Studied: Carleton Col, Northfield, MN; Herron AI; Munich, Germany; Florence, Italy. Teachers: Paul D. Dannowsky. Exhibited: Deluth A Cen. Note: Head A Dept, Dakota Wesleyan U, 1934-36.

HERTENSTEIN, DeWITT [P] Indianapolis, IN b. 16 Jul 1912, Terre Haute, IN. Studied: John Herron A Sch. Teachers: William Forsyth; Oakley Richey; Clifton Wheeler. Exhibited: Pen Women, 1983; Ind. AG, 1981. Prizes: A for Religion, 1977. Collections: Mobil Oil Corp.

HEYMAN, MARTHA J(osephine) [Ab, Ldscp. P, Print, Por. P] Indianapolis, IN b. 7 May 1927, Indianapolis, IN. Studied: Ind. U; John Herron A Sch. Teachers: Elmer Taflinger; George Jo Mess; Robert Berkshire; Loren Dunlap. Exhibited: IMA, 1987-89; Ball State U; Tippecanoe A Gal, Lafayette, IN; Mid-States A Show; Ind. AC; Herron A Show. Prizes: A for Religion; Indianapolis AL; Ind. State Fair.

HIBBEN, THOMAS E. [Print, Arch] Indianapolis/NYC b. 22 Oct 1860, Rushville, IN d. 6 Jul 1915. Studied: Butler Col; Ind. Sch A. Teachers: William Forsyth; R. Locke; Stark; Jaussley; Love; Gookins. Note: Partner, Hibben, Hollweg&Co. Dry Goods, Indianapolis. First sketch artist, *Indianapolis News*. Art patron and collector. He provided financial aid for William Forsyth's art study in Munich, Germany. Hibben's work exhibited posthumously in the first two Hoosier Salons.

HIBBS, RUTH KERLIN (Mrs. William G.) [P, S, Cer, T] Franklin, IN. Studied: Franklin Col; Herron AI; AIC; Chicago Acad FA. Exhibited: HS Gal, 1965. Prizes: HS, 1957, 59, 60. Collections: Frank Dailey A Collection, Bloomington, IN; Kappa Kappa Kappa Collection, Nashville, IN. Note: T, Franklin Col; Member, Brown Cnty AG.

HICKOK, CONDE WILSON [P] Berwyn, IL b. Batavia, IL. Studied: AIC. Teachers: C. P. Browne. Collections: Danville, IL; Chicago Col Cl.

HIGDON, PHIL Muncie, IN.

HIGGINS, BARBARA DUNCAN

HIGGINS, HERBERT C. [P, Por. P] Indianapolis, IN b. 11 Mar 1909, Stanford, KY. Studied: Manual Training H.S.; John Herron A Sch. Teachers: Gordon Fiscus; Harry Davis; Clayson Baker. Exhibited: Brown Cnty A Gal; Ball State Col, Muncie, IN; A&C Show, Montpelier, OH; A for Religion, Indianapolis; Ind. State Capital Rotunda. Prizes: Brown Cnty AG; Ind. State Fair; Ky. State Fair. Collections: Ind. State M; A.M.E. Church, Indianapolis.

HIGGINS, JULIETA [Ab, Dr, Ldscp. P, Print, Por. P] Evansville, IN b. 1 Mar 1945, China. Studied: Ind. State U; U of Evansville. Teachers: Virginia Cobb; Maxine Masterfield; Glen Bradshaw. Exhibited: Krempp Gal (solo), Jasper, IN, 1987; Evansville M Old Gal, 1988; Soaper A Cen, Henderson, KY, 1990. Prizes: Mid-Am Biennial Nat, 1986; Ky. WCS Aqueous '89; HS, 1990. Collections: Welborn Hospital, Evansville, IN; Southwest Mental Health Clinic, Jasper, IN.

HIGGINS, MARIAN

HIGGINS, REBECCA MOORE [P] Indianapolis, IN b. 4 Oct 1952, Winchester IN. Studied: Ind. U, Bloomington; John Herron A Sch. Exhibited: Ind. State Fair, 1985. Prizes: Ind. WCS, 1989; Ind. State Fair, 1989.

HIGGINS, (William) VICTOR [P, Print, T] Taos, NM b. 28 Jun 1884, Shelbyville, IN d. 23 Aug 1949. Studied: Chicago Acad FA; AIC; Grande Chaumière. Teachers: Robert Henri; René Ménard; Lucien Simon; Hans von Hyeck. Exhibited: CGA, 1935; PAFA; CI. Prizes: Chicago SA, 1917, 18, 28; Palette&Chisel Cl, 1914; NAD, 1918, 27, 32; HS, 1928, 1929; Municipal AL, 1915; AIC, 1915-17, 28, 32. Collections: AIC; Boston MFA; Terre Haute AA; Santa Fe Railroad; Chicago Union Lg Cl; Des Moines Assn FA; Los Angeles M; PAFA. Note: T, Chicago Acad FA, 1940. Member, Taos Society of Artists.

HILL, LARRY [P] Evansville, IN b. 28 Oct 1925, Carbondale, IL d. 16 Mar 1971. Self-taught. Exhibited: Red Spot Paint and Varnish Co., Evansville; U of Evansville. Prizes: Ohio State U, 1965; Abercrombie and Fitch Comp, NY, 1967. Collections: Evansville M. Note: Wildlife painter. Staff artist and outdoor editor, *Evansville Press*. First magazine cover, *The American Woodsman*, 1954.

HILL, LAURA [Dr] North Webster, IN b. 7 Sep 1930, Lewes, DE. Studied: Md. Inst, Baltimore. Exhibited: Ind. Wildlife A, 1984-87, 88; Northern Ind. A, 1985-87. Prizes: Ind. Wildlife A, 1988, 89; Starke Cnty Reg, 1989. Collections: General Electric Corp; Warsaw (Ind.) Public Sch Corp.

HILL, MARIAN J. [T] Franklin, IN. Deceased.

HILL, WAYNE W. [S, P] Minneapolis, MN. Studied: Herron Sch A; Butler U. Teachers: David Rubins; C. Curry Bohm.

HIMELICK, LUANA (Mrs. John) [P] Connersville, IN b. IN. Studied: Stephens Col; Northwestern U; Famous A Sch. Teachers: Merle Brandenburg. Exhibited: Richmond AA; Statehouse Exh, Indianapolis; Whitewater Valley A Assn; Kappa Kappa Kappa Exh; Cape Cod AA, Hyannis, MA. Collections: Fayette Bank&Trust Co, Connorsville; Connorsville Country Cl; Fayette Federal Savings&Loan, Connorsville.

HINDMARCH, ALAN W. LaGrange, IL d. c. 1972.

HINER, JOHN [MM] Indianapolis, IN.

HINKLE, BENJAMIN [Ldscp. P] Lafayette, IN b. 19 Jan 1911, St Paul Park, MN. Self-taught. Exhibited: Brown Cnty AG, 1980-89. Prizes: Ind. State Fair, 1984, 86. Collections: Lafayette Bank&Trust Co.

HINKLE, JAMES ROBERT [P] East Gary, IN.

HINNEFELD, A. JEAN Fortville, IN.

HIRSCH, CHARLES [P] Poseyville, IN b. 10 Dec 1920, Poseyville, IN. Studied: U of Evansville; Evansville M; Brown Cnty. Teachers: Loren Dunlap. Exhibited: Frame House Gal (solo), Louisville; Mid-States Show, Evansville, IN; Women's Cl, Louisville, KY. Prizes: HS, 1972. Collections: U of Evansville; Turner LTD, NYC; General Electric Plant.

HIRSCH, IONE [[Ldscp. P, SLP, Por. P, T] Indianapolis, IN. Exhibited: Ind. A Ann; Herron AM; Ind. AC; Ind. State Fair. Note: T, FA Dept, Arsenal Tech Sch. Taught for 34 years in Indianapolis high schools. T, Cape Girardeau, Mo. and Columbia, Mo.

HIRSHBURG, ROY [P, Photo] Richmond, IN b. Seymour, IN d. Mar 1957. Teachers: Lawrence McConaha, Richmond. Exhibited: Ind. State Fair. Prizes: HS, 1931.

HOBBS, FLORENCE RYAN [P] Muncie, IN.

HOCHMAN, JACQUIE

HOCKENSMITH, DAVID K. [P, Dr] Ft Wayne, IN/Bluffton, IN. Studied: Ft Wayne A Sch. Exhibited: Lyman Brothers, 1968. Prizes: HS, 1970-72.

HODAPP, MARY L. [P] Indianapolis, IN b. 1 Jun 1899, Seymour, IN. Studied: Indianapolis AL. Teachers: Paul Sweany; Floyd Hopper; Mary Dill; Frederick Rigley. Exhibited: Ind. AC; Southside A Exh. Prizes: 500 Festival A; Mile of A; Ind. State Fair, 1967-69; Indianapolis AL. Note: Librarian, Indianapolis Public Library.

HODGIN, JOHN T. [P, Print] Indianapolis, IN b. 22 May 1941, Winchester, IN. Studied: John Herron AI; Ind. Central U. Teachers: Gerald Boyce. Exhibited: Brown Cnty AA. Prizes: HS, 1980; Ind. State Fair. Collections: Indianapolis Power and Light Co; Weiss's Restaurant; Payne, Weiland, Wright&Fairchild Law Office.

HODGIN, MARSTON DEAN [P, T] Oxford, OH b. 3 Dec 1903, Cambridge, OH. Studied: Earlham Col; Ind. U; U of Chicago. Teachers: E. F. Brown; R. L. Coats; J. R. Hopkins; Hawthorne; T. C. Steele; W. Sargent. Exhibited: Ind. Exh, 1924; Butler AI, 1940. Prizes: Ind. Exh, 1925; Richmond (Ind.) AA, 1925, 27, 28, 33, 36, 41. Collections: Earlham Col; Miami U, Oxford, OH; Richmond AA. Note: T, Chairman A Dept, Miami U, 1927-1963.

HODSON, MILES R(AYMOND) [SLP, Por. P, T, Ab] Indianapolis, IN. Studied: Herron Sch A. Teachers: Yasuo Kuniyoshi. Exhibited: Anderson Civic AA, Anderson, IN; Marott Hotel, Indianapolis, 1955; Ind. A Exh; Creative Gal, NY; Butler Inst New Year Show, Springfield, IL. Prizes: Ind. State Fair, 1951, 53; HS, 1953, 55. Note: Head A Dept, Park Sch, Indianapolis.

HOERGER, GRACE E. (Mrs. Roy Ketcham) [S] b. 19 Sep 1888, Chicago, IL d. 1963. Studied: ASL; Provincetown, MA; Académie Julian, Paris, France. Teachers: Roy Ketcham. Note: Worked on Mem Bridge, Vincennes, IN.

HOFFLER, OTHMAR [P, Com. A] Chicago, IL b. Buffalo, NY. Studied: AIC; Albright A Sch, Buffalo; Acad Grande Chaumière and Acad Colarossi, both in Paris. Teachers: Karl A. Buehr; Urquhart Wilcox; Casteluchi; Nandin; Henry Rankin Poore; Morisset. Prizes: Palette and Chisel Acad FA; Albright A Gal; AIC, 1933, 39. Collections: City of Chicago Coll; Palette and Chisel Acad FA; Municipal AL, Chicago; Ill. State M; Purdue U; Iowa State Col; Ind. U.

HOFFMAN, ARTHUR

HOFFMAN, FRANK V. [SLP, P] Chicago, IL. Prizes: HS, 1941.

HOFFMAN, P. D. [Print] Indianapolis, IN.

HOFFMAN, ROBERT J. [Ldscp. P, Genre P, T] Merrillville, IN b. 26 Oct 1930, Gary, IN. Studied: Chicago Acad FA. Teachers: Hal Rogoff; Kay Pool; Frederick Rigley; Ken Gore; Franklin Jones; Jim Pollard. Exhibited: Art Camp '88. Prizes: Northern Ind. AA, 1985, 86; Art Camp '90; HS, 1986, 89. Collections: Northern Ind. Public Service; Hammand Clark Sch; Griffith Ind. Town Hall; Calumet H.S.

HOGUE, SARA JAYNE [SLP, T] Mooresville, IN b. 25 Jan 1916, Rosedale, IN. Teachers: William Ashby; Minnie Wiseman. Exhibited: Liebers Gal; Brown Cnty A Gal. Prizes: Brown Cnty A Gal; Ind. State Fair; Senior Citizen Sweepstake.

HOLIDAY, JOSEPH [P, Dr, T] Indianapolis, IN b. 1927, Chicago, IL d. Jun 1990. Studied: John Herron AI; AIC. Exhibited: Ky. State U; Ind. State U; Ind. Central Col; Marion Col, Indianapolis; Wesleyan U, Bloomington, IL. Prizes: John Herron AI; Ind. State Fair; AIC; Printing Industries of Am, Boston, MA.

HOLLETT, CLARE FERGUSON [P, Cer, MM] Indianapolis, IN. Studied: Bradford Jr. Col, Bradford, MA; U of Wis. Exhibited: Great Am Bowl Show, Newport, RI, 1982; Alliance Gal, IMA, 1983; Purdue U, 1981.

HOLLINGSWORTH, ALICE CLAIRE [I, Dr] Indianapolis, IN b. 12 Feb 1907, Indianapolis. Studied: Herron A Sch; Circle A Acad. Exhibited: Ind. A Exh, 1929.

HOLLINGSWORTH, JOSEPHINE A. *(See Poulson, Josephine Hollingsworth)* [Des, I] Chicago, IL. Studied: John Herron A Sch. Note. T, Shortridge H.S.

HOLLIS, FREDERIC LEE [S, Dr, P, T] Spencer, IN b. 27 Aug 1905, Terre Haute, IN. Studied: John Herron A Sch; Ind. U; Columbia U; Nat Acad; ASL. Teachers: Elmer Taflinger; Eliot O'Hara; Robert Brackman; Jerry Farnsworth; Frank Reilly. Exhibited: Ind. State Library, 1980; Ind. State Fair; Swope Gal; Herron Gal; Lieber Gal; Ind. U MA; Cumberland Col. Collections: *10 O'Clock Line,* Mem S, historical marker near Gosport; Huntington Col. Note: T, Indianapolis Public Sch, Huntington Col and Union Col, KY.

HOLME, MAUD [P] Ft Wayne, IN.

HOLMES, MARY J. Trafalgar, IN.

HOLMES, (Jr.), PALMER Z. [Ldscp. P, P] Terre Haute, IN b. c. 1896 d. 8 Mar 1955. Prizes: N.Y. Acad FA. Note: District Mgr, Mars Inc.

HOLSAPPLE, KERRY [Ldscp. P, SLP, Car, I, Por. P, T] New Castle, IN b. 10 Jun 1954, Greensboro, NC. Studied: John Herron AI; Atelier Lack; Fenway Studios. Teachers: Richard Lack; R. H. Ives Gammell. Exhibited: Henry Cnty Fall Show, 1981; Richmond Professional Show, 1983; Ind. State Fair, 1979. Prizes: HS, 1979, 81.

HOLT, FRANCIS E. [Com. A] Indianapolis/Carmel, IN b. NE. Teachers: Elmer Taflinger. Exhibited: HS (solo), 1957. Prizes: Ind AC 24th Expo; HS, 1950, 53, 57.

HOLTMAN, FLORENCE [P] Indianapolis, IN.

HOLTMAN, HOLLY Cincinnati, OH b. Indianapolis, IN.

HOLZAPFEL, ROBERT [Ldscp. P, Car, Genre P, I, Por. P] New Paris, OH b. 17 Jul 1922, Richmond, IN. Studied: Chicago Acad FA. Exhibited: Whitewater Valley Exh. Prizes: N.Y. Intl A Exh, 1970; Richmond (Ind.) AA, 1989, 90; HS, 1970.

HOOVER, TODD [S] Exhibited: 64th Ind. A Show.

HOPPER, FLOYD D. [P, Print, T] Noblesville, IN b. 1 Nov 1909, Martin Cnty, IN d. 2 Jul 1984. Studied: John Herron A Sch; PAFA; Ind. U Extension. Teachers: William Forsyth; Clifton Wheeler; Paul Hadley; Roy C. Nuse; Francis Speight; Donald M. Mattison; Eliot O'Hara; Francis Chapin; Max Kahn; Frank Schoonover. Exhibited: Am WCS Ann; South Shore AG; Ind. Soc Pr. M; Southern Pr. M Soc; Philadelphia WC Exh; Pa. Acad Ann; CI; Intl Exh of Lithography and Wood Engraving, Chicago; Michiana Biennial, South Bend; Aqua Chromatic, NY. Prizes: HS, 1942, 44, 58, 64-67, 69, 72, 77, 78, 80, 81, 83; Ind. A Ann; Nat Lithography Exh, Oklahoma City; Ind. AC; WC USA, Springfield, MO. Collections: Ind. U; DePauw U; Ft Wayne AM; Psi Iota Xi; Oklahoma City M; Ind. State U; Franklin Col; Wabash Col; Shortridge H.S.; IMA; Ball State U; Riley Hospital; Indianapolis Public Schs. Note: T, Indianapolis AL, 1963-84.

HORNE-KAPLAN, DENISE ANNE [P] North Manchester, IN. Prizes: HS, 1989.

HORTON, MARTHA L. POWELL *(See Powell, Martha L.)* [P]

HORWEDEL, ANNE [P, T] Otterbein, IN b. 1938, Ft Worth, TX. Studied: UCLA; Purdue U. Teachers: Rico LeBrun; Stanton McDonald-Wright. Exhibited: Lafayette A Cen (solo), Lafayette, IN; Southern Ohio M, Portsmouth, OH; Midwest M Am A, Elkhart, IN; Anderson FA Cen, Anderson, IN; New Harmony Gal Cont A; 35th Ann Salon Show Northern Ind. AA; Art 500, Indianapolis. Prizes: Tippecanoe Biennial, Artforms '79; 67th Ind. A Show, IMA; HS, 1981. Note: T, Lafayette (Ind.) A Cen.

HORWITZ, HAROLD I. Indianapolis, IN.

HOSACK, MARY (H.) [Dr] Newburgh, IN.

HOSTERMAN, NAOMI S. (Mrs. R. C.) [Por. P, I] Charleston, WV b. 13 Jan 1903, Elkhart, IN. Studied: Herron AI; Scott Carbee Sch, Boston; Ind. U; CM Sch. Teachers: William Forsyth; F. Stark; R. Grooms; C. Barnhorn; B. Keyes. Prizes: All. A, WV, 1938, 42, 46. Collections: First Presbyterian Church and Baptist Temple, Charleston, WV; Kanawha Cnty, WV. Note: I, *Greenbriar Pioneers and Their Homes.*

HOSTETLER, RENA A. [P] Nashville, IN b. Dallas, TX d. Mar 1982. Studied: CGA Sch, Washington, D.C.; Chicago Gal FA; Ringling Sch A, Sarasota, FL. Teachers: Frederick M. Grant; Frank Peyraude; Jesse Hobby; Arnold Turtle; Eliot O'Hara; Hilton Leech; Lauren Wilford. Prizes: HS, 1940, 45, 57. Note: Lived in Winnetka, IL; member Brown Cnty A Gal Assn.

HOUCK, ELIZABETH D.

HOUGH, BERENICE

HOUGLUM, JONATHON W. [P] Martinsville, IN.

HOUSE, MARTY [Silverpoint] Ft Wayne, IN.

HOWARD, (F.) MAX [Ldscp. P, T] Indianapolis, IN b. 21 Jun 1909, Clinton Cnty, IN. Studied: Herron Sch A; Ohio State U. Prizes: Ind. State Fair; HS, 1949, 75, 78, 79, 81, 83, 86. Collections: Mallory; Cummins Engine. Note: T and former head A Dept, Howe H.S., 1940-72. Created junk yard compositions.

HOWARD (Jr.), FRANK A. Indianapolis, IN b. c. 1923 d. Aug 1983. Studied: John Herron AI. Exhibited: 500 Festival Exh; Wabash Valley Show; Whitewater Valley Show.

HOWE, PHILIP (L.) [P] Indianapolis, IN.

HOWE, SUSAN R(osalind) [P] Hammond, IN b. 28 May 1873, Manchester. Prizes: Lake Cnty Fair, IN, 1936, 38, 39.

HUBBARD, J. F(rank) (Cap) [Ldscp. P, Por. P, Photo] Muncie, IN b. Piqua, OH. Note: President, Muncie AA; one of the founders of the Muncie Civic Theater.

HUBBARD, (Frank McKinney) KIN [Car, W, I] b. Bellefontaine, OH d. Dec 1930. Note: Car, *Indianapolis News.* Creator, Abe Martin cartoons which first appeared in the *News* in 1904.

HUBER, HELEN RUTH [W, Print, P] Gary, IN b. 19 Mar 1902, East Chicago, IN. Studied: Chicago Acad FA; U of Chicago; Northwestern U. Teachers: G. Bolande; R. Chase. Exhibited: Northern Ind. A, 1946; Gary, IN, 1945; East Chicago, IN, 1945. Note: T, Public Schs, Gary, IN; A Critic, *Gary Post-Tribune.*

HUDSON, BARBARA A. (Mrs. Phillip) [Por. P, SLP, Ldscp. P] Toledo, OH b. 1940, Franklin, IN. Studied:

Toledo AM. Teachers: Ruth Starlin. Exhibited: Ft Wayne Womens Cl; Ind. State Fair; Toledo AC Ann; Indianapolis 500. Note: Daughter of artist Ruth Starlin.

HUFFORD, BERNIECE M. (Mrs. Charles) [P, Dr] Brownsburg, IN b. 1 May 1920, Detroit, MI. Studied: Ind. U; Ind. U Extension; Indianapolis AL; Hendricks Cnty AL. Teachers: George Jo Mess; Ruth Anderson; Lois Davis. Exhibited: Wabash Valley Juried Exh, Swope A Gal, Terre Haute; Ind. AC. Prizes: A for Religion, Indianapolis; 500 Festival of A; Ind. State Fair. Collections: Terre Haute Sch; Plainfield Sch; Brownsburg Sch.

HUGHES, LEIGH E.

HULL, STEVE [Dr] Hancock Cnty, IN. Self-taught. Exhibited: Greenfield Banking Co; Penrod A Fair; Talbott Street A Fair.

HUMKE, CAROLYN J. [Ldscp. P, Ab] Indianapolis, IN b. 17 Sep 1933, Quincy, IL. Studied: Indianapolis AL. Teachers: Alice DeCaprio; Jeannie McLeish. Exhibited: Ind. WCS, 1990, 91.

HUMMEL, REBA LAYMAN Marion, IN.

HUMMER, ED(ward) J. Estes Park, CO.

HUMPHREY, HELEN [P] Indianapolis, IN b. Canton, OH. Teachers: Elmer Taflinger; Edmund Brucker; Ruth Anderson. Exhibited: Ind. State Fair; Ind. AC Show, L. S. Ayres, Indianapolis. Prizes: HS, 1955. Note: Injured in a car accident during her junior year at Shortridge H.S.; confined to a wheelchair.

HUNT, LOIS [P] Bloomington, IN.

HUNT, WILL HARVEY [Mur. P, Des, Dr] Indianapolis, IN b. 13 Jun 1910, Indianapolis. Studied: John Herron A Sch. Teachers: William Forsyth; Donald M. Mattison; Henrik M. Mayer. Prizes: HS, 1935; John Herron A Sch, 1935; Block Gal, Indianapolis, 1936. Collections: Northwestern U, Chicago; James Whitcomb Riley Hospital for Children, Ceiling Dec, Indianapolis. Note: Position, A Display Dept, H. P. Wasson&Co.

HUNTER, EDWIN E. [Pastel Dr, P] New Castle, IN b. 11 Nov 1905, New Castle, IN d. May 1981. Studied: Hanover Col; Mercer U, Macon, GA (Law Degree).

Teachers: Ruthven Byrum; Elizabeth Shaffer; Joe Henderson. Exhibited: Herron AM. Note: New Castle attorney.

HUNTER, MARY [P, S] Indianapolis, IN b. Springfield, OH. Studied: John Herron AI. Teachers: Clifton Wheeler; Elmer Taflinger; David Rubins. Exhibited: Ind. State Fair, 1952. Prizes: Ind. State Fair, 1953; HS, 1954, 59, 60; Ind. AC. Collections: DePauw U.

HURD, MAXINE [Dr, Por. P] Bedford, IN. Exhibited: Nashville A Gal; Spring Mill Inn, Spring Mill State Park; Bedford Medical Cen; Dunn Mem Hospital, Bedford, IN.

HURST, RALPH N. [S, T] Tallahassee, FL b. Decatur, IN. Studied: Ind. U. Teachers: Robert Laurent. Exhibited: First Am S Show, Metropolitan MA, NY; Barn Gal of the Ogunquit; Richmond AA Gal; Ind. A Exh; Herron AM. Prizes: HS, 1952, 56. Note: Asst. Professor A Education, Fla. State U.

HURT, SARAH (Miner) [Print, Col. A, P] Indianapolis, IN b. c. 1908 Ft Wayne, IN d. 3 May 1985. Studied: Ft Wayne A Sch; John Herron A Sch; Indianapolis AL. Exhibited: Indianapolis AL; Contemporary Pr. M, Birmingham, MI; Contemporary Am Pr. M, DePauw U; Jewish Community Cen (solo), 1963; A House, Cincinnati (solo), 1965-67; Ind. Central Col (solo), 1969; Ft Wayne AM Gal (solo), 1973. Prizes: Premiers Prix Internationaus, Cannes, France, 1969; Ind. A Exh; HS, 1960, 64; Ind. State Fair; Ind. AC; Wabash Valley Exh; Muncie AA; Nat Assn Women A; Whitewater Valley Reg; Mid-States A Exh; 500 Festival of the A; Tippecanoe Reg. Note: Included in Book #111 *Prize-Winning Graphics*.

HUTCHINSON, ROBERT F. Lebanon, IN. Note: Member, Brown Cnty A Gal.

HUTCHISON, CONNIE [P] Fostoria, OH. Note: Also worked in Muscatine, IA.

HUTTO, BLANCHE [T] b. Philadelphia, PA. Studied: Ball State TC; Columbia U. Teachers: Forrest Stark; Mrs. Walter McBride. Exhibited: Civic Theatre (solo), 1941-47. Prizes: Ft Wayne's Woman's Cl, 1942; Ind. A, 1947. Note: T, Southside H.S., Ft Wayne, IN.

HUTTON, ALBERT N.

IANUCILLI, FRANK J. Deceased.

ILES, MINNIE ELLEN Paris, IL d. c. 1969.

INCE, NANCY (Crockett) [Ldscp. P] Lafayette, IN b. 30 Oct 1927, Chicago, IL. Studied: Silvermine, Norwalk, CT; Indianapolis AL; Am Acad of A, Chicago; Montclair (N.J.) AM; Oakland and Laguna Beach A Schs, CA. Teachers: Rosemary Thomas. Exhibited: Ind. State Fair, 1990; Round the Fountain A Fair, Lafayette, IN.

IZOR, ESTELLE PEEL [P,T] Indianapolis, IN b. Centerville, Wayne Cnty, IN. Studied: Ind. A Sch; AIC. Teachers: William Forsyth; T. C. Steele; Frederick Freer; Fred Richardson; Arthur Dow; John C. Johansen; William M. Chase; Albert Herter; Herman Dudley Murphy; John Johanot; V. J. Cariani. Prizes: HS, 1929. Note: T, Head of FA Department, Emmerich Manual Training H.S. until 1938. Author, *Costume Designing and Home Planning.*

1952
Hoosier
Salon

JACKLEY, F. DANO [P, Print, Arch] Baltimore, MD b. 22 Jan 1900, Frankton, IN. Studied: Herron AI, Indianapolis; PAFA. Teachers: J. W. Smith. Exhibited: WC Ann, Baltimore, 1939; Md. Inst; Southern Pr. M.

JACKS, SUSAN [P]

JACKSON, CHIC (Charles Bacon) [I, Ldscp. P, Car] Indianapolis, IN b. 31 Dec 1880, Muncie, IN d. 3 Jun 1934. Studied: AIC. Prizes: HS, 1925. Teachers: J. Ottis Adams. Note: His newspaper career started with the *Muncie News,* continued with the *Muncie Star.* He went to the *Indianapolis Star* in 1907. Created the Bean Family comic strip, the originals of which are housed in the Lilly Library, Ind. U, Bloomington.

JACKSON, GERTRUDE [P] Chicago, IL b. Champaign, IL. Studied: AIC; Chicago A Acad. Teachers: Grant; St. John; Ruth Van Sickle; Ford. Note: Attended Rensselaer.

JACKSON, JOHN [S] Bedford, IN b. Scotland. Studied: Extension classes, South Kensington A Sch, London. Prizes: Ind. State Fair; HS, 1931.

JACKSON, LOIS M. [T] Indianapolis, IN. Studied: Herron Sch A, senior in 1951. Prizes: Ind. State Fair, 1951. Note: T, Indianapolis Public Sch.

JACQUES, EMIL [P, T, C] Notre Dame, IN b. 17 Jul 1874, Moorslede, Belgium d. 17 Aug 1937, Bellaire, MI. Studied: Institut Superieur des Beaux-Arts de Belgique, Antwerp. Prizes: HS, 1936. Collections: Wightman A Gal, U of Notre Dame; St Mary's Cathedral. Note: Established A Dept, Columbia U and Portland, OR. Dir, Sch FA, U of Notre Dame, since 1929.

JAGGER, FLORENCE Z. [P, T] Indianapolis, IN b. Racine, WI. Studied: Elmer Taflinger Life Drawing Studio; Indianapolis AL. Teachers: Elmer Taflinger; Helen Sawyer; G. Illingsworth; Harry Davis; Paul Sweany; Gene Lacy; Gianni Cilfone; Edward Manetta. Exhibited: Ann Drawing&Small S Nat Show, BSU; Miniature P, S&Gravers Soc of Washington, D. C.; Mid-States Exh, Evansville; Tippecanoe Reg, Lafayette. Prizes: Wabash Valley Reg, Terre Haute; Ind. AC; Indianapolis AL; Glendale Show; HS, 1979; Ind. State Fair. Collections: Franklin Col; Ind. State

TC; Lilly Clinic; Ind. Girl's Sch. Note: President, Ind. AC, 1973-74.

JAGODITS, CAROLYN [P, I] South Bend, IN b. 16 Jul, South Bend. Studied: St Mary's Col, Notre Dame, IN. Exhibited: South Bend A Cen Sales Gal, 1988. Prizes: Ind. Wildlife A, 1988; HS, 1988; Nat A Seminar, 1984; A Magazine 1990 Wildlife P Comp, finalist.

JAMES, ELIZABETH E. [Ldscp. P, Print, T] South Bend, IN b. IN. Studied: Ind. U; U of Notre Dame; St Mary's Col, Notre Dame, IN; South Bend A Cen. Teachers: Zygmund Jankowski; Karlyn Holman; Tony Couch. Exhibited: St Joe Valley WCS, Inc, 1990; Northern Ind. A, 1990. Prizes: Ft Wayne Women's Juried Exh, 1987; 100 Center A Fair, Mishawaka, IN; Midwest M of Am A, Elkhart, IN, 1982, 84, 85, 87; Leeper Park A Fair, South Bend, IN, 1982-90. Collections: South Bend A Cen. Note: T, South Bend A Cen and Elkhart AL; Owner, Studio d'Beaux Arts.

JAMES, EVA GERTRUDE [P, S, C, T] Brazil, IN b. 18 Jul 1871, Morgan Cnty, IN. Studied: Ind. U; St John's Acad. Teachers: R. E. Burke. Exhibited: Soc Ind. A; Ind. State Fair. Prizes: Brazil, IN. Collections: Oddfellows Hall, Eminence, IN.

JAMES, EVALYN GERTRUDE [P, C, T, W] Brazil, IN b. 22 May 1898, Chicago, IL d. Apr 1990. Studied: Herron AI; Earlham Col; Ind. U. Exhibited: Herron AI; Swope A Gal; Purdue U. Prizes: Ind. State Fair. Collections: Shortridge H.S., Indianapolis. Note: T, Dir, Studio Sch FA, Brazil, IN. Head FA Dept., Ind. State U.

JAMISON, BUD [Ldscp. P] Marion, IN b. 9 Jul 1957, Marion, IN. Self-taught. Prizes: HS, 1987. Collections: Eli Lilly Co, Indianapolis; Johnna Inst, Marion, IN.

JANKOWSKI, ZYGMUND S. [P, T] South Bend, IN. Exhibited: First Bank&Trust, South Bend, IN. Prizes: HS, 1966, 68. Collections: First Bank&Trust, South Bend. Note: T, Barn Sch P, Ind. U-South Bend, Niles A Cen and Breman A Cen.

JARRETT, JAMES E. [P] Nashville, IN b. 1923, Muncie, IN d. 21 May 1979. Studied: Am Acad FA, Chicago, IL; Chicago Professional Sch; Ball State U; Ind. U. Exhibited:

Ind. State Fair; A for Religion; Ball State Gal.

JARRETT, JUDY *(See Olive, Judy)* [P, I] Indianapolis, IN b. 18 Jul 1946, Indianapolis. Studied: Indianapolis AL; IUPUI. Teachers: Lois Davis; Harry Davis. Exhibited: Indianapolis AL, 1987; Ruschman A Gal, Indianapolis; Ind. State Fair; IMA; Indianapolis A Council. Prizes: Indianapolis A Council, Start With Art, 1990; HS, 1983. Note: Formerly, Judy Jarrett Olive.

JARRETT, KATHRYN [P] Terre Haute, IN. Prizes: HS, 1983.

JARVIS, Sr., LEON F.

JARVIS, PHILIP M. [P] Greenwood, IN.

JEFFERSON, ORVILLE [P] Kokomo, IN b. 8 Oct 1872, a farm south of Kokomo, IN d. 1941. Teachers: Edward Sitzman; William Forsyth. Exhibited: Ind. U.

JEFFRIES, HARRIET H. [Por. P, Ldscp. P, SLP, T] Carmel, IN b. Carmel, IN d. 3 Jun 1982. Studied: Herron Sch A. Teachers: Carl Graf; Edward Sitzman; Charles West; Edmund Brucker; George Jo Mess; Jerry Farnsworth. Exhibited: Herron AM, 1944; Nat Lg Am Pen Women, Washington, D.C., 1945. Note: T, Indianapolis ASL.

JENKINS, CONNIE S. Evansville, IN. Note: More current name, Connie Richmond.

JENKINS, Jr., F. RAYMOND [Dr, Ldscp. P, T] Tupper Lake, NY b. 4 Mar 1925, Richmond, IN. Studied: Earlham Col; Carnegie/Mellon U. Teachers: Elmira Kempton. Exhibited: Plattsburgh, NY, 1992. Prizes: HS, 1954; AWS Show, Old Forge, NY, 1991; 125th AWS Show, Salmagundi Club, NYC, 1992; NAPA Valley Nat Comp, 1992; Adirondack Centennial, 1992.

JENKINS, JAN [P] Indianapolis, IN.

JENNINGS, EDNA C. [Ldscp. P, T] Spencer, IN b. 27 Jul 1910, Jefferson Cnty, Canaan, IN d. 16 Oct 1987. Studied: Ft Wayne A Sch; St Francis Col, Ft Wayne; Grey Sch A, Aberdeen, Scotland. Teachers: James McBride; Floyd Hopper; Frederick Rigley; C. Curry Bohm; Kaye Poole; Clayson Baker. Exhibited: Auburn, IN; Owen Cnty AG; Hoosier Hills AG. Prizes: Ind. AC; Northeast Ind. A Show; Eastgate Plaza Show, Bloomington, IN. Collections: Spencer Senior Citizens Cen. Note: Mother of artist Margaret Kessler. Became Edna Jennings-McCutchan.

JILBURG, LLOYD [Dr, I, S] North Webster, IN b. 19 May 1936, Chicago, IL. Self-taught. Prizes: Peoples Choice, 1982-84.

JOHNS, MARY ANN [MM, S] Bloomington, IN.

JOHNSON, CAROLYN W. [P] Carmel, IN.

JOHNSON, FRANCES GOLDRICK [S] Columbus, OH.

JOHNSON, FRANCIS M. [P, S] Chicago, IL b. Bedford, IN. Teachers: William Forsyth; Clifton Wheeler; Myra R. Richards; James Weisman. Collections: Louisville Public Sch; Bedford H.S.

JOHNSON, GRACE [P] Indianapolis, IN. Exhibited: Evangelical and Reformed Church, Indianapolis.

JOHNSON, GUY D.

JOHNSON, JESSAMINE I(nglee) [P, T] Connorsville, IN b. 2 Dec 1874, Delphi, IN. Studied: Herron AI. Prizes: HS, Chicago, 1929.

JOHNSON, LOUISE [P, Ldscp. P, Ab, Por. P, T] Indianapolis, IN b. 8 Feb 1918, Whitesville, KY. Studied: Herron Sch A; Ind. Central Col; Indianapolis AL. Teachers: Elmer Taflinger; Floyd Hopper; Edward Manetta; George Jo Mess; Adolph Walters. Exhibited: Butler Inst Am A, Youngstown, OH, 1976; Chicago M of Sc&Industry, 1976; Evansville AM. Prizes: IMA, 1972; Indianaplis AL; HS, 1974; Ind. AC. Collections: Brown Cnty A Gal; First Nat Bank of Greenwood, Greenwood, IN; St James's Catholic Church, Indianapolis; Union Federal Savings&Loan, Indianapolis.

JOHNSON, MAXINE

JOHNSON, NEOLA [P, S, I, T] Gary, IN/Lindstrom, MN b. Chicago, IL. Teachers: A. Angarola; C. Booth. Exhibited: No Jury Show, Chicago, 1928.

JOHNSON, PAMELA [P] Evansville, IN.

JOHNSON, ROBERT R.

JOHNSON, THELMA [P]

JOHNSTON, F.

JONAS, TERI [P] San Antonio, TX b. 1942, Tucson, AZ. Teachers: Chen Chi; Christopher Schink; Jeanne Dobie; Marilyn Phyllis. Exhibited: Three Rivers A Festival, Pittsburg, PA; Butler Inst Am A, Youngstown, OH; Southern Ind. Exh. Prizes: Ind. State Fair; IHA; Ind. A Postcard Series; Anderson Winter Show; Totally Transparent; Phoenix&Dragon A Gal, Bloomington, 1989; HS, 1985. Collections: Indianapolis Power and Light Co; Cen for Mental Health, Anderson, IN; First Nat Bank, Bloomington. Note: Lived in Bloomington, Ind. from 1979-1989. Designed cards for Sunshine Greeting Cards.

JONES, ANNA M. [P, Print] Indianapolis, IN b. 16 Dec 1915, Kempton, IN. Studied: Shortridge H.S.; Indianapolis AL. Teachers: Paul Sweany; George Jo Mess; Edward Manetta; Gerald Boyce. Exhibited: Herron AM; Indianapolis AL; Butler Inst Am A, Youngstown, OH, 1965; IHA, 1979; Tippecanoe Reg, Lafayette, IN, 1967. Prizes: HS, 1962, 68, 75, 76, 84; Ind. State Fair, 1961, 65, 68, 69, 71, 78-82, 86, 89; 14th Whitewater Valley A Exh, Connersville, IN, 1973, 81; Anderson Winter Show, 1977, 78, 81. Collections: Ind. U Mem Union, Bloomington, IN; Lilly Endowment; Psi Iota Xi Sorority; Kappa Kappa Kappa Sorority.

JONES, BARBARA Indianapolis, IN b. 1932, Lafayette, IN. Studied: Purdue U. Exhibited: Purdue U, 1974; 68th Ind. A Show, 1981; 11th Biennial Michiana Reg, 1980. Prizes: HS, 1980, 83; Evansville M of A&Sc, 1974; Tippecanoe Cnty, 1974; Nashville A&C Exh, 1981; Sugar Creek, 1974, 79, 80, 81. Collections: Lafayette A Cen; Evansville M of A&Sc.

JONES, BEAUFORD FLOYD Chicago, IL.

JONES, CARL E. [Por. P, P] Ft Wayne, IN. Prizes: HS, 1954, 55.

JONES, CLIFFORD E(dgar) [Mur. P, I, T] Woodmont, CT b. 17 Jun 1915, Greentown, IN. Studied: John Herron AI; Am Acad, Rome; U of Iowa. Teachers: Donald Mattison; Henrik M. Mayer; J. Charlot. Exhibited: Ind. A, 1941; All-Iowa Exh, 1940; New Haven PCC, 1946; Ind. State Fair, 1936, 40, 41. Prizes: Prix de Rome, 1937; HS, 1941. Collections: St John's Church, Bridgeport, CT; Post Office, Cuyahoga Falls, OH. Note: T, Herron A Sch, U of Iowa.

JONES, DENNIS M(ichael) [Ldscp. P] Muncie, IN b. 2 Feb 1946, Shaker Heights, Cleveland, OH d. 15 Mar 1991. Teachers: Frederick Grue. Prizes: HS, 1987, 88.

JONES, DORIS D. [C, S] IN b. Bokchito, OK. Studied: Wabash Col; Lafayette A Cen. Teachers: Mary Johnson; Lee Seda; Audrey Rossman. Prizes: Old Jail A&C Show, 1977.

JONES, GLADYS [P] Shelbyville, IN b. Louisiana. Exhibited: Art 500, Indianapolis AL, 1972. Note: Artist, *Indianapolis News*, beginning1964.

JONES, HARRY DONALD [Mur. P, P] San Francisco, CA b. 13 Aug 1906, Vincennes, IN. Studied: Cumming Sch A; Child-Walker Sch Des; Iowa U; BMFA Sch; Harvard. Exhibited: AIC, 1935, 36; PAFA, 1936-38; Rockefeller Cen, 1937; Kansas City AI. Prizes: Carson Pirie Scott Co, Chicago; Des Moines, 1930, 32; Iowa State Fair, 1932, 33; All-Iowa Exh, Chicago, 1937. Collections: Des Moines Women's Cl; Iowa State TC; Des Moines Public Library; assisted on murals, Ames Col; Eli Lilly&Co, Indianapolis. Note: Iowa State Supv, Index Am Des, 1937-39; Director, Iowa A Program, 1939-41.

JONES, JACQUELYN JUDITH [S] West Palm Beach, FL/Marion, IN b. 5 Jun 1913, Blaine, IN. Studied: Chicago Sch S; John Herron AI. Teachers: R. Davidson. Prizes: Intl Soap S, NY, 1932, 33; Ind. State Fair, 1933, 34. Collections: Haines Mem, Portland; bust, Wabash Valley Trust Bank, Wabash, IN; Highland Country Cl, Indianapolis; Marion (Ind.) Col.

JONES, KENNETH Chicago, IL.

JONES, LORAN RAYMOND Chicago, IL.

JONES, MELVIN T.

JONES, MICHAEL L. [Ldscp. P] Danville, IN b. 21 Oct 1942, Indianapolis, IN. Teachers: Paul Sweany; Terry Wasson. Exhibited: Ind. WCS, 1984, 85; Ind. State Fair, 1975. Prizes: Prestwick A, 1984; HS, 1980; Ind. WCS, 1986. Collections: Ind. Nat Bank.

JONSON, JON MAGNUS [S, T] Frankfort, IN b. 18 Dec 1893, Upham, ND d. 1947. Studied: AIC; BAID. Teachers: Nadelman; Edward McCartan; A. Polásek; Lorado Taft; Partridge; Lawrie. Exhibited: Ind. State Fair. Prizes: Tiffany Foundation Fellowship, 1927; HS, 1931, 35, 37, 43, 49; Ind. AA, Herron AM, 1937, 42. Collections: Intl House, Chicago; public park, Frankfort, IN; State Col, Fargo, ND. Note: T, Cranbrook Acad A, Bloomfield Hills, MI.

JORDAN, J. E. [S] Bedford, IN. Prizes: HS, 1928.

JORDAN, JANE [P, Genre P, T] Evansville, IN b. 10 Nov 1923, Evansville, IN. Self-taught. Exhibited: Frame House Gal, Louisville, KY; Mid-States Exh, Evansville M, 1992; Realism Exhibition, Evansville M, 1987-89, 92; Ind. Realism, Ft Wayne, 1988. Collections: Ira Roberts Publishing, Beverly Hills, CA; Bristol Myers, Squibb, Evansville; Soldarbron Pointe, Evansville.

JOSEPH, Jr., ROBERT H. [Ldscp. P] Indianapolis, IN b. 18 Aug 1927, South Bend, IN. Studied: East Side A Cen. Teachers: William A. Eyden, Jr.; Fred Eilers; Robert Osborne. Exhibited: Richmond AA, Richmond, IN; Brown Cnty A Gal. Prizes: Tri Kappa; Fairwood Hills AA; Evansville AG Juried Show, 1983. Collections: Ford Motor Co.

JOSLIN, IRENE SHELLEY [I, Por. P] Nashville, IN b. 22 Aug 1952, Indianapolis, IN. Self-taught. Prizes: Heritage A '89.

JOSSEL, LEONARD [Print, P] Terre Haute, IN. Exhibited: Cornell Cl, NYC, 1975; Jefferson Nat Life Insurance Co, Indianapolis, 1976. Collections: First Nat Bank, Terre Haute.

JOURDAN, FRANCES [P] Evansville, IN.

JOYCE, PATRICK M(ichael) [C, P] Oxford, OH b. 1951, Indianapolis, IN. Studied: Herron Sch A; Pratt Inst; U of Md., European Campus Division. Exhibited: Am Consulate Library, Trieste, Italy; Ill. Quintesimo Extemporaneo Castello d'Auiano.

JUBELL, ALBERT E. [P] Michigan City, IN b. 8 Jan 1887, White Cloud, MI. Teachers: Karl Mattern. Exhibited: Michigan City, 1928.

JUDD, PATRICIA [P] Goshen, IN b. 17 Mar 1923, Lancaster Cnty, NE. Studied: AI, Denver, CO; South Bend A Cen. Teachers: Harriet Monteith. Exhibited: Goshen Public Library (solo), 1970, 73. Prizes: Lakeland AA, Warsaw, IN, 1960, 61, 62; Am A Gal, Syracuse, IN, 1962; 27th Ann Exh, Ft Wayne, IN, 1962; Nappanee A Festival, 1968; HS, 1973. Collections: First United Methodist Church, Goshen, IN.

JUERLING, GAIL [Ldscp. P] Indianapolis, IN b. 13 Oct 1938, St Petersburg, FL. Teachers: Barbara Gephart. Exhibited: Whitewater Valley, 1988; Nashville Heritage Exh, 1989.

JULIAN, JOHN D. [Dr] Franklin, IN. Prizes: 4th Fighter Interceptor Wing, Indianapolis, 1954; HS, 1963, 64, 67.

JUNGE, CARL S(teven) [Des, P, C, I] Oak Park, IL b. 5 Jun 1880, Stockton, CA. Studied: Hopkins AI; Partington Sch Illus, San Francisco; Sch of A, London; Académie Julian, Paris. Exhibited: AIC; CI; NAC; Toledo MA; Los Angeles MA. Prizes: Am Bookplate Soc, 1916, 17, 21, 22, 25; Bookplate Assn, 1926, 36. Collections: LOC; British M; MMA; BMFA; Toledo MA; Vanderpoel Coll. Note: I, *Bookplates, Ex Libris*.

KACHEL, NANCY JEAN [Cer] Richmond, IN.

KACKLEY, SALLY ANN [Por. P] Indianapolis, IN. Studied: Herron Sch A. Teachers: Frederick Hobbs, San Francisco. Exhibited: Community Service Library, Indianapolis, 1961.

KAESER, WILLIAM F. [Por. P, Ldscp. P, SLP, Des, T] Indianapolis, IN b. 31 Oct 1908, Durlach, Germany d. 17 Jul 1987. Studied: Herron A Sch; Ind. U; Leonardo da Vinci A Sch, NY. Teachers: William Forsyth; Clifton Wheeler; Eliot O'Hara; F. Piccirilli; Frank Schoonover; Oakley Richey. Exhibited: CGA, 1937; CM, 1935, 37; CI, 1941; PAFA, 1935, 37; Ind. A, 1936-46; WFNY, 1939. Prizes: HS, 1936, 39, 40, 51, 54, 64, 69, 70, 72; Culver Military Acad, 1939. Collections: Indianapolis Public Sch; Ind. Bell Telephone Co; Ind. State U; Ind. U; Indianapolis AL; Culver Military Acad; mural, USPO, Pendleton, IN. Note: WPA artist. One of the Indianapolis AL's first teachers.

KAKUTANI, MITSUO [Clay A]

KANE, ANN C. [P, T] Indianapolis, IN b. 2 Mar 1938, Indianapolis, IN. Studied: Marian Col; John Herron A Sch; Indianapolis AL. Teachers: Jean Vietor; Valfred Thelin, Sr.; Mary Jane Peine. Exhibited: CCA Gal; Ind. State Fair; Ind. State M; A For Religion; Art 500. Prizes: HS, 1977. Note: T, Immaculate Heart of Mary and Christ the King, 1970-76.

KANG, HELEN [S] Indianapolis, IN. Exhibited: Glendale Mall, Indianapolis, 1972.

KAPLAN, BARBARA [P, Print] Bloomington, IN b. 26 Apr 1939, Ashland, KY. Studied: U of Ill.; Yale Summer Sch A&Music; Atelier 17 and Atelier Desjobert, Paris, France. Teachers: S. W. Hayter. Exhibited: L'Estampe Contemporaine à la Bibliotheque Nationale, Paris, 1973; Boston PM 25th Anniversary Exh, De Cordova M, Lincoln, MA, 1973; Eight-State Print Exh, J. B. Speed AM, Louisville, KY, 1973; Indianapolis AL, 1973; IMA, 1972; Ind. PM, 1972; Mid-States A Exh, Evansville M of A&Sc, 1972. Collections: U of Ill., Champaign, IL; Bibliotheque Nationale, Paris; Atelier 17, Paris.

KARN, RON [P, T] Newburgh, IN b. Evansville, IN. Studied: U of Evansville. Exhibited: Swope Gal, Terre Haute, IN; Old National Bank Gal; Mid-States A Exh, Evansville M, 1972. Note: Layout and design artist, Creative Press, Inc., Evansville.

KASUBJAK, NAOMI WARD (Mrs. Michael A.) [P, T] Evansville, IN b. 28 Mar 1922, Butler Cnty, KY. Studied: U of Evansville. Exhibited: Mid-States Exh; Old Nat Bank Gal; Main Street Showcase of Evansville (solo); Evansville M of A&Sc. Note: T, Evansville M of A&Sc.

KECK, LOUISE HOPKINS (Lu) *(See Kek, Lu)* [P] Mt Vernon, IN. Prizes: HS, 1965. Note: President of a woman's art club in the early 1900s; charter member of Old Evansville AG. In later years, her brush signature was LuKek.

KEENE, MAXINE M. [S] Prizes: HS, 1968.

KEENER, ANNA ELIZABETH (Mrs. Wilton) [P, C, T, Print] Portales, NM b. 16 Oct 1895, Flaglor, CO. Studied: Bethany Col; AIC; Kansas City AI; Colo. State TC; U of N.M. Teachers: B. Sandzen; R. Davey. Exhibited: Museum N.M. Prizes: Kansas City AI. Collections: San Francisco Public Library; Vanderpoel Coll; Sul Ross State TC; Okla. U; Texas Hist Soc. Note: Author, *Spontaneity in Design*. T, Eastern N.M. Col.

KEESLING, ELIZABETH Winchester, IN.

KEK, LU *(See Keck, Louise Hopkins)*

KELLEY, BONNIE [P] Indianapolis, IN b. 8 Feb 1920, Brooklyn, IN. Self-taught. Exhibited: Brown Cnty AM. Prizes: Ind. State Fair, 1988; Marion Cnty Fair, 1989.

KELLEY, JOHN R. [Arch] Richmond, IN b. Richmond, IN. Studied: U of Mich. Teachers: Samuel Chamberlain; Leon Makielski; Jean Paul Slusser.

KELLOGG, JOAN HARLAN [Li]

KELLY, CLAY [P, Print, T] Chicago, IL b. 11 Jun 1874, Jeffersonville, IN. Studied: DePauw U. Exhibited: AIC, 1927, 40; Roullier Gal (solo), Chicago, 1936. Prizes: HS, 1938. Note: Director and Founder, South Shore A Sch, Chicago.

KELLY, GORDON R. [P] Indianapolis, IN.

KELLY, JOANNE [Genre P] Kokomo, IN b. 11 Jun 1964, Kokomo, IN. Studied: Ball State U. Exhibited: Kokomo AA Spring Show, 1990. Prizes: Kokomo AA Spring Show, 1987, 89; Green Town Glass Festival, 1987. Collections: Domino's Farm, Ann Arbor, MI.

KELLY, RUTH T. [P] Elkhart, IN.

KELSEY, CLAUDINE PALUZZI *(See Paluzzi, Claudine)* [S, P, Print, T] b. 1931, Jacksonburg, IN. Studied: John Herron Sch A; Ind. U; Butler U. Exhibited: Jewish Community Cen (solo), 1964, 67, 69, 73; North Central H.S. (solo), 1970-72; Indianapolis AL (solo), 1968, 70, 74; Lafayette A Cen (solo), 1968. Prizes: Anderson Winter Show, 1973; Richmond AA, 1958, 59, 62, 63, 72; Ind. State Fair, 1953, 55, 57, 61, 63, 67, 69, 71; HS, 1961, 64, 67; Evansville MA, 1963, 67; 500 Festival of A, 1967; Muncie AA, 1964, 65; Ind. A Exh, 1962; 50 Ind. Prints Show, 1960. Note: T, IUPUI and Indianapolis AL.

KEMPF, F. P. TUD [S, T, W] Chicago, IL b. 22 Oct 1886, Jasper, IN. Studied: Chicago Acad FA. Exhibited: Neo-Arlimuso Soc, Chicago, 1920s; AIC, 1925-1935; Ill. A Project Gal, 1940; Cincinnati M; IMA. Note: Contributed articles to *Popular Mechanics, Home Crafts*. Specialty, woodcarving.

KEMPF, ROMAN Chicago, IL.

KEMPF, THOMAS M. [P, S] Chicago, IL b. 1885, Jasper, IN. Studied: Syracuse (N.Y.) Col of FA. Exhibited: Neo-Arlimuso Soc, Chicago, 1924; AIC, 1926-31, 33; Maineger's Gal, Denver.

KEMPTON, ELMIRA [P, T] Richmond, IN b. 9 Aug 1892, Richmond, IN d. 20 Jun 1971. Studied: Cincinnati A Acad. Teachers: James R. Hopkins; Herman H. Wessel; Clement Barnhorn; L. H. Meakin; Albert Krehbiel; Eliot O'Hara; Wayman Adams. Exhibited: NAWA, 1944-46; Argent Gal, 1944 (solo); Ind. AC, 1944, 46; Richmond AA, 1944-46; Herron AM. Collections: Earlham Col; Richmond AA. Note: T of FA, Earlham Col, Richmond, IN.

KENADY, NANCY A.

KENDALL, YVONNE Crawfordsville, IN.

KENNEDY, MARGARET [Print, P, SG] Indianapolis, IN. Studied: Wells Col; Oberlin Col; U of Wis. Exhibited: 6th Nat Print Exh, New Canaan, CT; All-Ohio Graphics, Dayton AI, 1962, 63, 65; Richmond AA (solo), 1963. Prizes: Richmond (Ind.) AA, 1962, 64; HS, 1971. Collections: Stained glass for Christ Church, Oberlin, OH, St Peter's, Lakewood, OH and St Paul's, Aurora, NY.

KERCHEVAL, DALE O(wen) [Genre P] Noblesville, IN b. 2 May 1948, Medford, MA. Studied: John Herron A Sch. Teachers: Robert Berkshire; Robert Eagerton. Exhibited: Ind. State Fair, annually. Prizes: T. C. Steele M, 1990; Atlanta A Festival, 1985. Collections: IMA, Alliance Rental Gal; Continental Bank, Chicago; Hilton Hotel; Frankfort A Gal.

KERR, RUTH [S] Cincinnati, OH b. Dearborn Cnty, IN. Studied: Cincinnati AA. Teachers: Clement J. Barnhorn. Prizes: HS, 1928.

KERSEY, CONNIE Rockville, IN.

KERSTETTER, BARBARA A. Apollo, PA.

KESSLER, JAMES B. [P] Indianapolis, IN. Note: Professor, Political Science, Ind. U; Chief Aide to Governor Edgar D. Whitcomb; Ind. Higher Education Commissioner.

KESSLER, MARGARET [P, Ldscp. P, T, W] Richardson, TX b. 15 Aug 1944, Auburn, IN. Teachers: Edna Jennings-McCutchan; Carroll Collier. Prizes: Grand Nat Exh, SC, NYC, 1984; A&Craftsmen Associated, Dallas, TX; Grumbacher's Medals, 1982, 83; HS, 1983; Reg P&S Show, 1987. Note: Daughter of artist Edna Jennings-McCutchan. Author, *Painting Better Landscapes*, Watson-Guptill Publications.

KETCHAM, ROY ANDERSON [Por. P, I, P, T] Chicago, IL b. Sandborn. Studied: Herron Sch A; Chicago Acad FA; Académie Julian, Paris. Teachers: William Forsyth; Charles Hawthorne; Laurens. Prizes: HS, 1931, 37. Note: T, Chicago Acad FA.

KETCHAM, SUSAN M(errill) [Ldscp. P, P, T] NYC/Ogunquit, ME b. 1841, Indianapolis, IN d. 1 Feb 1930. Studied: Ind. Sch A; ASL; AIC. Teachers: John W. Love; James F. Gookins; William Merritt Chase; Bell; Charles H. Woodbury; Walter Shirlaw; Benjamin R. Fitz. Exhibited: World's Fair, Palace of A, Chicago, 1893; 50th Anniversary, ASL; Memorial Exh, Marott Hotel, 1930. Prizes: N.Y. Women's AC, 1908; HS, 1926. Collections: Herron AI, Indianapolis; Vincennes (Ind.) AA; Ind. High Schs. Note: Organized Intl Exh, AA of Indianapolis, 1883.

KIESS, G(race) M(argaret) [P, T, C] Cincinnati, OH b. Cincinnati. Studied: Cincinnati AA; U of Chicago; NYU; Columbia U; Herron AI. Teachers: William Forsyth; Myra Reynolds Richards; L. C. Lutz; L. H. Meakin; Vincent Nowottny; Walter Beck; Lillian Cushman; James Parton Haney; Otto Humann; George Cox.

KIGHTLINGER, HELEN E. [P, Dr, Print] Indianapolis, IN b. Brooklyn, NY. Studied: Ball State U; Ind. U. Teachers: Forrest Stark; Dorothy Hansen; Roger Costan. Exhibited: Ft Wayne AM; 13th Ann Small S&Dr, Ball State U. Prizes: John Herron AI; Ind. State Fair.

KILGORE, RUPERT

KILLY, EARL JAMES [S, T] Oxford, OH b. 20 Jun 1945, Toledo, OH. Studied: Columbus Col A&Des; U of Notre Dame. Exhibited: Hiestand Gal (solo), Oxford, OH, 1976; St Joseph A Cen (solo), St Joseph, MI, 1974; Sinclair Community Col, 1979. Prizes: Ball State Dr&Small S Show, Muncie, 1978; All-Ohio Exh, Canton AI, 1977; Salmonie A Exh, Warren, IN, 1973, 74; HS, 1972. Collections: Anchor Real Estate, South Bend, IN; Peat Marwick & Mitchell accounting firm, Chicago; Mt Mercy Col, Cedar Rapids, IA. Note: T, Miami U, Oxford, OH.

KIMBERLING, BRUCE [P, Por. P] Evanston, IL b. Shelbyville, IN. Studied: NAD; CGA. Prizes: HS, 1964.

KINCAID, JAMES A. Kokomo, IN. Prizes: Ind. State Fair; HS, 1974.

KINDER, HAL [Ldscp. P] Prizes: HS, 1969.

KING, CLARA W. [P] Richmond, IN.

KING, EDWIN W. River Forest, IL.

KING, EMMA B. [P] Indianapolis, IN b. 1858, Indianapolis d. 17 Jul 1933. Studied: ASL; Paris. Teachers: Jacob Cox, Indianapolis; Carroll Beckwith and William Merritt Chase, NY; Gustave Boulanger, Jules Lefebvre, Carolus-Duran, Frank E. Scott, Paris. Collections: Public Gal, Richmond, IN. Note: A published poet. Won a prize at the American Section of the Poetry Society of Great Britain.

KING, HELEN A. (Mrs. Alvin Hattorf) [Ldscp. P, T] Richmond, VA b. 12 Feb 1904, Huntington. Studied: AIC; ASL. Teachers: C. Hawthorne; R. Miller; W. Adams; R. Brackman; A. Brook; G. Bridgman; H. Hensche. Prizes: HS, 1930, 32, 35, 39. Note: T, Thomas Jefferson H.S., Richmond.

KING, JOHN M. [P, Por. P, T] Dayton, OH b. 1 Jul 1897, Richmond, IN d. 1977. Studied: Earlham Col; Cincinnati A Acad. Teachers: H. H. Wessel. Exhibited: Chicago, 1926-28. Prizes: HS, 1926-29, 33, 36; Chicago, 1929; Indianapolis AA, 1936. Collections: Purdue U; Administration Bldg, Oxford, OH; Nat Cash Register Co, Dayton; Municipal Bldg, Dayton; Miami U; Butler Col. Note: T, Dayton AI, 1927-46.

KING, MYRA P(arks) [S, P] Toledo, OH b. 1880, Martinsville, IN. Studied: Herron AI. Teachers: Rudolf Schwartz.

KING, PATRICK [Ldscp. P, Print] Indianapolis, IN b. 8 Nov 1951, St Joseph, MO. Studied: Kansas City AI and Sch Des; Parsons Sch Des, NYC; N.Y. Studio Sch, NYC; Mo. Western Col, St Joseph, MO. Teachers: Wilbur Niewald; Robert Kulick. Exhibited: Herron Gal Billboard Exh, 1980; N.Y. Studio Sch, 1975. Prizes: Nat Endowment for the A Fellowship, 1972. Collections: Albrecht MA, St Joseph, MO. Note: Owner, Patrick King Contemporary A Gal, Indianapolis.

KING, SHARON [P, T] Gosport, IN b. 13 May 1941, Indianapolis, IN. Studied: Herron Sch A. Teachers: Edward Manetta. Exhibited: Owen Cnty AG. Prizes: Ind. State Fair; Ind. A Education Assn. Note: Owner, Sharon King Gal and Studio.

KINGSBURY, EDNA A. [P] Indianapolis, IN b. 5 May 1888, Xenia, OH. Studied: John Herron AI. Teachers: J. Ottis Adams; Otto Stark; William Forsyth. Exhibited: Boston AC; Indianapolis, 1942-44; Ind. AC.

KINNAMAN, LISA A. [Print] Indianapolis, IN.

KINNEY, DAVID E. [P] Indianapolis, IN. Prizes: HS, 1973.

KINSEY, HORACE GAWAYNE [P] Grabill, IN. Exhibited: Brown Cnty A Gal; Am WCS Traveling Exh. Note: V.P., Bonsib Inc.

KINZ, ROBERT J. [Ab] Indianapolis, IN b. 27 Dec 1955, Indianapolis. Self-taught. Prizes: Strawberry A Festival, 1976, 77; Southside AL, 1977.

KIRBY, AMANDA ELLER [P, SLP, Por. P] Nashville, IN b. 31 Jul 1924, Noblesville, IN. Studied: Indianapolis AL; Positano, Italy; Herron A Sch; Madison Sch of A, CT. Teachers: Elmer Taflinger; Robert Brackman; Robert E. Wood; Herb Olsen; Tom Hill; Millard Sheets; Mario Cooper; Tom Nicholas; Frederick Rigley. Exhibited: Nat AC, NY, 1986; Ind. AC, 1969-81; Indianapolis AL; Ind. State Fair. Prizes: HS, 1964, 68, 70; Ind. AC, 1982; Ind. WCS, 1984, 85-89. Collections: Public Service Ind.; Ameritrust Nat Bank.

KIRK, MARY ELIZABETH [SLP] Indianapolis, IN b. 27 Mar 1921, Indianapolis, IN. Studied: Indianapolis AL. Teachers: Rosemary Browne Beck. Exhibited: 68th Ind. A Exh, IMA, 1981; Ind. AC, 1987-89. Prizes: Ind. State Poster Contest; Indianapolis AL, 1980; 39th Wabash Valley Exh, 1983. Collections: IMA, rental gal; Western Electric Co; Merchants Bank Gal; Hyatt Regency Hotel.

KIRKPATRICK, BLAINE E. Indianapolis, IN.

KIRN, FRANCIS EDWARD [I, Des] Whiting, IN b. 5 May 1903, Whiting. Studied: AIC. Teachers: Elmer Forsberg; DeForest Shook; Laura Pappelendam.

KIRSCHNER, HARRY A. [Ldscp. P, T] Greensburg, IN b. 2 Jan 1916, Indianapolis, IN. Exhibited: Whitewater Valley Exh; Brown Cnty A Gal. Prizes: Ind. State Fair, 1982; Decatur Cnty Fair; Oldenburg, IN. Collections: Union Bank&Trust, Greensburg, IN.

KISHEL, RICHARD F. [P, S, Cer, T] Muncie, IN. Studied: Cranbrook Acad A, Bloomfield Hills, MI; U of Minn., Deluth; U of Iowa. Exhibited: 10th Ann Newman A Show (solo), Muncie; Ind. Cer A, Herron AM, 1955; Ball State U, 1975. Prizes: HS, 1958. Note: Associate Prof A, Ball State U. T, Burris Lab Sch, Muncie.

KISKOWSKI, ROBERT G. South Bend, IN.

KISNER, JOAN KING [P, Col. A, C, T] Danville, IN b. Putnam Cnty, IN. Studied: Sullins Col, Bristol, VA; Ind. State U. Teachers: Stella Hendricks; Clayson Baker. Exhibited: Hendricks Cnty AL Show; Wabash Valley, Swope Gal, 1972, 73; 64th Ind. A Show, IMA, 1973; Blue Grass Open Acrylic, 1973. Prizes: Ind. State Fair; Mid-States Cr Exh.

KITKOWSKI, MICHAEL South Bend, IN. Prizes: HS, 1972.

KITTERMAN, ALMEDA H. (Mrs. Harry) [P] Indianapolis, IN b. 1900, NY d. 1978. Studied: Herron A Sch. Teachers: Earl Beyer; George Jo Mess; Garo Antreasian.

KLAUS, MAE B. CA. Deceased.

KLINE, DAVID [P] Decatur, IN.

KLINE, KEITH [I, P, Com. A] Ellettsville, IN b. 19 Jul 1956, Linton, IN. Self-taught. Exhibited: Ind. WCS, 1989, 90; Southside AL, 1986-90. Prizes: HS, 1989, 90; Southside AL, 1988; Ind. State Fair, 1987, 88. Collections: Owen Cnty State Bank; Arvin Corp. Note: Com. A, product illustrator for Cook Inc.

KLINTWORTH, ANNE SHIER [S] Greentown, IN.

KNARR, THELMA L. Indianapolis, IN. Exhibited: Village A Gal (solo), Indianapolis; Herron. Prizes: HS, 1970; Ind. U; Mile of A; Saranack Lakes, NY.

KNECHT, KARL KAE [Car, I, W] Evansville, IN b. 4 Dec 1883, Iroquois, SD. Studied: AIC. Prizes: Evansville, 1934. Collections: Evansville M of A⪼ Huntington Library, San Marino, CA; Press Cl Bldg, San Francisco, CA. Note: Author/Illustrator, *Surprise Puzzle Drawing Book*; Contributor, *Billboard* and *Variety*; Columnist/Car, *Evansville Courier*.

KNIESE, KATHERINE [P] Cambridge City, IN.

KNIGHT, KENNETH E. [Ldscp. P] Shelbyville, IN b. 26 Feb 1928, Shelbyville, IN. Exhibited: Ind. Heritage, 1986, 87, 89, 90; Brown Cnty A Gal, 1989-90. Prizes: Knauf Corp Christmas Card, 1983; Riley Festival, 1985-86; Brown Cnty A Gal Assn, 1988. Collections: Knauf Corp; K.C.L. Corp; Arby's (R.T.M. Inc); Shelby A Gal; Brown Cnty A Gal.

KOCH, ANDREA PORTER CARTER (Mrs. William) [P, Dr] Indianapolis, IN b. 4 Oct 1939, Lima, OH. Studied: Bowling Green State U, OH. Exhibited: Boston Pr. M Nat Show; Wabash Valley; Whitewater Valley; Ind. AC; Ind. State Fair. Prizes: HS, 1969, 70, 78.

KOCH, T(heo) J(ohn) [Dr, Ldscp. P] Columbus, IN b. 24 Aug 1881, Dusseldorf, Germany. Self-taught.

KOCHMAN, LEE A. [MM, P, Dr] Indianapolis, IN b. 4 Feb 1945, New Haven, CT. Studied: Wabash Col; ASL. Teachers: Harold McDonald; Federico Castellon; Peter Blume. Exhibited: Wabash Col Student Exh, 1963; ASL Student Exh, NY, 1967. Prizes: ASL Catalogue, 1967.

KORBLY, PATAREKA Indianapolis, IN.

KORCZYK, ANN-MARIE [Dr, S, T] Greenfield, IN b. 19 Dec 1962, Columbus, OH. Studied: Bradley U, Peoria, IL. Teachers: Nita Sunderland; Oscar Gillespie. Exhibited: Riverwalk A Show, 1988; Blue Moon Pottery, 1988. Prizes: HS, 1990; Kotteman S Scholarship, 1984-86; Nat A Merit Scholarship, 1981-85. Collections: Lakeview M, Peoria, IL; Oakbrook Country Cl, Oakbrook, IL.

KORMENDI, ELIZABETH [P, C] South Bend, IN b. Budapest, Hungary. Studied: Europe. Exhibited: Milwaukee AI (solo), 1940, 45; Renaissance Soc, U of Chicago, 1941; Oak Park AL, 1941; Herron AI, 1943; Norton Gal, 1944; Nuremburg, Germany; Venice, Italy; Barcelona, Spain; Budapest, Hungary. Note: T, St Mary's Col, South Bend, IN, 1946. Wife of artist Eugene Kormendi.

KORMENDI, EUGENE (Jeno) [S, T] South Bend, IN b. 12 Oct 1889, Budapest, Hungary d. 14 Aug 1959, Washington, D.C. Studied: Budapest A Acad; Paris. Exhibited: Milwaukee AI (solo), 1940, 45; Norton Gal, 1944; Renaissance Soc, U of Chicago, 1941; Oak Park AL, 1941; Herron AI, 1943; Audubon A, 1946; AIC, 1946. Prizes: Soc Four A, 1945; HS, 1946, 47, 49; Barcelona Intl Expo. Collections: Heeres M, Vienna; Budapest M; U of Notre Dame; Mt Mary Col, Milwaukee; Boys Town, NE. Note: T, U of Notre Dame, beginning 1941. Husband of artist Elizabeth Kormendi.

KRAFFT, ELTON G. [Ldscp. P] Lake Geneva, WI b. 15 Jan 1914, Elkhart, IN. Studied: Layton Sch A, Milwaukee, WI. Teachers: Gerrit Sinclair; Eva Cole; Robert Von Neumann; Martha Hayden. Exhibited: Rivertrace Gal, Galena IL; New Visions Gal, Marshfield, WI; Wustum MA Gal, Racine, WI; Pentagon, Washington, D. C. Prizes: HS, 1940, 71, 72, 78, 81; Oconomowoe, 1987. Collections: Intl Minerals Chemical Corp; Wheaten Franciscan Inst; A Independent Gal, Lake Geneva, WI; Katie Gingrass Gal, Milwaukee, WI.

KRINER, SALLY BRANT [Ldscp. P, SLP, Por. P] Nashville, IN b. 29 Jan 1911, Bradford, OH. Studied: John Herron A Sch; Ind. U, Indianapolis; Long Boat Key, Fla. Sch A; Indianapolis AL. Teachers: Robert E. Wood; Ilona Royce; V. J. Cariani; C. Curry Bohm; Harry Davis; Marilyn Bendell; Emile A. Gruppe. Exhibited: Ind. AC, 1964-90; Brown Cnty AG, 1967-90; Mid-States Exh; Indianapolis AL; Ind. State Fair. Collections: Riley Hospital, Indianapolis; Tri Kappa Sch Coll; Ind. Nat Bank.

KRUGER, MARILYN [P, T] Akron, IN b. 8 Jul 1938, Akron, IN. Studied: Cincinnati Acad of A; U of Southern Calif. Teachers: Robert Smith; Justin Fauve. Exhibited: Jack London Reg, Oakland, CA, 1970, 71; Elkhart Reg, 1988, 89. Prizes: HS, 1988; Northern Ind. A, 1989; Lakeland A, 1990. Collections: Corporate collections in San Diego, San Francisco Bay area and Northern Ind.

KUHN, DAVID PAUL [P] Albany, IN. Prizes: Arts Ind. Postcard Competition Series XII.

KULA, NANCY [Print, T] Evansville, IN b. Chicago, IL. Studied: Northeastern Ill. U; U of Southern Ind. Teachers: Michael Aakhus. Exhibited: Swope Gal, Terre Haute, 1989; Evansville M of A&Sc, 1985-90. Prizes: Henderson Soaper Gal, 1990; Graduate Student Award, U of Southern Ind., 1990. Collections: Henderson, KY.

KULIK, LUBA

KURTZ, AULIE [P] Indianapolis, IN b. 1888, Mosser, NE d. 1983. Teachers: Carl Graf; R. Beyer; George Jo Mess; Edmund Schildknect; Dick Jenders; Frederick Rigley; Elmer Taflinger; Charles Birchfield. Exhibited: DePauw Col; Ind. State Fair; IMA; Ball State U; Glendale Cinema I & II, Indianapolis, 1975. Prizes: Ind. AC; HS, 1951.

KYSAR, BARBARA JEAN COTTON [P, Ldscp. P, SLP] b. Marion Cnty, IN. Studied: Ind. U; Madison Sch A, Madison, CT; Indianapolis AL. Teachers: Elmer Taflinger; Robert Brackman; Paul Sweany; Robert Berkshire; Conrad Hudlow; Marilyn Price; Edward Manetta. Exhibited: Ind. AC; Lafayette Square Cinema, Indianapolis, 1971; Brown Cnty AG; IMA rental gal; Swope Gal; Mid-States Exh. Prizes: Indianapolis AL, 1964; HS, 1966; Ind. State Fair, 1969; Print Cl Show; 500 Show, 1972.

L

LABRUM, DAVID [Dr] Indianapolis, IN. Exhibited: Chesapeake Landing, Indianapolis, 1979. Prizes: HS, 1983.

LACEY, BERTHA J. [Por. P, Ldscp. P, T] Perrysville, IN b. 6 May 1878, Perrysville d. 25 Nov 1943. Studied: Cincinnati A Acad; AIC; Sch of Fine&App A, NY; Columbia U. Teachers: John Ottis Adams; Frank Duveneck; G. Bellows; J. Vanderpoel; Cechi, Italy. Prizes: HS, 1927. Collections: Covington Library; Clinton Library; Newport Library, all in Ind.; Courthouse, Fountain Cnty, Ind. Note: T, costume design, Washington Irving H.S., NYC.

LaCHANCE, GEORGES [Mur. P, Por. P, Ldscp. P] Nashville, IN b. 13 Oct 1888, Utica, NY d. 23 Jun 1964. Studied: St Louis A Sch. Exhibited: Swope Gal; Marshall Field Gal; Findlay Gal. Prizes: HS, 1939-41,45,48,57; AIC, 1940,41; Brown Cnty AA, 1941. Collections: Ind. U; DePauw U; Vincennes (Ind.) Jr H.S.; Old Territorial Hall, Cnty Courthouse, both in Vincennes; Toledo Scale Auditorium; Nashville House, IN; Bloomington (Ind.) Limestone Co; Fremont Nat Bank, OH; Lamson Bros. Co, Toledo.

LACY, GENE [Gra. A, Com. A, T] Indianapolis, IN b. IN c. 1918 d. 24 Sep 1990. Studied: Herron Sch A; Indianapolis Acad Com. A; U of Hawaii. Exhibited: Purdue U; Ind. U; Herron Sch A; Ind. A. Prizes: HS, 1948,52; Sagamore of the Wabash, 1984. Collections: Shortridge H.S.; IMA. Note: Former Chairman Dept, Visual Communications, John Herron A Sch. T, Indianapolis AL.

LAIDLAW, ROBERT CHARLES

LAIN, MAXINE [P] Edinburg, IN b. 2 May 1931, Brown Cnty, IN. Self-taught. Exhibited: Ind. State Fair. Prizes: Ky. State Fair, 1983; IHA. Collections: Galleria A, Inc; Brown Cnty A Barn; Wright-Hagerman Public Library, Edinburg. Note: Specialized in primitive-style paintings.

LAKE, MARY E. Connersville, IN.

LAMM, WILL [P, Ldscp. P] Winchester, VA b. 24 Dec 1917, Richmond, IN. Studied: CGA; Herron A Sch. Teachers: Richard Lahey; Donald Mattison; Harry Davis. Exhibited: MMA, NYC, 1950; Nat Acad, NYC, 1950; Minneapolis AI, 1953; Walker A Cen, 1953. Prizes: Ind. State Fair, 1956,67; Milliken Travel Award, John Herron A Sch, 1950; HS, 1968,69,80; 2nd Harrgarten, Nat Acad, 1950; Minneapolis AI, 1953. Collections: Minneapolis AI; Richmond (Ind.) AA; Ind. State Board of Health (mural). Note: Head Art Glass Dept, Stewart-Carey Glass Co.

LANDON, JOY [P, Ldscp. P] Anderson, IN b. 28 Feb 1924, Maryborough, Old Australia. Teachers: Floyd Hopper; Dorothy Drum; W. C. Shapiro; Jerry Meelish; Bridgett Austin. Exhibited: Indianapolis AL; Muncie Exh. Prizes: Ind. State Fair, 1969; 500 Festival of A, 1969; Pendleton AL; Redbud Exh; Anderson Soc A, 1968. Collections: Muncie Realty Co; Anderson Community Hospital.

LANE, MARSHALL H(auss) Chicago, IL.

LANGLAND, HAROLD (Tuck) R. [S, T] Granger, IN b. 6 Oct 1939, Minneapolis, MN. Studied: U of Mich. Teachers: Katherine Nash; Dennis Westwood; Bruno Lucchesi. Exhibited: Port of Hist M, Philadelphia, 1987,88; Royal Festival Hall, London, 1970; South Bend A Cen (solo), 1980. Prizes: HS, 1980,82,84-88,90; Nat S Soc; Northern Ind. A; Midwest M of Am A, Elkhart Juried Show, 1980. Collections: Midwest M of Am A, Elkhart; Minn. MA, St Paul; Beatrice Foods, Chicago. Note: T, Carlisle and Sheffield Colleges, England; T, Murray State U, KY; T, Ind. U, South Bend, chairman 1973-77.

LANGLEY, EDWARD [W] Los Angeles, CA/ Valparaiso, IN b. London, England. Studied: South Kensington A Sch, London. Note: Art Director for Douglas Fairbanks.

LANPHEAR, HELEN M.

LARKIN, ALAN [Dr, Print, T] South Bend, IN b. Minnesota. Studied: Pa. State U. Exhibited: Isis Gal, U of Notre Dame (solo), 1977; Alpha-Omega Gal (solo), Mishawaka, IN; Print and Rental Gal, Minneapolis IA, 1975; A Cen, South Bend, 1979. Prizes: HS, 1980; Minn. State Fair, 1974,77; Central Pa. AA, 1977; Tenth Biennial Reg A Comp, A Cen, Inc, South Bend, IN, 1978; Midwest M Am A, Elkhart, 1979. Collections: Carleton Col, Northfield, MN; Art Cen, Inc, South Bend; Anderson FA Cen, Anderson, IN; Western Ill. U Library, Macomb, IL. Note: T, Assistant Professor of FA in charge of printmaking program, Ind. U, South Bend.

LARKIN, TERI (D.) [P] South Bend, IN.

LARRANCE, WINNIFRED (E.) [P] Indianapolis, IN d. c. 1944.

LARROWE, HERMANN L. [P] New Castle, IN b. New Castle, IN. Note: Member Ind. AC.

LARSH, S. A. Indianapolis, IN.

LARSH, THEODORA (Mrs. Francis Dane Chase) [Min. P, Por. P, S] NYC b. Crawfordsville, IN d. 29 Oct 1955. Studied: Oberlin Col; AIC; ASL. Teachers: Johanson; Luks; Beaux; Vanderpoel; Bridgman; Hawthorne; Mme. LaForge, Paris. Exhibited: PAFA; ASMP; AWCS; CGA; AIC; AFA Traveling Exh; Pa. Soc Min P; NAWA; Brooklyn Soc Min P; Herron AI; Hollins Col; Paris. Prizes: HS, 1926; Crawfordsville AC.

LaRUE, GENE [P] Indianapolis, IN. Studied: Herron A Sch. Prizes: Ind. A Exh, 1950; Ind. State Fair, 1952.

LASKA, JOHN J. [Por. P, Ldscp. P, S, Print, T] Terre Haute, IN b. 1918 Port Chester, NY. Studied: AIC; U of Ill. Exhibited: HS (solo); Ind. State U (solo); New Haven Cen Gal (solo); Evansville U, 1966; DePauw U, 1966; Purdue U, 1966; Marion Col, 1967. Prizes: Mid-States A Exh, Evansville, 1961,63-65,67; Ind. State Fair, 1962,64,68; Tippecanoe Reg Exh, Lafayette, 1964; HS, 1960,61,63,65,66,70,86. Collections: Ind. State U; Kappa Kappa Kappa; Evansville M; Ind. U; Franklin Col. Note: Professor, Ind. State U, Terre Haute.

LATHROP, RUTH M.

LaTOOR, AL [P, Ldscp. P, C] Nashville, IN b. c. 1908 Orange Cnty, IN, near Orleans d. 1958. Teachers: S. F. Brasz, Calif. Exhibited: HS Gal, 1956. Prizes: HS, 1955; San Pedro AA, 1951,52. Collections: Tri Kappa; Dailey Collection, Ind. U Auditorium. Note: Member, Brown Cnty AG.

LATZ, WILLIAM [Por. P] Prizes: HS, 1939.

LAUCK, ANTHONY JOSEPH [S, Cer, T] Notre Dame, IN b. 30 Dec 1908, Indianapolis, IN. Studied: John Herron A Sch; ASL; CGA. Teachers: Richard Lahey; Heinz Warneke; Oronzio Maldarelli; Ivan Mestrovic; Hugo Robus. Exhibited: S Intl, Philadelphia MA, 1949; Ind. A, John Herron AI, 1954,55,58,61; 148th and 150th Ann, PAFA, Philadelphia. Prizes: PAFA, 1953; Ind. State Fair, 1954. Collections: CGA; IMA; Ball State U Gal; Grand Rapids MA; Butler Inst FA. Note: Full title, Reverend Anthony Lauck, C.S.C. Head A Dept, Notre Dame.

LAURENT, ROBERT [S, T] Cape Neddick, ME b. 29 Jun 1890, Concarneau, France d. 20 Apr 1970. Studied: British Acad, Rome, Italy; Paris. Teachers: Hamilton Easter Field; Frank Burty; M. Sterne. Exhibited: WMAA; MMA; WFNY, 1939; CGA (solo); Vassar Col (solo); John Herron AI (solo); PAFA. Prizes: BM, 1942; AIC, 1924,38; John Herron AI,1943-45,47,49,52; HS, 1945-49,52,53,61; Audubon Soc Award, NYC, 1945. Collections: WMAA; BM; AIC; Newark M; Fairmont Park, Philadelphia; Radio City Music Hall; Fed Trade Bldg, Washington, D.C.; MMA; Ind. U; USPO, Garfield, NJ; MOMA. Note: T, ASL; T, Brooklyn Inst A⪼ T, Corcoran Sch A; T, Vassar Col; T, Ind. U, 1942-c.1960. Dir, Ogunquit Sch P&S, ME. President, MA, Narrow Cove, Ogunquit, ME. Created the Showalter Fountain, Ind. U, Bloomington.

LAUTER, FLORA [P, Print, C] Indianapolis, IN b. NYC d. c. 1952. Studied: N.Y. Sch A; Herron Sch A. Teachers: T.

C. Steele; William Forsyth; J. Ottis Adams; William Merritt Chase; Robert Henri; F. Luis Mora; Kenneth Hayes Miller; Kenyon Cox; John Sloan. Exhibited: AIC; Herron AI; Midwestern A, St Louis. Prizes: Ind. AC, 1938. Collections: Christamore Settlement House, Indianapolis; Girl Scouts' Little House; St Vincent Hospital.

LAVENGOOD, GINEVRA J. [P] South Bend, IN. Exhibited: Marburger's (solo), Indianapolis, 1944.

LAWLOR, WILLIAM P. d. c. 1966.

LAWRENCE, MARIA A. [Ldscp. P, Por. P] Morgantown, IN b. 15 Aug 1949, Italy. Self-taught. Exhibited: Brown Cnty A Gal, 1986; IHA, 1986. Prizes: HS, 1984; IHA, 1981,82.

LAWRENCE, ROBERT D. [P] Brook, IN b. Rensselaer, IN.

LAWSON, LENORE CONDE [P, Print] Hammond, IN b. 27 May 1899, Batavia, IL. Studied: AIC; U of Ill. Teachers: M. M. Wetmore; C. E. Bradbury; F. F. Fursman; E. Rupprecht; C. W. Dahlgreen; C. Curry Bohm. Exhibited: WFNY, 1939. Prizes: Hammond A Exh, 1939; P&S Lg. Collections: Hammond H.S.; Hammond Jr H.S., Whiting; Roosevelt H.S., East Chicago; Public Sch, Munster, Ind.

LAY, GRACE L. (Mrs. Fred) [P] Indianapolis, IN b. Indianapolis d. 1983. Studied: Indianapolis AL; John Herron AI; Ohio U. Exhibited: Herron AI; Indianapolis AL; Ind. AC. Prizes: Ind. AC; Ind. State Fair; HS, 1953,62.

LEBHERZ, VICKI [Dr, Print] Indianapolis, IN b. 25 Feb 1946, Anderson, IN. Studied: Indianapolis AL; Ball State U. Teachers: Marilyn Price; Ned Griner. Prizes: A Ind. Postcard Series, 1984; Indianapolis AL, 1983.

LEDBETTER, DON [S] Evansville, IN.

LEE, GENNIE [P, I] Indianapolis, IN. Studied: Murray State U; Indianapolis AL. Teachers: Leah Traugott; Jean Vietor; Rob O'Dell; Floyd Hopper. Exhibited: Ind. State Fair, 1980,81; Indianapolis AL Ann Exh, 1979,81,82; Ind. Nat Bank Tower (solo), 1981. Prizes: Ind. State Fair, 1978,79.

LEE, MARIE [P] Indianapolis, IN.

LEE, NANCY [P] Zionsville, IN. Studied: Ind. U; John Herron Sch A.

LEE, ROSA [P] Chicago, IL b. Chicago, IL. Studied: AIC; Provincetown, MA. Teachers: Wayman Adams. Prizes: HS, 1947.

LEE, SHURLE [P] Ft Wayne, IN/Midland, MI. Exhibited: West Side A Cen, 1967; Les Galleries Raymond Duncan, Paris. Prizes: Prix de Paris, 1966,67; Ft Wayne AL Regional, 1965; Michiana Exh, 1966; HS, 1967.

LEECH, ANN [Ab, Ldscp. P] Fishers, IN b. 6 May 1938, Rensselaer, IN. Studied: U of Cincinnati; Indianapolis AL. Teachers: Floyd Hopper; Maxine Masterfield. Exhibited: Wabash Valley Reg, 1972,76,80,81; Mid-States Reg, 1972; Ind. AC Ann, 1984,86,90. Prizes: Ind. State Fair, 1967-69,1971; Indianapolis AL, 1969; Mid-States Reg, 1970; WFYI Show, 1980; Ind. WCS, 1988; HS, 1975. Collections: Evansville M of A⪼ Walker Research; Bank One; Eli Lilly Co; Carrier Corp.

LEFF, HENRY H. [Dr, Ldscp. P, Genre P] Muncie, IN b. 16 Jan 1921, Port Chester, NY. Studied: Private lessons, classes, seminars. Teachers: Marsha Saxon; Rosemary Lawton Thomas; John Goe; J. Bertaus. Prizes: Ind. WCS, 1989; Ind. AC, 1989. Collections: Psi Iota Xi Sorority; New Harmony, IN; Minnetrista Cultural Cen, Muncie, IN.

LEFFEL, DOROTHY S. [P, Col. A, MM] Zionsville, IN b. 25 Aug 1907, Stockwell, IN d. 23 Jan 1988. Studied: Indianapolis AL. Teachers: Simon Baus; Billie Cothran; Helen Woodward; Rosemary Browne Beck. Prizes: HS, 1972; Ind. State Fair.

LEFFLER, D. R. [P, Por. P, T] Studied: Purdue U. Exhibited: West Lafayette, 1977. Note: T, Twin Lakes Sch Corp, Monticello, IN.

LEHMAN, DIANE TRACY [Dr, Por. P] Peru, IN b. 24 Sep 1956, Bitburg, Germany. Studied: East Carolina U, Sch A.

LEHMAN, MAHREA CRAMER [P, Ldscp. P] Greenwood, MS b. 21 Mar 1896, near Fredonia, OH d. 5 Jul 1991. Studied: Acad FA, Chicago. Teachers: Otto Stark. Exhibited: HS Gal, 1942,49. Prizes: HS, 1944,45. Note: Married to artist Paul Lehman (died 1945). Artistic Editor, *Chicago Nightlife*.

LEICH, CHESTER [Print, P, T] Arlington, VA b. 31 Jan 1889, Evansville, IN. Studied: Columbia U. Teachers: H. Lesker, Munich; W. Oesterle, Berlin; G. Giacometti, Florence; Siebelist, Hamburg. Exhibited: SAE, annually; Chicago SE, annually; Ind. Soc Pr. M; AIC, 1934,36,38; WFNY, 1939; Nat M, Stockholm, Sweden, 1937; NAD; Montclair AM, 1933-37,39-46. Prizes: Paris Salon, 1937; Montclair AM, 1932,38; Tucson FA, 1938; AAPL, 1932,38. Collections: LOC; NGA; Newark Public Library; M, N.M.; Evansville M; Swope A Gal; Coll FA, Washington, D.C.; SAE; NAD; Central H.S., Evansville, IN.

LEIGH, HOWARD [P, Print, T] Mexico/Chicago, IL/Spiceland, IN b. 9 Aug 1896, Cecilia, KY d. 1981. Studied: Earlham Col, graduated in 1918; École des Beaux-Arts, Paris. Teachers: P. Mauron; J. A. Seaford. Exhibited: Paris Salon, 1927,31; NYC; Chicago; Indianapolis, 1920-21. Prizes: HS, 1931. Collections: Musée de la Guerre, Paris; NYPL; Boston Public Library; Henry Cnty Hist S; New Castle, IN; Dayton AI; John Herron AI; AIC. Note: He taught briefly at Earlham Col in the early thirties before leaving for Mexico in 1937.

LEIST, DORIS

LEMBERG, RICHARD I. [S, Cer] Syracuse, IN b. 1950, Evergreen Park, IL. Studied: Notre Dame. Exhibited: Ft Wayne MA. Prizes: Midwest MA; HS, 1980. Collections: Notre Dame; Midwest MA; Culver Military Acad.

LENHARDT, M. JOHN Charleston, SC.

LENNART, ESTHER Ft Wayne, IN.

LENNOX, JOHN C. [C] Indianapolis, IN b. 12 Dec 1918, Deming, NM. Self-taught. Note: Specialized in wood-carving and silver sculpture.

LENTZ, JAMES CURTIN [P, T] Indianapolis, IN b. 27 Feb 1947, Indianapolis, IN. Studied: Ind. U, Bloomington; Ind. State U; John Herron AI. Teachers: Earl Snellenberger; Jane Messick; Robert Eagerton. Exhibited: Alabama WCS, 1984; Ind. WCS, 1984-90; Ind. State Fair; Ind. AC; Evansville Mid-States Reg. Prizes: HS, 1972,77,79,81,85-87,90; Works on Paper, IMA, 1972; IMA P&S, 1971,73; Ind. WCS, 1987,89. Collections: Lacy Diversified; Shearson-Lehman Bros, Inc; American United Life Insurance Co; Dean Witter Reynolds, Inc; Indianapolis Athletic Cl. Note: T, Arlington H.S.

LENTZ, VIVIAN C. (Mrs. George) [P, Dr] Indianapolis, IN b. 1918, Waynesburg, PA. Studied: Indianapolis AL. Teachers: Rosemary Browne Beck. Exhibited: Ind. WCS; Ind. State Fair.

LEONARD, BEATRICE (Mrs. Arduino Laricci) [P] NYC b. 11 Jul 1889, Marion, IN. Studied: Chicago Acad FA.

LEONARD, GERALD L. [P, Col. A] Indianapolis, IN.

LEONARD, JAMES B. Bloomington, IN.

LETT, GLADYS B. (Mrs. Colin) [P, Cer] Indianapolis, IN b. Henderson Cnty, KY. Studied: Herron AI. Prizes: Ind. State Fair, 1949. Note: Specialized in hand-painted dinnerware.

LEVITON, FLORIE (Florence) *(See Williams, Florie)* [MM, Print, Col. A] Indianapolis, IN b. 10 Jul 1926, Chicago, IL. Studied: Carleton Col; Indianapolis AL. Teachers: Gretchen Sigmund; Robert Crutchfield; Bev Snodgrass; Conroy Hudlow. Exhibited: Whitewater Reg, 1968. Prizes: Indianapolis AL, 1990; Channel 20, 1990.

LEWIS, BETSE Lafayette, IN. Note: Wife of artist John Chase Lewis.

LEWIS, ELEANOR [P] Crown Point, IN b. c. 1930, Ft Wayne, IN. Studied: Ft Wayne AI; Ball State U; Ind. U, Bloomington. Teachers: Homer G. Davisson; Barry Gealt. Exhibited: HS (solo), Hyatt Eagle's Nest, 1975; Holiday Star Theatre (solo), Merrillville, IN, 1985; Ind. U Northwest Gal, Gary, IN, 1989. Prizes: Northern Ind. AA, 1961; Delta Kappa Gamma Intl A Scholarship and Award, 1977,78; HS, 1974,77,86,89. Collections: Ind. U; Ball State U; Anderson Col; Purdue U; Ft Wayne A Sch; Lowell Sch Corp; Bloomington and Crawfordsville Schs. Note: A Dept Chairperson, Merrillville H.S., Merrillville, IN.

LEWIS, JOHN CHASE [S, T] Lafayette, IN b. 15 Oct 1924. Studied: DePauw U; Ball State TC, Muncie, IN. Exhibited: Talbott Gal (solo), Indianapolis, 1966; Swope Gal, Terre Haute, 1948; Washington Gal, Miami Beach, FL; Feingarten Gal; Boutique Fastaque, Chicago; Ind. A Ann Exh, Herron AI, 1951,52,54-57,61-62. Prizes: HS, 1965,66. Note: Assistant Professor, A&Design, Purdue U. Husband of artist Betse Lewis.

LEWIS, LORENE S.

LEWTON, BONNIE Indianapolis, IN d. Mar 1987.

LEY, MARY HELEN [P, Des, I, T] Ft Wayne, IN/NYC b. Apr 1888, Leadville, CO. Studied: AIC; NYU; Columbia U. Teachers: D. C. Watson; A. Sterba. Note: Author, *Trees*, art textbook, 1937; T, Southside H.S., Ft Wayne.

LIAS, TOM [S] Exhibited: 47th Ann Ind. A Exh, 1954. Note: Dir, South Bend AA.

LICHTENSTEIN, ESTHER FRIEND [P, Por. P, I] Indianapolis, IN b. Chicago, IL. Studied: Vogue Sch; AIC; Paris. Exhibited: Civic Theatre, Indianapolis. Note: Under the name Esther Friend, she illustrated children's books for Rand McNally&Co.

LIDDELL, ALBERTA B. (Mrs. Fred R.) [P, T] LaPorte, IN b. 3 Nov 1887, LaPorte, IN. Studied: W. Adams; M. M. Hoffmaster; C. Curry Bohm; F. L. Allen. Prizes: Hammond, IN, 1946.

LIENERT, MARY SMYRNIS *(See Smyrnis, Mary)* [P, Por. P] b. Indianapolis, IN. Studied: Herron Sch A. Exhibited: Ind. State Fair. Prizes: HS, 1964. Note: Secretary to Mayor Phil Bayt.

LIEPSE, WILLIAM [Por. P, I, Ldscp. P] Concord, NH b. Marion, IN. Prizes: HS, 1935.

LIESS, TIM [P] Hobart, IN.

LIETZ, MATTIE [P, T] Dixon, IL b. 21 Jul 1893, Peoria, IL d. c. 1956. Studied: Butler Col, Irvington, IN; AIC. Teachers: F. Grant; G. E. Browne; J. T. Nolf; A. Hansen; Oberteufer. Exhibited: NAD; AIC; Chicago Gal Assn; P&S Assn, Chicago; Burpee A Gal, Rockford, IL. Prizes: HS, 1937,47,50; All-Ill. FA, 1946. Collections: Tipton (Ind.) Library; Norton A Gal, West Palm Beach, FL.

LIGOCKI, MICHAEL [P] Gary/Hammond, IN (until 1970s) b. 1913, Poland d. 1988. Exhibited: Southern Shores Exh; Michiana Biennial; Chesterton A Fair; Northern Ind. A Salons.

LIGOCKI, RAY

LIGOCKI, REGINA [P] Gary, IN b. 1912, Worcester, MA. Exhibited: Southern Shores Exh; Northern Ind. A Salons; Chesterton A Fair; Invitational Michiana Biennial, 1968; Congressional Exh, Washington, D.C., 1964. Note: Also worked in Mellen, WI.

LILLIE, ELLA FILLMORE (Mrs. Charles D.) [P, Print, C] Danby, VT b. 3 Oct 1887, Minneapolis, MN. Studied: Minneapolis Sch FA; AIC; N.Y. Sch FA; Cincinnati A Sch. Teachers: R. Koehler; K. H. Miller; A. Webster; W. Fry; A. Gunther. Exhibited: AIC, 1935,36,40; CGA, 1935,40; PAFA, 1936; Minneapolis IA, 1936; SFMA, 1937; Herron AI, 1946; Albright A Gal, 1940,43; SAM, 1939,40; CAFA, 1941,44; Okla. A Cen, 1939-41; Oakland A Gal, 1941; CI, 1945; Calif. PM; LOC, 1944-46. Prizes: HS, 1944-46,50,52,58; Southern PM, 1938; LOC, 1945. Collections: Fleming M, Burlington, VT; BMFA; LOC; Dayton AI; Calif. State Library; SAM.

LIMBACH, RAY(mond) THEODORE [Ldscp. P, Por. P] Indianapolis, IN b. 2 Dec 1913, Cumberland, IN d. 24 Jan 1988. Teachers: Michiko Boorman. Exhibited: Eastgate Mall, Indianapolis; Columbus (Ind.) Library.

LIMBAUGH, LORENE Indianapolis, IN b. 1932, Simpson Cnty, KY. Teachers: Daris Overman. Exhibited: Ind. State Fair, 1972.

LIND, JENNY [Print] Anchorage, AK. Prizes: HS, 1973. Note: Former Columbus, Ind., resident. She became Jenny Lind Hawley (Mrs. Charles).

LINDBERG, ARTHUR F. [Dr, Genre P, Por. P, Print] Muncie, IN b. 12 Jun 1906, St Paul, MN. Studied: U of Minn. Teachers: Chatwood Burton. Exhibited: Ind. State Fair; Northern Ind. AA. Prizes: HS, 1979; Muncie AG; Seasoned Eye 3, *Modern Maturity* Magazine. Collections: Butler U, Presidents' Portraits. Note: Architect by training. Worked with U.S. Nat Park Services. Butler U's architect, artist, engineer for 30 years, retired, 1976.

LINDLEY, AUDNA J.

LINDWALL, MARIE [P] Michigan City, IN.

LINK, JOHN J.

LITTELL, JUNE [P] Washington, IN. Note: She had a custom framing and matting business, Washington, IN.

LITTLE, SHIRLEY A. [Ldscp. P, SLP, T] Indianapolis, IN b. 14 Jul, Fargo, ND. Studied: Indianapolis AL; Arrowmont, Gatlinburg, TN; Bendel Sch A, Long Boat Key, FL. Teachers: Simon Baus; Rosemary Thomas; Billie Cothran; Bill Ashby; Helen W. Woods; Marilyn Bendel. Exhibited:

IHA, 1988; 1st Ann Reg, Southside AL, 1986; Brown Cnty A Gal (solo), 1987. Prizes: Ind. AC, 1974; Ind. A, 1978; Ind. A Fed, 1989; Fargo, N.D. Television Exh, 1978,83. Collections: Concept Marketing, Indianapolis, IN; Garret-Kosin, Winchester, VA; Farm Bureau Insurance, Indianapolis, IN.

LLOYD, ROSEMARY Indianapolis, IN.

LOBSIGER, EVELYN [Dr, Print, P] Marion, IN. Self-taught. Exhibited: Skokie A Show, Chicago, IL; Art 500, 1978. Prizes: Grant Cnty AA; Ventures in Creativity, Ft Wayne, IN, 1977; FA Gal, Anderson, IN; Michiana Reg, South Bend, IN.

LOBSTEIN, MIRIAM [Print, Li] West Lafayette, IN.

LOCHMUELLER, MICHAEL [S, Des, P] Studied: Herron Sch A. Note: Des, contemporary furniture. Des, Ello Manufacturing, Chicago; Des, General Electric; Des, Eli Lilly&Co; Des, Radio Corp of Am; Des, Silhouette Studio, Indianapolis.

LOCKER, THOMAS [P, Dr] b. c. 1937, NY. Studied: U of Chicago; Am U, Washington, D.C. Teachers: Mimi DuBois Bolton; Samuel Bookatz. Exhibited: Banfer Gal, NYC, 1964; Washington Gal A (solo), Georgetown, 1964; Gilma Gal, Chicago, 1964. Note: Head of A Dept, Franklin Col.

LOCKHART, GLADA TRENCHARD [P] Calumet City, IL b. 25 Sep 1892, Boone, IA. Studied: AIC. Teachers: Grant; Mrs. A. Oberteuffer; Alworthy. Prizes: PS Lg, Hammond, IN, 1939.

LOCKMAN, ROBERT H. [Ldscp. P] Indianapolis, IN b. 8 Apr 1914, Columbus, IN. Teachers: Leah Traugott; Rosemary Thomas; Elmer Taflinger. Exhibited: Ind. State Fair, 1983-85,88,89; Ind. Heritage, 1984-87.

LOGSDON, NICH(olas) [Dr, T, JA] Indianapolis, IN b. 28 Sep 1948, French Lick, IN. Studied: Herron A Sch; Ind. U, Bloomington; IUPUI. Exhibited: Ball State Dr Show; Remington Library Exh; Chicago A Cen; Anderson FA Cen; Swope Gal; Delphi Community. Prizes: 500 Festival. Note: T, Manual H.S., Indianapolis, IN.

LOHMAN, ROBERT [S, Cer, P] Indianapolis, IN b. 1919, Indianapolis, IN. Studied: John Herron A Sch; Yale U; Cranbrook Acad (asst. to Carl Milles); Washington U. Teachers: Maija Grotell; Gaetano Cecere. Exhibited: Am A Ann, Chicago, 1942; Mich. A Ann, 1946; Ind. A; St Louis AM, 1943; Soc of Medalists 73rd Issue, May, 1966; Intl Expo Des Arts Medailes, Athens, Greece, 1968, Breslau and Prague, 1969. Prizes: Prix de Rome, 1941. Collections: Harrison Lake, Columbus, IN; Bonlen&Sons Architects; Lutz Col (murals), Marion, IN; Red Cab Co.

LOKOTZKE, JOSEPHINE

LOMASNEY, ETHEL M. [Ldscp. P, SLP] Nashville, IN b. c. 1887, Chicago, IL d. 29 Sep 1959. Exhibited: Ind. AC. Collections: H. Lieber Co; Lyman Bros.

LONG, ESSIE [P, T] Carmel, IN b. Indianapolis, IN d. 1951. Studied: Herron A Sch. Teachers: William Forsyth; Clifton Wheeler; Paul Hadley. Prizes: Ind. AC, 1939; Ind. State Fair. Collections: Indianapolis Public Sch. Note: Wrote magazine articles on design. T, Shortridge H.S., Indianapolis.

LONSFORD, FLORENCE HUTCHINSON [Dr, Ldscp. P, Print, Li, S, I, Por. P, T] Lebanon, IN/NYC b. 7 Jan 1914, Lebanon, IN. Studied: Purdue U; ASL; Nat Acad,

NY; John Herron A Sch. Teachers: Edgar Whitney; John Howard Sanden; Mario Cooper. Exhibited: SC, NY, 1958-90; Ind. State Fair; Sotheby's, 1990. Prizes: Intl 22 Nations Show, Prix de Honneur, Monaco, 1966; Deauville and Cannes, finalist, 1973; *US ART* Magazine, 1989; Nat AL, NY; Oil Pastel Assn. Collections: Sheldon Swope M, Terre Haute, IN; Exxon Suite, Rockefeller Cen, NYC; Calvary Church, NY; Presbyterian Church, Lebanon, IN; Mary Manning Walsh Travelers' Lounge, NY; Lutheran Church, Ann Arbor, MI; Davidson Col, NC; Dennison U, OH; First Nat Bank, Chicago.

LOOP, LEOTA WILLIAMS [P, Ldscp. P, T] Nashville, IN b. 26 Oct 1893, Fountain City, IN d. 9 Sep 1961, Indianapolis. Teachers: Olive Rush; William Forsyth; Randolph L. Coats. Prizes: HS, 1939,46,53; Northern Ind. A Lg, South Bend, 1929. Collections: Tipton Library; Milwaukee Children's Home; Women's Dept Cl, Kokomo, IN; Governor's Mansion, Indianapolis; Mem Bldg, Purdue U; Public Lib, Marian and Kokomo, IN. Note: Spent her girlhood in Elwood before moving to Kokomo. T, Kokomo Women's Dept Cl and Brown Cnty.

LOPEZ, H. COURET

LOUDERBACK, WALTER S. [P, I] NYC b. 1887, Valparaiso, IN d. 15 Oct 1941, Socorro, NM. Studied: AIC. Prizes: HS, 1938,40; AM WCC, 1939. Collections: M des Beaux-Arts, Monte Carlo; Municipal Gal, Davenport, IA; U of Mich.

LOUNSBURY, LAVERGNE I. Chicago, IL.

LOVE, DANE L. [Ldscp. P, Car, I, Comp. A] Indianapolis, IN b. 16 Jan 1924, Marion, IN. Studied: Herron Sch A; Pratt Inst. Note: Executive A Dir, Pictorial, Inc, Indianapolis.

LOVE, EMMA JEAN [P, Weaver] Indianapolis, IN. Studied: Herron Sch A. Exhibited: Ind. Weavers Ann, 1977-79; Ind. State Fair; Broad Ripple and Talbott Street A Fairs.

LOVE, JOAN S. [S, Por. P] Noblesville, IN b. 25 Dec 1928, Lapel, IN. Teachers: Adolph Wolter; Harriet Jeffries; Floyd Hopper. Exhibited: Am Acad Equine A, 1986; M of the Horse, Ky. Horse Park, Lexington,1985. Collections: Intl Arabian Horse Assn, Inc. Note: Illustrated two books for Intl Arabian Horse Assn.

LOVETT, PEGGY [P, S] Indianapolis, IN b. NY. Studied: Herron Sch A; Ball State U. Exhibited: Major Ind. A, Invitational, Lafayette A Cen, 1980; 500 A, Indianapolis, 1977-80; Ind. Nat Bank (solo), 1978; 3 Women A, Marian Col, Indianapolis, 1977; Ind. AC, 1980; Gal, Entr'acte, Ind. Repertory Theatre (solo), Indianapolis, 1978. Prizes: Mid-States A Exh, Evansville, IN, 1978; 500 A, Indianapolis, 1977; Ind. State Fair, 1976; HS, 1979; Michiana Reg, 11th Biennial, South Bend, 1980.

LOWE, DON [P] South Bend, IN.

LOWENGRUB, CAROL [Dr] Bloomington, IN b. 23 Feb 1937, New York, NY. Teacher: B. Gealt. Exhibited: Linton A Show. Prizes: Swope Gal, Terre Haute, IN.

LOWES, SADIE H. [P, SLP] Chicago, IL b. 7 May 1870, Hamilton Cnty, IN d. c. 1945. Studied: Claude Buck; Mary B. Poull. Exhibited: Ind. AC, 1938,39.

LUCAS, GEORGETTA SNELL [Dr, Ldscp. P, Bat, T] Indianapolis, IN b. 25 Jul 1920, Harmony, IN. Studied: Ind. State U; IUPUI; Herron Sch A. Teachers: George Jo Mess; June Reynerson; Aloyce Saksedder. Exhibited: Nat

Acad Des, NY; NYWF; Nat Assn Women A Traveling Show, India, 1965-66 and France, 1965; Jersey City M, NJ; Purdue U, 1960; Intl A Exh, Washington, D.C. Prizes: IPA Silver Award, 1978; Ind. A Craftsmen Award, 1974; Nat Lg Am Pen Women, 1983. Collections: Ind. State U; IUPUI; Ind. U Med Cen, Indianapolis; General Motors Inst; Indianapolis Public Schs; Phi Delta Theta, DePauw U, Greencastle; Kappa Delta Pi Intl Headquarters, Kansas City, MO. Note: T, Public Schs, IN.

LUEDEMANN, DOROTHY

LUND, BELLE JENKS [P] Hammond, IN/Williams Bay, WI b. 22 Aug 1879, Alexandria, SD. Studied: AIC. Teachers: F. F. Fursman; E. A. Rupprecht; E. Cameron; J. Norton.

LUNDY, ROBERT [Photo, S, T] Muncie, IN b. c. 1931. Studied: San Bernardino Valley Col; U.C.L.A. Prizes: Mid-States Cr Exh, 1968. Note: T, Ball State U, beginning 1967. Known for his silver sculpture.

LUNN, W(illiam) H.W. b. 24 Mar 1933, Montreal, Quebec, Canada. Self-taught. Exhibited: Indianapolis AL, 1992. Note: Profession, research chemist.

LUPRESTO, JOYCE M. [Dr, Ldscp. P] Shelbyville, IN b. 15 Mar 1938, South Bend, IN. Studied: Indianapolis AL. Teachers: Gloria Fisher; Lois Davis; Paul Sweany; Jeanny Wassan.

LURIE, BARBARA

LUSHER, SUZANNE E. [Ldscp. P, Li] b. 21 Nov 1948, Kansas City, MO d. 29 Feb 1989. Studied: U of Mich. Prizes: Arts Ind. Postcard Comp, 1981.

LUTHER, W. STEVEN [Dr, P] Indianapolis, IN b. IN. Studied: Purdue U; John Herron A Sch. Exhibited: New Town A Fair, Chicago, 1973; Skokie Invitational A Fair, Chicago, 1973; Jeanne Gal (solo), Carmel, IN; Michigan City Dunes A Fair, IN, 1972. Prizes: HS, 1972; Ind. AC, 1972; Glendale A Exh, Indianapolis, 1971.

LUTTRELL, KAREN MILLER [P] Indianapolis, IN.

LUTZ, MARIE E. [P, T] Indianapolis, IN d. c. 1980. Exhibited: Ind. AC; Indianapolis AL; Herron AM; Brown Cnty A Gal; Culver Military Acad. Prizes: Indianapolis AL; Ft Wayne Women's Cl; Ind. A Exh; HS, 1963. Note: T, Poets Corner. Widow of Philip Lutz, former attorney general of Ind.

LUTZ, TIMOTHY GEORGE [P] Indianapolis, IN.

LUZZI, MARTHA M.

LYBARGER, JOHN T. Indianapolis, IN.

LYLES, JAMES L. [Dr] Valparaiso, IN.

LYNCH, JAMES [Dr, S, T] Indianapolis, IN b. 2 Sep 1941, Indianapolis, IN. Studied: John Herron A Sch; Ind. U; U of Iowa; U of Indianapolis. Teachers: Paul Sweany; Markman; Harry Davis. Exhibited: Exh 100, 1970s. Prizes: Ind. State Fair, 1969,72,87; Lilly Grant, 1989. Collections: Indianapolis Public Schs, Black Hist M and Athletic Coaches Hall of Fame.

LYNCH, KATHLEEN M. Lafayette, IN.

LYNN, KAY (Kathryn) [Ab, Ldscp. P, SLP, Cer] Indianapolis, IN b. 2 Dec 1919, Indianapolis. Studied: Ind. U, extension. Teachers: George Jo Mess; Harry Davis; Paul Sweany; Anita Giddings; Adolph Wolter; Elmer Taflinger;

Dee Schaad. Exhibited: Ind. A 100, 1972; Swope Gal, 1970. Prizes: Ind. State Fair, 1973; A for Religion, Bethlehem Lutheran, 1969,77; Mt St Joseph College, Cincinnati, OH, 1972. Collections: United Hospital Laundry; Weird Leaf, Greenwood, IN.

LYON, CHARLES K.

LYTLE, JOYCE EDWARDS [Dr, Genre P, T] Kokomo, IN b. 19 Nov 1950, Vincennes, IN. Studied: Herron Sch A. Teachers: Jan Tannenbaum; Richard Nicholson. Exhibited: Kokomo Public Library, 1990,91. Prizes: C. McKay Scholarship, Herron, 1988; Ho. Cnty Historical Soc, 1981; Kokomo AA Spring Exh, 1984. Collections: Kokomo Public Library Hoosier A Collection.

M

MacCOLLUM, ELIZABETH GETZ (Mrs. M. Speers) [P, Por. P] Indianapolis, IN b. Chicago, IL. Studied: Ohio State U; Grand Central A Sch. Teachers: Wayman Adams; James R. Hopkins; Charles Rosen; Edmund Graecen; George Pearse Ennis. Prizes: Ind. AC Exh, 1939; Grand Central A Sch, 1928.

MacDANIEL, DONALD L. [P] Connersville, IN b. 26 May 1922, Indianapolis, IN. Studied: Herron A Sch. Exhibited: Cincinnati AI; South Bend Biannual; Wabash Reg Exh, Lafayette, IN; Ball State Ann Dr&Small S Show; Herron AI; Jewish Community Cen, Indianapolis. Prizes: Ind. State Fair; Whitewater Valley Reg, Connersville; Ind. AC. Collections: Whitewater Valley AA. Note: Doctor of Optometry. Helped establish Whitewater Valley AA and Historic Connersville, Inc.

MacGINNIS, H(enry) R. [P, T] Trenton, NJ b. 25 Sep 1875, Morgan Cnty, IN d.1934. Teachers: J. Ottis Adams; T. C. Steele; William Forsyth; Carl Marr; Herman Obrist; Collin and Courtois, Paris; Weinholdt, Munich. Exhibited: Ball State U, 1932. Prizes: Royal Acad, Munich; HS, 1930. Note: T, Trenton Sch of Indst A.

MacINNIS, PATTY [Genre P] Noblesville, IN b. 27 May 1947, Columbus, OH. Studied: U of Dayton, OH; Indianapolis AL. Teachers: Floyd Hopper; Ruth Anderson. Exhibited: Indianapolis AL, 1974; Hamilton Cnty AA Ann Exh, 1973-91; Ind. State Fair, 1983, 88.

MACK, RONALD P. [Ldscp. P, SLP] Indianapolis, IN b. 10 Sep 1934, Indianapolis, IN. Studied: Indianapolis AL; East Side A Cen; Pro-A Studio. Teachers: Rosemary Browne Beck; Foster Caddell; Myron Finchum. Exhibited: Ind. State Fair, 1980-90; Ind. AC, 1987-89; IHA, 1987-89. Prizes: Sheldon Swope AM, 1989; HS, 1987; IHA, 1987.

MacKENZIE, JACQUELINE (Jackie) [Genre P] Elkhart, IN b. 22 Jan 1931, Athens, TN. Studied: Ind. U. Teachers: Edgar Whitney; Frank Webb; Tony Couch; Claude Croney; Albert Handell; Ben Konis. Exhibited: Midwest Pastel Nat Exh, Chicago, 1988, 89; 5 State Pastel, Krasl M, St Joseph, MI, 1989. Prizes: Midwest M of Am A, 1987; Northern Ind. A Ann, 1989; St Joseph Valley WCS, 1988.

Collections: Robert Weed Plywood Corp; Trustcorp Bank; Crowe Chizek&Co.

MacMILLAN, DAVID [P] Hammond, IN.

MacNABB, ELEANOR (S.) Indianapolis, IN.

MACOMBER, MICHAEL D. [P, Col. A] Indianapolis, IN b. c. 1929, Mineola, NY d. 11 Dec 1980. Studied: Indianapolis AL. Teachers: Leah Traugott. Exhibited: Jewish Community Cen, 1980; Indianapolis AL; Ind. State A Show, 1979. Prizes: HS, 1980.

MacPHERSON, MARIE M. [P] Chicago, IL b. Cincinnati, OH. Studied: AIC. Teachers: Frank Duveneck. Prizes: HS, 1930.

MacPHERSON, MARIE R.

MADINGER, SELENA (Mrs. George) [Ldscp. P, SLP] Indianapolis, IN. Teachers: Roda Selleck.

MAGAW, JEANNE [S] Boston, IN b. Centerville, IN. Note: Chainsaw A. Wife of artist William P. Magaw.

MAGAW, WILLIAM P. [S] Boston, IN b. 1932 on farm near Boston, IN. Self-taught. Exhibited: Richmond AA, 1972; McGuire A Gal, Richmond, IN; Galeria Juliana, San Miguel de Allende, Mexico. Note: Husband of artist Jeanne Magaw.

MAGLINGER, CALVIN [P, Ldscp. P, Gra. A] Evansville, IN b. Owensboro, KY. Studied: Kansas City AI, MO; Famous A Course. Exhibited: Louisville; Evansville; Memphis; Lexington. Note: Art Director, Evansville Printing Corp.

MAGNER, HELEN E. [P, Des, T] New Castle, IN b. c. 1888, Sioux Falls, SD d. May 1986. Studied: Acad of A, Chicago. Exhibited: Marshall Field&Co, Chicago; Milwaukee MA; Herron AM; Purdue AM; Ball State AM; Ft Wayne AM. Prizes: Ind. AC, 1939, 40. Note: Feature Writer/Art Critic, *New Castle Courier-Times*. Published poet. T, Kendall Col (now U of Tulsa, OK).

MAHLER, ANNEMARIE [Dr] Bloomington, IN.

MAHONEY, MURIEL Huntington, IN.

MAINES, MARIE [Dr, T] Carmel, IN. Studied: Indianapolis AL.

MAKIELSKI, BRONISLAW A(lexander) [P, T] Charlottesville, VA b. 13 Aug 1901, South Bend, IN. Studied: AIC. Teachers: Leon A. Makielski. Exhibited: Detroit IA, 1926-45. Collections: Church of the Holy Comforter, Charlottesville, VA; Lincoln Sch, Ypsilanti, MI; Royal Oak H.S., MI; Mich. State Col; McDonald Sch, Dearborn, MI; U of Mich., Ann Arbor.

MAKIELSKI, LEON A. [Por. P, T] Detroit, MI b. 17 May 1885, Morris Run, PA. Studied: AIC; Académie Julian and Grande Chaumière, both in Paris. Teachers: Lucien Simon; René Menard; Ralph Clarkson; Vanderpoel; H. Martin. Prizes: Detroit IA, 1917, 19, 21, 23, 25; Mich. State Fair, 1925; Scarab C, 1929; AIC, 1908. Collections: U of Mich.; Fordson H.S., Dearborn; Angel Sch, Ann Arbor, MI. Note: T, Community Cen, Detroit; Instructor in architecture, U of Mich.; T, Detroit Sch App A.

MAKIELSKI, THEODORA B. [P] South Bend, IN.

MALICOAT, PHILIP CECIL [P] Provincetown, MA b. 9 Dec 1908, Indianapolis, IN. Studied: John Herron A Sch. Teachers: Hawthorne; Hensche; Dickinson. Exhibited: PAFA, 1933; CGA, 1935, 37, 39; AIC, 1941; Philadelphia WCC, 1931, 35; Inst Modern A, Boston, 1939; NAD, 1936, 38-40; Provincetown AA, 1931-45.

MANETTA, EDWARD [Ab, T] Carmel, IN b. 26 Dec 1925, Export, PA. Studied: Herron Sch A; N.Y.U. Teachers: Harry Davis; Garo Antreasian; Estran Vincinte. Exhibited: Nat Hist M, 1979; U of Indianapolis, 1991; Indianapolis A Council, 1991; Intl Petroleum Festival, 1973; Academia di Belle Art, Perugia, Italy, 1980. Prizes: Milliken Travel&Study Scholarship, Herron, 1953; Ann Ind. A Exh, 1954; Huntington Hartford Fellowship, 1961; Fulbright Fellowship, Great Britain, 1959. Collections: HWA Kang MA, Taipei, Taiwan; RCA Corp, NY; Blue Box Toys Ltd., Hong Kong; Nat MA, Taipei, Taiwan; South Bend AM.

MANGUS, BARBARA (Mrs. Robert E.) [P] Indianapolis, IN b. Indianapolis. Studied: John Herron A Sch; Wendel Sch A; Indianapolis AL. Teachers: Paul Sweany; Kay Clay; Floyd Hopper. Prizes: Ind. State Fair; Red Mile Show; Indianapolis AL; 500 Festival of A. Collections: Library of Shelbyville; Ind. U Hospital; Christ Church, Indianapolis; Laughner's Cafeterias, Indianapolis.

MANN, Jr., JOHN L. [Print, P, T] Evansville, IN b. 1945, Oakland, CA. Studied: Ind. State TC; Ind. U. Note: First print, cover picture for Bowling Green, Ky., Bicentennial Celebration. T, Martinsville H.S. Worked at WFIE-TV, Evansville, "Travelin' Mann . . . Johnny Mann;" segment called "On the Road."

MAPEL, JEAN (Eugenia E) [P] Indianapolis, IN d. c. 1991.

MARCHETTI, VASCO Bedford, IN.

MARINE, RICHARD M. [S]

MARKER, ANNA S. [P] Chicago, IL b. Evansville, IN d. c. 1932. Studied: AIC; Acad FA, Chicago.

MARKEY, PATRICIA CONDO Indianapolis, IN.

MARKS, ELIZABETH

MARLOW, CHERI (L.) [P, Dr] Noblesville, IN.

MARLOW, LUCY DRAKE (Mrs. George A.) [P] Tucson, AZ/Erie, PA b. Erie. Studied: ASL; CI; PAFA. Teachers: G. E. Browne; E. Speicher; E. Blumenschein; B. Romag-

noli. Exhibited: Erie (Pa.) AC; Pittsburg AA; A Cen, Phoenix. Prizes: HS, 1936; Ariz. Expo, 1928, 31, 32; Erie AC, 1939. Collections: U of Ariz., Tucson; Pittsburg Board of Education.

MARSDEN, HELEN M. [P] b. 1926, Butte, MT. Studied: Indianapolis AL. Teachers: Louise Johnson; Floyd Hopper; Jean Vietor; Barbara Tompkins. Exhibited: Jefferson Nat Life Insurance Bldg, Indianapolis, 1975.

MARSH, ALIDA [Dr, T] Chicago, IL b. 1901, Muncie, IN. Studied: Chicago Acad A. Note: Sketched for Marshall Field&Co Advertising. I, syndicated column, "Designing Woman with Elizabeth Hiller." T, fashion design. Became Alida Marsh Smith.

MARSH, J. P. H. [Ldscp. P, S] Bloomington, IN b. 1886, Indianapolis, IN. Studied: Herron AI; Florence. Teachers: William Forsyth; Schwartz; William Allison. Exhibited: City Cl N.Y.; New Orleans AA.

MARSH, SUSAN R(yan) [P] Muncie, IN b. 1865, Winamac, IN d. 1959. Studied: Cincinnati; ASL. Exhibited: Ball State Gal. Note: Recognized for her miniature paintings on ivory.

MARSISCHKE, FLONA A. [SLP, P] Note: Member, Brown Cnty A Gal.

MARTENS, CHRISTIANE T. [S] South Bend, IN.

MARTIN, GAIL W. [P, Mur. P] Indianapolis, IN. Studied: Herron Sch A. Prizes: Mary Milliken Mem Fund Scholarship, 1937; HS, 1951. Collections: Mural, Danville Post Office.

MARTIN, JAN R(andolf) [P, S] Indianapolis, IN b. 10 Feb 1948, St Louis, MO. Studied: Purdue U; AIC; Bowling Green U. Exhibited: Ind. U, 1970; Bowling Green U, 1971; IMA. Prizes: HS, 1979. Note: V.P., Tarpenning-Lafollette Co.

MARTIN, LORINE [Ldscp. P] Indianapolis, IN b. 6 Mar 1916, Dana, IN. Studied: Indianapolis AL. Teachers: William Eyden; William Ashby; V. J. Cariani; Doris Overman. Exhibited: Ind. State Fair, 1966, 68-70, 73, 74; 500 Festival, 1966, 67. Prizes: Ind. State Fair; 500 Festival.

MARTIN, MARY E. [P] Indianapolis, IN. Studied: Herron Sch A; U of San Miguel, Mexico; Farnsworth Sch A, Sarasota, FL; Cortez Sch A, Bradenton, FL; Indianapolis AL. Teachers: Elmer Taflinger; Harry Davis; William Crutchfield; Jean White; Floyd Hopper; Frederick Rigley; George Jo Mess; Pedro Diaz; Jerry Farnsworth. Exhibited: Ind. State Fair; Ind. AC; Herron AI; Indianapolis AL; Muncie Print Show, Ball State; Nat WC Show; Whitewater Exh. Prizes: Ind. AC; Indianapolis AL; Bradenton A Show.

MARTIN, MICHAEL [Dr, Por. P] Lafayette, IN b. 23 Jan 1931, St Louis, MO. Studied: AIC; Carnegie AI, Carnegie Mellon U. Teachers: Boris Annisfield; Louis Rittman; Paul Wiegardt; Abbott Pattison; Robert Lifuendahl. Exhibited: Am Realist Gal (solo), NYC, 1981; MOMA, NYC; AIC, 1988. Prizes: NAD, 1964; Drawing USA Show, Minn. M, 1963; Old Orchard Exh, Skokie, IL, 1974; HS, 1978-80, 83, 85. Collections: Nat Gal, Washington, D.C.; NAD; Minn. M; Borg Warner; Ill. Bell Telephone; Jupitor Corp; Kemper Insurance Co; Ft Wayne M; AIC.

MARTIN, ROBERT E. [Li, Ldscp. P, I, Por. P, T] Indianapolis, IN b. 21 Jan 1914, Clear Creek, IN. Studied: Ind. U; Herron A Sch; Hawthorne Sch A, Cape Cod, MA. Teachers: Donald Mattison; David Rubins. Exhibited: Ind.

U, c. 1935; Grand Central A Gal, NY, 1940; Herron AM, 1940. Prizes: Ind. U, 1934; Nat Scholastic Award, Leather Des&Safety Poster, c. 1934; Ind. State Fair, 1985. Collections: Ind. U; Herron Sch A; Farm Bureau Insurance Co.

MARTIN, WES [Ldscp. P, Car] Indianapolis, IN b. 3 Apr 1918, Chicago, IL. Studied: AIC; U of Ill.; Indianapolis AL. Exhibited: Ind. WCS, 1989.

MARTIN, WILLIAM EDWARD

MARTINDALE, MONTA V. Indianapolis, IN b. Springfield, MO. Studied: Chicago Acad FA; Herron A Sch; John F. Carlson Sch, Woodstock, NY; Anna Hill Sch, Laguna, CA; Charles Hawthorne Sch, Provincetown, MA; Ind. U. Teachers: Carl C. Graf; C. Curry Bohm. Exhibited: Laguna AA; Herron AM; Ind. AC; Wawasee A Gal; Okla.

MASCHER, HERMINE E. [Com. A, I, P] Indianapolis, IN b. Indianapolis d. c. 1984. Studied: Circle A Acad; Herron A Sch; Ind. U. Teachers: Claude Croney; Tony Van Hasselt; Edward Manetta; William Ashby; Elmer Taflinger. Exhibited: Ind. AC; Ind. State Fair, 1976, 77, 79. Prizes: Sheldon Swope Gal, Terre Haute; Octoberfest; IHA. Collections: Citizens Bank, Portland, IN; Union Hospital, Terre Haute, IN. Note: Art director, L. S. Ayres&Co. and William H. Block Co.

MASON, GLADYS Indianapolis, IN.

MASSEY, DOROTHY HARDIN [Ldscp. P] Alexandria, VA b. 16 Mar 1919, Knightstown, IN. Teachers: Edgar Whitney. Exhibited: Audubon A, NY, 1966; Philadephia WCC, 1961; Nat Exh Realistic A, Springfield, MA, 1965. Prizes: HS, 1961, 63; Huntington Gal, Huntington, WV, 1958; Nat Bureau of Standards, Washington, D.C., 1971; Va. Highlands Festival. Collections: Vincent Price Coll; Sears, Roebuck&Co; Heineman Gal, Connersville, IN; General Electric Co, NY; Union Carbide Co, NY; Kidder, Peabody&Co, NY; Heineman Gal, Connersville, IN.

MAST, GERALD [P, T] Providence, RI b. 28 Jul 1908, Topeka, IN d. 1971. Studied: John Herron AI; Detroit Sch A&C. Teachers: J. Carroll. Exhibited: Great Lakes Exh, 1938; Albright A Gal; R.I. A. Prizes: Ind. AC, 1932; Detroit IA, 1938, 43; HS, 1930. Collections: murals, Franklin settlement, Detroit. Note: T, RISD.

MAST, S. P. [P] Kokomo, IN.

MATCHETTE, ADA B. Swayzee, IN b. Grant Cnty, IN. Studied: AIC.

MATHIS, A(manda) W(allace) [P] Morgantown, IN b. IN. Exhibited: Brown Cnty A Gal.

MATHIS, RUTH

MATTHEW, NEIL E. [P, Print, Photo] Indianapolis, IN b. 19 Jan 1925, Anderson, IN. Studied: Ariz. State U; Ind. U; U of Iowa; State Acad FA, Stuttgart (Fulbright Grant). Exhibited: John Herron Gal; Anderson Soc of A, 1971-73; Bergman Gal, U of Chicago, IL, 1971; Cincinnati Biennial, Cincinnati AM, 1967; Boston MFA; LOC; Ball State U; Seattle MA; Des Moines A Cen. Collections: South Bend A Cen; Public M, Ariz State Col; U of Iowa.

MATTHEWS, ROBERT [P] Indianapolis, IN. Prizes: HS, 1980.

MATTICE, HELEN Indianapolis, IN. Note: Also worked in Chicago, IL.

MATTINGLY, TOMMIE (Mary Agnes) (Mrs. Dan) [Ldscp. P, Por. P] Tipton, IN b. 2 Apr 1926, Frankfort, IN. Studied: Herron A Sch. Teachers: David Rubins; Donald Mattison; Edmund Brucker; Harry Davis. Exhibited: Ind. State Fair; Ind. A Invitational. Prizes: Ind. State Fair. Note: Owned and operated Atlanta Antiques and Gal, Atlanta, IN.

MATTISON, CATHERINE M(orrison) [Ldscp. P, SLP] Indianapolis, IN b. 1905, Newark, NJ d. 31 May 1961. Studied: Yale A Sch; N.Y. Sch of Fine&App A (Parsons); British Acad, Rome, Italy. Exhibited: Ind. A Ann; Herron AM. Prizes: HS, 1945, 47, 49, 54, 60. Note: Wife of artist Donald Mattison.

MATTISON, DONALD M. [Por. P, Ldscp. P, Mur. P, Li, T] Indianapolis, IN b. 24 Apr 1905, Beloit, WI d. 28 Jul 1975. Studied: Yale U; Am Acad, Rome. Teachers: E. F. Savage. Exhibited: NAD; MMA; Corcoran Gal, Washington, D.C.; PAFA; AIC. Prizes: Indianapolis AA, 1935; Prix de Rome, 1928; Ind. State Fair; Delgado M, New Orleans; HS, 1945, 47, 51, 52, 56. Collections: Yale MFA Sch; mural, Albert H. French Co, NYC; Cities Service Bldg, NYC; WPA mural, USPO, Tipton, Union City, both in Ind.; IMA. Note: Painted portraits of U.S. Supreme Court Justices Thurgood Marshall and Sherman Minton, Ind. governors Paul V. McNutt and Harold H. Handley, writer Booth Tarkington, among others. T, New York Sch Des; T, Columbia U; T, N.Y.U. Dir, Herron A Sch, 1957-1970. Husband of artist Catherine M. Mattison.

MAXAM, ROBERT A. [Ldscp. P, I, Des, Adv. A] Evansville, IN b. 26 Jul 1906, Princeton, IN. Studied: Ind. U; AIC; Am Acad, Chicago; Ruston Acad, Havana, Cuba. Teachers: T. C. Steele; H. Ruston; Frank Saunders. Exhibited: Old Nat Bank, Old Gal, Evansville, IN, 1980. Prizes: HS, 1989.

MAXWELL, CONSTANCE V. LaPorte, IN.

MAY, MARION E.

MAYBERRY, ELIZABETH S. [P] Bloomington, IN.

MAYBERRY, JOSEPH [SLP] Bloomington, IN b. 19 Jan 1917, Goshen, IN. Studied: Wabash Col. Teachers: Arthur Sprunger; Martin Stevens. Exhibited: Northern Ind. AA, 1972, 73, 75, 82. Prizes: HS, 1983; Ind. AC Exh 100, 1972; Midwest M of Am A, Reg Show, 1986. Collections: Libraries, Kokomo, Goshen, Middlebury, Bristol, all in Ind.; Banks, Goshen and Indianapolis, IN, and Jackson, MI. Note: Also drew architectural renderings.

MAYER, HENRIK M(artin) [Por. P, Mur. P, P, I, T] Essex, CT b. 24 Dec 1908, Nashua, NH. Studied: Manchester Inst A⪼ Yale U. Teachers: Maud Briggs Knowlton; Eugene Savage; Willy Pogany; Austin Purves. Exhibited: NAD, 1943-45; Herron AI, 1934-46; AIC, 1937; Toledo MA, 1938, 45; GGE, 1939; CGA, 1940, 43, 46; PAFA, 1941, 42, 44, 45; CI, 1938, 39, 45; Toronto M, 1940; Monteal M, 1940; CAM, 1939, 40; CM, 1941; Butler AI, 1945. Prizes: HS, 1935, 42-44, 47, 49, 51, 56; NAD, 1938, 41; Springfield AL, 1940; CAFA, 1941; Herron AI, 1937, 42, 43. Collections: Ind. U; Ind. State TC; Herron AI; murals, Women's Cosmopolitan Cl, NY and U.S. Marine Hospital, Louisville, KY; WPA murals, USPOs, Lafayette and Aurora, both in Ind. Note: T and Asst Dir, Herron AI, 1933-46; Dir, Hartford A Sch, Wadsworth Atheneum, beginning 1946.

MAYES, ANN (M.) [P] New Whiteland, IN.

MAYS, SUZANNE [Ldscp. P, T] Kokomo, IN b. 27 Oct

1942, Chicago, IL. Studied: Indianapolis AL. Teachers: Henry Bell; Rob O'Dell; Jerry Smith; Jeanne McLeish. Exhibited: Centre Gal, Carmel, IN; Anderson Winter Show, 1989, 90; Ind. State Fair, 1986-89; Indianapolis AL. Prizes: Ind. WCS, 1989, 90; Ind. State Fair, 1989; Kokomo AA Show, 1982, 83, 85-90; HS, 1990. Collections: Kokomo Public Library. Note: Featured, *Arts Indiana*, May, 1988.

McALLISTER, SUE [P] Brown Cnty, IN b. IN. Self-taught. Exhibited: Nashville Frame Co; Louise Kissling Gal.

McAULIFFE, MICHELLE [MM] Westport, IN.

McBRIDE, JAMES J. [P, Mur. P] Ft Wayne, IN b. Ft Wayne d. 1980. Studied: Ft Wayne A Sch; Cape Sch A, Provincetown, MA; PAFA. Teachers: Homer Davisson. Exhibited: Am WCS, 1975; Nat Soc of P in Acrylic, 1974; WC USA, 1972; Ind. AC, 1965, 66; Northern Ind. A Salon, 1960, 61, 65; Tri Kappa Reg, 1954, 57, 59, 60, 63, 67. Prizes: HS, 1955, 56, 58, 60, 69, 70, 74-76. Collections: Ft Wayne AI; Ind.-Purdue Reg Campus, Ft Wayne; State Collection, Tri Kappa Sorority; Ind. Nat Bank; Ind. State U; Psi Iota Xi Sorority, Ind.

McCAIN, SUSAN [Dr, I] Indianapolis, IN b. Crawfordsville, IN. Studied: Ind. U; Acad FA, Philadelphia. Teachers: Elmer Taflinger. Note: Educational Illustrator; designed film strips.

McCARTY, ARTHUR L. [SLP, Por. P]

McCARTY, PEGGY [Genre P] Portland, IN b. 9 May 1957, Canton, OH. Studied: U of Dayton; Ohio U. Teachers: Bernard Plugman. Exhibitions: Middletown FA Cen (solo), Middletown, OH, 1989; Anderson FA Cen, Anderson, IN, 1987. Prizes: Tri Kappa Show, Ft Wayne MA, 1989; Ind. State Fair, 1988; Minnetrista Ann Juried A Show, 1990; HS, 1983, 89. Collections: Nat Lincoln Life, Ft Wayne.

McCONAHA, LAWRENCE [P, Ldscp. P] Richmond, IN b. 8 Aug 1894, Centerville, IN d. 1962. Teachers: G. H. Baker; G. Wiggins. Prizes: Earlham Col, 1927; HS, 1927, 29-31, 33, 35; Richmond AA, 1929-31, 33, 34, 36; Ind. State Fair, 1938, 39; John Herron AI, 1929, 32, 34, 36, 37; CAFA, 1931, 33. Collections: Richmond AA; Public Library, Tipton, IN.

McCONNELL, EVELYN [Dr, P, Ldscp. P, T] Indianapolis, IN b. 17 Apr 1925, Indianapolis. Studied: John Herron A Sch; Butler U; Columbia U; U of Ill.; U of Colo. Exhibited: Ind. State M Cont Show, 1978; Ind. A Exh; Ball State Dr Show, 1969, 73. Prizes: HS, 1973, 74; Ind. State Fair, 1968, 70; Ind. AC Exh, 1971, 89; A for Religion; Anderson Winter Show, 1982. Collections: Kokomo Public Library; Carmel H.S.; IMA, rental gal; Alford House; Anderson FA Cen; Franklin Col; Vincennes U.

McCOY, MARTI [Cer, TA, T] Danville, IN.

McCRARY, KAY (Mrs. Robert) [P, C, Print] Morgantown, IN. Studied: Herron Sch A. Prizes: HS, 1971.

McCULLOCH, HARRIET F. [P] Muncie, IN b. Indianapolis, IN. Studied: Académie Julian, Paris; AIC; Summer Sch of Painting, Saugatuck MI. Exhibited: Muncie.

McCUTCHEON, JOHN T(inney) [Caric, Car, I, W] Chicago, IL b. 6 May 1870, near South Raub, Tippecanoe Cnty, IN d. 10 Jun 1949. Studied: Purdue U. Teachers: Ernest Knaufft. Prizes: Pulitzer Prize, 1931. Note: Staff, *Chicago Tribune*, from 1903-1946 and correspondent during Spanish War and WWI. W, *Stories of Filipino Warfare, Bird Center Cartoons, In Africa*. Illustrated several of George Ade's books. His cartoon, "Indiana Summer," was published each October for more than five decades on the front page of the *Chicago Tribune*.

McDERMED, ED [S] Indianapolis, IN b. Indianapolis. Studied: John Herron A Sch.

McDONALD, HAROLD [P, Mur. P] Indianapolis, IN b. Indianapolis. Studied: Herron Sch A. Teachers: William Forsyth; Clifton Wheeler; Ralph Sowell; Paul Hadley; Elmer E. Taflinger; Morris Davidson. Prizes: Ind. State Fair. Collections: Warren Central H.S.; Central Library, Indianapolis. Note: Dir, A Cen. Restored ceiling murals, Marion Cnty Courthouse.

McDONALD, VIRGINIA PERRY [P] Rising Sun, IN.

McDONNELL, GAIL CARNEFIX [P, T] IN. Prizes: HS, 1950. Note: T, Ind. Public Sch.

McDUFFEE, RUBY Muncie, IN.

McFARLAND, E. A. [P] Chicago, IL b. 1904, Wawaka, Noble Cnty, IN. Teachers: J. E. Phillips.

McGEE, JOSEPHINE HART *(See Hart, Josephine)*

McGREGOR, JAMES [P] Gary, IN.

McGRIFF, PAULETTE [Dr, Ldscp. P] Castine, OH b. 12 Apr 1951, Greenville, OH. Self-taught. Exhibited: HS, 1990 (Pr); IHA, Brown Cnty, 1986 (Pr), 89; Wassenberg A Cen, Van Wert, OH, 1986, 89 (Pr), 90. Collections: Richmond AM, Richmond, IN; George Eastman Intl Photography House, Rochester, NY; Greenville Technology, Inc; Darke Cnty Courthouse, OH; Greenville Ford, Lincoln, Mercury, Inc.

McGUINESS, ANN

McHUGH, JOHN W. [P] Wright Field, OH. Note: Served as sergeant in the military in 1945.

McILRATH, JAMES E. [P] Huntington, IN.

McINTOSH, P(leasant) R(ay) [P, T] Peoria, IL b. 4 Oct 1897, New Salisbury, IN. Studied: AIC; U of Chicago; Bradley Polytechnic Inst. Exhibited: Biarritz, France (solo), 1946; Paris, France (solo), 1946; Peoria, 1927, 33, 44, 45. Prizes: Peoria, 1929, 32; Columbus AL, 1925; Tiffany Fnd; HS, 1927. Note: T, Ohio State U, 1923-26; T, Bradley Polytechnic Inst, 1926-45; T, U.S. Army U, Biarritz, France, 1946.

McINTYRE, MARY HARRELL [P, Photo] Austin, TX b. Indianapolis, IN. Studied: Radcliffe Col; John Herron A Sch; Jerry Farnsworth Sch; Skowhegan Sch P&S; Brooklyn M Sch; ASL; Ind. U; U of Texas. Exhibited: 25th Ann Texas WC Show, McNay M, San Antonio, 1974; Cultural Activities Cen (solo), Temple, TX, 1972; Kilgore Jr Col (solo), Kilgore, TX, 1972; Texas P&S '71 Exh, Dallas MFA; Ind. A Exh, John Herron M, 1965. Prizes: Ind. AC Exh, 1968; HS, 1964. Collections: Skowhegan A Sch; U of Texas, Austin.

McKAIN, BRUCE [Ldscp. P, SLP] Provincetown, MA b. Freetown, IN. Studied: John Herron A Sch; Capetown Sch. Prizes: HS, 1955, 59.

McKEE, JOHN DUKES [I, P] Chicago, IL b. 4 Dec 1899, Kokomo, IN. Studied: AIC; Paris. Teachers: E. Forsberg; Colorossi. Prizes: HS, 1925, 26.

McKENZIE, RHEA [P] Brazil, IN.

McLAUGHLIN, ANN [Ldscp. P, Genre P, Por. P, T] Indianapolis, IN b. 19 May 1929, Ft Wayne, IN. Studied: Marion Col. Teachers: Rosemary Thomas; Jeanne McLeish; Lois Davis. Exhibited: Brebeuf Preparatory Sch, 1984; Lawrence Central Sch; Maple Creek Country Cl. Prizes: 500 Festival of A, 1977; Ind. State Fair, 1981; Indianapolis AL, 1983.

McLEISH, JEANNE [Ldscp. P, P, SLP, T] Monrovia, IN b. Clinton, IN. Exhibited: Ind. WCS; Ind. State Fair; Midwest WCS; IHA; Anderson Winter Show; Brown Cnty AG (solo); Marion Col (solo), 1983. Prizes: Ind. AC, 1982; HS, 1980.

McMANUS, ONNA Richmond, IN.

McMATH, NELLIE (Mrs. Griffin) [Por. P, SLP, Ldscp. P] Indianapolis, IN b. c. 1896 d. 7 Apr 1966. Teachers: William F. Kaeser. Exhibited: Herron AM; Ind. AC; ASL, Indianapolis.

McMILLAN, LAURA B(rown) [P, W, T] Kokomo, IN b. 23 Apr 1859, Malone, NY. Studied: John Herron AI; DePauw U. Teachers: Emma King; G. Innis; Edward Sitzman. Collections: Tipton Public Library; Kokomo Women's Cl House; YMCA Building.

McNAGNY, ROB R.

McNAMEE, DOROTHY DAVIS [P] Santa Fe, NM.

McNAUGHTON, JOHN W. [S, Des, T] Evansville, IN b. 1943, Winchester, IN. Studied: Ball State U; Bowling Green State U; Penland Crafts Sch. Exhibited: Workbench Gal, NY, 1983, 84; Furniture of the Nineties, Hokin Kaufman Gal, Chicago, 1993. Prizes: HS, 1971; Mid-States Crafts Exh, Evansville M, 1984; Nat Endowment for the Arts Grant, 1976, 92. Note: T, U of Southern Ind., Evansville, since 1970.

McNURNEY, PATRICK L. [P] Ft Lauderdale, FL.

McQUARIE, ELLEN (Mrs. Elbert Rawlinson) [Print, P, T] Indianapolis, IN. Studied: French Nat Sch FA, Beaux-Arts, Paris. Teachers: Lucien Simon. Exhibited: Lieber A Gal, 1954; John Herron AM, 1947, 50; La Camaraderie Francais. Note: Head of A Dept, Franklin Col.

McVEIGH, MIRIAM T. (Mrs. Robert) [Ab, P, T] St Petersburg, FL b. c. 1922, Wabash, IN d. 5 Feb 1993. Studied: Shortridge H.S. (graduated, 1939); Calif Col A&C; Paris Am Acad, France. Exhibited: Butler Inst, Youngstown, OH; Paris Am Acad, France; Gal Intl, N.Y. Prizes: HS, 1952; Grand Prix Legion d'Honneur for humanities. Note: Moved in 1956 from Indianapolis to Dunedin, Fl. After moving to St Petersburg, she became head of the A Dept, Shorecrest H.S. where she taught for more than 9 years.

McVEY, FRANCES HAINES (See Haines, Frances and Sweeney, Frances Haines)

McWHINNEY, HAROLD [Dec] Eaton, OH b. 17 Feb 1908, Campbellstown, OH. Teachers: Lawrence McConaha; Ross Moffett; John M. King. Exhibited: John Herron AI, 1934; Ind. State Fair; PAFA; Cincinnati AM; Denver AM. Prizes: HS, 1933; Richmond AA, 1934, 39; John Herron AI, 1939.

MEAD, AUGUST [Print] Prizes: HS, 1951, 52.

MEADOWS, HARVEY [P] Chicago, IL/Evansville, IN b. 1907, Evansville, IN. Studied: AIC.

MEADOWS, HELEN A. [Por. P, P] Indianapolis, IN. Prizes: Sarasota (Fla.) AA, 1952.

MEDERNACH, RUTH [S] Indianapolis, IN b. 25 Jan 1924, Lincoln, IL. Studied: William Woods Col; Ariz. State U; Instituto Allende, San Miguel de Allende, Mexico; Indianapolis AL; Springfield (Ill.) AA. Teachers: Ernest Freed; Ted Kurahara; Robert Berkshire; James Pinto. Exhibited: 17th Dr&Small S Show, Ball State U, 1971; 63rd Ind. A, IMA; Ill. State Fair; Ind. State Fair; 500 Exh. Prizes: Ind. State Fair, 1974, 75, 78, 83, 85, 88; Ind. AC, 1976, 80, 87, 88. Collections: Keller Collection, Chicago; Ind. Bell Telephone Co, Indianapolis; IMA, rental gal; Am Fletcher Nat Bank, Indianapolis.

MEEKER, BARBARA MILLER [P, MM, T] Munster, IN b. 31 Dec 1930, Peru, IN. Studied: DePauw U. Teachers: Miles G. Batt; Katherine Chang Liu; Don G. Kingman; Glen Bradshaw; Millard Sheets. Exhibited: WC USA, 1990; Rocky Mt Nat WC, 1987; Louisiana Nat WC, New Orleans, 1990; Ky. WCS Aqueous, 1989; Ft Wayne AM; Tri Kappa Exh. Prizes: Nat WC Okla., 1988; HS, 1983, 84, 86; Chicago AG, 1980; Outstanding Teacher, Purdue U, Calumet, 1971, 75, 76, 81. Collections: Indianapolis Public Sch; Lake Cnty Libraries; GTE; Ind. Bell; Mercantile Bank, Hammond, IN; Lafayette Nat Bank; Purdue U, Calumet; DePauw U. Note: Professor Emeritus, Purdue U, Calumet; T, Hammond Public Sch, 1952-57.

MEEKS, DONALD J(ennings) [Ldscp. P, I, T] Ft Wayne, IN b. 30 Jun 1925, Ft Wayne. Studied: Bamberg Sch A, Bamberg, Germany; Chicago Acad FA; Am Acad A, Chicago; AIC; Ft Wayne A Sch; Famous A Sch, Westport, CT. Exhibited: Central South Exh, Nashville, TN, 1966; Tri Kappa Exh, Ft Wayne, 1983. Prizes: Famous A Sch, 1963, 64; Ventures in Creativity Exh, Ft Wayne, 1982.

MEESE, MARYANN [Visual Communications, SLP] Indianapolis, IN b. 16 Jun 1954, Indianapolis. Studied: Cleveland AI; Herron Sch A. Teachers: Wilbur Meese; Rosemary Browne Beck; Henry Aguet. Prizes: Nat Scholarship, Scholastic A Awards, 1972; Valedictorian, Herron Sch A, 1977; A Director Cl Ind., 1980, 82, 83. Collections: North Central H.S. Note: Current name, Maryann Fletcher. Daughter of artist Wilbur Meese.

MEESE, WILBUR [Ldscp. P, SLP] Indianapolis, IN b. 25 Dec 1910, St Joseph, IL. Studied: Circle A Acad; Butler U, Indianapolis; Cleveland AI. Exhibited: Ky. Aqueous, 1987, 89; Marietta Ohio Ann, 1981; Ind. WCS. Prizes: Ky. WC Nat Show; Heritage Show, Nashville, IN; 500 FA Festival; Ind. State Fair; HS, 1968, 77, 78, 81, 82, 90; Ind. AC. Collections: Ind. U; Purdue U; Eli Lilly&Co; Ind. Bell Telephone Co; Ind. Nat Bank; P. R. Mallory; Inland Container Corp; Connor Prairie; Am United Life Insurance Co. Note: Com. A, Package Des, A Director for Eli Lilly&Co until retirement in 1973. Father of artist Maryann Meese Fletcher.

MEESE, WILLIAM

MEIS, BARBARA M. [P, S] Terre Haute, IN b. IL. Studied: Inst Allende, Mexico. Teachers: John Laska; Leroy Lamus; Fred Samuelson. Exhibited: Swope A Gal (solo), 1972; St Mary-of-the-Woods Col (solo). Prizes: Wabash Valley Exh; Tippecanoe Reg Exh; Paris Ill. AL Exh; Ind. State Fair. Collections: Swope Gal, Terre Haute.

MELCHIONE, HUGO Notre Dame, IN.

MELEVAGE, RAYMOND P. [I, Por. P, T] Indianapolis, IN b. 25 Feb 1949, Gary IN. Studied: Ind. State U; Ohio

State U; Ind. U; ASL. Teachers: John Howard Sanden; Daniel Greene. Prizes: Nat Citation for Excellence in A Education, 1981; Nat Portrait Seminar&Exh, 1980; HS, 1979. Collections: Richmond A Gal, Richmond, IN; Swope A Gal, Terre Haute, IN; Ind. Bell; Ind. State U. Note: T, Southmont Junior-Senior H.S., Crawfordsville IN.

MENDENHALL, MARY CHILTON GRAY *(See Gray, Mary Chilton)*

MERIDITH, I(ssac) W(att) [P] Chicago, IL b. 28 Mar 1878, Frankfort, IN d. c. 1954. Teachers: William Forsyth; Carl Graf. Collections: Board of Education, Chicago; Field House, Chicago Pk. Bd.; Union Chapel, St Paul.

MERKEL, ROGER [Genre P, I, Por. P] Indianapolis, IN b. 11 Jan 1949, East Chicago, IN. Self-taught. Exhibited: Ind. Penwomen's Exh; Ind. State Fair; IMA, rental gal. Prizes: Brown Cnty AG, 1988, 89; Brown Cnty A Gal, 1984. Collections: U.S. Marshals Hist Society; R. W. Armstrong & Assocs.

MERRILL, ALTA South Bend, IN.

MERRITT, OPAL [Dr, P] Anderson, IN b. New Albany, MS. Studied: Anderson FA Cen. Exhibited: Anderson; Ball State U. Prizes: Ind. State Fair; 500 Festival; HS, 1970. Collections: Pendleton and Anderson FA Cens.

MESS, BETTY (Elizabeth) JANE [Por. P, Dr, P] Indianapolis, IN b. 5 Jun 1917, Manistee, MI. Studied: École des Beaux-Arts, France. Teachers: Armeda Andre; Ellen LaBelle Martinague; Sister Mary Rosearium; Harry Waters Armstrong; Gordon Benjamin Mess; Emile Gruppe; Lucien Fontanarosa; M. La Montagne Saint-Hubert. Exhibited: Palace of Fontainebleau, France; Gavin Beaux Arts Gal, France; Mary Martha Guild, MI; Ind. State Fair. Note: Wife of artist Gordon Benjamin Mess; sister-in-law of George Jo Mess and Evelynne Mess Daily.

MESS, EVELYNNE C(harlien Bernloehr) *(See Daily, Evelynne Mess)*

MESS, GEORGE JO(seph) [Ldscp. P, Print, I, T] Indianapolis, IN/Brown Cnty, IN b. 30 Jun 1898, Cincinnati, OH d. 24 Jun 1962, Indianapolis. Studied: John Herron AI; Tiffany Fnd; Sch of Modern Des, Chicago; Columbia U; École des Beaux-Arts, Fountainebleau, France. Teachers: Otto Stark; William Forsyth; Andre Strauss; Robert Wolff; Arthur W. Dow; Wayman Adams; Achile Ouvre; Gaston Balande. Exhibited: CI, 1930; SAE, 1935, 37, 39-46; Wash. WCC; MMA, 1943; PAFA, 1940, 43-45; Herron AI; Ind. Soc Pr. M, 1936-46; Ohio Pr. M, 1940-46. Prizes: HS, 1931, 33, 44-47, 49, 50, 52, 54, 55, 56, 58, 62; Herron AI, 1931; LOC, 1945; Ind. AC, 1944-46; Ind. State Fair, 1932, 33, 36. Collections: IMA; LOC; Cleveland AM; Dayton AI; John Herron AI; CMA; MMA; Grand Rapids A Gal; Indianapolis Public Schs; Smithsonian Inst; Philadelphia MA; Princeton U AM; Richmond AA; Ind. U Medical Cen. Note: I, *Hoosier City*, 1943, *Living in Indiana*, 1946; Staff A, *Esquire*. First husband of artist Evelynne Mess Daily, brother of artist Gordon Mess and brother-in-law of artist Betty Mess.

MESS, GORDON BENJAMIN [P, Des, T] Indianapolis, IN b. 28 Sep 1900, Cincinnati, OH d. 1 Sep 1959. Studied: Herron AI; Fontainebleau Sch FA, France. Teachers: W. Adams; A. Thieme; E. Gruppe; R. Coats; R. E. Selleck; A. Strauss; J. Despujols; G. Balande. Exhibited: PAFA; Herron AI; CM; Richmond (Ind.) A Gal; Ball State TC; Ind. U; N.D. Col; Dayton AI; Palace of Fontainebleau,

France. Prizes: Richmond AA, 1931; Ind. State Fair, 1931; Ind. AC, 1938, 41. Collections: Indianapolis Public Schs; Valparaiso Public Schs; AA, Richmond, WV. Note: Dir, Circle A Acad, Indianapolis; President, Circle Engraving Co. Husband of artist Betty Jane Mess, brother of artist George Jo Mess and brother-in-law of Evelynne Mess Daily.

MESSER, LAURIE [MM] Connersville, IN.

MESSER, WILLIAM H. [HPA] Indianapolis, IN b. 23 Nov 1951, Beech Grove, IN. Studied: U of Indianapolis. Teachers: Gerald Boyce; Earl Shellenberger; Dee Schaad. Exhibited: Ind. Cr, Artlink, Ft Wayne, 1989; U of Indianapolis, 1986; Paper By Hand Studio, Summerspace Cont A, 1988; Mid-States Cr Exh, Evansville M of A&Sc, 1987. Prizes: Arts Ind. Postcard Series V, 1985; Ind. State Fair, 1983, 84. Collections: Am. Nat Bank, Muncie, IN; Am United Life Insurance Co, Indianapolis; CSO Architects, Inc, Indianapolis; Methodist Hospital, Indianapolis; St Vincent Hospital, Indianapolis; Simon and Assocs; Aviation, Inc, Indianapolis Intl Airport; Union Federal Savings Bank, Indianapolis.

MESSICK, (Elizabeth) JANE [P, Cer, T] Indianapolis, IN b. c. 1908, Columbus, OH d. Jan 1986. Studied: Butler U; Herron A Sch. Teachers: William Forsyth; Elmer Taflinger; George Pearse Ennis. Exhibited: Ind. AC, 1932, 33, 40-46, 48; Herron AM, 1928-30, 32, 35, 55; The 20, 1958-62; Woman's Dept Cl (solo), 1957, 59; Sherman Gal, Chicago, 1960. Prizes: HS, 1944, 45; Ind. State Fair, 1948, 49, 57, 60, 65. Note: T, Shortridge H.S., 1929-64; T, Arlington H.S., 1964-71.

METZGER, DAVID F. [P, T] Jamestown, IN b. 1924, Indianapolis, IN. Studied: John Herron A Sch; Am Acad A, Chicago; ASL; Académie Beaux-Arts, Paris, France. Teachers: Cliffton Wheeler; Jane Messick; T. Van Voorhees; Essie Long; O. Thundare; Edmund Schildnicht; Elmer Taflinger; Harry Davis; David Rubins; Edmund Brucker; Garo Antreasian; Robert Weaver. Exhibited: Ind. A Exh; Hudson Valley A Exh.

MEYER, THOMAS (K.) [Dr] Indianapolis, IN.

MEYNCKE, GRETCHEN D. [Ldscp. P, SLP] Indianapolis, IN b. 1893 d. 1941. Studied: Ind. U; U of Chicago; Herron Sch A. Teachers: William Forsyth; T. C. Steele. Prizes: Ind. State Fair, 1930s. Note: Occasionally signed her paintings "Menke."

MICHAU, MARY JOSSLYN BEMAN [Ab, Ldscp. P, Genre P] Indianapolis, IN b. 20 Apr 1918, Chicago, IL. Studied: Chicago; Indianapolis AL. Teachers: Roff Beman (father); Lester Bridaham; Edward Manetta; Ellie Siskind; Arturo Fallico; Emil Armin. Exhibited: Tri Kappa, Kendalville, IN, 1972. Prizes: HS, 1966; Amish Acres, Goshen, 1970.

MICHEL, DELBERT [P, Dr, T] b. Nov 1938, Libertyville, IN. Studied: DePauw U; U of Iowa. Teachers: Robert Knipschild; Mauricio Lasansky; Stuart Edie. Exhibited: All-Iowa Show; Park Ave Gal (two-person), 1964; Warehouse Gal (solo), Wilmington, DE; Washington Gal, Frankfort, 1974. Prizes: HS, 1970. Note: T, Hope Col.

MICHELE, MICHAEL [S] Bloomington, IN. Prizes: HS, 1982, 83.

MIDDENTS, JOHN R. [P]

MIDKIFF, THOMAS C. [P, Com. A] Evansville, IN/Newburgh, IN b. 10 Mar 1930, Ohio Cnty, KY d. c. 1989.

Studied: Am Acad A, Chicago, IL. Teachers: Irving Shapiro. Exhibited: Herron, rental gal, Indianapolis; Vincent Price Gal, Chicago; Evansville M, rental gal. Prizes: HS, 1970; Mid-States Reg, 1971. Note: Co-owner Newburgh Galleries, Inc, Newburgh, IN.

MIKUS, PAUL A.

MILES, MARIE A. (Mrs. James A.) [P, T] Pittsfield, IL/Indianapolis, IN b. Menomonie, WI. Studied: U of Ill. Extension; MacMurry Col, Jacksonville, IL. Teachers: W. F. Doolittle. Exhibited: IMA; Tippecanoe. Prizes: HS, 1970, 74; Ill. State Fair; Quincy (Ill.) A Show.

MILLER, DIANNA THORNHILL [S, MM] Ft Wayne, IN b. CA. Exhibited: 7th Intl Congress of Women Arch, West Berlin, Germany, 1984; L'Art Mural en France, Musée du Luxembourg, Paris, France; Saginaw MA, Saginaw, MI, 1983; Ball State U Gal, Muncie, IN, 1983; 12th Biennial Michiana Exh, A Cen, South Bend, IN; Sylvia Ullman American Craft Gal, Cleveland Heights, OH. Prizes: HS, 1981. Collections: General Telephone, Indianapolis; Lincoln Nat Life Insurance; Duke Mem Hospital, Peru, IN; Ft Wayne Municipal Airport; Summit Bank. Note: Worked in collaboration with husband, Jim Miller. They formed Omni-Art Design, architectonic art designed for specific environments.

MILLER, EMERY M. [S] Bedford, IN. Exhibited: Bedford A Show, 1963.

MILLER, ISABEL J. [P] Fountain City, IN. Collections: Mural, Covington Courthouse.

MILLER, JAMES GUY [Print] Bloomington, IN. Studied: U of Ind. Prizes: HS, 1971.

MILLER, JAMES H. [Arch] Ft Wayne, IN b. Ft Wayne, IN. Studied: Ill. Inst Technology. Teachers: Mies Van der Rohe. Exhibited: L'Art Mural en France, Musée du Luxembourg, Paris, France, 1984; Salon d'Automne, Paris, France, 1983; 68th and 69th Biannual Ind. A Exh, IMA, 1981, 83; Ball State U Gal, Muncie, 1982, 83; Invitational '81, Ft Wayne MA; Sylvia Ullman Am Cr Gal, Cleveland Heights, OH. Prizes: HS, 1981. Collections: Anthony Wayne Bank; Lincoln Nat Life Insurance; Ft Wayne Municipal Airport; Ind. Bank and Trust Co; Southwest Allen Cnty Schs; Cen for Mental Health, Anderson, IN; Performing A Cen, NYC; Mobil Oil Headquarters; Blue Cross, Indianapolis. Note: Worked in collaboration with wife, Dianna Thornhill Miller. They formed Omni-Art Design, architectonic art designed for specific environments.

MILLER, JOHN EDWARD [Arch, P, T] Cleveland, OH b. Cleveland. Teachers: C. Broemel. Prizes: HS, 1935. Note: T, U of Notre Dame.

MILLER, LEE E. [P] Indianapolis, IN. Note: Art Director, Art Therapist, Counselor, Raphouse, Indianapolis, 1973.

MILLER, MELVIN T. Ogden Dunes, IN b. 1924, Detroit, MI. Exhibited: Left Bank Gal, Saugatuck, MI; Gary Artists' Lg; Northern Ind. A Salons; Purdue U-Calumet; Ind. U-Northwest; Detroit Gal, Cleveland.

MILLER, MURILE [P] South Bend, IN b. 22 Sep 1887, Eaton, OH. Studied: Abroad. Teachers: James E. McBurney; Audubon Tyler. Collections: AA, Richmond, IN; Culver Military Acad; Women's Cl, South Bend, IN.

MILLESON, HOLLIS E. [Por. P, Ldscp. P] Columbus, IN b. Shelbyville, IN. Studied: AIC; Boston AM. Teachers:

Weitkamp, Amsterdam, Holland; Denman Ross. Exhibited: Herron AM; Ind. AC.

MILLHOLLAND, DORIS B. [Por. P] Indianapolis, IN b. 25 May 1924, Washington, D. C. Studied: Indianapolis AL. Teachers: Floyd Hopper; Paul Sweany; Irving Shapiro; Bill Smith. Exhibited: Indianapolis AL, 1990. Prizes: HS, 1990.

MILLS, PANSY Richmond, IN.

MILONADIS, KONSTANTIN [S, T] b. 1926. Studied: AIC; Tulane U. Exhibited: Detroit AI; Columbia M A⪼ New Orleans MA; Lexington Gal (solo), U of Chicago; Creative A Gal (solo), Central Mich. U. Prizes: AIC; IMA; Ft Wayne AM; South Bend A Cen. Collections: Western Ill. U; Swope A Gal; U of Notre Dame; Ball State U.

MILROY, HARRIE C. [P, S] Delphi, IN b. 13 Feb 1867, Delphi, IN. Studied: ASL. Teachers: George deForest Brush; William Merritt Chase; Kenyon Cox; W. L. Metcalf; A. St. Gaudens; Henry Siddons Mowbray; J. Carroll Beckwith. Exhibited: Herron AI. Collections: French Post Park, Carroll Cnty, IN.

MINKLER, THOMAS

MITCHELL, GLEN [P, I, T] NYC b. 9 Jun 1894, New Richmond, IN d. 1972. Studied: AIC; U of Ill.; Grande Chaumière, Paris; Chicago Acad FA; Italy; Egypt; Palestine. Exhibited: MOMA; WMAA; PAFA; NAD; AIC; W. R. Nelson Gal; SFMA; Oakland A Gal. Prizes: AIC, 1919-21; Minn AI, 1930, 36; Corcoran Gal, 1939; Milwaukee Women's Cl, 1939; HS, 1936, 40. Collections: First Methodist Episcopal Church, New Richmond, IN; Rotary Cl, Chicago. Note: T, Minneapolis Sch A.

MITCHELL, IRENE F. [P] Crawfordsville, IN b. Victoria, British Columbia. Studied: U of Chicago. Teachers: Harold MacDonald. Exhibited: Tippecanoe Cnty; Anderson; Swope Gal. Prizes: HS, 1968. Collections: Ind. State U, Terre Haute.

MITCHELL, JERRY L. [Ab, Dr, Ldscp. P, Genre P, Por. P] Culver, IN b. 17 May 1954, Plymouth, IN. Studied: IPFW, BFA, 1988. Teachers: Herb Eveland; Don Kitz; Noel Deuehenshon; Russel Oettel; Harold Zisla. Prizes: Blueberry Festival, 1987-89.

MITCHELL, LUCY [Por. P, T] Anderson, IN b. 1936, Cleveland, TN. Studied: Harris Advertising A Sch, Nashville, TN; Central Acad, Cincinnati, OH. Teachers: Gerald Martin, Minneapolis. Exhibited: Ind. State Fair; Marion Cnty AL; Ind. A Exh, IMA; Anderson Winter Show; 500 Festival. Prizes: HS; Whitewater Valley Exh. Collections: Pendleton A Gal; Stant Manufacturing Co, Connersville, IN.

MOCK, GEORGE A(ndrew) [P] Muncie, IN/FL b.18 May 1886, Muncie d. 2 Jun 1957. Studied: AIC. Exhibited: Brown Cnty AA, annually. Prizes: HS, 1934, 37; Ind. Fed Cls, 1942; Ind. U, 1945; Woman's Dept Cl, Indianapolis, 1946; Edward Rector Mem Pr. Note: One of the founders, Brown Cnty A Colony.

MOLL, MARY H(oyt) (Mrs. Alvin C.) Indianapolis, IN b. Delta, OH. Studied: Ohio State U; Herron A Sch; Ind. U; Indianapolis AL; A Acad, Cincinnati. Exhibited: Toledo MA Reg; Ind. AC Ann; Wabash Valley Exh; Evansville Mid-States A Exh; Eastern Ind. A Show, Ball State. Prizes: Tippecanoe Reg; Whitewater Valley Reg; Anderson Winter Show; Ind. State Fair. Collections: Lafayette A Cen,

Lafayette, IN; Psi Iota Xi, IN; L. S. Ayres&Co, Indianapolis; Bank of Portland, Portland, IN.

MONEY, JO [SLP, Por. P] Indianapolis, IN b. 13 Sep 1919, Odanah, WI. Studied: Indianapolis AL; John Herron A Sch. Teachers: Edmund Brucker; Elmer Taflinger; Bill Ashby; Marilyn Price; Lois Davis. Prizes: Indianapolis AL, 1964.

MONNINGER, IRENE [Por. P, T] Indianapolis, IN b. North Manchester, IN d. Jan 1962. Note: T, Veterans Hospital.

MONSMA, RONALD [P] South Bend, IN. Prizes: HS, 1989.

MONTAGUE, Jr., FRED H. [Dr] Monticello, IN b. 31 May 1945, Lafayette, IN. Studied: Purdue U. Exhibited: Lafayette A Cen; Watson's Crick Gal (solo), Purdue U; Ind. Wildlife A Exh, Ind. State M; Ann Arbor Street A Fair; Kansas City Country Cl Plaza A Fair; Cincinnati Creative A Festival; Wis. Festival A, Milwaukee. Prizes: HS, 1974; Tippecanoe Reg Exh; Sugar Creek Invitational Exh; Ind. Migratory Bird Hunting Stamp Comp. Collections: Tippecanoe Cnty Courthouse; Lafayette Savings Bank; Dept of Forestry and Natural Resources, Purdue U, West Lafayette, IN. Note: Asst Professor, Wildlife Biology, Dept of Forestry and Natural Resources, Purdue U. I, Nat Park Service, Washington, D.C.; I, *Outdoor Recreation*, Macmillian Co, Inc, NY.

MONTEITH, HARRIET E. (Mrs. Mark L.) [P, Dr, Por. P, T] Elkhart, IN b. 23 Feb 1903, Wakarusa, IN d. 19 Sep 1975. Studied: Notre Dame U; AIC. Teachers: Emil Jacques; Robert Brackman. Exhibited: HS A Gal, 1957; Brown Cnty AG. Prizes: HS, 1957, 58, 60, 62, 63, 68; Ft Wayne Woman's Cl; Palette and Chisel FA Acad, Chicago; Northern Ind. A, Inc, Hammond, 1956. Collections: Hotel Elkhart.

MONTEITH, PHILLIP E. [Print] Bristol, IN b. 26 Oct 1927, Elkhart, IN. Studied: Pastel Workshops. Teachers: Daniel Greene; Ben Konis. Exhibited: Midwest Pastel Soc, 1989; 11th Elkhart Juried Reg. Prizes: HS, 1986, 88; 10th Elkhart Juried Reg. Collections: Miles Lab, Inc, Elkhart, IN.

MONTGOMERY, MARTY [Dr, I, Por. P] Greenfield, IN b. 16 Nov 1947, Indianapolis, IN. Studied: John Herron A Sch. Exhibited: Greenfield Banking Co (solo), 1990. Prizes: HS, 1990. Collections: Greenfield Public Library.

MONTGOMERY, PATRICIA A. FENTON [P] Indianapolis, IN b. c. 1928, Terre Haute, IN. Studied: Herron Sch A. Exhibited: Ind. A Exh, IMA; Ind. AC; Sheldon Swope Gal; Wabash Valley Exh. Prizes: HS, 1967, 70; Ind. State Fair; 500 Festival. Collections: Tipton (Ind.) Public Library; Nora Elementary Sch, Indianapolis.

MONTGOMERY, SHARON J. [Print] Newburgh, IN. Prizes: HS, 1984.

MOODY, FRANCES JOHNSON [S] Abingdon, IL. Prizes: HS, 1940.

MOONEY, JOHN DAVID [Dr, Kinetic Light A, S, T] Chicago, IL b. 1941. Studied: U of Notre Dame; U of Ill. Exhibited: Grand et Jeunes D'Aujourd'hui, Grand Palais, Paris, 1975; Chicago Federal Cen Plaza, 1975; Purdue U, 1972; Metromedia, Inc, Los Angeles; M of Cont A, Chicago; IMA. Collections: MOMA; Purdue U; Murray State U; U of Ill.; South Bend A Cen. Note: T, U of Notre Dame; Purdue U; Murray State U, KY; U of Ill.; Villa Schifanoia, Florence, Italy; Hornsey Col A, London, England.

MOORE, DON [Cer, S, T] Indianapolis, IN. Studied: Ball State U. Prizes: Northern Ind. A Exh, 1968; HS, 1960, 64, 66, 67; Ind. State Fair, 1965. Note: Ind. State A Consultant. T, East Noble Sch Corp, 1960-70.

MOORE, HELEN ARNOLD (Mrs. Paul) [P] Chicago, IL b. 25 Apr 1889. Teachers: William Forsyth; Meakin; James Hopkins; George Bridgman. Collections: Richmond (Ind.) AA.

MOORE, M. JAYNE [P] Carmel, IN.

MOORE, MICHAEL J. [P] Waynetown, IN. Prizes: HS, 1979.

MOORE, W(endell) E. [S, T] Muncie, IN b. 28 Oct 1920, Muncie, IN. Studied: Ball State U. Prizes: Herron A Exh, 1954; HS, 1950, 51, 54, 56, 57; Ind. State Fair, 1951-53. Note: T, Wilson Jr. High, Muncie.

MOORMAN, BONNIE BAKER [Cer, Bat] Bluffton, IN b. Fairmount, IN. Studied: Purdue U; Bowling Green U; U of Hawaii; Brownville Sch FA, Brownville, MO. Teachers: Gordon Will; Nelson. Exhibited: Midland Invitational; Marion Col (solo). Prizes: Tri Kappa A Show; Forest Park, IL. Collections: La Maison 'd Art, Aspen, CO. Note: Owner, Boni Batik and Pottery, Bluffton, IN.

MOOTS, M. MAXINE

MORGAN, LYNN T(homas) [I, Print, P] NYC b. 24 Apr 1889, Richmond, IN. Studied: John Herron AI; Cincinnati A Acad; ASL. Teachers: William Forsyth; Clifton Wheeler; Meakin; J. Hopkins; G. Bridgman.

MORGAN, RANDALL [P, T] Italy b. Knightstown, IN. Studied: Am Acad Rome, Italy. Exhibited: New A Circle (solo), NY, 1951; Albert Landry Gal, NY, 1963; Grace Borgenicht Gal, NY, 1955. Prizes: HS, 1968. Note: T, Washington U, St Louis, MO.

MORGAN, ROSE ANN DAVIS Evanston, IL b. Corydon, IN. Studied: AIC; A Cen of Evanston. Teachers: Fredrick Grant; Edward Timmons.

MORLAN, DOROTHY [P, Ldscp. P] Indianapolis, IN b. 25 May 1882, Salem, OH (moved to Irvington, IN) d. 25 Oct 1967. Studied: Herron AI; PAFA. Teachers: William Forsyth; Otto Stark; Henri; Albert Morlan. Exhibited: Cincinnati AM; Herron AM; PAFA; Pettis Gal, Indianapolis, 1924; Carr Hall, Irvington; Irvington Union Social Clubs; Butler AI, Youngstown, OH, 1943. Prizes: Richmond, IN, 1908; HS, 1925; 26th Ann Exh Ind. A, Herron, 1933.

MORRIS, ELLWOOD [Ldscp. P] Richmond, IN b. 5 Jun 1848, Richmond, IN d. 20 Feb 1940. Self-taught. Collections: Earlham Col; Masonic Cl; St Mary's Sch, Richmond. Note: Oldest member, Richmond Group of Artists.

MORRIS, ELSA (L.) [P] Terre Haute, IN.

MORRIS, RAYMOND L. [P, Arch] Bloomington, IN b. 31 Dec 1897, Salem, IN. Studied: Herron AI. Collections: mural, USPO, Knightstown, IN. Note: WPA artist.

MORRIS, ROBERT C. [Ldscp. P, Por. P, SLP] Anderson, IN b. 6 Jan 1896, Anderson. Teachers: Edward R. Sitzman; Ruthven H. Byrum. Prizes: Ind. State Fair, 1929, 31; Anderson SA, 1932, 34, 35.

MOSER, LLOYD V. [Arch, P, T] Lafayette, IN b. Kokomo, IN. Studied: U of Cincinnati. Exhibited: Lafayette A Cen; Ind. AC. Prizes: HS, 1973; Sheldon Swope Gal. Collections: Lafayette A Cen. Note: T, Purdue U.

MOSIER, MARTHA HINKLE [P, SLP, Photo, T] Martinsville, IN b. Martinsville. Studied: Ind. U, Bloomington, 1950; AIC. Teachers: Clarence Staley; Adolph Shulz. Exhibited: DePauw U, 1956-60; Swope Gal, 1957-59; Brown Cnty A Gal Assn, 1953-60. Prizes: Ind. State Fair, 1945-50; Wabash Valley Show, Swope Gal, 1957; Monroe Cnty FA Exh, 1958; HS, 1947, 52. Collections: Ind. U; Brown Cnty A Gal Assn; Morgan Cnty Mem Hospital. Note: Nature photographer.

MOTZ, GRACE LESLIE [Por. P, SLP, Ldscp. P, S] Ft Wayne, IN b. 27 Aug 1911. Studied: Ft Wayne A Sch; AIC; Vienna. Teachers: Homer Davisson; Louis Ritman; Forrest F. Stark; Francis Chapin; F. V. Poole; Guy DuBois; Emmy Sweybruck. Exhibited: Herron AI, 1938, 39. Prizes: Ft Wayne and Vicinity Show, 1940. Collections: murals, hotel, IN; Masonic Cathedral, Indianapolis; Masonic Temples in Evansville, Ft Wayne and South Bend; St Patrick's Cathedral, Orcola, IN.

MOWREY, HELEN [P, Ldscp. P, T] Franklin, IN b. 28 Oct 1898, Lawrence, IN d. c. 1992. Studied: Herron Sch A; Winona Lake Summer Sch. Teachers: William Forsyth; Paul Hadley; Clifton Wheeler; Oakley Richey; Myra Richards. Exhibited: Ind. AC; Ind. Central Col; Methodist Home, Franklin, IN; Lafayette Square, Indianapolis; Brown Cnty A Gal. Collections: Franklin Col.

MUDGETT, MARCIA GARDNER [P] Wabash, IN.

MUELLER, JO FROHBIETER [SG, T, W] Evansville, IN b. 1934, Evansville. Studied: U of Evansville; Ind. U. Exhibited: Mid-States Fair, 1981; McCollough Library (solo), 1981; Evansville Day Sch (solo), 1981; New Harmony Gal, 1981; AG, 1981. Prizes: AG, 1980; A of Month, Evansville M, Oct 1980 and Mar 1981.

MUELLER, KARL [MM] Bloomington, IN.

MUELLER, LOUIS F. [P, Ldscp. P] Indianapolis, IN b. 29 Apr 1886, Indianapolis d. 8 Apr 1958. Studied: Royal Acad, Munich; Paris. Teachers: H. V. Zuegel; Heineriet; Hugo von Habermonn; Carl von Marr; Aman-Jean and Lucien Simon, Paris. Exhibited: Ind. A Ann; Ind. AC. Prizes: Royal Acad, cast prize. Note: Self-employed interior decorator.

MUHL, BETTY (Mrs. Robert) [P, Print] Richmond, IN b. 8 Jul 1919, Richmond. Studied: Earlham Col; Ind. U-East; Ind. U-extension. Teachers: Willliam Gaw; Robert Van Sickle; Esther Nusbaum; Eldon Rowland. Exhibited: Cincinnati and Vicinity Ann; Ft Wayne Ann. Prizes: Ind. State Fair; Richmond A Ann; HS, 1962, 75, 79; Whitewater Valley Reg; Eastern Ind. A Show. Collections: Richmond AA; First English Lutheran Church, Richmond; City Bldg, Richmond; Sheldon Swope Gal, Terre Haute, IN.

MUHL, ROBERT

MULLEN, MARK A. [Print] Winchester, IN b. 15 Apr 1958, Portland, IN. Studied: Herron A Sch. Teachers: Dena Stierwalt; Robert Farlow; Harry Davis. Exhibited: Am A '85, Santa Fe; Stockton Nat Print&Dr Exh, 1987; Curator's Choice, Ind. Exh, 1989. Prizes: HS, 1984, 85; Stockton Nat Print Exh, 1985; Ind. State Fair, 1986. Collections: City of Stockton, CA; Ind. Statewide Rural Electric, Indianapolis; Fayette Cnty Library, Connersville;

Anderson FA Cen, Anderson, IN; McGuire Mem Hall, Richmond, IN; Honeywell Cen, Wabash, IN.

MULLEN, NORMA [Ldscp. P, SLP, P, T] Indianapolis, IN b. 22 Apr 1927, Edinburg, IN. Studied: John Herron A Sch. Teachers: Simon Baus; William Eyden; George Jo Mess; Ruth Anderson. Exhibited: Lieber's (solo); Ind. State Fair; 500 Show. Prizes: Southside AL; Chautaugua, Madison, IN; Eastgate Mile of A. Collections: Central Nine Vocational Sch; Homecraft Elementary Sch; Madison Ind. Bank. Note: T, Shelby Cnty AL.

MULLIN, CHARLES EDWARD [P] Orland Park, IL.

MUNDY, C. W. [Dr, Ldscp. P, Por. P, I] Indianapolis, IN b. 1 Nov 1945, Indianapolis. Studied: Ball State U; Famous A Sch; Long Beach State. Teachers: Donald Putman; Jennifer Dixon. Prizes: HS, 1990; IHA, 1979, 90. Collections: GTE; U of Louisville; Ind. State M; Indianapolis 500 M; U.S. Golf Assn.

MURDOCK, VIRGINIA [P, SLP, Por. P] Logansport, IN. Prizes: HS, 1958.

MURPHY, MARIAN R. [P, T] Huntington, WV b. Cincinnati, OH. Studied: Cincinnati A Acad; John Herron A Sch. Teachers: Fletcher Martin; Edward Chavez; Hilton Leech; Arne Lindmark; William Gerhold. Exhibited: Women's Invitational WC Show, Morris Harvey Col, Charleston WV; West Texas Ann WC Show, Lubbock, TX; Zoo A Festival, Cincinnati, 1972. Prizes: HS, 1973; W. Va. Landmark, Charleston, WV, 1972; Cardinal Valley Exh, 1973. Collections: Ind. U, Bloomington. Note: Com. A, Indianapolis, IN, Columbus and Cincinnati, OH. T, U of Ky. Community Col, Ashland, KY; Huntington Gal.

MURPHY, WILLA [Ab, Por. P, I, P] Valparaiso, IN b. 9 Dec 1909, Tuscarawas, OH. Self-taught. Exhibited: Northern Ind. Patron's Assn, 1953; Southern Shores; Tri Kappa, 1960. Prizes: HS, 1948; Southern Shores, 1969; Gary Artists League, 1964. Note: Began signing her artwork Willa Hamady in 1966.

MURRAY, MARIA C. [P]

MURRAY, ROSANNE (Mrs. James L.) [Dr, Ldscp. P, I] Noblesville, IN b. 14 Mar 1926, Indianapolis, IN. Studied: John Herron AI; Indianapolis AL; Cincinnati Sch Fashion A. Teachers: Floyd Hopper; Paul Sweany; Jean Vietor; William Ashby. Exhibited: Frames and Things, 1983; Hamilton Cnty Theatre Guild, 1983; Hindman's A Cen, 1985; Ind. State Fair. Prizes: Signature Member, Ind. WCS, 1987; Elmer Taflinger-Morris Goodman Merit Award, 1983. Collections: Conner Prairie M; Noblesville Public Library.

MUSICK, W(illiam) E(arl) [P, I, T] Midlothian, IL b. 27 Nov 1896, Brashear, MO. Studied: AIC; PAFA; Chicago Acad FA; U of Ill. Teachers: J. Norton; Rivera. Exhibited: Am WCS, NY; AIC; Herron AI. Prizes: HS, 1927. Collections: Frescoes, Long Sch, St Louis; U of Ill.; Public H.S., Chicago. Note: T, Fenger H.S., Chicago.

MUSSELMAN, KEITH DON [Com. A] Chicago, IL b. Macy, IN. Teachers: William Forsyth.

MYERS, DORIS B. [Ldscp. P, P, T] Wheatfield, IN b. 24 Nov 1921, Shelby, IN. Studied: Valparaiso U; Ball State U. Teachers: Zoltan Szabo; Charles Movalli; Tom Lynch; Bruce McGrew. Exhibited: Carillion A Cen (solo), Houston, TX; Northern Ind. AA, 1987; Purdue Calumet (solo), Hammond, IN, 1990. Prizes: HS, 1987; Tri Kappa A Show; Chesterton Women's Show; AAA Juried Exh,

Michigan City, IN. Collections: Holiday Manor; Top O'Hill Restaurant; Jasper Cnty Library; Kokomo Library; Kankakee Valley Schs. Note: Owner, North Light Studio and Gal, Wheatfield, IN.

MYRICK, RUTH KEALING [P] Indianapolis, IN b. Indianapolis. Teachers: L. M. King.

MYSLIVE, FRANK RICHARD [P] Hammond, IN/Douglas, MI b. 5 Nov 1908, East Chicago, IN d. 1986. Studied: U of Wis.; Chicago Acad FA; Greason Sch Painting, Douglas, MI. Teachers: Frederick Taubes; Loomis; Schmidt; Kingdom; Greason. Exhibited: Hammond Public Library (solo); Dorchester Cl (solo), Dolton, IL; Lake Dalecarlia Country Cl (solo); Chicago Navy Pier; McCormick Place, Chicago. Prizes: Northern Ind. Salons; HS, 1957, 64; Kappa Kappa Kappa Exh; 4th Ann Munster Community Park Assn. Collections: St Catherine's Hospital, East Chicago, IN; Calumet Orphan Home for Boys, Hammond; Warsaw, Poland; Hoosier State Bank, Hammond, IN; Inland Steel Co. Note: Founding member, Hammond District AA, now Northern Ind. AA.

N

NASH, GRACE Chicago, IL d. c. 1938.

NATHAN, MARILYN [Litho-Embossment]

NAUMAN, HAZEL M. Milford, MI.

NAYLOR, ALICE L. [P] Indianapolis, IN.

NEEDHAM, RAY CLAY [P] Richmond, IN b. 5 Apr 1893, Owosso, MI. Studied: Earlham Col; Booth Bay A Colony. Teachers: John M. King; Edward Duffner; George H. Baker; Lawrence McConaha. Prizes: Richmond AA, 1931. Collections: Inter-mountain Union Col, Helena, MT; Masonic Home of Ind., Franklin; United Brethren Church, Richmond.

NEELD, C(larence) E(llsworth) [P] Glen Ellyn, IL b. 7 May 1895, New Albany, IN. Studied: Acad FA, Chicago; Sch App and Normal A. Teachers: Menoir; C. Buck; J. Topping.

NEFF, B. E. [P] New Albany, IN.

NELSON, GERTRUDE WISER [P, T] South Bend, IN b. 13 May 1898, Jonesboro, IN. Studied: AIC; Columbia U. Note: Formerly, Gertrude Wiser Butcher (Mrs. W. A.). Sister of artist Guy Brown Wiser.

NELSON, WILLIAM J. [P] Michigan City, IN.

NESSLAGE, F. HELEN

NETHERCUTT, RONNA A(llen) [Dr, P, S] Royal Center, IN b. 1929, Cass Cnty, IN. Exhibited: South Bend Mall; Logansport; Chicago. Note: Occupation, welder.

NEUFELD, LEO [P, Por. P] b. St Paul, MN. Studied: U of Wis.; ASL. Teachers: Harvey Dinnerstein; Ted Jacobs. Exhibited: NAD, 1984; Grand Central A Gal, NY, 1987; Union Gal, Purdue U, 1989. Note: Painting instructor, NAD, 1988-89.

NEWBERRY, W. L. Notre Dame, IN. Prize: HS, 1935.

NEWMAN, ANNA MARY [P, I, T] Richmond, IN b. Richmond, IN d. 15 Aug 1930. Studied: AIC; Sch App & Normal A, Chicago; Overbeck Sch Des Pottery, Cambridge City, IN. Teachers: Ralph Clarkson; John Vanderpoel; C. F. Browne; John E. Bundy. Prizes: Richmond AA, 1908; Ind.

State Fair, 1914. Collections: YMCA, Ft Wayne; Supreme Court, Indianapolis. Note: T, Ft Wayne H.S.

NEWMAN, CLARA G(rimes) [P, T, C] Richmond, IN b. 10 Sep 1870, Brownsville, NE. Studied: AIC; U of Chicago; Nat Sch Fine and App A, District of Columbia. Teachers: Overbeck; J. E. Forkner; F. Mahony; Coats; J. M. King; R. Byram. Prizes: Ind. State Fair, 1939.

NEWMAN, HELEN [P] Anderson, IN b. Anderson, IN. Studied: Indianapolis AL. Teachers: George Jo Mess; Garo Antreasian. Exhibited: Ind. Statehouse, Indianapolis. Note: Owner, Newman's A Supplies and Frame Shop.

NEWMAN, PAULA RANEY [P] Newton Highlands, MA b. Loogootee, IN. Studied: Ft Wayne; PAFA; Barnes Foundation; Cape Cod Sch A. Teachers: James King Bonnor; John Enser; George Dinkle. Prizes: HS, 1968.

NEWTON, KATHERINE West Hartford, CT.

NICHOLLS, MERLE R. [P] Gary, IN. Exhibited: Northern Ind. A Salon, 1946-60. Note: Lived in Gary, Ind., 1940s-1960s.

NICHOLSON, EDWARD (Horace) [Por. P, P, Print, T] Metamora, IL b. 13 Jun 1901, Lincoln, IL d. 1966. Studied: Chicago Acad FA; AIC; Grand Central Sch A, NY. Teachers: Wayman Adams. Exhibited: All-Ill. Soc FA, 1939, 40, 44; Faulkner Mem M, 1935, 36; Santa Barbara AA, 1936-38; Oakland A Gal, 1938, 39, 49; Peoria AL, 1941, 46; Nat Acad A Gal, NY, 1951. Prizes: HS, 1940, 44-46, 49-51, 56, 57, 59, 60, 64; All-Ill. Soc FA, 1940. Collections: Ebell Cl, Long Beach, CA; Bradley U; Peoria Public Library. Worked in Santa Barbara, Calif.

NICHOLSON, THURMAN [P] Michigan City, IN. Prizes: HS, 1949.

NICOLAI, C(harles) A. [Ldscp. P, Wood Engraver, Com. A] Chicago, IL b. 10 Jun 1856, Indianapolis, IN d. 19 Feb 1942. Studied: Ind. A Sch. Teachers: John Love; James F. Gookins; H. C. Chandler. Note: Last surviving member, Bohe Club. Member of Sketching Club whose members were pioneer discoverers of Brown Cnty's beauty.

NICOLAI, HELEN

NIESSE, MILDRED [Ldscp. P, Por. P, T] Indianapolis, IN b. 20 Dec 1915, Rushville, IN. Studied: Indianapolis AL. Teachers: George Jo Mess; Simon Baus; Garo Antreasian; Winnie Harvey; Gianni Cilfone. Exhibited: Ind. A Ann, John Herron and IMA, 1946-1975; Ind. State Fair; Swope Gal, Terre Haute, 1983; Whitewater Valley, Ind. U, Richmond, 1978; Ind. WCS, 1983-88; Brown Cnty A Gal, Nashville, IN. Prizes: HS, 1977; Ind. AC, 1966, 69, 76; Ind. State Fair, 1960, 66, 67, 71; John Herron AM, 1968; Tri Kappas of Terre Haute. Collections: Mem Union Bldg, Ind. U, Bloomington; Butler U; Banc One; Ind. Nat Bank, Speedway, IN; IBM; WISH-TV; Jacob Carciente Col, Caracas, Venezuela. Note: T, St Mary's. Self-taught primitive artist. By 1992, had 30 paintings accepted into HS.

NIXON, FLOYD

NOEL, A. [P] Prizes: HS, 1948.

NOËL, NANCY A. [Por. P, P] Zionsville, IN b. 29 Oct 1945, Indianapolis, IN. Studied: St Joseph Col, Cincinnati, OH. Prizes: 1990 Matrix Award (Woman of the Year); Addy Award, 1988-89; HS, 1972, 82. Collections: Kokomo-Howard Cnty Public Library; Sandoz Pharmaceutical Corporation; DuPont Foundation. Note: Her commemorative poster collection includes: 1987 Pan American Games, U.S.; Equestrian Team; Indianapolis Zoo. Associated with African Medical Research Foundation and South African Wildlife Federation, "Rhino Rescue" of Africa and England.

NOLF, JOHN T(homas) [P, I, Car] Grand Detour, IL b. 23 Jul 1872, Allentown, PA d. 1950, Dixon, IL. Studied: AIC; Smith A Acad, Chicago. Teachers: W. Reynolds; F. Smith; J. Vanderpoel; W. Ufer. Exhibited: PAFA; SFMA; NAD. Prizes: AIC, 1924, 29; Oak Park AA, 1928; Chicago Mun AL, 1929; Chicago Gal Assn, 1930. Collections: Chicago Public Schs; Union League Cl, Chicago; Public Schs, Gary, IN; Vanderpoel AA; Northwestern U; Lafayette AA, Ind. Note: I, *Chicago Tribune* and *Chicago Inter-Ocean.* Car, *Inland Printer*, 1920-40 or later.

NORTHWAY, ANN [P] Lebanon, IN.

NORTON, JAMES C. [Gra. A, I] Evansville, IN b. 1937, Evansville. Studied: U of Evansville; John Herron A Sch.

NUSBAUM, ESTHER COMMONS [P, T] Richmond, IN b. 12 Jan 1907, Richmond, IN. Studied: Gulf Park Col; U of Wis. Teachers: William Thon; Jon Corbin; Jerry Farnsworth; Hilton Leech; Edmund Brucker; Edwin Fulwider. Exhibited: Am WCS; Nat Assn Women A Ann; Dayton AM; Cincinnati AM; John Herron AM; Ball State AM; Ind. AC; Richmond AA Ann; Michiana Reg. Prizes: Ind. State Fair, 1934-35; Am Assn University Women; Virginia Highlands Festival; A for Religion; Richmond AA. Collections: Mural, First Federal Savings and Loan, Richmond, IN; Women's AL, Terre Haute; L. G. Balfour Co, Indianapolis; Richmond AA; YMCA.

OBER, ELEANOR VEE

OBERGFELL, MARY JANE [P, Print] Ft Wayne, IN b. Ft Wayne. Studied: Ft Wayne A Sch; St Francis Col. Teachers: James McBride. Exhibited: Shawnee Branch Library, Ft Wayne; Parkview Hospital; Linker's Gal; Ft Wayne Women's Cl; Ft Wayne MA; Wassenberg A Cen, Van Wert, OH; Noble Cnty A Cen, Albion, IN; Ind. AC; Ft Wayne AG. Prizes: Ft Wayne Women's Cl, 1973. Collections: Allen Cnty Crippled Children Assn.

OBERHOLTZER, TAMIKO [P, Dr] Bowling Green, IN b. 20 Oct 1928, Japan. Studied: Japan; U.S. Teachers: Gyokudo Kawai. Exhibited: Brown Cnty AG, 1987. Prizes: HS, 1990; Ind. Heritage, 1987; Nat A Gal, Tokyo, 1950. Collections: Rose Hulman Inst Technology; Heartland Automotive, Inc; Kamagawa Japan.

OBERMUELLER, STAN [P] Indiana b. 1945, Plainview, TX. Studied: Concordia TC, Seward, NE; Ft Wayne A Sch. Teachers: James McBride. Prizes: HS, 1978; Coldwater, MI.

O'BRIEN, BEA [P] Indianapolis, IN.

OCHS, ROBERT L. [P] Indianapolis, IN. Studied: Herron Sch A. Prizes: Wendell Color Mem Scholarship; Butler AI, Youngstown, OH; HS, 1952. Collections: Herron AI.

O'CONNELL, PATRICIA ELLIOTT [P] Indianapolis, IN.

O'CONNELL, PATSY (Patricia) SURH [P, T] Tacoma, WA b. 7 Feb 1943, Shanghai, China. Studied: Schaeffer Sch Des, San Francisco; Korea; Japan; U.S. Teachers: Kezo Sensai; Harold Holly; Floyd Hopper; Sadami Yamada; Kohei Aida. Exhibited: Intl Cen, Indianapolis, 1980; IMA, 1982; Am Cultural Cen, Korea. Prizes: Calif. State Fair, Monterey, 1978; Ind. Mid-Am Orchid Show, 1980; HS, 1983.

O'CONNOR, JOANNE [Intaglio A] Munster, IN.

O'CONNOR, KATIE C. [P] Indianapolis, IN b. Crawfordsville, IN.

O'CONNOR, VINCENT L. Chicago, IL.

O'DELL, ROB [Ldscp. P] Ladoga, IN b. 4 Jun 1938, Decatur, IL. Studied: Am Acad A, Chicago. Teachers: Irving Shapiro. Exhibited: IMA, 1980; Ky. WCS, 1981; Ind. AC. Prizes: HS, 1970-72, 74, 77, 80, 81, 87; WC USA, 1978; Ind. State M, 1978; Ill. State Fair. Collections: Ind. U; Purdue U; Ind. State U; Wabash Col; Stokely Van Camp; Ind. Bell; Lafayette A Cen; Sheldon Swope Gal; WISH-TV

O'FALLON, VIRGINIA (Mrs. Ray Anders) [P, S, T] Paoli, IN. Studied: Louisville A Cen. Teachers: Fayette Barnum. Prizes: Ky. State Fair, 1951. Note: T, Limerock A Cen, south of Paoli.

OFFUTT, LEE P. d. c. 1966.

O'HARA, MICHAEL [Silkscreen] Indianapolis, IN.

O'HAVER, MARIAN JOHNSON [T] Carmel, IN b. 8 Sep 1915, Indianapolis, IN. Studied: Ind. U; John Herron A Sch; Indianapolis AL. Exhibited: Ind.

OLIVE, JUDY *(See Jarrett, Judy)*

OLIVER, LOREN [P] Studied: Herron Sch A. Exhibited: Lieber Gal, 1957. Prizes: Milliken Award for Travel, 1954.

O'LOUGHLIN, THOMAS [P, Por. P] b. 24 Feb 1923, Saskatoon, Saskatchewan, Canada. Studied: Herron Sch A; Jerry Farnsworth Sch, Sarasota, FL. Teachers: Elmer Taflinger; Jerry Farnsworth; Helen Sawyer. Exhibited: Lyman Brothers Gal (solo), 1948; IMA, 1948; Cowie Gal, Los Angeles, 1952; 123rd Ann Exh of Nat Acad Des, NY. Collections: Mural, Children's Mus, Indianapolis.

OLSON, EARL B. LaPorte, IN.

OLSON, MILDRED A. [Plaster with Patina] Richmond, IN.

ORR, CAROLYN GRABHORN [P] Greenfield, IN b. Indianapolis, IN. Studied: Paris, France; U of Ariz.; U of Calif.; Calif. State. Exhibited: DeGrazia Gal, Tucson; Claremont Col; Paris Salon; Van Dyke Gal. Collections: San Bernadino M; Valley Col Collection, CA; Royal Family, England.

ORR, CYNTHIA A. [P, Photo] Indianapolis, IN b. 18 Feb 1948, Indianapolis. Studied: Greenfield, IN; Evreux,

France. Teachers: Siegfried Hahn; Carolyn Orr. Exhibited: Ind. State Fair; Tri Kappa A Auction, Greenfield; Am Fletcher Nat Bank; Riley Cen; Nat Lg Am Penwomen. Prizes: Ind. State Fair; Central Ind. Cer Assn.

ORR, Jr., R. B. [P] Greenfield, IN b. 1921 d. Aug 1985.

OSBORN, MARIAN [Ldscp. P, I] Indianapolis, IN b. 11 Mar 1924, Indianapolis. Studied: Earlham Col; Ind. U. Teachers: Elmira Kempton; Henry Hope. Exhibited: Ind. State Fair, 1968-70; 500 Festival Exh, 1969; Southside AL; East Side AL. Prizes: Mile of A, 1968; Ind. State Fair, 1968; 500 Festival Exh, 1970.

OSBORNE, BETTY LOCKE [P]

OSBORNE, ROBERT [P, S, T] Evansville, IN. Studied: Ind. U; U of Iowa. Teachers: Alton Pickens. Exhibited: 48th Ann Ind. A Exh, Herron AM, 1955.

OSBORNE, ROLAND DONOVAN [P, SLP, T] West Milton, OH b. 8 Sep 1904, Richmond, IN d. 1977. Teachers: Francis Focer Brown; Blanche Waite. Prizes: Ind. State Fair, 1936-39; HS, 1950, 56, 57, 62; AC Exh, 1961.

OSHIER, EARL [P] Anderson, IN b. c. 1938, Anderson. Self-taught. Prizes: HS, 1965, 67, 72; Ind. State Fair; Woman's Cl, Ft Wayne; Woman's Dept Cl, Terre Haute; Mid-States, Evansville M of A&Sc. Collections: DePauw U; Franklin Col; Vincennes U; Evansville M of A&Sc. Note: Employee of Guide Lamp Division, General Motors, Anderson.

OSHRAIN, JOAN

OSTEN, MARY Indianapolis, IN. Note: Associated with Ladywood Sch., Indianapolis.

OSTERDAY, MARY BOWE (*See Bowe, Mary E.*)

OVERHOLSER, JOAN F. Noblesville, IN b. Tipton, IA. Studied: U of Iowa; Indianapolis AL. Teachers: Sandy Ezell; Henry Bell; Shirley Carr; Joanne Cardwell; Jeanne McLeish; Sally Kenley.

OVERLEY, BRIAN D. [P, Print, S, Cer, T] Dallas, TX b. 25

Oct 1956, Denver, CO. Studied: Ind. U, Bloomington. Exhibited: San Antonio AI, 1986; Penegrine Gal, Dallas, 1986; Texas Christian U, Ft Worth; Red Studio, NY, 1984. Note: T, IMA.

OVERMAN, DARIS J.

OVERMAN, FRANCES [Print, P] St Petersburg, FL b. 27 Feb 1928, Bowling Green, OH. Studied: Herron Sch A. Teachers: William Ashby; Harry Davis; Peg Fierke; David Rubins. Exhibited: La. WC Intl, 1984; First Ann Penrod Soc. Note: Formerly of Indianapolis, IN.

OVERMAN, WENDELL F.

OVERPECK, (L.) GAIL [P, T] Speedway, IN. Studied: Herron Sch A.

OVERSTREET, ANNA

OWEN, NANCY R. [Ldscp. P] Carmel, IN b. Columbia, TN. Studied: MFA, Houston; Butler U, Indianapolis; Indianapolis AL. Teachers: Rosemary Lawton Thomas. Exhibited: Ind. State Fair, 1989. Prizes: HS, 1989, 90; Ind. State Fair, 1987. Collections: Noblesville City Hall, Noblesville, IN.

OWINGS, PATRICIA L. (Patte) [Ab] Indianapolis, IN b. 1 Nov 1954, Indianapolis. Self-taught. Exhibited: IMA, rental gal, 1988-91; Am States Insurance, 1990.

OZBUN, DONNA M(offett) [Print] Indianapolis, IN b. 13 Jan 1940, Indianapolis. Studied: Ft Wayne AI; Herron Sch A; Florence, Italy. Teachers: Roland Hobart. Exhibited: 25th Ann Juried Show, Acad of the A, Easton, MD, 1989; Arlington A Ann Juried Exh, Arlington M, Arlington, TX, 1988; Parkersburg Nat S&Print Comp, Parkersburg, WV, 1988; CCA Gal (solo), Indianapolis; Jewish Community Cen (solo), Indianapolis; IUPUI Law Sch (solo), Indianapolis. Prizes: Kansas Nat Small P&Dr Exh, Hays, Kansas, 1986; Salman River Nat A Comp, Riggins, ID, 1990; HS, 1990. Collections: Ft Hays State U, Hays, Kansas; City Press, Terre Haute, IN.

P

PADDACK, JULIE [P] Indianapolis, IN. Studied: Ind. U. Exhibited: Jefferson Nat Life Bldg, Indianapolis, 1978; Pro A Studio; Union Federal Savings&Loan Assn, Beech Grove, IN, 1979.

PAGE, CARRIE O'HARA [Ldscp. P, SLP, Por. P] Greensburg, IN b. 25 Jun 1915, Princeton, KY. Studied: Herron Sch A. Teachers: C. Curry Bohm; George Cheropov; Edmund Brucker; Frederick Rigley; Charles Movali. Exhibited: HS Gal (solo), 1967; George Coon Library, 1970, 73, 75-83; Ind. State Fair. Prizes: Tri Kappa State, 1971; IHA, Nashville, IN, yearly. Collections: Homer Gal; Greensburg A Cen; George Coon Library; Union Bank and Trust. Note: She has also painted under the name of Carrie O'Hara Morrison.

PAGE, EDSON WARD

PAGE, Jr., GROVER [I, Car, P] New Albany, IN b. 1892, Gastonia, NC. Studied: AIC; Acad FA, Chicago. Exhibited: Theobald Gal, Chicago. Note: Car, editorial page, *Louisville Courier-Journal.*

PAIDRICK, RUSSELL E. [P, Com. A, Des] Indianapolis, IN b. Indianapolis. Studied: Herron A Sch. Teachers: William Forsyth; Clifton Wheeler; Paul Hadley. Exhibited: Herron AM (solo); Prattlers; Ind. State Fair. Note: Founder, Prattlers. Asst Dir, FA Dept, Ind. State Fair.

PALUZZI, CLAUDINE (*See Kelsey, Claudine Paluzzi*)

PALUZZI, RINALDO R. [P, S] Alpera, Spain b. 1927, Greensburg, PA. Studied: Herron Sch A; Ind. U. Teachers: Garo Antreasian. Exhibited: XXXIV Intl Biennial Exh, Venice, Italy, 1968; IMA (solo), 1975; Colegio de Arquitecto (solo), Palma de Mallorca, 1976; Atrium Gal, Indianapolis, 1986. Prizes: Tiffany Grant, 1957. Collections: S, *Totem*, White River Park, Indianapolis; Banco Intl de Comercio.

PARCELS, SAM [P] Lebanon, IN.

PARKER, VIRGINIA RICE [P, T] Prizes: HS, 1947. Note: T, Ind. Public Sch.

PARKER, WENTWORTH [P, Print] Terre Haute, IN b. 11 Oct 1890, Terre Haute, IN. Teachers: William Forsyth.

PARKS, ROBERT OWEN [P, T] Lafayette, IN b. 25 Apr 1916, Richmond, IN. Studied: Herron AI; Cape Sch A, Provincetown, MA. Exhibited: Tiffany Fnd, 1938; Cincinnati M, 1938. Note: T, Purdue U. Dir, Smith Col MA. Lecturer, Smith Col.

PARSONS, DAVID G(oode) [S, T, P, I] Stoughton, WI b. 2 Mar 1911, Gary, IN. Studied: AIC; U of Wis. Exhibited: Wis. Salon, 1934-41, 43; Wis. PS, 1933, 36-40; AIC, 1935-40, 1946; PAFA, 1940, 46; WFNY, 1939; Grand Rapids A Gal, 1939; CI, 1940; U of Wis., 1940. Prizes: VMFA, 1943; HS, 1940; Wis. PS, 1941; Wis. Salon, 1938, 44, 45.

PATEL, DAKSHA J. [P] Ft Wayne, IN b. India. Studied: A in Government Col of FA and Architecture. Exhibited: Intl Women A Exh, Paris; U.S. Information Library (solo), Hyderabad, 1962; All-India FA&Cr Soc Gal, Rafi Marg, New Delhi, 1965; Intl Cen, NY, 1971; Ft Wayne AG, Glenbrook Mall, 1974; 10th Kenosha A Fair, Chicago, 1974. Prizes: All-India A Exh, 1957, 59, 67; Andhra Acad of A, 1964; 22nd Ann Exh Ind. A, Ft Wayne Women's Cl; Glenbrook Cen A '74, Ft Wayne; HS, 1978. Collections: Hyderabad M; Government Archeology M; Salarjung M; Madras M; Calcutta A Soc; Ft Wayne AM.

PATRICK, ALAN [Ldscp. P, Cer] Albany, IN b. 16 Jun 1942, Richmond, IN. Studied: Ball State U. Teachers: Roland Osborne; Byron Temple. Exhibited: A Forms '90, Lafayette, IN; Minnetrista Ann, Muncie, IN, 1990. Prizes: L. Carr Ldsp. Award, 1988-90; HS, 1963. Collections: Richmond AA; Ind. State U; Summit Bank, Muncie; Ball State U.

PATRICK, MILDRED [P, Print, Photo] Terre Haute, IN b. Morocco, IN. Studied: Famous A Painting Course; Ind. State U; Ind. U. Teachers: Whitaker Zornes. Exhibited: Swope A Gal; Brown Cnty A Gal; Evansville Gal; Louisville Bluegrass Acrylic Exh; U of Southern Ill.; Turman Gal, Ind. State U; Paris. Collections: Ind. State U; Cunningham Library, Ind. State U.

PATTERSON, JAMES K. [P, Dr] b. 1944, Indianapolis, IN. Studied: Herron Sch A. Exhibited: Ind. State Fair, 1973-78; 500 Festival, 1974; Blue Cross/Blue Shield Bldg (solo), 1976. Prizes: HS, 1978, 80; Ind. State Fair, 1973, 76. Note: Layout/Design, Mather, Dawson, Phelps, Inc.

PATTERSON, MARION L(ois) [P, T] Vincennes, IN b. 3 Nov 1909, Knox Cnty, IN. Studied: Ind. State TC; Syracuse U. Exhibited: AWCS, 1941; NAWA, 1943-45; Hoosier A Gal Mexican Exh, 1942; Ind. A, 1942, 44, 45; Syracuse U (solo), 1942; Vincennes Fortnightly Cl (solo), 1946. Prizes: HS, 1942, 48. Note: T, Vincennes City Sch, beginning 1937.

PATTERSON, RICHARD R. [Por. P, Print, T] Indianapolis, IN b. 27 Aug 1952. Studied: Manual H.S.; Herron Sch A; Tyler Sch A; Temple U. Exhibited: Temple U (solo), 1977; 55th Ann Traveling Print Exh, 1977-79; Print Cl, Philadelphia, 1977. Prizes: 500 A Festival, 1970; Gold Key Awards, Scholastic A Comp; Hallmark Prize, 1970; Young Am PM, 1976; HS, 1973.

PATTON, JACK D(esmond) [P, T] Upland, IN b. 1920, Huntington, WV. Studied: Columbus Sch FA, Ohio; Ohio State U; Taylor U, Upland, IN; Ball State U; Maranatha Sch A, Muskegon, MI. Exhibited: Grant Cnty AA Show; Blackford H.S. Exh; Ind. State Fair; Taylor U (solo). Collections: Upland Bank; Tulsa Okla. Bank; Henerson Furniture Store, Marion, IN. Note: T and A Dept Head, Taylor U, Upland, IN.

PAUL, DOROTHY SHORT [P] Prizes: HS, 1953.

PAUL, EVA E. [P] Cambridge City, IN.

PAUL, FRANK K. Chicago, IL.

PAULSON, REBECCA (J.) [Dr] Greenwood, IN.

PAXSON, CONNIE J. [Dr] Bluffton, IN.

PAYNE, GRACE (Mrs. Arthur) [P, T] Indianapolis, IN/FL b. 9 Jan 1918, Indianapolis. Studied: Herron Sch A; Butler U; Rockford Col, Rockford, IL. Teachers: Marques Reitzel; Elmer Taflinger. Exhibited: HS Gal (solo), 1969; Ind. AC; Bethleham A for Religion, Lafayette, IN; Sheldon Swope Gal, Terre Haute, IN. Prizes: HS, 1965. Note: T, evening staff, Broad Ripple H.S., Indianapolis.

PAYNE, MAHLON BAYLEY (Mrs. Paul T.) [S, P, W] Crawfordsville, IN b. Milwaukee, WI d. Nov 1983. Studied: Herron A Sch; PAFA; Cranbrook A Acad; Yale U. Teachers: Forrest Stark; Walter Hancock; Carl Millis; Marshall Fredericks. Exhibited: N.Y. Soc Cer A; Cranbrook A Acad, Bloomfield Hills, MI; Ind. A, Herron AI. Prizes: HS, 1937; Ind. AC, 1938, 39; Ind. Fed AC, 1939; Herron AM, 1937, 39; PAFA.

PAZOL, BETTY

PEABODY, RODNEY R. [Dr, Por. P, S, Cer, T] Plainfield, IN b. 1 Aug 1929, Blue Mound, IL. Studied: AIC. Exhibited: Marshall Field, 1956; IMA, rental gal. Prizes: HS, 1971, 75; Children's M, Indianapolis, 1973. Note: T, Tudor Hall and Park Tudor, Indianapolis, 1966-1972; T, Indianapolis AL, 1966-72.

PEARCY, GERALD [Ldscp. P, SLP] Ankeny, IA b. 27 Mar 1937, Charleston, IL. Studied: Am Acad A, Chicago. Exhibited: Brown Cnty AA; 500 Festival. Prizes: HS, 1987; Ind. Heritage, 1979-81; On Your Own Time, 1990.

PEARSON, THELMA FORSYTH [Ldscp. P] Prizes: HS, 1958.

PEDDLE, JULIET A. [P] Chicago, IL.

PEDEN, DONNA MOORE [P] Spencer, IN b. 27 Mar

1904, ID d. 11 Feb 1978. Note: Performer in Broadway musicals and Hollywood films.

PEED, WILLIAM B. [P, Ldscp. P, Car] Hollywood, CA b. Indianapolis. Studied: Herron A Sch. Teachers: William Forsyth; Clifton Wheeler; Oakley Richey; Donald M. Mattison; Henrik M. Mayer. Prizes: HS, 1937, 38; Ind. A Ann, Herron AM, 1935. Note: Sketch artist for Walt Disney Studio. Joined Disney, 1937. Created the cartoon character of "Dumbo." Also worked with Disney on "Song of the South, " "Snow White" and "Midnight and Jeremiah."

PEELER, MARJORIE M. [S, Cer] Reelsville, IN b. 9 May 1926, Indianapolis, IN. Studied: Arsenal Tech H.S., Indianapolis; U of Minneapolis. Teachers: Richard Peeler; John Rood; Sara Bard; John Simpson; Elizabeth Jasper; Karl Martz. Exhibited: Brown Cnty Cr Gal, 1983; The Gallery (two-person), Bloomington; IMA (two-person); Bicentennial Invitational, Ind. U, 1976; 40 Years Pottery&S, DePauw U, 1986; Women in Cer, Earlham U, 1987; Form and Function in Clay, Evansville M A&Sc, 1989. Prizes: HS, 1955. Note: Co-producer, eight art films on ceramics. Published in *Ceramics Monthly*. Since 1972, full-time occupation, making functional stoneware pottery. Works also in media such as fabric applique, quilting, basket-weaving, gourd painting. Wife of artist Richard Peeler.

PEELER, RICHARD [S, Cer, T, W] Reelsville, IN b. 8 Aug 1926, Indianapolis, IN. Studied: DePauw U; Ind. U. Teachers: Karl Martz; Robert Laurent. Exhibited: St Mary-of-the-Woods Col, 1974; Brown Cnty Cr Gal, 1983; Ind. Central Col, 1967; Syracuse Nat Cer S, 1964; 40 Years Pottery&S, DePauw U, 1986; IMA. Prizes: HS, 1951, 53, 61; Cer A USA, 1966; Ind. State Fair, 1959; Michiana Show, South Bend, 1963; Ind. Cer Show, Indianapolis, 1959; Mid-States Cr Exh, 1966, Evansville; Ind. A-Craftsmen, Lifetime Achievement, 1991. Note: T, Arsenal Tech H.S.; T, DePauw U. Producer of educational motion pictures made for McGraw Hill, distributed by Cer A Films. Published in *Ceramics Monthly*. Since 1972, full-time occupation, making functional stoneware pottery. Husband of artist Marjorie M. Peeler.

PEELING, FLORENCE M. (Mrs. James H.) [P, SLP, Ldscp. P, T] Indianapolis, IN d. Jun 1950. Studied: Indianapolis AL. Teachers: Earl Beyer. Note: T, Indianapolis AL. Also painted in Leland, MI.

PEGG, OLIF (Mrs. Harley) [Ldscp. P, SLP, T] Spencer, IN b. Greene Cnty, IN. Teachers: Charles Bergstrom, Chicago. Exhibited: Canyon Inn, McCormick's Creek State Park; Northern Ind. Salon, Hammond; Wabash Valley Reg, Swope Gal, Terre Haute; Ind. State Fair; A for Religion, Indianapolis; Owen Cnty State Fair, Spencer. Prizes: Wabash Reg; Owen Cnty Fair; HS, 1966.

PEKELSMA, JUDY [T, P] Lafayette, IN b. 2 Apr 1951, Chicago, IL. Studied: Purdue U. Exhibited: Bookstalls (solo), Purdue U, 1977, 79; The Stabilizer (solo), W. Lafayette, 1978.

PELHAM, ELEANOR Y. Indianapolis, IN.

PENN, EVA

PENNISTON, DAVID R. [P] Indianapolis, IN.

PEREIRA, MARGARET [Por. P, Com. A] Chicago, IL b. Oxford.

PERKINS, F. ALIDA Mishawaka, IN.

PERSELL, FRANK [P] Indianapolis, IN b. Indianapolis d.

c. 1990. Studied: Cleveland Inst A; John Herron Sch A. Teachers: Elmer Taflinger. Exhibited: Ohio Valley WC Shows; Ind. State Fair; Ind. A Exh; Anderson Winter Show; Wabash Valley Exh; IMA, rental gal. Prizes: Ind. State Fair, 1950, 72; HS, 1973; Ind. Central Col, 1969.

PERSOV, ANNEMARIE

PERSZYK, SY [P, S, T] Prizes: HS, 1949, 51. Note: T, Ind. Public Sch.

PESAVENTO, ERIN (Hope) [P, T] Carmel, IN b. c. 1947, Hamilton Cnty, IN. Studied: U of Evansville; Indianapolis AL; Ind. State U; John Herron Sch A. Teachers: Floyd Hopper; Jean Vietor; Rob O'Dell; Irving Shapiro. Exhibited: Ind. State Fair; Ind. WCS; Indianapolis AL; Hamilton Cnty AA; Hindman A Gal; Brown Cnty A Barn, Nashville, IN. Collections: Brown Cnty A Barn; Willow Wisp A Gal, Frankfort; Am Nat Bank; *Noblesville Daily Ledger;* Tri Kappa; F. C. Tucker Realty.

PESTA, MAUREEN [P, Dr] Vallonia, IN b. 4 Aug 1942, Philadelphia, PA. Studied: St Mary's Col; Notre Dame U. Teachers: Norman Laliberte. Exhibited: Southside AL Reg, 1989; Krempp Gal (solo), Jasper, IN, 1991. Prizes: 5-State Pastel Comp, Krasl A Cen, 1989; Floyd Cnty M 18th Ann, 1989. Collections: Am Water Co, IN; Jackson Cnty Bank.

PESTOW, FRANCES E. [Por. P, Ldscp. P, SLP, T, Ab] Elkhart, IN b. 14 Feb 1908, Goshen, IN d. 24 Feb 1983. Studied: U of Notre Dame; Ind. U, extension; South Bend A Cen. Exhibited: Hammond A Show; South Bend; Herron. Prizes: Motorola contest, 1962. Note: Helped found Elkhart AL. T, Elkhart AL.

PETERS, DONALD ALLEN [Dr] Studied: Herron Sch A. Exhibited: Combat A Exh, Wm. H. Block Co, Indianapolis, 1945. Prizes: HS, 1951. Collections: Mural, Milano Inn Restaurant, Indianapolis, 1983. Note: Worked at Disney Studios. Father of artist Steve Peters.

PETERS, DONOVAN W. [T] Indianapolis, IN b. 15 Jul 1917, Rosthern, Saskatchewan, Canada. Studied: John Herron A Sch. Teachers: David Rubins; Donald Mattison. Exhibited: Indianapolis AL; Ind. State Fair.

PETERS, MARI

PETERS, STEVE [Car, I] Studied: Herron Sch A. Note: Son of artist Donald Allen Peters.

PETERSON, ELIZABETH F.

PETERSON, HERMAN (J.) [Por. P] Winnetka, IL.

PETTY, MARGARET BALL [P, SLP] Muncie, IN b. 30 Jun 1898, Muncie d. 28 Dec 1984. Studied: AIC. Teachers: Otto Stark. Note: Niece of artists Winifred Brady Adams and J. Ottis Adams. President of Ball Stores, Muncie. President of Muncie AA, 1936-46.

PHEMISTER, LORENA [P, T] Studied: Herron Sch A; Iowa State U. Prizes: HS, 1947.

PHILLIPS, CONNIE L. [P, S] Morristown, IN b. 13 Mar 1942, Breckenridge, TX. Studied: Indianapolis AL. Teachers: Rosemary Lawton Thomas; Jean Vietor. Exhibited: Texas Women Western A, 1980; Two-Women Show, 1986. Prizes: HS; Beech Grove, 1975; TWWA, Texas. Collections: Ft Wayne Zoo; Desert Storm Mem, Indianapolis. Note: Currently, Connie Scott.

PICKENS, BARBARA ALLEN [Ab, Des] Muncie, IN b. 9 Oct 1955, Kansas City, MO. Studied: Kendall Sch Des, Grand Rapids, MI; Anderson U, Anderson, IN; Ball State

U. Teachers: Dr. Jean Murphy. Exhibited: Ft Wayne AM; Anderson Pen Women. Prizes: Pen Women. Collections: Reinhold Landscape, Pontiac, MI; Anderson U, Anderson, IN; Warner Gear, Muncie, IN.

PIEPER, LOIS [P] Ft Wayne, IN b. Butternut, WI. Studied: Famous A Course; Ft Wayne AI. Exhibited: Ft Wayne Woman's Cl (solo); The Gal, Ft Wayne AM (solo); Indianapolis 500; Tri-State Col; Huntington Gal; Ball State U; Michiana Mainstreams Intl. Prizes: Ft Wayne AM; Ind. A Exh; Indianapolis AL.

PIERCE, DIANA MILLER [P] Ft Wayne, IN b. 11 May 1954, Kokomo, IN. Studied: Indianapolis AL; Ind. U. Teachers: Rosemary Lawton Thomas; Floyd Hopper. Exhibited: Am WCS, 1989; Ind. AC, 1987-89. Prizes: HS, 1988; Ind. WCS, 1987; Ind. AC, 1987. Collections: Insurit Inc.

PIERCE, JENNIE S. [P] Indianapolis, IN.

PIERCY, DELITA ALVAREZ [Dr, Ldscp. P, T] Bloomington, IN b. 17 Apr 1936, Indianapolis, IN. Studied: Ind. U. Teachers: Barry Gealt; Bonnie Skylarski. Exhibited: Phoenix and Dragon Gal, 1988; Phoenix and Dragon Gal (solo), 1983, 87, 90; Nashville A Gal. Prizes: A for the Park, 1990; Midwest Pastel Soc; IHA, 1986; Brown Cnty AG, 1986. Collections: Ind. U; Ford Electronics; Coor Inc; Oliver Wineries. Note: T, Campus Community A Cen, Bloomington; T, Parks and Recreation Dept, Bloomington; T, Older Am Cen, Bloomington and Unionville.

PIERSOL, VIRGINIA [Print] Prizes: HS, 1968, 69, 71.

PIKER, HELEN B. [P] Monticello, IN.

PILLE, HELEN S. [P] Richmond, IN b. 1906, Richmond, IN.

PIPPENGER, ROBERT [S, Des, C, T] New Hope, PA b. 26 Apr 1912, Nappanee, IN. Studied: John Herron A Sch. Teachers: Donald Mattison; Henrik Mayer; David K. Rubins. Exhibited: Grand Central A Gal, 1937-39; PAFA, 1941; N.J. State M, Trenton, 1945. Prizes: Prix de Rome, 1938; Am Acad Rome; Herron AI, 1938; Ind. State Fair. Collections: S, Plymouth (Ind.) Library; Brookgreen Gardens, SC.

PIRKLE, (H.) B. Rockville, IN d. c. 1970.

PITLUCK, DORRIE [P] Bloomington, IN.

PIUNTI, KATHLEEN [P] Livonia, MI.

PLAAS, JOANNE Terre Haute, IN.

PLASCHKE, PAUL A. [P, Car, I] Chicago, IL b. 2 Feb 1880, Berlin, Germany. Studied: CUASch; ASL. Teachers: G. Luks. Prizes: Richmond (Ind.) AA, 1917; Nashville AA, 1925; HS, 1929, 34, 39; Louisville AA, 1932; SSAL, 1936. Collections: Attica (Ind.) Library; Lexington (Ky.) Library; Speed Mem M and Children's Free Hospital, both in Louisville; Vanderpoel AA. Note: I, humorous drawings for *Life;* Car, *Louisville Times; Chicago Herald Am; Sunday Courier-Journal,* 1913-36.

PLATT, TOM [Dr] Clarksville, IN. Prizes: HS, 1976.

PLATTER, LOUISE M. [P, T] Danville, IN b. Montezuma, IN. Studied: Herron A Sch; John Brady Sch, NC. Teachers: C. Curry Bohm; Hilton Leech; Tony Van Hasselt. Prizes: DePauw U; Swope Gal, Terre Haute; Paris (Ill.) Ann; Herron; Ind. State Fair; Ind. A. Collections: DePauw U; Danville State Bank; Farm Bureau Insurance, Indianapolis.

PLEASANT, GLENNA [Ldscp. P, Genre P, Por. P, T] Kokomo, IN b. 27 Feb 1940, Indianapolis, IN. Studied: Indianapolis AL. Teachers: William Ashby. Exhibited: Ind. State Fair, 1989; Logansport Iron Horse Festival, 1987. Prizes: Tipton Park Festival, 1986; KAA Spring Show, 1986, 87. Collections: Sheraton Inn, Lafayette, IN; St Joseph Hospital, Kokomo, IN.

PLOEGER, DOLORES [P] Evansville, IN b. Clinton, IA. Studied: Escuela Esmeralda, Mexico City; Instituto Allende, San Miguel, Mexico; ASL. Teachers: Don Kingman; Jerry Farnsworth. Exhibited: ASL; Louisville A Cen; Newburgh Gal; Old Gal, Old Nat Bank Building, Evansville, 1965.

PLUMMER, NELL (L.) Gary, IN.

PNEUMAN, MILDRED YOUNG (Mrs. Fred A.) [P, Print] Boulder, CO b. 15 Sep 1899, Oskaloosa, IA. Studied: U of Colo. Teachers: J. Rennell. Exhibited: Philadelphia Color Print Soc, 1945; Denver AM, 1944. Prizes: Gary Civic A Fnd, 1937. Collections: P.E.O. Mem Library, Mt Pleasant, IA.

POE, HUGH M. [P, Por. P] Indianapolis, IN b. 14 Dec 1902, Dallas, TX. Teachers: R. L. Mason; William Forsyth; C. Hawthorne. Prizes: Herron AI AA, 1923, 24; HS, 1925-27, 30, 48. Collections: Herron AI; Knoxville (Tenn.) Sketch Cl; 63 Portraits, Culver Military Acad.

POEHLMANN, THEODORE Indianapolis, IN.

POINTS, JERRY W. [Dr, P, Print, T] Evansville, IN b. 10 May 1942, Evansville. Studied: U of Evansville; Ind. State U; Southern Ill. U. Exhibited: 23rd Ann Wabash Valley Exh, Terre Haute, 1967; 62nd Ann Ind. A Exh, Indianapolis, 1969; Herron M, 1970; IMA, 1971; Louisville Biennial, J. B. Speed A Cen, KY, 1971. Prizes: Evansville M, 1967, 69; Swope Gal, 1968, 70; Mid-States Cr Exh, 1968; Mid-States Exh, 1968; Mid-South Exh, 1969; St Louis Print and Dr Exh, 1972; St Louis Guild Portrait Exh, 1973; Western N.M. U Nat Print Exh, 1973. Collections: Austin Peay U, Clarksville, TN; U of Evansville, Evansville, IN; Swope Gal, Terre Haute, IN; Carroll Reece M, East Tenn. U; Southern Ill. U, Edwardsville, IL. Note: T, Evansville Public Sch; T, U of Evansville; T, Southern Ill. U; T, Belleville Jr. Col, Belleville, IL.

POLK, MARY ALYS [P, I, T] Indianapolis, IN b. 29 Aug 1902, Greenwood, IN. Teachers: William Forsyth. Prizes: HS, 1927.

POLLEY, FREDERICK M. [P, Print, I, W, T] Indianapolis, IN b. 15 Aug 1875, Union City, IN d. 9 Sep 1957, Brown Cnty, IN. Studied: Ind. U; Corcoran A Sch, Washington, D.C. Teachers: James R. Hopkins; William Forsyth. Exhibited: Soc of Etchers, Brooklyn, NY; Philadelphia Soc of Etchers; LOC, 1944, 45; CI, 1945; Delgado M, annually. Prizes: HS, 1942, 43; Ind. AC, 1939, 43, 45; New Orleans AL, 1943; Herron AI, 1934. Collections: Herron AI; Nat M, Washington, D. C.; Iowa State U; U of Pittsburgh; Public Schs, Indianapolis. Note: Author/I, *Our America, Historic Churches in America*. I, *Indianapolis Old and New; Indianapolis Star*, Sundays, 1924-47; *Ladies Home Journal; Esquire*. T, Herron A Sch; T, Ind. U; T, Arsenal Tech H.S., 1917-41. Headed the graphic arts department of Arsenal Tech H.S. for many years.

POLOMCHAK, MARK [P] Crown Point, IN b. c. 1953, Gary, IN. Studied: Franklin Col, Franklin, IN; Ind. U, Bloomington. Teachers: Stephan Polomchak. Exhibited: Gold Coast Show, Chicago; St Joe's Mich. A Show. Prizes: HS, 1976, 82; Tri Kappa Ann, 1973. Note: Son of artist Stephan Polomchak.

POLOMCHAK, STEPHAN [P, T] Crown Point, IN b. c. 1927, NYC. Studied: Mich. State U; Ray Sch Des; AIC. Exhibited: AIC. Prizes: HS, 1965, 73, 74, 76, 82; Northern Ind. AA; Southern Shores; Ind. Women's Lg, Indianapolis. Collections: Tri Kappa; Ind. U; DePaul U; Nat Electric Des Comp. Note: A Dir, Federal Sign&Signal Corp, IL; T, Gary Artist's Lg, Northern Ind. AA. Note: Father of artist Mark Polomchak.

POMPA, GLADYS [P] Muncie, IN b. c. 1898, Muncie d. c. 1980. Studied: YMCA. Collections: Merchants Bank, Muncie. Note: Muncie's first draftsman. Worked at Warner Gear and Muncie Products.

PONADER, LEATHE CARMAN [Ldscp. P, S, T] Valparaiso, IN b. 21 Feb 1891, Perry, MI d. 1977. Studied: AIC; John Herron AI; Boothbay Harbor, ME; Ball State Col. Teachers: Frank Allen; Ernest Thurn; Frederick Grant; Ruth Van Sickle Ford. Note: Supervisor of A, Valparaiso public schs. Later became Leathe Anne Ponader-Worthington.

PONCE, ANN WALLS [P, Por. P] Wilmette, IL. b. Indianapolis, IN. Studied: Ind. U, Bloomington; Rocky Mt Sch A, Denver, CO. Prizes: Governor's Portrait Commission. Collections: Ball State U; Earlham Col; Concordia Theological Seminary, Ft Wayne, IN; Ind. U.

POOL, KAYE [Ldscp. P, SLP, T] Brown Cnty, IN b. Des Moines, IA. Studied: Frederick W. Rigley; Adolph Shulz; Leota Loop; Marilyn Bendell; George Burrows. Exhibited: Ft Wayne Women's Cl; Owen Cnty AL; Ind. State Fair; Tri Kappa, Paoli; IHA. Collections: Vincennes U.

POOR, BARBARA F(uson) [P] Greencastle, IN b. Greencastle, IN. Studied: DePauw U; Famous A Sch. Teachers: Reid Winsey; Floyd Hopper; Jim Hamil. Exhibited: Central Nat Bank, Greencastle, IN, 1978. Collections: Left Bank Gal.

POPE, W. L. [Dr] Fountaintown, IN.

PORTER, ELMER JOHNSON [C, P, Des, T] Cincinnati, OH b. 5 May 1907, Richmond, IN. Studied: AIC; Ohio State U; Earlham Col; Butler U. Exhibited: Columbus AL; Cincinnati. Prizes: Indianapolis AA, 1929; HS, 1939, 40; Richmond, IN, 1929; Ind. Exh, Herron AI, 1929. Collections: Richmond (Ind.) H.S. Coll; Earlham Col; mural, Shrine Temple dining room, Cedar Rapids, IA. Note: T, Hughes H.S., Cincinnati.

PORTER, MARY LOUISE

POSEY, LESLIE T(homas) [S, C, T, Arch, Dec] Sarasota, FL b. 20 Jan 1900, Harshaw, WI. Studied: PAFA; AIC; Wis. Sch F&App A. Teachers: F. Koenig; A. Laessle; C. Grafly; A. Polasek. Exhibited: Fla. Fed A, 1940-44; Sarasota AL, 1940-46. Prizes: Milwaukee AI, 1923; HS, 1931; Fla. Fed A, 1945; Ind. Arch Assn, 1928. Collections: Walker Theater; Granada Theater; Brightwood Community Bldg, Indianapolis. Note: Dir, Posey-Harmes Sch A, Sarasota, FL, 1944-46.

POTTENGER, ZEB E. [P] Richmond, IN.

POULSON, JOSEPHINE HOLLINGSWORTH (*See Hollingsworth, Josephine A.*)

POVALAC, JAN ERRINGTON [P] Ft Wayne, IN.

POWELL, MARGARET W. [Print, SLP] Prizes: HS, 1949, 50.

POWELL, MARTHA L. *(See Horton, Martha Powell)*

POWERS, JANET T. (Tommy) [Ldsp. P, SLP] Pisgah Forest, NC b. 7 Jan 1922, Westfield, NJ. Teachers: Kaye Pool, Nashville, IN. Exhibited: Ind. A, 1972-89. Prizes: Morgan Coal Co, 1983; Indianapolis Power and Light, 1983; James Houstan Purchase, 1983. Collections: Indianapolis Power and Light; Franklin Col; Acme Paving Co, Anderson, IN. Note: Lived for awhile in Fortville, IN.

PRASUHN, JOHN G. [S] Indianapolis, IN b. 25 Dec 1877, near Versailles, OH. Studied: AIC. Teachers: Lorado Taft; Charles J. Mulligan. Prizes: HS, 1927, 38, 39. Collections: Field M Natural History; Lincoln Park, Chicago; Lions on the Taft, Columbus Mem Foundation, Washington, D. C.

PRATT, ROSALIND JEAN [P] Indianapolis, IN.

PRETZ, RICHARD [P] Chicago, IL.

PRICE, CAROLYN [P] Anderson, IN.

PRICE, GENE [P]

PRICE, GLENN Glenview, IL.

PRICE, MARILYN [C, Print, TA, T] Indianapolis, IN b. 1938, Joplin, MO. Studied: Kansas State, Pittsburg, KS; Kansas City AI; U of Tenn. Sch of Cr; Instituto de Allende, Guanajuato, Mexico. Exhibited: Mid-Am Exh, Nelson Gal, Kansas City, MO; Springfield Ann Exh, Springfield, MO; Tippecanoe Reg Exh, Lafayette, IN; Mid-States Exh, Evansville, IN; Wabash Valley Ann, Terre Haute, IN; Ind. Prints, Dr, and WC, IMA; Ind. PM. Prizes: Whitewater Valley Exh, Connersville, IN; Anderson Winter Show, IN; HS, 1970; Indianapolis AL Ann Exh; State Fair FA Exh, Indianapolis. Collections: Kokomo Public Library; Lapel (Ind.) Public Library; Indianapolis Sch #70; Evansville M; IMA; Am States Insurance Co, Indianapolis; Methodist Hospital, Indianapolis. Note: T, Indianapolis AL.

PRICE, ROLLAND

PRILIK, CHARLES RAPHAEL [I, C, Print] Gary, IN/Miller, IN b. 8 Jan 1892, Odessa, Russia. Teachers: Forsberg; Philbrick.

PRITCHARD, RUTH W. [Ldscp. P, SLP] Indianapolis, IN b. 18 Jun 1926, Indianapolis, IN. Studied: Herron Sch A. Teachers: Edmund Brucker; R. B. Beck; Clifton Wheeler. Exhibited: Ind. State Fair; Ind. A. Prizes: HS, 1987. Collections: Indianapolis Power and Light; City of Franklin, IN.

PROUT, G(eorge) MORTON [P, Gra. A, I] Columbus, IN b. 1 Sep 1913, St Francisville, IL. Studied: Herron AI; PAFA. Teachers: Donald M. Mattison; Henrik M. Mayer; Alan Tompkins; David K. Rubins. Exhibited: Grand Central Gal, 1938; GGE, 1939. Prizes: Herron A Sch, 1939; Prix de Rome, 1938; Ind. A Ann, Herron AM, 1938. Collections: Herron AI.

PROW, HALLIE PACE (Mrs. Fred) [P, Ldscp. P, SLP] Bloomington, IN b. 25 Apr 1868, Salem, IN d. 11 Dec 1945. Studied: Herron AI; Ind. U, Bloomington. Teachers: Robert E. Burke; Tempe Tice; William Forsyth; Anna Hasselman; Blanche Stillson; Carl C. Graf; L. O. Griffith. Exhibited: Louisville; Tipton; Franklin; Ind. AC; Pettis Gal, Indianapolis; Salem (solo). Collections: Salem (Ind.) Public Library and Schs; Bloomfield H.S.; Principia Col, St Louis.

PRUITT, VERNISE IRENE Grand Rapids, MI.

PUCKETT, HENRY (Frank) [Por. P, Print, T] Chicago, IL b. 10 Aug 1914, Chicago. Studied: AIC. Teachers: Wellington J. Reynolds; James Swann; Albert Krehbiel; Antonin Sterba. Collections: St Procopius Abbey, Lisle, IL; Juvenile Court Bldg, Cook Cnty, IL; state of Ill. Note: T, Austin Evening H.S., Chicago.

PUTNAM, FANNY GIBBS Mt Carmel, IN.

PUTTY, HELEN [P] New Palestine, IN.

Q

QUAKENBUSH, SHIRLEY [P] Russiaville, IN b. 31 Oct 1927, Michigan City, IN. Studied: St Francis Sch A, Lafayette; Indianapolis AL. Teachers: Paul Sweany; Sister Rufinia. Exhibited: Northern Ind. AA. Prizes: Kokomo AA, 1989-91; Indianapolis AL Student Show, 1990, 91.

QUEAR, EDNA [P] Carmel, IN. Deceased. Studied: Indianapolis AL. Teachers: Ruth Anderson.

QUILLIN, EMERSON [Silkscreen]

QUILLIN, WILLIAM [P]

R

RAADE, KAY [P, Dr, C] Crawfordsville, IN b. MT. Studied: Mont. State U; Portland State U. Exhibited: Ind. State Fair, 1981. Prizes: Sugar Creek Juried A Show, 1979.

RAEMAEKERS, ANTOINE (Antonius) [P] Martinsville, IN b. Holland. Studied: Académie Royale des Beaux-Arts, Liège, Belgium. Teachers: Henri Jones.

RAFERT, MILLIE [MM] Pendleton, IN.

RAINEY, JUDITH A. [Fiber A] Franklin, IN b. 10 Mar 1955, Marion, IN. Studied: Ball State U. Teachers: Roberta Law; Marvin Reichle; Thomas Spoerner. Exhibited: Ind. A Show, 1983; Wabash Valley Exh, 1983, 86, 88, 90; Mid-States Cr Exh, 1988, 91. Prizes: Ind. State Fair, 1981, 82, 91, 92; Mid-States Cr Exh, 1985; IHA, 1984, 86-89. Collections: Rose-Hulman Inst Technology.

RAMSEY, SHERI J. [P] Indianapolis, IN. Exhibited: 12th Ann Benedictine A.

RANDALL, PAUL A. [Ldscp. P] Indianapolis, IN b. 28 Sep 1879, Warsaw, Poland d. 19 May 1933. Studied: Herron AI. Teachers: William Forsyth; Clifton A. Wheeler.

RANDALL, THEODORE [S] Indianapolis, IN. Prizes: HS, 1933.

RANS, JON W. [P] Nashville, IN.

RANSTEAD, PEARL Wilmette, IL.

RARICK, DOROTHY [Ldscp. P, SLP, Por. P] Nashville, IN. d. 18 Nov 1986. Exhibited: Brown Cnty A Gal.

RATLIFF, LOUISE G. [S] b. Indianapolis, IN. Studied: Manual H.S., Indianapolis. Teachers: Otto Stark; Estelle Igor; William Kaeger. Prizes: Indianapolis ASL; John Herron AM.

RATLIFF, PAT STAPF [P, Dr, Print] Indianapolis, IN. Studied: Purdue U; Prado MA, Madrid, Spain. Exhibited: Central Library, Indianapolis, 1982.

RAY, MELVILLE

RAYMOND, JO GREENE (See Greene, Jo)

REARICK, RUSSELL Detroit, MI.

REASON, MARILOU SMITH [P, Primitive A] Logansport, IN b. 21 May 1937, Logansport. Self-taught. Exhibited: Ind. State Fair, 1989; Logansport Public Library (solo), 1990. Prizes: Logansport Spring A Fair, 1988, 89. Collections: Logansport Public Library; Logansport H.S.

REASONER, DAVID [Por. P, Ldscp. P] Woodstock, NY b. Upland, IN. Teachers: Frank Benson; Phillip Hale; Abbott H. Thayer.

RECTOR, DONNA [SLP, P] Anderson, IN. Prizes: HS, 1961.

REDICK, JOHN [P] Valparaiso, IN.

REDICK, PAMELA LANG [P] Valparaiso, IN. Prizes: HS, 1975.

REDMAN, STEVEN [P, S] Indianapolis, IN b. 1 Jan 1944, Poseyville, IN. Studied: Herron Sch A; Ind. U; ASL. Teachers: Robert Berkshire; William Crutchfield; Arnold Blanch; Henry H. Smith. Exhibited: Mid-States Exh, Evansville, IN, 1983. Prizes: 64th Ind. A Exh, IMA, 1971; HS, 1990; Ind. State Fair, 1990. Collections: Bank One of Indianapolis; Sheldon Swope Gal, Terre Haute, IN; Melvin Simon & Assocs; Ind. U MFA.

REED, DOEL [Print, P, T, W] Taos, NM b. 21 May 1894, Logansport, IN. Studied: Cincinnati A Acad; France; Mexico. Teachers: Meakin; Hopkins; Wessel. Exhibited: SAE, 1930-46; 100 Etchings of the Year, 1932-44; NAD, 1934-46; CI, 1941; CGA, 1940; WMMA, 1942; AIC, 1934, 37, 39; 50 Am Prints, 1944; LOC, 1944-46; PAFA, 1944, 45; Herron AI, 1943; MMA, 1942; Paris Salon, 1937; Rome, Italy, 1937; Venice, Italy, 1940. Prizes: Philadelphia Print Cl, 1940; Chicago SE, 1938; Currier Gal A, 1942; Northwest Pr. M, 1942, 44; Tulsa AA, 1935; Philbrook A Cen, 1944; Laguna Beach AA, 1944; SSAL, 1944; Oakland A Gal, 1945; Kansas City AI, 1932. Collections: MFA, Houston; U of Mont.; U of Tulsa; Grinnell Col; Southern Methodist U; Okla. A Cen; Okla. AL; murals, Okla. State Office Bldg; Oklahoma City. Note: Author, *Doel Reed Makes an Aquatint*, 1967. T, Okla. A&M Col, 1942-59.

REED, FORREST J. [Dec] Logansport, IN b. 1907, Logansport. Studied: Ind. U; Ball State U. Prizes: Ind.

State Fair; Ind. A; Logansport A Show. Collections: Logansport Public Library; Calvary Presbyterian Church of Logansport.

REED, MATTHEW M. [P] b. 1958, Lafayette, IN. Studied: Ind. U. Exhibited: Washington Gal, Indianapolis, 1978; Art 500, Indianapolis AL, 1978; Mid-States Exh, Evansville, 1976, 78; Wells Library (solo), Lafayette. Prizes: Whitewater Valley Ann, Richmond, IN, 1978. Note: Son of artists Robert Browning Reed and Luanne I. Reed.

REED, MAY [Cer] Indianapolis, IN. Studied: Herron Sch A. Note: Worked in display department, Wm. H. Block Co, Indianapolis.

REED, ROBERT BROWNING [Print, P] Lafayette, IN b. 26 Feb 1922, Marion, IN. Studied: Ind. U; Escuela De Pintura&Escultura, Mexico, D. F. Exhibited: L. S. Ayres, 1948; Print Exh, Rochester, NY, 1947, 48; A.C.A. Gal, NYC, 1949; 1st Ind. Print Ann, Ind. U, 1948; 50 Ind. Prints, 1952. Note: Head of printmaking at Purdue U. Father of artist Matthew M. Reed.

REENTS, HENRY A. [Ldscp. P] Michigan City, IN b. 25 Mar 1892, Chicago. Studied: AIC. Teachers: A. Fleury; Edward Timmons; Carl Buhr. Collections: H.S.s in Harford, MI and Rockford, IL. Note: One of the founders, Businessmen's AC of Chicago.

REEVE, KENNETH J. [P, Ldscp. P, Print] Brown Cnty, IN b. Western Springs, IL. Studied: Chicago Acad of FA (graduated 1930). Exhibited: Brown Cnty A Gal; Tri-State Exh; Michiana Reg; Philadelphia Sketch Cl; U.S. Nat M; IHA; Wichita AL Am Graphics. Prizes: HS; Ind. State Fair; Ind. AC. Note: Worked in Chicago, 1930-49, artist and art director in advertising agencies. Produced a book on Brown Cnty cemeteries for the Brown Cnty Historical Society.

REEVES, LARRY GENE [P, T] Kentland, IN b. 10 Jul 1936, Huntington, IN. Studied: Ball State U. Teachers: Alice Nichols; Dr. Storey. Exhibited: Newton Cnty Fair, 1983. Prizes: First Premium A Show, 1983. Collections: Victory Knoll Chapel, Huntington, IN; Christian Church, Brook, IN.

REEVES, PAUL B. [P] Ft Lauderdale, FL b. 2 Apr 1889, Columbus, IN d. 25 Mar 1971. Studied: Herron AI; AIC; Robert Chase A Sch; Long Boat Key A Sch. Teachers: C. Curry Bohm; Eliot O'Hara; John Chetuti; Robert Chase; John Pike. Exhibited: Brown Cnty AG. Note: Retired industrialist. Mrs. Reeves dedicated a room to her husband in Brown Cnty AG, upstairs gallery.

REGAN, MARY [Ldscp. P] Lake Cicott, IN b. 27 Aug 1921, Logansport, IN. Teachers: Ray Loos; George Cherepou; Raleigh Kinney; Paul Sweany; Henry Bell. Exhibited: Edson Gal (solo), Logansport, 1988-89; Logansport Bicentennial, 1980. Prizes: Logansport, 1988; Winamac, 1986. Collections: Edson Gal and MacHale Auditorium, both Logansport.

REGESTER, ALICE (Mrs. Frank) [Ldscp. P, SLP] Bloomington, IN b. 16 Nov 1868, Morgan Cnty, IN d. 5 Mar 1952. Studied: Herron Sch A; Ind. U. Teachers: William Forsyth; Robert E. Burke; Harry Engel; L. O. Griffith; Anna Hasselman.

REIBEL, BERTRAM [Print, S, C] Chicago, IL b. 14 Jun 1901, New York, NY. Studied: AIC. Teachers: A. Archipenko. Exhibited: NAD; Intl PM; PAFA; MMA; CM; Oakland A Gal; Northwest PM; AIC; Kansas City AI; Detroit IA; Southern PM.

REICHARD, JOEL WARNER [P, Por. P, Ldscp. P] Silver Springs, FL b. 5 Dec 1909, Bourbon, IN. Studied: John Herron AI; AIC. Teachers: William Forsyth; Geisberg; Arsfeld; Jerry Farnsworth; Helen Sawyer; Robert Brackman. Exhibited: WC USA; AM WCS; South-Eastern Exh; AIC; Nat Acad; Smithsonian Inst; John Herron AI; High MA, Atlanta. Prizes: HS, 1946, 48, 50-55, 57-59, 61, 63-65, 68-70, 73, 79; Grand Central Gal, NYC. Collections: Ind. U; U of Fla.; DePauw U; Ind. State U; Sheldon Swope Gal, Terre Haute, IN; Loch Haven A Cen, Orlando, FL; Cummer Gal, Jacksonville, FL.

REID, JOANNE (F.) [P] Martinsville, IN.

REIDER, JOHN HENRY Indianapolis, IN.

REIFERS, ANNE d. c. 1969.

REIFFEL, CHARLES [Ldscp. P] San Diego, CA (since 1925) b. 9 Apr 1862, Indianapolis, IN d. 1942. Primarily self-taught. Teachers: C. von Marr, Munich, Germany. Exhibited: CAFA, 1920; Intl Expo, Pittsburg, 1922. Prizes: Buffalo SA, 1908; AIC, 1917; HS, 1925-28, 31, 38; Los Angeles M, 1926, 29; San Diego FA Gal, 1926, 27; Calif. AC, 1928; Sacramento AC, 1928, 30; John Herron AI, 1929; Richmond AA, 1930; Painters of the West, 1930; Pasadena A Gal, 1930; Los Angeles Exh, 1932. Collections: CGA; San Diego FA Gal; Santa Cruz AL; Mun Gal, Phoenix, AZ; Wood A Gal, Montpelier, VT; Los Angeles M; Herron AI.

REINES, BRUCE [S] b. c. 1958. Studied: North Central H.S., Indianapolis. Exhibited: Stouffer's Inn, 1979; Penrod Festival A, IMA. Prizes: Nichols Conn. A Show, 1973-75; Fairfield A Show, 1974; HS, 1980. Collections: Presidential Commemorative, Bicentennial; Nathan Hale Statue, State of Conn.; Art Foundry, Norwalk, Conn; General Electric.

REITH, LYLE [P, Print, Photo, Com. A] Marion, IN b. 1898, Marion d. 1979. Self-taught. Prizes: Nappanee, IN; Rochester, IN; Fairborn, OH, 1972, 73; Grant Cnty AC. Collections: Kokomo Library.

REITZEL, MARQUES E. [P, Print, T, I] San Jose, CA b. 13 Mar 1896, Fulton, IN. Studied: ASL; Ohio State U; AIC; Cleveland Col, Western Reserve U. Teachers: C. Buehr; Foster; Leopold Seyffert; G. Bellows; J. A. St John; Leon Kroll; James R. Hopkins. Exhibited: CI, 1929; CGA, 1929; PAFA, 1928, 29, 31; AIC, 1929, 31, 34; CMA, 1931; All-Calif. Exh, 1940, 41, 44; Oakland A Gal, 1941-43; CGE, 1939. Prizes: AIC, 1927, 28; HS, 1929, 40; Century of Progress, Chicago, 1934; San Jose AL, 1940, 41; Chicago Gal Assn, 1937, 43. Collections: Chicago Mun Coll for public schs; Chicago Public Schs; Hobart (Ind.) H.S.; Rockford Col; Dakota Boys' Sch; H.S. Rockford, IL; Belvidere Women's Col; Colo. State TC. Note: T, Rockford Col, Rockford, IL; Dir, Rockford AM; T, San Jose State Col.

REMLEY, ROXIE [Ab, P] Statesboro, GA b. 2 Oct 1910, Darlington, IN. Studied: Peabody Col, Vanderbilt U; Pratt Inst, NY; John Herron Sch A; Kennedy Sch A, Cape Cod. Teachers: Ernest Briggs; George MacNeil; Robert Richenburg. Exhibited: High M, Atlanta, GA; Soc of Four A, Palm Beach. Prizes: HS, 1971; Okefenokee Heritage Ann, 1986; Chattanooga; Macon, GA; Palm Beach; Winston-Salem; Evansville, IN; Nashville, TN. Collections: Ga. Col M; Stetson U; Ga. Southern U Library; Reg Library, Statesboro, GA. Note: Professor of A, Ga. Southern Col, 25 years.

RENNER, CHARLES H.

RENT, WILLIAM A(ustin) [P, Mur. P] Indianapolis, IN. Studied: John Herron A Sch. Exhibited: Penrod A Festival, IMA, 1990; Central Library, Indianapolis, 1986, 90; IMA, 1981; Ind. State Fair, 1960, 72, 74, 75. Prizes: Coalition of 100 Black Women, 1988; Ind. Black Expo, 1972; Ind. State Fair, 1969, 70, 71. Collections: New Liberty Missionary Baptist Church, Indianapolis.

REVEAL, JAMES RODNEY [P] Noblesville, IN.

REX, RUBY M. Anderson, IN.

REYNERSON, JUNE Terre Haute, IN.

RHOADES, JACK [Com. A] Indianapolis, IN.

RICH, GEORGE [Por. P, Ldscp. P] Chicago, IL b. 14 Nov 1891, Connersville, IN. Studied: AIC. Teachers: Harry Mills Walcott. Prizes: John Quincy Adams Foreign Scholarship, AIC, 1914; HS, 1926.

RICHARDS, MYRA REYNOLDS [S, P, T] Indianapolis, IN b. 31 Jan 1882, Indianapolis d. 28 Dec 1934, NYC. Studied: Herron AI. Teachers: J. Ottis Adams; R. Schwarz; G. J. Zolnay; Otto Stark; William Forsyth; Clifton Wheeler. Collections: statue, Greenfield, IN; bust, Ind. State Library, Indianapolis; Columbus (Ind.) H.S.; fountain figures, University Park, Indianapolis; Turkey Run State Park. Note: T, John Herron AI.

RICHARDS, VIOLET LINSON Hot Springs, AR b. 25 Aug 1908, Indianapolis, IN. Studied: Ind. Central U; Herron Sch A. Prizes: Southside AL; Red Mill Show, Boggstown; Southern A Show; Sun Festival Show, Hot Springs. Collections: FA Gal, Hot Springs; Bellevedere Country Cl, Hot Springs; Coronada Cen, Hot Springs; Desota Cen, Hot Springs. Note: Worked for 15 years at Am A Clay Co, Ind.

RICHARDSON, CONSTANCE COLEMAN (Mrs. E. P.) [P] Philadelphia, PA b. 18 Jan 1905, Indianapolis, IN. Studied: Vassar Col; PAFA. Exhibited: Detroit AI, 1945; AIC, 1940, 41, 45; CI, 1941, 43-45; CGA, 1945; WMAA, 1944, 45; PAFA, 1944, 45; Critics Choice, CM, 1945; Schaeffer Gal, NY, 1938; WFNY, 1939; Golden Gate Expo, 1939. Prizes: Mich. A Ann, 1937; Detroit AI, 1938. Collections: John Herron AI; Detroit AI; PAFA; Grand Rapids AM; New Britian Inst. Note: Lived also in Detroit, MI.

RICHARDSON, ESTHER RUBLE [P, T] Lockport, IL b. 8 Jun 1895, Nevada, MO. Studied: U of Chicago; AIC; Chicago Acad FA. Teachers: M. Sheets; F. M. Ganet; Walter Sargent. Exhibited: AIC, 1934-41; PAFA, 1935; Chicago Gal Assn; O'Brien's Gal, Chicago; Tower Town Gal, Chicago. Prizes: HS, 1941; Ill. Soc FA, 1936. Collections: Ill. Public Sch; Public Library, Iola, Kan. Note: T, Joilet H.S.&Jr. Col.

RICHARDSON, LaMONTA [P]

RICHARDSON, MILDRED [P] Plainfield, IN. Teachers: Luke Buck. Exhibited: Brown Cnty A Gal (solo), 1982.

RICHEY, OAKLEY E. [P, T, C, W] Indianapolis, IN b. 24 Mar 1902, Hancock Cnty, IN d. 20 Sep 1971. Studied: John Herron A Sch; Grand Central Sch A; ASL. Teachers: Frank V. DuMond; George B. Bridgeman; Willy Pogany. Exhibited: Herron AM; N.Y. Municipal Ann. Prizes: HS, 1948, 50, 53. Collections: Ball State Col; Colo. U; Purdue U; Richmond (Ind.) AA; Public Sch in Lafayette and Connersville. Note: T, Herron Sch A, 1924-35; T, Arsenal

Tech Sch; Director, FA Exh, Ind. State Fair, 1933-37; Lecturer, Ind. U.

RICHMAN, JEANNE P. [Ab, Dr, Ldscp. P, Por. P, Print, T] Indianapolis, IN b. 11 Jul 1928, Washington, PA d. 5 March 1993. Studied: Ohio State U; Herron Sch A; Northwestern U. Teachers: Edmund Brucker; Harry Davis; Sarah Burns; Robert Eagerton. Exhibited: Tippecanoe Reg; IMA Landmarks II; Ind. Fed A. Prizes: Ind. AC; Mid-States Exh; Ind. State Fair; A Religious Exh; Indianapolis AL; Ohio Graphic&Print.

RICHMAN, MARGARET A. VOGEL [Por. P] Lebanon, IN b. 26 Oct 1919, Evansville, IN. Studied: Herron Sch A; Georgetown Col, Lexington, KY; Indianapolis AL. Teachers: William Crutchfield; Edward Manetta; Elizabeth Schaeffer. Exhibited: Ind. State Fair; Indianapolis AL.

RIDGWAY, MARIFRANCES Indianapolis, IN b. IN. Studied: Dayton AI, Dayton, OH; Indianapolis AL. Exhibited: Mid-Am Nat A Exh, Owensboro, KY, 1980; Nat Dr&Small S Show, Ball State U, Muncie, IN, 1974; Works on Paper, Louisville AA, 1977; Tippecanoe Reg, Lafayette A Cen, 1968, 69, 71, 75, 77, 79; Whitewater Valley Ann Dr, Painting, Print Comp, Ind. U-East, Richmond, IN. Prizes: 38th Ann Ind. AC Exh, 1970, 73; Dayton Col, 1976; Nat Lg Am Pen Women's Ind. State Exh, 1980, 81. Collections: Ind. State U, Terre Haute; Grain Dealers Mutual Insurance Co, Indianapolis; Litho Press Inc, Indianapolis; Johnson Cnty Mem Hospital.

RIFFLE, ELBA L(ouisa) *(See Vernon, Elba Riffle)* [P, S] Indianapolis, IN b. 3 Jan 1906, Winamac, IN d. 8 Jul 1980. Studied: John Herron AI; Ind. U; Purdue U. Teachers: William Forsyth; Clifton Wheeler; Oakley Richey; Paul Hadley; Myra Richards. Exhibited: Ind. AC. Prizes: Northern Ind. A, 1931; Midwestern Exh, Wichita, KS, 1932; Ind. State Fair, 1930-32, 34, 35, 38. Collections: Christian Church, Winamac, IN; H.S., Winamac; Public Libraries, Winamac and Tipton; Ind. U; Women's Cl, Clay City, IN.

RIFNER, BEN O. [P, T] Lafayette, IN b. 26 May 1915, New Castle, IN. Studied: Ball State TC; Ohio State U; Herron Sch A. Teachers: Barbara Gersham; Dora Hegge; Garo Antreasian. Exhibited: Ind. WCS, 1956, 86(Pr); Ind. Now, Lafayette MA, 1986, 88, 89, 90. Collections: Lafayette Bank and Trust.

RIGLEY, FREDERICK W. [Ldscp. P, T] Nashville, IN. b. 1 Jul 1914, Owosso, MI. Studied: ASL; Ringling Sch A and Hilton Leech Sch, Sarasota, FL. Teachers: Adrian Pillars; Enrique Elferez; Emile A. Gruppe; Hilton Leech; John F. Carlson; Floyd Hopper; George Bridgman. Exhibited: Naples AA, 1980-82; North Shore AA, 1944-51. Prizes: HS, 1954, 58, 61, 77, 85; Ind. AC; Realist Cl, Terre Haute; Ind. State Fair; Wabash Valley Exh; Ft Wayne Women's Cl; Eastern Shore AA; Fairhope AL; North Shore AA, Gloucester; Ind. Heritage; Sarasota AA. Collections: Ind. Nat Bank; Indianapolis Public Schs; U of Delaware; Nat Bank, Easton, OH; Delco Remy and Guide Lamp, divisions of General Motors; Eastern Shore AA, AL.

RIGSBY, JON Evansville, IN b. 4 May 1925, Evansville. Studied: U of Wis.; Evansville M. Exhibited: Evansville; Madison, WI; KY; New Zealand; Australia; Germany. Collections: Mead Johnson Co.

RILEY, HARRIETT F. [P] Chicago, IL.

RITZ, JO [P, Dr] Evansville, IN b. Mexico. Studied: Otis AI; U of Evansville; Ind. State U. Teachers: Frederic Taubes;

Ray French; Bud Shackleford. Exhibited: Evansville; Terre Haute; MI; IL. Prizes: Bloomington; Terre Haute.

RITZI, ELLEN (N.) Greenwood, IN.

ROBBINS, BELLE BOGARDUS [Ldscp. P, Cer] b. 1888, Indianapolis, IN. Studied: Manual Training H.S.; TC, Indianapolis. Teachers: Otto Stark; Sister Rufinia. Exhibited: 7th Ann Exh, Lafayette AA, 1939. Prizes: Local A Show, GLMA, 1950. Collections: YWCA, Lafayette, IN.

ROBERTS, EDWARD J. [P] Indianapolis, IN.

ROBERTS, GEORGINA F.

ROBERTS, HERMINE (Maltilde) [Gra. A, P, Print, T] Billings, MT b. 6 Dec 1892, Cleveland, OH d. Mar 1962. Studied: App A Sch, Chicago; U of Ore.; Herron A Sch; Ind. U. Teachers: William Forsyth; E. Steinhof; Clifton Wheeler; Pedro Lemos; Karl Bolander. Note: Author, course of art study for Jr. H.S., state of Mont. T, Eastern Mont. State Normal Sch; Herron AI.

ROBERTS, J. ANNA [P] Brownsburg, IN b. 9 Jun 1953, Columbus, IN. Teachers: Rosemary Lawton Thomas. Exhibited: Wabash (solo), 1987. Prizes: HS, 1984; Anderson Winter Show, 1989; Ind. WCS. Collections: Kokomo Library; Cummins Engine; Anderson MFA.

ROBERTS, PATRICIA M.

ROBERTSON, DONALD L. [S] Indianapolis, IN. b. Indianapolis. Exhibited: Glendale Mall, 1972. Collections: Ind. U Law Sch; General Motors; Ford Motor Co; Keystone at the Crossing. Note: Started D. R. Design.

ROBERTSON, W(illiam) A. [S] Nashville, IN b. Ft Wayne, IN. Self-taught. Exhibited: Wabash Col; Ind. U; Franklin Col; Ind. Central U. Prizes: Ball State Dr&S, 1959; John Herron M, 1959; Ind. A, IMA, 1971. Collections: Ball State U; Swope M.

ROBINSON, R. H. [Por. P] Wolcott, IN.

ROCKE, GILBERT Chicago, IL.

RODGERS, DAVID L. [S] Bloomington, IN. Exhibited: Indianapolis AL, Claypool Court, Indianapolis. Prizes: HS, 1978. Note: President, Metaforms, Inc.

ROESENER, ELIZABETH TAUER Indianapolis, IN.

ROGERS, NELLE C. [P] Oak Park, IL. d. c. 1951.

ROHRMAN, JOE [S, Cer, T] Indianapolis, IN b. 17 Jan 1950, Indianapolis. Studied: Herron AI. Teachers: Harry Davis; Edmund Brucker. Exhibited: Middle Tenn. State U, 1989; Springfield, IL (Two-Person), 1990; Carlyn Gal (solo), NYC, 1988; Clayfest, Herron Sch A, 1988; Ruschman A Gal (Two-Person), Indianapolis, 1988. Prizes: Galeria Mesa, 1989; Art Forms '88, Lafayette M; Swope Gal, Terre Haute, IN; 39th Ann Wabash Valley Exh, 1983; HS, 1981. Collections: Sheldon Swope A Gal; McDonald's Corp. Note: T, Franklin Township Com Sch Corp, Acton, IN.

ROLLF, E. FIRTH [P] Richmond, IN.

ROOSE, ERNEST R. [P] b. Omaha, NE d. c. 1954, airplane crash. Studied: Am Acad, Chicago; AIC. Prizes: HS, 1944-48, 51, 54. Note: V.P., Keeling Co. Painted winners of Indianapolis 500 for L. Strauss.

ROPKEY, ERNEST C. [P] Indianapolis, IN b. McCordsville, IN. Teachers: T. C. Steele; William Forsyth; C. Curry Bohm. Exhibited: Herron AM; Ind. AC.

ROSE, PATRICIA E.

ROSEBROCK, WAHNITA C. [MM] Scottsburg, IN.

ROSENTHAL, NANCY GLOH Indianapolis, IN. Prizes: HS, 1971.

ROSS, CHARLES A.

ROSS, JOHN FREDERIC [P, T] Ft Wayne, IN b. 14 Jun 1912, Urbana, IL. Studied: John Herron A Sch; St Francis Col, Ft Wayne; Ft Wayne AI. Teachers: John von Wicht; William Thon. Exhibited: St Francis Col (solo), 1965; Ind. A Exh, Herron MA, 1954, 56, 59, 60-62; Ind. AC Ann Exh, 1955, 56, 58-62; Ft Wayne AM (solo), 1978. Prizes: Montpelier AA Ann, Montpelier, OH, 1961; Thieme A, Ft Wayne AI, 1972; HS, 1955; Ind. State Fair, 1952; Van Wert Ann Exh, 1961. Note: Curator, Ft Wayne AM, 1957-64.

ROSS, JOSEPH [Dr] Indianapolis, IN. Note: Employed by Handley & Miller Advertising Agency. Created cover, 1966 "500 Festival" souvenir program.

ROSSER, DONNA (Mrs. Richard) [P] Greencastle, IN. Studied: Ohio Wesleyan. Exhibited: Left Bank Gal (solo), Greencastle, 1979; DePauw A Gal (solo), 1984. Prizes: HS, 1985, 86. Note: Husband Richard Rosser was president of DePauw U.

ROTH, AMANDA

ROTHENBERGER, GARY L.

ROUSH, (Emma) CATHERINE [P, T] Morgantown, IN b. Brown Cnty, IN. Deceased. Studied: Ind. U; Europe. Teachers: Florentine Antonietti. Exhibited: Bradenton A Gal, Bradenton, FL. Prizes: Morgan Cnty Fall Foliage Festival A Show, 1974. Note: Had studio in Morgantown until her death. Specialized in floral studies.

ROUSH, J(esse) J. [P] Morgantown, IN. d. c. 1962.

ROYCE, JAN [Por. P, T] Indianapolis, IN b. 11 Nov 1946, Chicago, IL. Studied: Am Acad A, Chicago; AIC; Ind. U, Bloomington; Herron Sch A. Teachers: Ronald Markman; Robert Eagerton; Peg Fierke. Exhibited: Ind. AC, 1989; Boundaries Dr Exh, Herron Gal, 1989; Clowes Hall Exh, 1989. Prizes: Finalist, Governor's Portrait Commission, 1990; Emerging Woman A, 1987; Logo Des, Ind. Psychiatric Soc, 1987. Collections: Ind. Insurance Guaranty Corp, Indianapolis; Administrative Offices, IUPUI; Indianapolis City-Cnty Bldg.

ROYER, CATHERINE MILLS [P, T] Indianapolis, IN b. 1954, Peru, IN. Studied: Ball State U, Muncie, IN; Butler U, Indianapolis; Herron Sch A; Indianapolis AL. Exhibited: 69th Ind. A, IMA, 1983; Evansville M, 1983; Wabash Valley Exh, Sheldon Swope Gal, Terre Haute, IN, 1980; Dr&Small S, Ball State U A Gal, 1980; A 500, Indianapolis AL, 1980; Carmel Public Library (solo), Carmel, IN. Prizes: Ind. State Fair, 1981; HS, 1984.

ROYSTER, (Sr.), GEORGE M. Evansville, IN.

RUBENKOENIG, IRMA West Lafayette, IN b. Clebune, TX. Teachers: L. O. Griffith; V. J. Cariani. Exhibited: Ind. AC; Swope Gal; Purdue U.

RUBINS, DAVID K(resz) [S, Print, T, W] Indianapolis, IN b. 5 Sep 1902, Minneapolis, MN d. c. 1985. Studied: Dartmouth Col; BAID; École des Beaux-Arts, Paris, France; Académie Julian; Am Acad Rome. Teachers: J. E. Fraser. Exhibited: MMA, 1951; NAD, 1932; Ind. A, 1936, 38, 40, 42, 44, 46. Prizes: HS, 1942, 44; Sagamore of the

Wabash, 1964; Paris Prize, S, 1924; Prix de Rome, 1928; N.Y. Arch Lg, 1931; Ind. A Ann, Herron AM, 1935-40. Collections: IMA; Minneapolis IA; John Herron AI; Ind. U; Archives Bldg, Washington, D.C.; USPO, Courthouse, Indianapolis; WPA artist. Note: T, Herron A Sch; Head of Sculpture Dept until 1968. Author, *The Human Figure—An Anatomy for Artists,* 1953.

RUDDER, STEPHEN W(illiam) D(ouglas) [P, I, Print, W] Salem, IN b. 12 May 1906, Salem d. 27 Dec 1932, Chicago, IL. Studied: AIC. Teachers: Allen Philbrick; Antonin Sterba; Elmer Forsberg; F. DeForest Schook; Laura Van Pappelendam. Exhibited: AIC, 1925-27; ASL of Chicago, 1926, 27; Herron AI, 1928; Ind. AA. Note: Admitted to ASL of Chicago, an honorary organization.

RUDIN, ALBERT [Dr] Chicago, IL.

RUDMAN, JOAN COMBS [Ab, Ldscp. P, P, Genre P, T] Stamford, CT b. 7 Oct 1927, Owensburg, IN. Studied: Cincinnati AM; Mich. State U, East Lansing, MI. Teachers: Edgar A. Whitney; Walter DuBois Richards; Charles Reid; Diana Kan. Exhibited: NAD, 1986; Am WCS, 1974; Nat AC, NYC; Hudson Valley AA. Prizes: Pen Arts Grant, 1984; Pen&Brush Cl, NYC; Nat AL; Whiskey Painters of Am; HS, 1976. Collections: Combe Incorp, West Chester, NY; Kresge M; Mich. State U.

RUDOLPH, JOAN V.

RUEFF, JINI [Por. P, Figure P] Elkhart, IN b. 25 Dec 1928, Ames, IA. Studied: Goshen Col; Kansas U; Ind. U, South Bend. Teachers: Harold Zisla; Frederick Rigley; Charles Movalli; Albert Handell; Abner Hershberger. Exhibited: Five State Pastel Comp, Krasl A Cen, St Joseph, MI, 1989. Prizes: Midwest M Am A, 1990; Elkhart AL, 1988, 89. Collections: Bradley Vite FA, Elkhart, IN.

RUEL, TED [P] Logansport, IN.

RUMLEY, LUCILLE [P, T] Hagerstown, IN b. 9 Aug 1901, Preble Cnty, OH. Teachers: Marston D. Hodgin; John M. King; Guy Wiggins. Exhibited: Richmond AA, 1932; CAFA, 1933; Herron AI (solo), 1934.

RUNDELL, ORA E. [MM] New Richmond, IN.

RUSH, OLIVE [I, P, Por. P, Mur. P, T] Santa Fe, NM, b. 10 Jun 1873, Rush Hill (near Fairmont), IN d. 20 Aug 1966. Studied: Earlham Col; Corcoran Sch A; ASL; Howard Pyle Sch; Boston M Sch. Teachers: Frank Benson; William Paxton; John Elwood Bundy; John Twachtman; Augustus St. Gaudens; Henry Siddons Mowbray; Richard E. Miller. Exhibited: World's Columbian Expo, Chicago, 1893; CGA, 1912, 23-24; AIC, 1916; St Louis AM, 1917, 19; CI, 1911; Mus N.M., 1921, 26; Richmond AA, 1919; Denver, 1931; La. Purchase Exh, St Louis, MO, 1904; Lewis&Clark Centennial Expo, Portland, OR, 1905; MFA, NM (solo), Santa Fe, 1914, 57; Ferargil Gal (solo), NY, 1928; Allerton Gal (solo), Chicago, 1928; U of Colo. (solo), Boulder, 1936; Herron AI (solo), 1939; N.M. AL, Albuquerque, 1964. Prizes: HS, 1926, 30, 31, 49; Herron AI, 1919; Neb. AA; Wilmington Soc FA; Corcoran Sch A, 1892. Collections: WMA; BM; PMG; John Herron AI; Wilmington Soc FA; Witte Mem M; Neb AA; Sheldon A Gal, U of Neb, Lincoln; Mills Col, Oakland, CA; Glenbow M, Calgary (Alberta), Canada; Fairmount Public Library; MFA, Santa Fe, NM; murals, La Fonda Hotel&Public Library, Santa Fe; WPA murals, USPOs, Florence, CO and Pawhuska, OK; Phillips Coll, Washington, D.C.; Earlham Col, Richmond, IN. Note: Staff A, *New York Tribune,* beginning1897. T, U of Neb, 1922-23. I, *Collier's, Scribner's.* T, U of Neb., 1922-23. Received honorary degree of Doctor of FA, Earlham Col, Richmond, IN, 1947. Founding member, Women A Exhibiting Group, Santa Fe, 1949.

RUTSCHMANN, NANCY ANDER [Fiber A, Gra. A, P] Logansport, IN b. 16 Dec 1947, Dayton, OH. Studied: U of Ill.; Indianapolis AL. Teachers: Anne Mueller. Exhibited: Logansport/Cass Cnty Public Library (solo), 1985; Kokomo/Howard Cnty Public Library (solo), 1986. Prizes: Logansport AA, 1984, 85.

RYDEN, KENNETH G. Anderson, IN. Prizes: HS, 1989.

RYNERSON, HARRIET E. [Ldscp. P] Prairie Creek. IN. Prizes: HS, 1948, 49.

SAGER, GERALDINE [Ab, Ldscp. P] W. Terre Haute, IN b. 18 Apr 1925, Hagerman, NM. Teachers: Louise Hansen; Gale Waddell; Christopher Schink; Jean Vietor; Gaylen Gerber; Dorothy Voorhees; Barbara Nechis. Exhibited: Ind. WCS, 1990; New Mexico WCS, 1991. Prizes: Paris (Ill.) A Show, 1983, 86; Wabash Valley AG, 1992.

SALMON, CLORADEL D. [Ldscp. P, SLP] Indianapolis, IN. Studied: Indianapolis AL; Shortridge H.S. Teachers: Roda Selleck; Edmund Schildknecht.

SALTZ, LARRY Terre Haute, IN.

SAMPLE, ROSAMOND [Col. A] Corydon, IN. Exhibited: Ky. Guild Train. Prizes: Ky. State Fair.

SAMPSON, JOHN H. [Des, Ldscp. P] Chicago, IL b. 15 Jul 1896, Rush Cnty, IN. Note: Des, advertising and packages for merchandise.

SANBORN, JAMES [P, S, T] Sheridan, IN b. 27 Dec 1932, Shanghai, China. Studied: Maryville Col; Ball State U. Teachers: Ralph Beard; John Cavanaugh. Exhibited: Penrod, 1978.

SANDEFUR, JOHN COURTNEY [Print] Los Angeles, CA b. 26 May 1893, Alexandria, IN. Teachers: A. E. Philbrick. Prizes: HS, Chicago, 1928.

SANDERSON, HARRIET [Print, P] Indianapolis, IN. Studied: Purdue U; Herron A Sch; Indianapolis AL. Exhibited: Anderson Winter Show, 1977; 500 Festival A, 1978, 79; Tippecanoe Regional, 1973, 75; Red Barn Gal, 1972. Prizes: Indianapolis AL Ann, 1976, 77; Ind. State Fair, 1976.

SANFORD, W. DeLACEY

SANGERNEBO, EMMA EYLES (Mrs. Alexander) [S, Por. P] Indianapolis, IN b. 23 Jan 1877, Pittsburgh, PA. Studied: Herron Sch A. Teachers: William Forsyth; Otto Stark; Alexander Sangernebo; Rudolph Schwarz. Exhibited: Ind. State Fair; Herron AM; Ind. AC. Collections: S, Bloomington, IN, Evanston, IL and Akron, OH; portraits, Woman's Dept Cl, Carpenters and Joiners Assn and English Avenue Boys Cl, Indianapolis; figure panels, Loew's Theatre, historic panel, Washington H.S., Indianapolis. Note: Specialty, children's portraits.

SAN PIETRO, ALICE K. [P] Bloomington, IN b. 13 Jan 1931, Valley View, OH. Teachers: Edgar Whitney; Zoltan Szabo; Virginia Cobb; Robert Laessig. Exhibited: Wabash Valley Exh, Swope Gal, 1981, 83, 85; Anderson Winter Show, 1982; A Forms '82, Lafayette, IN; IHA, 1981-84, 86-90; By Hand Gal, Bloomington, IN, 1986-90; Nat Lg Am Pen Women Show, 1980, 81, 84, 85, 89; WC Ind., Indianapolis. Prizes: IHA, 1990. Collections: Merchants Nat Bank, Indianapolis; Bloomington Public Library; City of Bloomington Mayor's Office.

SARBER, HELEN I. [SLP] Muncie, IN. Prizes: HS, 1966.

SARGENT, PAUL T(urner) [P] Charleston, IL b. 23 Jul 1880, Hutton Township, Coles Cnty, IL d. 7 Feb 1946. Studied: AIC; Eastern Ill. State Normal Sch. Teachers: John M. Harlow; Anna Piper; Otis Caldwell; Charles Francis Browne; John H. Vanderpoel; Henry Wood Stevens. Exhibited: Henry Ford M (solo), Dearborn, MI; Eastern Ill. State TC (solo); Lieber A Gal (solo), Indianapolis; Sheldon Swope Gal (solo), Terre Haute; AIC, 1912-17; Brown Cnty AA; Wesleyan U; Ill. State M; U of Ill. Prizes: HS, 1945; Brown Cnty A Gal, 1934. Collections: Ind. U, Bloomington; Butler Sch, Chicago; Eastern Ill. U. Note: T, Eastern Ill. State TC, 1938-42.

SAUNDERS, JENNIE ROCHE [P] Indianapolis, IN b. c. 1890, near Bloomfield, IN d. c. 1975. Prizes: HS, 1971, 72.

SAVAGE, EUGENE FRANCIS [P, S, T, W] New Haven, CT b. 29 Mar 1883, Covington, IN. Studied: CGA; AIC; Am Acad in Rome; FA Acad, Chicago. Teachers: Reynolds; Henderson; Walcott; Groeber. Prizes: Am Acad in Rome Fellowship, 1912-15; N. Y. Arch Lg, 1921; AIC, 1922, 24; NAD, 1922, 24; Grand Central Gal, 1929; HS, 1925. Collections: Greenwich House, NYC; St Louis AM; Communications Bldg, WFNY, 1939; AIC; CAM; Los Angeles MA; Neb. State M; Herron AI; Oshkosh (Wis.) Public M; murals, Yale U and Columbia U; USPO, Washington, D.C. Note: Author, report on art schools for Carnegie Corp of N.Y. T, Yale U Sch FA.

SAVIDGE, HENRIETTA [P, T] Prizes: Milliken Memorial Fund Scholarship (first woman), 1941. Note: T, Ind. U, Bloomington.

SCAHILL, MARY MONSCHEIN [Dr, Pastels, T] Greenfield, IN b. 23 Nov 1946, Indianapolis, IN. Self-taught. Exhibited: Ind. A, 1987-89. Prizes: Pen Women, Ind. State Exh, 1984; Ind. State Fair, 1985. Collections: Merchants Nat Bank.

SCHAEFER, HAROLD [T] Greenfield, IN b. 6 May 1949, Long Island, NY. Studied: Ind. U; Herron Sch A. Teachers: Lance Baber; Lynn Thomsen Bradshaw. Prizes: Sursum Corda, A for Religion, Bethlehem Lutheran Church, Indianapolis, 1974. Collections: Indianapolis Public School #74; Ind. U A Dept.

SCHAEFER, LYDIA S. (Mrs. W. J.) [P] Gary, IN b. Lorain, OH. Studied: Am Acad A, Chicago. Teachers: John C. Templeton; Charles Untulis. Prizes: HS, 1971, 72.

SCHALDACH, WILLIAM J(oseph) [Print, P, I, W] West Hartford, VT (Tubac, AZ, 1964) b. 15 Feb 1896, Elkhart, IN. Studied: ASL. Teachers: John Sloan; Harry Wickey; George Bridgeman. Exhibited: NAD, 1935-44; PAFA, 1941; SAE, annually from 1928; Chicago SE, 1929, 30; WFNY, 1939; MMA (AV); Philadelphia Print Cl, 1930-36; Ind. S PM, 1938-46; Southern PM, 1939, 40; John Herron AI, 1946; Dartmouth, 1942, 46. Note: Author/Illustrator: *Fish*, 1937; I, *Coverts and Casts*, 1943, *Upland Gunning*, 1946. Articles and etchings in *Esquire, Field and Stream, Print Collectors Quarterly*.

SCHAUB, MARY HALL

SCHEERER, BILLIE MARIE Marion, IN. d. c. 1969.

SCHEID, RICHARD Prizes: HS, 1969.

SCHELL, J(ames) E. [Por. P, Ldscp. P] Westerville, OH b. 1877, Canada. Teachers: F. McGilvery Knowles; Frederich S. Challoner.

SCHEPMAN, FRANCES BERNHARDT NC. Studied: Herron Sch A, mid-1930s.

SCHERSCHEL, DORETTA (Dee) [P] Greenwood, IN. Exhibited: Ind. Fed A Cls.

SCHIEFER, C(harles) R. [S] Martinsville, IN b. 14 Sep 1925, Middletown, PA. Self-taught. Exhibited: IMA, 1980, 83; Studio, Champaign, IL, 1988; Ind. U, Student Union, Bloomington, 1987; By Hand Gal, Bloomington, 1989. Prizes: Miami Beach A Festival, 1989; Chicago Oak Brook Promenade, 1987; HS, 1979, 84, 86, 89; Milwaukee Winter A Festival; Columbus Fall A Fair; Indianapolis AL Ann Show; Northern Ind. AA Summer Show. Collections: City of Miami Beach; Public Fountain, Harmony Sch, Columbus, IN; Martinsville Bank; Martinsville Library.

SCHILDKNECHT, EDMUND G(ustav) [P, Print, T] Indianapolis, IN/Milwaukee, WI b. 9 Jul 1899, Chicago, IL. Studied: Wis. Sch A; PAFA; Académie Julian, Grande Chaumière, both in Paris. Teachers: Daniel Garber; George Oberteuffer. Exhibited: CGA, 1930; AIC, 1928, 29, 31, 34-36; PAFA, 1930-32, 35, 44; SAE, 1937, 38, 43; CM, 1931-34; Kansas City AI, 1935, 36; John Herron AI, 1924-46. Prizes: John Herron AI, 1932, 33, 39; HS, 1943, 44, 46, 47. Collections: John Herron AI; 600 paintings, U of Maine, Orono. Note: T, Arsenal Tech Sch, Indianapolis, from 1931-64.

SCHILL, ALICE E. [P] Richmond, IN. Exhibited: Richmond AA, 1939.

SCHILLER, DOROTHY C. Indianapolis, IN b. Newark, NJ. Studied: Hanes Community Cen, Winston-Salem, NC.

Teachers: Frederick Taubes; John Brady; Barclay Sheeks; Grace Freund. Exhibited: Art 500; Indianapolis AL, 1974; Nat Pen Women Show, Indianapolis; Gal of Contemporary A, Winston-Salem, NC; Sears Roebuck Comp, High Point, NC, 1967. Prizes: Assoc A of Winston-Salem, 1961; Indianapolis AG, 1978, 79.

SCHLEMMER, F(erdinand) LOUIS [P, T] Crawfordsville, IN/Provincetown, MA b. 26 Sep 1893, Crawfordsville d. c. 1947. Studied: AIC. Teachers: Hawthorne; H. M. Walcott. Exhibited: Ind. A, John Herron AM, 1927-31. Prizes: Ind. State Fair, 1930; Richmond (Ind.) AA, 1929. Collections: Miami Conservatory A, FL; Wabash Col, Crawfordsville.

SCHMIAT, WALT [Cer]

SCHMIDT, WALTER C. [S, Cer, Blacksmith] Bloomington, IN b. 29 Aug 1950, East Chicago, IN. Studied: Valparaiso U. Teachers: Flynn Sochen; Karl Martz. Exhibited: Buyers Market/Am Cr, 1986-93; Broad Ripple A Fair, 1992; Penrod, 1989-92. Prizes: Great Lakes Cer Invitational, 1972; Finlay, OH, 1990.

SCHOLER, WALTER [Arch] Lafayette, IN b. 8 May 1890 d. 29 Jan 1972. Studied: Columbia U. Note: Designed buildings at Purdue U, Ball State U, Franklin Col, Wabash Col and Manchester Col. Contributed also to the design of Greater Lafayette MA. Served on board and as president of Lafayette AA.

SCHROEDER, RICK [Dr] South Bend, IN. Prizes: HS, 1984.

SCHULTZ, GENE P. [Glass A] Richmond, IN.

SCHULTZ, JOSEPH L. [P] South Bend, IN.

SCHULTZ, TERRI [Dr, Print, I, Por. P] Nashville, IN b. 14 Dec 1952, Crawfordsville, IN. Teachers: Flora Burke. Exhibited: IHA, 1989 (Pr), 90.

SCHULZ, DOROTHY H(artman) [Ldscp. P] Indianapolis, IN b. 5 Dec 1933, New Kensington, PA. Studied: Indianapolis AL. Teachers: Charles Reid; Jeanne Dobie; Thelma Confer; Rosemary Lawton Thomas; Ruth Anderson; Katharine Chang Liu; Judy Betts; Alex Powers. Exhibited: Indianapolis AL Ann; Ind. WCS, 1985, 87, 88; IMA, rental gal, 1985-88. Prizes: Ind. AC, 1981; Brown Cnty Assn, 1981; Indianapolis AL, 1979.

SCHULZ, Jr., EDWIN A. [Ldscp. P, Genre P, Por. P] Indianapolis, IN b. 2 Aug 1908, Louisville, KY. Deceased. Studied: Atherstone Studio; Taflinger Studio. Teachers: Richard Genders; Elmer Taflinger. Exhibited: HS Building, 1977. Note: Husband of artist Marjorie D. Schulz.

SCHULZ, MARJORIE D. [Ldscp. P, SLP, Genre P, Por. P] Indianapolis, IN b. 27 Feb 1909, Indianapolis. Studied: Herron Sch A; Indianapolis AL. Teachers: William Forsyth; Elmer Taflinger; Gianni Cilfone; Earle Beeper. Exhibited: Michiana Reg, 1952. Prizes: HS, 1952; Ft Wayne, 1955; South Bend, 1952. Collections: Goshen General Hospital. Note: Wife of artist Edwin A. Schulz, Jr.

SCHUSTER, HELEN MARIE Deceased.

SCHWEHM, RAY F.

SCOTT, ANN [SLP, P] Indianapolis, IN b. Alexandria, VA. Teachers: Rosemary Browne Beck. Exhibited: IMA, 1971; Ind. A Show, Ind. State M, 1972; Ind. AC; Evansville Mid-States Exh; 500 Festival. Prizes: HS, 1972, 74; Ind. State Fair, 1970, 71, 73-75, 79, 81; A 500, 1976, 80; Mid-

States Exh, Evansville, 1970, 80; Whitewater Valley Exh, Ind. U-East, 1978.

SCOTT, DAVID O. [S] Indianapolis, IN.

SCOTT, GERALDINE ARMSTRONG [P, Dec, T] Kokomo, IN b. 1 Oct 1900, Elkhart, IN. Studied: Northwestern U; N.Y. Sch Fine&App A; Parsons Sch Des; Paris. Teachers: E. R. Sitzman. Exhibited: Ind. AC. Prizes: South Bend, 1928; Northern Ind. AL. Collections: Butler U; Carnegie Library, Kokomo; Carnegie Library, Tipton; Ind. Fed Cl; Northwestern U; Noblesville (Ind.) H.S. Note: T, Ind. U, Kokomo.

SCOTT, NANCIE [Por. P, T] Greenfield, IN b. 1 Jan, Ft Wayne, IN. Studied: Herron Sch A. Teachers: Clayson Baker. Exhibited: Central Library, Indianapolis, 1987; Toulouse Music/Art Festival, France, 1986. Prizes: HS, 1988; IHA, 1989; Brown Cnty A Gal, 1987. Collections: Eli Lilly&Co; Edward D. Jones&Co, Greenfield; Hancock Cnty Remc.

SCOTT, VERNON R. South Bend, IN.

SCOTT, WILLIAM EDOUARD [P, Mur. P, I, Dec] Chicago, IL/Indianapolis, IN b. 11 Mar 1884, Indianapolis d. May 1964, Chicago. Studied: AIC; Académie Julian and Colarossi Acad, Paris. Teachers: Otto Stark; J. Vanderpoel; Henry O. Tanner. Exhibited: Haiti, Port-au-Prince (solo), 1931; traveling exh, 1935; Autumn Salon, Paris, 1912; Royal Acad, London, 1913; AIC, 1915-27; Chicago AL, 1928; Findlay Gal, Chicago, 1935; Am Negro Expo, Chicago, 1940; Centennial Expo, Dallas, TX, 1936; FA Gal, Balboa Park, San Diego, CA, 1929. Prizes: Ind. State Fair, 1914; Harmon Fnd, 1927; Chicago AL, 1931; Legion of Honor, Government of Haiti; Rosenwall Fellow, 1931. Collections: Argentine Republic; First Presbyterian Church, Chicago; Government of Haiti; IMA; Ind. State M. Murals: Evanston, IL; Herron AI, Indianapolis; Ft Wayne (Ind.) Courthouse; Springfield (Ill.) Statehouse; Am Negro Expo; Indianapolis Public Sch, 1914; City Hospital (Wishard), Indianapolis, IN, 1915; Recorder of Deeds Bldg, Washington, D. C., 1943; NYPL; Carver M, Tuskegee Inst, Tuskegee, AL; Fisk U, Nashville, TN; Harmond Fnd Coll, Nat Archives, Washington, D.C.

SCUDDER, JANET [S, P, W] NYC/Paris, France b. 27 Oct 1873, Terre Haute, IN d. 10 Jun 1940, Rockport, MA. Studied: Cincinnati A Acad; Acad Vittie, Paris; Florence. Teachers: Rebisso; Lorado Taft; Macmonnies. Exhibited: Paris Salon, 1905, 10; CM, 1909, 18; PAFA, 1909; Nat S Soc, 1908; Albright M, Buffalo, 1916; NAD, 1918. Prizes: Columbian Expo, Chicago, 1893; Sun Dial Comp, NYC, 1898; St Louis Expo, 1904; Paris Salon, 1911; NAWPS, 1914; P.-P. Expo, San Francisco, 1915; AIC, 1922; Intl Exp, Paris, 1937; HS, 1926; Chevalier de la Legion d' Honneur, 1925. Collections: seal, Assn of the Bar, City of NYC; Brooklyn Inst M; public sch, Richmond, IN; Indianapolis AA; LOC; MMA; Peabody Inst; Musée du Luxembourg, Paris; RISD; fountains: MMA, AIC, Peabody Inst in Baltimore and BM. Note: Specialized in fountains. Author, *Modeling My Life.* First Am woman whose sculpture was purchased for the Luxembourg in Paris. Created the Indiana Medal commemorating the completion of a century of statehood, 1816-1916, under the direction of the Ind. Hist Commission.

SEAFORD, JOHN ALBERT [P, Ldscp. P, I, T] Richmond, IN/Boston, MA b. 1858, Salisbury, NC d. 3 Nov 1936, Boston. Collections: Boston Library; Bostonian Soc; New England Hist Soc; Richmond AA. Note: Lived in Spiceland, Ind., late 1890s-early 1900s. I, *Boston Herald.*

SEAMON, D(enzil) OMER [Com. A, P, Ldscp. P, T, W] Terre Haute, IN b. 1911, Gibson Cnty, IN. Teachers: Walter J. Wilwerding; Charles L. Bartholomew. Exhibited: Brown Cnty A Gal (solo), 1972; Sheldon Swope Gal, 1978; HS Gal, 1967. Prizes: Doctorate of Humanities, Rose-Hulman Inst Technology, Terre Haute, IN; Sagamore of the Wabash Valley; HS, 1948, 58, 61. Note: Art Dir, Thomson-Symon Co, Terre Haute, IN for 27 years. Specialized in travel posters. Published articles on poster techniques and how to paint watercolors. T, DePauw U, 1960.

SEARS, NELSON [Dr] Bedford, IN b. 2 Sep 1905, Mitchell, IN d. c. 1978. Studied: Franklin Col. Teachers: Ethel Frank. Prizes: HS, 1969; Ind. State Fair, 1968. Note: Was a draftsman, construction company estimator and plastering contractor. President, Lawrence Cnty AA.

SEET, MARY P(arrett) (Mrs. Carl W.) [P] Indianapolis, IN b. Newport, IN. Studied: Herron Sch A. Exhibited: Mid-States Show, Evansville; 500 Festival; 6th Eastern Ind. A Show; Ind. A Exh.

SEIFERT, BERTHA M. *(See Watkins, Bertha Seifert)* [Ldscp. P, Por. P, T] East Chicago, IN. Studied: AIC. Teachers: Willmaski; Giesbert.

SEIPEL, MARY

SEIPEL, VIRGINIA L. [Ldscp. P, Com. A] Anderson, IN b. 6 Jun 1922, Anderson. Studied: Am Acad, Chicago; John Herron A Sch; Indianapolis AL. Teachers: Ruthven Byrum. Prizes: Anderson Soc of A.

SEITZINGER, ARLENE MILLER [S] Portage, IN b. Chicago. Studied: AIC. Teachers: Eagan Weiner; Edouard Chassaing. Exhibited: IMA; Left Bank Gal, Saugatuck, MI; Joy Horwich Gal, Chicago; Nat Carver's M, Colorado Springs, CO. Prizes: AIC; Chicago Vicinity Show; HS, 1971; Chicago and Vicinity Show, 1973.

SELBY, ROBERT H. [P, T] Austin, TX b. 31 Jan 1909, Owensville, IN. Studied: John Herron AI; Hawthorne Cape Sch A, Provincetown, MA. Teachers: William Forsyth; P. Hadley; Charles Hawthorne. Exhibited: John Herron Ann; Montclair (N.J.) AA; Irvington A Exh; Art USA, Colosseum, NY. Prizes: HS, 1946-49, 51, 54, 58, 62, 65; Art USA; East Orange AA Ann; Indianapolis AA Ann; Ind. State Fair. Collections: IMA; Frank Dailey Col, Ind. U; Ft Wayne AM; N.J. Library, Madison. Note: T, Lifetime Learning Inst of Austin Community College. Son-in-law of artist William Forsyth and brother-in-law of artist Constance Forsyth.

SELFRIDGE, REYNOLDS L. [P, W, T] Indianapolis, IN b. 30 Sep 1898, Jasonville, IN. Studied: DePauw U. Teachers: Hawthorne; Forsyth. Prizes: John Herron AI, 1926, 29, 30; Richmond, IN, 1929; HS, 1926. Note: Owned and operated gas station, Indianapolis.

SELLERS, LYDIA ROBERT R. [SLP] Auburn, IN.

SEN St Mary-of-the-Woods, Terre Haute, IN.

SENSENY, SCOTT M. [P]

SENTER, GRACIE O(pal) [Ldscp. P, Por. P] Indianapolis, IN b. c. 1922, Putnam Cnty d. 27 Nov 1963. Studied: DePauw U; Herron AI; Brown Cnty.

SESSLER, STANLEY S(acha) [Por. P, P, Print, T, Des]

South Bend, IN b. 28 May 1905, St Petersburg, Russia. Studied: Mass. Sch A. Teachers: Ernest L. Major; Richard D. Andrew; Charles Woodbury; Wilbur D. Hamilton. Exhibited: Ind. AC, 1939-42; Northern Ind. A, 1929-46; Ogunquit A Cen, 1937, 38; Palm Beach A Cen, 1937, 38. Prizes: HS, 1935, 38, 39, 41; South Bend, IN, 1942. Collections: Wightman Gal, Notre Dame, IN; Midland A Acad, South Bend. Note: T, U of Notre Dame, South Bend, IN, 1928-46.

SEVIN, WHITNEY

SEYBERT, DIANE PIERCE [MM, Col. A, S, JA, W] Indianapolis, IN b. 24 Sep 1938, Warsaw, IN. Studied: Ind. U; Herron A Sch; Indianapolis AL. Teachers: Leon Golub; Rudy Pozatti; Alma Eikermann; Amanda Block; Joe Richardson. Exhibited: Ind. A, IMA; Ball State Small Dr&S; Ind. U East Regional, 1989. Prizes: Art 500, 1976. Collections: Ind. States Insurance; Suemma Coleman Home. Note: W, *Arts Indiana.*

SEYMOUR, HELEN *(See Baker, Helen Seymour and Baker, Seymour)*

SEYMOUR, RALPH FLETCHER [Print, Des, I, W, P, T] Chicago, IL b. 18 Mar 1876, Milan, IL d. 1966, Batavia, IL. Studied: Cincinnati A Acad. Teachers: Nowottny; Meakin. Prizes: Knox Col, Galesburg, IL; Chicago SE, 1934; Philadelphia Print Cl, 1936. Collections: AIC; Sorbonne, Paris; AFA; Knox Col, Galesburg, IL; Newberry Library, Chicago; NGA; Bibliotheque Nationale, Paris. Note: Author/Illustrator, *Across the Gulf, Some Went This Way.* T, AIC, 1909-18; Supervisor of publications, Knox Col, Galesburg, 1936-37.

SHAFFER, ELIZABETH DODDS *(See Dodds, Mary Elizabeth)*

SHAFFER, ELLEN E. [Dr] Rockville, IN b. 12 Aug 1934, Indianapolis, IN. Self-taught. Exhibited: Covered Bridge A Show, 1988, 89; Ind. State Fair. Prizes: Covered Bridge A Show, 1990; Parke Cnty Fair, 1989.

SHAND, KAREN L. [Bat] Flora, IN b. 1 Jan 1949, Peru, IN. Studied: Ball State U; St Francis Col; Ind. State U; Purdue U. Exhibited: World's Fair, Knoxville, TN, 1982; Ind. State Fair, 1986, 87. Prizes: HS, 1981, 82; Ind. State Fair, 1984, 85, 90; Logansport AA, 1985, 88-90; Art Train, 1986.

SHANNON, CLARA J. [P, SLP] Indianapolis, IN.

SHARP, EVERETT HILL [Por. P, P, Print, T] Muncie, IN b. 22 Feb 1907, Pendleton Cnty, KY. Studied: Ball State TC; John Herron AI; Académie Julian, Paris, France. Teachers: Wayman Adams; George Pearse Ennis; George Luks. Exhibited: VMFA, 1939; All A Am, 1939; Philadelphia Print Cl, 1939; Ind. A, 1929-46; Ind. AC, 1940-46. Prizes: Southern PM, 1940; HS, 1928, 29, 34, 36, 38, 41, 43; Ind. A, 1939; Ind. AC, 1942, 46; Ind. PM, 1946; Muncie AA, 1928, 29, 32; *Indianapolis Star*, 1936. Collections: Am Church, Paris; U of Wis.; University Cl, Madison, WI; Courthouse, Baraboo, WI; Ind. U; Ft Wayne AM; Ball State TC. Note: Worked for Muncie Gear Co until 1972; worked for Dek Identifications Co, Ft Wayne until 1983; designer for specialized cameras.

SHARP, G. MARTY [Silkscreen] Knightstown, IN.

SHARP, JAMES W. Indianapolis, IN.

SHATTUCK, JULIA C. [Ldscp. P] Indianapolis, IN b. 16 Dec 1912, Tell City, IN. Self-taught. Exhibited: Southside

AL Reg, 1986, 87; Ind. State Fair, 1981. Prizes: Southside AL, 1982; Ind. State Fair, 1986; Central Ind. A, 1990.

SHAVER, HELEN PUTNAM [P] Chicago, IL/Tucson, AZ. Prizes: HS, 1953. Note: Lived previously in Indianapolis and Hammond, IN.

SHAW, ROBERT M. [Ldscp. P, C] Marion, IN b. 2 Jul 1915, Marion. Teachers: Homer Davisson; C. Curry Bohm; G. Cleveland. Prizes: HS, 1937. Note: Manager, Pioneer Gal, Marion.

SHEARER, PEG (Margaret D.) [Ab, Ldscp. P, Por. P, T] Crawfordsville, IN b. 11 Jun 1917, Chicago, IL. Studied: La Grande Chaumiere, Paris, France, 1955; Samuel Fleischer Sch FA, Philadelphia, PA; Indianapolis AL. Teachers: Fritz Schlemmer; Harold McDonald; Philip Best; William Ashby; Rosemary Browne Beck. Exhibited: Old Jail M, Crawfordsville, IN, 1989; Anderson Rental Gal; Victoria's Gal, Carmel, IN; Ind. A, Herron M; Ind. AC; Ind. A Ann Exh; Ind. State Fair; Ind. State M; Pace Gal; Swope Gal, Terre Haute. Prizes: Ind. A Ann Exh, 1974; Sugar Creek Ann Juried A Exh, Crawfordsville, 1975; Swope Gal, Terre Haute, IN. Collections: Wabash Col; Crawfordsville Public Library.

SHEEHAN, EVELYN STEVENS

SHELINE, LEROY M.

SHELL, JOE [P] Hillsdale, IN b. 1 Jul 1936, Vermillion Cnty, near Newport, IN. Self-taught. Prizes: HS, 1972.

SHERLOCK, EDWARD W. [SLP, P] Lafayette, IN. Teachers: Randolph Coats.

SHERRILL, LOIS M. [P] Indianapolis, IN.

SHERROW, STEPHEN [Ldscp. P, T] Richmond, IN b. 15 Dec 1913, Marble Hill, MO. Teachers: Roland Osborne. Exhibited: Herron AI, 1950s; Ind. AC, 1960s. Collections: Mural, Metamora Canal Town, Metamora M. Note: Worked for 25 years in historical development, Metamora, IN.

SHERWOOD, IDA G.

SHICK, OLIVE J.

SHIDELER, PAUL [P, Print] Indianapolis, IN b. 16 Feb 1888, Indianapolis d. 1962. Teachers: William Forsyth, Randolph Coats. Exhibited: Woman's Dept Cl Gal, 1934. Note: Newspaperman by profession. As an artist, worked in etchings and aquatints.

SHIELDS, NANCY [Print] Indianapolis, IN.

SHORR, WINIFRED [S] New Buffalo, MI.

SHORT, BONNIE K. [P] Indianapolis, IN b. 4 Oct 1943, Hackensack, NJ. Studied: Indianapolis AL; Southside AL. Teachers: Judi Betts; Jo Ann Cardwell; Jeanne McLeish. Exhibited: Ind. State Fair, 1989; Southside AL Reg, 1990.

SHORT, JEANNE [Ldscp. P, P] Indianapolis, IN b. 10 Jul 1929, Indianapolis. Studied: Indianapolis AL. Teachers: Paul Sweany; Jo Ann Cardwell; Jeanne Wasson. Exhibited: Wabash Valley, 1989; Ind. State Fair, 1987.

SHOVER, EDNA MANN [P, Des, I, W, T] Indianapolis, IN b. 25 Sep 1885, Indianapolis. Studied: PMSchIA; ASL; Columbia U; PAFA. Teachers: Homer G. Davisson; Faber; Deigendesch; Thomas Scott; Philip Muhr; J. Frank Copeland. Prizes: PMSchIA Alumni Assn, 1931. Note: Author/Illustrator, *Art in Costume Design*, published by Milton Bradley Co. Principal, Herron AI Art Sch.

SHOWE, LOU-ELLEN CHATTIN *(See Chattin, Lou-Ellen)*

SHULER, DAVID b. Crawfordsville, IN. Studied: Crawfordsville; Chicago. Teachers: Heidinger. Exhibited: L. S. Ayres; Ross A Gal, Newark, NJ.

SHULZ, ADA WALTER [P] Nashville, IN b. 21 Oct 1870, Terre Haute, IN d. 4 May 1928. Studied: AIC; Vitti Acad, Paris; Munich. Teachers: Vanderpoel; Merson; Collin. Prizes: AIC, 1917; HS, 1926, 28, Chicago. Collections: Milwaukee AI; Municipal AL, Chicago Coll. Note: Founder, Brown Cnty Gal Assn. Specialty, portrayals of child life. First wife of artist Adolph Robert Shulz.

SHULZ, ADOLPH ROBERT [Por. P, Ldscp. P, T] Nashville, IN b. 12 Jun 1869, Delavan, WI d. 24 Jan 1963. Studied: AIC; ASL; Académie Julian and Colorossi, Paris; Munich. Teachers: Jules Lefebvre; Benjamin Constant; Paul Laurens. Prizes: Young Fortnightly Pr, Chicago, 1896; William Frederick Grower Pr, Chicago, 1898; AIC, 1900, 1904, 1908; Milwaukee AI, 1918; Brown Cnty Gal Assn, 1937; HS, 1926, 36. Note: One of the first artists to come to Brown Cnty, 1900. Came to stay in 1908. Generally credited with originating the Brown Cnty A Colony. Husband of artist Ada Walter Shulz and, later, artist Alberta Rehm Shulz. T, Ringling A Sch, Sarasota, FL. W, "The Story of the Brown County Art Colony," *Indiana Magazine of History*, Dec, 1935.

SHULZ, ALBERTA REHM [P, S] Nashville, IN b. 6 Jul 1892 Indianapolis, IN d. 7 Feb 1980, Bloomington, IN. Studied: Western Col for Women, Oxford, OH; Butler U; U of Texas; Ind. U; Herron AI; Ringling Sch A. Teachers: Adolph Shulz; C. Curry Bohm; Adrian Pillars; L. O. Griffith. Exhibited: Lieber's Gal (solo), Indianapolis; Brown Cnty A Gal; Swope A Gal, Terre Haute, IN; Brown Cnty A Gal, Nashville; Fla. Note: Second wife of artist Adolph Robert Shulz.

SHUMAN, OPAL F. [P] Anderson, IN. Deceased. Prizes: HS, 1970.

SHUMATE, ELLA A. [P] Lebanon, IN/Kansas City, MO b. 16 Aug 1879, Lebanon, IN. Studied: Provincetown; Kansas City AI; Cincinnati Inst; Paris, France; England. Teachers: Ambrose Webster; Andre L'Hote; Newland; Landsend. Exhibited: Ind. A Ann, Herron AM; Ind. AC, L.S. Ayres, Indianapolis.

SIDDIQ, PATRICIA FOLEY [Ldscp. P, I, T] Nashville, IN b. 1 Oct 1937, Indianapolis, IN. Studied: DePauw U; Ind. U; Northern Ill. U. Teachers: Ray French; Robert Hoffman; Frederick Rigley. Exhibited: IHA, 1982-90; U.S. Information Agency, 1972. Prizes: IHA, 1983, 85; HS Traveling Exh, 1970.

SIDMAN, CHARLOTTE [SLP, P] Indianapolis, IN b. 30 Apr 1884 d. 6 Oct 1977. Studied: Indianapolis ASL. Teachers: William F. Kaeser; Floyd Hopper; Eliot O'Hara; Charles M. West, Jr; Henrik Mayer; Edmund Brucker. Exhibited: Herron AM, 1945. Prizes: HS, 1943, 50; Ind. A Exh. Note: Mother of artist Joe Cox.

SILEIKIS, MICHAEL J(ustin) [P, W] Chicago, IL b. 15 Oct 1893, Lithuania. Studied: AIC. Teachers: L. Seyffert; L. Kroll. Exhibited: All-Ill. Soc FA. Prizes: AIC, 1925. Note: A Critic, *Lithuanian Daily News*, Chicago.

SILLS, ROGER [Print] Evansville, IN. Prizes: HS, 1977.

SILVER, IRENE [Ldscp. P]

SIMMONS, ROBERTA FAY [S, Cer, T] Noblesville, IN b. VA. Studied: Purdue U; Ball State U; Butler U. Exhibited: 500 Festival of A; Ind. State Fair. Note: T, Pendleton Jr High and H.S.

SIMPER, LEW [P] Indiana b. 1900, near Bury St Edmunds, England d. c. 1981. Prizes: Northern Ind. AA.

SIMPSON, HARRY West Lafayette, IN. Exhibited: Franklin Street Gal, Huntington, 1972.

SINCLAIR, BERNICE [P, T] Ft Wayne, IN b. 25 Nov 1888, Knox, IN. Teachers: Otto Stark; William Forsyth. Note: T, North Side H.S., Ft Wayne.

SINCLAIR, MARTHA WRIGHT

SINGH, K(anwal) P(rakash) [Dr] Indianapolis, IN b. 17 Jun 1939, Jaranwala, Pakistan. Self-taught. Exhibited: Jewish Community Center (solo); Butler U (solo); Wabash Col (solo); Intl Cen of Indianapolis (solo); President's Gal, Columbia Cl, Indianapolis, 1985, 88. Prizes: 500 A Festival, 1975; HS, 1985, 89; Marion Cnty-Indianapolis Hist Soc, 1988. Collections: IMA; Ind. Nat Bank; Bank One; Merchants Nat Bank; Wabash Col; Ind. State U; IUPUI; Notre Dame; Detroit Diesel Allison. Note: Bachelor of Architecture, Indian Inst of Technology, Kharagpur, India, 1963; Teaching Fellowship, Sch of Architecture and Des, U of Mich., 1965-66.

SINICK, GARY [Silkscreen] West Lafayette, IN.

SINNETT, LOIS BROWN [P] Indianapolis, IN. Studied: Herron Sch A; Ind. U; Indianapolis AL; East Side A Cen; Pro A Studio. Exhibited: Ind. State Fair; Hist Exh of Ohio; Wm. H. Block Co; Ind. Chamber of Commerce. Prizes: Ind. Reg; Mile of A; Southside AL; Beech Grove A Festival.

SIPE, IRENE BARLOW *(See Barlow, Irene)*

SIRKO, HELEN [Ab, Ldscp. P, Por. P, T, Col. A] Elkhart, IN b. 28 Dec 1935, Johnstown, PA. Studied: AIC. Teachers: Phil Austin; Nita Engle; Albert Handel; Val Thelin; Miles Batts; Virginia Cobb. Exhibited: Gold Coast A Fair, Chicago; Ann Arbor Summer A Show, MI; Del Bello Gal, Toronto, Canada; Park Forest A Cen, IL; South Bend A Cen. Prizes: Chesterton Spring A Show, 1990; Michigan City A Cen, 1988, 90; Midwest MA, 1987. Collections: Notre Dame U, South Bend, IN; Elkhart Public Sch; Columbus (Ind.) Public Sch; Ford Motor Corp, Detroit, MI; Northern Ind. Bank and Trust, Portage, IN.

SISKIND, ELLIE (Marie) [Dr, Por. P, P] Indianapolis, IN b. 16 Aug 1933, Oak Park, IL. Studied: Wichita AA, Wichita, KS; Kansas City AI, MO; Stephens Col, Columbia, MO; Herron Sch A. Teachers: Betty Dickerson; Pierre Montminy; Harry Davis. Exhibited: Faces of Racism, Evansville M A&Sc, 1993; Editions Limited (solo), 1993; Arc Gal (solo), Chicago, 1986; 431 Gal (solo), Indianapolis, 1986; South Bend A Cen (two-person), 1990; Anderson Winter Show; Art 500. Prizes: Am States Insurance, 1988; HS, 1981; Ft Wayne AM, 1979; Whitewater Valley Exh, 1985; Ind. State Fair, 1980-90; Michiana Reg, 1982; Sugar Creek; Hanson Merit Award; Tri-Kappa, Ft Wayne. Collections: Ft Wayne MA. Note: Specializes in art which addresses social issues.

SISTER CAMILLE, S.P. [Ldscp. P, Genre P, S, Cer, T] Indianapolis, IN/St Mary-of-the-Woods, IN b. 19 Jan 1901, Vincennes, IN d. 24 Mar 1985. Studied: St Mary-of-the-Woods; DePaul U, Chicago, IL; Corcoran Sch A;

AIC; Chicago Acad FA; Herron AI. Teachers: G. Mess. Exhibited: Herron AI; Ind. AC. Prizes: IMA, 1939. Collections: St Thomas More Church, Mooresville, IN; Ladywood Library, Indianapolis, IN. Note: Full name, Mary Catherine Ostendorf.

SISTER ESTHER, S.P. [P, Genre P, T, W, I] St Mary-of-the-Woods, IN b. 17 May 1901, Clinton, IN d. 9 Jul 1986. Studied: AIC; Syracuse U; Herron Sch of A; St Mary-of-the-Woods Col; Ind. U. Teachers: William Forsyth; O. Gross; F. Foy. Exhibited: Intl Exh Sacred A, Rome, Italy, 1950; Comer&Quint Gal Exh, Chicago, IL, 1958; Am&Intl Needlepoint Exh, Chicago, IL, 1974. Prizes: HS, 1937, 39, 43; St Mary's Col, LLD, Notre Dame, IN. Note: Full name, Catherine Newport. Author, *Diocese of Indianapolis*, 1936; Illustrator, *A Bible History*. T, St Mary's Col.

SISTER IMMACULEE, S.P. [Ab, Dr, Print, Genre P, S, Cer, Por. P, T] b. 26 Oct 1906, Ft Wayne, IN. Studied: St Mary-of-the-Woods Col; Notre Dame U; Columbia U, NYC; AIC; Catholic U, Washington, D.C.; Pius XII Inst FA, Florence, Italy. Exhibited: Villa Schiafonia (solo), Florence, Italy, 1957. Prizes: Scholarship, Pius XII Inst FA, 1956; St Mary-of-the-Woods, 1986; HS, 1939. Collections: Mother Theodore Guerin H.S., River Grove, IL; Our Lady of the Holy Cross, Trappist Monastery, Berryville, VA. Note: Full name, Mary Esther Krafthefer.

SISTER M. DOLORITA, O.S.F. [Ab, Ldscp. P, Print, S, Cer, Por. P, T] Oldenburg, IN b. 19 Apr 1911, Indianapolis, IN. Studied: AIC; Washington U, St Louis; Cincinnati A Acad; Ind. State U; Catholic U, Washington, D.C. Teachers: Constantine Pougialis; Leon Lippert; Clare Fontanini. Exhibited: Ind. Soc of Washington, Smithsonian Inst, 1949; Ind. State U, 1960; DePauw U A Cen, 1959. Prizes: HS, 1944, 48, 50, 52. Collections: Altrusa Cl, Gary, IN; Marian Col, Indianapolis, IN; Sisters of St Francis Convent, Oldenburg, IN. Note: Full name, Sister M. Dolorita Carper.

SISTER M. IMMACULATA, C.S.C. [P] Notre Dame, IN b. 1879, Cachville, CA. Studied: Saint Mary's Col, Notre Dame, IN; Baltimore; Washington, D.C.; Cape Cod. Note: Full name, Anna Maria DuChene.

SISTER M. ITTA, O.S.F. [Ldscp. P, T] b. 21 Jan 1889, Minank, IL d. 18 Oct 1974. Studied: Augsburg Sch, Chicago; A Acad, Cincinnati, Ohio; AIC; Ind. U. Prizes: HS, 1946, 50. Note: Full name, Sister M. Itta Lutomaki.

SISTER M(ary) LAUREEN, C.S.C. [P, Des, T] Holy Cross, IN b. 16 Jun 1893, Ft Wayne, IN. Studied: U of Chicago; AIC; U of Calif.; Notre Dame U; Catholic U, Washington, D.C. Prizes: HS, 1937. Note: Full name, Helen Hubler. T, St Mary's Col.

SISTER M. RUFINIA, O.S.F. [Por. P, SLP, Ldscp. P, Print, S, Cer, T] Mishawaka, IN/Lafayette, IN b. 24 Oct 1851, Kahlschlade, Rhineland, Germany d. 10 Oct 1959, Lafayette, IN. Studied: Acad A, Berlin; AIC; Syracuse U; Duchune Col; DePaul U, Chicago; Lewis Inst, Chicago; Ohio Sch FA. Teachers: Wayman Adams; Edna Ruby; Anna Lee Stacy; Walker; Hawley; Hese. Exhibited: Herron AI; Sacred Heart Church, Indianapolis; St Joseph Hospital, Omaha, NE; St Stanislaus Church, Columbus, NE; Sacred Heart Church, Peoria, IL; Lyman Gal, Indianapolis, 1936-38; Lieber's Gal, Indianapolis, 1951. Prizes: HS, 1936, 38-40, 43, 45, 52. Note: Full name: Sister M. Rufinia Kloke. A Dir, St Francis Sch A, Lafayette, IN.

SISTER MARIE ROSAIRE, C.S.C. [T] b. St Louis, MO. Studied: St Mary's Col; Pius XII Inst, Florence, Italy; Notre Dame U. Exhibited: Cincinnati AM. Collections: South Bend A Cen; Cleveland AI; Cincinnati AM. Note: Full name, Eleanor Blatterman.

SISTER MARY DePAUL SCHWEITZER, O.S.F. [Ab, T] Indianapolis, IN b. 19 May 1942, Cincinnati, OH. Studied: Marian Col, Indianapolis; Tyler Sch A, Temple U, Philadelphia. Teachers: Sister Dolorita Carper, O.S.F.; Margo Margolis. Exhibited: U of Pa. (two-woman), Philadelphia, 1974; Marian Col (solo), 1974; Mid-States A Exh, Evansville, IN, 1974; Nat A Auction, Am Kidney Fund, 1975. Prizes: NCCW North Deanery A Show, Indianapolis, 1972; A for Religion, Indianapolis, 1974. Note: Full name, Sister Sandra (Mary DePaul) Schweitzer. Chairman, A Dept, Marian Col. Dir since 1986, Liturgical A, R.C. Archdiocese, Indianapolis.

SISTER (Mary) EDNA, C.S.C. [T] b. 1891, South Bend, IN d. 1973. Studied: St Mary's Col, Notre Dame, IN; U of Notre Dame; AIC; Am Acad and Acad FA, Chicago; Broadmoor A Acad, Colorado Springs; Nat Sch Interior Dec, NYC. Prizes: HS, 1936, 48, 49, 51. Note: Full name, Helen Orzechowska.

SISTER MARY IGNATIA, S.P. [Print, MM, Mosiacs] Forest Park, IL b. 2 Mar 1917, LaPorte, IN. Studied: St Mary-of-the-Woods Col; Notre Dame U. Teachers: Sister Esther Newport, S.P.; Reverend Anthony Lauck, C.S.C.; Frederick Beckman. Exhibited: Tippecanoe Reg, Lafayette A Cen, 1965; A for Religion, Indianapolis Bethlehem Lutheran Church, 1964. Prizes: Rancho Mirage Calif., 1967; HS, 1965. Collections: Chamber of Commerce, Rancho Mirage, Calif.; St Mary-of-the-Woods Col.

SISTER MARY JANE, O.S.F. [Dr, SLP, T] b. 17 Aug 1893, Oldenburg, IN d. 10 Oct 1979. Studied: A Acad, Cincinnati, OH; Notre Dame U; Washington U, St Louis, MO; AIC; Butler U, Indianapolis. Teachers: Leon Lippert. Prizes: Peter Reilly Prize, HS, 1942. Note: Full name, Sister Mary Jane Peine.

SISTER RITA ANN ROETHELE, S.P. [Ldscp. P, Ab, T] St Mary-of-the-Woods, IN b. 25 Sep 1926, Ft Wayne, IN. Studied: Ind. State U; U of Notre Dame; Herron Sch A; St Francis Col, Ft Wayne; St Mary-of-the-Woods Col; Catholic U of Am, Washington, D.C. Teachers: Kenneth Nolan; John David Mooney. Exhibited: Canterbury A Cen, Ft Wayne, 1986; Cleo Rogers Mem Library, Columbus, IN, 1972; The Gal, Ft Wayne, 1979-80; Collector's Show Room, Chicago, 1970-72, 75-77; Ft Wayne MA, 1975, 78; Sheldon Swope A Gal, Terre Haute, 1976-77, 86; IMA, rental gal, 1968-76; Ball State U, Muncie, IN; Wabash Valley Exh, Sheldon Swope Gal, 1972, 73, 77, 78; A for Religion, 1967, 70, 71; Festival of A and Religion, 1969; Reg A Exh, Ft Wayne MA, 1967. Prizes: Wabash Valley Exh, Sheldon Swope Gal, 1975, 84; Indianapolis AL Reg, 1984; HS, 1974; A for Religion, 1968. Collections: Eli Lilly&Co, Indianapolis, IN; Am Fletcher Nat Bank, Indianapolis; Children's M, Indianapolis. Note: Full name, Rita Ann Roethele. Worked at St Mary-of-the-Woods, beginning 1970.

SITZMAN, EDWARD R. [P, T] Indianapolis, IN b. 31 Mar 1874, Cincinnati, OH d. 1949. Studied: Cincinnati A Acad; London; Munich. Teachers: Frank Duveneck. Exhibited: Ind. State Fair; Herron AM. Collections: Cincinnati AM; public libraries and schools, IN.

SKEMP, OLIVE H(ess) [P, Por. P, Des] Ogden Dunes, IN. b. Scottsdale, PA. Studied: Sch App A, Philadelphia; Paris, France. Teachers: C. H. Tillmanns. Prizes: HS, 1937. Note: Mother of artist Robert O. Skemp.

SKEMP, ROBERT O. [Mur. P, Por. P, Com. A, I] Gary, IN. b. Scottdale, PA. Studied: ASL; Grand Central A Sch. Teachers: Frank V. DuMond; George Bridgeman; Thomas Benton; H. R. Ballinger; Pruett Carter. Exhibited: Gary Civic Cen, Gary, IN. Note: Son of artist Olive Skemp.

SKINNER, R. CAROL [Dr, Ldscp. P, I, T] Carmel, IN b. 6 Aug 1942, Lexington, KY. Studied: Herron A Sch. Teachers: Harry Davis; William Crutchfield; Loren Dunlap; David Rubins. Prizes: HS, 1986, 87; Channel 20 Auction, Ardath Burkhart Award, 1986. Collections: GTE; AT&T; Eli Lilly&Co; Ind. Gas Co; Lilly Greenfield Labs.

SLAYMAKER, GENE [P, Print] Indianapolis, IN. Note: Public relations consultant. Once the husband of artist Martha Slaymaker.

SLAYMAKER, MARTHA [P, MM Relief S, Cast Paper Reliefs] New Mexico b. 1930, Randolph Cnty, Saratoga, IN. Studied: Ohio State U, Columbus; Edinboro Col, PA; Herron Sch A; Youngstown U, OH; Baldwin-Wallace U, Berea, OH. Exhibited: Editions Limited Gal, Indianapolis, 1991; Parma Philharmonic Orchestra Society, Parma, OH, 1959; Ft Wayne Gal, IN, 1966, 71; Vincent Price Gal, Chicago, IL, 1968; John Herron MA, 1969; Ball State U, Muncie, IN, 1973; Bedford Limestone Festival, Bedford, IN, 1971; Valparaiso U, Valparaiso, IN, 1972; Haslem Gal, Madison, WI, 1972; all solo. Prizes: HS, 1966, 72, 73, 76. Collections: IMA; U of Ill.; Columbia U, NYC; U of Western Ontario, London, Ontario; Ind. U Sch of Business, Bloomington, IN; Franklin Col, Franklin IN; Lafayette A Cen, Lafayette, IN; Brebeuf Preparatory Sch, Indianapolis; Valparaiso U; Eli Lilly Coll; Municipal Gal, Instanbul, Turkey.

SLUSSER, CECILIA [MM] Logansport, IN b. 31 Mar 1933, Logansport, IN. Teachers: Edward Betts; Raleigh Kinney; Paul Sweany; Marilou Crisman; Marion Allen. Exhibited: Anderson WC, 1982; Kokomo-Howard Public Library (solo), Kokomo, IN, 1983; Fordham U, Lincoln Center, NY, 1984; Inst for the A, Washington, D.C., 1986; Pacific FA, Seattle, WA, 1986. Prizes: HS, 1981-83; Iron Horse Festival, Logansport, IN, 1983, 84; Logansport A Show, 1985. Collections: Standard Life Insurance of Ind., Indianapolis; Kokomo-Howard Cnty Public Library; Indianapolis Power&Light; Kokomo Public Library; DePauw U.

SMALE, HOBART B. [S, Des] Bedford, IN b. Bedford, IN. Teachers: Ira A. Correll. Prizes: HS, 1930.

SMALTZ, CAROLYN [SLP, P] Prizes: HS, 1962.

SMEAD, VIRGINIA M. [P] FL. Studied: Herron Sch A. Teachers: Harry Davis; Lois Davis. Note: Paintings on religious themes.

SMILEY, WALLACE J.

SMIT, DERK [Ldscp. P, SLP, P] Santa Barbara, CA b. 29 Jan 1889, Netherlands d. c. 1985. Studied: Amsterdam, Holland; Hamburg, Germany; AIC; Chicago Acad FA. Teachers: Joseph Allworthy; C. Buck. Exhibited: Navy Pier, Chicago, 1939. Prizes: HS, 1954, 56, 60, 61, 64, 65; Wabash Valley, Swope Gal, Terre Haute, IN, 1954; Graphic Printing Co, 1959. Collections: Ind. U, Bloomington; Terre Haute AM; Butler U, Indianapolis. Note: President, D. Smit Interior Decorating Co, Chicago.

SMITH, CAROL LYNN [P] Bloomfield, IN. Prizes: HS, 1969. Note: Painted florals.

SMITH, CARRIE DYAR [P] Bloomfield, IN. Prizes: HS, 1963.

SMITH, DEBORAH A. [P] Greenfield, IN.

SMITH, DOROTHEA E. [P, S, Dr] St Paul, MN b. 31 Jan 1919, Rockford, IA. Studied: Pasadena City Col; Purdue U; Weaver's Guild, St Paul, MN; Walker A Cen, Minneapolis, MN; Alhambra A Sch, Alhambra, CA; A Barn Sch A, Salt Lake City, UT. Exhibited: Tweed Gal (solo), Duluth, MN; Gal Cl (solo), Jewish Community Cen, Minneapolis; Paul Whitney Larson Gal (solo), U of Minn., St Paul. Prizes: Dunes Reg, Michigan City, IN; Tippecanoe Reg, Lafayette, IN; A Barn Sch, Salt Lake City.

SMITH, DOROTHY [Ldscp. P, P, SLP] Frankfort, IN b. 3 May 1914, Salem, IN. Teachers: Ruth Anderson; William Eyden; Rosemary Lawton Thomas. Exhibited: Evansville A Show; Am Dream A Gal; Ind. State Fair. Prizes: Ind. State Fair.

SMITH, F. HAROLD

SMITH, HARRIET REX [P] Ashland, OR b. 1921, Montpelier, IN. Studied: John Herron Sch A; Notre Dame U. Exhibited: Southern Shores Exh; Michiana Reg; Dunes A Fnd; Valparaiso U; AIC, sales and rental gal. Prizes: Northern Ind. A Salons; HS, 1949, 56. Note: Lived in Valparaiso, IN, 1948-78. T, Purdue U-Westville, Valparaiso U, Ind. U-Northwest.

SMITH, HOWARD E. Universal City, TX.

SMITH, JERRY F. [Ldscp. P, T] Crawfordsville, IN b. 31 Jan 1944, Terre Haute, IN. Teachers: Louise Hansen; Floyd Hopper; Ray Loos; Don Stone. Exhibited: Evansville M of A⪼ Indianapolis AL; Ind. State Fair; Brown Cnty A Gal; Ind. Pen Women Exh; Ind. AC Exh. Prizes: HS, 1985, 86; Ind. AC, 1990; Ind. WCS; Leeper Park A Fair, 1987; Wabash Valley A Festival, 1987; Griffith A Fair, 1988. Collections: Ind. Bell; Indianapolis Water Co; Psi Iota Xi Sorority; Eli Lilly&Co; IBM.

SMITH, LUCILLE Maywood, IL.

SMITH, NELLE ADAMS [T] Chicago, IL. b. Union City, Randolph Cnty, IN. Studied: Winona Lake Summer Sch; Acad FA, Chicago; AIC; Columbia U. Teachers: Roda Selleck. Note: T, Oshkosh, WI and San Antonio, TX. Also a singer, mezzo-soprano.

SMITH, NORBERT [P] Valparaiso, IN. Prizes: HS, 1958.

SMITH, RICHARD F. [Ldscp. P] Indianapolis, IN b. 2 Jul 1933, Chariton, IA. Studied: U of Iowa. Teachers: Grant Wood; Claude Croney. Exhibited: Ind. A, 1982. Prizes: Always a River, 1990; Ind. WCS, 1990. Collections: Lever Brothers, NYC; Merchants Nat Bank.

SMITH, SAMUEL EDWARD [S] Indianapolis, IN. Studied: Herron Sch A, 1971. Prizes: Ind. A Exh, IMA, 1971.

SMITH, SHIRLEY

SMITH, TERRY LLOYD [Dr] Linton, IN b. 17 Dec 1953, Seoul, Korea. Self-taught. Prizes: HS, 1984, 86.

SMITH, THOMAS P. Columbus, IN.

SMITH, WILMA ALE Honolulu, HI.

SMITHBURN, FLORENCE BARTLEY [P, Print, Dr, T] NYC/New Augusta, IN b. 16 Oct 1904, New Augusta,

IN d. 31 Jan 1959. Studied: John Herron A Sch. Teachers: William Forsyth; R. Lahey; H. Sternberg; G. P. Ennis. Exhibited: Ind. A Exh, 1931. Prizes: Ind. State Fair, 1929-34; HS, 1929, 30. Note: T, Arsenal Technical H.S., Indianapolis.

SMOCK, WILLIAM D. Hebron, IN.

SMOOT, WILLIAM [Ldscp. P, Por. P] Crown Point, IN b. 27 Jun 1928, Gary, IN. Studied: Chicago Acad FA; Studio Sch A, Chicago. Exhibited: Salmagundi Cl, NYC, 1982; Academic A, Springfield, MA, 1983; *Artist's Magazine,* 1984. Prizes: HS, 1987; Patrons' WC Gala, Oklahoma City, OK, 1983. Collections: Northern Ind. Public Service Co, Merrillville, IN; Gainer Bank, Merrillville, IN; Porter Mem Hospital, Portage, IN.

SMYRNIS, MARY *(See Lienert, Mary Smyrnis)*

SNAPE, STEPHEN A. [S] Chicago, IL b. Birmingham, England. Prizes: HS, 1929. Teachers: Wogner; Saunders.

SNAPP, WILLIAM [Ldscp. P, S, I, Por. P, Com. A] Bloomington, IN b. 3 Oct 1921, Edwardsport, IN. Studied: Indianapolis Acad Com A. Prizes: Monroe Cnty Fair, 1969; Spring A Show, Morgan Cnty, 1970; HS, 1987. Note: *Courier Tribune,* Staff Artist, 1969-72.

SNETHEN, MERRILL F. [P, Com. A, I, T] Evansville, IN b. Evansville, IN. Studied: Carnegie Inst Technology, Pittsburgh; AIC; Amer Acad A; Evansville Col. Exhibited: AIC; Am WCS, NY; Butler AI, Youngstown, OH. Collections: Evansville M. Note: T, Bosse H.S.

SNIDER, DOLLY [Ldscp. P] Muncie, IN b. 20 Nov 1911, Circleville, OH. Studied: Ball State U. Teachers: Adelee Wendel; Alice Nichols; William Ashby; Floyd Hopper; Barbara Gray; Frank Frederico. Prizes: Randolph Cnty A Show; Muncie AG; Brown Cnty Gal Assn.

SNYDER, ROBIN A. [Por. P, SLP] Carmel, IN. Studied: Hillsdale Col; Ind. U. Teachers: Sam Knecht; Rosemary Lawton Thomas. Exhibited: Ind. A, 1989; Ind. WCS, 1988. Prizes: Ind. WCS, 1989; Ind. State Fair, 1988. Collections: Greenwood Public Library; Automatic Feed Co, Napoleon, OH.

SOHN, FRANK [Des, C, P, Gra. A] Toledo, OH b. 24 Jul 1888, Columbus, IN. Studied: U of Ill.; AIC. Teachers: A. Gunther; I. Manoir; A. Angarola; F. Grant. Exhibited: WMAA, 1933; MMA; AIC. Prizes: Toledo MA, 1946; HS, 1933. Note: Des, Libbey Owens Ford Glass Co.

SOLICH, LUCILLE KATHRYN

SOLOMON, A(nn) T. [P, I] Indianapolis, IN b. 21 Feb 1934, Henry Cnty, IN. Studied: Herron Sch A; Ind. U, South Bend. Teachers: Harold Zisla; John Pellew; George Cherepov. Exhibited: Flora 90, Chicago, IL, 1990; A for the Parks, Jackson, WY, 1990; Michiana Reg; Ind. AC; IMA, Alliance Gal. Prizes: HS, 1987, 90; AA of New Castle (Ind.); Tri Kappa A Exh, Auburn, IN; Ind. State Fair. Note: Co-illustrated a children's science book, published by Ohio State U, Col of Education.

SOMMERKAMP, SHERYL [P] Indianapolis, IN b. 26 Feb 1944, Sullivan, IN. Teachers: Rosemary Lawton Thomas. Exhibited: Ind. WCS; Southside AL, Reg Show VII; IHA; Ind. AC; Indianapolis AL. Prizes: Ind. State Fair, 1989; Central Ind. A, 1989, 90.

SONGER, GENE [P] Danville, IL.

SONNEFIELD, WILMA [T] Indianapolis, IN b. Indianapolis. Studied: U of Wis.; Herron AI; Butler U. Teachers: C. Curry Bohm. Exhibited: Jonesboro, IN (solo); Grant Cnty Federated Cls Convention. Note: T, Indianapolis Public Sch #69.

SORENSON, ERIC Evansville, IN.

SOTOLONGO, BERTHA C. [P] Indianapolis, IN.

SOWDER, DIANA [P] Huntington, IN b. Westerly, RI. Studied: Huntington Col; Ball State U; Dayton AI; Ft Wayne AI; St Francis Col. Exhibited: Tri Kappa Reg, 1970, 71, 73, 75-77, 80, 81; Midwest M of Am A, Elkhart, 1981. Prizes: HS, 1979. Collections: Huntington Col; Riverview H.S.; United Brethren Publishing Co; Huntington Laboratories; Ft Wayne Public Library.

SPANNUTH, SHARON F. W. [P] Indianapolis, IN b. 24 Nov 1952, Jacksonville, NC. Studied: Herron Sch A. Teachers: Robert Weaver; Aaron Law; Henry Aguet; Stanley Burford. Exhibited: Southside AL Reg, 1986-90; Ind. State Fair, 1987-90. Prizes: A Directors' Cl Ann, 1974-75; Ind. State Fair, 1986.

SPAULDING, WILLIAM A. French Lick, IN.

SPEAR, CHARLES [P] Peru, IN. Prizes: HS, 1978.

SPENCER, MARY(belle) J. [P, Des, T] Riverside, IL b. 14 Jan 1900, Terre Haute, IN. Studied: Ind. State TC; AIC; Chicago Acad FA; Otis AI. Teachers: Ruth Van Sickle Ford; Guy Wiggins. Exhibited: NAWA, 1937, 38; CAFA, 1939; AIC, 1936, 39; S.C. AA, 1943, 44. Prizes: HS, 1940. Collections: Chicago Public Schs. Note: T, Chicago Acad FA.

SPENNER, ELMER E(llsworth) [P] Indianapolis, IN b. NE, 1894. Studied: Herron A Sch; ASL. Teachers: William Forsyth; Clifton Wheeler; Frank Vincent DuMond; Wayman Adams; George Luks. Exhibited: Lieber A Gal (solo), Indianapolis; Los Angeles (solo); Pasadena (solo); South Bend (solo); Indianapolis (solo). Prizes: HS, 1947.

SPERL, GEORGE [P] Gary, IN. Self-taught. Exhibited: Gary, IN (solo); Southern Shores; Northern Ind. AA. Prizes: HS, 1969.

SPICKA, WALTER R. Michigan City, IN.

SPIEGEL, DOROTHY A. [P] Indianapolis, IN b. 8 Dec 1904, Shelbyville, IN. Studied: Ind. U; Herron AI; Butler U. Teachers: William Forsyth; Clifton Wheeler; Paul Hadley; Oakley Richey; Eliot O'Hara. Exhibited: Ind. Fed AC Traveling Exh; Herron AM. Prizes: Ind. State Fair, 1941; Goose Rocks Beach, MA, 1938; Ind. AC, 1937, 38. Collections: West Lafayette (Ind.) H.S.

SPIER, LINDA L. [Print] Carmel, IN b. 18 Apr 1940, Milan, IN. Studied: DePauw U. Teachers: Ray H. French; Amanda Block. Exhibited: Jefferson Life Gal, 1987; Ind. Repertory Theatre (solo), 1984, 86; Ind. Nat Bank (solo); Am States Insurance Co, 1990; Wabash Valley, 1985, 88. Prizes: DePauw U, 1962, 80; Indianapolis AL, 1975; Wabash Valley, 1986; Anderson Winter Show, 1985. Collections: DePauw U; Williams Plumbing&Heating, Terre Haute; Ermish Cleaners.

SPINKS, WAYNE F. Indianapolis, IN.

SPRAGUE, RACHEL J. [Ldscp. P, Por. P] Muncie, IN b. 6 Apr 1912, Monticello, IN. Studied: Ind. U; Ball State U. Teachers: Herbie Rose; Maralin Bendell; Bird Burns; Everett Hill Sharp; Joe Bertrand; John Gee. Exhibited: Manatee Cnty AL, 1989; Sarasota AL, 1985. Prizes: Ind.

State Fair, 1987; Brass Latch, Montpelier, IN, 1989; Randolph Cnty AA, 1990.

SPRAGUE, ROBERT B. [P, Des, Print, T, W] Dayton, OH b. 12 Jun 1904, Dayton. Prizes: Exh Mid-West A, 1934. Note: Director, Roswell M, NM.

SPRUNGER, ARTHUR L. [P, Print, C, T, Des] Goshen, IN b. 25 Apr 1897, Berne, IN. Studied: Goshen Col; Herron AI; AIC. Teachers: William Forsyth. Exhibited: PAFA; Albright A Gal; SAM; Philadelphia WCC; Ind. Soc Pr. M; Ind. A&Craftsmen; Indianapolis AA; Northern Ind. AL. Prizes: HS, 1931, 58, 61; Northern Ind. Artists' Lg, 1920; Friends of A, South Bend, 1929, 32-34, 37, 39; Ind. State Fair, 1939; Elkhart Cnty AL, 1939. Note: T, Goshen Col, beginning1926.

SPRUNGER, WARREN [P, T] Indianapolis, IN b. Adams Cnty, Monroe, IN. Studied: Herron AI; Ball State U; Butler U. Prizes: HS, 1977, 78. Note: T, Arlington H.S. for six years. Employed by Eli Lilly&Co.

SPURGEON, JOSEPH [Des] Chicago, IL b. 22 Oct 1903, Kokomo, IN. Studied: Cincinnati A Acad. Exhibited: All-Am Packaging Comp, 1935. Prizes: HS, 1936, 39; WC, 1939; Am Management Assn, 1939; All-Am Packaging Comp, 1939. Note: Des, packages and products.

St. HELENS, PAX [S] Indianapolis, IN.

St. JOHN, LOLA ALBERTA [P, C, Des] Albany, IN b. 16 Jul 1879, Albany d. 1972. Studied: Herron AI; Cincinnati Acad A. Teachers: Henry Ryan MacGinnis; Vincent Nowottny; L. H. Meakin; J. Ottis Adams; B. Steele. Prizes: Muncie AA; Ind. State Fair, 1933-35, 37. Collections: Montpelier (Ind.) Library; Tipton AA. Note: Speciality, china painting and design.

STAGE, ELIZABETH G. [Por. P] W. Lafayette, IN/Scottsdale, AZ. b. 25 May 1905, Chicago, IL. Studied: Ohio State U; Grand Central A Sch. Teachers: James R. Hopkins; Wayman Adams. Exhibited: Ind. A, 1940s. Collections: Purdue U; Tabernacle Presbyterian Church, Indianapolis.

STAIR, MARY ELI (Mrs. Mathews) [P] Chicago, IL. Note: Native, Mooresville, IN. Member, Daughters of Ind. of Chicago.

STALEY, CLARENCE W. [P, Ldscp. P] Martinsville, IN b. 19 Jan 1892, Sanborn, IN d. c. 1946. Studied: Herron A Sch. Teachers: William Forsyth. Exhibited: PAFA; Herron AM; Ind. AC. Prizes: HS, 1947.

STALEY, TERESA French Lick, IN b. c. 1950 d. 8 Jan 1990. Prizes: HS, 1989.

STARBUCK, JULIA MAGILL [P, Ldscp. P] Portland, IN b. 15 Jul 1912, Portland, IN d. 1957. Studied: Miami U, Oxford, OH; Herron AI. Teachers: Harry Engle; C. Curry Bohm; Eliot O'Hara; Wayman Adams; Carl Gaertner. Exhibited: Herron AM, 1936; Ohio WCS, 1944, 45; L. S. Ayres Anniversary Show, 1947; Ind. A, 1945, 46. Prizes: Ft Wayne M, 1946; Canton M, 1945, 46; Nat Assn Women A, NY, 1954.

STARK, BARBARA [P] Indianapolis, IN b. 28 Dec 1933, Indianapolis, IN. Studied: Ind. U. Teachers: Rosemary Lawton Thomas. Exhibited: Ind. WCS, 1990, 91; Ind. State Fair, 1989, 90. Prizes: Ind. State Fair, 1991.

STARK, FORREST F. [P, S, T] Ft Wayne, IN b. 29 May 1903, Milwaukee, WI. Studied: Milwaukee State TC; PAFA, 1927; ASL; A Sch, Chester Springs, PA. Teachers:

Leon Kroll; Charles Grafly; G. Harding; Albert Laessle; George Oberteuffer; Boardman Robinson. Exhibited: Ind. State Fair; PAFA, 1938; Ft Wayne AM. Prizes: Indianapolis AA, 1932; HS, 1934, 40, 53; Milwaukee AI, 1933; John Herron AI, 1932; Cresson Award for travel and study abroad, PAFA, 1927. Collections: Ft Wayne AM; John Herron AI; relief, Forsyth Mem, Indianapolis. Note: T, Ft Wayne A Sch; T, John Herron AI.

STARK, OTTO [Ldscp. P, Por. P, P, T, I] Indianapolis, IN b. 29 Jan 1859, Indianapolis d. 14 Apr 1926. Studied: Cincinnati A Acad; ASL; Académie Julian, Paris, France. Teachers: Jules Lefebvre; Gustave Boulanger; Fernand Cormon; William Merritt Chase; Carroll Beckwith; Walter Shirlaw. Exhibited: Paris Salon, 1886, 87; NAD, 1888; Columbian Exh, Chicago, 1893; La. Purchase Expo, St Louis, 1904; Intl Expo, Rome, Italy, 1912; P.-P. Expo, 1915; San Diego Exh, 1916; Brooklyn M, 1926; Chile; Argentina. Prizes: Richmond AA, Foulke Pr, Richmond, IN, 1908; Ind. A, 1915; Ind. State Fair, 1925. Collections: Herron AI; Cincinnati AM; City Hospital, Indianapolis; murals in public schools, Indianapolis; Ind. Statehouse; U of Kansas. Note: T, Herron AI. Supervisor of art, Emmerich Manual Training H.S., Indianapolis. First president, Indiana AC. Exhibited in 1894 in the Chicago exh, *Five Hoosier Painters,* along with T. C. Steele, Richard Gruelle, John Ottis Adams and William Forsyth. It was the first time the work of the five was exhibited together. Early in his career, he did illustrations for *Harper's Weekly* and *Scripner's Monthly.*

STARKEN, NADINE [P] Plainfield, IN b. 13 Sep 1907, Mt Vernon, IN. Studied: Herron A Sch; Ind. U extension; Indianapolis AL. Teachers: George Jo Mess; Ruth Anderson; Frederick Rigley; Edward Manetta; Paul Sweany. Exhibited: Wabash Valley; Evansville M of A⪼ 500 A Festival; Ind. State Fair. Prizes: Ind. State Fair; Hendricks Cnty AL. Note: Became Mrs. Raymond K. Tyson.

STARLIN, RUTH [Ldscp. P, I, Por. P, T] Portland, IN b. 23 Nov 1923, Thompson, MO. Studied: Ft Wayne A Sch; Herron Sch A; ASL; Ball State U. Teachers: John Sanden; Forrest F. Stark; Everett Hill Sharp; Max Howard; Francis Brown. Exhibited: Nat A Show, Chicago, 1984; Brown Cnty, Nashville, IN, 1965; Ft Wayne AM; AA Randolph Cnty, 1972, 73. Prizes: Ft Wayne Women's Cl; AIC; Ind. State Fair. Note: Became Ruth Starlin Schafer. Painted portrait of Ind. Governor Evan Bayh for his parents. Mother of artist Barbara Hudson.

STARR, JANE Anderson, IN.

STEADHAM, TERRY [I, P, Gra. A] Indianapolis, IN b. 4 Oct 1945, Indianapolis. Studied: Herron A Sch. Exhibited: Ind. A Show, 1968, 70, 72; N.Y. Soc Illus, 1974; 500 Festival A, 1973; Ind. State Fair, 1972; Lieber Gal (solo), 1968; Leah Ransburg Gal (solo), Ind. Central Col, 1974; Louisville Sch A (solo), Louisville, KY. Prizes: 500 Festival A, 1969; Ind. A Dir Show, 1971; N.Y. Soc Illus, 1967; Bardstown Invitational, 1973; IMA, Works on Paper, 1974. Collectons: IMA; Intl Center, Indianapolis; Montage Gal, Bloomington, IN. Note: Published pieces in *Illustration, Photography, Design, Saturday Evening Post, Holiday, New York Times Book Review, Ramparts, Design Magazine, Amateur Athlete, Interior Design Magazine.*

STEDRON, FRANK Bloomington, IN.

STEELE, SALLY [P, Ldscp. P, Por. P, T] Bloomington, IN b. 17 Mar 1937, Bloomington. Studied: Indianapolis AL. Teachers: Clay Kent; Kaye Pool; Joseph Fettingies. Exhibited: Wabash Valley Exh, 1977; Ind. State Fair, 1990. Collections: Lincoln Chiropractic Col, St Louis, MO.

STEELE, T(heodore) C(lement) [Ldscp. P, Por. P, P, T] Bloomington, IN/Brown Cnty, IN b. 11 Sep 1847, near Gosport, Owen Cnty, IN d. 24 Jul 1926, Brown Cnty, IN. Studied: Waveland Collegiate Inst; Chicago; Royal Acad, Munich, Germany. Teachers: Gyula Benczur; Ludwig von Loefftz; J. Frank Currier. Exhibited: World's Columbian Exh, Chicago, IL, 1893; Five Hoosier Painters, Chicago, IL, 1894; La. Purchase Expo, St Louis, MO, 1904; Intl Exh FA, Buenos Aires, Argentina and Santiago, Chile, 1910; P.-P. Expo, San Francisco, 1915. Prizes: Paris Expo, 1900; Royal Acad, Munich; Richmond AA, Foulke Prize, Richmond, IN, 1906; Soc of Western A Ann, FA Bldg Prize, 1909; Wabash Col, 1898; Ind. U, 1916; HS, 1925, 26. Collections: Cincinnati AM; Herron AI; St Louis AM; Richmond (Ind.) AA; U of Mo.; Christian Col, Columbia, MO; Richmond (Ind.) Gal; Boston AC. Note: Joined with John W. Love in 1877 in organization of Indianapolis AA. Joined with William Forsyth and J. Ottis Adams in organization of Society of Western A, 1896. Artist-in-residence, Ind. U, 1922-26. Member of "The Hoosier Group."

STEELE, W(illard) KARL [Por. P, SLP, Ldscp. P, Mur. P, T] Jackson, MI b. 16 Sep 1910, Willard, OH d. 23 Apr 1982. Studied: Herron A Sch. Teachers: Clifton Wheeler; Oakley Richey; Donald M. Mattison; Henrik M. Mayer; Thompson. Exhibited: Ind. AC, 1938, 41, 42; Smithsonian Inst; John Herron AM; Hackley AM, Muskegon, MI. Prizes: HS, 1936-38, 72; Ind. AC, 1936; Ind. A. Collections: Nashville M, Nashville, IN; Elkhart H.S.; Northwestern U. Note: T, Wheaton Col, Ill., beginning 1946.

STEFFEN, JOE Ft Wayne, IN b. Ft Wayne. Studied: Ind. U, Bloomington. Exhibited: Performing A Cen, Ft Wayne; Regional A Show, Ft Wayne; Penrod, IMA; Wassenberg A Cen, OH; Intl Design Resource, Miami. Collections: Phillips Petroleum; Lincoln Life Insurance; Meridian Life Insurance; Intl Design Resource.

STEFFLER, ALVA

STEINKRAUS, EDITH (Mrs. H. A.) [Sgraffito A, S, T] Peru, IN. Studied: Layton Sch A, Milwaukee, WI. Exhibited: Wis.; Minn.; Ind. Prizes: HS, 1967.

STEINMETZ, ALMA L. [P, Ldscp. P, SLP] Ft Lauderdale, FL b. 8 Jun 1887, Dearborn Cnty, IN d. 28 May 1983. Teachers: Edward R. Sitzman. Exhibited: Broward AL, FL, 1955. Prizes: HS, 1947. Note: Became Mrs. Harry Steinmetz-Bobbe. Lived for many years in Indianapolis.

STEKETEE, CRAIG ALLEN [S, I, T] Ft Wayne, IN b. 9 Jun 1947, Holland, MI. Studied: Kendall Sch Des, Grand Rapids, MI; Ft Wayne AI; Western Mich. U, Kalamazoo, MI. Exhibited: Goshen Col (solo), 1979; Huntington Col (solo), 1978; Tippecanoe Biennial Exh, Artforms '79. Prizes: 43rd Tri Kappa, Ft Wayne, 1978; Johnstown Allied A Exh, Johnstown, PA, 1976; 17th Ann A Exh, VanWert AA, VanWert, OH, 1973.

STEKETEE, SALLIE HALL (Mrs. Paul F.) [P] Grand Rapids, MI b. 11 Sep 1882, Brazil, IN. Studied: Cincinnati A Acad. Prizes: HS, 1926, 28, 29, 31. Collections: Daughters of Ind., Chicago.

STEPHANS, GEORGE [S] Prizes: HS, 1961.

STEPHENS, JERRY G. [Dr, SLP, T] Kokomo, IN b. 28 Dec 1937, Jasper, IN. Studied: Ind. State U, Terre Haute, IN. Teachers: Robert Montgomery; John Laska. Exhibited:

Ind. State U, 1965. Prizes: Kokomo AA, 1989; Burlington A Festival, 1987; Evansville Press, 1947. Collections: Kokomo Sch Corp; South Side Christian Church, Kokomo, IN. Note: T, Kokomo-Cen Schs.

STEPHENSON, GRIFFIN [P, T] Mesa, AZ b. 27 Jul 1903, Elwood, IN d. 1978. Studied: Herron AI, 1922, 23; Ball State U. Teachers: William Forsyth; Susan Trane; Francis F. Brown. Exhibited: H. Lieber Co, 1944; Ball State TC Gal, Muncie. Note: T, Muncie schools, 17 years. T, Ariz.

STEPHENSON, JOHN G. Stamford, CT.

STEUERWALD, DOROTHY SCHNITZIUS Mobile, AL d. 1990.

STEVENS, MARGI [Por. P, T] Middlebury, IN b. 1917, Cleveland, OH d. 29 Nov 1982. Note: She and husband, artist Martin Stevens, were nationally known puppeteers. Mrs. Stevens was a professional pastel portraitist and creative artist in monotype.

STEVENS, MARTIN [P, T] Middlebury, IN b. 8 Jun 1904, NY d. 27 Oct 1983. Note: He and wife, artist Margi Stevens, were nationally known puppeteers.

STEVENS, W. RAY [Ldscp. P, SLP, Print] Richmond, IN b. 14 Jan 1924, Richmond, IN. Studied: Ind. U-East; Indianapolis AL. Teachers: Robert Brubaker. Exhibited: Ind. AC, 1981-90; Richmond Area A, 1975-90; Whitewater Valley; Anderson Winter Show; Wabash Valley. Prizes: HS, 1980, 88; Ind. AC, 1990; Ind. WCS, 1987; Ind. State Fair. Collections: Richmond (Ind.) AM; Richmond Banking Co; Brady, Ware&Co; Bank One; Ind. U-East; U of Evansville.

STEVENS, WILL H(enry) [P, C, Dr, T] New Orleans, LA b. 28 Nov 1881, Vevay, IN. Studied: Cincinnati A Acad; NYC. Teachers: Nowottny; Caroline Lord; Duveneck; Meakin; Jonas Lie; Van Dearing Perrine. Exhibited: Delgado MA; New Orleans A&C Cl; Newcomb Col A Gal, 1945; Black Mountain Col, 1945. Prizes: Richmond, IN, 1914; Southern States AL, 1925. Collections: BMFA; J. B. Speed Mem MA, Louisville, KY; U of Okla., Norman. Note: T, Stevens Sch A, Gatlinburg, TN; T, Newcomb Sch A, New Orleans; Dir, Natchitoches (La.) A Colony. Dec, Rookwood Pottery.

STEVENSON, CLAUDIA [Por. P, P, T] Cicero, IL/Rochester, IN b. Bolivar, IN. Studied: AIC; N.Y. Sch F&APP A; Cape Cod Sch P. Teachers: C. Hawthorne; W. J. Reynolds. Exhibited: CGA; NAD; AIC. Note: A Dir, J. Sterling Morton H.S., Morton Jr Col, Cicero, IL, 1924-46.

STEVENSON, MARK (R) [Dr] Noblesville, IN. Prizes: HS, 1981.

STEVENSON, MARTHA [Ldscp. P, Li, Por. P, SLP] Noblesville, IN b. 17 Apr 1925, New Castle, IN. Studied: Iowa State U; Indianapolis AL. Teachers: Harriett Jeffries; Lois Davis; Jeanne McLeish; Floyd Hopper; Alex Powers. Exhibited: Ind. WCS, 1983-85, 90; Ind. AC, 1980-90. Prizes: Ind. State Fair; Ind. AC, 1980, 86, 88. Collections: Ameritrust Bank; Union State Bank; City of Noblesville City Bldg; Huntington Bank; Noblesville H.S.; GTE; Industrial Airport, Kansas City, KS.

STEWART, BIRGIT I. [Ab, Print] Evansville, IN b. 15 Jul 1941, Hamburg, Germany. Studied: Rochester Inst Technology, Rochester, NY. Exhibited: Mid-Am Biannual, 1989. Prizes: KWS Aqueous, 1982; HS, 1990; Evansville M, 1990.

STEWART, FENTON E. [P] Greenwood, IN b. c. 1902, Oxford, IN d. 11 Apr 1979. Studied: Herron AI; AIC. Teachers: Timmons. Exhibited: HS Gal, 1967; Lafayette; Ft Wayne. Collections: Delta Sigma Kappa; Tri Kappa. Note: Art Dir, *Indianapolis Star Sunday Magazine*, 28 years.

STEWART, MARIE H. [P, Des, C, T, W] Oxford, OH b. 20 Aug 1887, Eaton, OH d. 10 Apr 1963. Studied: PIASch; Butler U. Teachers: Harold Haven Brown; William Forsyth; Clifton Wheeler. Exhibited: Herron AM; Ind. AC. Prizes: HS, 1942; Lincoln Tablet of Bronze, 1907. Note: Supervisor of A in Public Schs, Indianapolis, 1918-40s. Des and I, publications by Mentzer Bush Co, Chicago.

STILLSON, BLANCHE [SLP, P, Print, W, T] Indianapolis, IN b. c. 1890, Indianapolis d. 4 Jan 1977. Studied: Herron Sch A; DePauw U, Greencastle, IN. Teachers: William Forsyth; Charles Hawthorne. Exhibited: Pettis Gal (solo), 1927; Woman's Dept Cl Gal, 1934. Note: T, Herron Sch A; T, Shortridge H.S.; T, DePauw U. Author, *Wings*, Bobbs-Merrill publisher.

STINEBURG, WILLIAM E. [S, P, Com. A] Indianapolis, IN b. 1920, Burlington, IA d. Oct 1985. Studied: Herron Sch A. Note: A Dir, Ind. Farm Bureau Co-op and Nat Retail Hardware Assn. For 20 years owned Stineburg Studios.

STIPANOVICH, DEBORAH [P, Ldscp. P, Ab, Print] Chesterton, IN b. 29 Apr 1956, Gary, IN. Studied: Valparaiso U; VU, Cambridge, England; AIC. Teachers: Matzie Stipanovich. Exhibited: Southern Shores A Exh, Gary Artists' Lg, 1975, 81; 38th Ann Salon Show, Northern Ind. AA, 1981. Prizes: Southern Shores A Exh, 1975; Pletchers's Village A Show, 1967, 69-72. Collections: Chesterton State Bank. Note: Also paints German-Dutch tole painting, freehand style. Daughter of artist Matzie Stipanovich.

STIPANOVICH, MATZIE [P, Ab, Ldscp. P, Print] Chesterton, IN b. 26 Oct 1925, Chicago, IL. Studied: Gary Artists' Lg; AIC. Teachers Dale Fleming; Connie Smith; Charles Untilus; Anna Sut. Exhibited Biennial Michiana Reg, South Bend, IN, 1974; Southern Shores A Exh, Gary, IN; Northern Ind. A Salon; A for Religion, Indianapolis, 1970. Prizes: Southern Shores A Exh, Gary, IN, 1975; Pletcher's Village A Show, 1967. Collections: Chesterton State Bank; Bailly Elementary Sch, Duneland Sch Corp. Note: Also paints German-Dutch tole painting, freehand style. Mother of artist Deborah Stipanovich.

STIPANUK, BARBARA [Dr] Portland, IN.

STIREWALT, MARY T. Indianapolis, IN.

STOCKING, CURTIS M. [Ldscp. P, P, T] West Lafayette, IN/Thousand Islands of the St Lawrence b. 1914, Ogdensburg, NY. Studied: Ohio State U. Exhibited: Plaza Gal (solo), Merchants Nat Bank, Indianapolis, IN. Note: T, Purdue U, beginning 1948.

STOCKWELL, JILL AULT [Bat, P, T] Crawfordsville, IN b. 21 Jan 1939, Rochester, IN. Studied: Ind. State Col; Ind. State U. Teachers: Robert Weaver; Elmer Porter; Wayne Taylor. Exhibited: Sugar Creek Juried A Exh, Crawfordsville, IN, 1971-79; Crawfordsville Public Library (solo), 1985; Ind. State Fair, 1979. Prizes: Old Jail M A&Cr Show, 1979. Collections: H-C Industries, Inc, Crawfordsville.

STODDARD, (Beatrice) MUSETTE OSLER [P, C, T] Nashville, IN b. Carson, IA. Studied: AIC; Herron AI. Teachers: Charles Hawthorne; Maud Mason; E. A. Webster; Franz Bischoff; Ralph Johonnot. Exhibited: Herron AM; Ind. AC; Brown Cnty A Gal; Prague Intl. Prizes: P.-P. Expo, 1915. Note: Head of A Dept, Hill Top Sch for Girls, Nashville, IN; A Supervisor, Marion Cnty Schs, 16 years. Head of A Dept, Ind. Central Col. T, Starkey Seminary.

STOEFFLER, AILEENE HOCH Indianapolis, IN.

STOKES, CRESTON [Ab, Ldscp. P, SLP, T] Cicero, IN b. 19 Oct 1937, Noblesville, IN. Studied: Butler U; Herron A Sch; Anderson U; Germany. Teachers: Floyd Hopper; Harry Davis; Edmund Brucker; Malcolm Black; David Rubins; Fritz Hoffman. Exhibited: Anderson FA Cen (solo), 1987; Butler U (solo), 1980; Marion U (solo), 1983. Prizes: Ind. State Fair, 1983; Ind. AC; Anderson Winter Show, 1984; Ind. WCS, 1988, 89. Collections: Anderson FA Cen; Ind. U; IPL.

STOKESBERRY, C(hester) L. [P] Indianapolis, IN b. Clinton, IN d. Jan 1985. Teachers: Edward R. Sitzman. Exhibited: Ind. AA, Herron M, 1952, 57; Festival in Ind. Show, L. Strauss&Co; East Side A Cen. Prizes: Tribute to the Arts, H. P. Wasson&Co, 1966. Note: Apprenticed with a watchmaker in 1915 and stayed with this profession. Worked for leading jewelers, including L. S. Ayres&Co, until he opened his own business where he remained until retirement in 1959.

STONGE, CARMEN [P] Greenwood, IN.

STOODY, CLYDE A. Bloomsburg, PA. Note: Also worked in Chicago, IL.

STOOPS, CAROL K. [P] Indianapolis, IN. Studied: C. S. Mott Community Col, Flint, MI; Herron Sch A; Indianapolis AL. Teachers: Joe Richardson. Exhibited: A 500, 1977.

STOTTS, RUSSELL [P, Arch] Morocco, IN. Studied: Purdue U. Teachers: Otto Stark; G. M. Kiess.

STOUDER, ELIZABETH CHENOWETH [P, Print, C, T] Evansville, IN b. 1903, Marion, IN d. Sep 1977. Studied: Ind. U; ASL; A Cen, U of Louisville; U of Ohio, Athens (summers). Teachers: Mary Nay Block; Eugene Leake; Connie Clark Willis; Nell Peterson; Boris Margo; Charles Burchfield; Ben Shahn; Paul Sample; Zoltan Sepeshy; Rudy Pozzatti; Arnold Blanche. Exhibited: Ohio Valley Color Show, Athens, OH; Tri-State Exh, Evansville, IN; A Cen Ann Show, Speed M, Louisville, KY; Ind. AC, Indianapolis; Tri Kappa A Show, Evansville, IN, 1962. Prizes: HS, 1955; Ky. Wesleyan Col, 1957; Tri-State A Exh, 1957; Ky. and Southern Ind. A Cen Ann, 1959; Thirty-third Ky. A Cen Ann, 1960; AC Prize Comp, 1962; Tri-Kappa Sesquicentennial A Show, Evansville M, 1962. Note: T, Evansville M and Evansville Col (Now the U of Evansville).

STOUDER, JOYCE A. [P] Kokomo, IN. Prizes: HS, 1978.

STOUFFER, WILLIAM PARKER [P] Wabash, IN b. 1946, Wabash, IN. Self-taught. Prizes: HS, 1973, 82; Tri Kappa, Ft Wayne, 1974; Rose Show, Wabash, 1972, 73. Collections: Wabash Carnegie Library.

STOUT, ETHEL [Ldscp. P] Plymouth, IN. Prizes: HS, 1941.

STOUT, FORREST A.

STOUT, KARYL DANIEL [Li] Sheridan, IN. b. 17 Jun

1947. Studied: Herron Sch A; Tyler Sch A, Temple U. Exhibited: Mid-States Exh, Evansville, 1969; Ind. U, 1969; Green Street Gal (solo), Philadelphia, PA, 1972.

STOVER, WALLACE P. [Por. P, P, I] Elkhart, IN b. 5 Jan 1903, Elkhart. Studied: Herron AI. Teachers: William Forsyth; Clifton Wheeler; Paul Hadley; Myra Richards. Prizes: Herron AI, 1925, 27.

STRACK, MARY ELLEN CALLAND [P, Dr, T] Indianapolis, IN b. 15 Oct 1953, Indianapolis, IN. Studied: Marion Col; Herron Sch A; Ind. U, Bloomington. Exhibited: IMA, rental gal.

STRANGE, JENNIFER A. [Ldscp. P, Genre P, T] Indianapolis, IN b. 18 May 1960, Indianapolis. Studied: Ind. U, Bloomington; U of Ga., Athens. Teachers: Barry Gealt; Mike Nicholson; Jim Herbert. Exhibited: Winthrop Place of A, Indianapolis, 1984; Palazzo Casali, Cortona, Italy, 1985; U of Ga., 1986. Prizes: 500 Festival of A, 1966. Collections: Indianapolis Intl Airport; Merchants Nat Bank; McDonalds Corp.

STREIT, FRANCES NORRIS [P, Por. P, Ldscp. P, SLP] Long Island, NY b. Indianapolis, IN. Studied: Herron Sch A; Iowa State U. Exhibited: Carnegie Show, Pittsburgh, 1941; CGA, 1941. Prizes: HS, 1949, 63; Ind. A Show, 1937. Collections: U of Iowa. Note: Painted portrait, Ind. Governor George Craig, 1955.

STRONG, CONSTANCE J. GILL [P, T] Gary, IN b. 13 May 1900, NYC. Studied: Pratt Inst; U of Pa. Prizes: Lake Cnty Fair, Crown Point, IN, 1926-28.

STROUSE, ELVA [P, T] Indianapolis, IN. Studied: Herron AI. Exhibited: Ind. A Exh. Note: T, Marion Cnty. Author, publisher, *Elva's Tips for Teachers.*

STUEBE, FRANCES [Ldscp. P] Indianapolis, IN b. 12 Apr 1907, Red Wing, MN. Studied: Indianapolis AL. Teachers: George Jo Mess; Edward Manetta. Exhibited: Sheldon Swope Gal, 1963, 75, 78; Anderson Winter Show, 1972, 74, 79; Muncie AA; Tippecanoe Reg; Ind. State Fair. Prizes: HS, 1970; Sugar Creek, Wabash Col, 1981; Anderson Winter Show, 1972; Ind. A, Herron M, 1965; Ind. AC, 1967; Indianapolis AL, 1960-73. Collections: Wabash Col; Stant Manufacturing Co, Connersville, IN; Harrington-Hock Insurance Co, Richmond, IN; Golden Rule Insurance, Indianapolis; Moore-Langen Printing&Publishing, Terre Haute, IN.

STUMP, CAROL [P] Noblesville, IN.

STURGEON, LEA A. [Ldscp. P, Por. P] Indianapolis, IN b. 1 Oct 1898, Portland, IN. Studied: Herron Sch A. Teachers: William Forsyth. Exhibited: Herron AI, 1928; Pettis Gal (solo), Indianapolis. Prizes: Ind. State Fair, 1929.

STURGEON, THELMA M. [P, T] Paris, IL b. Bloomington, IN. Studied: Paris (Ill.) AL. Teachers: Harold McDonald; John Laska; Laura Mason; Ernest DeSoto; Warren Doolittle; George Foster; Rob O'Dell; Irving Shapiro; Henry Bell. Exhibited: Associate Members' Exh, Brown Cnty A Gal, Nashville, IN; Bicentennial A Cen&M, Paris, IL; Wabash Valley AG (solo). Prizes: Wabash Valley A Exh, Sheldon Swope AM, Terre Haute, IN; Ann Paris A Show; Ill. Statewide Town and Country A Show. Note: Executive Coordinator, Bicentennial A Cen&M, Paris, IL, beginning in 1985.

STURGES, LEE [P, Print] Melrose Park, IL b. 13 Aug 1865. Studied: AIC; PAFA; Chicago Acad Des; Chicago

Soc Etchers; Calif PM Soc; Brooklyn Soc Etchers; Am Fed of Arts; Print Soc of England. Prizes: AIC, 1923. Collections: AIC; Smithsonian Inst; Calif. State Library. Note: Was president of Chicago Soc of Etchers. Also worked in Elmhurst, IL.

SUEBERKROP, HENRIK [S] Indianapolis, IN b. Shleswig-Holstein. Deceased. Prizes: HS, 1957-59. Note: Member, Ind. AC. Employed by Ind. State Conservation Dept.

SUGARMAN, S. JENNIFER [P, Print] Indianapolis, IN b. 27 Nov 1949, NYC. Studied: Northwestern U; U of Miss. Teachers: George Cohen; Betty Monroe. Exhibited: Am Painters in Paris, 1976; Small Works Nat Juried Exh, 1982; Nat '90 Small Works Juried Exh, 1990.

SUGGS, ISABELLE Kokomo, IN.

SULLIVAN, JANET [P] Valparaiso, IN.

SUMMERFIELD, BRUCE [Gouache] Ft Wayne, IN.

SUMMERS, MAURICE

SURENDORF, Jr., CHARLES FREDERICK [P, Print, Car, W] San Francisco, CA/Logansport, IN b. 9 Nov 1906, Richmond, IN. Studied: AIC; ASL; Ohio State U; Mills Col. Exhibited: CGA, 1933; PAFA, 1937; CM, 1933, 35, 36; SFMA, 1936-46; AV, 1942; DeYoung Mem Mus, 1946; Los Angeles MA, 1936; AIC, 1938, 40; NAD, 1941, 46; Albany Inst Hist&A, 1945; Philadelphia Print Cl, 1940, 46; Northwest PM, 1938, 41, 42, 44-46. Prizes: SFMA, 1937; Philadelphia Print Cl, 1941, 42; John Herron AI, 1933, 35, 38; SAM, 1938, 45; Ind. A, 1929-31, 33, 34, 40; HS, 1930, 49, 52, 54; San Francisco AA, 1938; Richmond AA, 1938. Collections: SFMA; Mills Col; LOC; Wichita AM; Richmond (Ind.) AM; public schs, Indianapolis; library, Logansport; Tahiti MA; Richmond (Ind.) A Gal. Note: I, *Mr. Pimney*, 1945.

SWABEY, LAURA C. Chicago, IL.

SWAN, RETA

SWANDER, DOROTHEA T.

SWARTZ, LESTER L. [P] Mishawaka, IN. d. 1991. Prizes: HS, 1981.

SWARTZ, LORNA R. [P] Monticello, IN b. 22 Oct 1942, Lafayette, IN. Self-taught. Exhibited: Pulaski Cnty AA, 1982-87; Monticello AA Exh, 1979-88. Prizes: HS, 1984.

SWEANY, PAUL J. [P, T] Indianapolis, IN b. 9 May 1927, Indianapolis. Studied: Herron Sch A. Teachers: David K. Rubins; Harry Davis; Robert Weaver. Exhibited: Am WCS, 1982; NIAA, Curator's Choice, Museum Opening, 1989; Watercolor USA, Springfield, 1986; Evansville Tri-State; Herron Ann; DePauw U Cer Ann. Prizes: Nature Interpreted, Cincinnati, OH; Ind. A Ann Exh, 1972; Nat Tour, Am WCS, 1982; HS, 1955, 89. Collections: Ball Coll, Muncie, IN; Ind. State TC, Terre Haute. Note: T, Park Tudor Sch; T, Orchard Country Day Sch; T, Herron Sch A; T, Indianapolis AL. Listed in *Arts Indiana*, Feb 1989, among eight of the decade's most influential Indiana artists.

SWEENEY, FRANCES HAINES *(See Haines, Frances and McVey, Frances Haines)*

SWIGGETT, JEAN (Mr.) [P, Print, Des, T] San Diego, CA b. 6 Jan 1910, Franklin, IN. Studied: Chouinard AI; San Diego State Col; U of Southern Calif. Exhibited: GGE, 1939; Los Angeles MA, 1935-41, 46; SAM, 1941; San

Diego FA Soc, 1937-39; SFMA, 1936, 38; Wichita AM. Prizes: Calif. State Fair, Sacramento, 1938; Los Angeles Cnty Fair, Pomona, 1938; HS, 1950. Collections: San Diego FA Soc; WPA mural; USPO, Franklin, IN; U of Southern Calif.; Polytech H.S., Long Beach. Note: T, U of Southern Calif., 1940-41; T, Washington State Col, 1941-42; T, San Diego State Col, from 1946.

SWITZER, JOHN E. [S] Indianapolis, IN.

SWOPE, H. VANCE [P] NYC/Ogunquit, ME b. 4 Mar 1879, Jefferson Cnty, IN d. 10 Aug 1926. Studied: Cincinnati A Acad; NAD; Académie Julian, Paris, France. Teachers: Constant. Collections: Public Library, Seymour, IN.

SYLVESTER, AGUSTUS M. [P, S, C] Anderson, IN b. 1908, Hamilton Cnty, IN. Teachers: Robert Youngman; Gerald Martin; Ralph M. Pearson. Exhibited: Ind. State Fair; Anderson Winter Show. Prizes: Anderson Soc of A. Collections: Pendleton A Gal; First Methodist Church, Anderson.

SYLVESTER, STEPHEN L. [Dr] Alexandria, IN.

SYMONS, LOUISE GRAY [Ldscp. P, SLP, T, W] Seymour, IN b. 1 Aug 1905, Brooklyn, NY d. 18 Oct 1992. Studied: Chautauqua Inst, NY; Upsala Col, East Orange, NJ; Brown Cnty; Provincetown; Rockport, MA; John Herron A Sch. Teachers: Garo Antreasian; George Jo Mess; Carl Graf; Maxwell Starr. Exhibited: Ind. AC; Ind. State Fair; IMA; Seymour Gal. Prizes: HS, 1965; Ind. AC, 1952; Chautauqua Inst, 1972; Upsala Medallion of Honor for her courage and achievement as a deaf person, 50th college reunion. Collections: Bates Col, Lewiston, MA; Merchants Bank; Mem Hospital, Seymour, IN. Note: W, *Indianapolis Times* and *Seymour Daily Tribune*. Dir, Ind. State Fair A Gal, 1958.

SZERDAHELYI, GEORGE V.

T

1963 *Hoosier Salon*

TAFLINGER, ELMER E(dward) [P, Mur. P, Por. P, T] Indianapolis, IN b. 3 Mar 1891, Indianapolis d. 13 Aug 1981. Studied: ASL. Teachers: G. Bridgeman; Otto Stark. Prizes: HS, 1926, 33, 45, 46; Ind. Painters, 1930; Sagamore of the Wabash, 1981; Adams Award. Collections: Mural, Manual Training H.S., Indianapolis. Note: Noted for his murals and pastels and for his art sch. Responsible for bringing "The Ruins" to Holliday Park, Indianapolis.

TAGGART, BARBARA (J.) [P] Zionsville, IN.

TAGGART, EDWIN LYNN [P, S, Print, I, Mur. P] San Mateo, CA/Richmond, IN b. 23 Apr 1905, Richmond, IN. Studied: Calif. Sch A&C; ASL; NAD. Teachers: R. L. Coats; F. F. Brown; B. Waite. Prizes: Wayne Cnty Fair; U.C.T. Art Medal, 1925. Collections: murals, Morton H.S., Richmond, IN.

TAGGART, LUCY M. [P, Por. P, Ldscp. P, T] Indianapolis, IN/Gloucester, MA b. 1880, Indianapolis d. 9 Oct 1960, Indianapolis. Studied: ASL; Smith Col, MA. Teachers: William Forsyth; William Merritt Chase; Charles Hawthorne. Prizes: J. I. Holcomb Award, 1922; HS, 1925, 26. Collections: Herron AI. Note: T, Herron AI.

TANNER, RUSSELL [P, MM] Kansas City, MO.

TARR, MARIE

TASKEY, HARRY LEROY [I, Print, T] NYC/Milford, NJ b. 12 Jun 1892, Rockford, IN. Studied: ASL; Grande Chaumière, Paris, France. Teachers: Henri; Bridgeman; Von Schlegell; H. Lever; H. Boss; B. Robinson; H. Sternberg. Exhibited: BM, 1931, 35; AIC, 1931, 35; NAD, 1935; Texas Centennial Expo, 1936; PAFA, 1935; Syracuse MFA, 1934; CGA, 1934; LOC, 1932; Am. Pr. M, 1932; WMAA, 1938. Collections: MMA; NYPL; Syracuse MFA; Montgomery MFA; City of N.Y.; John Herron AI; Wilmington Soc FA.

TAYLOR, B. L. [S] Columbus, IN b. 3 Jun 1933, Columbus, IN. Self-taught. Exhibited: Scholastic A Contest, 1949, 50; Columbus AL, 1977. Prizes: HS, 1972; Fair on the Square, Columbus, IN, 1977, 92. Collections: Noble Roman's Corporate Office; Ind. U, VIP Lounge; Circuit Court Room, Columbus, IN.

TAYLOR, D. CODER Chicago, IL.

TAYLOR, HAROLD E. Terre Haute, IN.

TAYLOR, JAMES EARL [P, Ldscp. P, Print] Boonton, NJ b. 17 Dec 1899, Greenfield, IN. Studied: Whittenberg Col; Ohio State U; Cincinnati AA. Exhibited: SAM, 1942; Butler AI, 1940, 43; CM, 1939-42. Note: Worked at Jones&Taylor Advertising, South Bend, IN.

TAYLOR, Jr., JAMES W(illiam) [P, Ldscp. P, Com. A] South Bend, IN b. 8 Jul 1902, South Bend. Studied: Dartmouth Col. Exhibited: John Herron AI, 1942, 43, 45, 46; Butler AI, 1943, 44; AIC, 1942-44. Prizes: HS, 1943, 44, 48. Note: Headed an advertising agency in South Bend.

TEMPLETON, J(ohn) C(owan) [Ldscp. P, T] East Chicago, IN b. 18 Apr 1880, Dunbar, PA d. 15 Dec 1958. Studied: Ind. U-East Chicago Extension; U of W. Va., Morgantown, W. VA; Saugatuck, MI; Positano, Italy. Teachers: Charles H. Keister; William Huettl; William Greason; Anthony Butcha. Exhibited: Ind. AC, 1953; Palette&Chisel Cl; Northern Ind. A Salon, 1945-55. Prizes: Lake Cnty Fair; Hammond P&S Lg; East Chicago Tri Kappa Exh; Northern Ind. A Salon, 1951, 53, 56. Collections: East Chicago Public Library; Ind. U; East Chicago Public Schs; Northern Ind. A. Note: Specialized in painting dunescapes. Worked as a steelworker for 29 years at Inland Steel Co. One of the founders, Northern Ind. A Salon.

TEMPLETON, LOIS MAIN [Ab, T] Indianapolis, IN b. 16 Jan 1928, Madison, WI. Studied: Canada Col, Redwood City, CA; Herron Sch A. Teachers: Robert Berkshire; Peg Fierke; Phillip Egan. Exhibited: Midwest M of Cont A, 1991; Bromfield Gal, Boston (solo), 1985; Patrick King Cont A, 1986, 90; Montalvo Cen for A, Saratoga, CA, 1985; Water Tower AA, Louisville, KY, 1985; Cincinnati Cont A Cen, 1984; Gallerie Hertz (solo), Louisville, 1992; Ind. U-South East (solo), New Albany, 1992. Prizes: Indianapolis AL Reg, 1988; 12th Biennial Michiana Reg, 1982; Dye Scholarship, Herron Sch A, 1981; HS, 1980, 91, 92. Collections: Am States Insurance Co, Inc, Indianapolis; Browning Investments, Inc; Merchants Nat Mortgage Corp.

TENENBAUM, JAN [Dr, Ldscp. P, Print, MM, T] Indianapolis, IN b. 18 Apr 1946, Birmingham, AL. Studied: U of Tenn.; U of Ill. Exhibited: 15th Nat Color Print USA; 52nd SAGA Nat Print Exh; Boston PM 25th Ann Exh; Works on Paper, IMA, 1972; Ind. PM, Ball State U, 1974. Prizes: Smithsonian Traveling Exh, 8th Nat Print&Dr Comp; 9th Biennial Michiana Regional A Comp; Black Forest Intl P&S Exh, 1980; 6th Ann Color Print USA, 1973; Print Cl, 1973; HS, 1982. Collections: IMA; Kemper Insurance. Note: T, Herron Sch A.

TERRY, WAYNE [P, Por. P] NYC. Studied: AIC; Herron Sch A. Teachers: Wayman Adams; Louis Bosa. Exhibited: PAFA, 1952; Butler Inst Ann, 1952; Portrait Show, San Francisco M; Ind. A Exh, 1949, 52. Prizes: AIC Ann, 1949.

THIERY, THOMAS [P, T] Onsted, MI b. 1940, St John, IN. Studied: AIC; Ind. U; Taylor U; Moody Bible Inst; Western Mich. U; Eastern Mich. U. Exhibited: WC USA; Mainstreams, 1971, 72, 74; Nat AC WC Nat; La. WCS Nat; N.M. AL; Academic A. Prizes: HS, 1969, 70, 73, 78; Randhurst A Festival, Chicago, 1969; Golf Mill A Festival, Chicago, 1969, 70; Toledo Tile Cl Nat P Show, 1969, 70; Jefferson A Council, New Orleans, 1969; Allied A, Nat Acad Gal, NYC; First Fed Bank Gal (solo), Chicago. Collections: Ferris State Col; Taylor U; Rothchild and Periwinkle Estate. Note: T, Adrian H.S., MI.

THOMAS, DIAN BUDKO

THOMAS, MARYBETH [Ldscp. P, I, Dr, T] Greenwood, IN b. 19 Mar 1923, Greenwood, IN. Studied: Ball State U; Chicago Acad FA; Ft Wayne A Col. Teachers: Elmer Taflinger; Floyd Hopper; Norman Hall; Otto Stark; Otto Hake; Ruth Van Sickleford; Francis Brown. Exhibited: Ind. State Fair; Anderson Winter Show, 1984; Am Pen Women, 1981, 83; Am United Insurance Co; Northern Ind. AA; Indianapolis AL; Ind. Heritage. Prizes: Nat Lg Am Pen Women, Boston, 1988; HS, 1981. Collections: Am References, 1991. Note: Did advertising layouts for over 6 years for the *Cleveland Press*.

THOMAS, ROSEMARY LAWTON [Ldscp. P, Genre P, Por. P, T] Indianapolis, IN b. 3 Jun 1919, Mulberry, IN. Studied: Ball State U; Herron Sch A. Teachers: Donald Mattison; Paul Wehr; David Rubins; Eliot O'Hara. Exhibited: Herron MA; Ind. AC; Ind. WCS. Prizes: HS, 1970, 88, 89; Ind. AC, 1989; Ind. State Fair, 1990. Collections: IMA; Herron MA; Ind. State M; Ind. Statehouse; IUPUI; Ball State U; U of Montreal; Oxford U, Oxford, England. Note: T, Indianapolis AL and Indianapolis Public Sch. Spent several years as head display artist, L. S. Ayres&Co, Indianapolis. Freelance Com. A and Interior Des.

THOMAS, SHIRLEY [P] Indianapolis, IN b. Memphis, MI. Studied: John Herron AI. Teachers: Adelee Wendel; Joseph Trover; Luther Buck. Exhibited: Ind. AC; Indy 500. Prizes: Ind. State Fair; Mile of A; Strawberry A Festival. Collections: Middletown (Ind.) Public Sch Library; Ind. Acad, Cicero, IN; Zionsville Gal, IN.

THOMAS, WILLIAM Marion, IN.

THOMPSON-SHOLTY, BEVERLY [Ab, Ldscp. P] Logansport, IN b. 6 Feb 1952, Louisville, KY. Studied: Herron Sch A. Teachers: Richard Nicholson; Robert Eagerton; Steve Mannheimer. Exhibited: Ft Wayne Women A Show, 1989; Logansport AA, 1989. Collections: Ind. Statewide REC.

THOMPSON, DOROTHY

THOMPSON, EDNA Indianapolis, IN b. Buffalo, NY. Exhibited: Indianapolis AL.

THOMPSON, ERNEST THORNE [Print, P, Mur. P, T, W] New Rochelle, NY b. 8 Nov 1897, St John, New Brunswick, Canada. Studied: Mass. Sch A; BMFA; Europe. Teachers: Major; Hamilton; Andrew; Bosley. Exhibited: 100 Prints of the Year, 1940, Bibliothèque Nationale, Paris; Victoria&Albert M, London. Prizes: Chicago, 1927; Fifty Prints of the Year, 1928; Cunningham Prize, 1929; New Rochelle, NY, 1937, 40, 46; HS, 1929. Collections: Bibliothèque Nationale, Paris; NYPL; U.S. Nat M; Wightman Mem Gal, U of Notre Dame; mural, St Patrick's Church, McHenry, IL; mural, Holy Cross Seminary, Notre Dame, IN; mural, Oliver Hotel, South Bend, IN; Nat Coll FA (Smithsonian Inst). Note: Dir, Sch FA, U of Notre Dame, 1922-29. T, Col New Rochelle, NY, beginning 1929. Author, *Technique of Modern Woodcuts*.

THOMPSON, FLORENCE M. Terre Haute, IN. Note: Also worked in South Bend. Included in *Who's Who of American Women*. Member, Brown Cnty A Gal, 1972.

THOMPSON, JEAN [Ldscp. P, P] Marshall, IN b. 16 Jun 1918, Homer, IL. Self-taught. Prizes: St Joseph's Catholic Church, 1990; Hoopeston AA, 1990; Brown Cnty A Gal, 1969. Collections: Kingman Community Health Cen.

THOMPSON, LAURA JONES (Mrs. Richard H.) [P, T] Winnetka, IL b. 18 Aug 1899, Muncie, IN. Studied: Northwestern U; Columbia U; AIC. Teachers: G. Buehr; C. Longabaugh. Exhibited: CGA, 1943; Denver AM, 1936; Evanston Woman's Cl, 1940, 43-46; Stevens Hotel (solo); Drake Hotel (solo), Chicago; Winnetka Community House, annually; Winnetka Woman's Cl, 1940-46. Prizes: Evanston Woman's Cl, 1941, 42; HS, 1953. Collections: Winnetka Woman's Cl.

THOMPSON, MABEL GRACE

THOMPSON, MARIE J. [Por. P, SLP, T] Nashville, IN b. 19 Dec 1921, St Paul, MN. Studied: Indianapolis AL; Farnsworth Sch, Sarasota, FL; Madison Sch, Madison, CT; Marilyn Bendell Sch A, Bradenton, FL. Teachers: Elmer Taflinger; Robert Brackman; Paul Strisik; Albert Handell; Daniel Green; Marilyn Bendell; Howard Sanden. Exhibited: Springfield Nat, Springfield, MA, 1963; Purdue Max, 1964; Kansas Pastel Soc, 1985, 88; 500 Festival A, 1972. Prizes: IHA, 1979; IALF, 1968; Purdue Max, 1975. Collections: Ind. U; Indianapolis Power&Light; Bartholomew Cnty Courthouse; Tri-Kappa; Cornell U; Brown Cnty A Gal Assn; Centre Gal, Carmel, IN.

THOMPSON, NORMAN E. Terre Haute, IN.

THOMPSON, RALPH F. [Ab, P] Indianapolis, IN b. St Louis, MO. Self-taught. Exhibited: Herron AM; Ind. AC. Collections: Ind. U. Note: Operated insurance agency.

THOMPSON, ROY F. [P] Prizes: HS, 1951.

THORNBER, MIRIAM H. Tucson, AZ.

THORNTON, H. LaVERNE [S] Hammond, IN b. 13 Jan 1906, Herrin, IL. Studied: AIC; Van Amburgh Sch, Chicago. Teachers: Raoul Josef; Jose Martin. Note: Technical Dir, Hammond Community Theatre.

THORWARD, CLARA SCHAFER [P, Bat, C, Print, T] West Orange, NJ b. 14 Jun 1887, South Bend, IN. Studied: AIC; Cleveland Sch A; ASL; Thurn Sch Modern A.

Teachers: H. Hofmann; Henry G. Keeler. Exhibited: AL of Northern Ind., 1932, 38; Montclair AM, 1939; Ringling AM, Sarasota, FL, 1939; Lock Gal (solo), Sarasota, 1939; Morton Gal, NY, 1940; Plaza Hotel, NY, 1940; Witte Mem M, 1944; Palace FA, Mexico City, D.F., 1946. Prizes: CMA, 1925, 26.

THUNDERE, O(rin) D. [P, Por. P] Indianapolis, IN. Studied: Herron Sch A. Teachers: William Forsyth.

THURMAN, TRACY J. [Dr] Marion, IN b. 12 Apr 1959, Marion, IN. Studied: Herron Sch A; Marion Col. Exhibited: Am A Pro League, NYC, 1983, 90; Catherine Lorillard Wolfe Women's Exh, NYC, 1985; Allegheny Intl Miniature Exh, WV, 1989. Prizes: HS, 1988; Ind. State Fair, 1988; Ft Wayne AG, 1986, 89; IHA, 1985-90.

TIMBERMAN, ANN GILLIS [Dr, P] Indianapolis, IN b. 27 Oct 1943 d. 30 Jan 1991. Studied: Herron Sch A; Ind. U; Ball State U. Prizes: Ford Fnd Scholarship; 500 Festival; Nat Hallmark Honor Prize.

TIMMINS, ABBIE [Ab, Ldscp. P, JA] Rensselaer, IN b. 30 Oct 1947, Washington, IA. Studied: Ft Wayne AI; Ind. U. Teachers: George McCullough; Norman Bradley. Exhibited: Ind. Now A Exh, 1985, 86. Prizes: Tri Kappa, Crown Point, 1989; Jasper Cnty Fair, 1990; Martha's Vineyard Island A Show, 1970. Collections: Washington Cnty Hospital, Washington, IA; *Washington Evening Journal*, Washington, IA; Westchester Savings Bank, Westchester, IA; Curtis Creek Country Cl, Rensselaer; Fagen Pharmacy, Rensselaer, IN and Demotte, IN.

TINGLEY, JOHN K. [P] Notre Dame, IN.

TIPTON, DAVID N. [Ldscp. P, T] Indianapolis, IN. Teachers: Luther Buck; Rob O'Dell; Jerry Smith. Exhibited: Ind. State Fair, 1985-89; Ind. WCS, 1985-87. Prizes: HS, 1988, 89; IHA, 1989. Collections: Wishard Mem Hospital, Indianapolis.

TIRMENSTEIN, MARTIN S.

TODD, AL [Ldscp. P] Prizes: HS, 1967.

TODD, DIANE [Dr, Intaglio]

TODDERUD, SARA [Ldscp. P, Genre P, Por. P, T] Indianapolis, IN b. 25 Apr 1924, Charlotte, NC. Studied: Catawaba Col, Salisbury, NC; Florence, Italy. Teachers: Floyd Hopper; Rosemary Lawton Thomas; Zoltan Szabo. Exhibited: Frames&Things, 1987; Hindman's Gal, 1978; Catawaba Col, 1983-89; Merchants Nat Bank, 1982-89; Jail House Gal, NC, 1982. Collections: Indianapolis Power&Light; Merchants Nat Bank; Psi Iota Sorority; Eli Lilly&Co.

TOEBES, INGRID [S] West Lafayette, IN. Prizes: HS, 1981.

TOMPKINS, BARBARA [Genre P] Carmel, IN b. Los Angeles, CA. Studied: AI of Pittsburgh; Carnegie-Mellon U; U of Ariz.; A Cen, Los Angeles; Brigham Young U. Exhibited: Merchants Bank Plaza (solo), 1982; Dr&Small S Show, Ball State U, 1981. Prizes: Ind. WCS, 1985; Ind. AC, 1988; Ind. Wildlife A, 1988. Collections: Indianapolis Water Co; Merchants Nat Bank.

TOOLE, DONALD C. [Com. A] Evansville, IN. Studied: Herron Sch A.

TOOLE, KATHERINE A. (Kathy) [P] Spirit Lake, IA.

TOPPING, JAMES [Ldscp. P, Li] Oak Park, IL b. 25 Feb 1879, Cleator Moor, Cumberland, England d. 24 Jul

1949. Studied: AIC; Cumberland Acad, England. Teachers: John Adamson; Louis Wilson. Exhibited: PAFA; Nat Exh Am A, NYC, 1936; Joslyn Mem; AIC, 1925-31; Brown Cnty AA; Businessmen's AC, Chicago, 1929; Boston AC; Omaha AI; Omaha Soc FA. Prizes: AIC, 1924, 26, 29; Chicago Gal Assn, 1927; HS, 1940; Palette&Chisel Acad, 1924, 27; Assn Chicago P&S, 1942; Oak Park AL, 1930. Collections: State M, Springfield, IL; Joslyn Mem; Oak Park Cl; Chicago Public Sch; Palette&Chisel Acad FA, Chicago; Chicago Gal Assn.

TORNOW, KENN Kokomo, IN.

TOTH, GENEVIEVE HARTIG Plainfield, IN. Deceased. Note: Also worked in South Bend, IN.

TOWN, CAROL M. [P, I] Indianapolis, IN b. 17 Dec 1937, Hannibal, MO. Studied: Christian Col; U of Mo.; Herron Sch A. Teachers: S. Larsen. Prizes: Soc of I, 1970s. Collections: Connor Prairie; DePaul U.

TOWNSEND, CHARLES [Ldscp. P] Cincinnati, OH. Prizes: HS, 1959.

TOWNSEND, HARRY R. [P] Richmond, IN b. Richmond, IN. Exhibited: Richmond AA.

TRACY, JAMES (Jim) LEON [P] Nashville, IN.

TRACY, RONALD R. [S] Prizes: HS, 1965.

TRANBARGER, FRANCES ROE [Ldscp. P, Por. P, P] Wiedman, MI. Prizes: HS, 1945.

TRAUGOTT, DALE ELLEN [S, T] Carrboro, NC b. 3 Jul 1951, Indianapolis, IN. Studied: U of Wis.; Ariz. State U, Tempe. Exhibited: Ariz. State U (solo), Tempe, AZ, 1976; Portnoy Gal (solo), NYC, 1981; Marietta Nat, Marietta, OH; Mid-States A Exh, Evansville M A⪼ Ind. A Exh, IMA. Prizes: 500 Festival, Indianapolis AL, 1980; Ind. State Fair, 1974-76; 21st and 23rd Ann Dr&Small S Show, Ball State U, Muncie, IN, 1975, 77. Note: Daughter of artist Leah Traugott and sister of artist Joseph Traugott.

TRAUGOTT, JOSEPH (Joe) HENRI [Li, S] Albuquerque, NM b. 3 Nov 1948, Indianapolis, IN. Studied: U of N.M., Albuquerque; Atlanta Col A; R.I. Sch Des; Philadelphia Col A. Teachers: Garo Antreasian. Exhibited: Santa Fe Festival of the A, 1983; Mariposa Gal, Albuquerque, 1983; Anderson Print and WC Show, 1981; Mid-States Exh, Evansville M A⪼ Purdue Small Print Exh, West Lafayette, IN. Prizes: Albuquerque United A, 1982; Ind. State A Exh, 1980, 82; 500 Festival, Indianapolis AL, 1980; Mid-States Exh, Evansville, 1979; Works on Paper, IMA, 1970; Purdue Small Print Nat, 1982; HS, 1979. Collections: South Street Seaport M, NYC; Purdue U; U of N.M., Albuquerque; Wabash Col; Indianapolis Children's M; IMA; Anderson FA Cen. Note: Son of artist Leah Traugott and brother of artist Dale Traugott.

TRAUGOTT, LEAH S. [P, T] Indianapolis, IN b. 16 Jan 1924, Cincinnati, OH. Studied: Herron Sch A. Teachers: Donald Mattison; David Rubins. Exhibited: WC USA, Springfield MA, Springfield, MO, 1982; Aqueous '86, Ky. WCS, Louisville, KY; Ind. A Exh, IMA, 1982; IMA, rental gal (solo); Indianapolis AL (solo); Ind. Repertory Theatre (solo); Jewish Community Cen (solo), Indianapolis; U of Indianapolis (solo). Prizes: Ind. A Exh, IMA, 1983; Aqueous '81, Ky. WCS; Ind. Mid-States Exh, Evansville M A⪼ HS, 1967, 68, 70, 72, 74, 75, 78, 86, 88, 89; Ind. State A Exh, 1981, 83; Ind. AC Exh, 1980, 82, 85, 86, 89; Whitewater Valley Reg, 1980, 81. Collections: IMA; Radisson Hotel, Orlando, FL; Ind. State M; Franklin Col;

Wabash Col; Evansville M; Lilly Endowment; Ind. Bell Telephone Co; Methodist Hospital, Indianapolis. Note: Mother of artists Dale Traugott and Joseph Traugott.

TREES, JULIA [P] Anderson, IN. Exhibited: Hoosier A Gal, 1945.

TRIMBLE, RAY [P] Crawfordsville, IN. b. Crawfordsville, IN. Studied: Ind. State U; Penn State U; Famous A Sch. Exhibited: L. S. Ayres Pavilion (solo), 1982; Crawfordsville Public Library (solo); House of A Gal, Champaign, IL, 1982; Patricia Keane Mason Gal (solo), NYC, 1982.

TRIPLETT, THELMA (Mrs. Harlow A.) [P] Columbus, IN b. La Grange, IL. Studied: Fla. Southern Col, Lakeland, FL; AIC. Teachers: Whitney Sevin; Conroy Hudlow. Exhibited: Ind. A Exh; Mid-States Exh, Evansville; Ind. Dr, Prints&WC. Prizes: A for Religion, Bethlehem Lutheran Church of Indianapolis; Tri Kappa. Collections: IMA, rental gal.

TRISSEL, LAWRENCE E. [P, Des, I] Indianapolis, IN b. 27 Jan 1917, Anderson, IN. Studied: Herron AI. Teachers: Eliot O'Hara; F. Chapin; M. Kahn. Exhibited: CM, 1940; CI, 1941; Oakland A Gal, 1940, 44; PAFA, 1941; VMFA, 1946; Butler AI, 1944. Prizes: BAID, 1938; Ind. AC, 1941, 44; Ohio Valley Exh, 1944; Ind. State Fair, 1941; HS, 1946, 48. Collections: U.S. Government.

TRITCH, FAITH Oklahoma City, OK.

TROBAUGH, (LE)ROY B. [Ldscp. P, P] Delphi, IN b. 21 Jan 1878, Delphi d. 4 Sep 1955. Studied: ASL. Teachers: John H. Twachtman; Douglas Volk; Kenyon Cox. Exhibited: Herron AM; Ind. AC. Prizes: HS, 1937, 44, 49. Collections: Columbia City H.S.; Greencastle (Ind.) H.S. Note: Telegrapher, Monon Railroad.

TROTTNOW, BERT MORRIS South Bend, IN b. Bradford, IL. Studied: AIC; U of Mich.; Columbia U. Teachers: C. J. Martin; Albert Heckman; George Oberteuffer.

TROVER, JOSEPH A. [P, Ldscp. P, SLP, T] Indianapolis, IN b. 1915. Teachers: Simon Baus; George Jo Mess; C. Curry Bohm; Edward Sitzman. Exhibited: U.S. Senate Office, Washington, D.C.; Westside A Cen, Indianapolis, 1966; Wabash Valley Show; Indianapolis AL; Ind. State Fair; Brown Cnty A Gal; HS A Gal (solo), 1969. Prizes: HS, 1961. Note: Owned a gallery in Bean Blossom, IN.

TRUCKSESS, F(rederick) CLEMENT (P, T) Boulder, CO b. 16 Aug 1895, Brownsburg, IN. Teachers: E. C. Taylor; Eugene Savage; William Forsyth. Prizes: Ind. State Fair, 1922; Denver AM, 1933. Collections: Jefferson Sch, Lafayette, IN; stage curtain and mural, U of Colo.

TRUE, VIRGINIA [P, T] Ithaca, NY b. 7 Feb 1900, St Louis, MO. Studied: John Herron AI; Cornell U. Teachers: William Forsyth; Daniel Garber; Richard S. Meryman; Hugh Breckenridge; Charles Grafly. Exhibited: AWCS; NAWA; CI; Cornell U; Kansas City AI; Am WCS; Rochester Mem A Gal. Prizes: Denver AM, 1932, 33; Kansas City AI, 1935; Rochester Mem A Gal, 1939; Ann Colo. A Exh, 1932-33. Collections: U of Colo.; Cornell U; State Col of Agriculture, Ft Collins, CO. Note: T, Herron AI (1926-28); T, U of Colo (1929-36); T, Cornell U, beginning 1936.

TRUEBLOOD, SUSAN [Ab] Terre Haute, IN. Studied: Butler U; Herron AI; Ind. State U. Exhibited: Thurman A Gal (solo), Terre Haute, 1979; Art 500, Indianapolis AL,

1978; Ind. Cr, IMA, 1978; Michiana Exh, 1976. Collections: Ind. State U Library Collection; Tirey Mem Union Board.

TRUEMPER, Jr., JOHN W. [P] Ft Wayne, IN.

TRUITT, JANE

TSCHAEGLE, ROBERT [S, T, W] Indianapolis, IN b. 17 Jan 1904, Indianapolis d. 1959. Studied: AIC; U of Chicago; U of London. Teachers: Lorado Taft. Exhibited: AIC; John Herron AI; NAD. Note: T, U of Mo., 1935-36; Asst Curator, John Herron AM, 1937-41.

TUCK, RICHARD [S, Dr, Print, Cer] Ft Wayne, IN b. 13 Feb 1948, Roanoke, VA. Exhibited: 35th Ann Tri Kappa Reg; Ft Wayne Public Library Gal (solo), 1972. Prizes: 33rd Ann Tri Kappa Reg; 19th, 20th, 23rd Ann Norfolk and Western Exh; 5th Ann Crossroads Exh; 7th Ann Nat Dr and Small S Show, Corpus Christi, TX.

TUCKER, IRENE W. [Ldscp. P, P] Indianapolis, IN b. 15 Aug 1924, Richmond, VA. Studied: Indianapolis AL. Teachers: Floyd Hopper; Valfred Thelin; Leah Traugott; Rob O'Dell; Henry Bell. Prizes: Ind. State Fair, 1986; IHA, 1987, 88; Ind. WCS, 1987. Collections: Eli Lilly&Co; U.S. Fidelity&Guarantee Co.

TURMAN, WILLIAM T(homas) [Por. P, SLP, Ldscp. P, T, Car] Terre Haute, IN b. 19 Jun 1867, Graysville, IN d. 20 Jun 1960. Studied: Union Christian Col; AIC; PAFA; Chicago Acad FA. Teachers: J. F. Smith; A. F. Brooks; D. Garber; A. Sterba; A. T. Van Laer. Exhibited: Ind. AC, 1939-45; Swope A Gal, 1943-46; Ind. State TC. Prizes: HS, 1932. Collections: Swope Gal, Terre Haute; Ind. State TC; Ind. Public Schs in Columbia City, Terre Haute, Jasonville and Harrison Township; Public Library, Thorntown, IN; Public Library, Merom, IN. Note: Head of FA Dept, Teachers' State Col, Terre Haute. Memorial in Turman's honor, Turman Gal of Ind. State U.

TURNBAUGH, DORIS O. [P, Ldscp. P, Genre P, Por. P, T] Richmond, IN/Eaton, OH b. 15 Feb 1927, Indianapolis, IN. Studied: Herron A Sch; Miami U, Oxford, OH; Ind. U-East. Teachers: Lawrence McConaha; Cesar Ciriliano; David Rubins; Jeanne Dobie; Marilyn Phillis. Exhibited: Harness Tracks of Amer, for 15 years; Ind. WCS, 1988, 89; Pastel Soc of Am, 1988; Cincinnati and Vicinity Exh; Ball State Dr&S Show; Nat Lg Am Pen Women, Washington D.C., 1992. Prizes: Ind. WCS, 1988; Intl Harness Track of Am Show, Lexington, KY, 1989-92; Lighthouse Gal Show, FL, 1988; Ind. State Fair; Ind. A Exh; Richmond and Area Show; Palm Beach WCS. Collections: Richmond (Ind.) AA; Chartwell Corp, Boston, MA; Harness Track of Am; Richmond (Ind.) AM.

TURNER, MARY CLEMENT [T, P, Ldscp. P, C] Waupaca, WI b. Central City, NE. Studied: Herron AI; Pratt Inst; AIC. Teachers: William Forsyth; Randolph Coats. Exhibited: Herron AM; Ind. State Fair; Library Rooms, Waupaca, WI. Note: Head of A Dept, Mrs. Blaker's TC, Indianapolis. Became Mrs. Francis Russell Gallagher.

TURTLE, ARNOLD E. [P] Chicago, IL b. England d. c. 1956. Exhibited: Nashville, IN. Collections: Dailey Mem Col, Ind. U, Bloomington, IN. Note: Worked as a public accountant. Handicapped by poor eyesight.

TYREE, JEANNINE Evansville, IN. Studied: Museum Classes; Community Col.

U

40th annual *Hoosier Salon* 1964

UHL, MARY A. [P, Print] Indianapolis, IN/Door Cnty, WI. Studied: U of Colo.; Indianapolis AL. Teachers: Floyd Hopper; Lois Davis; Marilyn Price; Beverly Snodgrass. Exhibited: Jewish Community Cen (solo), Indianapolis, 1977; Ind. Nat Bank, 1983; Whitewater Valley; Indianapolis AL; Mid-States Exh; Door Cnty Invitational. Prizes: Indianapolis AL. Collections: IMA.

UNTHANK, GERTRUDE [Print, Ldscp. P] Superior, WI b. Logansport, IN. Teachers: J. E. Bundy; Martha Walter; Knute Heldner; C. C. Rosencranz; P. J. Lemos.

UNTULIS, CHARLES R(aymond) [P, S, T] East Chicago, IN b. 1911, East Chicago d. 1971. Teachers: Arnold Turtle; Anthony Buchta; Marilyn Bendell; Charles Vickery. Exhibited: HS (solo), 1961; Rogers Park Women's Cl (solo), Chicago, 1960; Northern Ind. A Salon, 1940-70; Gary Artists' Lg; Ill. State Fair, 1969; Brown Cnty A Gal Assn; Cortez Gal, 1951-71, Cortez, FL. Prizes: Northern. Ind A Salon, 1956, 58, 60, 62, 63, 65; Union Lg Cl, Chicago; HS, 1960, 62.

UNVERSAW, JEAN [P, Por. P] Indianapolis, IN b. Indianapolis. Studied: John Herron A Sch; Indianapolis Acad Com A. Teachers: Elmer Taflinger; Stella Coler; George Jo

Mess; Frederick Rigley; Garo Antreasian; Harry Davis. Exhibited: Ind. AC, 1975. Prizes: HS, 1957, 78; Indianapolis AL; Ind. State Fair; Ind. AC; A for Religion; Michiana Biennial Reg A Exh. Collections: P. R. Mallory Co.

UPDEGRAFF, WILLIAM (Bill) R. [P, T] Vincennes, IN b. 23 Feb 1942, Columbus, OH. Studied: Am Acad A, Chicago. Teachers: Irving Shapiro; William Mosby. Exhibited: Ky. WCS Aqueous '83; Ala. WCS, 1990; Pittsburg WCS, 1986. Prizes: Ind. A, 1990; New Territory Show, 1990; Swope Gal, 1983. Collections: Swope Gal, Terre Haute, IN.

USHER, ALICE FRAVER (Mrs. Roland G.) [S, W] Indianapolis, IN. Studied: U of Mich.; PAFA; Herron Sch A. Exhibited: 43rd Ind. A Exh. Prizes: HS, 1960. Collections: Ind. Bell Telephone, Indianapolis; Merchants Bank, Hyatt Regency, Indianapolis. Note: Author, *The Sunny Hours*, illustrated by Sophie Kniffke, published by Green Tiger Press, La Jolla, CA.

USUL, NURUNNISA [P] Indianapolis, IN.

UUK, MARI

VAIL, DOROTHY MAKEPEACE (Mrs. C. B. Carlaw) [P] Greenwich, CT b. 13 Oct 1900, Madison, IN. Teachers: William Forsyth; Tucker; Nicoliades.

VanBRUNT, WILLA BOWEN [Ab, P, Photo, MM, Col. A, T] Indianapolis, IN b. Springfield, IL. Studied: Ind. U; IUPUI; Ind. Central; Indianapolis AL; U of Ill.; Butler U. Teachers: Floyd Hopper; Maxine Masterfield; Valfred Thelin; Laforce Baily; Jane Burnham; Marilyn Phillis; Gerald Brommer. Exhibited: Intl Juried MM Comp, Clary-Minor Gal, Buffalo, NY, 1989. Ind. State Fair; Ind. AC; Nat Lg Am Pen Women Biennial, 1988; Michiana Reg Biennial, South Bend, 1980; Ind. State M, 1982. Prizes: North Coast Collage Soc Exh, 1986, 87, 90; Nat Lg Am Pen Women Miniature, 1988, 89; IHA, 1987, 89; HS, 1990; Nevada WCS, 1990; Ind. State Pen Women Show, 1983; Intl Platform Assn Nat Convention A Show, 1990-92; 6th Ann Intl Exh Min A, Toronto, Canada, 1990, 91. Collections: Community Hospital, South, Indianapolis. Note: Retired T, Indianapolis Public Sch.

VANCE, FRED NELSON [Ldscp. P, Mur. P] Indianapolis, IN b. 1880, Crawfordsville, IN d. 21 Sep 1926. Studied: AIC; Smith Acad, Chicago; Académie Julian, Colarossi Acad, Vitti Acad, all in Paris. Teachers: Laurens; Gèrôme; Max Bohm; E. Vedder. Prizes: Smith Julien Concour, 1900. Collections: AAA Paris; Carnegie Library, Crawfordsville.

VANDERPOOL, EARL Marengo, IN.

VanHORNE, ANDREA MEIDINGER [P, Ldscp. P, T] Auburn, IN b. 11 Jul 1940, Lodi, CA. Studied: Minneapolis Sch A&Des; Macalester Col; Carleton Col; Banff Sch FA; U of Alberta; St Francis U; Herron Sch A. Teachers: Harry Davis; Roger Blakely; Robert Berkshire; Anthony Caponi. Exhibited: Ft Wayne AL, 1989-92; Auburn Tri Kappa, 1964-92. Prizes: Auburn Tri Kappa. Collections: DeKalb Mem Hospital; Betz's Nursing Home, Auburn; Mayor's Office, Auburn; Macalester Col, St Paul, MN.

VanLANDINGHAM, MARY (Mrs. Herman E.) [Ldscp. P] Winchester, IN. Exhibited: East Side A Cen Exh, Marott Hotel, Indianapolis, IN, 1962. Collections: Am United Life Insurance Co, Indianapolis. Note: Member of Randolph Cnty AA.

VANN, ESSE BALL [P, T] Richmond Beach, WA b. 21 Sep 1878, Lafayette, IN. Studied: U of Southern Calif. Teachers: Edgar Forkner; E. P. Ziegler.

VanSELL, PATRICIA ANN Indianapolis, IN b. c. 1943 d. 1 Jul 1979. Note: Found murdered, 1 Jul 1979.

VanSICKLE, JANE HEWITT [Ldscp. P] Indianapolis, IN b. 12 Dec 1919, Richmond, IN d. Apr 1974. Studied: John Herron A Sch. Exhibited: Richmond AA. Prizes: HS, 1952. Note: Married to artist Robert VanSickle.

VanSICKLE, JOSEPH L(ynn) [P, T] Studied: Herron Sch A (graduated 1943); Iowa State U, 1946. Note: Dir FA, T, Watkind Inst, Nashville, TN, beginning 1947.

VanSICKLE, ROBERT F. [P, Dr, T] Indianapolis, IN b. 11 Dec 1917, Anderson, IN d. 9 Nov 1982. Studied: John Herron A Sch; Ind. U; Syracuse U; U of N.Y. State. Teachers: John Taylor Arms; Thomas Hart Benton; Hobart Nichols; Eliot O'Hara; Max Kahn. Exhibited: Ind. State Fair; Albany, N.Y. Ann; Silvermine Ann, New Canaan, CT; AIC. Prizes: Tiffany Fnd Fellowship. Note: T, Ind. U, East, 1971-75. Married to artist Jane VanSickle.

VanVOORHIS, WILMA JEAN

VAWTER, J(ohn) WILL(iam) [P, I, Print] Nashville, IN b. 13 Apr 1871, Boone Cnty, W. VA d. 11 Feb 1941. Exhibited: Woman's Dept Cl Gal, Indianapolis, 1934; Lieber Gal (solo), Indianapolis, 1936, 37; Hoosier A Gal (solo), Chicago, 1939. Prizes: Marshall Field Gal, 1925; HS, 1925, 26, 28, 30, 35; Brown Cnty A Gal Assn, 1934; Nashville Gal, 1935. Note: I, the James Whitcomb Riley series of books, *The Rabbit's Ransom* and other books for children. Wrote and illustrated comic series for Cincinnati *Commercial Gazette*. He also contributed drawings to the *Indianapolis News* and *Sentinel* and made drawings for *Judge* and the old *Life* magazines. His first wife was artist Mary H. Murray Vawter. Vawter was one of the first members of the Brown Cnty A Gal Assn. He grew up in Greenfield, Ind., and lived in Brown Cnty from 1908 until his death.

VAWTER, MARY H(owey) MURRAY [Por. P, Ldscp. P, W] Nashville, IN b. 30 Jun 1871, Baltimore, MD d. 28 Mar 1950, Matthew, VA. Studied: ASL; Md. Inst and Charcoal Cl. Teachers: S. N. Randolph; Edwin S. Whiteman; Irving Wiles; T. C. Corner; L. Kroeger. Exhibited: Independent AA, 1931; Ind. A; J. B. Speed Mem M; Public Library, Mathews, VA. Collections: Nashville Public Library, Brown Cnty, IN; Courthouse, Franklin, IN. Note: First wife of artist J. Will Vawter.

VELSEY, SETH M. [S, P, T, Des] Dayton, OH b. 26 Sep 1903, Logansport, IN d. 12 Apr 1967. Studied: U of Ill.(Arch); AIC. Teachers: Albin Polasek; Lorado Taft. Exhibited: Herron AM; Chicago A Exh; Am P&S Exh; Philadelphia Acad; Palace of the Legion of Honor. Prizes: HS, 1928, 30, 33, 34, 36; Ind. A, 1931; Hickox Pr, 1934; Paris Salon, 1937. Collections: Dayton AI; Wright Field, Dayton; St Peter's Church, Chillicothe, OH; WPA reliefs; USPO, Pomeroy, OH. Note: T, Sch of S, Dayton (Ohio) M.

VELVICK-VIGNA, BERNICE [Dr] Indianapolis, IN. Studied: Indianapolis AL. Note: Courtroom artist.

VENN, ROBERT G. [S] South Bend, IN. Prizes: HS, 1971.

VERNON, ELBA L. RIFFLE *(See Riffle, Elba L.)*

VETETO, WILMA [Ab, Ldscp. P, SLP] Carmel, IN b. 1 Jan 1916, Portland, TN. Studied: Ind. U. Teachers: Neil Matthew. Exhibited: IHA; Warren Performing A Cen; Whitewater Valley Exh, 1965; N.M. AL Nat Exh, Albuquerque, 1971. Prizes: Ind. State Fair, 1965; Tribute to A, Indianapolis, 1966; Riley Festival, Greenfield, IN, 1980.

VICE, H(erman) STODDARD [P, I] Chicago, IL b. 21 Jun 1884, Jefferson, IN. Studied: Chicago Acad FA.

VICTOR, PATRICIA EBERHART Prizes: HS, 1970.

VIETOR, FRANK [Ldscp. P, I, Com. A] Indianapolis, IN b. 21 Dec 1919, Brazil, IN. Studied: John Herron A Sch. Teachers: Donald Mattison; Henrik Mayer; Edmund Brucker; Edwin Fulwider. Exhibited: Mainstreams USA, 1977; Ind. AC, 1978. Prizes: Ind. State Fair, 1976, 77; HS, 1973-76, 78, 79. Collections: Ind. State U; U of Evansville; Ind. State M. Note: Partner, Bradford&Vietor Advertising A since 1957. Husband of artist Jean Vietor. Served as an artist for Allied Intelligence in Europe during World War II.

VIETOR, JEAN F. [Ldscp. P, T] Indianapolis, IN b. 28 Jun 1933, Indianapolis, IN. Studied: Lindenwood Col; Ind. U. Teachers: Frank Vietor. Exhibited: WC USA, 1971; Am WCS, 1975; Butler Inst Am A, 1978; Ind. State Fair, 1969, 70, 71; Ind. AC, 1971; Indianapolis AL, 1971; Inaugural FA Exh, Ind. State M; Intl Women's Year Exh, State Capitol Bldg. Prizes: WC USA, 1974, 75; HS, 1972, 76, 90. Collections: Springfield (Mo.) AM; Ind. State M; Ind. Bell Telephone Co; Jefferson Nat Life Insurance; Indianapolis Power and Light Co. Note: Wife of artist Frank Vietor.

VINING, SHIRLEY [P, Print, S] Anderson, IN b. 16 Nov 1921, Spencer, MA. Teachers: Floyd Hopper; Edgar Whitney; Deane Keller; Dave Kayton; Barbara Gray. Exhibited: Whitewater Valley A; Ft Myers Beach AA. Prizes: Indianapolis AL; Ind. State Fair; Pendleton AL; Anderson Soc A; Madison Cnty Redbud Festival.

VOGL, DON [P, T] South Bend, IN b. Jul 1929, Milwaukee, WI. Studied: AIC; U of Chicago; U of Wis.; Cleveland Sch A; Calif. Col of A&C; Dayton Sch A. Exhibited: Chicago Vicinity Show, AIC, 1966; Springfield Mo. WC USA, 1967; Northern Ill. U, DeKalb, 1969; Ball State 13th Ann Dr&Small S Show; Ft Wayne Reg, 1966-68, 70; South Bend A Cen (solo), 1972; U of Notre Dame A Gal (solo), 1973. Prizes: Southern Shores A Salon, Gary AL, Gary, IN, 1979; South Bend A Cen, 11th Ann Michiana Show, 1980; Wis. P&S Vera Pohl Award, 1961; Niles A Cen, 1970; Nazareth Col, Kalamazoo, MI, 1970. Collections: St Marks Church, Niles, MI; Immaculate Conception Church, Hartford, MI; Alverno Col; Mount Mary Col. Note: T, U of Notre Dame, 1963-80; Ind. U, South Bend, 1965-66.

VOREIS, GARY E. [S] Indianapolis, IN. Studied: Ball State U, graduated in 1977. Prizes: HS, 1983, 85. Note: Worked as copywriter at William H. Block Co.

44th annual
Hoosier Salon
1968

WADE, BETTY S. [P] Martinsville, IN b. 8 Nov 1931, Lafayette, IN. Studied: Purdue U; Indianapolis AL. Teachers: Paul Sweany; Leah Traugott; Lois Davis; Virginia Cobb; Marilyn Phillis. Exhibited: Aqueous, Ky. WCS, 1987; Ind. WCS, 1983-87, 89. Prizes: Swope Gal, Terre Haute, IN, 1984; Ind. WCS, 1983; IHA, 1986. Collections: Kokomo Library; Merchants Bank.

WADE, ROSSIE S. [P] Indianapolis, IN. Exhibited: 50th Ann Ind. A Exh, Herron AM, 1957. Prizes: Naval Ordnance Plant Show, 1956. Note: Tech Illustrator, Naval Ordnance Plant.

WADE, TED

WAGNER, FRANK HUGH [P, S, I] Chicago, IL b. 4 Jan 1870, Milton, Wayne Cnty, IN. Studied: AIC. Teachers: William M. Chase; Frederick Freer; John Vanderpoel; Von Salza; Cara Campbell. Exhibited: P.-P. Exp, 1915. Prizes: HS, 1929. Collections: St Joseph's Chapel, West Pullman, IL; Chapel Hall and Danville Normal Sch, Danville, IN.

WAGNER, MARY NORTH [P, Por. P, W] Chicago, IL/Saugatuck, MI/Milford, IN b. 24 Dec 1875, Milford, IN. Studied: AIC. Teachers: John Vanderpoel; Frederick Freer; William Merritt Chase; Frederick Richardson; Mary Sylvia West; Von Saltza; Frank Hugh Wagner. Exhibited: Chicago Soc Min P, AIC; Herron AI; Ill. Cl; Woman's World's Fair, 1927, 28. Note: Author/I, *The Adventures of Jimmy Carrot*, 1911. I, *The Second Brownie Book* by A.B. Benson. Book plates, miniatures, decorative screens and portraits were her specialty.

WAITKUS, E. ALGERD Gary, IN.

WALDORF, BARBARA J. South Bend, IN.

WALKER, FERDINAND GRAHAM [P, Por. P, Ldscp. P] New Albany, IN b. 16 Feb 1859, Mitchell, IN d. 13 Jun 1927. Studied: Académie Colarossi, Paris, France. Teachers: Dagnan-Bouvert; Puvis de Chavannes; Blanche; Merson. Collections: Ky. State Hist. Soc; U of Ky., Lexington; Berea Col, KY; Agricultural Col, MI; Lincoln Inst; Simpsonville, KY; Ky. State Coll; Public libraries in Louisville and Lexington, KY; Evansville Col; Greenbrier Col; U of Louisville; public gallery, New Albany, IN; St Peter's Church, Louisville.

WALKER, INES D. South Bend, IN.

WALKER, JAMES A. [Print] Flint, MI. Prizes: HS, 1965-68.

WALKER, JUDITH [P]

WALKER, LEON R. [SLP] CA. Studied: Herron Sch A. Prizes: HS, 1952.

WALKER, MARGARET McKEE [P, Des] Wilmette, IL b. 12 Sep 1912. Studied: Northwestern U; ASL. Teachers: G. Grosz; Lhote. Exhibited: AIC, 1934-36, 38; Salon des Tuileries, Paris, 1939. Collections: Patten Gymnasium, Northwestern U.

WALKER, MILDRED K. [P, T] Ft Wayne, IN. Prizes: HS, 1942. Note: T, Ind. Public Sch.

WALLACE, MICHAELENE R.

WALLPE, CONNIE DEERING *(See Deering, Connie Jo)*

WALTERS, VAL [Dr, T] Kokomo, IN b. 25 Mar 1941, Mishawaka, IN. Studied: Ind. U; Ball State U. Teachers: William Baily. Exhibited: Ball State U Dr&Small S; Purdue Max 24/69; Mid-States Reg, Evansville, IN; Tri Kappa, Ft Wayne; Ind. U-Bloomington (solo); Ball State U (solo), Muncie; New Renaissance Gal (solo), Skokie, IL. Prizes: Wabash Valley Reg, Sheldon Swope Gal; Tippecanoe Reg, Lafayette; HS, 1971, 72, 77, 90; Michiana Biennial; A for Religion, Indianapolis; Four Flags Reg, Niles, MI, 1988. Collections: Greenville City Bldg, Greenville, MI; Moore Langen Printing and Publishing Co, Terre Haute, IN; Kokomo Public Library. Note: T, Kokomo H.S.; associate faculty member, Ind. U-Kokomo.

WALTON, LAWRENCE (Larry) A. [S] Indianapolis, IN. Note: Wood-carver. Project engineer, Allison Gas Turbine Division of General Motor Corp, Indianapolis.

WALTZ, ROBERT New Palestine, IN. Studied: Herron Sch A, diploma in Visual Communications, late-1940s.

WALWORTH, JOHN Nashville, IN.

WAMPLER, MARYROSE [P] Bloomington, IN b. New Harmony, IN. Studied: Ind. U. Exhibited: Hunt Botanical Exh, 1988. Note: Painted a series for Nature House, published as collector prints. Wampler's wildflower paintings were published in *Wildflowers of Indiana*, Ind. U Press, 1988.

WAPPLER, EDWIN Park Ridge, IL.

WARE, BILL SHANE [P, Print] Indianapolis, IN. Exhibited: Indianapolis Water Co, 1976. Prizes: HS, 1972.

WARE, JORDAN E.

WARFIELD, VIRGINIA [P, SLP] Shelbyville, IN b. 15 Dec 1914, South Pekin, IL. Studied: Studio of Fashion A, Cincinnati, OH. Teachers: Isabel Affleck; Mathias Noheimer; Rosemary Browne Beck. Exhibited: Eagle's Nest, Hyatt Regency (solo), Indianapolis, IN, 1978; Shelby A Council (solo), Shelbyville, IN, 1980. Prizes: Ind. State Fair, 1950, 52; HS, 1972.

WARNACUT, CREWES [P, Print] Inwood, IN b. 1 Jun 1900, Osman, IL. Teachers: William Forsyth; C. Hawthorne. Exhibited: Herron AI. Prizes: All-Ill. SFA, 1929; Lg Northern Ind., 1929.

WARNER, CLARA E. Syracuse, IN.

WARREN, KARL [P, T] Michigan City, IN b. Rich Hill, MO. Studied: AIC; Chicago Acad FA; Académie Colarossi, Paris, France. Exhibited: Chicago Gal Assn; Esquire Theatre, Chicago; Book Fair, Michigan City; Gilbert Gal, Chesterton, all solo. Prizes: *Chicago Tribune* Comp, 1952, 53; HS, 1955, 57, 58, 60; Chicago Gal Municipal AL, 1956; Northern Ind. A Salon, 1959, 64; 4th Ann Union Lg Cl, 1961; Michiana Reg Exh, South Bend, 1964. Collections: Michigan City Public Library; Purdue North Central. Note: T, Chicago Acad FA; T, Evanston Acad FA; T, Purdue North Central.

WASSON, CAROL STROCK [Ldscp. P] Union City, IN b. 20 May 1957, Muncie, IN. Teachers: Susan Kuznitsky; William Schultz. Exhibited: Midwest Pastel, 1992; 12th Ann Fla. Pastel Assn, 1992; Quincy Quad State A Show, 1991; Southside AL Reg A Show, 1989-91. Prizes: Quincy Quad State A Show, 1991; Richmond AA, 1988. Collections: Richmond AM.

WASSON, JEANNE BRUBECK [P, Dr, I, T] Indianapolis, IN b. 4 Jul 1931, Marion, IN. Studied: Ind. U. Teachers: A. Raemaekers; Adolph Wolter; Floyd Hopper; Valfred Thelin; Frank Webb; Irving Shapiro. Exhibited: IMA rental gal; Ind. AC; Ind. WCS; Anderson Winter Show. Prizes: Art 500; Ind. AC; Ind. WCS, 1983, 84; Arts Insight Postcard Series; Celebration in Creativity, 1985; Exhibit 20, Channel 20 Comp, 1986. Collections: White River Park, Indianapolis; Purdue U; Harcourt Management; Indianapolis Water Co.

WATHEN, JOHN ST. JUDE Native of Southern Ind. Studied: Oakland City Col; Ind. State U. Exhibited: A&C Show, 1971; Ind. Salon of Collegiate A; Northwestern Territorial A Gal, Vincennes, IN.

WATKINS, BERTHA SEIFERT (*See Seifert, Bertha*)

WATKINS, GERTRUDE MAY [P, S, T, W] Chicago, IL/Momence, IL b. 30 Aug 1890, Franklin, IN. Studied: AIC. Teachers: L. Van Pappelendam; P. de Lemos; A. W. Dow; A. Freman. Note: T, Chicago H.S.

WATKINS, MARY KAY (M. K.) [Dr, Ldscp. P, I, Por. P, T]

Anderson, IN b. 13 Feb 1941, Indianapolis, IN. Self-taught. Exhibited: Ind. State Fair, 1982-92; IMA, All Gal, 1988-90; Anderson FA Cen.

WATT, PHYLLIS HILLERMAN [Ldscp. P] Bloomington, IN b. 2 Sep 1927, South Bend, IN. Studied: Ind. U; Yokohama, Japan; Wayne State U, Detroit, MI; San Diego State U. Teachers: Kohei Aida; Frederick Rigley; Zoltan Szabo; Jeanne Dobie. Exhibited: 68th Ind. A Show, IMA, 1981; Ky. WCS, 1983. Prizes: Ind. AC, 1985; HS, 1984; Ind. WCS, 1985. Collections: Anderson Mental Health Center, Anderson, IN.

WAVRA, ROBERT J. [Ldscp. P] Kokomo, IN b. 19 May 1951, Ft Lewis, Washington. Self-taught. Exhibited: Ind. State Fair, 1980. Prizes: Kokomo AA, 1984, 88, 92. Collections: Kokomo-Howard Cnty Library; Ind. U, Kokomo; Delco Electronics Corp, Kokomo.

WEAVER, AVERY B. [P] Valparaiso, IN. Note: Employed by the *Vidette-Messenger.*

WEAVER, DOROTHY [P] Indianapolis, IN. Note: Physician and member of Ind. AC.

WEAVER, ELAINE HARTER Worthington, OH. Studied: Herron Sch A, BFA, 1946. Note: Married first to artist Robert Weaver and then to Ronald Rick.

WEAVER, JACKIE [Dr] Roann, IN.

WEAVER, JAMES W. [Car, I, Por. P] Indianapolis, IN b. 21 May 1940, Union City, IN. Studied: Herron Sch A. Teachers: David Rubins; Edmund Brucker; William Ashby; Aaron Shikler. Exhibited: Ind. State Fair, 1986, 88, 89; Southside AL Reg, 1987, 89. Collections: St Andrew Presbyterian Church, Indianapolis; M of Cartoon A, Rye Brook, NY.

WEAVER, MARGARITA W(eigle) [P] Chicago, IL/Brandon, VT b. 24 Nov 1889, Brandon, VT. Teachers: William Forsyth; L. Simon; H. Morriset; Bourdelle. Prizes: Hoosier A, Marshall Fields, 1925.

WEAVER, ROBERT E(dward) [P, I, Des, T] New Bern, NC. b. 15 Nov 1914, Peru, IN d. 18 Jul 1991. Studied: Herron Sch A; Skowhegan Sch P&S, Skowhegan, ME. Exhibited: PAFA; CGA, 1940; Preview '71, St Joseph Col; Studio San Guiseppe, Cincinnati, OH; Wabash Valley Exh; Illustrations 16 Show, NYC; Ind. U (solo), 1977; Ind. State M (solo), 1977-78; Ind. Nat Bank (solo), 1979. Prizes: Two Beaux-Arts Medals; NAD, 1938; Am Acad Rome, 1937; Paris Prize; Ind. AC; 500 Festival of A; Ind. State Fair; HS, 1950, 73-75, 78, 80, 81. Collections: Circus World M, Baraboo, WI; IMA; Intl Business Machines; Colesman Collection, NYC; Methodist Hospital, Indianapolis; Naval Air Station, Alameda, CA. Note: T, Herron Sch A until 1982. Married for a time to artist Elaine Weaver.

WEAVER, SYLVESTER V. [P] Indianapolis, IN. Studied: New London H.S. (graduated 1914); Intl Correspondence Schs, Arch. Exhibited: Herron AI, 1951.

WEBB, LORNA [P] Delphi, IN.

WEBER, BETTIE L.

WEBER, JAN [P] Albuquerque, NM.

WEEKS, LEO R(osco) [I, P] Chicago, IL b. 23 Jun 1903, LaCrosse, IN d. 1977. Studied: Am Acad A, Chicago. Teachers: G. Sheffer. Exhibited: Wawasee Gal. Prizes: Palette&Chisel Acad FA, 1943, 44; All-Ill. SFA, 1946.

Prizes: HS, 1948. Note: I, *Penny Wise*, 1942; I, children's books.

WEHR, PAUL A(dam) [I, Des, P, Print, T] Indianapolis, IN b. 16 May 1914, Mt Vernon, IN d. 2 Oct 1973. Studied: Herron Sch A. Exhibited: PAFA, 1940, 43; Adv A Exh, NY, 1945; Ind. A, 1937, 43; Ind. AC, 1944; Ind. State Fair, 1936; Am WCS; AIC; Philadelphia WCS. Prizes: Ind. A, 1942, 44, 69; Ind. State Fair, 1940, 41; HS, 1943, 44, 69; A Dir Cl, Chicago, 1945. Collections: Herron AI; DePauw U; Ind. U Sch Medicine, Indianapolis. Note: I, *Collier's, Cornet, Redbook, Country Gentleman, Sports Afield, Popular Mechanics*. T, John Herron AI, 1937-45.

WEISEL, JAN [P] Indianapolis, IN b. Holyoke, MA. Studied: Holyoke Jr Col; Memphis Acad A, Memphis, TN. Teachers: Edward Sanski; Clayson Baker; Adelee Wendel; Floyd Hopper; Dolph Smith; Steve Vee; Leah Traugott. Exhibited: Memphis Public Library (solo); Sheldon Swope Gal, Terre Haute, IN; Lafayette A Cen, Lafayette, IN; Whitewater Valley AA; Anderson FA Cen; Indianapolis AL. Prizes: Indianapolis AL, 1974; Greenwood Exh, 1974; Eastgate Mile of A, 1973; Mid-South Fair, Memphis, TN, 1966-69.

WELCH, WILLIE F. [Dr] Ft Wayne, IN.

WELSHANS, LOTAN [P] Maywood, IL b. 15 Jun 1905, Danville, IN. Studied: Chicago Acad FA. Teachers: Claude Buck. Exhibited: Lieber Gal (solo), Indianapolis, IN, 1927. Prizes: HS, 1930, 33; AIC, 1931. Collections: Stevens Hotel, Chicago. Note: I, *The Adventures of King Pansole*, by Pierre Louy.

WENDEL, ADELEE B. [P, T] Casselberry, FL b. ca. 1899, Maverick, TX d. 15 Aug 1990. Studied: South West Texas State TC; U of Texas; San Antonio Acad A. Exhibited: Ann Local A Exh; Witte M, San Antonio; N.J. AL; A Cen of the Oranges, East Orange, NJ; Ind. AC; Ind. U; Woman's Dept Cl. Collections: Wilking Music Co, Indianapolis, IN; Ind. U. Note: Dir, Wendel Sch A, Indianapolis. Founded East Side A Cen, 1951.

WENDT, JANE [P] Indianapolis, IN d. c. 1971. Prizes: HS, 1963.

WENGER, SUSAN [Dr, MM] Ft Wayne, IN.

WENTE, TRICIA HEISER [P, Ldscp. P, Por. P, T] Bloomington, IN b. 9 Oct 1946, Hamilton, OH. Studied: Marshall U, Huntington, WV; Miami U, Oxford, Ohio. Teachers: Daniel Greene; Edwin Fulwilder; Crossan Curry; Robert Wolf, Jr. Exhibited: Cincinnati Zoo Intl Show, 1983; Carnegie A Cen, Covington, KY. Prizes: Midwest Salute to the Masters, Fairview Heights, IL, 1989; Art Happenings, St Louis, 1988; Southside AL, 1986. Collections: Cincinnati Bell Information Systems; Miami U, Oxford and Hamilton Campus Coll; Cincinnati Commerce Cen.

WENTLAND, FRANK A. [P, Print, T] Michigan City, IN b. 28 Aug 1897, Rolling Prairie, IN. Teachers: A. C. Winn; A. H. Krehbiel.

WERNER, SHIRLEY J. (*See Carr, Shirley Werner*)

WESNER, KATHLEEN D. Wabash, IN.

WESSEL, BESSIE H(oover) [P, Ldscp. P, SLP, Por. P] Cincinnati, OH b. 7 Jan 1889, Brookville, IN d. 1973. Studied: Cincinnati A Acad. Teachers: Frank Duveneck. Exhibited: Ohio State Fair; CM, 1939; Cincinnati Professional A, annually. Prizes: Cincinnati Woman's AC, 1937,

39, 40; HS, 1943, 45, 47. Note: Wife of artist Herman Wessel.

WESSEL, HERMAN HENRY [P, Print, T] Cincinnati, OH b. 16 Jan 1878, Vincennes, IN d. 1969. Studied: Cincinnati A Acad; Académie Julian, Paris, France. Teachers: Frank Duveneck; J. P. Laurens. Prizes: South Western A, 1915; Atlanta, 1920; Columbus, 1922. Collections: CM; WPA murals; Scioto Cnty Courthouse; Federal Reserve Bank, Holmes Hospital, H.S., all in Cincinnati; Ohio State Office Bldg, Columbus; USPO, Springfield, OH. Note: T, Cincinnati A Acad. Husband of artist Bessie H. Wessel.

WEST, ANNE WARNER [P] Indianapolis, IN. Prizes: HS, 1943. Note: Wife of artist Charles M. West, Jr.

WEST, Jr., CHARLES MASSEY [P, T, S] Centreville, MD b. 5 Dec 1907, Centreville. Studied: PAFA; U of Iowa; Herron AI. Teachers: Ranzetti; George E. Harding; Francis Speight; Roy Nuse; John F. Carlson; Jean Charlott. Exhibited: CGA, 1941, 43; AIC, 1942; PAFA, 1941; BMA, 1941; Del. A, 1939-46; CM, 1942. Prizes: HS, 1942, 43; Del. A, 1942, 43; Ind. AA, 1940, 41. Note: T, Herron AI, Indianapolis, IN, 1939-43. Husband of artist Anne Warner West.

WEST, WILBUR WARNE [P] South Bend, IN.

WESTALL, T. C. [T] Indianapolis, IN. Studied: Herron Sch A. Teachers: William Forsyth; Clifton Wheeler; Paul Hadley. Exhibited: Ind. A Ann; Herron AM; Ind. State Fair; Ind. AC. Note: T, private class in A&C.

WESTCOTT, L. GEYER Gary, IN.

WESTFALL, SONYA A. [P] Indianapolis, IN.

WHEAT, STEPHEN PAUL [Dr, P] Indianapolis, IN b. 14 Sep 1951, Beech Grove, IN. Exhibited: Art 500, 1978. Prizes: HS, 1979, 82, 84, 87.

WHEELER, CLIFTON A. [P, Ldscp. P, T] Indianapolis, IN b. 4 Sep 1883, Hadley, IN d. 10 May 1953. Studied: Herron AI; N.Y. Sch A; Europe. Teachers: William Forsyth; William Merritt Chase; Robert Henri; Kenneth Hayes Miller. Exhibited: AWCS; PAFA; GGE, 1939; WFNY, 1939; VMFA, 1938; local & regional exhs, within Ind., annually. Prizes: Richmond, IN, 1917; Herron AI, 1921, 23; Ind. AA, 1924; Franklin Col, 1926; Rector Mem Prize, 1927, 32; Ind. U, 1928; HS, 1927, 28, 30, 33, 42, 43, 45, 48, 50, 51. Collections: IMA; Herron AI; Swope A Gal; Purdue U; DePauw U; Ind. U; Ball State Col; Rose Polytechnic Inst, Terre Haute, IN; Indianapolis Public Schs; Ind. Public Libraries in Thorntown, Mooresville and Syracuse; murals, City Hospital and Circle Theatre, Indianapolis. Note: T, Herron AI; T, Shortridge H.S.; T, U of Colo.; T, Butler U. Husband of artist Hilah Drake Wheeler and cousin of artist Paul Hadley.

WHEELER, HILAH DRAKE [P, I] Indianapolis, IN b. 1878, Newark, NJ d. 30 May 1970. Studied: ASL. Teachers: John Twachtman; George Bridgeman; Walter Appleton Clark; Frank Vincent DuMond; Henry Siddons Mowbray. Exhibited: Am WCS; Herron AM. Note: Wife of artist Clifton A. Wheeler.

WHEELER, RONALD [Dr] Roanoke, IN b. 16 Oct 1946, Kokomo, IN. Self-taught. Exhibited: Huntington Cnty Library, 1989; Spring A Exh, Grant Cnty, 1988; HS traveling exh, 1990. Prizes: Elwood Spring A Show, 1988; Montpelier A Show, 1989. Collections: Huntington Cnty Library, 1989; Elwood (Ind.) H.S.

THE HOOSIER SALON, 1925-1990

WHEELING, WILLIAM G. [P] New Palestine, IN.

WHIPPLE, KENNETH [Ldscp. P, Li] Greenfield, IN b. 7 Mar 1914, Crawfordsville, IN. Teachers: Clayson Baker; Luther Buck. Exhibited: Ind. State Fair, 1974; Art 500, 1974. Prizes: Red Mill, 1973; Beech Grove, 1976; HS, 1974.

WHITAKER, CHRIS(topher) [P] Wheatfield, IN.

WHITAKER, PETE [P, Dr] Indianapolis, IN.

WHITE, ALAN B. (Alan B. White, D.D.S.) [P] Westfield, IN b. 19 Jul 1938, Jackson, MI. Studied: Wabash Col; Butler U (Masters Degree, Music). Note: Husband of artist Barbara Brookie White. Proprietor, The Herb Barn, Westfield, IN. Pianist, Carmel Symphony.

WHITE, BARBARA BROOKIE [Por. P, P, Gra. A] Westfield, IN b. 15 Nov 1938, Indianapolis, IN. Studied: Herron Sch A. Teachers: David Rubins; Harry Davis. Exhibited: Ind. A, IMA and L. S. Ayres&Co. Prizes: HS, 1971; Ind. State Fair; Glendale A Exh; Swope Gal, Terre Haute, IN. Note: Wife of artist Alan B. White. Owner, Pennyroyal Papers and Publications, Westfield. Author, *Getting the Fresh Herb Habit.*

WHITE, CRAIG L. [S] Thorntown, IN.

WHITE, ELAINE [Dr] Indianapolis, IN.

WHITE, GRACE TYNER [Dec, Des] Chicago, IL b. Wabash, IN. Studied: AIC. Prizes: ASL, Chicago, 1912. Collections: Lafayette Cl.

WHITE, ISABEL [Ldscp. P] Decatur, IN. Prizes: HS, 1988. Note: Also worked in Longboat Key, FL.

WHITE, MAPHAJEAN [P] Nashville, IN b. 17 May 1931, Roundhill, KY. Studied: Herron Sch A; U of N.M.; Ind. U-Kokomo; IUPUI. Teachers: Frederick Rigley; George Cherpov; Sam Smith; Charles Movalls; Gerald Brommer; Irving Shapiro. Exhibited: Ind. and Ky. State Fairs; IHA; Hendricks Cnty AL. Prizes: Ind. AC, 1988; Brown Cnty AG; Brown Cnty A Gal. Collections: Brown Cnty A Gal; Ind. U-Kokomo.

WHITE, MARGUERITE G.

WHITE, MARY JANE *(See Bigler, Mary Jane White)*

WHITESEL, MILDRED A. [Ldscp. P, P] Union City, IN b. 21 Dec 1892, Randolph Cnty, north of Union City, IN d. 1987. Studied: Ball State U. Teachers: B. Muhl; E. Nusbaum. Exhibited: AA Randolph Cnty, yearly; Wayne Cnty AA; Annie Oakley Days, 1970s-80s. Collections: AA Randolph Cnty; Washington Township Library; Lynn (Ind.) M; Wayne Cnty Mun Bldg, Richmond, IN.

WHITLOCK, WALTER [Dr, Ldscp. P, Por. P, Car] Indianapolis, IN b. 19 Nov 1918, Christian, KY. Studied: Ind. Sch for the Deaf. Teachers: Matthews. Exhibited: Ind. State Fair, 1989; L. S. Ayres&Co, 1985; Greater Sanders Temple, 1989; Walker Theatre, Indianapolis; Central Library (solo), 1985. Prizes: Senior Citizens A Fair, Central Library, 1988; Ind. State Fair, 1988; *Indianapolis Recorder,* 1989.

WHITMIRE, LAVON [P, Print] Indianapolis, IN b. Hendricks Cnty, IN. Studied: Herron A Sch; Saugatuck, MI; Goose Rocks Beach, ME. Teachers: William Forsyth; Clifton Wheeler; Paul Hadley; Ralph Sowell; Francis Chapin; Frederick Fursman; Eliot O'Hara. Exhibited: Herron AI, 1937 (Pr), 39. Collections: Herron AI. Note: T, Washington H.S., Indianapolis.

WHITMORE, LENORE K. [P] New Jersey b. Lemont, PA. Studied: Penn. State U; Ind. U; Provincetown Workshop. Prizes: HS, 1963. Note: President Indianapolis AL, 1959-63.

WHITTED, BRYANT ALAN [Ab, Dr, Ldscp. P, I, Por. P, T] Marietta, GA b. 26 Nov 1959, New Castle, IN. Self-taught. Exhibited: Marietta/Cobb MA, Marietta, GA, 1990. Prizes: Juried A Show, Gainesville, FL, 1986; HS, 1979; Richmond (Ind.) AM, 1982. Collections: Standard Life of Ind., Indianapolis; Richmond (Ind.) AM.

WHITWORTH, PHYLLIS [Ldscp. P, SLP, I, Por. P, T, W] Middletown, IN b. 21 May, Sulphur Springs, IN. Studied: Swan Sch A, Toronto, Canada; Ill. U. Teachers: Dorothy Swan; William Ashby; Tom Lynch; John Pike. Exhibited: Mont. and N.M. Nationals, 1983-85. Prizes: 23rd Intl Grand Prix, Deaville, France, 1972; Prix de Rome, Palace of Beaux-Arts, Italy, 1972; Religious Reg, Indianapolis, 1976. Collections: Ind. State M; Rose Hulman Tech U; U of Mo.; Henry Cnty Hist Soc.

WICKARD, J(ohn) MURRY [P] West Los Angeles, CA b. 2 Oct 1898, Indianapolis, IN d. Jun 1948. Studied: Herron AI. Teachers: James R. Hopkins. Prizes: Herron AI, 1924; Ind. State Fair, 1923; HS, 1925, 27, 29, 30, 34.

WICKER, JAMES H.

WICKER, MARY H. [P, S] Chicago, IL b. Chicago. Studied: Académie Julian, Paris, France. Teachers: Brangwyn; Hawthorne; Pushman; Gaspard; Browne; Szukalski. Exhibited: AIC, 1923, 24.

WICKER, PHYLLIS JEANETTE [Por. P] Logansport, IN b. 1932, Twelve Mile, IN. Teachers: Daniel Greene. Exhibited: Tippecanoe Reg, 1971. Prizes: HS, 1977, 81; Ind. State Fair, 1966, 69, 76; Tri Kappa Spring Show, Crown Point, 1977. Collections: Logansport Library; Ind. U Union Bldg; Calvary Presbyterian Church.

WIEDENHOEFT, JANICE [P] Kokomo, IN b. 23 Mar 1947, Peru, IN. Studied: Indianapolis AL. Teachers: JoAnn Cardwell; Suzanne Mays; Henry Bell; Jerry Smith; Stephen Edwards. Exhibited: Ind. State Fair, 1989; Indianapolis AL, 1989. Prizes: Kokomo AA, 1988, 89; Mayor's Award, Kokomo, 1987. Collections: FA Cen, Kokomo; Fincher Photo&A Cen, Peru, IN.

WIGGINS, LINDA A. GLASS [Ldscp. P, SLP, Por. P] Indianapolis, IN b. 1 Feb 1957, Indianapolis. Teachers: Leanne DeWester; Jeanne McLeish; Christopher Schink. Exhibited: IHA, 1986. Prizes: Bears of Blue River Festival, Shelbyville, IN, 1990; Riley Day, Greenfield, IN.

WIGGS, CATHY E. [P] Indianapolis, IN b. c. 1941. Studied: St Mary-of-the-Woods Col (graduated 1963), Terre Haute, IN. Exhibited: St Mary-of-the-Woods Col, 1966.

WILCOX, ROBERT ALLEN [P] Michigan City, IN.

WILD, SYLVIA M.

WILDER, BETTY DeVERE [P] Evanston, IL.

WILDER, LOUISE [P] Gary, IN.

WILDMAN, E(lizabeth) G. [Genre P, T] Shelbyville, IN b. 1 Mar 1947, Sarasota, FL. Studied: BSU; Ind. U. Teachers: Carrie O'Hara Morrison; Alice Nichols; Rob O'Dell. Exhibited: IMA, Alliance Gal. Collections: Knauf Fiber Glass; Eli Lilly&Co.

WILDMAN, MARILYN [Ldscp. P, Por. P] Danville, IN b. 31 May 1933, Clinton, IN. Studied: Ind. State U. Teachers: Elmer Porter; Clay Kent; Joseph Fettingis; Rosemary Lawton Thomas; Mary Gaalema. Exhibited: Hendricks Cnty AL Spring Show, 1987; Covered Bridge AA, 1980-90.

WILLIAMS, C(harles) WARNER [S] Chicago, IL b. 23 Apr 1903, Henderson, KY d. Oct 1982. Studied: Berea Col; Butler U; AIC; Herron AI. Teachers: Albin Polasek; Emil Zettler; Alfonso Ianelli. Prizes: HS, 1928, 31, 32, 36, 39-41, 43, 47, 48; North Shore AA, 1937, 38; AIC, 1939; Daughters of Ind., 1937, 39; City of Chicago Prize, 1931. Collections: Courthouse, Frankfort, IN; Berea Col, KY; Logansport (Ind.) Public Sch; Bradwell Sch, Chicago; Riley Children's Hospital, Indianapolis; Kalamazoo (Mich.) Public Library; Ball State TC, Muncie; Three A Cen, Chicago; Ind. U; DePauw U. Note: T, Culver Military Acad, beginning 1940.

WILLIAMS, CHARLES SNEED [P, Por. P] Louisville, KY b. 24 May 1882, Evansville, IN. Studied: Allan Fraser Sch, Edinburgh, Scotland; London; Louisville. Teachers: George Harcourt; Edward Biedermann. Exhibited: Ackerman's Gal (solo), Chicago, 1931; Palette&Chisel Cl (solo), 1931; AIC, 1924-39; Paris Salon; Royal Soc Por P, London; Glasgow Inst; Belfast (Ireland) AM; NAD; PAFA; CGA; NGA; Paris (solo); London (solo); NYC (solo). Prizes: HS, 1927, 35, 38; SSAL, 1936. Collections: Am Col Surgeons, Chicago; State Capitol, Frankfort, KY; Northwestern U; Confederate M, Richmond, VA; Speed Mem M, Louisville, KY; Vanderpoel AA, Chicago.

WILLIAMS, EDWARD K. [P] Nashville, IN b. 5 Jun 1870, Greensburg, PA d. 1 Jan 1950. Studied: AIC. Teachers: John Vanderpoel; Frederick Freer; Albert Krehbeil; Frederick F. Fursman; H. A. MacNeil. Exhibited: Brown Cnty A Gal; Herron AI; AIC; N.Y. WCC; Am WCS; Baltimore WCC; CI, Pittsburgh; Toledo AM. Prizes: AIC, 1927, 28; HS, 1930, 34, 37, 38, 41, 45, 48; Brown Cnty A Gal Assn, 1939; Ind. AC, 1939-41; Chicago Gal Assn, 1940. Collections: Dailey Coll, Ind. U, Bloomington, IN. Note: Served as president, Ind. AC and Brown Cnty A Gal Assn. One of the founders of the Brown Cnty A Gal.

WILLIAMS, FLORENCE WHITE [P, I, W, T] Greenfield, MA b. Putney, VT d. 17 May 1953. Studied: Chicago Acad FA; AIC. Teachers: H. B. Snell; J. F. Carlson; A. Aldrich; F. Grant; K. Krafft. Exhibited: AIC; CGA; Baltimore WCC; Detroit Inst A; Milwaukee AI. Prizes: Ill. Fed Women's Cl; ASL, 1924; Boston Line Greeting Card Contest, Boston; Chicago Gal, 1927; All-Ill. SFA, 1932. Collections: Commission for Encouragement of Local A; Public Sch, Chicago. Note: I, children's books and magazines.

WILLIAMS, FLORIE (Florence) *(See Leviton, Florie)*

WILLIAMS, GAAR B. [Car, I] Glencoe, IL b. 12 Dec 1880, Richmond, IN d. 15 Jun 1935, Chicago. Studied: Cincinnati A Acad; AIC. Prizes: HS, 1925, 28. Note: He entered newspaper work as a staff cartoonist and illustrator for the *Chicago Daily News* in 1904. He came to Indianapolis five years later. I, *Indianapolis News;* front-page cartoonist for the *Indianapolis News* for 12 years before going to the *Chicago Tribune.* For 14 years his cartoons were distributed by the Chicago Tribune-N.Y. News Syndicate. Cartoon strips included "Just Plain Folks," "Among the Folks in History," "A Strain in the Family," "Wotta Life" and "Zipper." At the time of his death, his cartoons were being carried by thirty-nine newspapers.

WILLIAMS, JEAN [S]

WILLIAMS, PAULINE Muncie, IN.

WILLIAMS, ROBERT S. [Print, S] Indianapolis, IN b. 20 Apr 1948, New York, NY. Studied: Ind. U (graduated 1978), Bloomington. Exhibited: 34th Ann Wabash Valley Exh, Sheldon Swope Gal, Terre Haute, IN; Editions Limited, Indianapolis, Group Show, 1979 and Two-man show, 1982; Texas Tech Print Exh, 1977.

WILLIAMS, WALTER R(eid) [S, T] Chicago, IL b. 23 Nov 1885, Indianapolis, IN. Studied: Herron A Sch, Indianapolis, IN; AIC; École Colarossi and École des Beaux-Arts, Paris, France. Teachers: Rudolph Schwarz; Paul Bartlett; Mercie, Paris; Charles J. Mulligan; Bela Pratt, Boston. Exhibited: AIC; Women's Athletic Cl, Chicago. Prizes: HS, 1926; École Colarossi. Note: Director of Clay A Studio, Ridge Park Field House, Chicago.

WILLIAMSON, ARCHIE [Dr] Indianapolis, IN. Prizes: HS, 1981.

WILLIAMSON, L. L. VON [Ldscp. P, Cer, S] Nashville, IN b. 3 Aug 1924, Nashville, IN. Teachers: C. Curry Bohm; Frederick Rigley. Exhibited: Desch Studio, Brown Cnty; Brown Cnty A Gal, 1972.

WILLIAMSON, LESLIE (Lee) E. [P, Dr, I, T] Nashville, IN b. 4 May 1964, Nashville. Teachers: Marie Thompson; Lillian Dunnigan. Exhibited: Brown Cnty A Gal. Prizes: HS, 1987; Strathmore Greeting Card, 1989; "86, " Sheldon Swope Gal, Terre Haute, IN. Collections: First Nat Bank, Terre Haute, IN; Strathmore Greeting Card Coll. Note: Specializes in ornithological painting, insects and flowers.

WILLIS, WAYNE Indianapolis, IN.

WILLS, JAN [I, P, Com. A] Nashville, IN b. 1928, Des Plaines, IL, near Chicago. Studied: AIC. Exhibited: Merrill Chase Gal, Chicago; Joslyn M, Omaha; Galerie De Tours, San Francisco; Doth Gal, Minneapolis-St Paul; Ravens Gal, Ft Collins, CO; AIC. Prizes: Chicago Municipal AL Award; Ill. State Award. Note: Eighteen-year career in advertising illustration. Work published by Harper-Row, Scott Foresman, Field Enterprises and *Encyclopeadia Britannica.*

WILLS, VINETTA Pendleton, IN.

WILLSON, RALPH E. [S] Kokomo, IN. Prizes: HS, 1985.

WILSON, GILBERT B(rown) [P, S, I] Terre Haute, IN b. 4 Mar 1907, Terre Haute. Studied: AIC; Yale Sch FA; Ind. State TC. Teachers: Eugene Savage; Urbiel Soler; E. A. Frosburg; W. T. Turman. Prizes: HS, 1929, 33; BAID, 1930; Ind. State Kiwanis. Collections: murals, Woodrow Wilson Jr. H.S., Terre Haute; Ind. State TC; Antioch Col, Yellow Springs, OH; Hotel, Lake Wawasee, IN.

WILSON, GLENN L.

WILSON, JOHN H. Indianapolis, IN.

WILSON, JUDI [P] Camby, IN.

WILSON, KEVIN J. [I, P, Mur. P, Por. P] Indianapolis, IN. Studied: R.I. Sch Des. Exhibited: Talbott Street A Fair, 1983; Ind. Expo, 1982, 77; Centre Gal, Indianapolis, 1982; Collector's Corner, Indianapolis, 1981; Woods-Gerry Gal (solo), R.I. Sch Des, 1981; Washington Square Outdoor A Exh, NY, 1980.

WILSON, NELSON (D.) [P, Des, T] Evansville, IN b. 28

Jan 1880, Leopold, IN d. 5 May 1950. Studied: Chicago Acad FA. Exhibited: John Herron AI, 1926-28; Evansville MA (solo), 1930. Collections: Culver Grade Sch and Bosse H.S., Evansville, IN; Statehouse, Indianapolis; murals, Vanderburgh Cnty Coliseum and Evansville Bank, Evansville, IN.

WILSON, N(orman) B(adgley) [P, Print] Indianapolis, IN/Goshen, IN b. 1 Dec 1906, Arcadia, IN. Teachers: Turner B. Messick. Exhibited: PAFA, 1937; Butler AI, 1945, 46; Tri-State PM Exh, 1944, 45; Milwaukee AI, 1946; Herron AI, 1937, 39, 42, 44-46; Public Library, Ft Wayne, 1975. Note: Salesman for a manufacturer of work clothing in Indianapolis.

WILSON, WINIFRED Gary, IN.

WILSTACH, GEORGE L. [P, Des, C] Lafayette, IN/Gloucester, MA b. 1892, Lafayette, IN. Studied: ASL; AIC. Teachers: Ralph Clarkson; John C. Johansen; John Carlson. Exhibited: Ind. AC, L. S. Ayres&Co, Indianapolis. Collections: Lafayette AM. Note: Des/Manufacturer, hand-carved picture frames.

WIMMER, ETHEL THORNBURG Chicago, IL.

WINANS, FRANCILLE [P, T] Ft Wayne, IN b. 27 Mar 1912, Decatur, IN. Studied: Ind. U; Ft Wayne A Sch; St Francis Col, Ft Wayne. Teachers: Tony Von Hasselt; Clay Kent. Exhibited: Brown Cnty A Gal; Senior A Show, 1990; Ventures in Creativity, Ft Wayne AG, 1990. Prizes: Ft Wayne Woman's Cl, 1987; Ventures in Creativity, 1986; YWCA Juried Show, 1987. Collections: Banks in Indianapolis and Ft Wayne.

WINGERD, LOREEN [P, Print, C, T] Indianapolis, IN b. 2 Aug 1902, Delphi, IN. Studied: Herron AI; Chicago Acad FA. Teachers: William Forsyth. Exhibited: Herron AI (solo), 1933; Woman's Dept Cl Gal, 1934. Prizes: Ind. State Fair. Note: T, Arsenal Tech H.S., Indianapolis.

WINKLER, AGNES CLARK (Mrs. G. A. M.) [P, W] Chicago, IL b. 3 Apr 1893, Cincinnati, OH d. 15 Jan 1945. Studied: AIC. Teachers: L. Lundmark; E. James; Edward J. F. Timmons; Watson; Mary Helen Stubbs. Collections: La Revue-Moderne, Paris, France; Revue du Vrai et du Beau, Paris, France. Note: Contributor, Paris magazines.

WINN, ALICE COLLINSBOURNE [P] LaPorte, IN b. Milwaukee, WI. Studied: AIC; Capri; Amsterdam, Holland. Teachers: Sinibaldi; Eivert Pietut; Edwin Scott. Collections: Carnegie Library, Thorntown, IN.

WINSLOW, EDWARD L(ee) [Ldscp. P, P] Indianapolis, IN b. 28 Jun 1871, Tuscola, IL d. Dec 1952. Studied: Marion Normal Col. Teachers: Olive Rush. Exhibited: Herron AI; Ind. AC; A Review. Collections: Shortridge H.S., Indianapolis.

WINTON, EFFIE DILL [P] Detroit, MI.

WIPPERMAN, ELFRIEDA [SLP] Noble Cnty, IN b. c. 1867. Self-taught. Exhibited: Lieber Gal, Indianapolis. Note: Specialized in painting flowers.

WISE, BEULAH N. THOMPSON [P, Ldscp. P, SLP] Union City, IN b. 7 Jan 1902, near Liberty Center, Wells Cnty, IN. Studied: Ind. U. Teachers: Betty Muhl; Esther Nusbaum; Robert Brubaker; John Nartker. Exhibited: Ft Wayne Woman's Cl Exh; Richmond AA; Union City Depot (solo), 1991.

WISEMAN, MINNIE (Mrs. Earl C.) [P, T] Indianapolis, IN. Prizes: Indianapolis AL.

WISER, GUY BROWN [Por. P, P, I, W, T] Los Angeles, CA b. 10 Feb 1895, Marion, IN. Studied: Fontainebleau Sch of FA, France; PAFA. Teachers: Jean Despujols; Gorguet; H. H. Breckenridge; Charles Hawthorne; J. R. Hopkins. Prizes: PAFA, 1927; Northern Ind. AL, 1927; HS, 1927, 29, 30, 32-34; Richmond (Ind) AA, 1928; Columbus AL, 1929; Herron AI, 1930. Collections: Muskingum Col, New Concord, OH; Hospital and Law Sch, Ohio State U. Note: I, *Rambles in Europe*, Am Book Co, publisher; *Prose and Poetry*, L. W. Singer Co, publisher; *Ourselves and the World*, Whittlesey House, publisher. Brother of artist Gertrude Wiser Nelson.

WITHERSPOON, NORMA J. [P] Linton, IN b. 6 Aug 1926, Madison, IN. Teachers: Kaye Pool; Marie J. Thompson; Tony Couch; Nita Engle; Edgar Whitney. Exhibited: Ind. WCS, 1989; IHA; Southwestern Ind. A Exh. Prizes: Brown Cnty AG, 1990; Tri Kappa Province Convention, 1991; Brown Cnty A Gal. Collections: Camelot Care Cen, Seminole, FL; Eli Lilly Co; Citizens Nat Bank, Linton, IN; Linton-Stocking Sch Corp.

WITMER, MARY L. WRIGHT [Ldscp. P] Ardsley-on-the-Hudson, NY. Prizes: HS, 1945.

WITTENBERG, JET (Jeannette A.) [P] Portage, IN b. Bridgeport, OH. Studied: Ohio; W. Va. Exhibited: Chicago Press Cl; Covenant Cl of Chicago; Anderson A Cen; Ft Wayne MA; Gary AL.

WITTICH, WOLFGANG Chicago, IL.

WITTNER, RUTH

WOLTER, ADOLPH G. [S, C, T] Indianapolis, IN b. 7 Sep 1903, Reutlingen, Germany d. 15 Oct 1980. Studied: Herron AI; Acad FA, Stuttgart, Germany. Teachers: Donald M. Mattison; Henrik M. Mayer; David K. Rubins. Exhibited: Nat Exh Am A, NYC, 1938; Ind. State Fair, 1936; Herron AI, 1943, 45. Prizes: Ind. State Fair, 1935, 37-40; Herron AI, 1938; HS, 1946. Collections: Ind. State Library, Indianapolis; Washington Park Cemetery, Indianapolis; *Indianapolis Star;* Indianapolis Motor Speedway; World War II Mem, Detroit; Yale U; Purdue U; Butler U; DePauw U. Note: Full name, Adolph Gustave Wolter von Ruemelin. Gal Asst., Herron AI, 1945-46; T, Indianapolis AL.

WOOD, HARRY E. [Por. P, P, T] b. 1910, Indianapolis, IN d. c. 1950. Studied: U of Wis. Teachers: Harry Wood (father). Collections: Nat Por Gal, Washington, D.C., Por of George Santayana. Note: Played 2nd bassoon, Indianapolis Symphony Orchestra. Dean, Col FA, Bradley U, Peoria, IL. Painted Por, Ferdinand Schaefer of the Indianapolis Symphony Orchestra.

WOOD, MARJORY FARLEY [S] Chesterton, IN. Prizes: HS, 1977.

WOODRUFF, HALE A(spacio) [P, Mur. P, T, Print] NYC b. 26 Aug 1900, Cairo, IL d. Sep 1980. Studied: Herron AI; Paris; FMA Sch; Acad Scandinave; Acad Moderne; Mexico City. Teachers: Diego Rivera, fresco painting. Exhibited: IMA; VMFA, 1944; Studio M, Harlem, 1979 (retrospective); WFNY, 1939; Diamond Jubilee Expo, Chicago, 1940; High MA, 1940; Spiral, NYC, 1965; Morgan State Col, 1968. Prizes: Ind. State Fair, 1930s; Julius Rosenwald Fellow, 1943-44; NYU Great Teacher Award; Harmon Fnd, 1926; IUPUI, honorary degree, 1978. Collections: Smithsonian Inst; MMA; LOC; Newark M; Howard U; Atlanta U; John D. Rockefeller Coll. Murals: Talladega Col, AL; Howard H.S., Atlanta; Atlanta Sch Social Work; Golden State Mutual Life Insurance, Los Angeles, CA. Note: T, Atlanta U (1931-45); T, NYU (1945-1968).

WOODS, HELEN M. WOODWARD *(See Woodward, Helen M.)* [Por. P, SLP] Indianapolis, IN b. 28 Jul 1902, Orange Cnty, IN d. c. 1981. Studied: Herron AI; ASL; Butler U; Ind. U. Teachers: Wayman Adams; Jerry Farnsworth; Robert Brackman; Eliot O'Hara; Charles Hawthorne. Exhibited: Ball State Col (solo), Muncie, IN; Ind. U (solo); H. Lieber Gal (solo), Indianapolis. Prizes: HS, 1928, 29, 52, 53, 61; Herron AI, 1939; Ind. AC; Ind. State Fair. Collections: Riley Sch, Bedford H.S., IN; Purdue U; Finch Col, NY.

WOODWARD, HELEN M. *(See Woods, Helen M. Woodward)*

WOODWORTH, CHARLES H. [P] Indianapolis, IN.

WOOLDRIDGE, RUTH Indianapolis, IN b. 1941, Pigeon Roost, KY. Studied: AI of Minneapolis, correspondence. Exhibited: Marion Cnty AL; 500 Festival; Ind. State Fair.

WOOLDRIDGE, STEPHEN E. [S, Des, C] Sheridan, IN. Studied: Earlham Col, Richmond, IN; Dayton AI; Herron Sch A. Exhibited: Wabash Valley Exh, Terre Haute, IN, 1970; Penrod Soc, Indianapolis, 1970; Mid-States Show, Evansville, IN, 1970. Prizes: HS, 1970. Collections: State Life Insurance Bldg, Indianapolis; Ind. Nat Bank; Presbyterian Chapel, Purdue U; Ind. Nat Guard, War Mem Bldg; Forbes Bldg, NY.

WOOLF, AMELIA Greeley, CO.

WOOLSEY, CARL EDWARD [Ldscp. P] Taos, NM b. 24 Apr 1902, Chicago Heights, IL. Self-taught. Exhibited: Nat Acad, 1936; Pettis Gal (two-man), Indianapolis, IN, 1929. Prizes: HS, 1929, 35, 37, 39; William H. Block Prize, 1937-40; NAD, 1931; Southern Ind. A, 1939; Third Hallgarten Pr, 1931. Collections: Dailey Coll, Ind. U, Bloomington, IN; Kokomo (Ind.) AA. Note: Also worked in Taos, NM. Brother of artist Wood W. Woolsey.

WOOLSEY, WOOD W. [P, Por. P] Stroudsburg, PA b. 29 Jun 1899, Danville, IL. Self-taught. Exhibited: NAD, 1930, 32, 34; Pettis Gal (two-man), Indianapolis, IN, 1929. Prizes: HS, 1931, 32; Phoenix AA, 1932; Evansville AI, 1935. Collections: Dailey Coll, Ind. U, Bloomington, IN; Fed Woman's Cl, Kokomo, IN.; MFA, Evansville, IN; Lafayette (Ind.) AI; Danville, IL; Terre Haute, Evansville and Columbus H.S., all in Ind. Note: Also worked in Taos, NM. Brother of artist Carl Edward Woolsey.

WORMAN, SYLVIA [Print, P, Genre P, T] Evansville, IN b. 5 Sep 1935, Evansville, IN. Studied: U of Evansville; U of Southern Ind. Teachers: Miles Batt; Barbara Nechis; Gerald Brommer; Frank Webb; Tony Couch; Don Getz; Judi Betts; Doug Henry. Exhibited: Ky. WCS Aqueous, 1981, 83, 84; Mid-Am Biennial, 1988; Realism Today, 1987. Prizes: Franklin Col, 1982; HS, 1982, 85, 87; Ind. WCS, 1983; Eastland Mall Exh, 1984; Blue Grass Biennial; Ind. World Organization of China Painters; Evansville AG. Collections: Merchants Bank; Franklin Col; Indianapolis Power&Light; Bristol-Myers; Ronald McDonald House, Louisville, KY. Note: Watercolorist and porcelain artist who specialized in painting flowers.

WOTTON, JUNE MERKEL

WROBEL, JOSEPH [P] South Bend, IN. b. Poland. Studied: Chicago Acad FA; AIC. Exhibited: Am WCS; AIC.

WUNDERLICH, DIANE UBELHOR [P] Newburgh, IN b. Kincheloe AFB, MI. Studied: David Lipscomb U, Nashville, TN; Am Acad A, Chicago. Teachers: Irving Shapiro. Exhibited: Brown Cnty AG, 1987-91; Evansville AG, 1990. Prizes: HS, 1988; Evansville AG Ann; Garvin Park A Fair, 1987. Collections: Elwood Community H.S.

WYKOFF, LESTER D. [S] Bedford, IN.

WYNNE, BERNARD Prizes: HS, 1971.

Y

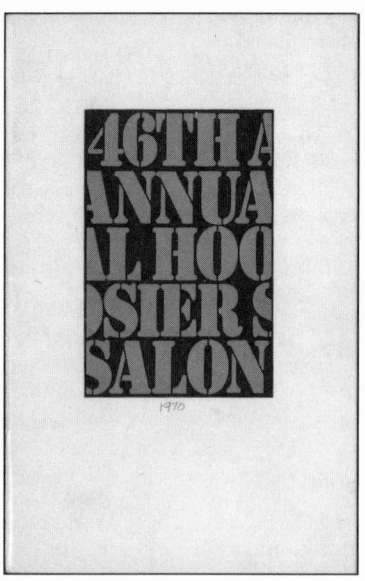

YATER, GEORGE DAVID [P, Des, W] Provincetown, MA b. 30 Nov 1910, Madison, IN. Studied: Herron AI; Cape Cod Sch A, Provincetown, MA. Teachers: William Forsyth; Henry Hensche; E. Dickinson. Exhibited: NAD, 1934, 40; AWCS, 1938, 45; PAFA, 1934, 37, 39, 43-45; WFNY, 1939; Currier Gal A, Manchester, NH, 1940; U of Ill., 1939; Inst Modern A, Boston, 1939; Provincetown AA, 1934-46; Ind. A, 1931-46; Hanover Col (solo), 1939; Babcock Gal (solo), NY; Herron AM. Prizes: HS, 1931, 36, 46, 54, 56. Note: Contributor, *Rudder, Motor Boating, Yachting.*

YAZEL, MIKE Mentone, IN.

YEAGER, CHARLES G(eorge) [C, Print, P, T] Indianapolis, IN b. 26 Jul 1910, Morgan Cnty, IN d. 1970. Studied: Herron A Sch; PAFA; Columbia U; Ohio State U; Butler U. Teachers: William Forsyth; Oakley Richey; Walter McBride; Clifton Wheeler; Paul Hadley; E. Miller; J. M. Thompson; A. Heckman; C. Martin. Exhibited: Am WCC; N.Y. WCC; Herron AM; H. Lieber&Co (solo). Prizes: Ind. A Exh, 1929; Ind. State Fair, 1929, 37; HS, 1937, 40, 43, 53. Collections: Ind. U. Note: Head FA Dept, Emmerich Manual Training H.S., Indianapolis.

YEAMANS, DAVID [Ldscp. P, Print, Genre P] Indianapolis, IN b. 21 Jun 1966, Anderson, IN. Studied: Wright State U, Dayton, OH. Teachers: Kim Kaiser; Thomas Mac-Cavlay; Ray Must. Exhibited: A Soc Intl, 1987; Dayton Soc P&S, 1987. Prizes: Ohio State Fair, 1985. Collections: Thurn Meats, Columbus, OH.

YODER, EVA MAY (Mrs. Worth N.) [Des, P] Tipton, IN b. TX. Studied: Cincinnati Acad FA. Prizes: HS, 1944, 45. Note: First to use the air-brush technique in work accepted by the Hoosier Salon jury.

YOHLER, KAREN [Dr]

YORGEN, DORRIE [Bat] Indianapolis, IN.

YOUNG, JUDITH [P] Ft Wayne, IN. Exhibited: Pletcher Village A Show, Nappanee, IN, 1972. Prizes: Ft Wayne AG Show, Nappanee, 1972; Wassenberg A Show, Van Wert, OH, 1973.

YOUNG, NUY [P] b. Shan Pao How, Kwungtung, China. Studied: Herron Sch A. Teachers: Edmund Brucker. Exhibited: Lyman Brothers Gal (solo), Indianapolis. Note: Painter for Lyman Brothers.

YOUNG, RUTH M. [P] Greenwood, IN. Note: Former SALI member, Greenwood, IN.

YUNG, JANE K(imball) [P, T] Terre Haute, IN b. Quincy, IL. Studied: AIC; Boston AM Sch; France; Germany. Teachers: Oliver D. Grover; J. C. Leyendecker; John H. Vanderpoel. Exhibited: Ruth Kealing's residence gal, Indianapolis; Fairbanks Gal, Terre Haute.

Z

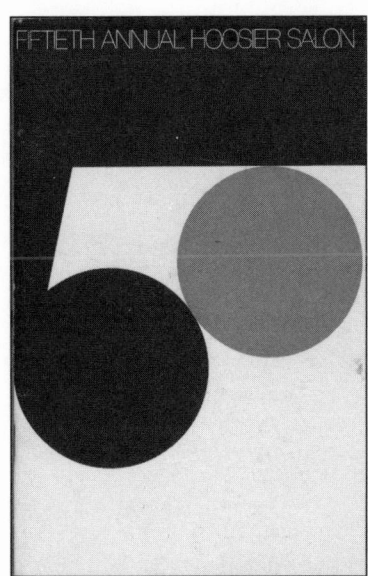

ZARING, LOUISE E(leanor) [P, S, C] Greencastle, IN b. Cincinnati, OH. Studied: Académie Vitti, Paris; ASL; Cape Cod A Sch. Teachers: Merson; John Twachtman; MacMonnies; L. R. Garrido; Charles Hawthorne; William Forsyth. Exhibited: Richmond AA, 1900, 19. Prizes: Académie Vitti; HS, 1925. Collections: Putnam Cnty (Ind.) Courthouse. Note: Worked in Evansville, Ind., for many years.

ZEIGLER, BILL [Dr, Print, Gra. A, Des, T] New Castle, IN b. 1925, Huntington, IN. Studied: Ohio Wesleyan; Ball State U. Note: T, Ind. public sch.

ZEIHER, MARGARET

ZERWEKH, BEATRICE [P] Peoria, IL.

ZIEGLER, JANE (Mrs. Fred F.) [P] Sarasota, FL b. MI d. c. 1961. Studied: Jordan Conservatory of Music, Indianapolis; U of Pittsburgh; Pa. Col for Women. Teachers: Jerry Farnsworth; Hilton Leech; Robert Chase. Exhibited: Nat Gal, Washington, D.C.; Nat Acad Des, NY; Carnegie M, Pittsburg; Michiana A, Detroit; Isaac Delgado M, New Orleans; Gulf Coast Nat Tour, Fla. A. Prizes: HS, 1953, 57.

ZIEGLER, MARY ADELE [P] Muncie, IN. b. IN. Prizes: HS, 1932.

ZIELS, VIRGINIA P. [P] Prizes: HS, 1966.

ZIESEMER, GREGORY A. [Dr, Genre P] Indianapolis, IN b. 4 Jun 1959, Indianapolis. Self-taught. Exhibited: 500 Festival A. Prizes: HS, 1983.

ZIGROSSI, DOROTHY [Ldscp. P, Genre P, I, Por. P, T, Min] Lebanon, IN b. 11 Nov 1916, Chicago, IL. Studied: A Cen Sch, Los Angeles, CA. Teachers: Rex Brandt; Robert E. Wood; Ruth VanSickle Ford; Marjorie MacDonald. Exhibited: Ind. WCS, 1988; Ind. AC, 1986. Prizes: Bowers M, Santa Ana, CA, 1980; Ind. WCS, 1985; Ga. Min Intl Show, 1988. Collections: Hist Soc, Orange Cnty, CA. Note: Original Tarot design in 1990 edition *Encyclopedia of Tarot* by Stuart Kaplan.

ZIMMERMAN, BEATRICE HARTIG [P] Osceola, IN b. Chicago, IL (moved to Ind., 1921). Studied: Com. A Sch, Chicago. Prizes: Northern Ind. A, South Bend; Northern Ind. A, Hammond.

ZIMMERMAN, HELEN M. [S, JA] Indianapolis, IN. Studied: U of Wis. Teachers: Emil Kronquist; Harold Milbrath; Sy Perszych; Bill Robertson. Prizes: Ind. State Fair. Collections: IMA.

ZIMMERMAN, PAUL W. [P, T] Hartford, CT b. Kokomo, IN. Studied: Herron Sch A, BFA in 1946. Exhibited: Herron AM; Wellons Gal, NY. Prizes: Norwich AA Gal, Norwich, CT, 1953; Mary Milliken Award, 1946; HS, 1955. Collections: St Philips Church, Indianapolis. Note: T, Hartford (Conn.) Sch A. Recognized for his semi-abstract landscapes.

ZIMMERMAN, WILLIAM [P] Nashville, IN b. c. 1938, Dearborn Cnty, IN (grew up in Dillsboro, IN). Studied: Cincinnati A Acad. Exhibited: Smithsonian Inst, Washington, D.C., 1980; Columbus Gal FA, Columbus, OH, 1975; Closson Gal, Cincinnati, OH, 1975; IHA, 1979. Prizes: HS, 1978. Note: Specialized in wildlife art. Collaborated with Dr. Russell E. Mumford and Charles Keller on *The Birds of Indiana*, Ind. U Press. Also wrote, *The Waterfowl of North America*.

ZIMPLEMAN, LARRY [Ldscp. P, Genre P, S, I] Indianapolis, IN b. 30 Aug 1953, Cleveland, OH. Self-taught. Exhibited: Nat Sports Festival, 1982; A of the Madonna, Chicago, 1987. Collections: Hallmark, Inc; Second Presbyterian Church, Indianapolis. Note: Paintings reproduced by Hallmark Cards, Inc, 1985, 86; Sculptures of children for *Saturday Evening Post*, 1985.

ZOUMIS, ELIAS

ZWARA, JOHN (Jan) [Ldscp. P, P, I, Car] Indianapolis, IN b. 27 Dec 1880, Stepahof, Orava-Stolica, Austria-Hungary d. c. 1951. Studied: Pupil of government schools in Prague for one year and in Poland for three years. Exhibited: Neb. A Sixth Ann Exh, AI of Omaha, 1927; Omaha SFA; Lyman Brothers, Indianapolis; H. L. Lieber Co., Indianapolis. Prizes: 2nd Prize, Salt Lake City, UT. Collections: Ind. Medical Hist M. Note: Zwara's name was changed from Jan to John after he immigrated to America in 1900. He lived in Neb. at least seven years, beginning in 1923. In 1938, he was diagnosed as suffering from schizophrenia at Central State Hospital, Indianapolis, IN.

NOTES TO THE TEXT

The Twenties

[1] Mrs. Henry Lester Smith, *The Hoosier Salon, 1925-1974: A Dream of Farsighted Men and Women* (Indianapolis: Hoosier Salon Patrons Association, 1974), 1. The Daughters of Indiana, a group of women who were born in Indiana but lived in the Chicago area, was organized in 1913 for the purpose of fostering interest in the history, literature and current events of Indiana. At their Art Tea in May of 1924, they decided to begin a study of the art in Indiana.

[2] Ruth G. Grimes, "The Hoosier Salon," *The Hoosier Magazine,* February 1930, 5.

[3] Lucille E. Morehouse, "Art Plus," *Indianapolis Star,* 3 August 1941.

[4] Daughters of Indiana, "Hoosier Salon," Circular, circa early 1925, Stout Reference Library, Indianapolis Museum of Art.

[5] Ibid.

[6] Lucille E. Morehouse, "Art Plus," *Indianapolis Sunday Star,* 16 February 1941.

[7] *Indianapolis Star,* 8 March 1925.

[8] E. V. Lucas, "Daniel Garber and Edward W. Redfield," *Ladies Home Journal,* May 1926, Indiana Room, Indiana State Library.

[9] *Art Digest,* 15 December 1932.

[10] Lucas, "Daniel Garber," *Journal.*

[11] Estella M. King to T. C. Steele, 19 August 1924, Selma N. Steele Collection, Indiana State Museum and Historic Sites.

[12] Estella M. King to T. C. Steele, 9 February 1925, Selma N. Steele Collection, Indiana State Museum and Historic Sites.

[13] *Indianapolis Star,* 8 March 1925.

[14] Judith O'Sullivan, *The Great American Comic Strip: One Hundred Years of Cartoon Art* (Boston, Toronto and London: Little, Brown & Co., 1990), 167.

[15] Arthur Asa Berger, "Little Orphan Annie: The Abandoned Years," *The Comic-Stripped American* (New York: Walker & Co., 1973), 83, 88-89.

[16] *Indianapolis Star,* 8 March 1925.

[17] *Indianapolis News,* 9 March 1925.

[18] Marguerite B. Williams, *Chicago Daily News,* circa mid-March 1925.

[19] Meredith Nicholson (1866-1947) was born in Crawfordsville, Indiana, and, during the first quarter of the twentieth century, was among the best-selling authors of the day. R. E. Banta, "Meredith Nicholson," *Indiana Authors and their Books, 1816-1916* (Crawfordsville, Indiana: Wabash College, 1949), 237-239.

[20] For the years 1900-1941, Indiana led the nation in the production of popular authors. See Steven J. Schmidt, "Do Hoosiers Sell Best?" *Indiana Libraries* 9.1 (1990): 5-6, for a discussion of the contribution of Indiana's writers to American literature. The Hoosier Salon Patrons Association would acknowledge the state's strong literary tradition when it took as its purpose in 1927: "Hoosier Art and Literature in Every American Home." This statement would appear on the cover of Salon catalogues from 1927 through 1941.

[21] Meredith Nicholson, "The Second Salon," *Catalogue of the Hoosier Salon* (March 1926): unpaginated.

[22] *Indianapolis News,* 8 March 1926.

[23] John T. McCutcheon, "The Hoosier Salon: 1927," *Fashions of the Hour* (January 1927).

[24] Newspaper accounts of the 1926 Hoosier Salon report that Janet Scudder, with a bronze figure entitled *Victory,* won the "Outstanding Piece of Sculpture" award. The 1926 Hoosier Salon catalogue, however, lists her single entry as being *Frog Fountain.* Perhaps the discrepancy is due to an additional entry by Miss Scudder that was not noted in the catalogue, or a substitution of *Victory* for *Frog Fountain* was made by the sculptor after the catalogue had been printed.

[25] *Indianapolis Star,* 7 March 1926.

[26] The painting was done in 1921, nearly seven years after the death of the fifth member of the Hoosier Group, R. B. Gruelle. Martin Krause, *The Passage: Return of Indiana Painters from Germany, 1880-1905* (Indianapolis: Indianapolis Museum of Art, 1990), 268.

[27] Charles Victor Knox, unidentified Chicago, Illinois, newspaper, 7 March 1926, Stout Reference Library, Indianapolis Museum of Art.

[28] Other African-American artists who exhibited work in the Salon during its early years were John Wesley Hardrick and Hale A. Woodruff.

[29] Judith V. Newton, *The Hoosier Group: Five American Painters* (Indianapolis: Eckert Publications, 1985), 52.

[30] *Catalogue of the Hoosier Salon* (March 1926): unpaginated.

[31] *Catalogue of the Hoosier Salon* (January 1927): unpaginated.

[32] Estella M. King to Mrs. Theodore C. Steele, 24 September 1926, Selma N. Steele Collection, Indiana State Museum and Historic Sites.

[33] McCutcheon, *Fashions of the Hour* (January 1927).

[34] George Ade (1866-1944) was born in Kentland, Indiana. After a stint on a Chicago newspaper where he was closely associated with his friend, cartoonist John T. McCutcheon, he expanded his writing to include books and plays. During the first decade of the twentieth century, these works were published and produced; later, they were in demand for motion pictures. R. E. Banta, "George Ade," *Indiana Authors and their Books, 1816-1916* (Crawfordsville, Indiana: Wabash College, 1949), 3.

[35] George Ade, "The Salon, An Institution," *Catalogue of the Hoosier Salon* (January 1927): unpaginated.

[36] *Indianapolis Star,* circa early-February, 1927.

[37] *Catalogue of the Hoosier Salon* (January 1927).

[38] Marguerite B. Williams, "Here and There in the Art World," *Chicago Daily News,* 2 February 1927.

[39] Ibid.

[40] Ibid.

[41] Margaret Doherty, "Three Indiana Cartoonists: Then and Now," *Mirages of Memory: 200 Years of Indiana Art* (South Bend, Indiana: University of Notre Dame, 1977), 134-136.

[42] Ibid., 127-130.

[43] McCutcheon, *Fashions of the Hour* (January 1927).

[44] Doherty, "Three Indiana Cartoonists," 131.

[45] O'Sullivan, *Great American Comic Strip,* 164.

[46] *Catalogue of the Hoosier Salon* (January 1928): unpaginated.

[47] *New Castle Courier-Times,* 1 February 1928.

[48] *Catalogue of the Hoosier Salon* (January 1928).

[49] Ibid.

[50] *Indianapolis News,* 31 January 1927.

[51] Lucille E. Morehouse, "In the World of Art," *Indianapolis Sunday Star,* 12 February 1928.

[52] Ibid.

[53] *Catalogue of the Hoosier Salon* (January 1929): unpaginated.

[54] Mrs. Clarence B. King, Report, Annual Meeting of the Hoosier Salon Patrons Association, Chicago, Illinois, 6 May 1929.

[55] Ibid.

[56] *Catalogue of the Hoosier Salon* (January 1929).

[57] "The Daughters of Indiana of Chicago," *Catalogue of the Hoosier Salon* (January 1940): unpaginated.

[58] *Indianapolis Star,* 27 January 1929.

[59] Julie Schimmel, "Chronology, 1879-1945," *Art in New Mexico, 1900-1945: Paths to Taos and Santa Fe* (Washington, D. C.: Natural Museum of American Art, 1986), 184.

[60] William H. Truettner, "The Art of Pueblo Life," *Art in New Mexico,* 67.

[61] *Indianapolis Star,* 31 January 1929.

[62] Ibid.

* * *

The Thirties

[1] Soon after the turn of the century, Chicago enjoyed a revival in miniature painting. By 1912, so many of the city's artists were working in this genre that the Chicago Society of Miniature Painting was organized. William H. Gerdts, *Art Across America: Two Centuries of Regional Painting, 1710-1920, Volume Two* (New York: Abbeville Press, 1990), 294.

[2] *Catalogue of the Hoosier Salon* (January 1930): unpaginated.

[3] Lucille E. Morehouse, *Indianapolis Star,* 19 February 1930.

[4] Wayne Guthrie, "Ringside in Hoosierland," *Indianapolis News,* 1 August 1972.

[5] Ibid.

[6] Gustave Baumann, "Hoosier Salon 1930, The Wood Block," *Fashions of the Hour* (New Year Number, 1930): 25.

[7] *Indianapolis Star,* 28 January 1930.

[8] Morehouse, *Star,* 19 February 1930.

[9] Ibid.

[10] Lucille E. Morehouse, "In the World of Art," *Indianapolis Sunday Star,* 2 February 1930.

[11] C. J. Bulliet, *New York Times,* 8 February 1931.

[12] Ibid.

[13] Lucille E. Morehouse, "In the World of Art," *Indianapolis Star,* 1 February 1931.

[14] Ibid.

[15] Ibid.

[16] William H. Truettner, "The Art of Pueblo Life," *Art in New Mexico, 1900-1945: Paths to Taos and Santa Fe* (New York: Abbeville Press, 1986), 72.

[17] Stanley L. Cuba, *Olive Rush: A Hoosier Artist in New Mexico* (Muncie, Indiana: Minnetrista Cultural Center, 1992), 74.

[18] Morehouse, *Star,* 1 February 1931.

[19] *Indianapolis Star,* 8 January 1929.

[20] *Indianapolis Star,* 5 May 1937.

[21] *Indianapolis Star,* 31 January 1932.

[22] James Ong, *The Hoosier Art Collection of the Kokomo-Howard County Public Library* (Kokomo, Indiana: Kokomo-Howard County Public Library, 1989), 3.

[23] *Indianapolis News,* 11 February 1941.

[24] *Star,* 31 January 1932.

[25] Lucille E. Morehouse, "In the World of Art," *Indianapolis Star,* 8 May 1932.

[26] Ibid.

[27] Eva Gough, "Foreword," *Catalogue of the Hoosier Salon* (January 1933): unpaginated.

[28] "Famous Artist Finds Subjects at Indiana Dunes State Park," *Outdoor Indiana,* September 1947, 15-16.

[29] Carl Lewis, "Painter of the Dunes," *Indianapolis Star Magazine,* undated, Indiana Room, Indiana State Library.

[30] *Indianapolis Star,* 12 March 1933.

[31] Ibid.

[32] *Indianapolis Sunday Star,* 28 January 1934.

[33] Dorothy Donald, "Foreword," *Catalogue of the Hoosier Salon* (January 1934): unpaginated.

[34] Estella M. King, "Tri Kappa Sorority of Indiana," *Catalogue of the Hoosier Salon* (January 1934).

[35] Lucille E. Morehouse, *Indianapolis Star,* 31 January 1932.

[36] "Feature Room of Beauty Spots of Indiana," *Catalogue of the Hoosier Salon* (January 1934).

[37] C. J. Bulliet, *Chicago Daily News,* 27 January 1934.

[38] Ibid.

[39] George T. Buckingham, "Welcome," *Catalogue of the Hoosier Salon* (January 1935): unpaginated.

[40] *Indianapolis Star,* 10 February 1935.

[41] "The Indiana Federation of Clubs," *Catalogue of the Hoosier Salon* (January 1935).

[42] Carolyn G. Bradley, "Report on the Experiences of a Visiting Professor of Art to Chile," University Archives, Ohio State University, Columbus, Ohio, 1946.

[43] Lucille E. Morehouse, *Indianapolis Star,* 4 February 1935.

[44] *Indianapolis Star,* 2 February 1936.

[45] See Judith V. Newton, "William Forsyth: 1854-1935," *The Hoosier Group: Five American Painters* (Indianapolis: Eckert Publications, 1985), 110-137, for a discussion of the painter's place among the Hoosier Group artists.

[46] George Chambers Calvert, "William Forsyth: 1854-1935," *Catalogue of the Hoosier Salon* (January 1936): unpaginated.

[47] "Gaar Williams," *Catalogue of the Hoosier Salon* (January 1936).

[48] Claude A. Mahoney, unidentified newspaper article, circa January 1936, Stout Reference Library, Indianapolis Museum of Art.

[49] *Indianapolis Star,* 19 July 1936.

[50] Ibid.

[51] Lucille E. Morehouse, *Indianapolis Star,* 28 June 1936.

[52] Lucille E. Morehouse, *Indianapolis Star,* 29 June 1936.

[53] "Indiana Federation of Art Clubs," *The First Summer Salon Catalogue* (June 1936): unpaginated, Hoosier Salon Patrons Association Papers.

[54] Lucille E. Morehouse, "In the World of Art," *Indianapolis Sunday Star,* 7 February 1937.

[55] "Gallery of Flower Paintings," *Catalogue of the Hoosier Salon* (January 1937): unpaginated.

[56] Lucille E. Morehouse, "In the World of Art," *Indianapolis Star,* 21 February 1937.

[57] Mrs. Henry Lester Smith, *The Hoosier Salon, 1925-1974: A Dream of Farsighted Men and Women* (Indianapolis: Hoosier Salon Patrons Association, 1974), 11.

[58] Lucille E. Morehouse, "In the World of Art," *Indianapolis Sunday Star,* 2 May 1937.

[59] Ibid.

[60] *Indianapolis Star,* 30 January 1938.

[61] Colonel F. L. Hunt, "Culver Military Academy," *Catalogue of the Hoosier Salon* (January 1938): unpaginated.

[62] Lucille E. Morehouse, *Indianapolis Star,* 8 February 1938.

[63] Helen Magner, *New Castle Courier-Times,* 31 January 1938.

[64] Eleanor Jewett, *Chicago Daily Tribune,* 31 January 1938.

[65] C. J. Bulliet, "Around the Galleries," *Chicago Daily News,* 31 January 1938.

[66] Jewett, *Chicago Tribune,* 31 January 1938.

[67] *Indianapolis Star,* 13 February 1938.

[68] *Indianapolis Sunday Star,* 20 March 1938.

[69] Smith, *Hoosier Salon,* 12.

[70] Ibid., 13.

[71] Helen Magner, *New Castle Courier-Times,* 1 February 1939.

[72] Circular, "Announcing the 15th Annual Hoosier Salon: January 28-February 11, 1939," Hoosier Salon Patrons Association Papers.

[73] "Gallery of Landscapes," *Catalogue of the Hoosier Salon* (January 1939): unpaginated.

[74] Eleanor Jewett, *Chicago Tribune,* 5 February 1939.

[75] Ibid.

[76] Ibid.

[77] *Indianapolis Star,* 29 January 1939.

[78] Magner, *Courier-Times,* 1 February 1939.

[79] "Announcing 15th Hoosier Salon," 1939.

[80] *Indianapolis Star,* circa late-March 1939, Hoosier Salon Patrons Association Papers.

* * *

The Forties

[1] Betty Foster, *Indianapolis News,* 29 January 1940.

[2] Betty Foster, *Indianapolis News,* 26 February 1940.

[3] Mrs. C. B. King to Helen Magner, 15 January 1940, Hoosier Salon Patrons Association Papers. James Irving Holcomb, owner of Holcomb and Hoke Manufacturing Company, was a leader among civic-minded figures in the Indianapolis community.

[4] Eleanor Jewett, *Chicago Sunday Tribune,* 28 January 1940.

[5] *Chicago Sunday Tribune,* 28 January 1940.

[6] Ibid.

[7] Jewett, *Tribune,* 28 January 1940.

[8] Foster, *News,* 26 February 1940.

[9] Lucille E. Morehouse, *Indianapolis Sunday Star,* 25 February 1940.

[10] C. J. Bulliet, "Foreword," *Catalogue of the Hoosier Salon* (January 1941): unpaginated.

[11] Ibid.

[12] C. J. Bulliet, "Artless Comment," *Chicago Daily News,* 1 February 1941.

[13] *Indianapolis News,* 27 January 1941.

[14] "Psi Iota Xi," *Catalogue of the Hoosier Salon* (January 1941).

[15] Lucille E. Morehouse, *Indianapolis Sunday Star,* 2 March 1941.

[16] Ibid.

[17] *Indianapolis Star,* 28 May 1939.

[18] "Hoosier Salon Patrons Association, 1924-1941," Pamphlet, Hoosier Salon Patrons Association Papers.

[19] Ibid.

[20] Lucille E. Morehouse, *Indianapolis Sunday Star,* 12 October 1941.

[21] Ibid.

[22] Ibid.

[23] W. F. Fox, Jr., *Indianapolis News,* 18 August 1941.

[24] "Hoosier Salon: The Mark C. Honeywell Garden Festival," Pamphlet, August 1941, Hoosier Salon Patrons Association Papers.

[25] Lucille E. Morehouse, "Art Plus," *Indianapolis Sunday Star*, 17 August 1941.

[26] Lucille E. Morehouse, *Indianapolis Star*, 15 August 1941.

[27] *Indianapolis News*, 19 January 1942.

[28] Kathryn E. Pickett, *Indianapolis Star*, 20 January 1942.

[29] *Indianapolis Star*, 21 January 1942.

[30] *Indianapolis Star*, 6 January 1942.

[31] Herman B Wells, "Foreword," *Catalogue of the Hoosier Salon* (January 1943): unpaginated.

[32] *Indianapolis Sunday Star*, 17 January 1943.

[33] Lucille E. Morehouse, "Books Plus Art," *Indianapolis Sunday Star*, 24 January 1943.

[34] Lucille E. Morehouse, "Books Plus Art," *Indianapolis Star*, 17 October 1943.

[35] *Indianapolis Star*, 10 October 1943. Shaffer's art collection included a number of works by John Elwood Bundy and four pieces by Theodore C. Steele: a portrait of James Whitcomb Riley, a portrait of Senator Beveridge and two Brown County scenes. Ruth G. Grimes, "The Hoosier Salon," *Hoosier Magazine*, February 1930, 6.

[36] Mabel Wheeler Shideler, *Indianapolis News*, 17 January 1944.

[37] *Indianapolis News*, 11 January 1944.

[38] *Catalogue of the Hoosier Salon* (January 1944): unpaginated.

[39] Unidentified newspaper article, circa late-January 1944, Hoosier Salon Patrons Association Papers. The painting was presented by American United Life Insurance Company to the art gallery of Rollins College in Winter Park, Florida, in honor of William R. O'Neal, secretary of the college and a member of the insurance company's board of directors. *Bradenton, Florida, Herald*, circa February 1944.

[40] Ralph W. Marks, *Chicago Sunday Tribune*, 26 March 1944, Letters to the Editor section.

[41] *Indianapolis Sunday Star*, 1 October 1944.

[42] Ibid.

[43] Lucille E. Morehouse, *Indianapolis Star*, 28 January 1945.

[44] Filomena Gould, "Information Plus," *Indianapolis News*, 24 January 1945.

[45] Lloyd B. Walton, "The Mystery Artist of Indianapolis," *Indianapolis Star Magazine*, 28 March 1976, 38-43.

[46] Charles A. Bonsett, M. D., "Medical Museum Notes," *Journal of the Indiana State Medical Association* (November 1980): 711.

[47] Walton, "Mystery Artist," 40.

[48] Unidentified newspaper article, circa early-February 1945, Hoosier Salon Patrons Association Papers.

[49] C. J. Bulliet, "Artless Comment," *Chicago Daily News*, 31 March 1945.

[50] *Indianapolis News*, 19 January 1946.

[51] Helen Magner, "Pencil Sketches," *New Castle Courier-Times*, circa late-January 1946, Hoosier Salon Patrons Association Papers.

[52] Anton Scherrer, *Indianapolis Times*, 21 January 1946.

[53] *Chicago Sunday Tribune*, 24 February 1946.

[54] "Randolph Coats," *The Cross Keys* (March 1941): 15-16.

[55] Helen Magner, "Pencil Sketches," *New Castle Courier-Times*, 18 July 1945.

[56] Filomena Gould, "Information Plus," *Indianapolis News*, 27 March 1946.

[57] Lucille E. Morehouse, "The Week in Local Art," *Indianapolis Star*, 26 January 1947.

[58] Helen Magner, *New Castle Courier-Times*, 6 February 1947.

[59] Lucille E. Morehouse, *Indianapolis Star*, 30 January 1947.

[60] Herbert P. Kenney, Jr., *Indianapolis News*, 27 January 1947.

[61] "The Art of Racing," *Indianapolis Star Magazine*, circa March 1948, Hoosier Salon Patrons Association Papers.

[62] *Indianapolis Times*, 4 February 1947.

[63] "A Tribute to Carl Graf," unpublished manuscript, author unknown, Ruth Anderson Papers.

[64] *Indianapolis News*, 17 January 1925.

[65] Ibid.

[66] *Indianapolis Star*, 5 July 1936.

[67] Lucille E. Morehouse, "This Week in Local Art," *Indianapolis Star*, 25 January 1948.

[68] Ibid.

[69] *Indianapolis Star*, 2 February 1948.

[70] Morehouse, *Star*, 25 January 1948.

[71] Helen Ruth Huber, *Gary Post-Tribune*, 6 April 1948.

[72] Ibid.

[73] *Indianapolis News*, 18 December 1948.

[74] Corbin Patrick, *Indianapolis Star*, 31 January 1949.

[75] Ibid.

[76] Ed Sovola, "Inside Indianapolis," *Indianapolis Times*, 2 February 1949.

[77] *Indianapolis News*, 23 March 1949.

[78] Martha Ellyn Slayback, *Indianapolis Star*, 27 February 1949.

[79] *Indianapolis Star*, 17 April 1949.

[80] *Washington, D. C., Sunday Star*, 17 April 1949.

[81] Jane Watson Crane, *Washington Post*, 17 April 1949.

* * *

The Fifties

[1] Lucille E. Morehouse, *Indianapolis Star*, 1 February 1950.

[2] Herbert Kenney, Jr., *Indianapolis News*, 30 January 1950.

[3] Corbin Patrick, *Indianapolis Star*, 30 January 1950.

[4] Marjorie Turk, *Indianapolis Times*, 30 January 1950.

[5] Lucille E. Morehouse, "The Week in Local Art," *Indianapolis Star*, 5 March 1950.

[6] *Gary Post-Tribune*, circa early-April 1950, Hoosier Salon Patrons Association Papers.

[7] Lucille E. Morehouse, "The Week in Local Art," *Indianapolis Star*, 8 January 1950.

[8] Ibid.

[9] "Welcome," *Catalogue of the Hoosier Salon* (January 1951): unpaginated.

[10] Lucille E. Morehouse, *Indianapolis Star,* 4 February 1951.

[11] Corbin Patrick, *Indianapolis Star,* 29 January 1951.

[12] Ibid.

[13] John Bernhardt, *Indianapolis News,* 20 February 1950, Letters to the Editor section.

[14] Ibid.

[15] Ibid.

[16] *Indianapolis Star,* 9 June 1927. Frederick Polley was not alone in his generosity to the Indianapolis public schools; a number of artists, including William Forsyth and Otto Stark, gave examples of their work to particular schools within the educational system.

[17] *Indianapolis Star,* 31 January 1952, Letters to the Editor section.

[18] Franz Schulze, *Indianapolis Star,* 5 February 1952, Letters to the Editor section.

[19] Corbin Patrick, "As the Day Begins," *Indianapolis Star,* 8 February 1952.

[20] Ed Sovola, "Inside Indianapolis," *Indianapolis Times,* 7 February 1952.

[21] Thelma Machael, *Indianapolis News,* 31 January 1952.

[22] Lucille Morehouse, *Indianapolis Star,* 10 February 1935.

[23] Sister M. Rufinia, O. S. F., "Reveries of an Artist," Sister Rufinia Art Club Papers, courtesy of Mary C. Craigmile of Lafayette, Indiana.

[24] Artist members of "The Twenty" in 1952 included: Simon P. Baus, Edmund Brucker, William Burden, David Dunlap, William Kaeser, Clifton Wheeler, Charles Yeager, Lillian Davidson, Elmira Kempton, Lawrence McConaha, Esther Nusbaum, Roland Osborne, Francis Clark Brown, Harold McDonald, Jane VanSickle and Norman B. Wilson.

[25] "The Twenty: A Group of Indiana Artists," Press Release, Hoosier Salon Patrons Association Papers.

[26] Walter Whitworth, *Indianapolis News,* 13 September 1952.

[27] Hal Jayar, "AMFOTOG," *Muncie Star,* 16 November 1952.

[28] Ibid.

[29] Corbin Patrick, *Indianapolis Star,* 26 January 1953.

[30] Walter Whitworth, *Indianapolis News,* 26 January 1953.

[31] Hertha Stein Duemling, *Fort Wayne News-Sentinel,* 26 January 1953.

[32] *Indianapolis News,* 29 January 1953.

[33] Wayne Guthrie, "Ringside in Hoosierland," *Indianapolis News,* 12 March 1954.

[34] Thelma Machael, *Indianapolis News,* circa early-February 1954, Hoosier Salon Patrons Association Papers.

[35] Ibid.

[36] "Helen Humphrey," *Indianapolis Star Magazine,* 21 February 1954.

[37] Betty Lane, "Clifton Wheeler: Rekindled Appreciation," *Indianapolis Star Magazine,* 2 November 1980, 46.

[38] "Library Notes," *Tipton Tribune,* 6 November 1930.

[39] Helen Vogt, President of the Daughters of Indiana of Chicago, to Whom It May Concern, 21 July 1954, Hoosier Salon Patrons Association Papers.

[40] Mrs. Leonidas F. Smith to Lilly Endowment, Inc., circa late summer, 1954, Hoosier Salon Patrons Association Papers.

[41] "Estimate of Additional Annual Expenditures," Grant proposal to Lilly Endowment, Inc., circa late summer, 1954, Hoosier Salon Patrons Association Papers.

[42] C. Curry Bohm to Mrs. Leonidas F. Smith, 10 July 1954, Hoosier Salon Patrons Association Papers.

[43] Johann Berthelsen to Mrs. Leonidas F. Smith, 13 July 1954, Hoosier Salon Patrons Association Papers.

[44] Gianni Cilfone to Mrs. Leonidas F. Smith, 12 July 1954, Hoosier Salon Patrons Association Papers.

[45] According to an official at Lilly Endowment, Inc., there is no record of either a grant application or a grant award having been made to the Hoosier Salon Patrons Association during the 1950s.

[46] Herbert P. Kenney, Jr., *Indianapolis News,* 7 February 1955.

[47] Ibid.

[48] Lotys Benning Stewart, *Indianapolis Star,* 5 February 1955.

[49] Ed Sovola, *Indianapolis Times,* 15 February 1955.

[50] Rosanna Hall, "Hoosier Artists: Donald M. Mattison," *Indianapolis Star Magazine,* 12 February 1961.

[51] Lucille E. Morehouse, *Indianapolis Star,* 10 December 1939.

[52] *Indianapolis Star,* 6 February 1956.

[53] *New York Herald-Tribune,* circa 1934, Stout Reference Room, Indianapolis Museum of Art.

[54] Ibid.

[55] Helen Ruth Huber, *Gary Post-Tribune,* 16 April 1956.

[56] Agnes H. Ostrom, *Indianapolis Times,* 27 January 1951.

[57] Louise Gray Symons, "Easel Jottings," *Indianapolis Times,* 16 September 1956.

[58] Helen Magner, "Pencil Sketches," *New Castle Courier-Times,* circa mid-February 1957, Hoosier Salon Patrons Association Papers.

[59] Cutline from photograph, *Indianapolis News,* circa early-February 1957, Hoosier Salon Patrons Association Papers.

[60] "Hoosier Artists: Louis W. Bonsib," *Indianapolis Star Magazine,* 28 February 1960.

[61] "Kappa Kappa Kappa Sorority," *Catalogue of the Hoosier Salon* (February 1957): unpaginated.

[62] Louise Symons, *Indianapolis Times,* circa May 1957, Hoosier Salon Patrons Association Papers.

[63] Ann Rein, *Indianapolis News,* 13 June 1958.

[64] Symons, *Times,* circa May 1957.

[65] "Special Days," *Catalogue of the Hoosier Salon* (February 1957).

[66] Louise Gray Symons, *Indianapolis Times*, 9 February 1958.

[67] Kathleen Van Nuys, *Indianapolis Times*, 10 February 1958.

[68] *Indianapolis Star*, 10 February 1958.

[69] Judith V. Newton, *The Hoosier Group: Five American Painters* (Indianapolis: Eckert Publications, 1985), 126, 136.

[70] *Star*, 10 February 1958.

[71] Helen Ruth Huber, *Gary Post-Tribune*, 12 March 1958.

[72] "Hoosier Artists: Robert Selby," *Indianapolis Star Magazine*, 25 May 1958.

[73] *Fort Wayne News-Sentinel*, circa January 1958, Hoosier Salon Patrons Association Papers.

[74] *Northside Topics*, 29 January 1959.

[75] Kathleen Van Nuys, *Indianapolis Times*, circa mid-January 1959, Hoosier Salon Patrons Association Papers.

[76] Edna Thayer, "Hoosier Artists: C. Curry Bohm," *Indianapolis Star Magazine*, 3 July 1966.

[77] Wayne Guthrie, "Ringside in Hoosierland," *Indianapolis News*, 3 June 1952.

[78] *Indianapolis Star*, 1 February 1959.

[79] Dorothy Knisely, *Indianapolis Star*, 13 December 1959.

* * *

The Sixties

[1] Kathleen Van Nuys, *Indianapolis Times*, 25 January 1960.

[2] Kathleen Van Nuys, *Indianapolis Times*, 10 January 1960.

[3] Miss Ruth Anderson, interview with co-author Judith V. Newton, Indianapolis, Indiana, 26 September 1990.

[4] Ibid.

[5] Mrs. Leonidas F. Smith, "Hoosier Artists: Anthony Buchta," *Indianapolis Star Magazine*, 7 February 1960.

[6] Ibid.

[7] *Fort Wayne Journal-Gazette*, 11 December 1960.

[8] Ibid.

[9] *Catalogue of the Hoosier Salon* (March 1925): unpaginated.

[10] Kathleen Van Nuys, *Indianapolis Times*, 22 January 1961.

[11] *Indianapolis Star*, circa June 1961, Hoosier Salon Patrons Association Papers.

[12] Van Nuys, *Times*, 22 January 1961.

[13] Herbert Kenney, Jr., *Indianapolis News*, 30 January 1961.

[14] Philip F. Clifford, "Hoosier Artists: Burling Boaz, Jr.," *Indianapolis Star Magazine*, 7 October 1962, 30.

[15] "Dedication of Showalter Fountain: The Birth of Venus," Pamphlet, Auditorium Plaza, Indiana University, Bloomington, Indiana, 22 October 1961.

[16] "What the Critics Say About the Art of Johann Berthelsen," undated, Hoosier Salon Patrons Association Papers.

[17] Ibid.

[18] Mrs. Hugh J. Baker, "Foreword," *Catalogue of the Hoosier Salon* (January 1962): unpaginated.

[19] Herbert Kenney, Jr., *Indianapolis News*, 29 January 1962.

[20] Ibid.

[21] Kathleen Van Nuys, *Indianapolis Times*, 29 January 1962.

[22] Ibid.

[23] One of the founders of Kappa Kappa Kappa Sorority was Beryl Showers—Mrs. J. E. P. Holland of Bloomington, Indiana—who was elected president of the Hoosier Salon Patrons Association in 1941. "Kappa Kappa Kappa, Inc.," *Catalogue of the Hoosier Salon* (January 1962).

[24] Ibid.

[25] Susan M. Ostrom, unidentified Indianapolis newspaper, 10 September 1962, Hoosier Salon Patrons Association Papers.

[26] Philip F. Clifford, "The Lure of the Hills," *Indianapolis Star Magazine*, 26 August 1962.

[27] Lotys Benning Stewart, *Indianapolis Star*, 31 October 1943.

[28] *Indianapolis Star*, 25 January 1963.

[29] Herbert Kenney, Jr., *Indianapolis News*, 26 January 1963.

[30] Ibid.

[31] Dorothy H. Weston, "Hoosier Artists: Joel Warner Reichard," *Indianapolis Star Magazine*, 13 October 1963.

[32] Ann Fellows, *Indianapolis Times*, 27 February 1963.

[33] The boy received a first-rate art education as the son of artist Josephine Davis and her husband, Dr. Merrill S. Davis. Dr. Joseph B. Davis, telephone interview with co-author Judith V. Newton, December 1992.

[34] Helen Magner, "Pencil Sketches," *New Castle Courier-Times*, 8 February 1964.

[35] Herbert Kenney, Jr., *Indianapolis News*, 27 January 1964.

[36] Ibid.

[37] "Today with Women," *Indianapolis News*, 23 January 1964.

[38] James Keeran, *Bloomington, Illinois, Pantagraph*, 18 July 1965.

[39] Donald L. Bandy, "Changing Lives through Art," *Indianapolis Star Magazine*, 15 October 1961.

[40] Mrs. Henry Lester Smith, *The Hoosier Salon, 1925-1974: A Dream of Farsighted Men and Women* (Indianapolis: Hoosier Salon Patrons Association, 1974), 16.

[41] "A Milestone in Indiana Culture," *Indianapolis Star Magazine*, 21 June 1964, 28.

[42] Elsie Irwin Sweeney, "Foreword," *Catalogue of the Hoosier Salon* (January 1965): unpaginated.

[43] Kathleen Van Nuys, *Indianapolis Times*, 21 January 1965.

[44] Helen Magner, "Pencil Sketches," *New Castle Courier-Times*, circa late-January, 1965, Hoosier Salon Patrons Association Papers.

[45] Unidentified newspaper article, 9 January 1965, Hoosier Salon Patrons Association Papers.

[46] Herbert P. Kenney, Jr., *Indianapolis News*, 1 February 1965.

[47] "Hoosier Artists: William A. Eyden," *Indianapolis Star Magazine,* 18 November 1962, 54.

[48] Ibid.

[49] Kenney, Jr., *News,* 1 February 1965.

[50] Ibid.

[51] *Indianapolis Star,* 31 January 1965.

[52] Mary Johnson, *Indianapolis News,* 2 February 1965.

[53] Ibid.

[54] Unidentified Indianapolis newspaper article, circa July 1965, Hoosier Salon Patrons Association Papers.

[55] Harold Sabin, *Indianapolis Star,* 26 June 1966.

[56] Ibid.

[57] Harold W. Jordan, "Foreword," *Catalogue of the Hoosier Salon* (January 1966): unpaginated.

[58] Kathleen Van Nuys, "Lightly Speaking," *Indianapolis News,* 31 January 1966.

[59] Ibid.

[60] Ibid.

[61] Gretchen Wolfram, "The Turned-on World of Martha Slaymaker," *Indianapolis Star Magazine,* 11 May 1969.

[62] Unidentified newspaper article, circa late-spring, 1966, Hoosier Salon Patrons Association Papers.

[63] Mary Waldon, *Indianapolis Star,* 5 June 1966.

[64] Helen Magner, "Pencil Sketches," *New Castle Courier-Times,* circa early-February 1967, Hoosier Salon Patrons Association Papers.

[65] Ibid.

[66] Bertha Scott, *Indianapolis News,* 26 January 1967.

[67] Ibid.

[68] Ibid.

[69] Ibid.

[70] *Indianapolis Star,* 30 January 1967.

[71] "Hoosier Artists: Lester W. Gallagher," *Indianapolis Star Magazine,* 5 November 1967.

[72] "This Week in Indiana Art," *Indianapolis Star,* circa 1967, Hoosier Salon Patrons Association Papers.

[73] "Salon's Best," *Indianapolis Star Magazine,* 3 March 1968.

[74] Corbin Patrick, "As the Day Begins," *Indianapolis Star,* circa early-February, 1968, Hoosier Salon Patrons Association Papers.

[75] Donna Snodgrass, *Indianapolis Star,* 26 January 1968.

[76] Ibid.

[77] Ibid.

[78] Ibid.

[79] Herbert P. Kenney, Jr., *Indianapolis News,* 29 January 1968.

[80] Lorraine Nelson, *Indianapolis Star,* 28 January 1968.

[81] Ibid.

[82] Ibid.

[83] Talitha Peat, "Foreword," *Catalogue of the Hoosier Salon* (January 1969): unpaginated.

[84] Unidentified Indianapolis newspaper, circa late-January 1969, Hoosier Salon Patrons Association Papers.

[85] Marion Simon Garmel, *Indianapolis News,* 24 February 1972.

[86] Among other African-American artists to have exhibited their work in the Salon were Hale A. Woodruff in 1927, William Edouard Scott in 1926-1928 and John Wesley Hardrick in 1929, 1931 and 1934.

[87] Garmel, *News,* 24 February 1972.

[88] "Cariani anglicized his middle name, Giuseppe which means Joseph. That explains the J." Excerpt from letter, Dorothy Crispino to Barbara Judd, circa September 1992, Brown County Public Library Collection.

[89] "Varaldo Giuseppe Cariani," Brown County Art Guild, Inc., Nashville, Indiana, Brown County Public Library.

[90] Lorraine Price, *Indianapolis News,* 17 January 1969.

[91] *Indianapolis Star,* 6 October 1969.

* * *

The Seventies

[1] Ian Fraser, "Art: News and Views," *Downtowner Indianapolis* (May 1970), 10.

[2] Ibid.

[3] Ibid.

[4] Ibid.

[5] *Indianapolis Star,* 26 January 1970.

[6] Ibid.

[7] Ibid.

[8] Marion Garmel, "Brush Strokes," *Indianapolis News,* circa 1973, Hoosier Salon Patrons Association Papers.

[9] Ibid.

[10] Ibid.

[11] Lowell Nussbaum, *Indianapolis Star,* 31 March 1970.

[12] Lloyd B. Walton, "Traditional Arts Advocate," *Indianapolis Star Magazine,* 30 August 1970.

[13] Ibid.

[14] Ibid.

[15] Mrs. Henry Lester Smith, *The Hoosier Salon, 1925-1974: A Dream of Farsighted Men and Women* (Indianapolis: Hoosier Salon Patrons Association, 1974), 19.

[16] Mrs. Leonidas F. Smith to Lilly Endowment, Inc., circa late summer, 1954, Hoosier Salon Patrons Association Papers.

[17] Smith, *Hoosier Salon,* 20.

[18] *Bloomington Herald-Telephone,* 20 August 1970.

[19] Ibid.

[20] Mrs. Victor C. Hackney to Mrs. Paul Tuerk, 21 September 1970, Hoosier Salon Patrons Association Papers.

[21] *Hoosier Salon Newsletter,* October 1970, Hoosier Salon Patrons Association Papers.

[22] Mrs. Victor C. Hackney, "Invitation to Join 'Volunteers for the Hoosier Salon,'" circa late summer, 1970, Hoosier Salon Patrons Association Papers.

[23] Kathleen Van Nuys, "Lightly Speaking," *Indianapolis News,* 27 September 1971.

[24] *Indianapolis Star,* 14 October 1970.

[25] Helen Magner, "Pencil Sketches," *New Castle Courier-Times,* circa November 1970, Hoosier Salon Patrons Association Papers.

[26] George S. Diener, "Foreword," *Catalogue of the Hoosier Salon* (January 1971): unpaginated.

[27] Susan Lennis, "Hoosier Artists: Elizabeth Dodds Shaffer," *Indianapolis Star Magazine,* 3 May 1970.

[28] *Indianapolis Star,* 24 January 1971.

[29] Corbin Patrick, "The Lively Arts," *Indianapolis Star,* 9 February 1971.

[30] *Indianapolis Star,* 21 February 1971.

[31] *Indianapolis Star,* 7 March 1971.

[32] *Star,* 21 February 1971.

[33] *Indianapolis Star,* 13 September 1971.

[34] Marion Adams, "Art: History of the Hoosier Salon," *Indianapolis Magazine* (September 1972), 17.

[35] Marion Garmel, *Indianapolis News,* 24 January 1972.

[36] Ibid.

[37] Riley Bertram, *Brown County Democrat,* 17 February 1972, Letters to the Editor section. This Nashville, Indiana, artist wrote two more letters to the *Democrat,* the second of which went unpublished. The newspaper's editor, Greg Temple, responded to Bertram's third letter: "The letter to which Mr. Bertram refers was one of only a few I have refused to publish during the last two years. It was a second broadside at the Hoosier Salon. And it was very long. I thought Mr. Bertram had made his point. Apparently, judging from the above (letter), he feels he has not. Okay, Riley, you've had your second chance . . . Now, enough is enough. Editor's Note, *Brown County Democrat,* 8 June 1972, Letters to the Editor section.

[38] Ibid.

[39] Harold W. Jordan, Memorandum to Hoosier Salon Patrons Association Officers, Board of Directors and Advisory Council, 6 March 1972, Hoosier Salon Patrons Association Papers.

[40] Harold W. Jordan, *Brown County Democrat,* 9 March 1972, Letters to the Editor section.

[41] Garmel, *News,* 24 January 1972.

[42] Unidentified newspaper article, circa January 1972, Hoosier Salon Patrons Association Papers.

[43] Garmel, *News,* 24 January 1972.

[44] Ibid.

[45] Marion Simon Garmel, "Brush Strokes," *Indianapolis News,* 3 February 1972.

[46] Ibid.

[47] Ibid.

[48] "Hoosier Artists: Rosemary Browne Beck," *Indianapolis Star Magazine,* 1 December 1968, 58-60.

[49] Ibid., 58.

[50] Otis R. Bowen, M. D., "Foreword," *Catalogue of the Hoosier Salon* (January 1973): unpaginated.

[51] Smith, *Hoosier Salon,* 21.

[52] Unidentified newspaper article, circa early-September 1973, Hoosier Salon Patrons Association Papers.

[53] Report issued by Study Committee of the Future of the Hoosier Salon Patrons Association, 8 February 1973, Hoosier Salon Patrons Association Papers.

[54] Marion Simon Garmel, *Indianapolis News,* 22 January 1973.

[55] *Indianapolis Star,* 6 November 1973.

[56] Ibid.

[57] David Mannweiler, "Don't Quote Me," *Indianapolis News,* 6 November 1973.

[58] Ibid.

[59] Marion Simon Garmel, "Brush Strokes," *Indianapolis News,* circa mid-November 1973, Hoosier Salon Patrons Association Papers.

[60] Ibid.

[61] Harold W. Jordan to Frank P. Thomas, 19 November 1973, Hoosier Salon Patrons Association Papers.

[62] Harold W. Jordan to Miss Katherine Wright, 20 November 1973, Hoosier Salon Patrons Association Papers.

[63] Emergency Grant #730199, Lilly Endowment, Inc., December 1973, Lilly Endowment, Inc., Archives, Indianapolis, Indiana.

[64] Harold W. Jordan to Members of the Hoosier Salon Patrons Association, Inc., 28 November 1973, Hoosier Salon Patrons Association Papers.

[65] Ibid.

[66] Harold W. Jordan, "Foreword," *Catalogue of the Hoosier Salon* (January 1974): unpaginated.

[67] Ibid.

[68] Marion Simon Garmel, "Brush Strokes," *Indianapolis News,* circa early-January, 1974, Hoosier Salon Patrons Association Papers.

[69] Unidentified newspaper article, circa January 1974, Hoosier Salon Patrons Association Papers.

[70] Garmel, *News,* circa early-January 1974.

[71] *Brown County Democrat,* circa January 1974, Hoosier Salon Patrons Association Papers.

[72] Henry Wood, "Portraits and Flowers," *Indianapolis Star Magazine,* 1 January 1951.

[73] Ibid.

[74] *Democrat,* circa January 1974.

[75] *Indianapolis News,* 3 November 1981.

[76] *Indianapolis Star,* 21 January 1974.

[77] *Indianapolis News,* 21 January 1974.

[78] Press Release, Hoosier Salon Patrons Association, January 1974, Hoosier Salon Patrons Association Papers.

[79] Kathleen Van Nuys, "Lightly Speaking," *Indianapolis News,* circa late-January 1974, Hoosier Salon Patrons Association Papers.

[80] Mrs. Thomas E. Husselman to Kenneth J. Reeve, 16 September 1974, Hoosier Salon Patrons Association Papers.

[81] Ibid.

[82] Kathleen Van Nuys, "Lightly Speaking," *Indianapolis News,* circa fall 1974, Hoosier Salon Patrons Association Papers.

[83] Ibid.

[84] Unidentified newspaper article, circa early-September 1974, Hoosier Salon Patrons Association Papers.

[85] Marion Simon Garmel, "Brush Strokes," *Indianapolis News,* 6 November 1974.

[86] Ibid.

[87] Philippa C. Hughes to Richard Ristine, 14 October 1974, Lilly Endowment, Inc., Archives, Indianapolis, Indiana.

[88] *Indianapolis Star,* 18 January 1975.

[89] Garmel, *News,* 6 November 1974.

[90] "Palette Patter," October 1974, Hoosier Salon Patrons Association Papers.

[91] Philippa C. Hughes, "Foreword," *Catalogue of the Hoosier Salon* (January 1975): unpaginated.

[92] Kathleen Van Nuys, "Lightly Speaking," *Indianapolis News,* 31 January 1975.

[93] Kathleen Van Nuys, "Lightly Speaking," *Indianapolis News,* circa mid-January 1975, Hoosier Salon Patrons Association Papers.

[94] Van Nuys, *News,* 31 January 1975.

[95] *Indianapolis Star,* 16 March 1975.

[96] *Catalogue of the Hoosier Salon* (January 1975).

[97] Marion Simon Garmel, *Indianapolis News,* 20 January 1975.

[98] Ibid.

[99] Ibid.

[100] Ibid.

[101] Ibid.

[102] *Brown County Democrat,* 15 January 1975.

[103] The Brown County coroner revealed that Miss Goth had been bitten by a poisonous brown recluse spider before she died. It is believed that she became ill and disoriented from the spider's bite, and this caused her to fall down a flight of steps in her home. Her death was caused by head injury and multiple fractures suffered in the fall. *Indianapolis Star,* 23 January 1975.

[104] Harold W. Jordan to Members of the 1973-1974 Hoosier Salon Patrons Association Board of Directors, 26 January 1975, Hoosier Salon Patrons Association Papers.

[105] *Indianapolis Star,* 14 February 1976.

[106] Marion Simon Garmel, *Indianapolis News,* 26 January 1976.

[107] *Hoosier Salon Newsletter,* April 1976, Hoosier Salon Patrons Association Papers.

[108] Sally Falk, "Concerning Women," *Indianapolis Star,* 8 May 1976.

[109] Unidentified Indianapolis newspaper article, 20 August 1975, Hoosier Salon Patrons Association Papers.

[110] Marion Simon Garmel, "Brush Strokes," *Indianapolis News,* circa August 1975, Hoosier Salon Patrons Association Papers.

[111] Falk, *Star,* 8 May 1976.

[112] Van Nuys, *News,* circa mid-January, 1975.

[113] *Hoosier Salon Newsletter,* October 1976, Hoosier Salon Patrons Association Papers.

[114] Ibid.

[115] Mrs. David A. Hicks to Members of the Hoosier Salon Patrons Association, Inc., 1 November 1976, Hoosier Salon Patrons Association Papers.

[116] Ibid.

[117] Kathleen Van Nuys, "Lightly Speaking," *Indianapolis News,* circa early-December 1976, Hoosier Salon Patrons Association Papers.

[118] "A Message from the President," *Hoosier Salon Newsletter,* January 1977, Hoosier Salon Patrons Association Papers.

[119] Marion Simon Garmel, "Brush Strokes," *Indianapolis News,* 24 January 1977.

[120] Ibid.

[121] Marion Simon Garmel, "Brush Strokes," *Indianapolis News,* circa 1973, Hoosier Salon Patrons Association Papers.

[122] Garmel, *News,* 24 January 1977.

[123] Betty J. Lane, "Hoosier Artists: Floyd Hopper," *Indianapolis Star Magazine,* 18 December 1966.

[124] Garmel, *News,* 24 January 1977.

[125] *Indianapolis Star,* 24 January 1977.

[126] Martha R. Van Sickle to Members of the Hoosier Salon Patrons Association, circa late summer, 1977, Hoosier Salon Patrons Association Papers.

[127] Ibid.

[128] Mrs. David A. Hicks, Special Announcement of Board of Directors Meeting, 1 September 1977, Hoosier Salon Patrons Association Papers.

[129] Ibid.

[130] "A Message from the President," *Hoosier Salon Newsletter,* October 1977, Hoosier Salon Patrons Association Papers.

[131] Ibid.

[132] Marion Simon Garmel, "Brush Strokes," *Indianapolis News,* 8 February 1978.

[133] Ibid.

[134] Ibid.

[135] Marion Simon Garmel, "Brush Strokes," *Indianapolis News,* 10 April 1978.

[136] *Indianapolis Star,* 10 April 1978.

[137] Garmel, *News,* 10 April 1978.

[138] Ibid.

[139] Lloyd B. Walton, "Under the Big Top with Bob Weaver," *Indianapolis Star Magazine,* 18 April 1971, 39.

[140] Ibid., 40.

[141] Ibid.

[142] *Indianapolis News,* undated, Hoosier Salon Patrons Association Papers.

[143] Ibid.

[144] Bill Pittman, *Indianapolis News,* 31 October 1984.

[145] Garmel, *News,* 10 April 1978.

[146] "Burkhart Bulletin," *Hoosier Salon Newsletter,* October 1978, Hoosier Salon Patrons Association Papers.

[147] Helen Magner, "Pencil Sketches," *New Castle Courier-Times,* circa late-December 1978, Hoosier Salon Patrons Association Papers.

[148] Kathleen Van Nuys, "Lightly Speaking," *Indianapolis News,* circa early 1979, Hoosier Salon Patrons Association Papers.

[149] *Hoosier Salon Newsletter,* July 1979, Hoosier Salon Patrons Association Papers.

[150] Marion Simon Garmel, "Brush Strokes," *Indianapolis News,* 30 April 1979.

[151] Ibid.

[152] "Special Days," *Catalogue of the Hoosier Salon* (April 1979): unpaginated.

[153] *Indianapolis Star,* 28 April 1979.

[154] Pam Hicks, Hoosier Salon Annual Exhibit Report, 11 June 1979, Hoosier Salon Patrons Association Papers.

[155] *Hoosier Salon Newsletter,* April 1979, Hoosier Salon Patrons Association Papers.

156 "Burkhart Bulletin," *Hoosier Salon Newsletter,* December 1979, Hoosier Salon Patrons Association Papers.

* * *

The Eighties

1 Marion Garmel, "Brush Strokes," *Indianapolis News,* 28 April 1980.

2 Ibid.

3 Ibid.

4 For years, the bust of Governor Henry Schricker was displayed in the Indiana State House, and the statue of young Abraham Lincoln was to be found in the Indiana State Office Building Plaza in downtown Indianapolis. *Indianapolis Star,* 3 May 1970.

5 *Indianapolis Star,* 16 December 1992. Some time after the purchase, and subsequent closing, of L. S. Ayres & Co. by May Department Stores Co., the new owner donated the sculpture to the city in December of 1992. *Indianapolis Star,* circa January 1993.

6 Garmel, *News,* 28 April 1980.

7 Press Release, Hoosier Salon Patrons Association, April 1980, Hoosier Salon Patrons Association Papers.

8 Garmel, *News,* 28 April 1980.

9 Charles A. Barnes, "Welcoming Letter," *Catalogue of the Hoosier Salon* (April 1980): unpaginated.

10 Carol Weiss, "Painter of People," *Arts Indiana* (October 1991), 22.

11 Ibid.

12 Marion Garmel, "Brush Strokes," *Indianapolis News,* 11 May 1981.

13 Ibid.

14 Ibid.

15 Ben Cole, "Washington Ripples," *Indianapolis Star,* 14 June 1981.

16 *Indianapolis Times Magazine,* 9 November 1981, 17.

17 Marion Garmel, "Brush Strokes," *Indianapolis News,* 24 October 1981.

18 Ibid.

19 Ibid.

20 Kathleen Van Nuys, *Indianapolis News,* 7 May 1981.

21 Unidentified newspaper article, circa mid-October 1981, Hoosier Salon Patrons Association Papers.

22 Marion Garmel, "Brush Strokes," *Indianapolis News,* 5 May 1982.

23 Kathleen Van Nuys, "Lightly Speaking," *Indianapolis News,* late-April 1982, Hoosier Salon Patrons Association Papers.

24 Helen Lair, unidentified New Castle, Indiana, newspaper, 6 May 1982, Hoosier Salon Patrons Association Papers.

25 "Executive Director's Report," *Hoosier Salon Newsletter,* September 1982, Hoosier Salon Patrons Association Papers.

26 Marion Garmel, "Brush Strokes," *Indianapolis News,* 3 May 1982.

27 Ibid.

28 Marion Garmel, "Brush Strokes," *Indianapolis News,* 19 May 1982.

29 Press Release, Nancy A. Noël, "Personal Statement," undated, Noël Studio, Zionsville, Indiana.

30 Van Nuys, *News,* late-April 1982.

31 "Special Thanks to the Daughters of Indiana," *Hoosier Salon Newsletter,* September 1982, Hoosier Salon Patrons Association Papers.

32 Marion Garmel, "Brush Strokes," *Indianapolis News,* 25 April 1983.

33 Carol Weiss, "Artists Explore Balance Between Money and Art," *Arts Insight* (February 1987), 8.

34 Ibid.

35 Ibid.

36 Steve Mannheimer, "Visual Arts," *Indianapolis Star,* 8 March 1992.

37 Garmel, *News,* 25 April 1983.

38 Kathleen Van Nuys, "Lightly Speaking," *Indianapolis News,* 18 April 1983.

39 Ibid.

40 *Hoosier Salon Newsletter,* February 1983, Hoosier Salon Patrons Association Papers.

41 *Hoosier Salon Newsletter,* August 1983, Hoosier Salon Patrons Association Papers.

42 Steve Mannheimer, *Indianapolis Star,* 18 May 1984.

43 *Catalogue of the Hoosier Salon* (May 1984): 46.

44 Kathleen Van Nuys, "Lightly Speaking," *Indianapolis News,* circa spring 1984, Hoosier Salon Patrons Association Papers.

45 Marion Garmel, "Brush Strokes," *Indianapolis News,* 14 May 1984.

46 Mannheimer, *Star,* 18 May 1984.

47 Marion Garmel, "Brush Strokes," *Indianapolis News,* 1 June 1984.

48 Mannheimer, *Star,* 18 May 1984.

49 Ibid.

50 Ibid.

51 Unidentified Indianapolis newspaper article, 3 July 1984, Hoosier Salon Patrons Association Papers.

52 Ibid.

53 "President's Message," *Hoosier Salon Newsletter,* October 1984, Hoosier Salon Patrons Association Papers.

54 Marion Garmel, "Brush Strokes," *Indianapolis News,* 29 April 1985.

55 Ibid.

56 Ibid.

57 See *Larousse Dictionary of Painters* (New York: Larousse and Co., Inc., 1981), 141-142 for a discussion about the artwork of François Gérard (1770-1837).

58 Garmel, *News,* 29 April 1985.

59 Ibid.

60 Ibid.

61 Kathleen Van Nuys, "Lightly Speaking," *Indianapolis News,* 20 February 1985.

62 Garmel, *News,* 29 April 1985.

63 Marion Garmel, "Brush Strokes," *Indianapolis News,* 21 April 1986.

64 Press Release, Hoosier Salon Patrons Association, April 1986, Hoosier Salon Patrons Association Papers.

65 Garmel, *News,* 21 April 1986.

66 Ibid.

67 Lori Sparger, *Topics Newspaper,* 11 January 1989.

68 Ibid.

69 Ibid.

70 *Wabash Plain Dealer,* 6 June 1986. The elegant three-story Honeywell Center, completed in 1952, is listed on the National Register of Historic Places; it was built by Mark C. Honeywell as a memorial to his first wife, Olive Lutz Honeywell, and to his parents. During the late-1930s and 1940s, Honeywell also erected—in the midst of his garden estate—a stone replica of a Norman-style château as a studio for making films. Today, the structure serves as the clubhouse for the Wabash Country Club. Pamphlet, *The Honeywell House,* Wabash, Indiana.

71 Press Release, *Hoosier Salon,* 21 April 1986.

72 "History," *Catalogue of the Hoosier Salon* (May 1987): 7.

73 Marion Garmel, "Brush Strokes," *Indianapolis News,* 21 January 1987.

74 *Indianapolis Star,* 11 May 1987.

75 Marion Garmel, "Brush Strokes," *Indianapolis News,* 11 May 1987.

76 Ibid.

77 Marion Garmel, "Brush Strokes," *Indianapolis News,* 28 May 1987.

78 Marion Garmel, "Brush Strokes," *Indianapolis News,* circa 1972, Hoosier Salon Patrons Association Papers.

79 Ibid.

80 Ibid.

81 Press Release, Hoosier Salon Patrons Association, May 1987, Hoosier Salon Patrons Association Papers.

82 Ken Ford, *Kokomo Tribune,* 9 July 1987.

83 Ibid.

84 "Executive Director's Report," *Hoosier Salon Newsletter,* October 1987, Hoosier Salon Patrons Association Papers.

85 Marion Garmel, "Brush Strokes," *Indianapolis News,* 8 October 1987.

86 Marion Garmel, "Brush Strokes," *Indianapolis News,* 29 December 1988.

87 Nancy E. DeBolt, *Chronicle-Tribune,* 4 April 1988.

88 "Hoosier Salon Guild," *Catalogue of the Hoosier Salon* (April 1988): unpaginated.

89 "Hoosier Salon Guild Report," *Hoosier Salon Newsletter,* April 1988, Hoosier Salon Patrons Association Papers.

90 Marion Garmel, "Brush Strokes," *Indianapolis News,* 6 May 1987.

91 Carol Weiss, "What Frees Creativity?" *Arts Indiana* (June 1988), 17.

92 Ibid.

93 Marion Garmel, "Brush Strokes," *Indianapolis News,* 25 April 1988.

94 Ibid.

95 Ibid.

96 Press Release, Hoosier Salon Patrons Association, April 1988, Hoosier Salon Patrons Association Papers.

97 "Executive Director's Report," *Hoosier Salon Newsletter,* September 1988, Hoosier Salon Patrons Association Papers.

98 Governor Evan Bayh, "Greetings," *Catalogue of the Hoosier Salon* (April 1989): 6.

99 Kathleen Van Nuys, "Lightly Speaking," *Indianapolis News,* 3 April 1989.

100 Ibid.

101 Ibid.

102 *Indianapolis Star,* 30 March 1969.

103 Ibid.

104 Marion Garmel, "Brush Strokes," *Indianapolis News,* 17 April 1989.

105 John Shaughnessy, *Indianapolis Star,* 5 October 1992.

106 Ibid.

107 "President's Message," *Hoosier Salon Newsletter,* August 1989, Hoosier Salon Patrons Association Papers.

108 Kathleen Van Nuys, "Lightly Speaking," *Indianapolis News,* 11 November 1989.

109 Marion Garmel, "Brush Strokes," *Indianapolis News,* 22 July 1983.

110 "President's Message," *Hoosier Salon Newsletter,* December 1989, Hoosier Salon Patrons Association Papers.

111 "Executive Director's Report," *Newsletter,* December 1989.

* * *

The Nineties

1 Marion Garmel, "Brush Strokes," *Indianapolis News,* 7 May 1990.

2 Ibid.

3 The Indiana State Museum building originally was constructed to serve as the Indianapolis City Hall. Completed in December of 1910, it is a fine example of Neo-classical revival architecture and is now listed in the National Register of Historic Places.

4 Richard A. Gantz, Ph.D., "Greetings," *Catalogue of the Hoosier Salon* (May 1990): 3.

5 Press Release, Hoosier Salon Patrons Association, 7 May 1990, Hoosier Salon Patrons Association Papers.

6 Garmel, *News,* 7 May 1990.

7 Ibid.

8 "Hoosier Artists: Wilbur Meese," *Indianapolis Star Magazine,* 15 March 1970.

9 "President's Message," *Hoosier Salon Newsletter,* Summer 1990.

10 Ibid.

11 Daughters of Indiana, "Hoosier Salon," Circular, circa early 1925, Stout Reference Library, Indianapolis Museum of Art.

12 Booth Tarkington, "Foreword," *Catalogue of the Hoosier Salon* (January 1940): unpaginated.

SELECTED BIBLIOGRAPHY

"A Milestone in Indiana Culture." *Indianapolis Star Magazine,* 21 June 1964.

"A Tribute to Carl Graf." Circa early-February 1947. Ruth Anderson Papers. Typewritten.

Adams, Marion. "History of the Hoosier Salon." *Indianapolis Magazine,* September 1972.

Anderson, Ruth. Series of interviews with co-author, Judith V. Newton. Indianapolis, Indiana, September and October, 1990.

Art Association of Richmond. *Art in Richmond: 1898-1978.* Richmond, Indiana: Art Association of Richmond, 1978.

Art Center, Inc. *Impressionistic Trends in Hoosier Painting.* South Bend, Indiana: Art Center, Inc., 1979. Exh. Cat.

Art Center, Inc. *The Work of George Ames Aldrich, L. Clarence Ball & Alexis Jean Fournier in South Bend Collections.* South Bend, Indiana: Art Center, Inc., 1982. Exh. Cat.

Art Institute of Omaha. *Nebraska Artists' Sixth Annual Exhibition.* Omaha, Nebraska: Art Institute of Omaha, 1927. Exh. Cat.

Bandy, Donald L. "Changing Lives Through Art." *Indianapolis Star Magazine,* 15 October 1961.

Banta, R. E., comp. *Indiana Authors and their Books: 1816-1916.* Crawfordsville, Indiana: Wabash College Press, 1949.

Barnes, Hope; and Sargent, Frances Petty. *Stone on Stone.* Muncie, Indiana: Ball State University Press, 1991.

Baumann, Gustave. "Hoosier Salon 1930: The Wood Block." *Fashions of the Hour,* January 1930.

Berger, Arthur Asa. "Little Orphan Annie: The Abandoned Years." *The Comic Stripped American.* New York: Walker & Co., 1973.

Bonsett, M. D., Charles A. "Medical Museum Notes." *Journal of the Indiana State Medical Association* (November 1980): 711.

Bradley, Carolyn G. "Report on the Experiences of a Visiting Professor of Art to Chile, 1946." Carolyn Bradley Papers. University Archives, Ohio State University, Columbus, Ohio. Photocopy.

Brown County Art Gallery Association. *Interesting Facts About the Artists.* Nashville, Indiana: Brown County Art Gallery Association, n. d.

Brown County Art Guild, Inc. "Carl Christopher Graf." *The Memorial Room of Marie Goth, Varaldo J. Cariani and Genevieve and Carl Graf.* Nashville, Indiana: Brown County Art Guild, Inc., n. d.

Brown County Art Guild, Inc. "Genevieve Goth Graf." *The Memorial Room of Marie Goth, Varaldo J. Cariani and Genevieve and Carl Graf.* Nashville, Indiana: Brown County Art Guild, Inc., n. d.

Brown County Art Guild, Inc. "Marie Goth." *The Memorial Room of Marie Goth, Varaldo J. Cariani and Genevieve and Carl Graf.* Nashville, Indiana: Brown County Art Guild, Inc., n. d.

Brown County Art Guild, Inc. "Varaldo Giuseppi Cariani." *The Memorial Room of Marie Goth, Varaldo J. Cariani and Genevieve and Carl Graf.* Nashville, Indiana: Brown County Art Guild, Inc., n. d.

Bucklin, Clarissa, ed. *Nebraska Art and Artists.* Lincoln, Nebraska: University of Nebraska Press, 1932.

Burnet, Mary Q. *Art and Artists of Indiana.* New York: The Century Co., 1921.

Carlisle, John C. "A Half Century of Public Art: The Heritage of Indiana Post Office Murals." *Traces of Indiana and Midwestern History* 4 (Summer 1992): 22-31.

Chavers, Susan O. *A Guide to Art Smart: Indiana.* Lafayette, Indiana: Greater Lafayette Museum of Art, 1986.

Cincinnati Art Galleries. *Frank Myslive.* Cincinnati, Ohio: Cincinnati Art Galleries, n. d.

Cincinnati Art Galleries. *Panorama of Cincinnati Art III, 1850-1950.* Cincinnati, Ohio: Cincinnati Art Galleries, 1988. Exh. Cat.

Cincinnati Art Galleries. *Stanley Bielecky: The American Scene.* Cincinnati, Ohio: Cincinnati Art Galleries, 1988.

Clifford, Philip F. "Hoosier Artists: Burling Boaz, Jr." *Indianapolis Star Magazine,* 7 October 1962.

Clifford, Philip F. "The Lure of the Hills." *Indianapolis Star Magazine,* 26 August 1962.

Cottman, George S. *Centennial History and Handbook of Indiana.* Indianapolis: Hollenbeck Press, 1915.

Couperie, Pierre; Horn, Maurice C.; Destefanis, Proto; François, Edouard; Moliterni, Claude; and Gassiot-Talabot, Gérald. *A History of the Comic Strip.* New York: Crown Publishing, Inc., 1968.

Crispino, Dorothy to Judd, Barbara, September 1992. Brown County Public Library Collection.

Cuba, Stanley L. *Olive Rush: A Hoosier Artist in New Mexico.* Muncie, Indiana: Minnetrista Cultural Foundation, Inc., 1992.

Dahlgreen, Charles to Shulz, Adolph R., 3 May 1955. Brown County Public Library Collection.

Dailey, Frank C. *Hoosier Paintings: The Dailey Family*

Memorial Collection. Indiana University Auditorium, Bloomington, Indiana, 1957. Typewritten.

Daily, Evelynne Mess. Interview with co-author Carol Weiss. Indianapolis, Indiana, 4 October 1990.

Daniel, Clifton, ed. *Chronicle of the 20th Century.* Mount Kisco, New York: Chronicle Publications, Inc., 1987.

"Daniel Garber." *The Art Digest,* 15 December 1932.

Daughters of Indiana. *Catalogue of the Hoosier Salon.* Chicago: Daughters of Indiana, 1926.

Daughters of Indiana, Earlham Alumni Association of Chicago and Indiana Society of Chicago. *Catalogue of the Hoosier Salon.* Chicago: Daughters of Indiana, Earlham Alumni Association of Chicago and Indiana Society of Chicago, 1925.

Daughters of Indiana of Chicago. *Hoosier Salon.* Chicago: Daughters of Indiana of Chicago, 1924. Promotional brochure.

"Dedication of Showalter Fountain: The Birth of Venus." Auditorium Plaza, Indiana University, Bloomington, Indiana, 22 October 1961. Pamphlet.

Doherty, Margaret. "Three Indiana Cartoonists: Then and Now." *Mirages of Memory: 200 Years of Indiana Art.* South Bend, Indiana: University of Notre Dame Press, 1977. Exh. Cat.

DuBois, June. *Indiana Artists George Jo and Evelynne Bernloehr Mess: A Story of Devotion.* Indianapolis: Indianapolis Historical Society, 1985.

Dunn, Jacob Piatt. *Greater Indianapolis: The History, The Industries, The Institutions and The People of a City of Homes.* Chicago: The Lewis Publishing Co., 1910.

Dunn, Jacob Piatt. *Indiana and Indianans: A History of Aboriginal and Territorial Indiana and the Century of Statehood.* Chicago and New York: The American Historical Society, 1919.

Eckert Fine Art. *William Forsyth (1854-1935).* Indianapolis: Eckert Fine Art, n. d.

Eldredge, Charles C.; Schimmel, Julie; and Truettner, William H. *Art in New Mexico, 1900-1945: Paths to Taos and Santa Fe.* New York: Abbeville Press, Inc., 1986. Exh. Cat.

Evelynne Mess Daily Papers. Indianapolis, Indiana. Collection includes correspondence, documents and newspaper articles concerning Hoosier artists.

Falk, Peter Hastings, ed. *Who Was Who in American Art.* Madison, Connecticut: Sound View Press, 1985.

"Famous Artist Finds Subjects at Indiana Dunes State Park." *Outdoor Indiana,* September 1947.

Fraser, Ian. "Art: News and Views." *Downtowner Indianapolis,* May 1970.

"Frederick Polley: Our Guest Artist." *Indiana Clubwoman,* January 1941.

"Gaar Williams." (Cover Information.) *Indiana History Bulletin* 35 (September 1958).

Gerdts, William H. *American Impressionism.* Seattle: The Henry Gallery Association, 1980.

Gerdts, William H. *Art Across America: Two Centuries of Regional Painting, 1710-1920.* New York: Abbeville Press, 1990.

Gerdts, William H.; and Frank, Peter. *Indiana Influence: The Golden Age of Indiana Landscape*

Painting and Indiana's Modern Legacy. Fort Wayne, Indiana: Fort Wayne Museum of Art, 1984. Exh. Cat.

Grimes, Ruth G. "The Hoosier Salon." *The Hoosier Magazine,* February 1930.

Griner, Ned H. *Side by Side with Coarser Plants: The Muncie Art Movement, 1885-1985.* Muncie, Indiana: Ball State University Press, 1985.

Haggar, Reginald G. *A Dictionary of Art Terms.* New York: Hawthorn Books, Inc., 1962.

Hall, Rosanna. "Hoosier Artists: Donald M. Mattison." *Indianapolis Star Magazine.*

Haskens, Mildred Stilz. Interview with co-author, Judith V. Newton. Indianapolis, Indiana, 16 March 1983.

Heritage, Louise; and Brown, Warren Wilmer. *Glen Cooper Henshaw.* Baltimore: The Monumental Press, 1945.

"Hoosier Artists: Katherine Groh Blasingham." *Indianapolis Star Magazine,* 4 May 1969.

"Hoosier Artists: Lester W. Gallagher." *Indianapolis Star Magazine,* 5 November 1967.

"Hoosier Artists: Louis W. Bonsib." *Indianapolis Star Magazine,* 28 February 1960.

"Hoosier Artists: Robert Selby." *Indianapolis Star Magazine,* 25 May 1958.

"Hoosier Artists: Rosemary Browne Beck." *Indianapolis Star Magazine,* 1 December 1968.

"Hoosier Artists: Wilbur Meese." *Indianapolis Star Magazine,* 15 March 1970.

"Hoosier Artists: William A. Eyden." *Indianapolis Star Magazine,* 18 November 1962.

Hoosier Salon Papers. Selma N. Steele Collection. Indiana State Museum and Historic Sites, Indianapolis, Indiana.

Hoosier Salon Patrons Association. *Catalogues of the Hoosier Salon.* Series, 1927-1990. Chicago and Indianapolis: Hoosier Salon Patrons Association, 1927-1990.

Hoosier Salon Patrons Association. *The Mark C. Honeywell Garden Festival.* Indianapolis: Hoosier Salon Patrons Association, August 1941.

Hoosier Salon Patrons Association Papers. Indianapolis, Indiana. Collection includes correspondence, documents, newspaper articles and photographs concerning the Hoosier Salon and its artists during the show's years in Chicago and Indianapolis.

Howard, Leland G. *Johann Berthelsen: An American Master Painter.* Terre Haute, Indiana: Sheldon Swope Art Museum, 1988.

"In Memory of a Hoosier Painter." *Indianapolis Star Magazine,* 29 September 1957.

Indiana Artist-Craftsmen, Inc. Directory, 1980-1981.

Indiana Federation of Art Clubs. "Art Guide to Indiana." *Bulletin of the Extension Division of Indiana University* 11 (April 1931): 3-179.

Indianapolis Art League. *The Edge of Town: Painting the Indiana Scene, 1932-1948.* Indianapolis: Indianapolis Art League, 1989. Exh. Cat.

Irvington Historical Society. *The Irvington Group: 1928-1937.* Indianapolis: Irvington Historical Society, 1984. Exh. Cat.

Janes, Paul N. "Portrait Painter: Randolph Coats." *Indianapolis Star Magazine*, 5 March 1950.

Judd, Barbara, comp.; and Nesbit, M. Joanne, ed. *Brown County's Art Colony: The Early Years*. Nashville, Indiana: Nana's Books, 1993.

Kokomo-Howard County Public Library. *The Hoosier Art Collection of the Kokomo-Howard County Public Library*. Kokomo, Indiana: Kokomo-Howard County Public Library, 1989.

Krause, Martin. *The Passage: Return of Indiana Painters from Germany, 1880-1905*. Indianapolis: Indianapolis Museum of Art, 1990. Exh. Cat.

Lane, Betty J. "Clifton Wheeler: Rekindled Appreciation." *Indianapolis Star Magazine*.

Lane, Betty J. "Hoosier Artists: Floyd Hopper." *Indianapolis Star Magazine*, 18 December 1966.

Larousse Dictionary of Painters. New York: Larousse and Co., Inc., 1981.

Lauter, Flora, comp. *Biographical Dictionary of Indiana Artists*. Indiana Artists Club, May 1937.

Lauter, Flora. *Indiana Artists (Active), 1940*. Spencer, Indiana: Samuel R. Guard & Co., Inc., 1941.

Lennis, Susan. "Hoosier Artists: Elizabeth Dodds Shaffer." *Indianapolis Star Magazine*, 3 May 1970.

Lewis, Carl. "Painter of the Dunes." *Indianapolis Star Magazine*.

Lucas, E. V. "Daniel Garber and Edward W. Redfield." *Ladies' Home Journal*, May 1926.

Madison, James H. *Indiana Through Tradition and Change: A History of the Hoosier State and its People, 1920-1945*. Indianapolis: Indiana Historical Society, 1982.

Mallett, Daniel Trowbridge. *Supplement to Mallett's Index of Artists*. New York: R. R. Bowker Company, 1948.

"Marie Goth: 1887-1975." Brochure. Brown County Public Library Collection.

Mayhill, Tom. "Polley: Indiana Artist." *Indianapolis Monthly*, October 1982.

McCutcheon, John T. "The Hoosier Salon, 1927." *Fashions of the Hour*. Chicago: Marshall Field & Co., 1927.

Mildred Niesse Papers. Indianapolis, Indiana. Collection includes documents and newspaper articles concerning Hoosier artists.

Minnetrista Cultural Center. *Frederik Grue*. Muncie, Indiana: Minnetrista Cultural Center, 1989. Exh. Cat.

Newton, Judith Vale. *The Hoosier Group: Five American Painters*. Indianapolis: Eckert Publications, 1985.

Nicholson, Edward. *Portraits in Oil or Charcoal*. Brochure.

Northern Indiana Arts Association. *Vintage Calumet: Regional Artwork, 1935-1965*. Munster, Indiana: Northern Indiana Arts Association, 1989. Exh. Cat.

Northway, Martin, ed. *The Artists of Brown County and Where to Find 'Em!* Nashville, Indiana: Northway & Reinwaldt Associates, 1979.

Oilar, John. "Forum: The Readers Corner." *Indianapolis Star Magazine*, 17 October 1982.

"One Man Show: "Indiana's Clifton Wheeler." *Indianapolis Star Magazine*, 11 April 1948.

Opitz, Glenn B., ed. *Mantle Fielding's Dictionary of American Painters, Sculptors & Engravers*. Poughkeepsie, New York: Apollo Book, 1988.

O'Sullivan, Judith. *The Great American Comic Strip: One Hundred Years of Cartoon Art*. Boston, Toronto and London: Bulfinch Press Book, Little, Brown & Co., 1990.

Pam Hicks Papers. Greenwood, Indiana. Collection includes documents, newspaper articles and photographs concerning the Hoosier Salon and Indiana's artists.

Parker, Lowell. "Brown County, Indiana: Hoosier." *Indianapolis Star Magazine*.

Peat, Wilbur D. *Pioneer Painters of Indiana*. Indianapolis: Art Association of Indianapolis, 1954.

Persinger, Joe. "Indiana Artist Loved Old Things." *Target*, 17 September 1967.

Phillips, Clifton J. *Indiana in Transition: The Emergence of an Industrial Commonwealth, 1880-1920*. Indianapolis: Indiana Historical Bureau and Indiana Historical Society, 1968.

Pisano, Ronald G. *A Leading Spirit in American Art: William Merritt Chase, 1849-1916*. Seattle: The Henry Gallery Association, 1983.

Pleasant Run Gallery. *The Forsyth Influence: The Students of William Forsyth*. Indianapolis: Pleasant Run Gallery, 1985. Exh. Cat.

Prologue to an Artist. Lafayette, Indiana: Sister Rufinia Art Club, 1 March 1976. Typewritten.

Psi Iota Xi Sorority. *Brown County Art and Artists*. Nashville, Indiana: Psi Iota Xi Sorority, 1971.

"Randolph Coats." *The Cross Keys*, March 1941.

Reichard, Joel. *Watercolors*. Brochure.

Ruth Anderson Papers. Indianapolis, Indiana. Collection includes correspondence, documents and newspaper articles concerning Hoosier artists.

Saint-Gaudens, Homer. *The American Artist and His Times*. New York: Dodd, Mead & Company, 1941.

"Salon's Best." *Indianapolis Star Magazine*, 3 March 1968.

Schmidt, Steven J. "Do Hoosiers Sell Best?" *Indiana Libraries* 9 (1990): 3-8.

Selma N. Steele Collection. Indiana State Museum and Historic Sites, Indianapolis, Indiana.

Sister Rufinia. *Reveries of an Artist*. Lafayette, Indiana: Sister Rufinia Art Club, 1 March 1976. Typewritten.

Smith, Mrs. Henry Lester. *The Hoosier Salon, 1925-1974: A Dream of Farsighted Men and Women*. Indianapolis: Hoosier Salon Patrons Association, 1974.

Smith, Mrs. Leonidas F. "Hoosier Artists: Charles R. Untulis." *Indianapolis Star Magazine*, 19 February 1961.

Smith, Mrs. Leonidas F. "Hoosier Artists: James McBride." *Indianapolis Star Magazine*, 4 October 1959.

Sparks, Esther. "A Biographical Dictionary of Painters and Sculptors in Illinois, 1808-1945." Ph. D. diss., Northwestern University, 1971. Microfilm.

Steele, Selma N.; Steele, Theodore L.; and Peat, Wilbur

D. *The House of the Singing Winds*. Indianapolis: Indiana Historical Society, 1966.

Thayer, Edna. "Hoosier Artists: C. Curry Bohm." *Indianapolis Star Magazine*, 3 July 1966.

The Old Masters of Taos: Selections from the Collection of Harrison Eiteljorg. Indianapolis, 1983. Exh. Cat.

The Twenty. *State House Art Salon for Hoosiers*. Indianapolis: The Twenty, June 1964. Exh. Cat. Ruth Anderson Papers.

Troyer, Byron L. *Yesterday's Indiana*. Miami, Florida: E. A. Seemann Publishing, Inc., 1975.

University of Southern Indiana and the Evansville Museum of Arts and Science. *The Hoosier Scene*. Evansville, Indiana: University of Southern Indiana Press and Evansville Museum of Arts and Science, 1989. Exh. Cat.

Walton, Lloyd B. "The Mystery Artist of Indianapolis." *Indianapolis Star Magazine*, 28 March 1976.

Walton, Lloyd B. "Traditional Arts Advocate." *Indianapolis Star Magazine*, 30 August 1970.

Walton, Lloyd B. "Under the Big Top with Bob Weaver." *Indianapolis Star Magazine*, 18 April 1971.

Weiss, Carol. "Artists Explore Balance Between Money and Art." *Arts Insight*, February 1987.

Weiss, Carol. "Painter of People." *Arts Indiana*, October 1991.

Weiss, Carol. "What Frees Creativity?" *Arts Indiana*, June 1988.

Weston, Dorothy H. "Hoosier Artists: Esther Commons Nusbaum." *Indianapolis Star Magazine*, 22 March 1964.

Weston, Dorothy H. "Hoosier Artists: Joel Warner Reichard." *Indianapolis Star Magazine*, 13 October 1963.

Weston, Dorothy H. "Katherine G. Blasingham." *Indianapolis Star Magazine*, 10 March 1963.

Wolfram, Gretchen. "The Turned-on World of Martha Slaymaker." *Indianapolis Star Magazine*, 11 May 1969.

Woman's Department Club. "Janet Scudder's Frog Fountain." Indianapolis: Woman's Department Club, October 1950. Photocopy.

Wood, Henry. "Portraits and Flowers." *Indianapolis Star Magazine*, 1 January 1951.

INDEX

(Numbers in italics refer to illustrations.)